Vol. 116 • No. 2 • April 2026

BSSA

Bulletin of the Seismological Society of America

SSA
Seismological Society of America

BSSA

Bulletin of the Seismological Society of America

Vol. 116 • No. 2 • April 2026

ARTICLES

Urban Seismology: A Homogenization Perspective on Site–City and Site–Foundation–City Interaction **535**
Agnès Maurel, Kim Pham, Jean-François Semblat, and Simon Félix

Effects of Topography on Ground-Motion Recordings at Short Wavelengths: The Case of a Cliff in Cephalonia, Western Greece **553**
Pauline Rischette, Zafeiria Roumelioti, Fabrice Hollender, Vincent Perron, Nikolaos Theodoulidis, Edward Cushing, Aline Bou Nassif, Emmanuel Chaljub, Fabien Lacroix, Paola Traversa, Emeline Maufroy, Pierre-Yves Bard, and Agisilaos Konidaris

A Direct Convergence Method for Computing Synthetic Seismograms for a Layered Half-Space with Sources and Receivers at Close Depths **576**
Dengda Zhu, Tao Xu, Jinlai Hao, and Zhenxing Yao

Decoding Intrinsic and Scattering Seismic Attenuation at the Conjunction of the Cocos, Nazca, Caribbean, and Panama Plates **589**
Daphne K. Sagel, Janire Prudencio, Edoardo Del Pezzo, Elisabetta Giampiccolo, Tiziana Tuvé, Eduardo Camacho Astigarrabía, Julissa Sanjur, Ariadna Flores, Néstor Luque, and Jesús M. Ibáñez

Moment Tensor Inversion of Microseismic Events Using Strain Waveforms Recorded by Multi-Well-Distributed Acoustic Sensing **603**
Avinash Nayak, Julia Correa, Jonathan Ajo-Franklin, Aleksei Titov, and Sireesh Dadi

ON THE COVER

On February 4, 1976, almost exactly 50 years ago from the publication date of this *BSSA* issue a powerful M_w 7.5 earthquake struck Guatemala, causing approximately 23,000 fatalities. The cover photo shows the collapse of the Hotel Terminal in Guatemala City, caused by the failure of reinforced concrete columns in its third story. In this issue, the review paper, "A Fiftieth Year Retrospective on the 1976 M_w 7.5 Motagua Earthquake in Guatemala," by Clark *et al.* (2026) summarizes five decades of research and recent investigations in Guatemala to synthesize the details of the rupture process and its consequences, to document the importance of this event for earthquake research, and to highlight the need to preserve essential datasets for future scientific analyses.

Image credit: *United States Geological Survey*

Time-Variable Moment Tensor Inversion of Seismic Data Collected at Blue Canyon Dome **624**
Andréa Darrh, Leiph Preston, and Adrian Christian Stanciu

Concentrated Rupture of the 2022 M_w 6.6 Luding Earthquake Bounded by Stress and Geometry Barriers **648**
Xinzhong Yin, Qibin Shi, Wenze Deng, Yingfeng Zhang, Zhangfeng Ma, Xiaoshu Li, Jiuhui Chen, Jinrong Su, and Shengji Wei

Stochastic Inversions for Source, Path, and Site Parameters from West Texas Earthquakes **663**
Bartik Pandel, Ellen M. Rathje, Alexandros Savvaidis, and Albert R. Kottke

HVSR-Based Peak Frequency Identification of S-Net Ocean-Bottom Stations for Site Characterization and Ground-Motion Prediction Models **680**
Tan Jingyang, Dai Mengqing, and Jinjun Hu

Do Earthquake-Induced Rotational Ground Motions Matter? A Case Study from the M_w 7.8 Pazarcık Earthquake **700**
Sergio E. Godínez, Mohamed Abdelmeguid, José I. Restrepo, and Ares J. Rosakis

Subduction or Crustal Faulting? Evaluating Ground-Motion Models to Characterize Haida Gwaii in the Canadian Seismic Hazard Model **720**
Alex Hughes, Tiegan E. Hobbs, Camille Brillon, Michael G. Bostock, and Simon Peacock

Vertical Ground-Motion Prediction Equation and Vertical-to-Horizontal Spectral Ratios of Peak Ground Acceleration, Peak Ground Velocity, and 5% Damped Response Spectra in Southwest China **738**
Bin Zhang, Xiaojian Lu, Jiamei Liu, Mianshui Rong, Yanxiang Yu, and Xiaojun Li

A Ground-Motion Model for the Vertical Ground-Motion Component Based on Empirical Data from the NGA-East Data Set **755**
Shahram Pezeshk, Ali Farhadi, and Mehran Davatgari-Tafreshi

MAILING & SUBSCRIPTION INFORMATION

Subscriptions to the *Bulletin of the Seismological Society of America (BSSA)*: Information regarding institutional subscriptions can be found at www.seismosoc.org/subscriptions. Eligible members of the Seismological Society of America receive online access to *BSSA*. Individuals may apply for membership or determine eligibility by visiting www.seismosoc.org.

Bulletin of the Seismological Society of America (BSSA) is the premier journal of advanced research in earthquake seismology and related disciplines. It first appeared in 1911. Each issue is composed of scientific papers on the various aspects of seismology, including investigation of specific earthquakes, theoretical and observational studies of seismic waves, inverse methods for determining the structure of the Earth or the dynamics of the earthquake source, seismometry, earthquake hazard and risk estimation, seismotectonics, and earthquake engineering. Special issues focus on important earthquakes or rapidly changing topics in seismology.

BSSA (ISSN 0037-1106) is published bimonthly in February, April, June, August, October, and December by the Seismological Society of America, 400 Evelyn Avenue, Suite 201, Albany, CA 94706- 1375. Periodicals postage paid at Berkeley, California and at additional mailing offices.

A Combined PGD–PGV Scaling Law with R_{proxy} Distance for the G-FAST Earthquake Early Warning Module **770**
Jensen V. DeGrande and Brendan W. Crowell

Capturing the Uncertainty of Seismicity Observations in Earthquake Rate Estimates: Implications for Probabilistic Seismic Hazard Analysis and the USGS National Seismic Hazard Model **786**
Andrew J. Michael and Andrea L. Llenos

Paleoseismology of the Zougahana Fault, Northern Aso Outer Rim, and Its Role in the Tectonics of Northern Kyushu **810**
Keitaro Komura, Hiroshi P. Sato, Hiroshi Yagi, Takayuki Nakano, and Hiroshi Une

ERRATUM

Erratum to Characterizing Lithospheric Transverse Isotropy Using Moment Tensors—On the Origin of the Non-Double-Couple Components of Global CMT Solutions **837**
Hitoshi Kawakatsu

Urban Seismology: A Homogenization Perspective on Site–City and Site–Foundation–City Interaction

Agnès Maurel[*1], Kim Pham[2], Jean-François Semblat[3], and Simon Félix[4]

ABSTRACT

We revisit site–city interaction (SCI) within the framework of a two-scale homogenization model verified through direct numerical simulations for an idealized geometry consisting of an infinite city and sedimentary basin. The proposed model extends previous investigations by systematically accounting for the collective influence of buildings on seismic wave propagation. We further generalize the homogenization approach to incorporate building foundations at various depths, highlighting their impact on resonance phenomena. These findings provide new insights into urban seismic wavefield and offer a simplified yet effective framework for assessing city-scale wave motion in complex site–foundation–city configurations.

KEY POINTS

- We revisit site–city interaction (SCI) using a homogenization model compared to a multimodal approach.
- The homogenized model replicates city-scale responses and captures foundation effects.
- Our model offers an efficient way to estimate the urban wavefield accounting for both SCI and site–foundation–city interaction.

INTRODUCTION

The concept of site–city interaction (SCI) emerged in the 90s (Wirgin and Bard, 1996), which is relatively recent when compared to the concept of dynamic soil–structure interaction proposed in the 50s for a single structure (Kausel, 2010). It relies on earlier studies investigating the interaction of a few buildings through the foundation soil (Housner, 1957; Luco and Contesse, 1973; Wong and Trifunac, 1975) and refers to the ability of a city—a dense ensemble of buildings—to strongly interact with seismic waves, particularly when the city is built on a sedimentary basin for which resonance frequency is comparable to that of the buildings (Wirgin and Bard, 1996; Guéguen *et al.*, 2000; Clouteau and Aubry, 2001; Tsogka and Wirgin, 2003; Guéguen and Bard, 2005; Kham *et al.*, 2006; Groby and Wirgin, 2008; Uenishi, 2010). The impact of a sedimentary basin or any layered deposit on seismic waves has long been referred to as seismic site effects; see, for example, Bard and Bouchon (1980). However, the influence of surface structures on seismic wave propagation remains underappreciated and is often overlooked in seismic hazard and risk assessments. This is why classical methods rely on computing the free field, which represents the ground motion in the absence of surface structures (Kausel *et al.*, 1978; Kausel, 2010). This free field is then used as input motion to calculate displacements within each structure considered as purely passive. The underlying assumption is that the energy radiated by a building is negligible and does not influence the seismic ground motion. However, this hypothesis was challenged after the analysis of certain earthquakes, such as the 1985 Mexico City earthquake, revealed amplification effects that could only be attributed to the global interaction with the city (Rosenblueth, 1986; Flores *et al.*, 1987; Wirgin and Bard, 1996; Guéguen *et al.*, 2002). Since then, this influence has been widely confirmed through numerical simulations as well as small- and medium-scale experiments (Wirgin and Bard, 1996; Guéguen *et al.*, 2000; Clouteau and Aubry, 2001; Tsogka and Wirgin, 2003; Guéguen and Bard, 2005; Kham *et al.*, 2006; Groby and Wirgin, 2008; Uenishi, 2010; Isbiliroglu *et al.*, 2014, 2015). It is now well established that the interaction between a whole city and the ground must be taken into account. Developing simplified models that effectively capture this interaction while identifying the key governing parameters remains a crucial challenge

1. Institut Langevin, ESPCI Paris, Université PSL, CNRS, Paris, France, https://orcid.org/0000-0001-8432-9871 (AM); 2. LMI, ENSTA, Institut Polytechnique de Paris, Palaiseau, France, https://orcid.org/0000-0001-8767-6457 (KP); 3. IMSIA (UMR 9219), CNRS, EDF, ENSTA, Institut Polytechnique de Paris, Palaiseau, France, https://orcid.org/0000-0002-8471-198X (J-FS); 4. Laboratoire d'Acoustique de l'Université du Mans (LAUM), UMR 6613, Institut d'Acoustique - Graduate School (IA-GS), CNRS, Le Mans Université, France, https://orcid.org/0000-0002-4951-9634 (SF)

*Corresponding author: agnes.maurel@espci.fr

Cite this article as Maurel, A., K. Pham, J.-F. Semblat, and S. Félix (2025). Urban Seismology: A Homogenization Perspective on Site–City and Site–Foundation–City Interaction, *Bull. Seismol. Soc. Am.* **116**, 535–552, doi: 10.1785/0120250151

(Brûlà *et al.*, 2020; Vicencio *et al.*, 2023; Singhai and Tiwari, 2024).

In wave physics, the collective effects of scatterers have been widely studied. In the 2000s, with the advent of metamaterials, such effects were used to achieve guided wave propagation (Achaoui *et al.*, 2011; Maznev and Gusev, 2015; Mercier *et al.*, 2015), trapping (Zhu *et al.*, 2013), and cloaking (Craster and Guenneau, 2012) in geometries that sometimes resemble idealized city configurations. Drawing parallels between physics and seismology, it has been proposed to use trees (Colombi *et al.*, 2016; Maurel *et al.*, 2018; Pham *et al.*, 2020), wind turbines (Pilz *et al.*, 2024), or artificial systems (Palermo and Marzani, 2018) to create urban protective shields (see reviews in Mu *et al.*, 2020). One of the theoretical tools used to characterize ensembles of scatterers is homogenization, which replaces a periodic or weakly nonperiodic set of elements with an effective medium. Initially developed in the 2000s by Boutin and coworkers (Boutin and Roussillon, 2004, 2006; Boutin *et al.*, 2015; Schwan *et al.*, 2016) for mass–spring systems, it has since been extended to include plate- and beamlike structures (Marigo *et al.*, 2020, 2021, 2024). This revealed the ability of resonant systems to influence scattering properties and generate controlled guided waves. These approaches are particularly advantageous because they circumvent cumbersome considerations on multiple scattering effects, which are unnecessary when the wavelength is much larger than the spacing between scatterers. In this regime, waves perceive a collective, mean effect from the scatterers, which homogenization precisely aims to capture. In the specific case of a city, which is the focus of this work, the urban region can be effectively modeled as an equivalent, homogeneous, anisotropic layer with a height corresponding to that of the buildings.

The present study aims to derive homogenized models to revisit and extend established findings on SCI, particularly in the presence of deep foundations. It will thus be named site–foundation–city interaction (SFCI). We focus on a 2D configuration for *SH* waves, assuming a linear, viscoelastic behavior for the soil, buildings, and foundations. Our reference configuration is the one considered in Kham *et al.* (2006), as illustrated in Figure 1, and we extend it to an infinite domain. First, we outline the scheme and present numerical results on SCI with and without foundations, which our homogenized models are designed to replicate. To lay the foundation for our model, we briefly review the principle of homogenization for a system of elastic blocks (representing the city) and for a composite soil (the foundations embedded in a soil). These theoretical results are then applied in the main sections investigating both SCI and SFCI. Specifically, for SCI, we demonstrate that our model faithfully reproduces the findings of Kham *et al.* (2006), showing that the dynamic responses remain identical at the center of the city, regardless of its width. The simplicity of the homogenized models allows us to characterize the key parameters governing SCI in both its classical form and its extension to more complex site–foundation–city configurations.

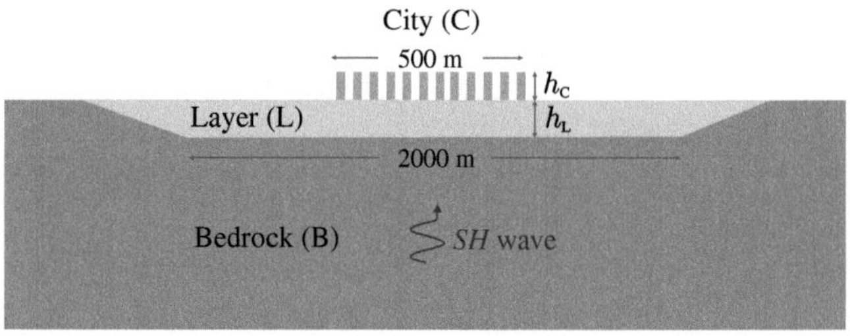

Figure 1. Configuration considered in Kham *et al.* (2006): a 2D city modeled as a periodic array of $\mathcal{N}$ buildings, each of width w_C and height h_C distributed over a 500-m-long region atop a sedimentary layer (L) of thickness h_L, itself overlying an elastic half-space (bedrock B). The color version of this figure is available only in the electronic edition.

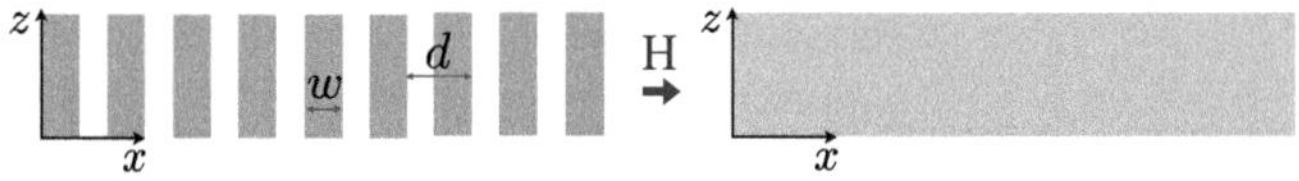

Figure 2. Homogenization procedure replaces the building array (left) with its homogenized counterpart (right), governed by equation (1). The color version of this figure is available only in the electronic edition.

HOMOGENIZED MODELS AND DIRECT SIMULATIONS

In this section, we introduce the homogenized models developed for the city region as well as for the sedimentary layer with embedded foundations. Originally formulated in the 1970s within the fields of mathematics and solid mechanics (Bensoussan *et al.*, 2011), the method of asymptotic homogenization has since become a standard tool in wave physics. Its purpose is to approximate the response of a heterogeneous medium characterized by subwavelength-scale variations through the derivation of an effective, homogeneous, and generally anisotropic representation obtained by asymptotic analysis. This framework is here employed to model the seismic response of an idealized city.

Homogenized site–city model

Homogenized version of the city. We consider a stratified medium composed of alternating elastic blocks C and air, representing an array of buildings (Fig. 2, left). The homogenization procedure can be applied in this context, while accounting for the stress-free boundary condition at the edges of the elastic blocks (Mercier *et al.*, 2015; Marigo and Maurel, 2017). As a result, the heterogeneous medium is replaced by an effective homogeneous medium (Fig. 2, right), which is infinitely anisotropic because wave propagation is restricted to the vertical z-direction. Within this framework, effective wave

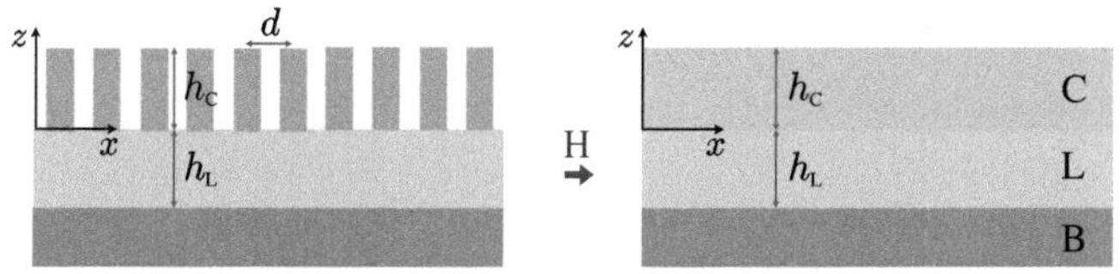

Figure 3. Effective site–city problem, where the city region (left) is replaced by a homogeneous, anisotropic layer of height h_C (right). The color version of this figure is available only in the electronic edition.

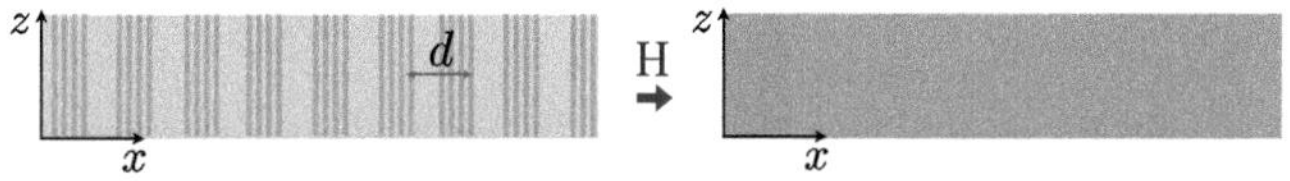

Figure 4. Homogenization procedure replaces the soil (sedimentary layer L or bedrock B) reinforced by the foundations with its homogenized counterpart (right), described by equations (4) and (5). The color version of this figure is available only in the electronic edition.

propagation is governed by the following propagation equation:

$$\Sigma = \mu_C \varphi_C \begin{pmatrix} 0 & 0 \\ 0 & 1 \end{pmatrix} \nabla U, \qquad \mathrm{div}\Sigma = \rho_C \varphi_C \frac{\partial^2 U}{\partial t^2}, \tag{1}$$

in which Σ and U denote the shear stress vector and the out-of-plane displacement, respectively. Here, (μ_C,ρ_C) represent the shear modulus and mass density of the elastic material, and φ_C is its filling fraction.

Homogenized site–city model. Thanks to the homogenization of the city region, the problem of wave propagation in the soil overlain by the sedimentary layer and ultimately by the city can be approximated by a three-layer structure, consisting of

- The bedrock half-space B, $z \in (-\infty, -h_L)$,
- the sedimentary layer L, $z \in (-h_L, 0)$, (2)
- the homogenized city region C, $z \in (0, h_C)$,

see Figure 3.

In both the bedrock and the sedimentary layer, which are treated as homogeneous layers, wave propagation is governed by the following equations:

$$\Sigma = \mu_X \nabla U, \qquad \mathrm{div}\Sigma = \rho_X \frac{\partial^2 U}{\partial t^2}, \tag{3}$$

with $(\mu_X,\rho_X) = (\mu_B,\rho_B)$ in the bedrock and $(\mu_X,\rho_X) = (\mu_L,\rho_L)$ in the sedimentary layer, whereas in the city region it is governed by equation (1). At each interface, namely at $z = -h_L$ and $z = 0$, continuity conditions for the displacement U and the normal stress $\Sigma \cdot \boldsymbol{e}_z$ are enforced. At $z = h_C$, corresponding to the interface between the city region and the air, a stress-free boundary condition applies with $\Sigma \cdot \boldsymbol{e}_z = 0$.

Homogenized site–foundation–city model

The presence of foundations partially or fully anchored in the sedimentary layer introduces an additional laminated layer that must be homogenized (the city region remains described by equation 1).

Homogenized version of the reinforced soil. Homogenization is a well-established technique for composite soils, including soft soils reinforced with rigid inclusions or mixed soils partially improved by various techniques (Hassen *et al.*, 2010). For a layered medium alternating between materials F (foundation) and X (the sedimentary layer or the bedrock), with a composition invariant along the z-direction, homogenized wave propagation is governed by the following equations:

$$\Sigma = \begin{pmatrix} \langle \mu^{-1} \rangle^{-1} & 0 \\ 0 & \langle \mu \rangle \end{pmatrix} \nabla U, \qquad \mathrm{div}\Sigma = \langle \rho \rangle \frac{\partial^2 U}{\partial t^2}, \tag{4}$$

in which the average of $a = \rho, \mu, \mu^{-1}$ is defined as

$$\langle a \rangle = \varphi_F a_F + (1 - \varphi_F) a_X, \tag{5}$$

with φ_F the filling fraction of material F and $\varphi_X = (1 - \varphi_F)$ the filling fraction of material X. Figure 4 illustrates the reinforced soil (left) and its homogenized counterpart (right). Note that equation (1) corresponds to a particular case of equation (4), where the air between buildings is modeled as a material with $\rho = \mu = 0$, that is, with negligible mass density and rigidity compared with those of the buildings.

In constructing the homogenized site–foundation–city model, we must distinguish between the cases $h_F \le h_L$ and $h_F \ge h_L$.

Homogenized site–foundation–city model for foundations partially embedded in the sedimentary layer ($h_F \le h_L$). In this case, the sedimentary layer is divided into two regions, one of which, denoted LF, is homogenized. The system is thus approximated as a four-layer structure, as illustrated in Figure 5a, consisting of

- The bedrock half-space B, $z \in (-\infty, -h_L)$,
- the part of the sedimentary layer, L, beneath the foundations, $z \in (-h_L, -h_F)$,
- the homogenized part of the layer, LF, in which the foundations are embedded, $z \in (-h_F, 0)$,
- the homogenized city region C, $z \in (0, h_C)$.

(6)

In B and L, which correspond to truly homogeneous regions, equation (3) applies. In contrast, in the homogenized city region and in the homogenized part of the sedimentary layer containing the foundations, equation (1) and equation (4) (with X = L in equation 5) apply, respectively. At each interface $z = -h_L, -h_F, 0$, continuity of displacement and normal stress is enforced, whereas at $z = 0$ the normal stress vanishes.

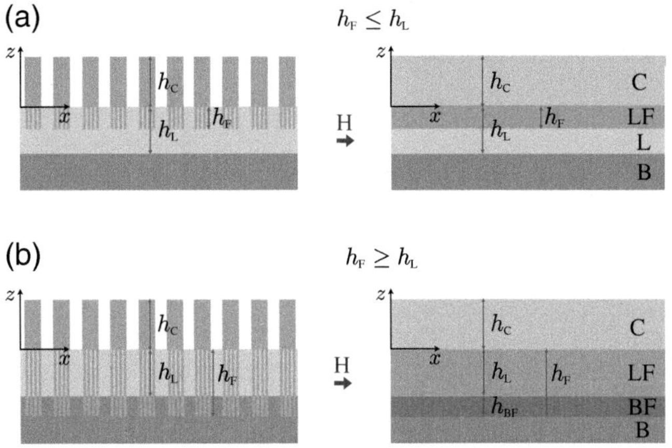

Figure 5. Effective site–foundation–city problem. (a) Foundations embedded in the sedimentary layer only. (b) Foundations embedded in the bedrock through the sedimentary layer. The color version of this figure is available only in the electronic edition.

Homogenized site–foundation–city model for foundations embedded in the bedrock ($h_F \geq h_L$). If the foundations cut through the entire sedimentary layer and penetrate the bedrock (Fig. 5b), the sedimentary layer L is replaced by an effective layer LF of thickness h_L, and a new layer BF must be introduced. This layer corresponds to the part of the bedrock occupied by the foundations and extends over $z \in (-h_F, -h_L)$. The system is then approximated as a four-layer structure consisting of

- the bedrock half-space B, $z \in (-\infty, -h_F)$,
- the part of the bedrock, BF, in which the foundations are embedded, $z \in (-h_F, -h_L)$,
- the homogenized sedimentary layer, LF, in which the foundations are embedded, $z \in (-h_L, 0)$,
- the homogenized city region C, $z \in (0, h_C)$. (7)

In B, which is now the only truly homogeneous region, equation (3) applies. As before, the homogenized city region is described by equation (1). In BF and LF, wave propagation is governed by equation (4), with X = B and X = L in equation (5), respectively. At each interface $z = -h_F, -h_L, 0$, continuity of displacement and normal stress is enforced, whereas at $z = 0$ the normal stress vanishes.

Direct numerical simulations

Boundary-element method (BEM). In our study, we make use of the numerical results reported by Kham *et al.* (2006), obtained with the BEM (Chaillat *et al.*, 2009; Delepine and Semblat, 2012) for a finite-size city, as illustrated in Figure 1. We do not implement the BEM ourselves; rather, we use these published results to compare with our homogenized models. This comparison (see the Finite-size effect, comparison with Kham *et al.* (2006) section) allows us to evaluate the relevance of the infinite-city approximation in a more realistic finite-city scenario.

Multimodal method (MM). Except in the Finite-size effect, comparison with Kham *et al.* (2006) section, the verification of the SCI and SFCI models is carried out by comparison with a multimodal numerical method that we have implemented for an infinitely periodic city, that is, consistent with the assumptions of our model. This method relies on decomposing the exact solution of the problem into elementary solutions. In the context of antiplane elasticity, these techniques have been described in detail, for example, in Wirgin (1988) and Wirgin and Bard (1996), and have been employed in previous studies (Marigo *et al.*, 2017; Pham *et al.*, 2017; Maurel *et al.*, 2018).

SITE–CITY INTERACTION

Homogenized scattering problem

We consider harmonic waves with time dependance $e^{-i\omega t}$ and solve the scattering problem for an incident wave enforcing a dependence $e^{i\beta x}$ of the solution. Thus, the displacement and stress field take the form

$$U(x,z) = e^{i\beta x} u(z), \tag{8}$$

and similarly for Σ, with

$$\Sigma_{yz}(x,z) = e^{i\beta x} \sigma(x). \tag{9}$$

According to equations (1)–(3), we have

$$\begin{cases} \sigma' + (\rho_B \omega^2 - \mu_B \beta^2) u = 0, & \sigma = \mu_B u', \quad \text{(bedrock)}, \\ \sigma' + (\rho_L \omega^2 - \mu_L \beta^2) u = 0, & \sigma = \mu_L u', \quad \text{(layer)}, \\ \sigma' + \varphi_C \rho_C \omega^2 u = 0, & \sigma = \varphi_C \mu_C u', \quad \text{(city)}, \end{cases} \tag{10}$$

in which the prime denotes the derivative with respect to z.

For notational convenience, we define the characteristic admittances

$$Y_B = i\mu_B \alpha_B, \quad Y_L = i\mu_L \alpha_L, \quad Y_C = i\varphi_C \mu_C k_C, \tag{11}$$

with

$$k_B = \frac{\omega}{c_B}, \quad k_L = \frac{\omega}{c_L}, \quad k_C = \frac{\omega}{c_C},$$
$$\alpha_B = \sqrt{k_B^2 - \beta^2}, \quad \alpha_L = \sqrt{k_L^2 - \beta^2}, \tag{12}$$

in which $c_B = \sqrt{\mu_B/\rho_B}$, $c_L = \sqrt{\mu_L/\rho_L}$, and $c_C = \sqrt{\mu_C/\rho_C}$. For an obliquely incident wave in the bedrock, we set

$$\beta = k_B \sin\theta, \tag{13}$$

in equation (8). We also define the generalized admittance $Y(z)$, satisfying

$$\sigma(z) = Y(z)u(z).$$

In the effective model, a stress-free condition applies at the top of the city region, $z = h_C$, yielding

$$Y(0) = -iY_C \tan k_C h_C. \quad (14)$$

and $Y(z)$ is continuous across all layers, in particular at the interfaces $z = 0$ and $z = -h_L$.

The solution for unit-amplitude incident wave, satisfying equation (10) and the boundary conditions, takes the form:

$$u(z) = \begin{cases} e^{i\alpha_B(z+h_L)} + re^{-i\alpha_B(z+h_L)}, & z \in (-\infty, -h_L), \\ (1+r)G_L(z), & z \in (-h_L, 0), \\ (1+r)G_L(0)G_C(z), & z \in (0, h_C), \end{cases} \quad (15)$$

with

$$G_L(z) = \frac{\cos\alpha_L z + C\sin\alpha_L z}{\cos\alpha_L h_L - C\sin\alpha_L h_L}, \qquad G_C(z) = \frac{\cos k_C(z-h_C)}{\cos k_C h_C},$$

and

$$C = \frac{Y_C}{Y_L}\tan k_C h_C,$$

in which C quantifies the coupling of the city with the sedimentary layer, and

$$r = \frac{1+i\hat{C}}{1-i\hat{C}}, \qquad \hat{C} = \frac{Y_L}{Y_B}\frac{\tan\alpha_L h_L + C}{1 - C\tan\alpha_L h_L}, \quad (16)$$

with $\hat{C}$ representing the combined coupling of the city and sedimentary layer with the bedrock. The displacements at ground level, $u_{bot} = u(0)$, and at the top of the city, $u_{top} = u(h_C)$, are given using equation (15), which leads to

$$u_{bot} = \frac{2}{\cos\alpha_L h_L\left(1 - i\frac{Y_L}{Y_B}\tan\alpha_L h_L - C\left(i\frac{Y_L}{Y_B} + \tan\alpha_L h_L\right)\right)},$$
$$u_{top} = \frac{u_{bot}}{\cos k_C h_C}. \quad (17)$$

For $h_C = 0$ (no city, so $C = 0$), this reduces to the exact solution for a sedimentary layer on bedrock; for $h_L = 0$ (no sedimentary layer), it corresponds to a city directly on the bedrock. The energy reflected in the soil is $|r|^2$ for a unitary energy carried out by the incident wave. Accordingly, the energy dissipated in the sedimentary layer and city is

$$\mathcal{E}_d = 1 - |r|^2. \quad (18)$$

We conclude this analysis by noting that u_{bot} and u_{top} are nondimensional quantities, computed for a unit-amplitude incident wave $U^{inc} = e^{i\alpha_B(z+h_L)}e^{i\beta x}$, according to equations (8) and (15). Similarly, the case $h_C = 0$ corresponds to the free-field solution for a unit-amplitude incident wave. Accordingly, the amplification factor is obtained by dividing u_{bot} in the presence of the city ($h_C \geq 0$) by u_{bot} in the free-field case ($h_C = 0$). Finally, for physical interpretation, one may also consider normalized quantities such as $(u_{top} - u_{bot})A^{inc}/h_C$, in which $A^{inc} = |U^{inc}|$ is the dimensional amplitude of the incident wave. This provides a driftlike measure, analogous to the interstory drift ratio in a building but applied here to the homogenized layer representing the city rather than to an individual structure.

TABLE 1
Material Parameters

B	L	C	F	(Unit)
$\mu_B = 2000$	$\mu_L = 72$	$\mu_C = 14.4$	$\mu_F = 15000$	(MPa)
$\rho_B = 2000$	$\rho_L = 1800$	$\rho_C = 250$	$\rho_F = 2500$	(kg.m^{-3})
$Q_B = 100$	$Q_L = 25$	$Q_C = 10$	$Q_F = 10$	

μ, shear modulus; ρ, mass density; B, bedrock; C, the city buildings; F, the foundations; L, the sedimentary layer; Q, loss quality factor.

Verification and assessment of homogenized SCI model

In the following, we use the material properties listed in Table 1, which are the same as those employed in Kham *et al.* (2006). Damping is included by replacing the density ρ with a complex-valued density $\rho(1 + i(2Q)^{-1})^2$, in which Q is the quality factor; see Grasso *et al.* (2012).

To begin with, we examine two key indicators that quantify wave interactions with the sedimentary layer (the site) and the city: the amplitude of relative displacements at the top and bottom of the buildings, $|u_{top} - u_{bot}|$ (for an incident wave of unitary displacement amplitude and at normal incidence $\theta = 0$), and the energy $\mathcal{E}_d$ dissipated by the sedimentary layer and the city, as defined in equation (18). These quantities were obtained numerically using MM computations and are reported in Figure 6. We considered both a city directly on the bedrock ($h_L = 0$, panel a) and a city above a sedimentary layer of thickness $h_L = 25$ m (panel b).

From Figure 6, we observe that the variations of these indicators align with previously reported patterns for dense building arrays:

- Interaction with the city in the absence of sedimentary layer (panel a): wave interaction with the city is generally weak, except at the building resonance frequencies, close to the fixed-base resonance frequencies of the buildings:

$$f_C^{(n)} = \frac{c_C}{2h_C}\left(n - \frac{1}{2}\right), \quad (19)$$

in which $n \geq 1$ is an integer. These frequencies are indicated by the black-dashed lines in Figure 6. At the fundamental

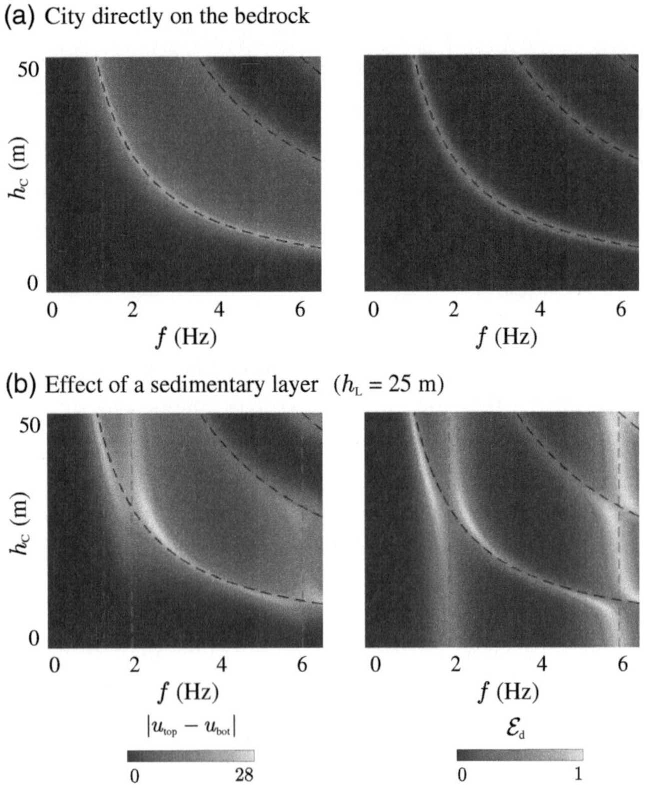

Figure 6. Variations of the relative displacement $|u_{top} - u_{bot}|$ within the buildings (left), and of the energy $\mathcal{E}_d$ dissipated in the sedimentary layer and the city (right), as functions of building height h_C and frequency f, for an incident wave of amplitude unity and normal incidence ($\theta = 0$). (a) No sedimentary layer ($h_L = 0$). (b) Sedimentary layer with $h_L = 25$ m. Building width is $w_C = 10$ m, with period $d = 20$ m, corresponding to a city density $\varphi_C = w_C/d = 0.5$. In (a,b), the black-dashed lines indicate $f_C^{(n)}$, $n = 1,2,3$, the resonance frequencies of the fixed-base building blocks, from equation (19), and in (b) the vertical red-dashed lines indicate the resonance frequencies of the sedimentary layer, $f_L^{(n)}$, $n = 1,2$, from equation (20). The color version of this figure is available only in the electronic edition.

resonance ($n = 1$), the energy dissipated by the city reaches about 50% of that of the incident wave, and the displacement at the building tops attains its maximum values.

- Amplification by the sedimentary layer (panel b): the sedimentary layer markedly amplifies wave interaction. This effect arises from the resonances of the layer, which, in the absence of buildings ($h_C = 0$), occur around frequencies

$$f_L^{(n)} = \frac{c_L}{2h_L}\left(n - \frac{1}{2}\right), \tag{20}$$

in which $n \geq 1$ is an integer and is indicated by the vertical red-dashed lines in panel (b) of Figure 6. Resonances at f = 2 Hz and 6 Hz (n = 1,2) are clearly visible in the results. It is noteworthy that the effects of the city and the sedimentary layer do not simply add up, especially when their respective resonance frequencies coincide. In such cases, avoided crossings, typical of interacting tuned resonators, broaden the regions of strong interaction. This leads to energy dissipation approaching 100% and significant amplification of displacements in both the soil and the buildings, with average factors of 2 and peaks up to 5 at resonances.

The homogenized model, using equations (15)–(17), shows excellent agreement with the numerical results: discrepancies are below 2% for the dissipated energy $\mathcal{E}_d$ and below 5% for the displacements across the entire range of frequencies and city heights h_C shown in Figure 6a,b. This comparison confirms the validity of the homogenized model in capturing the key features of SCI.

We now focus on the physical meaning of the homogenized solution in terms of the spatial displacement field and its relation to the field in the actual configuration. To illustrate this, Figure 7a–c compares the displacement fields $U(x,z)$ obtained numerically using the MM with those from the homogenized model defined in equations (15) and (16) (the real part of $U(x, z)$ is reported). The configuration corresponds to a sedimentary layer of height $h_L = 25$ m overlain by a city of height $h_C = 30$ m with a city density $\varphi_C = 0.5$. To better visualize the interference between incident and reflected waves, an oblique incidence of $\theta = 45°$ is chosen. The effect of wave incidence will be studied in more detail later; however, it is noted that the resonance frequencies, marked by maxima in $|u_{top} - u_{bot}|$, are almost identical for $\theta = 0°$ and $\theta = 45°$. Specifically, the first two resonances occur at $f \simeq 2$ Hz and $f \simeq 4$ Hz, corresponding to $f_L^{(n)} = f_C^{(n)}$, n = 1,2. At the first resonance, $|u_{top} - u_{bot}| \simeq 18$ in equation (17) and at the second resonance $|u_{top} - u_{bot}| \simeq 10$ in equation (9) for $\theta = 0°$ (45°), indicating that the overall SCI dominates over the effect of wave inclination.

Qualitative comparison of the fields in panels (a–c) shows that the homogenized model provides a faithful and continuous representation of the displacement within the city region, both far from resonance (panel b, f = 4 Hz), where displacements in the buildings, sedimentary layer, and bedrock have comparable amplitudes, and near the first two resonances (panels a, f = 2 Hz and c, f = 6 Hz), where wave amplification occurs in the resonant regions. Qualitative comparison of the fields in panels (a–c) shows that the homogenized model provides a faithful and continuous representation of the displacement within the city region, both far from resonance (panel b, f = 4 Hz), where displacements in the buildings, sedimentary layer, and bedrock have comparable amplitudes, and near the first two resonances (panels a, f = 2 Hz and c, f = 6 Hz), where wave amplification occurs in the two resonant regions. A quantitative comparison is given in Figure 7d–f, showing the displacement profiles $U_{bot}(x) = U(x,0)$ and $U_{top}(x) = U(x,h_C)$. In the MM simulations, $U_{bot}(x)$ is measured at the building bases (red in Fig. 7d, left panel) and at the free surface of the soil between two buildings (blue in Fig. 7d, left panel), with $w_C = 10$ m and d = 20 m. The top displacements $U_{top}(x)$

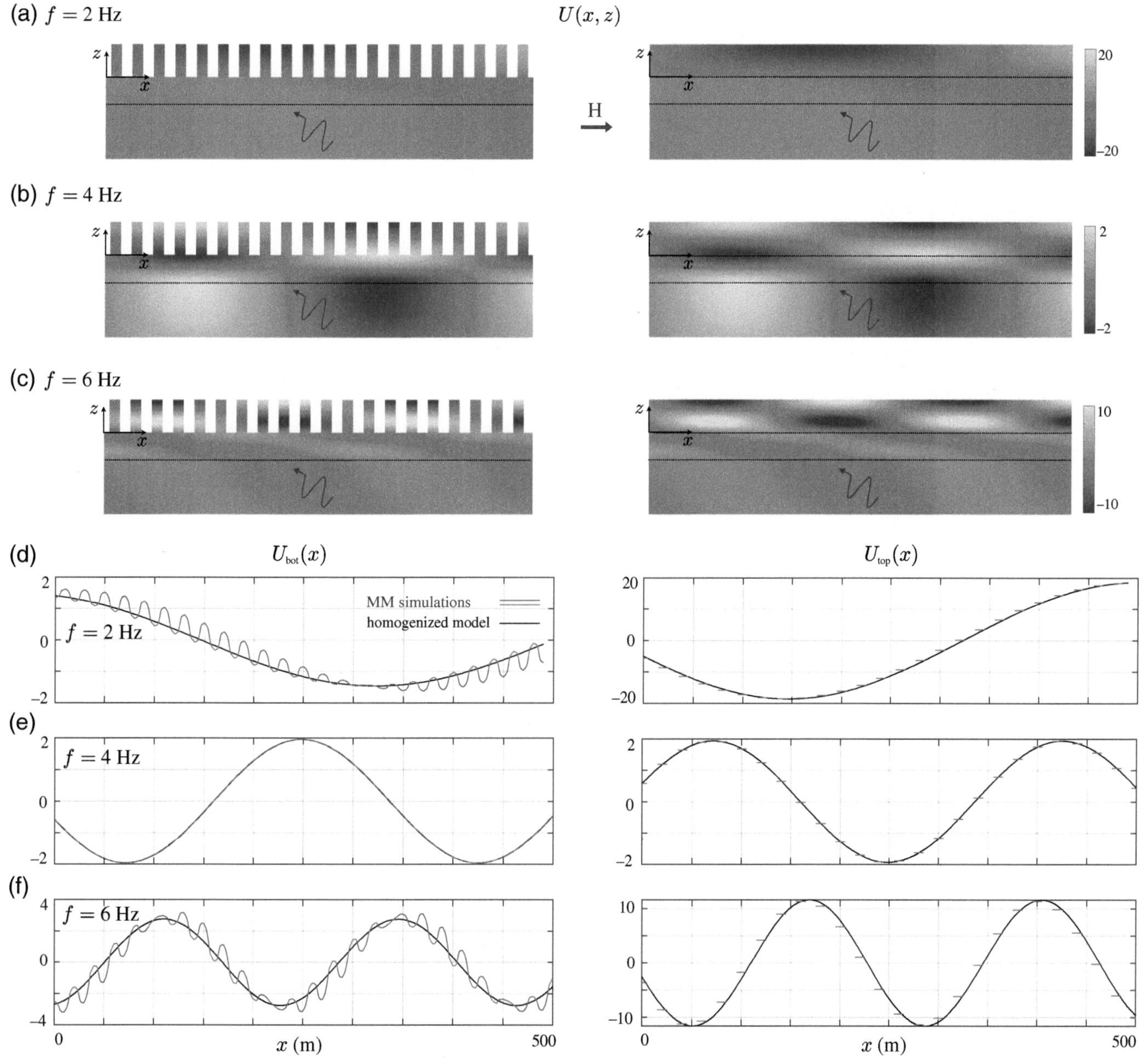

are defined only in the buildings (red in Fig. 7d, right panel). In the homogenized model, both profiles (black curves) are continuous over the interval $x \in (0{,}500)$ m, with $U_{\mathrm{bot}}(x) = u_{\mathrm{bot}} e^{i\beta x}$ and $U_{\mathrm{top}}(x) = u_{\mathrm{top}} e^{i\beta x}$, from equation (8), with $(u_{\mathrm{bot}}, u_{\mathrm{top}})$ given by equation (17). As expected, the homogenized displacements provide a smooth and continuous representation of the displacements computed in the buildings. Note that in the MM simulations, the displacements are piecewise constant at the top of the buildings, whereas at the building bases they vary significantly both within and between buildings, especially near resonance frequencies, due to a strong evanescent field triggered at the building-layer interfaces. Although the homogenized model does not capture the small, rapid oscillations due to evanescent fields, it accurately reproduces the underlying smooth curve of the displacements, representing the main variation along the city.

Figure 7. Illustration of the meaning of the homogenized solutions through comparison with multimodal method (MM) simulations, for an incident wave at 45° impinging on a city atop a soil composed of bedrock overlain by a sedimentary layer ($h_C = 30$ m, $\varphi_C = 0.5$, and $h_L = 25$ m) at frequencies $f = 2$ Hz, 4 Hz and 6 Hz. (a–c) Real part of the displacement field $U(x,y)$ obtained from MM simulation (left) and from the homogenized model (right). (d–f) left: Corresponding displacement profiles $U_{\mathrm{bot}}(x) = u_{\mathrm{bot}} e^{i\beta x}$ at the building bottom (blue lines) and free surface between two buildings (blue lines) and right: displacement profiles $U_{\mathrm{top}}(x) = u_{\mathrm{bot}} e^{i\beta x}$ at the building top, as given by the MM simulations (blue lines) and by the homogenized model (black curves). The homogenized solution is given by equation (8) along with equations (15)–(17). The color version of this figure is available only in the electronic edition.

Finite-size effect, comparison with Kham *et al.* (2006).

The homogenized (or effective) model assumes a city and a sedimentary layer of infinite extent. It is therefore important to assess

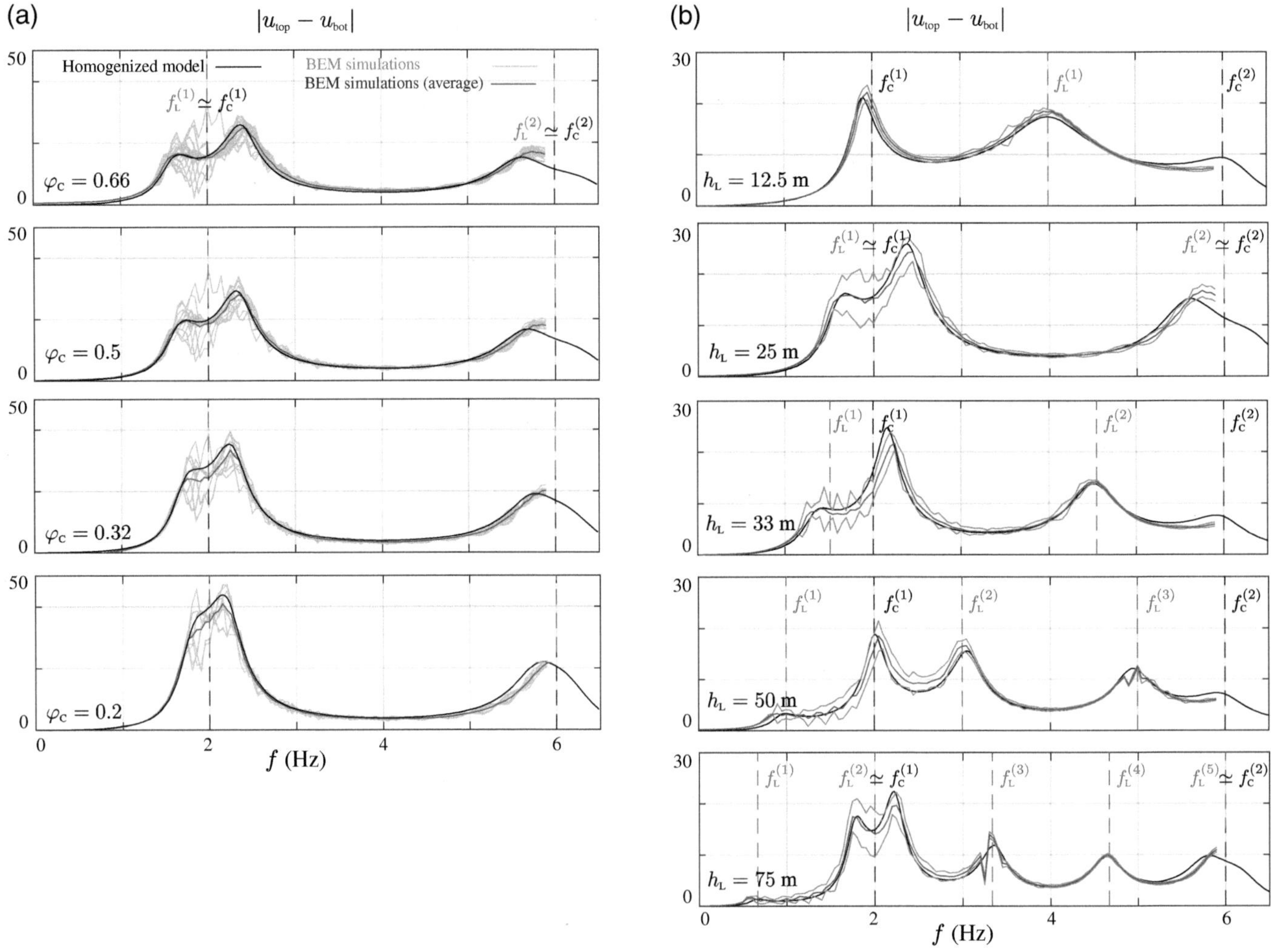

Figure 8. Finite-size effects—comparison with Kham *et al.* (2006). Variations of $|u_{\text{top}} - u_{\text{bot}}|$ as a function of frequency: (a) for varying urban density φ_C with fixed layer thickness $h_L = 25$ m; (b) for varying h_L for fixed urban density $\varphi_C = 0.66$. Data from Kham *et al.* (2006), computed at each building within a city of finite extent (light gray lines, boundary-element method [BEM] simulations), and their mean values (blue lines), are compared to our homogenized result from equation (17) (black lines). The vertical black-dashed (respectively red) lines indicate the resonance frequencies $f_C^{(n)}$, $n = 1,2$ from equation (19) (respectively $f_L^{(n)}$, $n = 1,\cdots,5$, from equation (20). The color version of this figure is available only in the electronic edition.

how closely the conclusions drawn from this idealized setting compare to a more realistic, finite-size configuration. To this end, we compare our model with the simulations computed by the BEM in Kham *et al.* (2006), which were conducted for a finite-size city, as illustrated in Figure 1. In that reference, the site and city response were numerically characterized in the frequency domain. Specifically, the displacements u_{bot} and u_{top} were computed at all points located at middistance between adjacent buildings, leading to a total of $\mathcal{N}$ measurements. In Figure 8, these measurements are shown as gray lines, with their averages represented by blue lines. Using the homogenized model, we predicted the same quantities based on equation (17), and these predictions are shown as black curves in the graphs displayed in Figure 8. It is noted that the homogenized model is expected to match the average response (blue lines) but does not capture the variability between individual buildings, particularly at the edges of the city. Compared to these average responses, a very good agreement is observed between the BEM simulations and the homogenized model, indicating that finite-size effects—whether due to the city or the sedimentary layer—are negligible in the city center. With this validation established, we can proceed to more detailed analysis of the city's influence on ground motion. We emphasize, however, that the comparison presented here focuses on the regular city configuration of Kham *et al.* (2006). For finite-size cities with irregular buildings, deviations from the purely periodic homogenized predictions may arise. Extensions of the model to such irregular city configurations are possible and are discussed in the conclusions; these extensions would allow one to distinguish the average response of the city, as captured here with the periodic homogenization, from highly local variations due to heterogeneities between buildings.

Coupling strength and dissipated energy. In the remainder of this section, we examine the parameters influencing the interaction between the city and the ground. According to equation (16), this interaction is encapsulated in the parameter $\hat{C}$. To begin, from equation (12), we can consider $\alpha_L \simeq k_L$ due to the strong velocity contrast between the layer and the bedrock ($c_L/c_B = 0.2$). The most significant parameter governing the interaction is thus the frequency, through variations in ($k_L h_L$,$k_C h_C$), particularly their proximity to resonances. The admittance ratios also play a role, depending on the city density φ_C and the wave incidence angle θ:

$$\frac{Y_C}{Y_L} \simeq \sqrt{\frac{\rho_C \mu_C}{\rho_L \mu_L}} \varphi_C \simeq 0.16\varphi_C, \quad \frac{Y_L}{Y_B} \simeq \sqrt{\frac{\rho_L \mu_L}{\rho_B \mu_B}} \frac{1}{\cos\theta} \simeq \frac{0.18}{\cos\theta}. \tag{21}$$

These ratios remain low except near grazing incidence angles, which we will specifically address later on. For $\theta = 0$, without the sedimentary layer (see Fig. 6a), $|\hat{C}|$ does not exceed 0.2. With the layer present, it reaches values close to 5. However, the highest values do not correspond to the strongest interactions, especially for the dissipated energy, which reaches 100% ($\mathcal{E}_d = 1$) at critical coupling when $\hat{C} = \mathrm{i}$ producing $r = 0$ in equation (16). The amplitudes of (u_{top},u_{bot}) align roughly with high $\mathcal{E}_d$ values, with differences seen in Figure 6. More specifically, the following trends can be identified for (u_{bot},u_{top}):

- Far from the resonances of the city and the sedimentary layer, waves are primarily reflected at the interface at $z = -h_L$ (with $r \simeq 1$). In this regime, both the layer and the city behave as passive structures, resulting in $u_{bot} \simeq u_{top} \simeq 2$. This behavior is particularly evident at low frequencies.
- At the city's resonances, u_{bot} decreases only slightly, whereas u_{top} increases significantly according to

$$u_{bot} \simeq \frac{2}{1 + \frac{Y_C}{Y_B} Q_C} \simeq 2, \quad u_{top} \simeq \frac{2Q_C}{1 + \frac{Y_C}{Y_B} Q_C} \simeq 20, \tag{22}$$

  at the fundamental frequency (the subsequent resonances $f_C^{(n)}$ produce lower maxima, with $u_{top} \simeq Q_C u_{bot}/(2n-1)$).
- At the sedimentary layer's resonance, the layer enforces a minimum displacement at $z = -h_L$ and a maximum displacement at $z = 0$, leading to

$$u_{bot} \simeq u_{top} \simeq \frac{2Q_L}{1 + \frac{Y_L}{Y_B} Q_L} \simeq 10. \tag{23}$$

- When the resonances of the sedimentary layer and the city coincide, the two effects compete, resulting in an avoided crossing. In particular, the city tends to decrease u_{bot}, whereas the sedimentary layer tends to increase it. This competition leads to a splitting of the maxima of u_{bot}, which shift to frequencies on either side of $f_C^{(1)} = f_L^{(1)} = c_C/4h_C$, following:

$$f^{\pm} = \frac{c_C}{4h_C}\left(1 \pm \frac{2}{\pi}\sqrt{\frac{Y_C}{Y_L}}\right), \tag{24}$$

  and leaves a local minimum of u_{bot}

$$|u_{bot}| \simeq \frac{2}{\frac{Y_L}{Y_B} + \frac{Y_C}{Y_L} Q_C} \simeq 2. \tag{25}$$

These estimates align well with the results shown in Figures 9 and 10, in which we revisit the data from Figure 8b, explicitly distinguishing between u_{bot} and u_{top}. The case $h_L = 2$ m has been added, in which only the city resonances are visible.

From Figure 10, we observe that, at the resonances, a larger proportion of the incident energy is dissipated. This is evident at the resonances of the sedimentary layer alone and, in the presence of the city, at frequencies of 2 and 6 Hz. It is at these frequencies that $|u_{top}|$ reaches its maximum; however, it is worth noting that although the displacement amplitudes are high at the resonances, they are actually significantly reduced due to the dissipation. This effect is well known and is the cause of the overestimation of u_{bot} (and consequently u_{top}) in two-step models, in which u_{bot} is computed while neglecting the presence of the city, hence the dissipation it induces.

The numerical estimates in equations (22)–(25) have been given for $\varphi_C = 0.5$ and $\theta = 0$. In the following, we inspect how these values change with φ_C and θ, and in the case of vanishing $\cos\theta$, how the trends can be modified.

Influence of the urban density. It was noticed in Kham *et al.* (2006) that decreasing the urban density φ_C results in an increase in $|u_{top} - u_{bot}|$, a phenomenon accurately reproduced by our model in Figure 8a. This observation is consistent with previous studies on the effect of the density in arrays of resonators: sparse arrays exhibit higher resonance quality factors, closer to that of a single resonator (Maurel *et al.*, 2019). In the present case, with $Y_C \propto \varphi_C$ from equation (21), the influence of φ_C is relatively limited at the city resonances resulting in $|u_{top}| \in (15,20)$ from equation (22), and it has no impact at the sedimentary layer resonances, according to equation (23). However, when the city and sedimentary layer resonances coincide, an increase in φ_C amplifies the city's effect in competition with the sedimentary layer, as illustrated in Figure 11 for $h_L = 25$ m and $h_C = 30$ m. Increasing $\varphi_C \in (0,1)$ produces a decrease in the dip of $|u_{bot}|$ at 2 Hz between 10 and 1 according to equation (25) (for $\theta = 0$), with $|u_{top}| = Q_C|u_{bot}|$, pushing the frequencies of larger displacement farther away from the resonance frequency and thus broadening the avoided crossing region, in agreement with equation (24). Notably, in this region, although the amplitudes, particularly u_{top}, are significantly reduced as the urban density increases, the interaction between the sedimentary layer and the city leads to strong energy dissipation, reaching up to 100%. In comparison, the sedimentary layer alone (gray lines) dissipates no more than 50% of the incident energy.

Note that, in the results presented in Figure 11, the MM simulations were performed by varying the building width w_C while keeping a constant spacing d, with $\varphi_C = w_C/d$. In

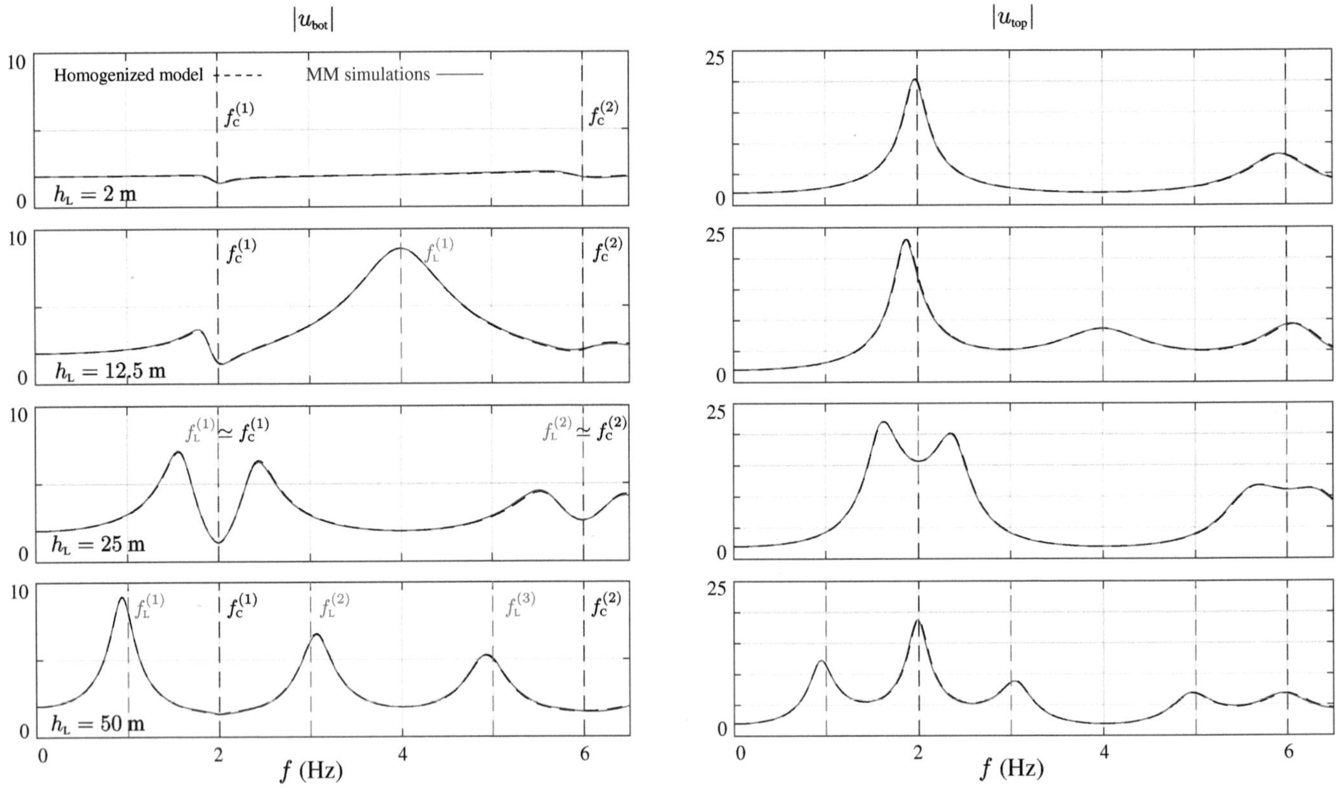

Figure 9. Variations of $|u_{bot}|$ (left) and $|u_{top}|$ (right) as a function of frequency, as in Figure 8b for $h_C = 30$ m. The case $h_L = 2$ m has been added, where only the city resonances are visible, at $f_C^{(1)} = 2$ Hz and $f_C^{(2)} = 6$ Hz (vertical black-dashed lines). The observations are consistent with the theoretical predictions: equation (22) at the city resonances and equation (23) at the sedimentary layer resonances $f_L^{(n)}$, $n = 1,2,3$ (vertical red-dashed lines). The color version of this figure is available only in the electronic edition.

Kham *et al.* (2006), w_C is kept constant while the spacing $d = 500/\mathcal{N}$ varies with $\mathcal{N}$, the number of buildings. This procedure leads to large interbuilding distances, resulting in the appearance of higher-order interference modes beyond the fundamental mode considered in the homogenized model, which constitutes a limitation of our approach.

Influence of the wave incidence and guided waves. It is often said that the interaction between the city and the soil is maximal at normal incidence, which is consistent with our model: from equation (21), increasing θ reduces $Y_B \propto \cos\theta$ and thus decreases the amplitudes of u_{bot} and u_{top} at the resonances, in accordance with equations (22) and (23), while leaving unchanged the frequency shift at the coincidence of the city and layer resonances, as given by equation (24). This is illustrated in Figure 12, where the variations of u_{bot} and u_{top} are presented for $\theta = 0°$ and 50°.

We also report these variations for larger angles, $\theta = 85°$ and 89°, revealing a distinct change in behavior, notably the disappearance of the avoided crossing and the appearance of local maxima at 4 Hz. This change is particularly evident when examining the dissipated energy $\mathcal{E}_d$, shown in Figure 12a. Because θ increases, the maxima of $\mathcal{E}_d$ shift from the frequencies satisfying $k_L h_L = \pi/2$ to those satisfying $k_L h_L = \pi$ (0 and 4 Hz), and this trend is independent of the presence or absence of the city. Again, this result is consistent with the critical coupling condition in equation (16). This shift occurs progressively for angles greater than 80° and because it only affects the resonance frequencies of the sedimentary layer, the city resonances remain at 2 and 6 Hz.

This property is of particular interest as it is related to the specificity of the grazing angle and its connection to guided waves. Indeed, with $\beta = k_B$ in equation (13), this grazing incidence corresponds to a wave propagating along x, living at the boundary between the radiative region of bulk waves (α_B real) and the region of Love-type waves (α_B imaginary). The ability of the model to describe guided wave behavior has been demonstrated in, for example, Maurel *et al.* (2018) and Pham *et al.* (2020). Therefore, it is unsurprising that we observe here a link with these guided waves.

SITE–FOUNDATION–CITY INTERACTION

Homogenized scattering problems

The scattering problems are formulated using equation (6) when $h_F \leq h_L$, and equation (7) when $h_F \geq h_L$. Using equation (4), and the same notations as in equations (8) and (9), the propagation in a region XF, alternating foundations (F) with filling fraction φ_F and material X, where X = L (the sedimentary material) or X = B (the bedrock), is governed by

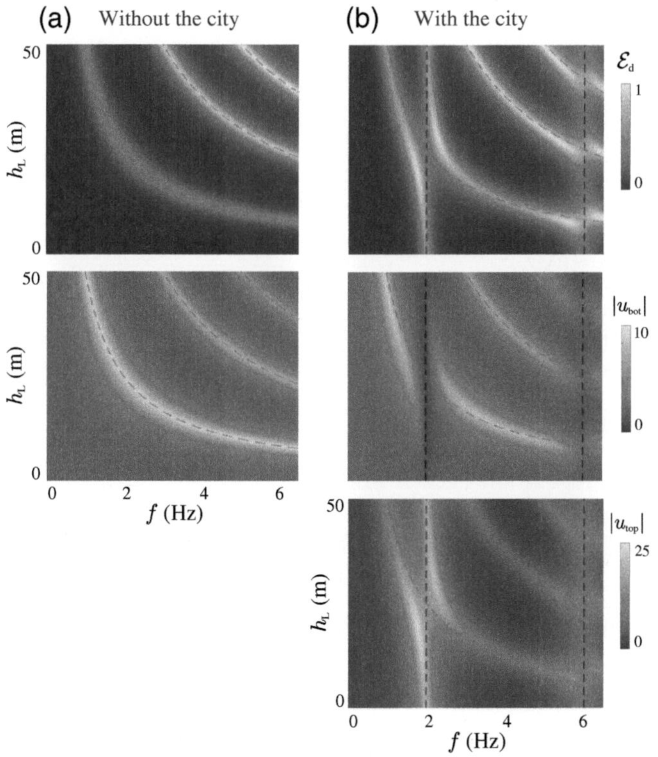

Figure 10. Variations of ($\mathcal{E}_d$,$|u_{bot}|$) in the absence of the city (a) and of ($\mathcal{E}_d$,$|u_{bot}|$,$|u_{top}|$) with a city (b) considering $h_C = 30$ m. The vertical black-dashed lines indicate the resonance frequencies $f_C^{(n)}$, $n = 1,2$ of the city (equation 19), and the red-dashed lines the resonance frequencies $f_L^{(n)}$, $n = 1,2,3$ of the sedimentary layer (equation 20). The color version of this figure is available only in the electronic edition.

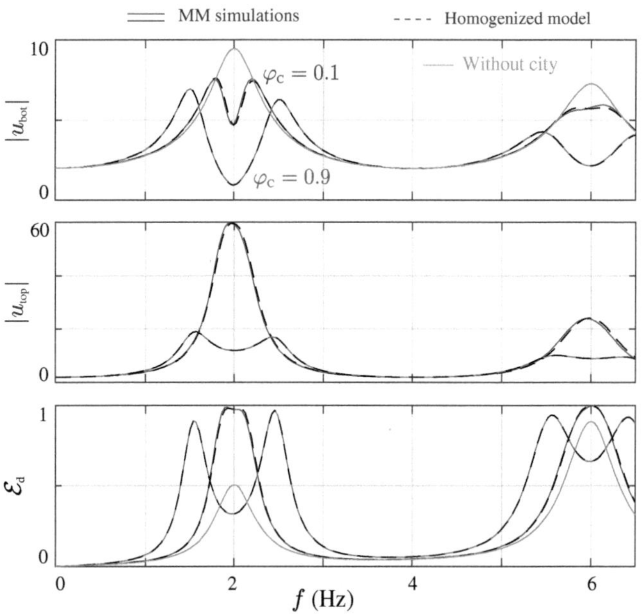

Figure 11. Influence of the urban density φ_C on the displacement amplitudes u_{bot} and u_{top} and on the dissipated energy $\mathcal{E}_d$, from MM simulations, for $\varphi_C = 0.1$ (blue line) and 0.9 (red line) and $h_L = 25$ m, $h_C = 30$ m. The black-dotted lines show the homogenized results, and for comparison, gray lines show the results in the absence of the city. The color version of this figure is available only in the electronic edition.

$$\sigma' + (\rho_{XF}\omega^2 - \hat{\mu}_{XF}\beta^2)u = 0, \quad \sigma = \mu_{XF}u', \quad \text{in XF region,} \tag{26}$$

with

$$\rho_{XF} = \varphi_F\rho_F + (1-\varphi_F)\rho_X, \quad \hat{\mu}_{XF} = \left(\frac{\varphi_F}{\mu_F} + \frac{1-\varphi_F}{\mu_X}\right)^{-1},$$
$$\mu_{XF} = \varphi_F\mu_F + (1-\varphi_F)\mu_X. \tag{27}$$

The characteristic admittance is defined as

$$Y_{XF} = \mathrm{i}\mu_{XF}\alpha_{XF}, \tag{28}$$

with $\alpha_{XF} = \sqrt{k_{XF}^2 - \frac{\hat{\mu}_{XF}}{\mu_{XF}}\beta^2}$ and $k_{XF} = \omega\sqrt{\rho_{XF}/\mu_{XF}}$.

Foundations partially embedded in the sedimentary layer ($h_F \le h_L$). In this case, following the same procedure as for equation (15), and using equation (6) together with equations (8), (9), and (26) for X = L, the displacement field in regions alternating layers B, L, LF, and C is obtained as

$$u(z) = \begin{cases} e^{i\alpha_B(z+h_L)} + re^{-i\alpha_B(z+h_L)}, & z \in (-\infty, -h_L), \\ (1+r)G_L(z), & z \in (-h_L, -h_F), \\ (1+r)G_L(-h_F)G_{LF}(z), & z \in (-h_F, 0), \\ (1+r)G_L(-h_F)G_{LF}(0)G_C(z), & z \in (0, h_C), \end{cases} \tag{29}$$

in which, denoting $\tilde{h}_L = (h_L - h_F)$,

$$G_L(z) = \frac{\cos\alpha_L(z+h_F) + \tilde{C}\sin\alpha_L(z+h_F)}{\cos\alpha_L\tilde{h}_L - \tilde{C}\sin\alpha_L\tilde{h}_L},$$
$$G_{LF}(z) = \frac{\cos\alpha_{LF}z + C\sin\alpha_{LF}z}{\cos\alpha_{LF}h_F - C\sin\alpha_{LF}h_F},$$
$$G_C(z) = \frac{\cos k_C(z-h_C)}{\cos k_C h_C},$$

and in which now

$$C = \mathrm{i}\frac{Y(0)}{Y_{LF}} = \frac{\varphi_C}{\cos\theta}\sqrt{\frac{\mu_C\rho_C}{\mu_{LF}\rho_{LF}}}\tan k_C h_C, \tag{30}$$

represents the coupling between the city and the composite soil (foundations embedded in the sedimentary layer), and

$$\tilde{C} = \mathrm{i}\frac{Y(-h_F)}{Y_L} = \frac{Y_{LF}}{Y_L}\,\frac{\tan\alpha_{LF}h_F + C}{1 - C\tan\alpha_{LF}h_F},$$

represents the coupling term between the combined system (city + composite soil) and the foundation-free part of the sedimentary layer (of reduced thickness $\tilde{h}_L$). Finally,

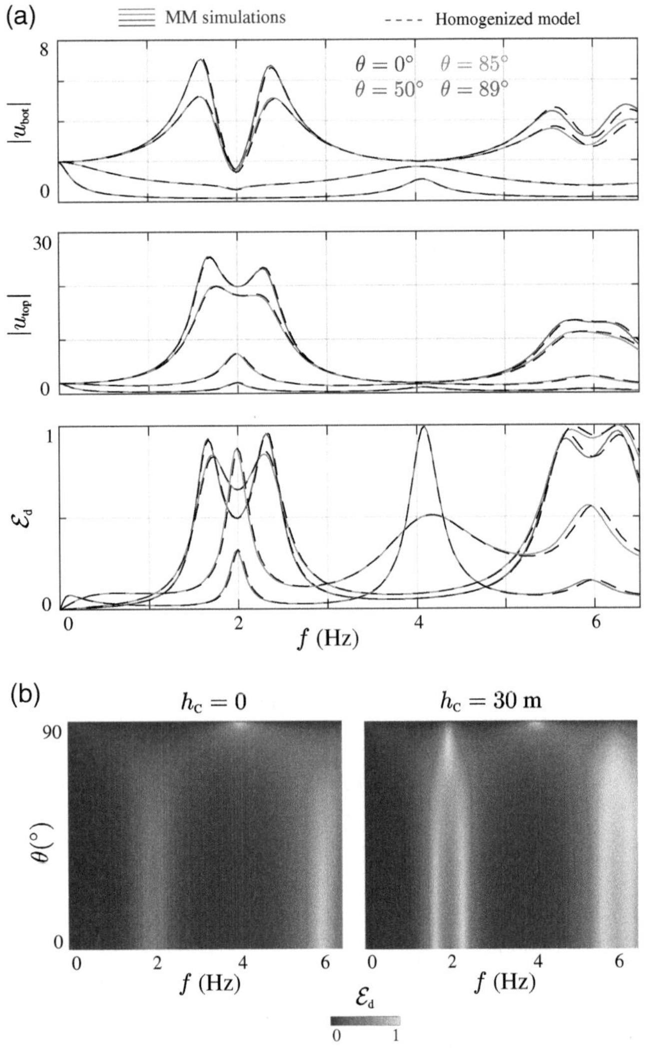

Figure 12. (a) Influence of the wave incidence θ on the displacement amplitudes of $(u_{\mathrm{bot}},u_{\mathrm{top}})$ and dissipated energy $\mathcal{E}_{\mathrm{d}}$ against frequency, for $\varphi_{\mathrm{C}} = 0.5$, $h_{\mathrm{C}} = 30$ m, and $h_{\mathrm{L}} = 25$ m. (b) Variations of $\mathcal{E}_{\mathrm{d}}$ in the plane (f,θ) for $h_{\mathrm{L}} = 25$ m and $h_{\mathrm{C}} = 0$ (left) and $h_{\mathrm{C}} = 30$ m (right). The color version of this figure is available only in the electronic edition.

$$r = \frac{1+\mathrm{i}\hat{C}}{1-\mathrm{i}\hat{C}}, \qquad \hat{C} = \frac{\mathrm{i}Y(-h_{\mathrm{L}})}{Y_{\mathrm{B}}} = \frac{Y_{\mathrm{L}}}{Y_{\mathrm{B}}}\frac{\tan\alpha_{\mathrm{L}}\tilde{h}_{\mathrm{L}} + \tilde{C}}{1-\tilde{C}\tan\alpha_{\mathrm{L}}\tilde{h}_{\mathrm{L}}}. \tag{31}$$

Foundations embedded in the bedrock ($h_{\mathrm{F}} \geq h_{\mathrm{L}}$). For foundations embedded in the bedrock ($h_{\mathrm{F}} \geq h_{\mathrm{L}}$), we follow the same procedure, but using equation (7) instead of equation (6), and equation (26) for X = L and for X = B, we obtain

$$u(z) = \begin{cases} e^{i\alpha_{\mathrm{B}}(z+h_{\mathrm{F}})} + re^{-i\alpha_{\mathrm{B}}(z+h_{\mathrm{F}})}, & z \in (-\infty, -h_{\mathrm{F}}), \\ (1+r)G_{\mathrm{BF}}(z), & z \in (-h_{\mathrm{F}}, -h_{\mathrm{L}}), \\ (1+r)G_{\mathrm{BF}}(-h_{\mathrm{L}})G_{\mathrm{LF}}(z), & z \in (-h_{\mathrm{L}},0), \\ (1+r)G_{\mathrm{BF}}(-h_{\mathrm{L}})G_{\mathrm{LF}}(0)G_{\mathrm{C}}(z), & z \in (0,h_{\mathrm{C}}), \end{cases} \tag{32}$$

with

$$G_{\mathrm{BF}}(z) = \frac{\cos\alpha_{\mathrm{BF}}(z+h_{\mathrm{L}}) + \tilde{C}\sin\alpha_{\mathrm{BF}}(z+h_{\mathrm{L}})}{\cos\alpha_{\mathrm{BF}}\tilde{h}_{\mathrm{B}} - \tilde{C}\sin\alpha_{\mathrm{BF}}\tilde{h}_{\mathrm{B}}},$$

$$G_{\mathrm{LF}}(z) = \frac{\cos\alpha_{\mathrm{LF}}z + C\sin\alpha_{\mathrm{LF}}z}{\cos\alpha_{\mathrm{LF}}h_{\mathrm{L}} - C\sin\alpha_{\mathrm{LF}}h_{\mathrm{L}}},$$

$$G_{\mathrm{C}}(z) = \frac{\cos k_{\mathrm{C}}(z-h_{\mathrm{C}})}{\cos k_{\mathrm{C}}h_{\mathrm{C}}},$$

in which C is the same as in equation (30), $\tilde{h}_{\mathrm{B}} = (h_{\mathrm{F}} - h_{\mathrm{L}})$ and

$$\tilde{C} = \mathrm{i}\frac{Y(-h_{\mathrm{L}})}{Y_{\mathrm{BF}}} = \frac{Y_{\mathrm{LF}}}{Y_{\mathrm{BF}}}\frac{\tan\alpha_{\mathrm{LF}}h_{\mathrm{L}} + C}{1 - C\tan\alpha_{\mathrm{LF}}h_{\mathrm{L}}},$$

represents the coupling between the combined system (city + composite soil) and the portion of the bedrock traversed by the foundations over a depth $\tilde{h}_{\mathrm{B}}$. Finally,

$$r = \frac{1+\mathrm{i}\hat{C}}{1-\mathrm{i}\hat{C}}, \qquad \hat{C} = \frac{\mathrm{i}Y(-h_{\mathrm{F}})}{Y_{\mathrm{B}}} = \frac{Y_{\mathrm{BF}}}{Y_{\mathrm{B}}}\frac{\tan\alpha_{\mathrm{BF}}\tilde{h}_{\mathrm{B}} + \tilde{C}}{1-\tilde{C}\tan\alpha_{\mathrm{BF}}\tilde{h}_{\mathrm{B}}}. \tag{33}$$

Limiting case $h_{\mathrm{F}} = h_{\mathrm{L}}$. This case corresponds to a rigidified layer. We obtain the solution similar to equations (15) and (16) as limiting cases of equation (29) disregarding G_{L} in equation (29) and G_{BF} in equation (32). This yields

$$u(z) = \begin{cases} e^{i\alpha_{\mathrm{B}}(z+h_{\mathrm{L}})} + re^{-i\alpha_{\mathrm{B}}(z+h_{\mathrm{L}})}, & z \in (-\infty, -h_{\mathrm{L}}), \\ (1+r)G_{\mathrm{LF}}(z), & z \in (-h_{\mathrm{L}},0), \\ (1+r)G_{\mathrm{LF}}(0)G_{\mathrm{C}}(z), & z \in (0,h_{\mathrm{C}}), \end{cases}$$

in which

$$G_{\mathrm{LF}}(z) = \frac{\cos\alpha_{\mathrm{LF}}z + C\sin\alpha_{\mathrm{LF}}z}{\cos\alpha_{\mathrm{LF}}h_{\mathrm{F}} - C\sin\alpha_{\mathrm{LF}}h_{\mathrm{F}}}, \qquad G_{\mathrm{C}}(z) = \frac{\cos k_{\mathrm{C}}(z-h_{\mathrm{C}})}{\cos k_{\mathrm{C}}h_{\mathrm{C}}},$$

with C in equation (30), and

$$r = \frac{1+\mathrm{i}\hat{C}}{1-\mathrm{i}\hat{C}}, \qquad \hat{C} = \frac{Y_{\mathrm{LF}}}{Y_{\mathrm{B}}}\frac{\tan\alpha_{\mathrm{LF}}h_{\mathrm{L}} + C}{1 - C\tan\alpha_{\mathrm{LF}}h_{\mathrm{L}}},$$

which coincides with equation (16) for a stiffened layer.

Verification and assessment of SFCI

With the values of the $(\rho_{\mathrm{F}},\mu_{\mathrm{F}})$ in Table 1, the effective material properties of the composite layers LF and BF are collected in Table 2. We considered six piles per building, each of width 0.5 m (hence $\varphi_{\mathrm{F}} = 0.15$ in equation 27 for both X = L and X = B). As expected, the composite layer LF exhibits strong anisotropy, owing to the large contrast in shear moduli between the sedimentary layer and the foundations. Its stiffness along the z-direction is significantly enhanced, approaching that of the bedrock.

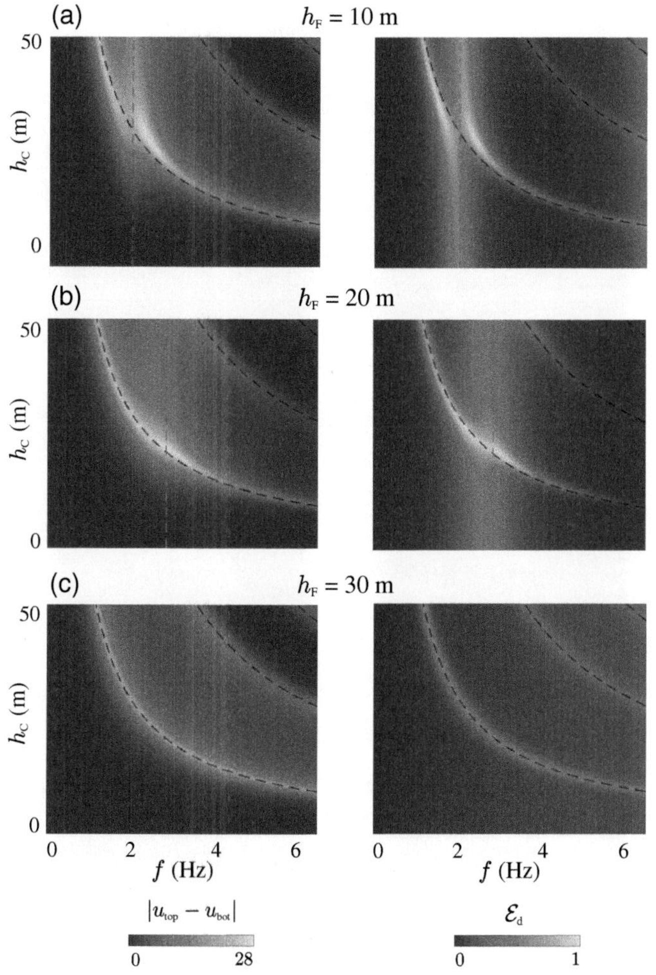

Figure 13. Variations of the relative displacement $|u_{top} - u_{bot}|$ within the buildings (left), and of the energy $\mathcal{E}_d$ dissipated in the sedimentary layer and the city (right), as functions of building height h_C and frequency f. (a) No sedimentary layer ($h_L = 0$). (b) Sedimentary layer of thickness with ($h_L = 25$ m), with foundations partially embedded in the layer ($h_F = 20$ m). (c) Same sedimentary layer ($h_L = 25$ m), with foundations fully crossing the layer and anchored in the bedrock ($h_F = 30$ m). Building width is $w_C = 10$ m, with period $d = 20$ m, corresponding to a city density $\varphi_C = w_C/d = 0.5$. The color version of this figure is available only in the electronic edition.

To evaluate the effect of the foundations, Figure 13 shows the variations of $|u_{top} - u_{bot}|$ and of the dissipated energy $\mathcal{E}_d$, computed numerically with the MM method, as functions of f and h_C. This corresponds to the same representation as in Figure 6 (without foundations). We considered a city built over a sedimentary layer of thickness $h_L = 25$ m, with foundations (1) partially embedded in the sedimentary layer (panels a and b, with $h_F = 10$ and 20 m, respectively), and (2) fully crossing the sedimentary layer and anchored in the bedrock (panel c, with $h_F = 30$ m). Compared to the case without foundations (see Fig. 6b), and as expected, stiffening the sedimentary layer —either partially or entirely—shifts its resonance frequencies to higher values, ultimately suppressing the amplification

TABLE 2
Effective Material Parameters of the Composite Layer Made of the Foundations Embedded in the Sedimentary Layer (LF) or Anchored in the Bedrock (BF)

LF	$\mu_{LF} = 2311$	$\hat{\mu}_{LF} = 84.7$	$\rho_{LF} = 1905$	$Q_{LF} = 19.3$
BF	$\mu_{BF} = 3950$	$\hat{\mu}_{BF} = 2300$	$\rho_{BF} = 2075$	$Q_{BF} = 38$

effects of the sedimentary layer. More specifically, for shallow foundations ($h_F < h_L$), the resonance frequencies of the sedimentary layer shift to higher values, as predicted by

$$\tan k_{LF} h_F \tan k_L \tilde{h}_L = \frac{Y_L}{Y_{LF}} = \sqrt{\frac{\rho_L \mu_L}{\rho_{LF} \mu_{LF}}} \simeq 0.17, \qquad (34)$$

in which $\tilde{h}_L = (h_L - h_F)$ denotes the height of the sedimentary portion intersected by the foundations. This condition produces strong coupling $\hat{C}$ in equation (31). For deep foundations ($h_F > h_L$), no resonances occur in the sedimentary layer and bedrock region traversed by the foundations because the corresponding frequencies, given by

$$\tan k_{LF} h_L \tan k_{BF} \tilde{h}_B = \frac{Y_{BF}}{Y_{LF}} = \sqrt{\frac{\rho_{BF} \mu_{BF}}{\rho_{LF} \mu_{LF}}} \simeq 1.36, \qquad (35)$$

fall outside the considered range $f \in (0,6.5)$ Hz. As previously, the condition equation (35) produces a large coupling $\hat{C}$ in equation (31), with $\tilde{h}_B = (h_F - h_L)$ the thickness of the bedrock penetrated by the foundations.

Figure 14a complements this analysis by displaying the displacement amplitudes (u_{bot},u_{top}) as functions of frequency f and foundation depth h_F for building heights $h_C = 15$, 30, and 50 m, with the sedimentary layer fixed at $h_L = 25$ m. As consistently observed throughout this study, city resonances reduce displacements $|u_{bot}|$ at the building base while amplifying those at the top $|u_{bot}|$. In contrast, sedimentary layer resonances amplify $|u_{bot}|$, with $|u_{top}| \simeq |u_{bot}|$ because the buildings essentially follow the ground motion. These trends remain visible even in the presence of foundations, as illustrated in panel (a) for $h_C = 15$ m, where the city resonance, at 4 Hz, is distinct from the sedimentary layer resonances (without foundations, $h_F = 0$) at 2 and 6 Hz. When foundations are present, however, the sedimentary layer resonance predicted by equation (34) shifts to higher values: from $f^{(1)} = c_L/(4h_L) = 2$ Hz at $h_F = 0$ to $f^{(1)} = c_{LF}/(4h_L) = 11$ Hz at $h_F = h_L = 25$ m (see red-dashed line in Fig. 14). For deep foundations, no resonances occur within the sedimentary layer and bedrock portion penetrated by the foundations. Consequently, the displacement amplitudes $|u_{bot}|$ and $|u_{top}|$ become essentially independent of h_F, behaving as if the city were resting on rigid bedrock. In particular, we note the disappearance of avoiding crossings for $h_C = 30$ m.

These trends remain valid for different urban densities φ_C, as illustrated in Figure 14b. The key effect is the frequency shift of sedimentary-layer resonances, caused by the stiffening

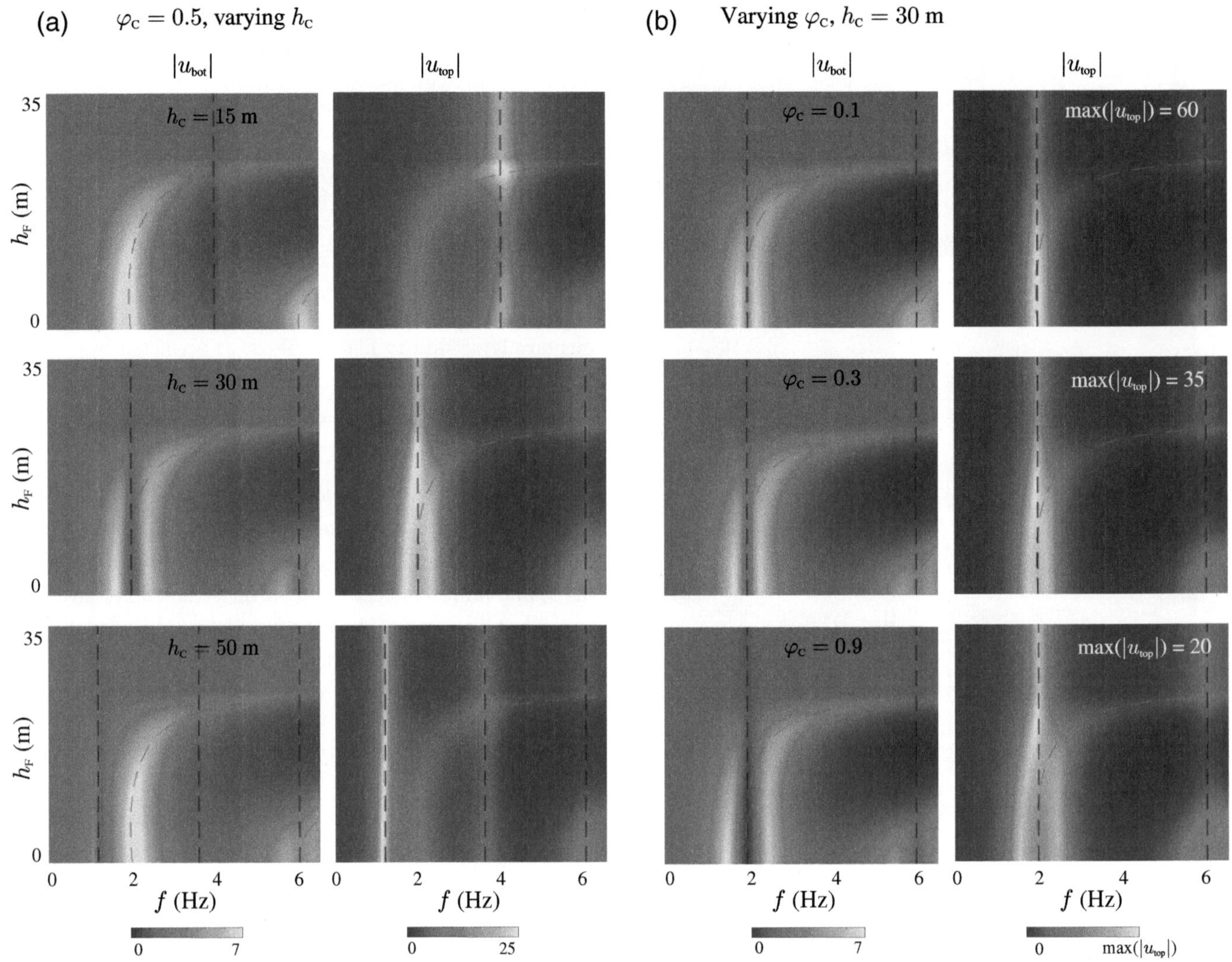

Figure 14. (a) Variations of $|u_{\text{bot}}|$ (left) and $|u_{\text{top}}|$ (right) as functions of frequency f and foundation depth h_F (with $\varphi_F = 0.15$), for different building heights h_C (with $\varphi_C = 0.5$). (b) Variations of $|u_{\text{bot}}|$ (left) and $|u_{\text{top}}|$ (right) as functions of frequency f and foundation depth h_F, for different urban densities φ_C (with $h_C = 30$ m). In (a,b) the vertical black-dashed lines indicate $f_C^{(n)}$, $n = 1,2,3$, the resonance frequencies of the fixed-base building blocks, from equation (19), and the red-dashed lines indicate the sedimentary-layer resonance predicted by equation (34) for $h_L = 25$ m. The color version of this figure is available only in the electronic edition.

induced by the foundations, which reduces or even eliminates amplification effects. As a consequence, when φ_C decreases, the peak displacement $|u_{\text{top}}|$ at the city resonance is significantly reduced: from 60 (for $\varphi_C = 0.1$) and 35 (for $\varphi_C = 0.3$) without foundations ($h_F = 0$), down to approximately 20 for deep foundations ($h_F > h_L$ m).

The results shown in Figures 13 and 14 are well reproduced by our analytical solutions equations (29)–(31) for $h_F \le h_L$ and equations (32) and (33) for $h_F \ge h_L$, with overall good agreement (within 2%–5%). However, a peak in the relative error—up to 14%—is observed for displacement amplitudes when h_F is close to h_L, partly due to modeling errors and partly to pronounced boundary layer effects.

At this stage, we make a short aside and point out that we are here using the resonance conditions equations (34) and (35) for a two-layer system. Although this relation was not written explicitly, it also applies to the bilayer system formed by the city and the sedimentary layer. In this case, the resonance condition reads:

$$\tan(k_C h_C)\tan(k_L h_L) = \frac{Y_L}{Y_C} = \sqrt{\frac{\rho_L \mu_L}{\rho_C \mu_C}} \simeq 13, \qquad (36)$$

which corresponds to a strong coupling $\hat{C}$ in equation (16). The relatively high value ratio Y_L/Y_C naturally implies that the resonance conditions of the two layers appear almost decoupled: $\tan(k_C h_C) = \infty$, corresponding to the fixed-based resonances of the city (equation 19), and $\tan(k_L h_L) = \infty$, corresponding to the resonance frequencies of the isolated sedimentary layer (equation 20). These are precisely the reference resonances used throughout the article, which thus naturally emerge from the high admittance contrast between the city and the sedimentary layer. In particular, at resonance coincidence ($k_C h_C = k_L h_L$), equation (36) provides the frequency width of the avoided

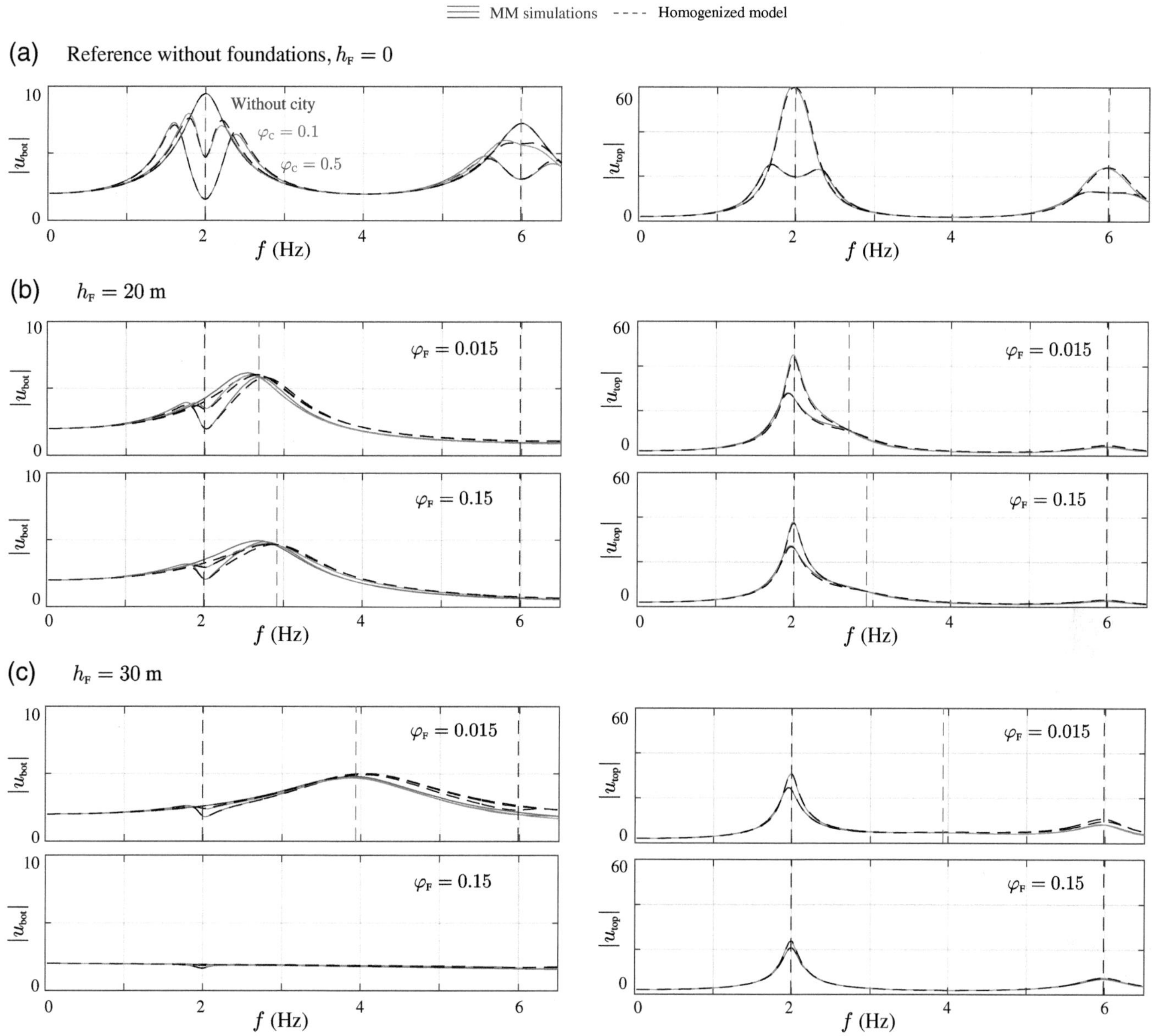

Figure 15. Effect of foundation density—Displacement amplitudes $|u_{bot}|$ (left panels) and $|u_{top}|$ (right panels) as functions of frequency. (a) Reference without foundations and (b,c) with foundations of depth $h_F = 20$ m and $h_F = 30$ m, respectively. MM simulations results for $h_C = 0$ (blue lines) and for $h_C = 30$ m (green lines for $\varphi_C = 0.1$ and red lines for $\varphi_C = 0.5$). In (b,c), we report the results for foundation densities $\varphi_F = 0.015$ and $\varphi_F = 0.15$, showing that low foundation density already significantly reduces resonance amplification. The color version of this figure is available only in the electronic edition.

crossing, with $\tan(k_C h_C) = \pm\sqrt{Y_L/Y_C}$, leading directly to the estimate given in equation (24).

In 2D geometry, foundation density can easily reach relatively high values (here, 15%, i.e., $\varphi_F = 0.15$), which substantially increases the stiffness of the sedimentary layer, bringing its effective properties close to those of the bedrock. Remarkably, however, such strong stiffening is not required to noticeably mitigate resonance effects. This is illustrated in Figure 15, which compares the frequency dependence of $|u_{bot}|$ and $|u_{top}|$ for two densities: $\varphi_F = 0.15$ (as in Fig. 14) and $\varphi_F = 0.015$, closer to values expected in three dimensions. The MM simulation results (colored curves) are compared with model predictions (black-dashed curves) using equations (29)–(31) and equations (32) and (33). The sedimentary layer has a depth of $h_L = 25$ m in all cases. Panel (a) recalls the reference case without foundations ($h_F = 0$): in the absence of buildings, layer resonances appear at 2 and 6 Hz. With buildings of height $h_C = 30$ m and urban density $\varphi_C = 0.1$ and 0.5, resonances for which coincide with those of the sedimentary layer, the avoided crossing is clearly visible, becoming more pronounced at higher density. Panels (b) and (c) show the influence of foundations for $h_F = 20$ m and $h_F = 30$ m, respectively. In both cases, results are shown for foundations densities $\varphi_F = 0.15$ and $\varphi_F = 0.015$. Despite the tenfold difference in density, the impact of foundations is qualitatively similar: in both cases, a strong reduction in $|u_{\mathrm{top}}|$ is observed. The only noticeable difference is that, for $\varphi_{\mathrm{F}} = 0.015$ and $h_{\mathrm{F}} = 30$ m, $|u_{\mathrm{bot}}|$ remains slightly affected by the resonance predicted by equation (35), close to $f^{(1)} = c_{\mathrm{LF}}/(4h_{\mathrm{L}}) = 4$ Hz, as $c_{\mathrm{LF}} = 400$ m/s in this case (compared to $c_{\mathrm{LF}} = 1100$ m/s for $\varphi_{\mathrm{F}} = 0.15$).

CONCLUDING REMARKS

In this work, we have investigated the ability of a homogenized model to reproduce the behavior of a set of buildings, or a city, within the framework of SCI with predictive accuracy comparable to that of direct numerical simulations. Reducing the city region to an effective homogeneous region simplifies the analysis, enabling clear identification of the physical parameters that govern the interaction. The coupling between the effective city region and the sedimentary layer mainly depends on two parameters: the admittance contrast and the existence of resonances of both layers within the considered frequency range. It also depends on the urban density and, to a lesser extent, on the incidence angle. We also investigated a homogenized model incorporating the presence of building foundations, which results in an additional effective layer to the problem and allows a straightforward assessment of SFCI. The main effect appears to be the stiffening of the homogenized layer.

Note that the model presented here, which simplifies a scattering problem, also simplifies guided wave propagation problems in a similar manner, as shown in Maurel *et al.* (2018) for two dimensions and Marigo *et al.* (2024) for three dimensions. In addition, homogenized models that account for more subtle structural effects of buildings are possible, as illustrated in Pham *et al.* (2020). Finally, the homogenization approach offers practical advantages for numerical implementation. Here, we focused on a scattering problem with an incident plane wave. For more general cases, the same analysis can be applied by "omitting" the city because its effect is captured by an effective boundary condition:

$$\Sigma_{yz}(x,0) = \varphi_{\mathrm{C}}\mu_{\mathrm{C}}k_{\mathrm{C}} \tan k_{\mathrm{C}}h_{\mathrm{C}}U(x,0),$$

which replaces the stress-free boundary condition for a free surface. This formulation allows the inclusion of the effects discussed earlier, for instance with characteristics φ_{C} or h_{C} varying as functions of x.

The configurations of this work are restricted to 2D geometries for an idealized city composed of a periodic array of identical buildings excited by plane *SH* waves in the context of linear elasticity. Extensions of this study to more realistic cases are possible, though they present different types of challenges and promises:

- 3D models already exist for buildings approximated as slender bodies, beams, or plates, involving flexural and compressional resonances (Marigo *et al.*, 2020, 2021). These models have been developed in the absence of a sedimentary layer, but accounting for the layer is evidently not a difficulty. Such models could be directly confronted with 3D simulations of building clusters, as proposed for instance in Isbiliroglu *et al.* (2014, 2015).
- Incorporating heterogeneities in building height, foundation depth, and local density is possible when considering a gradient of these quantities, see, for example, Pham *et al.* (2023), particularly for applications such as rainbow trapping with buildings of increasing height. Accounting for strong local heterogeneities, such as one or two buildings with characteristics that contrast sharply with their surroundings, remains to be addressed. In this respect, adaptations of the method presented here will have direct implications for realistic urban environments where variations in height and density are unavoidable. For such irregular configurations, deviations from the homogenized model used in this study are expected, but the approach nevertheless provides a robust baseline for quantifying the departure induced by these irregularities. In cities with buildings of varying heights and densities, the resulting effective layer obtained by homogenization would exhibit a spatially varying thickness, influence for which could be analyzed using approaches similar to those developed for sedimentary basins with variable depth (Semblat *et al.*, 2008).
- Considering finite-size effects remains an open question. Some studies have shown that it is possible to represent a finite-extent citylike region by considering its homogenized equivalent of the same extent; examples are reported in Maurel *et al.* (2018, 2024). Although this approach currently lacks theoretical justification, it would be interesting to systematically assess its validity.
- The polarization of the seismic wavefields is limited to antiplane *SH* waves. Various polarizations may be considered leading to more complex site–city and site–foundation–city effects including, for example, wave conversion, numerous critical angles, and multiple resonances. The link between multicomponent body waves and various types of surface waves with respect to SFCI should thus be considered in future works. In this regard, the normalized inner product method proposed by Meza-Fajardo *et al.* (2015) could help characterize the radiated wavefield by separating body- and surface-wave components, thereby improving the identification of the waves generated by buildings or basin edges.
- Another important limitation lies in the linear framework adopted throughout this study. Although linearity ensures analytical tractability and direct comparison with numerical reference models, it excludes important features such as soil and structural nonlinearities, which can significantly affect resonance amplitudes and energy dissipation during large seismic events. Therefore, the present analysis should be understood as a first-order benchmark, with nonlinear extensions representing a natural and necessary perspective for future research.

Despite these limitations and beyond the methodological perspectives, the present results provide qualitative insights for seismic design and analysis in urban environments. They highlight how collective effects related to buildings and foundations—such as density, height, foundation depth, or building characteristics—govern resonance shifts and amplification levels, thereby clarifying the key parameters that may control urban seismic response. Although not directly applicable as a design tool due to the simplifying assumptions adopted here, these results can nevertheless guide future investigations and help identify critical scenarios to be addressed in more detailed engineering models.

DATA AND RESOURCES

There are no new data or resources to report for this article. All results are based on numerical simulations performed with in-house codes.

DECLARATION OF COMPETING INTERESTS

The authors acknowledge that there are no conflicts of interest recorded.

ACKNOWLEDGMENTS

K. P. acknowledges the support of the French Agence Nationale de la Recherche (ANR) under Grant ANR-19-CE08-0006 MetaReso. The authors also thank the anonymous reviewers for their constructive comments and suggestions, which helped improve the quality of this article.

REFERENCES

Achaoui, Y., A. Khelif, S. Benchabane, L. Robert, and V. Laude (2011). Experimental observation of locally-resonant and Bragg band gaps for surface guided waves in a phononic crystal of pillars, *Phys. Rev. B* **83,** 104,201.

Bard, P.-Y., and M. Bouchon (1980). The seismic response of sediment-filled valleys. Part 1. The case of incident SH waves, *Bull. Seismol. Soc. Am.* **70,** 1263.

Bensoussan, A., J.-L. Lions, and G. Papanicolaou (2011). *Asymptotic Analysis for Periodic Structures,* Vol. 374, American Mathematical Society, Providence, Rhode Island.

Boutin, C., and P. Roussillon (2004). Assessment of the urbanization effect on seismic response, *Bull. Seismol. Soc. Am.* **94,** 251–268.

Boutin, C., and P. Roussillon (2006). Wave propagation in presence of oscillators on the free surface, *Int. J. Eng. Sci.* **44,** nos. 3/4, 180–204.

Boutin, C., L. Schwan, and M. Dietz (2015). Elastodynamic metasurface: Depolarization of mechanical waves and time effects, *J. Appl. Phys.* **117,** no. 6, 064,902.

Brûlé, S., S. Enoch, and S. Guenneau (2020). Emergence of seismic metamaterials: Current state and future perspectives, *Phys. Lett. A* **384,** no. 1, 126,034.

Chaillat, S., M. Bonnet, and J. F. Semblat (2009). A new fast multi-domain bem to model seismic wave propagation and amplification in 3-d geological structures, *Geophys. J. Int.* **177,** no. 2, 509–531.

Clouteau, D., and D. Aubry (2001). Modifications of the ground motion in dense urban areas, *J. Comput. Acoust.* **9,** 1659.

Colombi, A., D. Colquitt, P. Roux, S. Guenneau, and R. V. Craster (2016). A seismic metamaterial: The resonant metawedge, *Sci. Rep.* **6,** no. 1, 27,717.

Craster, R. V., and S. Guenneau (2012). *Acoustic Metamaterials: Negative Refraction, Imaging, Lensing and Cloaking,* Vol. 166, Springer Science and Business Media.

Delepine, N., and J.-F. Semblat (2012). Site effects in an alpine valley with strong velocity gradient: Interest and limitations of the 'classical' BEM, *Soil Dynam. Earthq. Eng.* **38,** 15–24.

Flores, J., O. Novaro, and T. Seligman (1987). Possible resonance effect in the distribution of earthquake damage in Mexico city, *Nature* **326,** no. 6115, 783–785.

Grasso, E., S. Chaillat, M. Bonnet, and J.-F. Semblat (2012). Application of the multi-level time-harmonic fast multipole BEM to 3-d visco-elastodynamics, *Eng. Anal. Bound. Elements* **36,** no. 5, 744–758.

Groby, J.-P., and A. Wirgin (2008). Seismic motion in urban sites consisting of blocks in welded contact with a soft layer overlying a hard half-space, *Geophys. J. Int.* **172,** no. 2, 725–758.

Guéguen, P., P. Bard, and J.-F. Semblat (2000). Engineering seismology: Seismic hazard and risk analysis: Seismic hazard analysis from soil-structure interaction to site-city interaction, *Proc. 12th World Conf. on Earthquake Engineering.*

Guéguen, P., and P.-Y. Bard (2005). Soil-structure and soil-structure-soil interaction: Experimental evidence at the Volvi test site, *J. Earthq. Eng.* **9,** no. 5, 657–693.

Guéguen, P., P.-Y. Bard, and F. J. Chavez-Garcia (2002). Site-city seismic interaction in Mexico city–like environments: An analytical study, *Bull. Seismol. Soc. Am.* **92,** no. 2, 794–811.

Hassen, G., P. de Buhan, and M. Abdelkrim (2010). Finite element implementation of a homogenized constitutive law for stone column-reinforced foundation soils, with application to the design of structures, *Comput. Geotech.* **37,** nos. 1/2, 40–49.

Housner, G. W. (1957). Interaction of building and ground during an earthquake, *Bull. Seismol. Soc. Am.* **47,** no. 3, 179–186.

Isbiliroglu, Y., R. Taborda, and J. Bielak (2014). Multiple structure-soil-structure interaction and coupling effects in building clusters, *Tenth U.S. National Conf. on Earthquake Engineering Frontiers of Earthquake Engineering July,* 21–25.

Isbiliroglu, Y., R. Taborda, and J. Bielak (2015). Coupled soil-structure interaction effects of building clusters during earthquakes, *Earthq. Spectra* **31,** no. 1, 463–500.

Kausel, E. (2010). Early history of soil–structure interaction, *Soil Dynam. Earthq. Eng.* **30,** no. 9, 822–832.

Kausel, E., R. V. Whitman, J. P. Morray, and F. Elsabee (1978). The spring method for embedded foundations, *Nucl. Eng. Des.* **48,** nos. 2/3, 377–392.

Kham, M., J.-F. Semblat, P.-Y. Bard, and P. Dangla (2006). Seismic site–city interaction: Main governing phenomena through simplified numerical models, *Bull. Seismol. Soc. Am.* **96,** no. 5, 1934–1951.

Luco, J. E., and L. Contesse (1973). Dynamic structure-soil-structure interaction, *Bull. Seismol. Soc. Am.* **63,** no. 4, 1289–1303.

Marigo, J.-J., and A. Maurel (2017). Second order homogenization of subwavelength stratified media including finite size effect, *SIAM J. Appl. Math.* **77,** no. 2, 721–743.

Marigo, J.-J., A. Maurel, K. Pham, and A. Sbitti (2017). Effective dynamic properties of a row of elastic inclusions: The case of scalar shear waves, *J. Elast.* **128,** no. 2, 265–289.

Marigo, J.-J., K. Pham, A. Maurel, and S. Guenneau (2020). Effective model for elastic waves propagating in a substrate supporting a dense array of plates/beams with flexural resonances, *J. Mech. Phys. Solids* **143,** 104,029.

Marigo, J.-J., K. Pham, A. Maurel, and S. Guenneau (2021). Effective model for elastic waves in a substrate supporting an array of plates/beams with flexural and longitudinal resonances, *J. Elast.* **146,** 143–177.

Marigo, J.-J., K. Pham, A. Maurel, and S. Guenneau (2024). Dispersion and ellipticity of Rayleigh waves in a soil substrate supporting resonant beams and plates, *Phys. Rev. B* **110,** no. 9, 094110.

Maurel, A., J.-J. Marigo, K. Pham, and S. Guenneau (2018). Conversion of Love waves in a forest of trees, *Phys. Rev. B* **98,** no. 13, 134311.

Maurel, A., J.-F. Mercier, K. Pham, J.-J. Marigo, and A. Ourir (2019). Enhanced resonance of sparse arrays of Helmholtz resonators–application to perfect absorption, *J. Acoust. Soc. Am.* **145,** no. 4, 2552–2560.

Maznev, A., and V. Gusev (2015). Waveguiding by a locally resonant metasurface, *Phys. Rev. B* **92,** no. 11, 115422.

Mercier, J.-F., M.-L. Cordero, S. Félix, A. Ourir, and A. Maurel (2015). Classical homogenization to analyse the dispersion relations of spoof plasmons with geometrical and compositional effects, *Proc. Math. Phys. Sci.* **471,** no. 2182, 20150472.

Meza-Fajardo, K. C., A. S. Papageorgiou, and J.-F. Semblat (2015). Identification and extraction of surface waves from three-component seismograms based on the normalized inner product, *Bull. Seismol. Soc. Am.* **105,** no. 1, 210–229.

Mu, D., H. Shu, L. Zhao, and S. An (2020). A review of research on seismic metamaterials, *Adv. Eng. Mater.* **22,** no. 4, 1901148.

Palermo, A., and A. Marzani (2018). Control of Love waves by resonant metasurfaces, *Sci. Rep.* **8,** no. 1, 7234.

Pham, K., N. Lebbe, and A. Maurel (2023). Diffraction grating with varying slit width: Quasi-periodic homogenization and its numerical implementation, *J. Comput. Phys.* **473,** 111,727.

Pham, K., A. Maurel, S. Félix, and S. Guenneau (2020). Hybridized Love waves in a guiding layer supporting an array of plates with decorative endings, *Materials* **13,** no. 7, 1632.

Pham, K., A. Maurel, and J.-J. Marigo (2017). Two scale homogenization of a row of locally resonant inclusions-the case of anti-plane shear waves, *J. Mech. Phys. Solids* **106,** 80–94.

Pilz, M., P. Roux, S. A. Mohammed, R. F. Garcia, R. Steinmann, C. Aubert, F. Bernauer, P. Guéguen, M. Ohrnberger, and F. Cotton (2024). Wind turbines as a metamaterial-like urban layer: An experimental investigation using a dense seismic array and complementary sensing technologies, *Front. Earth Sci.* **12,** 1352027.

Rosenblueth, E. (1986). The Mexican earthquake: A firsthand report, *Civil Eng. ASCE* **56,** no. 1, 38–40.

Schwan, L., C. Boutin, L. Padrón, M. Dietz, P.-Y. Bard, and C. Taylor (2016). Site-city interaction: Theoretical, numerical and experimental crossed-analysis, *Geophys. J. Int.* **205,** no. 2, 1006–1031.

Semblat, J.-F., M. Kham, and P.-Y. Bard (2008). Seismic-wave propagation in alluvial basins and influence of site-city interaction, *Bull. Seismol. Soc. Am.* **98,** no. 6, 2665–2678.

Singhai, K., and N. Tiwari (2024). A state-of-the-art review on earthquake soil-structure interaction including dynamic cross interaction (DCI) and site city interactions (SCI), *Earthq. Struct.* **27,** no. 5, 361–383.

Tsogka, C., and A. Wirgin (2003). Simulation of seismic response in an idealized city, *Soil Dynam. Earthq. Eng.* **23,** no. 5, 391–402.

Uenishi, K. (2010). The town effect: Dynamic interaction between a group of structures and waves in the ground, *Rock Mech. Rock Eng.* **43,** no. 6, 811–819.

Vicencio, F., N. A. Alexander, and E. I. S. Flores (2023). A state-of-the-art review on structure-soil-structure interaction (SSSI) and site-city interactions (SCI), *Structures* **56,** 105,002.

Wirgin, A. (1988). Love waves in a slab with rough boundaries, *Recent Developments in Surface Acoustic Waves: Proceedings of European Mechanics Colloquium 226*, University of Nottingham, United Kingdom, 2–5 September 1987, Springer, 145–155.

Wirgin, A., and P.-Y. Bard (1996). Effects of buildings on the duration and amplitude of ground motion in Mexico city, *Bull. Seismol. Soc. Am.* **86,** no. 3, 914–920.

Wong, H., and M. Trifunac (1975). Two-dimensional, antiplane, building-soil-building interaction for two or more buildings and for incident planet SH waves, *Bull. Seismol. Soc. Am.* **65,** no. 6, 1863–1885.

Zhu, J., Y. Chen, X. Zhu, F. J. Garcia-Vidal, X. Yin, W. Zhang, and X. Zhang (2013). Acoustic rainbow trapping, *Sci. Rep.* **3,** no. 1, 1728.

Manuscript received 21 June 2025
Published online 5 December 2025

Effects of Topography on Ground-Motion Recordings at Short Wavelengths: The Case of a Cliff in Cephalonia, Western Greece

Pauline Rischette*[1,2], Zafeiria Roumelioti[3], Fabrice Hollender[1,2], Vincent Perron[1], Nikolaos Theodoulidis[4], Edward Cushing[5], Aline Bou Nassif[2], Emmanuel Chaljub[2], Fabien Lacroix[6], Paola Traversa[7], Emeline Maufroy[2], Pierre-Yves Bard[1], and Agisilaos Konidaris[8]

ABSTRACT

OPEN ACCESS

Reliable ground-motion measurements are essential for seismic hazard assessment and require seismological stations to be installed in free-field conditions, away from structural interferences. However, global network analyses show diverse installation configurations that can affect measurements. Although topographic effects are natural, their influence can extend over several meters, making them closely related to operators' installation choices. Although summit effects are well studied and known to cause strong amplifications, the impact of cliffs or escarpments remains less explored. In this study, 16 SmartSolo IGU-16HR 3C nodes were placed on either side of a 30-m cliff located in Cephalonia (western Greece), for 4–10 months, recording 307 low-to-moderate-magnitude seismic events. The main results reveal that de-amplifications recorded at the cliff base are greater than amplifications determined at the cliff top, particularly between 5 and 15 Hz. This study shows that amplification and de-amplification are primarily driven by topography, whereas their directional dependence is likely shaped by both topographic and lithologic factors. Furthermore, the anisotropy related to cliff fracturing interacts with the effects of source back azimuth. Amplification and de-amplification can be correctly predicted using the frequency-scaled curvature (FSC) and illuminated FSC proxies, provided that an exponential functional form is used for determining de-amplifications at the base of near-vertical cliffs. Furthermore, the azimuthal dependence observed, inducing strong de-amplifications depending on the direction observed, seems related more to the anisotropy of geologic formations than to the cliff topography itself. These effects should be considered when using data from stations in similar topographic settings. Neglecting them can bias ground-motion models and underestimate earthquake magnitudes, particularly for stations at the base of cliffs. From these considerations, we strongly recommend installing future seismological stations a few tens of meters away from the bases and ridges of even small cliffs or escarpments.

KEY POINTS

- Topography effects on ground motion are examined at the top and base of a 30-m cliff.
- Cliff base de-amplifications exceed top amplifications, especially between 5 and 15 Hz.
- Stations near cliffs can bias ground-motion models and lead to inaccurate seismic hazard estimates.

Supplemental Material

INTRODUCTION

Reliable ground-motion measurements are essential for accurately estimating seismic hazard because these measurements serve as key inputs to ground-motion models (GMMs) that are fundamental to seismic hazard assessments. The free-field

1. French Alternative Energies and Atomic Energy Commission (CEA), DES, CEA Cadarache, Saint-Paul-lez-Durance, France, https://orcid.org/0009-0005-9616-4871 (PR); https://orcid.org/0000-0003-1440-6389 (FH); https://orcid.org/0000-0003-0283-7843 (VP); https://orcid.org/0000-0002-3018-1047 (P-YB); 2. University Grenoble Alpes, University Savoie Mont Blanc, CNRS, IRD, University Gustave Eiffel, ISTerre, Grenoble, France, https://orcid.org/0009-0002-6297-4807 (ABN); https://orcid.org/0000-0002-0995-5597 (EM); 3. Department of Geology, University of Patras, Patras, Greece, https://orcid.org/0000-0001-5038-3052 (ZR); 4. Institute of Engineering Seismology and Earthquake Engineering (ITSAK-EPPO), Thessaloniki, Greece, https://orcid.org/0000-0002-0169-9197 (NT); 5. Sorbonne Université, CY Cergy Paris Université, CNRS, Institut des Sciences de la Terre de Paris, ISTeP, Paris, France, https://orcid.org/0000-0002-1601-8323 (EC); 6. Osiris Environnement, Rustrel, France; 7. Electricité de France (EDF), DT-TEGG, Aix-en-Provence, France, https://orcid.org/0000-0002-9639-7342 (PT); 8. Department of Digital Media and Communication, TEI Ionion Nison, Argostoli, Greece

*Corresponding author: pauline.rischette@cea.fr

Cite this article as Rischette, P., Z. Roumelioti, F. Hollender, V. Perron, N. Theodoulidis, E. Cushing, A. Bou Nassif, E. Chaljub, F. Lacroix, P. Traversa, *et al.* (2025). Effects of Topography on Ground-Motion Recordings at Short Wavelengths: The Case of a Cliff in Cephalonia, Western Greece, *Bull. Seismol. Soc. Am.* **116**, 553–575, doi: 10.1785/0120250146 condition, defined as the installation of stations on the natural surface of the ground without disturbances from any neighboring structures, is necessary to allow an accurate measurement of the seismic waves reaching the ground surface. However, this condition is challenging to fulfil, particularly in urban areas where the need for instrumental stations with efficient functioning and easy maintenance is paramount (e.g., power supply, real-time data transmission). An inventory carried out on international seismological networks reveals the diversity of installation configurations and the various sensor-soil coupling techniques. These different installation conditions can have a significant impact on the measurement of ground motion within specific frequency ranges (e.g., Hollender *et al.*, 2020; Castellaro *et al.*, 2022). In addition to such operator- and configuration-dependent station installation conditions, the presence of topographic features in the vicinity of a seismic station can have an impact on the recorded ground motion.

The effect of topography on ground motion has been investigated for several years (e.g., Bouchon, 1973; Chávez-García *et al.*, 1996), and Massa *et al.* (2014) provide a review of relevant studies on the subject. The topographic site effect is known to cause significant amplification near summits and ridge crests (Nechtschein *et al.*, 1996; Maufroy *et al.*, 2015), as shown by the considerable damage to infrastructures located at the top of hills (e.g., Massa *et al.*, 2010; Pischiutta *et al.*, 2010). Furthermore, this is a mechanism for which complexity can make it challenging to separate the contribution of lithological effects from purely topographical site effects (Asimaki and Jeong, 2013). To enhance comprehension of this phenomenon, numerous numerical simulations have been performed (e.g., Sánchez-Sesma, 1985; Maufroy *et al.*, 2012), however, these tend to underestimate the observed amplifications (e.g., Geli *et al.*, 1988; Sánchez-Sesma and Campillo, 1993).

A significant number of studies have been conducted on the effect of strong positive (convex) curvatures of the Earth's surface, particularly the impact of summits that amplify the ground motion. However, although certain permanent seismological stations are installed at the base of escarpments and cliffs, there is a lack of studies on the impact of steep to vertical topographies on ground motion recorded at their base. This is the case for some stations of the French permanent accelerometric network (Réseau Accélérométrique Permanent [RAP]; RESIF, 1995), such as OGAN or OGMU and OGDF of the French permanent broadband network (Réseau Large Bande Permanent [RLBP]; Epos-France, 1995), installed at the foot of cliffs ranging from a few meters to a few dozen meters in height. The BSTF station of the RLBP network is installed near the edge at the top of a cliff. Consequently, it seems essential to characterize the impact of such topographies on the measurement of ground motion and to estimate their effects, including cases of strong negative curvatures.

This study presents the effects observed on both sides of a cliff about thirty meters high on the island of Cephalonia in Greece. For this, an experiment that involved the installation of stations at the summit and at the base of the cliff was carried out. The sensors were left in place for several months and recorded more than 300 earthquakes. First, the effects of the topographic feature on seismic motion are analyzed using conventional approaches such as the standard spectral ratio (SSR; Borcherdt, 1970) method according to several reference criteria. The results of this analysis are then compared with those obtained from seismic microtremors, for which the SSR technique applied on noise measurements (SSRn) is employed (e.g., Perron, Gélis, *et al.*, 2018). Subsequently, the distinction between lithological and topographical site effects is addressed through site condition characterization in the study area, performed by so-called passive ambient vibration array (AVA; e.g., Foti *et al.*, 2018; Hollender *et al.*, 2018) and active multichannel analysis of surface waves (MASW; Park *et al.*, 1999; Yong *et al.*, 2022) measurements. The empirical results are then compared with 1D and 2D numerical simulation results, and the use of frequency-scaled curvature (FSC) proxy (Maufroy *et al.*, 2015) and illuminated FSC (i-FSC) proxy (Bou Nassif *et al.*, 2025) for the prediction of amplifications and de-amplifications related to the curvature of the Earth's surface is discussed.

STUDY AREA AND EXPERIMENTAL DEVICE

Site description

Greece is one of the most earthquake-prone regions in Europe, with high seismicity recorded by permanent seismological networks. The island of Cephalonia, located in the western part of Greece (Fig. 1a), proved to be an ideal choice for hosting our experiment, allowing the collection of a large number of seismic events. The high seismicity of this area is particularly due to the proximity of the Cephalonia transform fault zone. This has facilitated the recording of a substantial number of low-to-moderate-magnitude earthquakes in less than a year. Our study area is located more precisely to the northeast (NE) of the Koutavos basin, near the town of Argostoli, which has already been the subject of numerous seismological, geophysical, and geotechnical measurements (e.g., Sbaa *et al.*, 2017; Theodoulidis, Cultrera, *et al.*, 2018; Perron, Hollender, *et al.*, 2018; Cushing *et al.*, 2020; Moiriat *et al.*, 2023). The study site is a former quarry, now giving way to a cliff of about 30 m high. The cliff face reveals fractured Upper Cretaceous limestone (Cushing *et al.*, 2020) and can be approximated as two slope segments: the first, oriented north–south, is about 20 m high, and the second, oriented northwest (NW)–southeast (SE), rises to 40 m. This geometry is clearly visible on the orthophoto obtained by drone in Figure 1b, which provides a high-resolution aerial image of the former quarry and the cliff.

Description of the experiment

All measurements were conducted using SmartSolo IGU-16HR 3C nodes. The nodes were configured with a sampling frequency of 250 Hz and continuously recorded the ambient

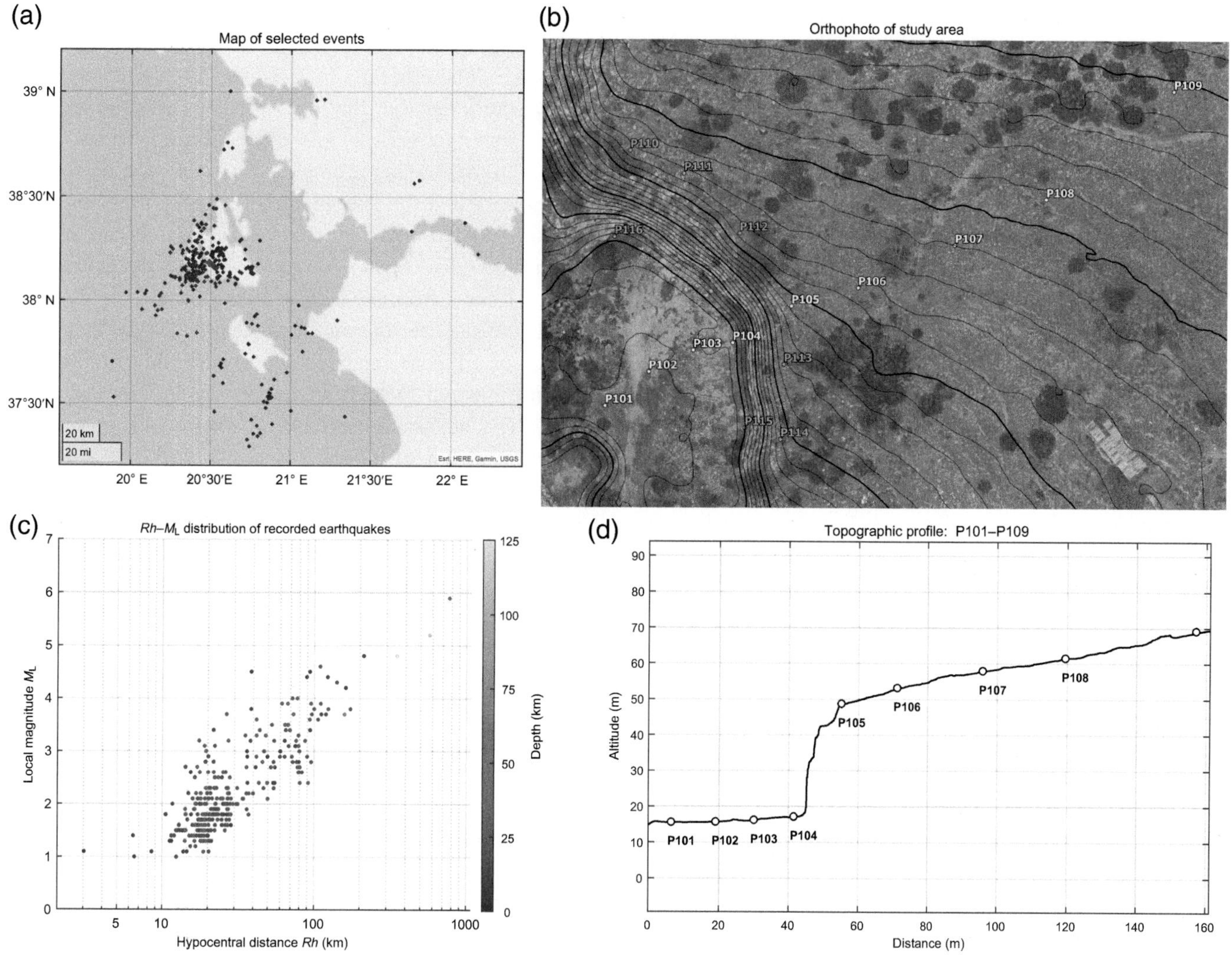

Figure 1. Presentation of the study area and the events constituting the database. (a) Map of the events recorded during the 10 months of acquisition. The small red line indicates the location of the cliff. (b) Drone-obtained orthophoto of the study area, with positions of stations P101–P116. The interval between black thin contour lines is 2 m, and thick contour lines are spaced 10 m apart. In panel (b), the white circles indicate the stations forming the topographic profile shown in panel (d), while the blue circles correspond to additional stations installed during the final acquisition phase. (c) Magnitude–distance distribution of recorded earthquakes. The color of each point indicates the depth of the considered event. (d) Topographic profile along the line delimited by stations P101–P109, made with a 1-m resolution digital terrain model. The color version of this figure is available only in the electronic edition.

vibrations over a period of several months. It was also possible to choose a preamplifier gain value ranging from 0 to 36 dB. Preliminary tests demonstrated that a gain setting of 0 dB provided satisfactory performances for recording low-to-moderate-magnitude earthquakes (up to 150–200 mg). Consequently, the nodes were configured with this gain value to avoid saturation in the case of weak-to-moderate motion. Furthermore, the SmartSolo IGU-16HR 3C nodes were qualified for ambient vibrations recording with an appropriate gain value.

In November 2022, eight nodes were installed, labeled P101–P108 (Fig. 1b,d), forming a profile perpendicular to the cliff face. Because real-time data transmission was not possible, data retrieval was carried out every three to four months. Following an initial analysis, additional SmartSolo IGU-16HR 3C nodes were deployed at both the top and base of the cliff to densify the monitoring of the study area. These additional sensors, corresponding to points P110–P116 in Figure 1b, were buried just below the surface. Point P109 was installed at a higher location along the initial profile, on flat ground. The topographic profile, delineated by points P101–P109, was extracted from a 1-m resolution digital elevation model (DEM) and an orthophoto acquired via drone surveying (Fig. 1d).

Nodes P101–P108 recorded ground motion from November 2022 to October 2023. The acquisition period, including all measurement points (up to P116), extended from July 2023 to October 2023 and included 110 recorded events. Most nodes were buried on the surface of the ground, connected to an external battery, which was itself connected to a solar panel, ensuring long-term autonomy. Both nodes and batteries were protected by boxes on which the solar panels were installed. The boxes were well stabilized to prevent disturbances in the measurements. Points P103 and P104 were installed on tripods due to the rigidity of the ground, with a metal strap around the nodes and bolted to the ground, securing the coupling.

Database

Intense seismic activity on the island of Cephalonia enabled the recording of 307 earthquakes from November 2022 to October 2023. To choose the earthquakes used in our analysis, we relied on the event selection procedure established for the nearby ARGONET network database (Theodoulidis, Hollender, *et al.*, 2018). The ARGONET database is populated by events for which peak ground acceleration exceeds a threshold of 0.2 mg at the deepest borehole station of the network. We followed the same procedure but lowered this threshold to 0.05 mg to include a greater number of events. Metadata associated with most of the earthquakes in our database (such as their location, depth, local magnitude, etc.) were extracted from the catalog of the National Observatory of Athens (NOA; see Data and Resources). For those events not listed in the NOA catalog, earthquake locations were determined specifically using the same velocity model and magnitude relation as NOA for maximum consistency.

Finally, we corrected any errors of station orientation related to the reinstallation of the sensors after each periodic data collection. To ensure consistent orientation, we chose the sensor at point P104 as a reference because it was installed on a tripod secured with a metal strap anchored to the ground, providing a fixed orientation marker throughout the entire experiment. For each acquisition period, all recordings from all sensors were reoriented according to the following procedure: (1) a low-frequency filter (0.2–0.6 Hz) was applied to the recordings of the 10 earthquakes with the highest signal-to-noise ratios (SNRs) in the low-frequency range; (2) for each event, signals from each sensor were rotated in 2° increments, and correlation coefficients were computed with respect to the reference sensor P104: the angle that provided the maximum correlation was retained; (3) a finer search was then performed around this angle (±2° in 0.1° increments) to refine the optimal rotation; and (4) these steps were repeated for each earthquake, and the median of the resulting optimal angles was retained for each sensor. Angle variations across events for a given sensor were minimal (<5°), reflecting the robustness of the procedure.

Our final database includes a total of 307 events, 110 of which were recorded by all the stations deployed around the cliff (P101–P116). Events are of low-to-moderate local magnitude, ranging from 1 to 4, as can be seen in the Rh–M_L distribution shown in Figure 1c. The database includes earthquake depths of up to 123 km in rare strong events, although most events occur at depths between 1 and 30 km (Fig. 1c). A few stronger events with hypocentral distances between 200 and 800 km were also recorded.

METHODOLOGICAL FRAMEWORK

The objective of this study is to evaluate the effects of a cliff on ground-motion recordings. To this end, the main analysis relies on the SSR reference method, which was originally introduced by Borcherdt (1970) and has since become widely employed. This technique is based on the calculation of the spectral ratios between the selected components recorded by a given sensor (target site) and those recorded by a reference sensor, thus delivering the empirical transfer function between the reference and the site. In such instances, the choice of a reference site exhibiting minimal site effects becomes paramount. Two reference sites were selected, both located at a substantial distance from the cliff, with one installed in the upper part (P108) and the other in the lower part (P101). To prevent reliance on reference stations, we also consider the median reference method (MRM) introduced by Wilson and Pavlis (2000). This statistical method involves the utilization of the median spectrum of all stations as the reference spectrum, thereby ensuring the independence of the reference from a single site. The efficacy of the MRM was first established for small areas with dense seismic arrays (Wilson and Pavlis, 2000), and Maufroy *et al.* (2012) demonstrated that the MRM reliably characterizes site effects in mountainous areas, and its effectiveness is not heavily dependent on the number of stations used. A comparison of the results obtained from the MRM with those from single reference stations then allows the evaluation of the impact of reference selections in such a context. This, in turn, will enhance the reliability of our interpretation.

Because of the nearly vertical topography considered in this study, the potential effects of the back azimuth of the sources are also analyzed. The recorded earthquakes are divided into four groups according to their back-azimuth values relative to point P105, which is located at the center of the experiment (see Fig. 1b). Applying the SSR method to each group of events and comparing the results with those calculated from all recorded earthquakes makes it possible to determine if the back azimuth of the sources—in other words, the propagation direction of incident waves, perpendicular or parallel to the main segment of the cliff—do impact the previously observed effects. Similarly, an effect of azimuthal dependence might influence the measurements due to the geometry of the studied topography. To investigate this, the SSR method is applied, but this time for one single station. The ratio between the rotated horizontal components (for each azimuth between N0°E and N180°E) and the average horizontal components of the station is computed, and referred to as $\mathrm{var}_{\mathrm{Az}}$.

Subsequently, we investigate whether the effects observed on earthquakes can be retrieved with ambient seismic noise measurements because, in some cases, only the latter can be conducted. To do this, the SSR technique is applied to ambient noise acquisitions, a method originally proposed by Irikura and Kawanaka (1980) and known as SSRn. In addition to comparing results from earthquake recordings and ambient seismic noise measurements, we also apply the horizontal-to-vertical spectral ratio (HVSR) method to both datasets. This standard method, promoted by Nakamura (1989), is based on computing the spectral ratios between the average of the horizontal components and the vertical component recorded simultaneously by the same station. The HVSR allows for the estimation of the fundamental (or resonance) frequency f_0 at a given station, identified as the frequency at which the HVSR reaches its maximum. It has been shown by Burjánek *et al.* (2014) to be of interest also for the amplification effects related to surface topography.

Then, we aim to determine whether the observed effects are primarily due to topography or if other factors, such as lithology, also play a significant role. Distinguishing purely topographic effects from lithological contributions is often difficult. To address this, we also conducted geophysical measurements to obtain *S*-wave velocity profiles at both the upper and lower parts of the cliff. These acquisitions result in combining the active method MASW (e.g., Park *et al.*, 1999; Yong *et al.*, 2022) with the passive AVA method (Foti *et al.*, 2018) by reproducing the acquisition geometry implemented for the characterization of RAP stations (RESIF, 1995) by Hollender *et al.* (2018). The resulting dispersion curves are used to analyze the anisotropy of the environment, thereby extending our earlier analysis of azimuthal dependence. Furthermore, these resulting velocity profiles allow us to estimate the potential pure lithological amplification through 1D simulation, which is compared with results from seismic motion measurements. To test the underlying phenomenology, we performed a 2D numerical simulation using SPECFEM2D (Komatitsch and Vilotte, 1998). The results of a simplified model of the cliff, represented as a step function within an assumed homogeneous medium, are compared with our instrumental results.

Finally, we intend to evaluate whether the observed amplifications and de-amplifications could be reliably predicted by topographic proxies, such as the FSC proxy developed by Maufroy *et al.* (2015), even in areas with highly pronounced topography. Moreover, we also test the i-FSC (Bou Nassif *et al.*, 2025) proxy, which takes into account for interactions between topographic irregularities and the incidence and back-azimuth angles of seismic waves from nearby sources. These proxies are relatively simple to apply because they only require DEMs and no measurements of earthquakes or ambient ground vibrations.

ANALYSIS OF GROUND-MOTION RECORDINGS

Study of ground-motion recording using the SSR technique

Reference method: SSR. To analyze ground-motion recordings, the SSR method, first proposed by Borcherdt (1970), has been employed. For this study, a preprocessing step consisting of the application of a cosine-taper window of 5% was applied to the edges of the windows containing both *P* and *S* waves, following the procedure of Perron, Laurendeau, *et al.* (2018). The selected windows start at the arrival time of *P* waves (T_P) and end according to the selection criteria defined by the same authors. These criteria are designed to include a significant portion of the *S*-wave energy. The minimum window duration is 10 s, and the maximum is 110 s, ensuring a reliable spectral analysis. The Fourier transforms of the specified windows were calculated and then smoothed according to the method of Konno and Ohmachi (1998) with a smoothing coefficient $b = 80$. Then, the ratios between the quadratic averages of the horizontal components of a target site and those of a reference site were determined. To guarantee the robustness of the results, only the SSR results at frequencies in which the associated recordings had an SNR greater than 3 were retained. The median was calculated when this criterion was met by at least three events at a given frequency, and the percentiles were determined when this threshold was reached by at least 10 events (Perron *et al.*, 2022).

As described in the Methodological framework section, the SSR method requires a reference site with minimal site amplification. Points P108 and P109 are located in a region where the earth's surface curvature values are very low, that is, on a relatively flat area compared with the other points of the profile. Thus, we expect less amplification related to the topographic site effect at these stations. In addition, our ambient noise analyses presented later in the Use of ambient vibrations by spectral ratio techniques section do not show any resonance frequency, particularly at point P108. We have therefore selected this measurement point as the reference site. Nevertheless, in the literature, the choice of the reference site for the study of topographic site effects is generally set at the foot of the studied topographic features (e.g., Pischiutta *et al.*, 2010; Stolte *et al.*, 2017). Consequently, we selected point P101 as a second reference site because it is the farthest measuring point from the cliff, making it less likely to be impacted by its effect. However, it should be noted that P101 is also a few meters from a small escarpment about 10 m high located farther west (Fig. 1b). Caution will therefore be required when interpreting the high-frequency results. Because these choices include a very strong dependence on the retained reference stations, we also applied the MRM introduced by Wilson and Pavlis (2000). The spectral ratios were then calculated, according to a reference spectrum considering the median spectrum of all stations as the reference (Maufroy *et al.*, 2012) as described in the Methodological framework section.

The SSR normalized by the MRM and by reference sites P101 and P108 are presented in Figure 2 for each measurement point, calculated from the average of the horizontal components. When comparing all selected references, the shape of the curves is generally similar. In particular, it appears that the SSR using P108 as the reference site closely follows those obtained with respect to the median of all the stations MRM (green and black curves, respectively). The P101 reference site (purple curves) provides SSR that diverges slightly from these first two references, showing weaker ratios beyond 10 Hz.

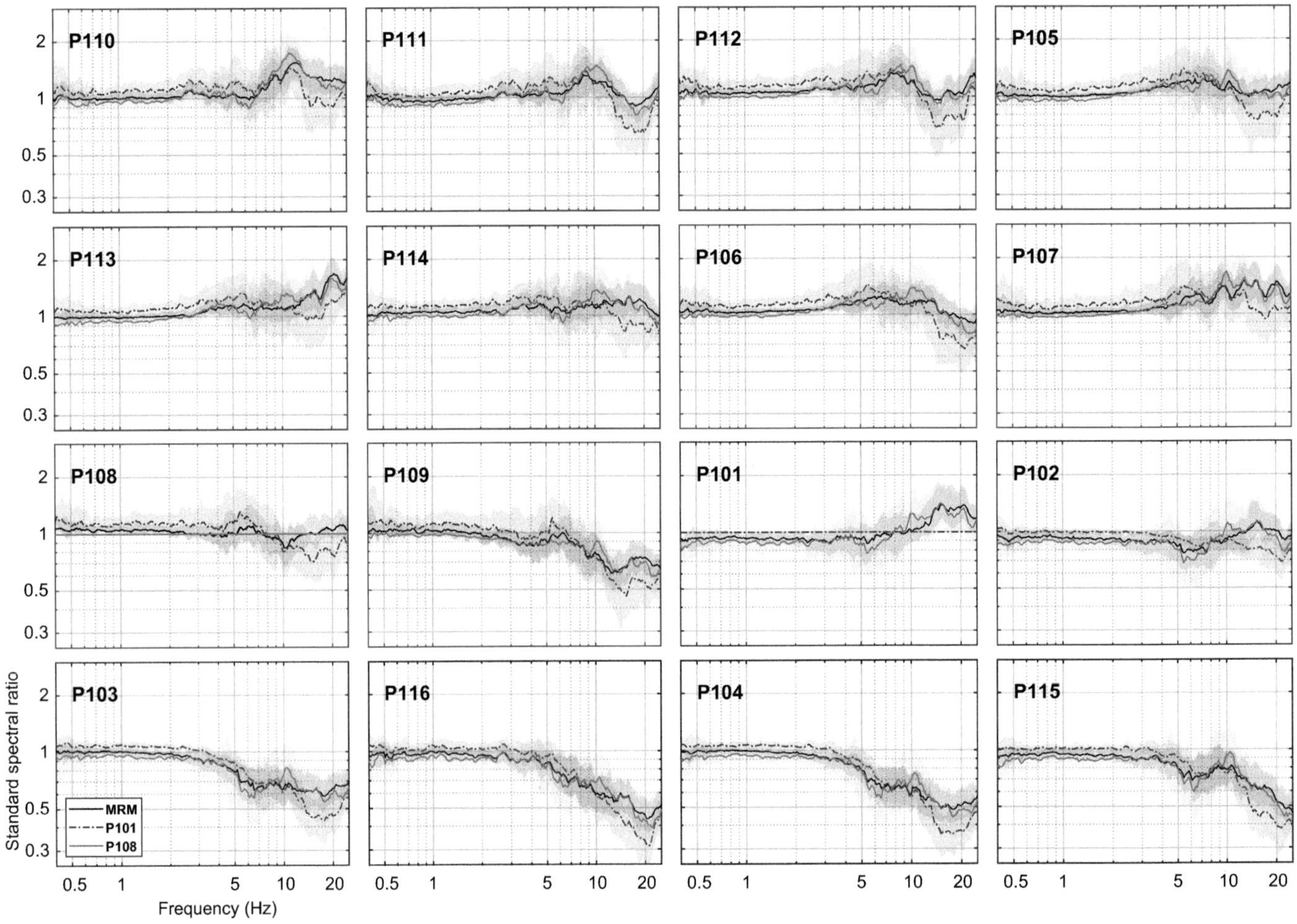

Figure 2. Standard spectral ratio (SSR) computed from the root mean square of horizontal components of each station with respect to several references: P101 (dashed–dotted purple) at the bottom of the cliff and farther from it (in the former quarry), P108 (green) at the edge and top of the cliff, and finally the median reference method (MRM; black). The solid lines correspond to the median of the SSR calculated over three months of acquisition, and the lighter patches represent the intervals defined by the 16th and 84th percentiles. From left to right: measurement points located from west to east, red boxes are stations at the top, blue at the bottom of the cliff. The thicker boxes indicate stations closest to the cliff (edge or foot). The color version of this figure is available only in the electronic edition.

In addition, a small constant amplification (<10%) is observed at low frequencies.

By first analyzing the results obtained by the stations at the top of the cliff (red boxes in Fig. 2), we observe a median SSR very close to 1 up to 5–7 Hz. From these frequencies up to around 12 Hz, some points at the edge of the cliff (P110, P111, and P112) show an amplification, which is, however, quite small because it does not reach a factor of 2. Furthermore, the points located at the foot of the cliff (blue thick boxes in Fig. 2) show a clear de-amplification beyond 5 Hz, reaching a factor of 2 at 20 Hz and up to a factor of 3 when the reference point is at the bottom of the cliff (P101).

Back-azimuth analysis of the sources. The topographic feature considered in this work is characterized by near-vertical slopes, with very pronounced curvatures at both the top and the base of the cliff, where the angle is close to 90° (compare with the topographic profile in Fig. 1d). Thus, the direction of seismic wave incidence from the various sources can significantly affect the site response at the cliff.

To study such an effect, the cliff is approximated by a segment with an orientation of N130°E centered on P105 located in the center of the study area (Fig. 1b) because this is the segment that constitutes the longest and highest part of the cliff. Based on these parameters, four zones were defined and are outlined in Figure 3. This breakdown was chosen so that the events contained in each zone originate from sources whose waves propagate perpendicular to the cliff (southwest [SW] and NE groups) and parallel to it (NW and SE groups).

In addition, we have only kept earthquakes for which epicentral distances are between 4 and 40 km. This range was chosen to avoid including events that are too close in distance, thus respecting the condition $R_e > 10\Delta d$, in which Δd is the distance between the site and the reference (so here the maximum intersensor distance). This range also ensures that the analysis remains relevant to the scale of the island of

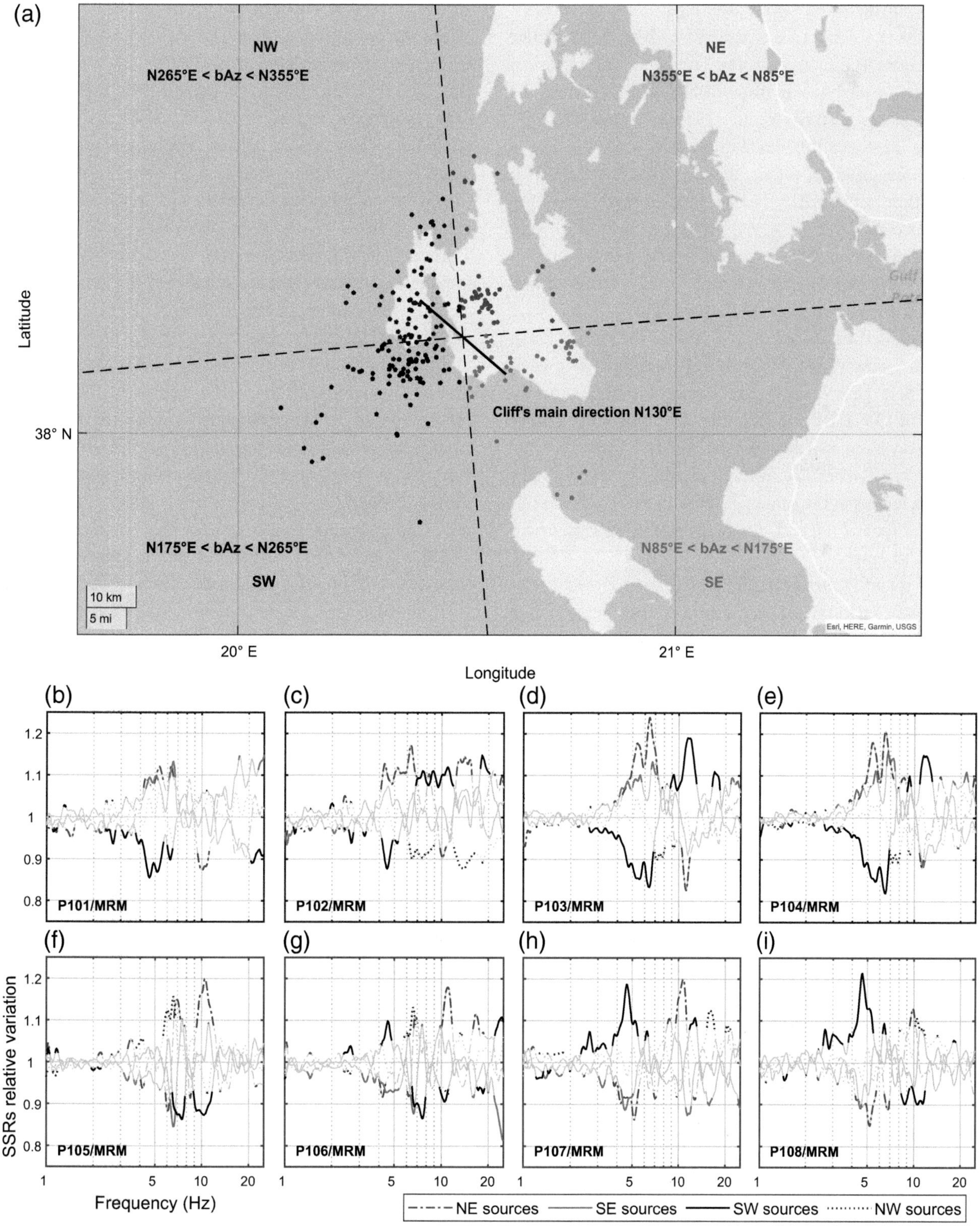

Figure 3. (a) Map of recorded earthquakes with an epicentral distance of between 4 and 40 km from station P105 located at the center of the experiment. The events are separated into four groups according to their back-azimuth (bAz) values. A black thick segment represents an approximation of the cliff orientation. (b–i) The curves represent the relative averages of SSR, calculated at each measurement point with respect to the MRM. These relative values correspond to the ratio of SSR computed for each group of events—classified according to their geographical distribution—to the SSR computed over the entire set of events. SSR is calculated from the root mean square of the horizontal components. The dashed–dotted, dotted, and solid colored segments indicate values exceeding 99% confidence intervals, and gray segments correspond to relative SSR average within confidence intervals. The colored boxes indicate the sensor positions relative to the cliff, as described in Figure 2. NE, northeast; NW, northwest; SE, southeast; SW, southwest. The color version of this figure is available only in the electronic edition.

Cephalonia. Furthermore, only the eight stations present throughout the experiment are considered here to have a greater number of events within each group. Thus, the four groups of events include: 74 earthquakes from the SW, 48 events from the NE, 43 earthquakes from the SE, then 63 events from the NW. Figure 3 also illustrates this distribution on a map.

For each new group of events, the SSRs of stations P101 to P108 in relation to the MRM (i.e., the median spectrum of the eight stations considered here, Wilson and Pavlis, 2000) were computed. The median SSR obtained is shown in Figure S1, available in the supplemental material to this article, and is superimposed on the median SSR calculated for the entire set of 307 recorded earthquakes. We present the results using the root mean square of the horizontal components of each station. At first glance, there are some variations, mainly between 4 and 15 Hz. It seems that the SW group (blue curves in Fig. S1), waves for which strike the cliff face more directly, diverges the most from the average of the SSR over all the events (black curves in the same figure) with greater de-amplification at the foot of the cliff. Apart from that, no clear trend really seems to emerge.

To better quantify these variations, we have adopted a statistical approach. Perron (2017) demonstrated that the variability of SSR results can be assimilated to a purely random phenomenon that follows a lognormal distribution (see Perron, 2017, for more details). Then, the established lognormal distribution of the SSR results means that the 99% confidence interval ($\boldsymbol{I}_{c99\%}$) can be used as a reliable parameter to determine whether there is epistemic uncertainty (related to incomplete knowledge of the model or data), rather than natural variability. Among the sets of events considered here, the smallest group comprises 43 earthquakes; therefore, we use a Student distribution that adequately reflects a moderate number of samples (Perron *et al.*, 2022), and approaches the normal distribution as the number of samples increases.

To investigate the influence of back azimuth, we calculated the average of the SSR of each back-azimuth group, relative to the overall average of the 307 events in our database. We determined these relative averages for each sensor on the mean of the horizontal components with respect to the MRM. We then plotted the $\boldsymbol{I}_{c99\%}$ as shown in Figure 3.

For most stations, the relative averages computed for the SW group (in black) and the NE group (dashed–dotted purple curves) exceed the $\boldsymbol{I}_{c99\%}$ between approximately 2 and 7 Hz, with variations that appear to be symmetric between the two groups. Above 7 Hz and up to around 12 Hz, this pattern seems to invert symmetrically, while still exceeding $\boldsymbol{I}_{c99\%}$ for both groups. These two groups exhibit deviations exceeding 20%, which are statistically significant. Furthermore, the probability that these exceedances are due to chance is less than 1% on a few successive frequencies. It is therefore very likely that they can be explained by the influence of the parameter being tested, in this case, the back azimuth.

Analysis of the directional dependence. The geometry of the studied topography suggests the possibility of an effect of directional dependence, consistent with previous studies that have reported directional site effects in areas with significant topographic features (Massa *et al.*, 2010; Pischiutta *et al.*, 2010; Burjánek *et al.*, 2014). This hypothesis was initially proposed based on certain observations from preliminary results, which led to the installation of additional SmartSolo IGU-16HR 3C nodes at the edge and foot of the cliff (Fig. 1b). To investigate this effect, we recalculated the SSR by computing, for the same station, the ratio between the rotated horizontal components (from azimuth N0°E to N180°E), and the average of its horizontal components, noted $\mathrm{var}_{\mathrm{Az}}$. The results were then multiplied by the SSR normalized by the MRM to obtain amplitudes comparable with those of a direct SSR. This formulation presents the advantage of defining the azimuthal variation of the studied site only, with no dependency on the reference site. The final results, which depend on both azimuth and frequency, are shown in Figure 4. The color scale is defined so that spectral ratios approaching 1 are represented in blue–green tones. Yellow has been used for the SSR values, suggesting amplification, and dark blue for de-amplification.

Figure 4 suggests slight variations around 1 below 5 Hz. However, between 1 and 2 Hz, around the azimuths N120°E and N160°E, a small decrease in amplification (~0.85) is systematically observed. Above 5 Hz, a clear directional dependence appears. Between approximately 5 and 15 Hz, amplitude variations are clearly observed as a function of azimuth. In this frequency band, our results show significant de-amplification factors of up to 3 for azimuths ranging from N10°E to N60°E, when the acquisitions were made at the foot of the cliff (P116, P104, and P115). This strong de-amplification gradually attenuates at points P103 and then P102 and is not found elsewhere. At the edge of the cliff, the spectral ratios tend to be greater than 1, particularly for orientations greater than N90° (red thick boxes in Fig. 4). When moving away from the cliff, azimuthal variations are still observed, but these seem to follow a more random pattern.

To better visualize these variations with respect to the studied topography, we isolated the 5–15 Hz frequency band, indicated by black lines in Figure 4, in which a significant polarization-related effect is observed. Then, we considered the maximum (>1) and minimum (<1) values of the $\mathrm{var}_{\mathrm{Az}}$ coefficient reached for each frequency between 5 and 15 Hz, for each station. In this way, we do not depend on the polarization of the reference. Then, for this same frequency band, we calculated the medians of the maximum and minimum $\mathrm{var}_{\mathrm{Az}}$ values retained, which thus corresponds to the highest average amplifications and de-amplifications between 5 and 15 Hz. These are represented by arrows in Figure 5, with the orientation of the arrows corresponding to the azimuths where these amplifications and de-amplifications occurred. The yellow arrows correspond to de-amplifications, and the black arrows to amplifications, which

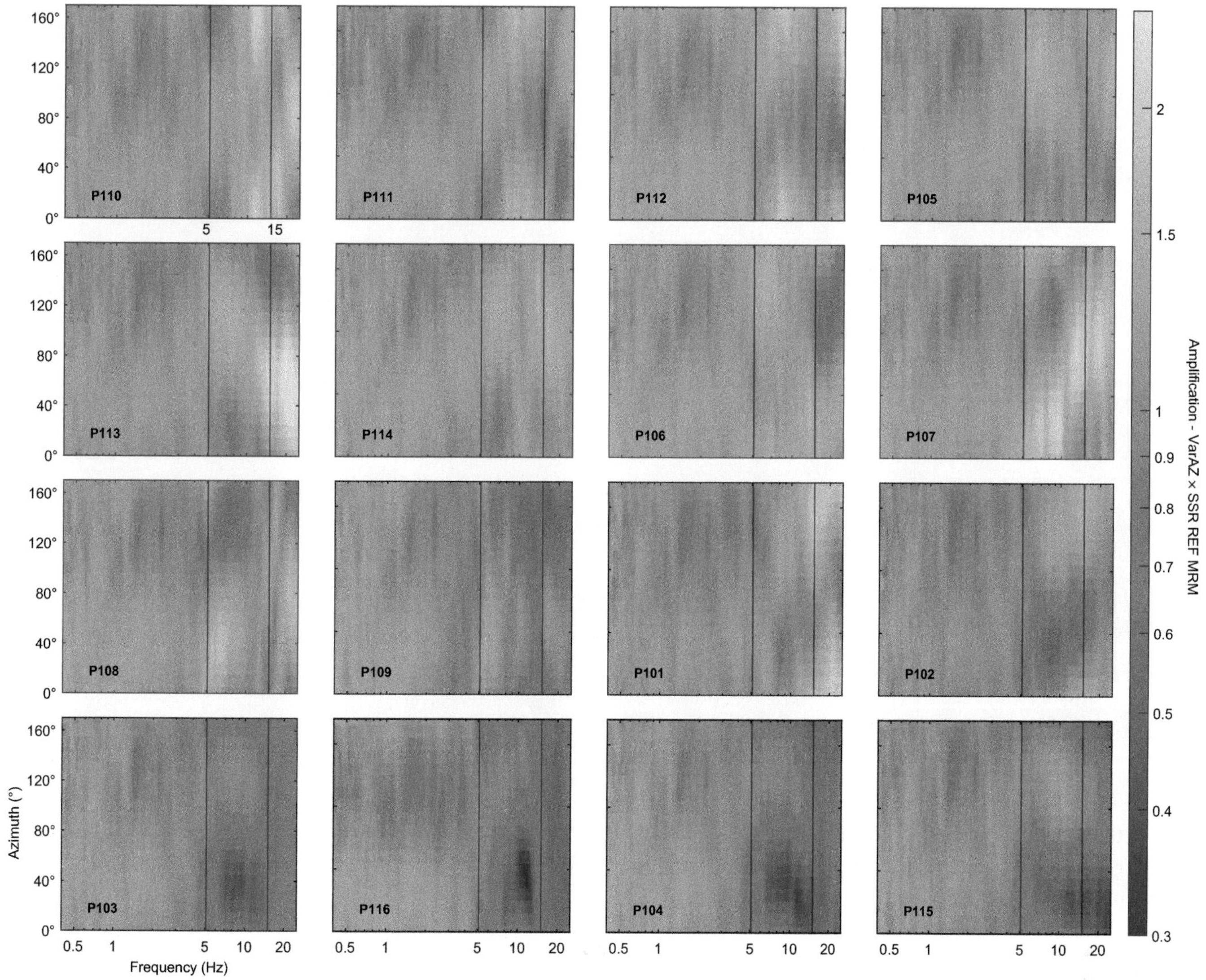

Figure 4. Spectral ratios between the signals recorded at each azimuth, ranging from N0°E to N180°E, relative to the average of the horizontal components of the same station (var_{AZ}). These results were then multiplied by the SSR normalized by the MRM. The 5–15 Hz frequency band is marked with dark gray lines, a band within which we observe significant azimuthal variations. The colored boxes indicate the sensor positions relative to the cliff, as described in Figure 2. The color version of this figure is available only in the electronic edition.

are superimposed on the orthophoto of Figure 1b. The yellow arrow standards correspond to the var_{Az} root mean square calculated between 5 and 15 Hz, normalized by the highest de-amplifications obtained. Conversely, the black arrow standards correspond to the highest amplifications normalized by the root mean square of var_{Az} over the same frequency band.

In Figure 5, we can see that stations P111, P112, and P116, located NW of the cliff, show amplifications for which directions seem to follow the orientation of the cliff. The points farther south, close to the cliff (P105 and P113–P115) and at the foot of the cliff (P101–P104), show amplifications that follow a direction systematically between N110°E and N130°E, and de-amplifications in transverse directions, between N20°E and N50°E, even N60°E for P101. In addition, an inversion of these directional patterns is observed for the most distant points (P107–P109) compared with the other stations. In fact, at these measurement points, the orientations of amplifications tend to evolve between N120°E to N150°E (and from N40°E to N60°E for the de-amplifications). Finally, the highest values are obtained at the bottom of the cliff, in the former quarry, where the arrow lengths are greater in this area in Figure 5, particularly for de-amplifications. These results confirm previous observations, in which stronger de-amplifications are observed at the bottom of the cliff (Figs. 2 and 4) compared with the amplification values reached at the top of the cliff. Although a clear dependence on the azimuth is observed, it does not appear to be due to the topography studied here. Indeed, the main directions followed do not systematically correspond to the longitudinal and transverse directions of the cliff face, which can be approximated by two main segments oriented according to N130°E and then according to the north–south

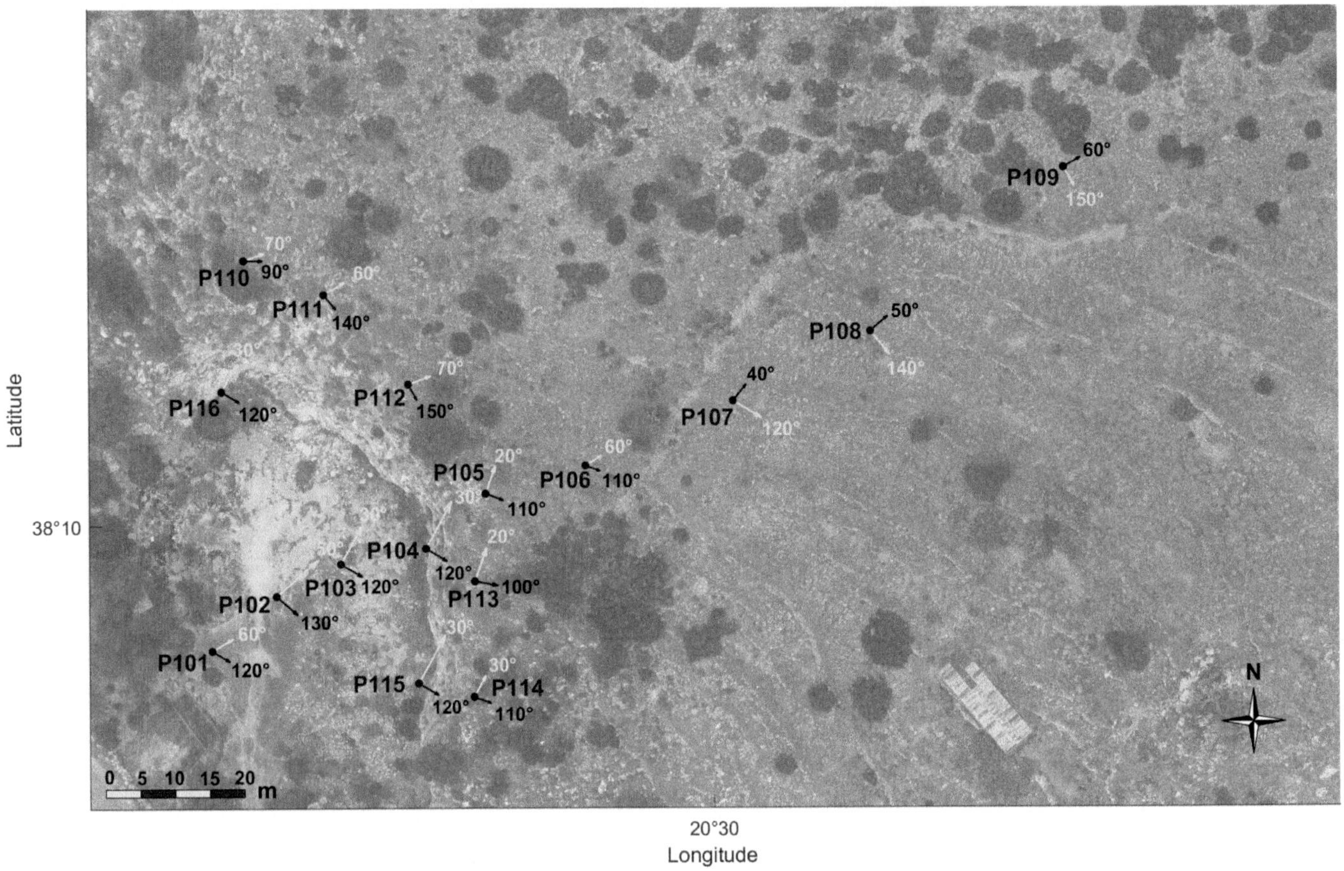

axis. On the contrary, they follow a relatively identical pattern, on average, according to the azimuths N130°E and N40°E for each point close to the cliff or in the quarry, regardless of the azimuth of the cliff face at the measurement points. It seems that this effect is rather dictated by an anisotropy of the medium, an observation to which we will return in the Origin of the observed amplifications and de-amplifications section.

Figure 5. Orthophoto of the study area with average maximum amplifications and de-amplifications of the var_{AZ} coefficient calculated over the 5–15 Hz frequency band. The black arrows correspond to amplifications: their length corresponds to the highest amplifications normalized by the root mean square of var_{AZ}. The yellow arrows indicates de-amplifications: arrow sizes correspond to var_{AZ} root mean square normalized by the highest de-amplifications. The arrows orientations indicate the azimuth at which these extreme values were reached. The color version of this figure is available only in the electronic edition.

Use of ambient vibrations by spectral ratio techniques

So far, our analyses have been carried out on recordings of earthquakes of low-to-moderate magnitude. However, some regions do not have significant seismic activity, and in some cases, only ambient seismic noise acquisitions can be conducted over a much shorter period of time. We have therefore investigated whether the effects observed on earthquakes were also found using ambient seismic noise measurements.

We applied the SSR method to ambient noise acquisitions, known as SSRn (Irikura and Kawanaka, 1980). This technique has been applied in several studies (e.g., Kagami *et al.*, 1982, 1986; Perron, Gélis, *et al.*, 2018) and its applications and limitations have been discussed in others (Bard, 1998; Perron, Gélis, *et al.*, 2018, among others).

As part of our experiment, the acquisitions were carried out continuously with SmartSolo IGU-16HR 3C nodes configured at 0 dB. Although this preamplifier gain value is low, a correction factor was applied, and power spectral density calculations showed noise levels recorded above the self-noise of the nodes determined with a gain of 0 dB, at least above 1 Hz. Ambient vibration acquisitions lasting three days were selected for SSRn calculations. Cosine-taper windows were applied to 180-s-long signal windows, and the resulting Fourier spectra were then smoothed (Konno and Ohmachi, 1998) with a smoothing coefficient of $b = 60$. Figure 6 superimposes the medians and 16th and 84th percentiles of the SSR and SSRn for each measurement point.

Concerning comparisons with the MRM, the SSR results obtained using earthquake recordings are generally in good agreement with those from the ambient vibrations SSRn up to 10 Hz. Above this frequency, for stations below the cliff (P101–P115, blue boxes in Fig. 6), the amplification indicated by noise measurements is often higher than the curves resulting from the SSR. In addition, we also performed the

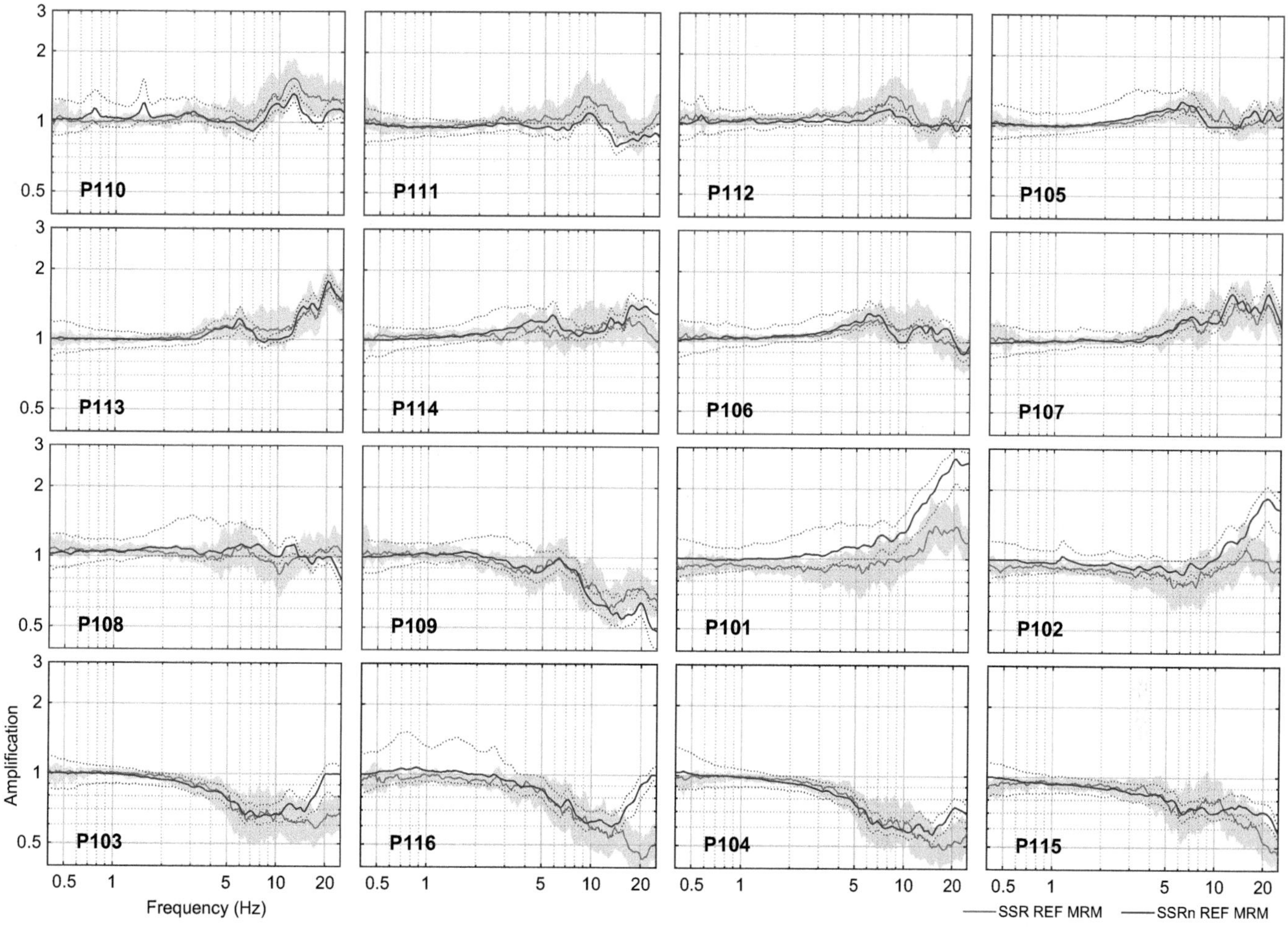

calculations by normalizing with the P108 reference station. These results are available in Figure S2. In this case, the SSRn approach aligns less closely with the SSR results. In particular, the SSRn technique underestimates the amplifications from ground-motion measurements for most stations located at the top of the cliff (red boxes in Fig. S2) from 7 to 20 Hz. For stations below the cliff and above 10 Hz, SSRn curves offer higher amplification than obtained with SSR calculations. However, it should be noted that the application of SSRn at high frequencies remains difficult. The use of this method assumes that noise sources are the same for the site under study and the chosen reference. However, at high frequencies, human activity is the main source of the ambient seismic field. To the SW of our experiment, a road passes at less than 30 m from station P101, and there is also a quarry still in operation to the NW: both are likely to have an impact on the recorded ambient seismic field. Given the distance between the sensors studied and the reference, in this case, the wavefield from these sources does not arrive via exactly the same path. Consequently, for the acquisition of ambient noise, the MRM smooths out these effects and is more reliable than a single reference, unlike earthquake measurements, for which the choice of reference did not appear to have a significant impact (see Fig. 2).

Figure 6. Comparison of the SSR (pink) and SSR technique applied on noise measurements' (SSRn; purple) reports on the root mean square of the horizontal components for each station, compared with the median reference. The solid lines represent the median, the dotted lines (SSRn curves), and pink patches (SSR curves) correspond to the 16th and 84th percentiles. The colored boxes indicate the position of the sensor relative to the cliff, as described in Figure 2. The color version of this figure is available only in the electronic edition.

Finally, when the MRM is used, the SSRn curves exhibit a close correspondence to the SSR values derived from earthquake recordings. This method thus appears as a valuable alternative for determining the amplification factors, especially in short-term acquisitions lacking sufficient earthquake data. Nevertheless, caution is advised when using this method with a single reference station because the effects may be overestimated above 10 Hz.

Moreover, as described in the Methodological Framework section, we applied the commonly used HVSR method proposed by Nakamura (1989). The fields of application and the limitations of this method have been commented on by numerous authors in recent years (e.g., Bonnefoy-Claudet *et al.*, 2006; Bard, 2008; Perron, Gélis, *et al.*, 2018; Xu and Wang, 2021, among others) and its use for the estimation of topographic site effects has been widely attempted (e.g., Chávez-García *et al.*, 1996; Massa *et al.*, 2014; Wood and Cox, 2016, among others), justifying our will to apply this method to both ambient seismic measurements (HVSR applied on noise measurements [HVSRn]) and ground-motion recordings (HVSR). The HVSR and HVSRn curves are compared in Figure S3. However, in most cases, the HVSR and HVSRn curves differ significantly with multiple peaks at low frequencies when computed on earthquakes, which leads to a difficult interpretation. It seems the use of the HVSR method does not yield significant results in this context, nor reveal key findings.

ORIGIN OF THE OBSERVED AMPLIFICATIONS AND DE-AMPLIFICATIONS

Geophysical measurements

Highlighting purely topographic effects is difficult because lithological effects often overlap and influence them (Asimaki and Jeong, 2013). It is not uncommon for amplifications that are initially attributed to topography to be mainly caused by lithological amplifications (Glinsky *et al.*, 2019). Generally, given the weathering of the rocks and their decompression close to the surface, the velocities of the waves tend to increase while propagating at deeper geological layers. In the case of the quarry that is the subject of our study, the rock excavation has stripped the naturally altered zone. It is therefore possible that at equivalent depth from the surface, the velocities are higher at the bottom of the quarry than at the top. The possibility that the observed de-amplification or amplification is due to this possible difference in velocity profile must be examined.

We therefore carried out geophysical measurements as described in the Methodological framework section, enabling us to establish *S*-wave velocity profiles. We applied surface-wave dispersion methods (Foti *et al.*, 2014), combining MASW (Park *et al.*, 1999; Yong *et al.*, 2022), and passive AVA (Foti *et al.*, 2018), using the acquisition geometry of RAP stations (RESIF, 1995) by Hollender *et al.* (2018).

At the summit of our study site, we set up three MASW lines (24 geophones spaced 2 m apart for one line and 1 m apart for two lines). We also implemented an AVA network with a total of 29 SmartSolo IGU-16HR 3C nodes arranged in groups of seven in circles with radii of 5, 15, 45, and 135 m, plus a central sensor. In the lower part of our study area, we set up one MASW line (24 geophones spaced 1 m apart) and an AVA network involving a total of 15 SmartSolo nodes, arranged in groups of seven in circles with radii of 5 and 15 m, plus a central sensor. For this ambient noise low-motion acquisition, the SmartSolo IGU-16HR 3C nodes were configured with a gain of 24 dB. Figure S4 shows the layout of these measurements. We followed the processing recommendations set out in the Interpacific Guidelines (Foti *et al.*, 2018), particularly with regard to the validity domains of the AVA networks and MASW lines (minimum and maximum interpretable wavelengths).

The AVA measurements were processed using the Rayleigh-wave three-component beamforming (RTBF) *f-k* processing (Wathelet *et al.*, 2018). We did not apply the RTBF processing simultaneously to all sensors but to pairs of consecutive circles (example for the top part: circles of 5 and 15 m, 15 and 45 m, and 45 and 135 m). A particular feature was observed during the initial processing tests. The dispersion curves obtained seemed to split (see Fig. S5a), a feature that cannot be explained here by the coexistence of different modes of the Rayleigh wave. We, therefore, considered the possibility that this feature was due to the anisotropy of the medium. To validate this hypothesis, we plotted the dispersion curve considering only the analysis windows associated with wavefields propagating in specific azimuths. We obtained the best results (clearest dispersion curve) by retaining windows corresponding to wavefields propagating in the azimuths 130° ± 30° (Fig. S5b) and 220° ± 30° (Fig. S5c). The hypothesis of anisotropy seems to be confirmed.

Analysis of environment anisotropy

To go further in this analysis, we first established a reference dispersion curve: the one obtained in the 130° and 220° directions mentioned earlier. We then plotted, for each analysis window (regardless of the propagation azimuth), the relationship between the measured phase velocities and the reference dispersion curve. These results are shown in Figure S6. The anisotropic nature of the phase velocities is clearly observed. A sine function adjustment suggests a maximum velocity direction of 137° and an average anisotropy rate of 41%. It can also be seen that the reference dispersion curve generally corresponds to the azimuth where the velocities are lowest.

The next step consisted of establishing a reference *S*-wave velocity profile, representative of the 130° azimuth (which we will call the slow direction or slow axis), consistent with the measured dispersion curves, for which depth is expressed from the top part of the study site. In line with the formulation of the velocity profiles proposed by Cushing *et al.* (2020), this velocity profile consists of a top layer of homogeneous velocity followed by different gradients of linear velocity with depth:

$$V_S(h) = \begin{cases} 300, & 0 \le h \le 2 \\ 7.25h + 695, & 2 < h \le 350 \\ 3230, & h > 350 \end{cases}.$$

At great depth (large wavelength), this profile matches the values proposed by Cushing *et al.* (2020), which themselves are based on the model of Haslinger *et al.* (1999). Considering the observations on the anisotropic nature of the environment, the reference profile for the fast direction is as follows:

$$V_S(h) = \begin{cases} 300, & 0 \le h \le 2 \\ 6.43h + 980, & 2 < h \le 350 \\ 3230, & h > 350 \end{cases}.$$

Note that we have chosen to keep an isotropic top layer (here we have no short-wavelength information on possible anisotropy values). Similarly, at great depth, we use an isotropic velocity. At the bottom of the quarry, the reference profile adopted in the slow direction is as follows:

$$V_S(h) = \begin{cases} 480, & 0 \le h \le 5 \\ 7.25h + 905, & 5 < h \le 320 \\ 3230, & h > 320 \end{cases}.$$

And in the fast direction:

$$V_S(h) = \begin{cases} 480, & 0 \le h \le 5 \\ 6.43h + 1170, & 5 < h \le 320 \\ 3230, & h > 320 \end{cases}.$$

In fact, these profiles correspond to the profiles expressed from the top part, offset by 30 m (approximate height of the cliff), except for the surface layer: $V_S = 300$ m/s and $h = 2$ m on the upper part; $V_S = 480$ m/s and $h = 5$ m on the lower part. These results are illustrated in Figure 7, which shows the following: the selected velocity profiles (Fig. 7a), the various dispersion curves calculated from these profiles, compared with the measured dispersion curves (Fig. 7b,c).

Comparison between the observed effects and the lithological effect

We then calculated the linear 1D ground response corresponding to these velocity profiles using the approach proposed by Kennett (1974) and implemented by Bard and Gariel (1986). It should be emphasized, however, that the previously identified anisotropy manifests itself in the horizontal plane. It applies to horizontally propagating waves, such as Rayleigh waves, which form the basis of passive and active geophysical measurements (AVA and MASW, respectively). However, we have no information on how this anisotropy might manifest itself in the vertical direction. In fact, the main purpose of performing vertical 1D simulations with the two reference profiles is to test extreme values, rather than to adopt a rigorous approach.

We then smoothed the results using the approach of Konno and Ohmachi (1998) with a smoothing parameter $b = 10$. This choice implies a fairly strong smoothing, but allows us to take into account the variability of the angles of incidence of the seismic motions used in the Back-Azimuth Analysis of the Sources section, as well as the smoothing effect of the heterogeneities of the medium (these two phenomena are not taken into account in our 1D simulation). These 1D site responses are given in Figure 8a. The ratios of site response between the top and bottom of the quarry, in the two characteristic directions, are given in Figure 8b. Overall, there is a little de-amplification (factor ~0.8) between 1 and 2 Hz, as well as a slight amplification centered at 20 Hz. These typologies of site response are nevertheless very different from those observed (for example, in Fig. 2). These results suggest that the average amplification and de-amplification (i.e., regardless of the direction considered), previously highlighted by the analysis of earthquake recordings (the Analysis of ground-motion recordings section, Figs. 2 and 4) cannot be attributed to lithological effects. On the other hand, the strong polarizations observed on the real data (Figs. 4 and 5) are probably attributable to the significant velocity anisotropy evidenced by geophysical measurements. Indeed, in Figure 5, it can be clearly seen that for all the stations located near the cliff and in the quarry, the average amplification and de-amplification do not really follow the changing direction of the cliff face but rather the 130° azimuth where the velocity anisotropy was identified earlier, as well as the perpendicular orientation (i.e., 40°). This can be explained by the former activities carried out in the quarry, which caused the fracturing of the rock, especially at the cliff level, because the quarry followed the directions of fracturing.

Comparison of the observed effects with the depth effect by 1D and 2D homogeneous numerical simulations

To deepen our analysis, a 2D numerical simulation was also performed using SPECFEM2D (Komatitsch and Vilotte, 1998), and the results were compared with our seismic motion analyses. A step function was used to simplify the cliff model, assuming a homogeneous medium. In addition, numerous receivers were simulated, some of which are shown in Figure 9. The parameters chosen for this simulation consist of a shear-wave velocity $V_S = 920$ m/s, corresponding to the average velocity over 30 m using the "fast" profile, and a step function height equal to 30 m, the approximate height of the cliff. Vertically incident *SV* and *SH* plane waves were applied to the bottom of the model.

Throughout the numerical simulation, a multitude of traces were obtained. Two of these were selected for further analysis because their locations corresponded to those of the two real stations located at the base and the summit of the cliff (P104 and P105, respectively). The fast Fourier transforms were calculated, and the resulting spectra were smoothed with a smoothing factor $b = 80$ (Konno and Ohmachi, 1998). We normalized these spectra to that of the receiver corresponding to point P108. Then, we computed the SSR on recorded seismic motion at these same two points, following the procedure described in the Reference method: SSR section, this time with respect to the P108 reference. These three points being present throughout the duration of the experiment, SSR were computed on the 307 seismic events recorded.

The SSR calculated on measured seismic motions shows amplifications at the top edge of the scarp (Fig. 9, P105/P108) that vary depending on the direction observed. In fact, very negligible variations are observed in a transversal direction (N40°E) to the orientation of the cliff face, whereas in a longitudinal direction (N130°E), the median SSR reaches a factor of 2–7 Hz. The SSR from the 2D numerical simulation

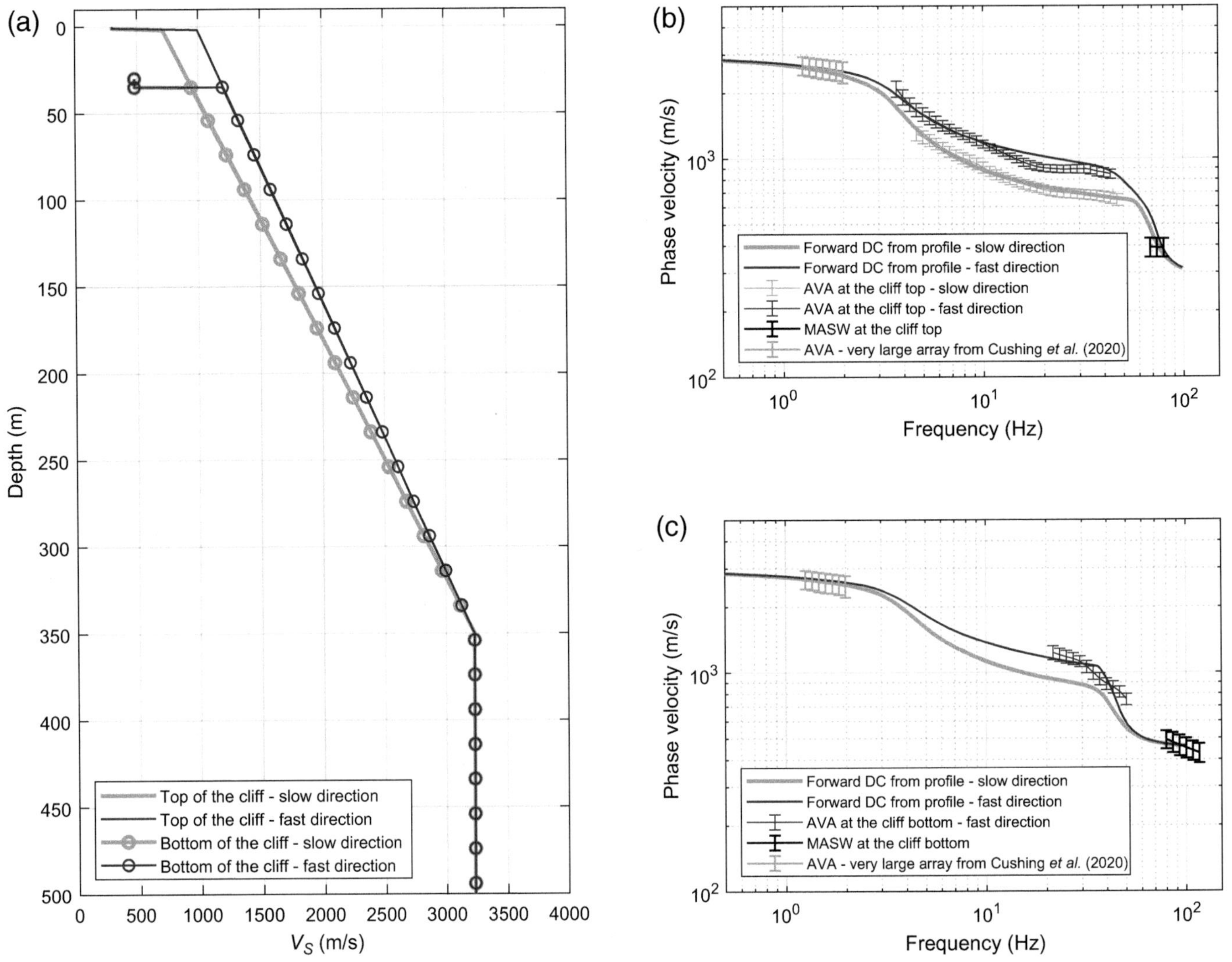

Figure 7. Results of geophysical measurements. (a) Velocity profiles obtained in the slow (orange) and fast (blue) directions, from the top in continuous lines and at the foot of the cliff in dotted lines. The equations of velocity profiles are detailed in the Origin of the Observed Amplifications and De-amplifications section. (b,c) Comparison of the dispersion curves (DCs) measured with the DCs calculated from the velocity profiles illustrated in (a), obtained at the top of the cliff (b) and at the foot of the cliff (c). AVA, ambient vibration array; MASW, multichannel analysis of surface waves. The color version of this figure is available only in the electronic edition.

shows amplifications at the top edge of the scarp that are less sensitive to the type of incident wave (*SH* or *SV*). In the *SH* case, the maximum amplification is approximately 1.6 and is reached at 6 Hz, which is slightly lower than that observed on the experimental SSR. In the case of a plane *SV* wave, the SSR reaches a factor of 2 at 6 Hz, whereas on actual measured data, almost no variations in the median SSR are observed.

Furthermore, the de-amplification observed at the foot of the cliff (Fig. 9, P104/P108) during real seismic events is clearly predicted by the numerical simulation. In the N40°E direction, there is a strong de-amplification reaching a factor of 3 at 7–8 Hz. In the longitudinal direction at the quarry face (N130°E), this only occurs from 10 Hz onward and reaches a maximum de-amplification of 0.5 at around 15 Hz. Numerical simulation shows that the SSR obtained in the *SH* and *SV* cases exhibits de-amplification in both cases, starting at 0.5 Hz. The minimum SSRs are 0.33 in the *SH* case and 0.4 in the *SV* case, reached at 6 and 4 Hz, respectively.

The general de-amplification observed at the base of the cliff on SSR derived from real seismic events is qualitatively reproduced by the 2D numerical simulation, although with a noticeable shift in frequency. This discrepancy can be explained by the highly simplified assumptions underlying the model. Indeed, the use of a homogeneous medium does not necessarily reflect all the properties of the real medium and the complexity of the real subsurface, nor does it account for the 3D effects. Nonetheless, the similarity in the shape of the simulated and measured curves suggests that the de-amplification at the cliff base results from interference between upgoing and downgoing waves, supporting the interpretation of a topographic effect. However, the directional dependence observed on the experimental SSR at the cliff top is not

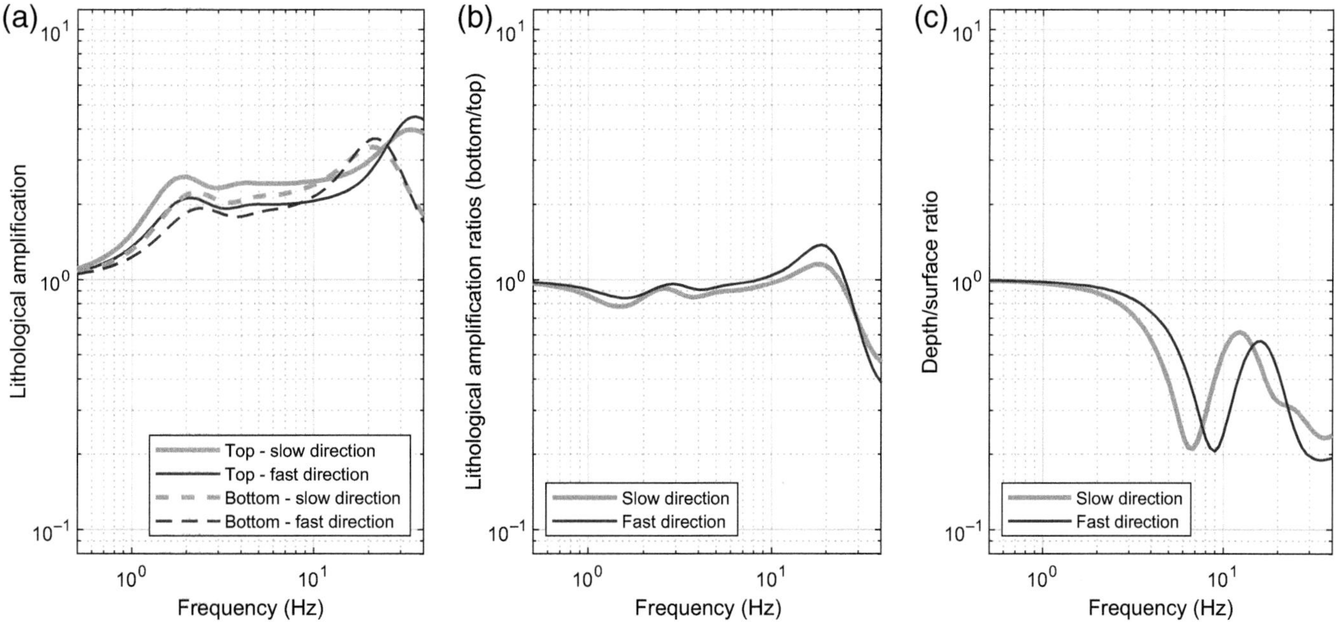

Figure 8. (a) Linear 1D soil responses in the slow (orange) and fast (blue) directions calculated at the top of the cliff in solid lines and at the base of the cliff in dotted lines. (b) Ratios of 1D site responses in the slow (orange) and fast (blue) directions. (c) 1D numerical simulation between a virtual sensor located on the surface and a sensor installed at a depth of 30 m, in the slow (orange) and fast (blue) directions. The color version of this figure is available only in the electronic edition.

reproduced by the 2D numerical simulation. This suggests that this directional effect is not explained by topography only, which is consistent with the findings from Burjánek *et al.* (2014), but is probably due to a combination of lithological and topographical effects.

In addition, we calculated, using 1D numerical simulation, the spectral ratio between a virtual sensor located at the surface and a virtual sensor located at a depth of 30 m. The results are shown in Figure 8c for the two reference profiles determined. Here, we note a clear de-amplification reaching a minimum at ~7 Hz in the slow direction and ~9 Hz in the fast direction. These de-amplifications are caused by destructive interference between the upgoing and downgoing waves. This type of spectral ratio is closer to what is observed at our study site for sensors located at the foot of the quarry.

Finally, the results from the 1D and 2D simulations are similar and suggest that the de-amplifications observed at the bottom of the quarry can be explained by a phenomenology similar to a depth effect. In the first case, the transfer function between a surface sensor and a sensor located at a depth of 30 m is calculated. In the second case, the spectral ratio is calculated between a receiver located 30 m above the cliff top and a receiver positioned at the surface (i.e., 0 m deep). The de-amplifications obtained in both situations are caused by destructive interference between the upgoing and downgoing waves. In both cases, the spectral ratios calculated from measured data from sensors located at the foot of the quarry are closer to the transfer functions obtained by 1D simulations and the SSR calculated from the 2D simulation than to the site responses obtained in Figure 8b. Therefore, although a topographic effect is clearly present, the observed directional dependence cannot be attributed solely to topography but may result from a combination of lithological and topographical effects.

EFFECTIVENESS OF FSC AND I-FSC PROXIES FOR THE PREDICTION OF OBSERVED AMPLIFICATIONS AND DE-AMPLIFICATIONS

Past studies have led several authors (Cauzzi *et al.*, 2010, 2012; Maufroy *et al.*, 2015; Rai *et al.*, 2016, 2017; Bou Nassif *et al.*, 2025) to propose some simple "site proxies" related to surface topography (based on DEMs) and to use available recordings or sets of synthetics to derive formulas allowing for the prediction of topographic amplification factors, linked exclusively to simple geometrical effects without any ground-motion measurement. The FSC proxy, developed by Maufroy *et al.* (2015), makes it possible to predict topographical effects based on the curvature of the Earth's surface, which is itself derived from DEMs. This proxy enables median amplification factors (MAFs) to be obtained by linking DEM and shear-wave velocities. As shown in equation (1), MAFs depend on λ_S the S waves wavelength and the smoothed topographic curvature C_S, which relies on the characteristic smoothing lengths L_S (which is wavelength dependent; see Maufroy *et al.*, 2015, for further information),

$$\mathrm{MAF}(f) = (0.0008 \times \lambda_S) \times C_S(L_S) + 1. \qquad (1)$$

A 1-m resolution DEM obtained over a 1 km × 1 km area centered on the cliff enabled us to extend the FSC proxy

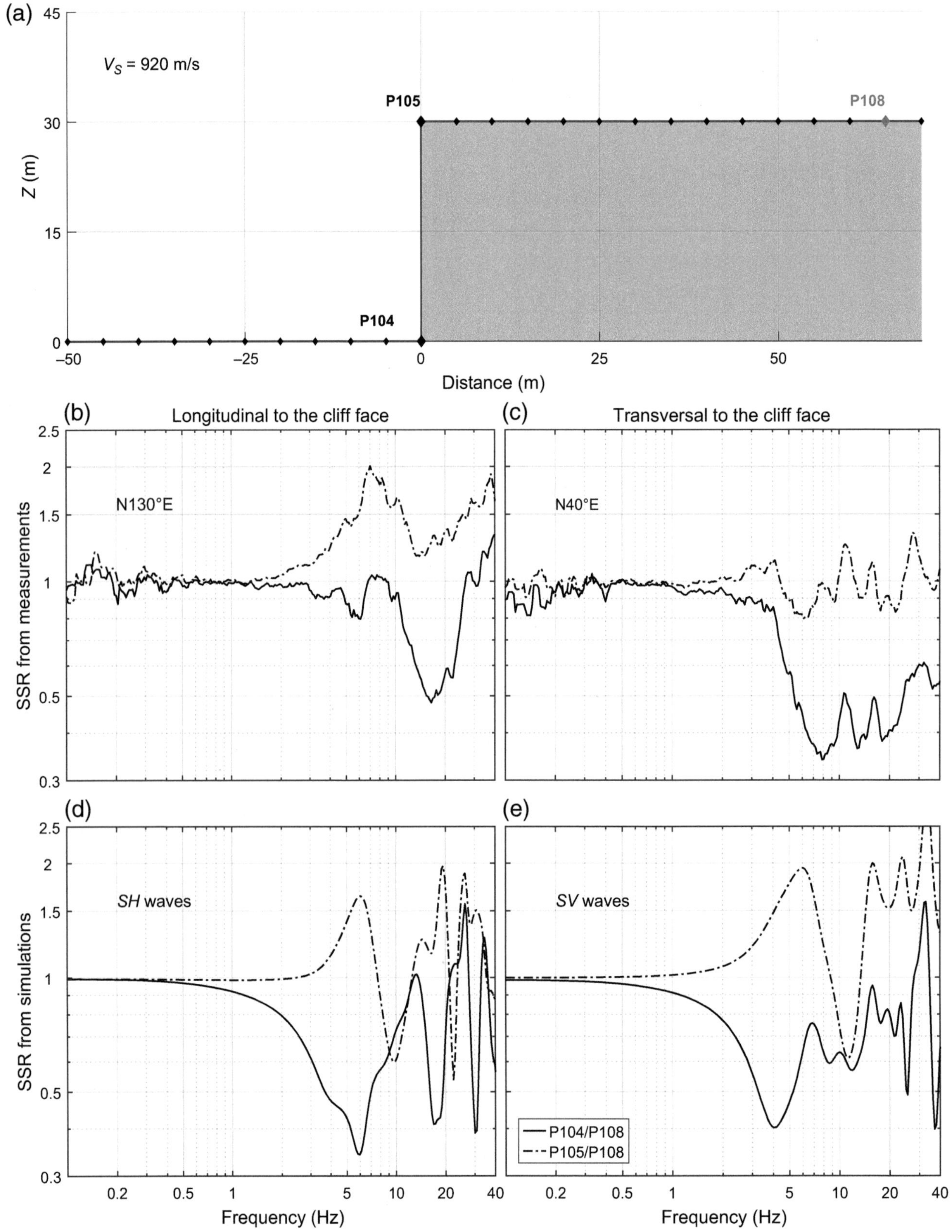

Figure 9. Comparison between experimental SSR and SSR resulting from a 2D digital simulation in a homogeneous environment, with a shear wave velocity equal to 920 m/s. (a) Geometry of the simulated receivers as well as of the cliff approximated by a 30-m high step function. (b,c) Median of SSR calculated on real measured seismic motion, in the longitudinal and then transverse directions to the cliff face. (d,e) SSR resulting from the 2D numerical simulation, for the case of plane waves with vertical incidence and *SH* excitation (left), then *SV* excitation (right). The spectral ratios were calculated for points P104 (solid lines) and P105 (dashed–dotted lines) and normalized by point P108. The color version of this figure is available only in the electronic edition.

calculations over a frequency band ranging from 0.4 to 25 Hz, using a shear-wave velocity of around 920 m/s (see the Origin of the observed amplifications and de-amplifications section). However, due to the extremely pronounced topography studied here, which is very different from that used for the initial simulation (Maufroy *et al.*, 2015), we aim to test truly extreme curvature values. In addition, the calculations were extrapolated to higher frequencies in this case study. Nonetheless, the linear form of equation (1) can yield negative MAFs values, which lack physical meaning, especially at high frequencies.

To address this, we adopted an improved exponential functional formulation developed alongside Bou Nassif *et al.* (2025) (see also Bou Nassif, 2023), as shown in equation (2), employing the same parameters as in equation (1),

$$\mathrm{MAF}(f) = \exp((0.00021 \times \lambda_S^{1.2}) \times C_S(L_S)). \qquad (2)$$

Thus, new calculations of the FSC proxy were performed using equation (2). Figure 10a compares maps of MAFs obtained from both linear and exponential functional forms of the FSC proxy, with a shear-wave velocity of 920 m/s at 5 Hz. The same behaviors are observed with both functional forms of the FSC proxy, which consist of a de-amplification at the base of the cliff, in the unused quarry, and a slight amplification at the top. At the top edge of the cliff, even if the linear form predicts slightly higher amplification with MAFs reaching approximately 1.5, whereas the exponential form predicts MAFs that do not exceed ~1.3, both functional forms give consistent results. However, at the lower part of the study area, MAFs computed with the linear form predict de-amplification by a factor of over 2 (MAFs ≤ 0.5), whereas with the exponential form, MAFs range from approximately 0.6 to 0.9. Moreover, de-amplification at the base of the cliff is more significant along the N130°E segment, where the cliff's height is greater.

We also computed the i-FSC proxy developed by Bou Nassif *et al.* (2025) on the study area. This proxy takes into account the interaction between topographic irregularities and incident seismic waves from nearby sources. The objective was to assess whether the i-FSC proxy predicts different site response behaviors for seismic sources located to the SW and NE, based on the previous Back-azimuth analysis of the sources section, which indicated greater de-amplification for the SW group and generally symmetrical behavior between the two source directions, as supported by the statistical approach. To investigate this, we computed the i-FSC Proxy using the developed exponential form for two representative events: one from the SW and one from the NE (Fig. 10b), at a frequency of 5 Hz. The resulting MAFs maps exhibit a clear contrast. At the cliff top, alongside the N130°E segment, MAFs for the SW source range between 1.2 and 1.5, whereas those for the NE source reach values up to 2. Conversely, the de-amplification predicted using an SW event, with waves illuminating the cliff's face, reaches nearly a factor of 2 between points P103 and P104, whereas MAFs from the NE source in the same area remain around 0.9. This latter observation is consistent with the SSR shown in Figure S1, which indicates stronger de-amplification at the cliff base for SW-originating seismic events around this.

In addition, i-FSC proxy maps were also computed for sources from all four cardinal directions, including NW and SE (see Fig. S7). The MAFs obtained from NW and SE sources, which correspond to waves propagating longitudinally along the cliff, are more similar. Among the four sources, the SW event yields the strongest de-amplification at the base of the cliff, which aligns well with the results on real seismic motion recordings.

Furthermore, Figure 10 also shows a comparison between experimental SSR and SSR evaluated using the MAF provided by the FSC proxy. We considered all the measurement points P101–P116 that were present during the last three months of acquisition. We calculated the SSR normalized by the MRM, that is, by the spectrum of the median of stations P101–P116. Similarly, we extracted the MAF from the FSC proxy at each measurement point. After that, we calculated the median of these values corresponding to the 16 stations considered. Then, at each calculation frequency, the MAF obtained at each of the 16 stations is normalized by the median of the MAF calculated previously. The results of this operation are superimposed on the experimental SSR of points P116 at the foot of the cliff and P110 at the top of Figure 10, obtained in the two developed functional forms, linear (in blue, compare with equation 1) and exponential (in black, compare with equation 2). It can be seen that at point P116, the SSR estimated from the FSC proxy in exponential form seems to follow the de-amplification observed on the experimental SSR, although they very slightly underestimate it. On the other hand, the linear functional form of the FSC proxy strongly overestimates the de-amplification measured on high-frequency seismic motion, with negative MAFs above 15 Hz. On the scarp, the two functional forms of the FSC proxy predict the amplification observed in recorded events relatively well, although the linear form predicts a slightly higher amplification above 15 Hz.

Finally, the FSC proxy seems to provide predictions that are consistent with the results obtained from ground-motion measurements. However, it is strongly recommended to calculate the FSC proxy in its two functional forms according to the typology of the studied topography, to avoid taking negative values in the very steep to sheer terrain. Furthermore, the influence of source back azimuth, which mainly increases de-amplification at the base of the cliff for SW-originating events, seems to be well predicted by the i-FSC proxy.

DISCUSSION AND CONCLUSIONS

This work investigated the effect of near-vertical topographic features on ground motion recorded at the top, at the base and in the vicinity of such features. To assess the impact of such steep to vertical topographies, 16 SmartSolo IGU-16HR 3C

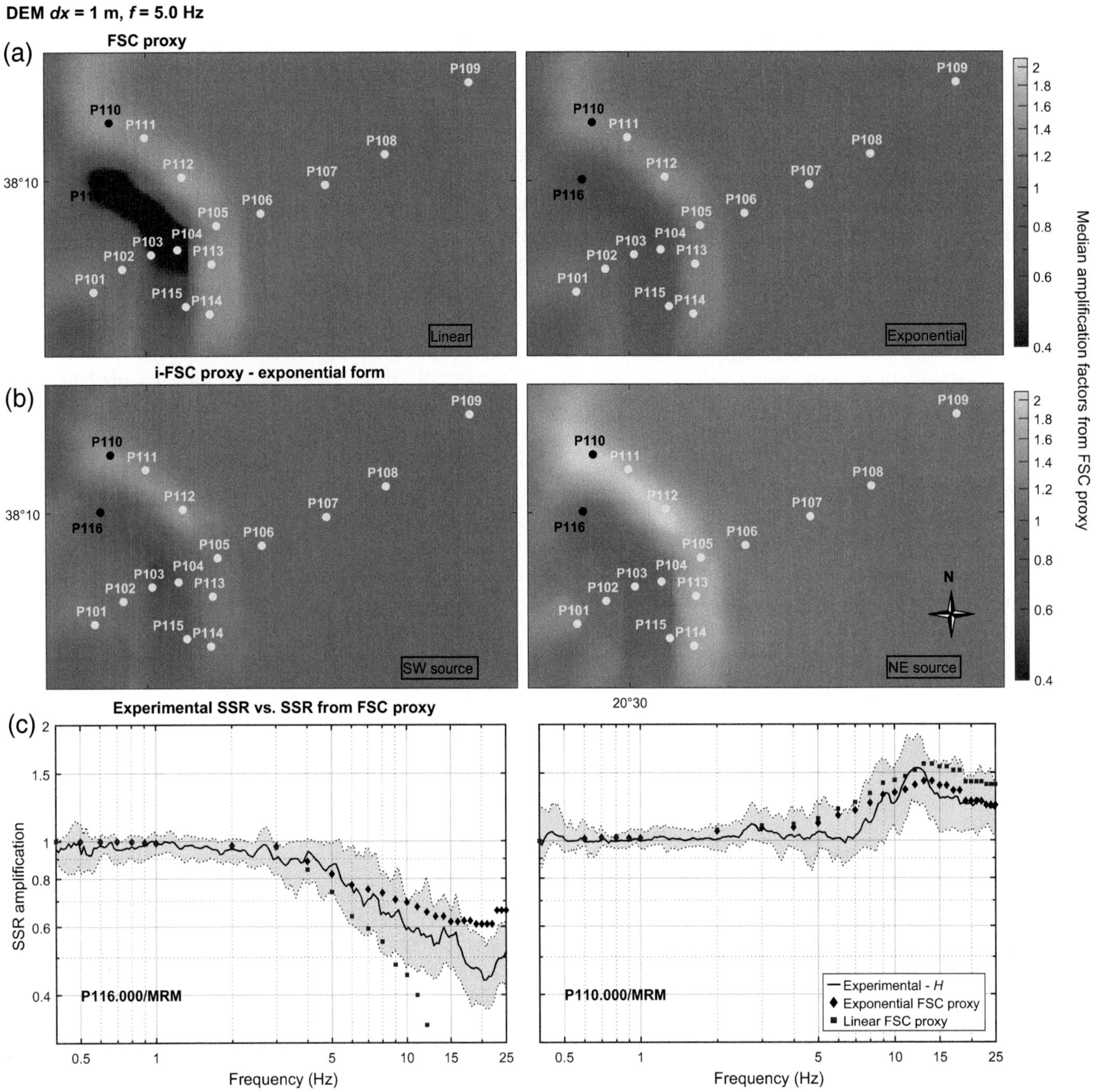

Figure 10. Frequency-scaled curvature (FSC) proxy calculated using a 1-m resolution digital elevation model (DEM) of the study area and a shear-wave velocity of 920 m/s. (a) Median amplification factor (MAF) maps computed with the linear (left) and exponential (right) functional forms of the FSC proxy. (b) Illuminated FSC (i-FSC) proxy computed with the optimized exponential form for a source located SW (left) and a source located NE (right). (a,b) The two black dots indicate the stations for which we show SSR amplification in panel (c). (c) Comparison between SSR calculated on the root mean square of the horizontal components of stations P116 on the left and P110 on the right, with SSR estimated from the amplifications derived from the FSC proxy. SSR values from the FSC proxy are calculated for frequencies ranging from 0.4 to 25 Hz, in linear functional form in blue squares and exponential in black diamonds. The SSR were normalized by the MRM for both methods. The solid lines and colored patches correspond to the median and the intervals delimited by the 16th and 84th percentiles of the SSR calculated on seismic motion. The color version of this figure is available only in the electronic edition.

nodes were set up on either side of a 30-m high cliff in Cephalonia, Western Greece. These stations, installed for 10 months, recorded more than 300 events of low-to-moderate magnitude, in addition to ambient vibrations.

Figure 11 compares the results of different methods applied and based on the SSR technique, with the MRM reference condition, that is, the median of all the spectra recorded at the considered stations. These results focus on the profile lying between points P101 and P108 crossing the cliff, so the MRM corresponds to the median spectrum of recordings at these eight stations, for each one of the methods. The SSR were calculated first on measured (1) earthquake ground motion and (2) ambient vibration recordings (SSRn), then on synthetic predictions (3) from a 2D numerical simulation and (4) from the FSC proxy assuming linear and exponential functional forms. We note that the results show an overall satisfactory agreement, regardless of the method used. De-amplifications are observed at the base of the cliff, with SSR values reaching approximately 0.45 beyond 10 Hz, and gradually decreasing with distance from the cliff. At the top of the scarp, amplification is observed, not exceeding a factor of 1.6. Depending on the method used, the frequency at which the main effects occur may vary.

The SSR technique, when applied to ambient seismic noise data, known as SSRn, provides yields results that are very similar to those of SSR derived from seismic motions up to 10 Hz in the quarry zone, and up to about 7 Hz for the stations at the top of the cliff P105 and P106 (black curves in Fig. 11). Above these frequencies, the use of ambient noise measurements tends to underestimate the effects obtained by SSR on seismic recordings (excepted for P101 and P102). However, it should be remembered that the application of high-frequency SSRn remains sometimes unreliable, especially on rock, because anthropogenic activity is the main source of the ambient vibration field in this case. Thus, the MRM smooths the effects related to such sources, and the method then results in larger variability when a single station is chosen as the reference site, which limits the use of this method at high frequency in our case study. The exponential FSC proxy (black diamonds in Fig. 11) results being a good indicator for predicting the de-amplifications observed on ground motion, in the case of negative curvature values. Indeed, the SSR estimated from the MAFs derived from this proxy closely follows the SSR curves obtained from the experiment (in red in Fig. 11), although from the FSC proxy, the strong de-amplification at the foot of the cliff (P104) and the amplification observed at the top (P105) are slightly underestimated at high frequencies. The SSR estimated from the FSC proxy in linear form is also consistent with the experimental results at the top of the cliff up to 7–10 Hz and for point P101. However, in some cases, the linear functional form FSC proxy (blue squares in Fig. 11) overestimates the de-amplifications (compare with P102 and P103), and can even take negative values beyond 15 Hz, like point P104 at the foot of the cliff. Nevertheless, it should be remembered that the typology of the topographical feature considered in this study is almost vertical, and the calculations were carried out up to very high frequencies in comparison with the initial simulation (Maufroy *et al.*, 2015). Finally, the SSR from the quadratic mean of *SV* and *SH* waves obtained by the 2D numerical simulation is also compared. For the four closest points to the cliff base and edge, that is, P103–P106, despite a shift toward lower frequencies, the 2D simulation (green curves, Fig. 11) predicts the observed amplifications and de-amplifications quite satisfactorily, at least qualitatively. For P101 and P102, the simulation overestimates the de-amplifications. These results should be interpreted with caution, given the highly simplified nature of the 2D model. In reality, a velocity gradient and heterogeneities likely exist that are not well captured by this overly simplified model, which also oversimplifies the actual 2D geometry (except the nearly vertical cliff base) and neglects potential 3D effects. Nevertheless, the 2D numerical simulation was primarily performed to assess the underlying phenomenology. All these results confirm that the observed de-amplification and amplification are consistent with a topographic effect.

The main effects observed consist of slight amplifications at the top of the cliff, for the stations installed at the edge of the cliff, and very strong de-amplifications at the foot of the cliff, occurring mainly between 5 and 15 Hz. The choice of reference condition does not seem to have a strong impact on this study (Fig. 2). The observed de-amplifications evolve by a factor of 2 from 7 Hz for stations at the foot of the cliff and can reach a factor of 3 in the direction perpendicular to the cliff face. However, this azimuthal dependence effect is likely related to the anisotropy of the environment, related to the fracturing of the rock within the cliff, rather than to the almost vertical slope that characterizes the studied topography. Such anisotropy was highlighted by analyses of geophysical measurements performed at the top and bottom of the cliff. In addition, a detailed microtectonic study was conducted in the quarry (Cushing and Roumelioti, 2025). This analysis revealed synsedimentary structures on the one hand, and a fractured zone on the other, both characterized by an N45° orientation and a 70° dip to the NW. The geometry of these structures is consistent with the results of seismological and geophysical investigations carried out on the site. Indeed, it appears that the wave propagation velocity is systematically lower in the direction perpendicular to the structural planes (N135°) than in the parallel direction. This velocity anisotropy directly reflects the influence of fracturing and synsedimentary discontinuities, which lead to a decrease in apparent stiffness and, consequently, a slowing of waves as they pass through these structures. Furthermore, these treatments have also shown that most of the observed effects on seismic motion are not of lithological origin, but are more likely to be related to the effect of the topography. Finally, the de-amplifications observed at the very bottom of the cliff remind closely the effect of the depth when the ground motion is recorded by a seismometer; they correspond to the effects of a seismometer installed at a depth of 30 m, the approximate height of the cliff studied here.

In summary, this study empirically confirms the amplification effects reported in many previous studies at the top of topographical features but mainly highlights that the de-amplifications obtained at the foot of a steep cliff are larger than the

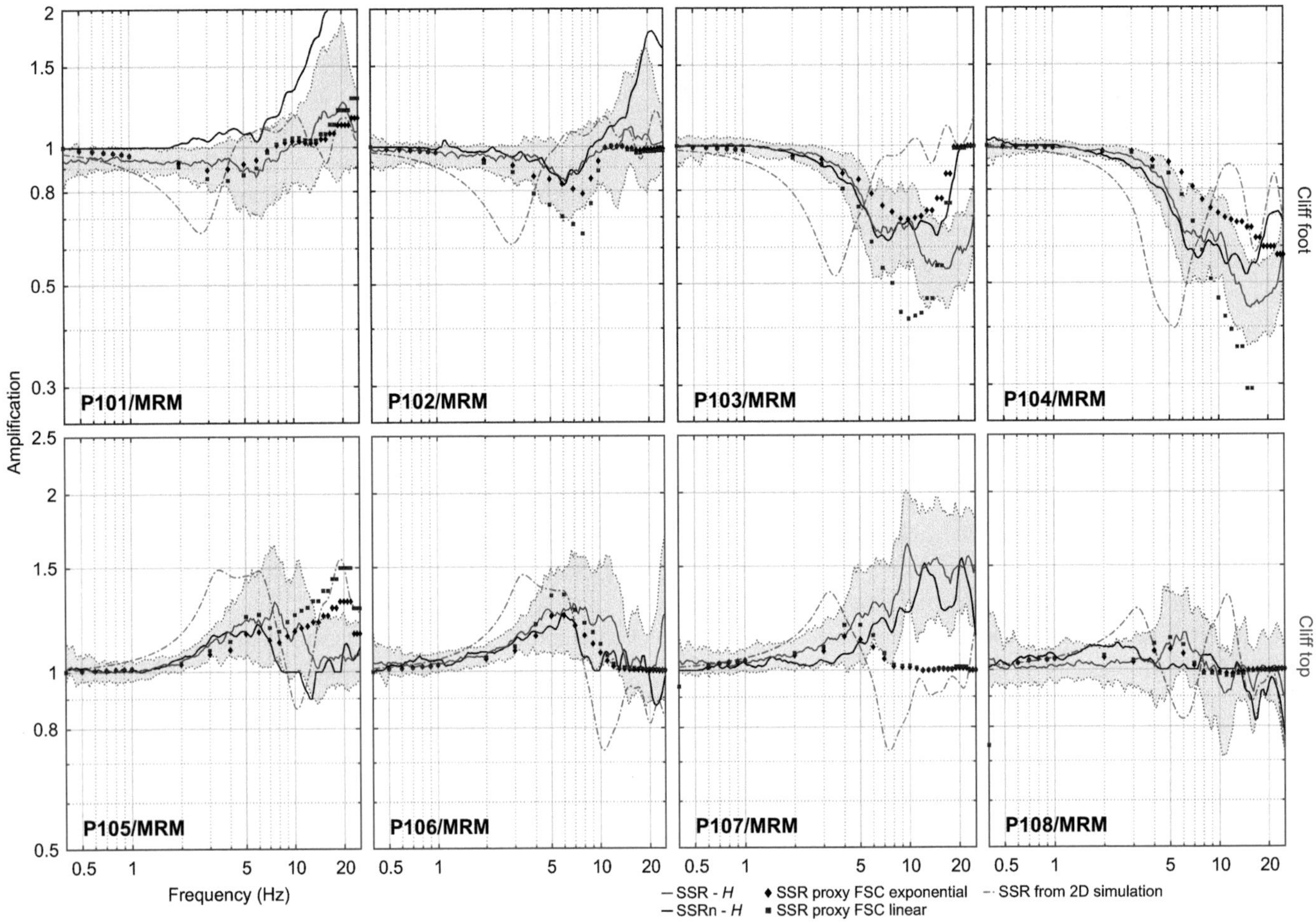

Figure 11. Comparison of the different methods used to estimate the amplifications at each measurement point located on the profile delimited by points P101–P108 and having thus recorded more than 300 events. The medians of the SSR and SSRn results are represented in red and black respectively, with a colored patch indicating the 16th and 84th percentiles of the SSR calculated on the quadratic mean of the horizontal components of each seismometer. The SSR determined from the MAF from the FSC proxy are represented by black diamonds when they have been calculated from the exponential functional form, and by blue squares when they have been calculated from the linear form. The green dashed–dotted curves correspond to the SSR from the quadratic mean of *SV* and *SH* waves obtained by the 2D numerical simulation. The SSR have been standardized by the MRM regardless of the technique applied, that is, by a reference spectrum taking the median of stations P101–P108 in this case. The measurements points at the top of the cliff are marked with red boxes (bottom), those installed at the bottom of the quarry with blue boxes (top). The color version of this figure is available only in the electronic edition.

amplifications obtained at the top. These effects can be satisfactorily predicted using the FSC proxy (Maufroy *et al.*, 2015) and i-FSC proxy (Bou Nassif *et al.*, 2025), provided that an exponential functional form is used for the determination of de-amplifications at the base of the cliff, where extremely steep to vertical topography is involved. Both amplifications at the top and de-amplifications at the foot of a topographic feature must be accounted for when using data recorded by stations installed on or near topographical features, and when choosing the installation site of a new station to be used as a reference site. Indeed, if such effects are not accounted for when determining GMM using data retrieved in such contexts, that is, if the ground motion is assumed representative of the free-field condition and free of amplification/de-amplification, the resulting models can lead to biased ground-motion estimates. By extension, this could lead to an inaccurate assessment of seismic hazard and increased associated uncertainties. These effects may also result in a misestimate of earthquake magnitudes if the considered reference stations are affected by topographic effects. For future seismic station deployments, all these results highlight the importance of keeping a minimum distance of at least tens of meters away from any topographic feature, even those of moderate elevations such as quarry cliffs. The FSC and i-FSC proxies can also help identify areas where significant topographic effects are unlikely, thereby supporting the selection of suitable locations for stations prior to installation.

DATA AND RESOURCES

The metadata extracted from the National Observatory of Athens (NOA) catalog are available at https://www.gein.noa.gr/ (last accessed May 2024). This study has used the event selection procedure from (Theodoulidis, Hollender, *et al.*, 2018) established for the ARGONET database. Data developed in this study may be available from the authors upon request. The supplemental material for this article includes Figures S1–S7, respectively presenting additional standard spectral ratio (SSR) curves illustrating source azimuth effects, comparisons of ground motion and microtremor analyses using P108 as reference, horizontal-to-vertical spectral ratio (HVSR) ambient seismic measurements (HVSRn) versus HVSR results, geophysical setup, and dispersion curves, anisotropy from azimuthal phase velocities, and cliff exposure evaluated through the illuminated frequency-scaled curvature (i-FSC) proxy.

DECLARATION OF COMPETING INTERESTS

The authors acknowledge that there are no conflicts of interest recorded.

ACKNOWLEDGMENTS

This work was supported by the French Atomic and Alternative Energies Commission (CEA) and Electricité de France (EDF), within the framework of the CASHIMA3 and SIGMA3 research programs on seismic hazard assessment. SIGMA3 (2024–2028, www.sigma-programs.com) is funded by an industrial consortium composed of EDF, CEA, České energetické závody (Czech Energy Company, CEZ) Group, Pacific Gas and Electric Company (PG&E), VTT research center, Swissnuclear, Central Research Institute of the Electric Power Industry (CRIEPI), Stük, Uniper, and Vattenfall. The authors would like to thank Dimitris Papadatos for allowing the installation of SmartSolo IGU-16HR 3C nodes in his quarry. The authors are also grateful to Harris Moustakas and Maria-Georgia Dasoula for their help in acquiring the geophysical measurements and for performing first stages of their treatment. Isabelle Douste-Bacqué and Margaux Buscetti provided valuable help and support during the initial logistical stages, as well as with the initial installation of the seismometers. The authors also thank Ioannis Grendas for his help with geophysical acquisitions, along with Ioanna Nikolopoulou and Panagiotis Tsigkanos, who ensured the experiment ran smoothly by retrieving several datasets in the field. The authors would like to sincerely thank John Douglas and Sadanori Higashi for their valuable feedback, insightful comments, and constructive suggestions, which greatly contributed to improving this article. Their reviews were carried out within the framework of the SeIsmic hazard and Ground Motion Assessment (SIGMA3) research program focused on seismic hazard assessment. A preliminary version of this work was initially prepared as a deliverable for that program. Finally, the authors thank the two anonymous reviewers for their insightful and constructive suggestions, which greatly contributed to improving the article.

REFERENCES

Asimaki, D., and S. Jeong (2013). Ground-motion observations at Hotel Montana during the M 7.0 2010 Haiti earthquake: Topography or soil amplification? *Bull. Seismol. Soc. Am.* **103,** no. 5, 2577–2590, doi: 10.1785/0120120242.

Bard, P. Y. (1998). Microtremor measurements: A tool for site effect estimation, *Proc. Effects of Surface Geology on Seismic Motion*, Vol. 3, 1251–1279.

Bard, P. Y. (2008). Foreword: The H/V technique: Capabilities and limitations based on the results of the SESAME project, *Bull. Earthq. Eng.* **6,** 1–2, doi: 10.1007/s10518-008-9059-4.

Bard, P. Y., and J.-C. Gariel (1986). The seismic response of two-dimensional sedimentary deposits with large velocity gradients, *Bull. Seismol. Soc. Am.* **76,** 343–366, doi: 10.1785/BSSA0760020343.

Bonnefoy-Claudet, S., C. Cornou, P.-Y. Bard, F. Cotton, P. Moczo, J. Kristek, and D. Fäh (2006). H/V ratio: A tool for site effects evaluation. Results from 1-D noise simulations, *Geophys. J. Int.* **167,** no. 2, 827–837.

Borcherdt, R. D. (1970). Effects of local geology on ground motion near San Francisco Bay, *Bull. Seismol. Soc. Am.* **60,** no. 1, 29–61.

Bou Nassif, A. (2023). Mouvements sismiques forts dans les régions montagneuses et mouvements de terrain induits, *Ph.D. Thesis*, Université Grenoble Alpes.

Bou Nassif, A., E. Maufroy, P. Lacroix, E. Chaljub, M. Causse, and P.-Y. Bard (2025). The i-FSC proxy for predicting inter-event and spatial variation of topographic site effects, *Bull. Earthq. Eng.* **23,** 671–692, doi: 10.1007/s10518-024-02042-4.

Bouchon, M. (1973). Effect of topography on surface motion, *Bull. Seismol. Soc. Am.* **63,** no. 2, 615–632, doi: 10.1785/BSSA0630020615.

Burjánek, J., B. Edwards, and D. Fäh (2014). Empirical evidence of local seismic effects at sites with pronounced topography: A systematic approach, *Geophys. J. Int.* **197,** no. 1, 608–619, doi: 10.1093/gji/ggu014.

Castellaro, S., G. Alessandrini, and G. Musinu (2022). Seismic station installations and their impact on the recorded signals and derived quantities, *Bull. Seismol. Soc. Am.* **93,** no. 6, 3348–3362, doi: 10.1785/0220220029.

Cauzzi, C., E. Faccioli, M. Stupazzini, and M. Villani (2010). Including topographic amplification factors in GMPEs by means of 3D simulations of ground motions, *Proc. of the 14th European Conf. of Earthquake Engineering*, Ohrid, Republic of Macedonia, 30 August–3 September, Paper No. 1382.

Cauzzi, C., D. Fäh, V. Pessina, E. Faccioli, and C. Smerzini (2012). Topographic amplification from recorded earthquake data and numerical simulations, *Proc. of the 15th World Conf. on Earthquake Engineering*, Lisbon, Portugal, Paper No. 5823.

Chávez-García, F. J., L. R. Sánchez, and D. Hatzfeld (1996). Topographic site effects and HVSR. A comparison between observations and theory, *Bull. Seismol. Soc. Am.* **86,** no. 5, 1559–1573, doi: 10.1785/BSSA0860051559.

Cushing, E. M., and Z. Roumelioti (2025). Study of ARGOSCARP experiment quarry fracturing regarding the seismological analysis of topographical effects, doi: 10.13140/RG.2.2.33137.54884.

Cushing, E. M., F. Hollender, D. Moiriat, C. Guyonnet-Benaize, N. Theodoulidis, E. Branchu-Pons, S. Sépulcre, P. Y. Bard, C. Cornou, A. Dechamp, *et al.* (2020). Building a three dimensional model of the active Plio-Quaternary basin of Argostoli (Cephalonia Island, Greece): An integrated geophysical and geological approach, *Eng. Geol.* **265,** 105,441.

Epos-France (1995). Epos-France Broad-band network (RLBP), Epos-France Seismological Data Centre, doi: 10.15778/resif.fr.

Foti, S., F. Hollender, F. Garofalo, D. Albarello, M. Asten, P. Y. Bard, C. Comina, C. Cornou, B. Cox, G. Di Giulio, *et al.* (2018). Guidelines for the good practice of surface wave analysis: A product of the InterPACIFIC project, *Bull. Earthq. Eng.* **16,** 2367–2420, doi: 10.1007/s10518-017-0206-7.

Foti, S., C. G. Lai, G. Rix, and C. Strobbia (2014). *Surface Wave Methods for Near-Surface Site Characterization*, CRC Press, Boca Raton, Florida.

Geli, L., P.-Y. Bard, and B. Jullien (1988). The effect of topography on earthquake ground motion: A review and new results, *Bull. Seismol. Soc. Am.* **78,** no. 1, 42–63, doi: 10.1785/BSSA0780010042.

Glinsky, N., E. Bertrand, and J. Régnier (2019). Numerical simulation of topographical and geological site effects. Applications to canonical topographies and Rognes hill, South East France, *Soil Dynam. Earthq. Eng.* **116,** 620–636, doi: 10.1016/j.soildyn.2018.10.020.

Haslinger, F., E. Kissling, J. Ansorge, D. Hatzfeld, E. Papadimitriou, V. Karakostas, K. Makropoulos, H.-G. Kahle, and Y. Peter (1999). 3D crustal structure from local earthquake tomography around the Gulf of Arta (Ionian region, NW Greece), *Tectonophysics.* **304,** no. 3, 201–218, doi: 10.1016/S0040-1951(98)00298-4.

Hollender, F., C. Cornou, A. Dechamp, K. Oghalaei, F. Renalier, E. Maufroy, C. Burnouf, S. Thomassin, M. Wathelet, P. Y. Bard, *et al.* (2018). Characterization of site conditions (soil class, VS30, velocity profiles) for 33 stations from the French permanent accelerometric network (RAP) using surface-wave methods, *Bull. Earthq. Eng.* **16,** no. 6, 2337–2365, doi: 10.1007/s10518-017-0135-5.

Hollender, F., Z. Roumelioti, E. Maufroy, P. Traversa, and A. Mariscal (2020). Can we trust high-frequency content in strong-motion database signals? Impact of housing, coupling, and installation depth of seismic sensors, *Bull. Seismol. Soc. Am.* **91,** no. 4, 2192–2205, doi: 10.1785/0220190163.

Irikura, K., and T. Kawanaka (1980). Characteristics of microtremors on ground with discontinuous underground structure, *Bull. Disaster Prev. Res. Inst.* **30,** 81–96.

Kagami, H., C. M. Duke, G. C. Liang, and Y. Ohta (1982). Observation of 1- to 5-second microtremors and their application to earthquake engineering. Part II. Evaluation of site effect upon seismic wave amplification due to extremely deep soil deposits, *Bull. Seismol. Soc. Am.* **72,** no. 3, 987–998.

Kagami, H., S. Okada, K. Shiono, M. Oner, M. Dravinski, and A. K. Mal (1986). Observation of 1- to 5-second microtremors and their application to earthquake engineering. Part III. A two-dimensional study of site effects in the San Fernando Valley, *Bull. Seismol. Soc. Am.* **76,** no. 6, 1801–1812, doi: 10.1785/BSSA0760061801.

Kennett, B. L. N. (1974). Reflections, rays, and reverberations, *Bull. Seismol. Soc. Am.* **64,** no. 6, 1685–1696, doi: 10.1785/BSSA0640061685.

Komatitsch, D., and J.-P. Vilotte (1998). The spectral element method: An efficient tool to simulate the seismic response of 2D and 3D geological structures, *Bull. Seismol. Soc. Am.* **88,** no. 2, 368–392, doi: 10.1785/BSSA0880020368.

Konno, K., and T. Ohmachi (1998). Ground-motion characteristics estimated from spectral ratio between horizontal and vertical components of microtremor, *Bull. Seismol. Soc. Am.* **88,** no. 1, 228–241, doi: 10.1785/BSSA0880010228.

Massa, M., S. Barani, and S. Lovati (2014). Overview of topographic effects based on experimental observations: Meaning, causes and possible interpretations, *Geophys. J. Int.* **197,** no. 3, 1537–1550, doi: 10.1093/gji/ggt341.

Massa, M., S. Lovati, E. D'Alema, G. Ferretti, and M. Bakavoli (2010). An experimental approach for estimating seismic amplification effects at the Top of a Ridge, and the implication for ground-motion predictions: The case of Narni, Central Italy, *Bull. Seismol. Soc. Am.* **100,** no. 6, 3020–3034, doi: 10.1785/0120090382.

Maufroy, E., V. M. Cruz-Atienza, F. Cotton, and S. Gaffet (2015). Frequency-scaled curvature as a proxy for topographic site-effect amplification and ground-motion variability, *Bull. Seismol. Soc. Am.* **105,** no. 1, 354–367, doi: 10.1785/0120140089.

Maufroy, E., V. M. Cruz-Atienza, and S. Gaffet (2012). A robust method for assessing 3-D topographic site effects: A case study at the LSBB underground laboratory, France, *Earthq. Spectra* **28,** no. 3, 1097–1115, doi: 10.1193/1.4000050.

Moiriat, D., M. Benz-Navarrete, E. Cushing, C. Gelis, P. Rischette, N. Theodoulidis, Z. Roumelioti, and F. Hollender (2023). Characterization of surface formations in the Koutavos sedimentary basin (Cephalonia, Greece), *Proc. of 11 ieme Colloque de l'AFPS (Association Française du Génie Parasismique),* Guadeloupe, French West Indies, 7–10 November 2023, 175–185.

Nakamura, Y. (1989). A method for dynamic characteristics estimation of subsurface using microtremor on the ground surface, *Q. Rep. Railway Tech. Res.* **30,** no. 1, 25–33.

Nechtschein, S., P.-Y. Bard, J.-C. Gariel, J. Meneroud, P. Dervin, E. Cushing, C. Gaubert, S. Vidal, and A.-M. Duval (1996). A topographic effect study in the Nice region, *Proc. of 5th Int. Conf. on Seismic Zonation*, 1074.

Park, C. B., R. D. Miller, and J. Xia (1999). Multichannel analysis of surface waves, *Geophysics* **64,** no. 3, 800–808, doi: 10.1190/1.1444590.

Perron, V. (2017). Apport des enregistrements de séismes et de bruit de fond pour l'évaluation site-spécifique de l'aléa sismique en zone de sismicité faible à modérée, *Ph.D. Thesis*, Université Grenoble Alpes.

Perron, V., P. Bergamo, and D. Fäh (2022). Evaluating the minimum number of earthquakes in empirical site response assessment: Input for new requirements for microzonation in the Swiss building codes, *Front. Earth Sci.* **10,** doi: 10.3389/feart.2022.917855.

Perron, V., C. Gélis, B. Froment, F. Hollender, P.-Y. Bard, G. Cultrera, and E. M. Cushing (2018). Can broad-band earthquake site responses be predicted by the ambient noise spectral ratio? Insight from observations at two sedimentary basins, *Geophys. J. Int.* **215**, no. 2, 1442–1454, doi: 10.1093/gji/ggy355.

Perron, V., F. Hollender, A. Mariscal, N. Theodoulidis, C. Andreou, P. Y. Bard, C. Cornou, R. Cottereau, E. M. Cushing, A. Frau, *et al.* (2018). Accelerometer, velocimeter dense-array, and rotation sensor datasets from the Sinaps@ postseismic survey (Cephalonia 2014–2015 aftershock sequence), *Bull. Seismol. Soc. Am.* **89,** no. 2A, 678–687, doi: 10.1785/0220170125.

Perron, V., A. Laurendeau, F. Hollender, P. Y. Bard, C. Gélis, P. Traversa, and S. Drouet (2018). Selecting time windows of seismic phases and noise for engineering seismology applications: A versatile methodology and algorithm, *Bull. Earthq. Eng.* **16,** no. 6, 2211–2225, doi: 10.1007/s10518-017-0131-9.

Pischiutta, M., G. Cultrera, A. Caserta, L. Luzi, and A. Rovelli (2010). Topographic effects on the Hill of Nocera Umbra, Central Italy, *Geophys. J. Int.* **182,** no. 2, 977–987, doi: 10.1111/j.1365-246X.2010.04654.x.

Rai, M., A. Rodriguez-Marek, and B. S. Chiou (2017). Empirical terrain-based topographic modification factors for use in ground motion prediction, *Earthq. Spectra* **33,** no. 1, 157–177.

Rai, M., A. Rodriguez-Marek, and A. Yong (2016). An empirical model to predict topographic effects in strong ground motion using California small- to medium-magnitude earthquake database, *Earthq. Spectra* **32,** no. 2, 1033–1054.

RESIF (1995). RESIF-RAP French accelerometric network, *RESIF - Réseau Sismologique et géodésique Français*, doi: 10.15778/resif.ra.

Sánchez-Sesma, F. J. (1985). Diffraction of elastic *SH* waves by wedges, *Bull. Seismol. Soc. Am.* **75,** 1435–1446.

Sánchez-Sesma, F. J., and M. Campillo (1993). Topographic effects for incident P, SV and Rayleigh waves, *Tectonophysics* **218,** no. 1, 113–125, doi: 10.1016/0040-1951(93)90263-J.

Sbaa, S., F. Hollender, V. Perron, A. Imtiaz, P.-Y. Bard, A. Mariscal, A. Cochard, and A. Dujardin (2017). Analysis of rotation sensor data from the SINAPS@ Kefalonia (Greece) post-seismic experiment—Link to surface geology and wavefield characteristics, *Earth Planets Space* **69,** no. 1, 124, doi: 10.1186/s40623-017-0711-6.

Stolte, A. C., B. R. Cox, and R. C. Lee (2017). An experimental topographic amplification study at Los Alamos National Laboratory using ambient vibrations, *Bull. Seismol. Soc. Am.* **107,** no. 3, 1386–1401, doi: 10.1785/0120160269.

Theodoulidis, N., G. Cultrera, C. Cornou, P. Y. Bard, T. Boxberger, G. DiGiulio, A. Imtiaz, D. Kementzetzidou, K. Makra, and Argostoli NERA Team, *et al.* (2018). Basin effects on ground motion: The case of a high-resolution experiment in Cephalonia (Greece), *Bull. Earthq. Eng.* **16,** no. 2, 529–560, doi: 10.1007/s10518-017-0225-4.

Theodoulidis, N., F. Hollender, A. Mariscal, D. Moiriat, P. Y. Bard, A. Konidaris, M. Cushing, K. Konstantinidou, and Z. Roumelioti (2018). The ARGONET (Greece) seismic observatory: An accelerometric vertical array and its data, *Seismol. Res. Lett.* **89,** 1555–1565.

Wathelet, M., B. Guillier, P. Roux, C. Cornou, and M. Ohrnberger (2018). Rayleigh wave three-component beamforming: Signed ellipticity assessment from high-resolution frequency-wavenumber processing of ambient vibration arrays, *Geophys. J. Int.* **215,** no. 1, 507–523, doi: 10.1093/gji/ggy286.

Wilson, D. C., and G. L. Pavlis (2000). Near-surface site effects in crystalline bedrock: A comprehensive analysis of spectral amplitudes determined from a dense, three-component seismic array, *Earth Interact.* **4,** 1–31.

Wood, C. M., and B. R. Cox (2016). Comparison of field data processing methods for the evaluation of topographic effects, *Earthq. Spectra* **32,** no. 4, 2127–2147, doi: 10.1193/111515EQS170M.

Xu, R., and L. Wang (2021). The horizontal-to-vertical spectral ratio and its applications, *EURASIP J. Adv. Signal Process.* **2021,** no. 1, 75, doi: 10.1186/s13634-021-00765-z.

Yong, A., A. Askan, J. Cassidy, S. D'Amico, S. Parolai, M. Pilz, and W. Stephenson (2022). Introduction to the special issue of the Consortium of Organizations for Strong Motion Observation Systems (COSMOS) international guidelines for applying noninvasive geophysical techniques to characterize seismic site conditions, *J. Seismol.* **26,** no. 4, 557–566, doi: 10.1007/s10950-022-10104-w.

Manuscript received 11 June 2025
Published online 18 December 2025

A Direct Convergence Method for Computing Synthetic Seismograms for a Layered Half-Space with Sources and Receivers at Close Depths

Dengda Zhu[1,2], Tao Xu*[1,2], Jinlai Hao[2,3], and Zhenxing Yao[3]

ABSTRACT

This study presents the direct convergence method (DCM), a novel numerical method for efficient computation of synthetic seismograms in a layered half-space when sources and receivers are at close depths. Conventional methods such as the discrete wavenumber method suffer from the slow convergence in such scenarios, which requires impractical wavenumber cutoffs. Although the semi-analytical method (SAM) and peak-trough averaging method (PTAM) offer improvements, SAM involves complex mathematical derivations, and PTAM demands an extra meticulous numerical implementation. DCM addresses these limitations by directly removing the slowly convergent component of the wavenumber-domain integrand over a finite interval and supplementing it with an analytically derived correction term. The method achieves higher accuracy and better stability than PTAM with minimal computational overhead—implementable in fewer than 20 lines of code in frameworks like PyGRT. Validation via the Sommerfeld integral and Lamb's problem confirms DCM's robustness and accuracy. Applications to soft sedimentary layers and far-field scenarios demonstrate its reliability. DCM provides a simple, efficient, and easily implementable solution for high-fidelity synthetic seismograms in challenging source–receiver configurations.

KEY POINTS

- Slow convergence in wavenumber integrals for shallow sources limits the calculation of synthetic seismograms.
- Direct convergence method accelerates convergence and achieves higher accuracy than peak-trough averaging method, only in less than 20 code lines.
- This plug-and-play algorithm enables efficient high-fidelity seismogram synthesis for challenging scenarios.

INTRODUCTION

The computation of synthetic seismograms for layered media serves as a fundamental and essential tool for researchers to understand Earth's internal structure and earthquake processes. Since the 1950s, advancements in computer technology have led to significant progress in the development of methods for calculating synthetic seismograms. Among these, the generalized reflection-transmission matrix (GRTM) method based on the discrete wavenumber method (DWM) has been widely adopted for its numerical efficiency in solving integral problems for layered media (Haskell, 1953; Kennett and Kerry, 1979; Luco and Apsel, 1983; Yao and Harkrider, 1983; Xie and Yao, 1989; Chen, 1993). However, when the source and receiver are at close depths, the integrand converges very slowly, requiring an impractically large wavenumber cutoff in DWM, which drastically reduces computational efficiency. The computation of synthetic seismograms for sources and receivers at close depths has critical applications in seismology, including monitoring induced seismicity, studying landslide dynamics, analyzing meteorite impacts, examining volcanic tremors, and monitoring nuclear explosions. To address the slow convergence, the semi-analytical method (SAM) was developed (Apsel and Luco, 1983; Herrmann and Wang, 1985; Hisada, 1994, 1995). In SAM, the integral is split into two parts: one is solved analytically, whereas the other, which benefits from the separation of the integrand, converges rapidly and can be evaluated numerically. Although

1. Key Laboratory of Deep Petroleum Intelligent Exploration and Development, Institute of Geology and Geophysics, Chinese Academy of Sciences, Beijing, China, https://orcid.org/0009-0004-7933-3357 (DZ); 2. University of Chinese Academy of Sciences, Beijing, China, https://orcid.org/0000-0002-9623-9221 (JH); 3. Key Laboratory of Planetary Science and Frontier Technology, Institute of Geology and Geophysics, Chinese Academy of Sciences, Beijing, China, https://orcid.org/0000-0002-4029-1266 (ZY)

*Corresponding author: xutao@mail.iggcas.ac.cn

Cite this article as Zhu, D., T. Xu, J. Hao, and Z. Yao (2025). A Direct Convergence Method for Computing Synthetic Seismograms for a Layered Half-Space with Sources and Receivers at Close Depths, *Bull. Seismol. Soc. Am.* **116**, 576–588, doi: 10.1785/0120250190

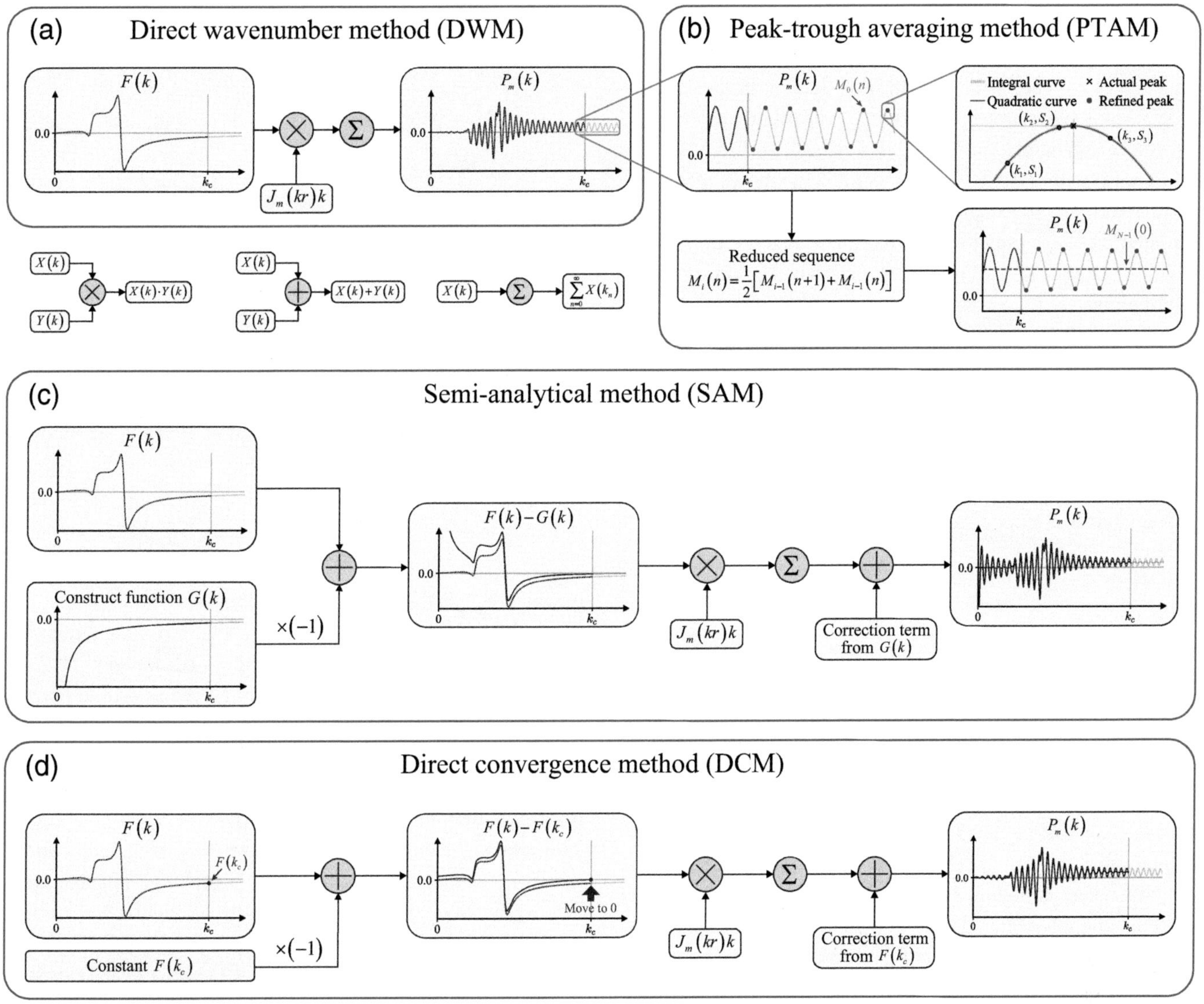

Figure 1. Schematic workflow of (a) discrete wavenumber method (DWM), (b) peak-trough averaging method (PTAM), (c) semi-analytical method (SAM), and (d) direct convergence method (DCM) for addressing slow convergence in integration. $F(k)$ is the kernel function, $J_m(kr)$ is the mth order Bessel function of the first kind, $P_m(k)$ is the integration result with upper limit k (defined in equation 4), k_c is the critical wavenumber. See the Method section for more details. The color version of this figure is available only in the electronic edition.

SAM effectively resolves the slow convergence, its mathematical treatment is cumbersome and requires a specialized numerical implementation. To reduce the complication of SAM, Greenfield (1995) developed the contour deformation method. This technique uses the asymptotic solutions of Hankel functions to obtain convergent results at large epicentral distances and has been applied to simulate strong ground motion near the fault plane in a layered half-space (Hisada and Bielak, 2003). Regarding the numerical method, Zhang *et al.* (2003) developed the peak-trough averaging method (PTAM) based on the repeated averaging method (RAM; Chang, 1988) to accelerate convergence for shallow sources. PTAM extracts peaks and troughs from the oscillatory integral to form a reduced sequence, then iteratively averages adjacent pairs to estimate the final convergence value. Compared to SAM, PTAM minimizes mathematical complexity and is more straightforward to implement numerically.

In this study, inspired by SAM and PTAM, we propose a new numerical integration method, the direct convergence method (DCM), to accelerate the convergence of wavenumber integrals. As the name suggests, DCM achieves improved convergence near the cutoff wavenumber by directly removing the slowly convergent component of the integrand through subtracting a constant term over a finite wavenumber interval, followed by adding an analytically derived correction term. Although this adjustment to the integral formula may resemble SAM in principle, DCM requires minimal mathematical complexity for implementation yet achieves high convergence accuracy. Figure 1 schematically illustrates the workflow of DWM, PTAM, SAM, and DCM for addressing the slow convergence issue. From the perspective of PTAM, DCM implicitly extracts an infinite series of peaks and troughs and automatically estimates their convergence limit. Unlike PTAM, which relies on careful curve fitting to locate the peaks and troughs, DCM is numerically straightforward to implement, introduces negligible computational overhead, and avoids additional memory demands. This simplicity allows researchers to easily adapt existing codes for synthetic seismogram computation with shallow sources. For example, in the PyGRT package (Zhu *et al.*, 2025; see Data and Resources), we implemented DCM by adding fewer than 20 lines of code to the original DWM framework. Numerical experiments confirm that DCM produces accurate synthetic seismograms with higher convergence accuracy and stability compared to PTAM.

In the following sections, we will first provide a brief introduction to DWM, SAM, and PTAM, then describe the implementation of DCM, and finally conduct a series of rigorous comparisons and application tests.

METHOD

Basic theory

According to Yao and Harkrider (1983), solving the Green's functions for layered media in the frequency domain requires solving the following integral:

$$I_m(\omega) = \int_0^{+\infty} F(k,\omega) J_m(kr) k\, dk, \quad m = 0,1,2, \tag{1}$$

in which ω is the angular frequency, k is the wavenumber, r is the epicentral distance, $J_m(kr)$ is the mth order Bessel function, and the kernel function $F(k,\omega)$ is the response of medium, which can be solved by GRTM. In this article, $F(k,\omega)$ generally denotes various types of kernel functions, whereas $g(k,\omega)$ specifically refers to the displacement kernel function, and $g_z(k,\omega)$ specifically refers to the kernel function for the derivative of displacement with respect to the receiver depth. The computation of stress, strain, and rotation tensors requires calculating the spatial derivatives of displacement with respect to the receiver coordinates. This involves replacing the displacement kernel function in equation (1) with $g_z(k,\omega)$, or replacing the Bessel function with its derivative. The resulting integral retains the same form as equation (1).

Bouchon (1981) proposed the DWM for the numerical evaluation of the integral in equation (1), expressed as

$$I_m(\omega) = \Delta k \sum_{n=1}^{\infty} F(k_n,\omega) J_m(k_n r) k_n, \tag{2}$$

in which $\Delta k = 2\pi/L$, $k_n = n\Delta k$, L is the characteristic length. Bouchon (1981) proposed that L must satisfy

$$\begin{cases} \sqrt{(L-r)^2 + |z|^2} > \alpha T \\ r < L/2 \end{cases}, \tag{3}$$

in which T is the time window length, $|z|$ is the depth gap between the source and receiver, α is the maximum P-wave velocity in the model. In practical computations, the integral in equation (1) is typically divided into two parts:

$$P_m(k,\omega) = \int_0^{k} F(s,\omega) J_m(sr) s\, ds, \tag{4}$$

$$I_m(\omega) = \lim_{k\to\infty} P_m(k,\omega). \tag{5}$$

The integral in equation (4) can be evaluated numerically using equation (2). To approximate the limit in equation (5), an empirical critical wavenumber k_c is selected as the upper bound in equation (4), ensuring the kernel function decays sufficiently close to zero beyond this point. Following Zhu and Rivera (2002) and Zhang *et al.* (2003), we can empirically set k_c as follows:

$$k_c = \sqrt{\left(s_1 \times \frac{\pi}{|z|}\right)^2 + \left(s_2 \times \frac{\omega}{v_{\min}}\right)^2}, \tag{6}$$

in which $v_{\min}$ is the minimum velocity of the model, and s_1 and s_2 are the scale factors, which can be adjusted manually to suit specific scenarios. Unless otherwise specified, we set $s_1 = 5$ and $s_2 = 1.15$ in the following tests. With a suitable k_c, the remaining contribution to the integral is then negligible and can be safely disregarded (Zhu and Rivera, 2002; Zhang *et al.*, 2003).

When the source and receiver are at close depths, the integral in equation (1) converges extremely slowly. Figure 1a shows how the integral oscillates severely with k_c when applying DWM, necessitating an impractically large upper limit to achieve satisfactory accuracy, which severely compromises computational efficiency. To address this issue, SAM was developed by decomposing equation (1) into two terms:

$$\begin{aligned} I_m &= \int_0^{+\infty} [F(k) - G(k) + G(k)] J_m(kr) k\, dk \\ &= \int_0^{+\infty} [F(k) - G(k)] J_m(kr) k\, dk + \int_0^{+\infty} G(k) J_m(kr) k\, dk, \end{aligned} \tag{7}$$

in which for notational simplicity, we omit the frequency parameter ω in the functions (i.e., $F(k,\omega)$ is abbreviated as $F(k)$, and $I_m(\omega)$ as I_m). Here, $G(k)$ is a kernel function constructed based on specific physical considerations, designed such that the first integral converges rapidly whereas the second admits an analytical solution. For instance, Apsel and Luco (1983) observed that the dynamic Green's functions asymptotically approach the static Green's functions (called the asymptotic solutions) as k increases. They thus approximated $G(k)$ using the static solution for a homogeneous half-space with the same material properties as the layer that includes the source. Herrmann and Wang (1985) improved upon the Apsel and Luco (1983) by employing numerical fitting with polynomial–exponential functions to derive a more accurate asymptotic approximation. Hisada (1994, 1995) further refined the GRTM proposed by Luco and Apsel (1983)

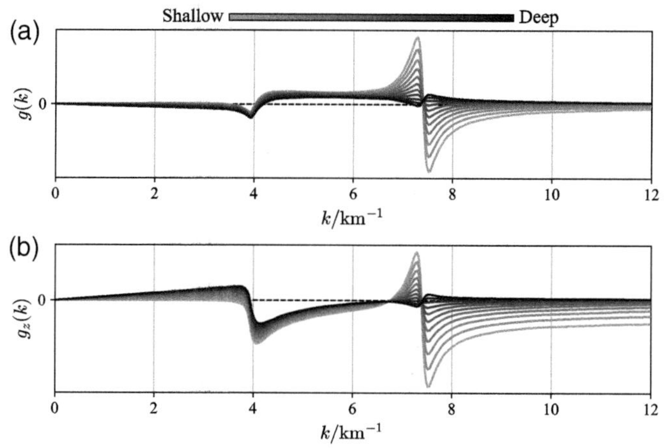

Figure 2. Morphological variations of the kernel functions (a) $g(k)$ and (b) $g_z(k)$ for the vertical displacement, with the depth of horizontal force sources varying from relatively deep (dark gray, 0.2 km) to shallow (light gray, 0 km). A half-space model (Table 1) is used. The receiver is at the surface, with an epicentral distance 10 km. The frequency is 5 Hz. Unless otherwise specified, all traces in the following figures are the real parts, and they are normalized using the maximum absolute value.

and incorporated contributions to the asymptotic solutions from direct, reflected, and transmitted waves between layers, significantly accelerating convergence. As noted explicitly by Hisada (1995), the more accurate the asymptotic solutions are, the faster the integral converges. However, this gain in efficiency comes at the cost of increased mathematical complexity and code implementation. Figure 1c shows the workflow of SAM. It can be seen that SAM effectively alleviates the integral oscillation problem existing in DWM, and the convergence speed has significantly increased.

The slow convergence issue can also be addressed using purely numerical methods. Zhang *et al.* (2003) proposed the PTAM to estimate the limit in equation (5). Figure 1b shows the workflow of PTAM. After reaching the critical wavenumber k_c, PTAM extracts consecutive peaks and troughs from the oscillatory integral curve to form a reduced sequence $M_0(n)$. The ith order reduced sequence is then defined as

$$M_i(n) = \frac{1}{2}[M_{i-1}(n+1) + M_{i-1}(n)], \quad i = 1,2,3\ldots \tag{8}$$

As $n \to \infty$, both M_i and M_0 converge to the same limit, with higher-order reduced sequences exhibiting faster convergence. The final PTAM convergence estimate is given by $M_{N-1}(0)$, in which N represents the number of extracted peaks and troughs. In practical implementation, the accuracy of PTAM's convergence estimate critically depends on accurate identification of peaks and troughs. To achieve this in discrete wavenumber sampling, Zhang *et al.* (2003) employed quadratic curve fitting using three consecutive sample points to estimate local extrema. Compared to the RAM, this approach demonstrates significantly improved accuracy.

Decay of the Kernel function

The Bessel function in equation (1) is an oscillatory function, which is the fundamental cause of the integral's oscillatory behavior. The convergence rate of the integral—that is, how the oscillation amplitude decays as k increases—depends on the decay rate of the kernel function $F(k)$ toward zero. Figure 2a illustrates the morphological changes in the displacement kernel function $g(k)$ as the source depth varies from deep to shallow. It can be observed that when the buried source is at some distance from the surface, $g(k)$ decays rapidly. However, as the source approaches the receiver at the surface, the decay of $g(k)$ slows significantly. This is the direct cause for the slow convergence of the integral.

Similar to the variation pattern of $g(k)$ shown in Figure 2a, $g_z(k)$ also exhibits slow decay characteristics (Fig. 2b). However, the decay rate of $g_z(k)$ is significantly slower than that of $g(k)$, causing the integrand in equation (1) to oscillate more irregularly. This makes it difficult for methods like PTAM to accurately compute physical quantities like stress. The decay rates of these functions can be analyzed through their asymptotic solutions. For large wavenumbers, the kernel functions approximate the following forms (Hisada, 1994):

$$\begin{aligned} g^R(k) &\approx (a_1 + a_2 k)e^{-k|z|}, \\ g_z^R(k) &\approx (a_3 + a_4 k)ke^{-k|z|}, \\ g^L(k) &\approx a_5 e^{-k|z|}, \\ g_z^L(k) &\approx a_6 ke^{-k|z|}, \end{aligned} \tag{9}$$

in which the superscript R denotes coupled P-SV waves (vertical and radial components), and L denotes SH waves (tangential component). $a_1 \sim a_6$ are constants estimated under the large-wavenumber approximation. It is evident that the long-term decay of the kernel functions is dominated by the exponential term $e^{-k|z|}$. When the depth gap $|z| \to 0$, the decay becomes extremely slow. Moreover, the asymptotic expression for $g_z(k)$ includes an additional linear factor k, which further delays its decay in the short to intermediate wavenumber range and can even cause local increases, making the corresponding integrals more challenging to evaluate.

DCM

To address the slow decay of the kernel function, DCM decomposes the integral in equation (1) into two terms:

$$I_m = \int_0^{+\infty} [F(k) - F(k_c) + F(k_c)]J_m(kr)k\,dk = \underbrace{\int_0^{+\infty} [F(k) - F(k_c)]J_m(kr)k\,dk}_{I_m^{(1)}} + F(k_c)\underbrace{\int_0^{+\infty} J_m(kr)k\,dk}_{I_m^{(2)}}. \tag{10}$$

This decomposition resembles SAM but differs in that DCM employs a constant term $F(k_c)$, avoiding the complex mathematical treatments required by SAM to construct asymptotic solutions. The first integral $I_m^{(1)}$ can still be evaluated using DWM by truncating the upper limit at a finite k_c and computing the numerical integral via equation (2). Although the second integral $I_m^{(2)}$ is divergent, its analytical solution can be derived under the Cauchy principal value (see the Appendix for details). The key advantage of this decomposition is that the integrand of $I_m^{(1)}$ vanishes at $k = k_c$, ensuring direct convergence of $I_m^{(1)}$ as the upper limit approaches k_c—hence the name "DCM." Meanwhile, $I_m^{(2)}$, serving as a correction term for I_m, is straightforward to implement in code due to its closed-form solution. Figure 1d shows the workflow of DCM. As shown, DCM achieves convergence during the integration phase through a simple shift of the kernel function, eliminating the need for the additional numerical computations required in PTAM.

NUMERICAL EXAMPLES

Validation

The Sommerfeld integral describes the potential of a spherical wave in an unbounded, homogeneous medium. This integral form exhibits slow convergence when the source and receiver are near the same depth—a key challenge in wave propagation modeling. Because of the availability of its closed-form solution, it is widely used to verify numerical integration techniques (Hisada, 1994; Zhang *et al.*, 2003). The Sommerfeld integral is defined as

$$\frac{e^{-ik^*R}}{R} = \int_0^\infty \frac{e^{-\gamma|z|}}{\gamma} J_0(kr)k\,dk, \tag{11}$$

in which $k^* = \omega/c$, $R = \sqrt{r^2 + z^2}$, and $\gamma = \sqrt{k^2 - k^{*2}}$ with $Re\{\gamma\} \geq 0$. The exponential term $e^{-\gamma|z|}$ effectively mimics the decay of kernel functions. Because the integrand in equation (11) has a pole at k^*, following Bouchon (1981), we introduce a small imaginary component to the angular frequency ω to slightly shift the integration path away from the real axis, ensuring numerical stability.

To better validate DCM, we derive two new integrals from the original Sommerfeld potential by taking its first and second derivative with respect to r. These are expressed as

$$\left(ik^* + \frac{1}{R}\right)\frac{r}{R^2}e^{-ik^*R} = \int_0^\infty \frac{k}{\gamma}e^{-\gamma|z|}J_1(kr)k\,dk, \tag{12}$$

and

$$-\left[\left(ik^* + \frac{1}{R}\right)\left(\frac{3r^2}{R^2} - 2\right) - \frac{k^{*2}r^2}{R}\right]\frac{1}{R^2}e^{-ik^*R} = \int_0^\infty \frac{k^2}{\gamma}e^{-\gamma|z|}J_0(kr)k\,dk. \tag{13}$$

These derived integrals share a similar form with equation (1). Their kernel functions, $\frac{k}{\gamma}e^{-\gamma|z|}$ and $\frac{k^2}{\gamma}e^{-\gamma|z|}$, effectively capture the asymptotic behavior of $g(k)$ and $g_z(k)$ at large wavenumbers. Using the equations (12) and (13) instead of equation (11) thus offers a more thorough test of DCM's performance in computing displacements and their spatial derivatives under slow convergence.

Given that DCM and SAM share a similar integral decomposition strategy, we also evaluate SAM's performance. In SAM, using the static solution ($\omega = 0$) (Apsel and Luco, 1983), the integral in equation (12) is decomposed as

$$\int_0^\infty \frac{k}{\gamma}e^{-\gamma|z|}J_1(kr)k\,dk = \int_0^\infty \left[\frac{k}{\gamma}e^{-\gamma|z|} - e^{-k|z|}\right]J_1(kr)k\,dk + \int_0^\infty e^{-k|z|}J_1(kr)k\,dk, \tag{14}$$

in which the second integral has an analytical solution,

$$\int_0^\infty e^{-k|z|}J_1(kr)k\,dk = \frac{r}{R^3}, \tag{15}$$

and the integral in equation (13) is decomposed as

$$\int_0^\infty \frac{k^2}{\gamma}e^{-\gamma|z|}J_0(kr)k\,dk = \int_0^\infty \left[\frac{k^2}{\gamma}e^{-\gamma|z|} - ke^{-k|z|}\right]J_0(kr)k\,dk + \int_0^\infty e^{-k|z|}J_0(kr)k^2\,dk, \tag{16}$$

in which the second integral has an analytical solution,

$$\int_0^\infty e^{-k|z|}J_0(kr)k^2\,dk = \frac{1}{R^3}\left(2 - \frac{3r^2}{R^2}\right). \tag{17}$$

Figures 3 and 4 demonstrate how integrals in equations (12) and (13) are solved using DWM, SAM, and DCM. We intentionally derived the integrals in equations (12) and (13) so that the process of solving them would be analogous to computing displacements and stresses in practical synthetic seismogram simulations. Therefore, to some extent, the test in Figure 3 reflects the capability of these three methods for computing displacements, whereas the test in Figure 4 reflects their capability for computing stresses. The conventional DWM produces results that oscillate continuously, failing to converge to a stable solution. This problem becomes particularly severe when computing the integral in equation (13) (Fig. 4), for which the oscillations grow stronger, making convergence even more challenging. In contrast, both DCM and SAM employ integral decomposition—through equation (10) for DCM and equations (14)–(17) for SAM—which causes their kernel functions to decay rapidly to zero. As a result, the oscillatory behavior of the integrands is quickly suppressed. The final converged values from DCM and SAM show excellent agreement with the theoretical solution, as represented by the black-dashed horizontal lines in panel (c) of both figures.

The critical wavenumber k_c plays a central role in numerical integration methods, directly controlling both the accuracy of results and computational speed. To compare the performance of different methods, we measured how their errors relative to

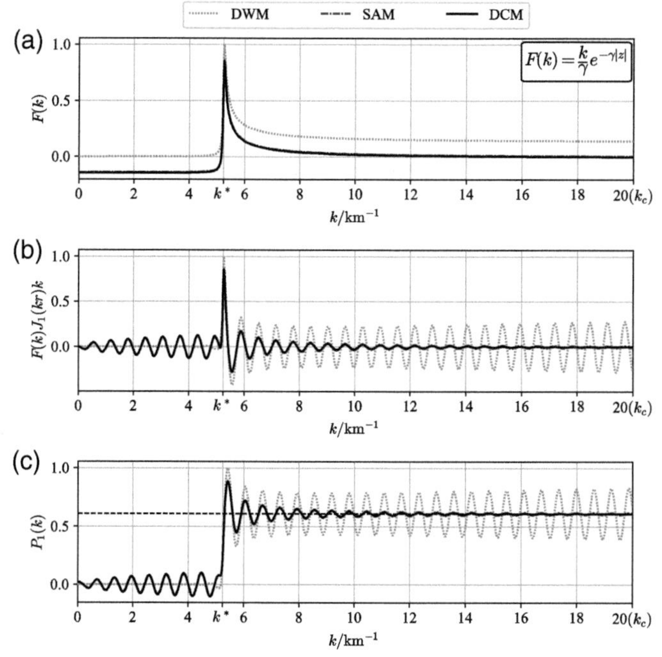

Figure 3. (a) The kernel function, (b) the integrand, and (c) the derived Sommerfeld integral in equation (12) versus wavenumber. In these panels, the curves of DCM and SAM almost overlap. The black-dashed horizontal line denotes the theoretical solution of the derived Sommerfeld integral. Here, $f = 5$ Hz, $c = 6$ km/s, $|z| = 1 \times 10^{-4}$ km, $k_c = 20$ km^{-1}, $k^* = \omega/c$, and $r = 10$ km. See the Validation section for details.

the theoretical solution change with k_c. As shown in Figure 5a, when the wavenumber exceeds a certain value ($k > k^*$), all methods initially show oscillating yet decreasing errors. However, the error for the DWM quickly levels off. The PTAM, which builds on DWM, achieves better accuracy but also stops improving with larger k_c. Although using more peaks and troughs in PTAM could reduce error further, it makes the method slower and less generally applicable. In contrast, both the SAM and the DCM maintain decreasing errors as k_c increases. Impressively, DCM achieves errors up to 100 times smaller than SAM. Figure 5b shows similar trends for a more difficult integral in equation (13). Here, errors for both DWM and PTAM even increase slightly at some points, reflecting the greater challenge of this case. Although DCM's error curve shows a small turning due to its approximation of the kernel function's decay, it still delivers the highest overall accuracy across the tested k_c range.

This test demonstrates that DCM, although employing an integral decomposition strategy similar to SAM, not only preserves SAM's advantage of rapid convergence but also achieves higher computational accuracy without requiring complex mathematical derivations.

Accuracy

To evaluate the accuracy of DCM in computing practical displacements and stresses, we applied both DCM and PTAM to

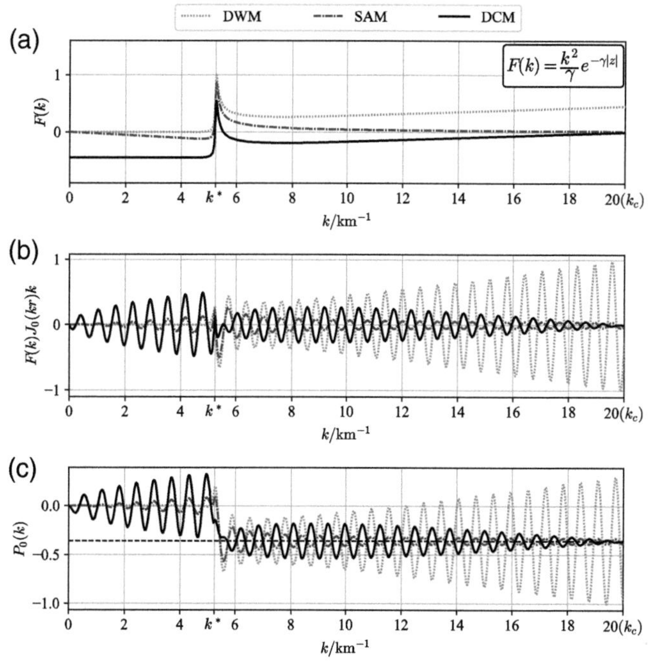

Figure 4. Same as Figure 3 but test the derived Sommerfeld integral in equation (13).

solve the Lamb (1904) problem in a half-space model (Table 1). We used synthetic seismograms calculated by the Cagniard–de Hoop method (CHM; Cagniard, 1939; de Hoop, 1960; Johnson, 1974) as reference solutions ("ground truth"). Following Chen and Zhang (2001), we defined the relative error function as

$$\Phi = \frac{\int_0^T |U(t) - U^*(t)| \, dt}{\int_0^T |U^*(t)| \, dt}, \tag{18}$$

in which $U^*(t)$ represents the reference seismogram, and T is the length of the time series.

We began by testing how well DCM and PTAM perform when the source is placed at different depths. As shown in Figure 6a, for vertical displacements recorded at the surface, both methods become more accurate as the source gets deeper. Although their error trends look similar, DCM consistently shows smaller errors than PTAM. It is worth noting that even when the source is very shallow (0.01 km deep), both methods keep errors down to about 3%. Figure 6b compares the synthetic waveforms, showing that results from both methods match the reference solution (CHM) quite well. The main difference appears in the strength of Rayleigh waves—likely due to inherent differences between frequency- and time-domain calculation methods. This confirms that both DCM and PTAM reliably calculate ground displacements with shallow sources.

Building on the previous analysis of displacement (Fig. 6a,b), Figure 6d,e shows how well each method calculates the derivative of vertical displacement with respect to the receiver

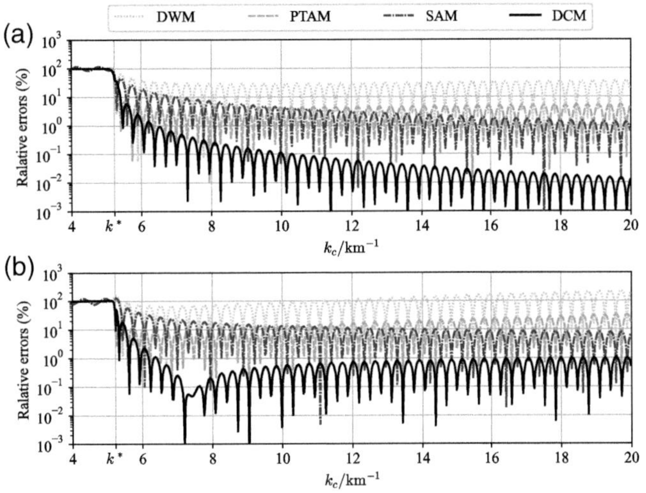

Figure 5. Relative errors between integral results of different methods and the theoretical solutions under different critical wavenumbers. The kernel function and the parameter settings are all consistent with those of (a) Figure 3 and (b) Figure 4.

depth—a key step for simulating stress. The results indicate that PTAM produces significant errors and struggles to accurately resolve near-surface stresses from a shallow source. In contrast, DCM maintains low relative errors, and its output closely matches the reference waveforms. This confirms that DCM reliably computes spatial derivatives of displacement, making it suitable for simulating related physical quantities such as stress.

The precision of the integration result is directly tied to the choice of the critical wavenumber k_c. We examined how the relative error of the 1 Hz frequency component changes as k_c varies. As seen in Figure 6c,f, the overall relative error decreases in an oscillatory manner for both methods—a pattern consistent with Figure 5. However, DCM produces lower errors with less fluctuation, showing it is less sensitive to the k_c than PTAM. In fact, when calculating the z-derivative, PTAM struggles to determine a suitable k_c at all. This confirms that DCM delivers higher accuracy alongside greater reliability.

Notably, Figure 6a reveals that both DCM and PTAM exhibit similar patterns in their relative errors. This indicates that the two methods are fundamentally guided by the same theoretical framework. In other words, both rely on the same key assumption: when $k = k_c$, the kernel function $F(k)$ has essentially converged to $F(k_c)$ (regardless of whether $F(k_c)$ equals zero), and for $k > k_c$, the kernel function $F(k)$ remains nearly constant. As a result, the integral in equation (4) oscillates symmetrically around an approximately fixed convergence value.

Under this assumption, PTAM explicitly extracts a series of peaks and troughs to compute reduced sequences, thereby achieving high-accuracy convergence estimated displacements. However, PTAM struggles when calculating stresses because the slower decay of the corresponding kernel function means the limited number of peaks and valleys no longer reliably follows the expected pattern. In contrast, DCM analytically decomposes these oscillations from the integral during the theoretical derivation phase and supplements them with a correction term derived from the integral's analytical solution. From this perspective, DCM can be viewed as implicitly extracting an infinite number of peaks and troughs while automatically estimating the convergence value. This makes DCM universally applicable for computing both displacements and their spatial derivatives. A key advantage is that DCM bypasses the need for PTAM's intricate process of numerically pinpointing peaks and troughs through curve fitting. This leads to a much simpler implementation and delivers more accurate results.

The assumption also explains the systematic variation of relative errors observed in Figure 6a,d. In practical implementations, we avoid using excessively large k_c values. Consequently, when the source and receiver depths are close, $F(k_c)$ represents merely an intermediate value in the kernel function's extremely slow decay process. The continued slow variation of the kernel function in the $k > k_c$ range still contributes to the final integral, which slightly deviates from the fundamental assumption of both methods and thus introduces errors. However, as demonstrated by the relative and absolute errors in Figure 6, this assumption does not significantly impact the results. In contrast, SAM aims to consider the contribution of the kernel function over the entire range, so it constructs an appropriate kernel function $G(k)$ with complex mathematical calculations. In practice, such errors are negligible, meaning DCM achieves greatest simplicity while sacrificing minimal accuracy.

TABLE 1
Parameters of the Half-Space Model

Thickness (km)	*P*-Wave Velocity (km/s)	*S*-Wave Velocity (km/s)	Density (g/cm³)
∞	8.0	4.62	3.3

Efficiency

Figure 1b,d demonstrates that PTAM requires more computational steps compared to DCM and theoretically demands more execution time. To better quantify this difference, we conducted an efficiency comparison test. Figure 7 presents the execution time for computing Green's functions using DCM and PTAM at different critical wavenumbers k_c. Because the k_c as defined in equation (6) depends on frequency, we simplified the test by setting $\omega = \omega_{max}$ in the k_c formula, ensuring a uniform wavenumber cutoff for all frequencies. For a fair comparison, we used a single-threaded version of the PyGRT program with standard optimizations (i.e., $-O$ in GNU compiler). All computations were performed on an Intel(R) Core(TM) Ultra 7 155 H processor.

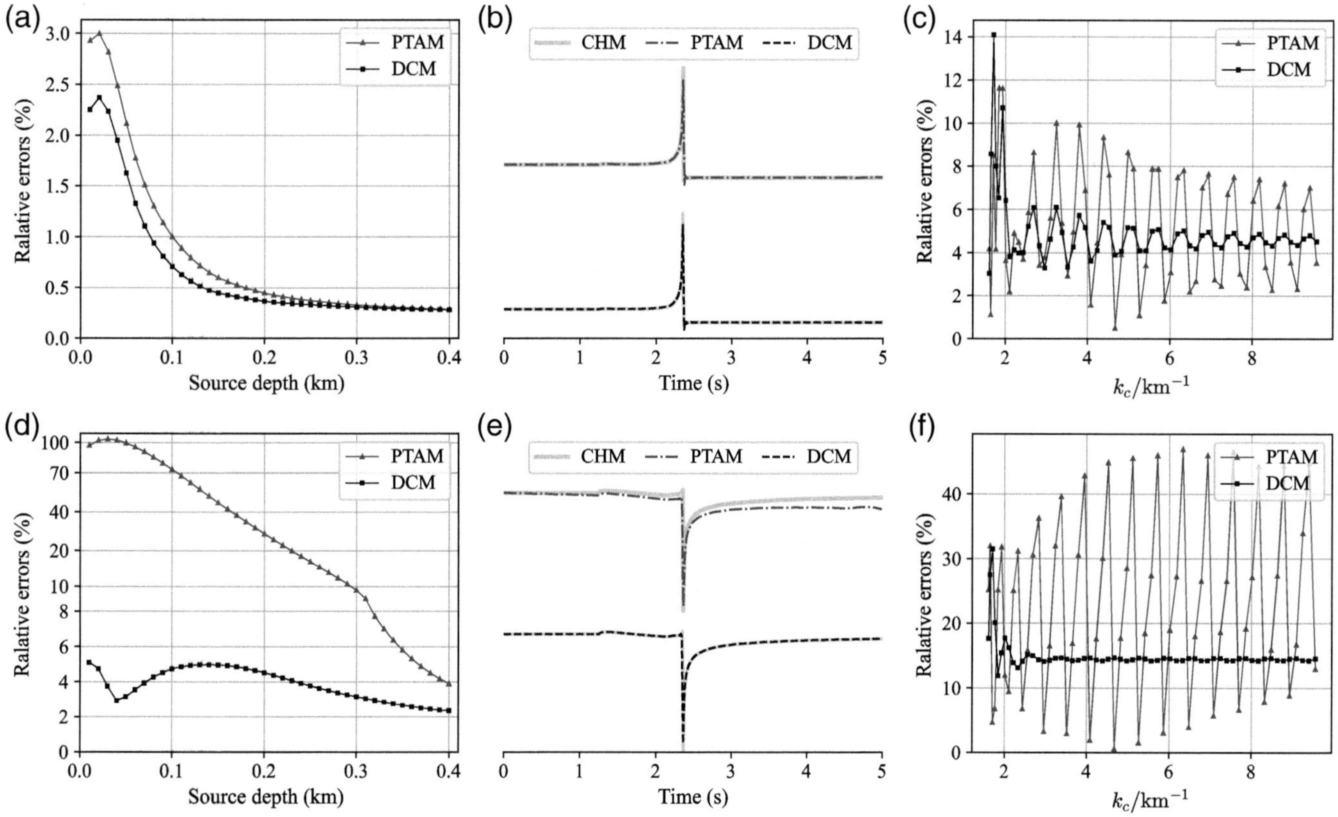

Figure 6. (a) Relative errors between the vertical displacements calculated by DCM and PTAM and the reference seismogram by the Cagniard–de Hoop method (CHM) across various source depths. (b) The waveform comparisons at a source depth of 0.01 km. (c) The relative errors of DCM and PTAM across various critical wavenumbers at frequency 1 Hz. Panels (d–f) are analogous to (a–c), respectively, but present results for the z-derivative of the vertical-component displacements. A half-space model (Table 1) is used. The source is a vertical downward force. The receiver is at the surface, with an epicentral distance 10 km. In panels (a–c), all traces are convolved with the step function, whereas in panels (d–f), all traces are convolved twice with the step function. The color version of this figure is available only in the electronic edition.

The results indicate that the execution time for both DCM and PTAM grows linearly with increasing critical wavenumber k_c. However, PTAM is globally slower than DCM, consistent with the operational differences illustrated in Figure 1b,d. Although modern computing technologies (including compiler optimizations and multicore processors) can substantially reduce this efficiency gap, DCM still maintains clear practical advantages. These include simpler code implementation, easier long-term maintenance, and better adaptability to different computing environments—all important factors when considering real-world efficiency.

Application

Through rigorous aforementioned testing, we have validated the correctness and computational accuracy of DCM. Next, we examine the performance of DCM under challenging physical conditions.

In earthquake engineering, near-surface velocity structures used for strong ground-motion simulation often include low-velocity, soft sedimentary layers. These layers, characterized by low density and low modulus, can significantly amplify ground vibrations due to intralayer multiples. In the first test, we computed synthetic seismograms for a sedimentary-layer model (Table 2) using both PTAM and DCM, with the source and receiver both located at the surface. The source type was a single-force point source, suitable for simulating events such as landslides, collapses, and tsunamis. As shown in Figure 8, the displacements computed by the two methods overlap well, without noticeable unphysical artifacts. The waveforms reveal that, with the source excited at the surface, the intralayer multiples within the low-velocity thin layer and the developed surface waves generate large-amplitude, long-duration coda signals, which can cause severe damage to buildings and other infrastructure. The displacement comparison demonstrates that both DCM and PTAM are capable of computing displacements in realistic low-velocity models.

Beyond the ground motion, the computed stress components are equally crucial, as they govern key engineering phenomena such as cyclic mobility in soils, foundation bearing capacity degradation, and the triggering of seismic liquefaction. Therefore, in addition to displacements, we computed all six independent components of the stress tensor. As shown in Figure 9, the three components $\sigma_{zz}, \sigma_{zr}, \sigma_{z\theta}$ computed by

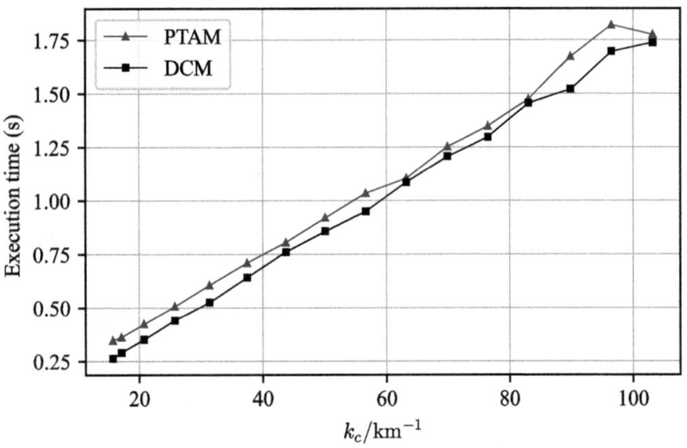

Figure 7. Execution time of DCM and PTAM at various critical wavenumbers. A half-space model (Table 1) is used. The source is at a depth of 0.01 km. The receiver is at the surface, with an epicentral distance 10 km. The number of sampling points is 1000, and the sampling frequency is 100 Hz. Each point is the average execution time of 10 repeated runs. The color version of this figure is available only in the electronic edition.

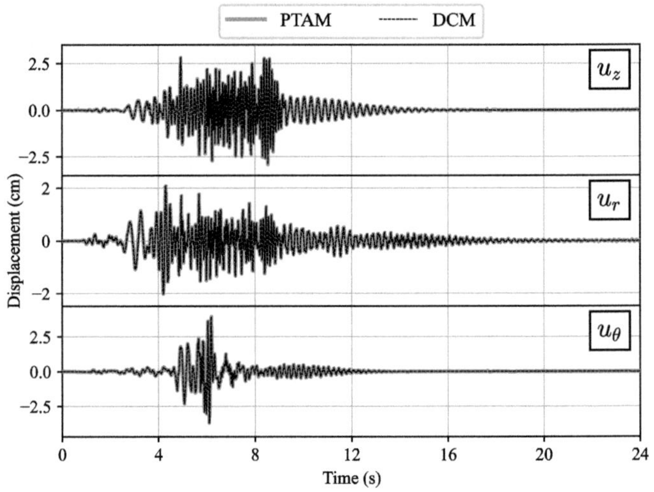

Figure 8. Comparison of the three-component displacements calculated by PTAM and DCM. A sedimentary-layer model (Table 2) is used. Both the point force ($(f_N, f_E, f_Z) = (1, 0.3, 1.5) \times 10^{15}$ dyne, defined in the north, east, and down coordinate systems) and receiver are at the surface, with an azimuth of 50° and an epicentral distance of 1 km. The sampling frequency is 50 Hz. All traces are convolved with the step function. The color version of this figure is available only in the electronic edition.

DCM remain zero over time, which correctly satisfies the free-surface boundary condition. In contrast, PTAM yields a significantly larger error in σ_{zz}. For the three nonzero components $\sigma_{rr}, \sigma_{r\theta}, \sigma_{\theta\theta}$, DCM produces stable results without noticeable numerical artifacts, whereas PTAM exhibits severe nonconvergence. Figure 10 schematically illustrates the kernel functions related in Figures 8 and 9. Consistent with the earlier validation analysis based on Lamb's problem, the kernel function $g_z(k)$ decays more slowly, and its local linear variations cause unstable oscillations in the integrand, leading to PTAM's failure in stress calculations. In other words, a larger critical wavenumber k_c is required for $g_z(k)$ to enter a stable decay, forcing PTAM to sample more peaks and troughs to achieve acceptable accuracy, which in turn diminishes its advantage. As a more robust numerical method, DCM remains insensitive to the choice of k_c and its direct convergence property ensures excellent stability in the results. The stress comparison confirms that DCM serves as a reliable solution for computing stresses in realistic low-velocity models.

In the second test, we computed far-field synthetic seismograms generated by an explosion within the crustal model of

TABLE 2
Parameters of the Sedimentary-Layer Model

Thickness (km)	P-Wave Velocity (km/s)	S-Wave Velocity (km/s)	Density (g/cm³)
0.01	1.5	0.18	1.78
0.01	1.7	0.35	1.85
0.02	1.6	0.25	1.80
0.20	2.6	1.20	2.10
∞	5.8	3.30	2.70

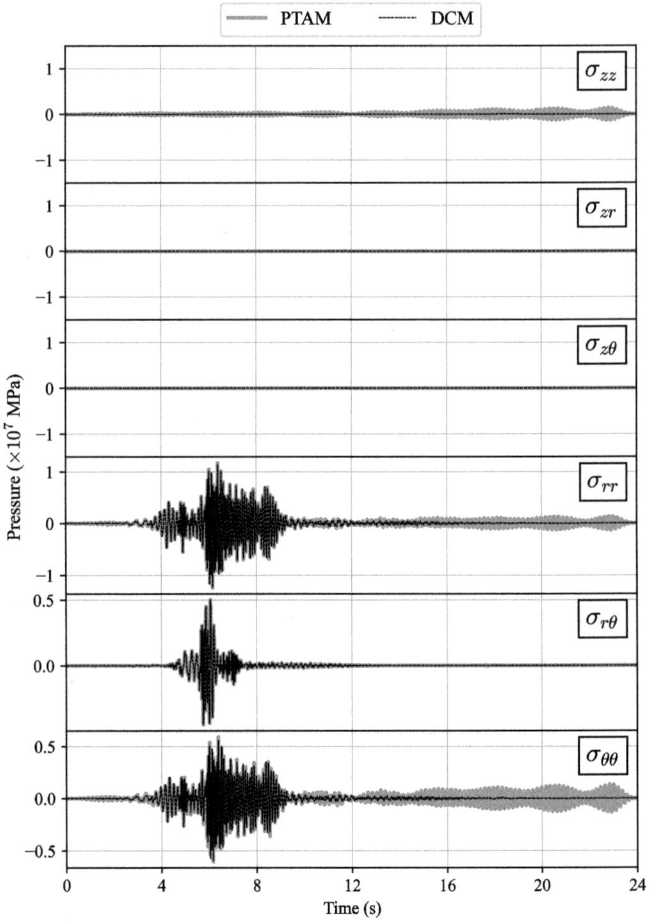

Figure 9. Comparison of the six-component stress tensor calculated by PTAM and DCM. All parameters are set the same as those in Figure 8. The color version of this figure is available only in the electronic edition.

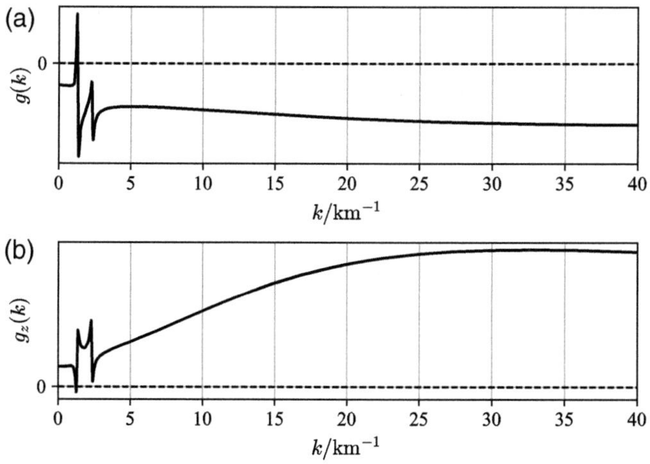

Figure 10. Kernel functions (a) $g(k)$ and (b) $g_z(k)$ for the vertical displacement. A sedimentary-layer model (Table 2) is used. Both the vertically downward force source and receiver are at the surface. The frequency is 1 Hz.

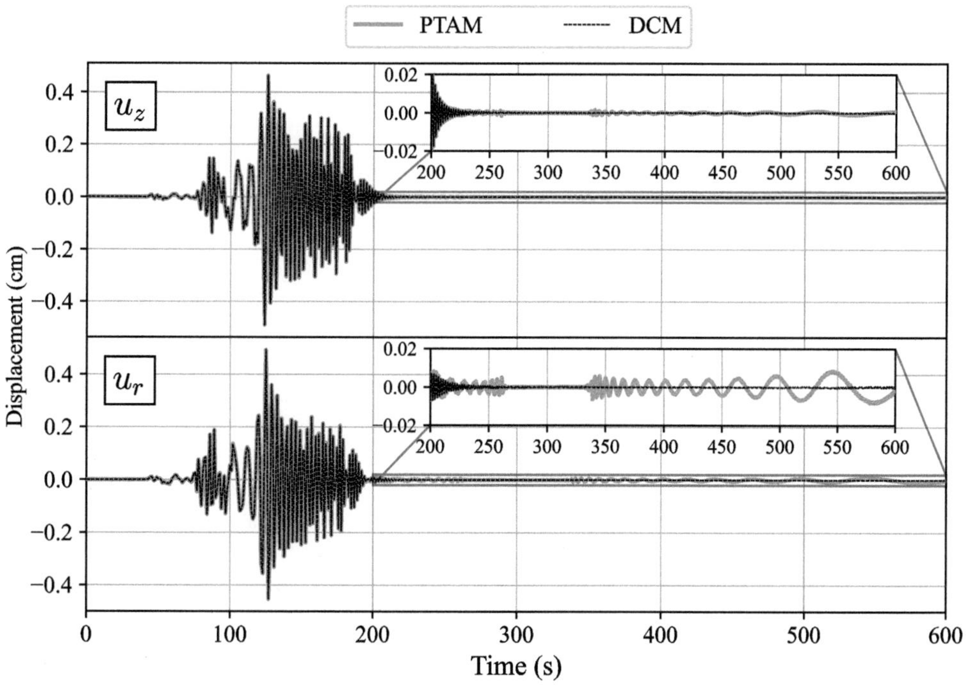

Figure 11. Comparison of the far-field displacements calculated by DCM and PTAM. The Amchitka crustal model (Table 3) is used. Both the explosion source (the scalar seismic moment $M_0 = 1 \times 10^{25}$ dyn · cm) and receiver are at the surface, with an epicentral distance of 300km. All traces are convolved with the step function. The color version of this figure is available only in the electronic edition.

the Amchitka region (Table 3). The model consists of eight layers and was used to simulate seismic recordings from the MILROW nuclear test. Both the source and the receiver are located at the surface. Because the explosive source is a dipole, the corresponding displacement can be represented by the spatial derivatives of the Green's functions with respect to the source coordinates. Consequently, the associated kernel function exhibits a decay characteristic similar to $g_z(k)$, making the solving process more challenging compared to the single-force source case. Figure 11 compares displacement results from PTAM and DCM. To avoid the low-frequency noise, in this far-field test, we set $s_1 = 0.1$ and $s_2 = 1.5$ in equation (6) and apply a high-pass filter with a corner frequency of 0.01 Hz. Although DCM produces a clean, well-converged waveform throughout, PTAM introduces significant artifacts in the coda portion where spurious oscillations reach amplitudes comparable to the body waves. Such artifacts could systematically bias subsequent analyses like signal filtering.

Besides the source type, two key factors explain the artifacts in PTAM's results (Fig. 11). First, as the epicentral distance increases, the Bessel function oscillates more rapidly. This makes it harder for PTAM's limited sampling of peaks and troughs to accurately determine the final converged value. Although using more peaks and troughs can improve accuracy, it comes at the cost of higher computational effort. In contrast, DCM remains accurate for far-field calculations because its approach depends only on the kernel function, which does not change with distance, making it unaffected by these Bessel function oscillations. Second, calculating seismograms in far-field scenarios or low-velocity models requires a longer signal duration. Equation (3) shows that this forces a very small integration step Δk. To save computation time, PTAM uses a much larger step Δk_2, based only on the epicentral distance (e.g., $\Delta k_2 = \frac{\pi}{8r}$) (Zhang *et al.*, 2003), in its stage of peak-trough collection. In this scenario, $\Delta k \ll \Delta k_2$, introducing errors into the numerical integration process. In contrast, DCM eliminates the need for PTAM's explicit second-stage convergence procedure by employing a single integration step throughout the entire integration, thereby avoiding such systematic errors.

Notably, the integration methods used in Figure 11 rely on a fixed Δk in equation (2), which becomes computationally expensive for large distances because it requires a very small Δk. To address this, Chen and Zhang (2001) developed the Self-Adaptive Filon's Integration Method (SAFIM), which dynamically adjusts the integration steps—sampling more points where

TABLE 3
Parameters of the Amchitka Crustal Model (Burdick *et al.*, 1984)

Thickness (km)	*P*-Wave Velocity (km/s)	*S*-Wave Velocity (km/s)	Density (g/cm^3)
0.2	3.4	1.7	2.3
0.6	3.7	1.9	2.4
0.5	4.2	2.1	2.4
0.5	4.6	2.3	2.5
0.7	4.9	2.8	2.6
0.5	5.1	2.9	2.7
6.0	5.9	3.3	2.7
28.0	6.9	4.0	2.8
∞	8.2	4.7	3.2

the kernel function changes rapidly and fewer where it varies slowly. This greatly improves efficiency in far-field scenarios. However, when dealing with both shallow sources and large distances, PTAM faces the same problem: it requires a separate step size during its convergence stage, which can introduce errors when combined with adaptive methods like SAFIM. In contrast, DCM's reformulation of the integral in equation (10) allows it to work naturally with SAFIM, thus avoiding such errors. Benefiting from its simplicity, DCM can be seamlessly integrated with various types of numerical techniques, establishing it as a stable, accurate, and general-purpose approach for computing synthetic seismograms from shallow sources.

CONCLUSION

The DCM effectively resolves the slow convergence of wavenumber integrals for synthetic seismograms when sources and receivers are at close depths in layered media. By decomposing the oscillatory kernel integral and analytically handling the divergent part via the Cauchy principal value, DCM eliminates the mathematical complexity of the SAM and bypasses the numerical peak-trough extraction of the PTAM. It achieves superior accuracy and stability with negligible coding effort. Rigorous validation and application tests confirm its reliability. The method's simplicity, efficiency, and seamless integration with existing codes (e.g., PyGRT) establish DCM as a general method for high-fidelity seismogram synthesis, particularly for shallow seismic sources.

DATA AND RESOURCES

The new PyGRT package with direct convergence method (DCM) was used to conduct the tests, which can be obtained at https://github.com/Dengda98/PyGRT (last accessed November 2025).

DECLARATION OF COMPETING INTERESTS

The authors acknowledge that there are no conflicts of interest recorded.

ACKNOWLEDGMENTS

The authors thank Associate Editor Martin Galis and two anonymous reviewers for their useful suggestions, which are crucial to the improvement of their article. The authors appreciate the technical support from Supercomputing Laboratory, Institute of Geology and Geophysics, Chinese Academy of Sciences (IGGCAS). This study was funded by the CAS Project for Young Scientists in Basic Research (YSBR-082) and the Deep Earth Probe and Mineral Resources Exploration-National Science and Technology Major Project (2024ZD1002905 and 2024ZD1000100).

REFERENCES

Apsel, R. J., and J. E. Luco (1983). On the Green's functions for a layered half-space. Part II, *Bull. Seismol. Soc. Am.* **73,** no. 4, 931–951, doi: 10.1785/BSSA0730040931.

Bouchon, M. (1981). A simple method to calculate Green's functions for elastic layered media, *Bull. Seismol. Soc. Am.* **71,** no. 4, 959–971, doi: 10.1785/BSSA0710040959.

Burdick, L. J., T. Wallace, and T. Lay (1984). Modeling near-field and teleseismic observations from the Amchitka Test Site, *J. Geophys. Res.* **89,** no. B6, 4373–4388, doi: 10.1029/JB089iB06p04373.

Cagniard, L. (1939). *Réflexion et réfraction des ondes séismiques progressives*, Gauthier-Villars, Paris (in French).

Chang, S. (1988). Complete wave field modeling and seismic inversion for lossy elastic layered half space due to surface force, *Ph.D. Thesis*, University of Southern California.

Chen, X. (1993). A systematic and efficient method of computing normal modes for multilayered half-space, *Geophys. J. Int.* **115,** no. 2, 391–409, doi: 10.1111/j.1365-246X.1993.tb01194.x.

Chen, X., and H. Zhang (2001). An Efficient method for computing Green's functions for a layered half-space at large epicentral distances, *Bull. Seismol. Soc. Am.* **91,** no. 4, 858–869, doi: 10.1785/0120000113.

de Hoop, A. T. (1960). A modification of cagniard's method for solving seismic pulse problems, *Appl. Sci. Res.* **8,** no. 1, 349–356, doi: 10.1007/BF02920068.

Gradshteĭn, I. S., and I. M. Ryzhik (2014). *Table of Integrals, Series, and Products*, Academic Press, London, United Kingdom.

Greenfield, R. J. (1995). Comment on "An efficient method for computing green's functions for a layered half-space with sources and receivers at close depths" by Y. Hisada, *Bull. Seismol. Soc. Am.* **85,** no. 5, 1523–1524, doi: 10.1785/BSSA0850051523.

Haskell, N. A. (1953). The dispersion of surface waves on multilayered media, *Bull. Seismol. Soc. Am.* **43,** no. 1, 17–34, doi: 10.1029/SP030p0086.

Herrmann, R. B., and C. Y. Wang (1985). A comparison of synthetic seismograms, *Bull. Seismol. Soc. Am.* **75,** no. 1, 41–56.

Hisada, Y. (1994). An efficient method for computing Green's functions for a layered half-space with sources and receivers at close depths, *Bull. Seismol. Soc. Am.* **84,** no. 5, 1456–1472, doi: 10.1785/BSSA0840051456.

Hisada, Y. (1995). An efficient method for computing Green's functions for a layered half-space with sources and receivers at close depths (part 2), *Bull. Seismol. Soc. Am.* **85,** no. 4, 1080–1093, doi: 10.1785/BSSA0850041080.

Hisada, Y., and J. Bielak (2003). A theoretical method for computing near-fault ground motions in layered half-spaces considering static offset due to surface faulting, with a physical interpretation of fling step and rupture directivity, *Bull. Seismol. Soc. Am.* **93,** no. 3, 1154–1168, doi: 10.1785/0120020165.

Johnson, L. R. (1974). Green's function for Lamb's Problem, *Geophys. J. Int.* **37,** no. 1, 99–131, doi: 10.1111/j.1365-246X.1974.tb02446.x.

Kennett, B. L. N., and N. J. Kerry (1979). Seismic waves in a stratified half space, *Geophys. J. Int.* **57,** no. 3, 557–583, doi: 10.1111/j.1365-246X.1979.tb06779.x.

Lamb, H. (1904). I. On the propagation of tremors over the surface of an elastic solid, *Phil. Trans. Roy. Soc. Lond. A* **203,** nos. 359/371, doi: 10.1098/rsta.1904.0013.

Luco, J. E., and R. J. Apsel (1983). On the Green's functions for a layered half-space. Part I, *Bull. Seismol. Soc. Am.* **73,** no. 4, 909–929.

Xie, X., and Z. Yao (1989). A generalized reflection-transmition coefficient matrix method to calculate static displacement field of a stratified half-space by dislocation source, *Acta Geophys. Sin.* **32,** no. 3, 270–280.

Yao, Z., and D. G. Harkrider (1983). A generalized reflection-transmission coefficient matrix and discrete wavenumber method for synthetic seismograms, *Bull. Seismol. Soc. Am.* **73,** no. 6A, 1685–1699.

Zhang, H., X. Chen, and S. Chang (2003). An efficient numerical method for computing synthetic seismograms for a layered half-space with sources and receivers at close or same depths, *Pure Appl. Geophys.* **160,** 467–486.

Zhu, D., J. Wang, J. Hao, S. Yao, Y. Xu, T. Xu, and Z. Yao (2025). PyGRT: An efficient and integrated python package for computing synthetic seismograms in a layered half-space model, *Seismol. Res. Lett.* doi: 10.1785/0220250057.

Zhu, L., and L. A. Rivera (2002). A note on the dynamic and static displacements from a point source in multilayered media: A note on the dynamic and static displacements from a point source, *Geophys. J. Int.* **148,** no. 3, 619–627, doi: 10.1046/j.1365-246X.2002.01610.x.

APPENDIX

In this appendix, we will provide a mathematical derivation of the analytical expression for the integral

$$I_m^{(2)} = \int_0^\infty J_m(kr)k\,dk, \tag{A1}$$

in which m is a nonnegative integer, $r > 0$, and $J_m(\cdot)$ denotes the Bessel function of the first kind of order m. The oscillatory nature of $J_m(kr)$ at infinity necessitates careful treatment to ensure convergence. Following standard regularization techniques, we introduce an exponential convergence factor e^{-ak} with $a > 0$, transforming the integral into a convergent form:

$$W_m(a) = \int_0^\infty e^{-ak}J_m(kr)k\,dk. \tag{A2}$$

The original integral is recovered through the limit $I_m^{(2)} = \lim_{a\to 0^+} W_m(a)$. This regularization is justified by the fact that the Laplace transform of $kJ_m(kr)$ converges for $\mathrm{Re}\{a\} > 0$, and the limit $a \to 0^+$ yields meaningful results under conditional convergence. The derivation employs formulas from Gradshteĭn and Ryzhik (2014; hereafter, G&R) in their section 6.623, which we now reproduce verbatim.

G&R formula 6.623.1 states:

$$\int_0^\infty e^{-\alpha x}J_\nu(bx)x^\nu\,dx = \frac{(2b)^\nu\Gamma\left(\nu+\frac{1}{2}\right)}{\sqrt{\pi}(\alpha^2+b^2)^{\nu+\frac{1}{2}}},\quad \left[\mathrm{Re}\{\nu\} > -\frac{1}{2}, \mathrm{Re}\{\alpha\} > |\mathrm{Im}\{b\}|\right]. \tag{A3}$$

G&R formula 6.623.2 states:

$$\int_0^\infty e^{-\alpha x}J_\nu(bx)x^{\nu+1}\,dx = \frac{2\alpha(2b)^\nu\Gamma\left(\nu+\frac{3}{2}\right)}{\sqrt{\pi}(\alpha^2+b^2)^{\nu+\frac{3}{2}}},\quad [\mathrm{Re}\{\nu\} > -1, \mathrm{Re}\{\alpha\} > |\mathrm{Im}\{b\}|]. \tag{A4}$$

For $m = 0$, we apply G&R 6.623.2 with $\nu = 0$, $\alpha = a$, and $b = r$. Substituting these parameters:

$$W_0(a) = \frac{2a(2r)^0\Gamma\left(\frac{3}{2}\right)}{\sqrt{\pi}(a^2+r^2)^{3/2}}. \tag{A5}$$

Simplifying the Gamma function $\Gamma(\frac{3}{2}) = \Gamma(1+\frac{1}{2}) = \frac{1}{2}\Gamma(\frac{1}{2}) = \frac{\sqrt{\pi}}{2}$ yields:

$$W_0(a) = \frac{2a \times 1 \times \frac{\sqrt{\pi}}{2}}{\sqrt{\pi}(a^2+r^2)^{3/2}} = \frac{a}{(a^2+r^2)^{3/2}}. \tag{A6}$$

For $m = 1$, we apply G&R 6.623.1 with $\nu = 1$, $\alpha = a$, and $b = r$:

$$W_1(a) = \frac{(2r)^1\Gamma\left(\frac{3}{2}\right)}{\sqrt{\pi}(a^2+r^2)^{3/2}}. \tag{A7}$$

Using $\Gamma(\frac{3}{2}) = \frac{\sqrt{\pi}}{2}$ simplifies this to

$$W_1(a) = \frac{2r \times \frac{\sqrt{\pi}}{2}}{\sqrt{\pi}(a^2+r^2)^{3/2}} = \frac{r}{(a^2+r^2)^{3/2}}. \tag{A8}$$

For $m = 2$, neither G&R formula directly applies. We employ the Bessel function recurrence relation:

$$J_2(kr) = \frac{2}{kr}J_1(kr) - J_0(kr). \tag{A9}$$

Substituting into $W_2(a)$ in

$$W_2(a) = \int_0^\infty e^{-ak}\left[\frac{2}{kr}J_1(kr) - J_0(kr)\right]k\,dk = \frac{2}{r}\int_0^\infty e^{-ak}J_1(kr)\,dk - \int_0^\infty e^{-ak}J_0(kr)k\,dk. \tag{A10}$$

The second integral is solved in equation (A6). The first integral uses G&R 6.611.1:

$$\int_0^\infty e^{-ak}J_1(kr)\,dk = \frac{\sqrt{a^2+r^2}-a}{r\sqrt{a^2+r^2}}, [a > 0]. \tag{A11}$$

Combining these

$$W_2(a) = \frac{2}{r}\left(\frac{\sqrt{a^2 + r^2} - a}{r\sqrt{a^2 + r^2}}\right) - \frac{a}{(a^2 + r^2)^{3/2}}. \quad \text{(A12)}$$

Evaluating the limit as $a \to 0^+$ for all cases:

$$\lim_{a\to 0^+} W_0(a) = \lim_{a\to 0^+} \frac{a}{r^3} = 0,$$

$$\lim_{a\to 0^+} W_1(a) = \lim_{a\to 0^+} \frac{r}{r^3} = \frac{1}{r^2},$$

$$\lim_{a\to 0^+} W_2(a) = \lim_{a\to 0^+} \frac{2r^3}{r^5} = \frac{2}{r^2}. \quad \text{(A13)}$$

Thus, the analytical expressions are

$$\int_0^\infty J_0(kr)k\,dk = 0,$$

$$\int_0^\infty J_1(kr)k\,dk = \frac{1}{r^2},$$

$$\int_0^\infty J_2(kr)k\,dk = \frac{2}{r^2}. \quad \text{(A14)}$$

Manuscript received 4 August 2025
Published online 24 December 2025

Decoding Intrinsic and Scattering Seismic Attenuation at the Conjunction of the Cocos, Nazca, Caribbean, and Panama Plates

Daphne K. Sagel[1,2], Janire Prudencio*[1,3], Edoardo Del Pezzo[1,4], Elisabetta Giampiccolo[5], Tiziana Tuvé[5], Eduardo Camacho Astigarrabía[6], Julissa Sanjur[7], Ariadna Flores[7], Néstor Luque[7], and Jesús M. Ibáñez[1,3]

ABSTRACT

Panama is located in a unique tectonic setting, the Panama triple junction, where the result of the interaction of the Cocos, Nazca, and Caribbean plates takes place. This interaction is characterized by high seismicity; therefore, seismic risk analysis is essential to understand the possible consequences derived from these earthquakes. Despite historical records of large-magnitude earthquakes and significant seismic hazard, seismic attenuation studies in this area have been largely absent. In this study, we applied the multiple lapse time window analysis method to quantify seismic attenuation parameters for the entirety of Panama. This approach allowed us to separately estimate intrinsic attenuation (Q_i) and scattering attenuation (Q_s), providing insights into energy dissipation mechanisms. We considered 288 local earthquakes with magnitudes between 2.5 and 4.5 and recorded from January 2014 to December 2019. Our results show that scattering attenuation dominates at low frequencies (1–2 Hz), whereas both attenuation mechanisms are comparable at higher frequencies. Spatially, seismicity and attenuation values are highest along the edges of the Panama microplate, decreasing toward the central region. These findings highlight the importance of incorporating regional attenuation models into ground-motion prediction equations to improve seismic hazard maps and strengthen earthquake-resistant infrastructure in Panama. This study represents the first comprehensive assessment of seismic attenuation for Panama and provides a framework for future regional seismic hazard analyses.

KEY POINTS

- We examine intrinsic and scattering attenuation mapped across the Panama triple junction.
- Scattering attenuation dominates at 1–2 Hz; both mechanisms are similar at higher frequencies.
- The first seismic attenuation model for Panama supports future improved seismic hazard assessment.

INTRODUCTION

In regions with high seismicity levels, including potentially destructive earthquakes, ground-motion prediction and seismic hazard analysis are essential to mitigate impacts, improve seismic engineering designs, and anticipate consequences for both population and infrastructure during future strong earthquakes. To achieve this goal, it is necessary to incorporate reliable descriptions of seismic-wave attenuation into hazard models. Attenuation directly controls how seismic energy decays with distance, influencing both the amplitude and the frequency content of ground motion at sites of interest. A key step in integrating attenuation values into regional ground-motion models (GMMs) or ground-motion prediction equations (GMPEs) is to parameterize the empirical regressions in terms of physically meaningful attenuation coefficients. Specifically, the frequency-dependent quality factor and geometric spreading functions obtained from seismogram analysis can be introduced as

1. Andalusian Institute of Geophysics, Campus de Cartuja, University of Granada, Granada, Spain, https://orcid.org/0000-0002-5481-3424 (DKS); https://orcid.org/0000-0003-1755-3771 (JP); https://orcid.org/0000-0002-6981-5967 (EDP); https://orcid.org/0000-0002-9846-8781 (JMI); 2. Departamento de Matemática y física, Ministerio de Educación, Escuela secundaria Benigno Tomás Argote, Chiriquí Province, Panama; 3. Department of Theoretical Physics and Cosmos, Science Faculty, University of Granada, Granada, Spain; 4. INGV Osservatorio Vesuviano, Naples, Italy; 5. INGV Observatotio Etneo, Catania, Italy, https://orcid.org/0000-0001-5203-7436 (EG); https://orcid.org/0000-0003-4111-8008 (TT); 6. Departamento de Física, Facultad de Ciencias Naturales, Exactas y Tecnologia, University of Panama, Panama City, Panama, https://orcid.org/0000-0001-7415-6786 (ECA); 7. Institute of Geociences, University of Panama, Panama City, Panama, https://orcid.org/0009-0000-1845-9651 (JS); https://orcid.org/0009-0002-4724-542X (AF); https://orcid.org/0000-0003-4564-1947 (NL)

*Corresponding author: janire@ugr.es

Cite this article as Sagel, D. K., J. Prudencio, E. Del Pezzo, E. Giampiccolo, T. Tuvé, E. Camacho Astigarrabía, J. Sanjur, A. Flores, N. Luque, and J. M. Ibáñez (2025). Decoding Intrinsic and Scattering Seismic Attenuation at the Conjunction of the Cocos, Nazca, Caribbean, and Panama Plates, *Bull. Seismol. Soc. Am.* **116**, 589–602, doi: 10.1785/0120250105 constraints in the functional form of the GMM. This allows the distance-decay terms and site or path corrections in the regression to be anchored to regionally observed attenuation properties rather than being estimated solely from regression residuals. In practice, the attenuation values enter the model through the anelastic and geometric spreading terms that govern the exponential decay of ground-motion amplitudes with distance. Therefore, attenuation studies are indispensable for obtaining realistic GMMs: the parameters reported here provide a physical basis for future regression analyses, serving as a starting point for the development of predictive models that more accurately capture regional propagation effects and strengthen seismic hazard assessments (Soham and Abhishek, 2016).

The Earth's crust and upper mantle constitute a highly heterogeneous system, from macroscopic to microscopic scales (Sato *et al.*, 2012). These heterogeneities, primarily defined by geological and tectonic structures, govern the propagation of seismic waves by influencing properties such as wave velocity, energy distribution, waveform shape, and signal duration (Del Pezzo, 2008). Seismologists use these propagation patterns to infer Earth structure at various scales, including large (e.g., Del Pezzo *et al.*, 1995; Levandowski *et al.*, 2021), medium (e.g., Bianco *et al.*, 2002, 2005; Giampiccolo *et al.*, 2006), small crustal scale (Prudencio *et al.*, 2017; Ibáñez *et al.*, 2020; Castro-Melgar *et al.*, 2021), and even centimeter to millimeter scale (Müller *et al.*, 2010). Seismic attenuation, which reflects the energy loss caused by these heterogeneities, allows for the differentiation of various geodynamic regimes, from tectonic (e.g., Biswas and Singh, 2020) to volcanic environments (e.g., Prudencio, Del Pezzo, *et al.*, 2013; Prudencio, Ibánez, *et al.*, 2013), or comparative analyses between them (e.g., Del Pezzo *et al.*, 1996; Eulenfeld and Wegler, 2016). Numerous studies highlight the strong depth dependence of seismic attenuation, revealing its relationship with wave velocity and the compressional state of the medium (e.g., Ibáñez *et al.*, 1990; Biswas and Singh, 2023). In general, attenuation studies consider both intrinsic attenuation (Q_i) related to energy loss via friction and scattering attenuation (Q_s) associated with energy redistribution caused by internal resonance of heterogeneities. Understanding the attenuation patterns of a region provides the best approximation for relating the physical properties of the medium to its structural characteristics (Sato *et al.*, 2012).

Most approaches and techniques to estimate seismic attenuation require extensive, high-quality datasets covering large spatial volumes—conditions that are often difficult to meet. Consequently, several seismically active regions still lack detailed attenuation studies. The spatial representation of attenuation values greatly aids interpretation, ideally enabling the identification of strong lateral variations in the propagation medium. Several techniques are available to produce attenuation maps (e.g., Prudencio, Del Pezzo, *et al.*, 2013; Del Pezzo *et al.*, 2016, 2018; Del Pezzo and Ibáñez, 2020; Sketsiou *et al.*, 2020). However, their application is limited because they require extensive high-quality datasets with complete spatial coverage and increasing the complexity of their implementation. Conversely, the multiple lapse time window analysis (MLTWA) method is a very reliable and well-known method for separating intrinsic attenuation (Q_i) and scattering attenuation (Q_s) and establishing good relationships between the average values and the tectonic and geomorphological structures of the region. It has been successfully applied in various regions (e.g., Fehler *et al.*, 1992; Akinci, Del Pezzo, and Ibáñez, 1995; Tuvè *et al.*, 2006; Carcolé and Sato, 2010; Meirova and Pinsky, 2014; Bachura and Fischer, 2016; Del Pezzo *et al.*, 2019; Padhy and Subhadra, 2021; Mahanama *et al.*, 2024). The technique is based on normalizing the direct *S*-wave energy with respect to the late coda energy, which shares the same source strength and site response (Aki, 1980).

Historical and instrumental seismic catalogs (e.g., Incorporated Research Institutions for Seismology and regional observatories in Panama, Colombia, and Costa Rica) show that over the past 150 yr, Panama has experienced earthquakes with magnitudes >7.5, along with numerous events with magnitudes >6.0. The largest recorded events include the estimated M_w 7.9 earthquake of 7 September 1882 and the M_w 7.6 earthquake of 18 July 1934, both of which caused extensive damage in southwestern Panama. The M_w 7.5 Limón–Costa Rica earthquake, associated with back-arc thrusting along faults of the North Panama deformed belt (Plafker and Ward, 1992), generated a tsunami and caused severe damage in northwestern Panama (Camacho, 1994). Other significant events in the Panama fracture zone (PFZ) include an estimated M_w 7.2 earthquake in 1879 (Peraldo *et al.*, 2006) and an M_w 7.6 earthquake in 1934 (Camacho, 2009). Despite the significant seismicity and its consequences in the region, seismic attenuation studies in and around Panama are scarce. Christeson *et al.* (2000) estimated *P*-wave attenuation values in the Costa Rica margin wedge, identifying high-attenuation regions associated with low-seismic velocity anomalies. Zhu *et al.* (2010) conducted a similar study in the central Pacific margin of Costa Rica, observing a clear relationship between Q_p and lithological variations across the marine fore-arc. Vargas *et al.* (2018) analyzed seismic attenuation in the Panama basin, bounded by the continental margins of Ecuador, Colombia, and Panama, and the Carnegie and Cocos ridges, to infer the thermal structure of the oceanic crust. They found a strong association between high attenuation (low Q) and areas of active magmatism and thermal anomalies, characterized by high heat flow. Vargas *et al.* (2019) also studied coda-wave attenuation (Q_c) in the Northern Andes (Colombia), reporting high attenuation associated with volcanic thermal anomalies and lower attenuation in cooler, less volcanically active regions.

Given the absence of attenuation studies in Panama, the primary objective of this study is to expand knowledge of *S*-wave attenuation properties in the region by providing estimates of Q_i and Q_s. These results will be compared with findings from other regions investigated using MLTWA, improving our

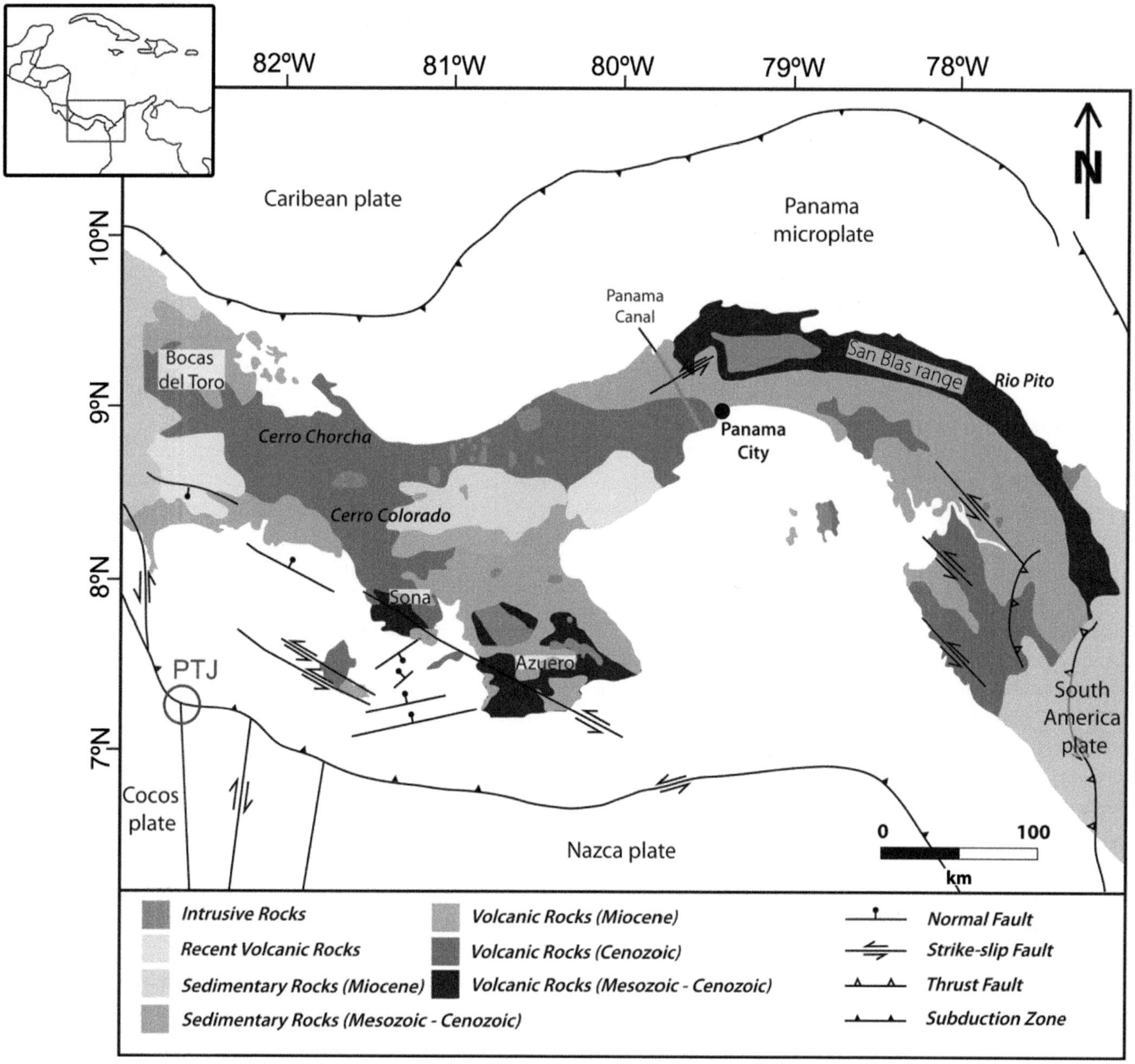

Figure 1. Simplified tectonic and geological map representing the main features of the area (modified from Sepp, 2016). There are large fault systems ranging from tens to hundreds of kilometers but also smaller structures, on the order of a few kilometers (e.g. San Blas Rance or Cerro Colorado volcanic zone), related to the heterogeneities obtained in this work. The inset in the top left corner corresponds to the location of Panama's location in relation to Central America. The color version of this figure is available only in the electronic edition.

interpretation. Moreover, the results will contribute to a better understanding of seismic risk in Panama, which is crucial for civil protection and infrastructure planning, as recently emphasized for neighboring Costa Rica by Hidalgo-Leiva *et al.* (2023), and will support future seismic hazard assessments.

Tectonic framework

Tectonically speaking, Panama is mainly characterized by the Panama triple junction (PTJ) (MacKay and Moore, 1990). This junction located at the western of Panama is the zone where the Cocos plate, the Nazca plate, the Caribbean plate, the fracture zone, and the microplate of Panama converge (Fig. 1; Camacho *et al.*, 2010). Some authors consider that this convergent margin region is a very interesting zone because it offers an unparalleled opportunity to study crustal deformation and other tectonic phenomena associated with the complex dynamics of the conjunction of different regimes, including the presence of subduction processes (Morell *et al.*, 2011). The triple junction of Panama steeply separates the subduction of the Nazca plate in the southeast, which is slow and oblique, from the Cocos plate to the northwest, which has a trace orthogonal to this first and fast convergence velocity (Bourke *et al.*, 2020, 2023). In addition, as Lemenkova and Debeir (2023) highlighted, the Cocos ridge, approximately 20 km thick, gives a bathymetric difference between both plates along the PFZ, which is the active plate boundary, giving this region special relevance from the tectonic point of view. In the center of the region is the Isthmus of Panama, with important left-lateral strike-slip faults, such as the Azuero fault zone, where on 2 May 1516 and 2 October 1913 earthquakes occurred, and right-lateral strike-slip faults such as the Pedro Miguel fault (central Panama), which generated a destructive event on 2 May 1621.

According to the recent results obtained by Lemenkova and Debeir (2023), the seismicity distribution is not homogeneous throughout the region; it is concentrated fundamentally in two regions, where the highest magnitudes also occur, and the highest seismicity rate occurs to the west, on the border with Costa Rica (in the PTJ zone). These authors' joint interpreting topographic, gravity anomaly, bathymetric maps, and satellite observations revealed that the seismicity of the region is influenced by the geodynamic complexity of the area, including magmatic and hydrothermal influence. Regarding the depth of these earthquakes, the seismicity in the Panama block occurs mostly at depths equal or shallower than 30 km depth. On the contrary, in the North Panama deformed belt in northeast Panama, earthquakes are located at depths up to 100 km depth along a well-determined Wadati–Benioff zone (Camacho *et al.*, 2010). Recently, Quintero *et al.* (2023), using the information of two moderate and close in time earthquakes (M_w 6.0 and 6.2) occurred in the strike slip to subduction transition zone in the Costa Rica–Panama border, concluded that the Cocos ridge and Nazca plate are largely accommodated by an outer-arc crustal block migration deforming the overriding Panama microplate. Active seismic source studies (Stevenhagen *et al.*, 1997) and receiver functions obtained in central and southern Costa Rica (Dzierma *et al.*, 2010, 2011) mapped the crust and Moho depth in southern Central America and placed the Moho at 35 km depth.

DATA

The data set analyzed in the present study comprises 1916 earthquakes with magnitudes ranging from 2.4 to 4.6, depths between 0.5 and 250 km, and source–receiver distances from 3.5 to 150 km. The earthquake were recorded at 15 broadband seismic stations operated by the Institute of Geosciences network of Panama, all equipped with three components and located throughout the Panamanian territory from 2000 to 2020. We performed a quality control to select high-quality signals based on signal-to-noise ratio, coda-to-noise ratio, and signal-to-coda ratio and removed waveforms with ratios <1.5. In addition, all saturated or clipped waveforms and seismograms that show overlapped events were not considered even if the ratios were over the threshold. Hence, the final dataset was composed of 288 earthquakes (see Fig. 2) and 1416 waveforms ranging from magnitude 2.5 to 4.5, depths from 0.5 to 30 km, and source–receiver distance from 10.0 to 130 km. We decided to set the maximum distance at 130, following the studies of Akinci, Del Pezzo, and Ibáñez (1995), in which they set a maximum distance of 170 km up to which the method has a good fit. At greater distances and as observed by Akinci, Ibáñez, *et al.* (1995) and Ibáñez *et al.* (1993), a conversion from body waves to surface waves occurs, and the geometrical spreading would have to be corrected.

METHOD: MLTWA

The MLTWA entails computation of the logarithm of the integral of seismic energy over designated time windows, with the objective of estimating the intrinsic (η_i) and scattering (η_s) coefficients (Fehler *et al.*, 1992; Hoshiba, 1993; Sato *et al.*, 2012). The estimation of η_i and η_s is performed through a comparison of empirical observations with synthetic predictions derived from a theoretical model, which assumes an infinitely extended medium with homogeneous properties and isotropic scattering (Carcolé and Sato, 2010; Sato *et al.*, 2012). The importance of quantifying the relative contribution of intrinsic and scattering attenuation helps in the synthesis of the seismograms, and because the scattering phenomena redistribute the seismic energy into the coda, they increase ground shaking, which is a crucial parameter in seismic risk studies (Del Pezzo *et al.* 2019).

The analysis was conducted using three discrete time intervals (E_1, E_2, and E_3), each of duration Δt, starting at the arrival of the *S* waves. In addition, a fourth interval (E_c) was selected within the coda of the seismogram, beginning at a fixed reference time (T_c), measured from the earthquake origin time. To minimize source, instrument, radiation pattern, and site effects, E_1, E_2, and E_3 were normalized by E_c. For each source–station pair, at an epicentral distance *r*, we computed the normalized values E_1/E_c, E_2/E_c, and E_3/E_c. These values were corrected for geometrical spreading by multiplying by $4\pi r^2$, assuming body-wave propagation.

Seismic energy in each window (E_1, E_2, E_3, and E_c) was estimated using the norm of the Fourier transform of the seismogram within each time window, averaged over the three components of ground motion. The windows for E_1, E_2, and E_3 were 15 s in duration, starting at the *S*-wave arrival, and the E_c window was 10 s in duration, starting 45 s after the origin time. This reference time ensured that the E_c window consistently sampled the coda, even for small events at short-epicentral distances. Analyses were performed in four frequency bands—1–2, 2–4, 4–8, and 8–16 Hz—using an eight-pole zero shift Butterworth band-pass filter. An example seismogram with the analysis windows is shown in Figure 3.

Then, the seismogram energy envelope, $E(r, t)$, in which *r* is the source–receiver distance and *t* is the lapse time (time elapsed from the earthquake origin), normalized and corrected by geometrical spreading, are plotted versus their associated

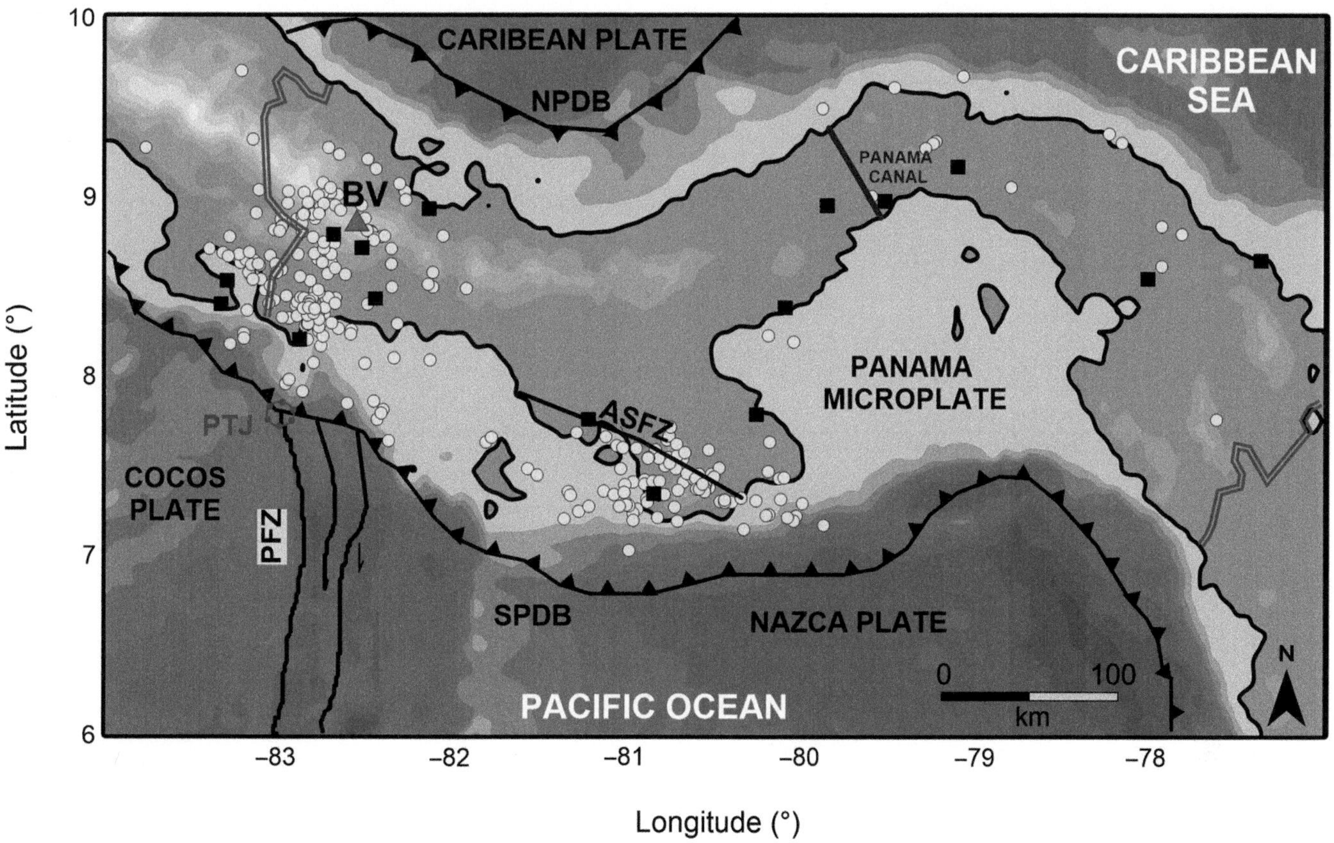

Figure 2. Map of Panama region with the main tectonic features and hypocenter distribution selected from the Institute of Geosciences (IGC) catalog between 2000 and 2020 (yellow dots). Black squares indicate the position of the 15 seismic stations used in this analysis. Double red lines are the border with Costa Rica to the west and Colombia to the east. The blue line marks the position of the Panamá Canal. The pink triangle is the position of the Barú volcano (BV). PMFVF represents the area of Pedro Miguel fault and volcanic field. ASFZ, Azuero Sona fault zone; NPDB, North Panamá deformed belt; PFZ, Panamá fault zone; PTJ, Panama Triple Junction; SPDB, South Panamá deformed belt. The color version of this figure is available only in the electronic edition.

source–receiver distance (Fig. 4) and fitted to the estimated theoretical values through the Paasschens solution of the energy transport equation (Paasschens, 1997) given by

$$E[r,t,B_0,L_e^{-1},v] = W_0 \frac{\mathrm{Exp}[-L_e^{-1}vt]}{4\pi r^2 v}\delta\left[t-\frac{r}{v}\right] + W_0 H\left[t-\frac{r}{v}\right] \times \frac{(1-\frac{r^2}{v^2t^2})^{1/8}}{(\frac{4\pi vt}{3B_0L_e^{-1}})^{3/2}} \times \exp[-L_e^{-1}vt] F\left[vtB_0L_e^{-1}\left(1-\frac{r^2}{v^2t^2}\right)^{3/4}\right], \quad (1)$$

in which $F(x) = \mathrm{Exp}(x)(1 + 2.026/x)1/2$, W_0 is the source intensity, L_e is the extinction length, v is the half-space velocity, H is the Heaviside function, δ is the Dirac's delta, and B_0 is the seismic albedo. In Figure 4, looking at the third window (green dots), you can see how from ~100 km onward, the adjustment is not as good as for shorter distances. Akinci, Del Pezzo, and Ibáñez (1995), observed that for a perfect fit, the geometrical spreading of body waves would have to be substituted for surface waves. By making this correction from body to surface waves, they observed that the fit is better, but there is no change in the attenuation values. Because it was demonstrated by Akinci, Del Pezzo, and Ibáñez (1995) that the attenuation values do not change, we decided not to repeat the fitting procedure by changing the geometrical spreading.

After the seismic albedo B_0 and the extinction length L_e are obtained, attenuation coefficients can be expressed as follows:

$$B_0 = \eta_s/(\eta_i + \eta_s) \text{ and } L_e^{-1} = \eta_i + \eta_s. \quad (2)$$

Alternatively, attenuation coefficients are commonly expressed as a function of the wave frequency f and seismic-wave velocity v and including intrinsic attenuation Q_i and scattering attenuation Q_s terms as follows (Hoshiba, 1995):

$$\eta_i = 2\pi f/vQ_i; \quad \eta_s = 2\pi f/vQ_s. \quad (3)$$

In this study, the nonlinear two-parameter fit was performed using a grid search to minimize the misfit function in parameter space (Fig. 5) to estimate the optimal B_0 and L_e^{-1} values and their uncertainties. This approach facilitates direct estimation of uncertainties and solution quality by analyzing the distribution of misfit values between theoretical predictions (for L_e^{-1} and B_0 parameters) and the observed data. The fit procedure was based on a grid of 20 × 30 parameter pairs,

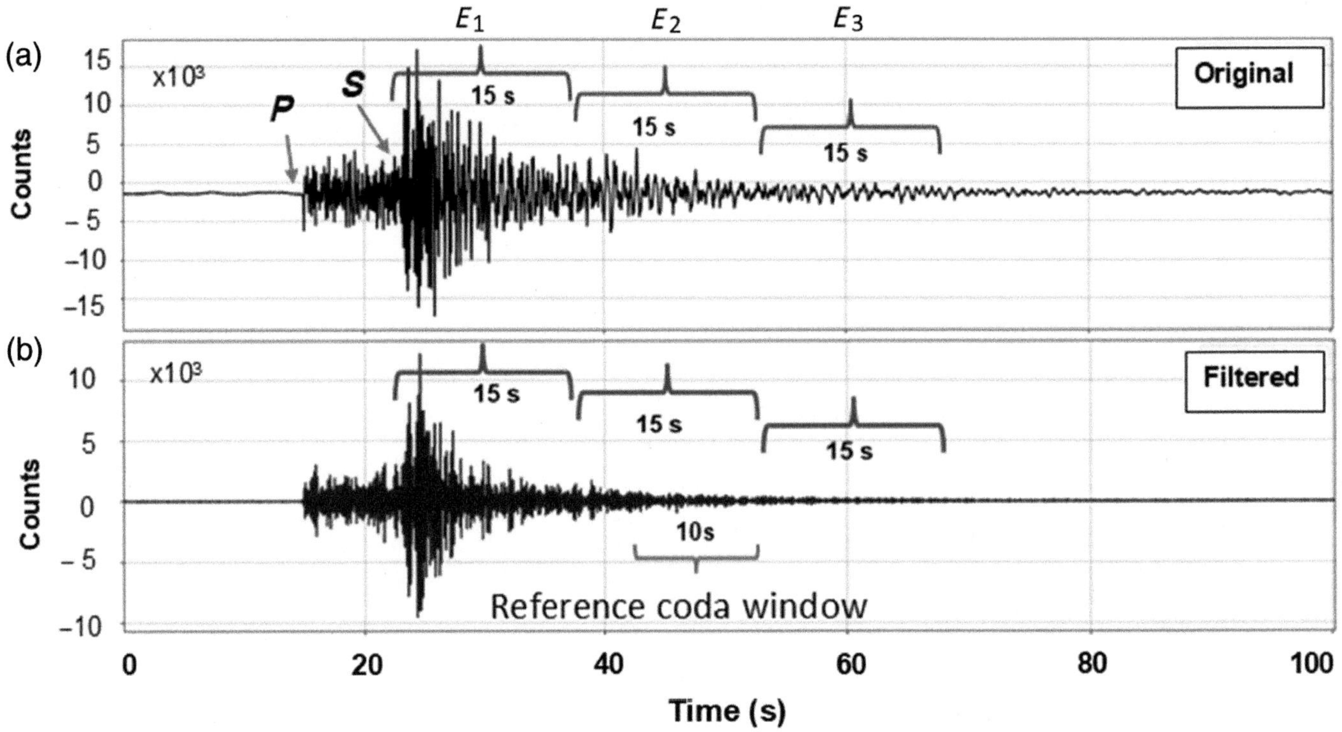

with B_0 ranging from 0.05 to 1.0 ($\Delta B_0 = 0.05$) and L_e^{-1} from 0.004 to 0.12 ($\Delta L_e^{-1} = 0.004$). These parameter ranges are consistent with values reported in previous studies for similar regions. For each pair (B_{0i}, L_{ei}^{-1}), we computed the misfit as the metric distance between the theoretical curve derived from equation (1) and the experimental data. The final solution corresponds to the parameter pair that yields the minimum misfit. Merit function values calculated at each grid point were normalized by their minimum to define the uncertainty region. Isolines of equal merit function values delineate confidence regions, with contours corresponding to $1-\sigma$, $2-\sigma$, and $3-\sigma$ intervals. These were computed using F-test statistics for two variables, with degrees of freedom $N-2$, in which N is the number of data points and 2 represents the number of fitted parameters. The dataset used in this study includes source–receiver pairs with epicentral distances ranging from 10 to 130 km. Table 1 summarizes the best-fit values of B_0 and L_e^{-1}, the corresponding $1-\sigma$ confidence intervals, and the derived Q_i (intrinsic quality factor), Q_s (scattering quality factor), and Q_t (total quality factor) values for all frequency bands across the 10–130 km distance range. The total quality factor (Q_t) can be estimated as $Q_t^{-1} = Q_s^{-1} + Q_i^{-1}$. The frequency column indicates the central value of each band: 1.5 (1–2), 3 (2–4), 6 (4–8), and 12 Hz (8–16 Hz). Because Q_i and Q_s are obtained from B_0 and L_e^{-1} following Hoshiba (1995), the uncertainties in Q_i and Q_s will be around the same uncertainty interval than B_0 and L_e^{-1} (around 12.5% in this case). Finally, Figure 6 shows the variation of Q_i, Q_s, and Q_t as a function of frequency.

Figure 3. Example of (a) original and (b) filtered at the 1–16 Hz frequency band, seismograms with the three successive time windows for energy estimation (E1–E3), and the reference coda window E_c centered at 45 s lapse time are reported. The color version of this figure is available only in the electronic edition.

DISCUSSION

In this study, we estimated the intrinsic and scattering attenuation parameters for the Panama region using the well-established MLTWA method. These parameters were obtained for four frequency bands centered at 1.5, 3, 6, and 12 Hz, across a range of epicentral distances from 10 to 130 km.

Looking at Table 1, a key observation is that for frequencies ≥3 Hz, the values of Q_i and Q_s are comparable and statistically indistinguishable within the margin of uncertainty. However, at the lowest frequency band (1.5 Hz), scattering attenuation (Q_s) clearly dominates over intrinsic attenuation (Q_i). This observation was corroborated by estimating the frequency dependence of intrinsic and scattering attenuation: $(f) = Q_0 f^n$, in which Q_0 is the value of Q at 1 Hz and n is the frequency-dependent parameter (Del Pezzo *et al.*, 1995). We obtained $Q_i = 338$ $f^{0.52}$ and $Q_s = 71 f^{1.33}$ frequency relationships, similar to those obtained by Del Pezzo *et al.* (1995, 1996) and Bianco *et al.*, (2002) in other tectonic regions. We observed that Q_i has a very low-frequency dependence, whereas the Q_0 values is relatively high compared with other regions. On the other hand, because the frequency dependence value of Q_s is very high, the scattering process at low frequencies is the dominant phenomena to

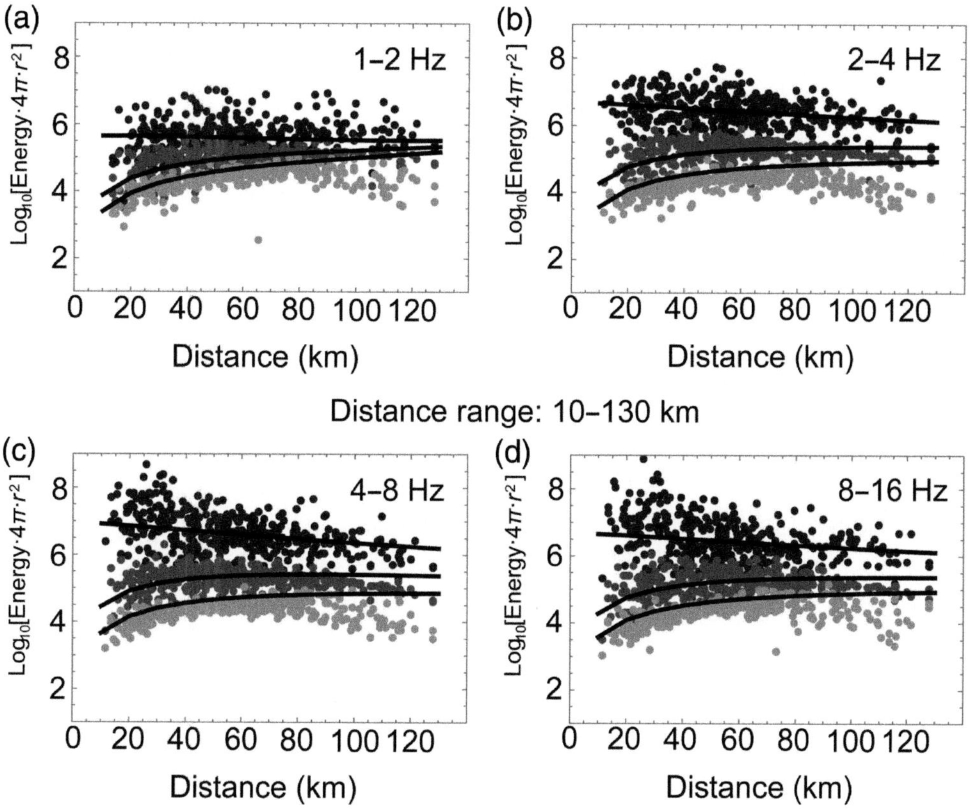

Figure 4. Example of multiple lapse time window analysis (MLTWA). Data and best-fitting curves are shown for the four frequency bands investigated (a) 1–2, (b) 2–4, (c) 4–8, and (d) 8–16 Hz at 10–130 km distance range. The blue, red, and green circles correspond to the first, second, and third windows, respectively. The black line is the best fit for each time window analysis. The color version of this figure is available only in the electronic edition.

produce attenuation effects, especially between 1 and 3 Hz. Similar patterns have been documented in other regions (e.g., Akinci, Del Pezzo, and Ibáñez, 1995; Del Pezzo *et al.*, 2019; Ibáñez *et al.*, 2020), where dominant scattering at low frequencies is interpreted as evidence of heterogeneities with characteristic sizes comparable to the seismic wavelength (λ). Assuming an average *S*-wave velocity of 3.5 km/s, the corresponding wavelengths (λ) range corresponds, approximately, between 2.3 and 2.5 km. This suggests the presence of structural heterogeneities, including faults and fractures, of similar dimensions in the upper crust that significantly affect *S*-wave propagation and are compatible with the magnitude of the average earthquakes that occur in the region. Looking at the geological and structural map in Figure 1, we can observe how the fault sizes are much larger, from tens to hundreds of kilometers, whereas we have observed that the scattering value is for structures on the order of a few kilometers in length. What we see in Figure 1 is the presence of a series of mountain and volcanic chains that are compatible with these structures that can produce scattering phenomena. That is, the San Blas range or the volcanic zones of Cerro Chorcha and Cerro Colorado are the ones that may be producing these scattering phenomena.

Figure 4 reveals that the energy–distance distributions are denser and more homogeneous for epicentral distances <100 km. Consequently, we reinverted the attenuation curves for two reduced distance ranges (10–60 and 10–80 km) to evaluate potential variations in attenuation parameters with distance (Figs. A1, A2). The resulting estimates of B_0, L_e^{-1} and their derived attenuation parameters are presented in Tables A1 and A2.

Comparison of Tables 1, A1, and A2 indicates that the qualitative relationship between Q_i and Q_s remains consistent across all distance ranges, and the absolute values are different, but the proportional relationship is practically the same.

Spatial variations in attenuation were also explored. Figure 2 shows two main seismic clusters: a larger one in the west near the PTJ and a smaller one in the southeast along Azuero Sona fault zone. Although data scarcity in the southeastern region prevents robust independent estimates of Q_i and Q_s, the western region provides a sufficiently large dataset to perform inversion. The resulting energy curves, uncertainty estimates, and derived parameters are presented in Figure A3 and Table A3.

Comparison between the entire region and the western subset reveals significant differences. In general, Q_i, Q_s, and Q_t values are lower in the west, indicating stronger attenuation, particularly caused by scattering. This correlates with the higher seismicity and greater tectonic complexity of the western region. Moreover, scattering dominates over intrinsic attenuation across most frequency bands, except 4–8 Hz, reinforcing the interpretation of abundant heterogeneities in the area.

All attenuation parameters in this study were estimated under the half-space assumption (i.e., constant velocity Earth model), which is an idealization. Previous works (Del Pezzo and Bianco, 2010; Del Pezzo *et al.*, 2011; Pisconti *et al.*, 2015) investigated the effects of realistic layered Earth models, for which an inhomogeneous crust overlies a transparent mantle, on synthetic energy envelopes. These studies demonstrated that MLTWA applied to such models yields estimates consistent with the input parameters, though parameters B_0 and L_e^{-1} tend to be overestimated relative to the half-space model.

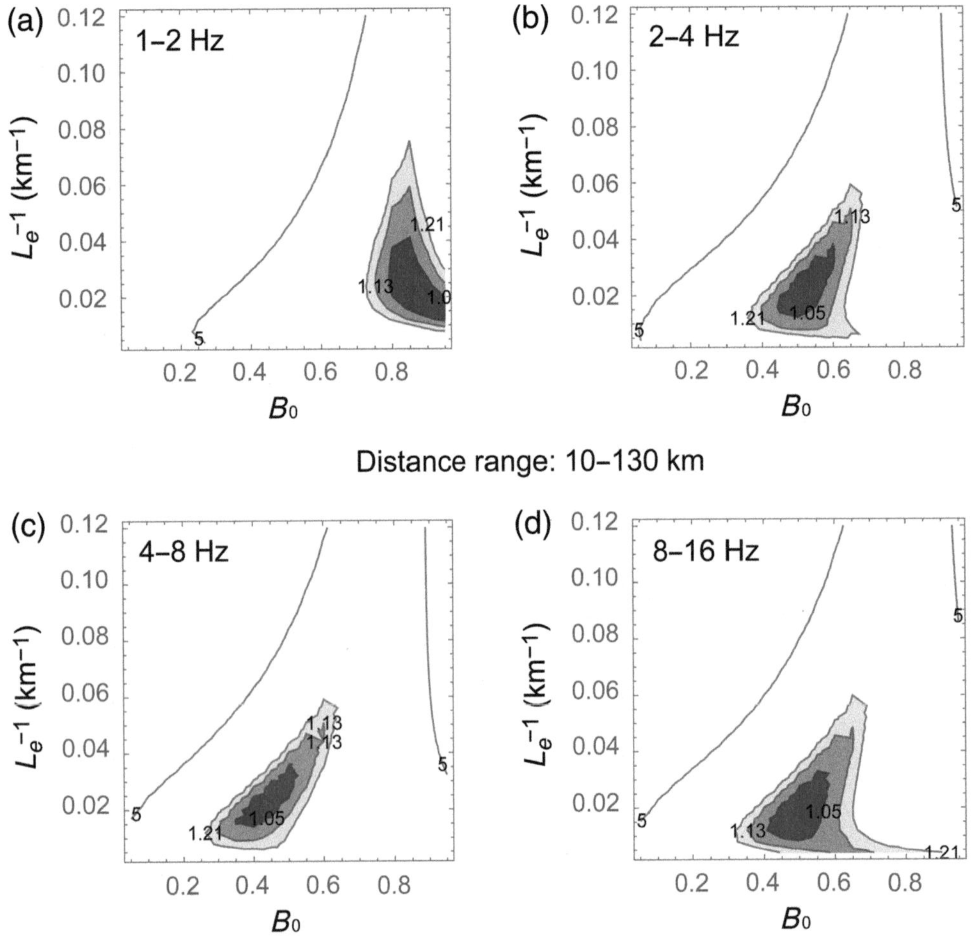

Figure 5. Residual map normalized at its minimum used for the estimation of the best parameter in the grid search and for the evaluation of the uncertainty associated with B_0 and L_e^{-1} at 10–130 km distance range. The three colored zones mark the $1-\sigma$ (red), the $2-\sigma$ (orange), and the $3-\sigma$ (yellow) confidence areas, respectively. Panels (a–d) correspond to 1–2, 2–4, 4–8 and 8–16 Hz, respectively. The color version of this figure is available only in the electronic edition.

Using correction nomograms from Del Pezzo and Bianco (2010), we estimate that B_0 decreases by ~20% at frequencies >1.5 Hz, with a larger reduction for L_e^{-1}. These corrected parameters are presented in Table A4.

Finally, Figures 7 and 8 compare our B_0, L_e^{-1}, Q_i^{-1}, and Q_s^{-1} results with those obtained in other tectonically active regions using the MLTWA method. In Figure 7, we can observe how obtained L_e values are lower than in other regions, which is compatible with the fact that we have a dominant effect of scattering at low frequencies. It is very interesting that the frequency dependence, which also represents the scattering value, is constant. Therefore, the L_e values are compatible with a strong scattering process and reinforce the idea that the geomorphology of the region is what significantly affects the attenuation effects. On the other hand, the B_0 values are comparable to those obtained in other tectonic regions. Because the Q_i^{-1} and Q_s^{-1} values are easier to relate to attenuation behavior, most studies use the inverse value to interpret their results. Because inverse attenuation values are easier to relate to study behavior, most studies use the inverse value to interpret their results. For this reason, inverse attenuation values are presented in Figure 8. Attenuation values (i.e., Q_s^{-1} and Q_i^{-1} values) for the Panama microplate are relatively low, especially Q_i^{-1}, which exceeds the average values from other regions. Despite the high seismicity and magnitudes, most seismicity is concentrated in the western sector. Given that the MLTWA method integrates paths traversing both active and stable areas, our average Q values are influenced by the broad stable regions in the central microplate (Figs. 1, 2). Therefore, the relatively low Q^{-1} (high Q) (i.e., low attenuation) values likely reflect contributions from tectonically stable areas, which are spatially more extensive than the active zones.

TABLE 1
Derived Attenuation Values for the Four Frequency Bands Analyzed at 10–130 km Distance Range

Frequency Band (Hz)	B_0	$1-\sigma$	L_e^{-1}	$1-\sigma$	Q_i	Q_s	Q_t
1–2	0.85	0.10	0.024	0.003	600	100	85
2–4	0.50	0.05	0.020	0.004	400	400	200
4–8	0.45	0.07	0.024	0.004	650	800	350
8–16	0.50	0.05	0.020	0.004	1700	1700	850

B_0, seismic albedo; L_e^{-1}, extinction length (km^{-1}); Q_i, intrinsic attenuation; Q_s, scattering attenuation; Q_t, total attenuation. $1-\sigma$ associated confidence areas for a standard $1-\sigma$ deviation.

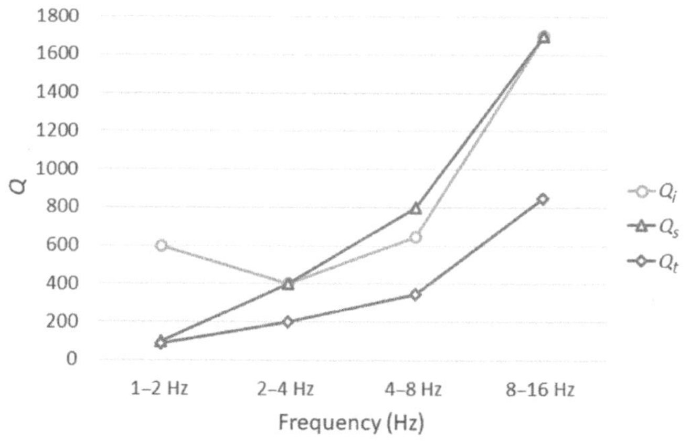

Figure 6. Graphical representation of the mean values of Q_i, Q_s, and Q_t for Panama using the MLTWA approach at 10–130 km distance range. The color version of this figure is available only in the electronic edition.

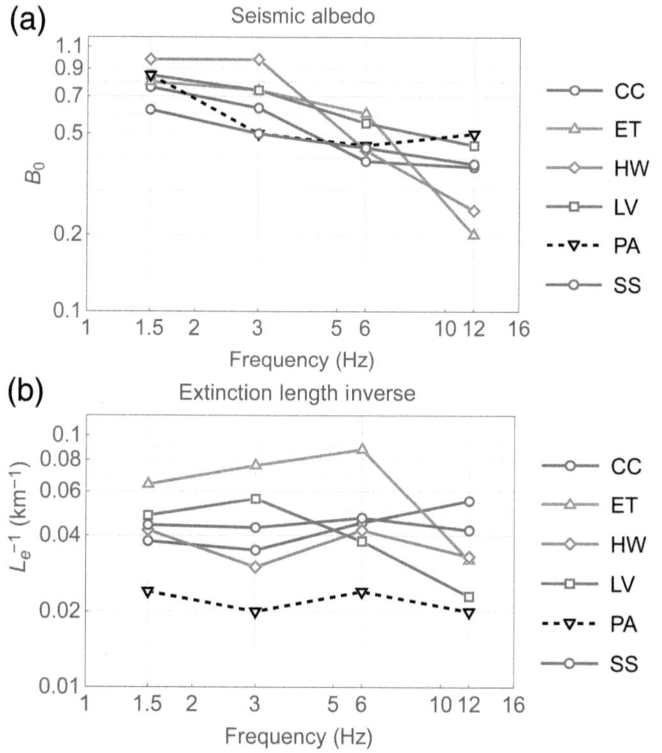

Figure 7. Graphical representation of average (a) seismic albedo and (b) extinction length versus frequency for Panama (PA) using the MLTWA approach at 10–130 km distance range and comparison with other tectonically active and volcanic regions of the world. CC, Central California (Mayeda *et al.*, 1992); ET, Etna (Del Pezzo *et al.*, 2019); HW, Hawaii (Mayeda *et al.*, 1992); LV, Long Valley (Mayeda *et al.*, 1992); SS, Southern Spain and Anatolia (Akinci, Del Pezzo, and Ibáñez, 1995). The color version of this figure is available only in the electronic edition.

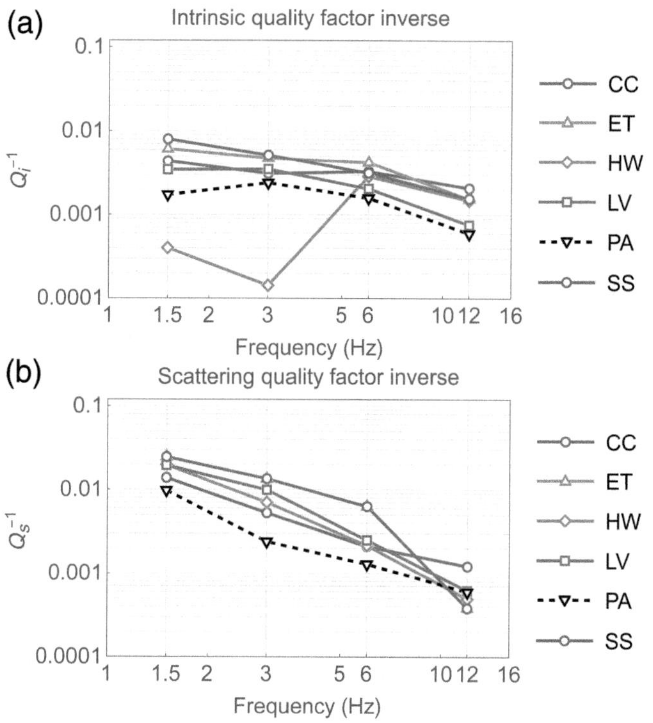

Figure 8. (a) Q_i^{-1} and (b) Q_s^{-1} versus frequency obtained using MLTWA in other tectonically active regions of the world. CC, Central California (Mayeda *et al.*, 1992); ET, Etna (Del Pezzo *et al.*, 2019); HW, Hawaii (Mayeda *et al.*, 1992); LV, Long Valley (Mayeda *et al.*, 1992); PA, Panama (this study); SS, Southern Spain and Anatolia (Akinci, Del Pezzo, and Ibáñez, 1995). The color version of this figure is available only in the electronic edition.

CONCLUSION

This study represents the first comprehensive analysis of seismic attenuation across Panama, a region characterized by complex tectonics and moderate to high seismicity within Central America. We applied the MLTWA method to estimate average attenuation parameters and to distinguish between intrinsic attenuation (anelastic absorption, reflecting rock rigidity) and scattering attenuation (wave dispersion caused by medium heterogeneities, reflecting heterogeneity scale).

Our results show that scattering attenuation predominates over intrinsic attenuation only at low frequencies (1–2 Hz). At higher frequencies, both attenuation mechanisms contribute similarly. The estimated parameters B_0 and L_e^{-1} and the derived Q_i and Q_s values consistently reflect this pattern. In addition, the additional analysis performed with the western subset reveals significant differences because Q_i, Q_s, and Q_t values are lower in the west, indicating stronger attenuation, particularly caused by scattering. This correlates with the higher seismicity and greater tectonic complexity (abundant heterogeneities) of the western region.

These findings highlight the need to apply additional attenuation analysis methods, when possible, to enable a more detailed spatial mapping and regionalization of seismic attenuation in Panama. The attenuation parameters derived in this study provide the physical basis needed to constrain future regional GMMs and GMPEs. Incorporating these values into the development and calibration of predictive models will lead to more reliable seismic hazard assessments in Panama, thereby supporting improved seismic-resistant design and more effective risk mitigation strategies.

DATA AND RESOURCES

The seismic waveforms analyzed in this study were recorded by 15 broadband seismic stations belonging to the Institute of Geosciences network of Panama and are available at https://zenodo.org/records/7248064 (last accessed October 2022). Their corresponding instrument responses and the seismic catalog were also provided from the same institution. The detection and segmentation of the seismic events together with the analysis of spectral characteristics were performed by two different software packages developed by Ligdamis Gutierrez from University of Granada available at doi: 10.5281/zenodo.7008075 and doi: 10.5281/zenodo.7268903, respectively. The multiple lapse time-window analysis (MLTWA) was performed using a Mathematica notebook.

DECLARATION OF COMPETING INTERESTS

The authors acknowledge that there are no conflicts of interest recorded.

ACKNOWLEDGMENTS

This work has been funded by the Spanish Project PID2022-143083NB-I00, "LEARNING" funded by MICIU/AEI/10.13039/501100011033 and by FEDER, UE, and by ALARM (C.EXP.022.UGR23). The authors thank the National Secretariat of Science, Technology, and Innovation and the Institute for the Training and Use of Human Resources, through the Program: Research Doctorate BBIDP-II-2019-03, for granting him the scholarship to be able to carry out the Doctorate in Earth Sciences at the University of Granada, Spain. The authors thank the Institute of Geosciences of Panama and University of Panama for providing them with the seismic data to carry out this research. The authors also thank the invaluable contribution of the editor and the high quality and complete revision the two anonymous reviewers.

REFERENCES

Aki, K. (1980). Attenuation of shear-waves in the lithosphere for frequencies from 0.05 to 25 Hz, *Phys. Earth Planet. In.* **21,** no. 1, 50–60, doi: 10.1016/0031-9201(80)90019-9.

Akinci, A., E. Del Pezzo, and J. M. Ibáñez (1995). Separation of scattering and intrinsic attenuation in southern Spain and western Anatolia (Turkey), *Geophys. J. Int.* **121,** no. 2, 337–353, doi: 10.1111/j.1365-246X.1995.tb05715.x.

Akinci, A., J. M. Ibáñez, E. Del Pezzo, and J. Morales (1995). Geometrical spreading and attenuation of Lg waves: A comparison between western Anatolia (Turkey) and southern Spain, *Tectonophysics* **250,** nos. 1/3, 47–60.

Bachura, M., and T. Fischer (2016). Coda attenuation analysis in the West Bohemia/Vogtland earthquake swarm area, *Pure Appl. Geophys.* **173,** 425–437, doi: 10.1007/s00024-015-1137-3.

Bianco, F., E. Del Pezzo, M. Castellano, J. M. Ibáñez, and F. Di Luccio (2002). Separation of intrinsic and scattering seismic attenuation in the Southern Apennine zone, Italy, *Geophys. J. Int.* **150,** no. 1, 10–22, doi: 10.1046/j.1365-246X.2002.01696.x.

Bianco, F., E. D. Pezzo, L. Malagnini, F. D. Luccio, and A. Akinci (2005). Separation of depth-dependent intrinsic and scattering seismic attenuation in the northeastern sector of the Italian Peninsula, *Geophys. J. Int.* **161,** no. 1, 130–142, doi: 10.1111/j.1365-246X.2005.02555.x.

Biswas, R., and C. Singh (2020). Seismic attenuation structure across the Karakoram fault in western Tibet, *Geophys. J. Int.* **223,** no. 2, 1418–1431.

Biswas, R., and C. Singh (2023). Variations of intrinsic and scattering seismic attenuation with depth in western Tibet, *Phys. Chem. Earth Parts A/B/C* **131,** 103454, doi: 10.1016/j.pce.2023.103454.

Bourke, J., V. Levin, L. Linkimer, and I. Arroyo (2020). A recent tear in subducting plate explains seismicity and upper mantle structure of southern Costa Rica, *Geochem. Geophys. Geosys.* **21,** no. 12, doi: 10.1029/2020GC009300.

Bourke, J. R., V. Levin, I. G. Arroyo, and L. Linkimer (2023). Evidence for Caribbean plate subduction in southern Costa Rica, *Geology* **51,** no. 4, 408–412, doi: 10.1130/G50796.1.

Camacho, E. (1994). El tsunami del 22 de abril de 1991 en Bocas del Toro, Panama. Volumen especial Terremoto de Limón, *Revista Geológica de América Central* 61–64, doi: 10.15517/rgac.v0i0.13422 (in Spanish).

Camacho, E. (2009). Sismicidad de las tierras altas de Chiriquí, *Revista Tecnociencia* **11,** no. 1, 119–130 (in Spanish).

Camacho, E., W. Hutton, and J. Pacheco (2010). A new look at evidence for a Wadati Benioff Zone and active convergence at the North Panama deformed belt, *Bull. Seismol. Soc Am.* **100,** 343–348, doi: 10.1785/0120090204.

Carcolé, E., and H. Sato (2010). Spatial distribution of scattering loss and intrinsic absorption of short-period S waves in the lithosphere of Japan on the basis of the multiple lapse time window analysis of Hi-net data, *Geophys. J. Int.* **180,** no. 1, 268–290, doi: 10.1111/j.1365-246X.2009.04394.x.

Castro-Melgar, I., J. Prudencio, A. Cannata, E. Del Pezzo, and J. M. Ibáñez (2021). Small-scale volcanic structures of the Aeolian volcanic arc revealed by seismic attenuation, *Front. Earth Sci.* **9,** 725402, doi: 10.3389/feart.2021.725402.

Christeson, G. L., K. D. McIntosh, and T. H. Shipley (2000). Seismic attenuation in the Costa Rica margin wedge: Amplitude modeling of ocean bottom hydrophone data, *Earth Planet. Sci. Lett.* **179,** no. 2, 391–405, doi: 10.1016/S0012-821X(00)00118-7.

Del Pezzo, E. (2008). Seismic wave scattering in volcanoes, *Adv. Geophys.* **50,** 353–371, doi: 10.1016/S0065-2687(08)00013-7.

Del Pezzo, E., and F. Bianco (2010). Two-layer earth model corrections to the MLTWA estimates of intrinsic-and scattering-attenuation obtained in a uniform half-space, *Geophys. J. Int.* **182,** no. 2, 949–955, doi: 10.1111/j.1365-246X.2010.04648.x.

Del Pezzo, E., and J. M. Ibáñez (2020). Seismic coda-waves imaging based on sensitivity kernels calculated using an Heuristic approach, *Geosciences* **10,** no. 8, 304, doi: 10.3390/geosciences10080304.

Del Pezzo, E., F. Bianco, S. Marzorati, P. Augliera, E. D'Alema, and M. Massa (2011). Depth-dependent intrinsic and scattering seismic attenuation in north central Italy, *Geophys. J. Int.* **186,** no. 1, 373–381, doi: 10.1111/j.1365-246X.2011.05053.x.

Del Pezzo, E., A. De La Torre, F. Bianco, J. Ibáñez, S. Gabrielli, and L. De Siena (2018). Numerically calculated 3D space-weighting functions to image crustal volcanic structures using diffuse coda waves, *Geosciences* **8,** no. 5, 175, doi: 10.3390/geosciences8050175.

Del Pezzo, E., E. Giampiccolo, E. Tuvé, G. Di Grazia, S. Gresta, and J. M. Ibáñez (2019). Study of the regional pattern of intrinsic and scattering seismic attenuation in Eastern Sicily (Italy) from local earthquakes, *Geophysics. J. Int.* **218,** 1456–1468, doi: 10.1093/gji/ggz208.

Del Pezzo, E., J. Ibáñez, J. Morales, A. Akinci, and R. Maresca (1995). Measurements of intrinsic and scattering seismic attenuation in the crust, *Bull. Seismol. Soc. Am.* **85,** no. 5, 1373–1380, doi: 10.1785/BSSA0850051373.

Del Pezzo, E., J. M. Ibáñez, J. Prudencio, F. Bianco, and L. De Siena (2016). Absorption and scattering 2-D volcano images from numerically calculated space-weighting functions, *Geophys. J. Int.* **206,** no. 2, 742–756, doi: 10.1093/gji/ggw171.

Del Pezzo, E., M. Simini, and J. M. Ibáñez (1996). Separation of intrinsic and scattering Q for volcanic areas: A comparison between Etna and Campi Flegrei, *J. Volcanol. Geoth. Res.* **70,** nos. 3/4, 213–219, doi: 10.1016/0377-0273(95)00056-9.

Dzierma, Y., W. Rabbel, M. M. Thorwart, E. R. Flueh, M. M. Mora, and G. E. Alvarado (2011). The steeply subducting edge of the Cocos Ridge: Evidence from receiver functions beneath the northern Talamanca Range, south-central Costa Rica, *Geochem. Geophys. Geosys.* **12,** 1–25, doi: 10.1029/2010GC003477.

Dzierma, Y., M. M. Thorwart, W. Rabbel, E. R. Flueh, G. E. Alvarado, and M. M. Mora (2010). Imaging crustal structure in South Central Costa Rica with receiver functions, *Geochem. Geophys. Geosys.* **11,** 1–21, doi: 10.1029/2009GC002936.

Eulenfeld, T., and U. Wegler (2016). Measurement of intrinsic and scattering attenuation of shear waves in two sedimentary basins and comparison to crystalline sites in Germany, *Geophys. J. Int.* **202,** 744–757, doi: 10.1093/gji/ggw035.

Fehler, M., M. Hoshiba, H. Sato, and K. Obara (1992). Separation of scattering and intrinsic attenuation for the Kanto-Tokai region, Japan, using measurements of S-wave energy versus hypocentral distance, *Geophys. J. Int.* **108,** no. 3, 787–800, doi: 10.1111/j.1365-246X.1992.tb03470.x.

Giampiccolo, E., T. Tuvè, S. Gresta, and D. Patanè (2006). S-waves attenuation and separation of scattering and intrinsic absorption of seismic energy in southeastern Sicily (Italy), *Geophys. J. Int.* **165,** no. 1, 211–222, doi: 10.1111/j.1365-246X.2006.02881.x.

Hidalgo-Leiva, D. A., L. Linkimer, I. G. Arroyo, M. Arroyo-Solórzano, R. Piedra, A. Climent, V. S. Díaz, L. C. Esquivel, G. E. Alvarado, R. Castillo, *et al.* (2023). The 2022 seismic hazard model for Costa Rica, *Bull. Seismol. Soc. Am.* **113,** no. 1, 23–40.

Hoshiba, M. (1993). Separation of scattering attenuation and intrinsic absorption in Japan using the multiple lapse time window analysis of full seismogram envelope, *J. Geophys. Res.* **98,** no. B9, 15,809–15,824, doi: 10.1029/93JB00347.

Hoshiba, M. (1995). Estimation of nonisotropic scattering in western Japan using coda wave envelopes: Application of a multiple nonisotropic scattering model, *J. Geophys. Res.* **100,** no. B1, 645–657.

Ibáñez, J. M., I. Castro-Melgar, O. Cocina, L. Zuccarello, S. Branca, E. Del Pezzo, and J. Prudencio (2020). First 2-D intrinsic and scattering attenuation images of Mt Etna volcano and surrounding region from active seismic data, *Geophys. J. Int.* **220,** no. 1, 267–277, doi: 10.1093/gji/ggz450.

Ibáñez, J. M., E. Del Pezzo, G. Alguacil, F. De Miguel, J. Morales, S. De Martino, C. Sabbarese, and A. M. Posadas (1993). Geometrical spreading function for short-period S and coda waves recorded in southern Spain, *Phys. Earth Planet. Int.* **80,** nos. 1/2, 25–36.

Ibáñez, J. M., E. Del Pezzo, F. De Miguel, M. Herraiz, G. Alguacil, and J. Morales (1990). Depth-dependent seismic attenuation in the Granada zone (Southern Spain), *Bull. Seismol. Soc. Am.* **80,** no. 5, 1232–1244, doi: 10.1785/BSSA0800051232.

Lemenkova, P., and O. Debeir (2023). Correlations between the topography-induced gravity, terrain structure and the seismicity in the Gulf of Panama, *Environ. Res. Eng. Manage.* **79,** no. 2, 64–76, doi: 10.5755/j01.erem.79.2.33500.

Levandowski, W., O. S. Boyd, D. AbdelHameid, and D. E. McNamara (2021). Crustal seismic attenuation of the central United States and Intermountain West, *J. Geophys. Res.* **126,** no. 12, e2021JB022097, doi: 10.1029/2021JB022097.

MacKay, M. E., and G. F. Moore (1990). Variation in deformation of the south Panama accretionary prism: Response to oblique subduction and trench sediment variation, *Tectonics* **9,** no. 4, 683–698, doi: 10.1029/TC009i004p00683.

Mahanama, A., S. Gabrielli, C. H. Cramer, and A. Akinci (2024). Separation of intrinsic and scattering seismic wave attenuation in the crust of central and south-central Alaska, *Bull. Seismol. Soc. Am.* **114,** no. 6, 2963–2977, doi: 10.1785/0120240094.

Mayeda, K., M. Hoshiba, K. Aki, and Y. Zng (1992). A comparative study of scattering, intrinsic and coda Q-1 for Hawaii, Long Valley, and Central California between 1.5 and 15.0 Hz, *J. Geophys. Res.* **97,** no. B5, 6643–6659, doi: 10.1029/91JB03094.

Meirova, T., and V. Pinsky (2014). Seismic wave attenuation in Israel region estimated from the multiple lapse time window analysis and S-wave coda decay rate, *Geophys. J. Int.* **197,** no. 1, 581–590, doi: 10.1093/gji/ggu005.

Morell, K. D., D. M. Fisher, T. W. Gardner, P. La Femina, D. Davidson, and A. Teletzke (2011). Quaternary outer fore-arc deformation and uplift inboard of the Panama Triple Junction, Burica Peninsula, *J. Geophys. Res.* **116,** no. B5, doi: 10.1029/2010JB007979.

Müller, T. M., B. Gurevich, and M. Lebedev (2010). Seismic wave attenuation and dispersion resulting from wave-induced flow in porous rocks—A review, *Geophysics* **75,** no. 5, 75A147–75A164, doi: 10.1190/1.3463417.

Paasschens, J. C. J. (1997). Solution of the time-dependent Boltzmann equation, *Phys. Rev. E* **56,** no. 1, 1135, doi: 10.1103/PhysRevE.56.1135.

Padhy, S., and N. Subhadra (2021). Frequency dependence of attenuation components including mantle leakage in Garhwal Himalaya based on a modified MLTWA method, *Geophys. J. Int.* **227,** no. 3, 2156–2179, doi: 10.1093/gji/ggab326.

Peraldo, G., W. Montero, and E. Camacho (2006). El terremoto del 29 de mayo de 1879: Una ruptura de magnitud Ms ≥ 7,0 en la zona limítrofe sur de Costa Rica y Panama, *Revista Geológica de America Central* **34/35,** 31–42 (in Spanish).

Pisconti, A., E. Del Pezzo, F. Bianco, and S. de Lorenzo (2015). Seismic Q estimates in Umbria Marche (Central Italy): Hints for the retrieval of a new attenuation law for seismic risk, *Geophys. J. Int.* **201,** no. 3, 1370–1382, doi: 10.1093/gji/ggv055.

Plafker, G., and S. N. Ward (1992). Backarc thrust faulting and tectonic uplift along the Caribbean Sea coast during the April 22, 1991 Costa Rica earthquake, *Tectonics* **11,** no. 4, 709–718, doi: 10.1029/92TC00609.

Prudencio, J., Y. Aoki, M. Takeo, J. M. Ibáñez, E. Del Pezzo, and W. Song (2017). Separation of scattering and intrinsic attenuation at Asama volcano (Japan): Evidence of high volcanic structural contrasts, *J. Volcanol. Geoth. Res.* **333,** 96–103, doi: 10.1016/j.jvolgeores.2017.01.014.

Prudencio, J., E. Del Pezzo, A. García-Yeguas, and J. M. Ibáñez (2013). Spatial distribution of intrinsic and scattering seismic attenuation in active volcanic islands–I: Model and the case of Tenerife Island, *Geophys. J. Int.* **195,** no. 3, 1942–1956, doi: 10.1093/gji/ggt361.

Prudencio, J., J. M. Ibánez, A. García-Yeguas, E. Del Pezzo, and A. M. Posadas (2013). Spatial distribution of intrinsic and scattering seismic attenuation in active volcanic islands–II: Deception Island images, *Geophys. J. Int.* **195,** no. 3, 1957–1969, doi: 10.1093/gji/ggt360.

Quintero, R., J. Zahradník, F. Güendel, D. Campos-Durán, G. E. Alvarado, and J. T. Boutet (2023). Subduction transition and relation to upper plate faults revealed by the 2019 Mw 6.0 and 6.2 Costa Rica-Panama border earthquakes, *Tectonophysics* **851,** 229759, doi: 10.1016/j.tecto.2023.229759.

Sato, H., M. C. Fehler, and T. Maeda (2012). *Seismic Wave Propagation and Scattering in the Heterogeneous Earth,* Second Ed., Vol. 496, Springer Science & Business Media, Berlin.

Sepp, M. D. (2016). Structural evolution, vein orientation, and paragenesis of the Botija Porphyry Cu-Mo-(Au) deposit, Colón, Panama, available at https://ir.library.oregonstate.edu/concern/graduate_thesis_or_dissertations/05741w340 (last accessed October 2022).

Sketsiou, P., F. Napolitano, A. Zenonos, and L. De Siena (2020). New insights into seismic absorption imaging, *Phys. Earth Planet. In.* **298,** 106337, doi: 10.1016/j.pepi.2019.106337.

Soham, B., and K. Abhishek (2016). Determination of seismic wave attenuation: A review, *Disaster Adv.* **9,** no. 6, 10–27.

Stevenhagen, A. U., E. R. Flueh, C. Ranero, K. D. McIntosh, T. Shipley, S. Augustin, G. Leandro, S. José, A. Schulze, and J. J. Danobeitia (1997). Seismic wide-angle investigations in Costa Rica-a crustal velocity model from the Pacific to the Caribbean coast, *Zentralblatt für Geologie und Paläontologie: Teil 1, Allgemeine, angewandte, regionale und historische Geologie* **3/6,** 393–408.

Tuvè, T., F. Bianco, J. Ibáñez, D. Patanè, E. Del Pezzo, and A. Bottari (2006). Attenuation study in the Straits of Messina area (southern Italy), *Tectonophysics* **421,** nos. 3/4, 173–185, doi: 10.1016/j.tecto.2006.04.005.

Vargas, C. A., L. H. Ochoa, and A. Caneva (2019). Estimation of the thermal structure beneath the volcanic arc of the Northern Andes by coda wave attenuation tomography, *Front. Earth Sci.* **7,** 208, doi: 10.3389/feart.2019.00208.

Vargas, C. A., J. E. Pulido, and R. W. Hobbs (2018). Thermal structure of the Panama Basin by analysis of seismic attenuation, *Tectonophysics* **730,** 81–99, doi: 10.1016/j.tecto.2018.02.017.

Zhu, J., H. Kopp, C. Papenberg, D. Klaeschen, E. R. Flueh, and L. Planert (2010). Margin architecture and seismic attenuation in the central Costa Rican forearc, *Marine Geol.* **276,** nos. 1/4, 30–41, doi: 10.1016/j.margeo.2010.07.004.

APPENDIX

This appendix provides supplementary material that supports and expands on the results discussed in the main article. It includes additional figures (Figs. A1–A3) and tables (Tables A1–A4) that offer detailed information, supplementary analyses, and visualizations that were not incorporated into the main body of the article for reasons of conciseness. These materials are intended to provide additional context and to facilitate the reproducibility of the results.

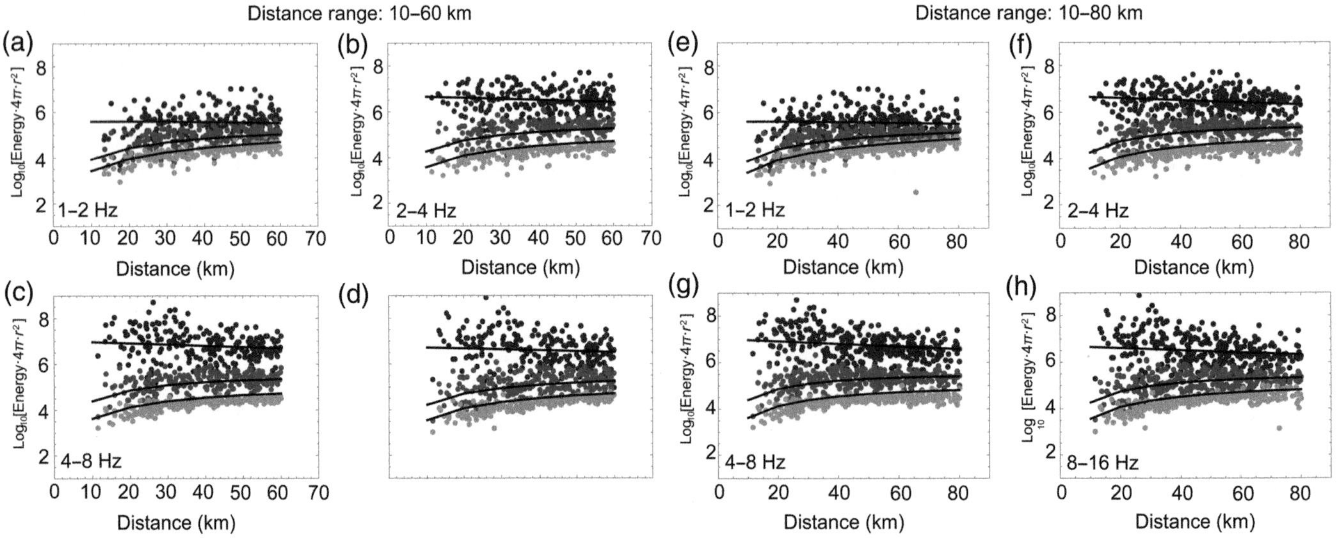

Figure A1. Example of MLTWA. Data and best-fitting curves are shown for 10–60 km distance range at the four frequency bands investigated (a) 1–2, (b) 2–4, (c) 4–8, and (d) 8–16 Hz and at 10–80 km distance range (e) 1–2, (f) 2–4, (g) 4–8, and (h) 8–16 Hz. The blue, red, and green circles correspond to the first, second, and third windows, respectively. The black line is the best fit for each time window analysis. The color version of this figure is available only in the electronic edition.

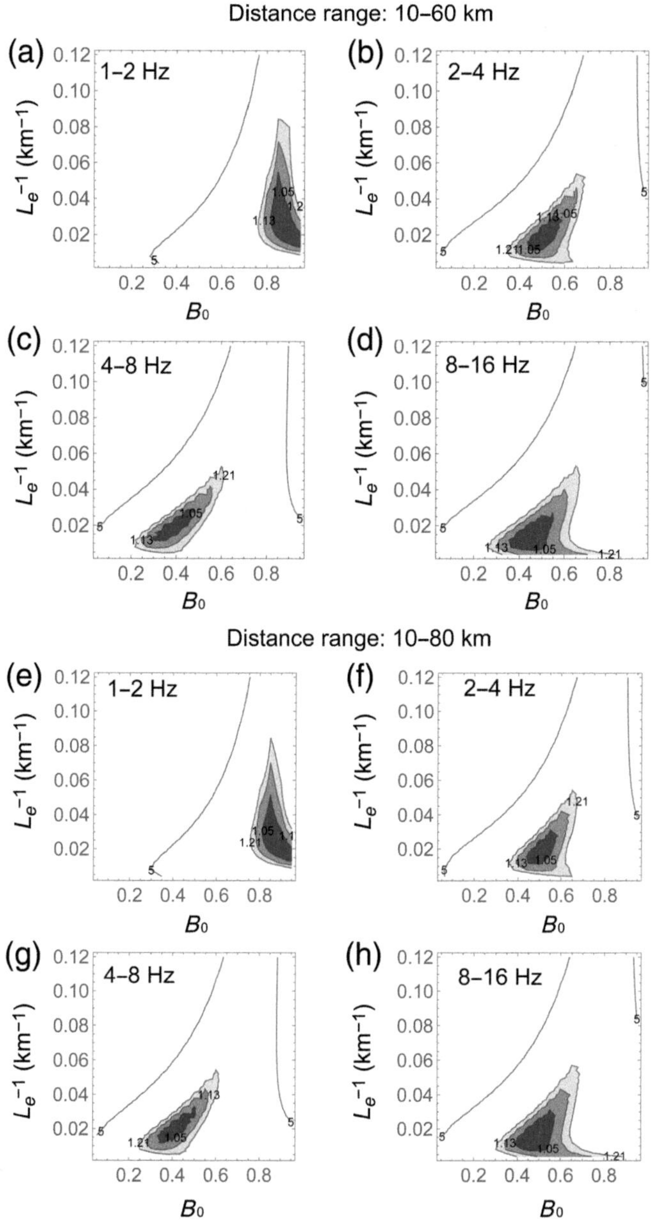

Figure A2. Residual map normalized at its minimum used for the estimation of the best parameter in the grid search and for the evaluation of the uncertainty associated with B_0 and L_e^{-1} at (a–d) 10–60 km distance range and at (e–h) 10–80 km distance range. The three colored zones mark the $1-\sigma$ (red), the $2-\sigma$ (orange), and the $3-\sigma$ (yellow) confidence areas. The color version of this figure is available only in the electronic edition.

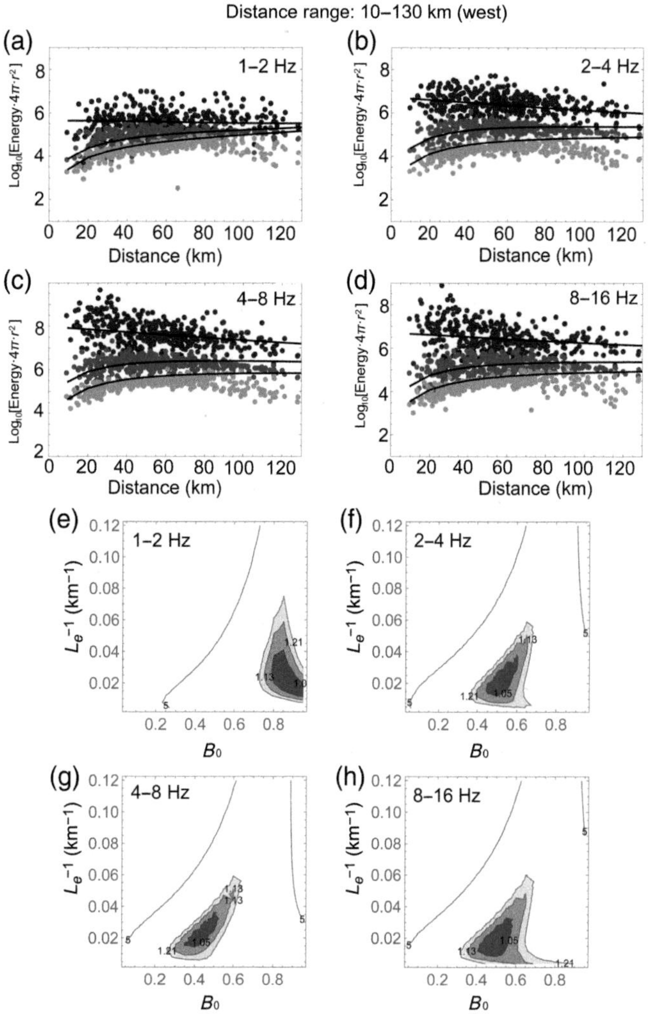

Figure A3. Example of MLTWA and residual map for western Panama region at 10–130 distance range. Best-fitting curves are shown for (a) 1–2, (b) 2–4, (c) 4–8, and (d) 8–16 Hz and the evaluation of the uncertainty associated with B_0 and L_e^{-1} for (e) 1–2, (f) 2–4, (g) 4–8, and (h) 8–16 Hz. The three colored zones mark the $1-\sigma$ (red), the $2-\sigma$ (orange), and the $3-\sigma$ (yellow) confidence areas. The color version of this figure is available only in the electronic edition.

TABLE A1

Derived Attenuation Values for the Four Frequency Bands Analyzed at 10–60 km Distance Range

Frequency Band (Hz)	B_0	1−σ	L_e^{-1}	1−σ	Q_i	Q_s	Q_t
1–2	0.85	0.10	0.031	0.003	450	80	65
2–4	0.50	0.05	0.020	0.004	400	400	200
4–8	0.40	0.07	0.020	0.003	700	1050	420
8–16	0.45	0.05	0.015	0.003	1900	2300	1050

B_0, seismic albedo; L_e^{-1}, extinction length (km^{-1}); Q_i, intrinsic attenuation; Q_s, scattering attenuation; Q_t, total attenuation. $1-\sigma$ associated confidence areas for a standard $1-\sigma$ deviation.

TABLE A2

Derived Attenuation Values for the Four Frequency Bands Analyzed at 10–80 km Distance Range

Frequency Band (Hz)	B_0	1−σ	L_e^{-1}	1−σ	Q_i	Q_s	Q_t
1–2	0.85	0.10	0.030	0.003	500	90	75
2–4	0.50	0.05	0.020	0.003	400	400	20
4–8	0.40	0.07	0.020	0.002	700	1050	420
8–16	0.50	0.05	0.020	0.002	1700	1700	850

B_0, seismic albedo; L_e^{-1}, extinction length (km^{-1}); Q_i, intrinsic attenuation; Q_s, scattering attenuation; Q_t, total attenuation. $1-\sigma$ associated confidence areas for a standard $1-\sigma$ deviation.

TABLE A3

Derived Attenuation Values for the Four Frequency Bands Analyzed at the Western Region of Panama at 10–130 km Distance Range

Frequency Band (Hz)	B_0	1−σ	L_e^{-1}	1−σ	Q_i	Q_s	Q_t
1–2	0.84	0.10	0.030	0.003	436	83	70
2–4	0.58	0.04	0.030	0.003	332	241	140
4–8	0.48	0.08	0.020	0.002	806	873	419
8–16	0.53	0.03	0.020	0.002	1782	1444	798

B_0, seismic albedo; L_e^{-1}, extinction length (km^{-1}); Q_i, intrinsic attenuation; Q_s, scattering attenuation; Q_t, total attenuation. $1-\sigma$ associated confidence areas for a standard $1-\sigma$ deviation.

TABLE A4

Derived Seismic Albedo (B_0) and Extinction Length (L_e^{-1}) (km^{-1}) for the Four Frequency Bands Analyzed at the Western Region of Panama at 10–130 km Distance Range And Its Corrected Values After Applying the Nomograms Obtained Del Pezzo and Bianco (2010)

Frequency Band (Hz)	B_0	B_0 Corrected	L_e^{-1}	L_e^{-1} Corrected
1–2	0.85	0.81	0.020	$1 \cdot 10^{-6}$
2–4	0.50	0.33	0.024	0.008
4–8	0.45	0.27	0.024	0.001
8–16	0.50	0.33	0.020	0.008

Manuscript received 9 May 2025
Published online 20 November 2025

Moment Tensor Inversion of Microseismic Events Using Strain Waveforms Recorded by Multi-Well-Distributed Acoustic Sensing

Avinash Nayak*[1], Julia Correa[1], Jonathan Ajo-Franklin[1,2], Aleksei Titov[3], and Sireesh Dadi[3]

ABSTRACT

Distributed acoustic sensing (DAS) array seismic data are now routinely acquired on fiber-optic cables in wells for downhole monitoring of microseismic events during geothermal and oil and gas operations. In an enhanced geothermal system experiment in Blue Mountain, Nevada, downhole DAS arrays operational in three different wells at all times provided unprecedented constraints on the locations and source radiation patterns of the microseismic events. We develop a simple framework for inverting low-frequency (~4 to 16 Hz) complete axial strain waveforms recorded by DAS for point-source moment tensors using axial strain Green's functions calculated for a 1D velocity model using frequency–wavenumber integration. We fit the strain waveforms recorded at two to three wells with a variance reduction of ~36% to 74%. We constrain the best-fitting source types to be strongly deviatoric; assuming a double-couple mechanism, we obtain predominantly normal faulting and right-lateral strike-slip faulting mechanisms on northwest to north-northwest-trending faults that agree with the geologic knowledge of the study area and the extensional Basin and Range tectonics prevalent in Nevada. We further validate magnitudes derived from low-frequency strain spectral amplitudes of far-field body waves by comparing them with magnitudes derived from moment tensors. Finally, for two of the larger events, we find the strike-slip focal mechanisms derived from the DAS data to be consistent with those estimated from low-frequency, vertical-component displacement waveforms recorded by a sparse network of surface seismometers. Moment tensor inversion applied to downhole DAS arrays helps characterize the size of the microseismic events that are relevant to induced seismicity, and the state of stress in the subsurface during geothermal, fracturing, and oil and gas operations. The inversion framework is general, and with a sufficiently accurate velocity model and good signal-to-noise ratio at frequencies lower than the corner frequency, it can be extended to dark fiber DAS arrays at the surface as well.

KEY POINTS

- Moment tensor inversion using low-frequency strain waveforms recorded by distributed acoustic sensing (DAS) arrays and a 1D velocity model.
- DAS arrays in three wells in the enhanced geothermal system experiment in Nevada strongly constrain the microseismic event source process.
- Normal and strike-slip focal mechanisms agree with tectonics. Magnitudes agree with magnitudes from spectral amplitudes.

Supplemental Material

INTRODUCTION

Microseismic events commonly occur during geothermal and hydraulic-fracturing operations, which involve the injection and extraction of fluids from the subsurface, and the process of creating permeable pathways by injection of high-pressure fluids. The seismic moment tensor is commonly used to characterize the source properties of these seismic events in terms of the focal mechanism and the scalar seismic moment (M_0) (Jost and Herrmann, 1989; Pasyanos *et al.*, 1996; Minson and

1. Earth and Environmental Science Area, Lawrence Berkeley National Laboratory, Berkeley, California, U.S.A., https://orcid.org/0000-0001-7913-7189 (AN); https://orcid.org/0000-0001-6005-3161 (JC); https://orcid.org/0000-0002-6666-4702 (JA-F); 2. Department of Earth, Environmental, and Planetary Sciences, Rice University, Houston, Texas, U.S.A.; 3. Fervo Energy, Houston, Texas, U.S.A., https://orcid.org/0000-0001-7699-7773 (AT); https://orcid.org/0009-0008-5747-2523 (SD)

*Corresponding author: anayak7@lbl.gov

Cite this article as Nayak, A., J. Correa, J. Ajo-Franklin, A. Titov, and S. Dadi (2025). Moment Tensor Inversion of Microseismic Events Using Strain Waveforms Recorded by Multi-Well-Distributed Acoustic Sensing, *Bull. Seismol. Soc. Am.* **116**, 603–623, doi: 10.1785/0120250099

Dreger, 2008; Eaton and Forouhideh, 2011; Song and Toksoz, 2011; Eyre and van der Baan, 2017). The focal mechanism describes the source radiation pattern and is used to infer the state of stress in the subsurface (Vavryčuk, 2014), which is crucial for evaluating the efficiency of injection and stimulation activities, and for guiding production. The scalar seismic moment, more commonly represented by the moment magnitude (M_w), provides an estimate of the size of the seismic events. The magnitude estimates are used for calculating the extent of the stimulated reservoir volume (Maxwell *et al.*, 2009; Shapiro *et al.*, 2011; Stork *et al.*, 2014) and for monitoring the induced seismicity for the potential occurrence of relatively larger magnitude seismic events that are relevant to seismic hazard (Bommer *et al.*, 2006; Utah FORGE, 2020). Moment tensors of microseismic events are typically determined by inverting displacement waveforms or displacement amplitudes and polarities of body waves recorded by geophones deployed in boreholes or on the surface (Eaton and Forouhideh, 2011; Song and Toksoz, 2011; Eyre and van der Baan, 2017). Wave propagation effects are corrected using Green's functions calculated assuming an appropriate seismic velocity model (Nayak and Dreger, 2018). The quality of the moment tensor solution strongly depends on the quality of the data, the quality of the velocity model, and coverage of the focal sphere or the radiation pattern.

Distributed acoustic sensing (DAS) seismic data are now routinely acquired on fiber-optic cables in wells for downhole monitoring of microseismic events during geothermal and oil and gas operations such as enhanced geothermal system (EGS) stimulation and hydraulic fracturing (Karrenbach *et al.*, 2018; Lellouch *et al.*, 2020). The technology transforms fiber-optic cables used in telecommunication into a linear array of axial strain-rate sensors that measure changes in Rayleigh scattering induced by extensional strain by applying coherent optical time-domain reflectometry (Daley *et al.*, 2013, 2016). The advantages of downhole DAS include—having a spatially dense array of seismic sensors close to the source depths of the microseismic events, thereby avoiding near-surface noise and near-surface heterogeneities, and improving resolution, and greater robustness to high-temperature conditions at depth compared to borehole geophones (Lellouch *et al.*, 2020), and improved coupling to the subsurface in case of fiber cemented behind the casing. Other applications of downhole DAS data include seismic imaging and monitoring of spatiotemporal changes in elastic properties of subsurface, fracture growth, and low-frequency strain (Mateeva *et al.*, 2014; Jin and Roy, 2017; Titov *et al.*, 2021; Norbeck *et al.*, 2023; Correa *et al.*, 2024). However, DAS is limited by measurement of only one component of strain (axial) for the most common type of fiber (single mode), and higher noise levels and saturation at lower ground motions compared to seismometers.

Whereas moment tensor inversion of microseismic events is traditionally performed using displacement data recorded by geophones, recent studies have established expressions of strain ground motions recorded by downhole DAS in terms of a moment tensor source (Vera Rodriguez and Wuestefeld, 2020; Luo *et al.*, 2021). The axial strain wavefield recorded by DAS is the spatial gradient of the displacement wavefield; therefore, we expect that the synthetic strain waveforms modeled to fit observed DAS waveforms are more sensitive to errors in source locations and the assumed velocity model. The limited aperture provided by a limited number of wells placed far away from the source region of the microseismic events can lead to large errors in event locations, making waveform inversion or modeling impractical (Shimony and Lellouch, 2024). However, many studies have been successful in directly modeling the strain waveforms. Baird *et al.* (2020) and Lecoulant *et al.* (2023) modeled DAS waveforms of far-field body waves radiated by microseismic events induced during hydraulic fracturing operations. Both studies assumed homogeneous anisotropic media that were sufficient for modeling data recorded by horizontal DAS arrays in wells. Luo *et al.* (2021) also assumed a homogeneous medium and a double-couple (DC) moment tensor source to forward model near-field and far-field body-wave components of the strain wavefield recorded by a horizontal DAS array during hydraulic fracturing operations.

In this study, we present location and moment tensor analysis of microseismic events during an EGS stimulation experiment at Blue Mountain, Nevada, that was monitored by downhole DAS arrays in four different wells, out of which three were operational at any given time. Unlike previous studies that used just one or two wells, *P*- and *S*-wave arrival times recorded on three wells in our study strongly constrain hypocenters of 74 events, both in the horizontal plane and in depth, and allow us to invert for a best-fitting 1D velocity model. Unlike previous studies that assumed homogeneous media, we use the 1D velocity model to calculate axial strain Green's functions for fundamental seismic sources using frequency–wavenumber integration (FKI), and directly invert the observed low-frequency axial strain wavefields recorded by the DAS arrays to calculate full moment tensors for a subset of 19 well-recorded events, with 10 events having observations in three wells. Hereinafter, "low-frequency" implies frequencies lower than the corner frequency of a seismic event (generally, few tens of hertz or higher for microseismic events), at which point-source assumption is valid and moment tensor inversion reduces to a simple linear inverse problem (Jost and Herrmann, 1989). This usage of the term differs from hydraulic fracturing studies in which "low-frequency" implies quasi-static signals of periods seconds to hours associated with fracture growth and evolution captured by DAS (low-frequency distributed acoustic sensing [LFDAS]; e.g., Jin and Roy, 2017). We model the complete low-frequency (~4 to 16 Hz) strain wavefield starting from the *P*-wave arrival time and extending up to and including the direct *S* wave, which also includes the near-field and intermediate-field components (Luo *et al.*, 2021). We fit the strain waveforms recorded at two to three wells with variance reduction (VR) of ~36% to 74%, including polarities of major components of the wavefield and the major polarity reversals. Despite an azimuthal gap exceeding 200°, observations at multiple azimuths and the coverage in take-off angle provided by a vertical DAS array helps constrain the best-fitting source types to be strongly deviatoric, and likely DC. We obtain predominantly normal and strike-slip focal mechanisms, consistent with local geology and the extensional Basin and Range tectonics prevalent in Nevada. We further calculate and validate seismic magnitudes derived from low-frequency strain spectral amplitudes of far-field body waves using the formulation of Nayak *et al.* (2024) by comparing with seismic magnitudes derived from the moment tensors. Finally, we estimate moment tensors for two of the larger events using low-frequency, vertical-component displacement waveforms recorded by a sparse network of surface seismometers. We find the strike-slip focal mechanisms derived from the DAS data to be consistent with those estimated from the seismometer data. In this study, we find the M_0 estimate from DAS to be systematically smaller than that from the surface seismometers, which we attribute to possibly reduced coupling with the subsurface. Our study is an advancement in application of downhole DAS arrays in characterization of source mechanisms and size of microseismic events, and the state of stress in the subsurface during geothermal, fracturing, and oil and gas operations. The formulation is general, similar to conventional point-source moment tensor inversion routinely applied to low-frequency displacement waveforms recorded by seismometers (Pasyanos *et al.*, 1996), and with sufficient coverage of the focal sphere and a 1D velocity model appropriate for fitting strain waveforms at frequencies lower than the corner frequency of seismic events, it can be applied to horizontal DAS arrays at the surface such as dark fiber DAS arrays as well (Ajo-Franklin *et al.*, 2022).

Study area

Blue Mountain (40.99° N, −118.09° E) is located in the Basin and Range extensional tectonic province in northern Nevada and rises to an elevation of ~2.2 km (Fig. 1). The geology of the study area is described in detail in Fercho *et al.* (2023) and is briefly summarized here. The mountain continues toward the west as basement under sedimentary basin fill, which is composed of Miocene to current alluvium. The basement rocks are primarily Mesozoic metasediments composed of interlayered phyllite and quartzite that have been intruded by diorite and granodiorite dike and sill swarms. In the geologic model, Blue Mountain is cut by a range-front fault system to the northwest, west, and southwest (Fig. 1a). The fault system toward the west is composed of multiple subparallel strands of arcuate normal and dextral-normal faults that splay from the fault system on the southwest side and wrap around to the fault system on the northwest side. The fault system to the southwest is dextral-normal and dies out into the basin toward the west; the dextral shear is transferred to multiple, subparallel, Quaternary-active, southwest-striking normal faults along the northwest side of

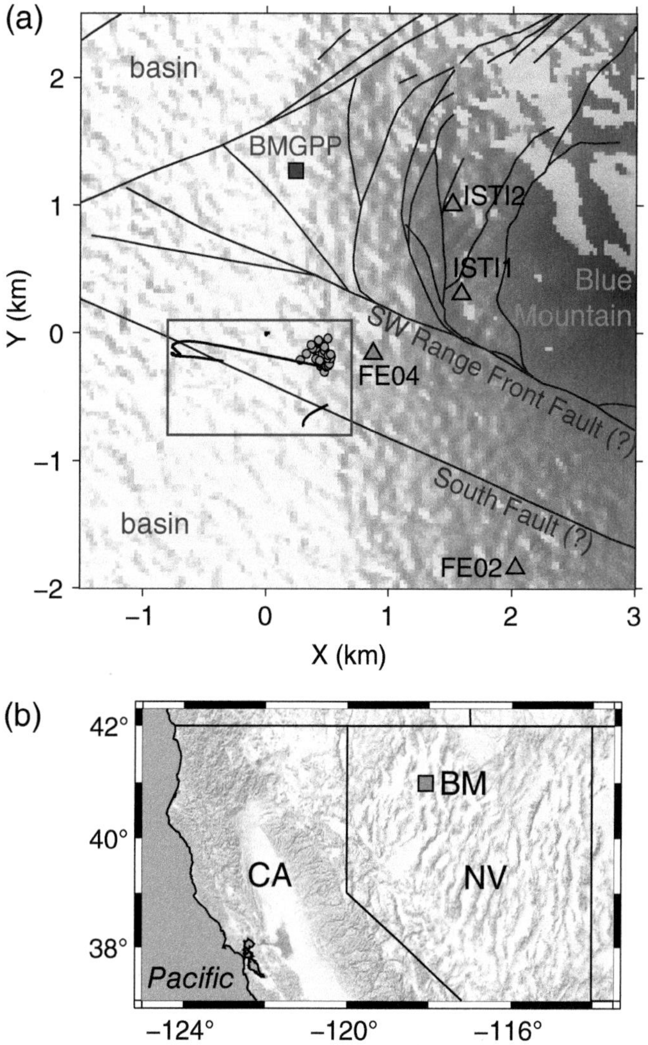

Figure 1. (a) Background color shows topography (elevation ~1.3 to ~1.8 km, white to black) around the study area (red rectangle, expanded in Fig. 2a) illuminated by topographic gradient. Blue curves mark certain, possible, or concealed fault traces in the geologic model of Fercho *et al.* (2023), manually digitized from Figure 5 in their study. Black curves (within the red rectangle) are projections of well trajectories along which distributed acoustic sensing (DAS) data were recorded. The red square is the Blue Mountain geothermal power plant (BMGPP). Cyan circles are the final locations of microseismic events analyzed in this study. Green triangles are local seismic stations for which data were used in this study. Other local stations not used in this study can be found in Dadi *et al.* (2024). (b) The location of the Blue Mountain study area (orange square, BM) is marked in Nevada (NV) state on a larger map of the western United States. The color version of this figure is available only in the electronic edition.

Blue Mountain, which accommodate northwest–southeast extension in the form of pure dip-slip motion. It is hypothesized that the intersection of north-, northwest- and northeast-trending faults controls deep circulation associated with a natural and active hydrothermal system that feeds the operational Blue Mountain geothermal power plant at the western edge of Blue Mountain. The subsurface in the region south of the southwest range-front fault exhibits elevated conductive temperatures,

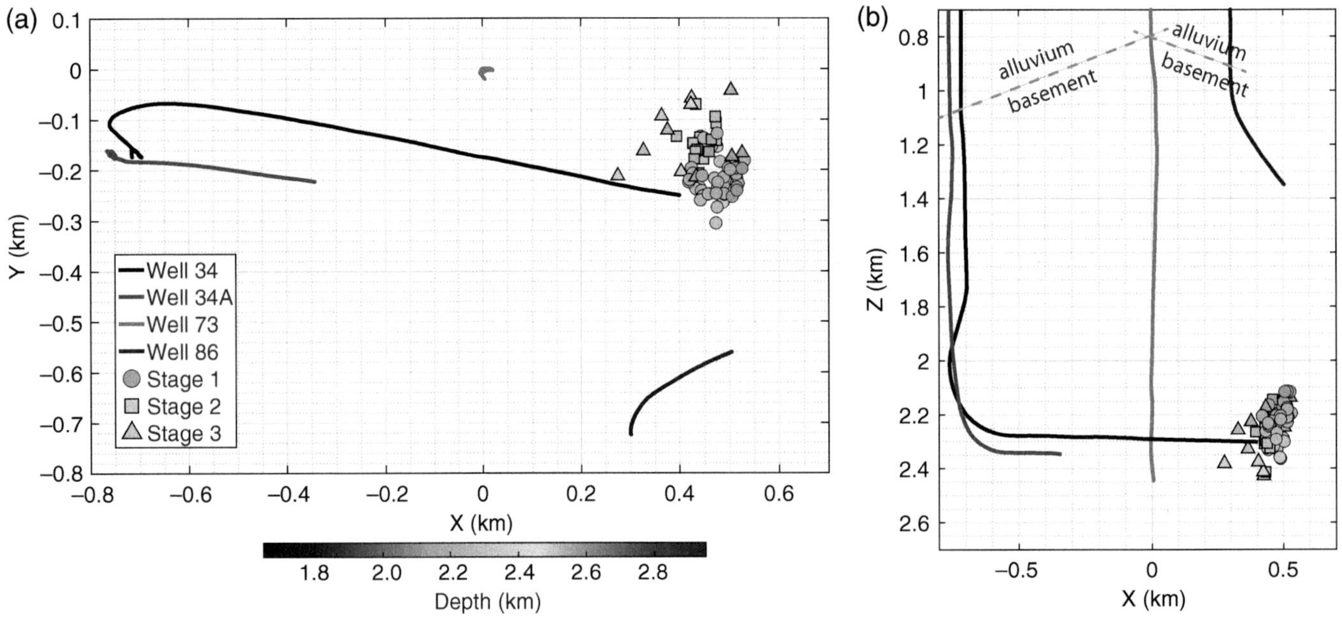

Figure 2. (a) Map view and (b) *X–Z* (east–west-depth) view of the study area showing the well geometry (solid color-coded lines) and final locations of microseismic events in this study (circles, squares, and triangles for stages 1, 2, and 3, respectively), color-coded by depth. Well 73 is located at ~(0,0) in panel (a). The gray dashed line in panel (b) indicates the approximate trend of the alluvium–basement interface (Dadi *et al.*, 2024). The color version of this figure is available only in the electronic edition.

likely radiating from the active hydrothermal reservoir to the north; however, it lacks deep permeability or connectivity to the main reservoir. This site was selected for an EGS experiment to demonstrate the feasibility of horizontal drilling and fracture creation using multistage stimulation. The operations may be considered similar to hydraulic fracturing in unconventional shale reservoirs but at high-temperature conditions in geothermal formations instead. Further details about the EGS experiment are provided in Fercho *et al.* (2023), Norbeck *et al.* (2023), Norbeck and Latimer (2023), Dadi *et al.* (2024), and Titov *et al.* (2024).

The study area hosts four wells: 34A, 34, 73, and 86 (Fig. 2). Wells 34A, 34, and 73 have fiber-optic cables cemented behind the casing; well 86 was a pre-existing shallow deviated well that was equipped with a fiber-optic cable during the experiment. In this study, all depths are with respect to the elevation at the well 73 wellhead. Well 73 is a vertical monitoring well extending from the surface to ~2.4 km depth, with fiber along the entire extent. Wells 34A and 34 are two parallel horizontal wells that acted as injection and production well, respectively, during the experiment; the horizontal portions are at depth ~2.3 km and are spaced ~100 m apart. In well 34A, the DAS array spans vertical section and the first ~0.3 km of the horizontal section from the heel (the limited portion shown in Fig. 2a). In well 34, the DAS array spans the vertical extent and the entire ~1.1 km horizontal extent. Well 86 extends vertically to ~1 km depth and then slopes to the northeast till ~1.4 km depth. The alluvium-basement contact is approximately at depths ~0.8, ~0.9, and ~1.1 km at wells 73, 86, and 34A/34, respectively. This study presents results from three stages of stimulation of well 34 in 2022. DAS data were acquired in wells 34A, 73, and 34 during stage 1, and in wells 34A, 73, and 86 during stages 2 and 3 using Optasense interrogators. The channel spacing, gauge length, and sample rate were 2 m, 16 m, and 2 kHz, respectively.

Event locations and velocity model

From an initial microseismic event catalog, we visually analyzed the records and selected 74 events that had clear *P* and *S* arrivals on at least a few channels of all three wells that were operational at any time (46, 17, and 11 events in stages 1, 2, and 3, respectively). For all analysis in this study, we first exclude all DAS data at channels shallower than 0.5 km depth due to low amplitudes with respect to the near-surface noise levels. For picking body-wave arrival times, we decimate the waveforms to 1 kHz, detrend the waveforms, and apply a three-channel-wide (~37% of gauge length) running spatial average to improve signal-to-noise ratio (SNR). DAS data recorded in well 34 were strongly contaminated with low-frequency tube-wave noise and required an additional causal Butterworth high-pass filter at 30 Hz before the spatial averaging step to identify body-wave arrivals. Finally, as a last preprocessing step for all analyses in this study, we remove common-mode noise by subtracting the median value over all channels from the data at each time sample. We manually reviewed *P*- and *S*-wave arrival times at every 10th channel (~20 m). Well 73 generally provides the best data, and for many events, it is possible to pick *P* and *S* waves over the entire vertical extent from depth ~0.5 to ~2.4 km. For well 34, it is generally possible to pick *P* and *S* waves only over the horizontal section for most events due to greater tube-wave noise in the vertical section. Figure 3 shows DAS record sections for

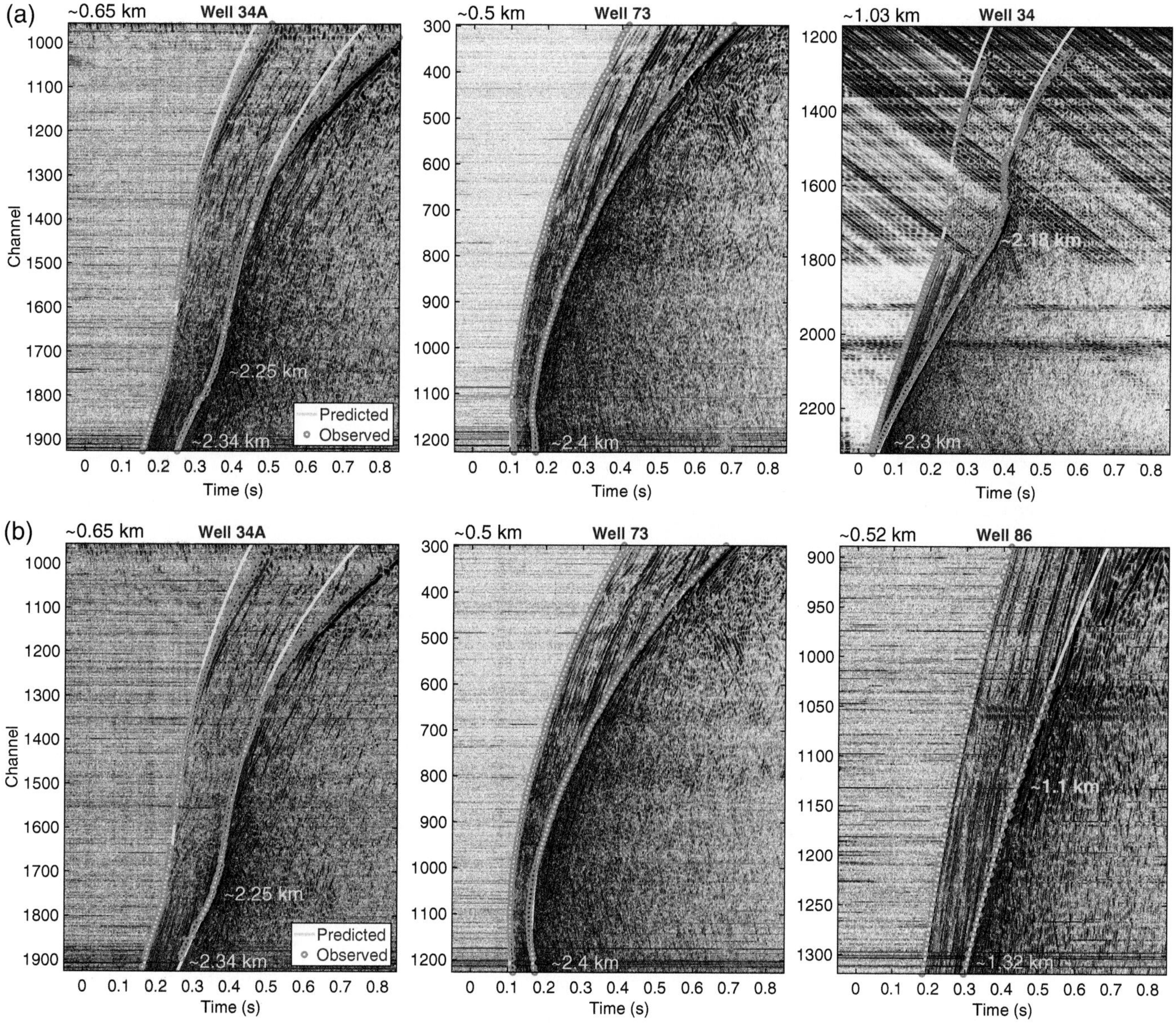

relatively larger magnitude events in stages 1 and 3, hereinafter referred to as events E1 and E31, respectively.

Figure 3. DAS record sections for (a) event E1 in stage 1 and (b) event E31 in stage 3. Different subplots correspond to different wells (indicated at top). Time is with respect to the estimated origin time. Picked (green circles) and predicted (yellow curves) arrival times from the revised locations and velocity model are marked. Waveforms of well 34 have been high-pass filtered at 30 Hz. The depths at the first and last channels of the record sections, the channels at the heels of wells 34 and 34A, and the channel near the transition of well 86 from vertical to deviated section are marked. The amplitudes are raw and range from red (negative) to blue (positive). The color version of this figure is available only in the electronic edition.

We invert the absolute *P*- and *S*-wave arrival times at the four wells for improved event locations, origin times, and best-fitting 1D *P*-wave velocity (V_P) and *S*-wave velocity (V_S) models using software tomoDD (Zhang and Thurber, 2003). Additional details and discussions are provided in the supplemental material section S1 and Figures S1–S5 available with this article. We assume 0.1 km grid spacing in the vertical dimension from depth 0.5 to 2.4 km with additional nodes at depth 2.7 and 3.0 km. We modified the inversion methodology to estimate a 1D model at each iteration. Based on Wadati plot analysis (Wadati, 1933), we tested uniform initial V_P/V_S values from 1.6 to 1.7. For the initial V_P, we use a smoothed version of a model derived from an acoustic log in well 73 between depths 0.8 and 2.4 km; the model was extrapolated to shallower and greater depths. Well 73 also contributes the largest amount of data to the inversion. Therefore, the least-squares inversion is slightly biased toward well 73 and results in best fits for the arrival times at the same well. Based on preliminary inversions, we further exclude arrival times at shallow sections of other wells for which the observed arrival times show systematic delay with respect to the arrival times predicted by the best-fitting 1D model (Fig. 3). These include *P* arrivals at depths < 1 km for well 34A and *S* arrivals at depths

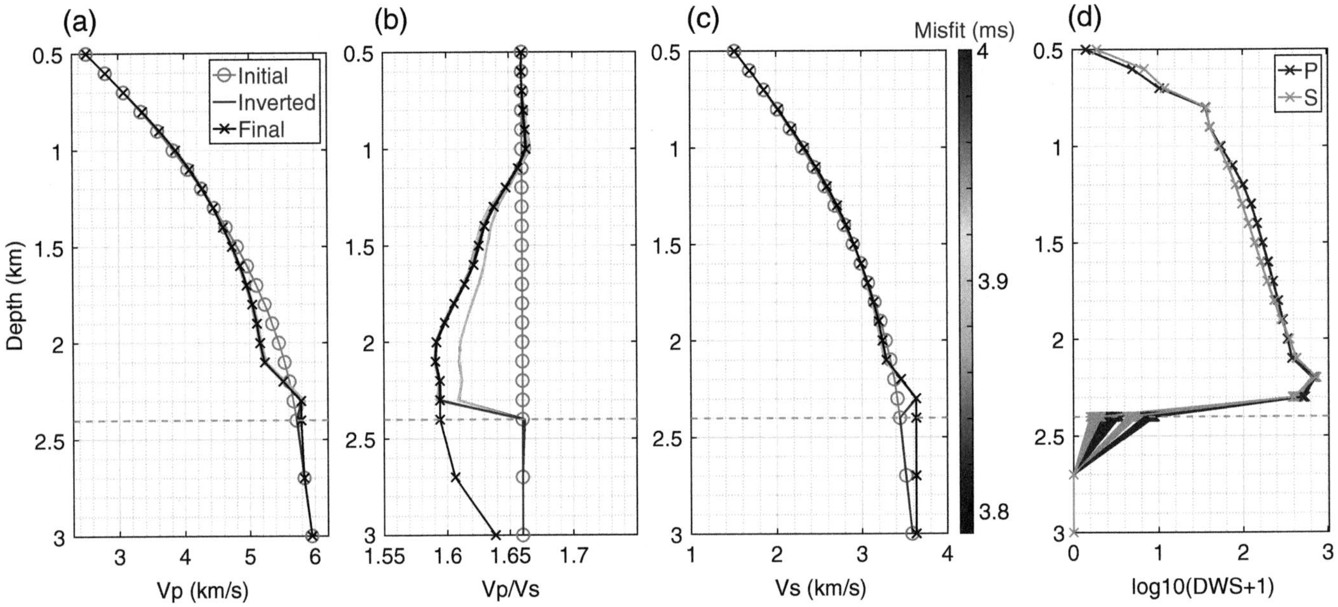

Figure 4. (a–c) Curves in jet color map show a subset of 1D models inverted assuming an initial V_P/V_S of 1.66 (preferred initial value): (a) V_P, (b) V_P/V_S, and (c) V_S. The models are color-coded by final misfit (color bar in panel c). The solid gray curve is the initial model, and the black curve is the final model adjusted to have velocities strictly increasing with depth. Circles and crosses on the gray and black curves, respectively, mark the model nodes. (d) Derivative weighted sum (DWS) on log10 scale as a function of depth. In all plots, the y axis is depth (km), and the gray dashed line indicates the depth below which the data have little or no sensitivity (2.4 km). The color version of this figure is available only in the electronic edition.

less than 1.2, 1.2, and 0.8 km for wells 34A, 34, and 86, respectively. The discrepancies are likely due to topographic variation in the basement-alluvium interface as well as 3D variations in seismic velocities within the lithologies. The small number of microseismic events and model parameters allows us to test many different combinations of regularization parameters.

We first downselect inversions in which only a small number of picks were automatically excluded as outliers (<0.3%), and the final misfit, defined as the weighted root mean square (RMS) value of residuals, was <4 ms (Fig. S2). The lowest misfit achieved was ~3.7 ms. A subset of final models inverted assuming an initial V_P/V_S of 1.66 is shown in Figure 4a–c. We quantify the sensitivity of the data to the model parameters using derivative weighted sum (DWS; Thurber and Eberhart-Phillips, 1999), which is shown for the subset of models in Figure 4d. The deepest receiver (in well 73) being at ~2.4 km depth, the data have little or no sensitivity to model parameters at depths ≥ 2.4 km. The final V_P models are similar to the initial V_P model derived from the well log (Fig. 4a and Fig. S2a). In the depth range ~1 to ~2.3 km, the gradient of V_P/V_S is better constrained than the average value, with a decrease of ~0.06 with increasing depth (Fig. S2b). The final V_P/V_S is close to the initially assumed value at shallower depths (<1 km), likely due to decreased sensitivity of rays at steeper incidence angles. Models inverted assuming initial V_P/V_S in the range ~1.62 to 1.66 result in similar low values of final misfit (~3.7 to 3.9 ms), accompanied by variations in the final event locations. Models assuming lower or higher values of initial V_P/V_S lead to a clear increase in final misfit. In Figure S3, we show the final locations for these models (Fig. S2) for five events from each stage with the highest number of phase picks, which highlights the effect of changing initial V_P/V_S, damping, and smoothing parameters on the final locations. The horizontal locations of the best events generally vary by ~100 m in the northeast–southwest direction, likely due to the coverage of the receivers being limited to west, northwest, and south directions (Fig. S3a and Fig. 2a). The locations exhibit a scatter of ~50 to 100 m in the vertical direction (Fig. S3b). *P*- and *S*-wave picks at receivers along the vertical well 73 from depth ~0.5 km down to event depths (~2.4 km) strongly constrain the 1D velocity model, as well as the depth of the microseismic events. We conclude that location errors for our best events are ≲150 m, which is significantly lower than location errors obtained if using DAS in one or two wells (Shimony and Lellouch, 2024).

For the final model and locations, we average a subset of models inverted assuming an initial V_P/V_S of 1.66. We artificially adjust the velocities at depths ≥ 2.4 km to get a simple 1D model with velocities strictly increasing with depth (Fig. 4) and relocate the events. The initial and final residuals are shown in Figure 5. Residuals of both *P*- and *S*-wave arrival times show a substantial reduction, with a ~40% decrease in both median and weighted RMS value; the final medians are less than 1 ms. The predicted arrival times agree well with the observed arrival times (Fig. 3). Figure S4 shows the residual distribution for each well separately. We plot the final event locations in Figure 2, with a zoomed-in view in Figure S5. The microseismic events are

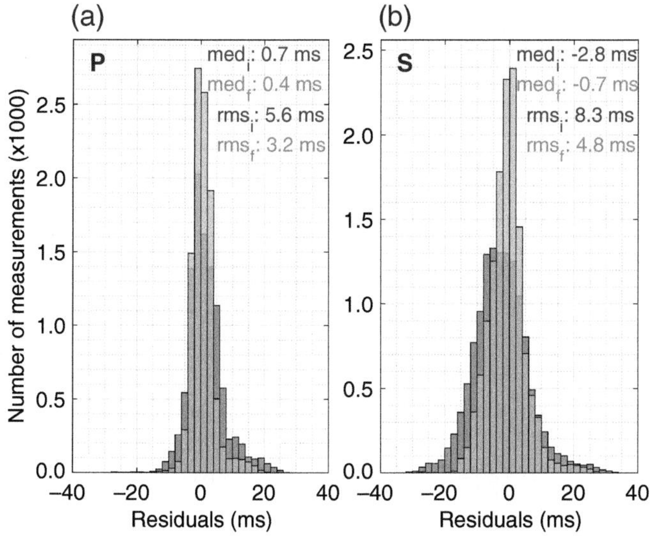

Figure 5. Initial (red) and final (green) residual distribution following the 1D model inversion and relocation for (a) *P*- and (b) *S*-wave arrival times. The color-coded median (med) and weighted root mean square (RMS) values of the initial (subscript *i*) and final (subscript *f*) distributions are mentioned on the plot. The color version of this figure is available only in the electronic edition.

located close to well 34, which was being stimulated. The events during the three stages are clearly separated by ~100 m along the direction of well 34 (west-northwest to east-southeast), with the stages moving toward the heel with time. The separation between event locations of different stages is in a direction distinct from the direction of highest location uncertainty (northeast–southwest, Fig. S3). The events are located in the depth range ~2.1 to 2.45 km, with most events at the same depth or slightly above the stimulated well. Events shallower than the deepest receiver of well 73 (~2.4 km depth) can be easily distinguished from deeper events by the observed vertex of the travel-time hyperbola; the channel corresponding to the vertex gives a direct estimate of event depth (event E31 in Fig. 3b).

Moment tensor inversion

We develop a framework for time-domain, point-source, full moment tensor inversion of low-frequency strain waveforms recorded by the DAS arrays in the wells. We first divide the raw DAS data in native units by $2^{15}/\pi$ (~10,430) to convert to phase in units of radians. We assume a frequency-independent instrument response for DAS (Lindsey *et al.*, 2020) and scale the phase data with the optical wavelength ($\lambda = 1550$ nm), refractive index of the fiber ($n = 1.468$), gauge length ($G_L = 16$ m), and the photo-elastic scaling factor ($\xi = 0.78$) to convert the values in radians to strain in units of strains:

$$\epsilon(\text{strains}) = \frac{\lambda}{(4\pi n G_L \xi)} (\phi_{\text{DAS}} \text{ in radians}). \quad (1)$$

The strain waveforms are detrended, decimated to 1 kHz, tapered, and filtered in the low-frequency passband of ~4 to 16 Hz using a causal Butterworth filter. Filtering to low frequencies is essential for satisfying the point-source assumption, that is, frequency range used is lower than the corner frequency or the seismic wavelengths are longer than the rupture dimensions. Filtering to low frequencies also reduces the observed DAS records to simple waveforms that can be easily fit with an approximate 1D velocity model. Thereafter, we apply three-channel-wide running spatial averaging and remove the common-mode noise. We selected waveform segments between 20 ms before the predicted *P*-wave arrival time and 0.23 s after the predicted *S*-wave arrival time. These waveform segments generally encompass the direct body waves as well as the near- and intermediate-field terms (e.g., Luo *et al.*, 2021). We visually identify and exclude a few DAS channels at the bottom of the wells that have highly dissimilar waveforms with anomalously very large amplitudes.

To calculate strain Green's functions, we interpolate the 1D velocity model derived from inverting body-wave arrival times to finer depth spacing and discretize it in layers of thickness 40 m. We derive density from V_P using the Brocher (2005) empirical relationship. We estimate Q_S from V_S using the Brocher (2008) relationship and assume Q_P to be $2Q_S$. We extrapolate the 1D velocity model from depth 0.5 km to the surface but assume that the top surface is a half-space because of uncertainties in the near-surface structure, and because our shallowest receiver is at 0.5 km depth and we do not attempt to model late arrivals after the direct *S* waves including reflections from the free surface. We use the relocated hypocenters for source location.

We develop a simple numerical scheme to calculate axial strain Green's functions for receivers placed at arbitrary distances and depths in an isotropic 1D medium using the widely used FKI method as provided in the software *Computer Programs in Seismology* (Haskell, 1964; Wang and Herrmann, 1980; Herrmann, 2013). We start with equations 6–8 in Minson and Dreger (2008) relating three-component displacements u_k, in which k is transverse (T), radial (R), or vertical (Z) direction, to a general point-source moment tensor and Green's functions in the T, R, and Z directions for the three fundamental faults (SS: vertical strike-slip fault, DS: vertical dip-slip fault, DD: 45° dip-slip fault) and an isotropic source (EX). The expressions for displacements and Green's functions in the cylindrical coordinate system can be easily reassembled into expressions in the Cartesian coordinate system:

$$u_k = M_{ij} G_{kij}, \quad (2)$$

in which M_{ij} and G_{kij} are moment tensor and Green's functions, respectively. i and j are Cartesian directions x, y, and z used in the standard moment tensor theory. Summation is implied over i and j in equation (2). u and G are waveforms. We provide the equation for the tangential component subsequently; the equations for the radial and vertical components can be framed similarly:

$$u_T = M_{xx}G_{Txx} + M_{yy}G_{Tyy} + M_{zz}G_{Tzz} + M_{xy}G_{Txy} + M_{xz}G_{Txz} + M_{yz}G_{Tyz}, \quad (3)$$

in which $G_{Txx} = \frac{TSS}{2}\sin(2az)$, $G_{Tyy} = -\frac{TSS}{2}\sin(2az)$, $G_{Tzz} = 0$, $G_{Txy} = -TSS\cos(2az)$, $G_{Txz} = TDS\sin(az)$, and $G_{Tyz} = -TDS\cos(az)$. az is the source–receiver azimuth. The Green's functions G_{kij} are rotated from the T–R–Z reference frame to the east (E)–north (N)–vertical (Z) reference frame using source–receiver azimuth (which is backazimuth—180° for small distances):

$$\begin{aligned} G_{Eij} &= G_{Tij}\cos(az) + G_{Rij}\sin(az), \\ G_{Nij} &= -G_{Tij}\sin(az) + G_{Rij}\cos(az), \\ G_{Zij} &= -G_{Zij}. \end{aligned} \quad (4)$$

The vertical components are flipped so that displacement is positive downward to be consistent with the positive direction of the vertical spatial dimension (depth). Equation (3) is reframed in the E–N–Z reference frame. For example, for the east–west direction,

$$u_E = M_{xx}G_{Exx} + M_{yy}G_{Eyy} + M_{zz}G_{Ezz} + M_{xy}G_{Exy} + M_{xz}G_{Exz} + M_{yz}G_{Eyz}. \quad (5)$$

In the following, we again express the equation in compact form, in which the right side consists of six terms associated with six moment tensor elements and k is E, N, or Z.

$$u_k = M_{ij}G_{kij}. \quad (6)$$

We aim to calculate axial strain Green's functions and invert axial strain waveforms at half a gauge length spacing along the fiber ($0.5G_L = 8$ m, every fourth channel). For every receiver location ($0.5G_L$ apart), we calculate the unit vector ($\hat{\eta}$) corresponding to the direction of the cable by differencing the spatial coordinates of the next and the previous receivers (next fourth channel or $0.5G_L$ distance ahead and previous fourth channel or $0.5G_L$ distance behind), which are one gauge length apart. The axial displacement Green's function in the direction of the cable ($G_{\eta ij}$) can be calculated from the dot product of the Green's function in E–N–Z reference frame with the unit vector corresponding to the direction of the cable (components η_E, η_N, η_Z in the E–N–Z reference frame):

$$G_{\eta ij} = G_{Eij}\eta_E + G_{Nij}\eta_N + G_{Zij}\eta_Z. \quad (7)$$

Equation (6) can be reframed in terms of the axial displacement (u_η) and axial displacement Green's functions in the direction of the cable.

$$u_\eta = M_{ij}G_{\eta ij}. \quad (8)$$

Finally, the axial strain Green's function in the direction of the cable ($G^{\varepsilon}_{\eta ij}$) at a receiver location $\boldsymbol{x}$ can be approximated by taking a central difference of axial displacement Green's function at two locations at equal distance h from the receiver in opposite directions along the cable.

$$G^{\varepsilon}_{\eta ij}(\boldsymbol{x}) \sim \frac{G_{\eta ij}(\boldsymbol{x} + h\hat{\eta}) - G_{\eta ij}(\boldsymbol{x} - h\hat{\eta})}{2h}. \quad (9)$$

$\hat{\eta}$ used to calculate the axial displacement Green's functions at $(\boldsymbol{x} + h\hat{\eta})$ and $(\boldsymbol{x} - h\hat{\eta})$ using equation (7) corresponds to the local cable direction at $\boldsymbol{x}$. It is straightforward to calculate $G_{\eta ij}(\boldsymbol{x} \pm h\hat{\eta})$ for all receiver locations corresponding to an epicentral distance and receiver depth combination using the FKI method. We use $h = 5$ m in this study. Equation (8) can be reframed in terms of axial strain ε_η and axial strain Green's functions in the direction of the cable.

$$\varepsilon_\eta \sim M_{ij}G^{\varepsilon}_{\eta ij}. \quad (10)$$

The steps in this section outline a simple numerical scheme for calculating axial strain Green's functions for a DAS array with an arbitrary but slowly varying geometry embedded in a 1D isotropic velocity model. The low-frequency axial strain waveforms recorded by the DAS arrays can be used as ε_η to invert equation (10) for M_{ij} using simple least-squares inversion. Our study was conducted using an older version of the *Computer Programs in Seismology* software. More recent versions can directly output waveforms rotated from the cylindrical coordinate system to a Cartesian coordinate system, with one of the axes being vertical. However, further rotations must be performed for deviated sections of the array that are not strictly vertical or horizontal.

We calculate displacement Green's functions at a sample rate of 800 Hz using a Dirac source time function, apply a spatial derivative to convert to strain, and filter the waveforms using the same low-frequency band-pass filter (4–16 Hz) used for observed DAS waveforms. Both observed waveforms and Green's functions are downsampled to 250 Hz prior to inversion. For waveform inversion, we use DAS waveforms recorded in wells 34A and 73 during stage 1 and those recorded in wells 34A, 73, and 86 during stages 2 and 3. We exclude well 34 data during stage 1 due to large amplitude tube-wave noise at low frequencies, possibly generated by activities related to stimulation in the same well (Schumann and Jin, 2022). We quantify the goodness of fit between observed waveforms and synthetic waveforms predicted by the inverted moment tensor using VR (Minson and Dreger, 2008). We also allow for a uniform time shift up to ±5 samples (20 ms) for each well (all channels in the well are assigned the same time shift), which is less than one-third of the shortest period (e.g., Ford *et al.*, 2009). We begin with an initial inversion without any additional time shifts; starting with the well with the highest VR, we repeat the inversions, shifting the window of observed waveforms by one sample each time. We keep the time shift that provides the highest VR, and repeat the process for the other wells arranged by descending values of VR. The necessary time shift could be due to errors in location or the velocity model, the difference between origin time and centroid time, or incorrect reference frequency assumed in calculating Green's functions. In particular, inversion of arrival times to estimate locations, origin time, and the velocity model was slightly biased toward *P* waves, whereas waveform inversion is dominated by large amplitude *S* waves.

Prior to inverting observed data, we test the developed inversion framework on synthetic waveforms at wells 34A, 34, and 73. We use the software SW4 (v.2.01) to forward model synthetic strain waveforms for two assumed moment tensor sources, a pure DC source and one with ~88% isotropic moment. SW4 is a node-based finite-difference seismic wave propagation code that solves the elastic wave equation in displacement formulation in 3D domains with fourth-order accuracy in space and time (Sjogreen and Petersson, 2012; Petersson and Sjogreen, 2015). The grid is of dimensions 2.44 km (east–west), 2 km (north–south), and 2.9 km (Z, from 0.1 to 3.0 km in depth) and includes a supergrid absorbing boundary of thickness 0.2 km on all faces. We interpolate the 1D velocity model on the 3D grid. The grid spacing is 4 m, which provides ~7.5 grid points per shortest wavelength for minimum $V_S \sim 1.2$ km/s in the model and assumed maximum frequency of ~40 Hz (2.5 times the upper corner frequency of ~16 Hz used in waveform inversion). For a Dirac source time function, we output three-component displacements up to 1.36 s duration at two points at distances ±8 m from the location of every fourth channel in the direction of the cable. The sampling interval is determined to be 6.56×10^{-4} s. We rotate the three-component displacement to axial displacement along the cable (similar to equation 7) and take the central difference of axial displacement at each pair of points to calculate synthetic axial strain along the cable (similar to equation 9). The synthetic waveforms are filtered and inverted using the framework established with Green's functions of fundamental seismic sources in a 1D medium calculated using the FKI method. The inverted moment tensors are close to the true moment tensors (VR of model parameters $\gtrsim$ 97.4%), and the waveform fits are of VR $\gtrsim$ 94.9% (Figs. S6 and S7). The residual differences can be primarily attributed to insufficient grid spacing for the finite-difference method and insufficient sampling in the wavenumber domain for the FKI method. In particular, SW4 outputs displacement at the closest grid point instead of the exact receiver location.

We initially selected ~25 relatively larger microseismic events for moment tensor inversion based on a visual quality check of their waveforms in the target frequency range (~4 to 16 Hz); we finally end up with ~19 events for which the overall VR is >30% and VR in all wells is >10% for interpretation of results. Figures 6 and 7 show record sections of observed and synthetic axial strain waveforms predicted by the best-fitting moment tensors for two relatively larger magnitude events —event E31 (same event as in Fig. 3b), and an event in stage 2, hereinafter referred to as event E2, respectively. Figure 8 shows the variation of minimum and maximum amplitudes of the observed and synthetic axial strain waveforms along the DAS arrays. Event E31 is a relatively shallower event (depth ~2.14 km) with good waveform fits on the three wells (VR ~57% to 73%). Polarity reversals in the observed *S*-wave strain at channels 900 and 1100, including the one at the closest channel, are well reproduced in the synthetic waveforms. The near-field strain observed between *P* and *S* arrival times at the closest section of well 73 (between channels 1000 and 1200) and the polarities of *P* and *S* waves over the entire DAS array are well reproduced in the synthetics. The vertical well samples take-off angles ranging from ~55° to ~150° based on ray tracing. We match the polarities of *S* waves in the employed sections of wells 34A and 86, as well as the polarity of faint *P* waves in well 86. We observe a strong *S-to-P* conversion and a reflection near channel ~1050 (~0.85 km depth), possibly due to the basement-sediment interface, in observed DAS data in well 86 that is not reproduced by our smooth 1D model. Frequency–wavenumber filtering may be applied to remove converted waves that are unlikely to be reproduced in the Green's functions by a smooth velocity model. At the shallow section of the DAS array in well 34A (channel < 1300) that was not used in waveform inversion, the polarities of *P* and *S* waves are correctly reproduced in the synthetic strain waveforms even though the observed body waves show a significant delay with respect to the 1D model. The moment tensor solution and the 1D velocity model can generally reproduce the variation of amplitudes along the DAS arrays in all three wells (Fig. 8a). The observed amplitudes in the shallowest section of well 73 (channels ~300 to 400, depth ~0.5 to 0.7 km) are greater than predicted, a feature observed in all analyzed events, possibly due to incorrect values of attenuation or the presence of an interface just below this depth range. Similarly, the observed amplitudes in a part of the horizontal section of well 34A (channels ~1700 to 1800) are greater than predicted, a feature that is observed in most but not all analyzed events. The horizontal section of well 34A is in a near-radial direction with respect to most events, leading to greater susceptibility to error due to errors in event locations and the geometry of the well. Short-distance fluctuations in observed strain amplitudes are likely due to variations in coupling along the wells. Figures 7 and 8b show results for event E2, which was the largest event in stage 2 and a relatively deeper event at depth ~2.41 km. The strain amplitudes at channels > 1000 in well 73 closest to the event were saturated upon *S*-wave arrival, and therefore, for this event alone, we detrend the waveforms based on the noise of duration 0.3 s prior to the origin time and use the waveform segments till the *S*-wave arrival for the saturated channels. Despite good SNR, the overall VR for this event is lower at ~45%, with lower VR for wells 34A and 86, possibly due to finite-source effects that are not accounted for in our analysis. We match the amplitude trends along the DAS array

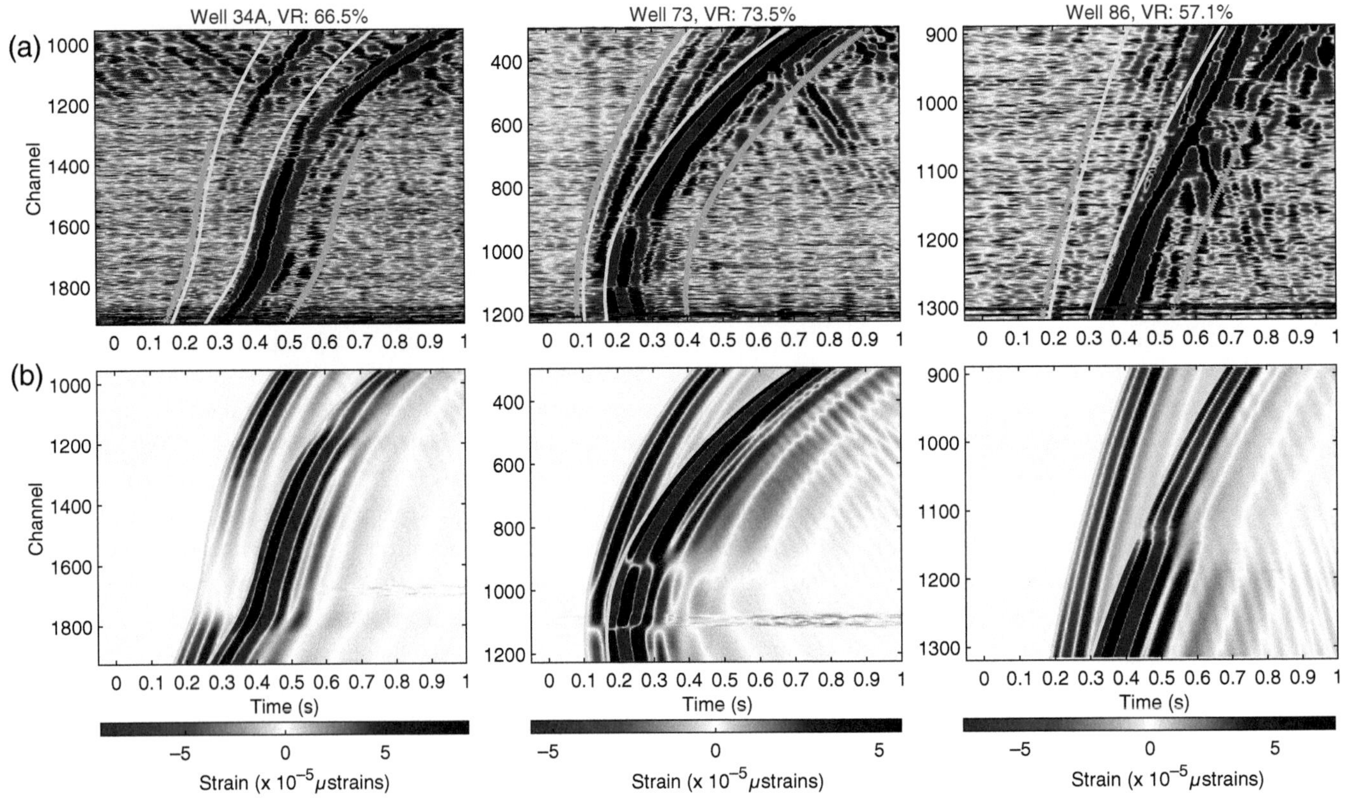

Figure 6. (a) Observed and (b) synthetic axial strain record sections at three wells (columns from left to right: 34A, 73, and 86) for event E31. The waveforms have been filtered in the passband ~4 to 16 Hz. The variance reduction (VR) between observed and synthetic waveforms predicted from the best-fitting moment tensor is mentioned at the top of the observed record sections, along with the name of the well. The yellow curves are the predicted *P*- and *S*-wave arrival times. The cyan curves on the observed record sections mark the beginning and end of the waveform segments used for waveform inversion. The color scale is the same for observed and synthetic record sections but different for each well, and is shown at the bottom of each column. The color version of this figure is available only in the electronic edition.

at wells 34A and 73, and in the deepest section of well 86. Figures S8 and S9 show similar results for event E1 (same event as in Fig. 3a), which was the largest event during stage 1, and shows excellent waveform fits (overall VR ~74%) at two wells. Overall VR of the 19 events in this study ranges from ~36% to ~74%, with a median of ~49%. The median overall VR for results using DAS arrays in two wells (stage 1, 9 events) and three wells (stages 2 and 3, 10 events) is ~48% and ~50%, respectively.

SOURCE-TYPE AND MAGNITUDE ESTIMATION

Nayak and Dreger (2015) developed a framework for inverting the best-fitting moment tensor for a specific source type, defined as ratios of eigenvalues of the moment tensor. A semi-uniform grid is assumed in the source-type space and at each source type on the grid, observed waveforms are inverted for the best-fitting moment tensor eigenvectors and a moment scale factor that characterizes the absolute size of the moment tensor eigenvalues, thereby resulting in the best-fitting moment tensor for that specific source type. The framework can be used to estimate the distribution of goodness of fit (VR) over the entire source-type space, known as the network sensitivity solution, which helps to assess the uniqueness and uncertainty of the inverted source type in terms of fit to the data. The eigenvalues are scaled to their absolute size by the moment scale factor, thereby providing an estimate of the best-fitting moment and magnitude for each source type. The framework, originally developed for displacement data, can be easily adapted to strain data by replacing the observed displacement waveforms and displacement Green's functions in equation 9 in Nayak and Dreger (2015) by observed axial strain waveforms and axial strain Green's functions from equation (10) in this study, respectively. We show the distribution of VR on Hudson source-type plots (Hudson *et al.*, 1989) for events E1, E2, and E31 in Figure 9a–c. To select a region of most probable source types on the source-type plot, we select a VR threshold 5% smaller than the VR of the best-fitting full moment tensor. More rigorous methods using observed noise and synthetic waveforms can be used to estimate this threshold statistically (Nayak and Dreger, 2018). Figure 9d shows a summary of best-fitting source types and VR threshold contours used as a proxy for source-type uncertainty for all 19 events. Even with an azimuthal gap > 200°, we are able to rule out isotropic volume increase or tensile opening crack-type source mechanisms that may be expected for seismic events induced by fluid injection in geothermal or hydraulic fracturing settings (Vavryčuk, 2011). The best-fitting source types and the region of high VR and the most probable source types for all events are

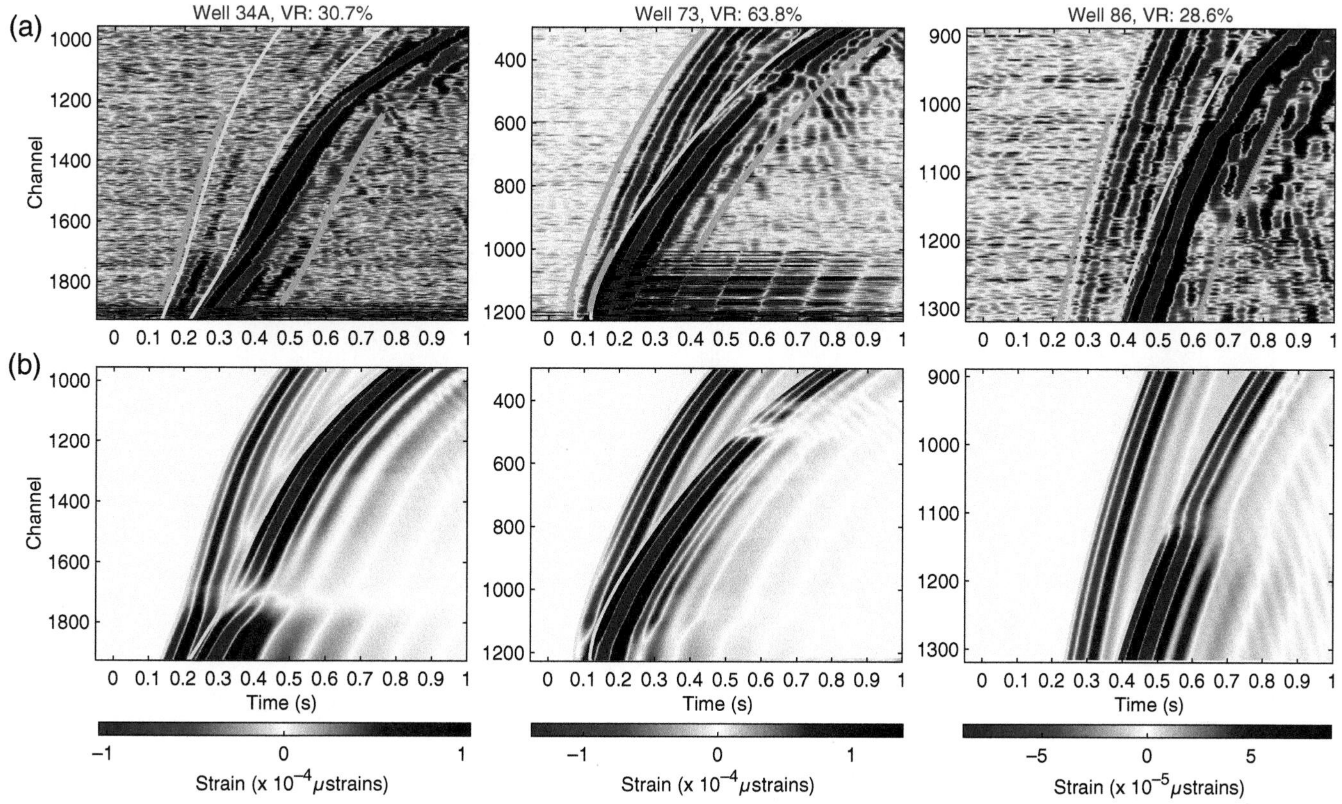

Figure 7. Similar to Figure 6, but for event E2 in stage 2. The color version of this figure is available only in the electronic edition.

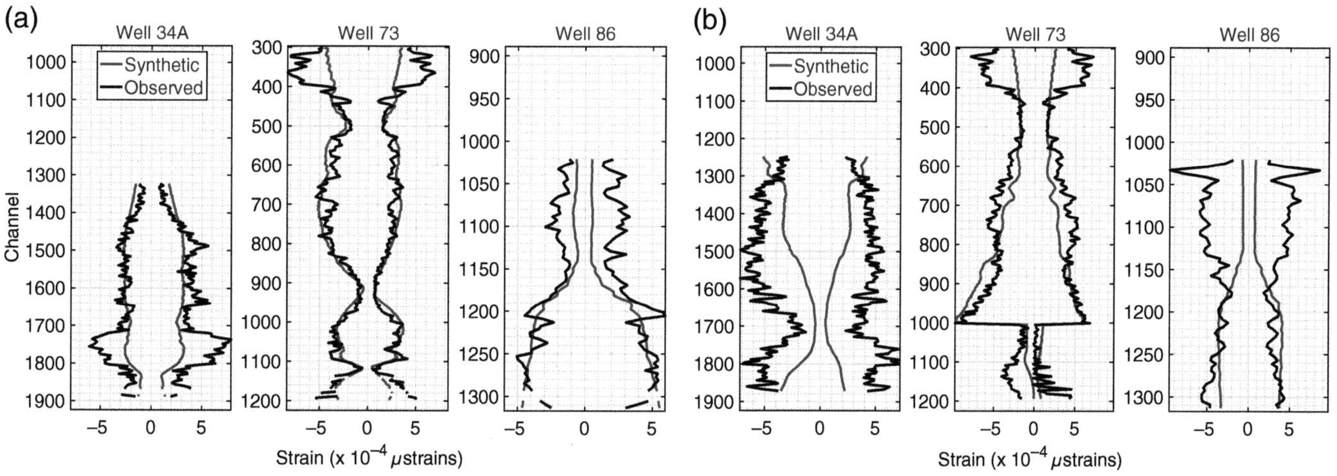

Figure 8. Curves show maximum (positive) and minimum (negative) amplitudes of observed axial strain waveform segments selected for inversion (black) and corresponding synthetic axial strain waveforms predicted by the best-fitting moment tensors (red). Panels (a,b) correspond to events E31 and E2 shown in Figures 6 and 7, respectively. The three subplots from left to right correspond to wells 34A, 73, and 86 (mentioned on top). In all plots, the *y* axis is the channel. The waveforms have been filtered in ~4 to 16 Hz. The color version of this figure is available only in the electronic edition.

spread around the deviatoric axis, with similar levels of fits for source types with large DC and large compensated linear vector dipole (CLVD) components. The spread is large, likely due to the poor azimuthal coverage of the focal sphere and strain data being limited to one component. Based on the small differences between VR of the best-fitting DC moment tensor and VR of the full moment tensor for most events ($\lesssim$2.5% for 15 out of 19 events, $\lesssim$4% for remaining events), the low waveform fits, and the large azimuthal gap, we assume that the events are dominantly DC mechanism for simplicity of interpretation.

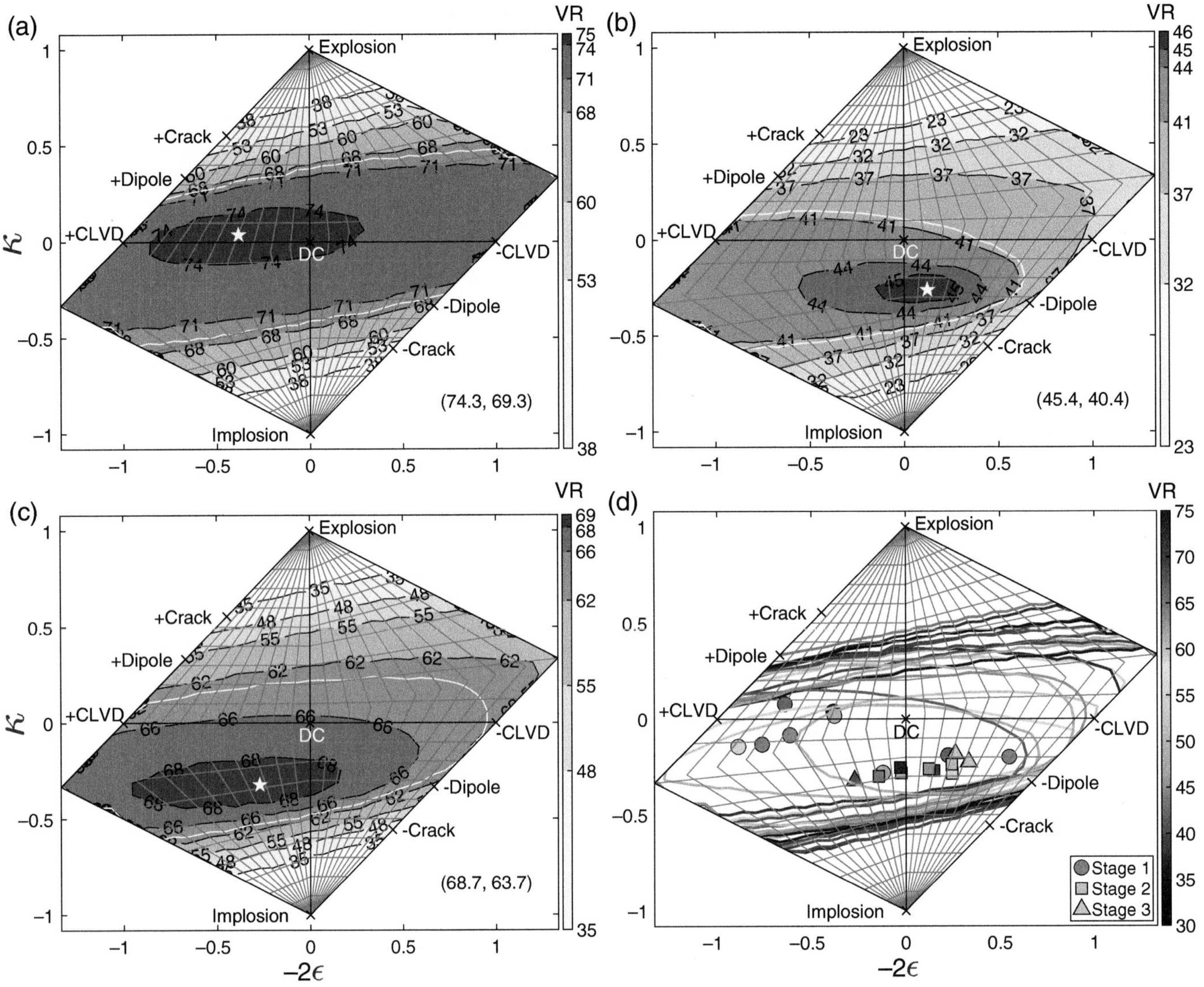

Figure 9. (a–c) Distribution (colors and contours) of VR on the Hudson source-type plot for three example events: (a) E1 (same as in Fig. 3a, Figs. S8 and S9), (b) E2 (same as in Figs. 7 and 8b), and (c) E31 (same as in Figs. 3b, 6, and 8a). The highest VR achieved and the VR threshold for selecting the most probable source types are indicated at the lower right corner in parentheses and correspond to the white star and the white contour, respectively. (d) Best-fitting source types (circles, squares, and triangles) and contours of the VR threshold (colored polygons) color-coded by VR for all 19 events analyzed in this study. In all plots, black crosses are the positions of major theoretical source types, and ϵ and κ are Hudson source-type parameters (Hudson *et al.*, 1989). CLVD, compensated linear vector dipole. The color version of this figure is available only in the electronic edition.

We further conduct synthetic tests to test the resolvability of isotropic and DC components with respect to the geometry of our DAS arrays and the contents of the employed strain wavefield. We use synthetic axial strain waveforms calculated for DAS arrays in well 73 and in the horizontal section of well 34A (stage 1 scenario) for the ~88% isotropic source in Figure S7. We invert the synthetic waveforms for the best-fitting moment tensors over the source-type space, similar to the evaluation for real events in Figure 9. We apply the inversion to both pure synthetic waveforms, as well as synthetic waveforms contaminated with real noise at a randomly selected time and filtered in the same passband. The noise waveform amplitudes are uniformly upscaled to get a similar level of VR (~76%) as the best stage 1 event (E1, Fig. S8). The waveform fits for the noise-contaminated synthetic waveforms are shown in Figure S10. Unlike the seismic events observed at Blue Mountain, a dominantly isotropic moment tensor source generates large amplitude low-frequency *P* waves (Figs. S7 and S10). The most probable source types have large isotropic components and are clearly separated from the deviatoric axis, for both noise-free synthetics and synthetics contaminated with noise (Fig. S11). Therefore, we conclude that our DAS geometry and selected wavefields are sufficient to resolve large isotropic components in seismic events, and the deviatoric nature of events observed during the stimulations at Blue Mountain is real.

Similarly, we use synthetic waveforms calculated for receivers along well 73, horizontal section of well 34A, and deeper section of well 86 (scenario of stages 2 and 3) for the pure DC source in

Figure S6. Whereas the deviatoric nature of the source is well resolved, inverting either noise-free or noise-contaminated synthetic axial strain waveforms returns relatively poor constraints on the DC component; source types with up to ~70% CLVD component provide waveform fits within VR ~5% of the VR achieved by a pure DC source (Figs. S12a and S13a,b). We get a similar spread on the deviatoric axis upon inverting synthetic axial displacement waveforms instead of axial strain waveforms (Figs. S12b and S13c), suggesting that the observed uncertainty may be due to the geometry of wells and composition of the bandlimited wavefield. Adding more information in the inversion using the complete synthetic three-component displacement wavefield leads to better resolution and a narrower region of most probable source types along the deviatoric axis; the CLVD component in source types that provide waveform fits within VR ~5% of the VR achieved by a pure DC source is limited to a maximum of ~50% (Fig. S13d). Unlike the synthetic tests, the best-fitting source types in observed events in Blue Mountain contain varying large contributions of DC and CLVD components (Fig. 9d). A future study will examine the role of geometry, mislocation, and errors in the assumed velocity model in errors in the recovered moment tensor.

In this study, we calculate M_0 from the eigenvalues of the moment tensor using the definition of Bowers and Hudson (1999) (e.g., Jiao *et al.*, 2014), which is further converted to M_w. To establish an uncertainty range for magnitudes derived from moment tensor inversion, we use the magnitudes of population of moment tensors on the source-type plot exceeding the VR threshold specific to each event (white contours in Fig. 9a–c and colored polygons in Fig. 9d). We define the uncertainty range as $\pm$ 1.5 standard deviation around the mean of the population; this range generally encompasses the magnitude from the best-fitting full moment tensor solution. We compare the moment tensor magnitudes with magnitudes derived from low-frequency spectral amplitudes of far-field body-wave strain using the methodology of Nayak *et al.* (2024). A similar methodology proposed and validated on horizontal DAS arrays at the surface can be found in Strumia *et al.* (2024). Nayak *et al.* (2024) applied the framework to horizontal well DAS recordings of microseismic events during a hydraulic fracturing experiment. In Nayak *et al.* (2024), because the events and receivers were roughly located at the same depth and were expected to have similar elastic properties in the vicinity, assuming a simple layered medium, simple expressions for a homogeneous medium were used. In this study, we correct the DAS strain spectral amplitudes for elastic parameters at event depth and DAS channel depths using the established 1D model:

$$M_w \sim \frac{2}{3}\log_{10}\left(\frac{4\pi(\rho_k\rho_o)^{0.5}V_{P,k}^{1.5}V_{P,o}^{2.5}}{0.52}\frac{r}{(\cos\theta)^2}\langle\frac{\epsilon_{ii,P}(f)}{(2\pi f)}\rangle\right)-10.73,$$
$$M_w \sim \frac{2}{3}\log_{10}\left(\frac{4\pi(\rho_k\rho_o)^{0.5}V_{S,k}^{1.5}V_{S,o}^{2.5}}{0.63}\frac{r}{(\sin\theta)(\cos\theta)}\langle\frac{\epsilon_{ii,S}(f)}{(2\pi f)}\rangle\right)-10.73, \quad (11)$$

in which $\epsilon_{ii,P}$ and $\epsilon_{ii,S}$ are low-frequency *P*- and *S*-wave strain spectral amplitudes, f is the frequency, subscripts k and o on elastic parameters (V_P, V_S, and density ρ) correspond to properties at channel and event depth, respectively, r is the hypocentral distance assumed for geometrical spreading correction, and θ is the angle between wavevector or the body-wave raypath and the direction of the cable at a specific channel. The inner-angle bracket implies averaging over low frequencies. Unlike Nayak *et al.* (2024), who estimated the final magnitude by averaging magnitude estimates from *P* and *S* waves recorded at different channels, we use the median of the estimates, which is less sensitive to outliers. Similarly, we use 1.5 times the median of the absolute deviation of all measurements from the median as uncertainty, which is equivalent to standard deviation for a normal distribution, and is less sensitive to outliers. For calculating *P*- and *S*-wave spectral amplitudes, we assume windows of duration 0.1 and 0.16 s starting 0.015 and 0.025 s, respectively, before the arrival times (t_P and t_S) predicted by the 1D model. We discard closer channels with $t_S - t_P < 0.095$ s to satisfy the far-field assumption and channels with low values of polarization factors (<0.02) to avoid division by small numbers. θ is calculated by ray tracing in the 1D model. The frequency search range for measuring spectral amplitudes spans the third sampled frequency ($2/T$, in which T is the duration of the time window) and the apparent corner frequency, and the passband used for measuring amplitudes is at least 1 octave and 3 sampled frequencies wide, with a minimum spectral SNR of 2. For records with lower apparent corner frequency, generally indicative of larger magnitude events, the frequency search range is allowed to start from the lowest frequency ($1/T$) with an imposed higher minimum spectral SNR of 2.5. We correct the spectral amplitudes for the average Q between event and receiver depths prior to averaging over low frequencies. Figure S14 shows strain spectra recorded by DAS, polarization factors along the wells, and magnitude estimates for event E2 (same event as in Figs. 7, 8b, and 9b).

Figure 10 shows a comparison of full moment tensor magnitudes and magnitudes derived from low-frequency spectral amplitudes. The estimates generally agree well with each other and cluster in the vicinity of a 1:1 line. Despite the narrow range of magnitudes (~ −0.2 to +0.5), an ordinary least-squares straight line fit to the data yields R^2 value of ~0.84, and a slope and intercept of 0.77 ± 0.16 and −0.13 ± 0.05, respectively, with the model parameter uncertainties represented by twice the standard deviation. The fit is biased toward smaller magnitude events due to their greater number; however, the error bars generally span the 1:1 line. The 95% confidence intervals of the prediction span ± ~0.15 magnitude units around the best-fitting line. The magnitudes from spectral amplitudes are smaller than moment tensor magnitudes by an average of ~0.17 units, with the absolute differences for 90% and all events being less than 0.29 and 0.35 units, respectively. We get a significantly better agreement in straight line fit if using magnitudes for the best-fitting DC moment tensor, with an R^2 value of

~0.87, and a slope and intercept of 0.80 ± 0.15 and −0.01 ± 0.03 (Fig. S15), likely due to the same assumption for the radiation pattern. In this comparison, the median difference between magnitudes from the best-fitting DC moment tensor and from spectral amplitudes is ~0.02 units, with the absolute differences for 90% and all events being less than 0.12 and 0.15 units, respectively. The framework of calculating magnitudes from low-frequency strain spectral amplitudes makes numerous assumptions and approximations—far-field body waves, an average of the radiation pattern over the focal sphere, dependence on elastic properties only at source and receiver locations, body-wave geometrical spreading for a homogeneous medium, and polarization factors. In contrast, the moment tensor inversion framework is physics-based, assuming only a 1D model. The good agreement with moment tensor magnitudes validates the framework of estimating magnitudes from low-frequency strain spectral amplitudes. The uncertainties for moment tensor magnitudes (median ~0.09 units) are smaller than those for magnitudes from spectral amplitudes (median ~0.23 units), likely because the former properly models the variation of amplitudes due to the radiation pattern, whereas the latter absorbs the variation of amplitudes into the uncertainty.

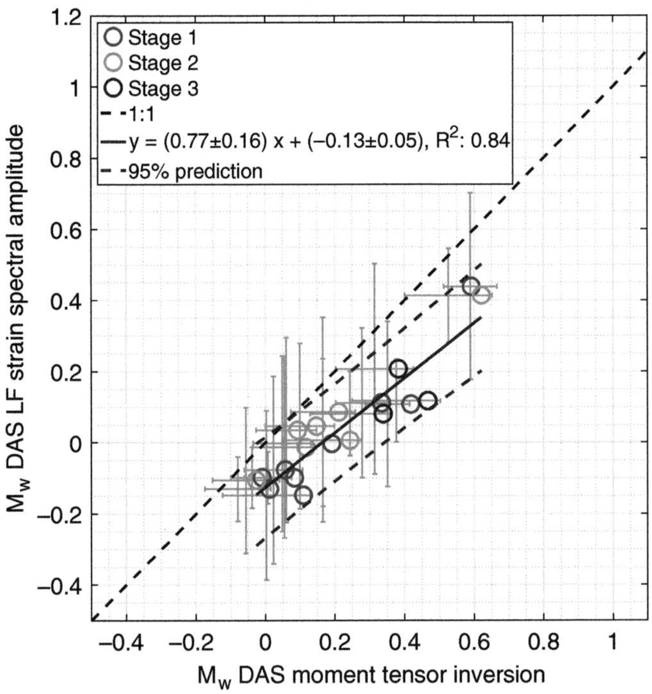

Figure 10. Comparison of magnitudes derived from moment tensor inversion of low-frequency (LF) strain waveforms with magnitudes estimated from low-frequency strain spectral amplitudes (circles). Different colors correspond to different stages. The error bars indicate uncertainties in magnitude estimates. For moment tensor inversion results, the marker's position on the *x* axis corresponds to the full moment tensor solution, whereas the error bar spans the uncertainty range as defined in the Source-type and magnitude estimation section. Solid and dashed blue lines are the best-fitting straight line and the 95% confidence intervals for the prediction, respectively. The color version of this figure is available only in the electronic edition.

Focal mechanisms

In the following, we assume that the microseismic events in our study area are of pure DC mechanism for simpler interpretation and examine the focal mechanisms and the constraints on the fault-plane parameters. We perform a grid search in strike, rake, and dip with 4° spacing to estimate the best-fitting DC moment tensor. For each combination of strike, rake, and dip, we invert the strain waveforms for best-fitting M_0 using linear least-squares inversion; for fault-plane parameters that return a negative M_0, the VR of waveform fits is set to zero. Figure 11a shows the lower hemisphere *P*-wave radiation pattern and magnitudes corresponding to the best-fitting DC moment tensor for most of the events analyzed in this study; the focal mechanisms of two other events are shown in the following figures. The estimated focal mechanisms are a mixture of predominantly normal, oblique, and strike-slip faulting. The normal-faulting mechanisms of larger events are primarily composed of a north-northwest-striking fault plane steeply dipping toward east-northeast and a south-southeast-striking fault plane, gently dipping toward west-southwest. We further check the resolvability of the fault-plane parameters and possible trade-offs between them by plotting VR as a function of two out of three parameters, utilizing the maximum VR obtained over all values of the third parameter. As expected, for the normal-faulting events such as event E1, we find a greater trade-off between the best-fitting strike and rake with respect to small variations in dip for the fault plane that is gently dipping (Fig. 11b). The large azimuthal gap, especially severe during stage 1 due to the absence of well 86 to the south, likely contributes to this uncertainty. The slip vector corresponding to the fault plane steeply dipping toward east-northeast is better constrained. Figures 12a,b and 13a,b show results for an event in stage 3, hereinafter referred to as event E32, and event E2, respectively; both events are of a dominant strike-slip mechanism. The strike-slip events generally occur in stages 2 and 3, tend to be slightly deeper at ~2.4 km, and are of relatively larger magnitudes. The sense of motion is right lateral or left lateral on northwest- or southwest-striking fault planes, respectively. The fault planes are almost vertical or steeply dipping toward the northeast or northwest, respectively. The difference in *S*-wave polarities at well 34A between events E31 and E2 (Figs. 6 and 7) supports a difference in source mechanism.

We did not find any earthquake with a focal mechanism solution within ~50 km of the study area in the Advanced National Seismic System (ANSS) Comprehensive Earthquake Catalog (Comcat; last accessed February 2025) for direct comparison. Focal mechanisms of regional earthquakes in the ANSS catalog, further away up to ~200 km distance, are shown in Figure S16. The north-northwest-striking normal-faulting and northwest-striking right-lateral strike-slip faulting mechanisms estimated in this study and the inferred east to east-

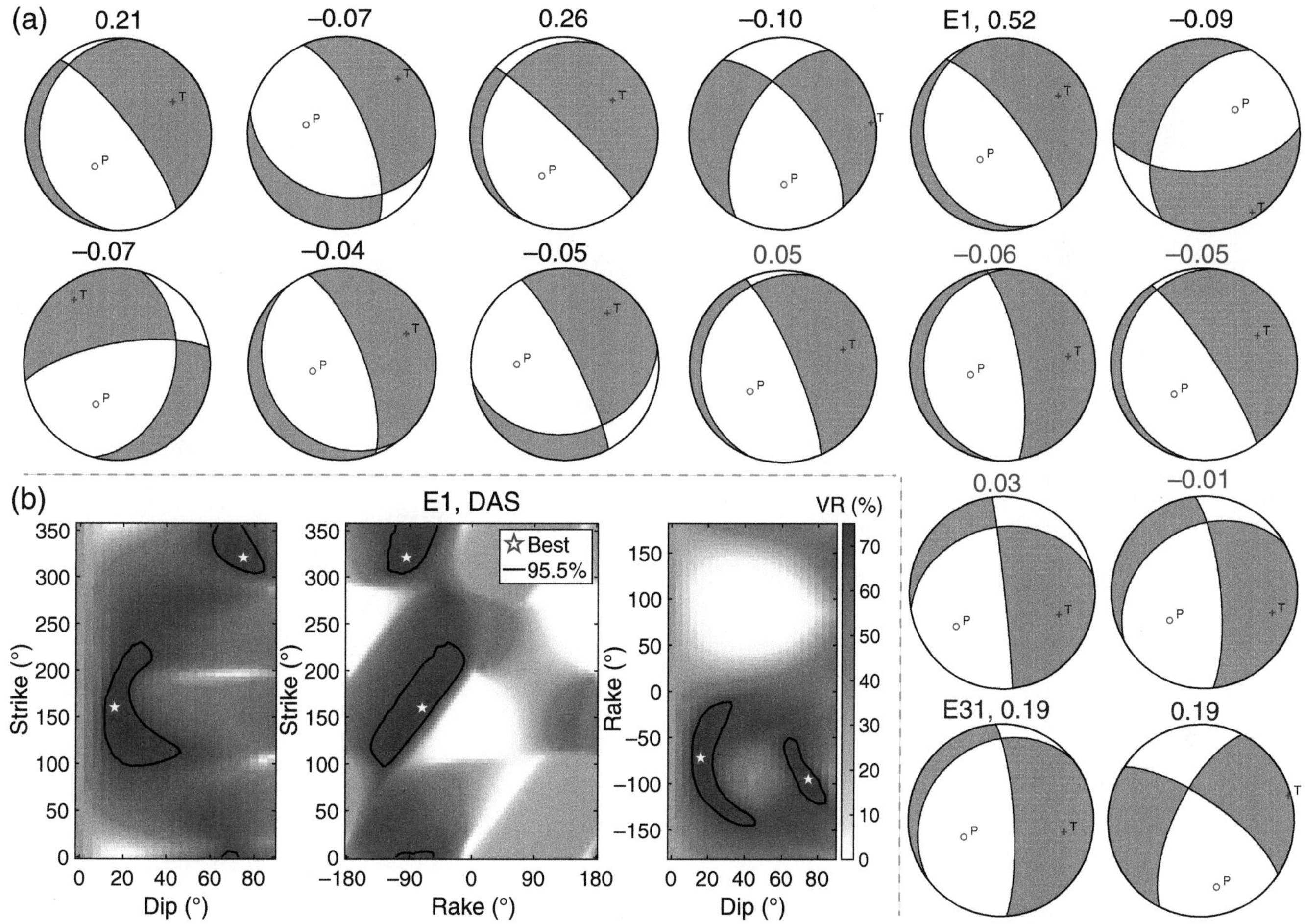

Figure 11. (a) Focal mechanism plots showing the lower hemisphere *P*-wave radiation pattern corresponding to the best-fitting double-couple (DC) moment tensor for most events analyzed in this study. The magnitude is listed on the top and color-coded by stage (black, red, and blue for stages 1, 2, and 3, respectively). Representative events E1 and E31 are marked. (b) VR of DAS waveforms as a function of fault-plane parameters for event E1. Left subplot: VR as a function of strike and dip, the maximum VR over all possible values of rake is considered; similarly, center subplot: VR as a function of strike and rake, the maximum VR over all possible values of dip is considered; right subplot: VR as a function of rake and dip, the maximum VR over all possible values of strike is considered. White stars mark best-fitting fault-plane parameters. Black polygons are contours corresponding to 95.5% of the highest VR achieved. The color version of this figure is available only in the electronic edition.

northeast direction of extension from the tension axes are consistent with the Basin and Range extensional tectonics prevalent in Nevada (Svarc *et al.*, 2002; Ichinose *et al.*, 2003; Reitman and Molnar, 2021). An M_L 3.1 earthquake in 2019 (event ID: nn00683614), ~130 km south-southwest of the study area, has a focal mechanism similar to the normal-faulting mechanisms in this study (Fig. S16). In the geological model of Fercho *et al.* (2023), the southwest range-front fault system bounding Blue Mountain to the southwest (Fig. 1a) is proposed to have dextral-normal motion. The normal and right-lateral strike-slip focal mechanisms recovered in this study for northwest to north-northwest-trending faults agree with the geological model. The greater north–south trend of the strike of the focal mechanisms is consistent with the general east–west trend of topographic gradient that may be interpreted as the direction of extension and the north–south trend of the range-front faults that bound Blue Mountain to the west (Fig. 1a).

Validation using surface seismometers

The seismicity at Blue Mountain has been monitored with an intermittently operating local seismic network comprising seven three-component wideband and broadband seismometers and a borehole seismometer of unknown instrument response, all recording data at 250 Hz. The network is described in detail in Dadi *et al.* (2024). The network was operational during a small portion of stage 1 and during the entire duration of stages 2 and 3 in this study; 51 out of 74 events analyzed in this study using DAS data were also recorded by the surface seismometers. We first examined the data filtered in different passbands. Despite the small magnitudes, two strike-slip events, E32 and E2 (Figs. 12 and 13, respectively) had simple waveforms with sufficient SNR at low frequencies at four surface stations to attempt waveform inversion. Two of the stations, ISTI1 and ISTI2, are on rock outcrops on Blue Mountain and sensors for the other two stations, FE02 and FE04, are in shallow holes in the foothills of the mountain (Fig. 1a). Because the surface seismic stations are located further away from the microseismic

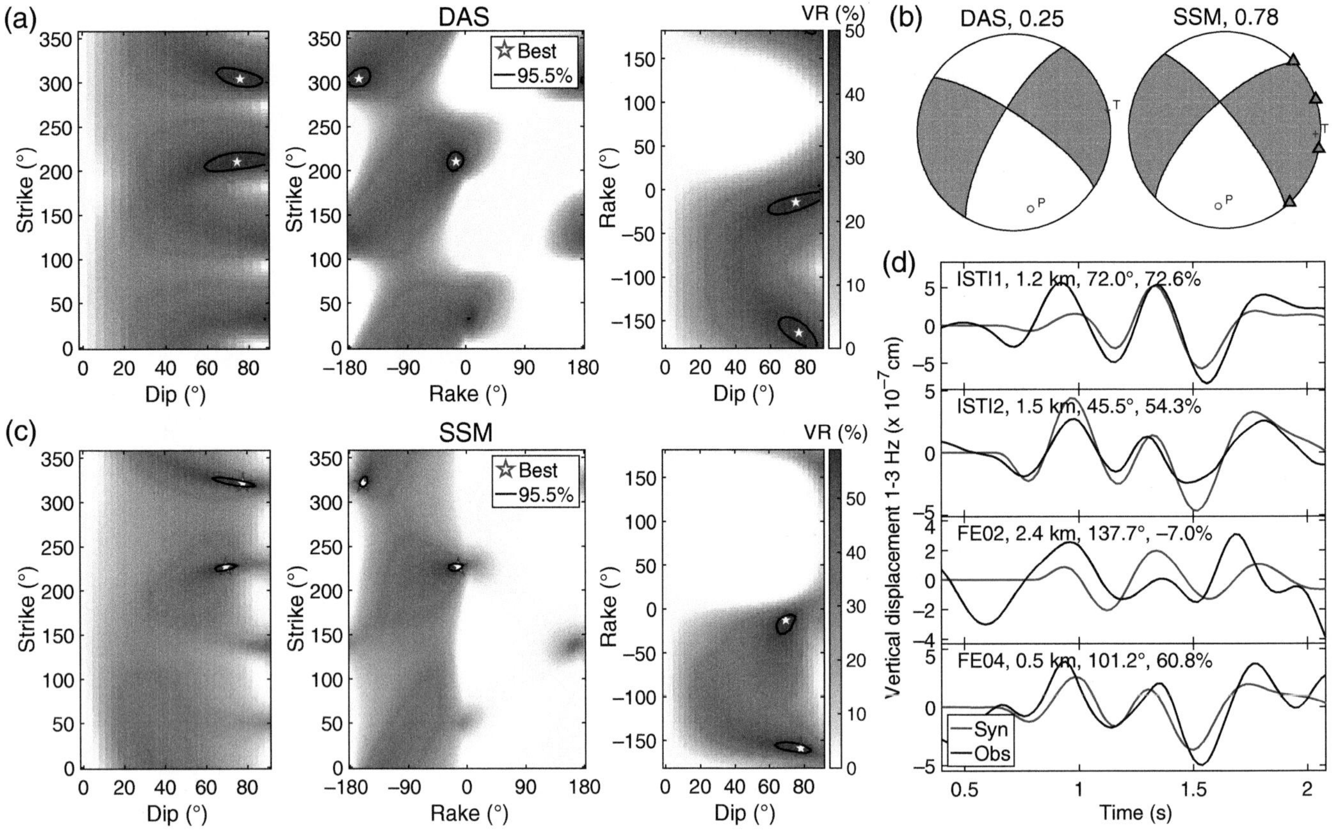

Figure 12. Focal mechanism results for event E32 in stage 3, assuming a pure DC source. (a) VR of DAS waveforms as a function of fault-plane parameters, similar to Figure 11b. (b) Focal mechanism plots corresponding to the best-fitting DC moment tensor derived from DAS waveforms (left, DAS) and surface seismometer waveforms (right, seismometer [SSM]). The green triangles mark the surface seismometer azimuths. The magnitude is listed at the top. (c) VR of seismometer waveforms as a function of fault-plane parameters, similar to panel (a). (d) Low-frequency (1–3 Hz) vertical-component observed displacement waveforms (black) and corresponding synthetic displacement waveforms (red) predicted by the best-fitting DC moment tensor. Each panel corresponds to a different station; the station name, epicentral distance (km), azimuth (°), and VR in percent are mentioned at the top. The color version of this figure is available only in the electronic edition.

events compared to the DAS arrays and the 1D velocity model derived from DAS arrays only extends up to 0.5 km depth, we develop station-specific 1D models by calibrating the near-surface velocity using static station corrections.

Example three-component seismometer waveforms of event E2 are shown in Figure S17. We were able to pick *P* waves on the vertical component for almost all events at stations ISTI1 and FE02 and ~78% and ~43% of the events at stations FE04 and ISTI2, respectively. Our *S*-wave picks on the horizontal components for the same events and stations are less certain and show greater scatter. We first extend the 1D model from 0.5 km depth to station elevation. The arrival times at the surface stations predicted from the hypocenters, origin times, and the 1D model derived from DAS data are generally delayed with respect to the observed arrival times, indicating that the model is slower than the actual velocities beneath the stations, which is consistent with the seismic stations being located closer to Blue Mountain than the DAS arrays (Fig. S18). The difference between observed and predicted arrival times has a narrow negative distribution, indicative of the difference originating near the receiver (Fig. S18). Because the velocities in our 1D model strictly increase with depth, we gradually strip the top layer and extend the velocity of the next deeper and faster layer to the station elevation, till the median of the residuals between observed and predicted arrival times, inferred to be static station correction, is reduced to <10 ms (Fig. S18). This simple workflow ensures that station-specific 1D models are consistent with each other at greater depths. Some deeper layers were slightly adjusted to have a slowly varying V_P/V_S. The final velocity models are shown in Figure S19, with the fastest velocities for stations ISTI1 and ISTI2 located on basement rock outcrops at Blue Mountain. We were unable to get a reasonable V_P/V_S for the surface layer at FE04, possibly due to systematic errors in picks (e.g., incorrectly picking a converted phase instead of the direct *S* wave), so its V_P/V_S is fixed to the original value.

For moment tensor inversion of surface seismometer data, we correct the waveforms for instrument response to ground velocity, integrate the data to displacement, filter the waveforms with a causal Butterworth band-pass filter (1–3 Hz), and decimate to 50 Hz. We calculate Green's functions using the station-specific 1D velocity models and the FKI method; the Green's functions are

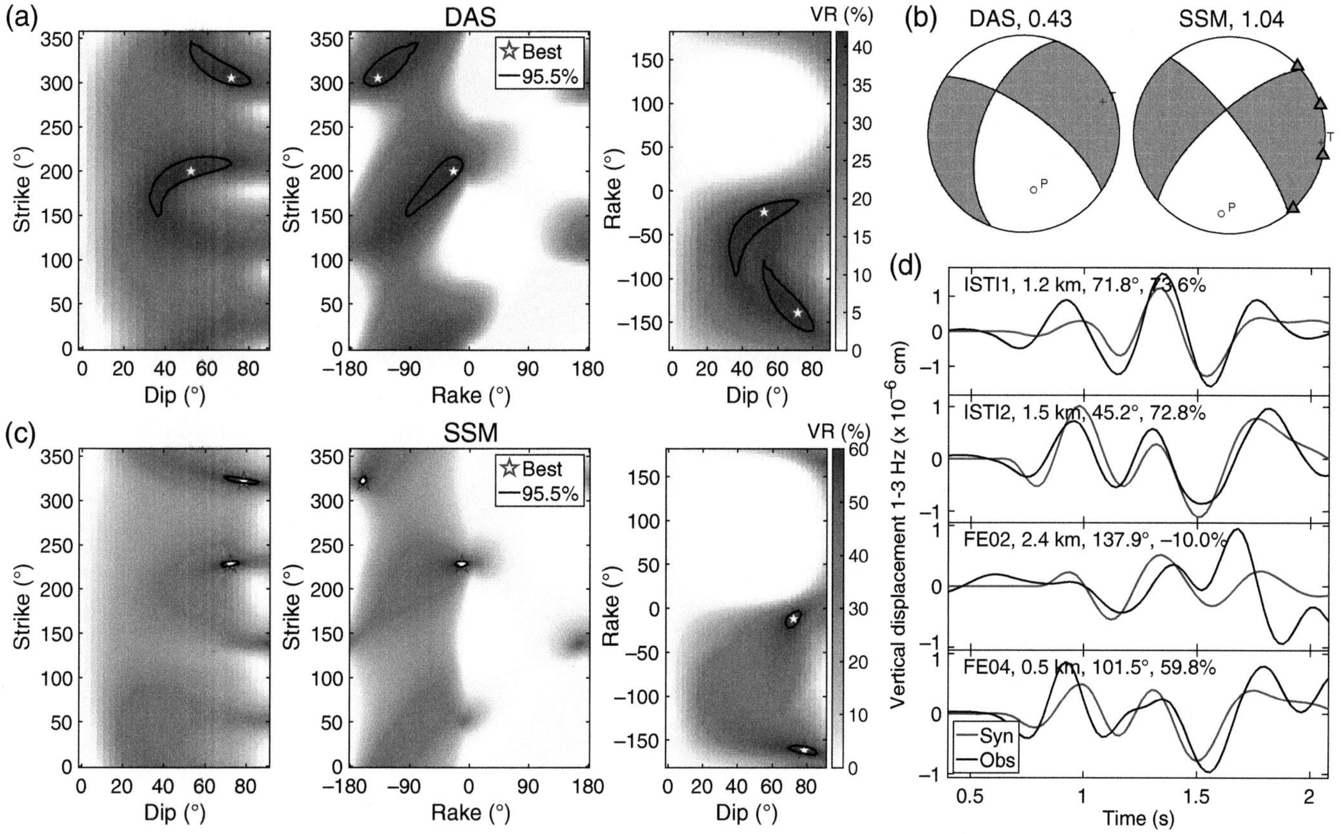

Figure 13. Similar to Figure 12 but for event E2 (same event as in Figs. 7, 8b, 9b, and Fig. S14). The color version of this figure is available only in the electronic edition.

processed the exact same way as observed waveforms. Even with the path calibration, we were unable to fit horizontal-component waveforms at all four stations simultaneously. Therefore, in the following, we work with vertical-component waveforms only. We invert low-frequency waveforms of duration ~1.7 s, that encompass body waves, as well as near-field and intermediate-field terms, while allowing up to 0.08 s time shifts to improve alignment between observed and synthetic waveforms. Because of the large azimuthal gap of ~270°, we assume a pure DC moment tensor, evaluate VR of waveform fits as a function of fault-plane parameters, and find the best-fitting parameters and M_0 similar to the procedure used for DAS data. Figure 12b–d shows the focal mechanism plot corresponding to the best-fitting DC moment tensor solution, VR as a function of fault-plane parameters, and observed and synthetic displacement waveforms for the best-fitting DC source, respectively, for event E32. Results for event E2 are shown in Figure 13b–d. Despite the azimuthal coverage opposite (toward east) to that provided by the DAS arrays (west to south), the strike-slip faulting focal mechanisms derived from seismometers agree with the focal mechanisms derived from DAS in terms of the sense of motion and strike of the two possible fault planes (Figs. 12a–c and 13a–c) for both events E32 and E2. We obtain generally good fits (overall VR ~58%) between observed and synthetic waveforms predicted by the DC moment tensor (Figs. 12d and 13d). The lower amplitudes and consequently poorer waveform fits at station FE02 are likely due to a greater distance from the event and its location in the direction of a node in the inverted *P*-wave radiation pattern.

The magnitudes derived from downhole DAS are smaller than the magnitudes derived from surface seismometers by ~0.5 to 0.6 units, indicating a relative amplitude discrepancy of a factor of ~6. Previous studies on the determination of magnitudes both from downhole DAS and dark fiber DAS arrays have found much better agreement with magnitudes derived from surface seismometers (Nayak *et al.*, 2024; Strumia *et al.*, 2024). We speculate on possible reasons for the discrepancy in our data and results. We first verified the instrument response of the surface seismometers by comparing recorded waveforms of large teleseismic earthquakes with those recorded by the closest permanent seismic stations. Most of the written code was verified by the retrieval of correct moment tensor elements in the synthetic tests (Figs. S6, S7, S10, and S12a) that applied the inversion framework to synthetic waveforms calculated using a different method (SW4) compared to the method used to calculate Green's functions (FKI). The simple 1D velocity models calibrated to fit body-wave arrival times at surface seismometers contain a thick layer of constant velocity at the surface, which may be unrealistic as velocities generally increase with depth in the near-surface weathered layer. However, we use a low-frequency (~1 to 3 Hz) vertical-component displacement wavefield that is generally less sensitive to small changes in the velocity structure. For example, introducing a thin ~100 m layer of low velocities ($V_P \sim 1.5$ km/s, $V_S \sim 0.5$ km/s) at the surface in the 1D velocity model for ISTI1 station, despite the knowledge that the station is located on rock outcrops, leads to a factor of ~2 increase in amplitudes of the ZSS component Green's functions, which would lead to only a ~0.2 unit decrease in magnitude. However, our inability to fit larger amplitude horizontal-component waveforms in this study indicates the need for further refinement of the near-surface velocity structure, possibly by ambient seismic noise imaging using a dense temporary array, which could lead to greater revision of the magnitude estimates derived from surface seismometers. Finally, we consider insufficient coupling of the fiber-optic cables to the subsurface as a possible reason. In a recent study of downhole DAS data, Boullenger *et al.* (2024) empirically determined a reduced downhole DAS amplitude response of ~ −10 to −20 dB in ~20 to 40 Hz frequency range, which is equivalent to a factor of ~3 to 10 reduction in amplitudes. We observe a similar reduction in amplitudes (factor of ~6) at lower frequencies (~4 to 16 Hz). A better velocity model and better azimuthal coverage provided by more seismic receivers, leading to stronger constraints on the source mechanism, and a different DAS interrogator using different acquisition parameters and writing data in a different file format, might shed further light on the reasons for the discrepancy between DAS and seismometer magnitudes at Blue Mountain.

DISCUSSIONS AND CONCLUSIONS

In this study, we analyze downhole DAS data of microseismic events during EGS operations at Blue Mountain, Nevada. DAS data in three wells provide strong constraints on the absolute locations of the microseismic events. The coverage provided by DAS in a vertical well extending down to event depths provides unprecedented constraints on event depths, which is generally difficult to achieve using surface seismometers. A 1D velocity model was found to be sufficient in fitting body-wave arrival times in multiple wells at greater depths to a reasonable degree (overall weighted RMS of residuals ~3.8 ms). Modeling body-wave arrival times at shallower depths may require a 3D velocity model.

The seismic data at depth captured by downhole DAS arrays contain relatively simple waveforms of body waves that may be easier to model compared to seismic records in horizontal DAS arrays at the surface that are dominated by surface waves and scattered waves, and are strongly influenced by greater heterogeneities in the near surface (Ajo-Franklin *et al.*, 2022). In this study, we develop a framework to invert low-frequency (~4 to 16 Hz) axial strain waveforms recorded by downhole DAS arrays with slowly varying geometries for a point-source moment tensor using axial strain Green's functions for a 1D velocity model calculated using the FKI method. The calculation of Green's functions using the FKI method has little computer memory requirements, even for a large number of distance–depth combinations, unlike grid-based numerical simulation of seismic wave propagation. We obtain generally good waveform fits at three wells (median overall VR ~48%) and are able to rule out isotropic and crack-type source mechanisms. The array geometry is not able to resolve moment tensors on the deviatoric source-type axis. Assuming a pure DC mechanism, we obtain normal-faulting and right-lateral strike-slip faulting mechanisms on northwest- to north-northwest-trending faults that agree with the geologic and tectonic knowledge of the study area. Microseismic event focal mechanisms shed light on the state of stress in the subsurface, which is important in geothermal and hydraulic fracturing operations. For two relatively larger magnitude strike-slip events, we invert low-frequency vertical-component displacement waveforms recorded by surface seismometers for DC moment tensors that agree with the fault-plane solutions determined from downhole DAS arrays despite different azimuthal coverage. The downhole DAS arrays proved valuable in constraining the locations and focal mechanisms of the microseismic events because data recorded at the surface by the sparse network of seismometers proved challenging to analyze due to noise, significant scattering observed in waveforms, and uncertainty in the near-surface velocity structure. However, surface seismometers can be deployed in dense arrays to reduce the noise floor by array processing and can provide greater azimuthal coverage. Unlike wells, surface seismic stations can be moved and redeployed in response to migrating seismicity for continued coverage. In addition, seismometers can record ground motions of larger events on scale unlike DAS, which is relevant for induced seismicity. The developed framework (equation 10) makes it straightforward to jointly invert low-frequency DAS and seismometer waveforms for stronger constraints on the source mechanisms; however, the velocity model used for calculating Green's functions should be appropriate for the paths and the frequency range.

Based on our experience, the requirements of moment tensor inversion of strain waveforms recorded by DAS arrays are similar to that for displacement waveforms recorded by seismometers—good SNR at low frequencies for which waveforms are simple and point-source assumption is valid (below the corner frequency), a good location, a velocity model good enough to fit low-frequency waveforms, good waveform fits, and a good coverage of focal sphere that increases reliability of the inverted moment tensor. The third and fifth requirements are likely a bit stricter for DAS strain waveforms than for displacement waveforms due to the gradient applied on the wavefield, observations being limited to one component, and directional dependence. If a reasonably good velocity model is available, automatic detection and estimation of centroid location and origin time of seismic events can be integrated into the moment tensor inversion workflow by performing a grid search over time and over a predefined grid of possible source locations (Nayak and Dreger, 2018). Outlier problematic channels with anomalously large amplitudes can be automatically identified based on median and median of absolute deviation criteria. The SNR of smaller events can be improved by array processing, taking advantage of the dense spatial sampling. The inversion framework developed in this study can be extended to horizontal dark fiber DAS arrays at the surface that are now routinely used for monitoring of local and regional earthquakes in areas of sparse seismic network coverage (Ajo-Franklin *et al.*, 2022), provided a good enough velocity model is available, and the geometry can provide meaningful coverage of the focal sphere. However, there are additional challenges. Dark fiber suffers from variable coupling with the subsurface due to varying installation conditions. For moment tensor inversion of displacement waveforms, it is generally recommended to invert lower frequencies that may be less sensitive to errors in the assumed velocity structure. However, unlike far-field body-wave displacement spectra that are proportional to source spectra and flat at frequencies lower than the corner frequency, the far-field body-wave strain spectral amplitudes decrease with decreasing frequency (Luo *et al.*, 2021), which could make achieving good SNR at low frequencies difficult.

DATA AND RESOURCES

The data of the hydraulic fracturing experiment were provided by Fervo Energy and are proprietary. ObsPy (Beyreuther *et al.*, 2010) and Seismic Analysis Code (SAC; Goldstein *et al.*, 2003) were used for basic analysis of seismograms. *Computer Programs in Seismology* software can be downloaded from https://www.eas.slu.edu/eqc/eqcsoftware.html (last accessed February 2025). The National Aeronautics and Space Administration (NASA) Shuttle Radar Topography Mission (SRTM, 2013) elevation data were downloaded from OpenTopography database (doi: 10.5069/G9445JDF). Some maps were prepared using Generic Mapping Tools (GMT; Wessel *et al.*, 2013). The supplemental material to this article includes additional details about the event locations and the velocity model, and figures showing Wadati plots of arrival times, final 1D velocity models with low misfit for all inversions, location uncertainties, arrival-time residual distribution for the wells individually, a zoomed-in-view of the final event locations, record sections in all synthetic tests, observed and synthetic distributed acoustic sensing (DAS) record sections and variation of peak amplitudes along the length of the wells for event E1, source-type uncertainty results for synthetic tests, far-field body-wave strain spectra, polarization factors and magnitude estimates from different channels for event E2, comparison of magnitudes for the best-fitting double-couple (DC) moment tensors and magnitudes estimated from low-frequency strain spectral amplitudes, regional focal mechanisms in the Advanced National Seismic System (ANSS) catalog, example records on the surface seismometers, body-wave arrival-time residual distributions at surface seismometers, and station-specific 1D velocity models.

DECLARATION OF COMPETING INTERESTS

The authors acknowledge that there are no conflicts of interest recorded.

ACKNOWLEDGMENTS

This project was funded by the U.S. Department of Energy, through Advanced Research Projects Agency – Energy (ARPA-E), under Contract Number DE-AC02-05CH11231 with Lawrence Berkeley National Laboratory (LBNL). The authors thank Fervo Energy for permission to publish this work. The authors thank Joern Kaven (U.S. Geological Survey [USGS]) for providing the surface seismometer data. The authors additionally thank Obinna Kanu (Fervo Energy) and Mike Hagerty (Instrumental Software Technologies Inc.) for their help in working with the data. The authors thank Associate Editor Václav Vavryčuk and two anonymous reviewers for their constructive comments and suggestions that significantly improved the quality of this research.

REFERENCES

Ajo-Franklin, J., V. Rodríguez Tribaldos, A. Nayak, F. Cheng, R. Mellors, B. Chi, T. Wood, M. Robertson, C. Rotermund, E. Matzel, *et al.* (2022). The Imperial Valley Dark Fiber Project: Toward seismic studies using DAS and telecom infrastructure for geothermal applications, *Seismol. Res. Lett.* **93,** no. 5, 2906–2919, doi: 10.1785/0220220072.

Baird, A. F., A. L. Stork, S. A. Horne, G. Naldrett, J.-M. Kendall, J. Wookey, J. P. Verdon, and A. Clarke (2020). Characteristics of microseismic data recorded by distributed acoustic sensing (DAS) systems in anisotropic media, *Geophysics* **85,** no. 4, KS139–KS147, doi: 10.1190/geo2019-0776.1.

Beyreuther, M., R. Barsch, L. Krischer, Y. B. T. Megies, and J. Wassermann (2010). ObsPy: A Python toolbox for seismology, *Seismol. Res. Lett.* **81,** no. 3, 530–533.

Bommer, J. J., S. Oates, J. M. Cepeda, C. Lindholm, J. Bird, R. Torres, G. Marroquín, and J. Rivas (2006). Control of hazard due to seismicity induced by a hot fractured rock geothermal project, *Eng. Geol.* **83,** no. 4, 287–306, doi: 10.1016/j.enggeo.2005.11.002.

Boullenger, B., A. Butcher, B. Paap, V. Vandeweijer, and A. L. Stork (2024). Distributed acoustic sensing, transfer functions and moment magnitude determination: application to high-frequency downhole data, *Geophysics* doi: 10.1190/geo2024-0059.1.

Bowers, D., and J. A. Hudson (1999). Defining the scalar moment of a seismic source with a general moment tensor, *Bull. Seismol. Soc. Am.* **89,** no. 5, 1390–1394.

Brocher, T. M. (2005). Empirical relations between elastic wavespeeds and density in the Earth's crust, *Bull. Seismol. Soc. Am.* **95,** no. 6, 2081–2092.

Brocher, T. M. (2008). Key elements of regional seismic velocity models for long period ground motion simulations, *J. Seismol.* **12,** 217–221, doi: 10.1007/s10950-007-9061-3.

Correa, J., S. Glubokovskikh, A. Nayak, L. Luo, T. Wood, X. Zhu, J. Ajo-Franklin, and B. Freifeld (2024). Revealing complex subsurface dynamics with continuous seismic monitoring: Observations using distributed acoustic sensing and surface orbital vibrators during hydraulic fracturing, *Geophysics* **89,** no. 6, P47–P56, doi: 10.1190/geo2023-0785.1.

Dadi, S., J. Norbeck, A. Titov, T. Payeur, S. Machovoe, K. Joern, and K. Chinaemerem (2024). Microseismic monitoring of a horizontal EGS system: case study and state of the art, *Proc. of the 49th Workshop on Geothermal Reservoir Engineering Stanford University*, Stanford, California, 12–14 February 2024, SGP-TR-227 pp.

Daley, T. M., B. M. Freifeld, J. Ajo-Franklin, S. Dou, R. Pevzner, V. Shulakova, S. Kashikar, D. E. Miller, J. Goetz, J. Henninges, *et al.* (2013). Field testing of fiber-optic distributed acoustic sensing (DAS) for subsurface seismic monitoring, *The Leading Edge* **32,** no. 6, 699–706, doi: 10.1190/tle32060699.1.

Daley, T. M., D. E. Miller, K. Dodds, P. Cook, and B. M. Freifeld (2016). Field testing of modular borehole monitoring with simultaneous distributed acoustic sensing and geophone vertical seismic profiles at Citronelle, Alabama, *Geophys. Prospect.* **64,** no. 5, 1318–1334, doi: 10.1111/1365-2478.12324.

Eaton, D. W., and F. Forouhideh (2011). Solid angle and the impact of receiver-array geometry on microseismic moment-tensor inversion, *Geophysics* **76,** no. 6, WC77–WC85, doi: 10.1190/GEO2011-0077.1.

Eyre, T. S., and M. van der Baan (2017). The reliability of microseismic moment-tensor solutions: surface versus borehole monitoring, *Geophysics* **82,** no. 6, KS113–KS125.

Fercho, S., J. Norbeck, E. McConville, N. Hinz, I. Wallis, A. Titov, S. Agarwal, S. Dadi, C. Gradl, H. Baca, *et al.* (2023). Geology, state of stress, and heat in place for a horizontal well geothermal development project at Blue Mountain, Nevada, *Proc. of the 48th Workshop on Geothermal Reservoir Engineering*, Stanford University, Stanford, California, 6–8 February 2023, SGP-TR-224 pp.

Ford, S. R., D. S. Dreger, and W. R. Walter (2009). Identifying isotropic events using a regional moment tensor inversion, *J. Geophys. Res.* **114,** no. B1, doi: 10.1029/2008JB005743.

Goldstein, P., D. Dodge, M. Firpo, and L. Minner (2003). SAC2000: Signal processing and analysis tools for seismologists and engineers, in *Invited Contribution to The IASPEI International Handbook of Earthquake and Engineering Seismology*, W. H. K. Lee, H. Kanamori, P. C. Jennings, and C. Kisslinger (Editors), Academic Press, London, United Kingdom.

Haskell, N. A. (1964). Radiation pattern of surface waves from point sources in a multi-layered medium, *Bull. Seismol. Soc. Am.* **54,** no. 1, 377–393.

Herrmann, R. B. (2013). Computer programs in seismology: An evolving tool for instruction and research, *Seismol. Res. Lett.* **84,** 1081–1088.

Hudson, J. A., R. G. Pearce, and R. M. Rogers (1989). Source type plot for inversion of the moment tensor, *J. Geophys. Res.* **94,** no. B1, 765–774.

Ichinose, G. A., J. G. Anderson, K. D. Smith, and Y. Zeng (2003). Source parameters of eastern California and western Nevada earthquakes from regional moment tensor inversion, *Bull. Seismol. Soc. Am.* **93,** no. 1, 61–84.

Jiao, W., M. Davidson, A. Sena, B. L. Bankhead, Y. Xia, S. Sil, and C. Zhou (2014). The matter of size: On the moment magnitude of microseismic events, *Geophysics* **79,** no. 3, KS31–KS41, doi: 10.1190/GEO2013-0194.1.

Jin, G., and B. Roy (2017). Hydraulic-fracture geometry characterization using low-frequency DAS signal, *The Leading Edge* **36,** 975–980, doi: 10.1190/tle36120975.1.

Jost, M. L., and R. B. Herrmann (1989). A student's guide to and review of moment tensors, *Seismol. Res. Lett.* **60,** no. 2, 37–57.

Karrenbach, M., S. Cole, A. Ridge, K. Boone, D. Kahn, J. Rich, K. Silver, and D. Langton (2018). Fiber-optic distributed acoustic sensing of microseismicity, strain and temperature during hydraulic fracturing, *Geophysics* **84,** no. 1, D11–D23, doi: 10.1190/geo2017-0396.1.

Lecoulant, J., Y. Ma, J. Dettmer, and D. Eaton (2023). Strain-based forward modeling and inversion of seismic moment tensors using distributed acoustic sensing (DAS) observations, *Front. Earth Sci.* **11,** 1176921, doi: 10.3389/feart.2023.1176921.

Lellouch, A., N. J. Lindsey, W. L. Ellsworth, and B. L. Biondi (2020). Comparison between distributed acoustic sensing and geophones: Downhole microseismic monitoring of the FORGE geothermal experiment, *Seismol. Res. Lett.* **91,** no. 6, 3256–3268, doi: 10.1785/0220200149.

Lindsey, N. J., H. Rademacher, and J. B. Ajo-Franklin (2020). On the broadband instrument response of fiber-optic DAS arrays, *J. Geophys. Res.* **125,** no. 2, 1–16, doi: 10.1029/2019JB018145.

Luo, B., G. Jin, and F. Stanek (2021). Near-field strain in distributed acoustic sensing-based microseismic observation, *Geophysics* **86,** no. 5, P49–P60, doi: 10.1190/geo2021-0031.1.

Mateeva, A., J. Lopez, H. Potters, J. Mestayer, B. Cox, D. Kiyashchenko, P. Wills, S. Grandi, K. Hornman, B. Kuvshinov, *et al.* (2014). Distributed acoustic sensing for reservoir monitoring with vertical seismic profiling, *Geophys. Prospect.* **62,** no. 4, 679–692, doi: 10.1111/1365-2478.12116.

Maxwell, S. C., C. K. Waltmann, N. R. Warpinski, M. J. Mayerhofer, and N. Boroumand (2009). Imaging seismic deformation induced by hydraulic fracture complexity, *SPE Reservoir Evaluation & Engineering*, Vol. 12, 48–52, doi: 10.2118/102801-PA.

Minson, S. E., and D. S Dreger (2008). Stable inversions for complete moment tensor, *Geophys. J. Int.* **174,** 585–592.

Nayak, A., and D. S. Dreger (2015). Source-type-specific inversion of moment tensors, *Bull. Seismol. Soc. Am.* **105,** no. 6, 2987–3000, doi: 10.1785/0120140334.

Nayak, A., and D. S. Dreger (2018). Source inversion of seismic events associated with the sinkhole at Napoleonville salt dome, Louisiana using a 3-D velocity model, *Geophys. J. Int.* **214,** 1808–1829, doi: 10.1093/gji/ggy202.

Nayak, A., J. Correa, and J. Ajo-Franklin (2024). Seismic magnitude estimation using low-frequency strain amplitudes recorded by DAS arrays at far-field distances, *Bull. Seismol. Soc. Am.* doi: 10.1785/0120230318.

Norbeck, J., and T. Latimer (2023). Commercial-scale demonstration of a first-of-a-kind Enhanced Geothermal System, Non-peer-reviewed manuscript submitted to EarthArXiv.

Norbeck, J., T. Latimer, C. Gradl, S. Agarwal, S. Dadi, E. Eddy, S. Fercho, C. Lang, E. McConville, A. Titov, *et al.* (2023). A review of drilling, completion, and stimulation of a horizontal geothermal well system in north-central Nevada, *Proceedings, 48th Workshop on Geothermal Reservoir Engineering Stanford University*, Stanford, California, 6–8 February 2023.

Pasyanos, M. E., D. S. Dreger, and B. Romanowicz (1996). Toward real-time estimation of regional moment tensors, *Bull. Seismol. Soc. Am.* **86,** no. 5, 1255–1269, doi: 10.1785/BSSA0860051255.

Petersson, N. A., and B. Sjogreen (2015). SW4-v1.18 Users Guide, available at https://github.com/geodynamics/sw4 (last accessed July 2017).

Reitman, N. G., and P. Molnar (2021). Strain and velocity across the Great Basin derived from 15-ka fault slip rates: Implications for continuous deformation and seismic hazard in the Walker Lane, California-Nevada, USA, *Tectonics* **40,** e2020TC006389, doi: 10.1029/2020TC006389.

Schumann, H., and G. Jin (2022). Inferring hydraulic connectivity of induced fractures in the near-wellbore region using distributed acoustic sensing-recorded tube waves excited by perforation shots, *Geophysics* **87,** no. 3, doi: 10.1190/GEO2021-0276.1.

Shapiro, S. A., O. S. Krüger, C. Dinske, and C. Langenbruch (2011). Magnitudes of induced earthquakes and geometric scales of fluid stimulated rock volumes, *Geophysics* **76,** WC55–WC63.

Shimony, E., and A. Lellouch (2024). Microseismic event location with dual vertical DAS arrays: Insights from the FORGE 2022 stimulation, *Seismol. Res. Lett.* **95,** no. 4, 2290–2304, doi: 10.1785/0220230128.

Sjogreen, B., and N. A. Petersson, 2012. A fourth order accurate finite difference scheme for the elastic wave equation in second order formulation, *J. Sci. Comput.* **52,** 17–48.

Song, F., and M. N. Toksoz (2011). Full-waveform based complete moment tensor inversion and source parameter estimation from downhole microseismic data for hydrofracture monitoring, *Geophysics* **76,** no. 6, WC103–WC116, doi: 10.1190/GEO2011-0027.1.

Stork, A. L., J. P. Verdon, and J. M. Kendall (2014). The robustness of seismic moment and magnitudes estimated using spectral analysis, *Geophys. Prospect.* **62,** no. 4, 862–878, doi: 10.1111/1365-2478.12134.

Strumia, C., A. Trabattoni, M. Supino, M. Baillet, D. Rivet, and G. Festa (2024). Sensing optical fibers for earthquake source characterization using raw DAS records, *J. Geophys. Res.* **129,** doi: 10.1029/2023JB027860.

Svarc, J. L., J. C. Savage, W. H. Prescott, and A. R. Ramelli (2002). Strain accumulation and rotation in western Nevada, 1993–2000, *J. Geophys. Res.* **107,** no. B5, 2090, doi: 10.1029/2001JB000579.

Thurber, C., and D. Eberhart-Phillips (1999). Local earthquake tomography with flexible gridding, *Comput. Geosci.* **25,** 809–818.

Titov, A., G. Binder, Y. Liu, G. Jin, J. Simmons, A. Tura, D. Monk, G. Byerley, and M. Yates (2021). Modeling and interpretation of scattered waves in interstage distributed acoustic sensing vertical seismic profiling survey, *Geophysics* **86,** no. 2, D93–D102, doi: 10.1190/geo2020-0293.1.

Titov, A., S. Dadi, G. Galban, J. Norbeck, M. Almasoodi, K. Pelton, C. Bowie, J. Haffener, and K. Haustveit (2024). Optimization of enhanced geothermal system operations using distributed fiber optic sensing and offset pressure monitoring, *Society of Petroleum Engineers Hydraulic Fracturing Technology Conference and Exhibition*, The Woodlands, Texas, 6–8 February 2024.

Utah FORGE (2020). Utah FORGE induced seismicity mitigation plan, *Report Prepared for U.S. Department of Energy*, Utah FORGE, University of Utah, Salt Lake City, Utah.

Vavryčuk, V. (2011). Tensile earthquakes: Theory, modeling, and inversion, *J. Geophys. Res.* **116,** no. B12, doi: 10.1029/2011JB008770.

Vavryčuk, V. (2014). Iterative joint inversion for stress and fault orientations from focal mechanisms, *Geophys. J. Int.* **199,** 69–77, doi: 10.1093/gji/ggu224.

Vera Rodriguez, I., and A. Wuestefeld (2020). Strain microseismics: Radiation patterns, synthetics, and moment tensor resolvability with distributed acoustic sensing in isotropic media, *Geophysics* **85,** no 3, KS101–KS114, doi: 10.1190/geo2019-0373.1.

Wadati, K. (1933). On the travel times of earthquake waves, Part-II, *Geophys. Mag.* **7,** 101–111.

Wang, C. Y., and R. B. Herrmann (1980). A numerical study of P-, SV- and SH-wave generation in a plane layered medium, *Bull. Seismol. Soc. Am.* **70,** no. 4, 1015–1036.

Wessel, P., W. H. F. Smith, R. Scharroo, J. Luis, and F. Wobbe (2013). Generic Mapping Tools: Improved version released, *Eos Trans. AGU* **94,** no. 45, 409–410, doi: 10.1002/2013EO450001.

Zhang, H., and C. H. Thurber (2003). Double-difference tomography: the method and its application to the Hayward Fault, California, *Bull. Seismol. Soc. Am.* **93,** no. 5, 1875–1889, doi: 10.1785/0120020190.

Manuscript received 1 May 2025
Published online 18 December 2025

Time-Variable Moment Tensor Inversion of Seismic Data Collected at Blue Canyon Dome

Andréa Darrh*[1], Leiph Preston[1], and Adrian Christian Stanciu[1]

ABSTRACT

We invert seismic data collected at Blue Canyon Dome, west of Socorro, New Mexico, to obtain a time-domain representation of the evolution of eight seismic sources from Blue Canyon Dome Phase II. This experiment consisted of eight chemical explosions (or shots), three with dry emplacements and five with wet emplacements. The three dry shots are co-located at depth with three of the wet shots. Seismic and distributed acoustic sensing data recorded at the site both show a polarity reversal in the dry shot data when compared with the wet shot data located at the same depth. This implies that there is a physical explanation for this polarity reversal because it is captured across two different data modalities. In addition, the moment functions (MFs) recovered from our inversions show source mechanisms consistent with the polarities present in the observed data. Inversion of 24 three-component seismic stations filtered in four frequency bands, 5–10, 9–15, 5–15, and 8–20 Hz, as well as inversions run using data from three different station geometries, resulted in an early-time net negative volumetric change in the MFs from the dry shots and a net positive volumetric change for the wet shots. The water in the near-source region, in which the wet shots were emplaced, appears to have a significant impact on the recovered yield for these shots.

KEY POINTS

- We invert seismic data for time-variable moment tensors to characterize seismic source parameters.
- The inversions recovered magnitudes and source evolution consistent with observed data polarities.
- Our inversions estimate source characteristics at local distances without a priori source time functions.

INTRODUCTION

An explosion is typically assumed to be composed of purely compressive energy radiating outward equally in all directions, resulting in higher amplitude *P*-wave arrivals and weaker *S*-wave arrivals recorded at seismic stations. Because earthquakes typically have higher *S*-wave amplitudes than *P*-wave arrivals, measurements of *P*- and *S*-wave amplitudes have historically been used to discriminate between earthquake and explosion sources (Taylor *et al.*, 1989; Kim *et al.*, 1993; Walter *et al.*, 1995; Fisk, 2006; Allmann *et al.*, 2008; Baruah *et al.*, 2016). However, there is a significant overlap between explosions and earthquakes when such discrimination tools are used, confounding the ability to differentiate between the source types (Ford and Walter, 2013; Stroujkova and Morozov, 2013; Rougier and Patton, 2015; Yang, 2016). Many factors can contribute to an explosion having the appearance of an earthquake with significant shear-wave energy in recorded seismic data. One such example is spall, in which the ground is upheaved by the explosion and falls back to the surface, resulting in vertically polarized shear waves and Rayleigh waves (Day *et al.*, 1983; Day and McLaughlin, 1991; Vorobiev, 2023). In addition, slip on near-source joints or pre-existing faults can result in significant shear energy (Wallace *et al.*, 1983; Day *et al.*, 1987; Stevens and Thompson, 2015). These "late-time" damages can result in observed seismic data different from the data that would typically be expected from an explosion and may result in a mischaracterization of the source (e.g., Stump, 1985; Patton, 1990, 2012; Patton and Taylor, 2011).

Historically, characterizing a seismic source is often done by inverting seismic data for a symmetric moment tensor matrix (e.g., Stump and Johnson, 1977; Dziewonski *et al.*, 1981; Ekström *et al.*, 2012; Pasyanos and Chiang, 2022). These inversions produce a time-independent moment tensor matrix in which a source time function (STF) is obtained by typically assuming a simple moment rate function (MRF), such as a delta or a triangle function, scaled by the moment tensor to describe the source. The inversion, therefore, is dependent

1. Sandia National Laboratories, Albuquerque, New Mexico, U.S.A., https://orcid.org/0000-0001-8560-2585 (AD); https://orcid.org/0009-0008-4905-2203 (LP); https://orcid.org/0000-0002-8768-2432 (ACS)

*Corresponding author: adarrh@sandia.gov

Cite this article as Darrh, A., L. Preston, and A. C. Stanciu (2025). Time-Variable Moment Tensor Inversion of Seismic Data Collected at Blue Canyon Dome, *Bull. Seismol. Soc. Am.* **116**, 624–647, doi: 10.1785/0120240268 on a simple function to describe the full complexity of the data being inverted. Thus, more complex sources, such as an explosion followed by slip on pre-existing joints, would not be accurately represented by a moment tensor inversion that has a predefined shape through time that is not allowed to vary in the inversion.

Recent work has been done to better characterize seismic sources by inverting for a time-varying moment function (MF) for each of the six unique components in the moment tensor, which describe the force couples comprising a seismic source. Time-varying moment tensor inversions can be conducted in either the frequency or the time domain. The frequency-domain approach involves inverting seismic data amplitude spectra for an STF amplitude spectra (Stump and Johnson, 1977, 1984; Yang *et al.*, 1999; Nakano *et al.*, 2008; Yang and Bonner, 2009; Yang, 2016; Kintner *et al.*, 2023). The STF spectra are then transformed into the time domain, resulting in an MRF or MF describing the moment tensor for a source at a given time. This implementation, therefore, can result in STFs that can be difficult to interpret without an additional step, such as implementing frequency content reconstruction via time-shifted elementary functions to better capture the characteristics of the unfiltered STF (Nakano *et al.*, 2008; Kintner *et al.*, 2023). The results of this inversion must assume elementary functions to estimate the unfiltered STF. Implementing the inversion in the time domain, however, allows for a direct estimation of the STF.

We implement a deterministic, regularized inversion similar to other studies (e.g., Poppeliers *et al.*, 2018; Poppeliers and Preston, 2020, 2021, 2022; Berg and Poppeliers, 2022) in which we invert directly for the six unique components of the MRFs used to describe a seismic source, but in the time domain (i.e., Preston and Eliassi, 2022; Harding *et al.*, 2023). We apply this inversion to seismic data collected at Blue Canyon Dome (BCD) near Socorro, New Mexico (Ingraham *et al.*, 2023). These data consist of eight chemical explosions with different emplacement conditions. We invert the seismic data recorded for each of these explosions to evaluate the source characteristics through time. We also introduce a method of reconstructing the source for bandlimited seismic data in which the corner frequency of the source is well above the frequency band present in the data.

EXPERIMENTAL DESIGN

The BCD experiments consisted of a series of subsurface tests conducted at the Energetic Materials Research and Testing Center near Socorro, New Mexico (Fig. 1), designed to investigate the effects of chemical explosions on geophysical properties (e.g., Ingraham *et al.*, 2023). The BCD testbed utilized various geophysical instrumentation, including subsurface and surface geophones and distributed acoustic sensing (DAS), to monitor seismic waves generated by downhole chemical explosions.

The host rock of the BCD site consists of rhyolitic rock with ~9 m of fanglomerate overlying welded rhyolitic tuff that extends at least ~46 m below the maximum depth of the ground zero (GZ) borehole (Bauer, 2021). There is a low-velocity zone that is apparent in borehole records at around ~50 m deep that extends for several meters, which is colloquially called the slow zone (Schneider *et al.*, 2024). The GZ borehole was 21.6 cm in diameter, with a casing depth of 24 m and a maximum depth of 76 m (Ingraham *et al.*, 2023). There were two phases to the experiments conducted at this site, Phases I and II, of which Phase II focused on varying emplacement conditions. The Phase II explosives all had an HMX/fluoropolymer composition, PBXN-5 (Robey *et al.*, 2023), and therefore had similar yields and were located at varying depths with either wet or dry emplacement (Table 1). During each shot, the explosive package was suspended in the borehole from a steel cable through a small hole in the wellhead with no backfilling or tamping (Ingraham *et al.*, 2023). Shots 1–3 were the "dry" shots in which the chemical explosive source was decoupled from the subsurface. Shots 4–8 were the coupled "wet" shots in which a water pump connected to the wellhead was used to maintain a constant flow of water through the GZ borehole. Shots 4, 7, and 8 were located at the same depths as the dry shots (Table 1). The bi-wing fracture, where shots 1 and 4 were located, is a near-vertical fracture caused by a previous experiment. Also caused by a previous experiment is the cavity damage where shots 2 and 7 were located, which is a cavity of at least 43.3 cm in diameter as the caliper used to measure the diameter of the borehole maxed out at this value. The virgin rock where shots 3 and 8 were located did not have previous experiments located at that depth (Schneider *et al.*, 2024).

In this study, we analyze seismic data from Phase II, which consisted of 57 shallowly buried Magseis Fairfield ZLand 3C nodes (at a depth of ~30.6 cm), operating at a sample rate of 1000 Hz, 49 of which were located within the bounds of our geologic model. The data were oriented with Z positive up and radial away from the source. Eight groups of geophones were co-located with the surface fiber cable to characterize the DAS response in the near and far field. Each group consisted of 4–5 3C Fairfield Zland Nodes with a maximum aperture of ~1.82 m. The seismic data were converted to physical units and gain corrected as well as band-pass filtered using an eighth-order Chebyshev filter between 5 and 15 Hz before being used in our inversion.

Over 1 km of fiber in a metal tube was deployed in a linear array encompassing both downhole and surface sections around eight monitoring boreholes. Standard single-mode and enhanced fiber optic (i.e., Silixa constellation) were utilized to record shot data between July 18 and 22 July 2022. The surface section was oriented approximately north-northwest–south-southeast across a 300 m distance, with an elevation change of approximately 5 m between the two end points

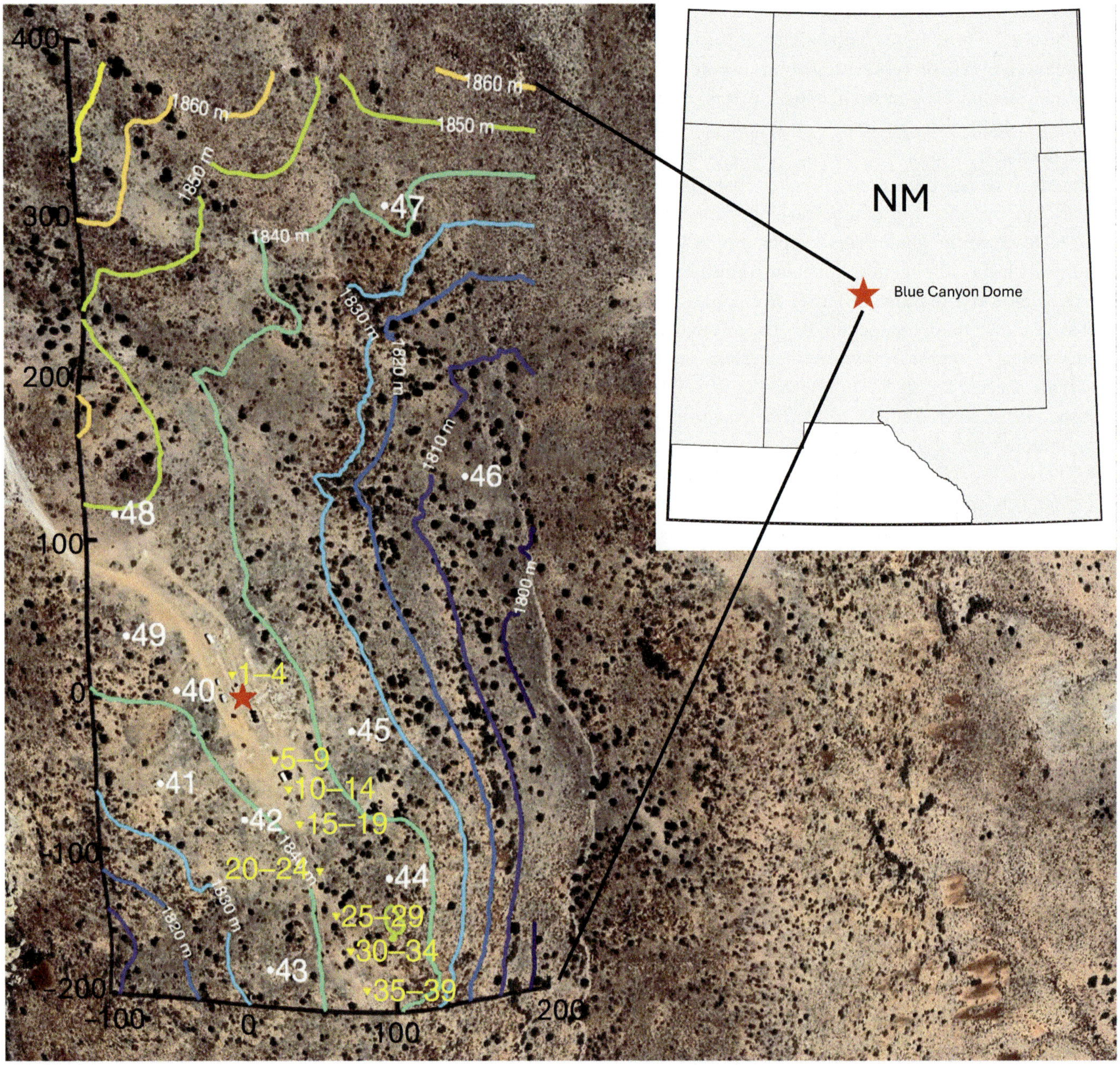

(see Fig. 1). Most of the cable was coupled to the ground using sandbags. Data were recorded at a sampling frequency of 40 kHz to maximize the dynamic range, with a spatial sampling of 1 m. The large volumes of data generated with these parameters required limiting the acquisition time windows to ~5 min around the shot times. For a gauge length of 2 m, the strain rate was averaged over a length of 2 m centered at each channel location. A linear correction was applied to raw amplitude data to convert it into values proportional to strain rate ($N \cdot m/m/s$). Timing was synchronized using the internal Global Positioning System clock connected to an external antenna, with timestamps recorded in UTC time. Several channels along the fiber were located using tap tests, and the location was interpolated for channels located between the tap test locations.

Figure 1. Map of Blue Canyon Dome located in New Mexico (NM), United States, and the Fairfield Zland 3C seismic station locations (Google Earth, 2023), there are eight groups of seismic stations which are co-located with the horizontal distributed acoustic sensing (DAS) cable, referenced herein as gradiometer stations, indicated by yellow inverted triangles, and labeled with the range of station numbers located in each gradiometer array. The axis shows the distance in meters away from ground zero, labeled as a red star; the non-gradiometer seismic stations are the labeled white dots, and the topography is shown as labeled contour lines.

METHODOLOGY

Inversion procedure

The inversion algorithm is constructed as a deterministic, regularized inverse problem, with the linear forward model equation describing the far-field seismic wavefield in the time

TABLE 1
Origin Time, Depth, Yield, and Emplacement for Each Shot

Shot	Origin Time (yyyy/mm/dd hh:mm:ss.sssssss) (UTC)	Depth (m)	Yield (kg TNT Equivalent)	Emplacement
Shot 1	2022/07/19 18:11:43.2291329	55.474	1.1474	Dry, bi-wing fracture
Shot 2	2022/07/19 20:33:34.2725697	43.967	1.1473	Dry, cavity damage
Shot 3	2022/07/20 16:31:47.6718671	37.948	1.1478	Dry, virgin rock shallow
Shot 4	2022/07/20 19:03:57.0934818	55.474	1.1463	Wet, bi-wing fracture
Shot 5	2022/07/21 17:26:41.3514921	51.054	1.1426	Wet, in slow zone
Shot 6	2022/07/21 19:58:51.4638557	49.530	1.1477	Wet, above slow zone
Shot 7	2022/07/21 21:30:39.4446339	43.967	1.1421	Wet, in cavity
Shot 8	2022/07/22 16:33:11.3620340	37.948	1.1466	Wet, virgin rock shallow

domain (Aki and Richards, 2002), assuming a point source,

$$d_k(\mathbf{x}',t') = \sum_{l=1}^{L} \int_{-\infty}^{\infty} g_{k,l}(\mathbf{x}',t';\mathbf{x},t) m_l(t) dt, \quad (1)$$

in which d_k is the seismic particle velocity at station k located at the observation point $\mathbf{x}' = [x',y',z']$ and source location $\mathbf{x}$. The Green's functions, $g_{k,l}$, are calculated for the lth source component located at $\mathbf{x}$ and at time t, recorded at the kth station, and m_l are the series of time-varying forces and/or force couples of which there are L total. We can simplify equation (1) to

$$\mathbf{d} = \mathbf{Gm} \text{ or } \begin{bmatrix} d_1(t) \\ d_2(t) \\ d_3(t) \\ \vdots \\ d_K(t) \end{bmatrix} = \begin{bmatrix} [\mathbf{G}_{1,1}] & [\mathbf{G}_{1,2}] & \cdots & [\mathbf{G}_{1,L}] \\ [\mathbf{G}_{2,1}] & [\mathbf{G}_{2,2}] & \cdots & [\mathbf{G}_{2,L}] \\ [\mathbf{G}_{3,1}] & [\mathbf{G}_{3,2}] & \cdots & [\mathbf{G}_{3,L}] \\ \vdots & \vdots & \ddots & \vdots \\ [\mathbf{G}_{K,1}] & [\mathbf{G}_{K,2}] & \cdots & [\mathbf{G}_{K,L}] \end{bmatrix} \begin{bmatrix} m_1(t) \\ m_2(t) \\ m_3(t) \\ \vdots \\ m_L(t) \end{bmatrix}, \quad (2)$$

in which $\mathbf{d}$ is a vector of length N containing the velocity time series at all K stations, $\mathbf{G}$ is the Green's functions matrix of size $N \times M$ in which each $\mathbf{G}_{k,l}$ matrix corresponds to the kth station and lth moment tensor component, and $\mathbf{m}$ is a model vector of length L composed of the six unique time-variable moment tensor M_{ij} rate functions. We use MRFs instead of MFs for our model because we find that solving for MRFs resulted in a more stable output due to the similarity in velocity units (Kintner *et al.*, 2023). In addition, the assumption of a zero mean, intrinsic to MRFs, allows the reference model in our model objective function formulation to be zero. The Green's function matrix for the kth station and lth moment tensor component is a lower triangular Toeplitz matrix representing the causal convolution with the lth moment tensor component:

$$\mathbf{G}_{k,l} = \begin{bmatrix} g_{k,n}(t_1) & 0 & \cdots & 0 & 0 \\ g_{k,n}(t_2) & g_{k,n}(t_1) & 0 & \cdots & 0 \\ g_{k,n}(t_3) & g_{k,n}(t_2) & g_{k,n}(t_1) & 0 & \vdots \\ \vdots & \vdots & \ddots & \ddots & 0 \\ g_{k,n}(t_T) & g_{k,n}(t_{T-1}) & \cdots & g_{k,n}(t_2) & g_{k,n}(t_1) \end{bmatrix}, \quad (3)$$

in which $\mathbf{G}_{k,l}$ is a $T \times T$ discrete convolution matrix, and T is the total number of samples in time of each waveform. With this formulation, there is an inherent assumption that there is no information past time sample T.

These Green's functions are calculated using a 3D finite-difference solver of the linear elastic wave equation, Parelasti (Poppeliers and Preston, 2021). We use a 3D model as an input to our Parelasti simulations, consisting of 11 layers following the topographic surface, the depths, and velocities of which are derived from a velocity well log at GZ (Fig. 2). Although this is an imperfect model, the scale of this survey is relatively small, with a maximum station offset of ~300 m, so a simple layered approximation of the geology is likely adequate for a first-order approximation of the wavefield.

This model has a node spacing of 1 m with a maximum frequency of 156 Hz, determined from the numerical dispersion relation given the requirement of at least ten grid nodes per wavelength, for synthetic data constructed from the simulated Green's functions. The seismic stations are located one node below the topographic layer, and the simulation is run for all six individual seismic source components.

We minimize an objective function consisting of a data objective function ϕ_d and a model object function ϕ_m that are regularized using a Lagrange parameter λ,

$$\min \phi = \phi_d + \lambda\phi_m = \|\mathbf{W_d}(\mathbf{Gm} - \mathbf{d_{obs}})\|^2 + \lambda\|\mathbf{W_m m}\|^2, \quad (4)$$

in which ϕ_d is the squared L2 norm of the product of the data weighting matrix and the data residual (observed minus predicted), and ϕ_m is the squared L2 norm of the product of the model weighting matrix $\mathbf{W_m}$ and the model. The data weighting matrix $\mathbf{W_d}$ is composed of a diagonal matrix that consists of a time-variable weighting function (Harding *et al.*, 2023), which begins at unity and downweights the data using a unit amplitude half-Gaussian with a standard deviation of σ_g, starting at a given time past the P-wave arrival pick for each station. The squared model weighting matrix is defined as $\mathbf{W_m^T W_m} = w_1^2\mathbf{I} + w_2^2\mathbf{L}^T\mathbf{L}$, representing a combined smallest and smoothest model norm with the smallest model weight w_1, smoothest model weight w_2, identity matrix, $\mathbf{I}$, and second-order finite-difference approximation of the Laplacian, $\mathbf{L}$. Matrix $\mathbf{L}$ is

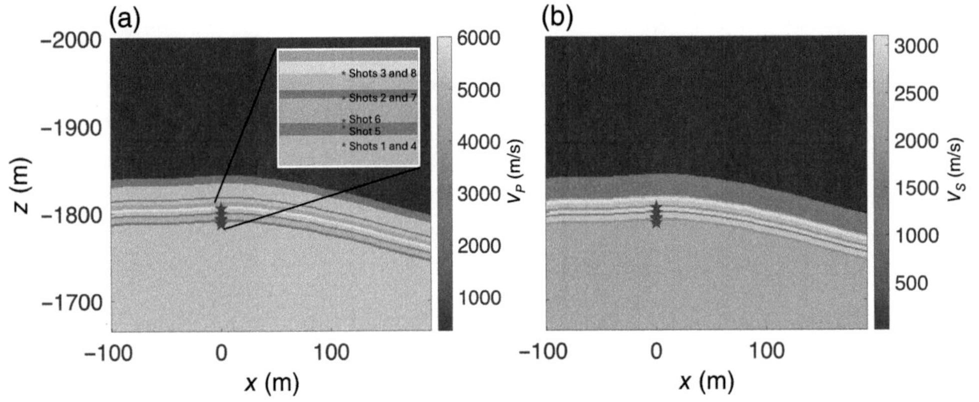

Figure 2. Cross-section of the velocities at the source location with depth, measured from sea level, labeled in meters on the vertical axis. Model velocities are selected using values from a velocity log at the source borehole. (a) *P*-wave velocities. (b) *S*-wave velocities. Sources are located at $x = 0$ m and denoted by red stars. The color version of this figure is available only in the electronic edition.

staggered at the length of each source component to prevent additional smoothing being applied to the first and last terms of adjacent source components. Taking the derivative of equation (4) with respect to $\mathbf{m}$ results in the solution:

$$\mathbf{m} = (\mathbf{G}^T\mathbf{W}_\mathbf{d}^T\mathbf{W}_\mathbf{d}\mathbf{G} + \lambda\mathbf{W}_\mathbf{m}^T\mathbf{W}_\mathbf{m})^{-1}\mathbf{G}^T\mathbf{W}_\mathbf{d}^T\mathbf{W}_\mathbf{d}\mathbf{d}_\mathbf{obs}. \quad (5)$$

We evaluate equation (5) for a range of λ values and select our output model through the use of the L-curve criterion.

Effect of filtering on the recovered MRF

Although the Green's functions are theoretically viable up to 156 Hz, the complexity of the real subsurface at the BCD site will limit the ability of our inversion to fit the data at higher frequencies than ~20 Hz because our earth model cannot capture the fine-scale variations that likely exist in the actual subsurface. Therefore, we need to limit the frequency content of our data to be within the range of frequencies our Green's functions, and subsequently our inversions, are sensitive to. For larger explosions, the corner frequency of the source can lie within this effective frequency band and we can directly recover an MRF without large filter effects. For very small explosions, such as the BCD explosions, filtering the data within this limited effective frequency band has the effect of only capturing a portion of the source at a much lower frequency than the true corner frequency of the source, effectively obscuring the true source characteristics. This limitation in frequency content results in an MRF with strong similarity to the impulse response (IR) of the filter used in the inversion, and an additional step is needed to reconstruct the higher-frequency MRF without the filter IR overwhelming the source information (Fig. 3).

The process to remove the IR can be demonstrated through a synthetic inversion (Fig. 3) in which the true MRF is modeled as a Mueller–Murphy source (Mueller and Murphy, 1971) with a corner frequency of 174 Hz convolved with our Green's functions to create synthetic data. We filter the synthetic data to 5–15 Hz using an eighth-order Chebyshev filter and are able to perfectly recover the synthetic data, but with an MRF that is dominated by the filter IR (Fig. 3a). Next, we up-sample the data using an antialiasing low-pass filter to a higher sample rate, 1200 Hz, which is selected to be well above the corner frequency of any realistically detectable source, assuming we do not know the exact frequency content of the true MRF. We then perform orthogonal matching pursuit (OMP), a greedy pursuit algorithm that is more efficient than other deconvolution methods like basic pursuit (Tropp and Gilbert, 2007), to recover the discrete impulses in time at which an IR is recovered by the inversion instead of the true, higher-frequency MRF, essentially a spiking deconvolution. OMP estimates the sparse representation of a signal given a representative "dictionary" of the wavelet convolved with the sparse points in time. For our purposes, we want to identify when in time and at what discrete amplitude the filter IR was recovered instead of the true MRF for each unique moment tensor component. We therefore construct a Toeplitz matrix using our filter IR as our dictionary $\mathbf{A}$,

$$\mathbf{A} = \begin{bmatrix} \mathrm{IR}_1 & 0 & \cdots & 0 & 0 \\ \mathrm{IR}_2 & \mathrm{IR}_1 & 0 & \cdots & 0 \\ \mathrm{IR}_3 & \mathrm{IR}_2 & \mathrm{IR}_1 & 0 & \vdots \\ \vdots & \vdots & \ddots & \ddots & 0 \\ \mathrm{IR}_6 & \mathrm{IR}_5 & \cdots & \mathrm{IR}_2 & \mathrm{IR}_1 \\ \mathrm{Pad} & \mathrm{Pad} & \cdots & \mathrm{Pad} & \mathrm{Pad} \end{bmatrix}, \quad (6)$$

in which IR_1 through IR_6 are all equal to the filter IR, numbered to show that the IR function is concatenated six times, one for each unique moment tensor component. In addition, zero padding (Pad) of length IR − 1 is added to the ends of the convolution matrix $\mathbf{A}$. We then use this dictionary for our OMP algorithm to get the sparse response o of our MRF (Fig. 3b).

To approximate the true MRF from the impulse at a discrete point in time, we reconstruct the MRF frequency so as to approximate the true MRF instead of an impulse at a discrete point in time. To do this, we calculate the amplitude spectrum of both the original recovered MRF contaminated with the IR and the amplitude spectrum of the IR. We then take the ratio of the original MRF and the IR amplitude spectrum and find the frequency that corresponds to the maximum ratio value between the two (Fig. 3c). In this synthetic example, this corresponds to

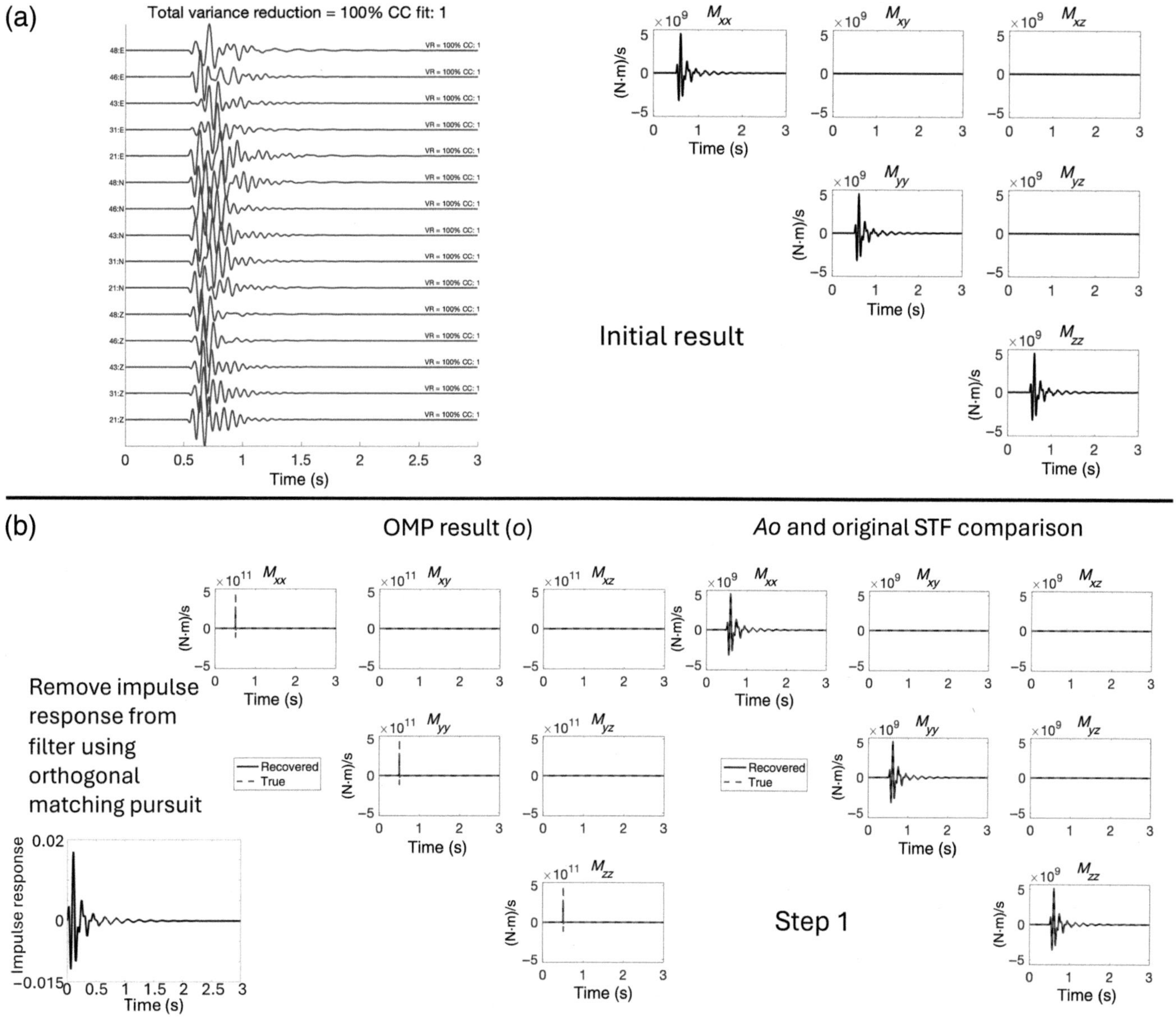

Figure 3. Process to remove the filter impulse response (IR) from an inversion using filtered synthetic data with a frequency band below the corner frequency of a source. (a) Initial inversion of synthetic data created by convolving Green's functions with a 174 Hz corner frequency Mueller–Murphy source, showing the moment rate functions (MRFs) contaminated by the filter IR. (b) Step 1 is the removal of the IR using orthogonal matching pursuit. (c) Step 2 is the process to reconstruct the corner frequency of the source and include the corner frequency in the reconstructed MRF. (d) The final result shows the reconstructed MRF and moment function (MF) after the IR has been removed. STF, source time function. The color version of this figure is available only in the electronic edition. (*Continued*)

103 Hz, which is lower than the true frequency, but the correct order of magnitude. We then convolve our sparse representation o with a Gaussian with unitary area at this frequency and with width $1/(\sqrt{2}f\pi)$ to obtain a reconstructed MRF. We also add in the residual between the original recovered MRF contaminated with the IR and the sparse signal convolved with the IR, Ao, scaled by the reciprocal of the norm of the IR to account for the fact that the convolution matrix composed of the IR is not orthogonal and therefore the inner product of the signal will not be preserved when the IR is convolved with the signal. This residual is added in to include any signal that was not part of the filter IR reconstruction but was still recovered in the initial inversion, resulting in the final reconstructed MRFs and MFs (Fig. 3d). This process does not retain the true amplitude of the MRFs, but is instead designed to respect the area under the curve of the reconstructed MRF so as to recover a realistic isotropic moment when integrating our MRF results to MFs, which are typically used to estimate yield and energy released.

Finally, we display these MFs on a fundamental lune (Tape and Tape, 2012, 2013). The fundamental lune allows for

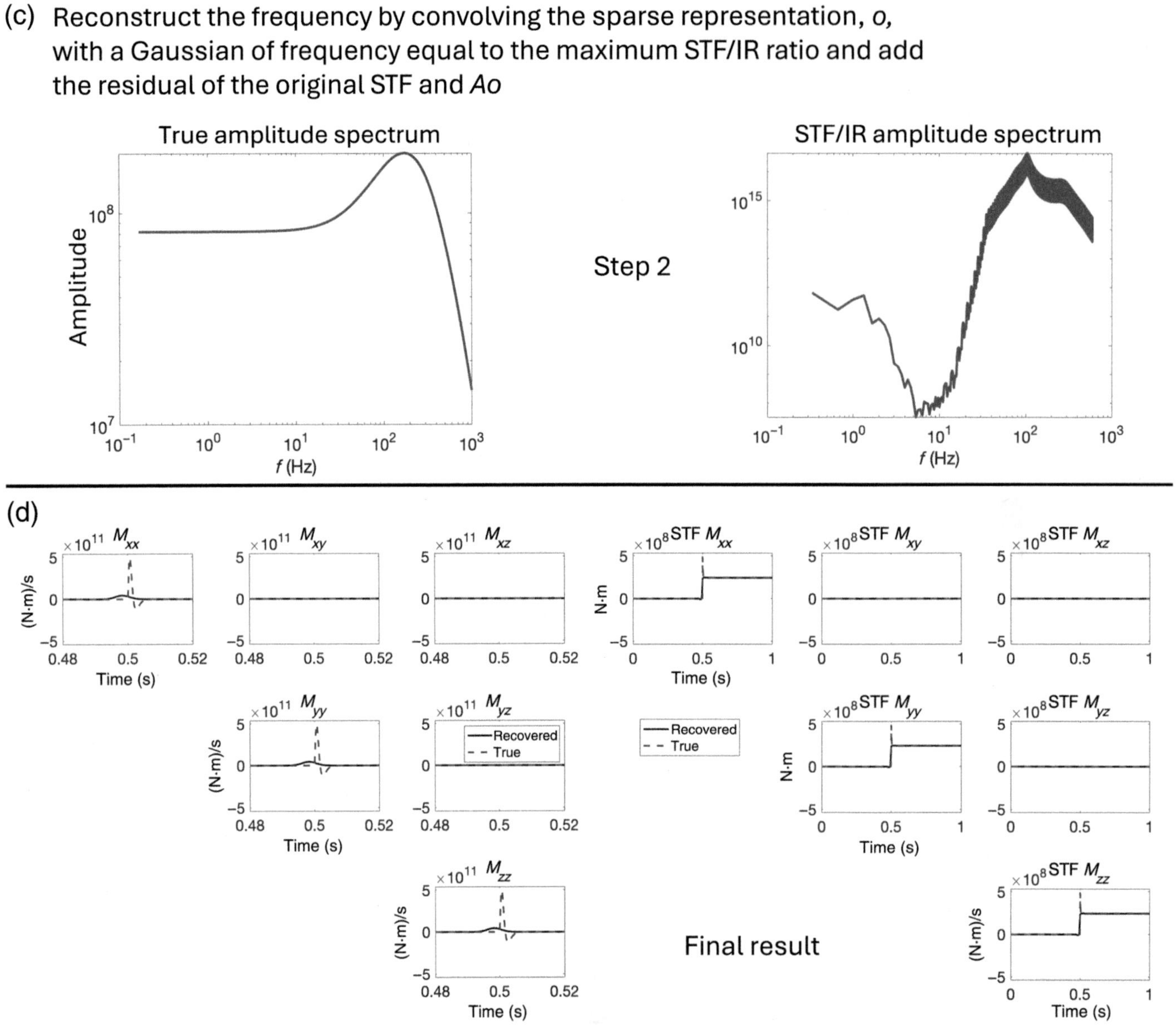

Figure 3. Continued

visualization of the source evolution through time by plotting the characteristic parameters of a source mapped onto a section of the unit sphere ranging from $-\pi/6$ to $\pi/6$ longitude and $-\pi/2$ to $\pi/2$ latitude. We also estimate the probability of the source mechanisms belonging to any one source type from multiple inversions on the fundamental lune by dividing the lune into bins with widths of approximately ~9°, summing the source mechanisms located within each bin, weighted by the variance reduction (VR) of the solution, and finally normalizing by the maximum weighted sum so the maximum probability of any given solution is 1.

Yield and energy analysis

In addition, for each of our results, we evaluate the ability of our inversion to recover an accurate isotropic moment by applying two different methods that use the isotropic moment as an input parameter. The first method uses a recently developed simplified yield relation (Ford *et al.*, 2023) that predicts yield W in kt from an isotropic moment M_0, bulk modulus κ, and gas porosity GP,

$$W = \kappa^{-1.4132} 10^{0.035626GP} M_0. \tag{7}$$

Because the scale of the BCD explosions is small, with a yield of ~1.14 kg TNT equivalent or ~4.8 MJ, and shots 4–8 are emplaced in water (Stanciu *et al.*, 2023), the assumption of the source region being primarily rock might be inaccurate because the water may have a large impact on the near-source characteristics. Therefore, we also use additional methods to compare the energy radiated from the explosion assuming different near-source material. The second method estimates the total radiated energy E_T of a vibrating sphere source in Joules, assuming a step function in radial stress,

$$E_T = \frac{\pi^2 f_c^3 M_0^2}{2\eta\rho\alpha^5}, \tag{8}$$

in which η is the ratio of the *S*-wave velocity over the *P*-wave velocity (β/α), f_c is the corner frequency, and ρ is density (Denny and Johnson, 1991). We evaluate the second method for a solid rhyolitic rock case and an averaged rock and water case.

As a third method, we estimate the total wavefield energy for a purely acoustic case because the water surrounding the charge may be a significant factor for such a small yield. Equation (8) is inappropriate in the limit $\beta \to 0$. Thus, we derive an analogous equation to equation (8) for the case $\beta = 0$ (Aldridge, 2000). We begin with the general kinetic energy density $\mathcal{K}(\mathbf{x},t)$ equation, which is true for an elastic or acoustic medium:

$$\mathcal{K}(\mathbf{x},t) = \frac{1}{2}\rho|\mathbf{v}(\mathbf{x},t)|^2, \tag{9}$$

in which $\mathbf{v}(\mathbf{x},t)$ is the particle velocity vector at position $\mathbf{x}$ and time t. We use the particle velocity from Aldridge (2000) for a homogeneous acoustic medium from an isotropic explosion, that is,

$$\mathbf{v} = \frac{M}{4\pi\rho}\left[\frac{1}{\alpha^3 r}w''\left(t-\frac{r}{\alpha}\right) + \frac{1}{\alpha^2 r^2}w'\left(t-\frac{r}{\alpha}\right)\right]\mathbf{e_r}, \tag{10}$$

in which M is the seismic moment of the explosion, $w(t-\frac{r}{\alpha})$ is the STF at retarded time, $\mathbf{e_r}$ is the unit vector in the radial, r is the direction, and prime symbols $'$ and $''$ indicate differentiation with respect to time. Using this particle velocity, equation (9) becomes

$$\mathcal{K}(\mathbf{x},t) = \frac{M^2}{32\pi^2\rho\alpha^6 r^2}\left[\left(w''\left(t-\frac{r}{\alpha}\right)\right)^2 + \frac{2\alpha}{r}w''\left(t-\frac{r}{\alpha}\right)w'\left(t-\frac{r}{\alpha}\right) + \frac{\alpha^2}{r^2}\left(w'\left(t-\frac{r}{\alpha}\right)\right)^2\right]. \tag{11}$$

Now integrating over space except for a small region near the source point to avoid the singularity there, we integrate from $r_{\min}$ to ∞ to obtain the partial kinetic energy,

$$K(t) = \int_{r_{\min}}^{\infty} 4\pi r^2 \mathcal{K}(\mathbf{x},t)dr = \frac{M^2}{8\pi\rho\alpha^6}\int_{r_{\min}}^{\infty}\left(w''\left(t-\frac{r}{\alpha}\right)\right)^2 + \frac{2\alpha}{r}w''\left(t-\frac{r}{\alpha}\right)w'\left(t-\frac{r}{\alpha}\right) + \frac{\alpha^2}{r^2}\left(w'\left(t-\frac{r}{\alpha}\right)\right)^2 dr. \tag{12}$$

Changing variables to retarded time, $\tau = t - \frac{r}{\alpha}$,

$$K(t) = \frac{M^2}{8\pi\rho\alpha^5}\int_{-\infty}^{t-r_{\min}/\alpha}(w''(\tau))^2 + \frac{2}{t-\tau}w''(\tau)w'(\tau) + \frac{1}{(t-\tau)^2}(w'(\tau))^2 d\tau. \tag{13}$$

We desire the total radiated kinetic energy at infinite time, so taking the limit $t \to \infty$ yields

$$K(\infty) = \frac{M^2}{8\pi\rho\alpha^5}\int_{-\infty}^{\infty}(w''(\tau))^2 d\tau. \tag{14}$$

At infinite time, the total radiated energy, E_w, is twice the kinetic energy due to energy equipartitioning, so

$$E_w = 2K(\infty) = \frac{M^2}{4\pi\rho\alpha^5}\int_{-\infty}^{\infty}(w''(\tau))^2 d\tau. \tag{15}$$

Now, we will assume a Gaussian STF; thus,

$$w(t) = e^{-(\pi f_p t)^2}, \tag{16}$$

in which f_p is the peak frequency of the source. Substituting this into equation (15) and making the substitution $x = \sqrt{2}\pi f_p t$ yields

$$E_w = \frac{M^2}{4\pi\rho\alpha^5}\frac{8\pi^3 f_p^3}{\sqrt{2}}\int_0^{\infty} e^{-x^2} - 2x^2 e^{-x^2} + x^4 e^{-x^2} dx. \tag{17}$$

Finally, after evaluating the integral assuming the peak frequency of the Gaussian function used in the derivation is approximate to the corner frequency (f_c) of the explosion of interest,

$$E_w = \frac{3M^2 f_c^3 \pi^2}{4\rho\alpha^5}\sqrt{\frac{\pi}{2}}. \tag{18}$$

We also calculate the averaged magnitude-squared coherence ($\mathcal{M}$) to identify the similarity of each nodal component to all others in the gradiometer array. The averaged magnitude-squared coherence of the ith east-component station ($\mathcal{M}_{E_i}$) against all other east-component station data would therefore be represented as

$$\mathcal{M}_{E_i} = \frac{1}{N-1}\sum_{N}^{i,j=1} C_{ij}(d_{E_i}, d_{E_j}), \text{ in which } i \neq j, \tag{19}$$

in which N is the number of stations, d_{E_i} and d_{E_j} are the eastern-component data at the ith and jth stations, respectively, and C_{ij} is the magnitude-squared coherence between the eastern component of the ith and jth stations as a function of time and frequency. This formulation is similarly defined for the north- and vertical-component data.

RESULTS

We will start with the results of our analysis of the polarity and coherence of the observations before proceeding to the results of our MRF inversions. We will then move to our investigation of the variability in our inversions due to station configuration and frequency content, and wrap up with results from the yield analysis of our MRF solutions.

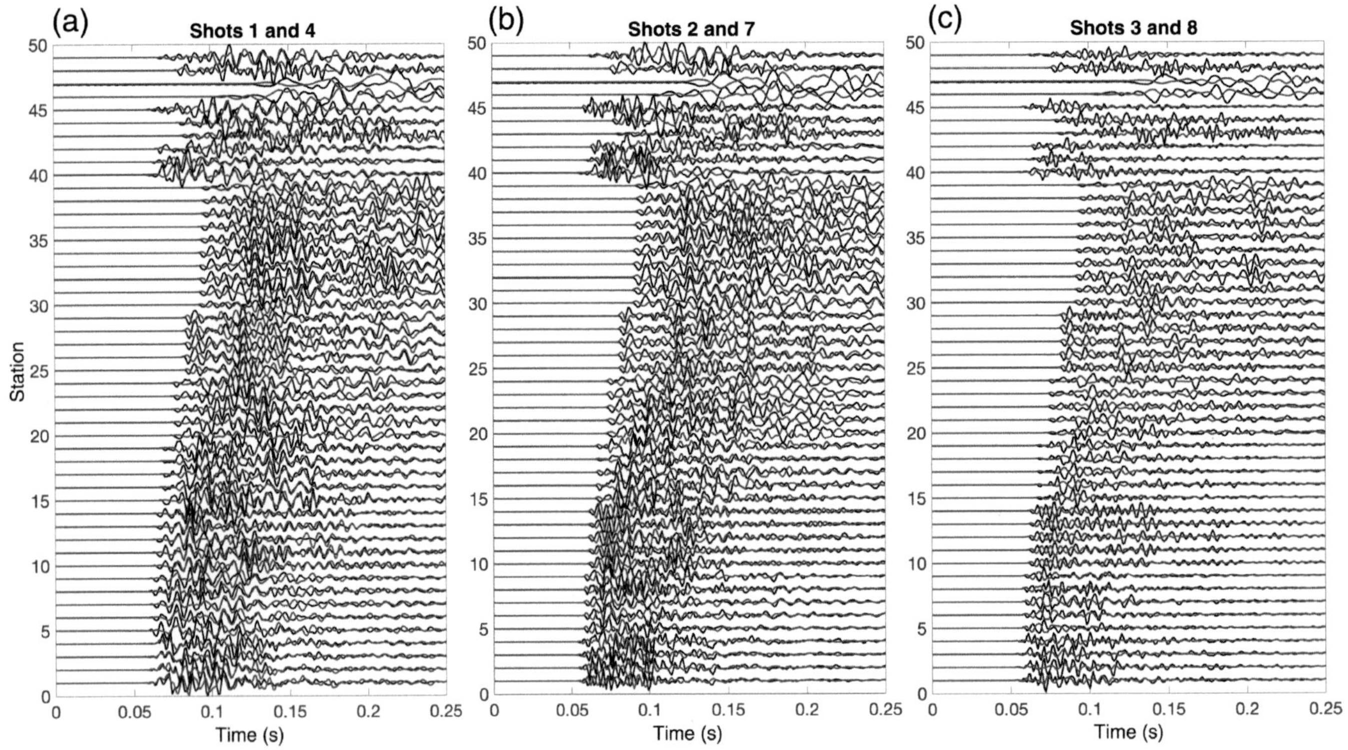

Figure 4. Comparison of vertical-component data normalized by the maximum for each trace for the co-located dry and wet shots starting at shot origin time. (a) Shot 1 (black) compared against shot 4 (red). (b) Shot 2 (black) compared against shot 7 (red). (c) Shot 3 (black) compared against shot 8 (red). The color version of this figure is available only in the electronic edition.

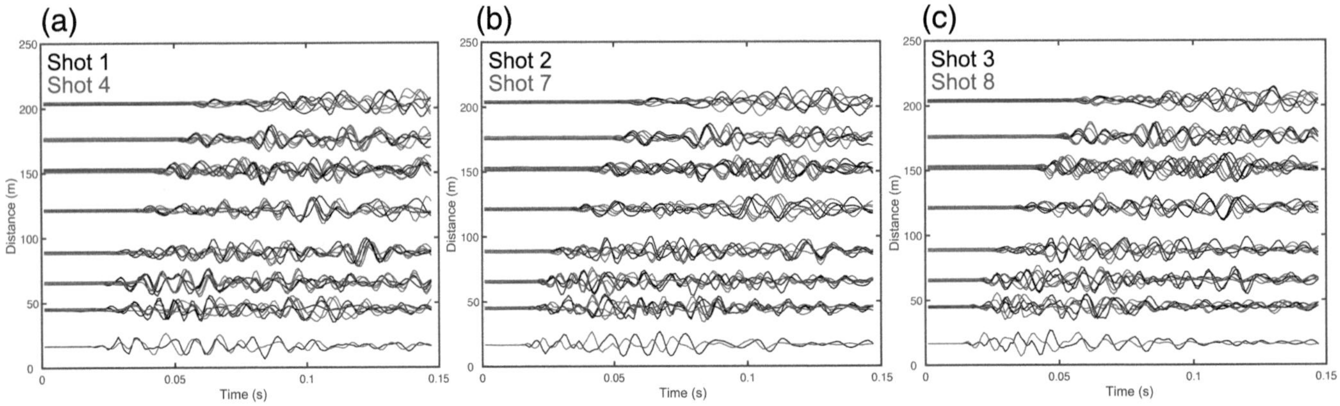

Figure 5. Comparison of the distributed acoustic sensing (DAS) dry and wet shot data channels, co-located at the node locations. (a) Dry shot 1 (black) and wet shot 4 (red) showing the polarity reversal between the dry and wet shots. (b) Dry shot 2 (black) and wet shot 7 (red). (c) Dry shot 3 (black) and wet shot 8 (red). The color version of this figure is available only in the electronic edition.

Waveform polarity and coherence

The raw data for all stations are shown in Figure 4 for the shots that were conducted at the same depths with different emplacement conditions. The depths of shots 1–3, which were dry, correspond to the same depths of wet shots 4, 7, and 8, respectively. All stations were left continuously monitoring between shots and were not moved or replaced; however, most of the stations in the dry shots have a reversed polarity for all three components when compared with the corresponding wet shots. This reversal in polarity is not the case for some stations, notably the closer offset stations in shots 1 and 3. This reversal is also present in the co-located DAS data recorded for these shots. Figure 5 shows the DAS data with the nodal horizontal component oriented toward GZ. The data were filtered with a

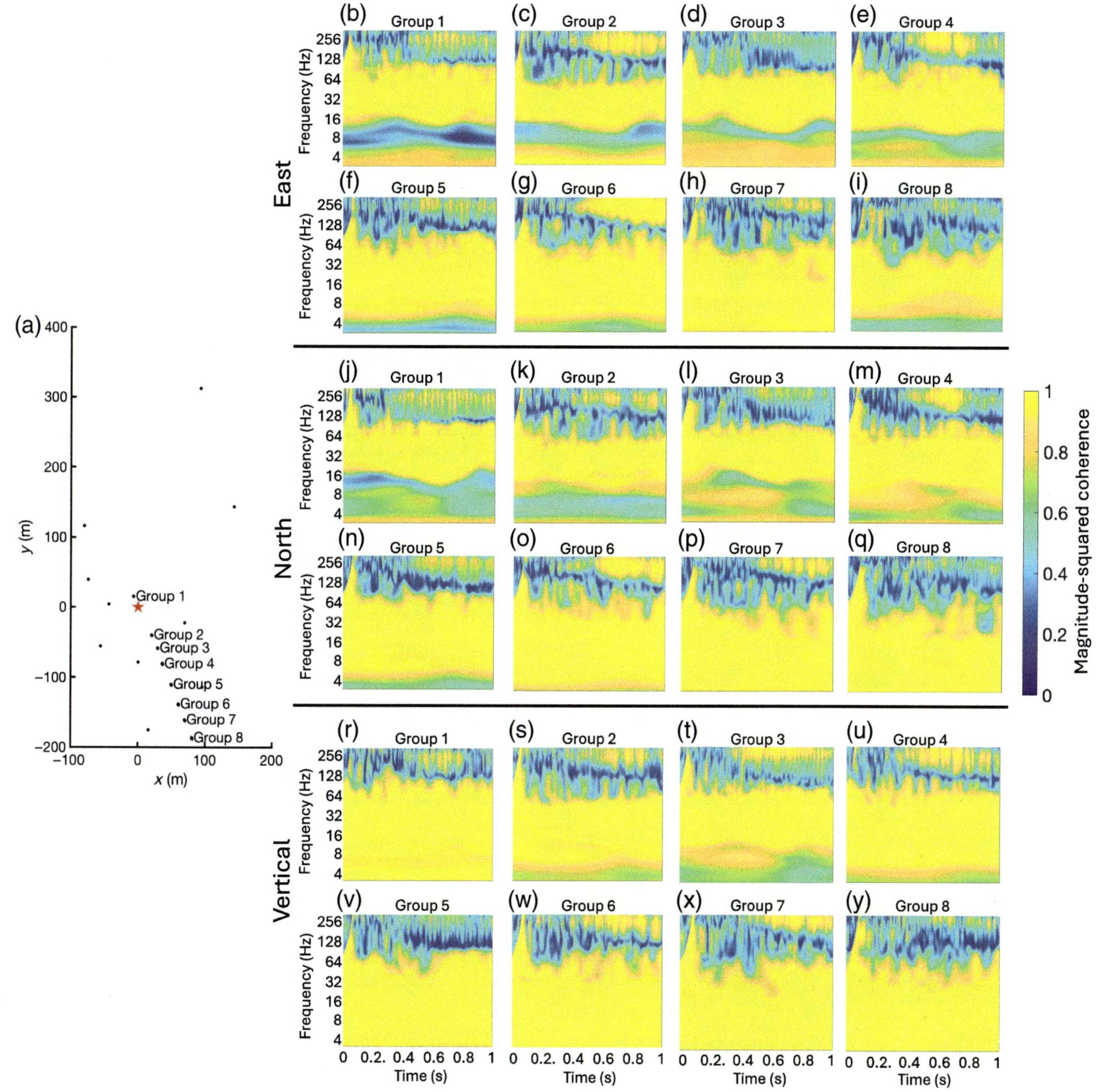

Figure 6. Average magnitude-squared coherence of the velocity data for shot 1 for each group of gradiometers. (a) Map showing the location of each gradiometer group where the magnitude-squared coherence was calculated. (b–i) Magnitude-squared coherence as a function of frequency through time for (b–i) east, (j–q) north, and (r–y) vertical components.

low-pass filter with a cutoff frequency of 100 Hz. The polarity reversal observed in the DAS data demonstrates consistent behavior across two different data modalities, suggesting a physical process near the source location is responsible for the observed polarity reversal in the dry shot data. In addition, there are large differences between data recorded at stations within the same gradiometer group when filtered below 16 Hz, notably at the gradiometer groups located closer to the source. This incoherency is present for all shots, and we show the average magnitude-squared coherence (equation 19) of the east-, north-, and vertical (Fig. 6)-component data of each gradiometer group as a function of frequency and time for shot 1 as a representative case. Figure 6 shows a region of high coherence for frequencies greater than 16 Hz and less than ~120 Hz. The coherence below 16 Hz is low at closer offset stations but increases in magnitude below 16 Hz with increasing offset. At larger offsets, the bottom of the coherence band lowers to ~6 Hz for the east components of group 5 (Fig. 6e,n), and then ~4 Hz for groups 6 and 8 (Fig. 6g,i).

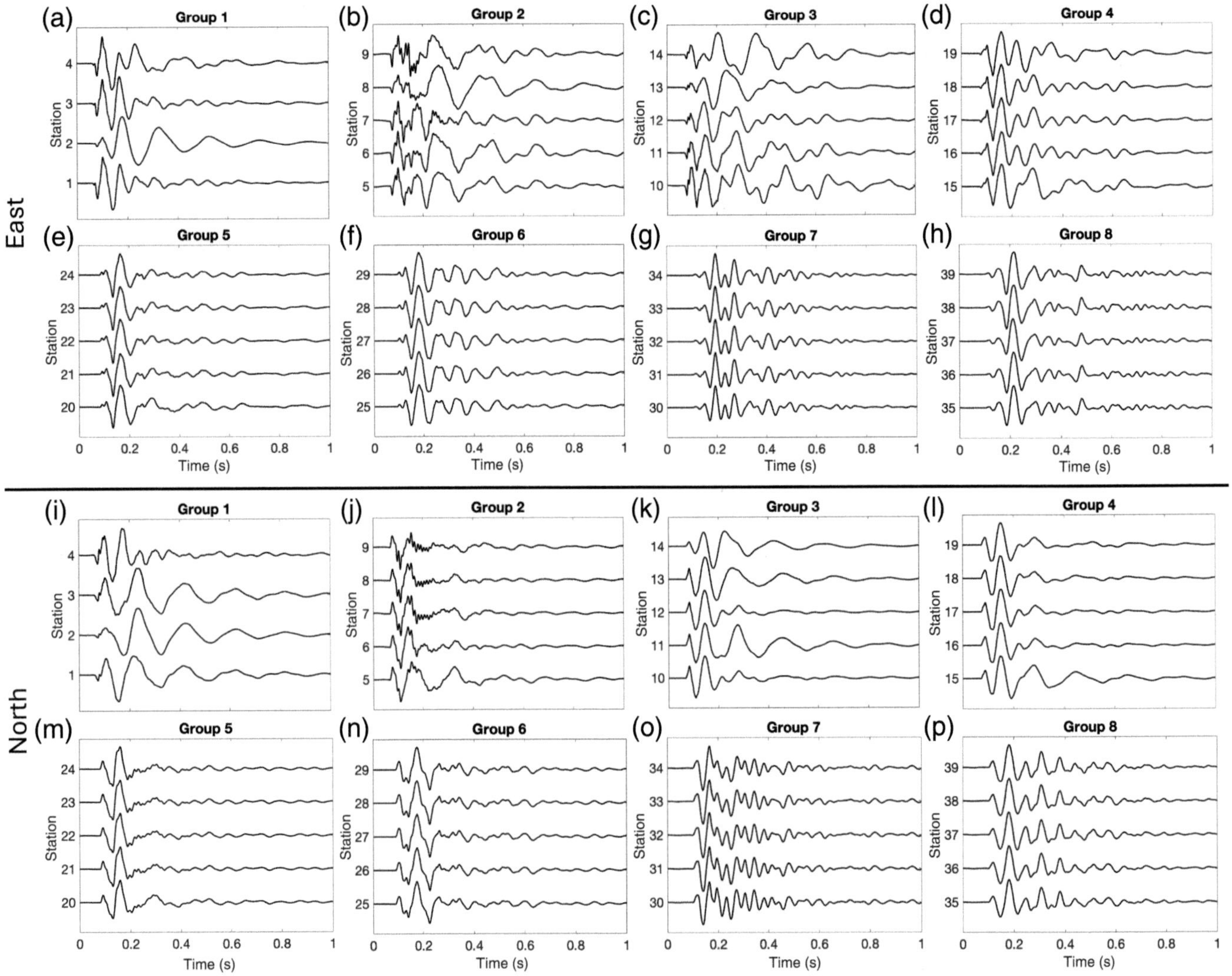

Figure 7. 5–15 Hz filtered (a–h) east- and (i–p) north-component data for shot 1 showing the variation in gradiometer groups at closer offsets.

In addition, the north-component coherence (Fig. 6j–q) follows a similar trend with increasing offset, with higher coherence in frequencies below 16 Hz. This trend is consistent for all horizontal-component data and all shots, with the closer offset stations more incoherent at lower frequencies and the farther offset stations more coherent at frequencies less than 16 Hz. The vertical-component data for all shots do not display this low-frequency incoherency to the same extent as the horizontal-component data (Fig. 6r–y). The vertical-component data for shot 1 and other shots have slightly lower coherence in the first four gradiometer groups below 16 Hz; however, the vertical-component coherence below 16 Hz is generally higher for all gradiometer groups when compared with the horizontal-component coherence, and around 1 for gradiometer groups located farther from the source (Fig. 6v–y).

To evaluate if any specific stations were consistently different, we examined the data for each gradiometer group filtered using a sixth-order Chebyshev filter from 5 to 15 Hz (Fig. 7). For all shots, the gradiometer groups with farther offsets have consistently coherent waveforms for all shots. Some stations in the gradiometer groups closer to the source are noticeably different from others, with some stations having different lower- (station 2, Fig. 7a) or higher-frequency (station 9, Fig. 7a and station 4, Fig. 7i) content than others. The same stations are not consistently variable between different shots, which, if they were consistently variable, would indicate an instrument problem. This instead implies that there is some degree of randomness in the seismic data recorded closest to the source in this frequency band.

Inversion results

Because of this variability, we limit our station selection to stations at least 120 m away from the source: stations 21–39, 43, 44, 46, 47, and 48, outside the range where the incoherency is occurring. We filter our data to a frequency band of 5–15 Hz using an eighth-order Chebyshev filter, resample our data and Green's functions to 200 samples per second, and invert for all six unique components of the moment tensor. We use the smallest model weighting parameter (w_1) of 10^{-5}, a smoothest model weighting parameter (w_2) of 10, and weight our data and Green's function matrix by the square root of the offset to encourage the inversion to fit all stations equally. We also use a time window of 0.1 s after the *P*-arrival pick, picked using a standard short-term average/long-term average algorithm with a Gaussian half-width of 0.8 s, therefore applying a slight taper to the later arrivals to encourage the inversion to fit the first arrivals. We always compare our predicted data from the inversion with the observed data without the taper to ensure that the later arrivals within the taper are captured in our predicted data. We invert 2 s of data to estimate how the source changes in that time. Although the corner frequency for shots this size is high, ~0.2–0.5 kHz and therefore on the order of milliseconds in duration, the signal observed at the receivers will be a low-passed version of that signal due to the signal traveling through the Earth. In addition, attempting to invert a signal less than a second would require very precise knowledge of the model that the Green's functions are generated from, information which is not feasible to obtain for most applications. Finally, traditional moment tensor inversions assume time invariance and recover a scalar value, therefore inherently assuming a zero-frequency low-pass filter. Given the previous, the choice of a two-second duration for recovering an MRF, while longer than a signal at the source corner frequency, is still a representative signal for what we could theoretically resolve in this frequency band, and which can be improved through the removal of the IR. The full predicted and observed data results for shot 1 are shown (Fig. 8), with the predicted data opacity corresponding to the time-variable weighting function applied in the inversion. The initial arrivals are fit well for the gradiometer stations 21–39, with the lowest VR for the vertical component at 33.6% and the correlation coefficient (CC) fit at 0.61, a VR of 31.7% and CC fit of 0.57 for the north-component data, and a VR of 37.7% and CC fit of 0.71 for the east-component data. The highest VR for the non-gradiometer stations is 74.3%, 29.2%, and −39.9% for the vertical-, north-, and east-component data, respectively. Station 48 is the best fit for the non-gradiometer vertical (VR: 74.3%), and north data (VR: 29.2%), and the next higher stations have a VR of 5.41% for the vertical-component data (station 46) and 8.3% for the north-component data (station 44).

The observed and predicted data for each shot are shown in Figure 9 for the three-component waveforms from station 44, along with a station in each linear gradiometer array. Shots 2–8 have similar data fits as shot 1, with the gradiometer data consistently containing the best data fits, with the lowest VR out of all shots at 12.5% for station 21:E in shot 5 (Fig. 9e) and CC fit at 0.48 for station 31:E in shot 3 (Fig. 9c). However, generally the VR and CC fits are reasonable for the stations as a whole, resulting in a total VR of 41.1% (Fig. 9d) to 53.5% (Fig. 9g) and CC fits of 0.66 (Fig. 9b) to 0.75 (Fig. 9g), indicating that the inversion is doing a good job fitting the phase with higher CCs closer to the maximum value of 1, but may be under- or overestimating amplitudes, likely within the non-gradiometer stations which have lower VR values.

The MRFs output from the OMP inversion are integrated and shown as MFs alongside their representation on a fundamental lune (Fig. 10). We sample the MFs in time using 20 equally spaced time intervals of length 0.08 s spanning from 0.01 to 2 s (red dots at the top of Fig. 10). The MFs for each component in these time intervals are averaged, and the resulting moment tensor is plotted on the fundamental lune. The dry shots 1–3 all start in the negative portion of the lune, with shot 2 resulting in the most negatively isotropic solution. The wet shots 4–8, all plot starting in the positive portion of the lune, with shot 8, the wet shot located at the same depth as dry shot 3, the most positively isotropic. Interestingly, each of the co-located dry and wet shots appears to show opposite behavior. Shot 1 starts negative, crosses a double couple (DC), and ends near a positive linear vector dipole (LVD)/crack solution (Fig. 10i). Shot 4 starts positive, near DC, moves toward a negative LVD solution, and ends near DC. Shots 2 and 7 both converge around a near-crack solution, with shot 2 a negative crack to near LVD solution (Fig. 10j) and shot 7 a positive LVD solution (Fig. 10o). Shot 3 moves toward a more negative solution (Fig. 10k) and shot 8 moves toward a positive solution (Fig. 10p). Shots 5 and 6 are between a positive LVD and DC solution (Fig. 10m,n).

Inversion variability

In addition to the results displayed in the previous section, we also run our inversion with observed data filtered with varying frequency bands, as well as using different station combinations to estimate the uncertainty in the STFs. We selected three frequency bands, 5–10, 9–15, and 8–15 Hz, to evaluate the inversion variability, which are subsets of and expand the upper frequency range of previous runs (5–15 Hz). We also vary the stations used in the inversion while filtering the data using a frequency band of 5–15 Hz. These station combinations use: (1) every other gradiometer station in the inversion: "every other" (stations 21, 23, 25, 27, 29, 31, 33, 35, 37, 39, 43, 44, 46, 47, and 48); (2) all non-gradiometer seismic stations: "Non-Grad." (stations 43, 44, 46, 47, and 48); and (3) one gradiometer station per gradiometer group: "1 Grad." (stations 24, 29, 34, 39, 43, 44, 46, 47, and 48). We show the recovered MRFs from each inversion in Figure 11, as well as the probability of the location of each MF (the integrated MRF) result on the fundamental lune. All MRF results are scaled in opacity by the squared average VR of each inversion result; therefore, darker solutions indicate a higher VR percent and better fit.

The MRFs recovered by each inversion are similar in phase, with impulses recovered at similar times and amplitudes in the early portions of the MRF. Generally, for each shot, there are two consistent impulses recovered at ~0.01 and 0.1 s, with some shots and moment tensor components containing more

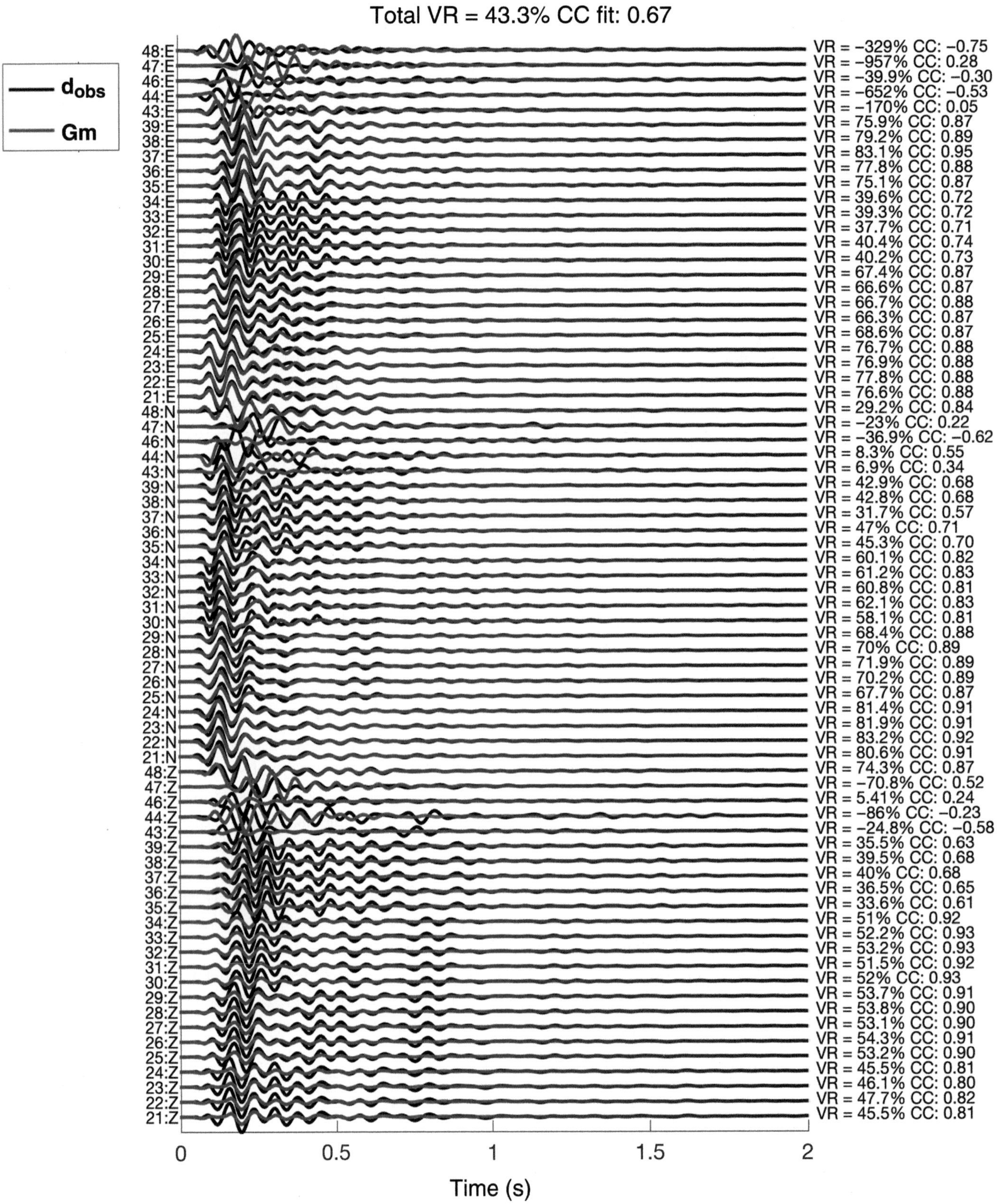

Figure 8. Predicted (red) and observed (black) data for shot 1 for each station component (y axis). Variance reduction (VR) and correlation coefficient (CC) fit are listed to the right of each waveform. The color version of this figure is available only in the electronic edition.

impulses around these times. For shots 1, 2, and 3, the first impulse is negative for M_{xx} (Fig. 11a–c). For shots 1 and 2, the first impulse is larger in amplitude for M_{yy} and M_{zz}, followed by a smaller, negative impulse at around 0.1 s. Shot 3 is similar but is missing the first impulse in M_{yy} (Fig. 11c). In

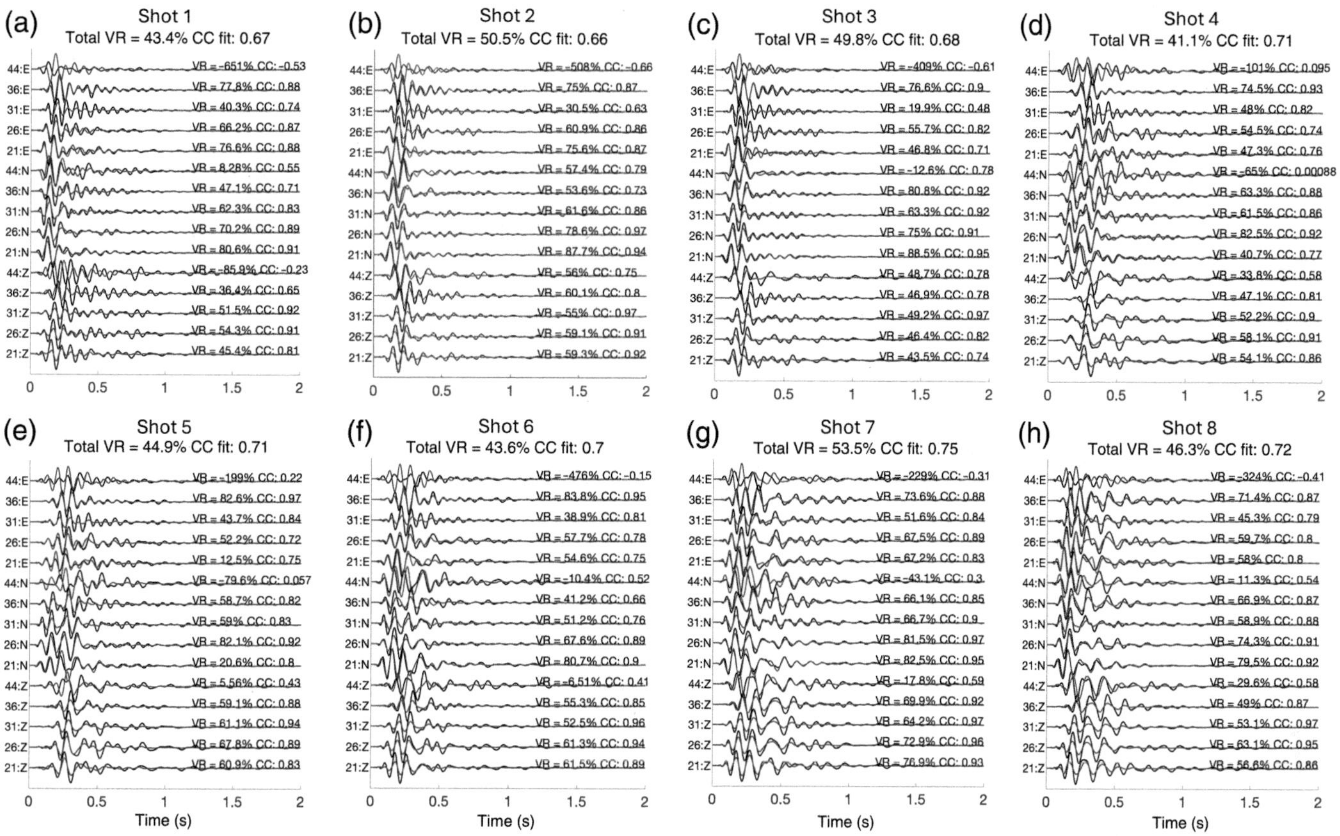

Figure 9. Predicted (red) and observed (black) data for every fifth station with station number and component shown on the y axis, starting from station 21 for shots 1–8. The color version of this figure is available only in the electronic edition.

addition, there are often negative impulses recovered surrounding the 0.1 s impulse, which, when integrated to an MF, pull the solution into the negative at late times for shots 2 and 3. This indicates that for the shots which display negative isotropic results, we do recover an explosion-like IR initially at 0.01 s, but a later, possibly lower-frequency collapse-like event occurring at around 0.1 s results in an overall negative source mechanism. Shot 4 has a slight positive first impulse for M_{xx} and M_{zz}; however, M_{yy} is missing the first impulse at 0.01 s (Fig. 11d). For shot 4, there is a large negative impulse at 0.1 s and a slight positive at 0.15 s for the diagonals. M_{zz} in shots 5–8 is the largest amplitude component, which has a positive impulse recovered at ~0.01 s for shots 5–7 (Fig. 11e–g). Shot 8 is largely missing the 0.01 s impulse, with the first impulse for most inversions coming in positive for all three diagonal components at 0.06 s instead. The inversion using only seismic data from outside the gradiometer groups is the only solution that recovers a negative first impulse for M_{yy} and M_{zz} and is the lone solution plotting solely in the negative portion of the lune with a low VR (Fig. 11h).

For the majority of the inversions, the fundamental lune representations of the STFs cluster in specific areas without much spread. Shot 1 generally starts at a positive crack solution or near DC, passes through DC, and ends at negative crack, with the solutions with the highest probability plotting in the negative portion of the fundamental lune (Fig. 11a). All solutions for shot 2 (Fig. 11b) plot in the negative portion of the lune, with the highest probability solution plotting just above negative isotropic. The majority of the solutions for shot 3 (Fig. 11c) are clustered in the negative portion of the lune. Two low VR runs, the one station per gradiometer group inversion (VR: 32.9%), as well as the inversion using only seismic data from outside the gradiometer groups (VR: 33.5%), plot toward the positive LVD and positive crack solution. Shot 4 (Fig. 11d), which is the wet shot located in the bi-wing fracture at the same depth as the dry shot 1, mirrors the source mechanisms of shot 1. In shot 4, the recovered STFs generally start negative or near DC and move to either a positive or negative crack. The highest total VR value for the inversion runs for shot 4 is the inversion using data filtered from 5 to 10 Hz, which results in a VR of at 68.97% and ends at DC. Except for two recovered STFs, the inversion solutions for shot 5 plot in the positive portion of the fundamental lune (Fig. 11e), with most just above DC. The highest VR inversion solutions for shot 6 (Fig. 11f) plot just above DC, similar to shot 5. Shot 7 (Fig. 11g), which was located at the same depth as the dry shot 2, resulted in recovered source mechanisms entirely in the positive portion of the fundamental lune. The cluster of solutions for shot 7 is a near-mirror image of the source mechanisms recovered for shot 2, which plot in the negative area of

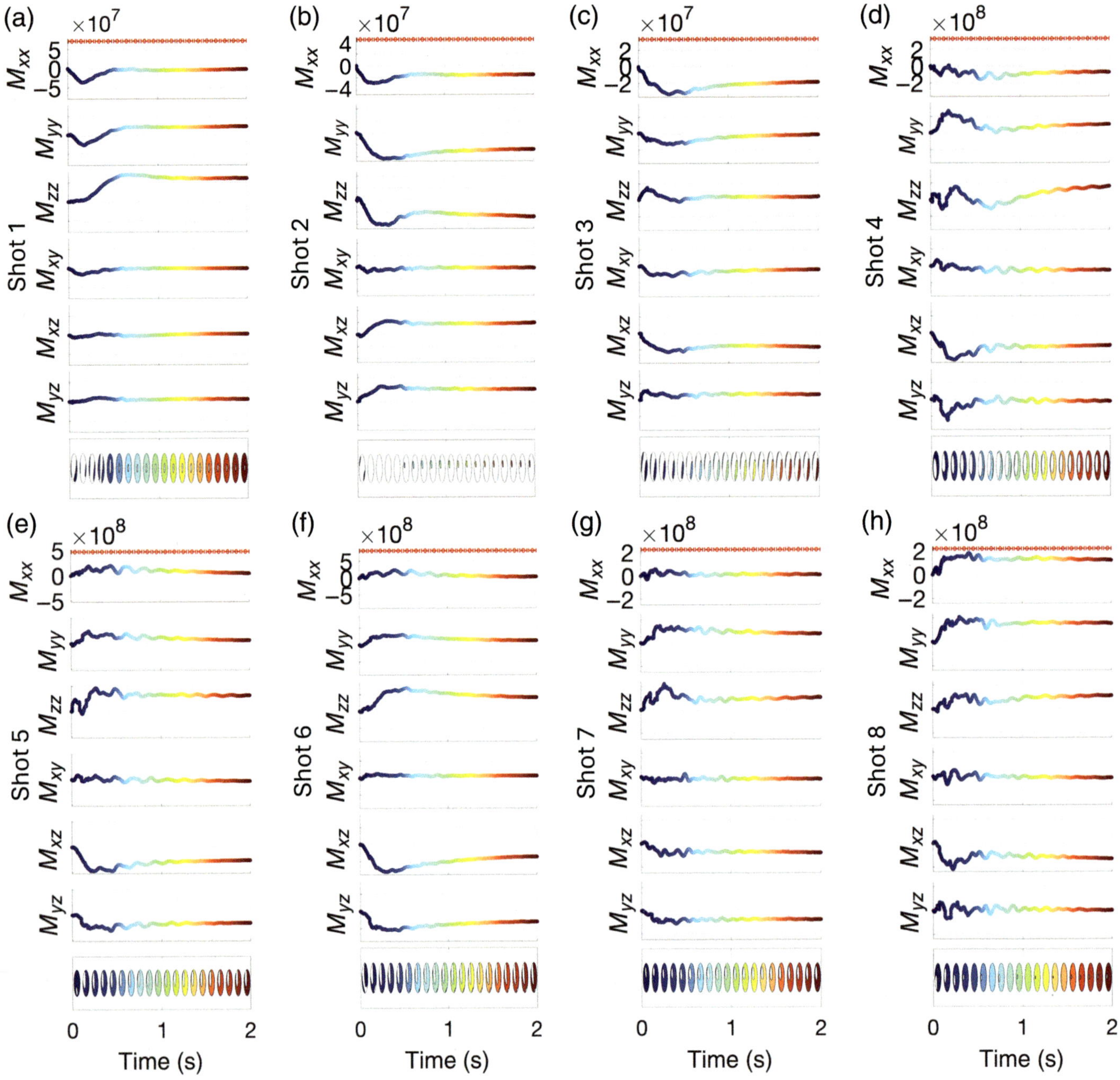

Figure 10. MF results and their representation on the fundamental lune. (a–h) MF solutions for shots 1–8 showing the six unique moment tensor components plotted in N · m using equivalent axes for components within the same shot, as well as the focal mechanism plot representations of the MF through time. A white or empty focal mechanism plot is indicative of an implosion; a solidly colored focal mechanism plot is indicative of an explosion. (i–p) Fundamental lune plots for shots 1–8 showing the dry shots, 1–3, to plot starting in the negative portion of the fundamental lune, and the wet shots, 4–8, plotting in the positive half of the fundamental lune. The points in time on the lune correspond to the average of the red bars shown at the top of M_{xx} in (a–h). CLVD, compensated linear vector dipole; ISO, isotropic; LVD, linear vector dipole. *(Continued)*

the lune. Finally, the highest VR solutions for shot 8 plot on the positive side of the fundamental lune, to the right near the positive crack solution, with the maximum total VR for these inversion runs at 50.2%. Similar to shots 2 and 7, shot 8 (Fig. 11h), which was at the same depth as shot 3, is also a near-mirror image of the recovered source mechanisms for shot 3. The lower VR solutions that plot in the negative portion of the fundamental lune for shot 8 are the 1 gradiometer station per gradiometer group inversion (VR: 31.6%), as well as the inversion using only seismic data from outside the gradiometer groups (VR: 26.7%).

To estimate the variability of the recovered STFs for each inversion, we also calculate the average CC for each moment tensor component against the same moment tensor

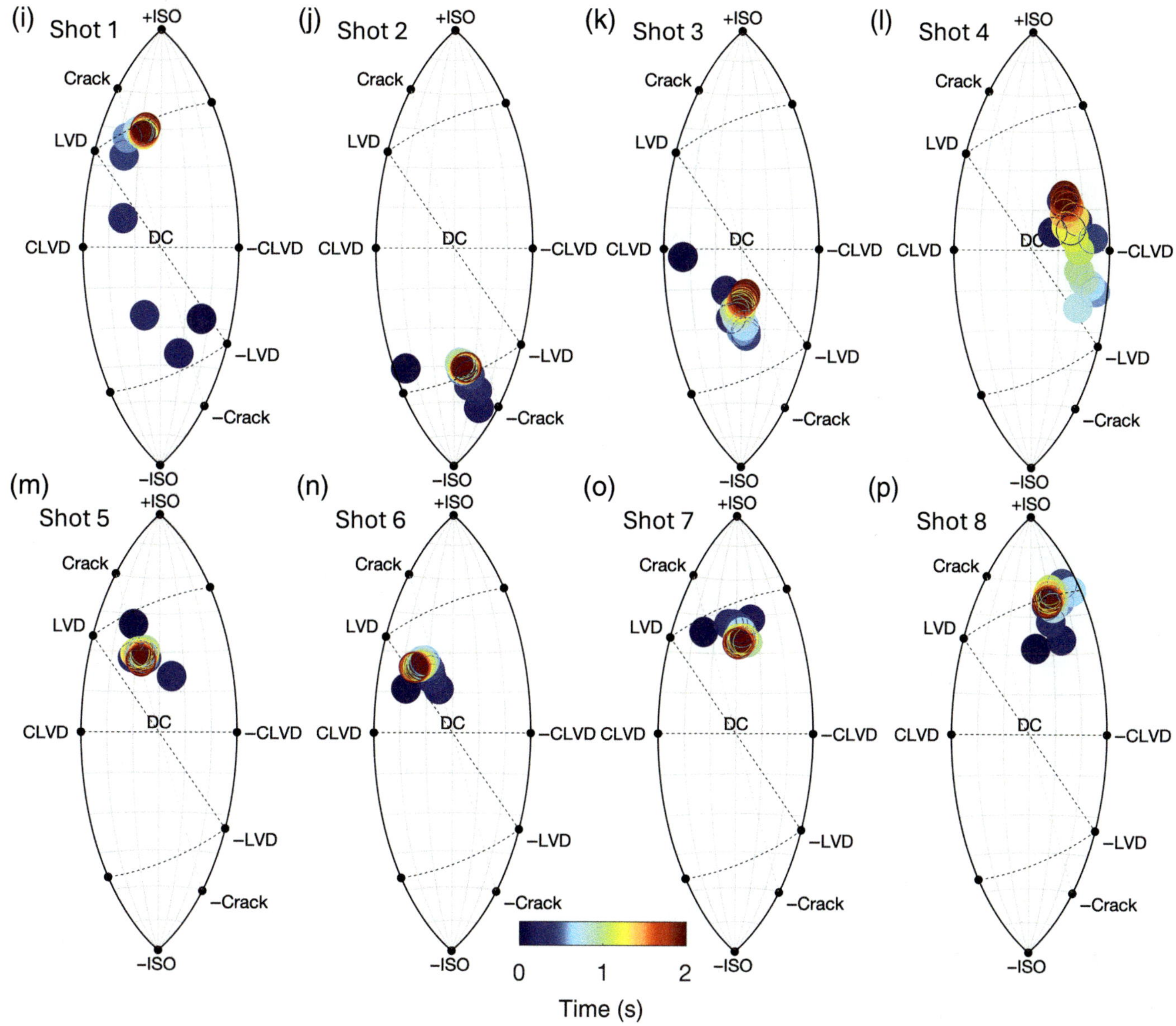

Figure 10. Continued

component from other inversion runs for a given shot. This is done for all inversion runs as well as for the varying frequency and station geometry runs (Fig. 12).

When correlated against the other inversions, the variable station inversions (Fig. 12c) were the most similar and consistent with each other, with CCs generally above 0.4 for the off-diagonal components and for the first three shots for the diagonal components. This indicates that even with different station configurations, the inversion was able to recover similar moment tensor solutions. M_{yy} has the lowest CCs, along with M_{xx} and the one Grad. solution for shot 8 in M_{zz}, which was inconsistent with the other solutions and poorly fit the data. The variable frequency runs (Fig. 12c) have a lower CC due to different phase information in each of the frequency bands; however, 9–15 Hz generally has the highest CCs, occasionally overtaken by 8–20 Hz in the diagonal components; 5–10 Hz has the lowest CC for most shots, generally, and is often negatively correlated and therefore not visible within the limits (Fig. 12b). This is likely due to the incoherency in the seismic stations, which can occasionally extend above 5 Hz even in the larger offset stations (Fig. 6f,g,i,n). The CCs in Figure 12a, which are calculated using all runs, follow the same trends as in the variable frequency inversion and the variable station inversion runs CC comparisons (Fig. 12b,c).

To evaluate the ability of the inversion to recover a stable solution from disparate groups of stations, we also conduct two inversions, one containing 30% of our viable seismic stations (stations 24, 29, 34, 39, 43, 46, and 48) and the other inversion

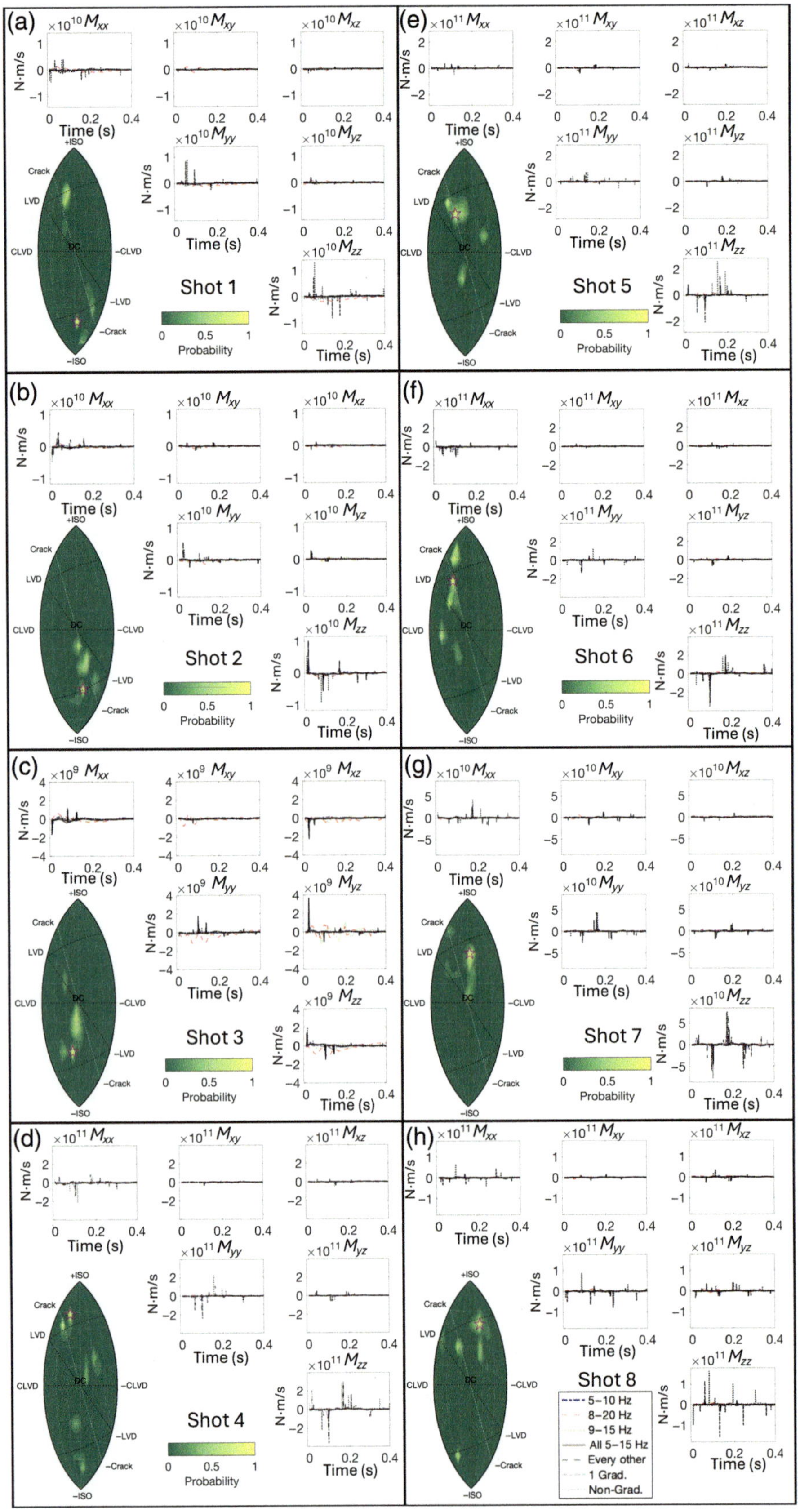

Figure 11. MRFs and their corresponding MF location on a fundamental lune as a function of probability when compared with other inversion runs for (a) shot 1, (b) shot 2, (c) shot 3, (d) shot 4, (e) shot 5, (f) shot 6, (g) shot 7, and (h) shot 8. The fundamental lunes were constructed using 10 time intervals from 0.01 to 2 s, with a width of 0.2 s, and the magenta stars indicate the locations of maximum probability for all inversion runs.

using the remaining 70% (stations 22, 23, 25–28, 30–33, 35–38, 44, and 47). We combine the 30% MRF solution with the Green's functions for the 70% stations that were not used in the 30% inversion as a cross-validation to see how well the inversion using a smaller subset of stations does with fitting data from completely different stations (Fig. 13).

The 30% MRF, when used to predict data for the 70% stations, results in a decrease in overall VR and CC (Fig. 13b) when compared with the 70% inversion, but is still able to sufficiently recover the main characteristics of each waveform. Figure 13c shows the VR and CC ratios for the 30% MRF compared against the 70% station data over the 70% station predicted data. The phase information recovered by each inversion, represented by the CC fit, is consistent between the 30% and 70% solutions for each shot, with the lowest being shot 1. For shot 1, the 30% inversion results in a solution with a CC fit of 0.85 of the 70% result. In addition, the VR values, measuring the amplitude of the MRF, are also consistent between shots but slightly lower than the CC fits. This indicates that, for this example, when using a smaller subset of stations, the inversion has more difficulty recovering the amplitude information than the phase information. This effect is also observed in the recovered MRF for shot 7 (Fig. 13d), where the impulses recovered for the inversion with 30% of the stations are larger than the MRF recovered from the 70% inversion. However, the timing and

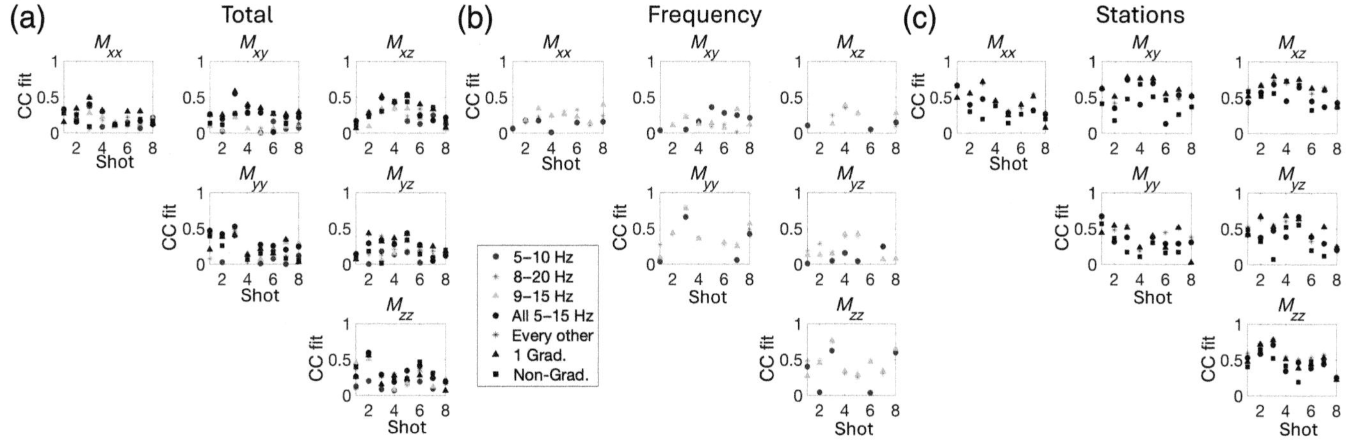

Figure 12. Average CCs for each moment tensor between inversion runs. Runs plotted in all three of the subplots are denoted in the central legend. (a) Average CCs for all inversion runs. (b) Average CCs using variable frequency bands to filter the data used in the inversion runs. (c) Average CCs varying the stations used in each inversion run.

number of impulses recovered are generally consistent between the two solutions. When looking at the overall drop in VR and CC for each shot, shots 2 and 3 have the highest ratios for both CC and VR, indicating that the station geometry has the least impact on the solutions for those inversions; however, station geometry does impact the solutions for shot 1 and, to a lesser extent, shots 4–6. These shots had the source mechanisms that ended closest to DC, which could explain why having more stations with ideally a greater azimuthal coverage is important for these shots in particular, because polarities for data at stations located at different azimuths from the source would be different for a source closer to DC.

Yield analysis

Finally, we use the isotropic moment from our MF results for each shot with a positive isotropic moment to estimate the yield using equation (7). We do not evaluate the dry shots 2 and 3 for this test because the negative isotropic moments would be nonphysical for this equation. However, we do include shot 1 as a point of comparison with the wet shots because the isotropic moment for shot 1 is positive for the 5–15 Hz inversion with all stations, despite a negative overall source mechanism (Fig. 11a), likely resulting from added complexity present in the recovered source mechanism due to movement on the bi-wing fracture at the location of the shot depth. Figure 14 shows the results of the Ford *et al.* (2023) yield equation, for a rhyolitic rock with a *P*-wave velocity (V_P) of 4500 m/s, an *S*-wave velocity (V_S) of 2600 m/s, and density (ρ) of 2300 kg/m^3. Velocity varies with depth (Fig. 2); therefore, shots located at different depths would vary slightly in recovered yield depending on the velocity used in the Ford *et al.* (2023) yield equation. Because the borehole and test bed were saturated for shots 4–8, we refer to the GP used here as an equivalent GP. With the isotropic moment from the MF solutions, we are able to recover the anticipated yield for shots 5–8 at reasonable GPs for a hard-rock like rhyolite, ranging from 13.7% for shot 6, located just above a "slow zone" where the *P*-wave velocity drops to 3000 m/s, to a larger value of 37.3% for shot 1, which was the dry shot located in a bi-wing fracture. Shot 8, located in virgin rock, and shot 5, located in the slow zone, resulted in the expected yield for both shots for GPs slightly higher than shot 6 (17.5% and 18.6%, respectively). Shot 7, which was located in a cavity, has the third highest GP, resulting in the expected yield with an equivalent GP of 26.7%. Shot 4, which was the wet shot located in the same location as shot 1 in a bi-wing fracture, had a similar GP as shot 7 at 27.5%.

Because the yield is small, ~1.14 kg TNT equivalent for all shots, and there is a significant amount of water in the near-source region, it is likely that the surrounding water would have an impact on the cumulative explosion and observed data, and a solid rhyolitic rock may not be an accurate assumption of realistic emplacement conditions. Therefore, we also evaluate the total energy radiating from the shots released for water (equation 18), assuming an ideal fluid whole space (after Aldridge, 2000) ($V_P = 1500$ m/s and $\rho = 1000$ kg/m^3), for a rhyolitic rock ($V_P = 4500$ m/s, $V_S = 2600$ m/s, and $\rho = 2300$ kg/m^3) (Bauer, 2021; Schneider *et al.*, 2024), and an averaged mixture of rhyolitic rock and water, assuming that the rhyolite rock matrix provides sufficient shear strength in the source region ($V_P = 3000$ m/s, $V_S = 1300$ m/s, and $\rho = 1650$ kg/m^3). The anticipated corner frequency we use is 500 Hz for a yield of 1.14 kg TNT-equivalent source (Denny and Johnson, 1991). The true total energy radiated from each source, as well as the total energy radiating from a source in these different conditions, are shown in Table 2, with the percent error between these values shown in the last three rows of Table 2.

A water emplacement results in the closest total energy values to the true total energy values for all shots. Shot 6, located above the slow zone, shows the closest agreement to a pure

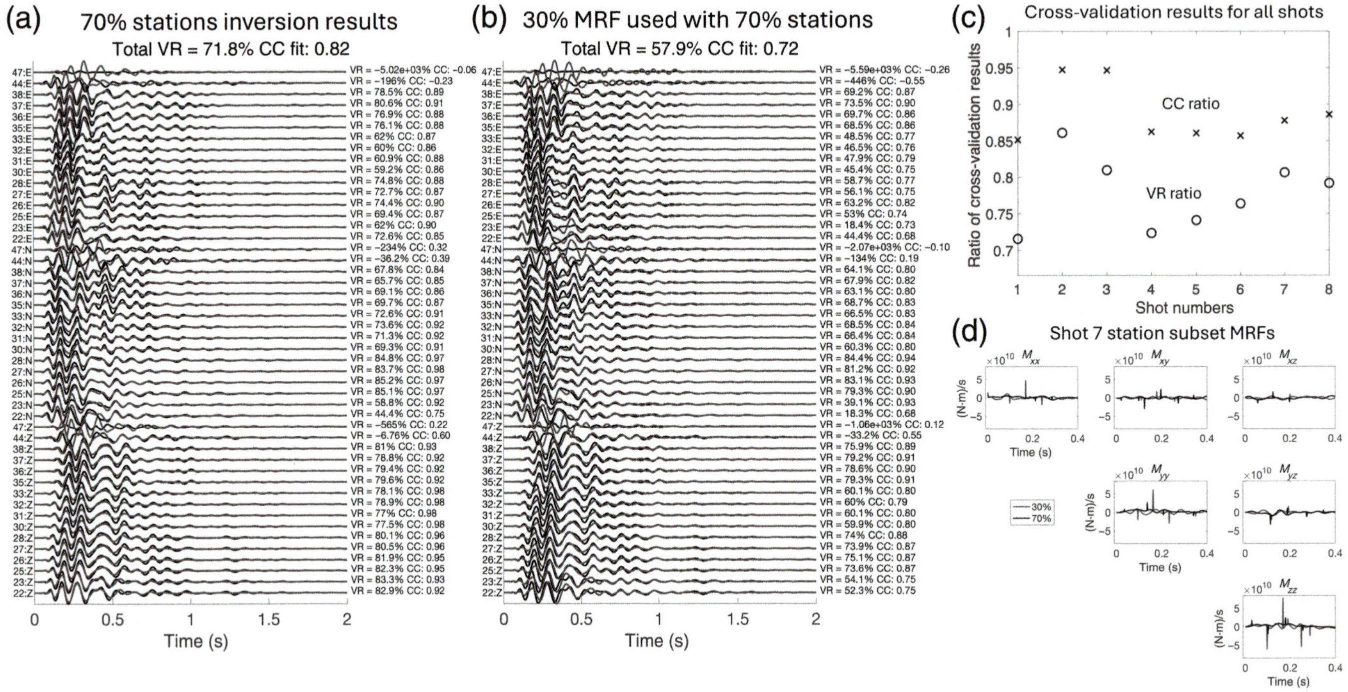

Figure 13. Cross-validation for the results of an inversion using 30% of stations used to predict data for data at the remaining 70% of stations. Predicted (red) and observed data (black) for shot 7 for the 70% station inversion (a), and the 30% inversion result used for the other 70% of stations (b). (c) Ratio of the 30% MRF predicted data overall VR (circles) and CC (×) over the 70% VR and CC for each shot. (d) The recovered MRFs for the 30% (red) and 70% (black) inversions. The color version of this figure is available only in the electronic edition.

emplacement in water with an error of 14.92%, followed by shot 5, located in the slow zone at 36.20%, and shot 8, with an error of 46.96%. Shot 4 has the largest error of the wet shots, with an 87.81% error from the total energy value predicted for a water emplacement. Shot 1, a dry shot emplaced in a bi-wing fracture at the same location as shot 4, has a large error for all three emplacement conditions, which is expected as air instead of water would be impacting this shot. A rhyolitic rock medium results in a much smaller total radiated energy than the true values for each of the shots, given the isotropic moment we invert from the data. To achieve the same order of magnitude of total energy, a much higher and unrealistic corner frequency would need to be used, at least an order of magnitude higher than what would be expected for this yield. This indicates that the water around these low-yield chemical explosions likely does have a strong effect on the total energy radiated out from the source, and treating the emplacement of the source as a solid rock is inaccurate.

DISCUSSION

The data recorded at Blue Canyon Dome for low-yield chemical explosives located at various depths and emplacement conditions display wide variation depending on source emplacement condition and station location. There were three co-located shots between the dry and wet shots, with the dry shots 1, 2, and 3 being co-located with the wet shots 4, 7, and 8. The data for the co-located dry shots appear to be reversed in polarity when compared with the wet shots, which have a polarity consistent with that of a positively isotropic explosion source. Because the stations were continuously recording through the entirety of the deployments for shots 1–8, the station orientations remained unchanged between shots. In

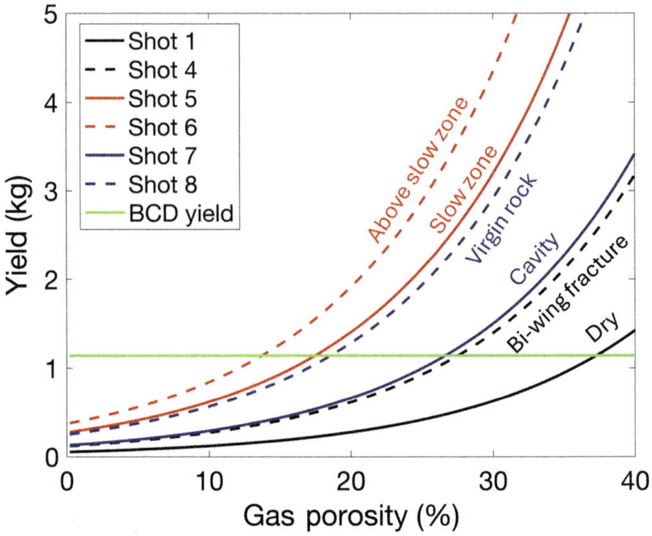

Figure 14. Yield estimated using a rhyolitic rock bulk modulus and the yield equation from Ford *et al.* (2023). The inversions for shot 1 and wet shots 4–8 are able to recover the exact anticipated yield with equivalent gas porosity (GP) values ranging from 13.7% (shot 6) to 37.3% (shot 1).

TABLE 2
Total Energy in Megajoules Radiated From Source Assuming Various Emplacement Conditions as Well as Total Energy Percent Error for Each Emplacement Condition

Emplacement	Shot 1	Shot 2	Shot 3	Shot 4	Shot 5	Shot 6	Shot 7	Shot 8
True	4.80×10^{00}	4.80×10^{00}	4.80×10^{00}	4.80×10^{00}	4.78×10^{00}	4.80×10^{00}	4.78×10^{00}	4.80×10^{00}
Rhyolite	1.94×10^{-04}	1.42×10^{-04}	7.24×10^{-06}	9.63×10^{-04}	5.02×10^{-03}	9.30×10^{-03}	1.11×10^{-03}	4.19×10^{-03}
Water	1.18×10^{-01}	8.64×10^{-02}	4.40×10^{-03}	5.85×10^{-01}	3.05×10^{00}	5.64×10^{00}	6.75×10^{-01}	2.54×10^{00}
Averaged	2.74×10^{-03}	2.01×10^{-03}	1.02×10^{-04}	1.36×10^{-02}	7.09×10^{-02}	1.31×10^{-01}	1.57×10^{-02}	5.92×10^{-02}
Rhyolite percent error	99.996	99.997	100.000	99.980	99.895	99.806	99.977	99.913
Water percent error	97.549	98.200	99.908	87.807	36.195	14.922	85.866	46.960
Averaged percent error	99.943	99.958	99.998	99.717	98.517	97.267	99.671	98.767

addition, DAS data recorded at this site show a similar reversal in polarity between the dry and wet shots. As an independent data modality, this consistent behavior suggests that the polarity reversal is a physical phenomenon. Because stations remained operational between all shots and two different modalities show this polarity reversal, we infer that the cause of this reversal is likely due to a combination of the low-yield chemical explosion and site characteristics, of which the emplacement is the dominant cause. The exact mechanism for this polarity reversal is a subject for future work and may be due to some combination of near-source mechanisms that would need to be explored in the nonlinear regime. Although not in relation to body-wave first motions like we observe here and at much different scales, several authors have noted reversed Rayleigh-wave polarities compared with expectations in certain circumstances from underground explosions, attributing the reversal to near-source-related phenomena such as cavity collapse, spall, or coincident DC release (e.g., Brune and Pomeroy, 1963; Toksöz and Kehrer, 1972; Rygg, 1979; Patton, 1991). We will first discuss the incoherency in low frequencies we observed in the data, followed by the inversion results and cross-validation of our results, and finish with a discussion on yield comparison with different methods.

Incoherency at low frequencies

Another phenomenon of interest in this dataset is a spike in incoherency for frequencies <16 Hz of the close-offset gradiometer stations. Because the stations are located within tens of centimeters of each other, they provide an opportunity to measure the relative coherence of the signals recorded at them, which should be consistent within the flat portion of the instrument response, which for the Fairfield nodes used in this survey is above 5 Hz. However, the stations in the gradiometer groups located at less than ~120 m from the source are highly variable, with varying frequency content present in stations located within the same gradiometer groups and with some later arrivals reversed in polarity. This variability decreases at farther offsets from the source and is worse for the horizontal station components. Discrepant stations are generally not consistent for a single-station component between shots, which would indicate an instrumentation problem. Different station components contrast with the rest of the data recorded in the gradiometer groups for different shots: stations that are consistent across an array for one shot can be inconsistent with the rest of the group during another shot. In addition, the incoherency is only present for low-frequency signals, the frequency content higher than 16 Hz has a coherence of near 1, indicating that, for frequencies higher than 16 Hz, the stations are recording nearly identical waveforms, so if an instrument problem is occurring, it would occur randomly per station at only those less than 120 m from the source for only a small portion of the frequency band. One explanation for this variability in stations closer to the source, outside of an instrument issue, is that the stations near the source could be influenced by imperfect coupling due to ground motion which would cause variability in the observed signals for those stations at close offsets. However, the ground displacement is small, on the order of 10^{-7} m for the dry shots and 10^{-6} m for the wet shots and so would not result in the differences observed in the data. In addition, within a gradiometer group, stations are located along the same azimuth with nearly identical take-off angles and therefore subject to the same portion of the source's radiation pattern; therefore, radiation pattern differences cannot explain the incoherency. Although small-scale heterogeneities can result in differences between waveforms recorded by adjacent stations, the wavelengths at the frequencies where the incoherency exists are much larger than the aperture of the gradiometer; thus, all components would be expected to measure the same portion of the wavefield. Improper filtering can result in artifacts not actually present in the data. To ensure we avoid any issues caused by filtering, we apply our filter to a six-minute-long data time series with the event starting at ~3 min to avoid filter issues caused by insufficiently long signal to ensure that the signal was sufficiently small at both ends to mitigate wrap around effects. We also use a large frequency band of 5–15 Hz to avoid artifacts caused by too narrow of a frequency band in the bandpass filter. In addition, because these incoherencies are present only in stations close to the source, this behavior could be the result of nonlinear effects that our linear forward model is unable to capture. Exploring the influence of nonlinear effects in the near-source region is the subject of future work.

Inversion results

The inversion results fit the data well with the lowest total VR of 41.1% and CC fit of 0.66. This indicates that even if the amplitude, measured best by the VR measure, is over- or underestimated, the phase information, measured by the CC measure, matches the observed data for the majority of stations. The inversion has consistent difficulty fitting the non-gradiometer east-component data for all shots, with the highest VR for the non-gradiometer east-component stations often negative. This may be due to additional variation located east and west of the source that is not captured in the earth model we use to generate our Green's functions, such as a fault that is known to run east of the source (Chamberlin, 1999). We assume a relatively simple layered velocity model with layers following the topography, which therefore means that any structural information that is not captured in this velocity model will not be represented in the Green's functions generated using that velocity model. This lack of complex structure information in the Green's functions may result in the inversion attempting to compensate for any significant errors introduced by an inaccurate model by recovering spurious and unrealistic MRFs. This is one of the reasons why we run multiple inversions with varying frequencies and station geometries, so we can attempt to isolate the invariant representation of the "true" STF that represents the source. In addition, there could be further uncertainty introduced by the station geometry because the majority of stations were deployed in a linear array co-located with the DAS data. This results in only a portion of the wavefield sampled and used in our inversions. We attempt to mitigate this effect by inverting the data for a variety of station geometries, including an inversion using only the stations located outside the linear array (Non-Grad). However, our results will be influenced by this low azimuthal coverage and would likely result in a lower sensitivity to east–west-directed source components because the majority of our stations are located to the south of the source.

By varying the frequency bands used to filter the observed data and the station locations included in the inversion, we can analyze the consistency of the MRFs recovered by each inversion. Overall, the STFs recovered by each of the inversions for a given shot are similar, with the MF representations on the fundamental lune generally clustering in the same area for a given shot. Shot 8 shows the most variability in source mechanisms between all wet inversion runs outside of shot 4; however, the two solutions that plot outside the cluster of inversion runs located in the upper right of the lune have low VR values. In addition, CCs between the inversion runs indicate that the recovered STFs for each shot and moment tensor component are similar (generally ~0.5) when using data from different stations in the inversion. To a lesser extent, the variable frequency band inversion runs are also similar, often resulting in CCs around 0.3 to just under 0.5. This indicates that the high-frequency features in the STFs recovered from the inversion runs are consistent with those using different data and frequency bands. In addition, removing the IR from the recovered MRFs through OMP also allows the use of data filtered at a much lower frequency than the corner frequency of a source. Without this step, the IR would dominate and additional potential sources, such as the multiple impulses recovered after 0.01 s in the inversion would be masked by the IR and not identified. With this process to reconstruct the MRFs, we observe an initially positive isotropic explosion at around 0.01 s for the inversion results for the dry shots which are then followed by a possibly lower frequency collapse-like event at around 0.1 s, which results in net negative isotropic moments for shots 2 and 3. Further examination of these results is required and will be the subject of future work.

The inversion results, when plotted on a fundamental lune, are consistent with the polarities present in the observed data, with the dry shots exhibiting early-time negative volume changes with a net negative trace of the moment tensor for shots 2 and 3, and the wet shots exhibiting an early-time positive volume change with a net positive trace of the moment tensor. In addition, as time progresses, the co-located shots of 1 and 4, 2 and 7, and 3 and 8 had quasi-mirrored patterns of source mechanism evolution. Shots 1 and 4 start on the negative and positive sides of the lune, respectively, cross DC and move to a net positive solution for shot 1 and a net positive solution back to DC for shot 4. Shots 2 and 7 are a negative and positive crack solution, respectively, and shots 3 and 8 move to a progressively more negative solution for shot 3 and a more positive solution for shot 8. This indicates that there is a symmetry in the co-located shot data that appears positive or negative based on the source emplacement, which may be the result of near-source interactions, which will be explored in future work.

Cross-validation

To assess the inversion's ability to recover consistent solutions with less data, we evaluate the effect of using a small subset of stations (in this case 30% of the stations) and using that solution to predict data for the remaining 70% of stations. Overall, the smaller 30% station inversion generally recovers similar phase information as the 70% inversion. However, using a more limited number of stations in our inversion results in much higher amplitude MRFs than those recovered from the 70% of stations inversion solution. This may mean that with a smaller number of stations, yield estimates may be impacted, with the 30%–70% station inversion VR ratios for all shots ranging from ~0.72 to ~0.86. However, the time variability of the source mechanism may be less impacted because the CC ratios for all shots were higher than the VR ratios between the 30% and 70% station inversions, ranging from ~0.85 to ~0.95. Future work is needed to further quantify the effect of station number and geometry on the recovered MRF for the time-variable moment tensor inversion approach.

Yield comparison

The magnitudes of the recovered STFs were evaluated using three different methods applied to the isotopic moments to calculate the yield and total energy of each shot. The Ford *et al.* (2023) yield equation results in the expected yield of 1.14 kg for all wet shots, with estimated GPs reasonable for rhyolite, ranging from 13.7% to 27.5%, which aligns with what would be expected for GPs for most materials (generally less than 25%) (Ford *et al.*, 2023). Because the wet shots have small yields, the effect of the water in the near-source region could have a large impact on the magnitudes of the observed data. Thus, we examine the total energy release for an emplacement in rhyolitic rock, an ideal fluid whole space, and for an averaged rhyolitic rock and water near-source composition. The rhyolite total energy is much smaller than the true total energy for all shots, which is expected, because the observed data magnitudes are much smaller than what would be expected if one assumes that each source was thoroughly coupled to the surrounding hard rock, resulting in a correspondingly small total energy prediction. The averaged emplacement assumption is around an order of magnitude closer to the true total energies than the pure rhyolite assumption; however, this assumption still results in total energy values that are an order of a magnitude off from the true total energy values, with the exception of shot 6. The water emplacement assumption results in the closest total energy predictions, with shots 5, 6, and 8 in particular on the same order as the true total energy and the estimate for shot 6 resulting in a percent error of around 14.9%. Thus, we infer that the water surrounding the chemical explosives in each wet shot is likely a large influence on the subsequent magnitudes of the observed data and therefore the isotropic moment of the recovered STFs.

One of the closest comparative explosions to the BCD shots is from the SPE-4Prime experiment, which was part of the SPE series. This tamped chemical explosion occurred in the Climax Stock granite in the northern portion of the Nevada National Security Site in 2015 with a TNT-equivalent yield of 89 kg at a depth of 87 m (Snelson *et al.*, 2022). Given that SPE-4Prime is nearly two orders of magnitude larger in yield, is ~2.5 times deeper scaled depth of burial, and has different emplacement conditions, it is difficult to do a detailed comparison between SPE-4Prime and the BCD shots. However, Kintner *et al.* (2023) performed a time-variable moment tensor inversion of the SPE-4Prime data. Because they also had to bandlimit the data below the corner frequency of the source due to errors in the earth model and challenges of the instrument response, they used weighted elementary functions to reconstruct the bandlimited MRFs. In the case of SPE-4Prime, their reconstructed MRFs are relatively smooth pulses, about a second in duration. The isotropic components M_{xx}, M_{yy}, and M_{zz} are all positive, within about a factor of two of each other in amplitude, and are roughly ten times the magnitude of the off-diagonal components, giving a strong explosion-type signature for the source. Although the authors do not give moment estimates based on their MRFs, an estimate of their final moment, based on a simple approximate integration of their MRFs, show that our results are roughly consistent with the two orders of magnitude difference in yields between SPE-4Prime and BCD. Although our results are not strongly positive isotropic, they generally show consistency of the source type with time with a consistent pattern of differences and similarities between the shots as described earlier. Because the BCD shots were not truly tamped, the near-source environment has a large impact on results as indicated by the water yield estimates giving the lowest overall error in general. Thus, the very near-source geologic conditions will imprint heavily on the recovered MFs.

CONCLUSIONS

We invert for the six unique MRFs from seismic data collected at Blue Canyon Dome from 24 three-component stations and consistently fit the data for eight different shots without *a priori* knowledge of STF shape or amplitude. In addition, we have developed a new method for reconstructing an MRF to identify high-frequency events within a time-variable moment tensor inversion MRF result that has been contaminated by the filter IR introduced when filtering the data. This method removes the filter IR and identifies higher-frequency events such as low-yield, high-corner frequency explosions that would otherwise be hidden by the filter IR. The time-variable moment tensor inversions are consistent with the polarities present in the observed data for each shot and indicate that further work needs to be done to explore the observed variability in polarity between dry and wet emplacement conditions observed in both the seismic and DAS data, as well as the incoherence present in the frequencies below 16 Hz in the near-source gradiometer stations. In addition, analysis of inversions using varying observed data frequency content and station locations indicate that the inversion returns consistent results that plot in specific portions of the fundamental lune for each shot. The use of different methods to calculate the yield and total energy for each wet shot indicates that the water that the chemical explosions were emplaced in does have a marked effect on the resulting total energy estimate. The time-variable moment tensor inversion shown here is a viable method to extract source mechanism and yield information from a seismic event. Furthermore, the results indicate that low-yield chemical explosions may have differences compared with higher-yield explosions that require further investigation, namely the reversal in polarities and low coherence found in frequencies less than 16 Hz for stations located close to the source.

DATA AND RESOURCES

The data used in this study are available upon reasonable request.

DECLARATION OF COMPETING INTERESTS

The authors acknowledge that there are no conflicts of interest recorded.

ACKNOWLEDGMENTS

The authors acknowledge Christian Poppeliers their work this study builds upon, Eric Robey for the technical review of this article, and Matt Ingraham for the providing a well log of the Blue Canyon Dome area. In addition, the authors acknowledge the anonymous reviewers their suggestions greatly improved this article. This Low-Yield Nuclear Monitoring (LYNM) research was funded by the National Nuclear Security Administration, Defense Nuclear Nonproliferation Research and Development (NNSA DNN R&D). The authors acknowledge important interdisciplinary collaboration with scientists and engineers from Los Alamos National Laboratory, Lawrence Livermore National Laboratory, Nevada National Security Site, Pacific Northwest National Laboratory, and Sandia National Laboratories. Sandia National Laboratories is a multimission laboratory managed and operated by National Technology & Engineering Solutions of Sandia, LLC, a wholly owned subsidiary of Honeywell International Inc., for the U.S. Department of Energy's National Nuclear Security Administration under contract DE-NA0003525. This article has been authored by an employee of National Technology & Engineering Solutions of Sandia, LLC under Contract Number DE-NA0003525 with the U.S. Department of Energy (DOE). The employee owns all right, title and interest in and to the article and is solely responsible for its contents. The United States Government retains and the publisher, by accepting the article for publication, acknowledges that the United States Government retains a non-exclusive, paid-up, irrevocable, world-wide license to publish or reproduce the published form of this article or allow others to do so, for United States Government purposes. The DOE will provide public access to these results of federally sponsored research in accordance with the DOE Public Access Plan available at https://www.energy.gov/downloads/doe-public-access-plan. This paper describes objective technical results and analysis. Any subjective views or opinions that might be expressed in the paper do not necessarily represent the views of the U.S. Department of Energy or the United States Government.

REFERENCES

Aki, K., and P. G. Richards (2002). *Quantitative Seismology*, Second Ed., University Science Books, Sausalito, California.

Aldridge, D. F. (2000). Radiation of elastic waves from point sources in a uniform wholespace, *Technical Rept. SAND2000-1767*, Sandia National Laboratory (SNL-NM), Albuquerque, New Mexico; Sandia National Laboratory (SNL-CA), Livermore, California.

Allmann, B. P., P. M. Shearer, and E. Hauksson (2008). Spectral discrimination between quarry blasts and earthquakes in Southern California, *Bull. Seismol. Soc. Am.* **98,** no. 4, 2073–2079.

Baruah, B., P. Kumar, and M. Ravi Kumar (2016). Discrimination of explosions and earthquakes: An example based on spectra and source parameters of the 11th May 1998 Pokhran explosion and the 9th April 2009 earthquake, *J. Geol. Soc. India* **88,** no. 1, 13–21.

Bauer, S. (2021). Laboratory measurements and field observations in support of blue canyon dome testing, *Technical Rept. SAND2021-6143*, Sandia National Laboratory (SNL-NM), Albuquerque, New Mexico.

Berg, E., and C. Poppeliers (2022). Unraveling the wrinkle in time-variable sources with lunes and synthetic seismic data, *Technical Rept. SAND2022-13242*, Sandia National Laboratory (SNL-NM), Albuquerque, New Mexico.

Brune, J. N., and P. W. Pomeroy (1963). Surface wave radiation patterns for underground nuclear explosions and small-magnitude earthquakes, *J. Geophys. Res.* **68,** no. 17, 5005–5028.

Chamberlin, R. M. (1999). Preliminary geologic map of the Socorro 7.5-minute quadrangle, *Open-File Geologic Map OF-GM-34*, New Mexico Bureau of Mines and Mineral Resources, Socorro County, New Mexico.

Day, S. M., and K. L. McLaughlin (1991). Seismic source representations for spall, *Bull. Seismol. Soc. Am.* **81,** no. 1, 191–201.

Day, S. M., J. T. Cherry, N. Rimer, and J. L. Stevens (1987). Nonlinear model of tectonic release from underground explosions, *Bull. Seismol. Soc. Am.* **77,** no. 3, 996–1016.

Day, S. M., N. Rimer, and J. T. Cherry (1983). Surface waves from underground explosions with spall: Analysis of elastic and nonlinear source models, *Bull. Seismol. Soc. Am.* **73,** no. 1, 247–264.

Denny, M. D., and L. R. Johnson (1991). The explosion seismic source function: Models and scaling laws reviewed, in *Explosion Source Phenomenology*, S. R. Taylor, H. Patton, and P. G. Richards (Editors), American Geophysical Union (AGU), Washington, D.C., 1–24.

Dziewonski, A. M., T.-A. Chou, and J. H. Woodhouse (1981). Determination of earthquake source parameters from waveform data for studies of global and regional seismicity, *J. Geophys. Res.* **86,** no. B4, 2825–2852.

Ekström, G., M. Nettles, and A. M. Dziewoński (2012). The global CMT project 2004–2010: Centroid-moment tensors for 13,017 earthquakes, *Phys. Earth Planet. In.* **200–201,** 1–9.

Fisk, M. D. (2006). Source spectral modeling of regional p/s discriminants at nuclear test sites in China and the former Soviet Union, *Bull. Seismol. Soc. Am.* **96,** no. 6, 2348–2367.

Ford, S. R., and W. R. Walter (2013). An explosion model comparison with insights from the source physics experiments, *Bull. Seismol. Soc. Am.* **103,** no. 5, 2937–2945.

Ford, S. R., M. E. Pasyanos, and A. Chiang (2023). Explosive yield estimation using regional seismic moment tensors, *Bull. Seismol. Soc. Am.* **113,** no. 5, 2211–2226.

Google Earth (2023). Blue canyon dome site, https://earth.google.com/web/search/34.059128880000000,-106.9563674000000/@34.0591289,-106.9563674,1843.08037472a,685.89279008d,35y,359.99999987h,0t,0r/data=CiwiJgokCfhAvlYO5UNAEfT2NcoG2y9AGShsdZlAvmRAId8JxGKzRVXAQgIIAQ (last accessed October 2024).

Harding, J. L., L. A. Preston, and M. Eliassi (2023). The influence of physical and algorithmic factors on simulated far-field waveforms and source–time functions of underground explosions using unsupervised machine learning, *Geophys. J. Int.* **233,** no. 2, 1399–1415.

Ingraham, M. D., H. A. Knox, K. Chojnicki, J. Feldman, J. Knox, C. Strickland, C. Johnson, T. Johnson, J. Lowrey, P. Sprinkle, *et al.* (2023). Blue canyon dome: Development of a small-scale testbed for monitoring underground explosions, *Technical Rept. No. SAND-2023-10965*, Sandia National Laboratory (SNL-NM), Albuquerque, New Mexico.

Kim, W.-Y., D. W. Simpson, and P. G. Richards (1993). Discrimination of earthquakes and explosions in the eastern United States using regional high-frequency data, *Geophys. Res. Lett.* **20,** no. 14, 1507–1510.

Kintner, J. A., K. Michael Cleveland, J. Eric Pippin, R. Thomas Modrak, and B. Delbridge (2023). Time-varying moment-tensor analysis with application to buried chemical explosions, *Seismol. Res. Lett.* **95,** no. 1, 352–366.

Mueller, R. A., and J. R. Murphy (1971). Seismic characteristics of underground nuclear detonations: Part I. Seismic spectrum scaling, *Bull. Seismol. Soc. Am.* **61,** no. 6, 1675–1692.

Nakano, M., H. Kumagai, and H. Inoue (2008). Waveform inversion in the frequency domain for the simultaneous determination of earthquake source mechanism and moment function, *Geophys. J. Int.* **173,** no. 3, 1000–1011.

Pasyanos, M. E., and A. Chiang (2022). Full moment tensor solutions of us underground nuclear tests for event screening and yield estimation, *Bull. Seismol. Soc. Am.* **112,** no. 1, 538–552.

Patton, H. J. (1990). Characterization of spall from observed strong ground motions on Pahute Mesa, *Bull. Seismol. Soc. Am.* **80,** no. 5, 1326–1345.

Patton, H. J. (1991). Seismic moment estimation and the scaling of the long-period explosion source spectrum, in *Explosion Source Phenomenology*, S. R. Taylor, H. Patton, and P. G. Richards (Editors), American Geophysical Union (AGU), Washington, D.C., 171–183.

Patton, H. J. (2012). Modeling Ms-yield scaling of Nevada test site nuclear explosions for constraints on volumetric moment due to source-medium damage, *Bull. Seismol. Soc. Am.* **102,** no. 4, 1373–1387.

Patton, H. J., and S. R. Taylor (2011). The apparent explosion moment: Inferences of volumetric moment due to source medium damage by underground nuclear explosions, *J. Geophys. Res.* **116,** no. B3, doi: 10.1029/2010JB007937.

Poppeliers, C., and L. Preston (2020). Inverting infrasound data for the seismoacoustic source time functions and surface spall at the source physics experiments phase II: Dry alluvium geology, *Technical Rept. SAND-2020-9217*, Sandia National Laboratory (SNL-NM), Albuquerque, New Mexico.

Poppeliers, C., and L. Preston (2021). The effects of earth model uncertainty on the inversion of seismic data for seismic source functions, *Geophys. J. Int.* **224,** no. 1, 100–120.

Poppeliers, C., and L. Preston (2022). An efficient method to propagate model uncertainty when inverting seismic data for time domain seismic moment tensors, *Geophys. J. Int.* **231,** no. 2, 1221–1232.

Poppeliers, C., K. Anderson Aur, and L. Preston (2018). The relative importance of assumed infrasound source terms and effects of atmospheric models on the linear inversion of infrasound time series at the source physics experiment, *Bull. Seismol. Soc. Am.* **109,** no. 1, 463–475.

Preston, L., and M. Eliassi (2022). Linear seismic source equivalents in 3D nonlinear models: Effects of embedded small-scale, near-source structures, *Technical Rept. SAND2022-11794*, Sandia National Laboratory (SNL-NM), Albuquerque, New Mexico.

Robey, R. E., B. A. Young, and M. D. Ingraham (2023). Characterization and response of three TNT equivalent materials in subsurface explosions, *Propellants Explos. Pyrotech.* **48,** no. 10, e202300078.

Rougier, E., and H. J. Patton (2015). Seismic source functions from free-field ground motions recorded on SPE: Implications for source models of small, shallow explosions, *J. Geophys. Res.* **120,** no. 5, 3459–3478.

Rygg, E. (1979). Anomalous surface waves from underground explosions, *Bull. Seismol. Soc. Am.* **69,** no. 6, 1995–2002.

Schneider, M. B., R. E. Robey, and S. L. Flores (2024). Blue canyon dome emplacement artifacts, *Technical Rept.*, Sandia National Laboratory (SNL-NM), Albuquerque, New Mexico, doi: 10.2172/2480069.

Snelson, C. M., C. R. Bradley, W. R. Walter, T. H. Antoun, R. A. Abbott, K. Jones, V. D. Chipman, and L. Montoya (2022). The source physics experiment (SPE) science plan, *Technical Rept.*, Lawrence Livermore National Laboratory (LLNL), Livermore, California, doi: 10.2172/1887003.

Stanciu, A. C., B. A. Young, and C. Poppeliers (2023). Comparing near and far field DAS fiber response for monitoring applications, *Technical Rept.*, Sandia National Laboratory (SNL-NM), Albuquerque, New Mexico, doi: 10.2172/2431493.

Stevens, J. L., and T. W. Thompson (2015). 3D numerical modeling of tectonic strain release from explosions, *Bull. Seismol. Soc. Am.* **105,** no. 2A, 612–621.

Stroujkova, A., and I. Morozov (2013). Seismic source studies for chemical explosions in granite, *Bull. Seismol. Soc. Am.* **104,** no. 1, 174–183.

Stump, B. W. (1985). Constraints on explosive sources with spall from near-source waveforms, *Bull. Seismol. Soc. Am.* **75,** no. 2, 361–377.

Stump, B. W., and L. R. Johnson (1977). The determination of source properties by the linear inversion of seismograms, *Bull. Seismol. Soc. Am.* **67,** no. 6, 1489–1502.

Stump, B. W., and L. R. Johnson (1984). Near-field source characterization of contained nuclear explosions in tuff, *Bull. Seismol. Soc. Am.* **74,** no. 1, 1–26.

Tape, W., and C. Tape (2012). A geometric setting for moment tensors, *Geophys. J. Int.* **190,** no. 1, 476–498.

Tape, W., and C. Tape (2013). The classical model for moment tensors, *Geophys. J. Int.* **195,** no. 3, 1701–1720.

Taylor, S. R., M. D. Denny, E. S. Vergino, and R. E. Glaser (1989). Regional discrimination between NTS explosions and western U.S. earthquakes, *Bull. Seismol. Soc. Am.* **79,** no. 4, 1142–1176.

Toksöz, M. N., and H. H. Kehrer (1972). Tectonic strain release by underground nuclear explosions and its effect on seismic discrimination, *Geophys. J. Int.* **31,** nos. 1/3, 141–161.

Tropp, J. A., and A. C. Gilbert (2007). Signal recovery from random measurements via orthogonal matching pursuit, *IEEE Trans. Inf. Theory* **53,** no. 12, 4655–4666.

Vorobiev, O. (2023). On various mechanisms of shear wave generation from underground chemical explosions in hard rocks, *Geophys. J. Int.* **232,** no. 3, 2133–2159.

Wallace, T. C., D. V. Helmberger, and G. R. Engen (1983). Evidence of tectonic release from underground nuclear explosions in long-period P waves, *Bull. Seismol. Soc. Am.* **73,** no. 2, 593–613.

Walter, W. R., K. M. Mayeda, and H. J. Patton (1995). Phase and spectral ratio discrimination between NTS earthquakes and explosions. Part I: Empirical observations, *Bull. Seismol. Soc. Am.* **85,** no. 4, 1050–1067.

Yang, X. (2016). Source spectra of the first four source physics experiments (SPE) explosions from the frequency-domain moment-tensor inversion, *Bull. Seismol. Soc. Am.* **106,** no. 4, 1637–1651.

Yang, X., and J. L. Bonner (2009). Characteristics of chemical explosive sources from time-dependent moment tensors, *Bull. Seismol. Soc. Am.* **99,** no. 1, 36–51.

Yang, X., B. W. Stump, and D. C. Pearson (1999). Moment tensor inversion of single-hole mining cast blasts, *Geophys. J. Int.* **139,** no. 3, 679–690.

Manuscript received 4 December 2024
Published online 31 December 2025

Concentrated Rupture of the 2022 M_w 6.6 Luding Earthquake Bounded by Stress and Geometry Barriers

Xinzhong Yin[1], Qibin Shi*[2], Wenze Deng[3], Yingfeng Zhang[1], Zhangfeng Ma[4], Xiaoshu Li[5], Jiuhui Chen[1], Jinrong Su[6], and Shengji Wei[7]

ABSTRACT

A comprehensive understanding of the earthquake rupture process and seismicity is crucial for revealing the physical mechanisms that govern fault behavior. The 2022 M_w 6.6 Luding earthquake occurred within the Xianshuihe fault system, a region where multiple geological block boundaries intersect and fault geometries remain poorly constrained. In this study, we investigate the mainshock rupture by integrating seismic and geodetic observations and analyze background and aftershock seismicity to better characterize this complex multifault system. Our results provide new insights into fault structures and their interactions. Kinematic modeling identifies three mainshock asperities, with spatial gaps filled by aftershocks and southward rupture propagation at ~1.5 km/s. The northern rupture segment dips westward, whereas the southern segment dips eastward. The rupture was spatially concentrated (~18 km along strike), contrasting with the broader ~60 km aftershock zone. Seismicity delineates the boundaries of the concentrated rupture zone along the Xianshuihe fault, whereas much off-fault seismicity occurred northwest of the main fault, along shallow left-lateral strike-slip faults to the north and normal faults to the west. These patterns align with Oligocene–Miocene geologic units rotated ~20° counter-clockwise relative to the Xianshuihe fault. North of the mainshock, seismicity outlines a deep conjugate fault intersecting the rupture near its northern termination, forming a potential stress barrier. South of the rupture, aftershocks confirm the east-dipping geometry of a branching segment, indicating a geometric barrier that limited further propagation. These findings highlight the importance of continuous seismological monitoring in complex fault systems, advancing our understanding of how heterogeneous fault properties and geological structure govern rupture dynamics and fault interactions.

KEY POINTS

- Joint seismic and geodetic observations reveal the 2022 M_w 6.6 Luding earthquake ruptured three asperities within a concentrated zone.
- The rupture terminated at stress and geometry barriers, highlighting the mechanical controls that confined its growth.
- An integrated conceptual model links geologic units, fault geometry, stress heterogeneity, slip concentration, and on- and off-fault seismicity into a unified framework.

Supplemental Material

INTRODUCTION

The M_w 6.6 Luding earthquake on 5 September 2022 occurred on the Moxi section of the ~350 km long Xianshuihe fault—a major left-lateral strike-slip fault extending southeast from Ganzi Tibetan Autonomous Prefecture to Shimian County in Sichuan Province, southwest China (Allen *et al.*, 1991; Bai *et al.*, 2021; Fig. 1). This fault system is part of the "escape

1. State Key Laboratory of Earthquake Dynamics and Forecasting, Institute of Geology, China Earthquake Administration, Beijing, China, https://orcid.org/0000-0003-2561-4028 (XY); https://orcid.org/0000-0001-5289-5705 (YZ); 2. Department of Earth, Environmental and Planetary Sciences, Rice University, Houston, Texas, U.S.A.; 3. China Earthquake Networks Center, China Earthquake Administration, Beijing, China, https://orcid.org/0000-0002-5360-3038 (WD); 4. Earth Observatory of Singapore, Nanyang Technological University, Singapore, Singapore, https://orcid.org/0000-0003-0044-7710 (ZM); 5. The Second Monitoring and Application Center, China Earthquake Administration, Xi'an, China; 6. Sichuan Earthquake Administration, Chengdu, China; 7. Key Laboratory of Deep Petroleum Intelligent Exploration and Development, Institute of Geology and Geophysics, Chinese Academy of Sciences, Beijing, China, https://orcid.org/0000-0002-0319-0714 (SW)

*Corresponding author: qs20@rice.edu

Cite this article as Yin, X., Q. Shi, W. Deng, Y. Zhang, Z. Ma, X. Li, J. Chen, J. Su, and S. Wei (2025). Concentrated Rupture of the 2022 M_w 6.6 Luding Earthquake Bounded by Stress and Geometry Barriers, *Bull. Seismol. Soc. Am.* **116**, 648–662, doi: 10.1785/0120240118

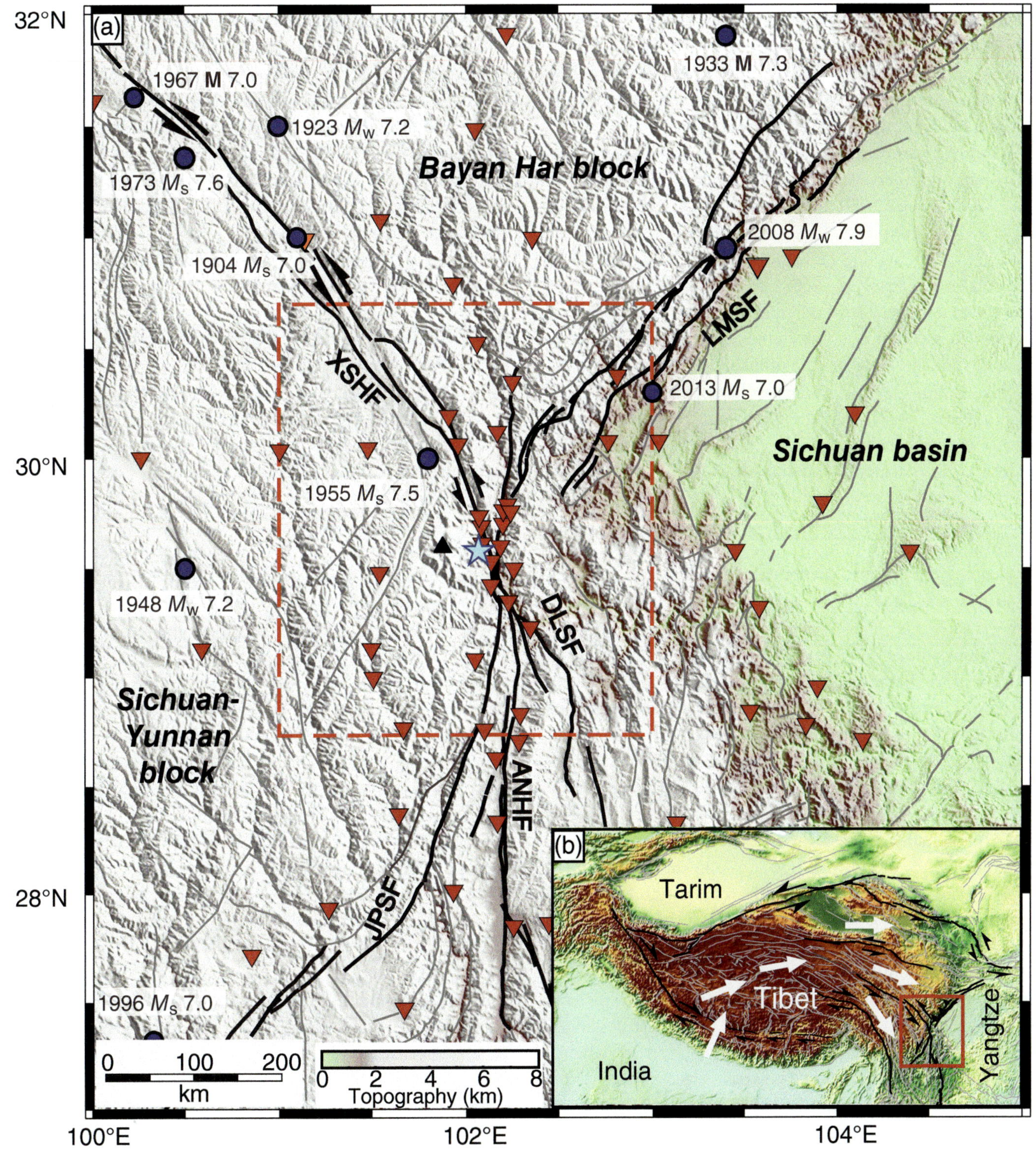

tectonics" regime along the eastern margin of the Tibetan Plateau and accommodates ~10 mm/yr of slip (Wang and Shen, 2020). Together with the Longmenshan and Anninghe faults, it forms the "Y-shaped" fault zone, delineating the boundaries of the Sichuan–Yunnan rhomboidal block, the Bayan Har block and the Yangtze block (Fig. 1a). The ongoing collision of the Indian and Eurasian plates (Fig. 1b) drives a shear strain rate of $\sim 10^{-6}$/yr along the eastern boundary of the Sichuan–Yunnan block, extending from Xianshuihe fault in

Figure 1. Regional tectonics near the Xianshuihe fault. (a) Major strike-slip faults (solid lines) form the Y-shaped block boundaries, with **M** >7.0 earthquakes (circles) documented between 1901 and 2022, before the 2022 M_w 6.6 Luding earthquake (star), which was recorded by regional seismic stations (inverse triangles). Gongga Mountain (black triangle) is located near fault intersections and the 2022 earthquake. The study of Figure 2 is indicated by the dashed box. ANHF, Anninghe fault; DLSF, Daliangshan fault; JPSF, Jinpingshan fault; LMSF, Longmenshan fault; and XSHF, Xianshuihe fault. (b) Escape tectonics of the Tibetan Plateau, with motion directions denoted by arrows and the area of panel (a) indicated by the red box.

the north to the Anninghe fault in the south (Wang and Shen, 2020). This strain is relatively uniform from ~30° to ~22° N, yet the fault system itself is structurally complex. Further south, the system diverges into four branches: the Daliangshan, Xianshuihe, Anninghe, and Jinpingshan faults.

Historically large earthquakes in this region display irregular recurrence intervals and a wide magnitude range (Wen *et al.*, 2008). Since 1700, the Xianshuihe fault has produced at least 16 earthquakes larger than **M** 6.5, including the 1786 M_s 7.75 Kangding-Luding and the 1973 M_s 7.6 Luhuo earthquakes (Wen *et al.*, 2008; Yi *et al.*, 2023). The 2008 Wenchuan and the 2013 Lushan earthquakes likely increased Coulomb stress near the Xianshuihe fault, potentially accelerating slip and elevating rupture probability (Wang *et al.*, 2009; Yi *et al.*, 2023). The 2022 Luding sequence, captured by dense seismic networks (Fig. 1 and Fig. S1, available in the supplemental material to this article), provides an opportunity to address two fundamental questions:

1. What controls the location and rupture extent of large earthquakes?
2. How are the mainshock rupture, seismicity, and geological structure related?

Previous studies have reached broad agreement on mainshock rupture directivity and the lateral extent of aftershocks (Fig. S2; Li *et al.*, 2022; Cai *et al.*, 2023; Guo *et al.*, 2023; Liu, Li, *et al.*, 2023; Xu *et al.*, 2023; Yi *et al.*, 2023; Zhang *et al.*, 2023; Zhao *et al.*, 2023). However, major discrepancies remain regarding the kinematic rupture process of the mainshock. For instance, Li *et al.* (2022), using Global Navigation Satellite System (GNSS) and Interferometric Synthetic Aperture Radar, proposed a ~50-km-long rupture including slip on a conjugate fault, whereas Han *et al.* (2023) reported a rupture of 20–30 km confined to the Xianshuihe fault with no evidence of conjugated slip. Asperity models also differ: some studies identified a single asperity (Guo *et al.*, 2023; Han *et al.*, 2023), whereas others suggested two (Zhang *et al.*, 2023; Zhao *et al.*, 2023) or even four (Li *et al.*, 2022). Similarly, the depth distribution of aftershocks is debated. Some clustered above the coseismic slip (Zhang *et al.*, 2023), others at greater depths (Yi *et al.*, 2023; Zhao *et al.*, 2023). Whether the rupture reached the surface also remains unresolved, given the challenges of geological mapping in this terrain. Crucially, the link between mainshock rupture, seismicity, and geological structure remains poorly understood.

To tackle these fundamental questions on mainshock rupture and its relation with seismicity and geological structure, we integrated decadal seismicity with modern geophysical observations, including teleseismic, strong-motion, and static GNSS data, to investigate the 2022 Luding mainshock and aftershocks. Our objectives are to: (1) robustly constrain rupture dimensions and asperity distribution, (2) link rupture processes to seismicity and fault structure, and (3) reconcile seismological and geological evidence to understand earthquake physics in this complex block boundary system.

To achieve these objectives, we constructed a refined earthquake catalog spanning 9.5 yr before and 2 months after the 2022 Luding event, using regional seismic networks. We then employed multiple-point-source and finite-fault inversions to characterize the mainshock rupture processes. The results are followed by analyses examining rupture characteristics, seismicity and fault geometries, and comparisons with prior models to provide plausible explanations for rupture dynamics.

BACKGROUND AND AFTERSHOCK SEISMICITY

Data integration

To obtain a clear overview of the seismic activity for this geologically complex region, we built a comprehensive earthquake catalog by combining 9.5 yr of analyst's phase picks before the mainshock with 10-day machine-learning (ML) phase picks of early aftershocks.

For background seismicity, we compiled 9360 manually picked events from 1 May 2013 to 31 October 2022, provided by the China Earthquake Networks Center (CENC). Because station configurations evolved over this 9.5 yr period, we relied on travel-time data to ensure consistency in location accuracy across the dataset.

For 10-day aftershocks, we collected *P*- and *S*-wave arrival times for 8572 aftershocks identified and picked with an ML algorithm (Liu, Li, *et al.*, 2023). On average, ML picks differed from manual analyst picks by 24.40 ms for *P* waves ($\sigma = 163.44$ ms) and 29.83 ms for *S* waves ($\sigma = 241.22$ ms). These accuracies satisfy the requirements for precise earthquake locations. The spatial distribution of relocated aftershocks agrees with the result obtained by the addition of interevent waveform cross-correlation (Liu, Li *et al.*, 2023), confirming that ML-derived picks reliably capture first-order seismicity patterns.

Relocation

We refined earthquake locations using the double-difference relocation algorithm HypoDD (Waldhauser and Ellsworth, 2000). To ensure robust earthquake pairing for HypoDD, we required each cluster to contain at least 10 events, with a maximum hypocentral separation of 10 km within a cluster. The selection criteria were designed to provide a sufficient number of events and clusters while maintaining strong constraints on the locations of individual events. To achieve this balance, only earthquakes recorded by ≥4 stations, with a maximum station distance < 200 km and azimuthal gap < 180°, were included. We then calculated travel-time differences for event pairs with a distance < 10 km. All events were relocated using a 1D velocity model (Table S1), modified from SWChinaCVM-V2.0 (Liu, Yu, *et al.*, 2023).

To quantify location uncertainties, we applied bootstrap resampling (Efron and Gong, 1983; Efron and Tibshirani,

1991; Li *et al.*, 2018). For each event, we resampled 90% of all double-pair differential times 100 times and computed the standard deviation as the relative location uncertainty. Median relative location uncertainties were 0.22 km in horizontal and 0.60 km in vertical dimensions for all events, 0.22 km (horizontal) and 0.53 km (vertical) for aftershocks, and 0.22 km (horizontal) and 0.94 km (vertical) for premainshock events, reflecting the limited number of permanent stations in earlier years. In total, we relocated 11,256 events (Figs. 2a and 3).

Seismicity before and after the mainshock

Pre- and post-mainshock seismicity broadly overlap, especially west of the main fault near Gongga Mountain. However, the 2022 sequence activated new clusters at northern and southern fault terminations.

Before the mainshock, seismicity was significant both along the Xianshuihe fault and on secondary faults (Fig. 3a). A prominent cluster ~5 km east of Gongga Mountain occupied a $20 \times 20 \times 15\ \text{km}^3$ volume, indicating a complex fault structure.

After the mainshock, seismicity intensified to the north and south, extending ~50 km along strike. Aftershocks revealed distinct seismic gaps (Fig. 3c), some attributable to coseismic rupture, others to additional processes (discussed later).

The aftershocks organize into four main clusters:

1. Cluster 1 (north of epicenter, 17–32 km): This cluster shows near-vertical faults intersecting the Xianshuihe fault at ~30° (Fig. 4, C–C′ profile). The cluster is shallow (2–8 km depth) and occurred mostly in the first days after the mainshock. Events align with Oligo–Miocene migmatite zones (Li *et al.*, 2016), suggesting reactivation of brittle structures, but field verification is needed to confirm this linkage.
2. Cluster 2 (near the epicenter): this cluster is sparse and is mainly distributed west of the Xianshuihe fault, consistent with a west-dipping rupture plane (Figs. 3c and 5b). Focal mechanisms (Yi *et al.*, 2023) indicate fault planes striking parallel to the Xianshuihe fault with dips of 65°–°85°. The limited aftershock density suggests the mainshock released much of accumulated stress locally.
3. Cluster 3 (west of epicenter, Gongga Mountain): This cluster exhibits complex spatial and temporal patterns (Figs. 3 and 5). The shallower events (2–10 km depth) follow northwest-trending migmatites zones, similar to cluster 1. The deeper events (10–13 km depth) form a northeast-trending alignment, consistent with right-lateral strike-slip activity (Fig. 2a). An M_w 4.9 normal-faulting event 47 days after the mainshock triggered extensive shallow aftershocks, implying a northeast-dipping plane (Fig. 5e,f) with a dip angle between 40° and 60°. Historical seismicity in this area also shows both northwest- and northeast-trending activities.

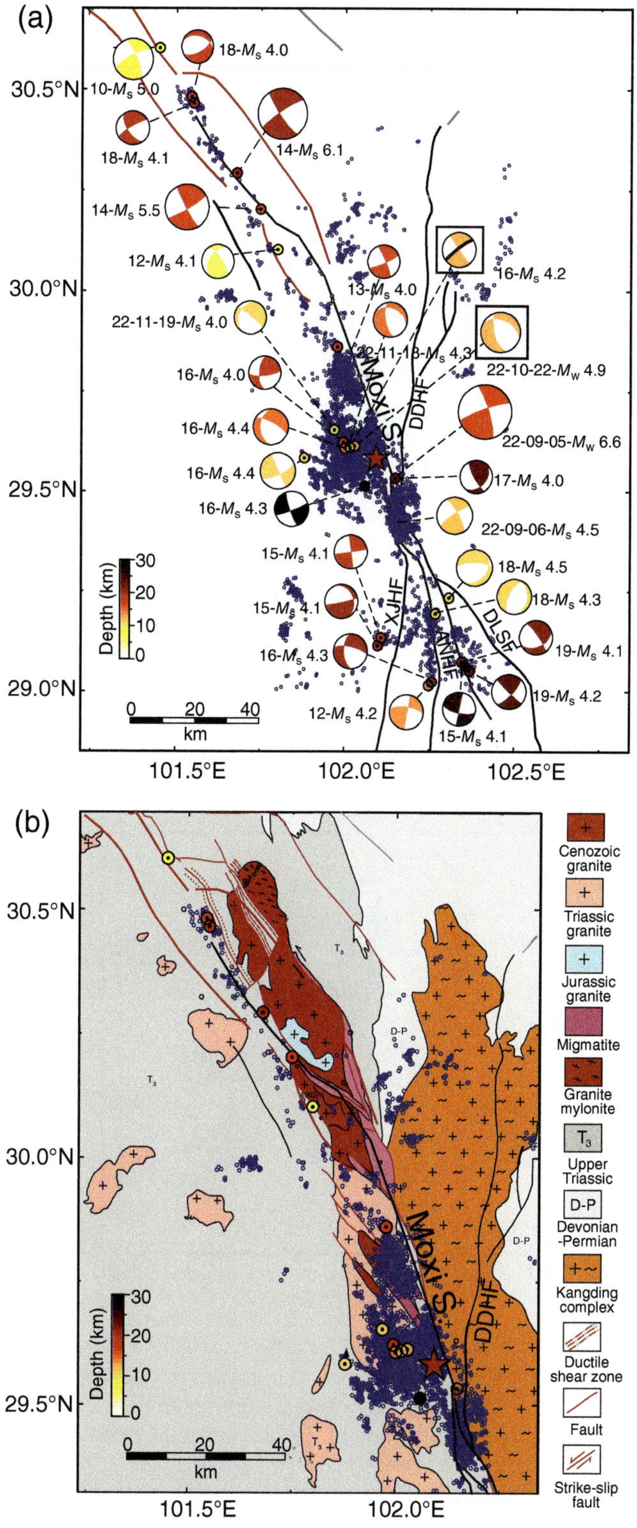

Figure 2. Seismic activity and geological structure. (a) Seismicity during 1 May 2013 to 15 September 2022 (blue circles), with **M** >4 earthquakes highlighted with their focal mechanisms (focal mechanism plots) that are scaled proportional to their magnitudes and color coded by depth. Major faults are plotted with solid lines. (b) Geological structure revised from Li *et al.* (2016) and Tang *et al.* (2022), labeled by rock types in the legend, overlapped by seismicity (circles) and fault traces (thick lines). ANHF, Anninghe fault; DDHF, Daduhe fault; JPSF, Jinpingshan fault; and Moxi S., Moxi segment of Xianshuihe fault.

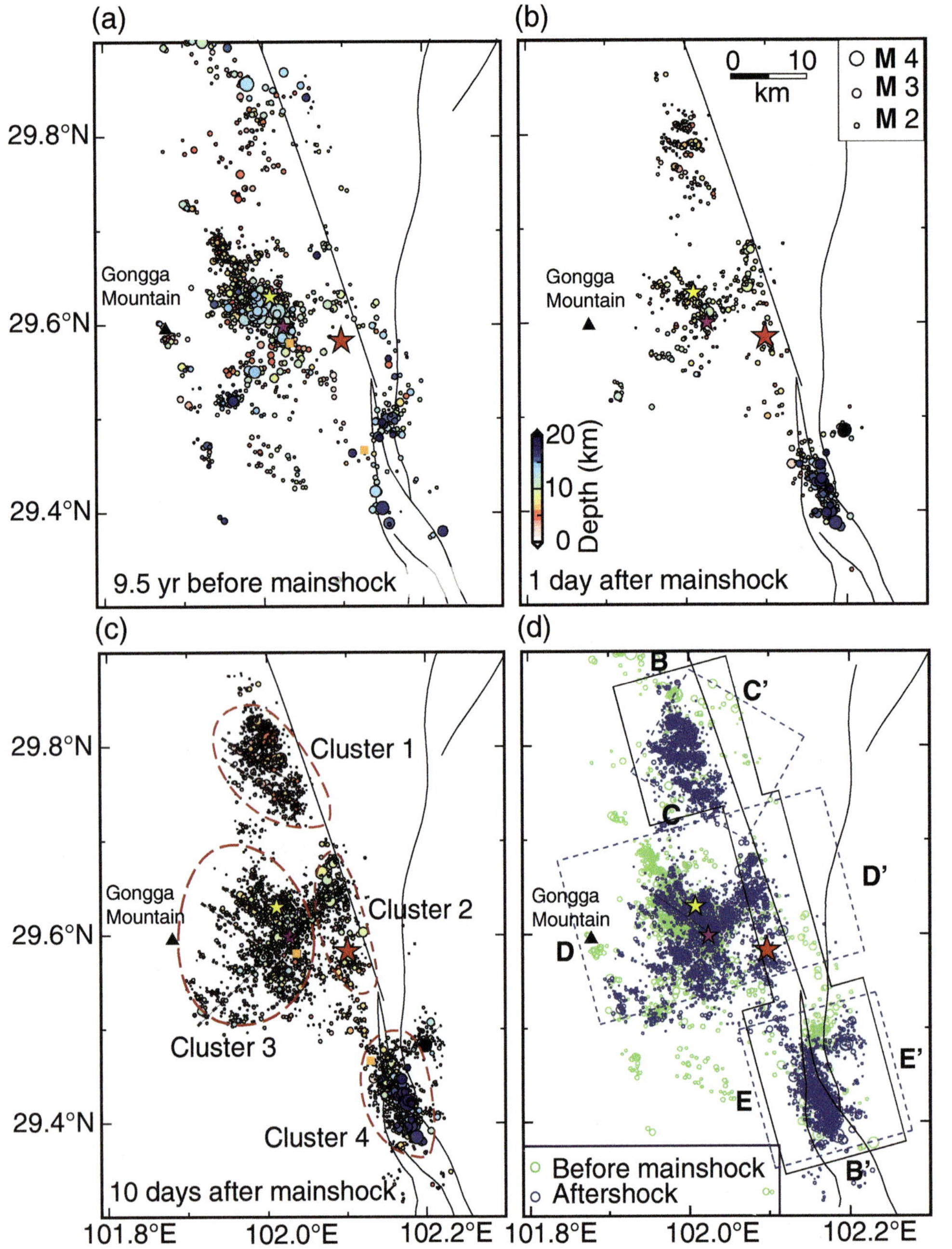

Figure 3. Relocated seismicity. (a) Background seismicity within 9.5 yr before the mainshock. (b) First 1-day aftershocks. (c) Aftershocks within 10 days of the mainshock. (d) Seismicity before and after the mainshock, combining panels (a–c). The seismicity in panels (a–c) is represented by circles with size proportional to magnitude and color coded by depth (color bar in panel b). The 2022 mainshock and two large aftershocks are marked by stars. Gongga Mountain is denoted by the black triangle. Fault traces are plotted as solid lines with inferred faults plotted as dashed lines. The profiles B–E are selected as boxes in panel (d). Box B combines seismicity of three subregions projected to a northwest-trending plane, whereas boxes C–E show separate sections on northeast-trending planes.

4. Cluster 4 (south of epicenter, 15–25 km): This cluster is near the junction of Jinpingshan, Anninghe, and Xianshuihe faults. The depth profile indicates one or two east-dipping faults (65°–85°), contrasting with the west-dipping Xianshuihe segment farther north (Fig. 6). The depth range spans >20 km, suggesting up-dip migration. A secondary northeast-trending seismicity trend matches the intersection of Xianshuihe and Daduhe faults (Fig. 3c).

Focal mechanisms

To validate fault geometries delineated by seismicity within the four clusters, we compiled focal mechanisms for $M_w > 4$ events from the CENC catalog (Fig. 2a). CENC applies quality control for first-motion and amplitude-ratio analysis: signal-to-noise ratio (SNR) > 3, source–receiver distance < 200 km, and azimuthal gap < 150°. First-motion polarities are routinely used as the primary input, whereas waveform inversions are performed for events with the highest SNR (manually selected). Among these high-SNR events, the "Cut-and-Paste" full-waveform inversion method (Zhu and Helmberger, 1996) and the Kiwi method developed by the Helmholtz Centre Potsdam (Cesca *et al.*, 2010; Heimann, 2011) are used for $M_s < 5.5$ and $M_s \geq 5.5$, respectively.

Relationship to the geological setting

The regional geology reflects multiple deformation episodes (Fig. 2b). Cenozoic granites and migmatites between the Moxi section and Gongga Mountain record intense left-lateral shearing and magmatism during 20–13 Ma (Tang *et al.*, 2022), whereas Triassic granites preserve evidence of later deformation after ~10 Ma, associated with block rotation and uplift. Seismicity north of the mainshock occurs along older fault traces, consistent with this inherited structure. Around Gongga Mountain, aftershocks align with northwest-trending normal faults inferred to exit beneath the glacial cover (Fig. 3). On the east side of the Xianshuihe fault, the Kangding

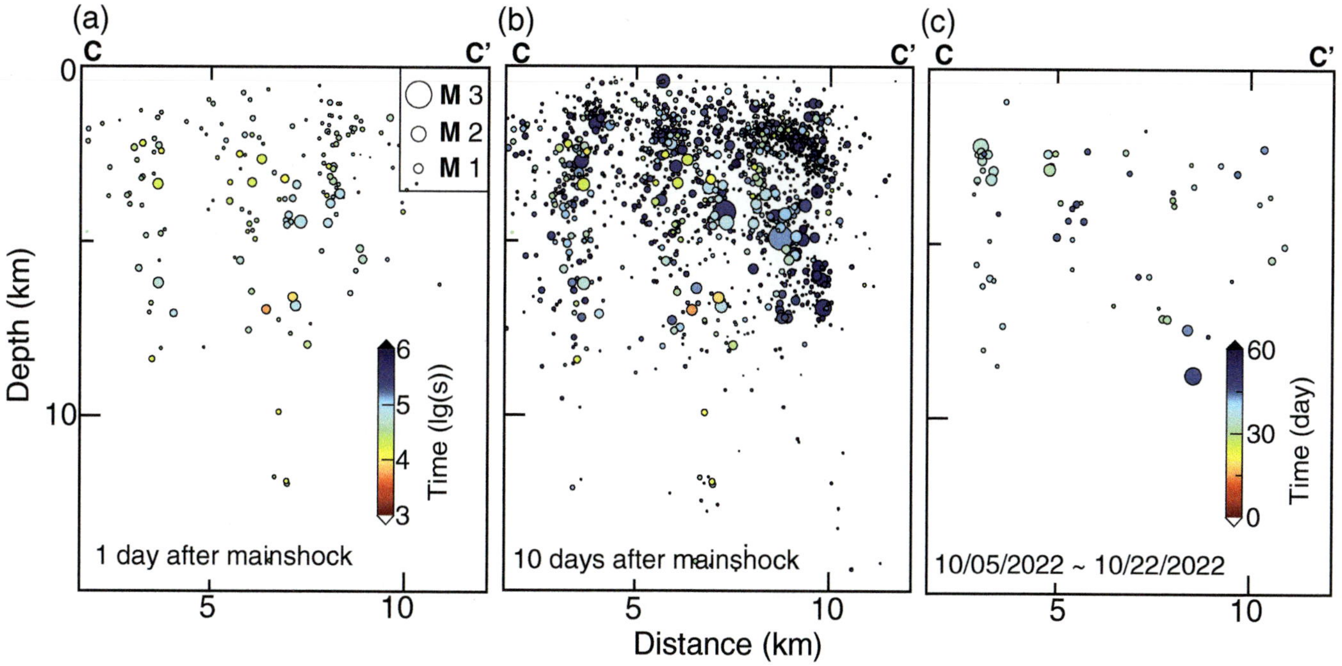

Figure 4. Seismicity of the vertical profile C. (a) First 1-day aftershocks. (b) Aftershocks within 10 days of the mainshock. (c) Late aftershocks starting from 1 month after the mainshock and ending right before the M_w 4.9 aftershock. Seismicity is projected to a northeast-trending vertical plane in which C′ represent the northeast side, with sizes of circles proportional to magnitudes and color coded by time taking the mainshock as 0. Panels (a) and (b) share the color bar in logarithmic scale.

Formation is predominantly composed of amphibolites, leptynites, granites, diorites, and basic dikes (Fig. 2b). The intersection of mixed and fractured migmatites, Triassic granites, and Cenozoic granites with the Kangding complex may be mechanically linked to the segmented fault strength, slip patch size, and stress variations along the strike, leading to distinct rupture styles which will be presented in the Kinematic rupture processes of the mainshock section.

KINEMATIC RUPTURE PROCESSES OF THE MAINSHOCK

With the distribution of seismicity as background knowledge, we resolved the rupture process of the Luding mainshock by performing multiple-point-source and finite-fault inversions based on seismic and GNSS observations.

Multiple-point-source inversion

We resolved first-order rupture complexity using the multiple-point-source inversion method (Shi *et al.*, 2018), which approximates the entire rupture process as a set of double-couple point sources. For each point source, this method optimizes location, depth, focal mechanism, source time function, and moment magnitude using a Markov chain Monte Carlo nonlinear algorithm. Unlike methods that assume a prescribed fault geometry, multiple-point-source inversion can independently identify ruptures on previously unmapped faults, allowing us to test whether the event ruptured a conjugate fault of the Xianshuihe fault.

We selected strong-motion and broadband stations within 500 km of the epicenter, removed instrument response, and converted the waveforms to velocity. Through visual inspection, 193 components from 66 regional stations were selected (Fig. S1), range from 0.01 to 0.40 Hz depending on station conditions.

Incrementally increasing the number of subevents, we found that three point sources adequately modeled the mainshock. On average, the final multiple-point-source synthetics provides 92% and 83% cross-correlation coefficients (CCs) to the observed *P* and *S* waves (Figs. S3 and S4a,b). The three subevents (Fig. 7) are as follows:

1. **M** 1, near the hypocenter (depth 6.5 km), west dipping,
2. **M** 2, ~8 km southeast of **M** 1, west dipping, and
3. **M** 3, ~12 km southeast of **M** 1, east dipping.

These subevents indicate southward rupture directivity. Their focal mechanisms are consistent, with one nodal plane (strike 162°) aligning closely with the mapped Xianshuihe fault, as determined by fault mapping (Deng *et al.*, 2003) and relocated seismicity (Fig. 3). Although the sense of dip varies, our solution does not require rupture on a conjugate fault.

Finite-fault inversion

Guided by first-order rupture complexity, we performed a finite-fault inversion assuming rupture on the Xianshuihe fault (strike 162°, dip 70°), consistent with Global Centroid Moment Tensor solution. The fault was discretized into 1.5 km × 1.5 km subfaults. Slip amplitude, rake, rise time, and rupture velocity were inverted using a simulated annealing algorithm (Ji *et al.*,

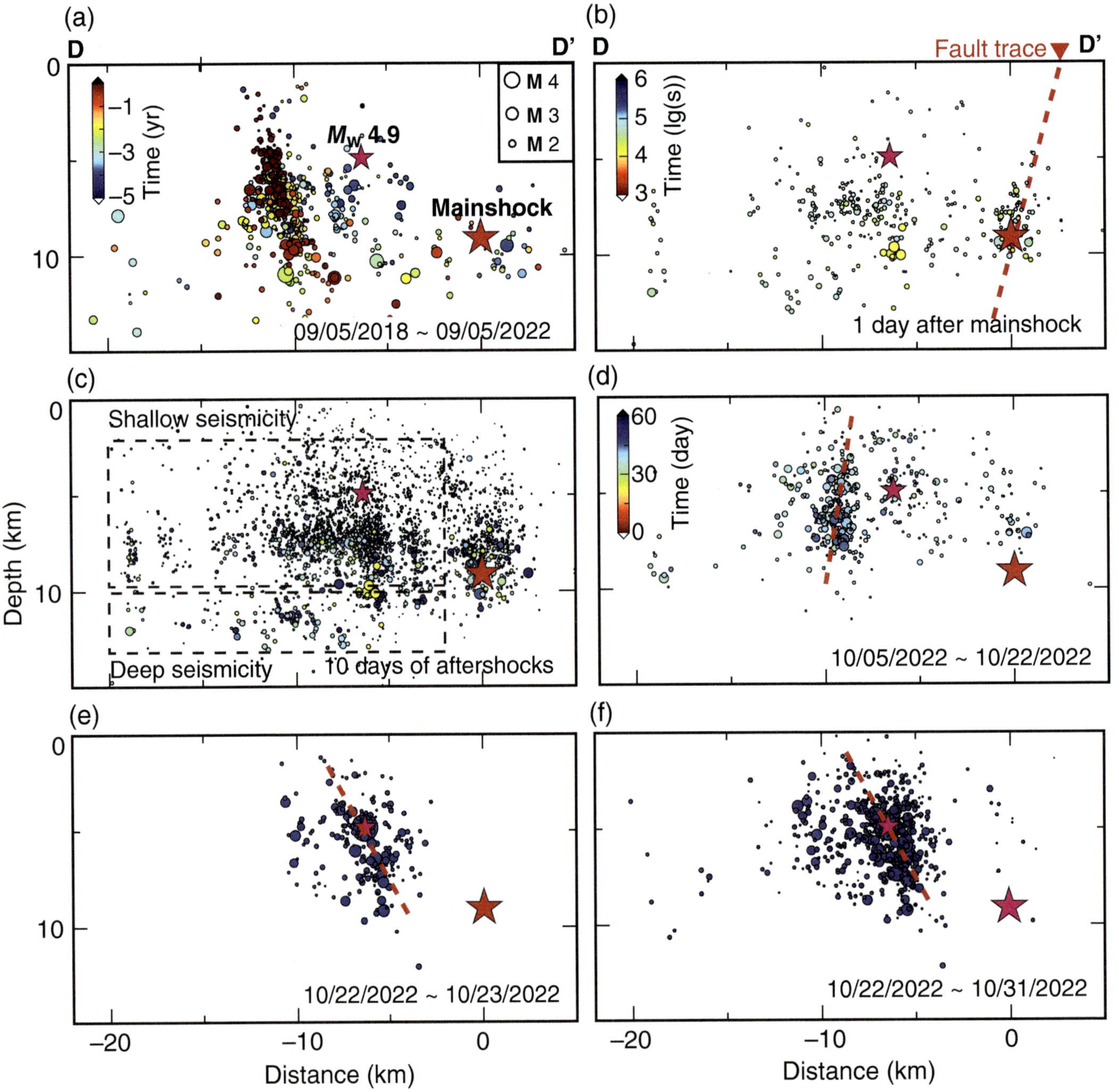

2002). A grid search was conducted to identify the optimal average rupture velocity.

The dataset included 23 strong-motion stations (Fig. S5), with five stations within 20 km of the rupture, which are critical for constraining rupture speed and asperity distribution. To further constrain asperity number and depth, we added 41 teleseismic *P* waves and 42 *SH* waves. Finally, static offsets (permanent displacements) from 74 GNSS stations (Li *et al.*, 2022) were incorporated with a weight equal to ~50% of the seismic data contribution, achieved by normalizing errors from separate inversions.

Our preferred finite-fault model (Fig. 7) achieves 73% and 81% average CCs to the observed strong-motion and teleseismic waveforms, respectively (Figs. S4c,d, S6, and S7) and a 13%

Figure 5. Seismicity of the vertical profile D. (a) Background seismicity (circles) color coded by year. (b) First 1-day aftershock (circles) color coded by logarithmic time counting from the mainshock. (c) Aftershocks within 10 days after the mainshock, color coded using the same time scale as panel (b). (d) Aftershocks starting from 1 month after the mainshock and ending before the M_w 4.9 aftershock, color coded by number of days after the mainshock. (e) Aftershocks within 1 day after the M_w 4.9 event, color coded using the same time scale as panel (d). (f) Aftershocks within 10 days after the M_w 4.9 event, color coded using the same time scale as panel (d). The mainshock and M_w 4.9 earthquake are plotted as stars. Seismicity is projected to a northeast-trending vertical plane in which D′ represent the northeast side, with sizes of symbols proportional to magnitudes. Inferred fault geometries are denoted by dashed lines.

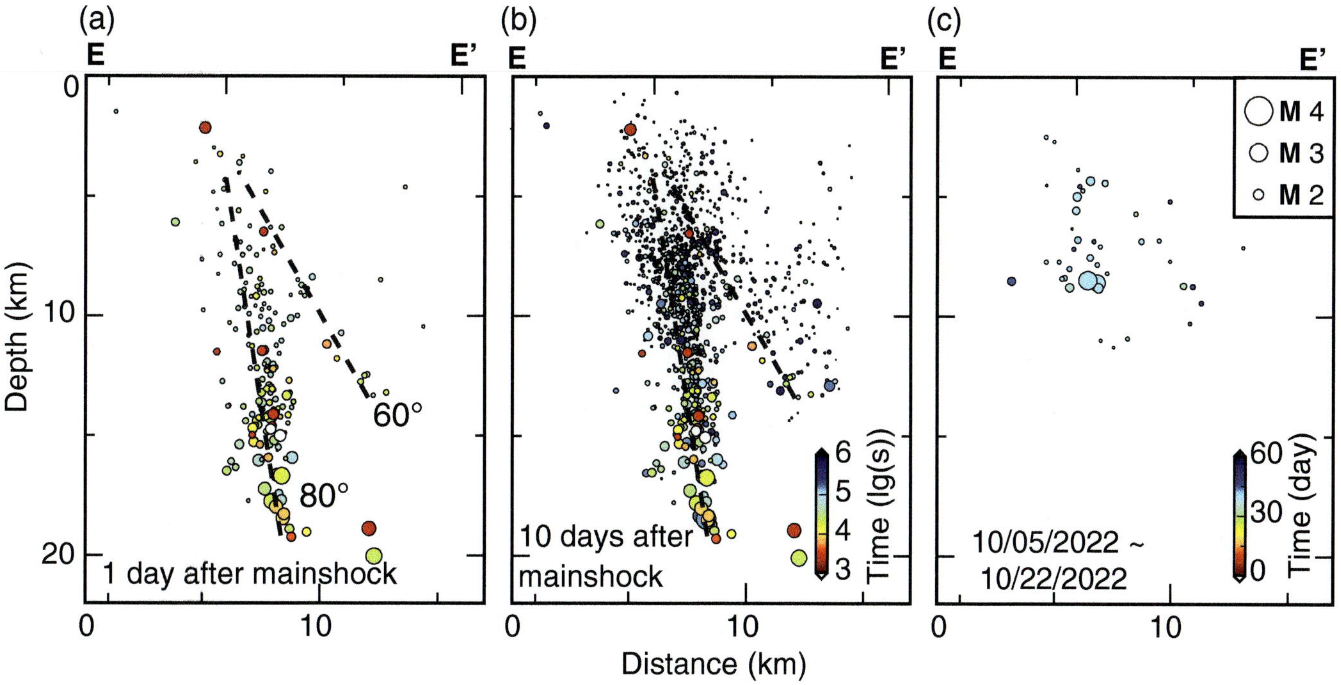

Figure 6. Seismicity of the vertical profile E. (a) First 1-day aftershocks color coded by logarithmic time (shared time scale with panel b). (b) Aftershocks within 10 days from the mainshock, color coded by logarithmic time. (c) Aftershocks starting from 1 month after the mainshock and ending right before the M_w 4.9 aftershock, color coded by number of days after the mainshock. Seismicity is projected to a northeast-trending vertical plane in which E′ represent the northeast side, with sizes of circles proportional to magnitudes. Inferred fault geometries are denoted by dashed lines.

misfit in GNSS amplitudes relative to the mean observed values (Fig. S4e). The model confirms a unilateral southward rupture with a relatively slow rupture speed of 1.5 ± 0.5 km/s (Fig. 7b) and a well-constrained source duration of ~10 s (Fig. 8a). A unilateral rupture propagation at 1.5 km/s extends the total rupture length to ~15 km in 10 s. The finite-fault inversion resolves three asperities:

1. asperity 1, near the hypocenter (~8 km depth),
2. asperity 2, ~10 km southeast of the hypocenter, and
3. asperity 3, beneath asperity 2.

Spatiotemporal distribution

Temporally, all asperities produce evident pulses in displacement waveforms (Fig. 8b), which are shown in both observed and synthetic waveforms. For example, broadband displacement at station YAK shows three pulses (black). The first pulse corresponds to asperity 1, the second corresponds to asperity 2, and the third pulse corresponds to asperity 3. Nearby strong-motion stations (see Fig. 7 for locations) confirm these patterns: stations XXXJ and VL002 (closest to asperity 1) both have their first pulses dominated by radiation from asperity 1, whereas T2402, T2404, and V2201 (closest to asperity 2) have their strongest contributions from asperity 2. At XXXJ and VL002, asperities 2 and 3 contribute equally to their second pulses. In terms of frequency, asperity 1 generates higher-frequency energy (i.e., narrower pulses) than asperities 2 and 3 at all stations (Fig. 8b,c) and thus in moment rate functions (Fig. 8a), implying smaller isolated slip patches and more heterogeneous stress conditions associated with asperity 1.

Spatially, asperity 1 does not reach the surface, whereas asperity 2 does. The finite-fault model yields slip up to ~100 cm in asperity 2, although no field measurements have been available to date. We estimated the rupture extent using the same method as Brengman *et al.* (2019), using 15% of the peak slip as the boundary (Fig. S8) after background slip calibration. This threshold of 15% has been used in previous studies (Allen and Hayes, 2017; Brengman *et al.*, 2019; Neo *et al.*, 2021), mainly to compensate for the smoothed slip beyond the true spatial extent due to inversion regularization. Our estimated extent of 18 ± 1.5 km indicates that the rupture was concentrated along strike, shorter than the empirical 30 ± 10 km rupture length expected for M_w 6.6 earthquakes (Fig. 9; Leonard, 2010; Brengman *et al.*, 2019), and toward the low end of the range observed for strike-slip earthquakes of similar magnitude (Mai and Beroza, 2000, 2002; Thingbaijam *et al.*, 2017). The peak slip of ~2.5 m is relatively high for an intraplate event of this size. Static stress-drop calculations, using the method by Ripperger and Mai (2004), identify two high-value patches associated with asperity 1 (Fig. S9), with an average static stress drop of ~9.3 MPa, ~50% higher than the global intraplate average (Kanamori and Anderson, 1975), consistent with the relatively concentrated stress release.

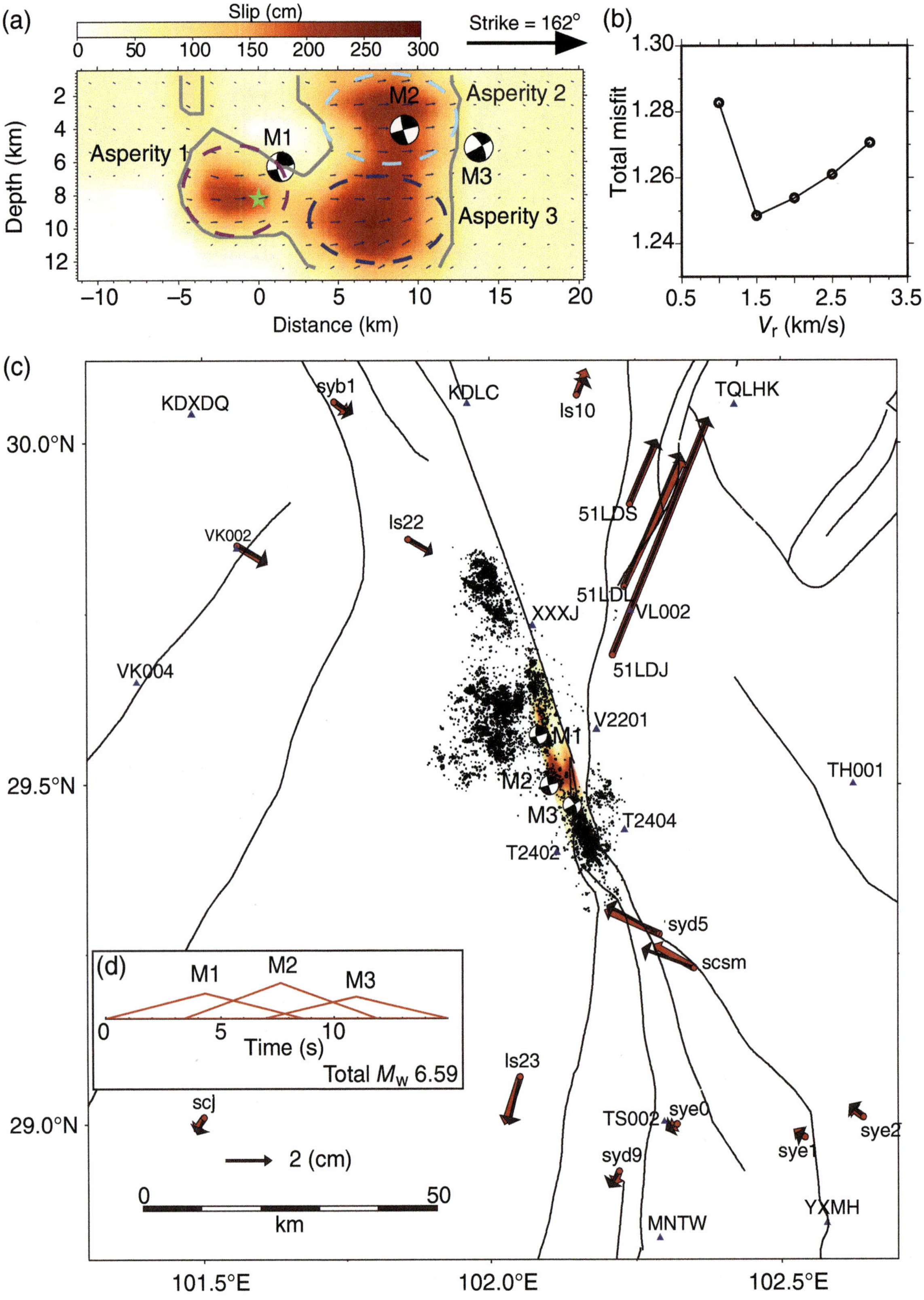

Figure 7. Kinematic source model of the mainshock. (a) Finite-fault model (background) color coded by slip distance and multiple-point-source (focal mechanism plots) models of the mainshock, with the star denoting the hypocenter, gray line indicating 15% of the peak slip, and arrows showing rake angle. (b) Comparison of misfit using different baseline rupture speeds in finite-fault inversions. (c) Map view of the kinematic models in panel (a), overlapped with aftershocks (dots) within 10 days after the mainshock and fits between synthetic (red arrows) and observed (black arrows) Global Navigation Satellite System (GNSS) offsets. Faults are plotted as black lines. (d) Source time functions of three subevents obtained from the multiple-point-source inversion.

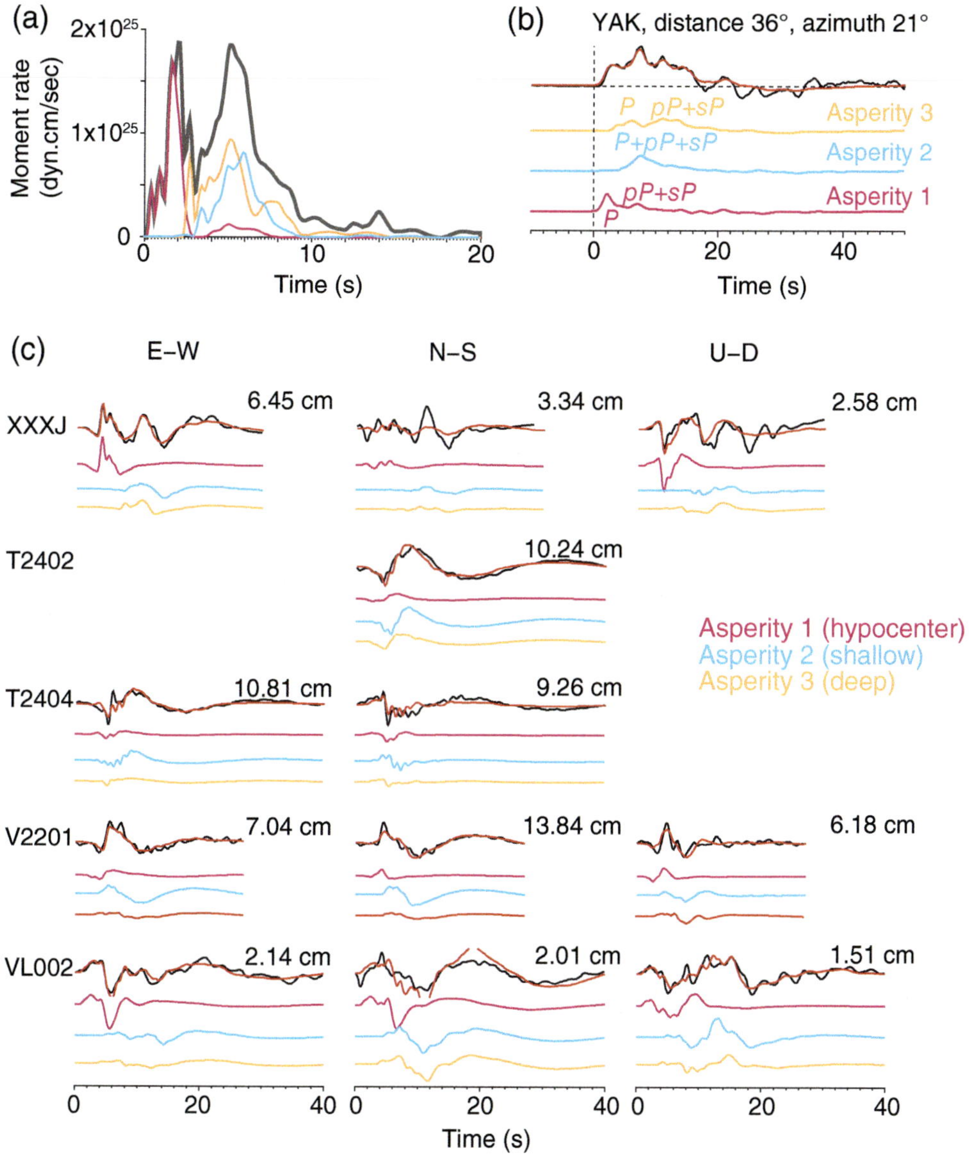

Figure 8. Contribution of three asperities. (a) Moment rate functions of total slip (gray) and individual asperities (red, blue, and orange). (b) Contribution of three asperities on the teleseismic *P*-wave pack at station YAK, with direct *P*, reflected *pP*, and *sP* phases indicated above each waveform. (c) Contribution of three asperities on nearby stations with station codes labeled on the left and peak displacements (in centimeters) labeled on the top right. All the waveforms are low-pass filtered to 1 Hz.

Relationship to seismicity

To understand the three asperities in the context of seismicity on the Xianshuihe fault, we projected seismicity of clusters 1, 2, and 4 onto profile B–B′ (Fig. 10). The seismicity extends laterally for ~60 km, with a clear gap (between −18 and −12 km) between the on- and off-fault events (Fig. 10).

The on-fault events mainly belong to clusters 2 and 4, with a lateral extent two times longer than the rupture extent of the mainshock rupture (red area). The aftershocks complement the slip distribution of individual asperities. Taking asperity 1 as an example, ~100 early aftershocks occupy a low- or no-slip zone near the hypocenter at 5–10 km depth (distance between −10 and 5 km in Fig. 10c). Background seismicity also shows gaps coincident with the mainshock rupture (Fig. 10a), implying asperities were fully locked during the interseismic period. South of the mainshock, aftershocks reveal an east-dipping fault with a dip angle of ~75° (Fig. 6), contrasting with the west-dipping northern rupture (Fig. 5). The off-fault seismicity (distance between −30 and −20 km in Fig. 10) was substantially more active after the mainshock.

PROPOSED FAULT STRUCTURE

To reconcile the distribution of seismicity, mainshock rupture, surface fault traces, and geologic units, we propose a simplified fault structural model (Fig. 11). In this model, the focal mechanisms of strike-slip and normal faults are compatible with the regional stress field (Fig. 2). The stress regime is characterized by a northwest–southeast-oriented maximum compressional principal axis, consistent with the rotation of the Sichuan–Yunnan rhombic block and the relative motion along the Xianshuihe fault (Xu *et al.*, 2003).

A key feature of this model is the presence of pervasive active faults within the Sichuan–Yunnan rhombic block. These secondary faults include: (1) northwest-trending shallow normal faults east of the Gongga Mountain; and (2) left-lateral strike-slip faults located 20–30 km north of the mainshock epicenter, intersecting the Xianshuihe fault at angles of 20°–30°. These faults bound migmatite units that formed 27–25 Ma. In addition, deeper right-lateral strike-slip faults trending northeast are also present. The relationship between the deep strike-slip faults and the overlying normal faults can be explained by the "bookshelf" fault model that has been supported by Li *et al.* (2016), which predicts northwest striking, northeast dipping of the normal faults.

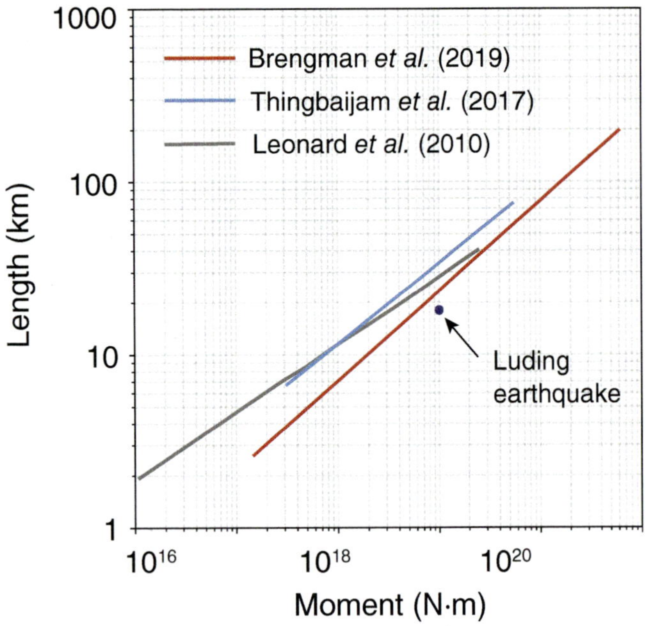

Figure 9. Comparison between empirical rupture length and moment relationships for strike-slip earthquakes and that of the 2022 M_w 6.6 Luding earthquake (18 km).

The convex boundary of the Sichuan–Yunnan rhombic block promotes stress diffusion into the more compliant block, reactivating secondary faults both before and after the mainshock. Stress transfer from the Xianshuihe fault likely occurs at depth and propagates upward, activating shallow normal faults through the bookshelf mechanism. These secondary faults are absent in the Sichuan block, which is a more rigid craton compared to the Sichuan–Yunnan block.

DISCUSSION

Stress and geometry barrier

The sharp terminations of the mainshock slip coincide with the boundaries of aftershock clusters and the southern cluster of background seismicity, implying strong stress or geometric barriers that constrained rupture propagation.

At the northern end, the conjugate fault intersects the Xianshuihe fault at ~70° (blue line in Fig. 11). Long-term loading of this right-lateral fault increases the normal stress on the Xianshuihe fault segment north of this intersection, thereby strengthening the fault and impeding northward rupture propagation.

At the southern end, seismicity indicates a change in fault-dipping direction accompanied by a clockwise rotation of fault strike (black-dashed line in Fig. 11). This geometric barrier likely contributed to halting the southward propagation of the rupture. However, neither stress nor geometric barriers completely arrest rupture during a large earthquake; rather, they may delay rupture or cause slip deficit, ultimately triggering aftershocks beyond the boundary and contributing to interseismic stress accumulation. Alternatively, two overlapping strands may exist, though the absence of southern west-dipping seismicity makes this explanation less likely.

Seismicity and rupture kinematics

Our study reveals complex faulting activity associated with the Xianshuihe fault and the 2022 M_w 6.6 Luding earthquake based on several technical improvements from previous work. First, we incorporated the ML phase picks, which show low deviation (only 2–3 samples in digital seismograms) from analysts' manual picks, contributing to consistent distributions of background seismicity and aftershocks. Second, our combined earthquake catalog of background seismicity and aftershocks lowered the completeness threshold from M_L 1.0 to 0.5 compared with previous studies (Liu, Li, *et al.*, 2023), yielding an order of magnitude more events for both the main fault and smaller secondary faults. Third, we use the multiple-point-source model to guide the development of a more comprehensive finite-fault model, reducing the uncertainties surrounding fault geometries and asperity sizes, and eliminating the possibility of conjugate fault rupture during the mainshock. Fourth, our joint inversion combining regional seismic, GNSS, and teleseismic data provides an effective constraint on depths, locations, distinct frequency content, and moment release of individual asperities. Our rupture model differs from several published models, as outlined subsequently (Fig. S2). We resolved three major asperities, whereas previous studies reported one (Guo *et al.*, 2023; Han *et al.*, 2023) or two (Zhao *et al.*, 2023; Zhang *et al.*, 2023). Zhang *et al.* (2023) suggested a deeper slip patch (~15 km), whereas Zhao *et al.* (2023) reported faster rupture speed (2.0–3.4 km/s) and greater moment release at their second asperity (Fig. S2). Synthetic waveform comparisons (Fig. 12) show that our three-point-source model improved the average CC to the nearest 12 strong-motion stations by 33% compared to Zhao *et al.* (2023), despite that our model requires an order of magnitude fewer parameters. Unlike the well-isolated asperity 1, asperities 2 and 3 exhibit less distinct spatial separation, implying a more gradual and smoother progression of rupture from the near-surface zone to greater depths.

These advances enable us to gain new insights into fault properties associated with this earthquake sequence, as well as the interplay between the Xianshuihe fault and secondary fault structures.

Heterogeneous fault properties

Spatially, the early aftershock zone extends two to four times beyond the concentrated mainshock slip zone, an atypical contrast for crustal earthquakes (Neo *et al.*, 2021). The fact that the majority of abundant early aftershocks complement slip distribution and fill the gaps between asperities supports the conclusion that the mainshock may have fully released the slip deficit within the asperities, thus producing a high stress drop.

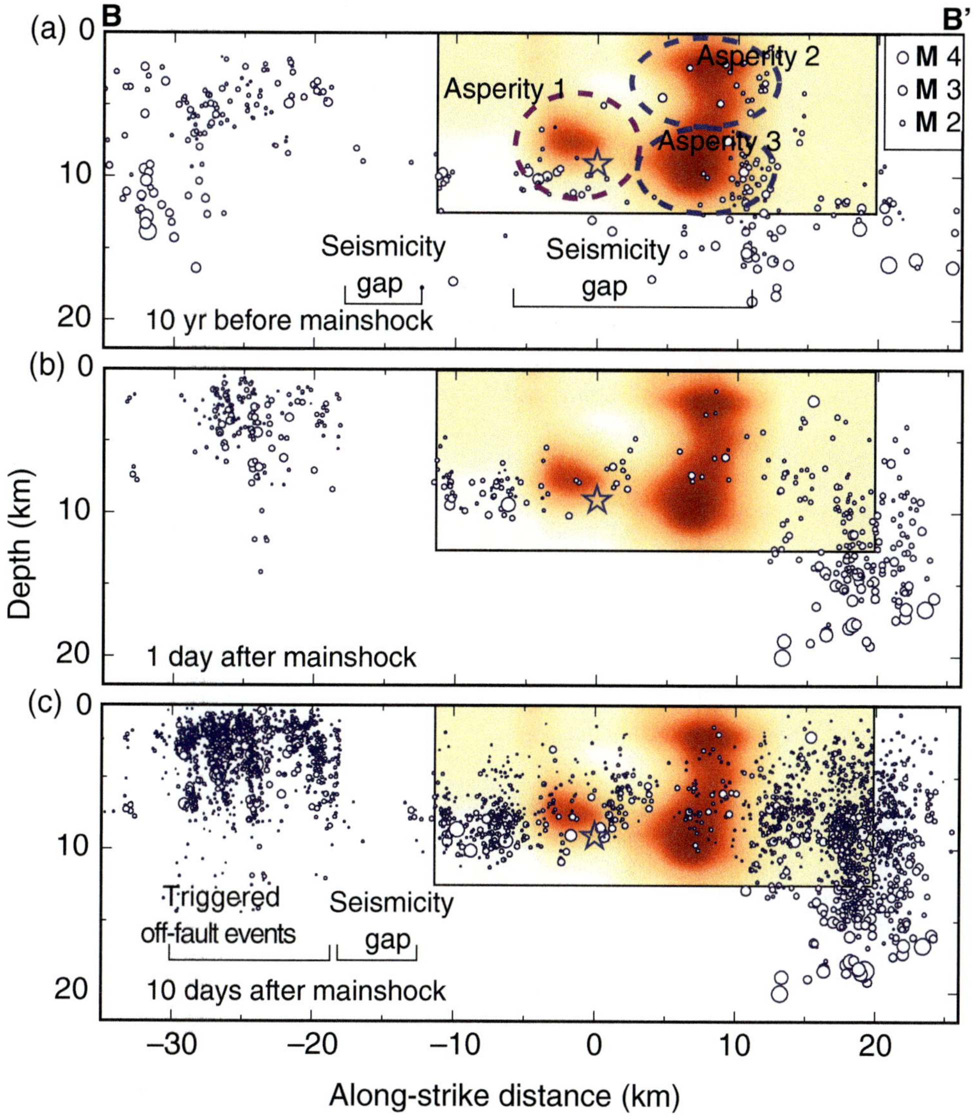

Figure 10. Seismicity of profile B and its relation with mainshock slip. (a) 9.5-yr background seismicity overlapped with the three-asperity slip distribution of the mainshock (background color in red to yellow). (b) The first 1-day aftershocks overlapped with the mainshock slip distribution. (c) Aftershocks 10 days after the mainshock overlapped with the mainshock slip distribution. The mainshock hypocenter is marked as a star, and other events are plotted in circles with sizes proportional to magnitudes.

The frictional properties of mainshock asperities show along-strike variations. Asperity 1 presents a shorter source duration (~3 s) that is 50% of the duration of asperities 2 and 3 (Fig. 8a), although their spatial extent and total slip distance are similar. This contrast indicates asperity 1 experienced relatively faster slip velocity, which radiated higher-frequency energy. Although the literature we reviewed does not provide a lithological explanation for the higher rupture velocity observed along asperity 1, high stress concentration is likely the cause of faster energy release at the initial stage of the rupture.

Besides potential stress barriers separating the mainshock asperity and seismicity, heterogeneous frictional properties may contribute to variabilities of friction properties, and overall size of slip patches within individual zones on the fault. These frictional properties may be controlled by geological structures (Shi *et al.*, 2020). For example, the fault surface formed by fractured migmatite and Triassic granite may be associated with smaller isolated slip patches, linked to abundant seismicity, whereas the Upper Triassic layer is more continuous, associated with larger mainshock asperities. Moreover, such heterogeneity is persistent, as evidenced by the consistent distribution between the 9.5 yr background seismicity and early aftershocks.

Rupture dynamics

Our observed stress and geometry barriers are intrinsically connected. Dynamic earthquake simulations (Harris *et al.*, 1991) show that stepovers or changes in dip can slow or arrest rupture propagation depending on prestress and geometric variation, though such barriers are not always effective (e.g., 2010 M_w 7.2 El Mayor–Cucapah; Wei *et al.*, 2011). For the 2022 Luding earthquake, stress accumulation near a fault jog, combined with geometric complexity, likely increased stress heterogeneity and created potential nucleation zones for future earthquakes (Wesnousky, 2006).

Topography also influenced rupture dynamics. The Xianshuihe fault separates the Sichuan basin from the high Gongga Mountain (7556 m). We used the method of Liu and Zoback (1992), implemented via an open-source package (Styron and Hetland, 2015), to estimate topographic stresses at fault grid points in our finite-fault model (Fig. S10). Our stress profiles show strong gradients in both normal (~10 MPa) and strike-slip (~2.5 MPa) stresses near the Luding hypocenter, with normal stress exhibiting the largest amplitude. This concentrated rupture and stress heterogeneity highlight the role of topography on both the earthquake nucleation and rupture termination processes.

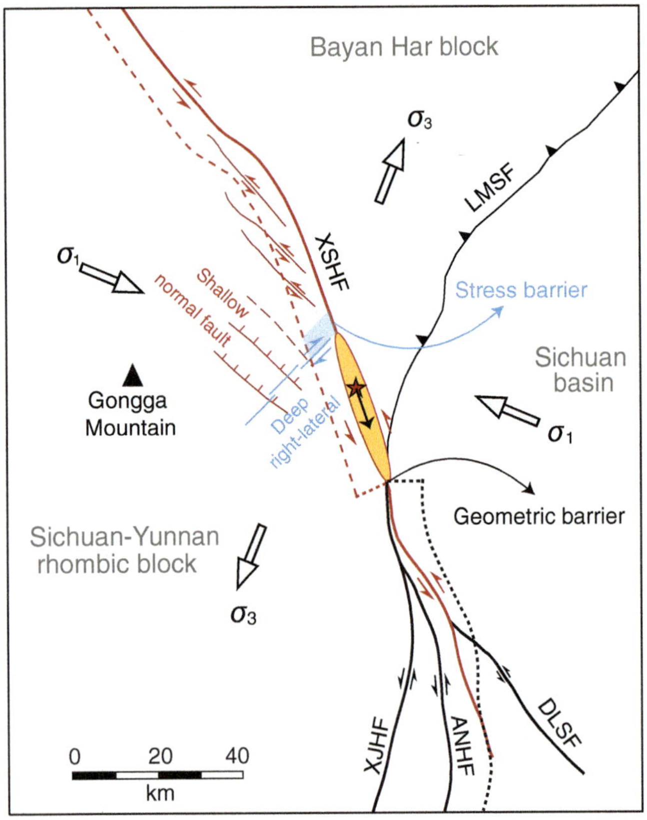

Figure 11. Conceptual model of fault structure near the Luding earthquake. Surface fault traces are shown as solid lines, and inferred geometries at depth are indicated by dashed lines. The Xianshuihe is colored in red with an orange ellipse denoting the approximate ruptured extent during the 2022 Luding mainshock, within which the red star is the hypocenter and the black arrow implies rupture directivity. Sense of motion is shown for strike-slip (arrows), normal (ticks), and reverse (sawteeth) faults. Regional stress field (Wang and Shen, 2020) is indicated by open arrows. See Figure 1 for abbreviations.

Additional factors affecting rupture dynamics involve pore-fluid pressure, secondary faulting, and velocity structure, which could be associated with geological structures. Hot springs along the Xianshuihe fault suggest fluid involvement, potentially a source of changes in effective normal stress. Our fault structure model highlights pervasive secondary faults that contribute to stress complexity. Furthermore, seismicity correlates with Poisson's ratio anomalies (Cai *et al.*, 2023), with the Luding hypocenter located at the boundary of low-V_P and low-Poisson's ratio zones (Fig. S11), coinciding with topographic gradients. These observations emphasize the interplay of geological structure, fluids, and topography in concentrating stress and promoting unstable slip.

The mainshock rupture also influences secondary faults through stress transfer. Coulomb stress changes for vertical faults striking 315° (Fig. S12a) explain aftershocks in clusters 1 and 3 as triggered events. Similar analysis (Zhang *et al.*, 2023) using the main-fault geometry shows consistency in aftershock distribution.

CONCLUSION

We present a fault structure model for the Xianshuihe fault system that integrates relocated seismicity (both historical events and the 2022 sequence), the regional stress field, the coseismic rupture characteristics, and fault geometries. This framework provides new insights into the seismotectonics of a geologically complex region, although the detailed structures near Gongga Mountain remain unresolved. Future high-resolution observations and fault mapping will be crucial for addressing these complexities, advancing our understanding of earthquake physics, and refining seismic hazard assessments.

Using both near-field and teleseismic data, we derived a first-order coseismic rupture model through a multiple-point-source scheme, which served as the foundation for a detailed finite-fault model validated against both seismic and geodetic observations. By integrating these geophysical results with available geological mapping, we developed a self-consistent interpretation of the regional seismotectonics. Our multidisciplinary approach—combining seismicity catalogs, waveform inversions, geodesy, stress modeling, and topographic analysis—marks a significant step forward from previous studies of the 2022 Luding earthquake.

DATA AND RESOURCES

The teleseismic data used here are downloaded using the Standing Order for Data (Owens *et al.*, 2004). The mainshock data used here are available at https://researchdata.ntu.edu.sg/dataset.xhtml?persistentId=doi:10.21979/N9/LXOYVL (last accessed September 2022). The regional seismic data were last accessed in October 2022 from the Earthquake Science Data Center, Institute of Geophysics, China Earthquake Administration (http://esdc.ac.cn/, last accessed October 2022). The original aftershock catalog data are available at http://www.cses.ac.cn/detail/showDetail.shtml?id=ff80808183e9b7830186b6f6238f601e (last accessed March 2023). The original catalog data are manually reviewed and provided by China Earthquake Networks Center (CENC), China Earthquake Administration. Geological data and focal mechanisms data for $M_w > 3.5$ events are available at the National Earthquake Data Center of China (http://data.earthquake.cn, last accessed January 2023). The near-field seismic data are provided by the CENC. The supplemental material contains regional maps (Figs. S1 and S5); slip models (Fig. S2); waveform comparison (Figs. S3, S4, S6, and S7); mainshock rupture extent (Fig. S8); stress drop (Fig. S9); topographic stress (Fig. S10); tomographic velocity structure (Fig. S11); Coulomb stress change (Fig. S12); additional seismicity profiles (Figs. S13 and S14); and the 1D velocity model for earthquake relocation (Table S1). A separate file is uploaded as Table S2. The code package for topographic stress can be found in Styron and Hetland (2015).

DECLARATION OF COMPETING INTERESTS

The authors acknowledge that there are no conflicts of interest recorded.

ACKNOWLEDGMENTS

The authors thank the Associate Editor Thomas M. Brocher and the two anonymous reviewers for their constructive review, which has

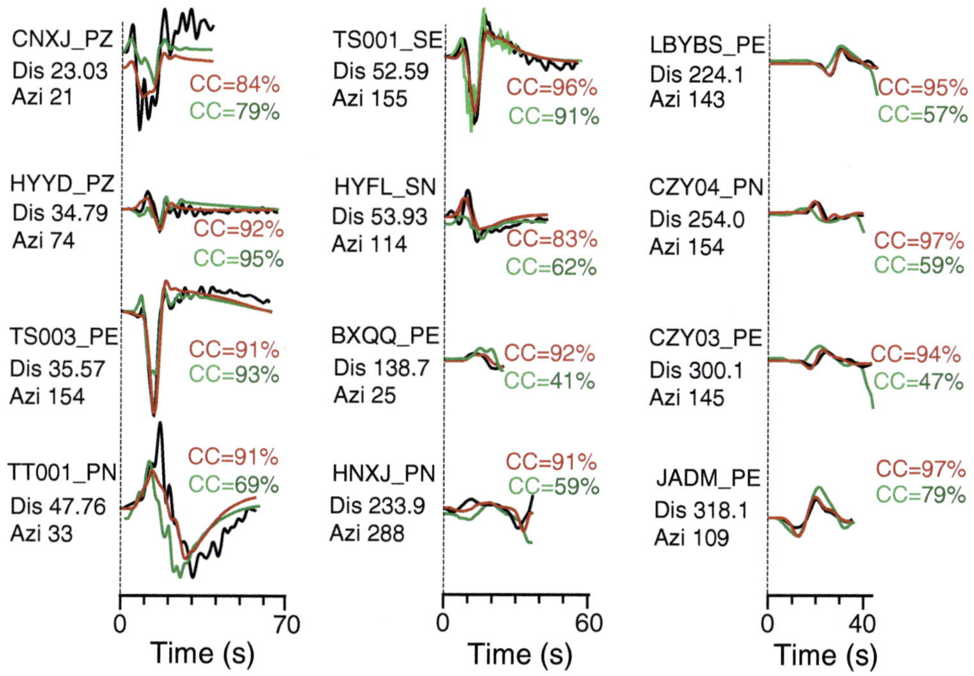

Figure 12. Comparison between the observed waveforms for the Luding mainshock at nearest stations (black lines), the synthetic waveforms using Zhao *et al.* (2023; green lines), and this study (red lines). The station code, distance (dis; in kilometers), and azimuth (azi; in degrees) are indicated on the left side. CC, cross-correlation coefficient.

improved this summary. The figures in the article are plotted using the Generic Mapping Tools (GMT; Wessel *et al.*, 2019). The seismic waveforms are processed using Seismic Analysis Code (SAC) (Goldstein and Snoke, 2005). The project benefits from discussion with Feng Jiang and Feng Long. This work is supported by the Chinese Academy of Sciences (Grant Number E4515401), State Key Laboratory of Earthquake Dynamics and Forecasting (LED2021A07), the Poh-Hsi Pan Postdoctoral Fellowship, and the National Natural Science Foundation of China (42174078).

REFERENCES

Allen, C. R., Z. Luo, H. Qian, X. Wen, H. Zhou, and W. Huang (1991). Field study of a highly active fault zone: The Xianshuihe fault of southwestern China, *Geol. Soc. Am. Bull.* **103,** no. 9, 1178–1199.

Allen, T. I., and G. P. Hayes (2017). Alternative rupture-scaling relationships for subduction interface and other offshore environments, *Bull. Seismol. Soc. Am.* **107,** no. 3, 1240–1253.

Bai, M., M. L. Chevalier, P. H. Leloup, H. Li, J. Pan, A. Replumaz, S. Wang, K. Li, Q. Wu, and F. Liu (2021). Spatial slip rate distribution along the SE Xianshuihe fault, eastern Tibet, and earthquake hazard assessment, *Tectonics* **40,** no. 11, e2021TC006985, doi: 10.1029/2021TC006985.

Brengman, C. M. J., W. D. Barnhart, E. H. Mankin, and C. N. Miller (2019). Earthquake-scaling relationships from geodetically derived slip distributions, *Bull. Seismol. Soc. Am.* **109,** no. 5, 1701–1715, doi: 10.1785/0120190048.

Cai, G., W. Wang, J. Wu, J. Su, G. Lai, P. Wu, L. Chen, and J. Su (2023). Three-dimensional body wave velocity structure and seismogenic structure for the 2022 MS 6.8 Luding earthquake sequence in Sichuan, China, *Front. Earth Sci.* **11,** 1099744, doi: 10.3389/feart.2023.1099744.

Cesca, S., S. Heimann, K. Stammler, and T. Dahm (2010). Automated procedure for point and kinematic source inversion at regional distances, *J. Geophys. Res.* **115,** no. B6304, doi: 10.1029/2009JB006450.

Deng, Q. D., P. Z. Zhang, Y. K. Ran, X. P. Yang, W. Min, and L. C. Chen (2003). Active tectonics and earthquake activities in China, *Earth Sci. Front.* **10,** no. S1, 66–73.

Efron, B., and G. Gong (1983). A leisurely look at the bootstrap, the jackknife, and. cross-validation, *Am. Stat.* **37,** no. 1, 36–48.

Efron, B., and R. Tibshirani (1991). Statistics data analysis in the computer age, *Science* **253,** 390–395.

Goldstein, P., and A. Snoke (2005). SAC availability for the IRIS community, *Incorporated Research Institutions for Seismology Newsletter*, Vol. 7, UCRL-JRNL-211140.

Guo, R., L. Li, W. Zhang, Y. Zhang, X. Tang, K. Dai, Y. Di, L. Zhang, and J. Wang (2023). Kinematic slip evolution during the 2022 Ms 6.8 Luding, China, earthquake: Compatible with the preseismic locked patch, *Geophys. Res. Lett.* **50,** no. 5, e2023GL103164, doi: 10.1029/2023GL103164.

Han, B., Z. Liu, B. Chen, Z. Li, C. Yu, Y. Zhang, and J. Peng (2023). Coseismic deformation and slip distribution of the 2022 Luding Mw 6.6 earthquake revealed by InSAR observations, *Geo. Inform. Sci. Wuhan Univ.* **48,** no. 1, 36–46.

Harris, R. A., R. J. Archuleta, and S. M. Day (1991). Fault steps and the dynamic rupture process: 2-D numerical simulations of a spontaneously propagating shear fracture, *Geophys. Res. Lett.* **18,** no. 5, 893–896.

Heimann, S. (2011). A robust method to estimate kinematic earthquake source parameters, *Ph.D. Thesis*, University of Hamburg, Hamburg, Germany.

Ji, C., D. J. Wald, and D. V. Helmberger (2002). Source description of the 1999 Hector Mine, California, earthquake, part I: Wavelet domain inversion theory and resolution analysis, *Bull. Seismol. Soc. Am.* **92,** no. 4, 1192–1207, doi: 10.1785/0120000916.

Kanamori, H., and D. L. Anderson (1975). Theoretical basis of some empirical relations in seismology, *Bull. Seismol. Soc. Am.* **65,** no. 5, 1073–1095.

Leonard, M. (2010). Earthquake fault scaling: Self-consistent relating of rupture length, width, average displacement, and moment release, *Bull. Seismol. Soc. Am.* **100,** no. 5A, 1971–1988, doi: 10.1785/0120090189.

Li, C., Z. Peng, D. Yao, H. Guo, Z. Zhan, and H. Zhang (2018). Abundant aftershock sequence of the 2015 Mw 7.5 Hindu Kush intermediate-depth earthquake, *Geophys. J. Int.* **213,** no. 2, 1121–1134.

Li, H., Y. Zhang, C. Zhang, and J. Wang (2016). Zircon U-Pb study of two-staged Oligo-Miocene migmatization along the Xianshuihe fault zone, East Tibet Plateau, *Earth Sci. Front.* **23,** no. 2, 222.

Li, Y., D. Zhao, X. Shan, Z. Gao, X. Huang, and W. Gong (2022). Coseismic slip model of the 2022 Mw6.7 Luding (Tibet) earthquake: Pre and post-earthquake interactions with surrounding major faults, *Geophys. Res. Lett.* **49,** e2022GL102043, doi: 10.1029/2022GL102043.

Liu, L., and M. D. Zoback (1992). The effect of topography on the state of stress in the crust: Application to the site of the Cajon Pass Scientific Drilling Project, *J. Geophys. Res.: Solid Earth* **97,** no. B4, 5095–5108.

Liu, Y., Z. Yu, Z. Zhang, H. Yao, W. Wang, H. Zhang, H. Fang, and L. Fang (2023). The high-resolution community velocity model V2.0 of southwest China, constructed by joint body and surface wave tomography of data recorded at temporary dense arrays, *Sci. China Earth Sci.* doi: 10.1007/s11430-022-1161-7.

Liu, Z., J. Li, J. Su, Z. Yu, C. Huang, Y. Qi, Y. Chen, and W. Wang (2023). Auto-building of aftershock sequence and seismicity analysis for the 2022 Luding, Sichuan, MS 6.8 earthquake, *Chin. J. Geophys.* **66,** no. 5, 1976–1990.

Mai, P. M., and G. C. Beroza (2000). Source-scaling properties from finite-fault rupture models, *Bull. Seismol. Soc. Am.* **90,** 604–615.

Mai, P. M., and G. C. Beroza (2002). A spatial random-field model to characterize complexity in earthquake slip, *J. Geophys. Res.* **107,** no. B11, 2308, doi: 10.1029/2001JB000588.

Neo, J. C., Y. Huang, D. Yao, and S. Wei (2021). Is the aftershock zone area a good proxy for the mainshock rupture area? *Bull. Seismol. Soc. Am.* **111,** no. 1, 424–438.

Owens, T. J., H. P. Crotwell, C. Groves, and P. Oliver-Paul (2004). SOD: Standing order for data, *Seismol. Res. Lett.* **75,** no. 4, 515–520, doi: 10.1785/gssrl.75.4.515-a.

Ripperger, J., and P. M. Mai (2004). Fast computation of static stress changes on 2D faults from final slip distributions, *Geophys. Res. Lett.* **31,** no. 18, doi: 10.1029/2004GL020594.

Shi, Q., S. Barbot, S. Wei, P. Tapponnier, T. Matsuzawa, and B. Shibazaki (2020). Structural control and system-level behavior of the seismic cycle at the Nankai Trough, *Earth Planets Space* **72,** no. 1, 27.

Shi, Q., S. Wei, and M. Chen (2018). An MCMC multiple point sources inversion scheme and its application to the 2016 Kumamoto Mw 6.2 earthquake, *Geophys. J. Int.* **215,** no. 2, 737–752, doi: 10.1093/gji/ggy302.

Styron, R. H., and E. A. Hetland (2015). The weight of the mountains: Constraints on tectonic stress, friction, and fluid pressure in the 2008 Wenchuan earthquake from estimates of topographic loading, *J. Geophys. Res.: Solid Earth* **120,** 2697–2716, doi: 10.1002/2014JB011338.

Tang, Y., P. Wang, H. Deng, Y. Liu, and W. Tang (2022). Petrological records of major tectono-magmatic events since Oligocene in the southeastern segment of Xianshuihe fault zone in the eastern margin of Tibetan Plateau[J], *Geol. Bull. China* **41,** no. 7, 1121–1143, doi: 10.12097/j.issn.1671-2552.2022.07.001.

Thingbaijam, K. K. S., P. M. Mai, and K. Goda (2017). New empirical earthquake source scaling laws, *Bull. Seismol. Soc. Am.* **107,** no. 5, 2225–2246, doi: 10.1785/0120170017.

Waldhauser, F., and W. A. Ellsworth (2000). Double-difference earthquake location algorithm: Method and application to the northern Hayward fault, California., *Bull. Seismol. Soc. Am.* **90,** 1353–1368.

Wang, H., M. Liu, X.-H. Shen, and J. Liu (2009). Balance of seismic moment in the Songpan-Ganze region, eastern Tibet: Implications for the 2008 Great Wenchuan earthquake, *Tectonophysics* doi: 10.1016/j.tecto.2009.09.022.

Wang, M., and Z. Shen (2020). Present-day crustal deformation of continental China derived from GPS and its tectonic implications, *J. Geophys. Res.: Solid Earth* **125,** no. 2, doi: 10.1029/2019JB018774.

Wei, S., E. Fielding, S. Leprince, A. Sladen, J. P. Avouac, D. Helmberger, E. Hauksson, R Chu, M. Simons, K. Hudnut, *et al.* (2011). Superficial simplicity of the 2010 Mw 7.2 El Mayor-Cucapah earthquake of Baja California, Mexico, *Nature Geosci.* 4, 615–618.

Wen, X., S. Ma, X. Xu, and Y. He (2008). Historical pattern and behavior of earthquake ruptures along the eastern boundary of the Sichuan-Yunnan faulted-block, southwestern China, *Phys. Earth Planet. In.* **168,** nos. 1/2, 16–36, doi: 10.1016/j.pepi.2008.04.013.

Wesnousky, S. G. (2006). Predicting the endpoints of earthquake ruptures, *Nature* **444,** no. 7117, 358–360.

Wessel, P., J. Luis, L. Uieda, R. Scharroo, F. Wobbe, W. Smith, and D. Tian (2019). The generic mapping tools version 6, *Geochem. Geophys. Geosys.* **20,** no. 11, 5556–5564, doi: 10.1029/2019gc008515.

Xu, C., Y. Zhang, R. Wang, S. Hua, Y. Xu, D. Dai, Y. Pang, and J. Su (2023). Application of MEMS data to fast inversion of rupture process: Tests with recordings from the IRREEW network, *Seismol. Res. Lett.* **94,** no. 4, doi: 10.1785/0220220369.

Xu, X., X. Wen, R. Zheng, W. Ma, F. Song, and G. Yu (2003). Pattern of latest tectonic motion and its dynamics for active blocks in Sichuan-Yunnan region, China, *Sci. China Earth Sci.* **46,** no. Suppl 2, 210–226.

Yi, G., F. Long, M. Liang, M. Zhao, H. Zhang, R. Zhou, Y. Li, H. Liu, P. Wu, S. Wang, *et al.* (2023). Seismogenic structure of the 5 September 2022 Sichuan Luding M S 6.8 earthquake sequence, *Chin. J. Geophys.* **66,** no. 4, 1363–1384.

Zhang, L., Y. Zhou, X. Zhang, A. Zhu, B. Li, S. Wang, S. Liang, C. Jiang, J. Wu, Y. Li, *et al.* (2023). 2022 Mw 6.6 Luding, China, earthquake: A strong continental event illuminating the Moxi seismic gap, *Seismol. Res. Lett.* **95,** no. 5, doi: 10.1785/0220220383.

Zhao, X., Z. Xiao, W. Wang, J. Li, M. Zhao, S. Chen, and L. Tang (2023). Fine seismogenic fault structures and complex rupture characteristics of the 2022 M6.8 Luding, Sichuan earthquake sequence revealed by deep learning and waveform modeling, *Geophys. Res. Lett.* **50,** e2023GL102976, doi: 10.1029/2023GL102976.

Zhu, L., and D. V. Helmberger (1996). Advancement in source estimation techniques using broadband regional seismograms, *Bull. Seismol. Soc. Am.* **86,** 1634–1641.

Manuscript received 30 May 2024
Published online 31 December 2025

Stochastic Inversions for Source, Path, and Site Parameters from West Texas Earthquakes

Bartik Pandel[*1], Ellen M. Rathje[2], Alexandros Savvaidis[3], and Albert R. Kottke[4]

ABSTRACT

This study utilizes recorded ground motions from West Texas to evaluate the source, path, and site effects in this region. We analyze the Fourier amplitude spectra from 354 earthquakes in the Delaware basin recorded by the TexNet seismic network at 49 sites. The magnitudes of the earthquakes range from ~3.0 to 5.0, with hypocentral distances up to 300 km. Using a Bayesian parametric inversion on 6479 records, we simulate the spectra as a combination of source, path, and site effects from a stochastic point-source model. The inverted moment magnitudes were comparable to the catalog moment magnitudes, and the stress parameter ($\Delta\sigma$) ranged from 5 to 134 bar, increasing with magnitude. The geometrical spreading was characterized by a smooth bilinear function, yielding a near-field γ of 1.15 and a frequency-dependent quality factor of $Q = 837 \cdot f^{0.59}$. The inverted site amplification functions revealed six distinct clusters of response, with three clusters located in the western part of the study area and the other three scattered to the east. The inverted high-frequency decay parameter (κ_0) ranged from 0.005 to 0.056 s, with no clear relationship to shear-wave velocity but systematic variation with cluster and location. Correlation between parameters was observed, but only the prior distribution of $\Delta\sigma$ strongly influenced the other inverted parameters.

KEY POINTS

- Seismological parameters in West Texas are derived via stochastic inversions of recorded ground motions.
- The parameters together capture magnitude and distance scaling, and site amplification and site attenuation.
- The parameters can be used to develop region-specific ground-motion models via the hybrid empirical approach.

Supplemental Material

INTRODUCTION

In West Texas, particularly in the Delaware basin, a discernible increase in seismic activity has prompted extensive research into its origins and characteristics. The prevailing consensus attributes this phenomenon to oil and gas production, with fluid disposal and hydraulic fracturing being recognized as the main sources of this induced seismicity (Savvaidis *et al.*, 2020; Grigoratos *et al.*, 2022). Noteworthy findings from prior investigations in the Fort Worth basin of Texas emphasize the role of stress changes resulting from fluid disposal in triggering earthquakes (Jeong *et al.*, 2021). This mechanism weakens the shear strength of faults, leading to slip events. Hydraulic fracturing, a technique that involves injecting fluids to fracture rock and enhance permeability, also contributes to stress changes and has been linked to seismic activity in various regions (Butcher *et al.*, 2020). In the broader Central and Eastern North America (CENA), earthquakes exceeding a magnitude of 3.5 have been linked to fluid disposal from oil and gas production (Ellsworth, 2013; Grigoratos *et al.*, 2022). Induced earthquakes typically exhibit shallow depths and smaller magnitudes, in contrast to tectonic earthquakes that tend to occur at greater depths and produce larger magnitudes (Boyd *et al.*, 2017).

Of particular concern in West Texas is the elevated frequency of moderate earthquakes ($M \geq 4.0$) that have the potential to induce damage to infrastructure. Between 1 January 2017 and 23 July 2024, the region experienced 45 earthquakes with magnitudes greater than or equal to 4.0, underscoring the urgency for improved understanding of the ground shaking generated by these events and the potential for damage to infrastructure that has not been designed to withstand earthquake shaking due to the low rates of natural seismicity in the area.

The stochastic point-source method is a widely used approach for predicting ground shaking, particularly in stable

1. GeoEngineers, Tacoma, Washington, U.S.A., https://orcid.org/0009-0005-7136-6717 (BP); 2. Fariborz Maseeh Department of Civil, Architectural, and Environmental Engineering, The University of Texas at Austin, Austin, Texas, U.S.A., https://orcid.org/0000-0002-4169-7153 (EMR); 3. Bureau of Economic Geology, The University of Texas at Austin, Austin, Texas, U.S.A., https://orcid.org/0000-0001-6373-5256 (AS); 4. Pacific Gas and Electric Company, Oakland, California, U.S.A., https://orcid.org/0000-0002-1861-5682 (ARK)

*Corresponding author: bartikpandel@utexas.edu

Cite this article as Pandel, B., E. M. Rathje, A. Savvaidis, and A. R. Kottke (2025). Stochastic Inversions for Source, Path, and Site Parameters from West Texas Earthquakes, *Bull. Seismol. Soc. Am.* **116**, 663–679, doi: 10.1785/0120250078 continental regions with limited seismicity. This method, as elucidated by Boore (2003), utilizes simple physics-based formulations and parameters that capture the characteristics of seismic source properties, seismic-wave attenuation through the travel path, and near-surface site effects from shallow geological layers to determine the intensity of shaking. Recorded ground motions can be analyzed through inversion techniques to determine the seismic source, path, and site parameters and better understand their contributions to the observed shaking. These methods have been widely used globally for this purpose. In Texas, Jeong *et al.* (2021, 2022) applied stochastic inversions to study induced seismicity in the Dallas-Fort Worth area. However, a significant research gap remains in West Texas, where the geology is more complex and heterogeneous. Combined with a notably higher frequency and magnitude of events, these distinct geological conditions highlight the need for further investigation in the West Texas region.

The Texas Seismological Network (TexNet) has installed a dense array of seismometers in West Texas, and these data form the basis for the present study on ground-motion characteristics. This article focuses on the spectral characteristics of ground motions in West Texas, utilizing a parametric inversion technique to derive source properties, attenuation characteristics, and site response functions through predefined functional forms. The study emphasizes understanding the key parameters influencing ground motion in the region, exploring potential trade-offs and uncertainties, and aims to contribute to the future development of ground-motion prediction equations.

DATA SET AND PROCESSING

This study utilizes ground-motion records collected from stations in West Texas. These stations are equipped with broadband (BB) seismometers recording at sampling frequencies of either 100 or 200 Hz. The data collection spans from 1 January 2017 to 8 August 2023, focusing on earthquakes with local magnitude (M_L) ≥ 3.0 and hypocentral distances (R_{hyp}) up to 300 km. This initial data set consists of 13,009 records, each consisting of three components, from 360 earthquakes in the Delaware basin region of West Texas and recorded at 74 stations. The M_L values, epicentral locations, and depths are reported by TexNet (Bureau of Economic Geology, The University of Texas at Austin, 2016), and R_{hyp} values are computed from the station locations using the epicentral distance (R_{epi}) and depth.

To enhance the accuracy of our inversions, we performed an in-depth relocation of earthquake events starting with the locations provided by the TexNet web catalog (Bureau of Economic Geology, The University of Texas at Austin, 2016). This process involved employing a local 1D Earth model specific to the study area (see the supplemental material, available to this article, for the 1D Earth model employed) and applying the relocation method described by Lomax and Savvaidis (2022). The updated earthquake depths were typically 3.5–5.5 km shallower than the original values. These refined locations and depths were subsequently utilized in our inversion analysis.

Seismometer time-series data were downloaded from 30 s before to 150 s after the catalog origin time. For data processing, we utilized the gmprocess Python library developed by the U.S. Geological Survey (USGS; Thompson *et al.*, 2024a,b). Traces were screened for clipping, zero-crossing issues, and short signal or noise durations, and rejected if they failed quality checks. The instrument response was removed from the Fourier amplitudes of the raw velocity recordings, and the resulting velocity spectra were converted to acceleration by differentiating in the frequency domain. A combination of linear, demean, and pre-event detrending was applied, along with a Hann taper (5% width) on both ends. Signal and noise windows were defined using a travel-time model (iasp91) to estimate the *P*-wave arrival. The noise window spanned from the start of the trace to 1 s before the predicted *P*-wave arrival and was required to be at least 1.0 s in duration. The signal window began 1 s before the *P*-arrival time and was required to have a minimum length of 5.0 s.

Subsequently, the acceleration Fourier amplitude spectra (FAS) for the noise and signal components of each horizontal record were computed, smoothing it with a Konno–Ohmachi filter with $b = 40$ (Konno and Ohmachi, 1998). The frequency-dependent signal-to-noise ratio (SNR) was computed as the ratio of the smoothed signal and noise spectra. A band-pass filter was applied, with filter frequencies determined based on a minimum SNR of 3.0. In addition, the low-pass filter frequency (f_{LP}) was restricted to not exceed 80% of the Nyquist frequency (f_{Nyq}). If both horizontal components passed the SNR check, their intersecting frequency band was used to compute the geometric mean of the FAS at each frequency, resulting in a single FAS per record. A representative example is shown in Figure 1.

To ensure a reliable and stable inversion, we utilized events with a minimum of 10 records and stations with at least 5 records. Following these criteria, our final data set consisted of 6479 records from 354 earthquakes recorded at 49 stations. Furthermore, we set the usable frequency range for each record in the inversion to $1.2f_{HP}$ to $0.8f_{LP}$ to avoid the effects of filtering at the ends.

Figure 2 illustrates the spatial distribution of the stations and events for the final data set, and Figure 3 provides an overview of the data set characteristics. The events are concentrated on the western edge of the Delaware basin, a region of dense seismicity that has generated the largest magnitude earthquakes in the area. Events from other parts of the Delaware and Midland basins (also shown in Fig. 2) were excluded from the study due to the unavailability of relocated depths for the Midland basin events and the smaller magnitudes of events (< 3.5) in the southeastern Delaware basin, which produced very noisy records. The stations are distributed across the Delaware and Midland basins, as well as the Central Basin Platform, but with the highest density of stations in the Delaware basin. The time-averaged

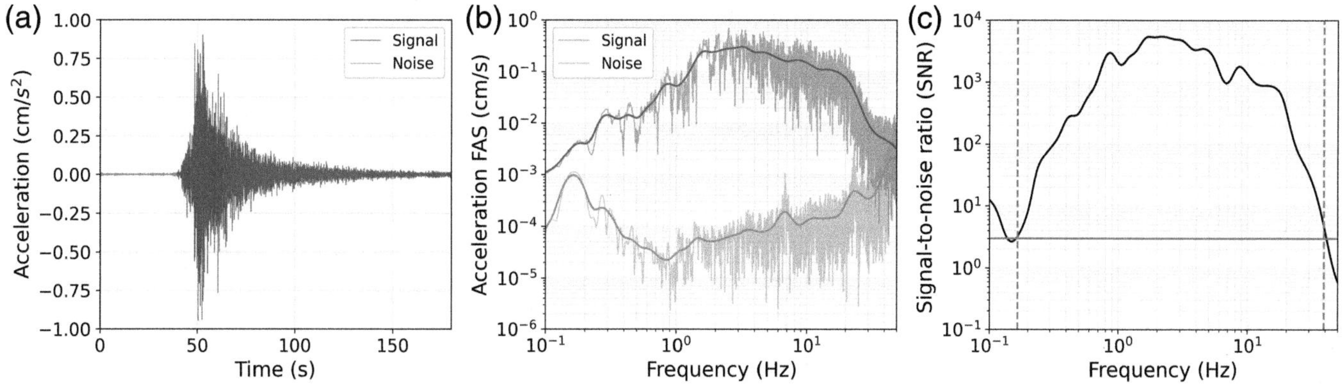

Figure 1. (a) Acceleration time series with noise (orange) and signal (blue) windows. (b) Corresponding Fourier amplitude spectrum (FAS) of the noise and signal. (c) Signal-to-noise ratio (SNR) with threshold of 3.0 (horizontal line) and selected frequency band (f_{HP}, f_{LP}) shown using vertical dashed lines. The color version of this figure is available only in the electronic edition.

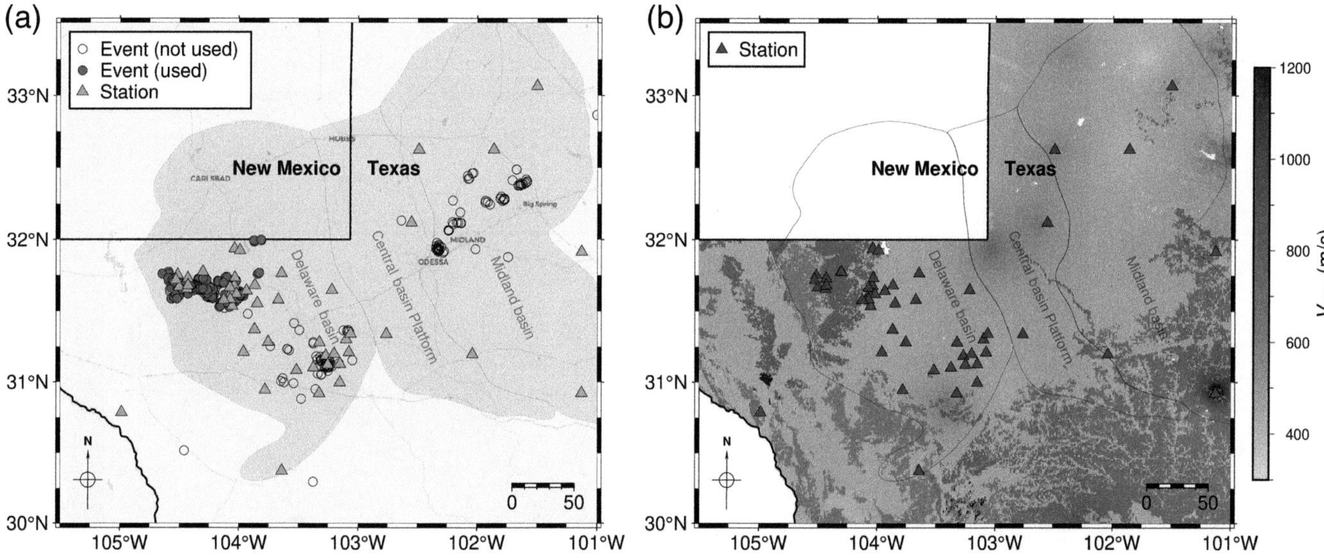

Figure 2. (a) Overview of the research area in West Texas, with basins highlighted in blue (from Dutton *et al.*, 2004), along with earthquake events and ground-motion recording stations used in the study. (b) Basin extents and stations from the Li *et al.* (2022) V_{S30} map of Texas. The color version of this figure is available only in the electronic edition.

shear-wave velocity in the top 30 m (V_{S30}) across the study region is generally within the range of 400–1000 m/s (Fig. 2b, Li *et al.*, 2022). It is notable that the V_{S30} along the edges of the Delaware and Midland basins exceed 700 m/s in some locations, which is due to the presence of Paleozoic and Mesozoic limestone and clastic sedimentary rocks at the surface (Li *et al.*, 2022).

The magnitude–distance distribution of the data set (Fig. 3a) shows that most of the data are associated with distances between 30 and 170 km and M_L values ranging from 3.0 to 3.5. The depth distribution of the events (Fig. 3b) indicates that all events have focal depths shallower than 10 km, with the majority concentrated around 2 km. Li *et al.* (2022) developed a V_{S30} map for Texas (Fig. 2b) using multiple methods, including the *P*-wave seismogram method, in situ V_{S30} values derived from measured V_S profiles, and a geologic proxy based on rock type and geologic age. For seven stations (ALPN, ODSA, PB01, PB05, PB11, PECS, and VHRN), direct shear-wave velocity profiles were available from Yust (2018) and used to calculate V_{S30}. For the remaining 42 stations, we used the Li *et al.* (2022) V_{S30} map to estimate the site conditions. All the stations have V_{S30} greater than 400 m/s and one station has V_{S30} ~1400 m/s. The distribution of the recordings with respect to V_{S30} is shown in Figure 3c. A significant portion (over 50%) of the recordings is from stiff soil sites, with V_{S30} values ranging between 400 and 500 m/s. In addition, approximately 30% of the recordings are from rock sites, with V_{S30} values between 700 and 1000 m/s.

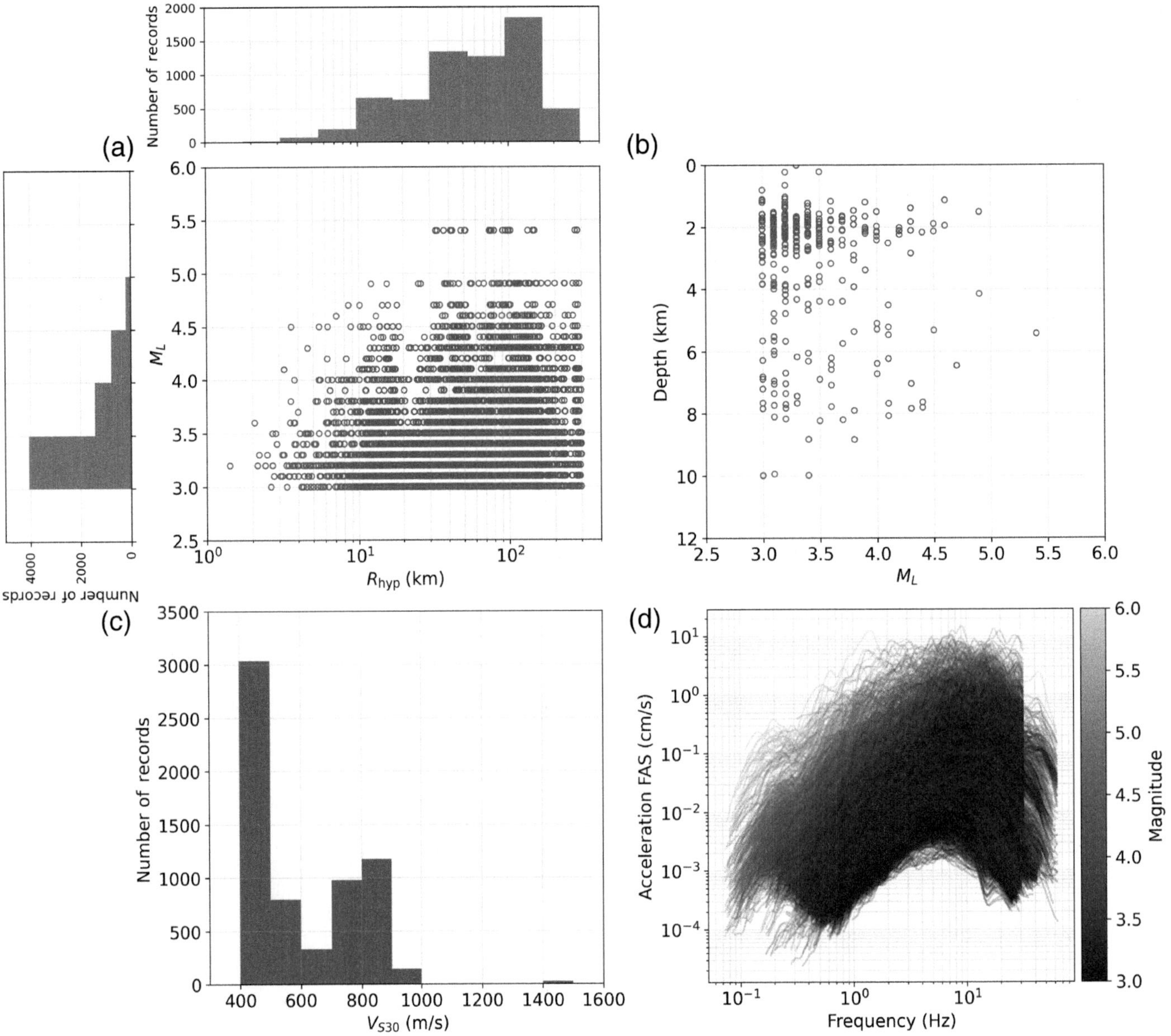

Figure 3. Data set used in this study. (a) Local magnitude (M_L) versus hypocentral distance (R_{hyp}) plot for all 6479 records, with the top and left panels displaying the distributions of records in terms of R_{hyp} and M_L. (b) Hypocentral depth versus M_L plot for the 354 earthquakes used in the inversions. (c) Distribution of records as a function of V_{S30} at the station. (d) FAS plotted as a function of frequency for all records, color coded by M_L. The color version of this figure is available only in the electronic edition.

Finally, the FAS for the complete data set are shown in Figure 3d, demonstrating that the bandwidth for the recordings is broad enough to resolve source, path, and site effects.

BB INVERSION

The BB inversion method relies on the point-source seismological model for FAS (Boore, 2003). Central to this approach is the ω^2 model, which defines the amplitude of the acceleration FAS (A) as the product of three frequency-dependent components: source (E), path (P), and site (S) terms:

$$A(R_{hyp}, f) = E(f) \times P(R_{hyp}, f) \times S(f). \quad (1)$$

The source term $E(f)$ is defined as

$$E(f) = \frac{CM_0 f^2}{1 + \left(\frac{f}{f_c}\right)^2}, \quad (2)$$

in which C represents the source constant, M_0 denotes the seismic moment (dyn·cm), f_c is the corner frequency (Hz), and f represents frequency (Hz). The constant C is given by

$$C = \frac{R_{\theta\varnothing} VF}{4\pi\rho\beta^3}, \quad (3)$$

in which $R_{\theta\varnothing}$ is the average shear-wave radiation pattern set at 0.55, $V = 1/\sqrt{2}$ accounts for the division of total S-wave energy into two horizontal components, and $F = 2$ relates to the free surface amplification factor (Boore and Boatwright, 1984). Here, ρ is the density (2.8 g/cm^3) and β is the shear-wave velocity (3.5 km/s) at the source depth.

The seismic moment M_0 is computed from the moment magnitude **M** using the Hanks and Kanamori (1979) equation:

$$M_0 = 10^{1.5(\mathbf{M}+10.7)}. \tag{4}$$

Following Brune (1970), the corner frequency is determined to be

$$f_c = 4.9058 \times 10^6 \times \beta\left(\frac{\Delta\sigma}{M_0}\right)^{1/3}, \tag{5}$$

in which $\Delta\sigma$ denotes the stress parameter (bar).

The path term P can be decomposed into geometrical spreading (G) and anelastic attenuation (L) functions:

$$P(R_{\text{hyp}},f) = G(R_{\text{hyp}}) \times L(R_{\text{hyp}},f). \tag{6}$$

We utilize the Stafford *et al.* (2022) model to describe the geometrical spreading function, characterized as a smooth bilinear function:

$$G(R_{\text{hyp}}) = \frac{1}{R_{\text{hyp}}^{\gamma}}\left(\frac{R_{\text{hyp}}^2 + R_t^2}{1^2 + R_t^2}\right)^{(\gamma-\gamma_f)/2}, \tag{7}$$

in which γ is the near-field spreading rate, γ_f is the far-field spreading rate (fixed at its theoretical value of 0.5 in this work, in accordance with Aki and Richards 2002), and R_t denotes the transition distance where the geometrical spreading rate changes from spherical in the near field to cylindrical in the far field.

Anelastic attenuation describes the attenuation of seismic waves, and it is modeled as

$$L(R_{\text{hyp}},f) = \exp\left(\frac{-\pi R_{\text{hyp}} f}{\beta Q(f)}\right), \tag{8}$$

in which $Q(f)$ is the frequency-dependent quality factor, an inverse measure of anelastic attenuation. It is typically modeled by the equation $Q(f) = Q_0 f^{\eta}$, in which Q_0 is the Q value at 1 Hz, and η represents the frequency dependence of Q (e.g., Boore, 2003; Bayless, 2021). Although some studies have incorporated depth and location dependence for the attenuation (e.g., Atkinson, 2004; Bindi *et al.*, 2021), these effects were not included in this study.

The site term component $S(f)$ combines site amplification (SA) and site-specific attenuation:

$$S(f) = \text{SA}(f)\exp(-\pi\kappa_0 f), \tag{9}$$

in which $SA(f)$ represents the frequency-dependent SA, whereas the high-frequency decay parameter (κ_0) models the site-specific attenuation (Anderson and Hough, 1984).

The analysis employs a Bayesian parametric inversion model using the PyMC Python library. This approach utilizes Markov chain Monte Carlo (MCMC) regression, which enables flexible modeling of complex relationships between variables while integrating prior information. The inversion simultaneously estimates two event-specific parameters (**M**, $\Delta\sigma$), four path parameters (Q_0, η, γ, and R_t) and the site-specific parameters κ_0 and amplification at each frequency $SA(f)$. The equations are converted to log-space, transforming the multiplicative formulation of the stochastic model into an additive one and allowing the source, path, and site terms to be expressed as sums plus residuals. The likelihood is constructed independently at each frequency using a Student's t-distribution for robustness to outliers, with the assumption that, for a given frequency, the FAS amplitudes follow a log-normal distribution.

Each reported parameter estimate is the mean of the respective posterior distribution for each parameter. The posterior distribution is proportional to the likelihood of the observed data given the model parameters, combined with the prior distributions of those parameters. The program minimizes the negative log-posterior, which is the sum of the negative log likelihood of the observed data and the negative log-prior of the parameters. This process identifies the parameter values that best explain the data while balancing the likelihood with the prior information. Posterior sampling was performed in PyMC using the No-U-Turn Sampler with 200 samples across four parallel chains. To quantify the uncertainty in the inverted parameters, we plotted the posterior distributions and computed the ratio of the 97% to 3% values of the posterior distribution as a measure of variability in the distribution of the parameter. The 97% to –3% ratio was used in lieu of a standard deviation because MCMC does not assume a specific statistical distribution. The posterior distributions are discussed in the sections for each of the inverted parameters.

Earthquake ground-motion models are poorly constrained by data. In the development of empirical ground-motion models, coefficients are iteratively fit to the data (e.g., Boore *et al.*, 2014) with constraints imposed by functional forms or in the regression. In generalized inversion techniques (Andrews, 1986), constraints are placed through the selection of reference sites that have unit site terms. In Bayesian techniques, prior estimates play a critical role in the effectiveness of the inversion process. To establish priors, we estimated means and standard deviations based on commonly used values for the limited regional information available for West Texas or expert judgment. Prior distributions for each parameter are listed in Table 1, and they primarily employ lognormal distributions due to their realistic constraints, such as nonnegative values. The selection of the standard deviation values for each distribution was guided by visualizing the full range covered by each distribution to ensure all viable parameter values were included. For parameters such as $\Delta\sigma$, Q_0, R_t, and κ_0, a standard deviation (ln units) of 0.4 was required to capture the broader

TABLE 1
Seismological Parameters and Their Corresponding Prior Distributions Used in the Inversion, with the Mean and Standard Deviation (σ) Presented in Their Respective Scales

Parameter	Distribution [μ, σ]
M	Normal [M_L, 0.1]
$\Delta\sigma$ (bar)	Lognormal [ln(50), 0.4]
Q_0	Lognormal [ln(150), 0.4]
η	Lognormal [ln(0.4), 0.2]
γ	Lognormal [ln(1.0), 0.2]
R_t (km)	Lognormal [ln(50), 0.4]
κ_0 (s)	Lognormal [ln(0.03), 0.4]
SA(f)	Lognormal [ln(interpolated V_{S30} based site amplification (SA) from Fig. 4), 0.2]

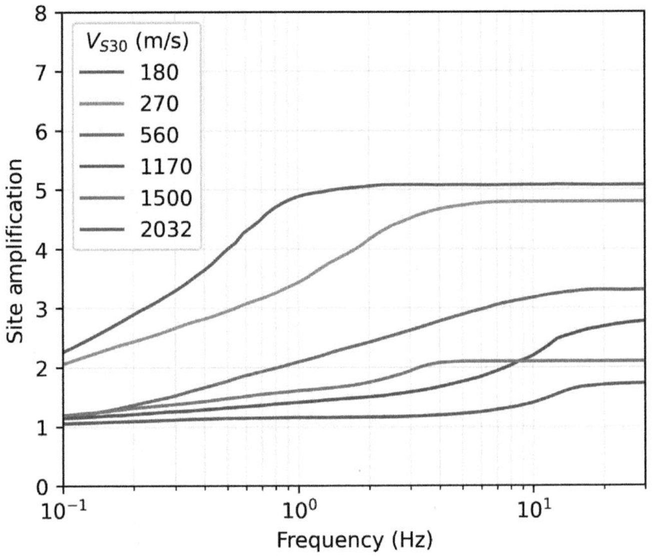

Figure 4. Site amplification (SA) factors used to assign prior distributions in the inversions. The color version of this figure is available only in the electronic edition.

range of potential values. In contrast, for more constrained parameters such as η and γ, a standard deviation (ln units) of 0.2 was sufficient because the expected range of these values is narrower and more well defined. For magnitude, uncertainty was modeled using a normal distribution with a standard deviation similar to the uncertainty provided in the catalog.

The prior distribution of SA(f) for each site is based on the assigned V_{S30} and the generic SA functions developed by Pacific Engineering and Analysis (personal comm.). These SA functions are categorized based on V_{S30} site classes (Fig. 4) and have been used by Pacific Engineering and Analysis in their inversions for ground-motion studies at various nuclear facilities. The prior amplification function used for each site is interpolated from those in Figure 4 based on the assigned V_{S30} for each site.

The input data, data processing and inversion scripts, and the output results are published on DesignSafe and available at Pandel *et al.* (2025).

To evaluate the inversions, we first investigate the FAS residuals. Figure 5a plots the computed FAS residuals and their standard deviation (in natural log units) as a function of frequency between 0.3 and 30 Hz. We calculate these residuals across all records using the inverted event-specific source parameters (**M**, $\Delta\sigma$), region-specific path parameters (Q_0, η, γ, R_t), and site-specific site parameters (SA(f), κ_0). Figure 5a illustrates that the average residuals are close to zero with a $\sigma_{\ln}$ of about 0.3 over most frequencies. Residuals are also investigated as a function of magnitude, distance, and V_{S30}, and there is no systematic variation of the mean residuals with M, R_{hyp}, or V_{S30}, as shown in Figure 5 for three frequencies (0.5, 3, and 20 Hz).

SOURCE PARAMETERS

The stochastic inversion yields an event-specific moment magnitude ($\mathbf{M}_{inv}$) and $\Delta\sigma$ for each earthquake. The inverted $\mathbf{M}_{inv}$ were very stable, with the posterior distributions indicating 97% to 3% ratios of 1.01. Figure 6a compares our M_{inv} values with the reported local magnitude (M_L) values in the TexNet catalog. The results indicate a consistent trend in which inverted $\mathbf{M}_{inv}$ tends to be smaller than M_L, particularly at larger M_L, following the relationship $\mathbf{M}_{inv} = 0.84M_L + 0.46$. As shown in Figure 6a, our findings are consistent with Trugman and Savvaidis (2021) who established also a linear relationship between M_L and **M** for the Delaware basin for events within the magnitude range $1.7 \le M_L \le 4.0$ using the low-frequency amplitudes of the *S*-wave spectra. Similar trends of moment magnitudes smaller than the local magnitudes have been documented in other studies as well (e.g., Drouet *et al.*, 2008).

In addition, we compared our $\mathbf{M}_{inv}$ estimates with the catalog moment magnitudes ($\mathbf{M}_{cat}$) derived from moment tensor inversions provided by TexNet and USGS for available events (Fig. 6b). We prioritized the use of the TexNet catalog for each event; however, when data were unavailable, we utilized the USGS catalog. Of the 87 events common between our data set and the moment magnitude catalog, 34 events (~39%) have $\mathbf{M}_{cat}$ values from the TexNet catalog, whereas the remaining events have $\mathbf{M}_{cat}$ values from the USGS catalog. As illustrated in the figure, our inverted $\mathbf{M}_{inv}$ values are comparable to those from the TexNet and USGS catalogs, although the $\mathbf{M}_{inv}$ are slightly larger. Figure 6c presents these data as the difference between the $\mathbf{M}_{inv}$ and $\mathbf{M}_{cat}$ ($\Delta\mathbf{M}$) as a function of the $\mathbf{M}_{cat}$. The $\mathbf{M}_{inv}$ values exhibit an average difference of ~+0.085 for $\mathbf{M}_{cat} < 4.5$, but the difference becomes ~−0.1 for the few events with $\mathbf{M}_{cat} > 4.5$.

Figure 7a illustrates the relationship between the inverted $\Delta\sigma$ and inverted **M**, with the inverted $\Delta\sigma$ ranging from approximately 5–134 bar and increasing with **M**. The average $\Delta\sigma$, as computed from magnitude bins ~0.5 units wide (except the last bin, which is 1 unit wide), increases from about 22 bar at **M** 3.25 to about 41 bar at **M** 4.25. The $\Delta\sigma$ continues to increase with M (the largest $\Delta\sigma$ of 134 bar is associated with

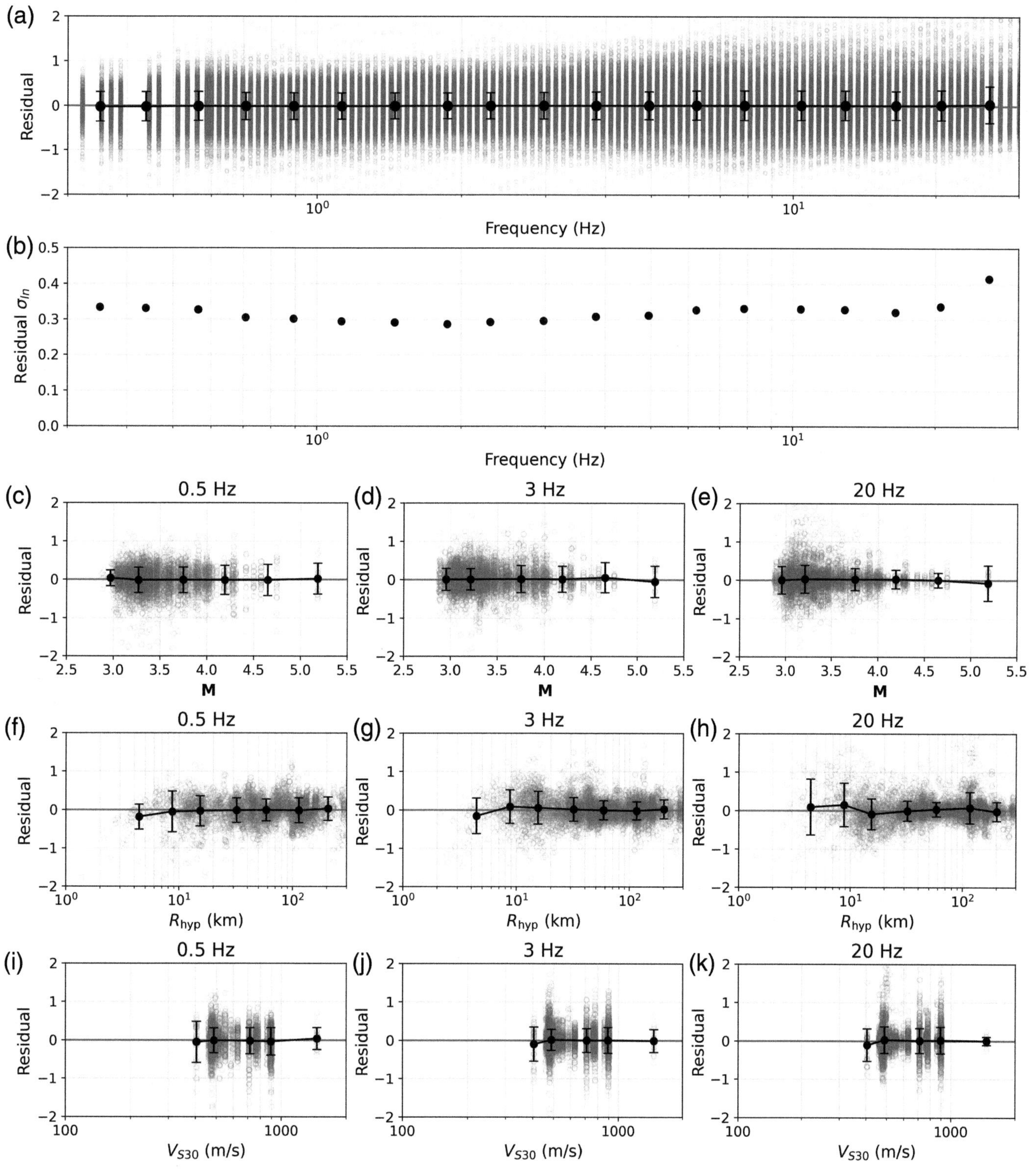

the largest event M 5.2), although the data are sparse. We plotted $\Delta\sigma$ against hypocentral depth to examine potential depth effects (Fig. 7b). However, no clear correlation was observed across event depths, a result that differs from other studies that suggest an increase in $\Delta\sigma$ with depth (e.g., Boyd *et al.*, 2017; Huang *et al.*, 2017; Trugman *et al.*, 2017) attributing this trend to rising overburden pressure (e.g., Boyd *et al.*, 2017) or decreasing pore pressure (e.g., Huang *et al.*, 2017; Trugman

Figure 5. (a) Residuals (ln units) from the overall inversion plotted against frequency. (b) Standard deviation of residuals as a function of frequency. Residuals for 0.5, 3, and 20 Hz as a function of: (c–e) inverted moment magnitude M; (f–h) hypocentral distance R_{hyp}; and (i–k) V_{S30}. The binned mean and standard deviation are shown in black in each plot.

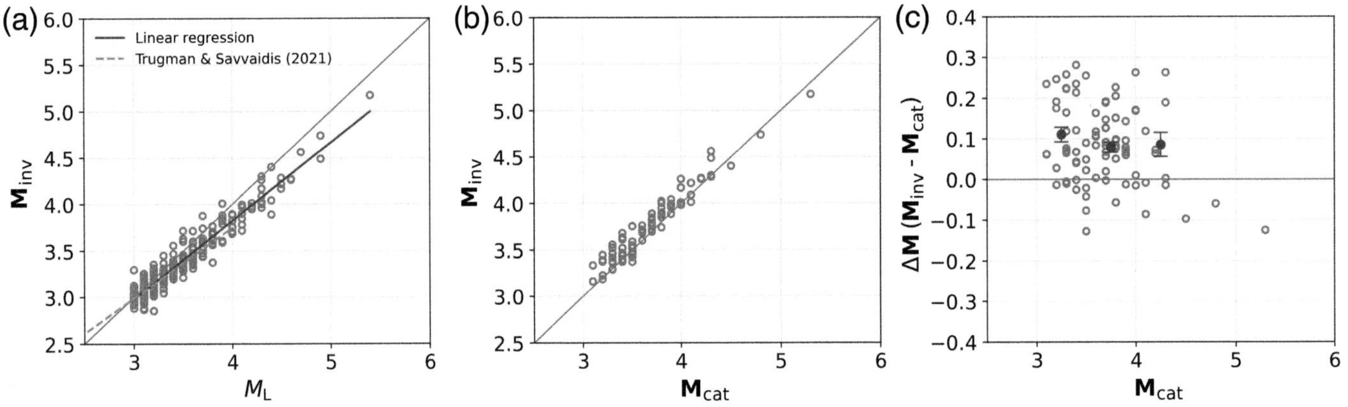

Figure 6. (a) Inverted $\mathbf{M}_{inv}$ versus M_L from the TexNet catalog. (b) $\mathbf{M}_{inv}$ values from this study versus moment tensor $\mathbf{M}_{cat}$ values from cross-listed events in the TexNet and U.S. Geological Survey (USGS) catalogs. (c) $\Delta\mathbf{M}$ ($\mathbf{M}_{inv} - \mathbf{M}_{cat}$) versus $\mathbf{M}_{cat}$. The color version of this figure is available only in the electronic edition.

et al., 2017) with depth. Our results did not reveal such a trend.

Figure 7c presents a comparison of our $\Delta\sigma$ versus **M** results with those from recent studies on induced seismicity in Oklahoma and West Texas. These other studies employed different methods for estimating $\Delta\sigma$, with the main differences associated with how f_c was identified. For example, Huang *et al.* (2017), Boyd *et al.* (2017), and Wu *et al.* (2018) used the spectral ratio method to derive f_c, whereas Cramer (2017) relied on subjective estimation of f_c from the velocity spectrum. Trugman and Savvaidis (2021) applied the Brune model to fit the source spectrum of each earthquake, enabling them to estimate f_c. Each study converted these corner frequencies to $\Delta\sigma$ using the f_c–$\Delta\sigma$ relationship (equation 5). Distinct from these other studies, Yenier *et al.* (2017) estimated $\Delta\sigma$ by calibrating an adjustable ground-motion model to fit observed ground motions from the 2011 Prague, Oklahoma, earthquake sequence.

For the comparison shown in Figure 7c, we collected data from each study directly from the publication or their supplemental materials, organized it into **M** bins according to data availability, and computed statistics for each **M** bin. The standard error for each bin is also computed and shown in Figure 7c. Our $\Delta\sigma$ estimates

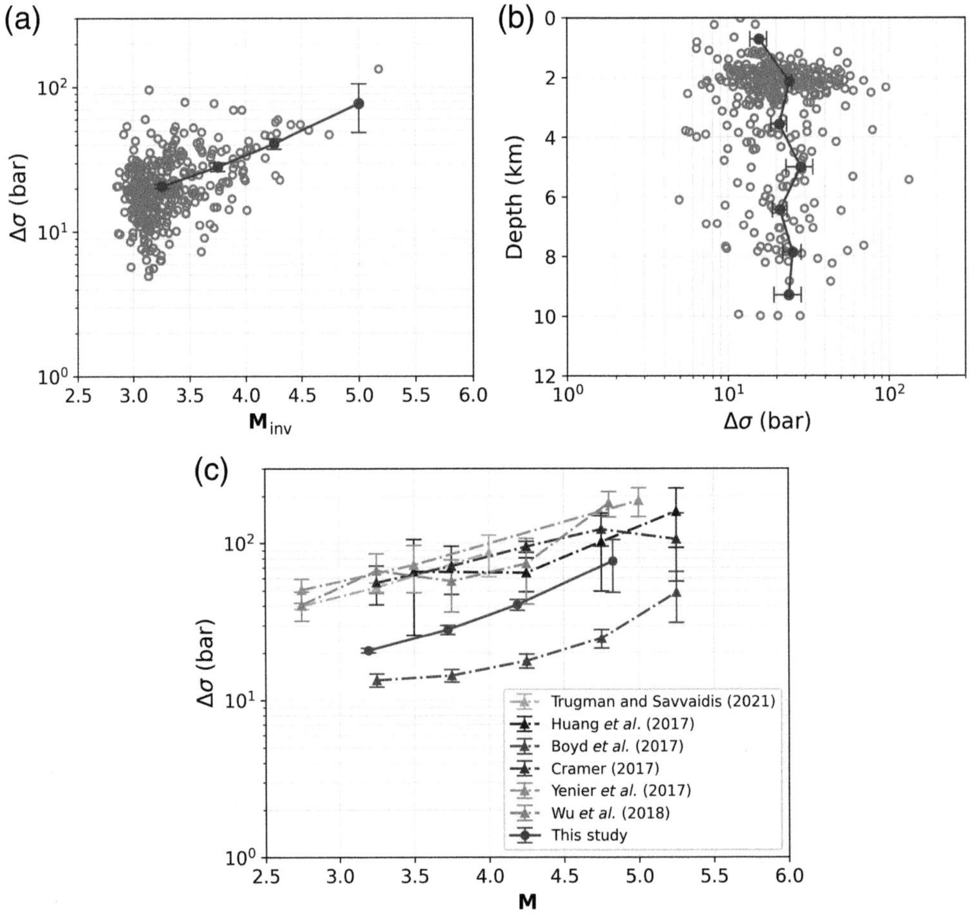

Figure 7. (a) Inverted $\Delta\sigma$ versus inverted moment magnitude ($\mathbf{M}_{inv}$), with binned mean and standard error shown in red. (b) Inverted $\Delta\sigma$ versus hypocentral depth. (c) Comparison of $\Delta\sigma$ estimates from this study with those from other studies of induced earthquakes in Central and Eastern North America (CENA). The color version of this figure is available only in the electronic edition.

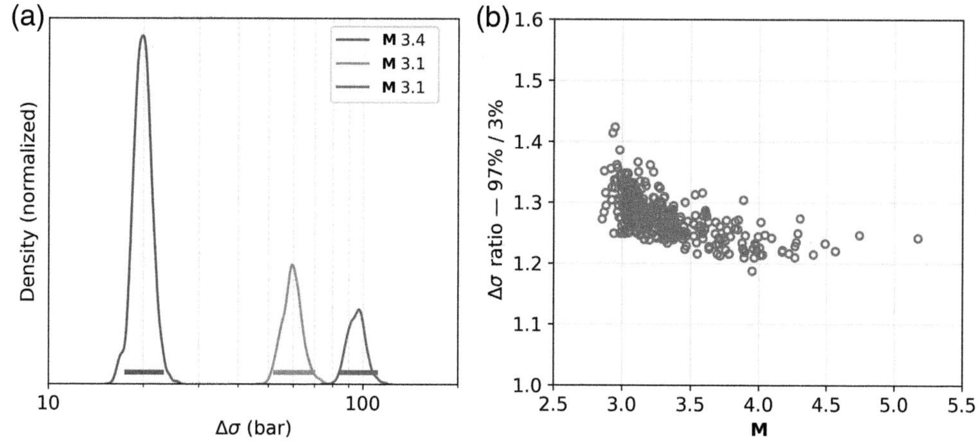

Figure 8. (a) Posterior distributions of $\Delta\sigma$ for three representative events; horizontal lines indicate the 3% to 97% range. (b) Ratio of 97%–3% $\Delta\sigma$ values from the posterior distribution of each event. The color version of this figure is available only in the electronic edition.

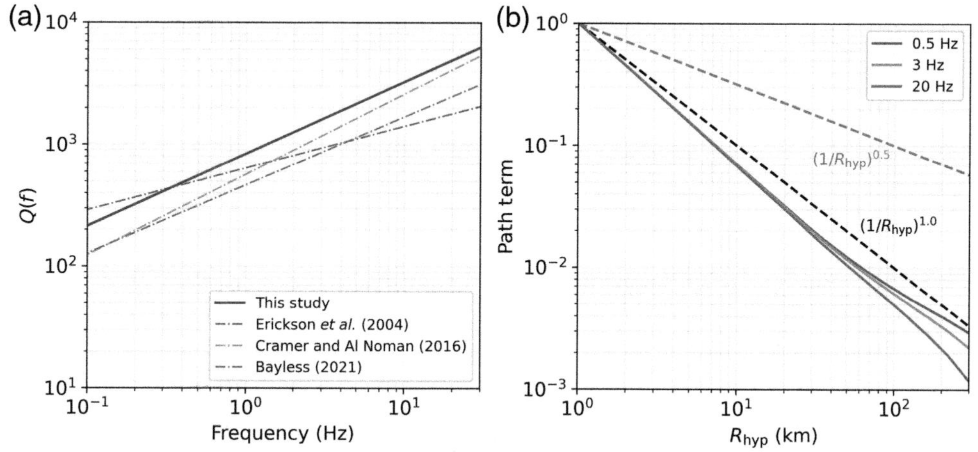

Figure 9. (a) Comparison of $Q(f)$ model from this study with those from previous studies. (b) Path term (anelastic attenuation and geometrical spreading) curves for selected frequencies (0.5, 3, and 20 Hz) computed from the inverted $Q(f)$ and γ parameters from this study. The color version of this figure is available only in the electronic edition.

trend lower than those from other studies (except for Boyd *et al.*, 2017) but exhibit a similar scaling relationship with *M*. Comparing absolute values of $\Delta\sigma$ across studies is particularly challenging because these estimates are significantly influenced by the various assumptions and methods employed. For example, Wu *et al.* (2018) noted that for moderate earthquakes, for which regional moment tensor solutions are commonly available, moment magnitudes often differ by about 0.2 units between catalogs, leading to a factor of 2 variation in both M_0 and $\Delta\sigma$. In addition, f_c itself is a major contributor to $\Delta\sigma$ uncertainty due to its cubic relationship with $\Delta\sigma$ (equation 5), such that minor variations in the estimated f_c for an event can lead to significant differences in the computed $\Delta\sigma$.

Figure 8 displays results from the posterior distributions for $\Delta\sigma$. The posterior distributions for three representative events (Fig. 8a) reveal smooth distributions with a distinct peak, and the range between 3% and 97% is shown. The ratio of 97% to 3% values for $\Delta\sigma$ are plotted as a function of **M** in Figure 8b. The ratios are generally between 1.20 and 1.30 for **M** > 3.5 and increase to above 1.3 for smaller **M**. These results indicate stable estimates of $\Delta\sigma$ with somewhat more uncertainty at smaller **M**.

PATH PARAMETERS

The combined effects of geometrical spreading and anelastic attenuation define the overall path attenuation characteristics of seismic waves. Geometrical spreading primarily influences ground motions at near-source distances, whereas anelastic attenuation becomes predominant beyond approximately 100 km (Bayless, 2021). Although the geometrical spreading rate (γ) is widely accepted to be around 0.5 at regional distances (R > 100 km), variability exists in short-distance rates (Atkinson and Mereu, 1992; Atkinson and Boore, 1995; Atkinson, 2004; Erickson *et al.*, 2004; Boatwright and Seekins, 2011). In our study, we employed a smooth bilinear parametrization (equation 7) with the far-field γ_f set to 0.5, which yielded an inverted value of $\gamma = 1.15$ at short distances and a transition distance to $R_t = 68$ km. The value of $\gamma = 1.15$ is larger than the theoretical 1.0 for spherical wave spreading, but values larger than 1.0 have been reported in other studies (e.g., Atkinson and Mereu, 1992; Boore, 2018; Atkinson, 2024).

The anelastic attenuation term (equation 8) quantifies the distance-dependent effects of intrinsic and scattering attenuation on seismic-wave propagation through the crust. Larger Q_0 indicates better seismic-wave transmission (i.e., less damping) within crustal layers is typically accompanied by weaker frequency dependence (i.e., smaller η) and is common in tectonically stable regions. In contrast, active regions often exhibit lower Q_0 with stronger frequency dependence (Cramer and Al Noman, 2016; Bayless, 2021). In our analysis, we estimated

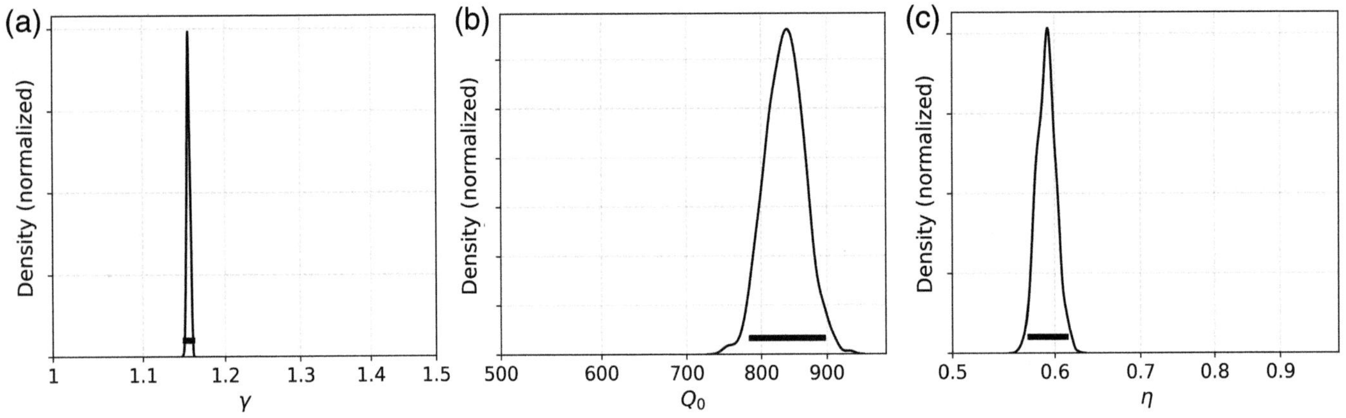

Figure 10. Poster distributions for path parameters (a) γ, (b) Q_0, and (c) η; horizontal lines indicate the 3%–97% range.

$Q_0 = 837$ and $\eta = 0.59$. Figure 9a visually compares the $Q(f)$ function derived from our analysis with those from other studies of the CENA region. Although our inverted anelastic attenuation function falls slightly above the others, it is still within the same range as those derived for the broader CENA region. Figure 9b plots the combined path term (equation 6) as a function of distance for three frequencies. For distances less than 20 km, the geometrical spreading term dominates, and the three frequencies decay similarly with distance. At larger distances, the higher frequencies decay more quickly than the lower frequencies due to the frequency-dependent effects of Q.

Figure 10 shows the posterior distributions for the three path parameters (γ, Q_0, and η), along with the 3% and 97% values. Each distribution displays a narrow peak, with γ displaying very small uncertainty (97% to 3% ratio = 1.007) and Q_0 and η displaying larger uncertainty (97% to 3% ratios of 1.14 and 1.07, respectively). The variability in the path parameters is smaller than for the source parameter $\Delta\sigma$, for which the smallest 97% to 3% ratio was about 1.2 (Fig. 8).

SITE PARAMETERS

The site component encompasses both the effects of amplification and diminution (i.e., high-frequency spectral decay κ_0), both of which are a function of frequency. Amplification effects are influenced by the velocity gradient and subsurface layering at a given site (Boore and Joyner, 1991), whereas diminution effects manifest as a consistent linear decrease in the logarithm of spectral amplitude as frequency increases (Ktenidou *et al.*, 2014). The inversion solves simultaneously for both the SA (SA(f)) and κ_0 for each site, and here we investigate first SA(f) and then κ_0.

To identify sites with similar inverted SA, we apply a spectral clustering technique to group the sites based on the amplitude and shape characteristics of SA(f). We utilized the SpectralClustering algorithm from the scikit-learn library (v.1.3.2) and manually evaluated the clusters based on the shapes of the SA(f) in each cluster and the associated standard deviation. Ultimately, the analysis yielded six distinct clusters with site counts for the clusters ranging from 5 to 16 (Table 2).

Figure 11 illustrates the individual inverted SA(f) across the six clusters, highlighting their distinct characteristics. Clusters 1 and 2 display relatively flat amplification at lower frequencies and larger amplification at higher frequencies, with cluster 2 starting its increase in amplification at lower frequencies than cluster 1. These shapes suggest the presence of a shallow, stiff layer. Cluster 3, on average, has a broad peak between 1 and 10 Hz, but also appears to consist of two subgroups with three stations displaying larger amplitudes between 1 and 2 Hz and the others not. Cluster 4 displays a strong peak at ~0.7 Hz, indicating a softer site response, whereas clusters 5 and 6 lack distinct peaks. The $\sigma_{\ln}$ for each cluster (Fig. 8h) reveals values generally below 0.4 across most of the frequency range.

To investigate the spatial distribution of the clusters, Figure 12 displays the SA clusters on a V_{S30} map of the region. Clusters 1–3 are primarily situated in the western part of the Delaware basin (near the locations of the earthquake events, Fig. 2), whereas stations in clusters 4–6 are dispersed across the Delaware basin, Central Basin Platform, and Midland basin. The western part of the Delaware basin is characterized by Paleozoic sandstones with V_{S30} ~700 m/s and Paleozoic limestones, anhydrite, and gypsum with V_{S30} ~900 m/s surrounded by stiff Quaternary deposits with V_{S30} ~500 m/s

TABLE 2
Results of Spectral Clustering Analysis

Cluster	Number of Stations	Stations
1	6	PB04, PB09, PB20, PB35, PB36, PB38
2	5	PB14, PB23, PB28, PB29, PB37
3	8	PB25, PB31, PB33, PB34, PB40, PB42, PB43, PB44
4	5	PB07, PB10, PB12, PB13, PB22
5	16	MB04, MB05, ODSA, OZNA, PB01, PB03, PB05, PB06, PB17, PB19, PB21, PB24, PB30, PECS, POST, SGCY
6	9	ALPN, MB02, MNHN, PB11, PB16, PB18, PB26, PB32, VHRN

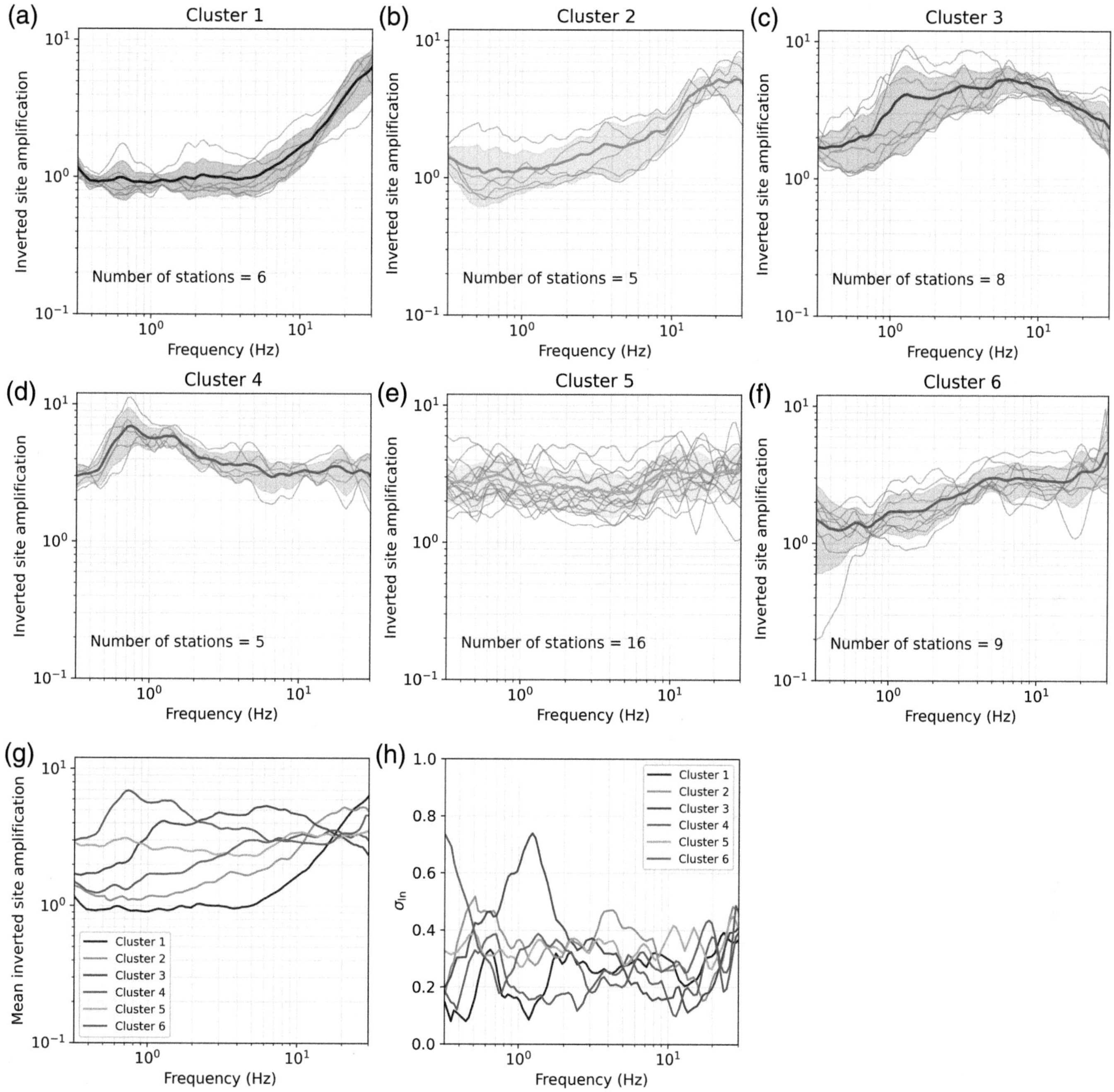

Figure 11. Spectral clustering of the 49 West Texas sites based on inverted SA. Plots (a–f) display individual stations within each cluster in gray, alongside their corresponding mean represented by a thick-colored line and ± one standard deviation as the shaded region ($\sigma_{\ln}$). Plot (g) shows the mean SA for each cluster, whereas plot (h) presents the corresponding $\sigma_{\ln}$ values for each cluster. The color version of this figure is available only in the electronic edition.

(Li *et al.*, 2022). This area is also characterized by variations in the depth to crystalline basement, with the basement ~3 km deep in the western part of the Delaware basin and increasing to ~6 km deep in the central part of the basin (Huang *et al.*, 2019). Across the Central Basin Platform and Midland basin the V_{S30} is ~500 m/s, and the depth of the basement is ~3 km (Huang *et al.*, 2019).

Broadly speaking, cluster 1 is generally associated with Paleozoic limestone with V_{S30} ~900 m/s, cluster 2 is associated with Paleozoic sandstone with $V_{S30} \sim 700$ m/s, and cluster 3 is predominantly found along the eastern edge of the V_{S30} ~900 m/s area in a region that transitions into Quaternary deposits with V_{S30} ~500 m/s (Fig. 12b). The larger V_{S30} in the regions of clusters 1 and 2 is consistent with their relatively flat inverted SA at low frequencies and amplification at higher frequencies (Fig. 11). The smaller V_{S30} in the region of cluster 3 is consistent with their larger SA at moderate frequencies (Fig. 11). However, it should be noted that the mapped V_{S30} values in Figure 12b for the sites located at the western edge of the Delaware basin are somewhat uncertain due to the presence

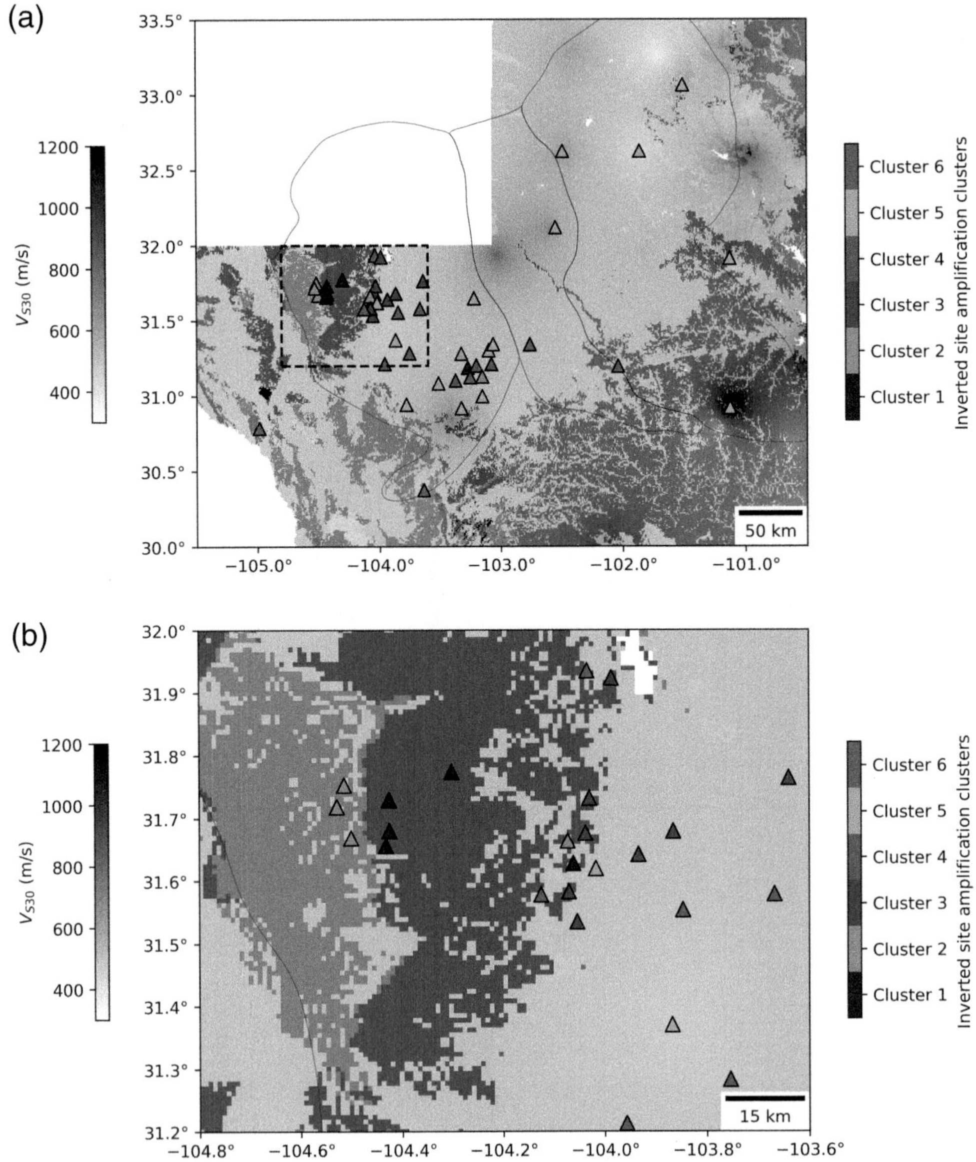

Figure 12. (a) Inverted SA clusters displayed on a V_{S30} map (white areas indicate regions outside the study area or where no V_S data are available). (b) Zoomed-in view of the western Delaware basin. The color version of this figure is available only in the electronic edition.

of multiple geologic units and the uncertainty in the boundaries between these geologic units at a regional scale.

The factors influencing the SA for clusters 4–6 are less clear. The sites associated with these clusters are scattered across all three basins and are mostly associated with V_{S30} ~500 m/s, except for sites located along the margins of the basins that have larger V_{S30}. Cluster 4, with its large peak in site term at low frequencies, is exclusively located in the Delaware basin, but sites associated with clusters 5 and 6 are located across all three basins.

The inverted κ_0 values range from 0.005 to 0.056 s and are displayed spatially in Figure 13a and grouped according to cluster in Figure 13b. Spatially, the smaller κ_0 (< 0.02 s) are located predominantly in the western part of the Delaware basin close to the earthquake events, whereas the moderate κ_0 (~0.02 to 0.04 s) are located across the broad region of all three basins to the east. The largest κ_0 (> 0.04 s) are found near the boundaries of the study area, farthest from the earthquake events. When considering the κ_0 grouped by cluster (Fig. 13b), clusters 2 and 3 are associated with the smaller κ_0 (< 0.02 s), clusters 5 and 6 are characterized with larger κ_0 (~0.03 to 0.06 s), and clusters 1 and 4 are primarily associated with moderate κ_0 (~0.02 to 0.04 s), although one station in cluster 1 has κ_0 ~0.01 s. The κ_0 data in Figure 13b are color coded based on the V_{S30} of each site. Because of the large number of sites with V_{S30} values between 400 and 600 m/s, all clusters contain sites within this V_{S30} range. Cluster 1 is the only group with a majority of sites with $V_{S30} > 800$ m/s, but this cluster does not have the smallest κ_0. In addition, sites with $V_{S30} > 800$ m/s are found in clusters 3, 5, and 6 but their κ_0 range from 0.005 to 0.04 s. Thus, the observations in Figure 13b indicate no strong relationship between the assigned V_{S30} and either κ_0 or the SA cluster.

Figure 14 plots results from the posterior distributions of κ_0 and SA(f). The κ_0 distributions for two representative sites are shown in Figure 14a, with station PB43 displaying more uncertainty than PB17 (i.e., 97% to 3% ratio = 1.22 and 1.078, respectively). Across all of the stations, the uncertainty in κ_0 (as quantified by the 97% to 3% ratio) is related most strongly to the mean value of κ_0, with smaller values of κ_0 associated with more uncertainty (Fig. 14b). Values of the 97% to 3% ratio are as large as 1.2–1.6 for sites with $\kappa_0 < 0.015$ s. Given that κ_0 represents the high-frequency decay of the FAS, it makes sense that smaller κ_0 values with less decay would be harder to resolve. SA(f) plots for the same two sites are shown in Figure 14c with the 94% confidence interval displayed as a function of frequency. Here, the SA(f) at PB17 shows more uncertainty than PB43. Across all of the stations, the uncertainty in SA(f) is most strongly related to the number of records

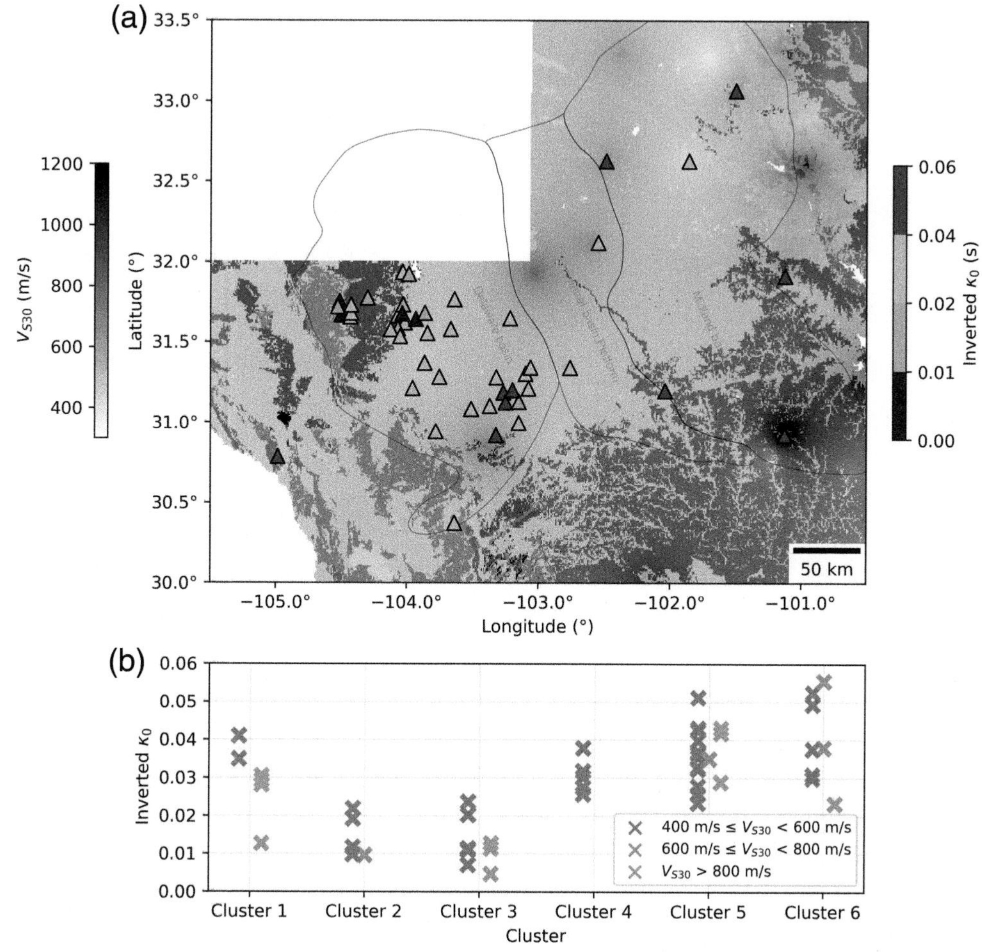

Figure 13. (a) Inverted κ_0 displayed on a V_{S30} map (white areas indicate regions outside the study area or where no V_S data are available). (b) Inverted κ_0 values within each SA cluster color coded according to their V_{S30} values. The color version of this figure is available only in the electronic edition.

available at a site, as shown by the 97% to 3% ratio for SA(f) at 3 Hz in Figure 14d (similar results are obtained for other frequencies). The 97% to 3% ratio is generally smaller than 1.2 when the number of records exceeds 30 but can reach values as high as 1.6 when the number of records is less than 10.

PARAMETER TRADE-OFFS

The inverted parameters carry inherent uncertainties due to trade-offs among various parameters, such as Q_0 and η, or between different effects, such as source and site effects (Hassani *et al.*, 2011). We analyzed the posterior distributions of the inverted parameters and computed the correlation matrix, as shown in Figure 15. The strongest positive correlation ($\sim +0.7$) is observed between **M** and γ, and between $\Delta\sigma$ and κ_0, whereas the strongest negative correlation (~ -0.8) is observed between Q_0 and η. The strong positive correlation between M and γ is a result of geometrical spreading playing a substantial role at near-source distances, where a more rapid decay in amplitude necessitates a higher magnitude to accurately fit a given spectrum. The strong positive correlation between $\Delta\sigma$ and κ_0 is due to larger $\Delta\sigma$ generating larger f_c and associated high-frequency FAS that need to be counteracted by a larger κ_0. Finally, the negative correlation between Q_0 and η indicates that similar levels of attenuation can be achieved with larger Q_0 and a flatter η. In addition, we observed a correlation of −0.68 between R_t and γ, which is consistent with the idea that for a smaller γ, seismic waves must attenuate at a rate of γ for a greater distance to match the amplitude at larger distances.

Given the strong correlations among these parameters, we sought to understand the impact of varying priors on our final inversion results. We adjusted the mean priors for Q_0 (originally 150, modified to 300, 600, and 1000), for η (originally 0.4, modified to 0.2 and 0.6), for R_t (originally 50 km, modified to 100 km) and for $\Delta\sigma$ originally 50 bar, modified to 30 and 100 bar), testing each one individually to assess their effect on the inversion outcomes. We did not modify γ, as its theoretical value should be close to 1.0, and we had already considered a wide range of values in the initial inversion. The variations in the mean priors for Q_0, η, and R_t did not result in meaningful changes in the inverted parameters. However, modifying the mean prior for $\Delta\sigma$ significantly influenced the inverted parameters, while maintaining the same unbiased fit to the data.

To understand the impact of the mean prior $\Delta\sigma$, we plotted the inverted $\Delta\sigma$ values for the three priors and computed the inverted source, path, and site terms relative to the baseline case of $\Delta\sigma = 50$ bar. The inverted $\Delta\sigma$ values for the three priors (Fig. 16a) indicate that higher prior values lead to larger inverted $\Delta\sigma$ across the full magnitude range, although $\Delta\sigma$ still follows a similar scaling relationship with **M**. The ratios of the event-specific source terms (Fig. 16b) demonstrate that a larger $\Delta\sigma$ prior generates a larger source term at frequencies greater than 1 Hz due to the associated larger f_c (equation 5). The opposite trend occurs for a smaller $\Delta\sigma$ prior. The ratio of path terms (Fig. 16c), encompassing both anelastic attenuation and geometrical spreading, show minimal sensitivity to the $\Delta\sigma$ prior as the path parameters did not change substantially.

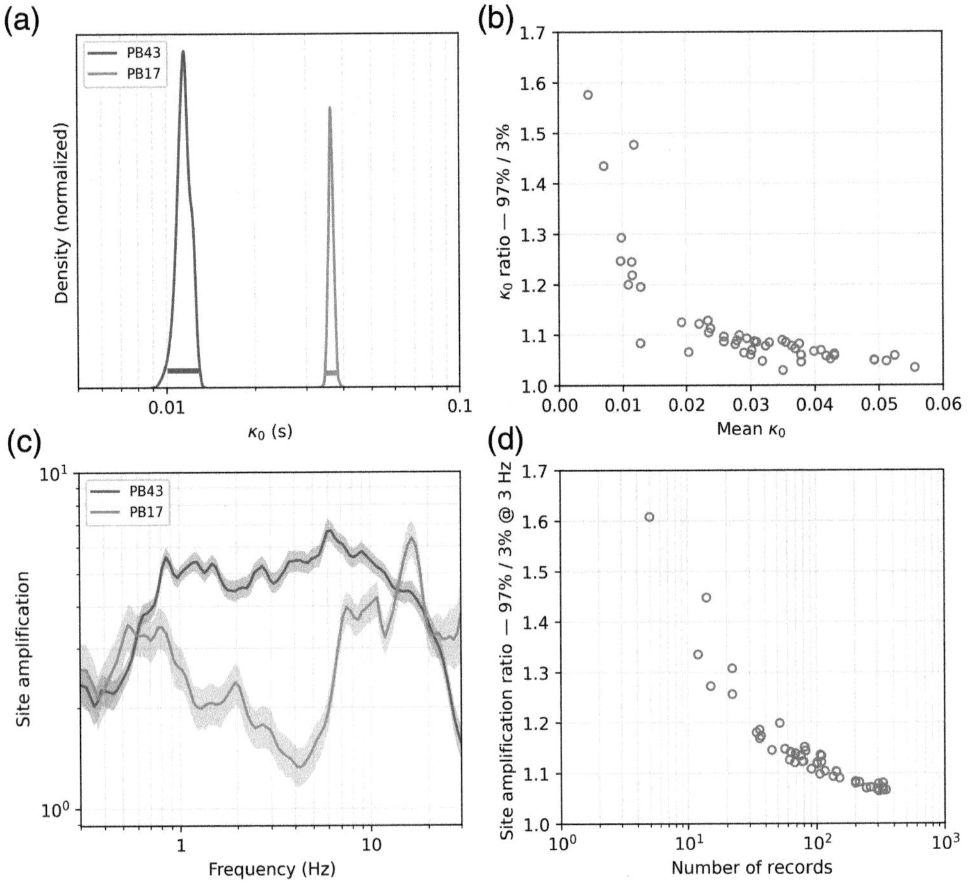

Figure 14. (a) Posterior distributions of κ_0 for two representative sites; horizontal lines indicate the 3%–97% range. (b) Ratio of 97% to 3% κ_0 values from the posterior distributions for all stations as a function of the mean κ_0. (c) Posterior distributions of SA(f) for two representative sites; shaded bands show 3%–97% range at each frequency. (d) Ratio of 97% to 3% SA(f) values at 3 Hz for each station as a function of the number of records per station. The color version of this figure is available only in the electronic edition.

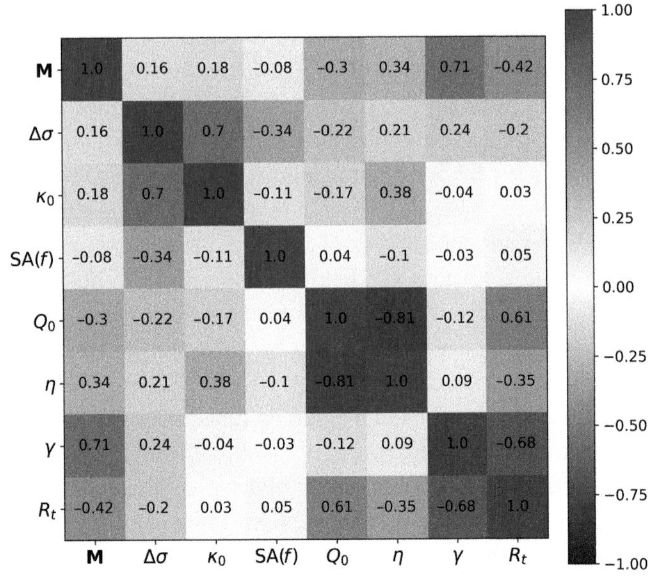

Figure 15. Correlation matrix between the inverted parameters. The correlation of SA(f) represents the correlation of the mean SA(f) over all frequencies. The color version of this figure is available only in the electronic edition.

More notably, the ratio of the site-specific inverted site terms (Fig. 16d) follows a trend that is opposite of the ratio of source term (Fig. 16b), with the larger $\Delta\sigma$ prior generating a smaller site term at high frequencies. The change in site term is due predominantly to changes in κ_0, for which the inverted κ_0 for the different $\Delta\sigma$ priors consistently shift up and down relative to the inverted κ_0 for $\Delta\sigma = 50$ bar (Fig. 16e).

The results in Figure 16 reveal that the prior distribution for $\Delta\sigma$ significantly influences the inverted parameters. The larger source terms at high frequencies for a larger $\Delta\sigma$ prior are offset by smaller site terms and larger κ_0. Together, these different combinations of stochastic parameters maintain consistency with the observed FAS with a similar statistical fit. This issue makes it difficult to compare individual stochastic parameters derived from different studies because it is the combined set of stochastic parameters together that fit the ground-motion recordings. The trade-off between $\Delta\sigma$ and the site term could be reduced through independent assessment of the site term using measured velocity profiles and site response analyses.

CONCLUSIONS

This study examines the seismological parameters influencing earthquake ground shaking in West Texas, a region where earthquake research is still developing within the context of induced seismicity. Recorded earthquake motions are used in stochastic inversions to characterize the source, path, and site parameters in the region, which can be used to better understand ground shaking in regions impacted by induced seismicity.

Our results for the source parameters reveal that the inverted moment magnitudes (**M**) are similar to those from the TexNet and USGS catalogs, although the inverted M were slightly larger on average, with a mean difference of 0.085 magnitude units. Regarding $\Delta\sigma$ estimates, we observed an increase in $\Delta\sigma$ with **M**, consistent with previous studies. However, our values were somewhat smaller than those reported in other studies for induced events in CENA, likely due to differences in the

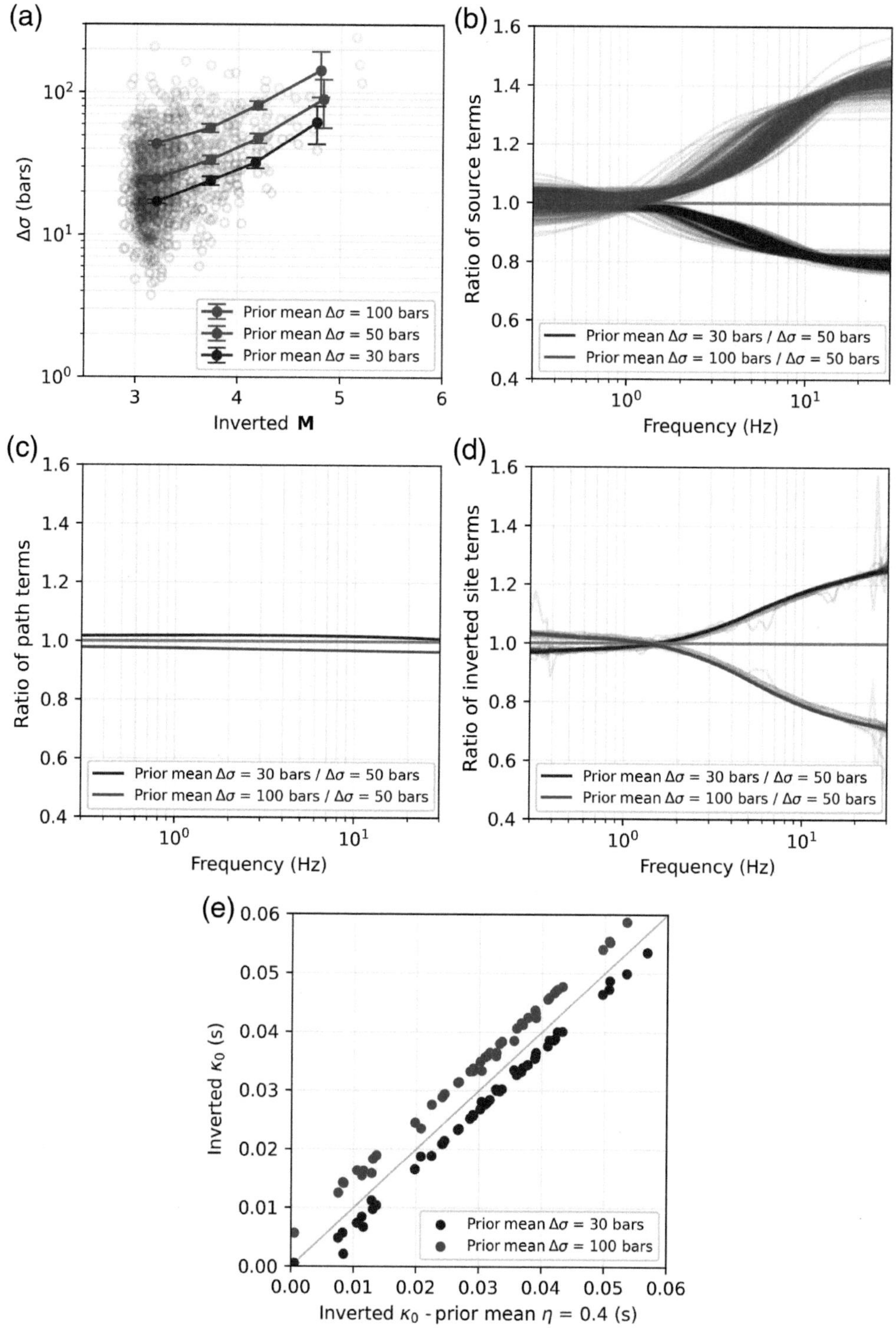

Figure 16. Influence of prior $\Delta\sigma$ on inversion results. (a) Inverted $\Delta\sigma$ for different mean prior $\Delta\sigma$. Ratio of inverted (b) source terms, (c) path terms, and (d) site terms from inversions with different mean prior $\Delta\sigma$. (e) Inverted κ_0 values from inversions with different mean prior $\Delta\sigma$. The color version of this figure is available only in the electronic edition.

For the path parameters, we estimated a geometrical spreading rate (γ) of 1.15 at short distances, which is slightly larger than the theoretical value of 1.0, and a transition distance to far-field geometrical spreading (R_t) of 68 km. Our frequency-dependent quality factor was determined as $Q(f) = 837 f^{0.59}$, which aligns with values observed in the CENA, suggesting similar attenuation behavior.

Through spectral clustering, we identified six clusters of sites with similar inverted SA functions SA(f). The characteristics of SA(f) for these clusters vary from relatively flat responses to responses with broad peaks at moderate frequencies to responses with low-frequency peaks. The sites with flat responses are located in the western part of the Delaware basin, an area associated with stiffer materials and shallower basement depth, whereas the other sites are scattered across the basins to the east. The inverted κ_0 values systematically vary between clusters, but do not correlate well with V_{S30}.

The posterior distributions of the inverted parameters revealed robust inversions, although each parameter revealed different levels of uncertainty. The parameters with the least uncertainty were γ, **M**, η, and Q_0, with 97% to 3% ratios less than 1.15. Values of $\Delta\sigma$, κ_0, and SA(f) were more uncertain with 97% to 3% ratios between 1.2 and 1.6. However, the uncertainty in these parameters varied systematically with different variables. The uncertainty in $\Delta\sigma$ decreased with increasing **M**, the uncertainty in κ_0 decreased with increasing κ_0, and the uncertainty in SA(f) decreased with increasing number of records at a station. Further analysis of the posterior distribution revealed strong correlations between some

approaches used to estimate $\Delta\sigma$. The shallower depths of the relocated events in our study relative to those in other studies may also have contributed to the differences, although we found no relationship between $\Delta\sigma$ and hypocentral depth within our data set.

model parameters, highlighting the inherent trade-offs in the inversion process. However, sensitivity analyses on the prior distributions of these parameters showed that only the prior distribution of $\Delta\sigma$ significantly influenced the inverted model parameters. For $\Delta\sigma$, the inverted $\Delta\sigma$ values shifted systematically based on the assumed prior, and these shifts were compensated by corresponding changes in κ_0.

The results of our study provide a consistent set of stochastic parameters that represent ground shaking in West Texas over the magnitude range of ~3.0 to 5.0. These stochastic parameters provide insights into the region-specific source, path, and site characteristics, and they can be used to develop region-specific ground-motion models through host-to-target conversions using the hybrid empirical method (Campbell, 2003). Finally, the inverted site terms provide insights into the local site effects and can be related to specific geotechnical and geologic conditions in the region.

DATA AND RESOURCES

The earthquake waveform data used in this study were sourced from the Texas Seismological Network (TexNet) server (https://www.fdsn.org/networks/detail/TX, last accessed August 2023), operated by the Bureau of Economic Geology. Moment magnitude (**M**) values for comparison were obtained from both the TexNet and U.S. Geological Survey (USGS) catalogs. Figure 1, depicting the geographic distribution of seismic events, was generated using Generic Mapping Tools (GMT). In addition, Matplotlib, a Python-based plotting library, was used to create various figures throughout the study. The input data, scripts, and output results are published on DesignSafe (Pandel *et al.*, 2025; doi: 10.17603/ds2-s7sx-7z83). The supplemental material for this article includes the local 1D velocity model (depth relative to mean sea level in meters, with corresponding *P*-wave [V_P] and *S*-wave [V_S] velocities in kilometers per second) used for earthquake relocation and to refine hypocentral depths incorporated into the inversion analysis.

DECLARATION OF COMPETING INTERESTS

The authors acknowledge that there are no conflicts of interest recorded.

ACKNOWLEDGMENTS

The author(s) would like to thank the Texas Seismological Network and Seismology Research program funded by the State of Texas that provided financial support for this research under the University of Texas at Austin Award Number 201503664. The author(s) also thank the reviewers and Associate Editor Sanjay Singh Bora for their insightful comments and suggestions, which helped improve the quality and clarity of this article.

REFERENCES

Aki, K., and P. G. Richards (2002). *Quantitative Seismology*, University Science Books, Sausalito, California.

Anderson, J. G., and S. E. Hough (1984). A model for the shape of the Fourier amplitude spectrum of acceleration at high frequencies, *Bull. Seismol. Soc. Am.* **74,** no. 5, 1969–1993, doi: 10.1785/BSSA0740051969.

Andrews, D. J. (1986). Objective determination of source parameters and similarity of earthquakes of different size, in *Earthquake Source Mechanics*, American Geophysical Union (AGU), Washington, D.C., 259–267, doi: 10.1029/GM037p0259.

Atkinson, G. M. (2004). Empirical attenuation of ground-motion spectral amplitudes in Southeastern Canada and the Northeastern United States, *Bull. Seismol. Soc. Am.* **94,** no. 3, 1079–1095, doi: 10.1785/0120030175.

Atkinson, G. M. (2024). Impact of geometric spreading in the Fourier domain on source spectra: Observations of steep amplitude decay and frequency dependence from the 2019 Ridgecrest, California, earthquake, sequence, *Bull. Seismol. Soc. Am.* doi: 10.1785/0120240005.

Atkinson, G. M., and D. M. Boore (1995). Ground-motion relations for eastern North America, *Bull. Seismol. Soc. Am.* **85,** no. 1, 17–30, doi: 10.1785/BSSA0850010017.

Atkinson, G. M., and R. F. Mereu (1992). The shape of ground motion attenuation curves in southeastern Canada, *Bull. Seismol. Soc. Am.* **82,** no. 5, 2014–2031, doi: 10.1785/BSSA0820052014.

Bayless, J. (2021). Regional attenuation models in Central and Eastern North America using the NGA-East database, *Earthq. Spectra* **37,** no. 1_suppl, 1460–1486, doi: 10.1177/87552930211018704.

Bindi, D., H. N. T. Razafindrakoto, M. Picozzi, and A. Oth (2021). Stress drop derived from spectral analysis considering the hypocentral depth in the attenuation model: Application to the Ridgecrest Region, California, *Bull. Seismol. Soc. Am.* **111,** no. 6, 3175–3188, doi: 10.1785/0120210039.

Boatwright, J., and L. Seekins (2011). Regional spectral analysis of three moderate earthquakes in Northeastern North America, *Bull. Seismol. Soc. Am.* **101,** no. 4, 1769–1782, doi: 10.1785/0120100225.

Boore, D. M. (2003). Simulation of ground motion using the stochastic method, *Pure Appl. Geophys.* **160,** 635–676.

Boore, D. M. (2018). Ground-motion models for very-hard-rock sites in eastern North America: An update, *Seismol. Res. Lett.* **89,** no. 3, 1172–1184, doi: 10.1785/0220170218.

Boore, D. M., and J. Boatwright (1984). Average body-wave radiation coefficients, *Bull. Seismol. Soc. Am.* **74,** no. 5, 1615–1621, doi: 10.1785/BSSA0740051615.

Boore, D. M., and W. B. Joyner (1991). Estimation of ground motion at deep-soil sites in eastern North America, *Bull. Seismol. Soc. Am.* **81,** no. 6, 2167–2185, doi: 10.1785/BSSA0810062167.

Boore, D. M., J. P. Stewart, E. Seyhan, and G. M. Atkinson (2014). NGA-West2 equations for predicting PGA, PGV, and 5% damped PSA for shallow crustal earthquakes, *Earthq. Spectra* **30,** no. 3, 1057–1085, doi: 10.1193/070113EQS184M.

Boyd, O. S., D. E. McNamara, S. Hartzell, and G. Choy (2017). Influence of lithostatic stress on earthquake stress drops in North America, *Bull. Seismol. Soc. Am.* **107,** no. 2, 856–868, doi: 10.1785/0120160219.

Brune, J. N. (1970). Tectonic stress and the spectra of seismic shear waves from earthquakes, *J. Geophys. Res.* **75,** no. 26, 4997–5009, doi: 10.1029/JB075i026p04997.

Bureau of Economic Geology, The University of Texas at Austin (2016). Texas seismological network, *International Federation of Digital Seismograph Networks*, doi: 10.7914/SN/TX.

Butcher, A., R. Luckett, J.-M. Kendall, and B. Baptie (2020). Seismic magnitudes, corner frequencies, and microseismicity: Using ambient noise to correct for high-frequency attenuation, *Bull. Seismol. Soc. Am.* **110,** no. 3, 1260–1275, doi: 10.1785/0120190032.

Campbell, K. W. (2003). Prediction of strong ground motion using the hybrid empirical method and its use in the development of ground-motion (attenuation) relations in Eastern North America, *Bull. Seismol. Soc. Am.* **93,** no. 3, 1012–1033, doi: 10.1785/0120020002.

Cramer, C. H. (2017). Brune stress parameter estimates for the 2016 Mw 5.8 Pawnee and other Oklahoma earthquakes, *Seismol. Res. Lett.* **88,** no. 4, 1005–1016, doi: 10.1785/0220160224.

Cramer, C. H., and N. Al Noman (2016). Improving regional ground motion attenuation boundaries and models in the CEUS and developing a Gulf Coast empirical GMPE using EarthScope USArray data for use in the National Seismic Hazards Mapping Project, Center for Earthquake Research and Information, University of Memphis.

Drouet, S., S. Chevrot, F. Cotton, and A. Souriau (2008). Simultaneous inversion of source spectra, attenuation parameters, and site responses: Application to the data of the French accelerometric network, *Bull. Seismol. Soc. Am.* **98,** no. 1, 198–219, doi: 10.1785/0120060215.

Dutton, S., E. Kim, R. Broadhead, C. Breton, W. Raatz, S. Ruppel, and C. Kerans (2004) Play analysis and digital portfolio of major oil reservoirs in the Permian Basin: Application and transfer of advanced geological and engineering technologies for incremental production opportunities, Bureau of Economic Geology, doi: 10.2172/828411.

Ellsworth, W. L. (2013). Injection-induced earthquakes, *Science* **341,** no. 6142, 1225942, doi: 10.1126/science.1225942.

Erickson, D., D. E. McNamara, and H. M. Benz (2004). Frequency-dependent Lg Q within the Continental United States, *Bull. Seismol. Soc. Am.* **94,** no. 5, 1630–1643, doi: 10.1785/012003218.

Grigoratos, I., A. Savvaidis, and E. Rathje (2022). Distinguishing the causal factors of induced seismicity in the Delaware Basin: Hydraulic fracturing or wastewater disposal? *Seismol. Res. Lett.* **93,** no. 5, 2640–2658, doi: 10.1785/0220210320.

Hanks, T. C., and H. Kanamori (1979). A moment magnitude scale, *J. Geophys. Res.* **84,** no. B5, 2348–2350, doi: 10.1029/JB084iB05p02348.

Hassani, B., H. Zafarani, J. Farjoodi, and A. Ansari (2011). Estimation of site amplification, attenuation and source spectra of S-waves in the East-Central Iran, *Soil Dynam. Earthq. Eng.* **31,** no. 10, 1397–1413, doi: 10.1016/j.soildyn.2011.05.017.

Huang, G. D., A. Savvaidis, and J. I. Walter (2019). Mapping the 3-D lithospheric structure of the Greater Permian Basin in West Texas and Southeast New Mexico for earthquake monitoring, *J. Geophys. Res.* **124,** no. 11, 11,466–11,488, doi: 10.1029/2019JB018351.

Huang, Y., W. L. Ellsworth, and G. C. Beroza (2017). Stress drops of induced and tectonic earthquakes in the central United States are indistinguishable, *Sci. Adv.* **3,** no. 8, e1700772, doi: 10.1126/sciadv.1700772.

Jeong, S. J., B. W. Stump, and H. R. DeShon (2022). Stress drop variations of induced earthquakes near the Dallas–Fort Worth Airport, Texas, *Seism. Record* **2,** no. 2, 68–77, doi: 10.1785/0320220003.

Jeong, S. J., B. W. Stump, H. R. DeShon, and L. Quinones (2021). Stress-drop estimates for induced seismic events in the Fort Worth Basin, Texas, *Bull. Seismol. Soc. Am.* **111,** no. 3, 1405–1421, doi: 10.1785/0120200268.

Konno, K., and T. Ohmachi (1998). Ground-motion characteristics estimated from spectral ratio between horizontal and vertical components of microtremor, *Bull. Seismol. Soc. Am.* **88,** no. 1, 228–241, doi: 10.1785/BSSA0880010228.

Ktenidou, O., F. Cotton, N. A. Abrahamson, and J. G. Anderson (2014). Taxonomy of κ: A review of definitions and estimation approaches targeted to applications, *Seismol. Res. Lett.* **85,** no. 1, 135–146, doi: 10.1785/0220130027.

Li, M., E. M. Rathje, B. R. Cox, and M. Yust (2022). A Texas-specific VS30 map incorporating geology and VS30 observations, *Earthq. Spectra* **38,** no. 1, 521–542, doi: 10.1177/87552930211033622.

Lomax, A., and A. Savvaidis (2022). High-precision earthquake location using source-specific station terms and inter-event waveform similarity, *J. Geophys. Res.* **127,** no. 1, e2021JB023190, doi: 10.1029/2021JB023190.

Pandel, B., E. Rathje, A. Savvaidis, and A. Kottke (2025). Stochastic inversions for source, path, and site parameters from West Texas earthquakes [Dataset], *Designsafe-CI*, doi: 10.17603/DS2-S7SX-7Z83.

Savvaidis, A., A. Lomax, and C. Breton (2020). Induced seismicity in the Delaware Basin, West Texas, is caused by hydraulic fracturing and wastewater disposal, *Bull. Seismol. Soc. Am.* **110,** no. 5, 2225–2241, doi: 10.1785/0120200087.

Stafford, P. J., D. M. Boore, R. R. Youngs, and J. J. Bommer (2022). Host-region parameters for an adjustable model for crustal earthquakes to facilitate the implementation of the backbone approach to building ground-motion logic trees in probabilistic seismic hazard analysis, *Earthq. Spectra* **38,** no. 2, 917–949, doi: 10.1177/87552930211063221.

Thompson, E. M., M. Hearne, B. T. Aagaard, J. M. Rekoske, C. B. Worden, M. P. Moschetti, H. E. Hunsinger, G. C. Ferragut, G. A. Parker, J. A. Smith, *et al.* (2024a). Automated, near real-time ground-motion processing at the U.S. Geological Survey, *Seismol. Res. Lett.* **96,** no. 1, 538–553, doi: 10.1785/0220240021.

Thompson, E. M., M. Hearne, B. T. Aagaard, J. M. Rekoske, C. B. Worden, M. P. Moschetti, H. E. Hunsinger, G. C. Ferragut, G. A. Parker, J. A. Smith, *et al.* (2024b). USGS automated ground motion processing software version 2 [Computer software], *U.S. Geol. Surv.*, doi: 10.5066/P13HMKFJ.

Trugman, D. T., and A. Savvaidis (2021). Source spectral properties of earthquakes in the Delaware Basin of West Texas, *Seismol. Res. Lett.* **92,** no. 4, 2477–2489, doi: 10.1785/0220200461.

Trugman, D. T., S. L. Dougherty, E. S. Cochran, and P. M. Shearer (2017). Source spectral properties of small to moderate earthquakes in Southern Kansas, *J. Geophys. Res.* **122,** no. 10, 8021–8034, doi: 10.1002/2017JB014649.

Wu, Q., M. Chapman, and X. Chen (2018). Stress-drop variations of induced earthquakes in Oklahoma, *Bull. Seismol. Soc. Am.* **108,** no. 3A, 1107–1123, doi: 10.1785/0120170335.

Yenier, E., G. M. Atkinson, and D. F. Sumy (2017). Ground motions for induced earthquakes in Oklahoma, *Bull. Seismol. Soc. Am.* **107,** no. 1, 198–215, doi: 10.1785/0120160114.

Yust, M. B. S. (2018). Dynamic site characterization of TexNet ground motion stations, *Master's thesis*, The University of Texas, Austin, Texas, available at http://hdl.handle.net/2152/68144.

Manuscript received 3 April 2025
Published online 9 December 2025

HVSR-Based Peak Frequency Identification of S-Net Ocean-Bottom Stations for Site Characterization and Ground-Motion Prediction Models

Tan Jingyang[1,2,3,4], Dai Mengqing[3,4], and Jinjun Hu[*1,5]

ABSTRACT

The horizontal-to-vertical spectral ratio (HVSR) technique is widely used to estimate the site resonant frequency. This technique is particularly valuable for ocean-bottom stations where shallow site information and reference sites are unavailable, providing reliable site resonant frequency and characteristics. Several critical aspects of the HVSR require careful consideration, including the selection of response spectra and Fourier spectra, as well as the choice of smoothing functions for Fourier spectra. Evaluating the reliability and superiority of various identification results is essential. In this study, weak motion earthquake records (peak ground acceleration ≤ 50 cm/s^2) from the S-net ocean-bottom sites in Japan Trench area were analyzed to investigate the correlation between different identification results for first and highest peak frequencies and the single-station site terms of the ocean-bottom sites, thereby assessing the applicability of the HVSR for ocean-bottom site characterization. By applying various HVSR identification schemes to 150 ocean-bottom stations, the applicability and uncertainty of the H/V Fourier spectral ratio (HVFSR) and the H/V response spectral ratio (HVRSR) were explored. The results show that the highest peak frequency identified by the HVFRS smoothed with the Parzen window exhibits the strongest correlation with the amplification site term of unburied ocean-bottom sites. In addition, it shows a strong correlation with buried sites in the short-period range. Furthermore, as an effective explanatory variable for site amplification, the correlation analysis of the HVRSR with the site terms reveals that HVRSR has a relatively significant correlation with both buried and unburied ocean-bottom sites. Therefore, it is recommended to use the HVFRS smoothed with the Parzen window for identifying the highest peak frequency and constructing a site effect model based on either the highest peak frequency or the amplitude of HVRSR, providing a valuable reference for the development of offshore ground-motion models.

KEY POINTS

- We examine the applicability of HVSR in detecting resonant for ocean-bottom site.
- Fourier spectra by Parzen window are preferred, and the highest peak frequency is the optimal.
- The peak frequency represents the offshore site effect more accurately than water and sediment.

Supplemental Material

INTRODUCTION

The marine structure is highly susceptible to damage under the influence of strong earthquakes, especially in regions such as the West Coast of United States, the eastern and southern offshore areas of China, and nearly all offshore areas of Japan, where seismic activities are prevalent (Hu *et al.*, 2020; Zhang and Zheng, 2020). With the exploitation of global

1. Key Laboratory of Earthquake Engineering and Engineering Vibration, Institute of Engineering Mechanics, China Earthquake Administration, Harbin, China, https://orcid.org/0000-0001-7549-3063 (TJ); https://orcid.org/0000-0001-7151-0049 (JH); 2. Key Laboratory of Earthquake Disaster Mitigation, Ministry of Emergency Management, Harbin, China; 3. Hubei Key Laboratory of Disaster Prevention and Mitigation, China Three Gorges University, Yichang, China; 4. College of Civil Engineering and Architecture, China Three Gorges University, Yichang, China; 5. State Key Laboratory of Precision Blasting, Jianghan University, Wuhan, China

*Corresponding author: hujinjun@iem.ac.cn

Cite this article as Jingyang, T., D. Mengqing, and J. Hu (2025). HVSR-Based Peak Frequency Identification of S-Net Ocean-Bottom Stations for Site Characterization and Ground-Motion Prediction Models, *Bull. Seismol. Soc. Am.* **116**, 680–699, doi: 10.1785/0120250156

marine resources and advancements in marine engineering, research on seismic zoning in offshore areas (Li *et al.*, 2021) and structural seismic fortification (Chen *et al.*, 2021) have gained significant attention. As marine engineering systems such as offshore oil platforms, underwater pipelines, and cross-sea bridges contribute to develop (Chen *et al.*, 2023), studying the characteristics of strong earthquakes and the attenuation patterns of offshore ground motions provides a fundamental basis for offshore seismic zoning and marine seismic hazard analysis. This is especially critical for ensuring the safety of major marine structures (Chen *et al.*, 2023; Fu *et al.*, 2024). With the construction of the ocean-bottom observation network and the accumulation of seafloor seismic motion records, research on offshore site effects is gradually progressing. Because of the limited availability of shallow site information at ocean-bottom sites, commonly used site parameters such as the average shear-wave velocity within the top 30 m (V_{S30}) and the fundamental period T_n, which are widely used in onshore strong earthquake observations, cannot be directly obtained in offshore seismic engineering studies. Consequently, identifying alternative site parameters for offshore site characterization holds great significance for evaluating the offshore site effects and developing accurate offshore site effect models. Previous studies have demonstrated that the site amplification of offshore ground motions differ significantly from those of onshore motions, particularly in the long-period ranges (Diao *et al.*, 2014; Hu *et al.*, 2020; Dhakal *et al.*, 2021; Tan and Hu, 2024). Nevertheless, research on the rational assessment of the offshore site effects and the identification of peak frequency for ocean-bottom sites remains limited. Furthermore, the applicability of Fourier spectral ratios or response spectral ratios for identifying the peak frequency of the offshore sites requires further evaluation.

The ground-motion model (GMM) plays a critical role in earthquake disaster assessment and seismic probabilistic hazard analysis. Typically, the GMM incorporates the effects of earthquake sources, propagation paths, and local site effects. A reasonable evaluation of the local site amplification effect is essential for ensuring the overall accuracy and reliability of the GMM (Hou and Zhao, 2023). For onshore sites, the commonly used site parameter V_{S30} can be obtained through borehole data to evaluate the onshore site effect (Abrahamson *et al.*, 2014; Parker *et al.*, 2021). However, several studies have highlighted the limitations of V_{S30}, indicating that its correlation with site amplification is not always strong (Castellaro *et al.*, 2008; Arteta *et al.*, 2023). Obtaining shallow site information (i.e., V_{S30}) remains challenging for numerous onshore and offshore stations globally (Hu *et al.*, 2020; Zhu *et al.*, 2022). Given the challenges associated with obtaining V_{S30} and its limited predictive capability, researchers have actively sought alternative site parameters to evaluate site effects, such as the site resonant period or fundamental period (Zhao *et al.*, 2006; Hassani and Atkinson, 2016; Hou and Zhao, 2023; Mercado *et al.*, 2023). Hassani and Atkinson (2016, 2018), and have used the fundamental frequency of the onshore site as a site parameter to account for site resonance effects and characterize the site amplification model. Pinilla-Ramos *et al.* (2022) assessed the effectiveness of the horizontal-to-vertical spectral ratio (HVSR) of microtremors as site terms by using the Next Generation Attenuation-West2 Project database, revealing a significant correlation between the normalized HVSR and site terms. In addition, researchers have explored the potential of the HVSR for site classification, assuming that sites within the same category exhibit similar resonant periods and seismic-induced site amplifications (Arteta *et al.*, 2023). Studies on the onshore site effects indicate that site classification based on HVSR or a linear effect model based on the resonant frequency can effectively reduce the uncertainties in GMMs (Di Alessandro *et al.*, 2012; Idini *et al.*, 2017; Zhao and Xu, 2013; Zhu *et al.*, 2019) and provide smaller within-event residuals (Arteta *et al.*, 2021; Mercado *et al.*, 2023). Therefore, using the HVSR technique to evaluate site effects is especially essential for sites lacking fundamental site information, offering an economical and convenient solution (Zhu *et al.*, 2020; Wang *et al.*, 2023). Because of the substantial differences in site effects between offshore and onshore ground motions (Diao *et al.*, 2014; Fu *et al.*, 2025), several researchers have previously classified ocean-bottom sites through the H/V response spectral ratio (HVRSR; Hu, Zhang, *et al.*, 2023; Hu *et al.*, 2024). Nonetheless, the applicability of various HVSR techniques in identifying the resonant frequencies of ocean-bottom sites and their capacity to characterize offshore site effects still warrant further investigating.

The HVSR is currently recognized as the most economical and convenient method for obtaining the site resonant frequency (Nakamura, 2019; Zhu *et al.*, 2020). Proposed by Nakamura (1989), this technique has been extensively applied in site effect evaluation and site classification. Compared with the standard spectral ratio (SSR) technique, the level of ground-motion amplification derived from the HVSR is generally smaller; however, the peak frequencies obtained by SSR and HVSR are relatively consistent. Consequently, the HVSR is frequently used to estimate the site resonant period or frequency (Zhu *et al.*, 2020; Hassani and Atkinson, 2016; Pinilla-Ramos *et al.*, 2022; Mercado *et al.*, 2024). Zhu *et al.* (2020) investigated the goodness of the first peak and the highest peak frequencies identified by the HVRSR and the H/V Fourier spectral ratio (HVFSR, smoothing with the Konno–Ohmachi window, Konno and Ohmachi, 1998) in characterizing site effects using 207 Kik-net onshore sites in Japan. They found that the highest peak frequency identified using the Konno–Ohmachi window had the best performance. Mercado *et al.* (2024) used HVFSR and HVRSR to analyze the site effects in northern South America and assess optimal site parameters. Both HVRSR and HVFSR have proven practical and reliable for characterizing the peak frequency of onshore sites. However, there remains a lack of in-depth analysis regarding the application of the HVSR for evaluating the site effects of ocean-bottom sites, and it remains uncertain whether the identification results of HVFSR and HVRSR can effectively represent the site effects of offshore areas.

This article analyzes and evaluates the effectiveness of various HVSR schemes for identifying the peak frequency of S-net ocean-bottom sites in the Japan trench area. In addition, it explores the correlation between offshore site amplification and the first and highest peak frequencies, providing a foundation for ocean-bottom site classification in aspects such as offshore seismic zoning. In this study, the peak frequencies of S-net offshore sites are identified using both HVFSR and HVRSR technique. The applicability of the HVRSR and HVFSR is examined, including the selection of the smoothing window functions and the optimal identification scheme for multipeak spectral ratios. Furthermore, the influence of the layout of ocean-bottom stations on the offshore site effects is investigated. The identified peak frequencies are compared with the offshore site terms obtained from the random effects model based on the site layout method to assess the goodness of fit. The feasibility of various ocean-bottom site peak frequencies in characterizing the linear offshore site effect is examined, and the strengths and limitation of different schemes for identifying the offshore site peak frequencies are determined, thereby providing offshore site parameters for developing the offshore site effect model.

SEAFLOOR GROUND-MOTION DATASET

The Seafloor Observation Network for Earthquakes and Tsunamis along the Japan trench (S-net) is currently the largest seafloor observation network in Japan (Aoi *et al.*, 2020; Dhakal *et al.*, 2021). Real-time observations began in May 2016 (Aoi *et al.*, 2020). It is deployed on the seafloor in the Pacific Ocean off eastern Japan, consisting of a total of 150 ocean-bottom observation stations (Aoi *et al.*, 2020). The S-net ocean-bottom stations are distributed across water depths ranging from 102 to 7830 m. To minimize interference from fishing activities, reduce noise, and enhance coupling with the seabed, stations located at water depths shallower than 1500 m are placed in a 1-m-deep excavation trench. These stations, referenced to as buried stations, total 41. In contrast, stations located at water depths deeper than 1500 m are freely placed on the seabed and are termed unburied stations, totaling 109 (Dhakal *et al.*, 2021). Because the sensors of the S-net stations are housed in cylindrical containers, the coupling with the seabed is relatively weak. Consequently, the S-net sensors are prone to rotation during strong earthquakes (Takagi *et al.*, 2019; Dhakal and Kunugi, 2023a). Therefore, seafloor ground-motion records in the S-net network must be processed using the matrix transformation method by Takagi *et al.* (2019). For a detailed description of the calculation of the sensor rotation and pitch angles, as well as the matrix operations required to obtain the horizontal and vertical components from the original ground-motion records, refer to Takagi *et al.* (2019).

It is commonly accepted that ground motion with peak ground acceleration (PGA) below 50 cm/s^2 generally does not induce the nonlinear site response (Ren *et al.*, 2017; Dhakal and Kunugi, 2023b). Consequently, this study selects a weak earthquake dataset to investigate the linear site effect of offshore sites. The criteria for selecting offshore ground-motion records are as follows: (1) offshore ground-motion records from the S-net network in subduction zones are selected, with moment magnitudes M_w ranging from 3.5 to 6, hypocentral distances R of 10–300 km, and $0.01\ cm/s^2 < PGA \leq 50\ cm/s^2$. The distance truncation is performed based on the magnitude. (2) Records with sensor rotation angles exceeding 0.1° are excluded to mitigate the influence of strong rotation (Dhakal *et al.*, 2021) (3) Baseline correction and filtering are performed, and records with unsatisfactory waveforms (e.g., waveform errors, incompleteness, or containing multiple earthquake events) are removed. (4) Three-component offshore records with signal-to-noise ratios <3 for any component within the frequency range of 0.1–20 Hz are excluded. The data are statistically analyzed, and only earthquake events with at least seven qualified three-component records are retained. In addition, it is ensured that each station has at least seven records. In this study, a total of 17,727 three-component offshore ground-motion records from 618 earthquakes were collected from the S-net network along the Japan trench area. The distribution of the earthquake epicenters used in this study is shown in Figure 1. The distributions of magnitude, distance, and PGA for the selected offshore ground motions in this study are presented in Figure 2. In Figure 2c,d, the relationships of PGA with magnitude and distance for buried and unburied stations are examined separately. It is observed that under the same magnitude and distance conditions, the ground-motion amplitudes of unburied stations are larger. Overall, the data distribution is relatively uniform. Consequently, the single-station HVFSR and HVRSR of all ocean-bottom stations is calculated using the ground-motion database in this section.

CALCULATION OF HVSR

The methods for seismic site response analysis based on strong-motion data can be classified into two categories: the reference site method and the nonreference site method, depending on whether a reference site is used (Wang, 2011). The reference site method involves selecting a bedrock reference site; however, identifying an appropriate reference site is often challenging. Therefore, researchers have extensively explored the nonreference site method. Among these approaches, the HVSR method has been widely adopted (Rong *et al.*, 2017; Wang *et al.*, 2023). The HVSR does not depend on a bedrock reference site and enables the estimation of a reasonable peak frequency of the site using either single-station ground-motion records or ambient vibration records (Hassani and Atkinson, 2016; Ren *et al.*,

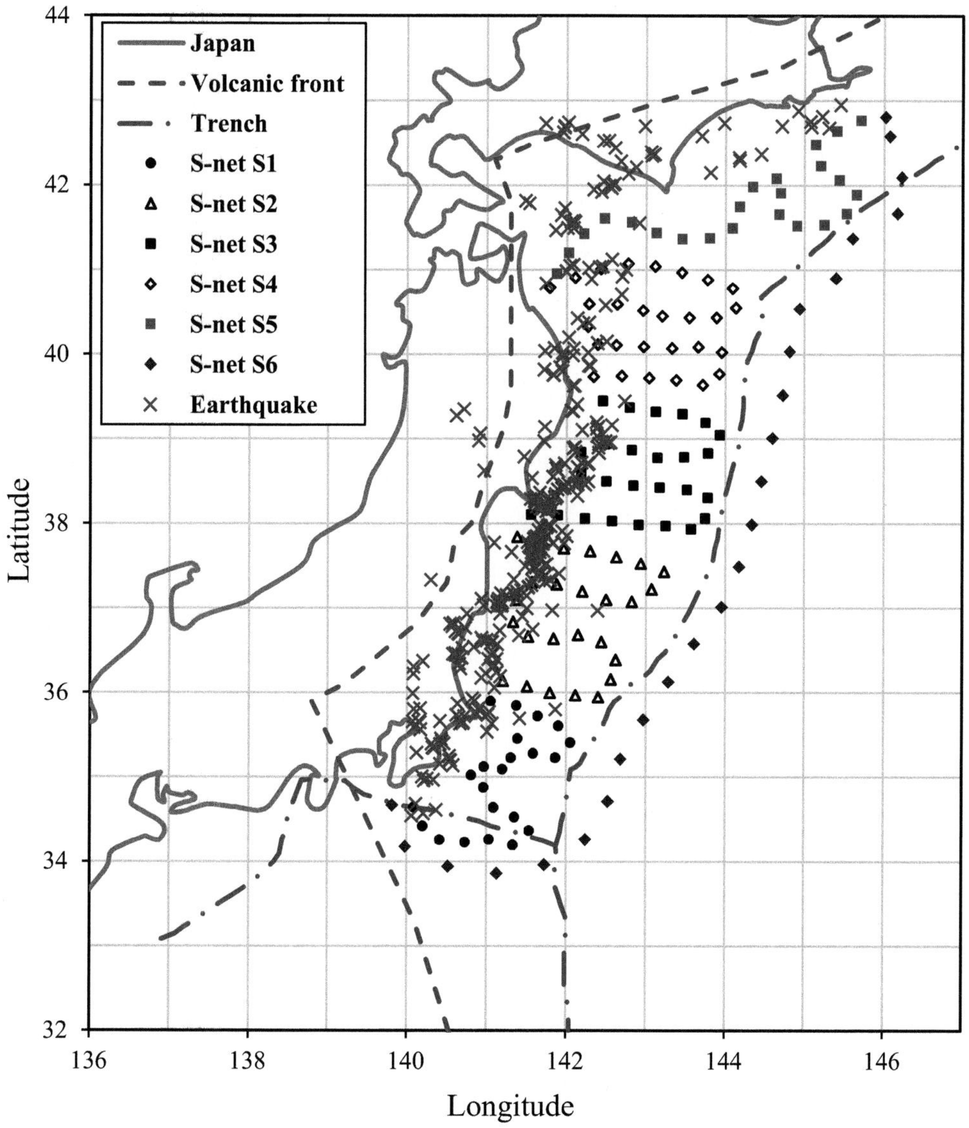

Figure 1. Distribution of the south-northeast ocean-bottom stations and epicenters of earthquakes (2016–2024) used in this study. The color version of this figure is available only in the electronic edition.

2017; Zhu *et al.*, 2022; Mercado *et al.*, 2024). Although the HVSR method effectively identifies the reasonable peak frequency of most onshore sites, it tends to underestimate the linear site response compared with the SSR method, which uses a reference site (Zhu *et al.*, 2020).

Because the calculation of HVFSR is computationally intensive and requires spectral smoothing, many researchers have explored the use of the response spectral ratio as an alternative to the smoothed Fourier spectral ratio. The HVRSR is derived directly by computing the 5% damped elastic response spectra of a single-degree-of-freedom (SDOF) system (Yamazaki and Ansary, 1997; Zhao *et al.*, 2006; Hu, Hu, *et al.*, 2023; Hu, Zhang, *et al.*, 2023). To identify the peak frequency using the Fourier spectral ratio, the main procedure involves cutting the *S* wave of ground motion and performing smoothing and then obtaining the HVFSR. Different researchers use distinct smoothing functions for the Fourier spectral window. For instance, Zhu *et al.* (2020) and Mercado *et al.* (2024) selected the logarithmic window function, the Konno–Ohmachi window (Konno and Ohmachi, 1998), whereas Wang *et al.* (2022), Dhakal *et al.* (2017), and Kubo *et al.* (2019) adopted the Parzen window. Therefore, it is essential to evaluate the identification performance of different window functions when selecting the Fourier spectrum ratio for identifying the peak frequency of ocean-bottom sites. In this study, the computed HVSRs include the HVRSR, the HVFSR smoothed by the Parzen window ($HVFSR_{Parzen}$), and HVFSR smoothed by the Konno–Ohmachi window ($HVFSR_{KO}$). During the identification process for each spectral ratio, the first peak frequency f_0 and the highest peak frequency f_p of offshore stations are identified.

The main steps for identifying the first and highest peak frequency of offshore sites by the HVSR in various schemes are outlined subsequently. The calculation framework is shown in Figure 3.

1. Perform baseline correction and filtering on offshore ground motions. Compute the acceleration response spectrum (SA) and the Fourier amplitude spectrum (FAS) of the *S* wave. When calculating the FAS, it is necessary to pick the *S* wave from the offshore ground motion, perform taper processing, and then compute the FAS. The *S*-wave window is defined by determining the arrival and end times of the *S* wave, aiming to capture the energy distribution throughout the entire acceleration time history. The *S*-wave arrival time, denoted as t_s, is identified using the Husid function (Husid, 1967), which characterizes the temporal evolution of cumulative seismic energy. Specifically, t_s corresponds to the moment when the energy begins to increase sharply. The Husid function is expressed as

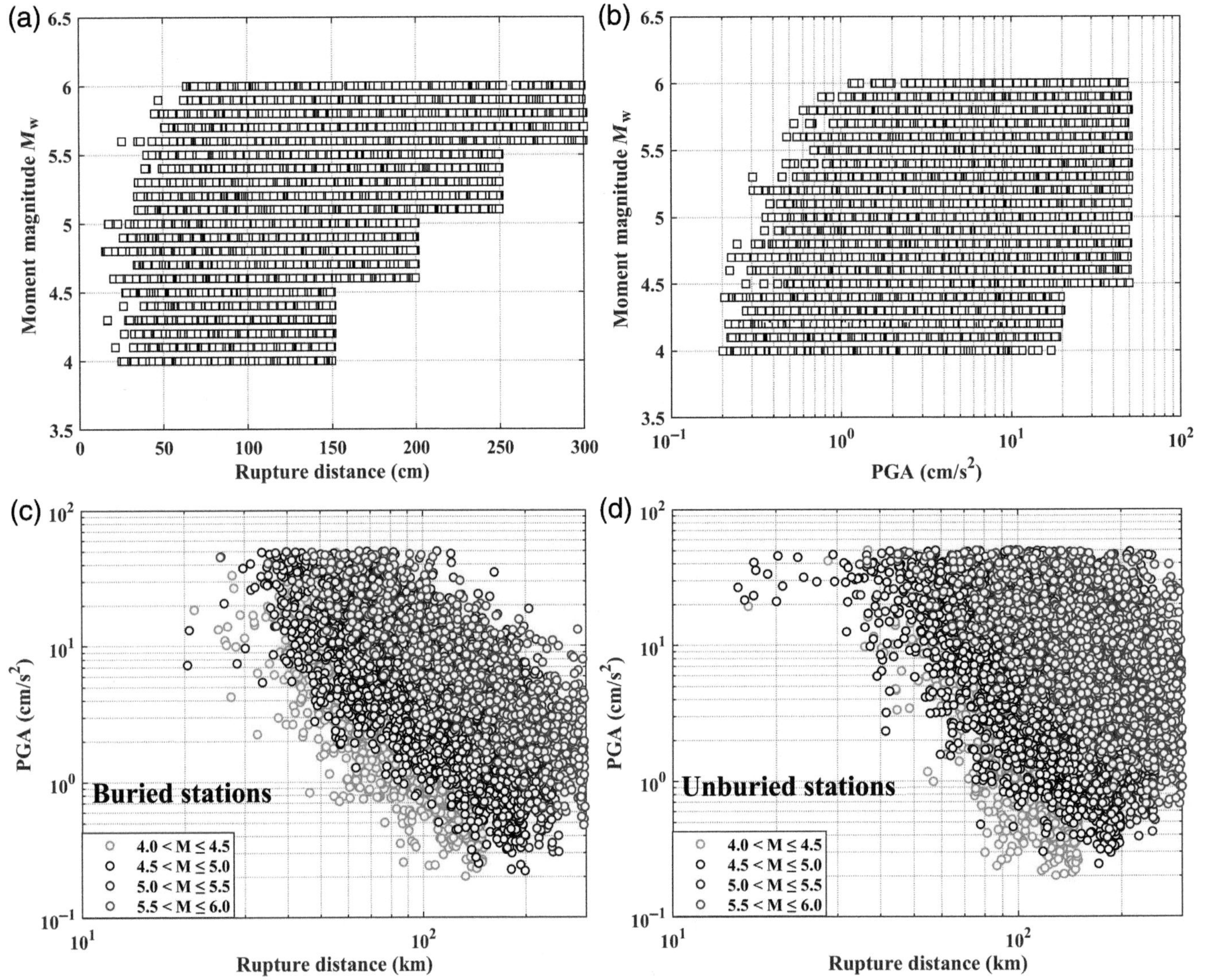

Figure 2. (a) Distribution of earthquake magnitude and distance of offshore ground motion in the study, (b) distribution of earthquake magnitude and peak ground acceleration (PGA) (PGA < 50 gal), (c) distribution of the PGA and distance of buried site, and (d) distribution of the PGA and distance of unburied sites. The color version of this figure is available only in the electronic edition.

$$Hn(t) = \frac{\int_0^t [a(t)]^2 dt}{\int_0^\infty [a(t)]^2 dt}. \quad (1)$$

The end time of the *S* wave is determined using the cumulative root mean square (CRMS) function (McCann and Shah, 1979). Specifically, the *S* wave end time t_e is defined as the moment when the CRMS function begins to decrease, marking the transition from strong shaking to energy dissipation. The CRMS function is expressed as follows:

$$\text{CRMS} = \sqrt{\frac{1}{T}\int_0^T |a(t)|^2 dt}, \quad (2)$$

in which $a(t)$ denotes the acceleration time history and T represents the total duration of the seismic record. The *S* wave is defined as the time interval between the *S*-wave arrival time and end time, as illustrated in Figure S1.

2. Smooth the FAS using either the Parzen window or the Konno–Ohmachi window. Through systematic evaluation of various smoothing parameters, it is demonstrated that using band = 0.4 for the Parzen window and b = 20 for the Konno–Ohmachi window ensures consistently high correlation across the entire period range for both smoothing methods. Therefore, these parameter settings enable reliable identification of prominent frequencies of ocean-bottom stations (see supporting evidence in Figs. S2–S10).
3. For three-component offshore ground motions, calculate the HVSR(f) by taking the ratio of the geometric mean of the two horizontal components to the vertical spectral value. When averaging HVSR, the spectral ratio is regarded as a function of the frequency f, that is

$$\log \overline{\text{HVSR}}_j(f) = \frac{\sum_{i=1}^{n_j} \log \text{HVSR}_{ij}(f)}{n_j}. \quad (3)$$

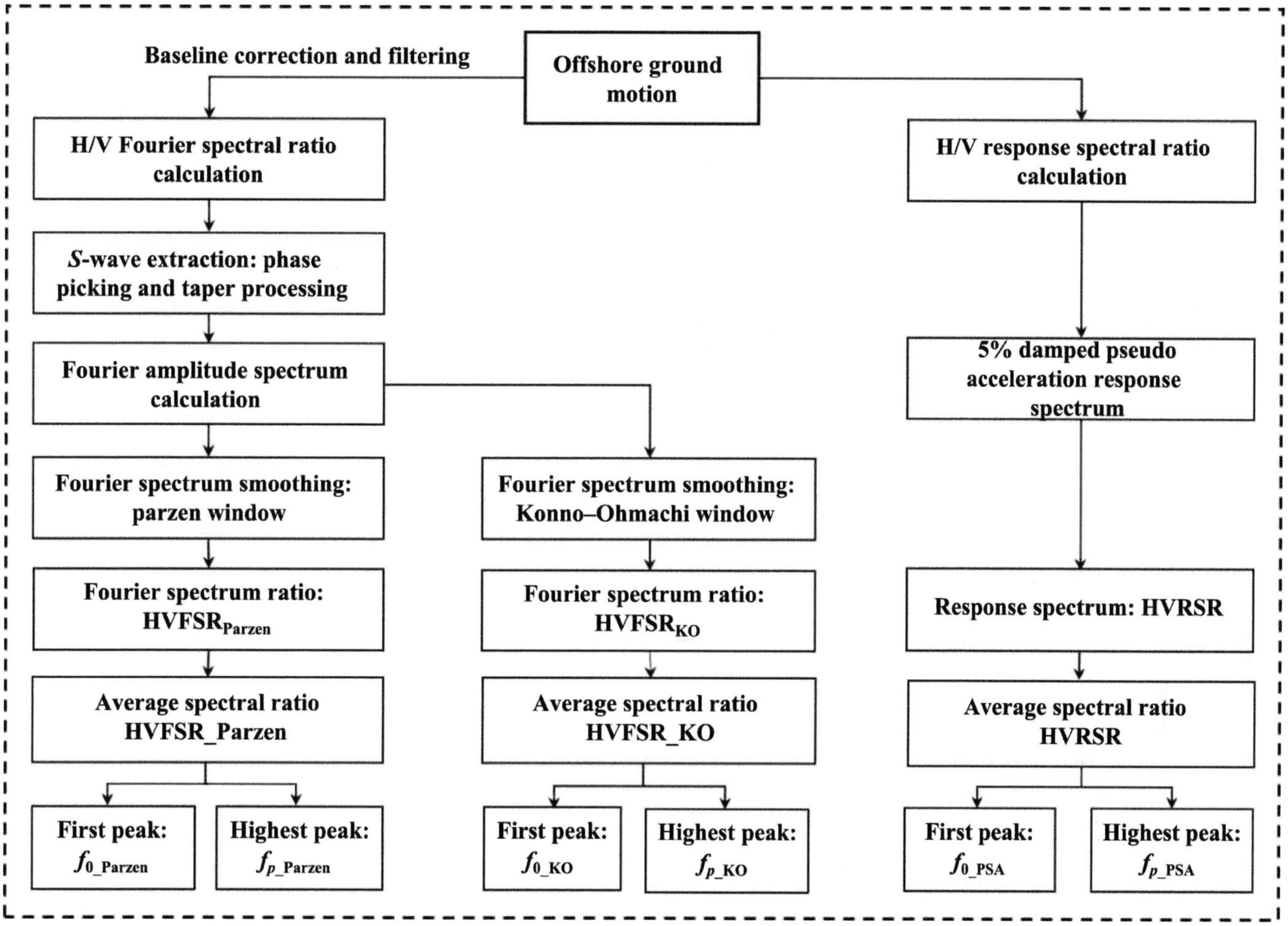

Figure 3. Processes for calculating the first and highest peak frequencies of S-net ocean-bottom stations using the horizontal-to-vertical spectral ratio (HVSR) technique. HVFSR, H/V Fourier spectral ratio.

For the 150 ocean-bottom sites, six distinct peak frequencies and their corresponding amplitude HVSR(f) were computed respectively following the procedure outlined in Figure 3. These data were subsequently used to analyze the correlation between the single-station site term and the peak frequency.

The amplitude of the HVSR of offshore stations is generally much larger than that of onshore motions. This phenomenon primarily arises because the vertical high-frequency component of offshore ground motions is suppressed by the seawater layer (Diao *et al.*, 2014; Chen *et al.*, 2015; Hu *et al.*, 2020; Dhakal and Kunugi, 2021). Therefore, the verification criteria requiring an amplitude amplification factor >2 for identifying the peak frequency of the onshore HVSR are satisfied. However, for ocean-bottom sites, stricter verification criteria should be established in the future to more accurately identify the peak frequency of offshore sites. In this study, the highest peak frequency was identified as the point corresponding to the maximum amplitude within the frequency band. The first peak frequency is primarily used to identify the presence of distinct peaks preceding the highest peak in multipeak HVSR curves. Figure 4 shows the identification process for ocean-bottom station S1N01. Figure 4a–c depicts the HVFSR smoothed by the Parzen window, the Konno–Ohmachi window, and HVSR, respectively. The smoothness of the results varies significantly among these three schemes, with the HVRSR exhibiting the highest smoothness and the HVFSR smoothed by Parzen window showing lower smoothness. For station S1N01, the peak frequencies identified as the first peak and the highest peak are consistent across all three schemes, as shown in Figure 4d. Figure 5 presents the identification results of station S2N01. Figure 5a–c illustrates schematic diagrams of various identification outcomes. Figure 5d shows the results of identifying six peak frequencies (three f_0s and three f_ps). The first peak frequency aligns with the highest peak frequency for HVRSR. Conversely, for HVFSR, the highest peak frequency considerably surpasses the first peak frequency. Differences in smoothness are evident across different identification schemes within varying frequency ranges. Whereas the Parzen window has the best effect under natural coordinates, the Konno–Ohmachi window smoothing is mainly more effective for smoothing in logarithmic coordinates, and the overall smoothness of the response spectrum is the highest. However, because of the relatively broad smoothing width of the response spectrum ratio and the Konno–Ohmachi window smoothing in the high-

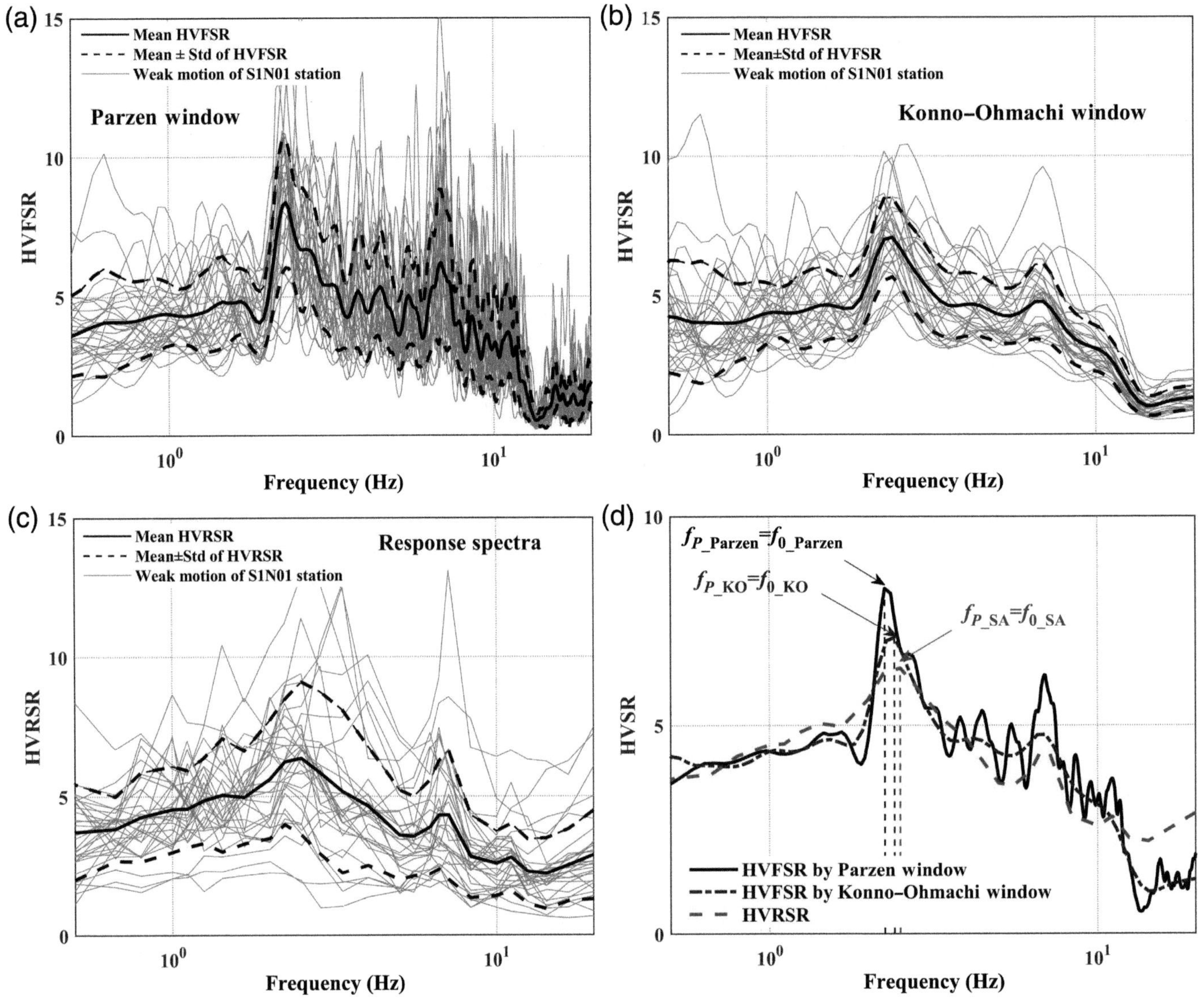

Figure 4. Identification of the peak frequency at station S1N01 using different HVSR techniques. (a) Parzen window smoothing; (b) Konno–Ohmachi window smoothing; (c) response spectrum smoothing; and (d) a comparative analysis of the three smoothing techniques with clear identification of the corresponding peak frequencies. The color version of this figure is available only in the electronic edition.

frequency range, excessive smoothing causes some ocean-bottom sites to identify the first peak frequency as the highest peak frequency in the high-frequency range, as shown in Figure 5.

The results of identifying the peak frequencies using the steps in Figure 3 are summarized in Table S1. For each offshore site, the three first peak frequencies and three highest peak frequencies identified are listed according to the station name. In addition, the water depth and sedimentary thickness for each station are provided as reference information. Figure 6 shows the overall distribution of the six identified peak frequencies. The red boxes denote buried sites, and the black dots represent the unburied sitess. Figure 6a depicts the distribution of the highest peak frequencies of $HVFSR_{Parzen}$ and HVRSR. For most sites, the deviation between the highest peak frequencies of HVRSR and $HVFSR_{Parzen}$ is relatively small. Figure 6b shows the distribution of the highest peak frequencies of $HVFSR_{Parzen}$ and $HVFSR_{KO}$. The identification results obtained using the Konno–Ohmachi window are notably lower than those obtained using the Parzen window at certain offshore sites, though the overall deviation remains small for most sites. Figure 6c presents a comparison between the first peak frequencies identified by the $HVFSR_{Parzen}$ and $HVFSR_{KO}$. Overall, the first peak frequency is significantly smaller than the highest peak frequency, and the first frequencies of $HVFSR_{KO}$ is smaller than those of $HVFSR_{Parzen}$. Figure 6d presents the proportions of single-peak and multi-peak cases, along with the frequency of first peak identification, under the three identification methods. It also illustrates instances in which the first identified frequency differs from the dominant (highest amplitude) frequency. Although such discrepancies are generally infrequent across all methods, they

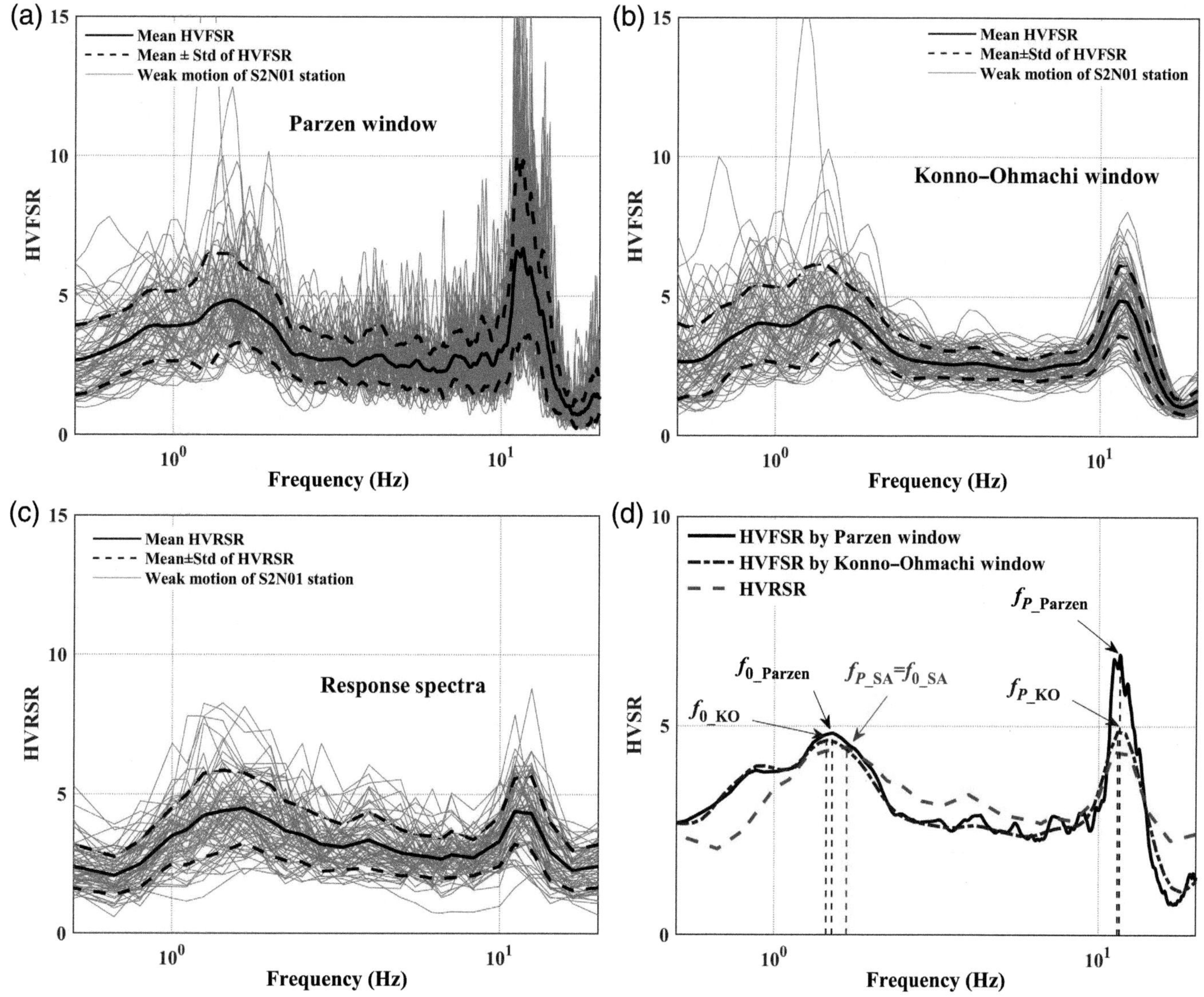

Figure 5. Identification of the peak frequency at station S2N01 using different HVSR techniques: (a) Parzen window smoothing; (b) Konno-Ohmachi window smoothing; (c) response spectrum smoothing; and (d) a comparative analysis of the three smoothing techniques with clear identification of the corresponding peak frequencies. HVRSR, H/V response spectral ratio. The color version of this figure is available only in the electronic edition.

occur more frequently with the Parzen window. This is primarily due to the smaller smoothing interval used by the Parzen window in the high-frequency range during the identification process, which increases the likelihood of misalignment between the first peak and the highest-amplitude peak.

CORRELATION BETWEEN PEAK FREQUENCY AND OFFSHORE SITE PARAMETERS

This section primarily evaluates six types of peak frequencies, station water depth, and sedimentary thickness to investigate which type of peak frequency best characterizes the site effects of 150 ocean-bottom sites of S-net. Therefore, the single-station site term of the offshore motion database is derived through regression analysis, and the correlations of the peak frequencies are analyzed separately for buried and unburied sites. The interrelationship between different site parameters within the ground-motion database is a critical concern. Figure 7 presents the correlation coefficients between offshore site parameters for buried and unburied sites. As shown in Figure 7a, the selected offshore site parameters include the sedimentary thickness $Z_{1.4}$ (the thickness of the seafloor sedimentary layer when the shear-wave velocity of the soil exceeds 1.4 km/s, from the Japan Earthquake Disaster Information Station), the water depth of the ocean-bottom station (obtained from the Japan Seafloor Seismic Wave Observation Network), the highest peak frequencies f_{pSA}, $f_{pParzen}$, and f_{pKO} identified in the present study, and the amplitudes of HVRSR at different periods (T = 0.2, 0.8, and 1.0 s). Sedimentary thicknesses at shear-wave velocities of 1.4 km/s ($Z_{1.4}$) and 2.7 km/s ($Z_{2.7}$) were selected for subsequent analysis. Although $Z_{1.4}$ is a commonly used site parameter in prior studies (Dhakal *et al.*, 2023; Hu, Hu, *et al.*, 2023), $Z_{2.7}$ demonstrates a higher correlation with site terms in this study. (See Fig. S12 for correlation

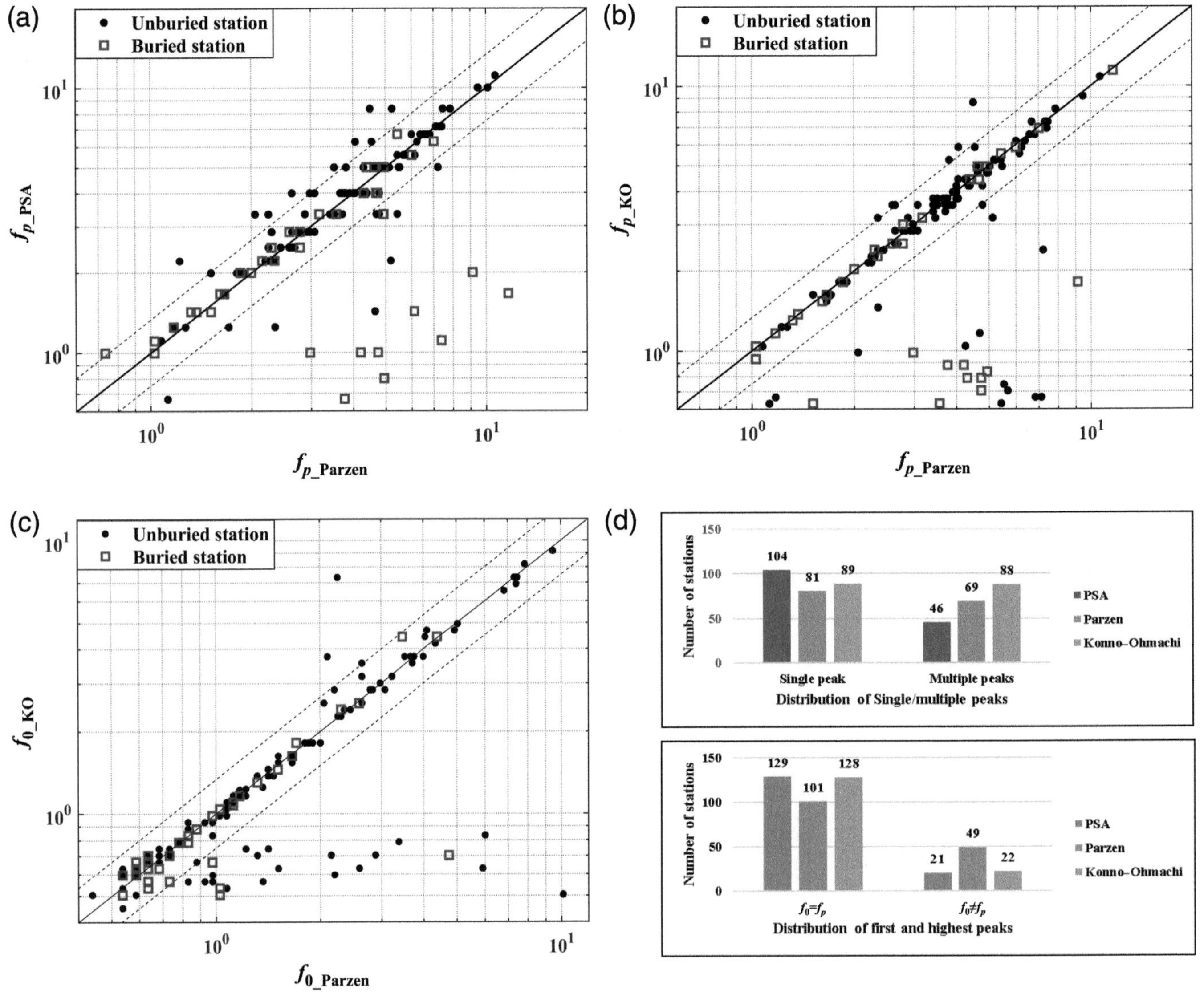

Figure 6. Comparison of peak frequencies and spectral ratios identified by different techniques for buried and unburied ocean-bottom sites. (a) f_{pPSA} versus $f_{pParzen}$; (b) f_{pKO} versus $f_{pParzen}$; (c) f_{0KO} versus $f_{0Parzen}$; and (d) the statistical results of single/multiple peaks and the identification of the first versus highest peak frequency. The color version of this figure is available only in the electronic edition.

coefficients between individual sediment layer thicknesses and site terms.) It can be observed that the sedimentary thickness $Z_{1.4}$ exhibits the strongest correlation with HVSR (T = 1.0 s) but with a relatively low R of 0.3. In addition, whereas the correlation between water depth and the sedimentary layer is −0.27, the highest correlation of water depth with HVSR (T = 1.0 s) is −0.46. The correlations among the three highest peak frequencies are very high, with the correlation between f_{pPSA} and $f_{pParzen}$ being the highest of 0.85. Similarly, the correlations among the HVSR amplitudes are also relatively strong, which is expected given their frequency characteristics. For the buried offshore site, as shown in Figure 7b, there is a weak negative correlation between the sedimentary thickness $Z_{1.4}$ and water depth. The correlations among the highest peak frequencies are slightly lower than those of unburied offshore sites, with the correlation between $f_{pParzen}$ and f_{pKO} is the highest of 0.61. Currently, the primary site parameters for the ocean-bottom sites include water depth, sedimentary thickness, and site peak frequency. The correlations among these parameters are not substantial, with only a weak correlation observed between the sedimentary thickness and water depth. The water depth influences the vertical component of offshore ground motions in marine environments (Diao *et al.*, 2014; Hu *et al.*, 2020). Although the P-wave resonance frequency in seawater can be expressed as $f_1 = V_P/4H$, no clear correlation is observed between this resonance frequency and the predominant frequency. Seawater effectively attenuates vertically propagating S waves, thereby suppressing their transmission; consequently, the overall amplitude of the vertical ground-motion component remains small. The relationship between water depth and P-wave resonance frequency is further illustrated in Figure S11. Consequently, water depth, sedimentary thickness, and peak frequency can all be treated as independent variables for site parameters.

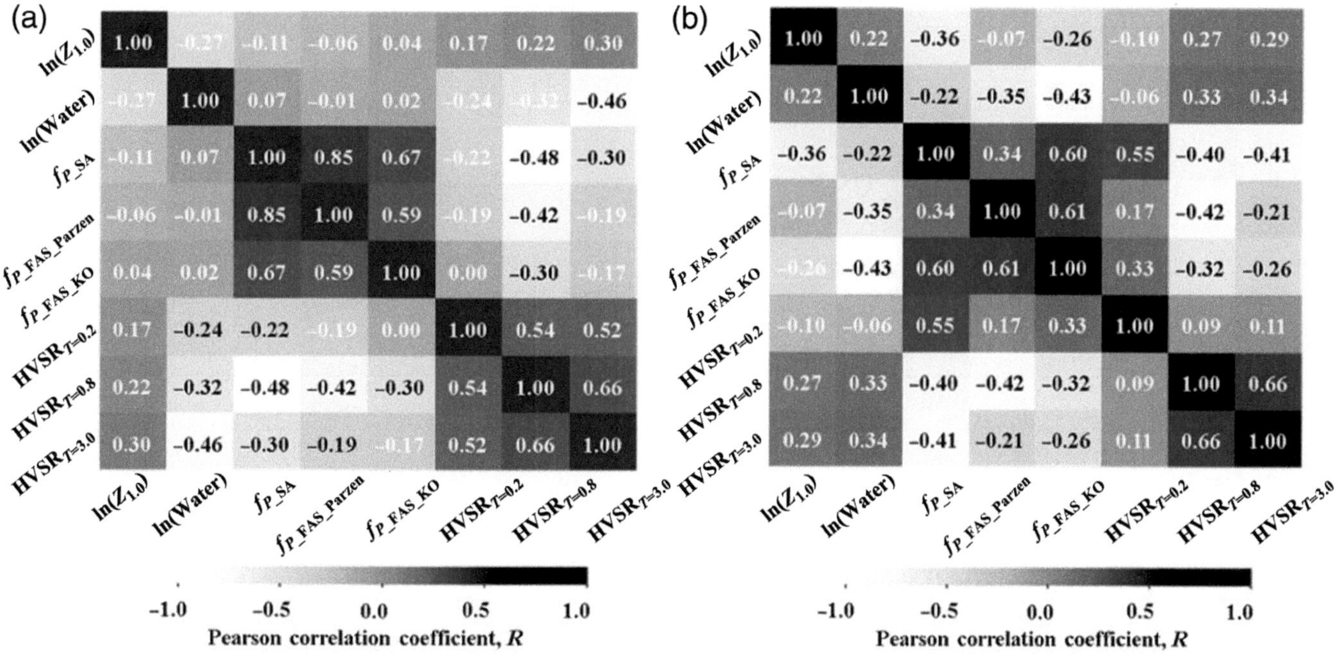

Figure 7. Correlation coefficient matrix of site parameters for offshore sites: (a) unburied ocean-bottom sites and (b) buried ocean-bottom sites.

Based on six distinct definitions of the peak frequency, 150 offshore sites within the S-net network were systematically analyzed. The results indicate that the correlation of the first peak frequency with site terms is generally weak. Therefore, the focus shifts to the outcomes related to the highest peak frequency in the subsequent section. The site term S_k for an individual station was determined using the random-effects model proposed by Abrahamson and Youngs (1992). Here, the site term S_k represents the variability in site effects for a single ocean-bottom site. For the weak earthquake database used in this study, the ground-motion prediction equation (GMPE) can be expressed as follows:

$$\ln(Y_{i,j}) = f_M + f_R + a_1 + \delta S2S_s + \delta WS_{ij} + \delta B_i, \quad (4)$$

in which $Y_{i,j}$ is either PGA (cm/s^2) or 5% damped SA (cm/s^2) at spectral period T for the offshore ground motion and f_M and f_R represent the source term and the path term, respectively. The functional form of magnitude and path term discussed by Tan and Hu (2024) was primarily used to determine the GMPE of the weak earthquake database in this study; a_1 denotes the constant term, $\delta S2Ss$ presents the between-site residual (also referred to as the site term; Pinilla-Ramos *et al.*, 2022), δWS_{ij} is the within-site residual, and δB_i indicates the between-event residual. Through regression analysis, the single-station site terms of 150 ocean-bottom sites in the weak earthquake database of this study were determined. Subsequently, correlations between the site terms and various offshore site parameters were analyzed to evaluate the performance of these site parameters in characterizing the offshore site effects.

Analysis of unburied ocean-bottom site effects

Multiple peak frequencies can be obtained through the HVSR, with the HVSR amplitude serving as a variable. In this section, we primarily compare the correlations of these variables as site interpretation variables and evaluate their identification effects through various schemes. The analysis focuses on comparing the correlations of different peak frequencies and assessing the goodness-of-fit between site parameters (f_ps, HVRSR, water depth, and sedimentary thickness) and site terms to ultimately determine the optimal site parameters for the entire periods. Figure 8 shows the correlation between the single-site term $\delta S2Ss$ of 109 unburied ocean-bottom sites and the highest peak frequency $f_{p\text{Parzen}}$. To comprehensively evaluate the performance of the peak frequency, quadratic fitting is used for the peak frequency (Zhu *et al.*, 2020). The correlation in Figure 8a is significantly weaker than those in Figure 8b–d. However, the highest peak frequency $f_{p\text{Parzen}}$ overall has the best-fitting effect for the site term in the medium and long periods, effectively characterizing the variation characteristics of the unburied site with respect to the highest peak frequency $f_{p\text{Parzen}}$. Specifically, a higher peak frequency corresponds to a smaller site class and reduced site response, indicating a negative correlation between $\delta S2Ss$ and the $f_{p\text{Parzen}}$. Figure 9 shows the variation of the single-site term of unburied ocean-bottom sites with $\ln(\text{HVFSR}(f_p))$. Overall, the ln(HVFSR(*fp*)) exhibits a positive correlation with the site term of unburied sites. Notably, the $\ln(\text{HVFSR}(f_p))$ only shows a good correlation with the site term at the frequency $f = 2$ and 4 Hz, with the overall performance being relatively poor. The correlation analysis of the remaining site parameters for unburied sites is presented in Figures S10–S15.

To comprehensively evaluate the performance of various offshore site parameters in characterizing the offshore site

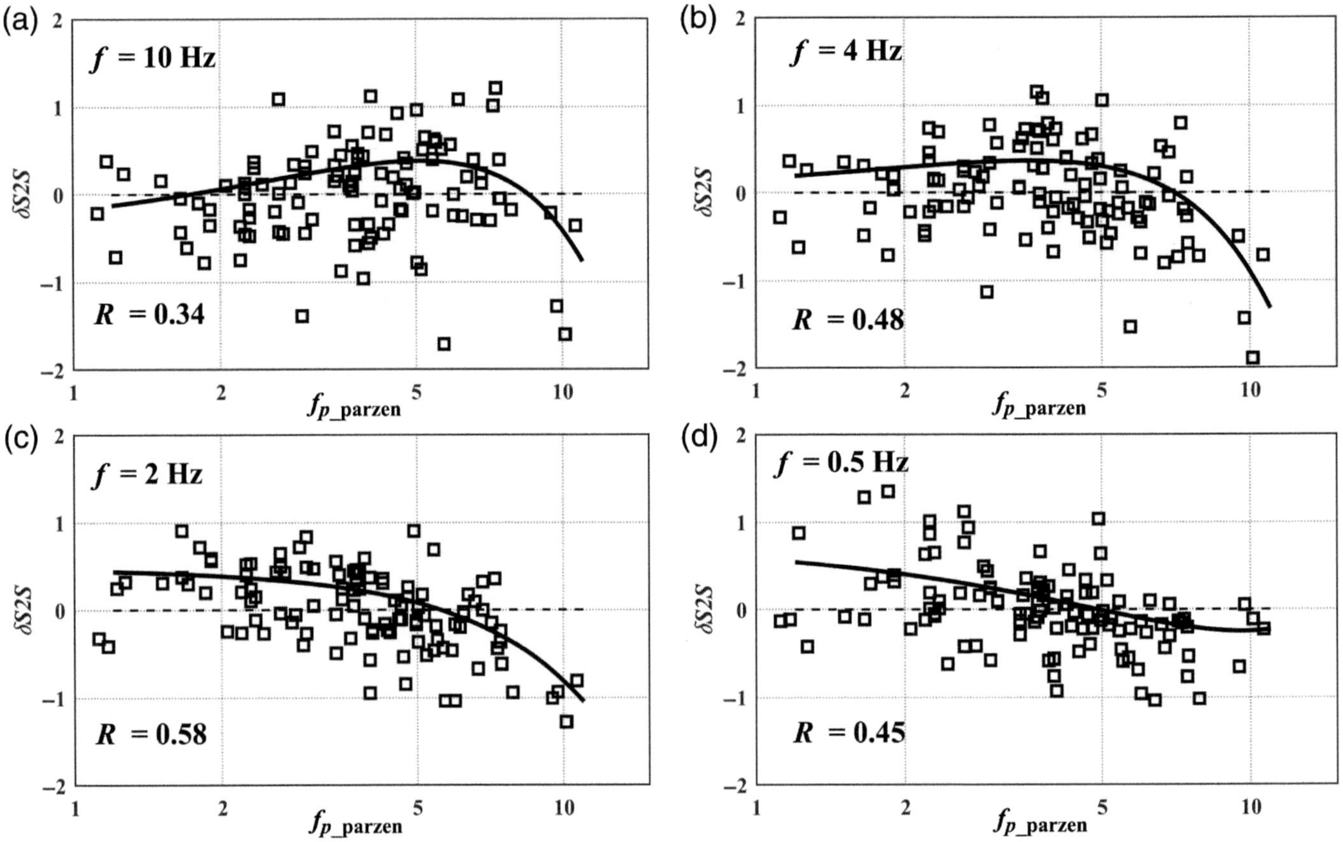

Figure 8. Correlation analysis between the highest peak frequency $f_{p\mathrm{Parzen}}$ and the single-station site term for unburied ocean-bottom sites at spectral frequency: (a) f = 10 Hz; (b) f = 4 Hz; (c) f = 2 Hz; and (d) f = 0.5 Hz.

effect, correlations among water depth, sedimentary thickness, the three first and three highest peak frequencies, the HVSR amplitude, and the site term of unburied sites were analyzed, as summarized in Figure 10. Because of the relatively weak overall correlation of the first peak frequency, this study primarily focuses on presenting the analysis results for the highest peak frequency. This finding is consistent with the analysis of the peak frequency of the Japanese onshore sites (Zhu *et al.*, 2020). Figure 10a presents the correlation analysis between the highest peak frequency by $\mathrm{HVFSR}_{\mathrm{Parzen}}$ ($f_{p\mathrm{Parzen}}$), sedimentary thickness of ln(Sediment), site water depth of ln(Water), HVFSR amplitude of $f_{p\mathrm{Parzen}}$, and the site term of unburied sites. The correlation between sedimentary thickness and the site term is very low and remains essentially uncorrelated across the entire periods. In contrast, the overall correlations of ln(Water) and HVFSR(f_p) are significantly weaker than the $f_{p\mathrm{Parzen}}$. Therefore, when a single site parameter is used to characterize the offshore site term, the highest peak frequency demonstrates significantly greater superiority compared with water depth and sedimentary thickness used in previous studies (Hu, Zhang, *et al.*, 2023; Tan and Hu, 2024). Figure 10b compares three highest peak frequencies with the HVRSR amplitude, which exhibits overall good performance. The HVRSR amplitude notably outperforms HVFSR in the short-period ranges, but there is minimal difference in the long-period range. In the short periods, the correlation of $f_{p\mathrm{KO}}$ is the highest, but in the long periods, the correlation of $f_{p\mathrm{Parzen}}$ is the highest and markedly exceeds that of several other site parameters. Three distinct smoothing methods are used, and differences in their performance across frequency bands are inevitable. Response spectrum is performed using an SDOF system with a 5% damping ratio, which effectively averages the entire response spectrum. In contrast, Fourier spectrum smoothing operates directly on the spectral components in the frequency domain. The key difference between these two approaches lies in their smoothing efficacy at high and low frequencies, which in turn affects the consistency and reliability of identified frequency peaks. Given that offshore ground motions generally exhibit higher-frequency content compared with those on land (Hu *et al.*, 2020; Dhakal *et al.*, 2023), the choice of smoothing method becomes particularly important and may vary accordingly.

The performance of the site parameters was further assessed using the residual standard deviation associated with the site term, for which a lower value reflects reduced prediction error and thus indicates superior model performance (Zhu *et al.*, 2020). Here, $\ln(\mathrm{AF}(T))$ represents the site term, denoted as $\delta S2Ss$. The highest peak frequency or other site parameters can be used to quantify and evaluate the performance in characterizing site amplification, as illustrated in the following equations:

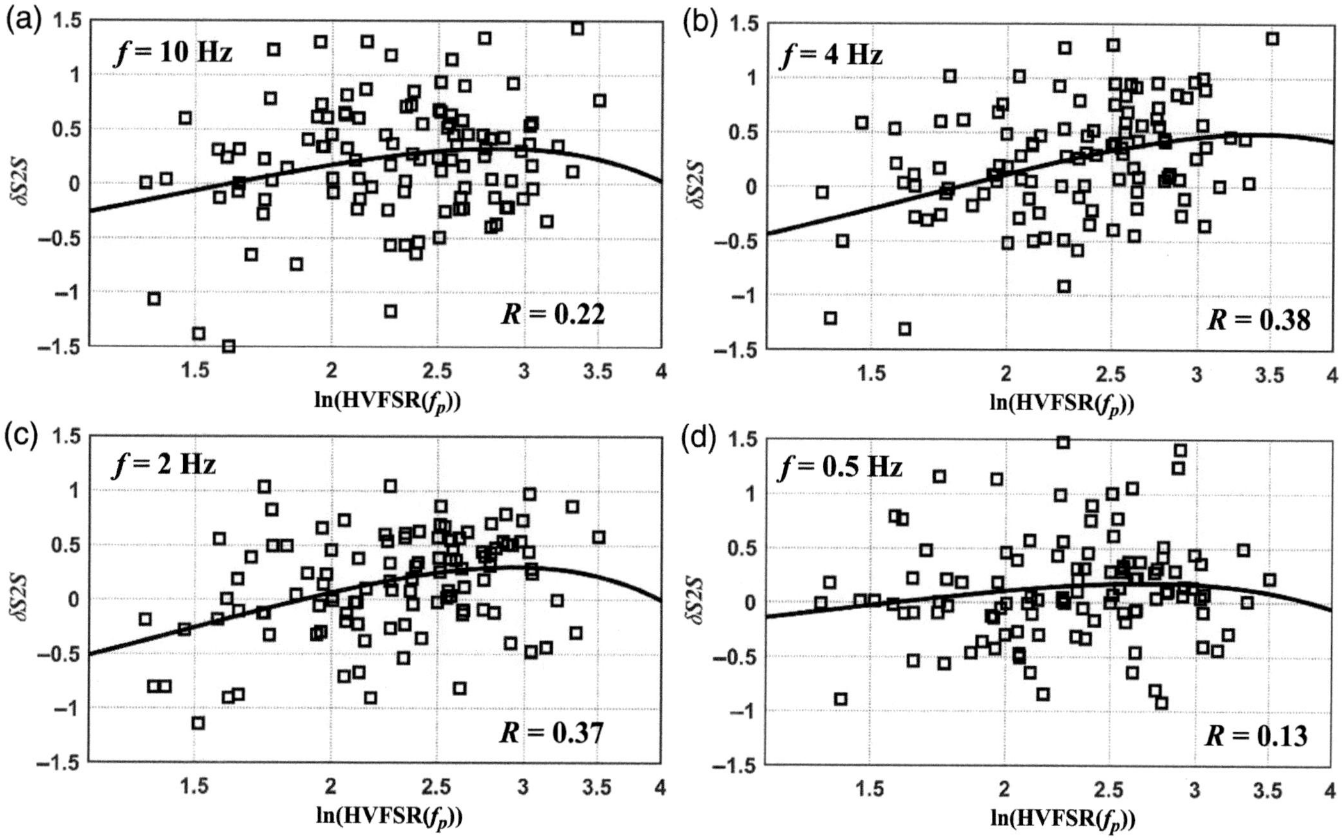

Figure 9. Correlation analysis between the HVFSR amplitude $\ln(\mathrm{HVFSR}(f_p))$ at $f_{p\mathrm{Parzen}}$ and the single-station site term for unburied ocean-bottom sites at spectral frequency: (a) $f = 10$ Hz; (b) $f = 4$ Hz; (c) $f = 2$ Hz; and (d) $f = 0.5$ Hz.

$$\ln(\mathrm{AF}(f_p)) = c_0 + c_1 f_p + c_2 f_p^2, \quad (5)$$

$$\mathrm{Res} = \ln(\mathrm{AF}_{\mathrm{obs}}) - \ln(\mathrm{AF}_{\mathrm{pre}}), \quad (6)$$

$$\sigma_{\mathrm{Res}} = \sqrt{\frac{\sum_1^N (\ln(\mathrm{AF}_{\mathrm{obs}}) - \ln(\mathrm{AF}_{\mathrm{pre}}))^2}{N}}, \quad (7)$$

in which f_p represents the offshore site parameter, $\ln(\mathrm{AF}_{\mathrm{obs}})$ denotes the site term derived from regression analysis, $\ln(\mathrm{AF}_{\mathrm{pre}})$ indicates the site term predicted by equation (3), and N represents the total number of offshore sites included in the computation.

Figure 11a shows the variations in the residual standard deviation of the site term with varying spectral period when $f_{p\mathrm{Parzen}}$, $\ln(Z_{1.4})$, $\ln(Z_{2.7})$, ln(Water), and $\ln(\mathrm{HVFSR}(f_p))$ are used as site parameters. The trends observed in Figure 11a are consistent with those in Figure 10a: higher correlations correspond to smaller residual standard deviations (σ_{Res}). Across the entire period range, $f_{p\mathrm{Parzen}}$ exhibits the lowest standard deviation compared with the other three site parameters, particularly in the long-period range, for which the reduction in standard deviation is notably pronounced. Figure 11b further examines the discrepancies in various highest peak frequencies of offshore sites derived using different schemes. In the short-period range, $f_{p\mathrm{Parzen}}$ demonstrates the highest standard deviation; however, overall, the residual standard deviations of parameters such as $f_{p\mathrm{Parzen}}$ and $f_{p\mathrm{PSA}}$ remain relatively consistent. In the long-period range, $f_{p\mathrm{Parzen}}$ not only achieves the lowest standard deviation but also shows substantial improvement relative to the other three site parameters. Based on the comparative analyses presented in Figures 10 and 11, $f_{p\mathrm{Parzen}}$ stands out as the optimal single site parameter for the 109 unburied sites analyzed in this section, consistently representing the site term of unburied sites with the lowest residual standard deviation.

Analysis of buried ocean-bottom site effects

Because of the distinct burial methods of buried and unburied sites, significant differences in response spectrum amplitudes are observed across the entire period range. Specifically, the response spectra for buried ocean-bottom sites are considerably lower than those for unburied sites (Hu, Zhang, *et al.*, 2023; Tan and Hu, 2024). These variations can also be identified through the distribution of offshore site terms. As shown in Figures 12 and 13, the mean site term for buried sites is ~−0.5, whereas the mean site term for unburied sites (Figs. 8 and 9) is close to zero. These variations can also be identified through the distribution of offshore site terms, which is

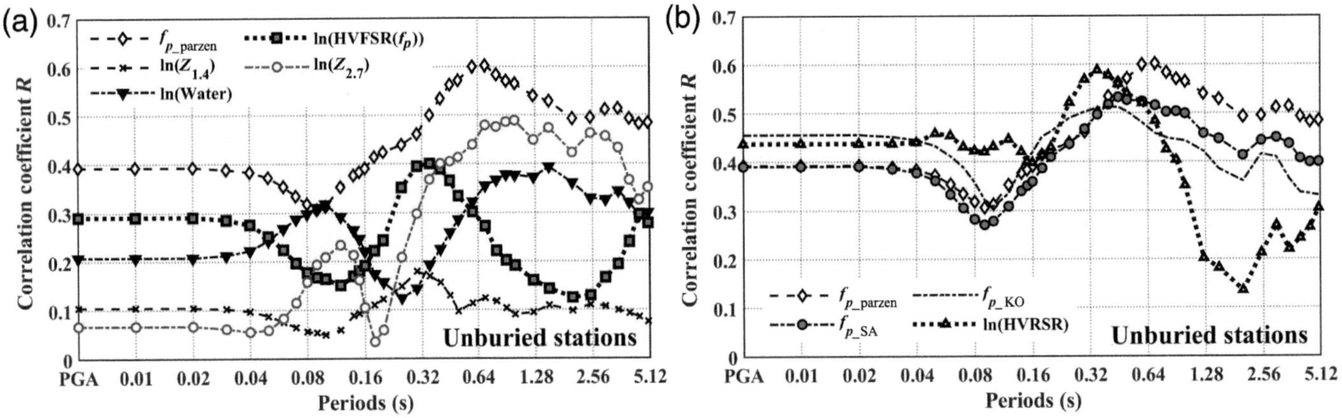

Figure 10. Distribution of correlation coefficients between various site parameters and the spectral period for unburied ocean-bottom sites: (a) site parameters $f_{pParzen}$, $\ln(Z_{1.4})$, $\ln(Z_{2.7})$, ln(Water), and $\ln(HVFSR(f_p))$ and (b) site parameters $f_{pParzen}$, f_{pKO}, f_{pSA}, and ln(HVRSR). The color version of this figure is available only in the electronic edition.

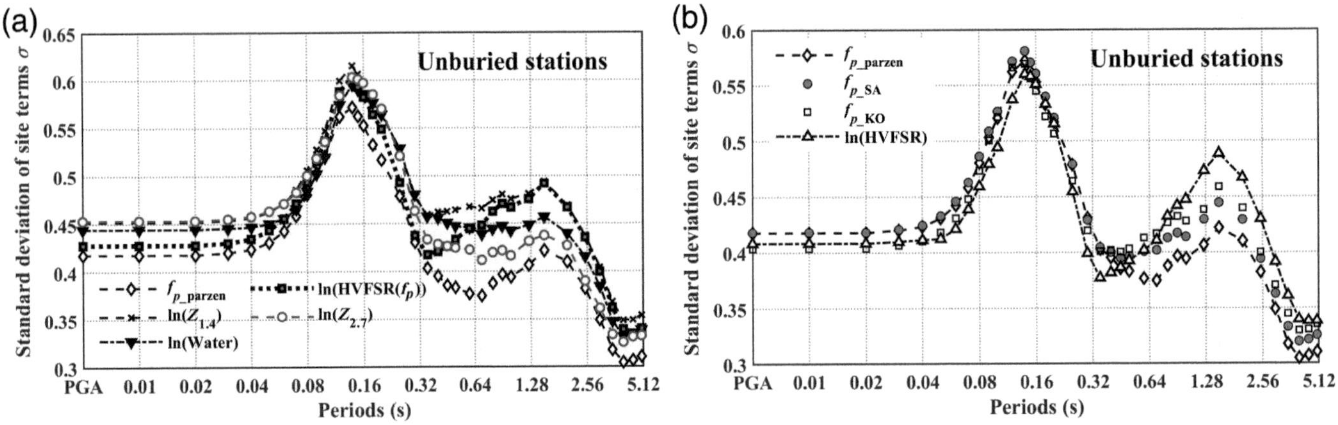

Figure 11. Distribution of residual standard deviation between various site parameters and the spectral period for unburied ocean-bottom sites: (a) site parameters $f_{pParzen}$, $\ln(Z_{1.4})$, $\ln(Z_{2.7})$, ln(Water), and $\ln(HVFSR(f_p))$ and (b) site parameters $f_{pParzen}$, f_{pKO}, f_{pSA}, and ln(HVRSR). The color version of this figure is available only in the electronic edition.

consistent with the findings shown in Dhakal *et al.* (2024). This indicates that buried sites generally exhibit an inhibitory effect compared with unburied sites. In this study, the same site parameters used in the analysis of unburied sites were applied to analyze the 41 buried ocean-bottom sites. Figure 12 presents the correlation analysis between the site term of buried sites and the HVRSR(T). The results show a strong correlation between the buried site term and HVRSR(T), consistent with the findings of Pinilla-Ramos *et al.* (2022), who used the normalized HVSR(T) as the site term. This suggests that the HVRSR(T) is strongly correlated with the site term at the corresponding period. Notably, this correlation is more pronounced for buried sites than for unburied sites. The correlation analysis of the remaining site parameters for buried sites is presented in Figures S4–S6.

Figure 13 shows correlation analysis between water depth and the buried site term. Specifically, ln(Water) shows relatively low correlation with the site term in the short-period range but shows higher correlation in the long-period range. Figure 14 presents the variations of various site parameters and the site term of buried sites with respect to the spectral period. In Figure 14a, the water depth, sedimentary thickness, HVSR corresponding to the peak frequency, and HVRSR(T) are analyzed. For periods not exceeding 3.5 s, ln(HVRSR) shows the highest correlation with the buried site term. When the period exceeds 3.5 s, ln(Water) exhibits the strongest correlation. Figure 14b compares the correlation analysis results of $f_{pParzen}$, f_{pPSA}, f_{pKO}, and ln(HVRSR) with the buried site term. Within the period range of 0.08–3.5 s, the correlations of the three types of highest peak frequencies with the

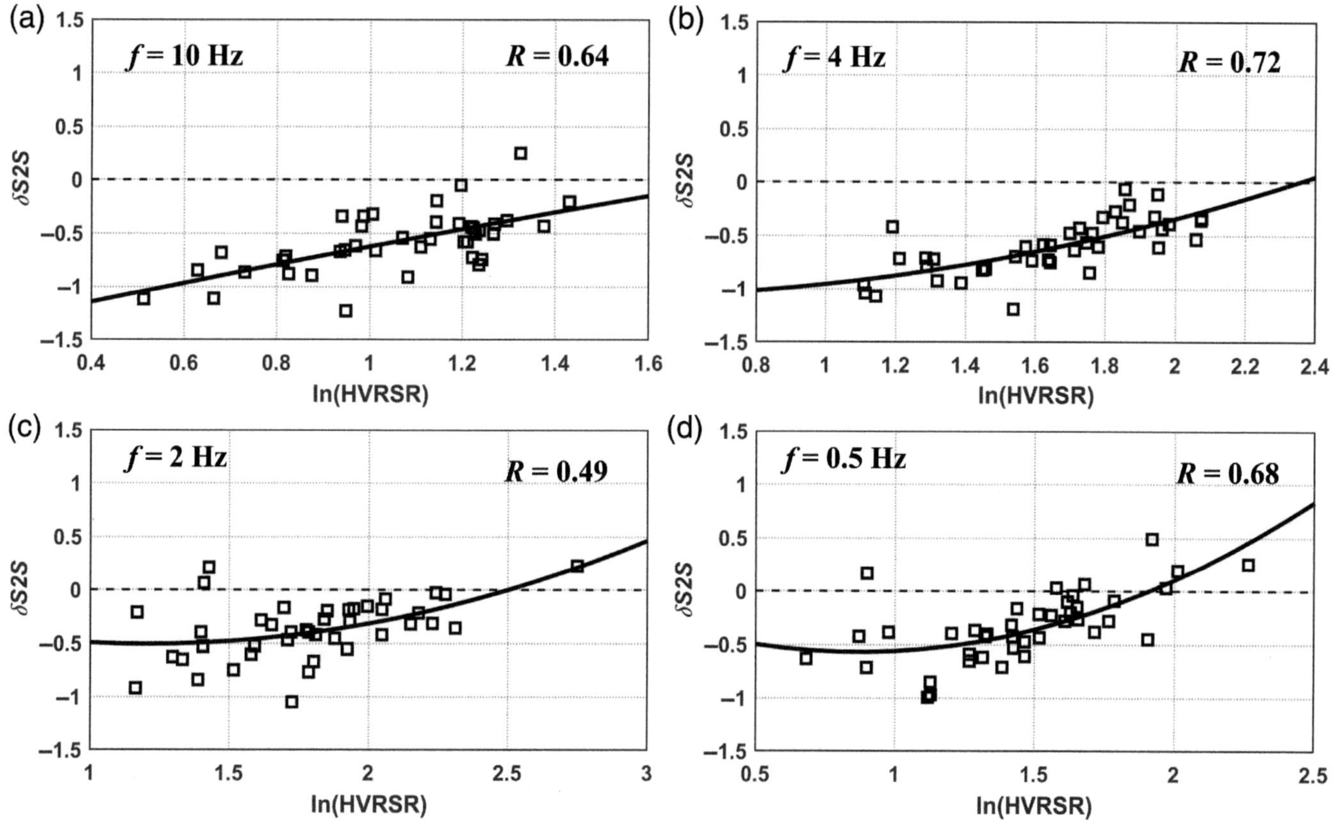

Figure 12. Correlation analysis between the HVRSR amplitude ln(HVRSR) and the single-station site term for buried ocean-bottom sites at spectral frequency: (a) f = 10 Hz; (b) f = 4 Hz; (c) f = 2 Hz; and (d) f = 0.5 Hz.

buried site term are similar and lower than that of ln(HVRSR).

Figure 15 shows the distribution of the residual standard deviation for various site parameters in presenting the site term. The site parameters analyzed in Figure 15a are consistent with those in Figure 14a, whereas Figure 15b aligns with Figure 14b. Overall, the standard deviation of HVRSR(T) is the smallest, and the standard deviations of the three highest peak frequencies show minimal variation. When developing site effect models using a single site parameter, HVRSR(T) is the optimal choice for buried ocean-bottom sites, followed closely by the three highest peak frequencies $f_{p\mathrm{Parzen}}$, $f_{p\mathrm{PSA}}$, and $f_{p\mathrm{KO}}$. However, the correlation performance using the peak frequency is less effective for buried sites than for unburied ones. Dhakal *et al.* (2023) investigated the absolute site amplification factors of both seabed-buried and unburied stations in the S-net network using a generalized inversion technique. Differences between buried and unburied stations were attributed to the effects of sediment layer thickness and seismic-wave propagation paths. Nevertheless, given the limited number of buried sites, it is essential to further assess the adequacy of the selected parameters within the broader context of combining site terms for both buried and unburied sites and for developing offshore GMMs.

PERFORMANCE OF VARIOUS SITE TERMS IN THE OFFSHORE GMPE

The highest peak frequency identified by HVFSR smoothing with a Parzen window, $f_{p\mathrm{Parzen}}$, shows the strongest performance in analyzing the correlation of site parameters and offshore unburied site terms. In contrast, ln(HVRSR(T)) exhibits superior performance for buried ocean-bottom sites. However, using HVRSR(T) requires each station to provide the corresponding HVSR, which is more complex and less convenient than directly using the site peak frequency. Furthermore, the highest peak frequency f_p shows strong correlations for both buried and unburied stations. Because of the number of unburied sites significantly larger than that of buried sites, the results of unburied site terms are more representative. Consequently, this section evaluates the strengths and limitations of the highest peak frequencies in presenting the offshore site effects (Hassani and Atkinson, 2016; Zhu *et al.*, 2020). To further validate the applicability of the offshore site peak frequency in GMMs, this section selects three highest peak frequencies, along with water depth and sedimentary thickness (Hu, Zhang, *et al.*, 2023; Tan and Hu, 2024) as site models, conducts regression analysis on the weak earthquake database, and compares the performance of different peak frequencies in offshore GMMs.

Using the offshore ground-motion database in this study (Fig. 2), site effect models with different peak frequencies are developed. Specifically, single-station site terms are

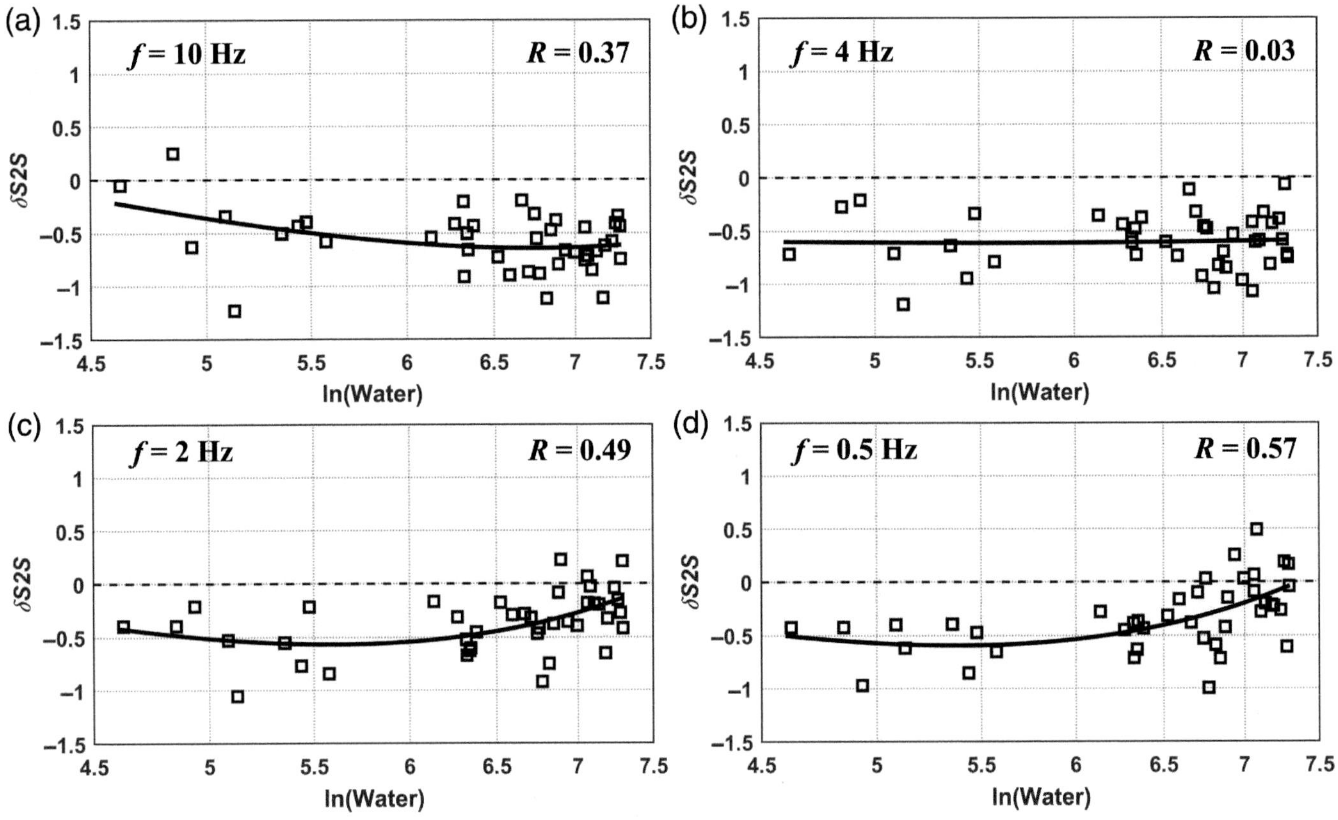

Figure 13. Correlation analysis between the water depth ln(Water) and the single-station site term for buried ocean-bottom sites at spectral frequency: (a) $f = 10$ Hz; (b) $f = 4$ Hz; (c) $f = 2$ Hz; and (d) $f = 0.5$ Hz.

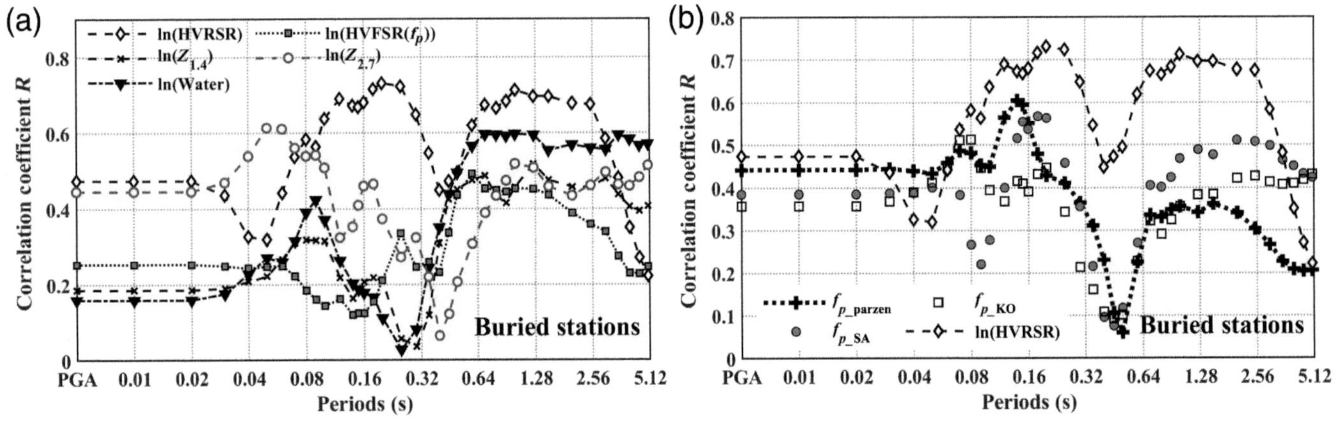

Figure 14. Distribution of correlation coefficients between various site parameters and the spectral period for buried ocean-bottom sites: (a) site parameters ln(HVRSR), ln($Z_{1.4}$), ln($Z_{2.7}$), ln(Water), and ln(HVFSR(f_p)) and (b) site parameters $f_{pParzen}$, f_{pKO}, f_{pSA}, and ln(HVRSR). The color version of this figure is available only in the electronic edition.

modeled through quadratic fitting of f_p, thereby facilitating an evaluation of the advantages of developing the offshore site effects based on the peak frequency. This approach contrasts with methods that rely on the HVSR as the parameter; instead, it uses a single site parameter (Hassani and Atkinson, 2018). The source and path terms of the offshore GMMs adhere to the functional form proposed by Tan and Hu (2024), whereas the site term is explicitly formulated using the peak frequency as the site parameter, as presented in the following equations:

$$\ln(Y_{i,j}) = f_m(m_i,h_i) + g\ln(r_{i,j}) + g_L\ln(x_{i,j} + 200.0) + ex_{i,j} + \gamma + F_i + F_s + f_{\text{site}} + \xi_{i,j} + \eta_i, \quad (8)$$

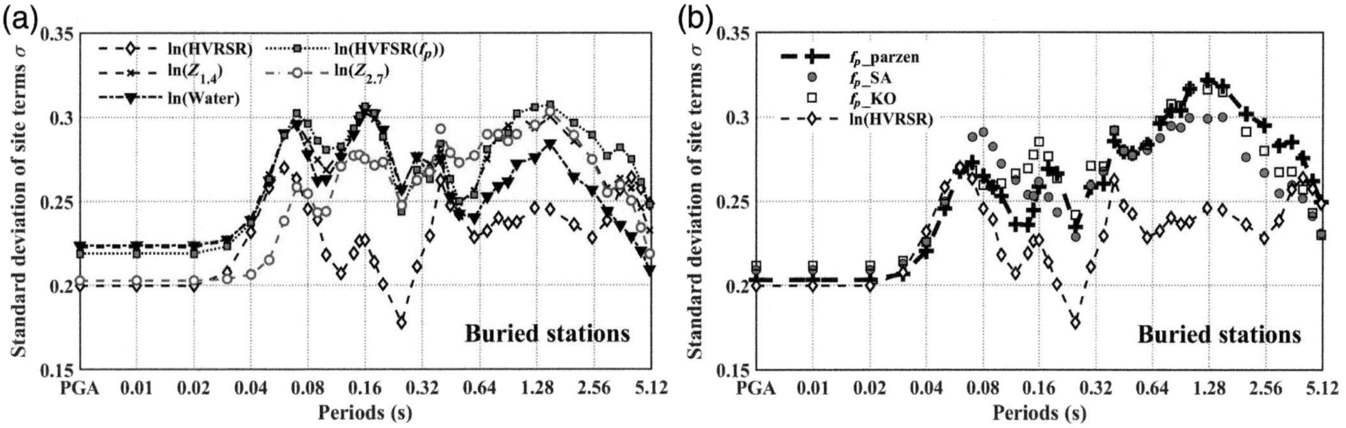

Figure 15. Distribution of residual standard deviation between various site parameters and the spectral period for buried ocean-bottom sites: (a) site parameters ln(HVRSR), ln($Z_{1.4}$), ln($Z_{2.7}$), ln(Water), and ln(HVFSR(f_p)) and (b) site parameters $f_{pParzen}$, f_{pKO}, f_{pSA}, and ln(HVRSR). The color version of this figure is available only in the electronic edition.

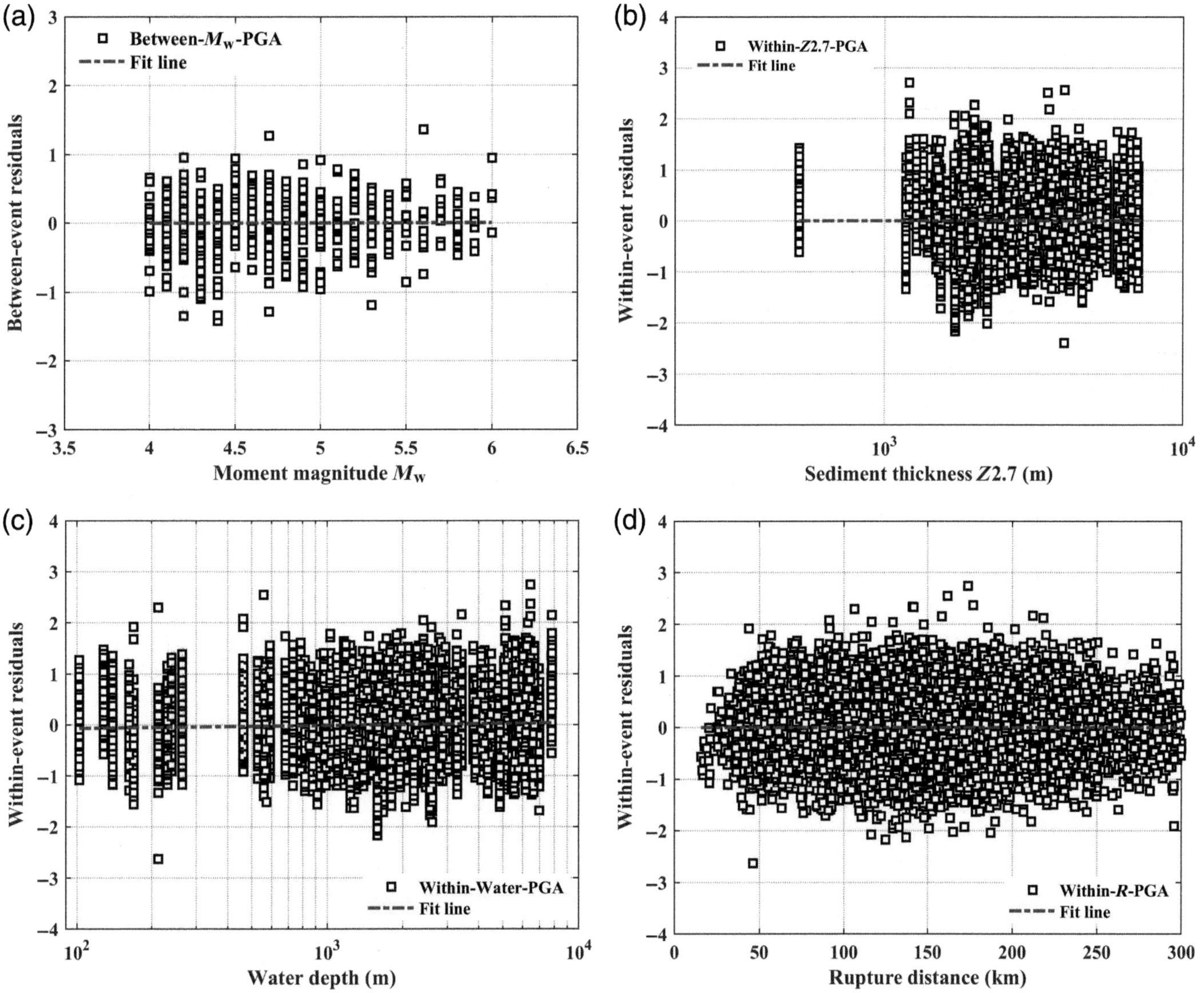

Figure 16. Residual analysis of the regression results using $f_{pParzen}$ as an explanatory variable for constructing the site effect model: (a) between-event residuals versus M_w; within-event residuals versus $Z_{2.7}$; within-event residuals versus water depth; and (d) within-event residuals versus rupture distance. The color version of this figure is available only in the electronic edition.

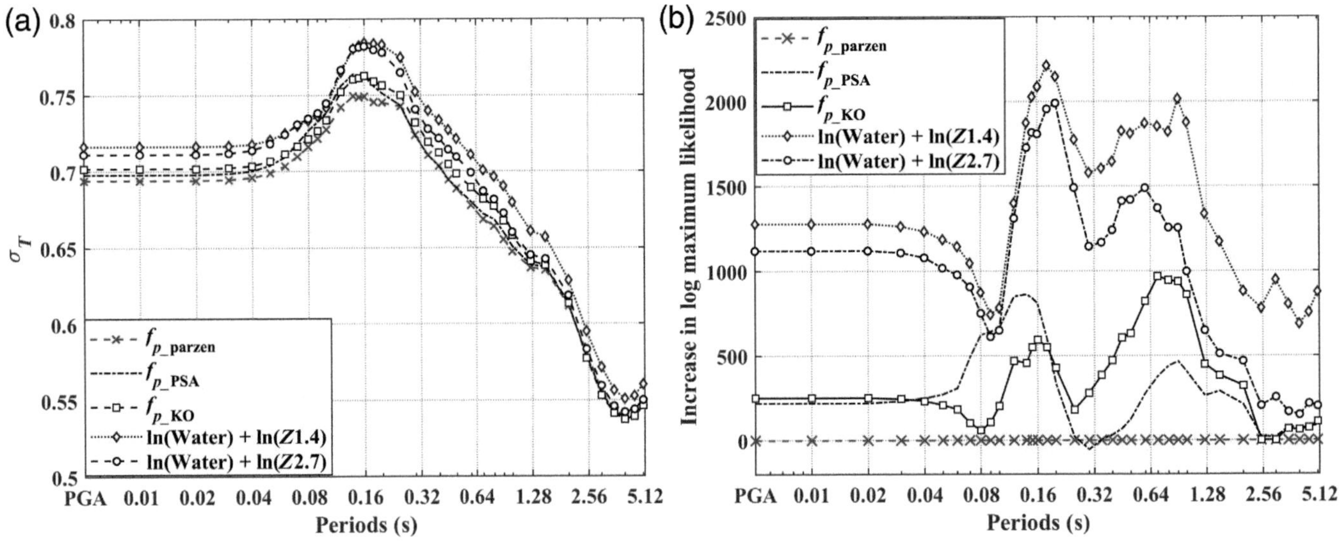

Figure 17. Comparison of the total standard deviation for offshore ground-motion models (GMMs) when different site parameters are used as (a) site terms and the (b) Akaike information criterion (AIC) differences among the models. The color version of this figure is available only in the electronic edition.

$$f_m(m_i,h_i) = bh_i + c_1 m_i + c_2(m_i - m_{sc})^2, \quad (9)$$

$$r_{i,j} = x_{i,j} + \exp(c_1 + c_2 m_i), \quad (10)$$

in which m_i denotes the earthquake magnitude, h_i denotes the focal depth, x_i denotes the distance to the fault, F_i is the dummy variable for interface earthquakes, F_s is the dummy variable for slab earthquakes, and f_{site} represents the offshore site effect. The site effect f_{site} is formulated based on the peak frequency as shown in the following equation:

$$f_{\text{site}} = \begin{cases} \gamma_b + s_{b1} f_{\text{peak}} + s_{b2} f_{\text{peak}}^2 & \text{buried stations} \\ \gamma_u + s_{u1} f_{\text{peak}} + s_{u2} f_{\text{peak}}^2 & \text{unburied stations} \end{cases}, \quad (11)$$

in which f_{peak} represent the highest peak frequency, specifically $f_{p\text{Parzen}}$, $f_{p\text{PSA}}$, and $f_{p\text{KO}}$. In addition, water depth and sedimentary thickness are used as site parameters for comparison (Hu, Zhang, *et al.*, 2023; Tan and Hu, 2024), as presented in the following equation:

$$f_{\text{site}}(\text{WD},S) = \begin{cases} w_b \ln(\text{WD}/\text{WD}_0) + s_b \ln(S/S_0), & \text{buried stations, WD} < 1500 \\ w_u \ln(\text{WD}/\text{WD}_0) + s_u \ln(S/S_0), & \text{unburied stations, WD} > 1200, S > 400 \end{cases}, \quad (12)$$

in which WD and S denote the water depth and sedimentary thickness (Z1.4 and Z2.7) of the offshore sites, respectively. Regression analyses were performed on offshore response spectra using various forms of site effect models. Taking the regression analysis results of $f_{p\text{Parzen}}$ as an example, as shown in Figure 16, after incorporating the site-effect model of the peak frequency $f_{p\text{Parzen}}$, the within-event residuals exhibit minimal bias with respect to both sediment layer thickness and water depth. The residual analysis results for $f_{p\text{KO}}$ and $f_{p\text{PSA}}$ are consistent with these findings.

Figure 17 evaluates the effectiveness of various site parameters in developing offshore GMMs as site terms. Figure 17a illustrates the distribution of the total standard deviation of the model across the spectral period following regression analysis for four distinct site-effect models. Figure 17b presents the Akaike information criterion (AIC) differences between different site forms and the $f_{p\text{Parzen}}$ model. The AIC criterion is widely recognized for assessing the goodness of fit of GMMs (Jiang and Zhao, 2017). A regression model with the smallest AIC value demonstrates the best fit. As shown in Figure 17, when $f_{p\text{Parzen}}$ is used as the site parameter, both the total standard deviation of the model and the AIC value are minimized. This suggests that $f_{p\text{Parzen}}$ is more appropriate than $f_{p\text{KO}}$ and $f_{p\text{PSA}}$ for developing the offshore site effect. In addition, site effects constructed using site peak frequency can substantially reduce model uncertainty compared with those based on water depth or sedimentary thickness.

Unlike previous studies on offshore GMMs (Hu, Zhang, *et al.*, 2023; Tan and Hu, 2024), which lacked reliable estimates of site amplification, researchers are now exploring improved site parameters to assess seafloor site amplification (Hu *et al.*, 2024). Because of the scarcity of shallow site information for ocean-bottom stations, this study suggests that constructing the site-effect models using the highest peak frequency $f_{p\mathrm{Parzen}}$ or classifying ocean-bottom stations based on their peak frequency could serve as a viable approach, offering valuable insights for further investigation into the attenuation characteristics of offshore ground motions.

DISCUSSION

The application of the HVSR technique in site characterization and seismic hazard assessment is of significant importance for marine infrastructure development. However, many ocean-bottom stations in the S-net are located in far offshore regions, well beyond the typical zones of current marine infrastructure deployment. Consequently, the HVSR-based identification and analysis results from this study may have limited direct applicability to offshore engineering projects. Nevertheless, these findings hold substantial potential for improving earthquake early warning systems and enhancing the accuracy of magnitude estimation, particularly in offshore regions.

Ocean-bottom stations are typically deployed on or within shallow sediment layers, where local site conditions are dominated by water-saturated seafloor sediments. These sediments exhibit pronounced amplification effects on both horizontal and vertical components of offshore ground motions (Hu *et al.*, 2020). In addition, water depth exerts a damping influence on high-frequency components of vertical offshore ground motion (Diao *et al.*, 2014), leading to fundamental differences between offshore and onshore site response characteristics. As a result, HVSR curves observed at ocean-bottom stations differ markedly from their onshore counterparts in both shape and peak behavior. Correlation analyses indicate that for both buried and unburied ocean-bottom sites, the first peak frequency generally exhibits weaker correlation with site effects than the highest peak frequency, suggesting that the latter more effectively captures the dynamic characteristics of ocean-bottom sites. Furthermore, correlation assessments stratified by station burial type reveal no statistically significant relationships among water depth, sediment thickness, and peak frequencies, implying that all three parameters can serve as independent explanatory variables in modeling offshore site effects.

Further investigation into the relationship between peak frequencies and site amplification reveals distinct behaviors between buried and unburied stations. For unburied stations, $f_{p\mathrm{Parzen}}$ exhibits the strongest correlation with the site term, highlighting its effectiveness as a predictive variable. In contrast, correlations with sedimentary thickness and water depth remain relatively weak. For buried stations, the three peak frequency metrics show comparable correlation levels with site term, though all are generally lower than $\ln(\mathrm{HVRSR}(T))$. Given the limited number of buried stations ($n = 41$), regression analysis primarily relies on data from the 109 unburied stations. Although $\ln(\mathrm{HVRSR}(T))$ offers greater practicality and stability as a composite site proxy, the use of a single peak frequency retains strong physical interpretability and modeling efficiency, making it especially suitable for developing offshore GMMs.

CONCLUSIONS

This study uses the HVSR to identify the first and highest peak frequencies for 109 unburied and 41 buried ocean-bottom sites of S-net in the Japan trench area. It explores the correlation between the peak frequencies of different identification schemes and the site terms and evaluates the superiority of these identification schemes, with the aim of obtaining the optimal peak frequency that best characterizes the site effects of ocean-bottom sites. The main conclusions are as follows.

1. The first and highest peak frequencies of the response spectrum for offshore sites ($f_{0\mathrm{PSA}}$ and $f_{p\mathrm{PSA}}$), the first and highest peak frequencies of the *S*-wave Fourier spectrum ratio smoothed by the Parzen window ($f_{0\mathrm{Parzen}}$ and $f_{p\mathrm{Parzen}}$), and the first and highest peak frequencies of *S*-wave Fourier spectral ratio smoothed by the Konno–Ohmachi window ($f_{0\mathrm{KO}}$ and $f_{p\mathrm{KO}}$) were determined using a weak earthquake dataset from the S-net. Correlation analysis for buried and unburied ocean-bottom sites revealed that the correlation for the first peak frequency is generally weaker than that for the highest peak frequency.
2. Correlations among site parameters were evaluated based on burial methods. No significant correlation was observed among water depth, sedimentary thickness, and peak frequencies, suggesting that all three kinds of site parameters can serve as explanatory variables for the offshore site effect. The highest peak frequency shows significantly greater effectiveness than the first peak frequency in characterizing the offshore site effect.
3. The feasibility of developing an offshore site effect model using various highest peak frequencies as explanatory variables was investigated. By comparing the standard deviations and AIC values among regression models with different site terms, it was determined that the site term constructed using $f_{p\mathrm{Parzen}}$ exhibited the lowest standard deviation and the smallest AIC across the entire period range. This indicates that $f_{p\mathrm{Parzen}}$, as a single explanatory variable, provides the best fit for offshore GMMs. Therefore, the highest peak frequency $f_{p\mathrm{Parzen}}$ is identified as the optimal explanatory variable for characterizing the offshore site term for the S-net in this study.

DATA AND RESOURCES

The offshore earthquake ground motions of the S-net are from the Hi-net (https://www.hinet.bosai.go.jp). The moment magnitude, focal depth, and longitude and latitude of the earthquake locations were all collected from the high-precision Japan Meteorological Agency (JMA; https://www.jma.go.jp) data in Japan, and the rupture model used to calculate the rupture distance was derived from the Natural Research Institute for Earth Science and Disaster Prevention (NIED; https://www.bosai.go.jp). All websites were last accessed in April 2025. The supplemental material includes the detailed peak frequency information for 150 offshore stations from the S-net, figures of *S* wave, smoothing process for H/V Fourier spectral ratio (HVFSR) curves, correlation analysis for all selected site parameters, and figures of residual analysis for the offshore ground-motion models (GMMs) with the $f_{pParzen}$ model.

DECLARATION OF COMPETING INTERESTS

The authors acknowledge that there are no conflicts of interest recorded.

ACKNOWLEDGMENTS

This work was financially supported by the Scientific Research Fund of Institute of Engineering Mechanics, China Earthquake Administration (Grant Number 2024D10), and National Natural Science Foundation of China (52079072). The authors specially thank the anonymous reviewers and the Editor-in-Chief Martin Mai for their valuable comments. The authors are grateful to the K-NET and Hi-net for providing valuable offshore ground motions.

REFERENCES

Abrahamson, N. A., and R. R. Youngs (1992). A stable algorithm for regression analyses using the random effects model, *Bull. Seismol. Soc. Am.* **82,** no. 1, 505–510.

Abrahamson, N. A., W. J. Silva, and R. Kamai (2014). Summary of the ASK14 ground motion relation for active crustal regions, *Earthq. Spectra* **30,** no. 3, 1025–1055.

Aoi, S, Y. Asano, T. Kunugi, T. Kimura, K. Uehira, N. Takahashi, H. Ueda, K. Shiomi, T. Matsumoto, and H. Fujiwara (2020). MOWLAS: NIED observation network for earthquake, tsunami and volcano, *Earth Planets Space* **72,** 126.

Arteta, C. A., C. A. Pajaro, V. Mercado, J. Montejo, M. Arcila, and N. A. Abrahamson (2023). Ground-motion model (GMM) for crustal earthquakes in Northern South America (NoSAm crustal GMM), *Bull. Seismol. Soc. Am.* **113,** no. 1, 186–203.

Arteta, C. A., C. A. Pajaro, V. Mercado, J. Montejo, M. Arcila, and N. A. Abrahamson (2021). Ground-motion model for subduction earthquakes in northern South America, *Earthq. Spectra* **37,** no. 4, 2419–2452.

Castellaro, S., F. Mulargia, and P. L. Rossi (2008). VS30: Proxy for seismic amplification? *Seismol. Res. Lett.* **79,** 540–543.

Chen, B., B. Wang, Z. Ma, Y. Du, and C. Li (2023). Influence of seawater depth on offshore ground motion characteristics and seismic responses of sea-crossing cable-stayed bridges, *Ocean Eng.* **280,** no. 3, 114853, doi: 10.1016/j.oceaneng.2023.114853.

Chen, B., D. Wang, S. Chen, and S. Hu (2021). Influence of site factors on offshore ground motions: Observed results and numerical simulation, *Soil Dynam. Earthq. Eng.* **145,** 106,729.

Chen, B., D. Wang, H. Li, Z. Sun, and Y. Shi (2015). Characteristics of earthquake ground motion on the seafloor, *J. Earthq. Eng.* **19,** no. 6, 874–904.

Dhakal, Y. P., and T. Kunugi (2021). An evaluation of strong-motion parameters at the S-net ocean-bottom seismograph sites near the Kanto basin for earthquake early warning, *Front. Earth Sci.* **9,** 699439.

Dhakal, Y. P., and T. Kunugi (2023a). Analysis of orientation changes of s-net accelerometers due to earthquake motion, *J. Disaster Res.* **18,** no. 7, 730–739.

Dhakal, Y. P., and T. Kunugi (2023b). Preliminary analysis of nonlinear site response at the S-net seafloor sites during three Mw 7 class earthquakes, *Front. Earth Sci.* **11,** 1180289, doi: 10.3389/feart.2023.1180289.

Dhakal, Y. P., S. Aoi, T. Kunugi, W. Suzuki, and T. Kimura (2017). Assessment of nonlinear site response at ocean bottom seismograph sites based on S-wave horizontal-to-vertical spectral ratios: A study at the Sagami Bay area K-NET sites in Japan, *Earth Planets Space* **69,** no. 1, 1–7.

Dhakal, Y. P., H. Kubo, and T. Kunugi (2024). Prediction equations for peak-ground accelerations and velocities in northeast Japan using the S-net data, *J. Disaster Res.* **19,** no. 5, 760–771, doi: 10.20965/jdr.2024.p0760.

Dhakal, Y. P., T. Kunugi, H. Yamanaka, A. Wakai, S. Aoi, and A. Nishizawa (2023). Estimation of source, path, and site factors of S waves recorded at the S-net sites in the Japan Trench area using the spectral inversion technique, *Earth Planets Space* **75,** 1.

Dhakal, Y. P., T. Kunugi, W. Suzuki, T. Kimura, N. Morikawa, and S. Aoi (2021). Strong motions on land and ocean bottom: Comparison of horizontal PGA, PGV, and 5% damped acceleration response spectra in Northeast Japan and the Japan Trench Area, *Bull. Seismol. Soc. Am.* **111,** no. 6, 3237–3260.

Di Alessandro, C., L. F. Bonilla, D. M. Boore, A. Rovelli, and O. Scotti (2012). Predominant-period site classification for response spectra prediction equations in Italy, *Bull. Seismol. Soc. Am.* **102,** no. 2, 680–95.

Diao, H., J. Hu, and L. Xie (2014). Effect of seawater on incident plane P and SV waves at ocean bottom and engineering characteristics of offshore ground motion records off the coast of southern California, USA, *Earthq. Eng. Eng Vib.* **13,** no. 2, 181–194.

Fu, L., S. Chen, L. Jin, X. Liu, and X. Li (2024). Seismic response characteristics of offshore sites in the Sagami Bay, Japan – Part I: Comparison of spectral inversion and ratio under weak motions, *Soil Dynam. Earthq. Eng.* **185,** 108909.

Fu, L., S. Chen, Z. Xie, S. Wang, J. Chen, and X. Li (2025). Seismic response characteristics of offshore sites in the Sagami Bay, Japan – Part II: Nonlinear behaviors and stochastic simulation of subduction zone earthquakes, *Soil Dynam. Earthq. Eng.* **188,** 109081.

Hassani, B., and G. M. Atkinson (2016). Applicability of the site fundamental frequency as a VS30 proxy for Central and Eastern North America, *Bull. Seismol. Soc. Am.* **106,** no. 2, 653–664.

Hassani, B., and G. M. Atkinson (2018). Site-effects model for central and Eastern North America based on peak frequency and average shear-wave velocity, *Bull. Seismol. Soc. Am.* **108,** no. 1, 338–50.

Hou, R., and J. X. Zhao (2023). Ground motion prediction equations for the horizontal component from shallow crustal and upper mantle earthquakes in Japan using site period as site parameter, *Bull. Earthq. Eng.* **106,** no. 4, 1518–1534.

Hu, J., L. Hu, C. Jin, Z. Wang, Y. Ding, and C. Tang (2023). Offshore ground motion models for Arias Intensity and Cumulative absolute velocity in the Japan Trench Area, *J. Earthq. Eng.* **27,** no. 14, 4005–4023.

Hu, J., J. Tan, and J. X. Zhao (2020). New GMPEs for the Sagami bay region in Japan for moderate magnitude events with emphasis on differences on site amplifications at the seafloor and land seismic stations of K-NET, *Bull. Seismol. Soc. Am.* **110,** no. 5, 2577–2597.

Hu, J., W. Zhang, L. Hu, L. Ding, and J. Tan (2023). Regional offshore ground motion prediction equation model from a referenced empirical approach: A case study in the Japan Trench area, *Soil Dynam. Earthq. Eng.* **174,** 108196.

Hu, L., Y. Li, and S. Ji (2024). An offshore non-ergodic ground motion model for subduction earthquakes in Japan Trench area, *Earthq. Spectra* **40,** no. 1, 379–419.

Husid, R. (1967). *Gravity Effects on the Earthquake Response of Yielding Structures*, California Institute of Technology, Pasadena, California, doi: 10.7907/9XAB-6V59.

Idini, B., F. Rojas, S. Ruiz, and C. Pastén (2017). Ground motion prediction equations for the Chilean subduction zone, *Bull. Earthq. Eng.* **15,** no. 5, 1853–1880.

Jiang, F., and J. X. Zhao (2017). A ground-motion prediction equation for vertical spectra of the strong-motion records from the subduction slab events in Japan using site class as the site term, *Bull. Seismol. Soc. Am.* **107,** no. 5, 2328–2341.

Konno, K., and T. Ohmachi (1998). Ground-motion characteristics estimated from spectral ratio between horizontal and vertical components of microtremor, *Bull. Seismol. Soc. Am.* **88,** 228–241.

Kubo, H., T. Nakamura, W. Suzuki, Y. P. Dhakal, T. Kimura, T. Kunugi, N. Takahashi, and S. Aoi (2019). Ground-motion characteristics and nonlinear soil response observed by DONET1 seafloor observation network during the 2016 southeast Off-Mie, Japan, earthquake, *Bull. Seismol. Soc. Am.* **109,** no. 3, 976–986.

Li, X., N. Li, and S. Chen (2021). Study on seismic zoning in China Sea area and its key issues, *Technol. Earthq. Disaster Prev.* **16,** no. 1, 1-10 (in Chinses)

McCann, M. W., and H. C. Shah (1979). Determination strong-motion duration of earthquakes, *Bull. Seismol. Soc. Am.* **69,** no. 4, 1253–1265.

Mercado, V., F. Diaz-Parra, C. A. Pajaro, J. Montejo, G. Posada, M. Arcila, and C. A. Arteta (2024). Performance evaluation of parameters as estimators of seismic site effects in northern South America, *Soil Dynam. Earthq. Eng.* **180,** 108584.

Mercado, V., C. A. Pajaro, C. A. Arteta, F. J. Díaz, J. Montejo, M. Arcila, and N. A. Abrahamson (2023). Semiempirical model for the estimation of site amplification in Northern South America, *Earthq. Spectra* **39,** no. 2, 1109–1139.

Nakamura, Y. (1989). A method for dynamic characteristics estimation of subsurface using microtremor on ground surface *Q. Rep. Railway Tech. Res. Inst.* **30,** 25–33.

Nakamura, Y. (2019). What is the Nakamura method? *Seismol. Res. Lett.* **90,** 1437–1443.

Parker, G. A., J. P. Stewart, D. M. Boore, G. M. Atkinson, and B. Hassani (2021). NGA-subduction global ground motion models with regional adjustment factors, *Earthq. Spectra* **38,** no. 1, 456–493.

Pinilla-Ramos, C., N. A. Abrahamson, and R. Kayen (2022). Estimation of site terms in ground-motion models for California using horizontal-to-vertical spectral ratios from microtremor, *Bull. Seismol. Soc. Am.* **112,** no. 6, 3016–3036.

Ren, Y., R. Wen, X. Yao, and K. Ji (2017). Five parameters for the evaluation of the soil nonlinearity during the Ms 8.0 Wenchuan Earthquake using the HVSR method, *Earth Planets Space* **69,** 116.

Rong, M., L. Fu, Z. Wang, X. Li, N. S. Carpenter, E. W. Woolery, and Y. Lyu (2017). On the amplitude discrepancy of HVSR and site amplification from strong-motion observations, *Bull. Seismol. Soc. Am.* **107,** no. 6, 2873–2884.

Takagi, R., U. Uchida, T. Nakayama, R. Azuma, A. Ishigami, T. Okada, T. Nakamura, and K. Shiomi (2019). Estimation of the orientations of the S-net cabled ocean-bottom sensors, *Seismol. Res. Lett.* **90,** no. 6, 2175–2187.

Tan, J., and J. Hu (2024). Horizontal ground-motion model for subduction slab earthquakes using offshore ground motions in the Japan Trench area, *Earthq. Spectra* **40,** no. 3, 1653–1682.

Wang, H. (2011). Amplification effects of soil sites on ground motion in the Weihe basin, *Chin. J. Geophys.* **54,** no. 1, 137–150 (in Chinese).

Wang, Z., K. Nakano, E. Ito, H. Kawase, and S. Matsushima (2023). A hybrid approach for deriving horizontal site amplification factors considering both the similarity of HVSRE and the vertical amplification correction function, *Earthq. Eng. Struct. Dynam.* **52,** no. 1, 128–146.

Yamazaki, F., and M. A. Ansary (1997). Horizontal-to-vertical spectrum ratio of earthquake ground motion for site characterization, *Earthq. Eng. Struct. Dynam.* **26,** no. 7, 671–689.

Zhang, Q., and X. Y. Zheng (2020). Temporal and spectral characteristics of seismic ground motions: Offshore versus onshore, *Mar. Struct.* **74,** no. 1, 102812.

Zhao, J. X., K. Irikura, J. Zhang, Y. Fukushima, P. G. Somerville, A. Asano, Y. Ohno, T. Oouchi, T. Takahashi, and H. Ogawa (2006). An empirical site-classification method for strong-motion stations in Japan using H/V response spectral ratio, *Bull. Seismol. Soc. Am.* **96,** no. 3, 914–925.

Zhao, J. X., and H. Xu (2013). A comparison of Vs30 and site period as site-effect parameters in response spectral ground-motion prediction equations, *Bull. Seismol. Soc. Am.* **103,** 1–18.

Zhu, C., F. Cotton, H. Kawase, A. Haendel, M. Pilz, and K. Nakano (2022). How well can we predict earthquake site response so far? Site-specific approaches, *Earthq. Spectra* **38,** no. 2, 1047–1075.

Zhu, C., F. Cotton, and M. Pilz (2020). Detecting site resonant frequency using HVSR: Fourier versus response spectrum and the first versus the highest peak frequency, *Bull. Seismol. Soc. Am.* **110,** no. 2, 427–440.

Zhu, C., M. Pilz, and F. Cotton (2019). Which is a better proxy, site period or depth to bedrock, in modelling linear site response in addition to the average shear-wave velocity? *Bull. Earthq. Eng.* **18,** 797–820.

Manuscript received 25 June 2025
Published online 18 December 2025

Do Earthquake-Induced Rotational Ground Motions Matter? A Case Study from the M_w 7.8 Pazarcık Earthquake

Sergio E. Godínez*[1], Mohamed Abdelmeguid[2], José I. Restrepo[1], and Ares J. Rosakis[2]

ABSTRACT

This article investigates the influence of the rotational components of ground motion on the seismic response of structures. Two independent seismic stations, located 30 m apart and within 1 km of the fault rupture, recorded the near-field motions of the 6 February 2023 M_w 7.8 Kahramanmaraş–Pazarcık earthquake. A third, synthetic station was generated using a stochastic frequency-domain approach to estimate the complete set of rotational components. The synthetic records assume that spatial variations in motion depend solely on the interstation separation distance. The resulting rotational response spectra indicate limited sensitivity to the random variability introduced by the synthetic station. For the first time, near-fault rotational ground-motion components—pitch, roll, and yaw—derived from a major earthquake are estimated and used as an input in nonlinear response-history analyses of 3D reinforced concrete building models. The case studies show that including rotational components increases peak core-wall shear forces by 5.3% and peak interstory drift by 13.3%. These findings underscore the importance of measuring and incorporating rotational ground-motion effects in seismic design codes and guidelines to better mitigate the vulnerability of structures near active faults.

KEY POINTS

- We evaluate the effect of near-fault rotational ground motions on the nonlinear performance of structures.
- Including rotational components increases the displacement demands and shear forces in concrete elements.
- There is a need to measure and include the effects of rotational ground motions in design codes.

INTRODUCTION

On 6 February 2023, an M_w 7.8 seismic event, now referred to as the Kahramanmaraş–Pazarcık earthquake, struck southeastern Türkiye and northern Syria. Based on teleseismic data and multiple seismic inversions, the rupture began at 01:17:355 Coordinated Universal Time (UTC) along a splay fault, specifically the Narli fault, located near the East Anatolian fault (EAF) (Disaster and Emergency Management Authority [AFAD], 1973; Jia *et al.*, 2023; Liu *et al.*, 2023; U.S. Geological Survey [USGS], 2023; Ren *et al.*, 2024). The estimated hypocenter is located at 37.230° N, 37.019° E, at a depth of 10 km (AFAD, 1973; USGS, 2023; Ren *et al.*, 2024). The rupture propagated northeast, transitioning onto the EAF, and triggering a series of subsequent earthquakes. Preliminary geodetic inversions further confirmed the multisegment nature of the M_w 7.8 rupture (Barbot *et al.*, 2023). Figure 1a presents a detailed map of the Kahramanmaraş–Pazarcık earthquake, showing the fault trace (Reitman *et al.*, 2023; USGS, 2023), and the locations of major cities.

Geological characteristics of the fault system likely contributed to the extensive damage caused by the Kahramanmaraş–Pazarcık earthquake, which proved to be more destructive than what historical records indicate (Taymaz *et al.*, 1991; Emre *et al.*, 2018; Xu *et al.*, 2023). The orientation of the EAF relative to the principal stress directions places its segments within a highly stressed regime, making them susceptible to dynamic stress transfer and rotational effects (Güvercin *et al.*, 2022). The fault network's complexity, including multiple segmentations, kinks, and bends, plays a critical role in controlling rupture dynamics (Bhat *et al.*, 2007; Biegel *et al.*, 2007; Ma and Elbanna, 2019; Goldberg *et al.*, 2023; Mai *et al.*, 2023;

1. Department of Structural Engineering, University of California San Diego, San Diego, California, U.S.A., https://orcid.org/0000-0003-2063-1259 (SEG); https://orcid.org/0000-0001-7968-166X (JIR); 2. Graduate Aerospace Laboratories, California Institute of Technology, Pasadena, California, U.S.A., https://orcid.org/0000-0002-3985-1721 (MA); https://orcid.org/0000-0003-0559-0794 (AJR)

*Corresponding author: segodine@ucsd.edu; sergiog.2392@gmail.com

Cite this article as Godínez, S. E., M. Abdelmeguid, J. I. Restrepo, and A. J. Rosakis (2026). Do Earthquake-Induced Rotational Ground Motions Matter? A Case Study from the M_w 7.8 Pazarcık Earthquake, *Bull. Seismol. Soc. Am.* **116**, 700–719, doi: 10.1785/0120250096

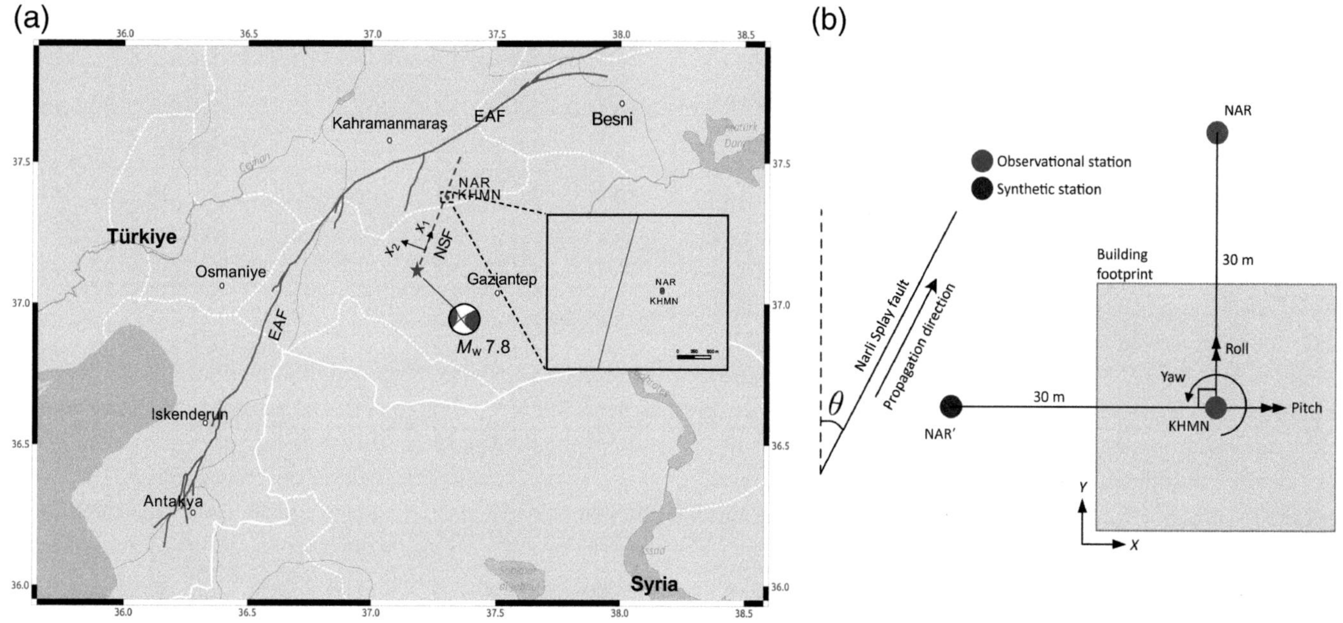

Figure 1. Map of the East Anatolian fault (EAF), highlighting the estimated location of the hypocenter of the M_w 7.8 Kahramanmaraş-Pazarcık earthquake, and locations of major cities and towns. (a) The location of seismic stations utilized in this study is highlighted by filled circles on the map. The two stations are NAR and KHMN, located approximately 30 m apart. (b) Schematic of ground station distribution, including station NAR′. NAR′ is placed such that the distance between KHMN and NAR is the same as KHMN to NAR′, creating a vertical plane that is orthogonal to the one created by KHMN and NAR. The three rotational components (pitch, roll, and yaw) are included with the base reference of the location of KHMN. The color version of this figure is available only in the electronic edition.

Reitman *et al.*, 2023). This geometric irregularity, when combined with elevated stress conditions, can amplify rupture complexity, resulting in high stress concentrations, rupture arrest, backpropagation, or transient supershear propagation. Multiple studies have shown that the rupture temporarily transitioned to supershear at various locations along the fault trace (Abdelmeguid *et al.*, 2023; Liu *et al.*, 2023; Delouis *et al.*, 2024; Ren *et al.*, 2024; Rosakis *et al.*, 2025).

The magnitude, duration, and geographic extent of the event resulted in the loss of more than 48,000 lives, damage to over half a million structures, and an estimated financial burden of 103.6 billion USD (Republic of Türkiye Presidency of Strategy and Budget, 2023). Some field investigations reported several casualties exceeding 50,000 (Ozturk *et al.*, 2023; Hu *et al.*, 2025). Several factors likely contributed to the widespread structural failures, including excessive seismic demands and substandard construction quality. Although this article does not focus on construction practices from a structural engineering standpoint, ground excitation during the Kahramanmaraş–Pazarcık earthquake exceeded the demands prescribed in the Turkish seismic code (Mertol *et al.*, 2023; Ozturk *et al.*, 2023; Papazafeiropoulos and Plevris, 2023; Wang *et al.*, 2023; Hu *et al.*, 2025; Vuran *et al.*, 2025).

Türkiye's building stock, particularly in urban regions, primarily comprises cast-in-place reinforced concrete (RC) structures (Ozturk *et al.*, 2023; Vuran *et al.*, 2025). The most used lateral force resisting system (LFRS) is a dual system consisting of RC frames and walls. Most of the buildings that experienced severe damage or collapse during the Kahramanmara–Pazarcık earthquake had that lateral system (Wang *et al.*, 2023). Notably, failures were documented in thirteen-story and sixteen-story buildings featuring U-shaped RC walls (Vuran *et al.*, 2025). The prevalent use of infilled joist slab system limits beam depth to that of the slab, reducing frame action. Field investigators attribute many structural failures to this limited frame action, which restricts interaction between frames and walls and reduces both ductility and redundancy (Ozturk *et al.*, 2023; Vuran *et al.*, 2025).

Accurately evaluating the performance of RC structures requires a faithful physical representation and reliable demand estimates. Nonlinear response history analysis (NRHA) of a structural model using two orthogonal horizontal ground motions is the standard method for assessing seismic performance. Vertical ground motion must also be considered when vertical elements of the gravity system are discontinuous (LATBSDC, 2024). Although the importance of measuring and incorporating rotational motions has been acknowledged (Lee *et al.*, 2009), such components are commonly neglected in practice, primarily due to the assumption that translational motions dominate and the limited availability of rotational data from past earthquakes. In addition, capturing rotational components requires special seismic sensors (Nigbor, 1994; Takeo, 1998; Igel *et al.*, 2005; Yin *et al.*, 2016), or alternatively, seismic arrays capable of accurately measuring motion gradients (Huang, 2003; Suryanto *et al.*, 2006), both of which are scarce and expensive to implement.

The deployment of two independent seismic stations located 30 m apart enabled the estimation of ground rotations induced by the seismic source within 1 km of the fault. These estimated rotations were used as an input in a nonlinear structural analysis model. The station spacing is comparable to the footprint of many buildings, making the setup particularly relevant for structural response evaluation. Previous studies have investigated the effect of torsional ground motions on single-story structures (Awad and Humar, 1984; De la Llera and Chopra, 1994), idealized multistory buildings (Ghafory-Ashtiany and Singh, 1986; Gupta and Trifunac, 1991; Vicencio and Alexander, 2019), and on tall slender chimneys (Bońkowski *et al.*, 2018), all using linear models. A consistent finding across these studies is that rotational input influences structural response. To the authors' knowledge, this is the first 3D NRHA of an RC structure subjected to simultaneous translational and estimated rotational ground motions in a near-fault setting.

In addition to examining the influence of rotational ground motion, this study also evaluates the impact of torsional irregularities on structural response. The proposed approach emphasizes the importance of incorporating ground rotations into building design and seismic performance assessment. These insights can support future updates to design codes aimed at reducing structural vulnerability and enhancing the resilience of communities located near active fault zones.

GROUND-MOTION ANALYSIS

Ground-motion analysis was carried out using strong-motion records obtained from Turkey's Disaster and Emergency Management Presidency (AFAD) and Kandilli Observatory and Earthquake Research Institute for stations TK:NAR and KO:KHMN, hereafter referred to as NAR and KHMN, respectively. The station locations are shown in Figure 1a. Both stations are situated approximately 22 km from the hypocenter, and ~700 m from the mapped fault surface (Reitman *et al.*, 2023; U.S. Geological Survey [USGS], 2023). Geographically, the stations are separated by 30 m, with coordinates of 37.3919° N 37.1574° E for NAR, and 37.3916° N 37.1574° E for KHMN (Kandilli Observatory And Earthquake Research Institute Boğaziçi University, 1971; AFAD, 1973). Their proximity to each other and to the fault surface makes them well-suited for assessing the influence of rotational ground motions on structural response in the near field. Notably, both stations recorded a larger fault-parallel (FP) velocity jump relative to the fault-normal (FN) component, an observation consistent with supershear rupture behavior documented in previous studies (Abdelmeguid *et al.*, 2023; Rosakis *et al.*, 2025).

The raw, unfiltered acceleration records were numerically integrated to obtain velocity and displacement time histories. To eliminate integration constants arising from instrumental noise, a baseline correction (Boore, 2001) was applied to the vertical component of the NAR station only because it exhibited a pronounced drift near the end of the displacement record. This correction ensured that the final velocity averaged to zero. A linear polynomial fit was applied over a selected portion of the time series, in this case, for times greater than 34 s (well beyond the strong shaking phase, see Fig. A1) to avoid introducing any bias into the key signature of the earthquake source. This process yields the three translational motion components at each station. The FP and FN ground-motion records derived from these components are shown in Figure A1. Peak ground acceleration (PGA) and peak ground velocity (PGV) values for both stations are reported in Table 1, using the strike of the estimated Narli splay fault of 28° (Reitman *et al.*, 2023; USGS, 2023) as a reference. As expected for supershear rupture propagation, both PGA and PGV values are higher in the FP direction compared to the FN direction.

TABLE 1
Peak Ground Acceleration (PGA) and Peak Ground Velocity (PGV) from Ground Motions

	PGA (*g*)			PGV (m/s)		
Station	**FP**	**FN**	**Vertical**	**FP**	**FN**	**Vertical**
KHMN	0.647	0.521	0.481	1.217	0.883	0.453
NAR	0.652	0.611	0.478	1.19	0.815	0.462

FN, fault normal; FP, fault parallel.

Figure 2 presents a comparison of the velocity time histories for the *X*, *Y*, and *Z* (vertical) directions, including records from stations KHMN and NAR, as well as a synthetic tertiary station, NAR′. The NAR′ station record was generated using the procedure detailed in the following paragraphs. The velocity time histories from KHMN and NAR exhibit strong similarity, particularly within the window corresponding to PGV, which is highlighted in the figure. A time lag is evident between the two records. The lag at which the cross-correlation of both the records is maximized is determined to be 0.03 s.

In addition to the translational ground motion at the stations, rotational components were also estimated. These components were computed in local coordinates (x_1, x_2, and x_3), using the rotation tensor, defined as the skew-symmetric part of the deformation gradient (Aki and Richards, 2002):

$$\Omega_{ij} = \frac{1}{2}(u_{i,j} - u_{j,i}), \tag{1}$$

which u_i denotes translational displacement. It is assumed that the tangential strain is zero at the free surface and, consequently, that all variations with respect to the x_3 direction are zero, that is, $u_{i,3} = 0$. Under this assumption, the rotation tensor can be represented by three distinct components: yaw, $\Omega_{12} = \frac{1}{2}[u_{1,2} - u_{2,1}]$, roll $u_{3,1}$, and pitch $u_{3,2}$.

To obtain the values of these three components, a finite-difference approximation was employed for the gradients, such that:

$$u_{i,j} = \Delta u_i / \Delta x_j, \tag{2}$$

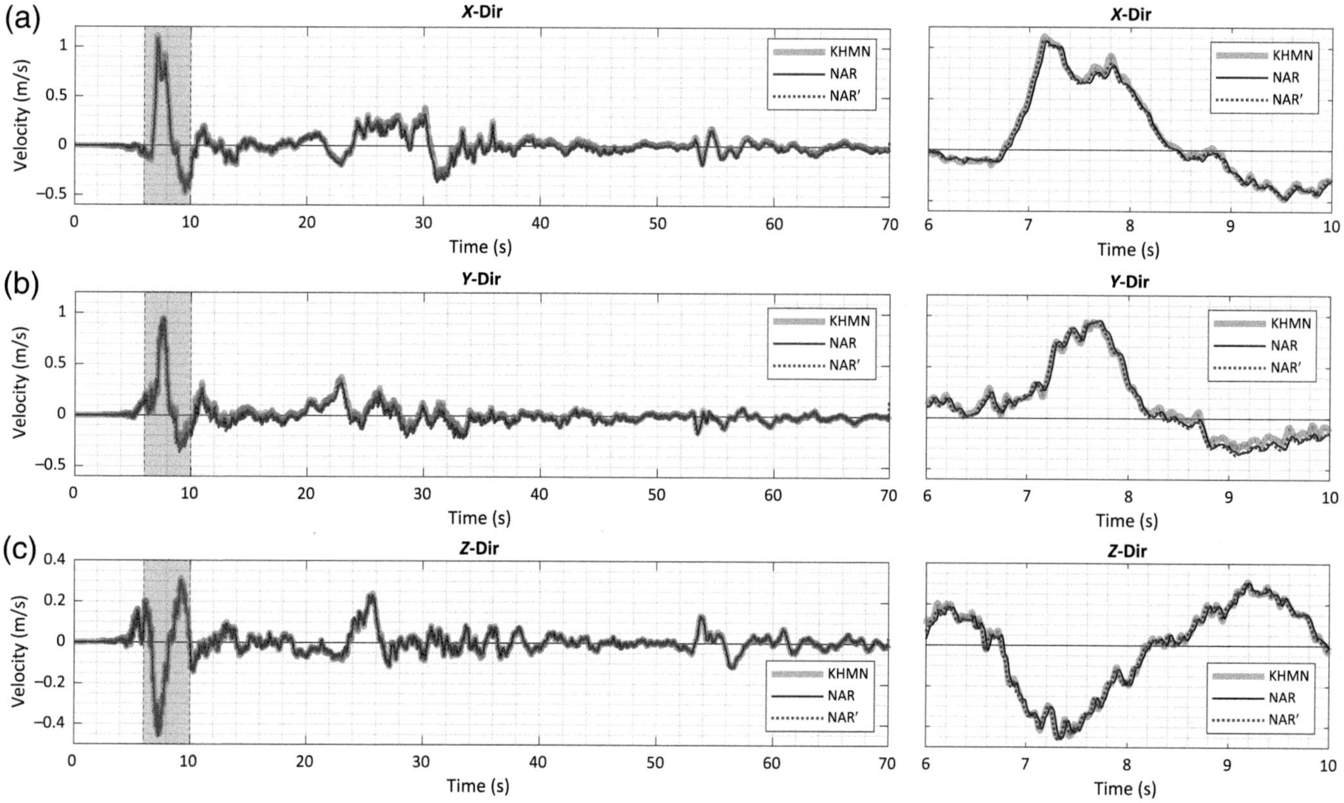

Figure 2. Velocity records of KHMN and NAR stations. Velocity records and window in which peak ground velocity (PGV) is found in KHMN and NAR stations, in the (a) *X*-Dir, (b) *Y*-Dir, and (c) vertical component. Both stations result in a similar velocity record, with a time delay between them. The color version of this figure is available only in the electronic edition.

in which Δu_i represents the difference in displacement between two grid points, and Δx_j is the distance between the points. To resolve all three rotational components uniquely, three distinct stations are required. In this case, only two strong ground motion stations (NAR and KHMN) were available. To obtain the full set of rotational components, it is assumed that a tertiary station, denoted as NAR′ and shown in Figure 1b, existed. Station NAR′ was positioned orthogonally to the vertical plane defined by KHMN and NAR and is located 30 m from KHMN, the same separation distance as between KHMN and NAR. It was further assumed that the spatial variability between KHMN and NAR was similar to that between KHMN and NAR′, and that all motion variations were governed solely by the separation distance between stations (Zerva and Zervas, 2002). Although near-fault rupture propagation physics and soil anisotropy could influence ground motions differently at the synthetic station, the analysis was deliberately limited to this assumption, based on array observations that exhibit no directionality bias (EPRI, 2007).

The following discussion focuses on the generation of the vertical ground-motion component for NAR′ because it was required to compute the missing rotational component. First, the signals of KHMN and NAR were compared in the frequency domain to evaluate differences in amplitude and phase. Figure 3a presents the amplitude comparison between both signals in the frequency domain, whereas Figure 3b shows the amplitude ratio of KHMN to NAR. Figure 3a,b also indicates the frequencies corresponding to the first, second, and third effective translational modes of the primary case study discussed later in this article. The amplitudes are nearly identical at low frequencies (0.01–3 Hz) but begin to diverge significantly at frequencies above 7 Hz. Previous researchers have found that at higher frequencies (> 8 Hz), the coherency between ground motions, even at closely spaced stations, is increasingly chaotic (Abrahamson *et al.*, 1991; Vernon *et al.*, 1991, 1998).

Although the frequency range of primary interest for the building case studies is 0.01–8 Hz, the signal analysis was extended to 20 Hz to capture higher frequency variations. After comparing the two signals, a piecewise linear model was fitted to represent the mean of the differences in amplitude and phase between them. For the amplitude difference, the model assumed no variation between 0.01 and 1.25 Hz, followed by an increase proportional to the frequency (see Fig. 3c). For the phase difference, a linear increase was observed up to 16 Hz, after which the difference remained constant (see Fig. 3d). Because a linear phase shift with frequency corresponds to a constant time shift, applying a constant time shift Δt to the time series results in a phase change given by $\Delta\phi(f) = -2\pi\Delta tf$. The slope of the fitted phase model from 0 to 16 Hz shown in Figure 3d is $0.0567\ \mathrm{rad}/\pi/\mathrm{Hz}$ ($0.0567\ \mathrm{rad}/\pi/\mathrm{Hz} = -2\pi\Delta tf$), resulting in a Δt of 0.028 s,

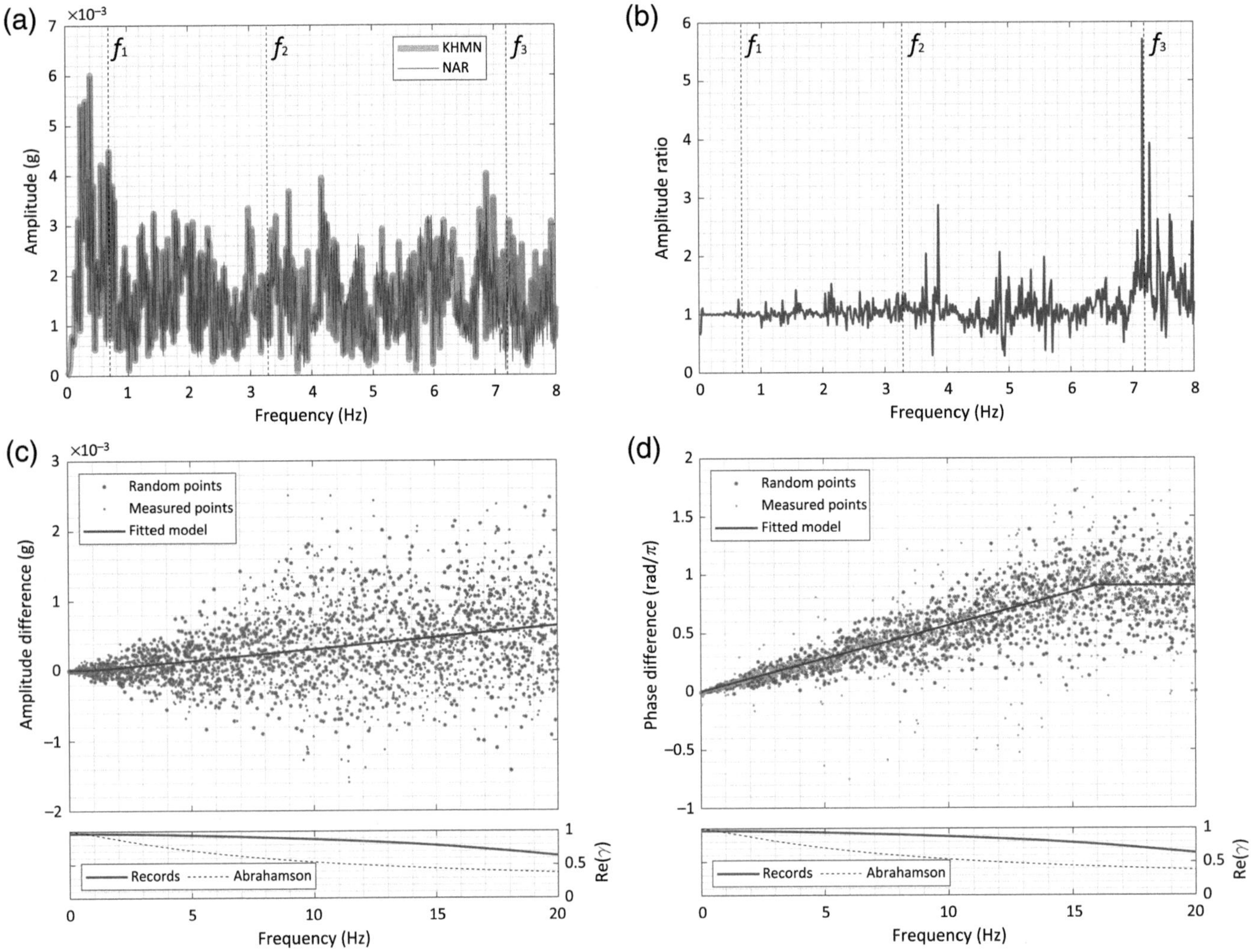

Figure 3. Vertical ground-motion comparison between KHMN and NAR. (a) Comparison of amplitudes of both signals in the frequency domain, (b) ratio of the amplitudes of KHMN to NAR for a frequency range of 0–8 Hz. The frequencies corresponding to the first, second, and third effective translational modes are indicated with vertical dashed lines. Based on the signal analysis, a model to estimate the variation in amplitude (c) and phase (d) as a function of frequency to randomly generate station NAR′ was created. The plane-wave coherency of both signals is shown in (c) and (d), as well as the soil coherency model for plane-wave coherency proposed by Abrahamson (EPRI, 2007). The color version of this figure is available only in the electronic edition.

which matches the time shift that maximizes the cross correlation between the two records.

The plane-wave coherency of the two signals (KHMN and NAR) using an 11-point Hamming window for the frequency smoothing is included in Figure 3c,d. The results indicate high coherence at frequencies up to 10 Hz. The NAR time series were shifted by 0.03 s before computing the plane-wave coherency; further discussion of this time shift is included subsequently. A 10 s time window capturing the strongest portion of the acceleration and velocity time series was used for the computation of the plane-wave coherency. The soil coherency model proposed by Abrahamson (EPRI, 2007) for vertical components is also plotted for reference. The same analysis was performed on the horizontal components, which also exhibited high coherence. Vertical and horizontal acceleration records from these two stations, separated 30 m, show higher coherency values than those computed using the empirical models proposed by Abrahamson (EPRI, 2007); the cause of the high coherency for these particular records remains unknown and warrants further evaluation.

Four frequency ranges were defined to determine the distribution of residuals from the fitted model: (0–2) Hz, [2–8) Hz, [8–14) Hz, and [14–20] Hz. The distribution of the residuals was found to be approximately normal for both amplitude and phase across these frequency ranges. The mean and standard deviation for each range were used to generate random realizations of the tertiary station based on one of the observed stations. To avoid abrupt discontinuities and bias in the third signal, a continuous model for the standard deviation, dependent on the frequency, was developed for the amplitude and phase residuals. The cumulative distribution functions for the residuals and the random realizations were then compared to verify that the selected distribution type and statistical parameters were adequate.

Once the fitted model and the distribution of the residuals for the amplitude and phase differences were established, random variations in amplitude and phase were introduced according to the defined models for the frequency range of interest (0.01–20 Hz). The random points for a single realization are shown in Figure 3c,d, together with the measured data points, demonstrating that the random points follow the same general pattern as the observations. In this case, a third station at the same distance from KHMN as NAR was generated under the assumption that the spatial variability between KHMN and NAR is like that between KHMN and NAR′. Accordingly, a frequency-domain perturbation was applied to KHMN so that the resulting NAR′ record reflected the modeled amplitude and phase difference distributions between KHMN and NAR that could not be physically modeled. In reality, the generation of the ground motion at NAR′ should also consider the differences in amplitude and phase between NAR and NAR′, as well as between NAR′ and KHMN. This could be achieved by incorporating both NAR and KHMN in the estimation of NAR′, and extrapolating the differences in amplitude and phase difference relationships from the 30 m separation to 42 m, which is the distance between NAR′ and NAR.

As shown in Figure 1a,b, the epicenter is located south-southwest of stations KHMN and NAR; thus, the waves arrived at KHMN before reaching NAR. This timing is also observed in the velocity time histories for both stations (Fig. 2), which display a clear lag between the two signals. Consequently, the waves would also reach NAR′ prior to NAR. A cross-correlation analysis of the KHMN and NAR acceleration time history signals was performed to determine the time shift t_s that maximizes the cross correlation, resulting in $t_s = 0.03$ s. This value of 0.03 s matches the estimated time shift that corresponds to the constant phase shift shown in Figure 3c, approximated as 0.028 s. This time perturbation of 0.03 s was applied to the third station NAR′ after converting to the time domain, as shown in Figure 2.

The models used to estimate the amplitude and phase differences are relatively simple and have inherent limitations. Other researchers have performed multiparameter analyses of the strong ground motion data from the M_w 7.8 Kahramanmaraş–Pazarcık earthquake (Tang *et al.*, 2024). The objective of this analysis is not to reproduce the exact differences observed between the KHMN and NAR signals, but rather to account for the spatial variability in estimating the tertiary station, which has the same spacing distance to KHMN as NAR. The principal limitation is that only a single event and set of recordings are available. The analysis assumed that all variations between motions depend solely on the separation distance between stations (Zerva and Zervas, 2002). However, the generation of ground motions at the third station, NAR′, should consider the differences in amplitude and phase between NAR′ and both existing stations, as well as their covariance. Furthermore, the interfrequency correlation was neglected. Although the generation of NAR′ introduces some uncertainty, the approach remains a practical way to investigate the influence of rotational ground motions on medium- and high-rise structures, given the scarcity of direct rotational measurements of strong ground motions in near-fault regions. To isolate the effect of rotational ground motions, independent of the assumptions used to create NAR′, a separate set of analyses was performed using only the measured rotational components from the observational stations.

With the known gradients, all three additional rotational components were obtained. The displacement time histories of these components are plotted in Figure A2. These three components, in addition to the horizontal translational motions, represent the input ground motions for performing the nonlinear structural analysis. Rotation about the X axis (pitch) was derived directly using the data from the observational stations, whereas the rotation about the Y axis (roll) was computed using data from KHMN and the synthetic station NAR′, using the stochastic process described previously. Because the objective of this article is to evaluate the effects of the rotational components of the ground motion on the response of a structure, a single realization of the stochastic process defined previously was used as an input for the 3D NRHA. However, to better understand the variability of the stochastic process, the rotational response spectra of one hundred realizations were analyzed.

The response spectra for elastic response and a viscous damping ratio $\xi = 5\%$ of the resulting ground-motion components are plotted in Figure 4. The spectra of the two horizontal translational components are presented in Figure 4a, obtained by rotating the components and enveloping the spectra into the RotD100 spectrum (Boore, 2010). The pseudo-acceleration and displacement spectra are shown in the upper and lower rows, respectively. The ratio of RotD100 to RotD50 is a way to define the level of directionality of the spectral response (Poulos *et al.*, 2022) and is used to illustrate the directionality of the records used in this study. The ratio $SA_{RotD100}/SA_{RotD50}$ has an upper limit of $\sqrt{2}$ and a lower limit of 1, the latter indicating low polarization. The ground motion has large directionality in the period range of 1.5 s < T < 8.0 s, in which the ratio of $SA_{RotD100}/SA_{RotD50}$ is larger than 1.35 throughout. At a period range of 2.8 s < T < 4.2 s the value of $SA_{RotD100}/SA_{RotD50}$ exceeds 1.39. As a comparison, the geometric mean of this ratio from a subset of the Next Generation Attenuation-West2 database ranged from 1.24 to 1.28 at 1.5 s < T < 8.0 s (Shahi and Baker, 2014). Thus, this indicates that the record has large directionality within those periods. The FP component dominates the response in the period range mentioned, characteristic of supershear ground motions (Rosakis *et al.*, 2025). The directionality of the ground motion is also large between 0.7 s < T < 1.0 s, but with the FN

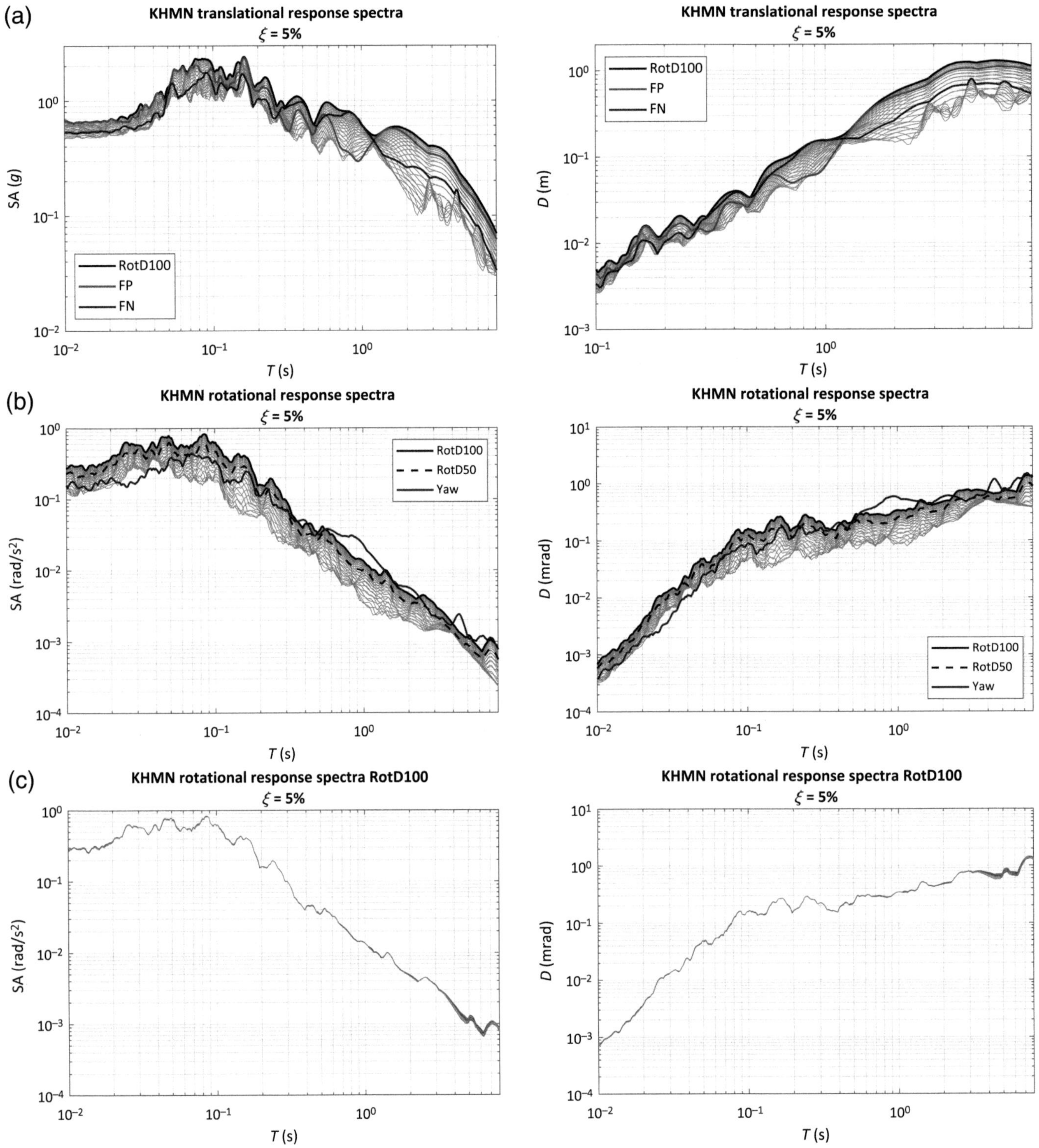

component dominating in this range. At long periods, the translational displacement spectra range from $D_{\mathrm{RotD100}} = 0.34$ m at $T = 6$ s to $D_{\mathrm{RotD100}} = 1.28$ m at $T = 5.6$ s. The response spectra for elastic response of the rotational components (Fig. 4b) show the spectra from the two orthogonal-component records combined into single records corresponding to a rotation angle and their corresponding envelope (RotD100) and median (RotD50) (Boore, 2010). The yaw (rotation about the vertical axis) is also included. The spectral acceleration

Figure 4. Response spectra for the elastic response of ground motions used in analyses. (a) The response spectra of the translational components of the ground motion: fault-parallel (FP), fault-normal (FN), combined orthogonal components corresponding to increments of rotation angle, and corresponding envelope (RotD100). (b) Response spectra of the rotational components of the ground motion: combined orthogonal components (pitch and roll) corresponding to increments of rotation angle and corresponding envelope (RotD100) and median (RotD50), and yaw (rotation about the vertical axis). (c) RotD100 response spectra of the pitch and roll components corresponding to 100 random samples of NAR′. The color version of this figure is available only in the electronic edition.

values at short periods of $T = 0.2$ s are 0.16 rad/s^2 for the RotD100 of the out-of-plane rotational components and 0.11 rad/s^2 for the yaw component; the acceleration values decrease exponentially at $T > 0.1$ s. Regarding the displacements at $T = 1.0$ s, the values range from $D_{\mathrm{RotD0}} =$ 0.09 mrad to $D_{\mathrm{RotD100}} = 0.34$ mrad, with the yaw rotation resulting in 0.57 mrad. For longer periods ($T > 8$ s), the RotD100 spectral out-of-plane and in-plane rotation is > 1.4 mrad.

To evaluate the variability of the stochastic process used to generate the records from the synthetic station NAR′, 100 realizations were done to obtain 100 different NAR′ vertical records and evaluate the variability in the response spectra. Figure 4c shows the RotD100 for each of the rotational components resulting from the 100 realizations. The overall variability in the spectral demands is limited, with the largest deviations occurring at very short periods (0.01–0.02 s) and at longer periods ($T > 3.0$ s).

The peak ground rotational acceleration values are 0.233 rad/s^2 and 0.117 rad/s^2 for the pitch and roll components, respectively (Fig. 1b), and 0.140 rad/s^2 for the yaw component, that is, the rotation about the vertical axis. The corresponding peak ground rotational velocities of the pitch, roll, and yaw components are 2.98×10^{-03}, 1.34×10^{-03}, and 2.85×10^{-03} rad/s, respectively.

CASE STUDIES

The primary case presented in this article is a medium-rise, 14-story RC building with an overall height of 51.6 m. The first story is 4.8 m high, and each of the remaining thirteen stories is 3.6 m high. The LFRS consists of a pair of U-shaped walls coupled by diagonally reinforced coupling beams. The gravity system comprises flat slabs and vertical rectangular columns, which do not contribute significantly to the building's lateral stiffness. The initial design was performed using a linear model with effective stiffness modifiers, and seismic demands were estimated through modal response spectrum analysis. The spectral parameters were $\mathrm{Sa}(T = 0.2\ \mathrm{s}, \xi = 5\%) = 0.99g$ and $\mathrm{Sa}(T = 1\ \mathrm{s}, \xi = 5\%) = 0.60g$. For reference, the RotD100 (Boore, 2010) for station KHMN (Fig. 4a) has seismic parameters $\mathrm{Sa}(T = 0.2\ \mathrm{s}, \xi = 5\%) = 1.41g$ and $\mathrm{Sa}(T = 1\ \mathrm{s}, \xi = 5\%) = 0.62g$. The design considerations are representative of typical Turkish RC building stock and follow the provisions of the American Society of Civil Engineers (ASCE 7-16, ASCE 2017) and the American Concrete Institute (ACI 318-19, ACI 2019) code requirements.

One of the main concerns in structural behavior is torsional irregularity in a building. To evaluate its effects, several cases of the same building with different eccentricities were analyzed. Case 1 is the building with eccentricity in both directions, case 2 has an eccentricity in the Y direction, case 3 has an eccentricity in the X direction, and case 4 has no eccentricity between the center of mass and the center of rigidity. The eccentricities were introduced by changing the mass distribution on the plane but keeping the same total mass for all cases. The plan view and geometry of the four cases are shown in Figure A3.

A nonlinear model of each case was created in the open-source nonlinear analysis program OpenSees (McKenna, 2011). All models included nonlinear material and were run with geometric nonlinearity (i.e., $P - \Delta$ effects). The U-shaped walls and coupling beams were modeled using the Beam-Truss Model (BTM) (Lu and Panagiotou, 2016; Lu *et al.*, 2016; Álvarez *et al.*, 2019, 2020; Mavros *et al.*, 2022, 2023). The BTM is a widely validated methodology that naturally captures the shear-flexure interaction in concrete elements and does not have the kinematic constraint of plane sections remaining plane. The gravity columns were modeled using elastic beam-column elements with effective stiffness properties. The slabs were modeled using a linear stringer-panel model (Godínez and Restrepo, 2023). After applying the gravity loads, the fundamental period of the nonlinear models was 0.91, 0.89, 0.89, and 0.82 s for cases 1–4, respectively. These values are consistent with the estimated period range of 0.5–1.5 s reported for most buildings that collapsed during the Kahramanmaraş–Pazarcık earthquake (Ozturk *et al.*, 2023). A detailed description of the nonlinear models is included in the Nonlinear building analysis section.

To highlight the importance of considering rotational motion regardless of structural characteristics, an additional design and analysis of a high-rise building was performed, hereafter referred to as case high-rise (HR). Case HR is a 36-story building with 3 basements, 8 podiums, and 25 tower levels, with all floors exhibiting eccentricity between the center of mass and rigidity. The building height is 116.4 m, of which 9.6 m are below the ground surface. The LFRS consists of two RC U-shaped walls coupled with diagonally reinforced coupling beams throughout the entire height of the building. Additional rectangular RC structural walls are incorporated in the basement and podium levels to control the torsional response. The gravity system consists of square RC columns and posttensioned flat slabs. After applying the gravity loads, the fundamental period was found to be 3.44 s.

All case studies were assumed to be located at station KHMN (see Fig. 1b). Each nonlinear model was subjected to two analyses: one using only horizontal input ground motions, and another incorporating the two horizontal and the three rotational ground-motion components (pitch, roll, and yaw). The ground-motion components were assigned as an imposed motion to a master node at the base, to which all nodes at the base were constrained by the use of rigid elements. Thus, there is a rigid body component of the deformation of the building during the analyses (see Fig. 5). The effect of the soil–foundation–structure interaction was out of the scope of this current study. The building was assumed to have a stiff mat foundation and be on-site class C per ASCE 7-16.

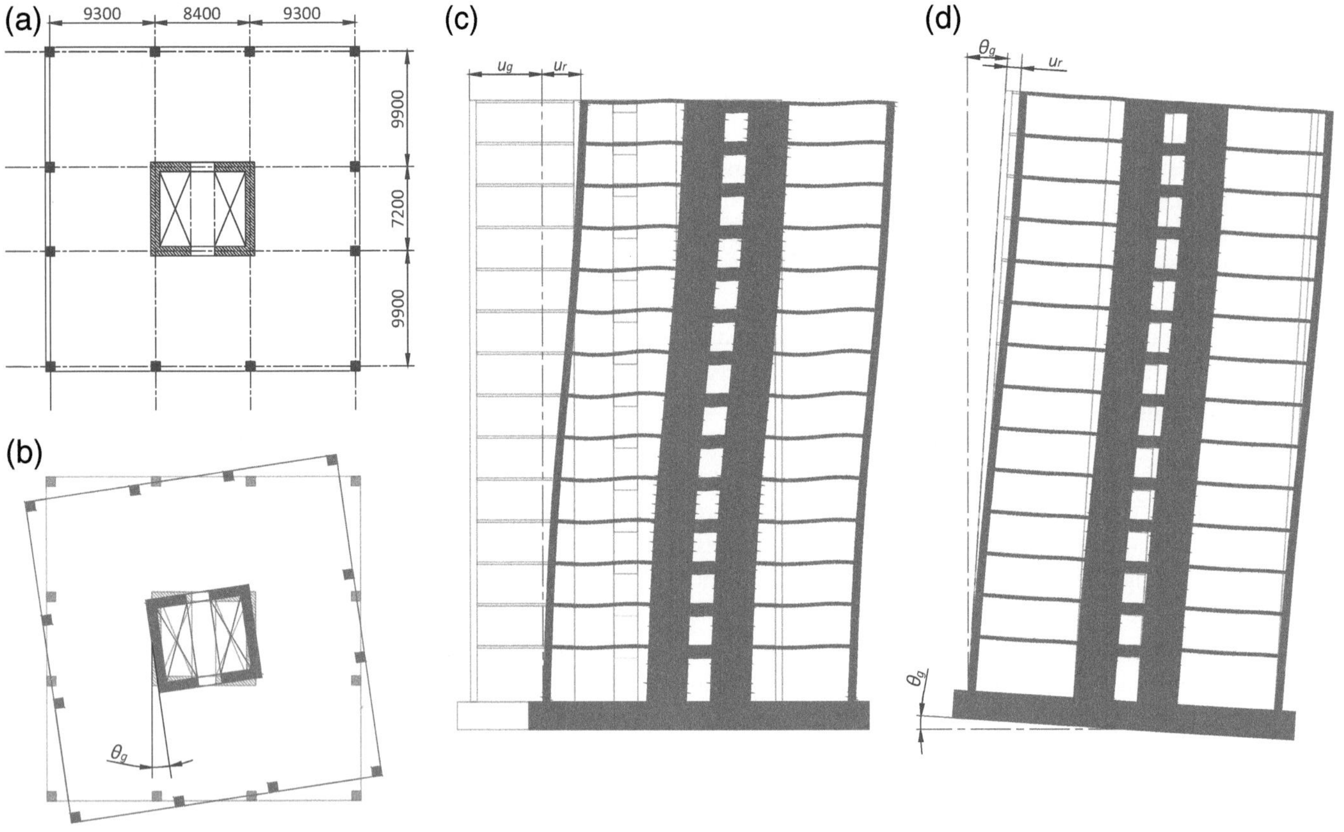

Figure 5. Building model kinematics when subjected to ground motions. (a) Plan view of case study without any eccentricities, building deformation when subjected to a (b) yaw rotation, (c) horizontal motion, and (d) pitch or roll rotation.

NONLINEAR RESPONSE HISTORY ANALYSES RESULTS

To study the difference between horizontal ground motion input and horizontal plus pitch, roll, and yaw input on the structural response, the shear force at the core wall and the displacement demands of the structure were examined. The shear force of the two flanges—oriented in the X direction (X-Dir)—and the web—oriented in the Y direction (Y-Dir)—of each U-shaped wall was computed separately. The maximum force out of the four flanges and the maximum force out of the two webs at each story are plotted. The shear forces are normalized by the in-plane shear capacity based on the equation from ACI 318 (ACI, 2019) using expected material properties for the concrete (f'_{ce}) and for the steel (f_{ye}); no reduction factors are included in the capacity. The interstory drifts and displacements are adjusted for the rigid body component of the deformation of the structure due to the imposed ground motion.

The comparison of the responses from the NRHA, including only the horizontal ground motions (HOR) and the analysis including the horizontal and the pitch, roll, and yaw ground motions (HOR + ROT), is shown in Figure 6. Including the ground-motion rotational components results in a change of the maximum shear force at the core: 5.3% increase in the X-Dir and a 1.2% reduction in the Y-Dir (Fig. 6c). The shear force increases at upper stories as well, with a maximum increment of 7.1% in the X-Dir. The maximum interstory drift (Fig. 6d) increases by 7.8% in the X-Dir and by 0.6% in the Y-Dir. The roof displacement increases by 3.4% in the X-Dir and by 0.6% in the Y-Dir (Fig. 6e). The rotational components have a larger effect on the upper stories regarding the interstory drift as shown in Figure 6d; at the upper stories, the interstory drift increases 10.2%. The maximum vertical tensile strains at the core are plotted in (Fig. 6b); the color map scale ranges from 0 to the yield strain of the reinforcing steel (0.0024). The peak vertical tensile strain measured at the centerline of the core is reduced by 6.8% when including the rotational components of the ground motion; however, the region in which the strain exceeds the yield strain extends when including the rotational components of the ground motion.

The deformed configuration of the core wall at different time steps of the nonlinear response history analyses is shown in Figure 7. The deformations are scaled by the same factor of 30 for visualization purposes and consider the absolute displacements of the analyses. Figure 7a shows the undeformed configuration of the core wall and the deformed configuration at four timesteps: t_1 and t_2 are early stages of the analyses at which the differences between the analyses are already significant, and t_3 and t_4 are the timesteps at which the maximum

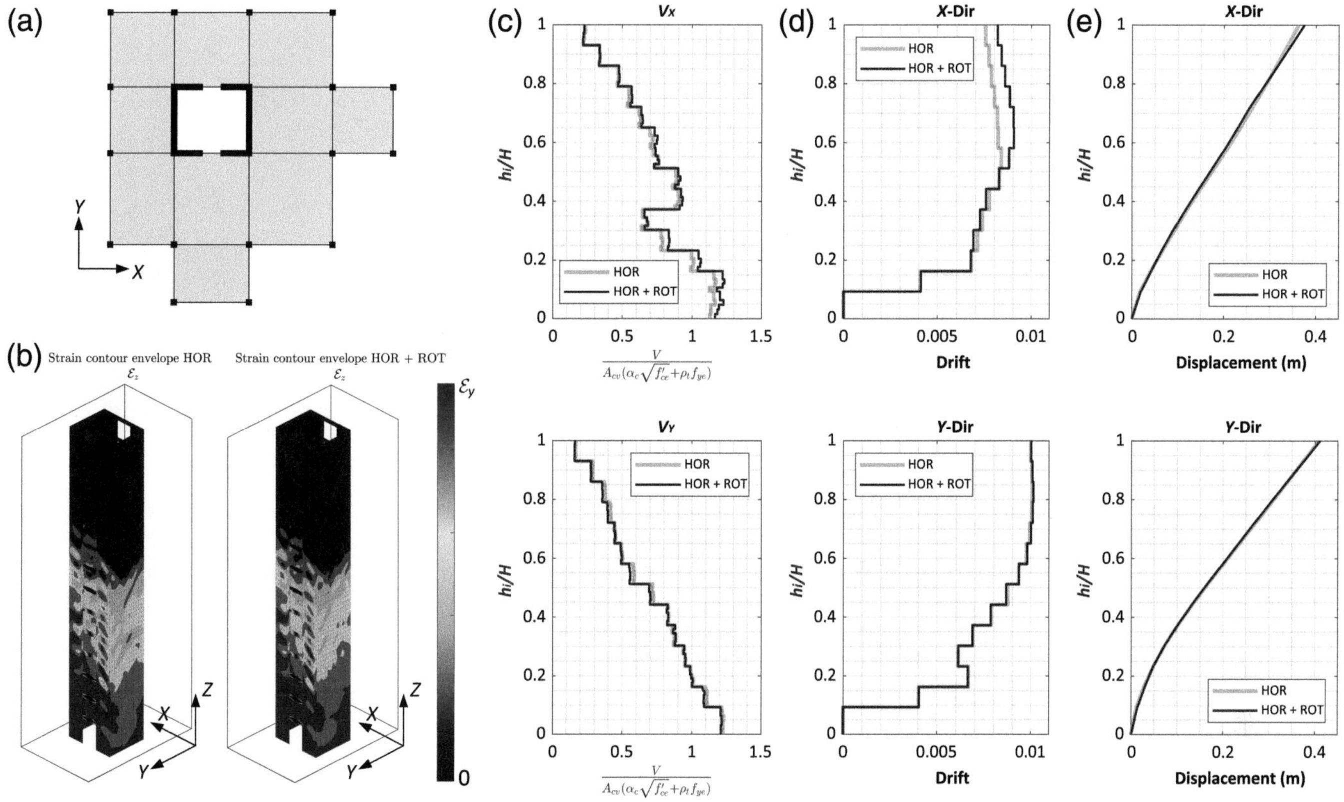

Figure 6. Response of the case 1 nonlinear model. The responses shown are for the nonlinear model with only horizontal ground motions (HOR) and with horizontal plus the three rotational components of the ground motion (HOR + ROT), in the X-Dir and Y-Dir. (a) Plan view of case 1, (b) maximum vertical tensile strains at core wall, (c) envelope of shear forces at the core wall normalized by the wall's shear capacity (units of f'_{ce} in MPa), (d) envelope of interstory drift, and (e) envelope of lateral displacement of the structure in meters. The color version of this figure is available only in the electronic edition.

roof displacements in the X-Dir and Y-Dir occur in the HOR analysis, respectively. The deformed configuration of the structure at the end of the analyses is presented in Figure 7b, the undeformed configuration is also included for reference. The effect of the rigid body rotation of the structure is the main cause of such a large visual difference. The differences between the analyses after correcting for the rigid body rotation were already established. A residual displacement is observed, which is more noticeable in the analysis that considers the rotational components. The roof displacement time history normalized by the building height (roof drift) is plotted in Figure 7c; the four steps included in Figure 7a are highlighted. The roof drift plotted in Figure 7c is after correcting for the rigid body components of the deformation of the building due to the imposed ground motion.

An additional set of analyses using only the pitch and the yaw components was performed. These two rotational components are obtained through the measured data from KHMN and NAR directly, without the tertiary station NAR′. The results for case 1 of the medium-rise 14-story building are described in this paragraph. When including the rotational components, the peak interstory drift increases by 4.0% and 3.3% in the X-Dir and Y-Dir, respectively. However, at upper stories, the interstory drift increases by up to 7.8%. The peak shear stress increases by 3.3% and 2.4% in the X-Dir and Y-Dir, respectively. Finally, the peak roof displacement increases by 3.5% and 3.0% in the X-Dir and Y-Dir, respectively. These results highlight that, regardless of the tertiary station, there is an effect of the ground-motion rotational components. Furthermore, the results indicate that the pitch component has more influence on the response of the case studies presented compared to the yaw component. Analyses using only the pitch component were performed, and the results by less than 1% compared to when both the pitch and the yaw components were included.

As described in the previous section, a high-rise building (case HR) was also analyzed. The comparison of the response for case HR is shown in Figure 8. Including the ground-motion rotational components in the analysis results in minimal differences of the shear stresses at the core (Fig. 8b); the maximum shear stress is reduced by 1.0% in the X-Dir, and increases by 1.8% in the Y-Dir. The maximum shear stress increase at upper stories is 5.5% in the X-Dir and 11.3% in the Y-Dir. The largest difference is in the displacement demands. The maximum interstory drift is 13.3% larger in the X-Dir, and the peak roof displacement increases by 12.8%. In the Y-Dir, the maximum interstory drift increases by 2.8%, and the roof displacement reduces by 0.2%. The vertical tensile strains at the

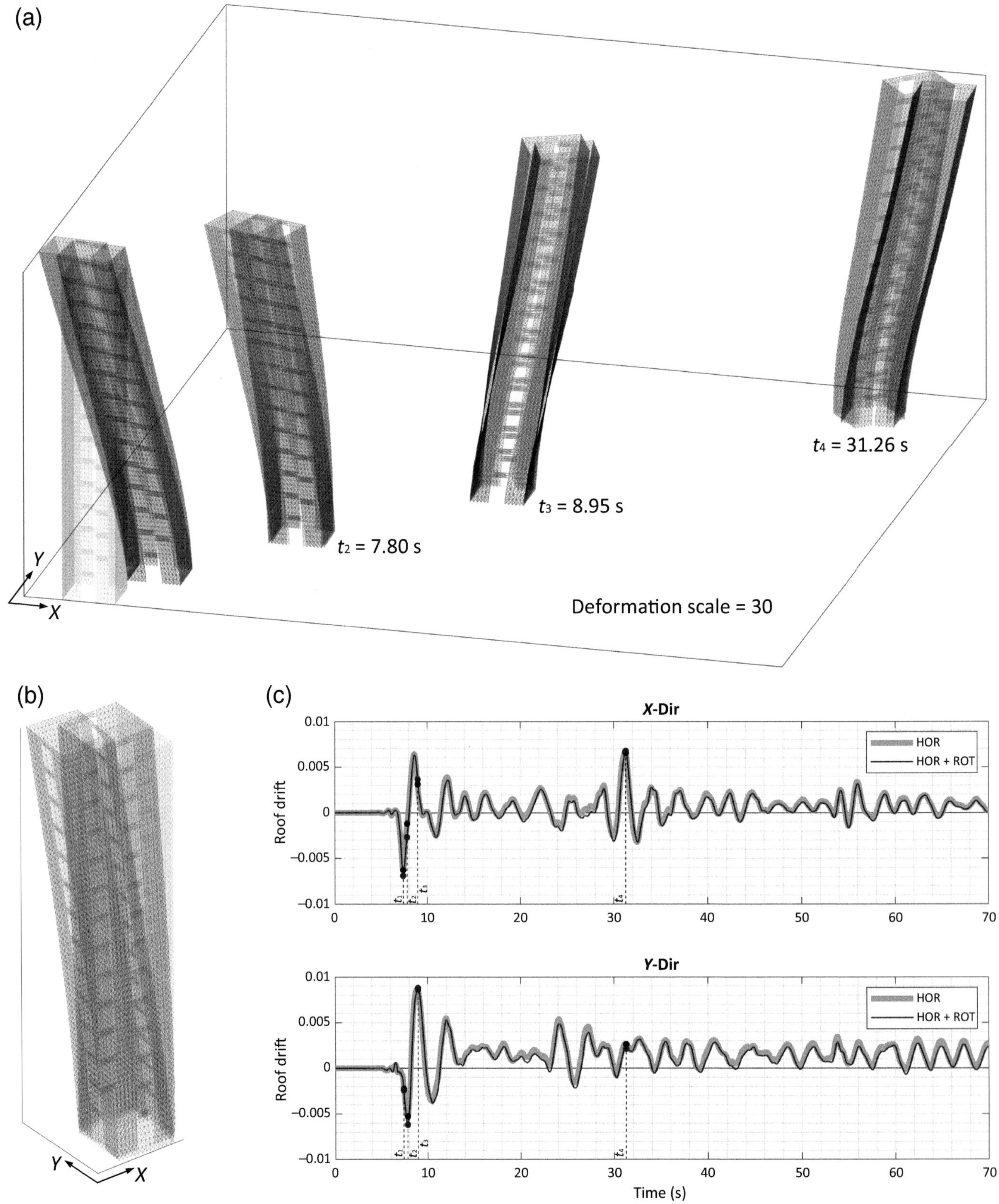

Figure 7. Deflected shape comparison. The displacement response of the nonlinear models with the horizontal ground motions as input (HOR) in black and with the horizontal and rotational ground motions as input (HOR + ROT) in blue. (a) The deflected shape considering the absolute displacement at the nodes of the nonlinear models at different timesteps of the analysis (scale factor of 30), timestep t_3 is when the maximum relative roof displacement in the X-Dir occurs, timestep t_4 is when the maximum relative roof displacement in the Y-Dir occurs. (b) Deflected shape at the end of the analysis (scale factor of 30). (c) Relative roof displacement time history normalized by the building height in the X-Dir and Y-Dir. The color version of this figure is available only in the electronic edition.

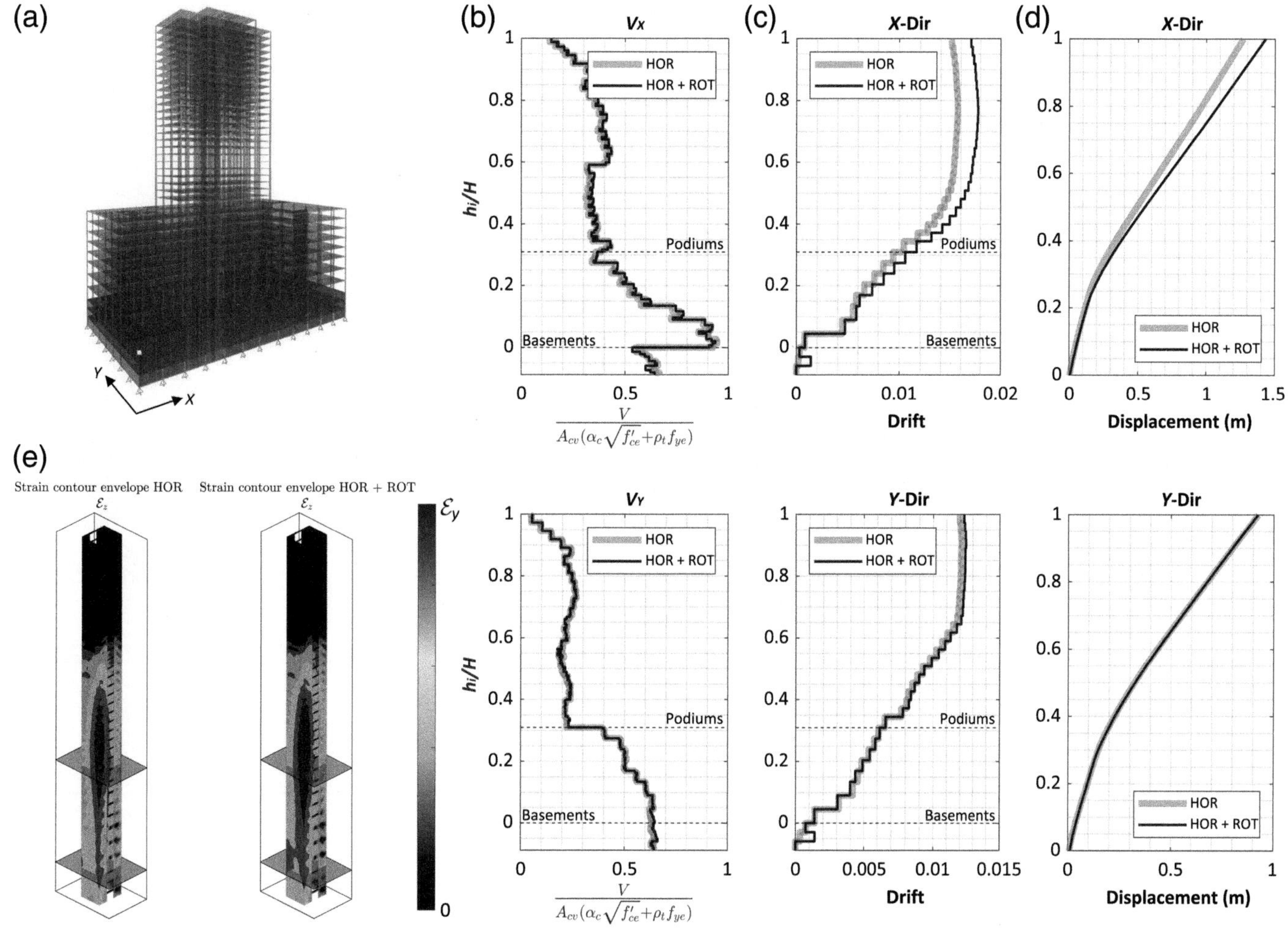

Figure 8. Response of a high-rise building nonlinear model. The responses shown are for the nonlinear model with only horizontal ground motions (HOR) and with horizontal plus the three rotational components of the ground motion (HOR + ROT), in the X and Y directions. (a) 3D view of the building, (b) envelope of shear forces at the core wall normalized by the wall's shear capacity (units of f'_{ce} in MPa), (c) envelope of interstory drift, (d) envelope of lateral displacement in meters, and (e) maximum vertical tensile strains at the core wall. The height at which there is a discontinuity in the lateral stiffness is marked in (b), (c), and (e). These levels are at the top of the basements and at the top of the podiums. The color version of this figure is available only in the electronic edition.

centerline of the core are presented in Figure 8e; the maximum value of the scale is the yield strain of the reinforcing steel ($\mathcal{E}_y$). The region where the reinforcing steel yields increases considerably when including the ground-motion rotational components, particularly above the podiums. This suggests that the effect of the rotation has a greater influence on the higher modes, which also explains the larger increase in shear forces at upper stories.

The building slabs are subjected to rotation demands at the slab-wall interface consistent with deformation compatibility of the structure's lateral drifts. An increase in the drifts increases the rotations. The slabs must be properly detailed to meet the rotation demands and the in-plane stresses due to the inertial loads and transfer these forces to the LFRS; failure to do so can lead to catastrophic collapse of buildings (Canterbury Earthquakes Royal Commission, 2012). The deformed configuration considering the absolute displacements of the core wall of case HR is shown in Figure 9a; the deformations are scaled by a factor of 20 for visualization purposes. Timestep t_1 is when the maximum relative roof displacement occurs in the X-Dir, and t_2 is when the maximum roof displacement occurs in the Y-Dir. Timestep t_3 shows a large variation in the deformed shape of both analyses, represented visually in Figure 9a and relatively in Figure 9c. The deformed configurations at the end of both analyses are shown in Figure 9b. A residual displacement is observed in the HOR + ROT analysis that is not observed in the analysis with only translational input ground motions. When comparing the roof drift time history, the residual roof drift in the X-Dir is 0.12% in the HOR + ROT analysis, whereas in the HOR analysis the value is 0.01%. The differences between both analyses are more noticeable than in the case shown in Figure 7, even considering that a smaller-scale factor is being used. Although the medium-rise building had residual displacements (see Fig. 7c), this

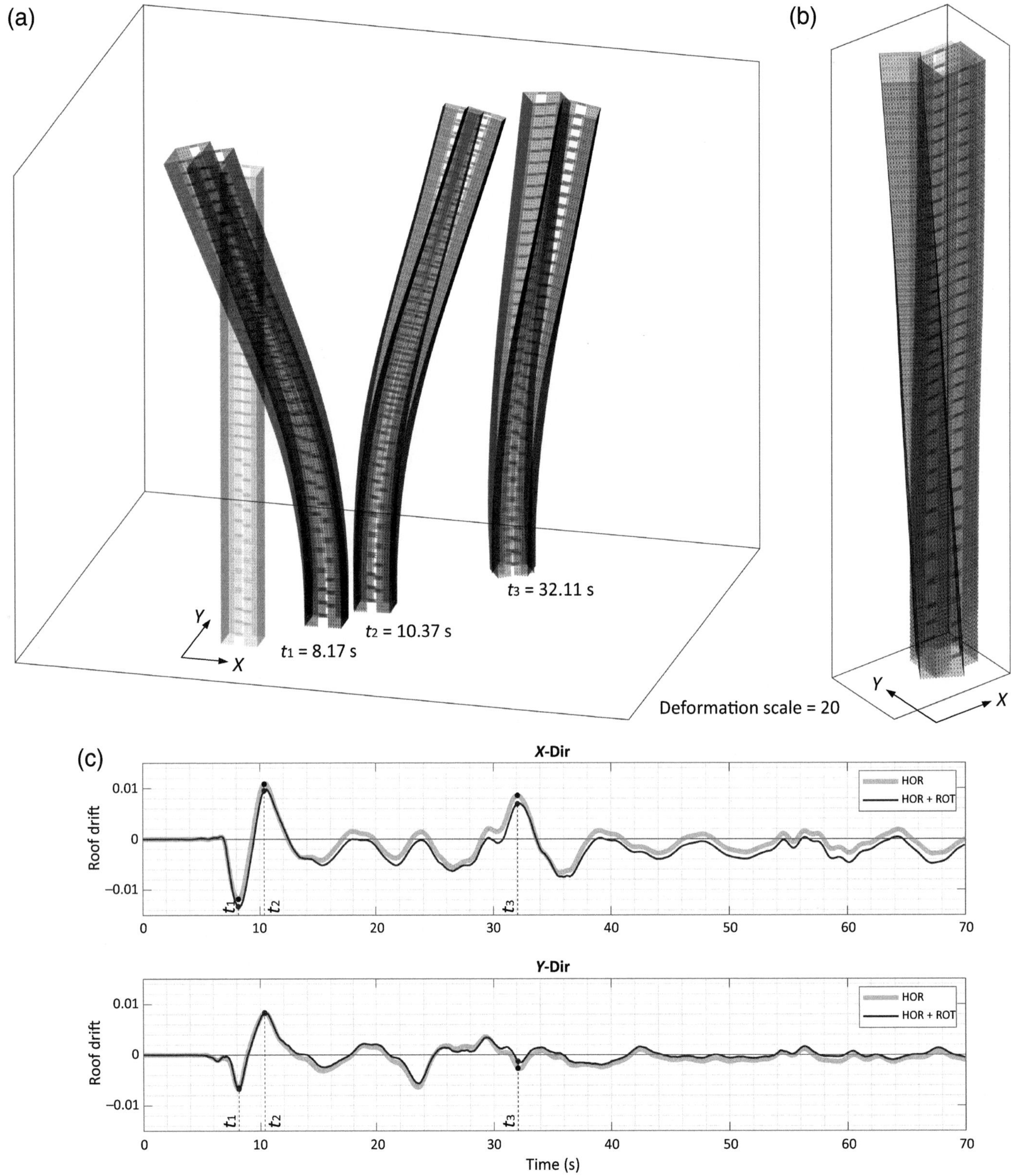

Figure 9. Deflected shape comparison of a high-rise building. The displacement response of the nonlinear model of a high-rise building with the horizontal ground motions as input (HOR) in black and with the horizontal and rotational ground motions as input (HOR + ROT) in blue. (a) The deflected shape considering the absolute displacement at the nodes of the nonlinear models at different timesteps of the analysis (scale factor of 20), timestep t_1 is when the maximum relative roof displacement occurs in the *X*-Dir, t_2 is when the maximum relative roof displacement in the *Y*-Dir occurs, and at t_3 there is a large variation in the deformed shape of both analyses. (b) Deflected shape at the end of the analysis (scale factor of 20). (c) Roof drift time history considering the relative displacements and adjusting for the rigid body rotation of the building. The color version of this figure is available only in the electronic edition.

TABLE 2
Changes in the Peak Responses of the Structure When Including Rotational Ground Motions

Case Study	Drift		Displacement		Shear	
	X-Dir	Y-Dir	X-Dir	Y-Dir	X-Dir	Y-Dir
Case 1	7.9%	0.6%	3.4%	0.6%	5.3%	−1.3%
Case 2	10.2%	−2.0%	5.2%	−1.0%	5.3%	1.6%
Case 3	3.0%	−1.3%	1.0%	−1.0%	5.0%	5.3%
Case 4	3.3%	−2.4%	2.5%	−3.5%	4.4%	−0.8%
Case HR	13.3%	2.8%	12.8%	−0.2%	−1.0%	1.8%

Case HR, additional design and analysis of a high-rise building; Dir, direction.

occurred for both analyses (HOR and HOR + ROT), suggesting that the rotational component was not relevant to the residual displacements of that case study. The explicit consideration of the rotations at the ground and consequent rigid body rotation of the building will increase the $P-\Delta$ effects in the structure, which will have a larger impact on taller structures because the total lateral displacement due to the rigid body rotation increases with the height.

The changes in the peak responses of the structure for all case studies are summarized in Table 2. The peak responses from all cases are presented in Tables A1 and A2. For cases 1–4, the trend is similar. Even the response of a structure without eccentricities (case 4) is affected when considering the ground-motion rotational components in the analysis; in the X-Dir, the maximum interstory drift increases 3.3% and the maximum shear stress increases 4.4%. For this same case, the shear stress increases by as much as 7.2% and 8.8% in the X-Dir and Y-Dir, respectively, at upper stories. The maximum shear stress with the largest increment is case 3 (eccentricity in the X-Dir), with an increase of 5.0% and 5.3% in the X-Dir and Y-Dir, respectively. The case with the largest increment in the interstory drift is case 2 (eccentricity in the Y-Dir), with an increase of 10.2% in the maximum interstory drift in the X-Dir.

DISCUSSION

Two independent seismic stations located 30 m and less than 1 km from the fault were used to estimate ground-motion rotational components and evaluate the effect that these components have on the nonlinear response of structures. To estimate the full set of rotational components, three distinct stations are required. To create the third station, a stochastic frequency-domain procedure that introduces amplitude and phase variability consistent with array observations was used. The main assumption in creating the third station was that variations between motions are dependent only on the separation distance between stations. The effect of the variability in the stochastic process used in creating the third station was studied by performing spectral analyses using the resulting records of rotational accelerations from 100 realizations of the stochastic process. The main observation was that there is no significant variability in the overall elastic spectral demands, and thus a lack of sensitivity to the third station. The observed lack of sensitivity justifies the use of a relatively simple stochastic process. To study the effect of rotational motions on a structure, the full set of rotational components and translational components was applied to a 3D nonlinear model. This is the first time that near-fault rotational ground-motion records are estimated from a strong earthquake and used as an input in a nonlinear analysis of 3D buildings. Because of the computational resources required to run the nonlinear analyses, the resulting rotational components from a single realization of the stochastic process were considered. A set of medium-rise RC buildings and a high-rise RC building were analyzed. The input ground motions were applied as a displacement boundary condition at the base of the structure; thus, when the pitch, roll, and yaw components were applied, the structure explicitly tilted, increasing the second-order effects. The results obtained in this study indicate that the rotational components of the ground motion have a non-negligible effect on the response of structures. When including the three rotational components, the medium-rise building displacement demands increase by up to 10.2%, whereas the high-rise building's interstory drifts increase by as much as 13.3%. The drift and displacement demands reported are relative to the ground displacement, that is, after adjusting for the rigid body rotation of the structure. The maximum shear demands in the medium-rise buildings increase by 5.3% in the case with the largest difference. For the high-rise building, the maximum shear demands reduce by 0.2% in the X-Dir and increase by 1.8% in the Y-Dir. For these specific records and case studies, the yaw component had a negligible effect on the structural response compared to the pitch and roll components. The increase in the drifts and consequent increase in the rotation demands at the slab-wall interface due to deformation compatibility would result in slab yielding. The underestimation of the shear demands in an RC wall at the design stage increases the probability of brittle failures. The inclusion of ground-motion rotational components resulted in larger vertical strains.

The M_w 7.8 Kahramanmaraş–Pazarcık earthquake resulted in significant structural damage. A common conclusion from field investigations after the earthquake is that the structures were not capable of accommodating the large imposed displacements. Displacements are the cause of damage in structural and nonstructural components. The current structural design practice and code philosophy is to design elements based on estimated forces and to limit deformations. Displacement-based design procedures have been established (Moehle, 1992; Priestley and Kowalsky, 2000; Priestley *et al.*, 2007) but are not widely implemented. Another common conclusion from the Kahramanmaraş–Pazarcık earthquake is that it exceeded the code-prescribed values. Analysis procedures used in design are also based on simplifications. This study demonstrates that an analysis of a building using the current state-of-the-art practice in performance-based seismic design may underestimate the displacement and force demands on a structure if the input is incomplete. The structural responses that increase when including the rotational components are related to the hypotheses of the structural failure of buildings in Türkiye: insufficient development length at the beam-column joints, bond-slip failure at the foundation, limited shear reinforcement in the walls, and out-of-plane bending failure of structural walls (Mertol *et al.*, 2023; Ozturk *et al.*, 2023; Wang *et al.*, 2023; Vuran *et al.*, 2025).

CONCLUSION

Two principal conclusions result from this study: (1) the need to gather more data to further investigate the effect of ground-motion rotational components on structural performance, and (2) that this effect is not negligible. Although the dataset is limited to a single near-fault rotational record, this study is the first of its kind and is intended to stimulate greater interest in investigating rotational ground-motion effects. Eurocode 8 part 6: Towers, masts, and chimneys, specifies that the pitch and roll components of the ground motion should be taken into account for the design of tall structures in regions of high seismicity. This study shows that not only tall structures are sensitive to rotational motion input. A dense array of stations and equipment to measure rotational components is needed to obtain more data, particularly in the near field of active faults, and use that data to further investigate the effect that these components have on the behavior of structures. Although the occurrence of a large earthquake at a given fault may not occur within this generation's lifespan, it is still important to invest in this data acquisition. An alternative would be to deploy equipment near a fault after the occurrence of a large earthquake and gather data from the aftershocks. With further data and research, the effect of rotational ground motions should be implemented on design codes and performance-based seismic design guidelines.

In addition to the limitations posed by introducing a tertiary station to construct the ground-motion records needed for computing rotational components, our conclusions are based on data from a single event. A more comprehensive analysis of the effect of rotational ground motion on near-fault structures during large events requires additional datasets with sufficient resolution. One potential approach to expand the currently sparse dataset is through combining high-resolution velocity structures obtained from dense array measurements with physics-based modeling, which can incorporate realistic physical processes to generate ground motions consistent with updated empirical models. Although progress has been made in this area (McCallen *et al.*, 2021), the significant computational demands and the lack of accuracy of the 3D velocity structure limit the inclusion of high-resolution physics that influence near-fault response. Furthermore, this study focused on the structural responses of two archetypal building designs; future efforts will investigate additional design archetypes to provide a broader perspective on the impact of rotational ground motion and to inform design considerations. Finally, future work is required to incorporate soil–structure interaction in the nonlinear response history analysis.

DATA AND RESOURCES

The mapped surface rupture data are from doi: 10.5066/P985I7U2 (Reitman *et al.*, 2023). All the ground-motion records used in this study are obtained from the Disaster and Emergency Management Authority (AFAD) and Kandilli Observatory and Earthquake Research Institute (KEORI; AFAD, 1973; Kandilli Observatory and Earthquake Research Institute Boğaziçi University, 1971). Figure 1 was produced using QGIS (quantum geographic information system) based on map data from Natural Earth. The nonlinear models used to obtain the results discussed in this article are available to download in the following repository (https://github.com/SGodinez92/RotationalGM, last accessed December 2025).

DECLARATION OF COMPETING INTERESTS

The authors acknowledge that there are no conflicts of interest recorded.

ACKNOWLEDGMENTS

The authors thank Associate Editor Ivan G. Wong, the Editor-in-Chief P. Martin-Mai, Norman Abrahamson, and an anonymous reviewer for their invaluable feedback that improved this article. The ground-motion data used in this study can be obtained from the Turkish Disaster and Emergency Management Authority (AFAD). The authors would like to thank the Turkish AFAD for setting up dense near-fault observatories, and for immediately publishing a huge number of openly accessible accelerometers during these trying times for Türkiye. A. J. R. acknowledges support by the Caltech/Mechanical and Civil Engineering (MCE) Big Ideas Fund (BIF), as well as the Caltech Terrestrial Hazard Observation and Reporting Center (THOR). A. J. R. would also like to acknowledge the support of the National Science Foundation (NSF) (Grant EAR-2045285).

REFERENCES

Abdelmeguid, M., C. Zhao, E. Yalcinkaya, G. Gazetas, A. Elbanna, and A. Rosakis (2023). Dynamics of episodic supershear in the 2023 M7.8 Kahramanmaraş/Pazarcik earthquake, revealed by near-field records and computational modeling, *Commun. Earth Environ.* **4,** 456.

Abrahamson, N., J. Schneider, and J. Stepp (1991). Empirical spatial coherency functions for application to soil-structure interaction analyses, *Earthq. Spectra* **7,** no. 1, 1–27.

ACI (2019). *Building Code Requirements for Structural Concrete (ACI 318-19) and Commentary (ACI 318R-19),* American Concrete Institute, Michigan.

Aki, K., and P. G. Richards (2002). *Quantitative Seismology,* University Science Books.

Álvarez, R., J. I. Restrepo, M. Panagiotou, and S. E. Godínez (2020). Analysis of reinforced concrete coupled structural walls via the beam-truss model, *Eng. Struct.* **220,** 111005.

Álvarez, R., J. I. Restrepo, M. Panagiotou, and A. R. Santhakumar (2019). Nonlinear cyclic truss model for analysis of reinforced concrete coupled structural walls, *Bull. Earthq. Eng.* **17,** no. 12, 6419–6436.

ASCE (2017). *Minimum Design Loads and Associated Criteria for Buildings and Other Structures,* American Society of Civil Engineers, Reston, Virginia.

Awad, A. M., and J. L. Humar (1984). Dynamic response of buildings to ground rotational motion, *Can. J. Civ. Eng.* **11,** 48–56.

Barbot, S., H. Luo, T. Wang, Y. Hamiel, O. Piatibratova, M. T. Javed, C. Braitenberg, and G. Gurbuz (2023). Slip distribution of the February 6, 2023 M_w 7.8 and M_w 7.6, Kahramanmaraş, Turkey earthquake sequence in the East Anatolian fault zone, *Seismica* **2,** no. 3, doi: 10.26443/seismica.v2i3.502.

Bhat, H. S., M. Olives, R. Dmowska, and J. R. Rice (2007). Role of fault branches in earthquake rupture dynamics, *J. Geophys. Res.: Solid Earth* **112,** no. 11, doi: 10.1029/2007JB005027.

Biegel, R. L., C. G. Sammis, and A. J. Rosakis (2007). Interaction of a dynamic rupture on a fault plane with short frictionless fault branches, *Pure Appl. Geophys.* **164,** no. 10, 1881–1904.

Bońkowski, P. A., Z. Zembaty, and M. Y. Minch (2018). Time history response analysis of a slender tower under translational-rocking seismic excitations, *Eng. Struct.* **155,** 387–393.

Boore, D. M. (2001). Effect of baseline corrections on displacements and response spectra for several recordings of the 1999 Chi-Chi, Taiwan, earthquake, *Bull. Seismol. Soc. Am.* **91,** no. 5, 1199–1211.

Boore, D. M. (2010). Orientation-independent, nongeometric-mean measures of seismic intensity from two horizontal components of motion, *Bull. Seismol. Soc. Am.* **100,** 1830–1835.

Canterbury Earthquakes Royal Commission (2012). Volume 6: Canterbury television building (CTV), Canterbury Earthquakes Royal Commission.

De la Llera, J. C., and A. K. Chopra (1994). Accidental torsion in buildings due to base rotational excitation, *Earthq. Eng. Struct. Dynam.* **23,** 1003–1021.

Delouis, B., M. van den Ende, and J.-P. Ampuero (2024). Kinematic rupture model of the 6 February 2023 M_w 7.8 Türkiye earthquake from a large set of near-source strong-motion records combined with GNSS offsets reveals intermittent supershear rupture, *Bull. Seismol. Soc. Am.* **114,** no. 2, 726–740.

Disaster and Emergency Management Authority (AFAD) (1973). Turkish national strong motion network, Department of Earthquake, Disaster and Emergency Management Authority, doi: 10.7914/SN/TK.

Emre, O., T. Duman, S. Özalp, F. Şaroğlu, Ş. Olgun, H. Elmaci, and T. Can (2018). Active fault database of Turkey, *Bull. Earthq. Eng.* **16,** 3229–3275.

EPRI (2007). Program on technology innovation: Effects of spatial incoherence on seismic ground motions, EPRI, Palo Alto, California, 1015110.

Ghafory-Ashtiany, M., and M. P. Singh (1986). Structural response for six correlated earthquake components, *Earthq. Eng. Struct. Dynam.* **14,** 103–119.

Godínez, S. E., and J. I. Restrepo (2023). Stringer-panel model to support the seismic design and response verification of building diaphragms, *Resilient Cities Struct.* **2,** 46–67.

Godínez, S. E., R. Álvarez, and J. I. Restrepo (2024). Nonlinear dynamic seismic analysis of a high-rise concrete core wall building with podiums using the beam-truss model, *Bull. Earthq. Eng.* 1–44.

Goldberg, D. E., T. Taymaz, N. G. Reitman, A. E. Hatem, S. Yolsal-Çevikbilen, W. D. Barnhart, T. S. Irmak, D. J. Wald, T. Öcalan, W. L. Yeck, *et al.* (2023). Rapid characterization of the February 2023 Kahramanmaraş, Türkiye, earthquake sequence, *Seism. Rec.* **3,** no. 2, 156–167.

Gupta, V. K., and M. D. Trifunac (1991). Effects of ground rocking on dynamic response of multistoried buildings during earthquakes, *Struct. Eng.* **8,** 87–94.

Güvercin, S. E., H. Karabulut, A. O. Konca, U. Doğan, and S. Ergintav (2022). Active seismotectonics of the East Anatolian Fault, *Geophys. J. Int.* **230,** no. 1, 50–69.

Hu, J., M. Liu, T. Taymaz, L. Ding, and T. S. Irmak (2025). Characteristics of strong ground motion from the 2023 M_w 7.8 and M_w 7.6 Kahramanmaraş earthquake sequence, *Bull. Earthq. Eng.* **23,** 1225–1254.

Huang, B. S. (2003). Ground rotational motions of the 1999 Chi-Chi, Taiwan earthquake as inferred from dense array observations, *Geophys. Res. Lett.* **30,** doi: 10.1029/2002GL015157.

Igel, H., U. Schreiber, A. Flaws, B. Schuberth, A. Velikoseltsev, and A. Cochard (2005). Rotational motions induced by the M 8.1 Tokachi-oki earthquake, September 25, 2003, *Geophys. Res. Lett.* **32,** 1–5.

Jia, Z., Z. Jin, M. Marchandon, T. Ulrich, A.-A. Gabriel, W. Fan, P. Shearer, X. Zou, J. Rekoske, F. Bulut, *et al.* (2023). The complex dynamics of the 2023 Kahramanmaraş, Turkey, M_w 7.8-7.7 earthquake doublet, *Science* **381,** no. 6661, 985–990.

Kandilli Observatory And Earthquake Research Institute Boğaziçi University (1971). Kandilli Observatory and Earthquake Research Institute (KOERI), *International Federation of Digital Seismograph Networks,* doi: 10.7914/SN/KO.

LATBSDC (2024). *An alternative Procedure for Seismic Analysis and Design of Tall Buildings,* Los Angeles Tall Buildings Structural Design Council.

Lee, W. K., M. Celebi, M. Todorovska, and H. Igel (2009). Introduction to the special issue on rotational seismology and engineering applications, *Bull. Seismol. Soc. Am.* **99,** no. 2B, 945–957.

Liu, C., T. Lay, R. Wang, T. Taymaz, Z. Xie, X. Xiong, T. S. Irmak, M. Kahraman, and C. Erman (2023). Complex multi-fault rupture and triggering during the 2023 earthquake doublet in southeastern Türkiye, *Nat. Commun.* **14,** no. 1, 5564.

Lu, Y., and M. Panagiotou (2016). Three-dimensional beam–truss model for reinforced concrete walls and slabs–part 2: Modeling approach and validation for slabs and coupled walls, *Earthq. Eng. Struct. Dynam.* **45,** no. 11, 1707–1724.

Lu, Y., M. Panagiotou, and I. Koutromanos (2016). Three-dimensional beam-truss model for reinforced concrete walls and slabs – part 1: Modeling approach, validation, and parametric study for individual reinforced concrete walls, *Earthq. Eng. Struct. Dynam.* **45,** 1495–1513.

Ma, X., and A. Elbanna (2019). Dynamic rupture propagation on fault planes with explicit representation of short branches, *Earth Planet. Sci. Lett.* **523,** 115702.

Mai, P., T. Aspiotis, T. Aquib, E. Cano, D. Castro Cruz, A. Espíndola-Carmona, B. Li, X. Li, J. Liu, R. Matrau, *et al.* (2023). The destructive earthquake doublet of 6 February 2023 in south-central Türkiye and northwestern Syria: Initial observations and analyses, *Seism. Rec.* **3,** 105–115.

Mavros, M., M. Panagiotou, I. Koutromanos, R. Alvarez, and J. I. Restrepo (2022). Seismic analysis of a modern 14-story reinforced concrete core wall building system using the btm-shell methodology, *Earthq. Eng. Struct. Dynam.* **51,** 1540–1562.

Mavros, M., M. Panagiotou, I. Koutromanos, and J. I. Restrepo (2023). Nonlinear dynamic seismic analysis of a modern concrete core wall building in Los Angeles using the BTM-shell methodology, *Earthq. Eng. Struct. Dynam.* **52,** 4416–4441.

McCallen, D., A. Petersson, A. Rodgers, A. Pitarka, M. Miah, F. Petrone, B. Sjogreen, N. Abrahamson, and H. Tang (2021). EQSIM—A multidisciplinary framework for fault-to-structure earthquake simulations on exascale computers part i: Computational models and workflow, *Earthq. Spectra* **37,** no. 2, 707–735.

McKenna, F. (2011). OpenSees: A framework for earthquake engineering simulation, *Comput. Sci. Eng.* **13,** no. 4, 58–66.

Mertol, H. C., G. Tunç, T. Akış, Y. Kantekin, and İshak Can Aydın (2023). Investigation of RC buildings after 6 February 2023, Kahramanmaraş, Türkiye earthquakes, *Buildings* **13,** no. 7, 1789.

Moehle, J. (1992). Displacement-based design of RC structures subjected to earthquakes, *Earthq. Spectra* **8,** 403–428.

Nigbor, R. L. (1994). Six-degree-of-freedom ground-motion measurement, *Bull. Seismol. Soc. Am.* **84,** 1665–1669.

Ozturk, M., M. H. Arslan, and H. H. Korkmaz (2023). Effect on RC buildings of 6 February 2023 Turkey earthquake doublets and new doctrines for seismic design, *Eng. Fail. Anal.* **153,** 107521.

Papazafeiropoulos, G., and V. Plevris (2023). Kahramanmaraş—Gaziantep, Türkiye M_w 7.8 earthquake on 6 February 2023: Strong ground motion and building response estimations, *Buildings* **13,** no. 5, 1194.

Poulos, A., E. Miranda, and J. W. Baker (2022). Evaluation of earthquake response spectra directionality using stochastic simulations, *Bull. Seismol. Soc. Am.* **112,** no. 1, 307–315.

Priestley, M., G. Calvi, and M. Kowalsky (2007). *Displacement-Based Seismic Design of Structures*, IUSS Press, Italy.

Priestley, M. J. N., and M. J. Kowalsky (2000). Direct displacement-based seismic design of concrete buildings, *Bull. New Zeal. Soc. Earthq. Eng.* **33,** 421–444.

Reitman, N. G., R. W. Briggs, W. D. Barnhart, A. E. Hatem, J. A. Thompson Jobe, C. B. DuRoss, R. D. Gold, J. D. Mejstrik, C. Collett, R. D. Koehler, *et al.* (2023). Rapid surface rupture mapping from satellite data: The 2023 Kahramanmaraş, Turkey (Türkiye), earthquake sequence, *Seism. Rec.* **3,** no. 4, 289–298.

Ren, C., Z. Wang, T. Taymaz, N. Hu, H. Luo, Z. Zhao, H. Yue, X. Song, Z. Shen, H. Xu, *et al.* (2024). Supershear triggering and cascading fault ruptures of the 2023 Kahramanmaraş, Türkiye, earthquake doublet, *Science* **383,** no. 6680, 305–311.

Republic of Turkey Presidency of Strategy and Budget (2023). 2023 Kahramanmaraş and Hatay Earthquakes Report, available at https://www.sbb.gov.tr/wp-content/uploads/2023/03/2023-Kahramanmaras-and-Hatay-Earthquakes-Report.pdf (last accessed June 2024).

Rosakis, A., M. Abdelmeguid, and A. Elbanna (2025). Near-field evidence for early supershear rupture of the M_w 7.8 Kahramanmaraş earthquake in Turkey, *Nature Geosci.* **18,** no. 6, 534–541.

Shahi, S. K., and J. W. Baker (2014). NGA-West2 models for ground motion directionality, *Earthq. Spectra* **30,** no. 3, 1285–1300.

Suryanto, W., H. Igel, J. Wassermann, A. Cochard, B. Schuberth, D. Vollmer, F. Scherbaum, U. Schreiber, and A. Velikoseltsev (2006). First comparison of array-derived rotational ground motions with direct ring laser measurements, *Bull. Seismol. Soc. Am.* **96,** 2059–2071.

Takeo, M. (1998). Ground rotational motions recorded in near-source region of earthquakes, *Geophys. Res. Lett.* **25,** 789–792.

Tang, Y., K. Şeşetyan, and P. M. Mai (2024). Comprehensive ground-motion characterization of the 6 February 2023 7.8 Pazarcık earthquake in Kahramanmaraş, Türkiye: Insights into attenuation effects, site responses and source properties, *Bull. Earthq. Eng.* **22,** no. 14, 6829–6857.

Taymaz, T., H. Eyidoğan, and J. Jackson (1991). Source parameters of large earthquakes in the East Anatolian fault zone (Türkiye), *Geophys. J. Int.* **106,** no. 3, 537–550.

U.S. Geological Survey (USGS) (2023). M 7.8-27 km E of Nurdağı, Turkey, available at https://earthquake.usgs.gov/earthquakes/eventpage/us6000jllz/executive (last accessed December 2025).

Vernon, F. L., J. Fletcher, L. Carroll, A. Chave, and E. Sembera (1991). Coherence of seismic body waves from local events as measured by a small-aperture array, *J. Geophys. Res. Solid Earth* **96,** no. B7, 11,981–11,996.

Vernon, F. L., G. L. Pavlis, T. J. Owens, D. E. McNamara, and P. N. Anderson (1998). Near-surface scattering effects observed with a high-frequency phased array at pinyon flats, California, *Bull. Seismol. Soc. Am.* **88,** no. 6, 1548–1560.

Vicencio, F., and N. A. Alexander (2019). A parametric study on the effect of rotational ground motions on building structural responses, *Soil Dynam. Earthq. Eng.* **118,** 191–206.

Vuran, E., C. Serhatoğlu, M. Ömer Timurağaoğlu, E. Smyrou, İhsan E. Bal, and R. Livaoğlu (2025). Damage observations of RC buildings from 2023 Kahramanmaraş earthquake sequence and discussion on the seismic code regulations, *Bull. Earthq. Eng.* **23,** no. 3, 1153–1182.

Wang, Z., W. Zhang, T. Taymaz, Z. He, T. Xu, and Z. Zhang (2023). Dynamic Rupture Process of the 2023 M_w 7.8 Kahramanmaraş earthquake (SE Türkiye): Variable rupture speed and implications for seismic hazard, *Geophys. Res. Lett.* **50,** no. 15, e2023GL104787, doi: 10.1029/2023GL104787.

Xu, C., Y. Zhang, S. Hua, X. Zhang, L. Xu, Y. Chen, and T. Taymaz (2023). Rapid source inversions of the 2023 SE Türkiye earthquakes with teleseismic and strong-motion data, *Earthq. Sci.* **36,** no. 4, 316–327.

Yin, J., R. L. Nigbor, Q. Chen, and J. Steidl (2016). Engineering analysis of measured rotational ground motions at GVDA, *Soil Dynam. Earthq. Eng.* **87,** 125–137.

Zerva, A., and V. Zervas (2002). Spatial variation of seismic ground motions: An overview, *Appl. Mech. Rev.* **55,** no. 3, 271–297.

Zhang, P., J. I. Restrepo, J. P. Conte, and J. Ou (2017). Nonlinear finite element modeling and response analysis of the collapsed Alto Rio Building in the 2010 Chile Maule earthquake, *Struct. Design Tall Special Build.* **26,** no. 16, e1364, doi: 10.1002/tal.1364.

APPENDIX

The technical details of the models created for the nonlinear response history analyses are described in depth in this section. Further information on the peak structural response values in

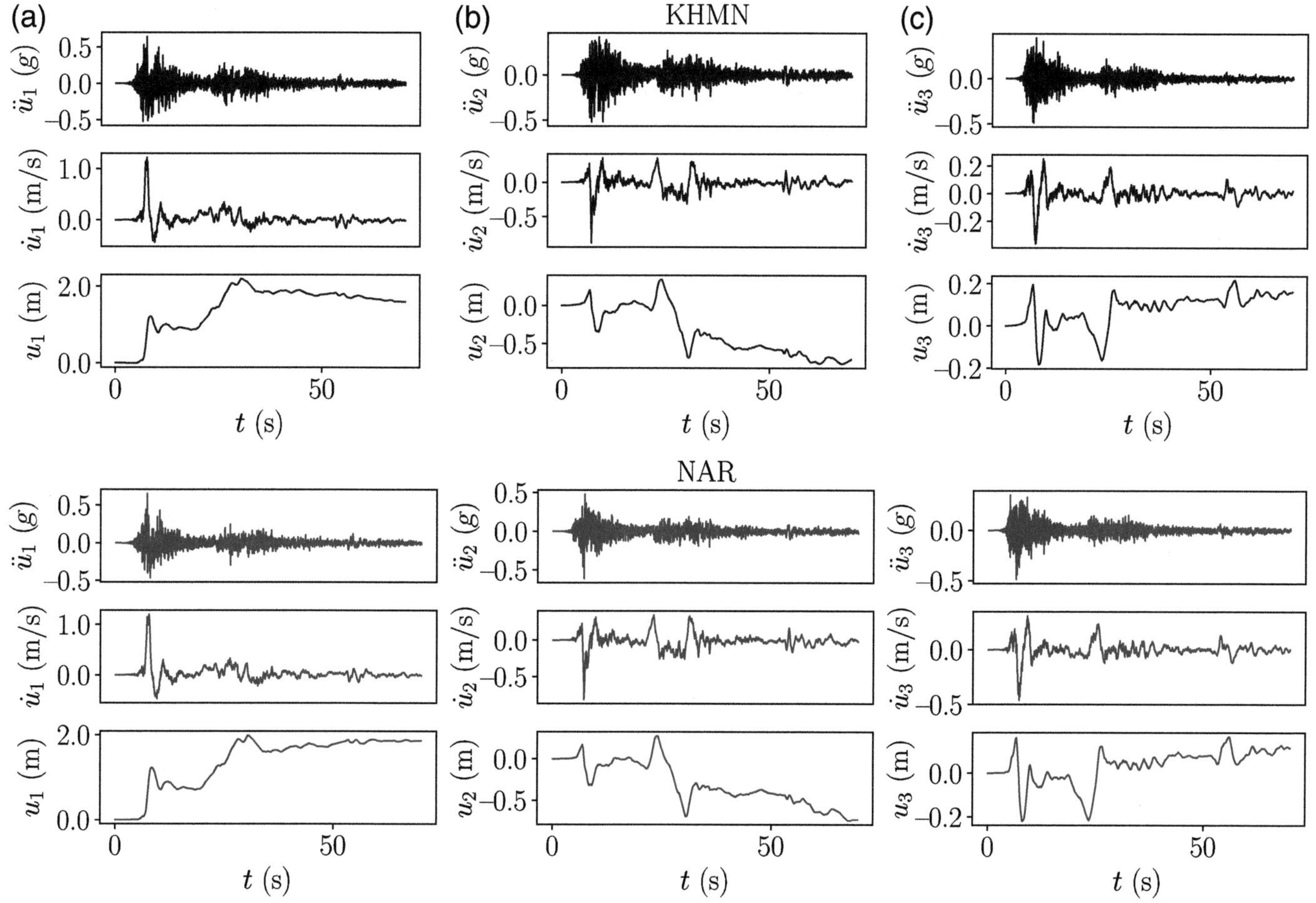

the X-Dir and Y-Dir for all case studies are shown in Tables A1 and A2, respectively. Figures supporting the main body of the article such as the baseline corrected near-field records of KHMN and NAR (Fig. A1), the resulting rotational ground motions used in the analyses (Fig. A2), and the geometry of the case studies (Fig. A3) are included.

Figure A1. The baseline corrected near-field records at stations (a) KHMN and (b) NAR. (a) The first column shows the fault-parallel particle acceleration, velocity, and displacement for both stations. (b) The second column shows the fault-normal particle acceleration, velocity, and displacement for both stations. (c) The third column shows the vertical particle acceleration, velocity, and displacement for both stations. The color version of this figure is available only in the electronic edition.

Nonlinear building analysis

The nonlinear models used for the analyses were created in the free open-source software Open System for Earthquake Engineering Simulation (OpenSees) (McKenna, 2011). The methodology used to model U-shaped reinforced concrete (RC) walls and the diagonally reinforced coupling beams was the Beam-Truss model (BTM) (Lu and Panagiotou, 2016; Lu *et al.*, 2016; Álvarez *et al.*, 2019, 2020). The BTM has been widely validated and used to model and analyze complete buildings (Zhang *et al.*, 2017; Mavros *et al.*, 2022, 2023). For cases 1–4, the BTM of the U-shaped wall was discretized into six vertical divisions in the first story and five vertical divisions in the remaining stories. The flanges have five horizontal divisions, and the webs have fourteen. Considering the coupling beams, the core wall is composed of a total of 14,502 elements. The uniaxial constitutive laws used for the concrete and reinforcing steel are *ConcretewBeta* and *Steel02*, respectively.

TABLE A1
Peak Structural Response Values *X*-Dir

	***X*-Dir**					
	Interstory Drift		**Roof Drift**		**Shear Ratio***	
Case Study	**HOR**	**HOR + ROT**	**HOR**	**HOR + ROT**	**HOR**	**HOR + ROT**
Case 1	0.84%	0.90%	0.70%	0.73%	1.17	1.23
Case 2	0.82%	0.91%	0.70%	0.73%	1.19	1.25
Case 3	0.89%	0.92%	0.75%	0.76%	1.17	1.23
Case 4	0.87%	0.90%	0.73%	0.75%	1.19	1.24
Case HR	1.78%	1.57%	1.19%	1.34%	1.036	1.027

*Shear demand to capacity ratio, considering the in-plane shear capacity in ACI 318-19 using expected material properties. Case HR, additional design and analysis of a high-rise building; HOR, horizontal ground motions; HOR+ROT, horizontal plus the three rotational components of the ground motion.

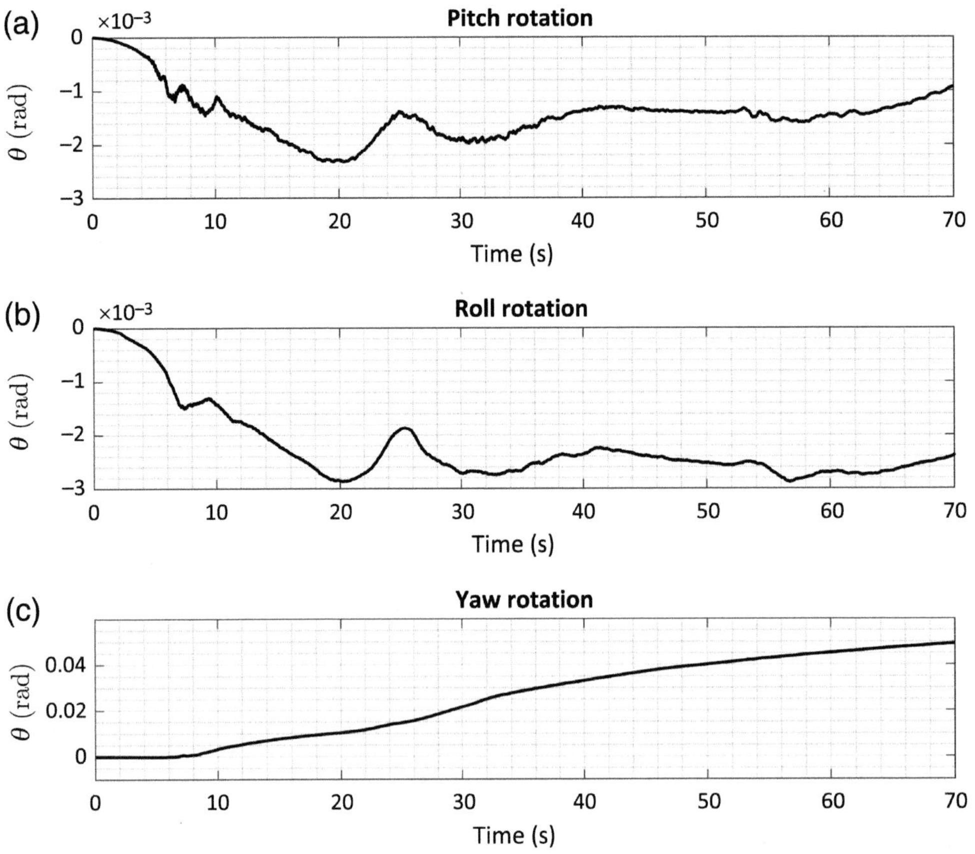

Figure A2. Rotational ground motions used for nonlinear response history analysis. The baseline corrected rotational motions records obtained from records of stations KHMN, NAR, and NAR′ are shown in Figure 1.

TABLE A2
Peak Structural Response Values *Y*-Dir

	***Y*-Dir**					
	Interstory Drift		**Roof Drift**		**Shear Ratio***	
Case Study	**HOR**	**HOR + ROT**	**HOR**	**HOR + ROT**	**HOR**	**HOR + ROT**
Case 1	1.01%	1.01%	0.79%	0.80%	1.23	1.22
Case 2	1.05%	1.03%	0.83%	0.83%	1.28	1.30
Case 3	0.96%	0.95%	0.79%	0.79%	1.21	1.28
Case 4	1.00%	0.97%	0.83%	0.80%	1.29	1.28
Case HR	1.21%	1.25%	0.86%	0.86%	0.712	0.725

*Shear demand to capacity ratio, considering the in-plane shear capacity in ACI 318-19 using expected material properties. Case HR, additional design and analysis of a high-rise building; HOR, horizontal ground motions; HOR+ROT, horizontal plus the three rotational components of the ground motion.

ConcretewBeta accounts for the biaxial strain field on the concrete compressive behavior in the diagonal elements of the model. Although the BTM can also be used to model the slabs, this research uses the computationally less expensive Stringer-Panel Model (SPM) (Godínez and Restrepo, 2023) to represent the in-plane stiffness of the diaphragm at each story and avoid the common assumption of a rigid diaphragm. The SPM does not consider out-of-plane stiffness of the slab; thus, no frame action is represented between the columns and the walls. The gravity columns are all modeled using elastic beam-column elements with effective stiffness properties. In case HR, the perimeter walls in the basement levels were modeled using the shell element *ShellMITC4*. The effect of the soil stiffness, lateral pressure, and soil–structure interaction is out of the scope of this study. The gravity loads are applied as nodal loads to the columns and to the core wall and rectangular walls based on the tributary area. The mathematical model of case 1 has a total of 24,552 degrees of freedom. The mathematical model of case HR has a total of 38,323 elements and 66,624 degrees of freedom. A more detailed description of the case HR model can be found elsewhere (Godínez *et al.*, 2024). Constant equivalent viscous damping is considered by the classical Rayleigh damping model. For cases 1–4, the value for the mass proportional coefficient was $\alpha = 0.24141/\text{s}$ and the stiffness proportional coefficient was $\beta = 0.0011$ s. For case HR, the value for the mass proportional coefficient was $\alpha = 0.06681/\text{s}$ and the stiffness proportional coefficient was $\beta = 0.0036$ s. These sets of parameters used to define the Rayleigh damping model consider a damping ratio of $\xi = 2\%$ for the average of the first translational modes in each direction, and $\xi = 2\%$ for the largest second translational mode. The rocking modes are highly coupled with the translational modes, and thus have the same damping associated with them. Whereas the first torsional mode is the third overall mode in all case studies presented, and thus a damping ratio lower than $\xi = 2\%$ is associated with it.

The ground-motion input was applied to a master node at the geometrical centroid at the base of the structure as an *imposedMotion* through the *MultipleSupport* command in OpenSees with a timestep of $dt = 0.01$ s. The nodes at the base of the columns were connected to the master node through the *rigidLink* command. To properly transfer the forces to the U-shaped walls, a node was modeled at the centroid of the wall at the base level, an elastic beam-column element with artificially

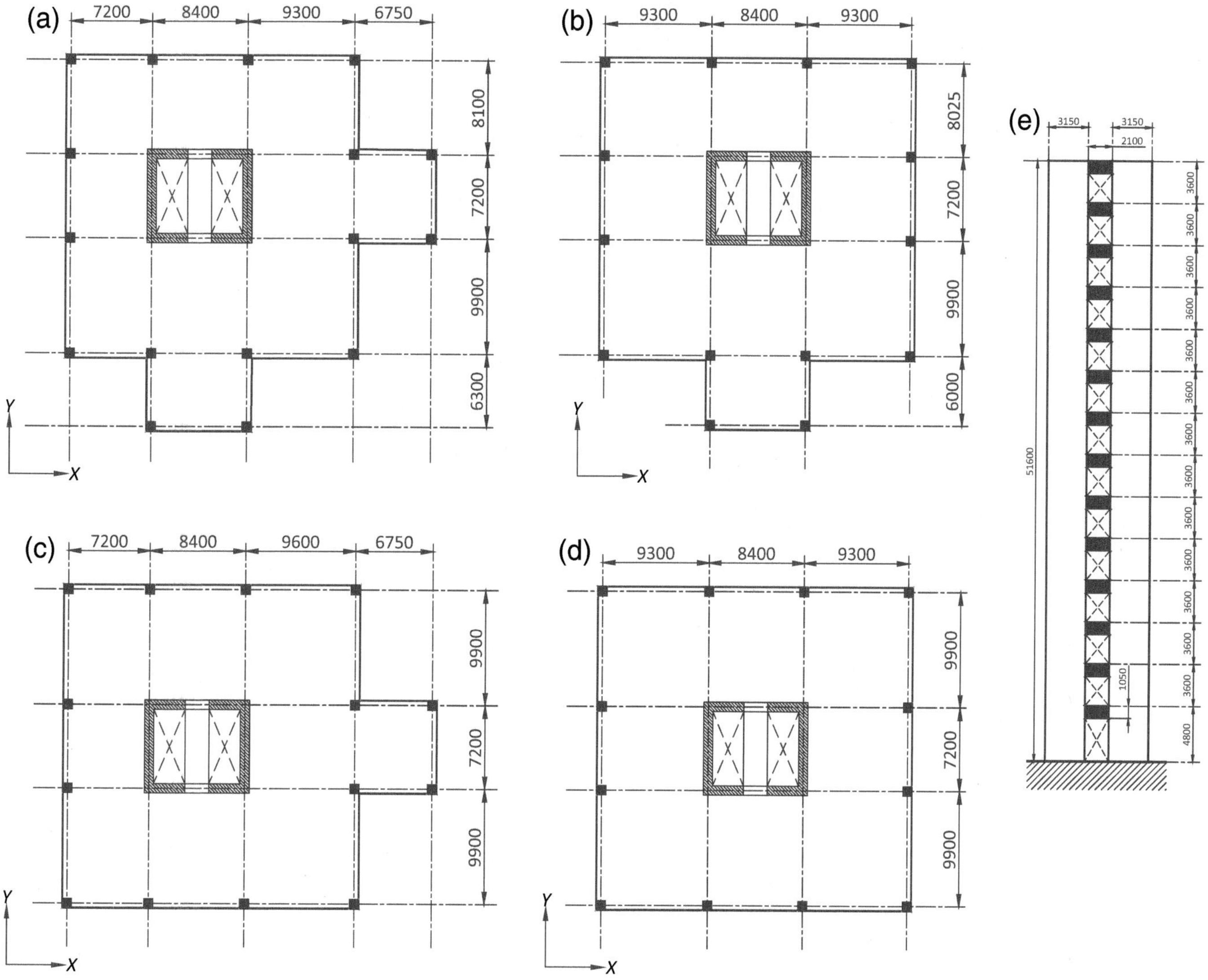

Figure A3. Geometry of case studies. (a) Case 1 plan view, eccentricity in both directions. (b) Case 2 plan view, eccentricity in the *Y*-Dir. (c) Case 3 plan view, eccentricity in the *X*-Dir. (d) Case 4 plan view, no eccentricities. (e) Elevation of the core wall.

large stiffness was modeled from this centroidal node to the four corners of the wall, as well as at the perimeter of the U-shaped wall at the base level. The wall's centroidal node was then constrained to the master node through a *rigidLink*. The average constant acceleration method was used to solve the equation of motion. The *KrylovNewton* algorithm was used to solve the nonlinear equation.

Manuscript received 14 April 2025
Published online 8 January 2026

Subduction or Crustal Faulting? Evaluating Ground-Motion Models to Characterize Haida Gwaii in the Canadian Seismic Hazard Model

Alex Hughes[1], Tiegan E. Hobbs[*1,2,3], Camille Brillon[4], Michael G. Bostock[1], and Simon Peacock[1]

ABSTRACT

The tectonic classification of the Haida Gwaii thrust fault (HGT) as either a subduction interface or a crustal fault is important for seismic hazard assessment in northwest British Columbia. To inform future versions of the Canadian Seismic Hazard Model (CanadaSHM), we reviewed evidence from the literature for subduction beneath Haida Gwaii, and found that various independent geophysical datasets suggest localized incipient underthrusting along an ∼180 km segment, roughly corresponding to the 2012 rupture plane. We evaluate the performance of newly developed ground-motion prediction equations (GMPEs) for Haida Gwaii by analyzing instrumental ground motion and shaking intensity data from the 2012 Haida Gwaii earthquake, considering two magnitudes for the event (M_w 7.8 from teleseismic data and M_w 7.4 from a regional seismicity catalog). We also assess GMPE performance for another reverse-faulting earthquake that could plausibly have occurred on the HGT. Our results show that the GMPEs predict horizontal ground motions reasonably well, especially for the 2012 mainshock. On average, GMPEs overestimate shaking by a factor of 1.1 (M_w 7.4) or 1.6 (M_w 7.8), improving on earlier estimates of overprediction by a factor of two or more. Although residuals for roughly half the data overlap with the zero-residual line within uncertainty, residuals for all GMPEs tested overlap within the aleatory uncertainty of active crustal GMPEs. Therefore, ground motions are not diagnostic in terms of a crustal faulting or subduction interface designation for the HGT. We recommend that the HGT remain classified as a subduction interface in future versions of CanadaSHM, consistent with previous hazard assessments and recent studies that advocate for incipient subduction, while noting that reclassifying the HGT as an active crustal fault would have minimal impact on ground-motion simulations.

KEY POINTS

- Ground-motion prediction equations (GMPEs) make reasonable predictions of horizontal ground motions for the 2012 Haida Gwaii earthquake.
- Ground-motion analyses alone do not favor an active crustal or subduction interface designation for the Haida Gwaii thrust.
- Recent literature indicates incipient underthrusting beneath Haida Gwaii, consistent with subduction interface models.

Supplemental Material

INTRODUCTION

On 27 October 2012 at 08:04 p.m. local time (28 October 03:04 UTC), a moment magnitude (M_w) 7.8 earthquake occurred on a low-angle thrust fault offshore from southern Haida Gwaii (herein referred to as the "Haida Gwaii thrust" or HGT: Fig. 1) and triggered a large tsunami. Although the damage was relatively light for such a large earthquake due to the sparse population in this part of northwestern British Columbia (Bird and Lamontagne, 2015), the resulting tsunami was the largest globally in 2012 (Leonard and Bednarski, 2014). The 2012 Haida Gwaii

1. Department of Earth, Ocean, and Atmospheric Sciences, University of British Columbia, Vancouver, British Columbia, Canada, https://orcid.org/0000-0002-4866-1006 (AH); https://orcid.org/0000-0002-6174-632X (TEH); https://orcid.org/0000-0002-2532-543X (SP); 2. Geological Survey of Canada, Pacific Division, Natural Resources Canada, Vancouver, British Columbia, Canada; 3. School of Earth and Ocean Science, Bob Wright Centre A405, University of Victoria, Victoria, British Columbia, Canada; 4. Geological Survey of Canada, Pacific Division, Natural Resources Canada, Sidney, British Columbia, Canada, https://orcid.org/0009-0001-9548-1390 (CB)

*Corresponding author: tiegan.hobbs@nrcan-rncan.gc.ca

Cite this article as Hughes, A., T. E. Hobbs, C. Brillon, M. G. Bostock, and S. Peacock (2025). Subduction or Crustal Faulting? Evaluating Ground-Motion Models to Characterize Haida Gwaii in the Canadian Seismic Hazard Model, *Bull. Seismol. Soc. Am.* **116**, 720–737, doi: 10.1785/0120250061

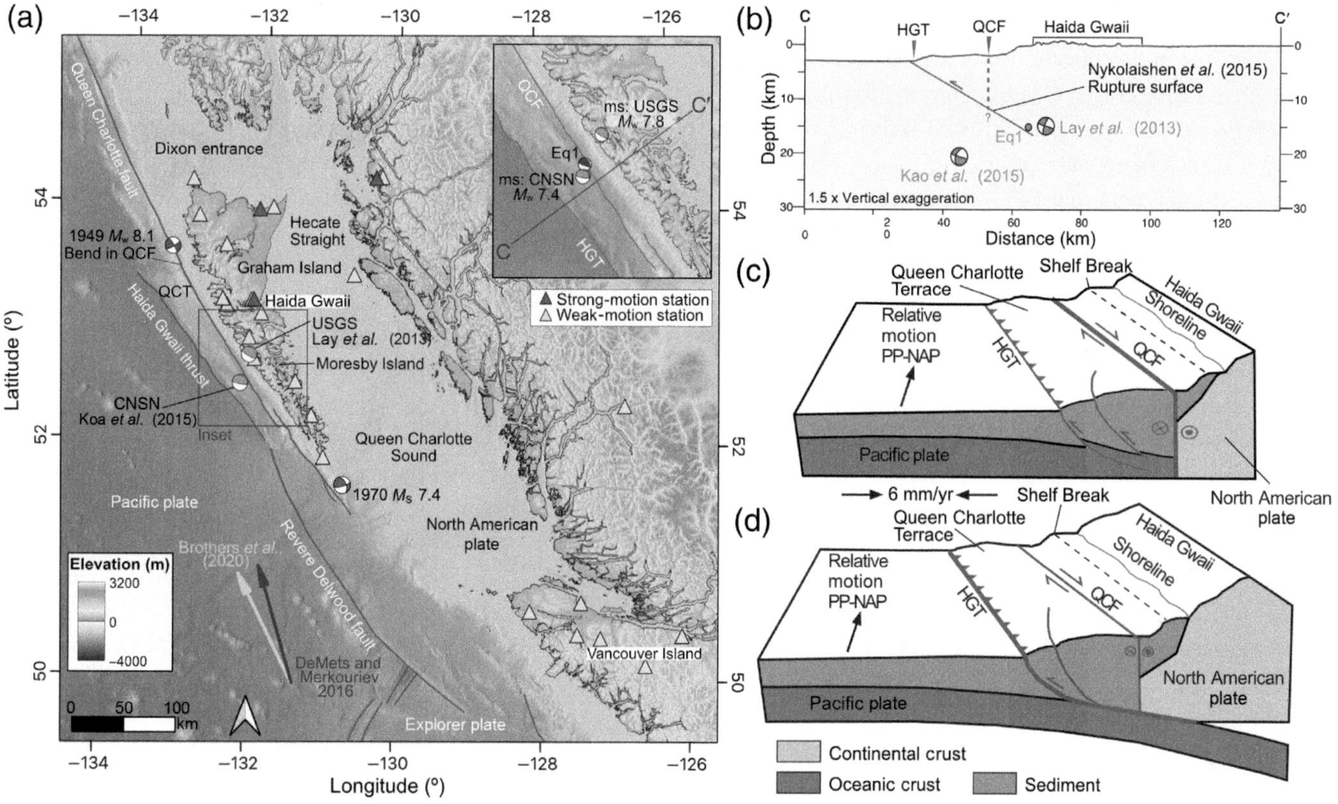

Figure 1. (a) Map showing the location of major faults (red lines) and stations in the Canadian National Seismic Network (CNSN) that were active for the period of the data used for this study (i.e., up to 2013). The fault-plane solutions are from the U.S. Geological Survey (USGS) (Lay *et al.*, 2013) and the Natural Resources Canada regional catalog. The colored arrows are the Pacific plate motion vectors. The inset shows the epicenters and moment tensors of the earthquakes analyzed in this study based on the regional fault-plane solution from Kao *et al.* (2015) and the locations of Oliva *et al.* (2024) (green indicates mainshock [ms], blue indicates EQ1). (b) Cross-section along the line C–C′ showing the dip of the Haida Gwaii thrust (HGT) based on the rupture surface of Nykolaishen *et al.* (2015) in relation to the various earthquakes included in this work. (c) Schematic diagram for the active crust model adapted from Brothers *et al.* (2020). Here, shortening is accommodated by internal deformation within the Pacific plate (PP) because it is buttressed against the Queen Charlotte fault (QCF), and the HGT does not penetrate eastward of the QCF. (d) The subduction model where the PP is underthrust beneath the North American plate (NAP) via slip on the HGT, with the QCF acting as a sliver-bounding fault (after Hyndman, 2015). The red thick line in each model represents the primary plate boundary fault. The color version of this figure is available only in the electronic edition.

earthquake confirmed that large, tsunamigenic earthquakes are possible offshore from Haida Gwaii and raised speculation about how strain is partitioned between the HGT and the adjacent, subvertical, strike-slip Queen Charlotte fault (QCF). Scientific literature is divided between considering the HGT as (1) a true subduction interface with underthrusting of oceanic crust beneath a continental fore-arc and overriding plate (e.g., Hyndman, 2015), and (2) a low-angle thrust fault that allows for compression and shortening just outboard of the oblique transpressional QCF (e.g., Rohr *et al.*, 2000).

The difference between these two end members has potentially broad implications for regional seismic hazards. The Canadian Seismic Hazard Model (CanadaSHM; Kolaj *et al.*, 2019, 2020) underpins the seismic provisions in the building code of Canada and is a key input to the Canadian Seismic Risk Model (Hobbs *et al.*, 2023). In the 2020 CanadaSHM, the HGT is treated as a subduction interface, based on previous studies comparing observed ground motions to predicted shaking from ground-motion prediction equations (GMPEs) used in older versions of the hazard model (Rosenberger *et al.*, 2013; Allen and Brillon, 2015). Recently updated fragility functions show significantly increased risk to infrastructure on Haida Gwaii if a subduction interface model is adopted for the HGT (Abraham, 2023). The increased risk is due, in part, to higher damage expected from long-duration seismic shaking produced during megathrust events. Therefore, treating the HGT as a subduction interface rather than a crustal fault potentially increases both the assessed hazard and subsequent risk for Haida Gwaii.

GMPEs, which relate an earthquake source to shaking at a site of interest, are often constructed using regression analysis on global earthquake catalogs (e.g., Power *et al.*, 2008; Bozorgnia *et al.*, 2014, 2022). GMPEs are critical inputs for seismic hazard models, which undergo periodic updates to the choice of GMPEs based on new data and analyses (e.g., Power *et al.*, 2008; Bozorgnia *et al.*, 2014). The HGT was initially designated a subduction interface in CanadaSHM5 (Adams *et al.*, 2015). This designation was based on the observation that strong-motion recordings at three stations from the 2012 Haida Gwaii earthquake matched more closely with the subduction interface GMPEs than active crustal GMPEs from the fourth-generation CanadaSHM (Rosenberger *et al.*, 2013). Based on residual analysis from a catalog of 56 earthquakes with $M_w > 4.6$, Allen and Brillon (2015) observed that all GMPEs overestimated ground shaking and concluded that no single GMPE is appropriate for the northern coastal area of British Columbia. Of these two studies, the low number of data points in the former and the uncertainty in the latter merit further analysis to designate an appropriate tectonic setting for the HGT for use in future generations of CanadaSHM. This also presents an opportunity to consider over a decade's worth of research into the fundamental tectonics and geomorphic expression of the HGT and QCT since the 2012 earthquake.

Here, we attempt to identify the most appropriate tectonic designation of the HGT within CanadaSHM. We first review the literature arguing for and against the HGT as a subduction interface or crustal fault to provide context for an analysis of newly developed GMPEs applied to the HGT. We then model horizontal ground motions for the 2012 M_w 7.8 mainshock and a 2001 M_w 6.1 foreshock from the catalog of Allen and Brillon (2015) that could plausibly have occurred on the HGT (Fig. 1b). Instead of individual GMPEs, we model ground motions using sets of GMPEs for active crustal and subduction interface models within the sixth generation of CanadaSHM and sets of GMPEs under consideration for the seventh generation of CanadaSHM. We compare modeled ground motions to instrumental ground motions recorded at both strong- and weak-motion stations. As an additional data source, we also compare modeled shaking intensity data from GMPEs and reported shaking intensity reports from "Did You Feel It?" data for the 2012 mainshock. Finally, we compare data from the literature with our model results to help determine an appropriate designation for the HGT in future versions of CanadaSHM.

TECTONIC SETTING

The QCF extends for ~800 km northward from southern Moresby Island (Fig. 1a) to near the Alaska border, where it transitions to the Fairweather fault (e.g., Hyndman and Hamilton, 1993; Rohr and Furlong, 1995; Brothers *et al.*, 2020). The right-lateral strike-slip QCF is the primary structure that accommodates north-northwesterly motion of the Pacific plate relative to North America at rates of 50–57 mm/yr (DeMets *et al.*, 2010; DeMets and Merkouriev, 2016). Along most of its length, plate boundary strain along the QCF is localized along the fault with minimal off-fault deformation (Hyndman and Hamilton, 1993; Rohr and Furlong, 1995; Brothers *et al.*, 2020). At its southern end, the QCF overlaps with the Revere Dellwood fault, which forms part of a complex triple junction between the Pacific, Explorer, and North American plates (Rohr and Tryon, 2010; Littel *et al.*, 2023; Fig. 1a). Offshore Moresby Island at 53.2° N, there is a subtle change in strike of the surface trace of the QCF, which results in obliquity of the northwestward Pacific–North American plate motion vector relative to the mapped surface trace of the QCF (Rohr *et al.*, 2000; Tréhu *et al.*, 2015). This relative obliquity is manifest in additional convergence toward the southern end of the QCF, in the range of 6°–21° when measured clockwise from the strike of the QCF (Rohr *et al.*, 2000; DeMets *et al.*, 2010; Tréhu *et al.*, 2015; DeMets and Merkouriev, 2016; ten Brink *et al.*, 2018; Brothers *et al.*, 2020). Offshore western Haida Gwaii, this southern section of the QCF coincides with the Queen Charlotte Terrace (Fig. 1), which some researchers have likened to an accretionary prism along a subduction margin (e.g., Hyndman, 2015).

Canada's largest instrumentally recorded earthquake, an M_s 8.1 event in 1949, occurred on the QCF just offshore from northern Graham Island (Rogers, 1983), and seven $M_w > 7$ events have occurred on the entire fault system in the last hundred years (Nishenko and Jacob, 1990). The 2012 M_w 7.8 thrust earthquake occurred beneath the Queen Charlotte Terrace and highlighted the north/south variation in plate boundary mechanics along the QCF (Lay *et al.*, 2013; Cassidy *et al.*, 2014; Nykolaishen *et al.*, 2015), with dominant strike-slip motion to the north and thrusting to the south. The occurrence of a large thrust earthquake offshore from Haida Gwaii resolved long-standing questions about the suggested presence of the HGT (e.g., Cassidy *et al.*, 2014, and references therein). Nevertheless, questions remain about the geometry of the HGT, the subsurface structure of the Queen Charlotte terrace, and the extent of potential underthrusting beneath Haida Gwaii.

Haida Gwaii thrust as a subduction interface or crustal fault

Two competing models exist to explain the accommodation of oblique convergence along the southern QCF (Fig. 1c–d): (1) a crustal fault model for the HGT where convergence is accommodated by shortening of the Pacific plate or within-plate deformation in both the Pacific and North American plates (Fig. 1c; Bérubé *et al.*, 1989; Rohr *et al.*, 2000; Tréhu *et al.*, 2015; Brothers *et al.*, 2020) and (2) a subduction model where shortening is accommodated by incipient subduction or underthrusting of the Pacific plate beneath Haida Gwaii (Fig. 1d; Yorath and Hyndman, 1983; Hyndman and Hamilton, 1993; Hyndman, 2015; Walton *et al.*, 2015; Wang *et al.*, 2015; ten Brink *et al.*, 2018; Oliva *et al.*, 2024).

Some of the earliest suggestions for the crustal fault model were based on an offshore seismic refraction profile across northern Moresby Island collected in 1983 (Dehler and Clowes, 1988; Bérubé *et al.*, 1989; Mackie *et al.*, 1989). The data showed oceanic crust overlain by a sedimented terrace, which was separated from continental crust by the QCF. Although they believed that the data pointed toward the QCF being the main transform plate boundary, these authors acknowledged that a subduction model was also plausible (Dehler and Clowes, 1988). The most comprehensive arguments for the crustal fault model are from Rohr *et al.* (2000), who used multichannel seismic reflection data from the Dixon Entrance and the Hecate Strait (Fig. 1) to describe the geometry of the QCF in relation to the characteristics of the Pacific and North American plates. The main arguments for the active crust model suggested by Rohr *et al.* (2000) are as follows. First, the QCF is thought to be a vertical fault that acts as a clean break between the Pacific and North American plates based on flexural analysis (Prims *et al.*, 1997) and glacial sea-level fluctuations (Barrie *et al.*, 1991). Based on thermal modeling, the plates on either side of the QCF are both thought to be warm and thin and have similar mechanical properties (Chen and Morgan, 1990; Lewis *et al.*, 1991). These conditions are thought to facilitate internal deformation within the North American and Pacific plates in the vicinity of the QCF and farther afield within the Pacific plate (Rohr *et al.*, 2000). In this model, flexure of the Pacific plate is thought to result from the weight of the overlying terrace (Prims *et al.*, 1997). These interpretations were supported by Tréhu *et al.* (2015), who also noted an increase in obliquity of the QCF to >15° south of 53.2° N (Fig. 1a), which they suggest is related to a southward transition from dominantly strike-slip deformation to oblique shear expressed as a combination of strike-slip and reverse faulting. Recent work added further support to the crustal model by recalculating the Pacific–North American Euler pole using the relative plate motion from the trace of the northern QCF (Brothers *et al.*, 2020). With the recalculated Euler pole, average obliquity for the southern section of the QCF (i.e., south of the U.S./Canada border) is 7.4° ± 7.1°, lower than previous estimates of >15°. This lower obliquity implies cumulative convergence over 4 Myr of 26 km, which agrees with the average width of the Queen Charlotte Terrace and implies that no subduction is necessary to create the terrace (Brothers *et al.*, 2020).

The arguments for subduction or underthrusting of the Pacific plate beneath Haida Gwaii were summarized by Hyndman (2015). Central to the argument is the observation that the plate boundary offshore from Haida Gwaii shares several characteristics with subduction zones elsewhere. For example, there is a forebulge in the Pacific plate known as the Oshawa rise (e.g., Chase *et al.*, 1975), and the Pacific plate is warped downward as it approaches the Queen Charlotte Terrace, creating the Queen Charlotte trough (e.g., Yorath and Hyndman, 1983). The terrace itself is interpreted as a fold-and-thrust belt due to the similarity in velocity structure to the accretionary prism of the Cascadia subduction zone offshore from Vancouver Island (Smith, 1999; Smith *et al.*, 2003). A pronounced linear low in the gravity structure beneath the Queen Charlotte trough contrasts with a gravity high over western Haida Gwaii, a pattern characteristic of subduction zones (Dehler and Clowes, 1988; Spence and Long, 1995). However, a similar gravity high is present farther north along the QCF in Alaska, where deformation is purely strike slip (ten Brink *et al.*, 2018). Heat flow models using a subduction configuration show a better fit to observations than models using a crustal thickening configuration (Smith *et al.*, 2003), and the landward decrease in heat flow is characteristic of subduction zones (Smith *et al.*, 2003; Wang *et al.*, 2015).

Receiver function analyses for five teleseismic stations on Haida Gwaii identified a positive velocity contrast at 18–26 km depth and a 12–17 km thick low shear-wave velocity zone increasing in depth from 25 to 42 km eastward (Gosselin *et al.*, 2015). The velocity contrast is thought to represent a shallow continental Moho, and the low-velocity zone is interpreted to be the subducting oceanic plate, where the eastward increase in depth is consistent with subduction of the Pacific plate beneath Haida Gwaii (Smith *et al.*, 2003; Bustin *et al.*, 2007; Gosselin *et al.*, 2015). More recently, ten Brink *et al.* (2018) calculated the trajectory of the Pacific slab beneath North America using the stage poles (axes of rotation) of DeMets and Merkouriev (2016). In their preferred model based on a 15° convergence angle, they predict that underthrusting commenced at ~6 Ma and that the slab extends almost exactly beneath the land area of Haida Gwaii (ten Brink *et al.*, 2018). Recent work relocating a catalog of ~50,000 earthquakes from offshore Haida Gwaii from 1998 and 2020 shows two distinct clusters of deep (>20 km) earthquakes beneath Moresby Island (Oliva *et al.*, 2024). These deep clusters are consistent with the geometry of a subducting slab from receiver functions (e.g., Gosselin *et al.*, 2015) interpreted to be the underthrust Pacific plate beneath Haida Gwaii. Recent analysis of 17 seismic reflection profiles collected offshore from Haida Gwaii images the HGT, the overlying Queen Charlotte terrace, and the QCF in detail (Brandl *et al.*, 2025). The Queen Charlotte terrace is interpreted as a crustal sliver bounded by the QCF and underlain by the HGT, where the HGT acts as a décollement that facilitates underthrusting as the main mechanism of plate convergence between the Pacific and North American plates (Brandl *et al.*, 2025).

In summary, though there have been compelling arguments made for and against the subduction hypothesis, there is convincing evidence for some degree of underthrusting beneath Haida Gwaii. Most of the primary data arguing for the crustal model is located north of the Queen Charlotte Terrace. Ocean-bottom seismometer deployments are ongoing between 2023 and at least 2025 as part of the Pacific Coast Seismic Assessment for Faults and Earthquakes (PACSAFE). These data will continue to shed light on this important issue in years to come.

DATA AND METHODS

To compare how well GMPEs reflect instrumentally recorded ground motions for the HGT, we updated and augmented the work of Rosenberger *et al.* (2013) and Allen and Brillon (2015). We compared the observed ground-motion parameters (pseudospectral accelerations [PSA], SA, at 0.3, 0.6, and 1.0 m/s and reported shaking intensity data) with modeled ground motions from sets of GMPEs from the OpenQuake Engine software. The

TABLE 1
Sets of Ground-Motion Prediction Equations (GMPEs) Used in This Study

Tectonic Regime	Ground-Motion Model	Weight	Ground Motions
CanadaSHM6			
Active crust	Abrahamson *et al.* (2014)	0.25	Horizontal
	Boore *et al.* (2014)	0.25	Horizontal
	Campbell and Bozorgnia (2014)	0.25	Horizontal
	Chiou and Youngs (2014)	0.25	Horizontal
Subduction interface	Abrahamson *et al.* (2016)	0.25	Horizontal
	Atkinson and Macias (2009)	0.25	Horizontal
	Ghofrani and Atkinson (2014)	0.25	Horizontal
	Zhao *et al.* (2006)	0.25	Horizontal
Models under consideration for CanadaSHM7			
NGA-Subduction			
Subduction interface	Abrahamson and Gulerce (2022)	0.25	Not explicitly stated. Described as "All azimuths"
	Kuehn *et al.* (2020)	0.25	Horizontal and vertical
	Parker *et al.* (2022)	0.25	Horizontal
	Si *et al.* (2020)	0.25	Horizontal
USGS NGA-Subduction			
Subduction interface	Abrahamson and Gulerce (2022)	0.25	See above
	Atkinson and Macias (2009)	0.125	Horizontal
	Kuehn *et al.* (2020)	0.25	See above
	Parker *et al.* (2022)	0.25	Horizontal
	Zhao *et al.* (2006)	0.125	Horizontal

CanadaSHM, Canadian Seismic Hazard Model.

goal was to assess if either active crustal or subduction interface GMPEs show a better fit to observed ground-motion data.

GMPEs for CanadaSHM

Our analysis focused on crustal and subduction GMPEs used in the sixth Generation CanadaSHM (CanadaSHM6; Kolaj *et al.*, 2019, 2020) and subduction GMPEs under consideration for the seventh Generation CanadaSHM (CanadaSHM7). The GMPEs for the hazard models are summarized in Table 1, along with their respective weights. The active crustal GMPEs in CanadaSHM6 are based on equal weighting of four GMPEs from the Next Generation Attenuation (NGA)-West2 models for shallow crustal earthquakes, which itself is based on a global dataset of earthquakes ranging from M_w 3.0 to 7.9 (Bozorgnia *et al.*, 2014). There have been no recent updates to NGA-West 2, so a similar model will likely be applied in CanadaSHM7. Therefore, the active crustal model for CanadaSHM6 is the only active crustal model we considered in this analysis.

The subduction interface model in CanadaSHM6 also consists of four GMPEs with equal weights (Table 1). Two variations of subduction interface GMPEs are currently under consideration for CanadaSHM7: NGA-Subduction (NGA-Sub; Bozorgnia *et al.*, 2022) and the suite of GMPEs from the 2023 U.S. National Seismic Hazard model for the Cascadia subduction zone, which is also based on GMPEs from the NGA-Sub project (herein referred to as U.S. Geological Survey [USGS] NGA-Sub; Moschetti *et al.*, 2024). The two models differ in the specific choice of composite GMPEs. NGA-Sub consists of four GMPEs with equal weights, and USGS NGA-Sub consists of five GMPEs, where three are assigned a weighting of 0.25 and two are assigned a weighting of 0.125 (Table 1).

We note that here we focus on horizontal ground accelerations only to be consistent with many of the subduction interface GMPEs described earlier, which are mostly based on horizontal records (Table 1). We also note that other GMPEs may be considered for CanadaSHM7, and the choices used herein are not meant to represent the opinions of the CanadaSHM7 working group.

Measured ground-motion values

Allen and Brillon (2015) assessed GMPEs for 56 earthquakes between M_w 4.6 and 7.8 that occurred between 1996 and 2014 offshore from Haida Gwaii. From the 56 events, we identified a single reverse slip earthquake (in addition to the 2012 mainshock) with multiple horizontal weak-motion records that could potentially have occurred on the HGT (Fig. 1). This event was a 2001 M_w 6.1 earthquake with horizontal records at five stations within 500 km that we herein term earthquake 1 (EQ1). We also searched the Natural Resources Canada (NRCan) regional earthquake catalog for additional events, but identified no supplemental reverse earthquakes from between 2014 and 2023 that were sufficiently large ($M_w > 5$), potentially located on the HGT, and recorded on multiple stations. For this study, we used the processed waveform data from Allen and Brillon (2015). The waveform data were initially extracted from the archive of the Canadian National Seismic Network (CNSN) and, for the mainshock, records

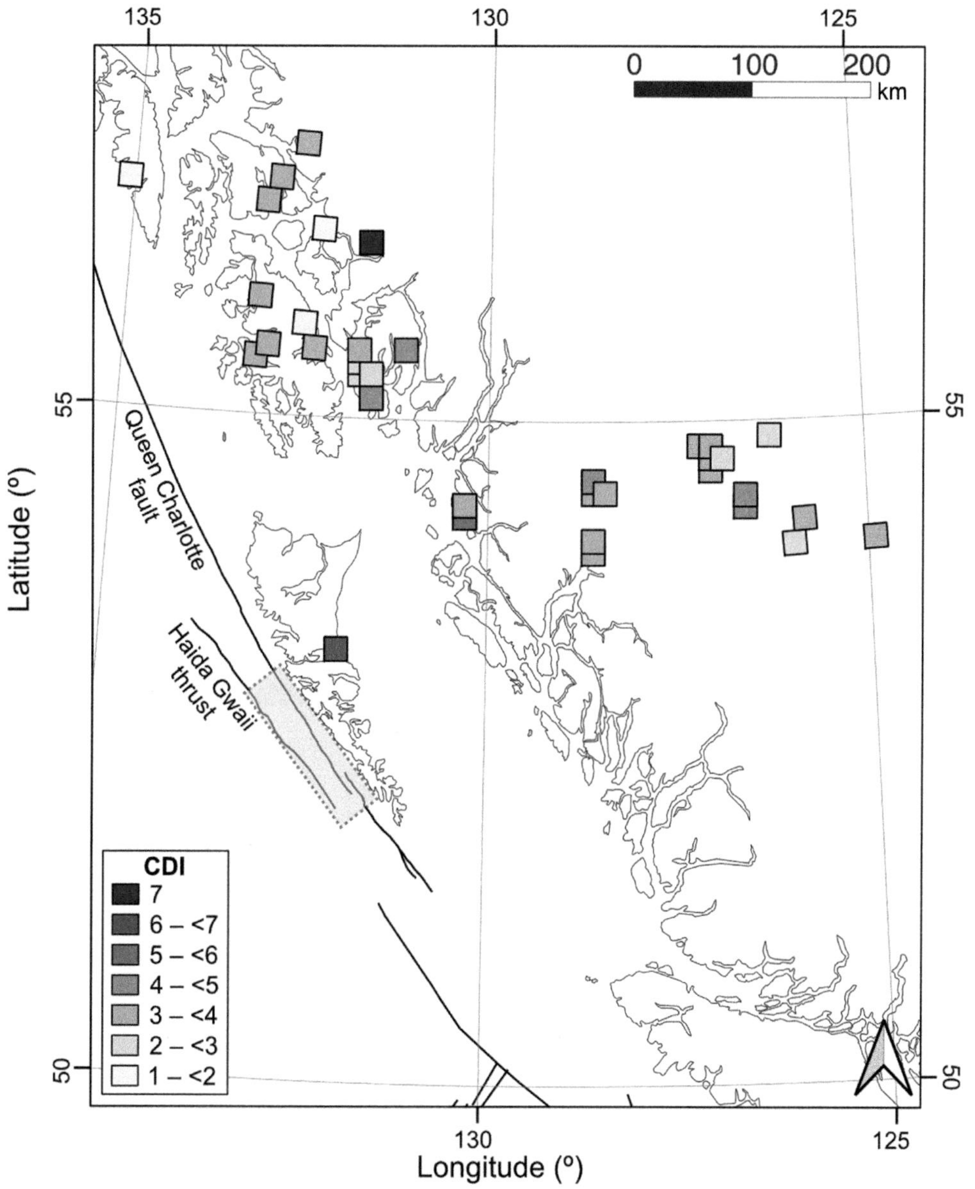

Figure 2. "Did You Feel It?" (DYFI) data from the USGS for the 2012 mainshock. The polygons are shaded by Community Density Intensity (CDI). The large rectangle is the 2012 rupture surface from Nykolaishen *et al.* (2015). The DYFI data are provided in 10 km polygons. For visualization purposes, we have increased the size of the polygons using a 5 km buffer.

from three internet accelerometers were obtained from the British Columbia Ministry of Transportation and Infrastructure Internet Accelerometer network (at the time run by NRCan; Rosenberger *et al.*, 2006). Raw time-series data were corrected for instrument response, and velocity records were baseline corrected and differentiated to acceleration. A full explanation of the data processing approach is included in Allen and Brillon (2015). To compare with the sets of GMPEs and to be consistent with values considered in the Canadian Seismic Risk Model (Hobbs *et al.*, 2023), we used the geometric mean of two-component, horizontal, 5% damped PSAs at 0.3, 0.6, and 1 s.

In situ data to characterize site conditions at the individual stations are not available. Accordingly, we scaled instrumental ground accelerations using the average shear-wave velocity to 30 m depth (V_{S30}) from the location of the stations within the global V_{S30} mosaic from the USGS (Allen and Wald, 2009; Heath *et al.*, 2020). The global V_{S30} compilation is based primarily on topographic slope and has a resolution of 30 arcsec. Ground accelerations were corrected from a reference value of 760 m/s using the equations in Seyhan and Stewart (2014) and a reference peak ground acceleration (PGAr) from Akkar *et al.* (2014).

"Did You Feel It?" data

Reported shaking intensity data are available for the 2012 mainshock from the U.S. Geological Survey (USGS) via their "Did You Feel It?" (DYFI) program (Fig. 2). Shaking intensity is recorded in the aggregated bins as community density intensity (CDI), which is equivalent to modified Mercalli intensity (MMI). The USGS DYFI data are binned in 1 and 10 km aggregated bins, based on UTM coordinates (Fig. 3b; Quitoriano and Wald, 2020). In total for the 2012 mainshock, the USGS received 1043 individual DYFI reports, which are prescribed to 176 aggregated bins of 10 km^2. CDI ranged from 1.0 to 7.9, and the farthest report was 2491 km from the epicenter. We considered DYFI reports within 500 km rupture distance (R_{rup}) from the epicenter to compare with predicted shaking intensities, which amounts to 36 bins including 279 individual reports (Fig. 2).

Modeling and residual analysis

We ran ground motion predictions for all four sets of GMPEs (CanadaSHM6 Active Crust, CanadaSHM6 Subduction, NGA-Sub, USGS NGA-Sub) using the OpenQuake engine version 3.19 (Pagani *et al.*, 2014). For the 2012 M_w 7.8 mainshock (MS in Table 2), we used the fault plane of Nykolaishen

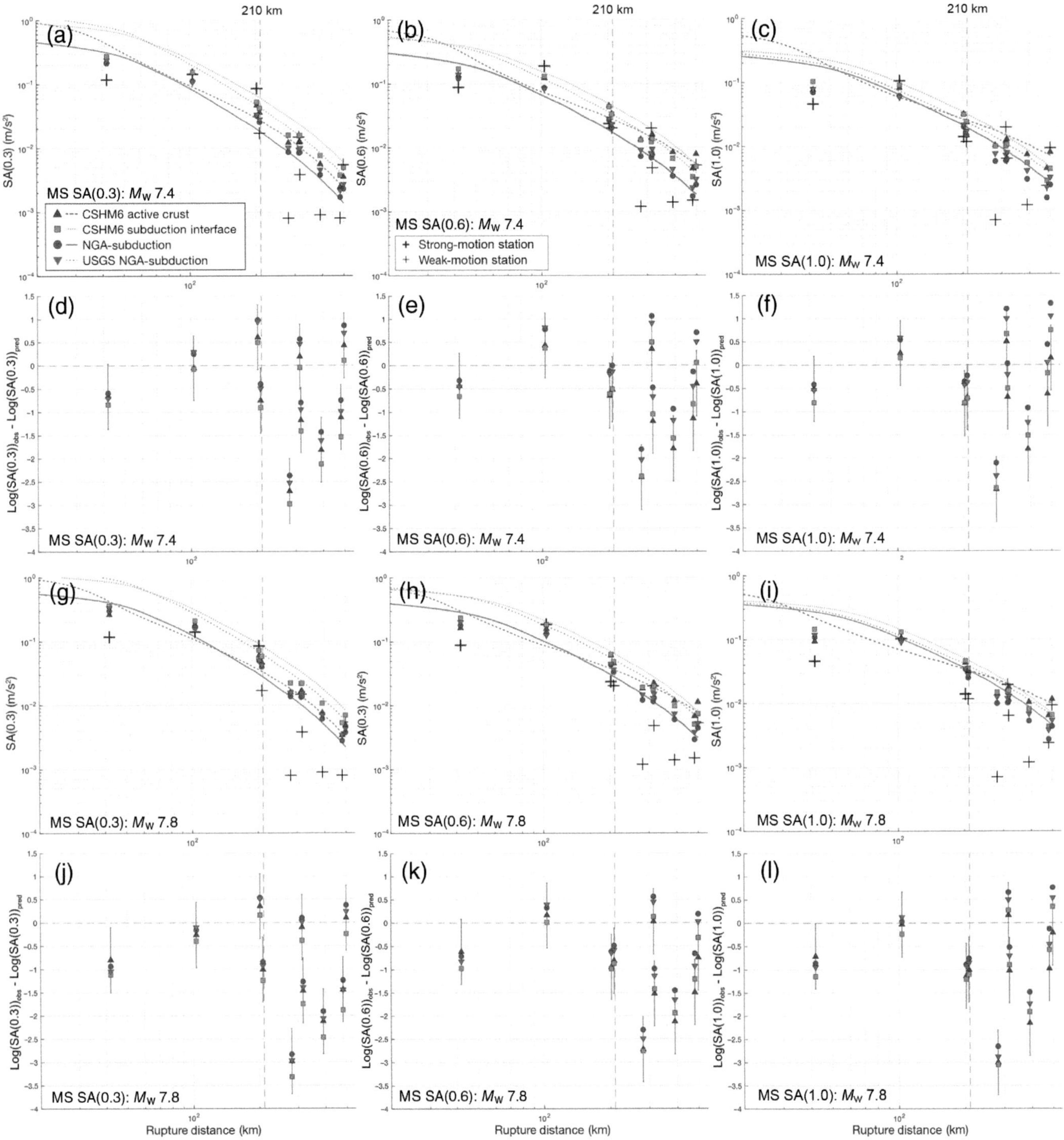

Figure 3. (a–c, g–i) Attenuation of the geometric mean of 5% damped pseudospectral accelerations (PSA) for the 2012 mainshock at periods of (a,g) SA(0.3), (b,h) SA(0.6), and (c,i) SA(1.0). Parts (a) and (b) use M_w 7.4 based on the Natural Resources Canada regional hypocenter (Kao *et al.*, 2015) and (g–i) use M_w 7.8 based on the hypocenter of the USGS (Lay *et al.*, 2013) and the Global Moment Tensor catalog (Ekström *et al.*, 2012). All stations are broadband seismometers. Instrumental data are corrected for site conditions using V_{S30} values from the USGS global V_{S30} compilation and the equations of Seyhan and Stewart (2014), assuming a reference peak ground acceleration from Akkar *et al.* (2014). The curved lines are ground-motion attenuation for the various sets of GMPEs using an average V_{S30} of 760 m/s. These lines are for reference and not used for data analysis. (d–f, j–l) Ground-motion residuals in natural log units of 5% damped PSAs with increasing distance (R_{rup}) for the 2012 Haida Gwaii earthquake at (d,j) SA(0.3), (e,k) SA(0.6), and (f,l) SA(1.0) relative to various sets of GMPEs. The dashed line is zero residual, and the error bars show the average aleatoric uncertainty for the active crust GMPEs from Kolaj *et al.* (2019). All models use the fault rupture plane from Nykolaishen *et al.* (2015). AC, active crust; CSHM6, sixth Generation of Canada Seismic Hazard model; NGA-Sub, Next Generation Attenuation-Subduction model; Sub, subduction interface; and USGS NGA-Sub, USGS interpretation of NGA-Sub equations. The color version of this figure is available only in the electronic edition.

TABLE 2
Earthquake Parameters

EQ ID	Date (yyyy/mm/dd) Origin Time (hh:mm) (UTC)	Latitude	Longitude	Depth (km)	M_w	Strike (°)	Dip (°)	Rake (°)	Strike Alt. (°)	Dip Alt. (°)	Rake Alt. (°)	No. of Stations ≤ 210 km*	No. of Stations ≤ 500 km*	Total Stations
MS CNSN†	2012/10/28 03:04	52.547	−132.243	21.00	7.4	312	17.09	121	99	75.42	81	4	6	10
MS USGS/Lay‡		52.788	−132.101	14.00	7.8	317	18.50	103	–	–	–			
MS Global CMT§		52.940	132.330	12.00	7.8	318	25.00	104	122	66.00	83			
EQ1‖	2001/10/12 05:02	52.629	−132.217	15.17	6.1	330	23.30	128	110	71.80	75	1	3	4

*Distance for station categorization for the mainshock (MS) is rupture distance relative to the surface projection of the fault plane from Nykolaishen *et al.* (2015). Distance for EQ1 is the hypocentral distance. <500 km used all data at rupture distances less than 500 km, including data <210.
†Mainshock hypocenter from Kao *et al.* (2015).
‡Mainshock hypocenter from the U.S. Geological Survey (USGS) with the focal mechanism solution from Lay *et al.* (2013).
§Mainshock from Global Centroid Moment Tensor (Global CMT) catalog (Ekström *et al.*, 2012).
‖Hypocenter location from Oliva *et al.* (2024) with the focal mechanism solutions from Kao *et al.* (2015).

et al. (2015) for the HGT. We computed two estimates of ground motions using either M_w 7.4 based on the NRCan regional moment tensor solution (Kao *et al.*, 2015) or M_w 7.8 consistent with the solutions of the Lay *et al.* (2013) and the Global Centroid Moment Tensor solution (Ekström *et al.*, 2012). For EQ1, we used the moment tensor solution and moment magnitude from the NRCan regional earthquake catalog (Kao *et al.*, 2015) with the relocated hypocentral location from Oliva *et al.* (2024). The ground-motion predictions do not account for directivity effects, which could alter measured ground motions near the source (<50 km) and at periods of 0.6 s or greater (e.g., Somerville *et al.*, 1997).

For each earthquake scenario, we predicted ground motions at the locations of the CNSN stations that recorded the event. At each point, we subtracted the log of modeled ground motion from the log of measured ground motion to calculate natural log residuals. Residuals were plotted against distance for a semi-quantitative assessment of each suite of GMPEs. For predictions of the mainshock ground motions, we used R_{rup} as the distance parameter. We separated results into distance bins of <210 km and <500 km, where 210 km was selected to increase the data in each bin based on R_{rup} of the stations (Table 1). No published rupture model is available for EQ1, so we used hypocentral distance as the distance parameter for this event. To be consistent with the measured ground motions, ground-motion predictions were scaled using V_{S30} values from the Global V_{S30} Mosaic from the USGS (Allen and Wald, 2009; Heath *et al.*, 2020).

For a more quantitative comparison, we performed a likelihood goodness-of-fit test (Scherbaum *et al.*, 2004; Allen and Brillon, 2015) to attempt to rank each suite of GMPEs for CanadaSHM. The likelihood (LH) value represents the likelihood that a given observed ground motion could be modeled by a given GMPE and assumes a normal distribution with unit variance. LH can range between 0 and 1, with values approaching 1 indicating an observation coincides with the mean value from the model. To calculate *LH*, we used the following equation (Scherbaum *et al.*, 2004):

$$\mathrm{LH}(|z|) = \mathrm{erf}\left(\frac{|z|}{\sqrt{2}},\infty\right) = \frac{2}{\sqrt{2\pi}}\int_{|z|}^{\infty} \exp\left(\frac{-z^2}{2}\right)dz, \quad (1)$$

in which z is the ground-motion residual normalized by the standard deviation of the GMPE (in natural log units), and Erf is the error function.

For comparison of the DYFI data with modeled ground motions, we assumed CDI is equivalent to MMI and converted modeled PGA to MMI using the following equation from Worden *et al.* (2012):

$$\mathrm{MMI} = 1.78 + 1.55(\log(\mathrm{PGA})) - 0.91 + 1.02\log(R_{rup}) + 0.17M_w \text{for MMI} \le 4.22, \quad (2)$$

$$\mathrm{MMI} = -1.60 + 3.70(\log(\mathrm{PGA})) - 0.91 + 1.02\log(R_{rup}) + 0.17M_w \text{for MMI} > 4.22, \quad (3)$$

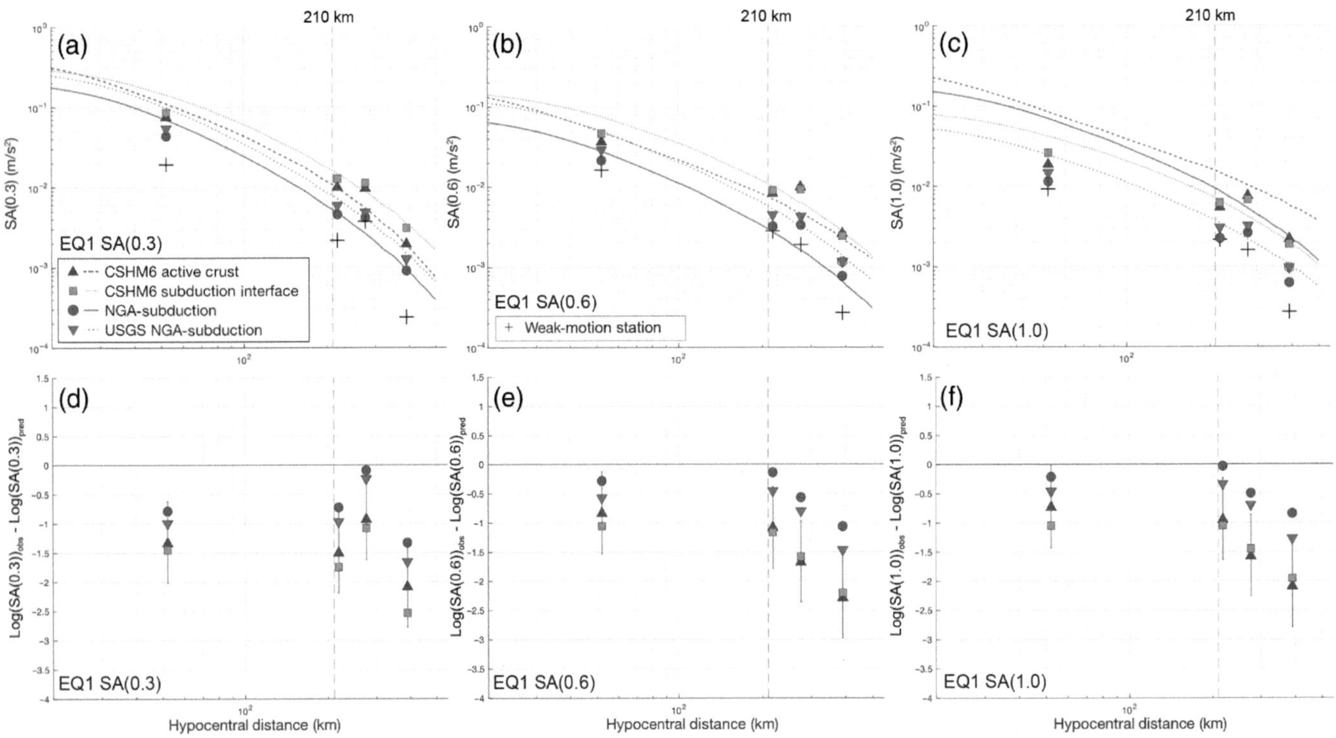

Figure 4. (a–c) Attenuation of the geometric mean of 5% damped PSAs for earthquake 1 (EQ1) at periods of (a) SA(0.3), (b) SA(0.6), and (c) SA(1.0). All stations are broadband seismometers. Instrumental data are corrected for site conditions using V_{S30} values from the USGS global V_{S30} compilation and the equations of Seyhan and Stewart (2014), assuming a reference peak ground acceleration from Akkar *et al.* (2014). The lines are ground-motion attenuation for the various sets of GMPEs using an average V_{S30} of 760 m/s. These lines are for reference and not used for data analysis. (d–f) Ground-motion residuals in natural log units of 5% damped PSA with increasing distance for EQ1 at (d) SA(0.3), (e) SA(0.6), and (f) SA(1.0) relative to various sets of GMPEs. The dashed horizontal line is zero residual, and the error bars show the average aleatoric uncertainty for the active crust GMPEs from Kolaj *et al.* (2019). All models use the regional fault-plane solution from Kao *et al.* (2015) with the location of Oliva *et al.* (2024). AC, active crust; CSHM6, sixth Generation of Canada Seismic Hazard model; NGA-Sub, Next Generation Attenuation-Subduction model; Sub, subduction interface; and USGS NGA-Sub, USGS interpretation of NGA-Sub equations. The color version of this figure is available only in the electronic edition.

in which PGA is measured in centimeters per second square. We predicted ground motions at the center point of the DYFI polygons and calculated residuals by subtracting the predicted CDI from the reported CDI for each bin. We note that the regressions used to derive equations (2) and (3) are based on shallow crustal earthquakes in California (Worden *et al.*, 2012). Therefore, equations (2) and (3) may be better suited to the active crust GMPEs than the subduction interface GMPEs at Haida Gwaii. We note, however, that the magnitude (M_w 3.0–7.0), distance range (up to 400 km), and periods (PGA, SA(0.3), SA(1.0)) of the earthquakes used to derive equations (2) and (3) are similar to the earthquakes used in regressions to derive the various GMPEs used here (Table 1). We also capped modelled CDI at seven because reported shaking intensities become unreliable above CDI VII (Dengler and Dewey, 1998).

RESULTS AND DISCUSSION

The 2012 Haida Gwaii mainshock was recorded by three strong-motion stations and seven weak-motion stations, each with three orthogonal-component records within 500 km rupture distance. EQ1 was recorded by four weak-motion stations, also with three orthogonal-component records, within 500 km of the hypocenter (Table 1). Here, we compare the performance of various GMPE sets against both the horizontal components of ground motions and the shaking intensity data. We begin with a semiquantitative assessment based on mean absolute residuals, followed by a more detailed goodness-of-fit analysis. Key data are presented in Figures 3–5, and complete results for all scenarios are included in Tables 3–5.

Residual analysis

The GMPEs generally overestimate ground shaking, but this is nonsystematic, and several stations have near-zero or positive residuals (Figs. 3 and 4). On average, the GMPEs overpredict instrumental ground motions by a factor of 1.7. However, this average is skewed by data from EQ1, where the overestimation is on average a factor of 2.5 (Fig. 4). For the 2012 mainshock, the GMPEs perform reasonably well (Fig. 3). Assuming a moment magnitude of M_w 7.4 for the mainshock, the GMPEs overestimate ground motions by a factor of only 1.1, on average (Fig. 3a–f). In this case, the NGA-Sub and USGS NGA-Sub

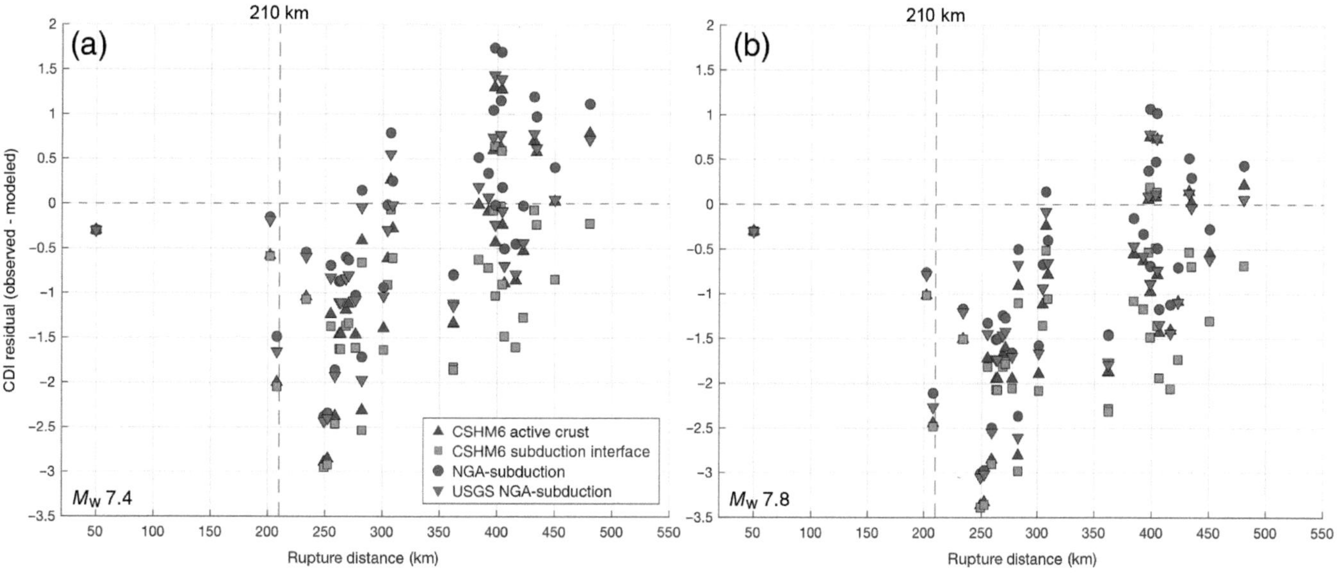

Figure 5. CDI residuals from ground shaking intensity reports from the USGS "Did You Feel It?" (DYFI) data for various sets of GMPEs plotted against rupture distance. (a) CDI residuals for the 2012 mainshock using M_w 7.4 based on the hypocenter from the NRCan regional catalog (Kao *et al.*, 2015). (b) CDI residuals for the 2012 mainshock using M_w 7.8 based on the USGS and Global Centroid Moment Tensor catalogue hypocenters (Lay *et al.*, 2013; Ekström *et al.*, 2012). The dashed horizontal line is zero residual. AC, active crust; CSHM6, sixth Generation of Canada Seismic Hazard model; NGA-Sub, Next Generation Attenuation-Subduction model; Sub, subduction interface; and USGS NGA-Sub, USGS interpretation of NGA-Sub equations. The color version of this figure is available only in the electronic edition.

models slightly underpredict ground motions at longer periods (SA(0.6) and SA(1.0)). Applying M_w 7.8 for the mainshock, the average overestimation increases to a factor of 1.6 (Fig. 3g–l), indicating that M_w 7.4 yields slightly better agreement with observations. Previous analyses for northwest British Columbia found that GMPEs often overestimate ground shaking by a factor of two or more (Allen and Brillon, 2015). However, that analysis potentially included vertical component data. The improved fit seen in our results likely reflects both the exclusion of vertical data and a modified approach to accounting for site response.

Residuals are also generally higher and have greater scatter farther from the rupture (Figs. 3 and 4). The increase in scatter with increasing distance is likely due to varying attenuation effects and several of the constituent GMPEs having a distance range of <500 km (e.g., Bozorgnia *et al.*, 2014; Si *et al.*, 2020). The weak-motion stations on Haida Gwaii did not remain on scale during the 2012 mainshock, and so no stations that experienced wave clipping were included in our analysis. Moreover, the three strong-motion stations were all within 210 km of the rupture plane (Fig. 3), so the increased scatter beyond 210 km also probably results from our reliance on weak-motion data at large distances from the rupture.

The average aleatoric uncertainty (sigma) associated with both the active crust and subduction interface sets of GMPEs from CanadaSHM6 is ~0.7 natural log units for SA(0.3), SA(0.6), and SA(1.0) (Kolaj *et al.*, 2019). The sigma for the active crust GMPEs is plotted as gray bars on Figures 3 and 4. To further highlight the performance of the GMPEs relative to the instrumental recordings, the predicted values for the active crust GMPEs overlap with zero residual in roughly half of the data points for the mainshock (Fig. 3). Residuals for the NGA-Sub and USGS NGA-Sub GMPEs are generally lower than for the CanadaSHM6 GMPEs but, in most cases, the average residual for the subduction interface GMPEs fall within the sigma of the active crust GMPEs (Table 3; Fig. 3). The only exceptions are for EQ1 at SA(0.6) and SA(1.0) where the NGA-Sub GMPEs are ~1 log unit lower than the active crust GMPEs (Table 3; Fig. 4). We note, however, that we do not have average aleatoric uncertainty data for the NGA-Sub and USGS NGA-Sub GMPEs.

In reality, we cannot confirm that EQ1 occurred on the HGT. Although the hypocentral location and preferred strike 330)°), dip (23°), and rake (128°) have similar kinematics to the mainshock (Table 2), the alternative fault-plane solution (strike: 110°, dip: 72°, and rake: 75°) indicates that this event could possibly have occurred on steeply seaward-dipping reverse faults within the Queen Charlotte terrace (Riedel *et al.*, 2021). Nevertheless, because the preferred fault-plane solution is broadly consistent with the mainshock and the results in terms of relative performance of log residuals and attenuation are similar to the results for the mainshock (Figs. 3 and 4), we feel it is justified to assume that this event occurred on the HGT and include it in our analysis.

Did-You-Feel-It? data

The results of the comparative analysis using DYFI data for the 2012 mainshock generally agree with the results from the

TABLE 3

Residuals from Ground-Motion Analysis, in Mean Absolute Residuals (MAR) of Ground Accelerations in Natural Log Units

Model	Tectonic Regime	Moment Magnitude (M_w)*	MAR SA(0.3) ≤210 km†	MAR SA(0.3) ≤500 km†	MAR SA(0.6) ≤210 km†	MAR SA(0.6) ≤500 km†	MAR SA(1.0) ≤210 km†	MAR SA(1.0) ≤500 km†
Mainshock								
CanadaSHM6	AC	7.4	0.52	0.95	0.51	0.93	0.57	0.88
CanadaSHM6	SI	7.4	0.58	1.05	0.54	0.85	0.62	0.88
NGA-Sub	SI	7.4	0.55	0.90	0.31	0.64	0.39	0.76
USGS NGA-Sub	SI	7.4	0.61	0.97	0.40	0.74	0.48	0.79
CanadaSHM6	AC	7.8	0.61	1.06	0.64	1.12	0.72	1.04
CanadaSHM6	SI	7.8	0.73	1.30	0.71	1.06	0.92	1.08
NGA-Sub	SI	7.8	0.62	1.02	0.54	0.83	0.64	0.88
USGS NGA-Sub	SI	7.8	0.65	1.07	0.61	0.91	0.71	0.97
EQ 1								
CanadaSHM6	AC	6.1	1.32	1.45	0.82	1.46	0.73	1.33
CanadaSHM6	SI	6.1	1.45	1.70	1.05	1.50	1.05	1.37
NGA-Sub	SI	6.1	0.78	0.77	0.28	0.49	0.22	0.37
USGS NGA-Sub	SI	6.1	1.00	0.97	0.57	0.82	0.46	0.69

First column acronyms: CanadaSHM6, sixth Generation of the Canada Seismic Hazard model; NGA-Sub, Next Generation Attenuation-Subduction model; USGS NGA-Sub, U.S. Geological Survey interpretation of NGA-Sub equations.
The second column acrnoyms: AC, active crust; and SI, subduction interface.
*For the mainshock, all results use the fault model from Nykolaishen *et al.* (2015). The moment magnitude (M_w) of 7.4 is based on the Natural Resources Canada regional earthquake catalog and M_w 7.8 is based on the solutions from both the Global Centroid Moment Tensor catalog and the USGS. Earthquake 1 is based on hypocentral locations from Oliva *et al.* (2024) and magnitude and fault-plane solutions from Kao *et al.* (2015).
†Distance for the mainshock is rupture distance based on the rupture plane of Nykolaishen *et al.* (2015), and distance for EQ1 is hypocentral distance. <500 km used all data at rupture distances less than 500 km, including data <210.

TABLE 4

Residuals from the "Did You Feel It?" Analysis of Mean Absolute Residuals (MAR) of Community Density Intensity

Model	Tectonic Regime	Moment Magnitude (M_w)*	Average MAR < 210 km†	Average MAR < 500 km†	LH Score
CanadaSHM6	AC	7.4	0.96	1.02	0.41
CanadaSHM6	SI	7.4	0.98	1.16	0.11
NGA-Sub	SI	7.4	0.65	0.85	0.68
USGS NGA-Sub	SI	7.4	0.71	0.85	0.51
CanadaSHM6	AC	7.8	1.25	1.29	0.20
CanadaSHM6	SI	7.8	1.27	1.54	0.01
NGA-Sub	SI	7.8	1.06	1.08	0.27
USGS NGA-Sub	SI	7.8	1.11	1.16	0.20

First column acronyms: CanadaSHM6, sixth Generation of Canada Seismic Hazard model; NGA-Sub, Next Generation Attenuation-Subduction model; and USGS NGA-Sub, U.S. Geological Survey interpretation of NGA-Sub equations.
The second column acronyms: AC, active crust; and SI, subduction interface.
*All results use the fault model from Nykolaishen *et al.* (2015). The moment magnitude (M_w) of 7.4 is based on the Natural Resources Canada regional earthquake catalog and M_w 7.8 is based on the solutions from both the Global Centroid Moment Tensor catalog and the USGS.
†Distance is rupture distance. <500 km used all data at rupture distances less than 500 km, including data <210.

instrumental recordings (Fig. 5; Table 4). Most of the CDI bins are between 210 and 500 km rupture distance (32/36 total bins). At rupture distances <300 km the predicted CDI results generally overestimate reported shaking intensity values by 0.5–2.5 CDI units using both M_w 7.4 and 7.8 for the mainshock (Fig. 5). Beyond 300 km rupture distance, the predicted CDI values overestimate and underestimate reported shaking intensities by ± 1.5 CDI unit (Fig. 5). Using M_w 7.8 for the mainshock results in slightly higher average CDI residuals than using M_w 7.4 (1.3 versus 1.0 CDI units, respectively). Like the ground-motion analysis, the NGA-Sub and USGS NGA-Sub GMPEs perform slightly better than the active crust GMPEs, but only by 0.1–0.2 CDI units. The standard deviation of the CDI residuals for most GMPEs is ~1 CDI unit, so this small decrease in performance for the active crust GMPEs is well within the overall uncertainty.

Goodness-of-fit analysis

We calculated median LH scores for each set of GMPEs from the ground-motion analysis using various earthquake scenarios

TABLE 5
LH Values from Ground-Motion Analysis

Model	Tectonic Regime	LH Score SA(0.3)	LH Score SA(0.6)	LH Score SA(1.0)
M_w 7.4 for MS and EQ1*				
CanadaSHM6_AC	AC	0.20	0.14	0.12
CanadaSHM6_Sub	SI	0.19	0.16	0.20
NGA_Sub	SI	0.24	0.37	0.40
USGS_NGA_Sub	SI	0.23	0.21	0.25
M_w 7.8 for MS and EQ1*				
CanadaSHM6_AC	AC	0.22	0.13	0.19
CanadaSHM6_Sub	SI	0.18	0.18	0.25
NGA_Sub	SI	0.25	0.28	0.33
USGS_NGA_Sub	SI	0.22	0.27	0.31
MS only with M_w 7.4*				
CanadaSHM6_AC	AC	0.24	0.18	0.29
CanadaSHM6_Sub	SI	0.20	0.25	0.40
NGA_Sub	SI	0.18	0.33	0.41
USGS_NGA_Sub	SI	0.23	0.24	0.37
MS only with M_w 7.8*				
CanadaSHM6_AC	AC	0.23	0.09	0.23
CanadaSHM6_Sub	SI	0.22	0.17	0.37
NGA_Sub	SI	0.24	0.27	0.41
USGS_NGA_Sub	SI	0.19	0.28	0.40
EQ1*				
CanadaSHM6_AC	AC	0.32	0.14	0.11
CanadaSHM6_Sub	SI	0.20	0.17	0.17
NGA_Sub	SI	0.43	0.39	0.43
USGS_NGA_Sub	SI	0.41	0.35	0.37

First column acronyms: CanadaSHM6, sixth Generation of Canada Seismic Hazard model; MS, Mainshock; NGA-Sub, Next Generation Attenuation-Subduction model; USGS NGA-Sub, U.S. Geological Survey interpretation of NGA-Sub equations.
The second column acronyms: AC, active crust; and SI, subduction interface.
*For the mainshock, all results use the fault model from Nykolaishen *et al.* (2015). The moment magnitude (M_w) of 7.4 is based on the Natural Resource Canada regional earthquake catalog, and M_w 7.8 is based on the solutions from both the Global Centroid Moment Tensor catalog and the USGS. EQ1 is based on hypocentral location from Oliva *et al.* (2024) and magnitude and fault-plane solution from Kao *et al.* (2015).

(i.e., combinations of different earthquakes: Table 5). A median LH score approaching 0.5 suggests that the model's predicted mean and variance align closely with the observed data, indicating a good fit. Because of limited data at distances <210 km, we are unable to calculate reliable median LH scores in that range. However, when considering all available data, median LH scores are all below 0.5, indicating that the GMPEs generally overpredict ground motions relative to observations, consistent with the semiquantitative analysis above (Table 5). At SA(0.3), median LH scores typically fall between 0.20 and 0.25, with little distinction between active crust and subduction interface GMPEs. At SA(0.6), the NGA-Sub and USGS-NGA-Sub GMPEs perform moderately well, with median LH scores approaching 0.3, whereas the active crust GMPEs perform less favorably, yielding values between 0.09 and 0.18 (Table 5). Performance improves further for the NGA-Sub and USGS-NGA-Sub GMPEs at SA(1.0), where median LH scores reach around 0.4. In contrast, the active crust GMPEs continue to perform relatively poorly, with median LH scores ranging from 0.12 to 0.29 (Table 5).

The LH scores for the DYFI data do not record a decrease in performance for the active crust GMPEs. Using M_w 7.4 for the mainshock returns high median LH scores for the active crust (LH score: 0.41), NGA-Sub (0.68), and USGS NGA-Sub (0.51) GMPEs (Table 4). With M_w 7.8 for the mainshock, median LH scores are between 0.20 and 0.27 for the three aforementioned GMPEs, indicating an overall overprediction of shaking intensity. The subduction interface GMPEs from CanadaSHM6 perform poorly for both M_w 7.4 (0.11) and M_w 7.8 (0.01), with low median LH scores indicating large overprediction of shaking intensity (Table 4).

Overall suitability of GMPEs at Haida Gwaii

The GMPEs show a reasonable fit to instrumentally recorded, horizontal, ground motions, albeit with some scatter beyond >210 km. For roughly half of the data points for the mainshock, the predicted ground motions for the active crust GMPEs overlap within the aleatoric uncertainty with the zero-log residual line. This is an important finding for seismic hazard analysis in northwestern British Columbia because it suggests that applying either subduction interface or active crust GMPEs in hazard models may produce realistic forecasts. We caveat this finding by noting that our approach is slightly restricted because we only have horizontal records from two events on the HGT, so we cannot quantify or assess intra-event variability. For the most part, log residuals for the subduction interface GMPEs overlap within the aleatoric uncertainty of the active crust GMPEs. By contrast, the goodness-of-fit analysis indicates a slightly better relative performance of the NGA-Sub and USGS NGA-Sub GMPEs compared to the active crust GMPEs, especially at longer periods. However, the goodness-of-fit analysis is somewhat limited by the sparsity of data for the HGT, particularly for the instrumental data. In summary, given the large aleatoric uncertainty associated with the active crust GMPEs and the small number of horizontal records available for the HGT, it is difficult to assign a tectonic designation for the HGT based on ground-motion analysis alone. The comparison could be improved with more three-component strong-motion stations on Haida Gwaii to record future reverse earthquakes and/or regionally calibrated ground-motion models for use in hazard assessment.

DESIGNATION OF THE HAIDA GWAII THRUST IN THE CANADASHM

In light of the uncertainty associated with the ground-motion analysis described earlier and to guide future seismic hazard analyses in northwest British Columbia, we now discuss the results in context, reviewing the evidence for and against underthrusting presented in the Tectonic Setting section.

A key argument against subduction is the near-vertical nature of the QCF, which is thought to act as an efficient backstop that facilitates internal deformation in the oceanic plate (e.g., Rohr *et al.*, 2000; Brothers *et al.*, 2020). The QCF appears subvertical north of 53.2° based on the fault-plane solutions for the 1949 M_w 8.1 earthquake (dip 82°; Rogers, 1983) and the 2013 M_w 7.5 Craig earthquake (dip 75°: Lay *et al.*, 2013; Fig. 6a), in addition to seismic reflection profiles from the Dixon Entrance (Rohr *et al.*, 2000). However, south of 53.2°, the geomorphology of the QCF is complex (Barrie *et al.*, 2013; Rohr, 2015; Brothers *et al.*, 2020; Oliva *et al.*, 2024). In this area, an east–west elongate patch of seismicity exists between 10 and 20 km depth and immediately east of the QCF (Fig. 6c). We propose two possible interpretations for this patch of seismicity. First, the seismicity could be occurring on the base of the QCF (Fig. 6d). In this case, matching the seismicity at depth with the surface trace of the fault would result in a listric or eastward-dipping QCF, which is inconsistent with the vertical backstop implied to the north. In the alternative interpretation, the seismicity between 10 and 20 km depth records down-dip aftershocks due to stress interactions on the underthrust slab toward the base of the 2012 rupture plane (Lay *et al.*, 2013; Oliva *et al.*, 2024; Brandl *et al.*, 2025). In this model, a vertical QCF would be undercut by the subducting Pacific plate at ~12 km depth (Fig. 6e). Neither model is consistent with a vertical QCF acting as a clean break between the Pacific and North American plates offshore of Moresby Island. Although, we note that the patches of seismicity east and west of the QCF in Figure 6 are consistent with active deformation of both the Pacific and North American plates as suggested by Rohr *et al.* (2000). However, such deformation would be expected in the fore-arc of a subduction zone, so seismicity east and west of the QCF is not discriminatory between the models. In addition, vertical faults hosting strike-slip motion often accommodate strain partitioning in oblique subduction zones (Jarrard, 1986). Examples of this can be found in Sumatra (Sieh and Natawidjaja, 2000), Costa Rica (Hobbs *et al.*, 2019), and Ecuador (Alvarado *et al.*, 2016).

The low obliquity of 7.4° ± 7.1° for the southern QCF south of 53.2° measured between the QCF strike and Pacific–North American plate motion is a compelling observation that favors an active crustal model because the convergence angle is potentially too low to initiate subduction (Brothers *et al.*, 2020). Nevertheless, the uncertainty in the obliquity values quoted for the southern QCF allows for up to 14.5°, and the obliquity values in the region of the Nykolaishen *et al.* (2015) rupture plane approach 15° (Brothers *et al.*, 2020). These values may still be too low to initiate subduction (e.g., McClay *et al*, 2004), although it has been argued that the elastic properties of the crust beneath Haida Gwaii may act to decrease the obliquity threshold required for subduction initiation (ten Brink *et al.*, 2018).

Some of the most compelling data arguing for underthrusting along the HGT comes from seismicity data and receiver functions. The low-velocity zone identified in receiver functions beneath Haida Gwaii (Smith *et al.*, 2003; Bustin *et al.*, 2007; Gosselin *et al.*, 2015) is consistent with the down-dip projection of the thrust (Nykolaishen *et al.*, 2015), and also roughly aligns with the patch of seismicity between 10 and 20 km depth and landward of the QCF surface trace (Fig. 6c; Oliva *et al.*, 2024). Furthermore, two small clusters of seismicity beneath Haida Gwaii at depths between 15 and 20 km (C2 and C3 in Fig. 6c) are consistent with the geometry of an underthrust Pacific plate (Oliva *et al.*, 2024; Brandl *et al.*, 2025). Another simple observation in support of the subduction interface model is the large magnitude of the 2012 earthquake. Using standard regressions (e.g., Wells and Coppersmith, 1994), an M_w 7.8 earthquake requires a well-developed fault plane approaching 4500 km^2, consistent with the size of fault planes suggested by finite fault models and GPS inversion (Lay *et al.*, 2013; Nykolaishen *et al.*, 2015). A fault plane of this size would have to project landward of the QCF surface trace and undercut the QCF at depth, like the subduction interface example in Figure 6e. We note, however, that if the 2012 Haida Gwaii earthquake was M_w 7.4, as suggested by the regional catalog, the fault plane could be confined seaward of the QCF surface trace (Fig. 6d).

Considering the above, we favor a model with limited incipient subduction (or underthrusting) beneath Haida Gwaii (e.g., Hyndman, 2015; Oliva *et al.*, 2024; Brandl *et al.*, 2025). Clearly, the HGT is not a mature subduction zone, but the seismicity data, receiver functions, and interpretations

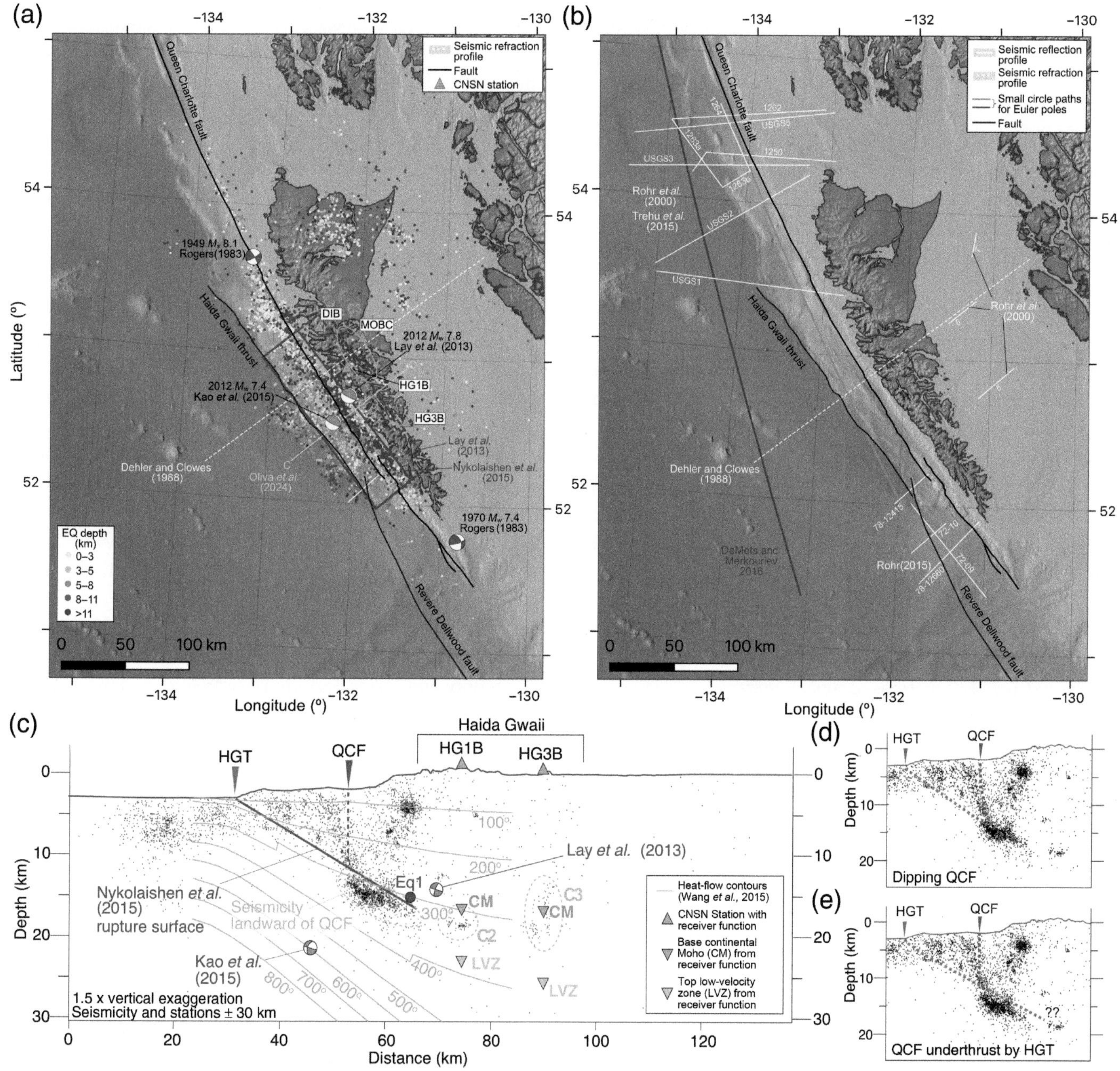

Figure 6. (a) Summary of seismicity and receiver function data used to argue in favor of underthrusting along the Haida Gwaii thrust (HGT). The blue box shows the rupture plane from Nykolaishen *et al.* (2015). Colored dots are relocated seismicity from 1995 to 2020 from Oliva *et al.* (2024). The white-dashed line is the line of a seismic refraction study (Dehler and Clowes, 1988). C–C′ is the line of the cross-section in panel (c), and C2 and C3 refer to clusters of seismicity identified in Oliva *et al.* (2024), also shown in panel (c). The red focal mechanism plots are historical large magnitude (>M_w 7) historical seismicity on the Queen Charlotte fault (QCF), and green focal mechanism plots are interpretations of the 2012 Haida Gwaii earthquake. (b) Seismic reflection data used to argue for an active crust model for the HGT. The purple and green lines show two interpretations of small circle paths of plate motion, which are used to characterize the angle of relative Pacific–North American plate motion relative to the strike of major faults. (c) Cross-section with geophysical data beneath southern Haida Gwaii adapted from Oliva *et al.* (2024). The black dots are relocated seismicity from Oliva *et al.* (2024) projected onto the line of section from within 30 km. The red dashed line denotes a vertical QCF. The orange dashed ellipses are deep seismicity clusters C2 and C3 from Oliva *et al.* (2024). Receiver function data from Gosselin *et al.* (2015). (d) Schematic interpretation of the active crustal model. (e) Schematic interpretation for the subduction interface model. The color version of this figure is available only in the electronic edition.

of seismic reflection data from the Queen Charlotte terrace appear to provide evidence for some underthrusting of the Pacific plate in the area of the HGT. Crucially, these observations are based on in situ data from beneath Haida Gwaii, in the area of the 2012 Haida Gwaii earthquake, and the location of the HGT (Fig. 6). Gravity data and a seismic refraction profile across central Haida Gwaii (Dehler and Clowes, 1988) have been used to argue both for (e.g., Hyndman, 2015) and against underthrusting (e.g., Rohr *et al.*, 2000). Therefore, the remaining primary data for studies arguing for crustal thickening without underthrusting are located in the Dixon entrance (Fig. 6b; e.g., Prims *et al.*, 1997; Rohr *et al.*, 2000; Tréhu *et al.*, 2015). Although with limited underthrusting (e.g., tens of kilometers), the HGT could be viewed as either a large crustal fault or an incipient subduction zone, and this transient nature is in keeping with the similarity in results for the active crustal GMPEs versus the subduction interface GMPEs.

Previous work arguing for the active crust model provides good constraints on the extent of underthrusting, with little evidence for underthrusting north of Haida Gwaii (Rohr *et al.*, 2000; Tréhu *et al.*, 2015). Likewise, subduction may have been occurring along the southward extension of the QCF between southern Haida Gwaii and Vancouver Island before 6 Ma, but subsequent plate reorganization caused the QCF to retreat northward (Davis and Riddihough, 1982; Rohr and Furlong, 1995; Hyndman, 2015). Although obliquity increases south of Haida Gwaii, there is no thought to be active subduction south of southern Haida Gwaii (Rohr and Tryon, 2010). In this area, convergence is accommodated by a trans-tensional stepover resulting in leaky-transform tectonics (Littel *et al.*, 2023). Any potential underthrusting probably has its southern limit at ~52° N, where strain is transferred to the Revere Dellwood fault (Rohr, 2015). This leaves an ~180 km section from ~52.0° to 53.2° N where incipient underthrusting may be occurring, approximately coincident with the rupture plane of the 2012 mainshock (Lay *et al.*, 2013; Nykolaishen *et al.*, 2015) and in the area of seismicity, receiver function, and seismic reflection studies (Smith *et al.*, 2003; Bustin *et al.*, 2007; Gosselin *et al.*, 2015; Oliva *et al.*, 2024).

We choose to advocate for the designation of the HGT as a subduction interface in future versions of CanadaSHM. Although the ground-motion analysis does not allow us to assign a tectonic designation, a subduction interface designation is consistent with previous versions of the Canadian Seismic hazard models (e.g., Rosenberger *et al.*, 2013; Kolaj *et al.*, 2019, 2020) and with the proposed limited underthrusting beneath Haida Gwaii from recent literature (e.g., Oliva *et al.*, 2024; Brandl *et al.*, 2025). A subduction interface designation is also conservative, given that recently revised fragility functions indicate a substantially higher risk to local infrastructure if the HGT is modeled as a subduction interface fault (Abraham, 2023). Important next steps will be to better constrain the geometry of the HGT and assign an appropriate maximum magnitude to better understand the hazard and risk posed to communities in northwestern British Columbia.

CONCLUSION

To improve future and existing seismic hazard models along the northwestern margin of British Columbia, we compared instrumental ground motions to modelled ground motions using recently developed sets of GMPEs from CanadaSHM6 and those under consideration for future versions of CanadaSHM. Supplemented by shaking intensity data and a review of recent literature on the tectonics beneath Haida Gwaii, the goal was to provide a tectonic designation for the Haida Gwaii thrust, the source of the 2012 M_w 7.8 Haida Gwaii earthquake, in future versions of the CanadaSHM. We examined instrumental ground-motion data and shaking intensity reports for the Haida Gwaii earthquake and ground motions for another reverse-slip earthquake with a moment tensor solution that likely occurred on the Haida Gwaii thrust. The results of a semiquantitative residual analysis and a goodness-of-fit analysis show that the various GMPEs do a decent job of predicting horizontal ground motions, especially for the 2012 mainshock. GMPEs overestimate horizontal ground shaking for the Haida Gwaii earthquake by a factor of just 1.1, on average, if M_w 7.4 is applied for the mainshock and by a factor of 1.6, on average, if M_w 7.8 is applied. Moreover, predicted ground-motion residuals overlap with the zero-residual line within the large aleatoric uncertainty of the active crust GMPEs for roughly half the data, with some predictable scatter at distances beyond 210 km.

Unfortunately, due to insufficient data to assess intra-event uncertainty and large aleatoric uncertainty, we cannot speculate on whether an active crust or subduction interface designation is more appropriate for the HGT on ground-motion analysis alone. We therefore augmented the ground-motion analysis with a literature review on the tectonics of the HGT. We note that evidence from seismicity and receiver functions from stations on Haida Gwaii points to some incipient underthrusting. Most recent studies that argue against subduction are based on primary data from north and south of the HGT. These studies provide potential bounds on the spatial extent of underthrusting, which appears limited to a ~180 km long section roughly coincident with the rupture plane for the 2012 Haida Gwaii earthquake. For consistency, we advocate that the Haida Gwaii thrust remain treated as a subduction interface in current and future versions of CanadaSHM, but note that using an active crust designation would not significantly alter the resulting ground-motion estimates.

DATA AND RESOURCES

The V_{S30} maps used in this study are available from the U.S. Geological Survey at https://earthquake.usgs.gov/data/vs30/ along with the Did-You-Feel-It? data at https://earthquake.usgs.gov/earthquakes/search/. OpenQuake is available to download from the Global Earthquake Model Foundation at https://docs.openquake.org/oq-engine/3.19/manual/getting-started/installation-instructions/index.html. The weak-motion instrumental data are available to download from the International Federation of Digital Seismograph Networks at https://www.fdsn.org/networks/. The strong-motion records for the 2012 mainshock will be made publicly available at https://geo.ca and/or the original publication (Allen and Brillon, 2015). All sites were last accessed in June 2025. The supplemental material includes one additional table with the V_{S30} values applied for each station in the study.

DECLARATION OF COMPETING INTERESTS

The authors acknowledge that there are no conflicts of interest recorded.

ACKNOWLEDGMENTS

The authors are grateful to John Cassidy for constructive comments on the article and to Michael Kolaj for advice on shaking intensity data. This article was significantly improved based up on the thoughtful feedback from Gail Atkinson, an anonymous reviewer, and Associate Editor Aybige Akinci. This work was conducted with funding from the Pacific Rim Ocean Data Mobilization and Technology (PRODIGY) program and the Emergency Management Strategy of Public Safety Canada, through the Geological Survey of Canada.

REFERENCES

Abraham, A. (2023). Effect of subduction ground motions on regional seismic risk assessment in selected localities in British Columbia, Doctoral dissertation, University of British Columbia.

Abrahamson, N., N. Gregor, and K. Addo (2016). BC Hydro ground motion prediction equations for subduction earthquakes, *Earthq. Spectra* **32,** no. 1, 23–44, doi: 10.1193/051712EQS188MR.

Abrahamson, N. A., and Z. Gulerce (2022). Summary of the Abrahamson and Gulerce NGA-SUB ground-motion model for subduction earthquakes, *Earthq. Spectra* **38,** no. 4, 2638–2681.

Abrahamson, N. A., W. J. Silva, and R. Kamai (2014). Summary of the ASK14 ground motion relation for active crustal regions, *Earthq. Spectra* **30,** no. 3, 1025–1055, doi: 10.1193/070913EQS198M.

Adams, J., S. Halchuk, T. Allen, and G. Rogers (2015). Canada's 5th generation seismic hazard model, as prepared for the 2015 National Building Code of Canada, *11th Canadian Conf. on Earthquake Engineering*, 21–24.

Akkar, S., M. A. Sandıkkaya, and J. J. Bommer (2014). Empirical ground-motion models for point-and extended-source crustal earthquake scenarios in Europe and the Middle East, *Bull. Earthq. Eng.* **12,** 359–387.

Allen, T. I., and C. Brillon (2015). Assessment of ground-motion models for use in the British Columbia North Coast region, Canada, *Bull. Seismol. Soc. Am.* **105,** no. 2B, 1193–1205.

Allen, T. I., and D. J. Wald (2009). On the use of high-resolution topographic data as a proxy for seismic site conditions (VS 30), *Bull. Seismol. Soc. Am.* **99,** no. 2A, 935–943.

Alvarado, A., L. Audin, J. M. Nocquet, E. Jaillard, P. Mothes, P. Jarrín, M. Segovia, F. Rolandone, and D. Cisneros (2016). Partitioning of oblique convergence in the Northern Andes subduction zone: Migration history and the present-day boundary of the North Andean Sliver in Ecuador, *Tectonics* **35,** no. 5, 1048–1065.

Atkinson, G. M., and M. Macias (2009). Predicted ground motions for great interface earthquakes in the Cascadia subduction zone, *Bull. Seismol. Soc. Am.* **99,** no. 3, 1552–1578, doi: 10.1785/0120080147.

Barrie, J. V., B. D. Bornhold, K. W. Conway, and J. L. Luternauer (1991). Surficial geology of the northwestern Canadian continental shelf, *Cont. Shelf Res.* **11,** nos. 8/10, 701–715.

Barrie, J. V., K. W. Conway, and P. T. Harris (2013). The Queen Charlotte fault, British Columbia: Seafloor anatomy of a transform fault and its influence on sediment processes, *Geo-Mar. Lett.* **33,** 311–318.

Bérubé, J., G. C. Rogers, R. M. Ellis, and F. O. Hasselgren (1989). A micro- seismicity survey of the Queen Charlotte Islands region, *Can. J. Earth Sci.* **26,** 2556–2566.

Bird, A. L., and M. Lamontagne (2015). Impacts of the October 2012 magnitude 7.8 earthquake near Haida Gwaii, Canada, *Bull. Seismol. Soc. Am.* **105,** no. 2B, 1178–1192.

Boore, D. M., J. P. Stewart, E. Seyhan, and G. M. Atkinson (2014). NGA-West 2 equations for predicting PGA, PGV, and 5%-damped PSA for shallow crustal earthquakes, *Earthq. Spectra* **30,** no. 3, 1057–1085, doi: 10.1193/070113EQS184M.

Bozorgnia, Y., N. A. Abrahamson, S. K. Ahdi, T. D. Ancheta, L. A. Atik, R. J. Archuleta, G. M. Atkinson, D. M. Boore, K. W. Campbell, B. S. J. B. Chiou, and V. Contreras (2022). NGA-Subduction research program, *Earthq. Spectra* **38,** no. 2, 783–798.

Bozorgnia, Y., N. A. Abrahamson, L. Al Atik, T. D. Ancheta, G. M. Atkinson, J. W. Baker, A. Baltay, D. M. Boore, K. W. Campbell, B.S.-J. Chiou, *et al.* (2014). NGA-West2 research project, *Earthq. Spectra* **30,** 973–987.

Brandl, C. C., L. L. Worthington, E. C. Roland, M. A. Walton, M. R. Nedimović, A. C. Gase, O. Adedeji, J. C. Castellanos, B. J. Phrampus, M. G. Bostock, and K. Wang (2025). Seismic imaging reveals a strain-partitioned sliver and nascent megathrust at an incipient subduction zone in the northeast Pacific, *Sci. Adv.* **11,** no. 29, eadt3003.

Brothers, D. S., N. C. Miller, J. V. Barrie, P. J. Haeussler, H. G. Greene, B. D. Andrews, O. Zielke, J. Watt, and P. Dartnell (2020). Plate boundary localization, slip-rates and rupture segmentation of the Queen Charlotte fault based on submarine tectonic geomorphology, *Earth Planet. Sci. Lett.* **530,** 115,882.

Bustin, A. M. M., R. D. Hyndman, H. Kao, and J. F. Cassidy (2007). Evidence for underthrusting beneath the Queen Charlotte margin, British Columbia, from teleseismic receiver function analysis, *Geophys. J. Int.* **171,** 1198–1211.

Campbell, K. W., and Y. Bozorgnia (2014): NGA-West2 ground motion model for the average horizontal components of PGA, PGV, and 5% damped linear acceleration response spectra, *Earthq. Spectra* **30,** no. 3, 1087–1115.

Cassidy, J., G. C. Rogers, and R. D. Hyndman (2014). An Overview of the 28 October 2012 M_w 7.7 earthquake in Haida Gwaii, Canada: A tsunamigenic thrust event along a predominantly strike-slip margin, *Pure Appl. Geophys.*, doi: 10.1007/s00024-014-0775-1.

Chase, R. L., D. L. Tiffin, and J. W. Murray (1975). The western Canadian continental margin, in Canada's continental margins and offshore petroleum exploration, *AAPG Mem.*, **4,** 701–721.

Chen, Y., and J. W. Morgan (1990). A non-linear rheology model for mid-ocean ridge axis topography, *J. Geophys. Res.* **95,** 17,583–17,604.

Chiou, B.S.-J., and R. R. Youngs (2014). Update of the Chiou and Youngs NGA model for the average horizontal component of peak ground motion and response spectra, *Earthq. Spectra* **30,** no. 3, 1117–1153, doi: 10.1193/072813EQS219M.

Davis, E. E., and R. P. Riddihough (1982). The Winona basin: Structure and tectonics, *Canadian J. Earth Sci.* **19,** 767–788.

Dehler, S. A., and R. M. Clowes (1988). The Queen Charlotte Islands refraction project. Part 1. The Queen Charlotte fault zone, *Can. J. Earth Sci.* **25,** 1857–1870.

DeMets, C., and S. Merkouriev (2016). High-resolution reconstructions of Pacific–North America plate motion: 20 Ma to present, *Geophys. J. Int.* **207,** no. 2, 741–773.

DeMets, C., R. G. Gordon, and D. F. Argus (2010). Geologically current plate motions, *Geophys. J. Int.* **181,** no. 1, 1–80.

Dengler, L. A., and J. W. Dewey (1998). An intensity survey of households affected by the Northridge, California, earthquake of 17 January 1994, *Bull. Seismol. Soc. Am.* **88,** no. 2, 441–462.

Ekström, G., M. Nettles, and A. M. Dziewoński (2012). The Global CMT project 2004–2010: Centroid-moment tensors for 13,017 earthquakes, *Phys. Earth Planet. Int.* **200,** 1–9, doi: 10.1016/j.pepi.2012.04.002.

Ghofrani, H, and G. M. Atkinson (2014). Ground-motion prediction equations for interface earthquakes of M 7 to M 9 based on empirical data from Japan, *Bull. Earthq. Eng.* **12,** 549–571, doi: 10.1007/s10518-013-9533-5.

Gosselin, J. M., J. F. Cassidy, and S. E. Dosso (2015). Shear wave velocity structure in the vicinity of the 2012 M_w 7.8 Haida Gwaii earthquake from receiver function inversions, *Bull. Seismol. Soc. Am.* **105,** no. 2B, doi: 10.1785/0120140171.

Heath, D. C., D. J. Wald, C. B. Worden, E. M. Thompson, and G. M. Smoczyk (2020). A global hybrid V_{S30} map with a topographic slope-based default and regional map insets, *Earthq. Spectra* **36,** no. 3, 1570–1584.

Hobbs, T. E., J. M. Journeay, A. S. Rao, M. Kolaj, L. Martins, P. LeSueur, M. Simionato, V. Silva, M. Pagani, K. Johnson, and D. Rotheram (2023). A national seismic risk model for Canada: Methodology and scientific basis, *Earthq. Spectra* **39,** no. 3, 1410–1434.

Hobbs, T. E., A. V. Newman, and M. Protti (2019). Enigmatic upper-plate sliver transport paused by megathrust earthquake and afterslip, *Earth Planet. Sci. Lett.* **520,** 87–93.

Hyndman, R. D. (2015). Tectonics and structure of the Queen Charlotte fault zone, Haida Gwaii, and large thrust earthquakes, *Bull. Seismol. Soc. Am.* **105,** no. 2B, 1058–1075.

Hyndman, R. D., and T. S. Hamilton (1993). Queen Charlotte area Cenozoic tectonics and volcanism and their association with relative plate motions along the northeastern Pacific margin, *J. Geophys. Res.* **98,** 14,257–14,277.

Jarrard, R. D. (1986). Relations among subduction parameters, *Rev. Geophys.* **24,** no. 2, 217–284.

Kao, H., S. J. Shan, and A. M. Farahbod (2015). Source characteristics of the 2012 Haida Gwaii earthquake sequence, *Bull. Seismol. Soc. Am.* **105,** no. 2B, 1206–1218.

Kolaj, M., J. Adams, and S. Halchuk (2020). The 6th generation seismic hazard model of Canada, *17th World Conf. on Earthquake Engineering*, 1–12.

Kolaj, M., T. Allen, R. Mayfield, J. Adams, and S. Halchuk (2019). Ground-motion models for the 6th Generation Seismic Hazard Model of Canada, *12th Canadian Conf. on Earthquake Engineering.*

Kuehn, N., Y. Bozorgnia, K. Campbell, and N. Gregor (2020). *Partially Non-Ergodic Ground-Motion Model for Subduction Regions Using NGA-Subduction Database, PEER Report 2020/04*, Pacific Earthquake Engineering Research Center, University of California, Berkeley, California.

Lay, T., L. Ye, H. Kanamori, Y. Yamazaki, K. F. Cheung, K. Kwong, and K. D. Koper (2013). The October 28, 2012 M_w 7.8 Haida Gwaii underthrusting earthquake and tsunami: Slip partitioning along the Queen Charlotte fault transpressional plate boundary, *Earth Planet. Sci. Lett.* **375,** 57–70.

Leonard, L. J., and J. M. Bednarski (2014). Field survey following the 28 October 2012 Haida Gwaii tsunami, *Pure Appl. Geophys.* **171,** 3467–3482.

Lewis, P. D., J. W. Haggart, R. G. Anderson, C. J. Hickson, R. I. Thompson, J. R. Dietrich, and K. M. M. Rohr (1991). Triassic to Neogene geologic evolution of the Queen Charlotte region, *Can. J. Earth Sci.* **28,** no. 6, 854–869.

Littel, G. F., M. G. Bostock, A. Schaeffer, and S. Roecker (2023). Microplate evolution in the Queen Charlotte triple junction and explorer region: New insights from microseismicity, *Tectonics* **42,** no. 6, e2022TC007494.

Mackie, D. J., R. M. Clowes, S. A. Dehler, R. M. Ellis, and P. Morel-À-l'Huissier (1989). The Queen Charlotte Islands refraction project. Part II. Structural model for transition from Pacific plate to North American plate, *Can. J. Earth Sci.* **26,** no. 9, 1713–1725.

McClay, K., P. Whitehouse, T. Dooley, and M. Richards (2004). 3D evolution of fold and thrust belts formed by oblique convergence, *Mar. Pet. Geol.* **21,** no. 7, 857–877, doi: 10.1016/j.marpetgeo.2004.03.009.

Moschetti, M. P., B. T. Aagaard, S. K. Ahdi, J. Altekruse, O. S. Boyd, A. D. Frankel, J. Herrick, M. D. Petersen, P. M. Powers, S. Rezaeian, and A. M. Shumway (2024). The 2023 US national seismic hazard model: Ground-motion characterization for the conterminous United States, *Earthq. Spectra* **40,** no. 2, 1158–1190.

Nishenko, S. P., and K. H. Jacob (1990). Seismic potential of the Queen Charlotte-Alaska-Aleutian seismic zone, *J. Geophys. Res.* **95,** no. B3, 2511–2532.

Nykolaishen, L., H. Dragert, K. Wang, T. S. James, and M. Schmidt (2015). GPS observations of crustal deformation associated with the 2012 M_w 7.8 Haida Gwaii earthquake, *Bull. Seismol. Soc. Am.* **105**, no. 2B, 1241–1252.

Oliva, S. J., M. G. Bostock, A. J. Schaeffer, E. Nissen, R. Merrill, A. Hughes, S. W. Roecker, M. R. Nedimovic, E. Roland, L. L. Worthington, and M. A. L. Walton (2024). Incipient subduction and slip partitioning at high obliquity: The Haida Gwaii plate boundary, *J. Geophys. Res.* **129,** no. 5, p.e2024JB028752.

Pagani, M., D. Monelli, G. Weatherill, L. Danciu, H. Crowley, V. Silva, P. Henshaw, L. Butler, M. Nastasi, L. Panzeri, and M. Simionato (2014). OpenQuake engine: An open hazard (and risk) software for the global earthquake model, *Seismol. Res. Lett.* **85,** no. 3, 692–702.

Parker, G. A., J. P. Stewart, D. M. Boore, G. M. Atkinson, and B. Hassani (2022). NGA-subduction global ground motion models with regional adjustment factors, *Earthq. Spectra* **38,** no. 1, 456–493.

Power, M., B. Chiou, N. Abrahamson, Y. Bozorgnia, T. Shantz, and C. Roblee (2008). An overview of the NGA project, *Earthq. Spectra* **24,** no. 1, 3–21.

Prims, J., K. P. Furlong, K. M. M. Rohr, and R. Govers (1997). Lithospheric structure along the Queen Charlotte margin in western Canada: Constraints from flexural modeling, *Geo-Mar. Lett.* **17,** 94–99.

Quitoriano, V., and D. J. Wald (2020). USGS "Did You Feel It?"—Science and lessons from 20 years of citizen science-based macroseismology, *Front. Earth Sci.* **8,** 120.

Riedel, M., S. Yelisetti, C. Papenberg, K. M. M. Rohr, M. M. Côté, G. D. Spence, R. D. Hyndman, and T. James (2021). Seismic velocity structure of the Queen Charlotte terrace off western Canada in the region of the 2012 Haida Gwaii M_w 7.8 thrust earthquake, *Geosphere* **17,** no. 1, 23–38, doi: 10.1130/GES02258.1.

Rogers, G. C. (1983). Seismotectonics of British Columbia, Doctoral dissertation, University of British Columbia, doi: 10.14288/1.0052938.

Rohr, K. M. (2015). Plate boundary adjustments of the southernmost Queen Charlotte fault, *Bull. Seismol. Soc. Am.* **105,** no. 2B, 1076–1089.

Rohr, K. M., and K. P. Furlong (1995). Ephemeral plate tectonics at the Queen Charlotte triple junction, *Geology* **23,** no. 11, 1035–1038.

Rohr, K. M., M. Scheidhauer, and A. M. Trehu (2000). Transpression between two warm mafic plates: The Queen Charlotte fault revisited, *J. Geophys. Res.* **105,** no. B4, 8147–8172.

Rohr, K. M. M., and A. J. Tryon (2010). Pacific-North America plate boundary reorganization in response to a change in relative plate motion: Offshore Canada, *Geochem. Geophys. Geosyst.* **11,** no. 6.

Rosenberger, A., A. Bird, M. E. Turek, S. Huffman, G. Rogers, J. Cassidy, and T. Mulder (2013). Strong motion data from the magnitude 7.7 "Haida Gwaii" earthquake on October 27, 2012 (local time), *Geological Survey of Canada, Open File 7324*, 34 pp.

Rosenberger, A., G. Rogers, and S. Huffman (2006). Real-time ground motion from the new strong motion seismic network in British Columbia, Canada, *First European Conf. on Earthquake Engineering and Seismology*, pp. 3–8.

Scherbaum, F., F. Cotton, and P. Smit (2004). On the use of response spectral-reference data for the selection and ranking of ground-motion models for seismic-hazard analysis in regions of moderate seismicity: The case of rock motion, *Bull. Seismol. Soc. Am.* **94,** no. 6, 2164–2185.

Seyhan, E., and J. P. Stewart (2014). Semi-empirical nonlinear site amplification from NGA-West2 data and simulations, *Earthq. Spectra* **30,** no. 3, 1241–1256.

Si, H., S. Midorikawa, and T. Kishida (2020). *Development of NGA-Sub Ground Motion Model of 5%- Damped Pseudo-Spectral Acceleration Based on Database for Subduction Earthquakes in Japan, PEER Report 2020/06*, Pacific Earthquake Engineering Research Center, University of California, Berkeley, Berkeley, California.

Sieh, K., and D. Natawidjaja (2000). Neotectonics of the Sumatran fault, Indonesia, *J. Geophys. Res.* **105,** no. B12, 28,295–28,326.

Smith, A. J. (1999). Structure, deformation, and thermal regime of the Queen Charlotte Transform margin, Master's Thesis, University of Victoria, Victoria, British Columbia, 179 pp.

Smith, A. J., R. D. Hyndman, J. F. Cassiday, and K. Wang (2003). Structure, seismicity, and thermal regime of the Queen Charlotte Transform margin, *J. Geophys. Res.* **108,** doi: 10.1029/2002JB002247.

Somerville, P. G., N. F. Smith, R. W. Graves, and N. A. Abrahamson (1997). Modification of empirical strong ground motion attenuation relations to include the amplitude and duration effects of rupture directivity, *Seismol. Res. Lett.* **68,** no. 1, 199–222.

Spence, G. D., and D. T. Long (1995). Transition from oceanic to continental crustal structure: Seismic and gravity models at the Queen Charlotte transform margin, *Can. J. Earth Sci.* **32,** 699–717.

ten Brink, U.S., N. C. Miller, B. D. Andrews, D. S. Brothers, and P. J. Haeussler (2018). Deformation of the Pacific/North America plate boundary at Queen Charlotte fault: The possible role of rheology, *J. Geophys. Res.* **123,** no. 5, 4223–4242.

Tréhu, A. M., M. Scheidhauer, K. M. Rohr, B. Tikoff, M. A. Walton, S. P. Gulick, and E. C. Roland (2015). An abrupt transition in the mechanical response of the upper crust to transpression along the Queen Charlotte fault, *Bull. Seismol. Soc. Am.* **105,** 1114–1128.

Walton, M. A., S. P. Gulick, P. J. Haeussler, E. C. Roland, and A. M. Tréhu (2015). Basement and regional structure along strike of the Queen Charlotte fault in the context of modern and historical earthquake ruptures, *Bull. Seismol. Soc. Am.* **105,** no. 2B, 1090–1105.

Wang, K., J. He, F. Schulzeck, R. D. Hyndman, and M. Riedel (2015). Thermal condition of the 27 October 2012 M 7.8 Haida Gwaii subduction earthquake at the obliquely convergent Queen Charlotte margin, *Bull. Seismol. Soc. Am.* **105,** no. 2B, doi: 10.1785/0120140183.

Wells, D. L., and K. J. Coppersmith (1994). New empirical relationships among magnitude, rupture length, rupture width, rupture area, and surface displacement, *Bull. Seismol. Soc. Am.* **84,** no. 4, 974–1002.

Worden, C. B., M. C. Gerstenberger, D. A. Rhoades, and D. J. Wald (2012). Probabilistic relationships between ground-motion parameters and modified Mercalli intensity in California, *Bull. Seismol. Soc. Am.* **102,** no. 1, 204–221.

Yorath, C. J., and R. D. Hyndman (1983). Subsidence and thermal history of Queen Charlotte basin, *Can. J. Earth Science.* **20,** 135–159.

Zhao, J. X., J. Zhang, A. Asano, Y. Ohno, T. Oouchi, T. Takahashi, H. Ogawa, K. Irikura, H. K. Thio, P. G. Somerville, Y. Fukushima, and Y. Fukushima (2006). Attenuation relations of strong ground motion in Japan using site classification based on predominant period, *Bull. Seismol. Soc. Am.* **96,** no. 3, 898–913, doi: 10.1785/0120050122.

Manuscript received 21 March 2025
Published online 26 November 2025

Vertical Ground-Motion Prediction Equation and Vertical-to-Horizontal Spectral Ratios of Peak Ground Acceleration, Peak Ground Velocity, and 5% Damped Response Spectra in Southwest China

Bin Zhang[1,2], Xiaojian Lu*[1,2], Jiamei Liu[3], Mianshui Rong[2,4], Yanxiang Yu[5], and Xiaojun Li[2,4]

ABSTRACT

Using strong ground-motion records from 116 mainshocks with moment magnitude (M_w) ranging from 4.0 to 7.9 in the active tectonic regions of southwest China, a vertical ground-motion prediction equation (V-GMPE) was developed. This V-GMPE estimates the vertical peak ground acceleration (PGA), peak ground velocity (PGV), and 5% damped absolute spectral acceleration (SA) for periods ranging from 0.01 to 8 s for shallow crustal earthquakes. To enable an unbiased estimation of the vertical-to-horizontal (V/H) spectral ratio, this V-GMPE adopts the same functional form as the horizontal GMPE (V-GMPE) developed by Zhang *et al.* (2022). The V-GMPE is effective in predicting the vertical ground motion of earthquakes with M_w between 4.0 and 7.9, considering faulting styles, rupture distance (R_{rup}) ≤ 300 km related to M_w, and sites with V_{S30} values ranging from 140 to 1130 m/s in southwest China. Compared with the horizontal component, the vertical component demonstrates stronger anelastic attenuation. The influence of the nonlinear site response on the V/H spectral ratio is particularly prominent at short periods. When estimating the V/H spectral ratio, equal aleatory variability exists in both the vertical and horizontal components. The V/H spectral ratio in southwest China is significantly influenced by factors such as M_w, R_{rup}, site type, and period. There are also significant regional differences compared with the findings in regions such as the western United States and Taiwan. These factors should be considered when developing a vertical design spectrum suitable for southwest China.

KEY POINTS

- A new vertical ground-motion prediction equation (V-GMPE) that adopts the same functional form as horizontal GMPE in southwest China is developed.
- The proposed V-GMPE is effective in predicting the vertical ground motions of mainshocks in southwest China.
- The vertical-to-horizontal spectral ratio is affected by moment magnitude, rupture distance, site type, and spectral period.

Supplemental Material

INTRODUCTION

Owing to the P-delta effect, when the horizontal displacement reaches a critical value, the overturning moment suddenly increases because of the vertical axial force, which may potentially cause severe damage to engineering structures. Therefore, vertical ground motion is of crucial significance in the earthquake-resistant design of high-rise buildings, long-span bridges, and other engineering structures (Campbell and Bozorgnia, 2003; Kunnath *et al.*, 2008; Gülerce and Abrahamson, 2011;

1. Institute of Earthquake Forecasting, China Earthquake Administration, Beijing, China, https://orcid.org/0000-0003-0466-9193 (BZ); 2. Key Laboratory of Earthquake Forecasting and Risk Assessment, Ministry of Emergency Management, Beijing, China, https://orcid.org/0000-0002-9820-0312 (MR); https://orcid.org/0000-0002-7526-0558 (XL); 3. Institute of Geomechanics, Chinese Academy of Geological Sciences, Beijing, China, https://orcid.org/0000-0003-0543-9867 (JL); 4. Key Laboratory of Urban Security and Disaster Engineering of China Ministry of Education, Beijing University of Technology, Beijing, China; 5. Institute of Geophysics, China Earthquake Administration, Beijing, China, https://orcid.org/0000-0001-7430-8110 (YY)

*Corresponding author: lxj@ief.ac.cn

Cite this article as Zhang, B., X. Lu, J. Liu, M. Rong, Y. Yu, and X. Li (2025). Vertical Ground-Motion Prediction Equation and Vertical-to-Horizontal Spectral Ratios of Peak Ground Acceleration, Peak Ground Velocity, and 5% Damped Response Spectra in Southwest China, *Bull. Seismol. Soc. Am.* **116**, 738–754, doi: 10.1785/0120250063

Akkar *et al.*, 2014; Stewart *et al.*, 2016; Gülerce *et al.*, 2017; Laouami, 2019; Xing and Zhao, 2021; Phung *et al.*, 2022). Studies on destructive earthquakes, such as the 1994 M_w 6.7 Northridge earthquake in California, the 1995 M_w 6.9 Kobe earthquake in Japan, and the 1999 M_w 7.6 Chi-Chi earthquake in Taiwan, indicate that the vertical ground motion in the near-source region of large earthquakes can be equivalent to or exceed the horizontal ground motion (Haji-Soltani *et al.*, 2017). This phenomenon can result in significant damage to engineering structures such as long-span bridges, dams, large oil storage tanks, highways, and nuclear power plants (Papazoglou and Elnashai, 1996; Kunnath *et al.*, 2008; Gülerce and Abrahamson, 2011; Haji-Soltani *et al.*, 2017). An investigation of the 2008 M_w 7.9 Wenchuan earthquake in southwest China revealed that the vertical ground motion had a significant impact on many bridges in mountainous areas (Du *et al.*, 2008). For instance, at the Wolong station, which is close to the earthquake's epicenter, the vertical-to-horizontal (V/H) ratio of peak ground acceleration (PGA) reached 1.18 (Han and Zhou, 2012).

Thus, vertical ground motion must be carefully considered in the seismic design of long-span bridges, dams, large liquid storage tanks, and nuclear power plants. Globally, many seismic design codes globally initially adopted the assumption proposed by Newmark and Hall (1982) that the vertical component of an earthquake is two-thirds of the horizontal component. In China, current seismic design codes typically specify the vertical design ground motion as 0.5–1 times the horizontal design ground motion (Ministry of Transport of the People's Republic of China, 2013; China National Energy Administration, 2015). However, existing studies have demonstrated that the two-thirds rule for the V/H spectral ratio is nonconservative in near-source regions and is excessively conservative in distant-source scenarios (Bommer *et al.*, 2011; Akkar *et al.*, 2014; Bozorgnia and Campbell, 2016a; Stewart *et al.*, 2016).

Currently, the vertical design spectrum is primarily obtained by scaling the horizontal design spectrum, which is derived from probabilistic seismic hazard analysis of the horizontal component, using the V/H spectral ratio. This method preserves the seismic scenario governing the hazards of the horizontal component and ensures alignment between the vertical and horizontal spectra (Phung *et al.*, 2022). The V/H spectral ratio can be determined via two different methods. The first method involves developing ground-motion prediction equations (GMPEs) directly for V/H spectral ratios derived from empirical data (Bommer *et al.*, 2011; Gülerce and Abrahamson, 2011; Akkar *et al.*, 2014; Ramadan *et al.*, 2021; Tan and Hu, 2021). However, the vertical response spectrum obtained by multiplying the horizontal response spectrum by the V/H spectral ratio from such GMPEs does not consistently align with the observed vertical response spectrum (Bozorgnia and Campbell, 2016a). Furthermore, because many applications of V/H spectral ratio GMPEs fail to consider the standard deviation of the V/H spectral ratio, the seismic risk associated with vertical ground motion may be underestimated (Phung *et al.*, 2022). The second method derives the V/H spectral ratio by dividing the vertical ground motion by the median horizontal ground motion, which are obtained from a pair of vertical and horizontal GMPEs (Bozorgnia and Campbell, 2016a; Stewart *et al.*, 2016; Laouami, 2019; Phung *et al.*, 2022). Bozorgnia and Campbell (2016a) demonstrated that the predicted V/H spectral ratio, obtained from corresponding vertical and horizontal GMPEs, is unbiased compared with empirical data.

In recent years, researchers have developed horizontal GMPEs for southwest China using strong-motion records from this region (Li, Zhai, *et al.*, 2020; Zhang *et al.*, 2022). However, research on vertical GMPEs for this region remains limited. Liu *et al.* (2020) developed a vertical GMPE specifically for the 2008 M_w 7.9 Wenchuan earthquake, incorporating geometric attenuation, anelastic attenuation, site effects, and hanging-wall (HW) effects. Xing and Zhao (2021) further advanced a vertical GMPE for southwest China by calibrating models with strong-motion records from local earthquakes in the region and large earthquakes from the Pacific Earthquake Engineering Research Center (PEER) Next Generation Attenuation-West2 (NGA-West2) dataset. Critically, no paired set of horizontal and vertical GMPEs has been developed for southwest China to enable unbiased calculation of the V/H spectral ratio.

Based on 1324 average horizontal ground motions from 70 mainshocks with $4.2 \le M_w \le 7.9$ in southwest China, Zhang *et al.* (2022) developed a horizontal GMPE, hereafter referred to as the ZYLW22 H-GMPE. This H-GMPE incorporates terms for magnitude, distance, HW effect, faulting style, linear and nonlinear site effects, and anelastic attenuation. It was developed to estimate the median and standard deviation of PGA, peak ground velocity (PGV), and 5% damped spectral acceleration (SA) over periods ranging from 0.033 to 8 s. The objective of this study is to develop a vertical GMPE (V-GMPE) for southwest China, adopting the same functional form as the ZYLW22 H-GMPE. This consistency enables the calculation of the V/H spectral ratio, laying the groundwork for constructing a vertical design spectrum tailored to southwest China. The ultimate goal is to effectively mitigate seismic disaster risks for critical infrastructure, such as large-span bridges, dams, highways, and nuclear power plants.

STRONG-MOTION DATASET

We used the same earthquake and record selection criteria as Zhang *et al.* (2022), selecting 1935 vertical strong ground motion records. These records were obtained from 116 mainshocks with moment magnitude (M_w) ranging from 4.0 to 7.9 that occurred in the active tectonic regions of southwest China between 2008 and 2022; all had a rupture distance (R_{rup}) of <300 km. Details of these earthquakes are presented in Figure 1 and Table S1, available in the supplemental material to this article. Finite-fault models for the 12 earthquakes with $5.8 \le M_w \le 7.9$ were sourced from published literature (Zhang *et al.*, 2008, 2014, 2015;

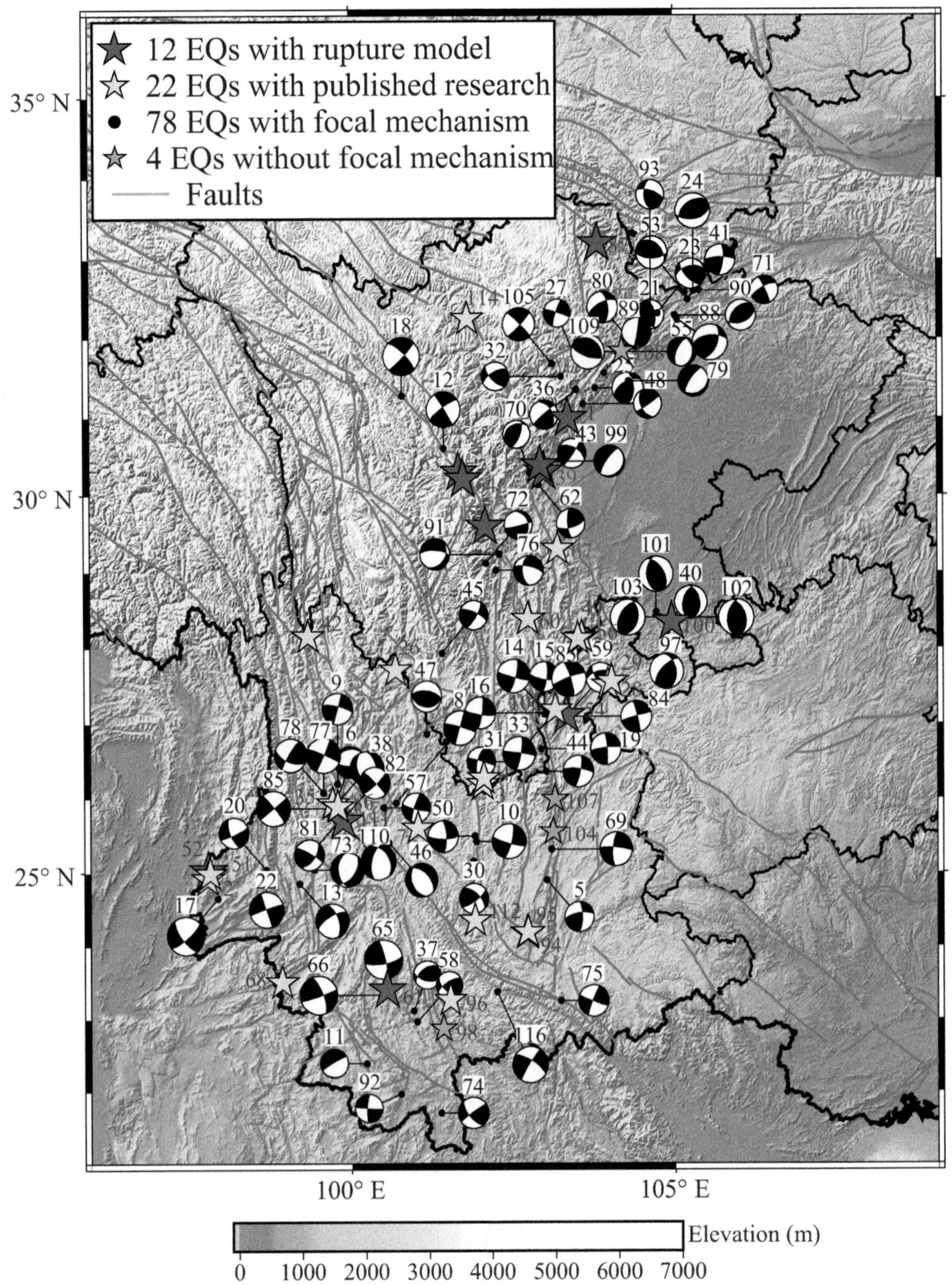

Figure 1. Distribution of the epicenters and faults. The magenta stars indicate 12 earthquakes for $5.8 \le M_w \le 7.9$ that the rupture models have known. The yellow stars indicate 22 earthquakes for $4.6 \le M_w \le 6.0$ that the seismogenic structure, faulting style, and M_w obtained from published and frequently cited research results in China. The black circles indicate 78 earthquakes for $4.0 \le M_w \le 5.6$ with the focal sphere. The cyan stars indicate 4 earthquakes for $4.2 \le M_w \le 4.5$ without the focal sphere. The black focal sphere represents earthquakes with a hypocentral depth of ≤20 km. The color version of this figure is available only in the electronic edition.

Yang *et al.*, 2016; Li *et al.*, 2017; Wang *et al.*, 2020; Zhang, Feng, *et al.*, 2021; Zhang, Xu, *et al.*, 2021; Lu *et al.*, 2022; Zhu *et al.*, 2022; Zhang *et al.*, 2023). For the 22 earthquakes with $4.6 \le M_w \le 6.0$, their seismogenic structure, faulting style, and M_w were obtained from peer-reviewed studies published in Chinese academic journals (Chang *et al.*, 2013; Lv *et al.*, 2013; Qin *et al.*, 2014; Huang, Wu, Jiang, *et al.*, 2015; Huang, Wu, Zhao, *et al.*, 2015; Luo *et al.*, 2015, 2020; Xu *et al.*, 2015; Yi *et al.*, 2016; Shi *et al.*, 2018; Wang *et al.*, 2018; Gong *et al.*, 2019, 2024; Pan *et al.*, 2019; Li, Wan, *et al.*, 2020; Xiao *et al.*, 2020; Song *et al.*, 2022; Fan *et al.*, 2023). For the 24 earthquakes with $4.7 \le M_w \le 5.6$, their M_w and focal mechanisms were obtained from the U.S. Geological Survey (USGS) and the Global Centroid Moment Tensor (Global CMT) project. For the 54 earthquakes with $4.0 \le M_w \le 5.0$, their focal mechanisms were obtained from a comprehensive open-access database (Wang *et al.*, 2025). The strike, dip, and rake angles, along with the geometric dimensions of the fault rupture plane, were determined using the method proposed by Zhang *et al.* (2022). For the 4 remaining earthquakes ($4.2 \le M_w \le 4.5$) that lacked focal mechanism solutions, these events were assumed to be strike-slip earthquakes, with the dip angle set to 90° and the rake angle set to 180°; they were treated as point sources. A simple classification of faulting style was performed based on the rake angle (Boore *et al.*, 1997). Hypocentral depths of all earthquakes were uniformly derived from the China Seismic Network Center.

Low-frequency errors primarily refer to the phenomenon where, because of factors such as instrument noise, background noise, and processing errors, nonsignal components other than the signal itself are mixed into the low-frequency segment of the recorded data, thereby causing baseline shifts in the data. The NGA-West2 data processing workflow (Ancheta *et al.*, 2014) was adopted to process the selected records, addressing low-frequency errors and baseline drifts. This processing workflow involved applying a five-pole acausal Butterworth band-pass filter. The high-pass filter frequency (f_{hp}) was selected following the steps

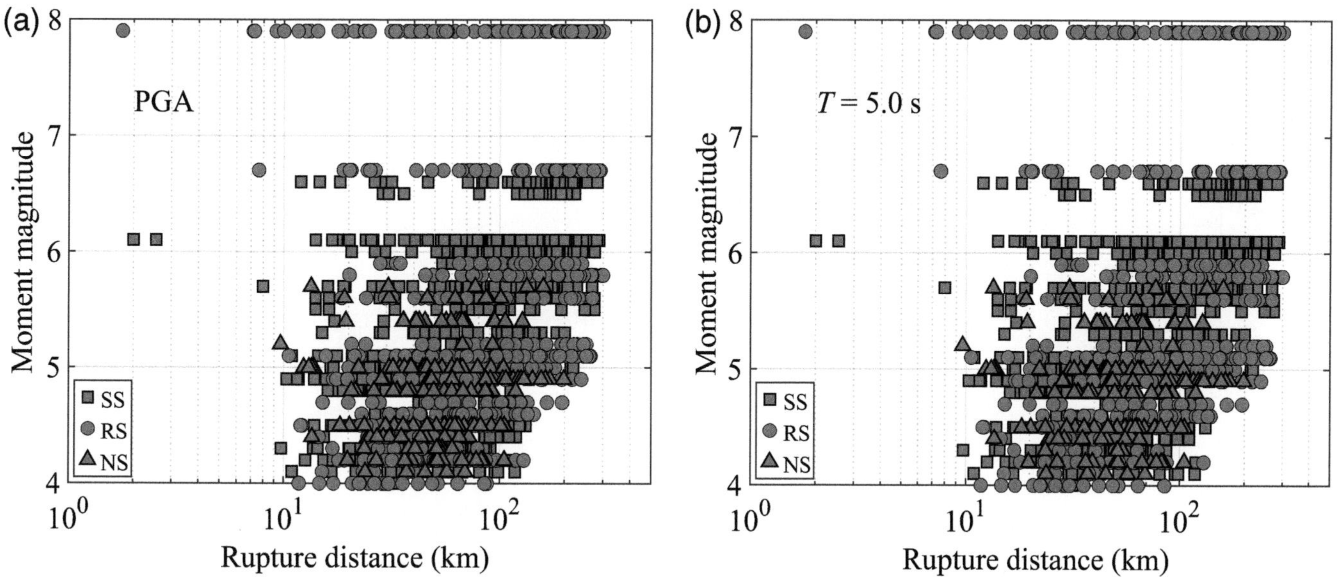

Figure 2. Distribution of (a) peak ground acceleration (PGA) and (b) spectral acceleration (SA) (T = 5.0 s) data in relation to M_w and R_{rup} according to faulting style used in this study. NS, normal-slip earthquakes; RS, reverse-slip earthquakes; SS, strike-slip earthquakes.

outlined in Zhang *et al.* (2022): (1) the theoretical frequency of the source spectrum model, (2) a signal-to-noise ratio (SNR) of ≥3, and (3) the processed velocity and displacement time series converging to zero at their end. According to $1/(1.5 \times f_{hp})$ (Chiou *et al.*, 2008), the processed data typically had a maximum usable period of 8.0 s. In addition, the low-pass filter frequency was set to 30 Hz because the SNR of most strong-motion records exceeded 3 at frequencies below this threshold. In this study, the data truncation and maximum available distance (R_{max}) method proposed by Chiou and Youngs (2014) was used for data screening. After this screening process, the R_{max} value for each seismic event was determined; these values are listed in Table S1. Figure 2 illustrates the PGA and SA (T 5.0 s) data distribution with respect to M_w and R_{rup}, categorized by the faulting style used in this study. Figure 3 shows the number of available records and earthquakes for each period.

The final dataset also incorporates key parameters essential for developing the V-GMPE, including M_w, R_{rup}, Joyner–Boore distance (R_{JB}), depths from the surface to the top of fault rupture plane (Z_{TOR}), focal mechanism solution, and time-averaged shear-wave velocity in the upper 30 m (V_{S30}). The parameters R_{rup}, R_{JB}, and Z_{TOR} were computed using the method proposed by Kaklamanos *et al.* (2011). Figure 4a illustrates the distribution of site V_{S30} sources for the 536 strong-motion stations used in this study. Specifically, 72.76% of these stations obtained their site V_{S30} values from Xie *et al.* (2022). In addition, for 57 stations (10.63%) located on rock sites, including both rock and slightly hard-rock sites, the V_{S30} values were assigned as 760 and 1130 m/s, respectively, based on the minimum and median values of the V_{S30} range for National Earthquake Hazards Reduction Program (NEHRP) class B (Building Seismic Safety Council, 2003). For the remaining 89 stations (16.61%) lacking borehole data, site V_{S30} values were derived from a recently published open-access V_{S30} database for China (Ji *et al.*, 2024). Figure 4b illustrates the distribution of V_{S30} data across the dataset, indicating an absence of data from hard-rock sites (NEHRP class A; $V_{S30} >$ 1500 m/s) and limited data from rock sites (NEHRP class B; $760 < V_{S30} \le 1500$ m/s). The majority of the data originates from NEHRP class C ($360 < V_{S30} \le 760$ m/s) and class D ($180 \le V_{S30} \le 360$ m/s) sites, which correspond to very dense soil and soft rock and stiff soil, respectively. The substantial volume of data with $V_{S30} < 360$ m/s corresponds to sites located in basins, plains, or valleys.

FUNCTIONAL FORMS

The V-GMPE adopts the same functional form as the ZYLW22 H-GMPE, which was modified from the functional form of the Campbell and Bozorgnia (2008) GMPE (hereafter referred to as the CB08 GMPE). Specifically, the functional forms of the magnitude term (f_{mag}), distance term (f_{dis}), faulting style term (f_{flt}), HW term (f_{hng}), and site term (f_{site}) are consistent with those of the CB08 GMPE and the ZYLW22 H-GMPE. The functional form of the anelastic attenuation term (f_{atn}) is consistent with that of the ZYLW22 H-GMPE.

The function form is given as follows:

$$\ln Y_{ij} = f_{mag} + f_{dis} + f_{flt} + f_{hng} + f_{site} + f_{atn} + \eta_i + \varepsilon_{ij}, \quad (1)$$

in which Y_{ij} is the observed vertical PGA (g), PGV (cm/s), and 5% damped SA (g) from event i recorded at station j; η_i represents the between-event residual; and ε_{ij} represents the within-event residuals.

f_{mag} uses a three-segment linear model. The piecewise linear scaling model for $M_w > 6.5$ provides enhanced control over

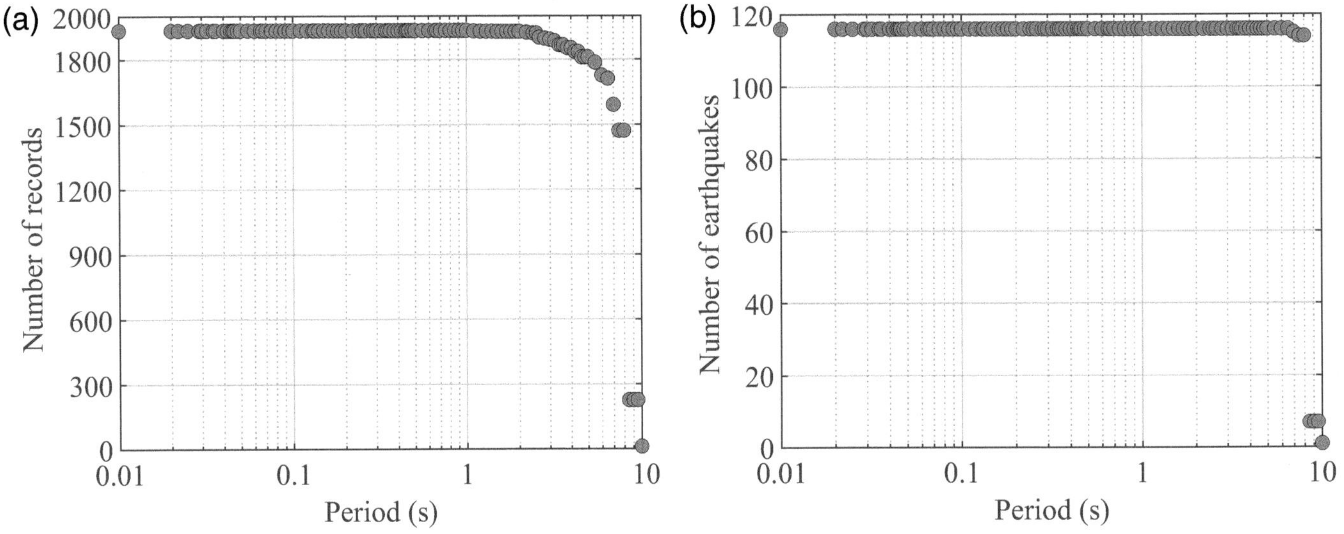

Figure 3. Number of (a) records and (b) earthquakes available at each period for the vertical component used in this study.

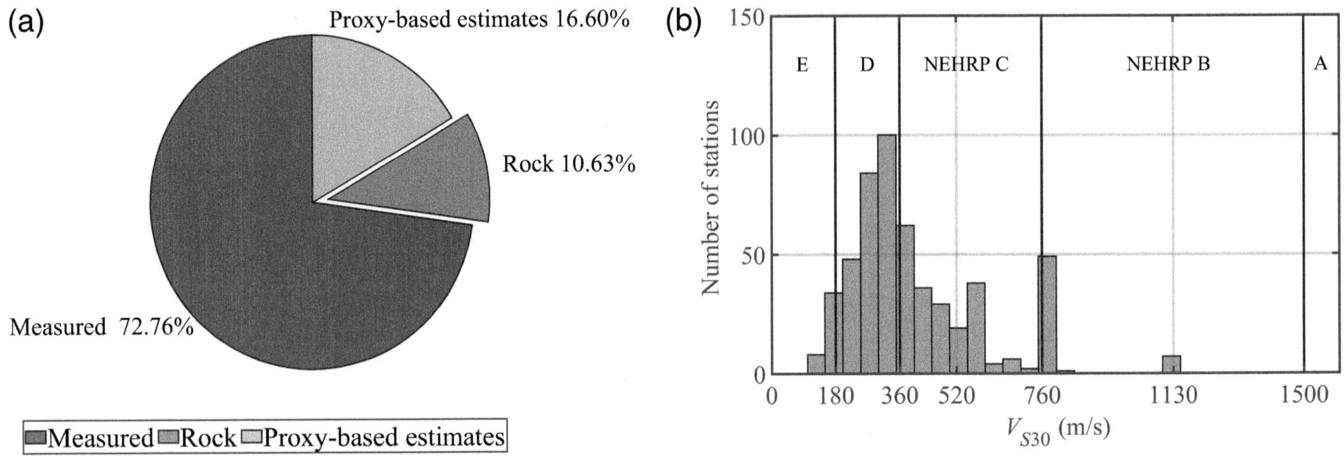

Figure 4. (a) Site V_{S30} pie chart of strong-motion stations from measured, rock, and proxy-based estimates and (b) histogram of site V_{S30} for strong-motion stations used in this study. NEHRP, National Earthquake Hazards Reduction Program.

large-magnitude scaling by decoupling it from smaller-magnitude scaling. This approach significantly improves the flexibility in modeling how ground-motions scale with earthquake size. The magnitude term is given by

$$f_{\text{mag}} = \begin{cases} c_0 + c_1 M_w & M_w \le 5.5 \\ c_0 + c_1 M_w + c_2(M_w - 5.5) & 5.5 < M_w \le 6.5, \\ c_0 + c_1 M_w + c_2(M_w - 5.5) + c_3(M_w - 6.5) & M_w > 6.5 \end{cases} \quad (2)$$

f_{dis} incorporates a geometric attenuation term dependent on M_w and relocates the magnitude-dependent attenuation component from inside to outside the square-root term. This adjustment not only enhances the model's capacity to fit both small- and large-magnitude records but also improves the stability of nonlinear regression analyses (Campbell and Bozorgnia, 2007),

$$f_{\text{dis}} = (c_4 + c_5 M_w) \ln\left(\sqrt{R_{\text{rup}}^2 + c_6^2}\right), \quad (3)$$

f_{flt} is defined by equations (4) and (5):

$$f_{\text{flt}} = c_7 F_{\text{RV}} f_{\text{flt},Z} + c_8 F_{\text{NM}}, \quad (4)$$

$$f_{\text{flt},Z} = \begin{cases} Z_{\text{TOR}}; & Z_{\text{TOR}} < 1 \\ 1; & Z_{\text{TOR}} \ge 1, \end{cases} \quad (5)$$

f_{hng} takes into account the effects of R_{JB}, M_w, Z_{TOR}, and δ (dip angle of the rupture plane). Its functional form is described by equations (6)–(10):

$$f_{\text{hng}} = c_9 f_{\text{hng},R} f_{\text{hng},M} f_{\text{hng},Z} f_{\text{hng},\delta}, \quad (6)$$

$$f_{\text{hng},R} = \begin{cases} 1; & R_{\text{JB}} = 0 \\ [\max(R_{\text{rup}}, \sqrt{R_{\text{JB}}^2 + 1} - R_{\text{JB}})] / \max(R_{\text{rup}}, \sqrt{R_{\text{JB}}^2 + 1}); & R_{\text{JB}} > 0, Z_{\text{TOR}} < 1 \\ (R_{\text{rup}} - R_{\text{JB}}) / R_{\text{rup}}; & R_{\text{JB}} > 0, Z_{\text{TOR}} \geq 1 \end{cases}, \quad (7)$$

$$f_{\text{hng},M} = \begin{cases} 0; & M_{\text{w}} \leq 6 \\ 2(M_{\text{w}} - 6); & 6 < M_{\text{w}} < 6.5 \\ 1; & M_{\text{w}} \geq 6.5 \end{cases}, \quad (8)$$

$$f_{\text{hng},Z} = \begin{cases} 0; & Z_{\text{TOR}} \geq 20 \\ (20 - Z_{\text{TOR}})/20; & 0 \leq Z_{\text{TOR}} < 20 \end{cases}, \quad (9)$$

$$f_{\text{hng},\delta} = \begin{cases} 1; & \delta \leq 70 \\ (90 - \delta)/20; & \delta > 70 \end{cases}, \quad (10)$$

f_{site} comprises both linear and nonlinear site response models (Walling *et al.*, 2008),

$$f_{\text{site}} = \begin{cases} c_{10} \ln\left(\frac{V_{S30}}{V_{\text{Lin}}}\right) + k_2 \left(\ln\left(\text{PGA}_{\text{rock}} + c \left(\frac{V_{S30}}{V_{\text{Lin}}}\right)^n \right) - \ln(\text{PGA}_{\text{rock}} + c) \right); & V_{S30} < V_{\text{Lin}} \\ (c_{10} + k_2 n) \ln\left(\frac{V_{S30}}{V_{\text{Lin}}}\right); & V_{\text{Lin}} \leq V_{S30} < 1100 \\ (c_{10} + k_2 n) \ln\left(\frac{1100}{V_{\text{Lin}}}\right); & V_{S30} \geq 1100 \end{cases}, \quad (11)$$

in which PGA_{rock} represents the vertical PGA at a reference site with $V_{S30} = 1100$ m/s. As the site becomes softer ($V_{S30} < V_{\text{Lin}}$), nonlinear site amplification occurs. For sites with $V_{\text{Lin}} \leq V_{S30} < 1100$ m/s, linear site amplification occurs; for $V_{\text{Lin}} \geq 1100$ m/s, constant site amplification is observed. The NGA-West2 vertical and V/H models showed minimal nonlinear site response for the vertical component (Bozorgnia and Campbell, 2016a,b; Stewart *et al.*, 2016). Consequently, the effects of nonlinear soil response on the vertical component were not considered in the V-GMPE, and k_2 was thus set to 0. Because the soil response of the vertical component is assumed to be linear, the parameter PGA_{rock} is unnecessary.

Campbell and Bozorgnia (2013) identified a strong regional dependence of ground-motion attenuation at distances >80 km during the development of their near-source NGA-West2 model. Farajpour *et al.* (2019) emphasized that ground-motion behavior at distances >80 km is predominantly influenced by anelastic attenuation. Given the critical role of the near-source region in seismic hazard analysis and seismic fortification, a boundary distance of 80 km was selected to distinguish between near-source and far-source regions. The V-GMPE incorporates f_{atn} for data in which $R_{\text{rup}} > 80$ km,

$$f_{\text{atn}} = \begin{cases} 0; & R_{\text{rup}} \leq 80 \text{ km} \\ c_{11}(R_{\text{rup}} - 80); & R_{\text{rup}} > 80 \text{ km} \end{cases}. \quad (12)$$

After determining the functional forms of all terms, the coefficients and standard deviations of the f_{mag}, f_{dis}, f_{flt}, f_{hng}, and f_{site} terms were derived via random-effects regression (Abrahamson and Youngs, 1992) using the vertical strong-motion database. After these coefficients were fixed, the coefficient of f_{atn} was determined through nonlinear regression based on data with $R_{\text{rup}} > 80$ km.

The total residual (r_{ij}) is decomposed into between-event (η_i) and within-event (ε_{ij}) residuals for the random-effects model. The variables η_i and ε_{ij} follow a normal distribution with a mean of zero. As specified in the random-effects regression, which are defined in accordance with equations (13) and (14) (Abrahamson and Youngs, 1992),

$$\eta_i = \tau^2 \sum_{j=1}^{N_i} r_{ij} / (N_i \tau^2 + \phi^2), \quad (13)$$

$$\varepsilon_{ij} = r_{ij} - \eta_i, \quad (14)$$

in which N_i is the number of data for event i, τ and ϕ are the standard deviations of η_i and ε_{ij}, respectively. The total standard deviation (σ) is calculated as

$$\sigma = \sqrt{\phi^2 + \tau^2}. \quad (15)$$

The predictor variables used in equations (2)–(12) include M_{w}, R_{rup}, R_{JB}, Z_{TOR}, V_{S30}, δ, and λ. Here, λ represents the average rake angle of the rupture plane. F_{RV} represents reverse-fault earthquake, defined as 1 for $30° \leq \lambda \leq 150°$ and 0 for otherwise, and F_{NM} represents normal-fault earthquake, defined as 1 for $-150° \leq \lambda \leq -30°$ and 0 for otherwise. The regression coefficients c_0–c_{11} are period-dependent coefficients. The coefficients n, c, and V_{Lin} are the period-independent coefficients. Owing to $k_2 = 0$, the values for n and c are not provided.

MODEL REGRESSION ANALYSIS

Regression results

To develop a V-GMPE aligned with the ZYLW22 H-GMPE for southwest China, the model coefficients were determined using a random-effects regression algorithm. Table 1 presents the coefficients c_0–c_{11} and V_{LIN} for PGA, PGV, and SA ($T = 0.01$–8 s). It is noteworthy that because k_2 was set to 0, the values of the coefficients c and n for the nonlinear shallow site response term have no impact on the results and are therefore not listed in Table 1.

TABLE 1
Model Coefficients for the Vertical Ground-Motion Prediction Equation (V-GMPE) in Southwest China

T (s)	c_0	c_1	c_2	c_3	c_4	c_5	c_6	c_7	c_8	c_9	c_{10}	c_{11}	V_{LIN}
PGA	−0.3230	0.2018	0.3529	−0.3823	−2.1282	0.1181	4.7000	0.4927	0.0702	1.2048	−0.3374	−0.0023	865
PGV	1.8874	0.3463	0.0126	−0.3293	−2.4032	0.2272	3.1000	0.2091	−0.0903	0.6941	−0.3697	−0.0052	400
0.01	−0.3408	0.2044	0.3531	−0.3824	−2.1245	0.1176	4.7000	0.4936	0.0714	1.2042	−0.3374	−0.0023	865
0.02	0.1039	0.1594	0.3720	−0.3891	−2.1968	0.1242	4.8000	0.5156	0.0636	1.3135	−0.3335	−0.0020	865
0.03	1.6393	−0.0088	0.4511	−0.3710	−2.4909	0.1547	5.3000	0.5754	0.0726	1.8698	−0.3587	−0.0019	926
0.04	1.8263	0.0269	0.5412	−0.4378	−2.4495	0.1350	5.9000	0.6267	0.0797	1.8041	−0.3623	−0.0013	995
0.05	1.5227	0.1112	0.5921	−0.4694	−2.3029	0.1069	6.1000	0.6421	0.0950	1.6057	−0.3214	−0.0003	1054
0.075	1.0462	0.2354	0.6011	−0.4986	−2.1081	0.0752	7.9000	0.5974	0.1120	1.3937	−0.2407	−0.0010	1086
0.10	0.0477	0.3337	0.5787	−0.5002	−1.8401	0.0495	6.8000	0.5471	0.1335	1.2565	−0.2291	−0.0016	1032
0.15	−1.3982	0.5350	0.3075	−0.3601	−1.7084	0.0445	6.8000	0.4020	0.1100	1.0740	−0.2673	−0.0018	878
0.20	−2.2648	0.6293	0.1272	−0.3145	−1.7124	0.0602	6.2000	0.3064	0.0458	0.9765	−0.3161	−0.0027	748
0.25	−2.8223	0.6942	−0.1482	−0.2253	−1.8449	0.0921	5.2000	0.2959	−0.0098	0.9441	−0.3820	−0.0032	654
0.30	-3.7669	0.8205	−0.3096	−0.0837	−1.7660	0.0873	5.0000	0.2294	−0.0426	0.8776	−0.4029	−0.0035	587
0.40	−4.8920	0.9757	−0.4987	−0.0611	−1.7475	0.0931	4.6000	0.1235	−0.1096	0.6024	−0.3959	−0.0044	503
0.50	−5.6995	1.0577	−0.7350	−0.0018	−1.7986	0.1140	4.2000	0.0842	−0.1418	0.4543	−0.4314	−0.0052	457
0.75	−7.2660	1.2433	−1.0038	−0.0032	−1.8869	0.1410	3.1000	0.0284	−0.1842	0.0959	−0.3944	−0.0071	410
1.0	−8.3307	1.3455	−1.0591	−0.0662	−1.9703	0.1642	3.1000	0.0369	−0.2316	0.0344	−0.3877	−0.0065	400
1.5	−9.8065	1.4276	−1.0952	−0.0972	−1.9985	0.1862	3.1000	0.0930	−0.1588	0.1740	−0.3241	−0.0061	400
2.0	−10.7242	1.4988	−0.9131	−0.3405	−2.0224	0.1886	3.1000	0.1670	−0.1022	0.2276	−0.2905	−0.0057	400
3.0	−11.4880	1.4903	−0.4985	−0.9660	−2.0605	0.1978	3.1000	0.1665	−0.0295	0.4750	−0.1921	−0.0052	400
4.0	−11.9315	1.4303	−0.3957	−0.8858	−2.0271	0.2053	3.1000	0.0721	0.0031	0.8948	−0.1282	−0.0034	400
5.0	−12.2111	1.3763	−0.1953	−0.8607	−1.9524	0.1998	3.1000	0.0249	−0.0296	0.9175	−0.1426	−0.0033	400
6.0	−12.3221	1.3198	0.0283	−0.9074	−1.9179	0.1950	3.1000	0.0868	−0.0287	0.9325	−0.1652	−0.0032	400
7.0	−11.8008	1.1554	0.2396	−0.9543	−2.0089	0.2120	3.1000	0.1635	−0.0036	0.7789	−0.1624	−0.0036	400
8.0	−11.5124	1.0467	0.3777	−0.9590	−1.9936	0.2098	3.1000	0.2129	−0.0173	0.5850	−0.1781	−0.0052	400

PGA, peak ground acceleration; PGV, peak ground velocity.

Table 2 presents the standard deviations ϕ, τ, and σ as a function of period.

Residual analysis

In this study, residuals were used to evaluate the performance of the V-GMPE against the predictor variables (M_w, Z_{TOR}, R_{rup}, and V_{S30}). The accuracy of the V-GMPE relative to empirical data was evaluated by analyzing the residuals trends associated with these predictor variables. To illustrate these residual trends, the segmented means and 95th percentile confidence limits were plotted together with the residuals.

Figures 5 and 6 depict the between-event residuals of PGA, PGV, and SA ($T = 0.1$, 1.0, 3.0, and 5.0 s) against M_w (checking M_w scaling) and Z_{TOR} (checking depth scaling), respectively. These figures demonstrate that the between-event residuals are distributed between −1 and 1 near zero values and exhibit no systematic trends with respect to M_w and Z_{TOR}. Although the V-GMPE slightly overestimates ground motions for earthquakes with $M_w \geq 7.0$, likely because of the limited data from only the 2008 M_w 7.9 Wenchuan earthquake included in our model, the impact on the average predictions of the V-GMPE remains negligible.

Figures 7 and 8 present the within-event residuals of PGA, PGV, and SA ($T = 0.1$, 1.0, 3.0, and 5.0 s) plotted against R_{rup} and V_{S30}, respectively. Results from these figures indicate that the within-event residuals predominantly fall within the range of −2 to 2 around zero and exhibit no systematic trends with respect to R_{rup} and V_{S30}. Figures S1 and S2 further present the predicted PGA, PGV, and SA ($T = 0.1$, 1.0, 3.0, and 5.0 s) from the V-GMPE plotted against M_w (Fig. S1) and R_{rup} (Fig. S2), respectively, alongside the observed data. Comparisons were performed for rock sites ($V_{S30} = 760m/s$), reverse earthquakes ($F_{RV} = 1$, $F_{NM} = 0$), and $Z_{TOR} = 1.0$ km. The observed data were extracted from reverse earthquakes in the dataset and corrected to rock sites ($V_{S30} = 760$ m/s) using the method proposed by Seyhan and Stewart (2014). Results indicate that the prediction curves for each distance or magnitude match the observed data well within their corresponding distance or magnitude interval. Collectively, these findings demonstrate that the predicted values of the V-GMPE are consistent with the observed data, thereby confirming the model's reliability.

Figure 9 compares the standard deviations (σ, ϕ, and τ) as a function of period between the V-GMPE and the ZYLW22 H-GMPE. The figure demonstrates that both horizontal and vertical components exhibit higher σ than ϕ, with τ being the smallest. Across all periods, τ values of the V-GMPE are larger than those of the H-GMPE. For periods ranging from 0.06 to 8 s, ϕ values of the V-GMPE are smaller than those of the H-GMPE. However, for periods ranging from 0.08 to 8 s, σvalues of the H-GMPE and V-GMPE are comparable and

TABLE 2
Between-Event, Within-Event, and Total Residual Standard Deviations for the Vertical Ground-Motion Prediction Equation (V-GMPE)

T(s)	ϕ	τ	σ
PGA	0.6297	0.5461	0.8335
PGV	0.5874	0.5254	0.7881
0.01	0.6293	0.5462	0.8333
0.02	0.6347	0.5557	0.8435
0.03	0.6671	0.5807	0.8844
0.04	0.6825	0.5991	0.9081
0.05	0.6850	0.5860	0.9015
0.075	0.6964	0.5781	0.9051
0.10	0.6900	0.5635	0.8909
0.15	0.6970	0.5658	0.8978
0.20	0.6834	0.5514	0.8781
0.25	0.6671	0.5667	0.8753
0.30	0.6593	0.5712	0.8723
0.40	0.6680	0.5462	0.8629
0.50	0.6686	0.5493	0.8654
0.75	0.6656	0.5583	0.8688
1.0	0.6786	0.5716	0.8872
1.5	0.6749	0.5893	0.8960
2.0	0.6558	0.5972	0.8870
3.0	0.6042	0.6003	0.8518
4.0	0.5841	0.5851	0.8267
5.0	0.5738	0.5752	0.8125
6.0	0.5596	0.5570	0.7896
7.0	0.5660	0.5529	0.7913
8.0	0.5628	0.5641	0.7969

PGA, peak ground acceleration; PGV, peak ground velocity.

exhibit consistent variation trends with period. This finding is particularly critical for the application of the V/H spectral ratio to scenario spectra because it indicates that the V/H spectral ratio is associated with an equivalent degree of aleatory variability for both vertical and horizontal components (Bommer *et al.*, 2011). However, between periods of 0.033 and 0.08 s, σ values of the V-GMPE are slightly larger than those of the H-GMPE.

Predicted ground motion

Figures 10 and 11 present the vertical PGA, PGV, and SA (T = 0.1, 1.0, 3.0, and 5.0 s) predicted by the V-GMPE, scaled with respect to R_{rup} and M_w. Evaluations were conducted at rock sites ($V_{S30} = 760$ m/s), strike-slip earthquakes ($F_{RV} = F_{NM} = 0$), and $Z_{TOR} = 1$ km. The scaling characteristics of predicted ground motions from the V-GMPE with respect to M_w and R_{rup} are consistent with those of the ZYLW22 H-GMPE. At short periods, the attenuation rates of vertical ground motions for M_w 5, 6, 7, and 8 are consistent across all distances. At moderate to long periods, the larger the M_w, the slower the attenuation rate of vertical ground motions with distance; this is attributed to geometric spreading associated with M_w and anelastic attenuation. As R_{rup} decreases, the increasing rate of vertical PGA, PGV, and SA (T = 0.1, 1.0, 3.0, and 5.0 s) predicted by the V-GMPE slows down. This indicates that the V-GMPE effectively captures the magnitude and distance saturation effects in the near-fault region of large earthquakes in southwest China. However, compared with

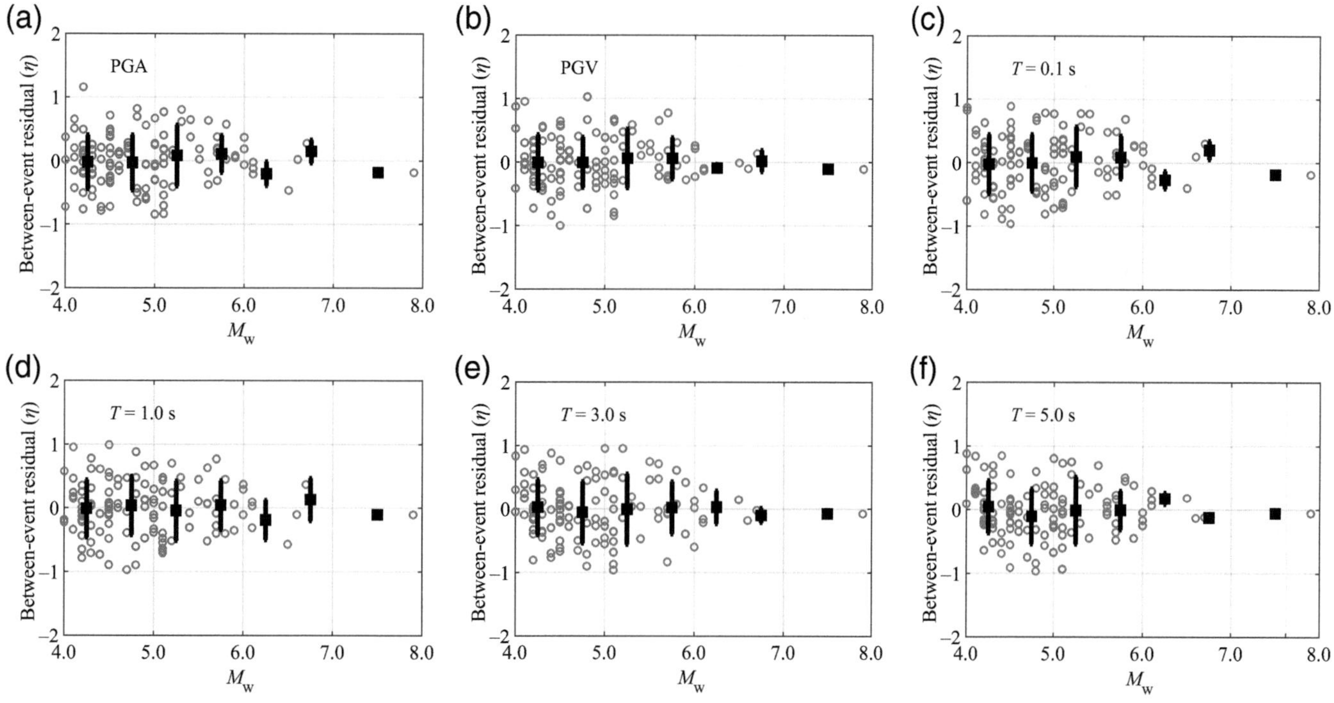

Figure 5. Correlation of between-event residuals and M_w for (a) PGA, (b) peak ground velocity (PGV), and (c–f) SA (T = 0.1, 1.0, 3.0, and 5.0 s). The black squares and error bars represent the mean and 95th percentile confidence limits of mean binned residuals, respectively.

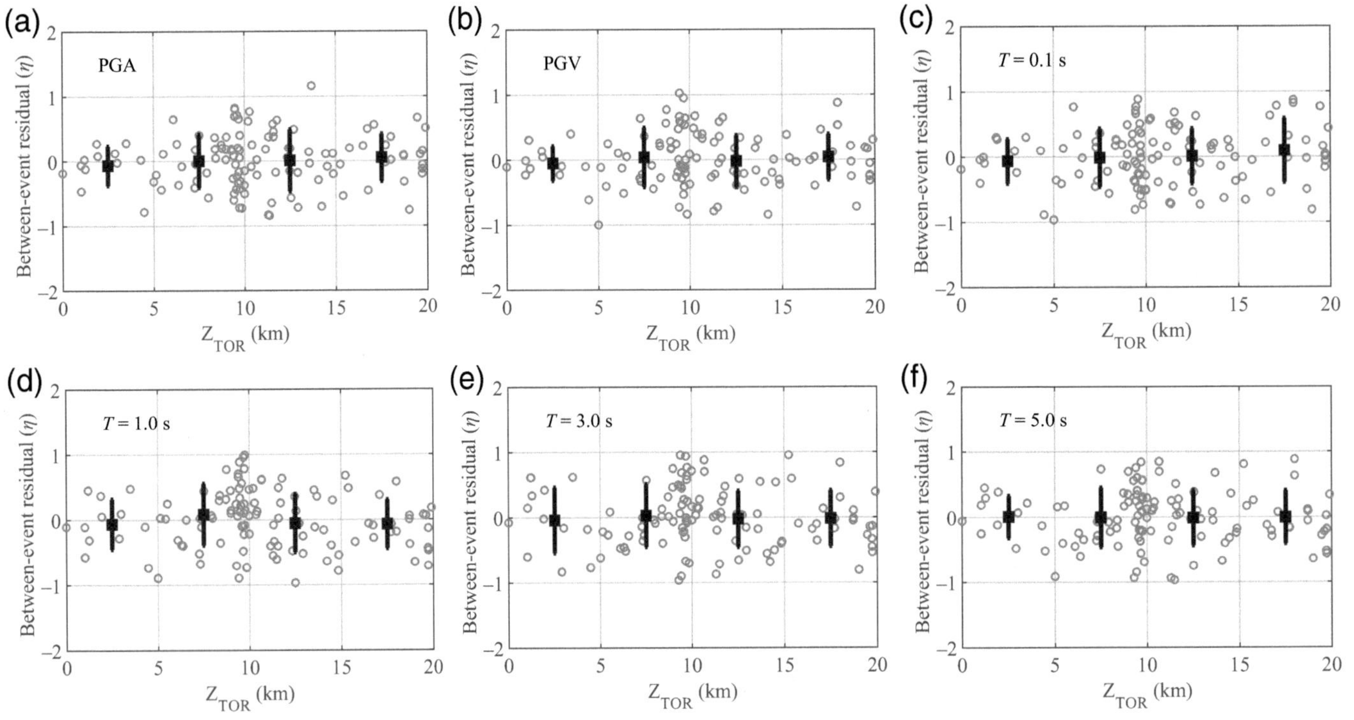

Figure 6. Correlation of between-event residuals and Z_{TOR} for (a) PGA, (b) PGV, and (c–f) SA (T = 0.1, 1.0, 3.0, and 5.0 s). The black squares and error bars represent the mean and 95th percentile confidence limits of mean binned residuals, respectively.

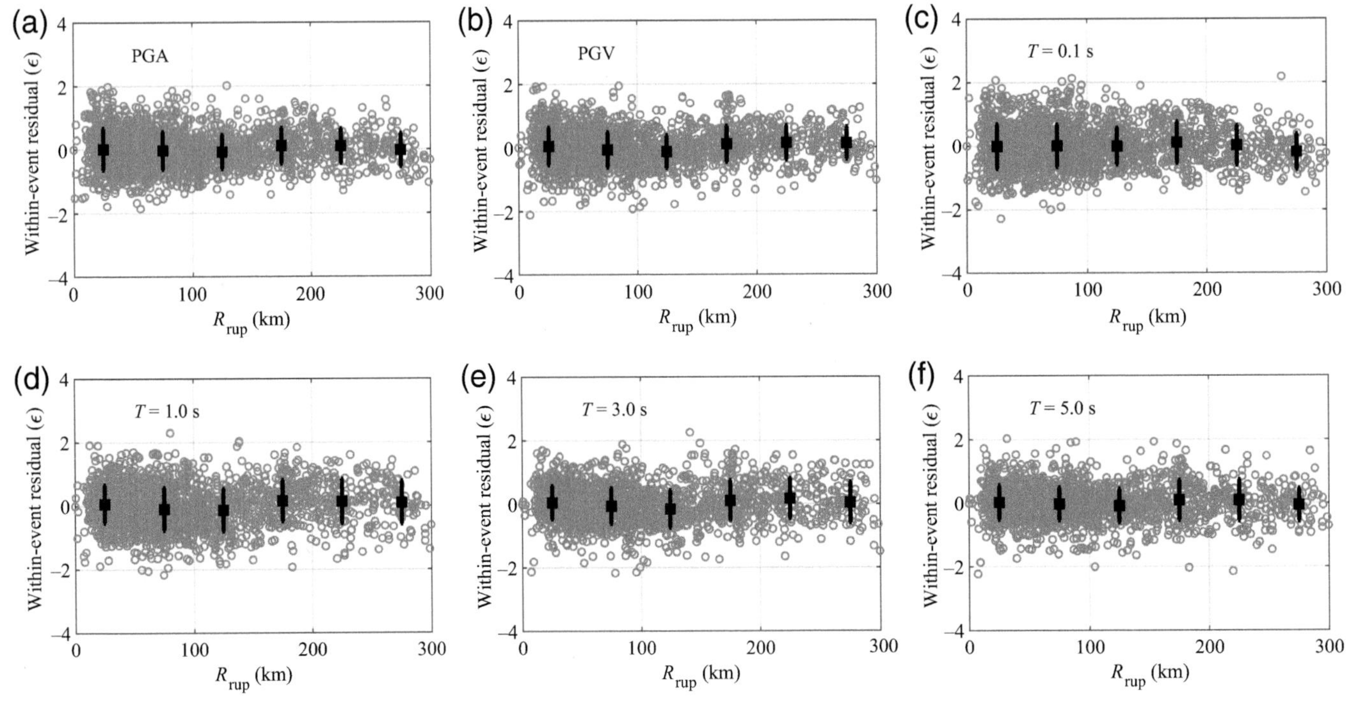

Figure 7. Correlation of within-event residuals and R_{rup} for (a) PGA, (b) PGV, and (c–f) SA (T = 0.1, 1.0, 3.0, and 5.0 s). The black squares and error bars represent the mean and 95th percentile confidence limits of mean binned residuals, respectively.

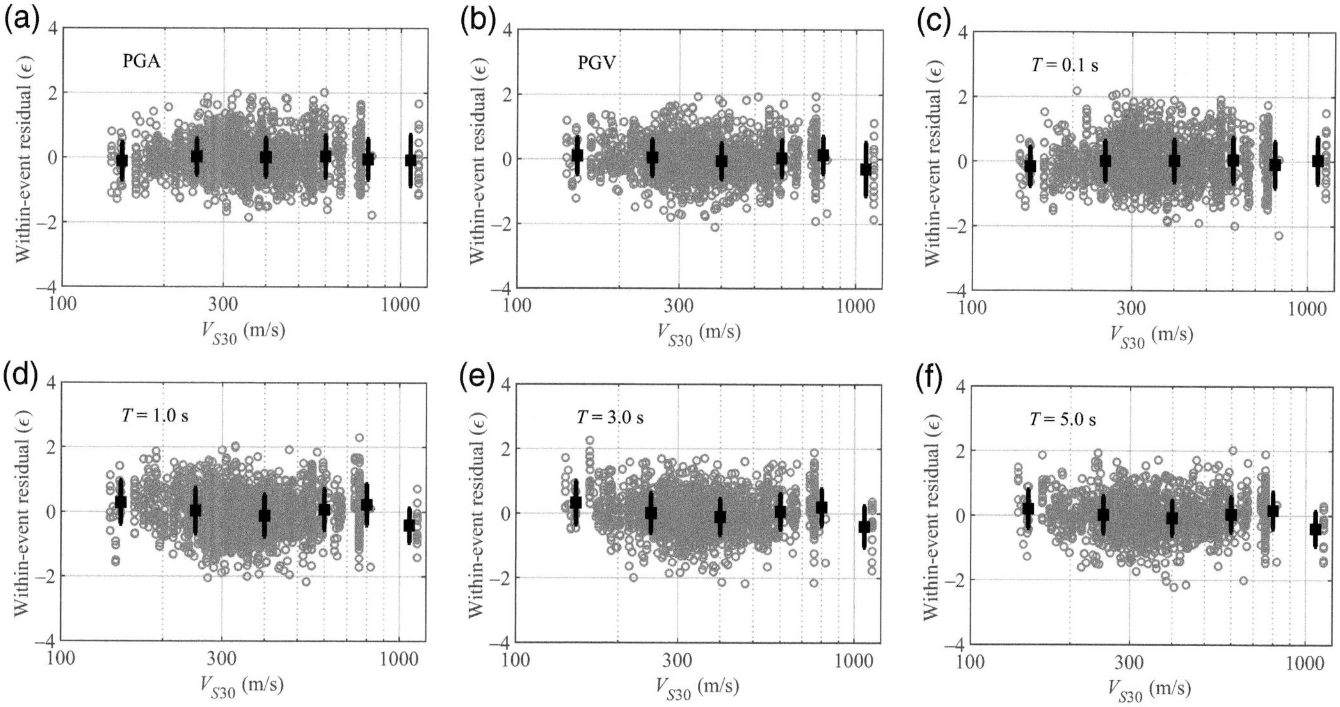

Figure 8. Correlation of within-event residuals and V_{S30} for (a) PGA, (b) PGV, and (c–f) SA (T = 0.1, 1.0, 3.0, and 5.0 s). The black squares and error bars represent the mean and 95th percentile confidence limits of mean binned residuals, respectively.

the H-GMPE, the V-GMPE exhibits larger absolute values of anelastic attenuation coefficients, indicating stronger anelastic attenuation for the vertical component.

Figure 12 presents the predicted acceleration response spectra from the V-GMPE. This figure was conducted for M_w 5, 6, 7, and 8, strike-slip earthquakes ($F_{RV} = F_{NM} = 0$), $Z_{TOR} =$ 1 km, $R_{rup} = 10$, 100 km), rock sites ($V_{S30} = 760$ m/s), and soil sites ($V_{S30} = 270$ m/s). At $R_{rup} = 10$ km, the peak of the vertical response spectrum occurs at 0.075 s for M_w 5, 6, 7, and 8, and $V_{S30} = 270$, 760 m/s. However, at $R_{rup} = 100$ km, the peak of the vertical response spectrum is largely affected by M_w and site conditions. This characteristic is consistent with findings from the ZYLW22 H-GMPE, where the peak of horizontal ground motion shifts to longer periods and increases systematically with increasing M_w and decreasing V_{S30}. Figure 12 further demonstrates that long-period ground motions undergo significant amplification in both soil and rock sites. This phenomenon is speculated to be associated with the basin amplification effect in southwest China.

Figure S3 presents the effect of faulting style, including strike-slip faults (90° dip), reverse faults (45° dip), and normal faults (−45° dip), on the vertical response spectra at HW and footwall (FW) sites with $V_{S30} = 270$ and 760 m/s. For FW sites, strike-slip, normal, and reverse faults exhibit nearly identical effects on SA for periods $T > 0.2$ s. However, for $T < 0.2$ s, the estimated short-period SA for reverse faults is slightly larger than that for normal faults, with strike-slip faults yielding the smallest values. Figure S3 further demonstrates that the HW effect on the vertical component is significant, particularly at short periods, which is qualitatively consistent with observations on the horizontal component.

The predicted response spectra and standard deviations of the proposed V-GMPE were also compared with those of the BC16 (Bozorgnia and Campbell, 2016b) and XZ21 (Xing and Zhao, 2021) V-GMPEs, as shown in Figure 13 and Figure S4, respectively. Figure 13 shows that for a strike-slip earthquake

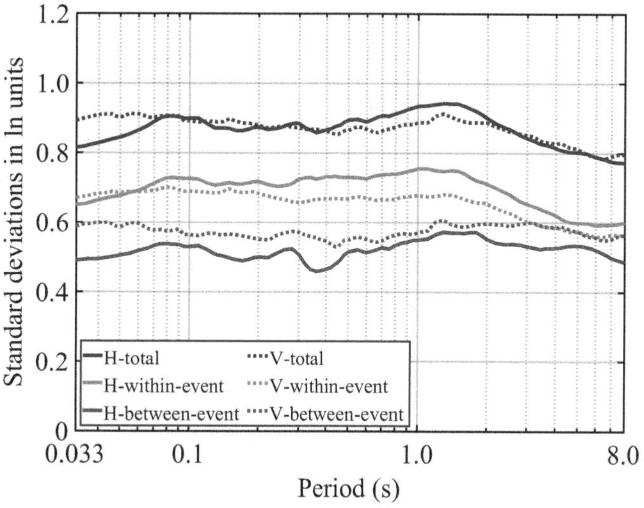

Figure 9. Comparison of standard deviations σ (top), ϕ (middle), and τ (bottom) between the proposed vertical ground-motion prediction equation (V-GMPE) and the ZYLW22 horizontal ground-motion prediction equation (H-GMPE). The color version of this figure is available only in the electronic edition.

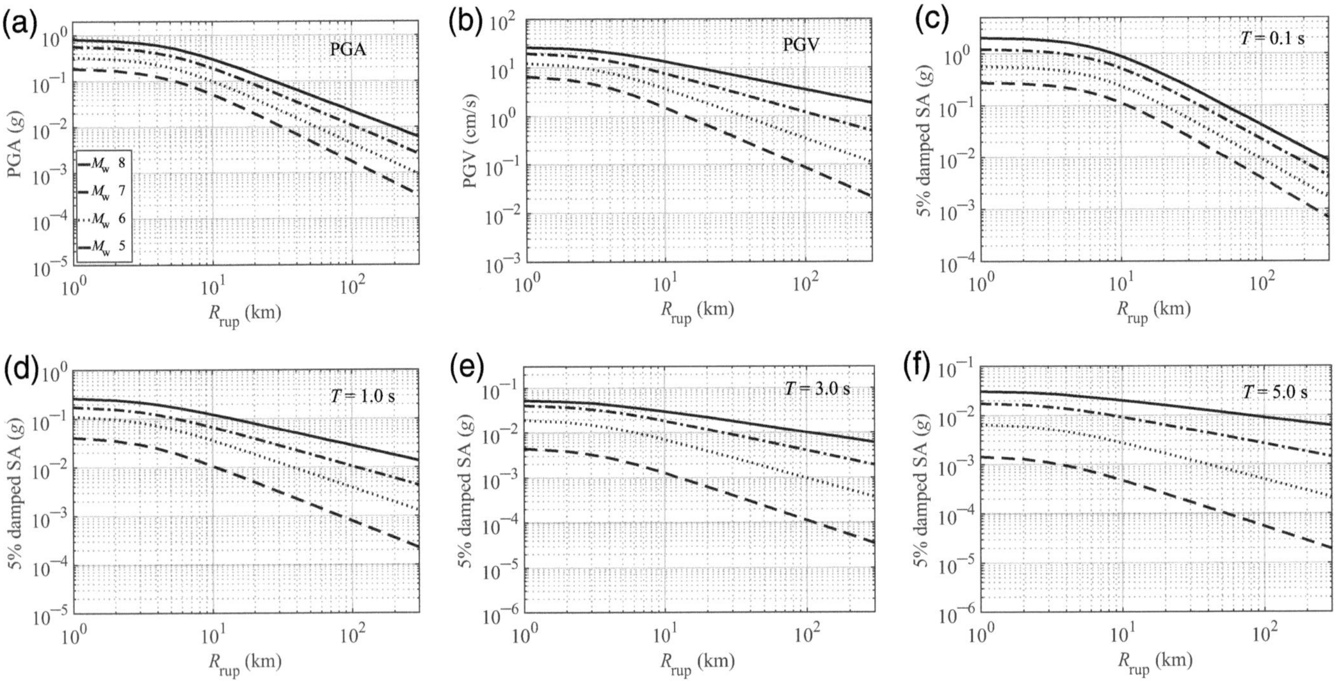

Figure 10. Attenuation of vertical (a) PGA, (b) PGV, and (c–f) SA (T = 0.1, 1.0, 3.0, and 5.0 s) with respect to R_{rup} for M_w 5, 6, 7, and 8, strike-slip earthquakes ($F_{RV} = 0$, $F_{NM} = 0$), rock sites ($V_{S30} = 760$ m/s), and $Z_{TOR} = 1.0$ km.

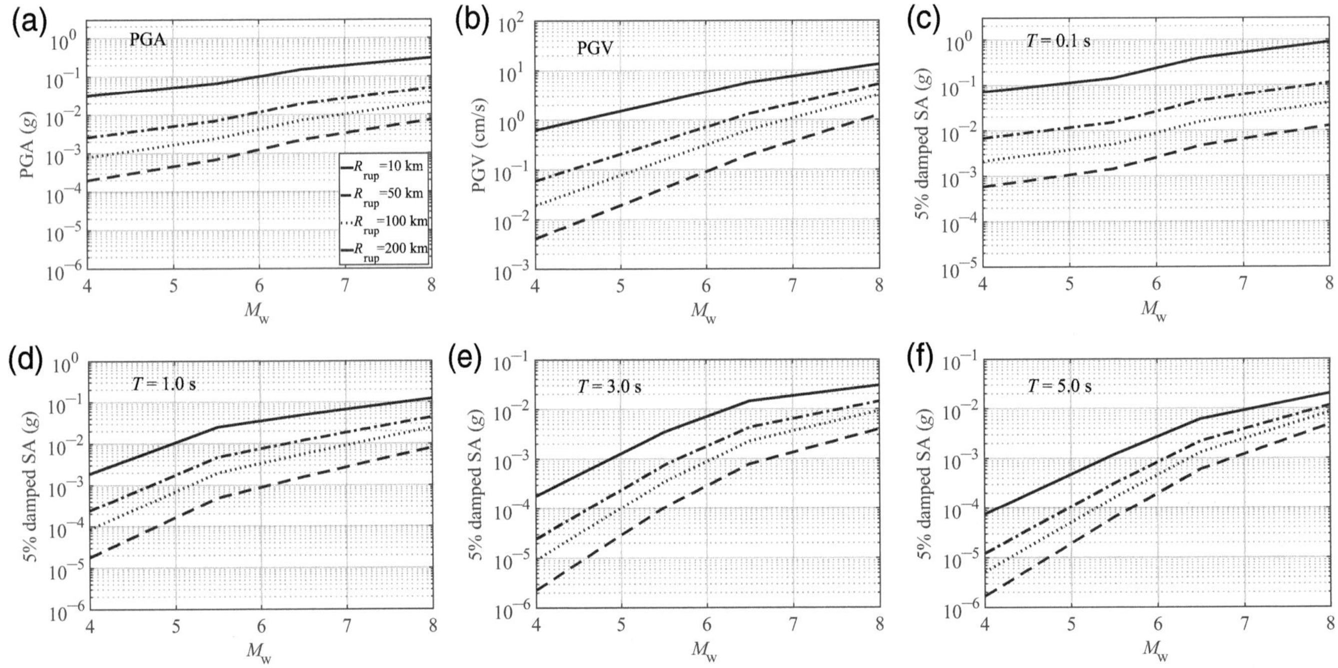

Figure 11. Magnitude scaling of vertical (a) PGA, (b) PGV, and (c–f) SA (T = 0.1, 1.0, 3.0, and 5.0 s) with respect to M_w for R_{rup} = 10, 50, 100, and 200 km, strike-slip earthquakes ($F_{RV} = 0$, $F_{NM} = 0$), rock sites ($V_{S30} = 760$ m/s), and $Z_{TOR} = 1.0$ km.

with M_w 7 at near-fault ($R_{rup} = 20$ km) soil sites ($V_{S30} = 270$ m/s), (1) for $0.02 < T < 0.075$ s, the predicted response spectra of the proposed V-GMPE are slightly larger than those of the BC16 V-GMPE but slightly smaller than those of the XZ21 V-GMPE, and (2) for $T < 0.02$ s and $T > 0.075$ s, the predicted response spectra are consistently smaller

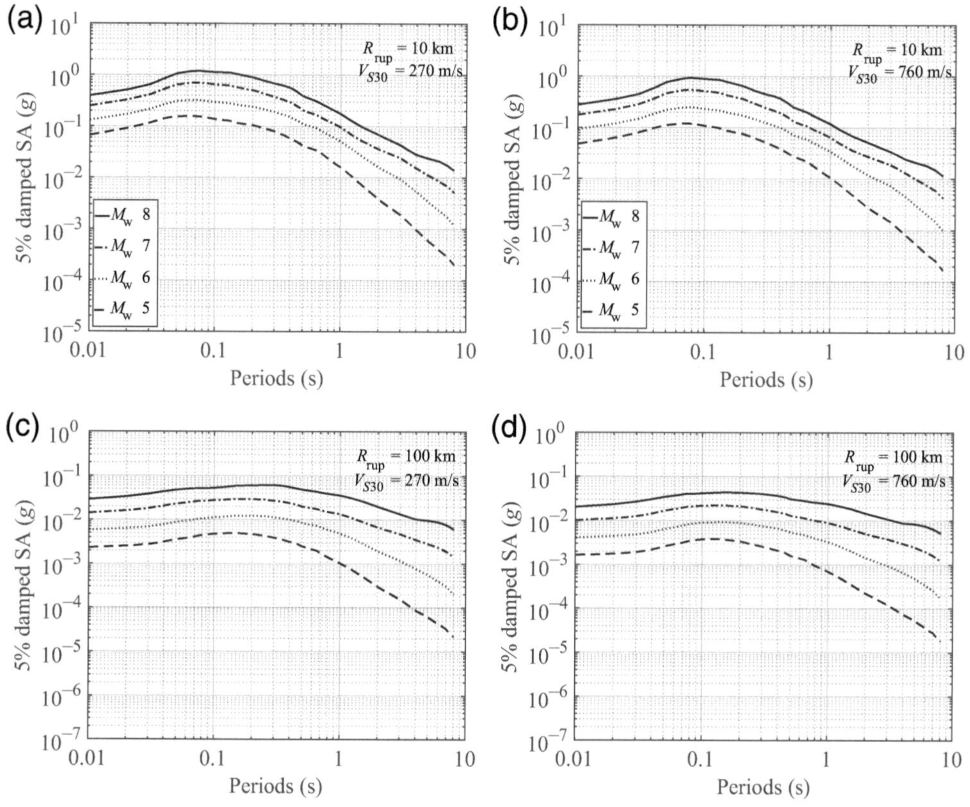

Figure 12. Predicted acceleration response spectra from the vertical GMPE for M_w 5, 6, 7, and 8, strike-slip earthquakes ($F_{RV} = 0$, $F_{NM} = 0$), $Z_{TOR} = 1$ km, (a) $R_{rup} = 10$ km, soil sites ($V_{S30} = 270$ m/s), (b) $R_{rup} = 10$ km, rock sites ($V_{S30} = 760$ m/s), (c) $R_{rup} = 100$ km, soil sites, and (d) $R_{rup} = 100$ km, rock sites.

than those of both the BC16 and XZ21 V-GMPEs. However, at near-fault rock sites ($V_{S30} = 760$ m/s), the comparison results differ: (1) for $0.04 < T < 0.1$ s, the predicted response spectra of the proposed V-GMPE are slightly larger than those of the BC16 V-GMPE but slightly smaller than those of the XZ21 V-GMPE, and (2) for $T < 0.04$ s and $T > 0.1$ s, the predicted response spectra are consistently smaller than those of both the BC16 and XZ21 V-GMPEs. At far-source ($R_{rup} = 100$ km) soil sites, the predicted response spectra of the proposed V-GMPE are smaller than those of the BC16 and XZ21 V-GMPEs for $T < 6$ s but larger than those of the BC16 V-GMPE for $T > 6$ s. For far-source rock sites, however, this transition period shifts to 3 s.

Figure S4 demonstrates that φ values of the proposed V-GMPE are nearly identical to those of the XZ21 V-GMPE for $T < 1$ s but exceed those of the XZ21 V-GMPE for $T > 1$ s. For the BC16 V-GMPE, comparisons vary with M_w and T: (1) for $M_w \leq 4.5$, φ values of the proposed V-GMPE are smaller than those of the BC16 V-GMPE for $T < 0.3$ s but larger for $T > 0.3$ s, and (2) for $M_w \geq 5.5$, φ values of the proposed V-GMPE are larger than those of the BC16 V-GMPE across all periods. The τ values of the proposed V-GMPE are larger than those of the BC16 and XZ21 V-GMPEs across all periods, except for $T > 5$ s, in which case they are smaller than those of the BC16 V-GMPE for $M_w \leq 4.5$. The σ values of the proposed V-GMPE are larger than those of the BC16 and XZ21 V-GMPEs across all periods, except for $T < 0.075$ s, in which case they are slightly smaller than those of the BC16 V-GMPE for $M_w \leq 4.5$.

V/H SPECTRAL RATIOS

Figure 14a,b presents the dependence of V/H spectral ratios on period for soil and rock sites, respectively, under reverse earthquakes with M_w 4.5, 5.5, 6.5, and 7.5 and $R_{rup} = 10$ and 100 km. The V/H spectral ratio is defined as the ratio of ground motions predicted by the V-GMPE to those predicted by the ZYLW22 H-GMPE. These figures clearly demonstrate the effects of M_w, R_{rup}, and site conditions on the V/H spectral ratio.

At $R_{rup} = 10$ km, the V/H spectral ratio decreases consistently with increasing M_w across all periods. For soil sites, the V/H spectral ratios for M_w 4.5, 5.5, 6.5, and 7.5 range from 1.00–2.68, 0.96–2.24, 0.67–1.63, and 0.32–1.36, respectively. For rock sites, the V/H spectral ratios for M_w 4.5, 5.5, 6.5, and 7.5 are distributed between 0.61–2.0, 0.63–1.83, 0.37–1.79, and 0.18–1.71, respectively. However, at $R_{rup} = 100$ km, the M_w dependence of the V/H spectral ratio varies with period: (1) for $T < 1$ s, the V/H spectral ratio is the highest for M_w 5.5, followed by M_w 6.5 and 4.5, with the lowest value observed for M_w 7.5, and (2) for $T > 1$ s, the V/H spectral ratio is the highest for M_w 7.5, followed by M_w 6.5, 5.5, and the lowest value observed for M_w 4.5. For soil sites, the V/H spectral ratios for M_w 4.5, 5.5, 6.5, and 7.5 fall within the ranges of 0.61–1.14, 0.71–1.36, 0.79–1.41, and 0.61–1.50, respectively. For rock sites, the V/H spectral ratios for M_w 4.5, 5.5, 6.5, and 7.5 are distributed between 0.36–1.36, 0.55–1.41, 0.50–1.53, and 0.34–1.76, respectively.

Figure 14 also shows that for both soil and rock sites, the variation trends of the V/H spectral ratio with period demonstrate remarkable consistency at different distances for M_w 4.5, 5.5, 6.5, and 7.5. Specifically, the trend initially decreases, then increases, and finally decreases again. In addition, the figure reveals that, regardless of near-fault or far-fault conditions, under reverse earthquakes ($F_{RV} = 1$, $F_{NM} = 0$) at short periods, the V/H spectral ratios at soil sites ($V_{S30} = 270$ m/s) are

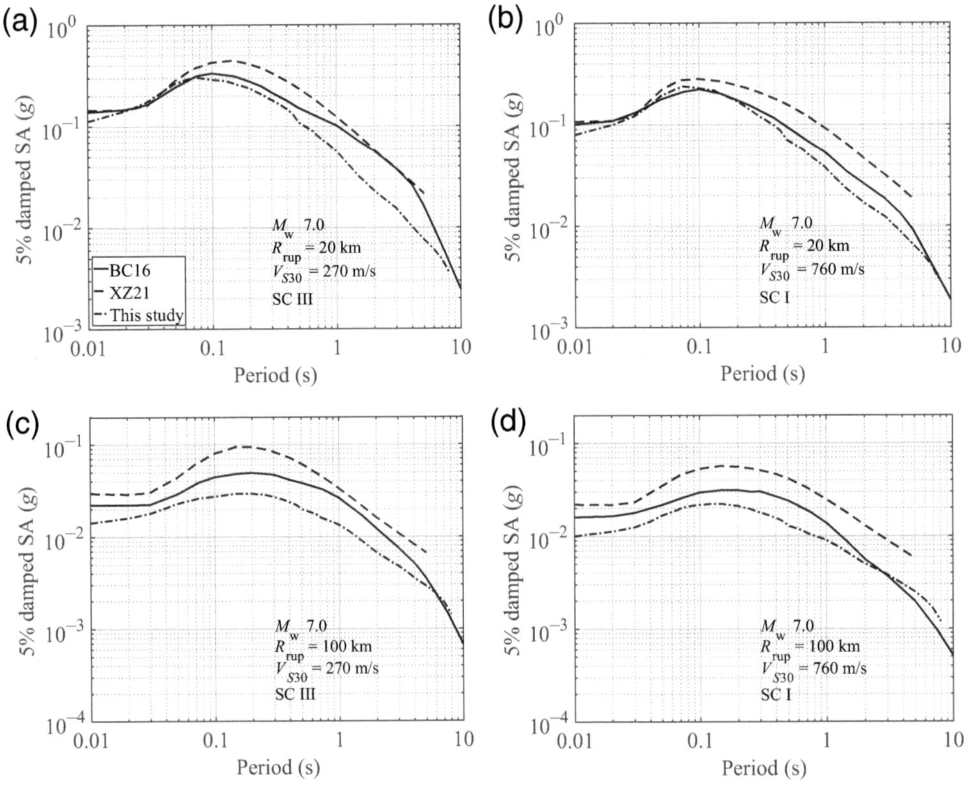

Figure 13. Comparison of predicted spectral acceleration between the proposed V-GMPE and those of the BC16 and XZ21 V-GMPEs. The GMPEs are evaluated for M_w 7, strike-slip earthquakes ($F_{RV} = F_{NM} = 0$), $Z_{TOR} = 1$ km, (a) $R_{rup} = 20$ km, $V_{S30} = 270$ m/s, (b) $R_{rup} = 20$ km, $V_{S30} = 760$ m/s, (c) $R_{rup} = 100$ km, $V_{S30} = 270$ m/s, and (d) $R_{rup} = 100$ km, $V_{S30} = 760$ m/s.

significantly larger than those at rock sites ($V_{S30} = 760$ m/s) for M_w 4.5, 5.5, 6.5, and 7.5, indicating a distinct site amplification effect. This discrepancy can be attributed to the stronger attenuation of the horizontal ground-motion component compared with the vertical component at short periods, suggesting that the nonlinear effects of the soil layer on the horizontal component of ground motion are particularly prominent in southwest China at short periods. However, at long periods, the V/H spectral ratios of rock sites exceed those of soil sites. This observation differs significantly from previous findings reported by Bozorgnia and Campbell (2016a) and Phung *et al.* (2022), likely because of the differences in tectonic environments between southwest China and the western United States and Taiwan regions.

SUMMARY AND CONCLUSION

Using 1935 vertical ground-motion records from 116 mainshocks (with M_w ranging from 4.0 to 7.9, and $R_{rup} < 300$ km) that occurred in southwest China between 2008 and 2022, a V-GMPE was developed to estimate the vertical PGA, PGV, and SA ($T = 0.01$–8 s) of mainshocks in this region. To maintain consistency with the ZYLW22 H-GMPE, the V-GMPE adopts the same functional form as the ZYLW22 H-GMPE, thereby ensuring an unbiased estimation of the V/H spectral ratio.

The between-event and within-event residuals of the V-GMPE are found to be around zero with respect to the predictor variables M_w, R_{rup}, Z_{TOR}, and V_{S30}. No discernible trend was observed, indicating good consistency between the predicted values of the V-GMPE and the observed data. Within the period range of 0.08–8 s, the total standard deviations of the H-GMPE and the V-GMPE are comparable, and their period-dependent variation trends are also roughly similar. This finding suggests that the V/H spectral ratio is estimated with equivalent aleatory variability for both vertical and horizontal components (Bommer *et al.*, 2011). Therefore, when using the predicted V/H values, the total standard deviations from the V-GMPE and the ZYLW22 GMPE can be used optionally.

The scaling behavior of predicted ground motions in the V-GMPE with respect to M_w and R_{rup} is consistent with that of the ZYLW22 H-GMPE. The predicted ground motions from the V-GMPE are influenced by M_w-dependent geometric spreading and anelastic attenuation, which effectively captures the magnitude and distance saturation effect in the near-fault region of large earthquakes in southwest China. However, the anelastic attenuation of the vertical component is generally stronger than that of the horizontal component.

In the near-fault region, the peak of the vertical response spectrum occurs at 0.075 s for M_w 5, 6, 7, and 8, and $V_{S30} = 270$ and 760 m/s. However, in the far-fault region, the peak position of the vertical response spectrum is largely affected by M_w and site conditions. This characteristic is consistent with findings from the ZYLW22 H-GMPE, where the peak position of horizontal ground motion shifts to longer periods and increases systematically with increasing M_w and decreasing V_{S30} values. In the far-fault region, long-period ground motions are significantly amplified at both soil and rock sites. This phenomenon may be associated with the basin amplification effect in southwest China. Consequently, similar to the H-GMPE, the basin amplification effect should also be incorporated into subsequent research on the V-GMPE in southwest China. Furthermore, regardless of soil or rock site conditions, the V-GMPE distinctly captures the HW effect in the near-fault region of large earthquakes.

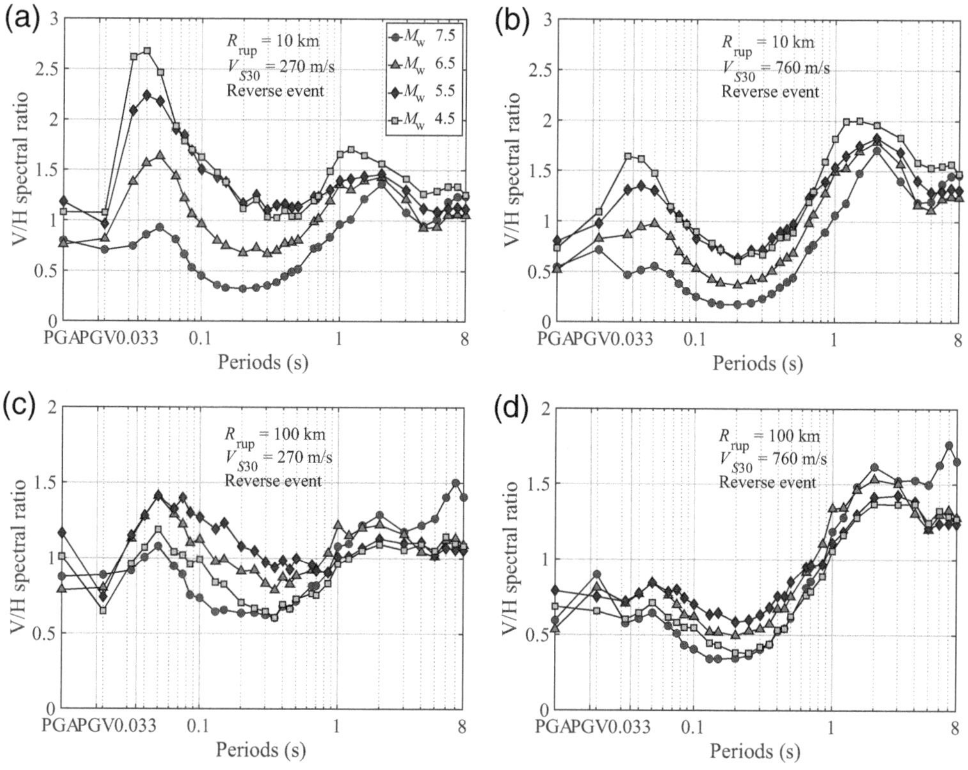

Figure 14. Dependence of the vertical-to-horizontal (V/H) spectral ratios on period for M_w 4.5, 5.5, 6.5, and 7.5, reverse events ($F_{RV} = 1$, $F_{NM} = 0$), (a) $R_{rup} = 10$ km, soil sites ($V_{S30} = 270$ m/s), (b) $R_{rup} = 10$ km, rock sites ($V_{S30} = 760$ m/s), (c) $R_{rup} = 100$ km, soil sites, and (d) $R_{rup} = 100$ km, rock sites. The color version of this figure is available only in the electronic edition.

We recommend applying the V-GMPE to estimate the vertical ground-motion parameters (PGA, PGV, and SA (T = 0.01–8 s)) for mainshocks in southwest China within the following predictor variables range: (1) $M_w \geq 4.0$; (2) $M_w \leq 7.9$ for reverse fault, $M_w \leq 5.7$ for normal fault, *and* $M_w \leq 6.6$ for strike-slip fault; (3) $R_{rup} = 10$–300 km related to M_w; (4) $V_{S30} = 140$–1130 m/s; (5) $Z_{TOR} = 0$–20 km; and (6) $\delta = 20°$–90°.

The predicted response spectra of the proposed V-GMPE exhibit slight differences from those of the BC16 and XZ21 V-GMPEs. For a strike-slip earthquake with M_w 7, at near-fault soil sites, the predicted response spectra of the proposed V-GMPE are slightly larger than those of the BC16 V-GMPE and slightly smaller than those of the XZ21 V-GMPE for $0.02 < T < 0.075°$s; for $T < 0.02°$s and $T > 0.075°$s, they are uniformly smaller than those of both the BC16 and XZ21 V-GMPEs. However, at near-fault rock sites, the predicted response spectra of the proposed V-GMPE are slightly larger than those of the BC16 V-GMPE and are slightly smaller than those of the XZ21 V-GMPE for $0.03 < T < 0.1°$s; for $T < 0.03°$s and $T > 0.1°$ s, they are uniformly smaller than those of both the BC16 and XZ21 V-GMPEs. At far-fault soil sites, the predicted response spectra of the proposed V-GMPE are smaller than those of the BC16 and XZ21 V-GMPEs for $T < 6$ s, and larger than those of the BC16 V-GMPE for $T > 6$ s. However, at far-fault rock sites, this transition period shifts to 3 s.

The predicted ground motions from the V-GMPE and the ZYLW22 H-GMPE were used to estimate the V/H spectral ratio. At near-fault distances, the V/H spectral ratios decrease consistently with increasing M_w across all periods. For soil sites, the V/H spectral ratios for M_w 4.5, 5.5, 6.5, and 7.5 range from 1.00 to 2.68, 0.96 to 2.24, 0.67 to 1.63, and 0.32 to 1.36, respectively. For rock sites, the V/H spectral ratios for these four magnitudes range from 0.61 to 2.00, 0.63 to 1.83, 0.37 to 1.79, and 0.18 to 1.71, respectively. However, at far-fault distances, the magnitude dependence of the V/H spectral ratios varies with period. For soil sites, the V/H spectral ratios for the four magnitudes fall within the ranges of 0.61–1.14, 0.71–1.36, 0.79–1.41, and 0.61–1.50, respectively. For rock sites, the V/H spectral ratios for the four magnitudes range from 0.36 to 1.36, 0.55 to 1.41, 0.50 to 1.53, and 0.34 to 1.76, respectively.

For both soil and rock sites, the variation trend of the V/H spectral ratio with period shows remarkable consistency at different distances for M_w 4.5, 5.5, 6.5, and 7.5. Specifically, this trend initially decreases, then increases, and finally decreases again. In addition, under reverse earthquakes, the V/H spectral ratios at soil sites are significantly larger than those at rock sites for the four magnitudes at short periods, regardless of near-fault or far-fault conditions. This indicates a distinct site amplification effect. Such a difference can be attributed to the stronger attenuation of the horizontal component compared to the vertical component at short periods. This further implies that the nonlinear effects of the soil layer on the horizontal component of ground motion are particularly prominent in southwest China at short periods. However, at long periods, the V/H spectral ratios of rock sites are larger than those of soil sites. This observation differs significantly from previous findings reported by Bozorgnia and Campbell (2016a) and Phung *et al.* (2022). This is likely because of the difference in tectonic environments between southwest China and the western United States and Taiwan regions.

For rock sites in the near-fault region with M_w 7.5, the V/H spectral ratios range from 0.5 to 1 for $T < 0.06$ s and $0.5 < T < 1$ s. For $0.06 < T < 0.5$ s, the V/H spectral ratios span 0–0.5. For $T > 1$ s, the V/H spectral ratios exceed 1, peaking at $T = 2$ s with a maximum value of 1.71. For soil sites in the near-fault region with M_w 7.5, the V/H spectral ratios exhibit similar patterns but with distinct threshold values. Specifically, the V/H spectral ratios range from 0.5 to 1 for $T < 0.1$ s and $0.5 < T < 1$ s; for $0.1 < T < 0.5$ s, they span 0–0.5; for $T > 1$ s, the V/H spectral ratios exceed 1, peaking at $T = 2$ s with a maximum value of 1.36. Therefore, the current seismic design codes for most structures in China, including Ministry of Transport of the People's Republic of China (2013) and China National Energy Administration (2015), which typically assume the vertical design ground motion to be 0.5–1 times the horizontal design ground motion, are partially justified. Nevertheless, these assumptions should still incorporate earthquake magnitude, distance, site type, and spectral period for a more comprehensive assessment. Notably, this assumption is not applicable to engineering structures with long natural vibration periods that may be subjected to strong ground motions from distant sources of large earthquakes.

The study of the vertical GMPE and V/H spectral ratio in southwest China in this article can lay the foundation for the subsequent development of vertical design spectrum suitable for southwest China. This development is crucial for effectively reducing the earthquake disaster risk of engineering structures such as long-span bridges, dams, highways, and nuclear power plants in southwest China.

DATA AND RESOURCES

Strong-motion data for this study are provided by Engineering Mechanics, China Earthquake Administration (offline application). Focal mechanism solution and M_w of 24 earthquakes for $4.7 \le M_w \le 5.6$ in southwest China are obtained from Global Centroid Moment Tensor (Global CMT), available at www.globalcmt.org and U.S. Geological Survey (USGS) Earthquake Hazards Program, available at www.earthquake.usgs.gov. The hypocentral depth is uniformly obtained from the China Seismic Network Center, available at www.ceic.ac.cn. All the websites were last accessed in July 2024. The supplemental material for this article includes a Word file containing one table and four figures.

DECLARATION OF COMPETING INTERESTS

The authors acknowledge that there are no conflicts of interest recorded.

ACKNOWLEDGMENTS

This work was supported by research grants from the Central Public-interest Scientific Institution Basal Research Fund (Number CEAIEF20250202), the National Key R&D Program of China (2022YFC3003502), and the National Key R&D Program of China (2022YFC3003503). The random-effects regression used in this study was implemented through the MATLAB software (MathWorks, 2019). The authors thank two anonymous reviewers, the associate editor, and the editor-in-chief for their kind review and constructive comments. Bin Zhang supported through the methodology, writing of the original draft, and visualization. Xiaojian Lu supported with conceptualization, writing, review, and editing. Jiamei Liu supported with data curation and formal analysis. Mianshui Rong supported with investigation, writing, review, and editing. Yanxiang Yu supported with writing, review, and editing. Xiaojun Li supported with writing, review, and editing.

REFERENCES

Abrahamson, N. A., and R. R. Youngs (1992). A stable algorithm for regression analyses using the random effects model, *Bull. Seismol. Soc. Am.* **82,** no. 1, 505–510.

Akkar, S., M. A. Sandikkaya, and B. Ö. Ay (2014). Compatible ground-motion prediction equations for damping scaling factors and vertical-to-horizontal spectral amplitude ratios for the broader European region, *Bull. Earthq. Eng.* **12,** 517–547.

Ancheta, T. D., R. B. Darragh, J. P. Stewart, E. Seyhan, W. J. Silva, B. S. J. Chiou, K. E. Wooddell, R. W. Graves, A. R. Kottke, D. M. Boore, *et al.* (2014). NGA-West2 database, *Earthq. Spectra* 30**,** no. 3, 989–1005.

Bommer, J. J., S. Akkar, and Ö. Kale (2011). A model for vertical-to-horizontal response spectral ratios for Europe and the Middle East, *Bull. Seismol. Soc. Am.* **101,** 1783–1806.

Boore, D. M., W. B. Joyner, and T. E. Fumal (1997). Equations for estimating horizontal response spectra and peak acceleration from western North American earthquakes: A summary of recent work, *Seismol. Res. Lett.* **68,** no. 1, 128–153.

Bozorgnia, Y., and K. W. Campbell (2016a). Ground motion model for the vertical-to-horizontal (V/H) ratios of PGA, PGV, and response spectra, *Earthq. Spectra* **32,** no. 2, 951–978.

Bozorgnia, Y., and K. W. Campbell (2016b). Vertical ground motion model for PGA, PGV, and linear response spectra using the NGA-West2 database, *Earthq. Spectra* **32,** no. 2, 979–1004.

Building Seismic Safety Council (BSSC) (2003). *The 2003 NEHRP Recommended Provisions for New Buildings and Other Structures, Part I (Provisions) and Part II (Commentary),* FEMA 368/369, Washington, D.C.

Campbell, K. W., and Y. Bozorgnia (2003). Updated far ground-motion (attenuation) relations for the horizontal and vertical components of peak ground acceleration and acceleration response spectra, *Bull. Seismol. Soc. Am.* **93,** no. 1, 314–331.

Campbell, K. W., and Y. Bozorgnia (2007). *Campbell-Bozorgnia NGA Ground Motion Relations for the Geometric Mean Horizontal Component of Peak and Spectral Ground Motion Parameters,* Pacific Earthquake Engineering Research Center, California, Berkeley.

Campbell, K. W., and Y. Bozorgnia (2008). NGA ground motion model for the geometric mean horizontal component of PGA, PGV, PGD and 5% damped linear elastic response spectra for periods ranging from 0.01 to 10 s, *Earthq. Spectra* **24,** no. 1, 139–171.

Campbell, K. W., and Y. Bozorgnia (2013). *NGA-West2 Campbell-Bozorgnia Ground Motion Model for the Horizontal Components of PGA, PGV, and 5%-Damped Elastic Pseudo-Acceleration Response Spectra for Periods Ranging from 0.01 to 10 s, PEER Rept. No. 2013/06,* Pacific Earthquake Engineering Research Center, University of California, Berkeley, California, 238 pp.

Chang, Z. F., S. Y. Yang, Q. Y. Zhou, Y. F. Zhang, and Y. Q. Xie (2013). Discussion of seismogenic structure of the June 24, 2012 Ninglang-

Yanyuan M_s 5.7 earthquake, *Seismol. Geol.* **35,** no. 1, 37–49 (in Chinese).
China National Energy Administration (2015). *Code for Seismic Design of Hydraulic Structures of Hydropower Project (NB 35047-2015)*, China Electric Power Press, Beijing (in Chinese).
Chiou, B., and R. Youngs (2014). Update of the Chiou and Youngs NGA model for the average horizontal component of peak ground motion and response spectra, *Earthq. Spectra* **30,** no. 3, 1117–1153.
Chiou, B., R. Darragh, N. Gregor, and W. Silva (2008). NGA project strong-motion database, *Earthq. Spectra* **24,** no. 1, 23–44.
Du, X. L., Q. Han, and Z. X. Li (2008). The seismic damage of bridges in the 2008 Wenchuan earthquake and lessons from its damage, *J. Beijing Univ. Technol.* **34,** no. 12, 1270–1279 (in Chinese).
Fan, W. J., K. Z. Zuo, C. P. Zhao, and G. M. Wang (2023). Analysis of seismogenic structure of Yunnan Shuangbai earthquake sequence on June 10, 2021, *Chinese J. Geophys.* **66,** no. 5, 1991–2006 (in Chinese).
Farajpour, Z., S. Pezeshk, and M. Zare (2019). A new empirical ground-motion model for Iran, *Bull. Seismol. Soc. Am.* **109,** no. 2, 732–744.
Gong, Y., F. Long, M. J. Liang, G. X. Yi, Y. X. Wang, and G. S. Zhai (2019). Seismogenic structure of the Jinkouhe M_S 5.0 earthquake in 2015, *Earthq. Res. China* **35,** no. 3, 445–454 (in Chinese).
Gong, Y., F. Long, M. Zhao, P. Yang, Y. X. Wang, M. J. Liang, H. Z. Qiao, and Y. H. Wang (2024). The spatio-temporal evolution characteristics of the M_S 6.0 Barkam earthquake in Sichuan on June 10, 2022, *Acta Seismol. Sinica* **46,** no. 2, 173–191 (in Chinese).
Gülerce, Z., and N. A. Abrahamson (2011). Site-specific design spectra for vertical ground motion, *Earthq. Spectra* **27,** no. 4, 1023–1047.
Gülerce, Z., R. Kamai, N. A. Abrahamson, and W. J. Silva (2017). Ground motion prediction equations for the vertical ground motion component based on the NGA-W2 database, *Earthq. Spectra* **33,** no. 2, 499–528.
Haji-Soltani, A., S. Pezeshk, M. Malekmohammadi, and A. Zandieh (2017). A study of vertical-to-horizontal ratio of earthquake components in the Gulf Coast region, *Bull. Seismol. Soc. Am.* **107,** no. 5, 2055–2066.
Han, J. P., and W. Zhou (2012). Preliminary investigation on characteristics of vertical ground motion during Wenchuan earthquake, *Eng. Mech.* **29,** no. 12, 211–219 (in Chinese).
Huang, X. L., Z. H. Wu, Y. Jiang, T. T. Tian, and Y. H. Liu (2015). Seismic intensity distribution and seismogenic structure analysis of the March 3, 2013 Eryuan M_s 5.5 earthquake in Dali, Yunnan Province, *Geol. Bull. China* **34,** no. 1, 135–145 (in Chinese).
Huang, X. L., Z. H. Wu, X. Y. Zhao, K. G. Wu, X. J. Huang, and J. J. Du (2015). Seismogenic structure of 2014 *Ms* 5.6 and *Ms* 6.1 earthquake in Yingjiang, Yunnan Province, *Acta Geosci. Sinica* **36,** no. 6, 761–770 (in Chinese).
Ji, K., Y. F. Ren, C. B. Zhu, Y. T. Zhang, X. X. Yao, D. R. Wang, P. Zhang, H. J. Si, T. Kishida, Y. Liu, *et al.* (2024). Site database for national strong motion stations in mainland China, *Eng. Geol.* **339,** 107,651, doi: 10.1016/j.enggeo.2024.107651.
Kaklamanos, J., L. G. Baise, and D. M. Boore (2011). Estimating unknown input parameters when implementing the NGA ground-motion prediction equations in engineering practice, *Earthq. Spectra* **27,** no. 4, 1219–1235.
Kunnath, S. K., E. Erduran, Y. H. Chai, and M. Yashinsky (2008). Effect of near-fault vertical ground motions on seismic response of highway overcrossings, *J. Bridge Eng.* **13,** no. 3, 282–290.
Laouami, N. (2019). Vertical ground motion prediction equations and vertical-to-horizontal (V/H) ratios of PGA and PSA for Algeria and surrounding region, *Bull. Earthq. Eng.* **17,** no. 7, 3637–3660.
Li, D. N., Y. Gao, H. Y. Zhu, M. Qin, H. Y. Zhang, and Y. Xu (2017). Research on double - difference relocations and focal mechanism solutions of the 2014 Yunnan Jinggu M_S 6.6 earthquake sequence, *J. Seismol. Res.* **40,** no. 3, 465–473 (in Chinese).
Li, X. L., C. H. Zhai, W. P. Wen, and L. L. Xie (2020). Ground motion prediction model for horizontal PGA, 5% damped response spectrum in Sichuan-Yunnan region of China, *J. Earthq. Eng.* **24,** no. 11, 1829–1866.
Li, Z. X., Y. G. Wan, H. W. Cui, Z. Y. Li, X. H. Hu, J. C. Huang, and Z. T. Jin (2020). Characteristics analysis of tectonic stress field around the Mojiang earthquake and its adjacent areas on September 8, 2018, *Chin. J. Geophys.* **63,** no. 4, 1431–1443 (in Chinese).
Liu, P., Q. F. Luo, and X. Z. Chen (2020). Vertical ground motion attenuation relationship of Wenchuan earthquake, *J. Harbin Inst. Technol.* **52,** no. 2, 119–127 (in Chinese).
Lu, R. Q., L. H. Fang, Z. Guo, J. Y. Zhang, W. Wang, P. Su, W. Tao, X. Sun, G. S. Liu, X. J. Shan, and H. L. He (2022). Detailed structural characteristics of the 1 June 2022 M_S 6.1 Sichuan Lushan strong earthquake, *Chin. J. Geophys.* **65,** no. 11, 4299–4310 (in Chinese).
Luo, J., C. P. Zhao, and L. Q. Zhou (2015). Focal mechanisms and stress field of Shangri-La Deqen, Yunnan province-Derong Sichuan Province M_S 5.9 earthquake sequence in August, 2013, *Chin. J. Geophys.* **58,** no. 2, 424–435 (in Chinese).
Luo, Y., L. Zhao, and J. Tian (2020). The focal depths of the 2008 Panzhihua earthquake sequence and the stress field in the source region, *Sci. China Earth Sci.* **63,** 439–451 (in Chinese).
Lv, J., X. F. Zheng, J. Xiao, Z. J. Xie, X. F. Zeng, B. Li, and F. F. Dong (2013). Rupture characteristics and seismogenic structures of the M_S 5.7 and M_S 5.6 Yiliang earthquake of Sep.7, 2012, *Chin. J. Geophys.* **56,** no. 8, 2645–2654 (in Chinese).
MathWorks (2019). *MATLAB (Version R2019b) [Computer software]*, available at https://www.mathworks.com/products/matlab.html (last accessed August 2025).
Ministry of Transport of the People's Republic of China (2013). *Specification of Seismic Design for Highway Engineering (JTG B02-2013)*, China Communications Press, Beijing (in Chinese).
Newmark, N. M., and W. J. Hall (1982). Earthquake spectra and design, Engineering monographs on earthquake criteria, available at https://kupdf.net/download/1982-newmark-amp-hall-eeri-earthquake-spectra-and-design_5900ac9ddc0d60a04e959e90_pdf (last accessed August 2025).
Pan, R., J. Z. Jiang, H. Fu, and J. Li (2019). Focal mechanism and focal depth determination of Yunnan Yangbi M_S 5.1 and M_S 4.8 earthquakes in 2017, *J. Seismol. Res.* **42,** no. 3, 338–348 (in Chinese).
Papazoglou, A. J., and A. S. Elnashai (1996). Analytical and field evidence of the damaging effect of vertical earthquake ground motion, *Earthq. Eng. Struct. Dynam.* **25,** 1109–1137.
Phung, V. B., N. A. Abrahamson, B. S. Huang, and H. L. Chin (2022). Vertical ground-motion prediction equation and the vertical-to-horizontal spectral ratio for crustal earthquakes in Taiwan, *Earthq. Spectra* **38,** no. 2, 1189–1222.
Qin, L. B., W. W. Chen, S. D. Ni, L. B. Han, and Y. Luo (2014). A method of resolving earthquake rupture directivity with relative

centroid location and it's application to 2008 Yingjiang Ms 6.0 earthquake, *Chin J. Geophys.* **57,** no. 10, 3259–3269 (in Chinese).

Ramadan, F., C. Smerzini, G. Lanzano, and P. Francesca (2021). An empirical model for the vertical-to-horizontal spectral ratios for Italy, *Earthq. Eng. Struct. Dynam.* **50,** no. 15, 4121–4141.

Seyhan, E., and J. P. Stewart (2014). Semi-empirical nonlinear site amplification from NGA-West2 data and simulations, *Earthq. Spectra* **30,** no. 3, 1241–1256.

Shi, C. H., X. H. He, and S. D. Ni (2018). Rupture directivity of the July 9, 2009 Yao'an MS 6.0 earthquake, *Earthq. Res. China* **34,** no. 2, 293–302 (in Chinese).

Song, Q., S. S. Liang, X. W. Yu, W. B. Zhang, and C. L. Li (2022). Seismogenic mechanism of the 2020 Qiaojia M_S 5.0 earthquake sequence and its relationship with the 2014 Ludian M_S 6.5 earthquake in Yunnan, *Chin. J. Geophys.* **65,** no. 4, 1303–1324 (in Chinese).

Stewart, J. P., D. M. Boore, E. Seyhan, and G. M. Atkinson (2016). NGA-West2 equations for predicting vertical-component PGA, PGV, and 5%-damped PSA from shallow crustal earthquakes, *Earthq. Spectra* **32,** 1005–1031.

Tan, J. Y., and J. J. Hu (2021). A prediction model for vertical-to-horizontal spectral ratios of ground motions on the seafloor for moderate magnitude events for the Sagami Bay region in Japan, *J. Seismol.* **25,** 181–199.

Walling, M., W. J. Silva, and N. A. Abrahamson (2008). Nonlinear site amplification factors for constraining the NGA models, *Earthq. Spectra* **24,** no. 1, 243–255.

Wang, G. M., Z. F. Liu, X. Y. Zhao, W. J. Fan, Y. L. Li, G. L. Peng, and N. Sun (2018). Relocation of Tonghai M_S 5.0 earthquake sequence in 2018 and discussion of it's seismogenic fault, *J. Seismol. Res.* **41,** no. 4, 503–510+657 (in Chinese).

Wang, H. W., H. R. Li, Y. F. Ren, and R. Z. Wen (2025). A comprehensive earthquake source database for China's strong-motion flatfile (2007–2020), *Earthq. Res. Adv.* **5,** no. 2, 100,346, doi: 10.1016/j.eqrea.2024.100346.

Wang, S., G. Jiang, M. Weingarten, and Y. F. Niu (2020). InSAR evidence indicates a link between fluid injection for salt mining and the 2019 Changning (China) earthquake sequence, *Geophys. Res. Lett.* **46,** e2020GL087603.

Xiao, B. F., Y. P. Qi, F. Long, Y. Shen, H. L. Liang, and Y. P. Tian (2020). Focal mechanism solutions and seismogenic structure of $M \geq 4.7$ earthquakes since 2014 in Yongshan, Yunnan, *North China Earthq. Sci.* **38,** no. 3, 13–18 (in Chinese).

Xie, J. J., X. J. Li, Z. P. Wen, L. Jia, Z. An, J. Cui, G. Lin, Q. Zhang, P. Jiang, Q. Xie, *et al.* (2022). Soil profile database and site classification for national strong-motion stations in western China, *Seismol. Res. Lett.* **93,** no. 3, 1930–1942.

Xing, H., and J. X. Zhao (2021). A ground-motion prediction equation for the western and the southwestern parts of China based on local strong-motion records and an overseas reference model for the vertical component, *Bull. Seismol. Soc. Am.* **111,** no. 6, 3314–3331.

Xu, F. K., Z. F. Liu, N. Sun, J. J. He, and X. Y. Zhao (2015). Distribution and temporal evaluation characteristic of Cangyuan M_S 5.5 earthquake sequences in Yunnan in 2015, *J. Seismol. Res.* **38,** no. 3, 333–340 (in Chinese).

Yang, T., J. P. Wu, L. H. Fang, and W. L. Wang (2016). Relocation of main shock and aftershocks of the 2014 Yingjiang M_S 5.6 and M_S 6.1 earthquakes in Yunnan, *Seismol. Geol.* **38,** no. 4, 1047–1057 (in Chinese).

Yi, G. X., F. Long, M. Zhao, Y. Gong, Z. W. Zhang, and H. Z. Qiao (2016). Focal mechanism and seismogenic structure of the M 5.0 Yuexi earthquake on 1 Oct. 2014, southwestern China, *Seismol. Geol.* **38,** no. 4, 1124–1136 (in Chinese).

Zhang, B., Y. X. Yu, X. J. Li, and Y. S. Wang (2022). Ground motion prediction equation for the average horizontal component of PGA, PGV, and 5% damped acceleration response spectra at periods ranging from 0.033 to 8.0 s in southwest China, *Soil Dynam. Earthq. Eng.* **159,** 107,297.

Zhang, L., Y. Zhou, X. Zhang, A. Zhu, B. Li, S. Wang, S. Liang, C. Jiang, J. Wu, Y. Li, *et al.* (2023). 2022 M_W 6.6 Luding, China, earthquake: A strong continental event illuminating the Moxi seismic gap, *Seismol. Res. Lett.* **94,** 2129–2142.

Zhang, X., W. P. Feng, D. H. Li, F. L. Feng, and Y. Lei (2021). Diverse rupture process of the 2014 Kangding, China, earthquake doublet (M_W 6.0 and 5.7) and driving mechanisms of aftershocks, *Tectonophysics* **820,** 229,118.

Zhang, X., L. Xu, L. Yi, and W. P. Feng (2021). Confirmation and characterization of the rupture model of the 2017 M_S 7.0 Jiuzhaigou, China, earthquake, *Seismol. Res. Lett.* **92,** 2927–2942.

Zhang, Y., Y. T. Chen, L. S. Xu, X. Wei, P. M. Jin, and S. Zhang (2015). The 2014 M_W 6.1 Ludian, Yunnan, earthquake: A complex conjugated ruptured earthquake, *Chin J. Geophys.* **58,** no. 1, 153–162 (in Chinese).

Zhang, Y., W. P. Feng, L. S. Xu, C. H. Zhou, and Y. T. Chen (2008). Spatio-temporal rupture process of the 2008 great Wenchuan earthquake, *Sci. China Earth Sci.* **38,** no. 10, 1186–1194 (in Chinese).

Zhang, Y., R. Wang, Y.-T. Chen, L. S. Xu, F. Du, M. P. Jin, H. W. Tu, and T. Dahm (2014). Kinematic rupture model and hypocenter relocation of the 2013 M_W 6.6 Lushan earthquake constrained by strong-motion and teleseismic data, *Seismol. Res. Lett.* **85,** no. 1, 15–22.

Zhu, Y. J., Y. Luo, L. Zhao, and J. H. Tian (2022). Rupture process of Yunnan Yangbi M_S 6.4 earthquake constrained by regional broadband seismograms, *Chin. J. Geophys.* **65,** no. 3, 1021–1031 (in Chinese).

Manuscript received 23 March 2025
Published online 3 December 2025

A Ground-Motion Model for the Vertical Ground-Motion Component Based on Empirical Data from the NGA-East Data Set

Shahram Pezeshk*[1], Ali Farhadi[2], and Mehran Davatgari-Tafreshi[1]

ABSTRACT

In this study, we propose a ground-motion model (GMM) to estimate vertical ground-motion components in central and eastern North America (CENA) using the referenced empirical method (REM) introduced by Atkinson (2008). The GMM developed in this study is the first vertical GMM for CENA using REM. To account for epistemic uncertainty in choosing a reference model, we considered three alternative models for the host region: Stewart *et al.* (2016), Gülerce *et al.* (2017), and Bozorgnia and Campbell (2016). We began by computing the vertical response spectrum for recorded motions in the Next Generation Attenuation-East Project data set. Next, we calculated residuals between the vertical-component pseudo-spectral accelerations from 0.01 to 10.00 s and the average predictions of the three reference models. We then applied a mixed-effects regression technique to derive adjustment factors for refining these predictions and to estimate the standard deviation components. The proposed GMM is assessed through residual analyses and comparisons with recorded data as a final step. The proposed GMM does not exhibit any discernible residual trends with distance and magnitude and appropriately accounts for site effects.

KEY POINTS

- The vertical component of earthquakes can cause damaging effects on short-period critical structures.
- We used referenced empirical method to develop a ground-motion model (GMM) for estimating the vertical ground-motion component for central and eastern North America.
- The proposed GMM is assessed through residual analyses and comparisons with recorded data as a final step.

Supplemental Material

INTRODUCTION

A sequence of devastating earthquakes, including Bam, Iran (2003); Chi-Chi, Taiwan (1999); Kobe, Japan (1995); and Northridge, California (1994), highlighted the destructive impact of vertical ground-motion components on short-period critical structures, including lifeline systems, highway bridges, ordinary buildings near causative faults, dams, and nuclear power plants (Elnashai and Papazoglou, 1997; Campbell and Bozorgnia, 2003, ; Kunnath *et al.*, 2008; Bommer *et al.*, 2011; Gülerce and Abrahamson, 2011). Over the past 30 yr, numerous studies have aimed to better understand the vertical ground motion and its impact on seismic design and geotechnical structures. Bozorgnia and Campbell (2004, 2016) and Bommer *et al.* (2011) have shown that vertical-to-horizontal (V/H) ratios vary with source-to-site distance (e.g., rupture distance) and spectral period, exhibiting higher values at closer distances and shorter periods.

Ground-motion models (GMMs) or ground-motion prediction equations are considered an important element in probabilistic seismic hazard analysis (PSHA). Two methodologies have been employed to establish the vertical design spectrum for critical structures (Gülerce and Abrahamson, 2011). In the first approach, PSHA is carried out with vertical GMMs, whereas the second approach modifies horizontal design spectra using V/H ratios. However, discrepancies arise between these approaches due to differences in the scaling behavior of vertical and horizontal components with respect to seismological parameters, such as distance and magnitude. Although V/H ratio models attempt to capture these differences, recently developed GMMs suggest distinct scaling characteristics for vertical and horizontal components, making the second methodology a good alternative. Considering these challenges, this

1. Department of Civil Engineering, The University of Memphis, Memphis, Tennessee, U.S.A., https://orcid.org/0000-0002-4367-1184 (SP); https://orcid.org/0000-0002-4646-4156 (MD-T); 2. Tigerrisk Partners, Durham, North Carolina, U.S.A.

*Corresponding author: spezeshk@memphis.edu

Cite this article as Pezeshk, S., A. Farhadi, and M. Davatgari-Tafreshi (2026). A Ground-Motion Model for the Vertical Ground-Motion Component Based on Empirical Data from the NGA-East Data Set, *Bull. Seismol. Soc. Am.* **116**, 755–769, doi: 10.1785/0120250145 study implements the first method and proposes a standalone GMM to estimate vertical ground motion in central and eastern North America (CENA). Despite extensive studies on V/H ratios in CENA, no prior research has directly characterized the vertical ground-motion component. Notable studies on V/H ratios in CENA include those by McGuire *et al.* (2001), Haji-Soltani *et al.* (2017), and Pezeshk *et al.* (2022). In this study, we develop a GMM for the vertical component instead of the V/H ratio because models for the V/H ratio are already available (e.g., Haji-Soltani *et al.*, 2017; Pezeshk *et al.*, 2022). In contrast, no model currently exists for the vertical component. We also select the referenced empirical method (REM) because it uses data to adjust the host model, providing residuals and standard deviation components based on the empirical data set.

In this study, we employed REM to propose a new GMM for predicting the vertical component of ground motion in CENA. This approach is essential because the limited availability of strong-motion data across a broad range of engineering-interest magnitudes and distances hinders the direct development of vertical GMMs. The REM adjusts GMM predictions from a data-rich (host) region to a data-scarce (target) region using adjustment factors. This approach defines adjustment factors as the ratio of observed ground motion in the target region to the GMM-predicted values in the host region. In this approach, three GMMs, Stewart *et al.* (2016; hereafter, SBSA16), Gülerce *et al.* (2017; hereafter, GKAS17), and Bozorgnia and Campbell (2016; hereafter, BC16), are considered as reference models for the western United States (WUS), the host region. Successful applications of this method include horizontal GMMs for Puerto Rico, eastern North America, and Hawaii (Atkinson, 2008, 2010; Atkinson and Boore, 2011; Atkinson and Motazedian, 2013; Hassani and Atkinson, 2015). The hybrid empirical method (HEM) can be considered an alternative to the REM (Campbell, 2003; Tavakoli and Pezeshk, 2005; Pezeshk *et al.*, 2011, 2018; Shahjouei and Pezeshk, 2016). Similar to REM, HEM links predictions from a data-rich (host) region to a data-poor (target) region using adjustment factors. However, unlike REM, HEM derives these adjustment factors from synthetic ground-motion simulations (stochastic simulations) rather than observed data. Several researchers have successfully applied HEM in GMM development (e.g., Campbell, 2003; Douglas *et al.*, 2006; Douglas *et al.*, 2024; Pezeshk *et al.*, 2024; Davatgari-Tafreshi and Pezeshk, 2025a,b). In addition, the stochastic simulation approach (Atkinson and Boore, 1995, 2006, 2011; Toro *et al.*, 1997; Silva *et al.*, 2002) has been used in ground-motion modeling in data-poor regions. In this study, we utilized REM and the Next Generation Attenuation-East Project (NGA-East) data set to develop a new GMM for the vertical component of ground motion, with CENA as the target region and WUS as the host region. However, we acknowledge the value of alternative approaches in generating multiple models to enhance the quantification of epistemic uncertainty.

Developing localized GMMs is essential for regions (such as CENA) where earthquake-resistant design or structural safety assessments are necessary (Lin *et al.*, 2011). CENA is classified as a stable continental regime with a rich data set of recorded ground motions from distant small-to-moderate earthquakes but lacks sufficient near-source recordings of large-magnitude events, which are of primary engineering interest. The seismotectonic and geological features of CENA differ significantly from those of WUS because CENA exhibits less topographic variation and is tectonically stable, being an intracontinental region. The geological and seismotectonic background of CENA has influenced the formation of large-scale structures with common geomorphological and geological characteristics, such as the Gulf Coast and the Interior Highlands. In addition, the main conventional difference between the CENA and WUS regions is typically related to event stress drop and the rate of attenuation with distance.

Strong-motion data set

The data set used in this study is derived from NGA-East (Goulet *et al.*, 2014), which contains approximately 29,000 strong-motion records from 81 earthquake events recorded at 1379 stations in CENA. This data set comprises earthquakes with moment magnitudes (**M**) exceeding 2.5 and rupture distances (R_{rup}) up to 1500 km. It is important to note that the NGA-East data set does not include vertical components of the response spectrum. To address this, we derived vertical response spectra from the recorded time series in the NGA-East data set. To this end, we performed standard signal processing protocols using the NGA-East raw data set. Baseline correction was applied by removing the mean and linear trend from the raw acceleration records. For each record, we selected the pre-event noise for the vertical component and calculated the signal-to-noise ratio (SNR). The estimated SNR values were then used to determine the low-cut frequency. We also compared our low-cut frequencies with the NGA-East metadata to ensure that precise values were used. We applied a 5% cosine taper on each side of the signal (Dawood *et al.*, 2016), added zeros to both ends of the signals (zero padding; Boore, 2005), and applied a Butterworth band-pass filter (Boore and Akkar, 2003). The spectral acceleration for the vertical component, for periods ranging from 0.01 to 10 s, was then calculated.

The three reference models used in this study have different applicability ranges. The Bozorgnia and Campbell (2016) model applies to events with $\mathbf{M} \geq 3.3$, whereas Gülerce *et al.* (2017) and Stewart *et al.* (2016) apply to $\mathbf{M} \geq 3.0$. These models also have different minimum V_{S30} (time-averaged shear-wave velocity in the top 30 m) applicability thresholds: 150 m/s for Bozorgnia and Campbell (2016), 180 m/s for Gülerce *et al.* (2017), and 200 m/s for Stewart *et al.* (2016). To ensure consistency across models, we selected NGA-East records with $M_w \geq 3.3$, $R_{rup} < 300$ km, and $V_{S30} > 200$ m/s for developing our GMM. In addition, we did not consider events and stations

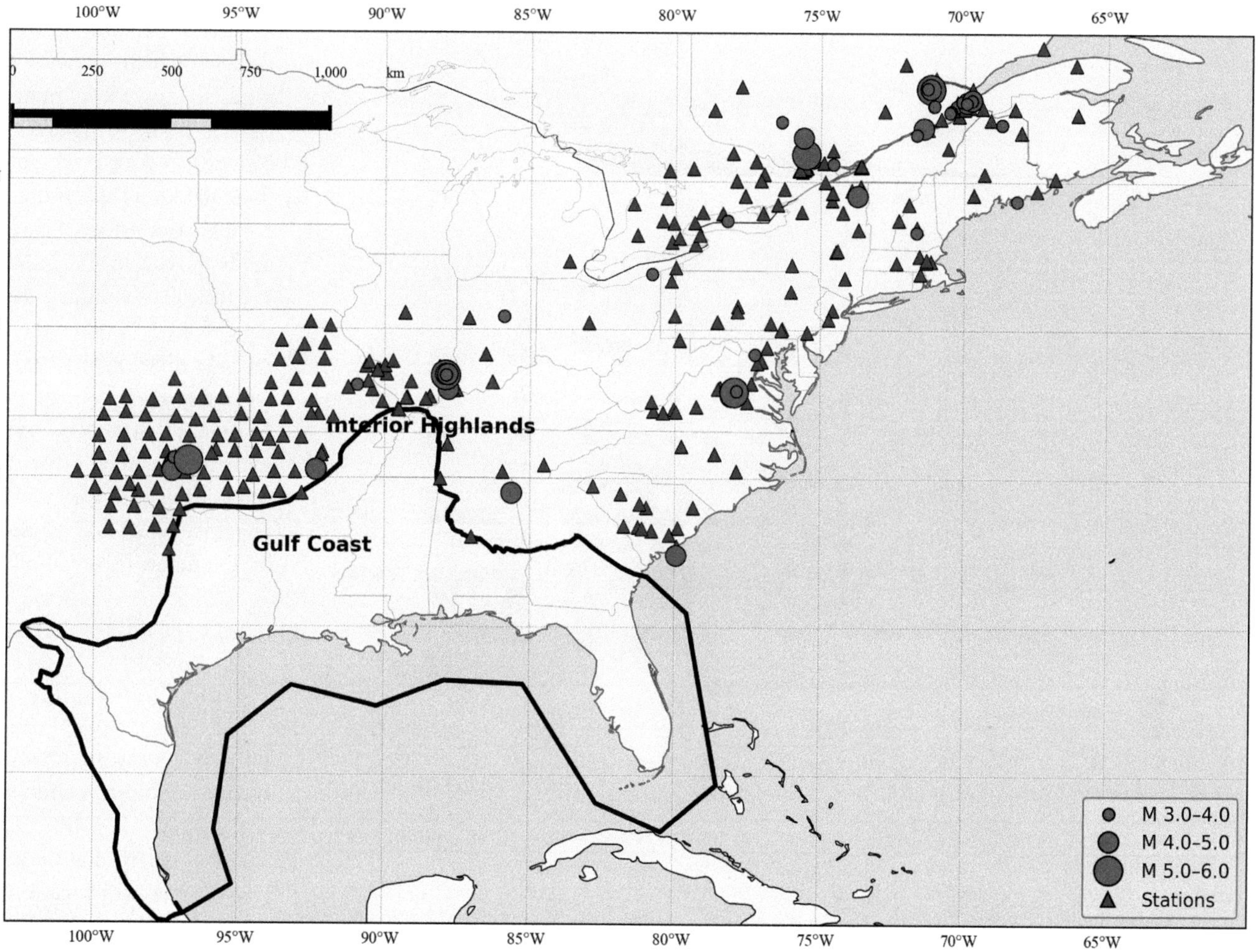

Figure 1. Geographical distribution of earthquakes and stations. The Gulf Coast boundary is shown as a solid-black line. The color version of this figure is available only in the electronic edition.

in the Gulf Coast region because of their distinct attenuation characteristics influenced by thick sediments (Dreiling *et al.*, 2014). Significant differences are observed between the amplitude and the Fourier amplitude spectrum of ground motions recorded inside the Gulf Coast region and those recorded outside it (Goulet, Kishida, *et al.*, 2021; Akhani *et al.*, 2024). The thick sediments in the Gulf Coast region contribute to both attenuation (reduction) and amplification of ground shaking (Hollenback *et al.*, 2015; Goulet *et al.*, 2018). Akhani *et al.* (2024) reported that, relative to the GMM developed by Pezeshk *et al.* (2018) for regions outside the Gulf Coast region, their corrected model for sites within the Gulf Coast region predicts lower values at shorter periods and higher values at longer periods. These discrepancies become more pronounced with increasing sediment thickness, particularly for events of larger magnitude. We also retained only events with at least three recorded motions. The final data set comprises 747 ground-motion records from 44 earthquakes, recorded at 259 stations, as detailed in Table S1, available in the supplemental material to this article. This table includes event dates, magnitudes, the number of records per event, and earthquake coordinates.

Figure 1 depicts the geographical distribution of the selected earthquakes and stations. The Gulf Coast boundary follows Dreiling *et al.* (2014) because it was used to divide CENA into subregions in the NGA-East data set. This boundary has also been widely adopted in the development of the CENA GMM. Figure 2 illustrates the magnitude versus rupture distance distribution to further characterize the data set, with data points categorized by National Earthquake Hazard Reduction Program (NEHRP) site classifications. NEHRP defines five site classes based on V_{S30}: class A (greater than 1500 m/s), class B (between 760 and 1500 m/s), class C (between 360 and 760 m/s), and class D (between 180 and 360 m/s). For the V_{S30} values, we used the NGA-East metadata (Goulet, Kishida, *et al.*, 2021). In the NGA-East data set (Goulet, Kishida, *et al.*, 2021), only 6% of stations have measured V_{S30} values, whereas at the remaining sites, V_{S30} is estimated from proxies, most commonly topographic slope. The data set lacks sufficient coverage of large magnitude at short distances, and recordings from softer sites are less frequent than those from stiffer ones.

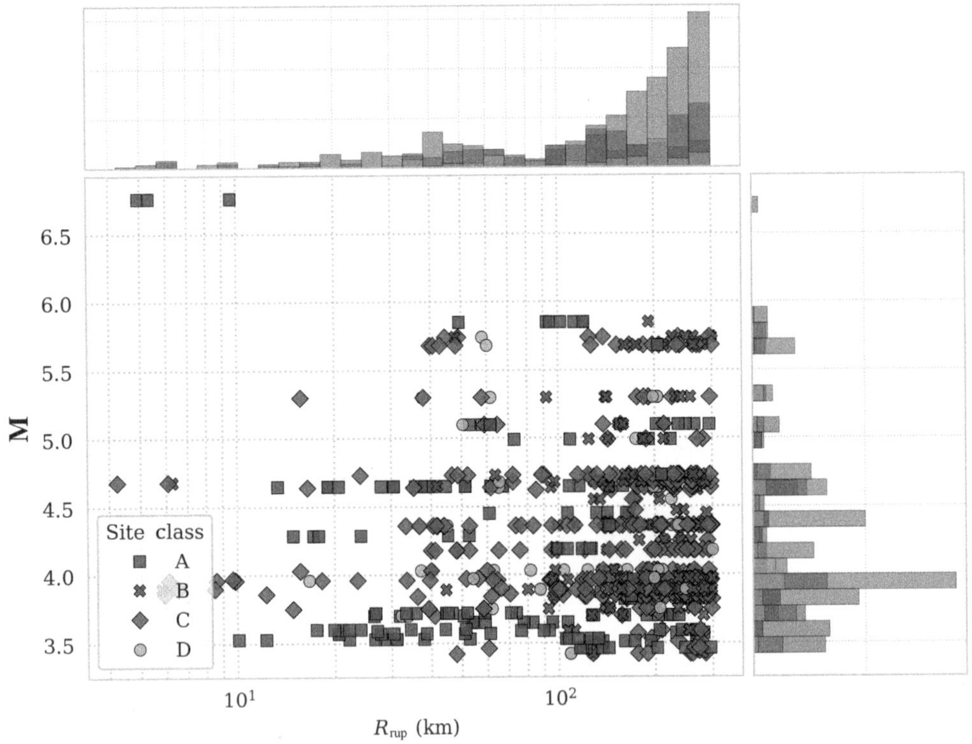

Figure 2. Magnitude–distance distribution of the data set. The color version of this figure is available only in the electronic edition.

In addition, the NGA-West2 data set, which underlies these models, includes numerous records from earthquakes with $\mathbf{M} \geq 3.0$ and distances of less than 300 km. This ensures that comparisons with CENA data are both reliable and insightful. We calculate residuals (Δ) as the difference between the natural logarithm of observed data (strong-motion records in the NGA-East data set) and the natural logarithm of predicted values (the mean of the three reference GMMs), as defined by the following equation:

$$\Delta = \ln\left(\frac{\text{Obs}_{ij}}{\text{Pre}_{ij}}\right) = \ln(\text{Obs}_{ij}) - \ln(\text{Pre}_{ij}), \quad (1)$$

in which Obs_{ij} represents the observed ground-motion intensity measure (GMIM) for the ith event recorded at the jth station in the target region and Pre_{ij} denotes the mean prediction from the three selected reference GMMs for the corresponding observation. Because residuals (Δ) are defined as the ratio of observed data in the target region to their corresponding predictions in the host region, these values can be used to develop adjustment factors that enhance predictions.

It is essential to note that the three reference GMMs are ergodic (global) models, which can be applied in shallow crustal regions such as California, Japan, Türkiye, Italy, and China. Bozorgnia and Campbell (2016) and Gülerce *et al.* (2017) require specific input parameters, such as depth to the top of rupture and depth to a shear-wave velocity of 2.5 km/s, which are not well established in the NGA-East data set. However, these models allow users to estimate missing parameters using empirical relations provided by Campbell and Bozorgnia (2014) and Chiou and Youngs (2014). Because the empirical relations provided by Campbell and Bozorgnia (2014) and Chiou and Youngs (2014) are primarily based on California data, we implicitly assume that average effects are region independent, at least to a first approximation. However, this assumption may be invalid due to regional variability. Therefore, its validity is evaluated through residual analysis, with deviations expected to appear as systematic residual trends. In other words, we believe this assumption introduces additional uncertainty, which is reflected in the corresponding residuals and standard deviation components. Making acceptable assumptions for these

Model development

We applied the Atkinson (2008) REM to develop a GMM to predict the vertical component of ground motion in CENA. This method adapts well-established GMMs from a data-rich host region to develop GMMs for a data-scarce target region. In REM, adjustment factors are calculated as the ratio of observed data from the target region to the corresponding GMM predictions from the host region. For this study, CENA serves as the target region, whereas WUS is selected as the host region due to its extensive strong-motion records and well-developed vertical GMMs. A key step in the REM involves selecting a reliable GMM from those developed for the host region. As part of the Next Generation Attenuation-West2 (NGA-West2) Project (Bozorgnia *et al.*, 2014), four GMMs have been developed for the vertical ground-motion component in WUS, authored by Chiou and Youngs (2013), Bozorgnia and Campbell (2013), Stewart *et al.* (2013), and Gülerce *et al.* (2013). The models by Bozorgnia and Campbell (2016), Stewart *et al.* (2016), and Gülerce *et al.* (2017) were published in Earthquake Spectra. We use their published versions (Bozorgnia and Campbell, 2016; Stewart *et al.*, 2016; Gülerce *et al.*, 2017) as alternative reference models to address epistemic uncertainty in model selection. These GMMs incorporate a broad range of seismological sources, paths, and site parameters, effectively capturing complex ground-motion scaling effects.

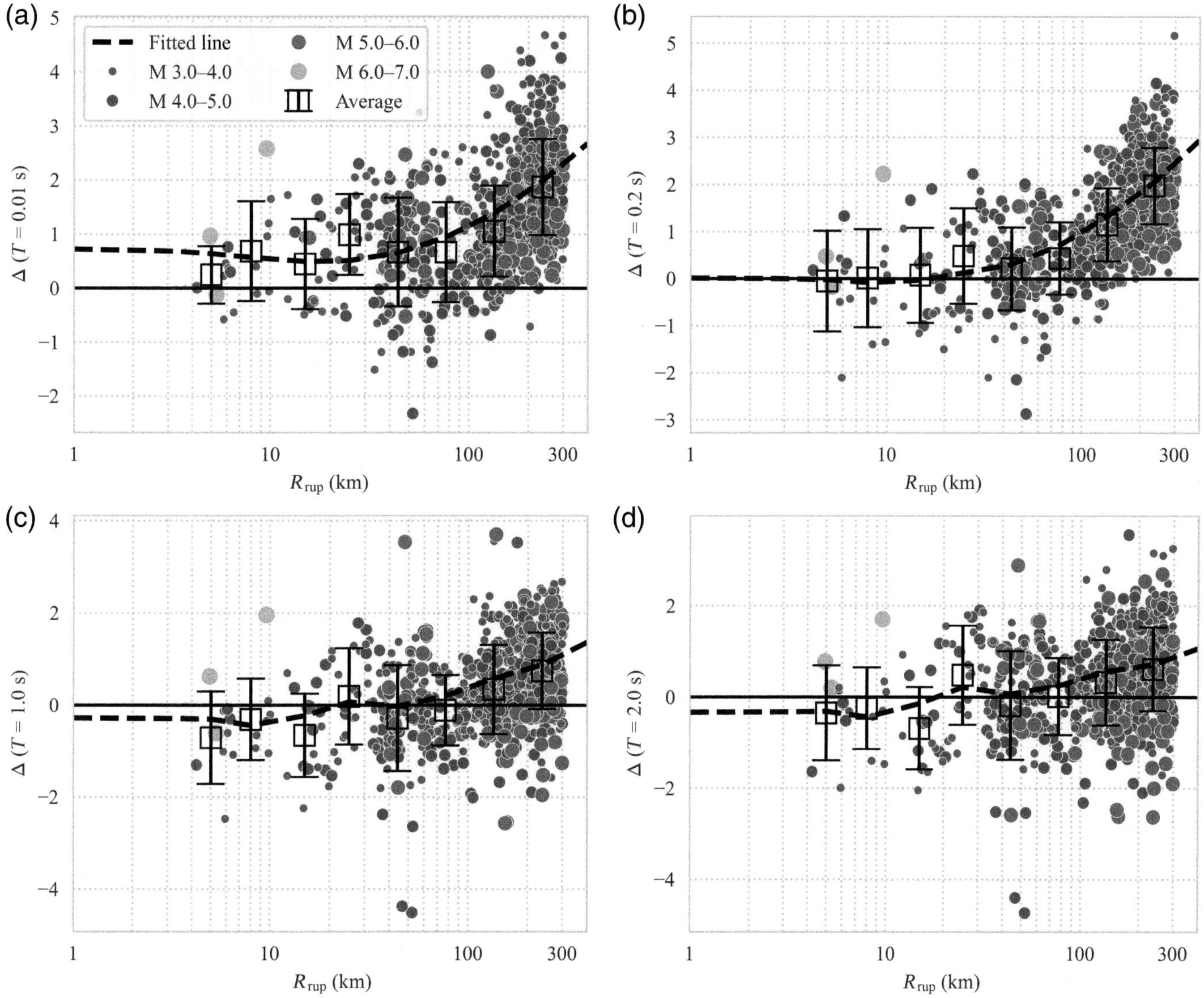

Figure 3. Total residuals for spectral periods (a) 0.01, (b) 0.20, (c) 1.00, and (d) 2.00 s. Residuals are color coded based on magnitude. Squares and vertical bars (error bars) represent the average residuals within equally log-spaced distance bins and their corresponding standard deviations, whereas dashed lines depict the fitted residual trend based on equation (2). The color version of this figure is available only in the electronic edition.

unknown parameters helps mitigate potential biases in the predictions.

Figure 3 illustrates total residuals (Δ) as a function of distance for spectral accelerations at periods of 0.01, 0.2, 1.0, and 2.0 s. The residuals are categorized into four magnitude ranges and eight distance intervals. Figures S1–S4 illustrate Δ as a function of distance for spectral accelerations at periods of 0.01 (Fig. S1), 0.2 (Fig. S2), 1.0 (Fig. S3), and 2.0 (Fig. S4). A simple functional form can be fitted to the residuals to derive adjustment factors. The functional form was determined through a trial-and-error process. Several functional forms were tested, starting with more complex expressions and progressively eliminating statistically insignificant terms to identify the best fit for the residuals. The following equation gives the resulting mathematical expression for the best-fit residual adjustment:

$$\ln(F_{\mathrm{CENA}})_{ij} = C_0 + C_1 \times \ln\left(\sqrt{R_{ij}^2 + h^2}\right) + C_2 \times \left(\ln\sqrt{R_{ij}^2 + h^2}\right)^2 + C_3 \times \ln(V_{S30}) + \delta B_e + \delta W_{es}, \quad (2)$$

in which F_{CENA} denotes the adjustment factor that adjusts the reference GMM's predictions for CENA, V_{S30} represents the timed-average shear-wave velocity in the upper 30 m, and R is the closest distance from the site to the rupture plane (R_{rup}). We expect that C_1 and C_2 capture attenuation with distance, whereas C_3 captures site effects. We used the mixed-effects regression approach (Pinheiro and Bates, 1996; Bates *et al.*, 2015) to estimate the fixed-effects coefficients (C_0, C_1, C_2, and C_3) and residual components. The indices i and j correspond to individual earthquakes and recording stations. Regarding the pseudodepth term h, we considered several approaches for

TABLE 1
Regression Coefficients and Standard Deviations Derived from the Mixed-Effects Regression

IM	C_0	C_1	C_2	C_3	τ	ϕ_{S2S}	ϕ_{SS}	ϕ	σ_{SS}	σ
0.01	2.161	−1.153	0.210	0	0.53	0.47	0.43	0.70	0.74	0.88
0.02	2.493	−1.246	0.216	0	0.55	0.49	0.44	0.71	0.75	0.90
0.03	2.824	−1.409	0.236	0	0.58	0.53	0.47	0.74	0.78	0.94
0.05	2.967	−1.462	0.251	0	0.58	0.61	0.49	0.76	0.74	0.95
0.075	2.793	−1.511	0.267	0	0.53	0.56	0.44	0.77	0.75	0.94
0.1	2.377	−1.425	0.265	0	0.48	0.52	0.44	0.74	0.71	0.88
0.15	1.310	−1.299	0.251	0.070	0.45	0.44	0.42	0.70	0.71	0.84
0.2	0.636	−1.246	0.242	0.138	0.44	0.38	0.45	0.67	0.71	0.80
0.25	0	−1.163	0.227	0.205	0.43	0.36	0.47	0.65	0.69	0.77
0.3	0	−1.151	0.217	0.206	0.42	0.36	0.48	0.63	0.67	0.76
0.4	0	−1.159	0.210	0.213	0.42	0.33	0.52	0.61	0.66	0.74
0.5	−0.745	−1.009	0.186	0.274	0.40	0.32	0.54	0.62	0.66	0.74
0.75	−1.572	−0.844	0.161	0.342	0.39	0.32	0.57	0.65	0.69	0.75
1	−2.377	−0.707	0.140	0.417	0.40	0.29	0.58	0.68	0.73	0.79
1.5	−2.969	−0.479	0.109	0.442	0.43	0.31	0.58	0.69	0.75	0.82
2	−3.328	−0.258	0.081	0.428	0.47	0.31	0.59	0.69	0.78	0.84
3	−3.642	0	0.050	0.393	0.48	0.3	0.59	0.68	0.78	0.83
4	−3.256	0	0.046	0.334	0.48	0.3	0.57	0.66	0.76	0.81
5	−2.699	0	0.039	0.264	0.47	0.29	0.56	0.64	0.74	0.79
7.5	−1.886	0	0.029	0.163	0.46	0.27	0.55	0.61	0.71	0.76
10	−1.107	0	0.023	0.076	0.44	0.26	0.54	0.60	0.70	0.74

IM, intensity measure.

developing the GMM: (1) using nonlinear mixed-effects regression for the estimation of all coefficients, (2) implementing a two-step regression in which h is first estimated from nonlinear mixed-effects regression and then fixed in the second step whereas the other coefficients are estimated using linear mixed-effects regression, (3) fixing h to the value from the host model, and (4) fixing h to a constant value. Numerous initial regressions and visual inspections were performed, and the residual trends, standard deviations, confidence interval bands, Bayesian information criterion, log-likelihood, and Akaike information criterion were compared. The pseudodepth term h is fixed to be equal to 6.

In equation (2), δB_e denotes the between-event residual, whereas δW_{es} represents the within-event residual. δB_e and δW_{es} are normally distributed with zero means and standard deviations of τ and φ, respectively. The total standard deviation (σ) is calculated using the following equation:

$$\sigma = \sqrt{\tau^2 + \varphi^2}. \quad (3)$$

Table 1 summarizes the regression coefficients and standard deviation components for various spectral periods in the developed GMM. In this table, the standard deviation components are represented in terms of natural logarithms. The derived standard deviation values align with those of the reference models for regions with small-to-moderate earthquakes. Given that our data set consists primarily of earthquakes with small-to-moderate magnitude at considerable distances, slightly larger model standard deviations are expected (Boore *et al.*, 2014; Campbell and Bozorgnia, 2014). The sigma values reported in Table 1 are also comparable to those found in previous studies, such as Pezeshk *et al.* (2018) and Hassani and Atkinson (2015), for the horizontal ground-motion component. In PSHA, GMMs express ground motion as functions of source, path, and site parameters, characterized by a median and standard deviation (Strasser *et al.*, 2009; Douglas and Edwards, 2016). The standard deviation quantifies residual variability between observations and predictions and strongly influences hazard estimates, particularly at low-exceedance probabilities, for which it controls the slope of the hazard curve (Bommer and Abrahamson, 2006). Figure S5 presents a comparison of the sigma estimated in this study with those reported by previous studies, including BC16, GKSA17, SBAS16, and Hassani and Atkinson (2015). Figure S6 and Table S2 show the regression coefficients as a function of period, together with their 95% confidence intervals.

Evaluation of the developed model

Residual analyses. In this section, we assess the effectiveness of the proposed GMM using residual analysis. The adjustment factors derived from equation (2) must first be multiplied by the GMIM predicted by the reference model (the average of the three selected reference models) to generate ground-motion predictions for CENA. The following equation describes this process:

$$Y_{\mathrm{CENA}} = Y_{\mathrm{WUS}} \times F_{\mathrm{CENA}}, \quad (4)$$

in which Y_{CENA} represents the predicted vertical GMIM for CENA whereas Y_{WUS} denotes the parameter's predicted value

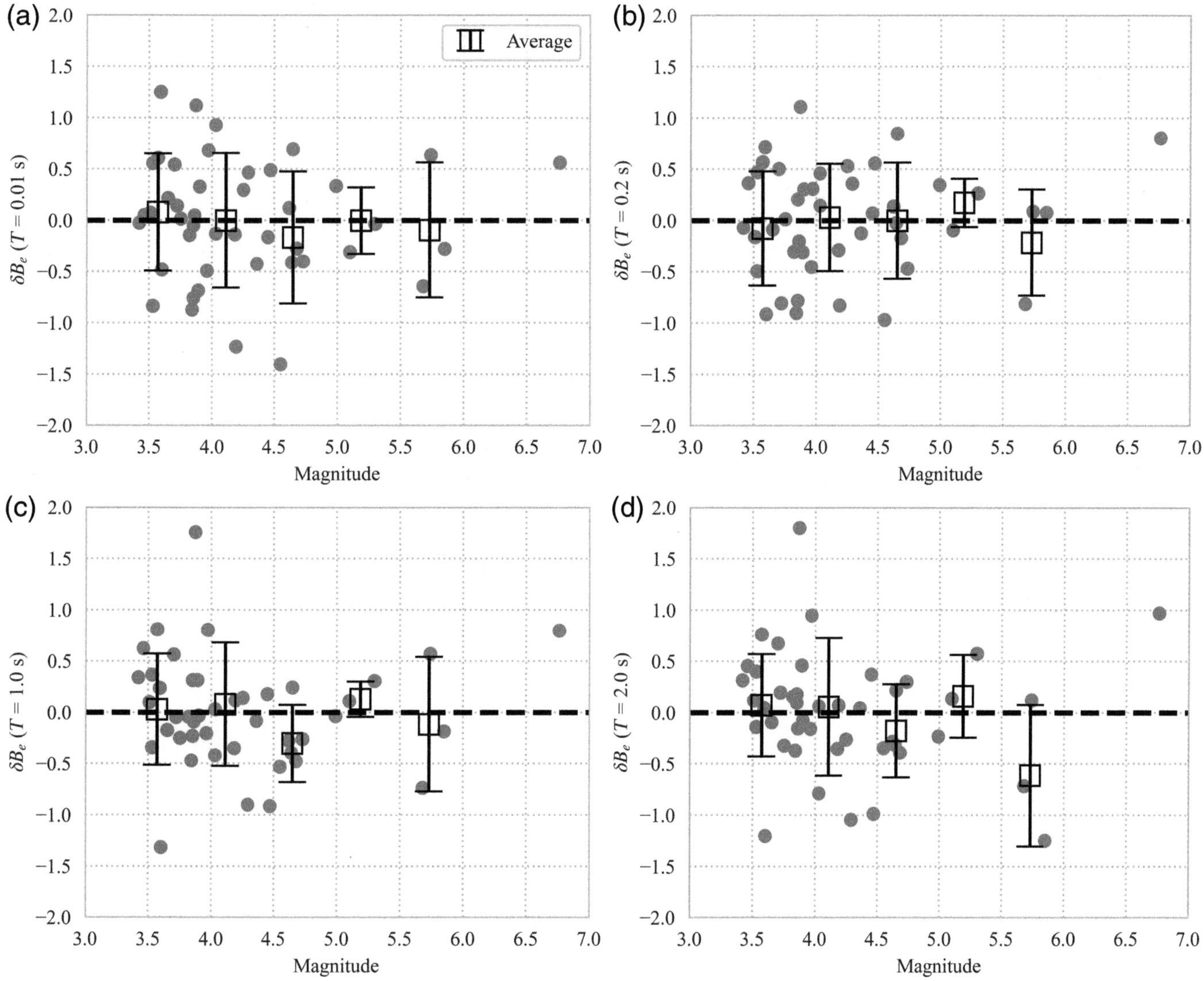

Figure 4. δB_e as a function of magnitude for spectral periods (a) 0.01, (b) 0.20, (c) 1.00, and (d) 2.00 s. Squares and vertical bars (error bars) represent the average residuals within equally linear-spaced magnitude bins and their corresponding standard deviations.

based on the three selected reference models developed for the western U.S. (BC16, GKSA17, and SBAS16). F_{CENA} is the adjustment factor introduced in equation (2) of this study.

Figures 4, 5 and Figure S7 display the residuals of the proposed GMM relative to the average of the three selected reference models, plotted against magnitude, distance, and V_{S30}, respectively. These figures cover periods of 0.01, 0.20, 1.00, and 2.00 s to assess the performance of the proposed GMM. Figure 4 shows the between-event residuals as a function of magnitude, whereas Figure 5 and Figure S7 illustrate the within-event residuals plotted as a function of distance and V_{S30}, respectively. In Figure 4, magnitude data are grouped into five bins, with residuals averaged for each bin. Similarly, distance data are divided into eight bins in Figure 5; and in Figure 6, recording motions are categorized according to four NEHRP site classifications. Our binning strategy required each bin to contain at least three earthquakes for δB_e and at least 10 records for δW_{es}. Overall, no discernible trend in the residuals is observed in these figures, supporting the validity of the proposed model. At longer periods (e.g., T = 1.0 and 2.0 s), δB_e shows slight overprediction at magnitudes between 4.5 and 5.0, and slight underprediction at all periods (except $T = 0.01$ s) for magnitudes between 5.0 and 5.5. At a period of $T = 2.0$ s, δB_e shows slight overprediction at magnitudes between 5.5 and 6.0. One possible reason for these under- and overpredictions is the sparsity of the data set, particularly for earthquakes larger than **M** 5.0. δW_{es} shows slight overprediction at distances less than 8 km for all periods (except T = 2.0 s), slight overprediction at distances between 80 and 100 km for $T = 0.2$ s, and slight underprediction at distances between 20 and 30 km for T = 2.0 s.

Partially nonergodic model and single-station standard deviation.

Nonergodic and partially nonergodic GMMs can be constructed either using an ergodic GMM as the backbone model (Kuehn *et al.*, 2019) or by deriving them directly from observed

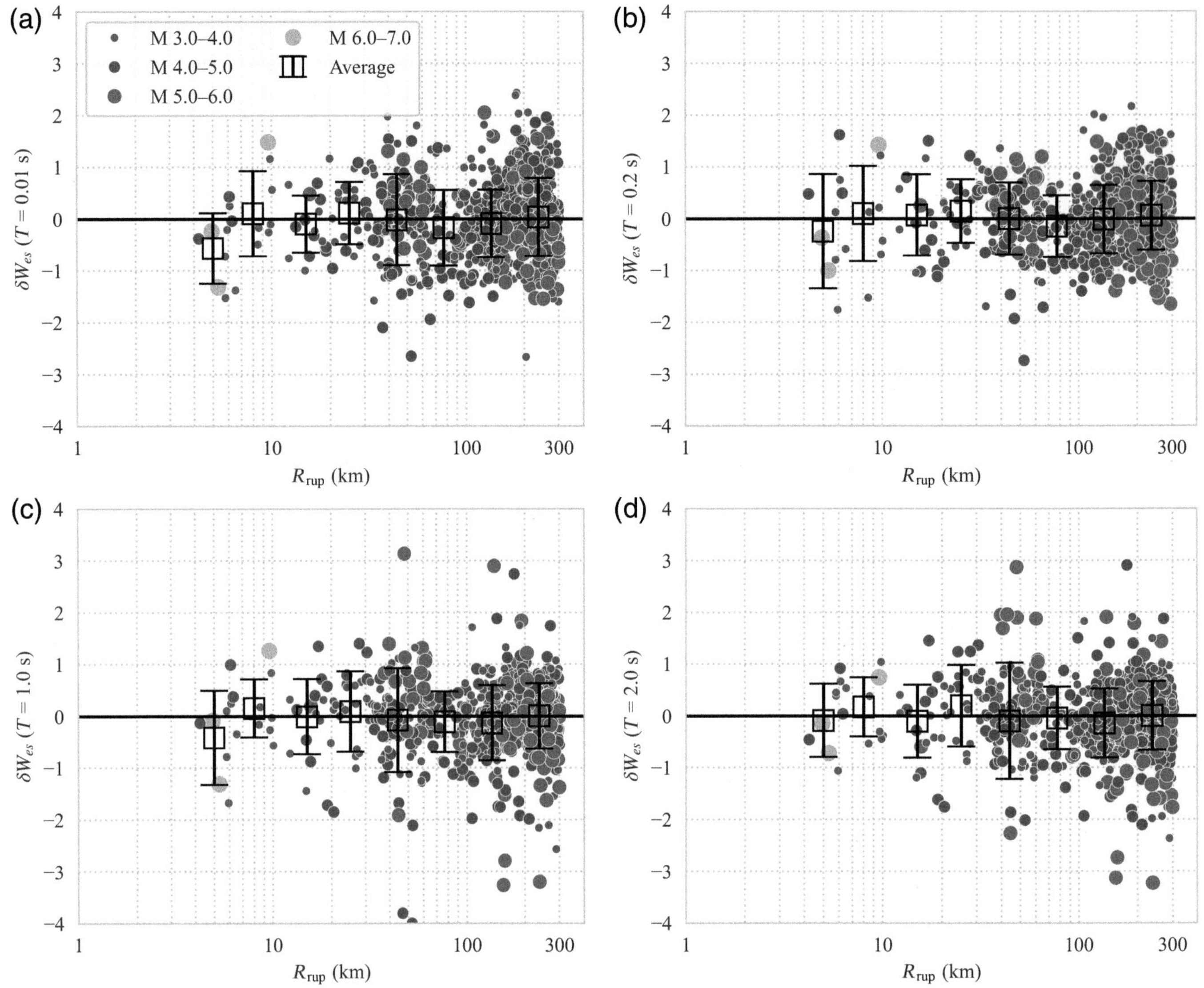

Figure 5. δW_{es} as a function of distance for spectral periods (a) 0.01, (b) 0.20, (c) 1.00, and (d) 2.00 s. Squares and vertical bars (error bars) represent the average residuals within equally log-spaced distance bins and their corresponding standard deviations. The color version of this figure is available only in the electronic edition.

ground-motion data (e.g., Landwehr *et al.*, 2016). Nonergodic and partially nonergodic GMMs are often developed using an ergodic backbone GMM, for which the median scaling is taken from the backbone model and the nonergodic component is derived from residuals, an approach shown to be advantageous in regions with sparse data sets (e.g., central and eastern United States [CEUS]; Lavrentiadis *et al.*, 2023). For the purpose of developing a partially nonergodic GMM by removing the ergodic assumption on site response, we further decompose δW_{es} into between-station ($\delta S2S_s$) and event-site corrected (δWS_{es}) residuals, with zero means and standard deviations of ϕ_{S2S} and ϕ_{SS}, using a mixed-effects regression approach (Pinheiro and Bates, 1996; Bates *et al.*, 2015) as follows (Atik *et al.*, 2010):

$$\delta W_{es} = \delta S2S_s + \delta WS_{es}. \tag{5}$$

Figure 7 depicts $\delta S2S_s$ as a function of V_{S30} for the selected periods, showing no discernible trend or bias. $\delta S2S_s$ shows slight overprediction at V_{S30} values between 200 and 300 m/s for all periods (except T = 2.0 s), and slight underprediction at V_{S30} values between 800 and 1200 m/s for all periods. Figure 8 depicts δWS_{es} as a function of R_{rup} for the selected periods, showing no discernible trend or bias. Our binning strategy required each bin to contain at least five records for $\delta S2S_s$ and at least 10 records for δWS_{es}. The single-station standard deviation is calculated as a combination of τ and ϕ_{SS}, as follows:

$$\sigma_{SS} = \sqrt{\tau^2 + \phi_{SS}^2}. \tag{6}$$

The resulting standard deviation components are reported in Table 1. We calculated the standard error (SE) of $\delta S2S_s$ using the following formula (Villani and Abrahamson, 2015):

$$\mathrm{SE}(\delta S2S_S) = \frac{\phi_{S2S}}{\sqrt{N_{es}}}, \tag{7}$$

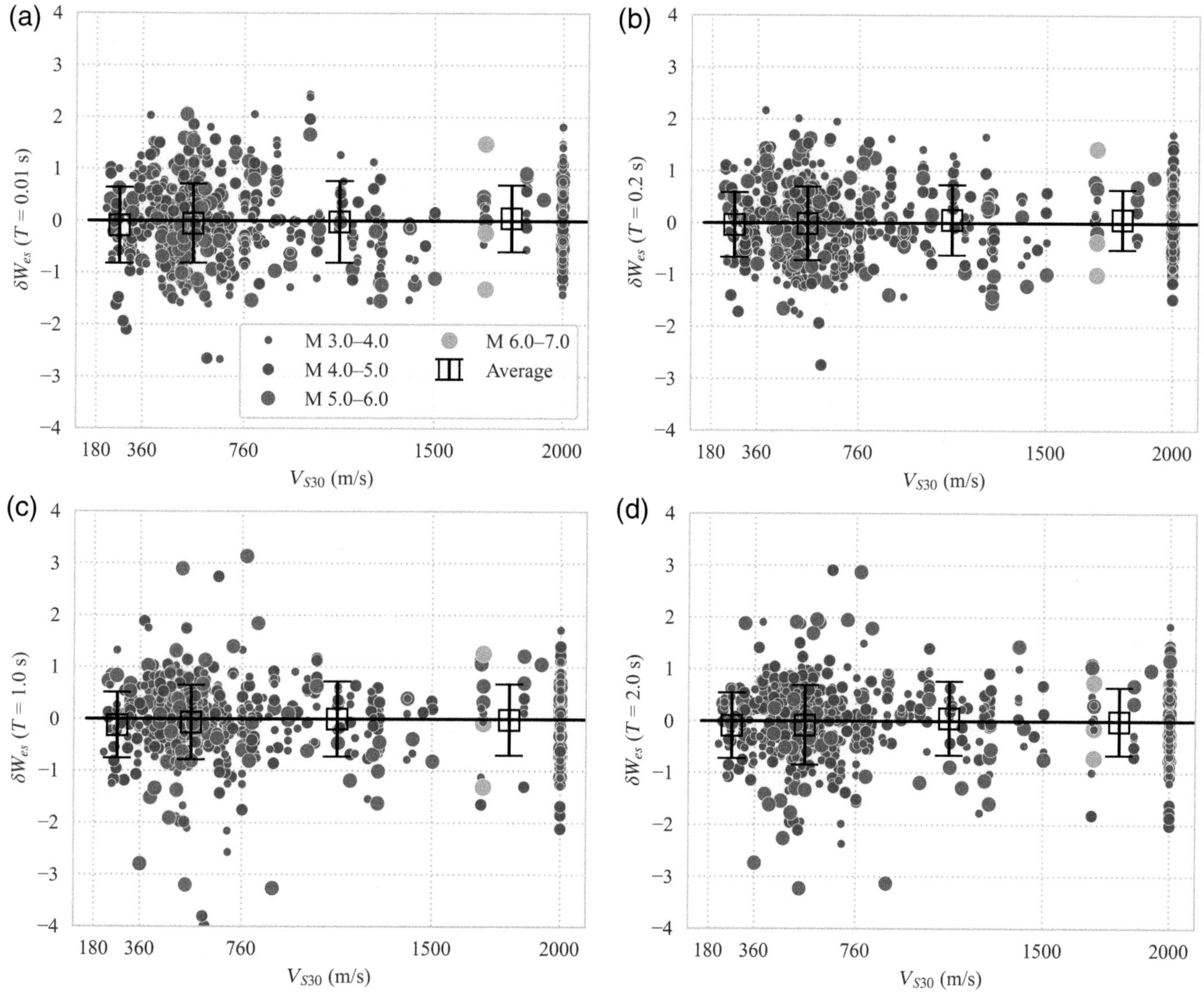

Figure 6. δW_{es} as a function of V_{S30} for spectral periods (a) 0.01, (b) 0.20, (c) 1.00, and (d) 2.00 s. Squares and vertical bars (error bars) represent the average residuals within equally log-spaced V_{S30} bins and their corresponding standard deviations. The bin widths are 30, 180, 400, 740, and 600, and the sample sizes are 10, 59, 373, 139, and 166 records for the respective bins. The color version of this figure is available only in the electronic edition.

in which N_{es} is defined as the number of earthquakes recorded at station s. Based on the recommendation of Villani and Abrahamson (2015), the SE of $\delta S2S_s$ can be considered an epistemic uncertainty in the site term. Several formulations and methods exist for characterizing epistemic uncertainty and the SE of the mean standard deviation. Equation (7) was employed to account for differences between locations with and without nearby recordings by incorporating increased epistemic uncertainty (Villani and Abrahamson, 2015). Figures S7 and S8 depict the spatial distribution of $\delta S2S_s$ and the SE of $\delta S2S_s$ (SE($\delta S2S_s$)) for selected spectral periods in CENA. It should be noted that Figures S7 and S8 present spatially smoothed results.

Single-station standard deviation estimation relaxes the ergodic assumption for site response (Rodriguez-Marek *et al.*, 2011) and has been widely applied in seismic hazard studies, particularly for critical facilities and dams. In partially nonergodic PSHA, the site term is removed from the aleatory component (reducing aleatory variability) and treated as epistemic uncertainty (Davatgari-Tafreshi and Pezeshk, 2025d). The median GMIM predicted by the GMM (Y) is replaced by $\bar{Y} = Y\delta S2S_s$, in which $\delta S2S_s$ is estimated for each station, and the single-station standard deviation represents the aleatory variability. This can either decrease or increase the calculated hazard at the site. Recently, Davatgari-Tafreshi and Pezeshk (2025c) estimated the single-station standard deviations using a data set from the CEUS for the horizontal component of ground motion. Davatgari-Tafreshi and Pezeshk (2025c) estimated a ϕ_{S2S} of ~0.48 to 0.81 for CEUS, whereas Atik (2015) reported ~0.30 to 0.70 for CENA. In this study, we estimate ϕ_{S2S} to be ~0.26 to 0.61 for CENA. Our estimates fall within the range of Atik (2015) but are lower than those

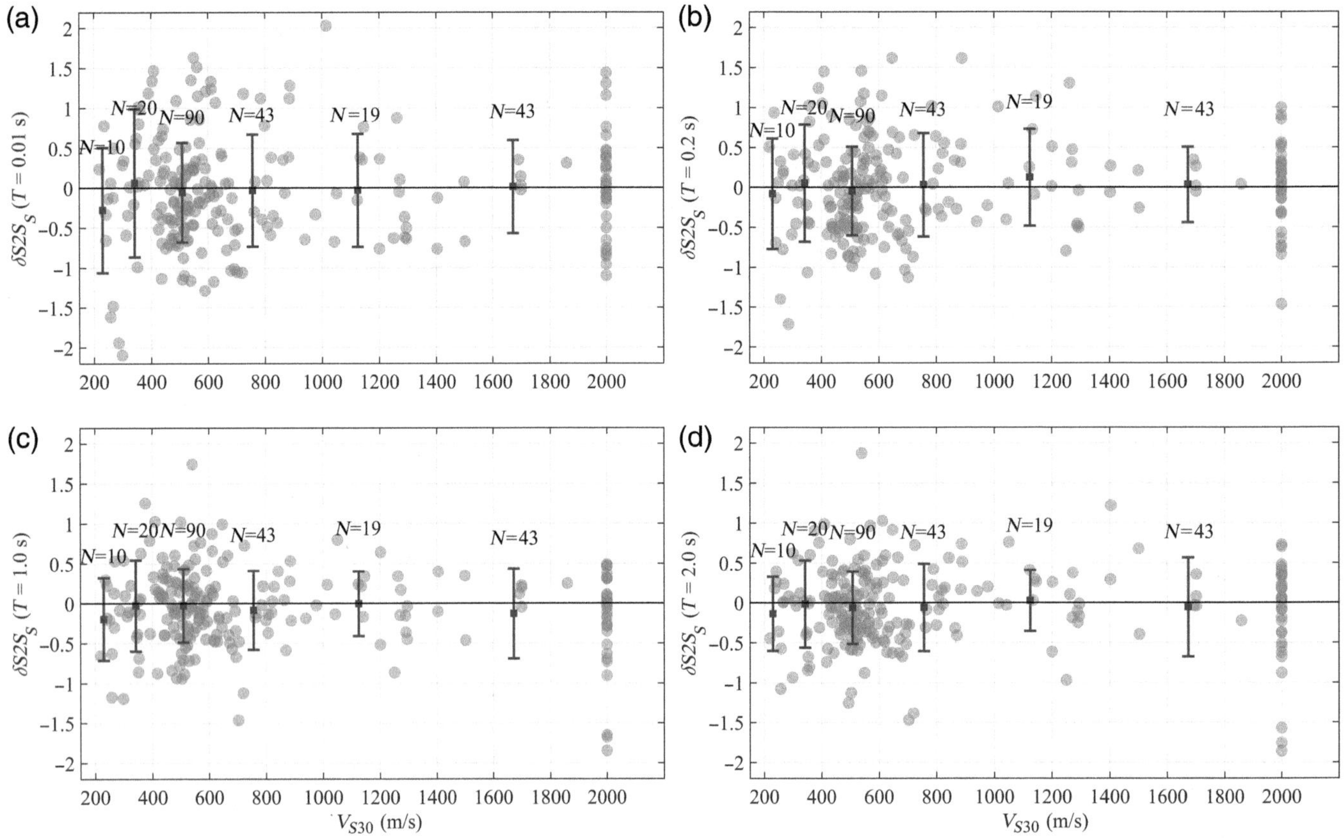

Figure 7. $\delta S2S_S$ as a function of V_{S30} for spectral periods (a) 0.01, (b) 0.20, (c) 1.00, and (d) 2.00 s. Red circles and vertical bars (error bars) represent the average residuals within equally log-spaced V_{S30} bins and their corresponding standard deviations. The color version of this figure is available only in the electronic edition.

of Davatgari-Tafreshi and Pezeshk (2025c). It is important to note that data set differences may explain this variation, as we used ~259 stations, whereas Davatgari-Tafreshi and Pezeshk (2025c) analyzed a data set with more than 2000 stations. For CENA, Goulet, Bozorgnia, *et al.* (2021) recommended σ_{SS} values of 0.42–0.82 at T = 0.3 s and 0.45–0.77 at T = 1.0 s, whereas Atik (2015) reported ~0.40 to 0.83 at T =0.01 s, 0.41–0.81 at T = 0.2 s, and 0.47–0.80 at T = 1.0 s. Davatgari-Tafreshi and Pezeshk (2025c) recommended σ_{SS} values of ~1.2 at T = 0.01 s, 0.86 at T = 0.2 s, and 0.87 at T = 1.0 s for CEUS. In this study, we estimated σ_{SS} values of ~0.74 at T = 0.01 s, 0.71 at T = 0.2 s, and 0.73 at T = 1.0 s for CENA. The σ_{SS} values estimated in this study fall within the ranges of Atik (2015) and Goulet, Bozorgnia, *et al.* (2021) but are lower than those of Davatgari-Tafreshi and Pezeshk (2025c). Data set differences may explain this variation, as we used ~747 records, whereas Davatgari-Tafreshi and Pezeshk (2025c) analyzed more than 20,000 records. It should also be noted that the estimates of Atik (2015), Goulet, Bozorgnia, *et al.* (2021), and Davatgari-Tafreshi and Pezeshk (2025c) are for horizontal components.

Median predictions. Figure 9 and Figures S9 and S10 compare the distance scaling of the proposed GMM, the reference model (average of the three selected reference models), and observed data across various magnitudes. The selected magnitudes are 4, 5, and 7, and a standard deviation of 0.25 magnitude units is assumed for the observed data in each figure. The V_{S30} values are taken as the mean of the observed data, and the other parameters are calculated using empirical relations provided in the literature (Campbell and Bozorgnia, 2014; Chiou and Youngs, 2014). Figure 9 and Figures S9 and S10 show the comparisons based on the median values of magnitude bins (**M** 4.0, 5.0, and 7.0) and the corresponding average V_{S30} within each bin. As the magnitude increases, the observed data sharply decrease. For instance, Figure S10, representing magnitudes ranging from 6.75 to 7.25, contains only three recorded motions from the 1985 Nahanni earthquake. Figure 9 and Figure S10 demonstrate that the proposed GMM aligns well with the empirical data in CENA across different periods and magnitude–distance intervals. This validates the suitability of the adjustment factors applied to the average of the three reference models for the CENA empirical data set. The model exhibits varying behavior based on period and R_{rup}. It generally predicts higher vertical ground motion at greater distances and shorter periods while yielding lower predictions at closer distances and longer periods than the reference models' average. Overall, the proposed GMM more closely follows the trends of the reference models for larger magnitudes at shorter distances.

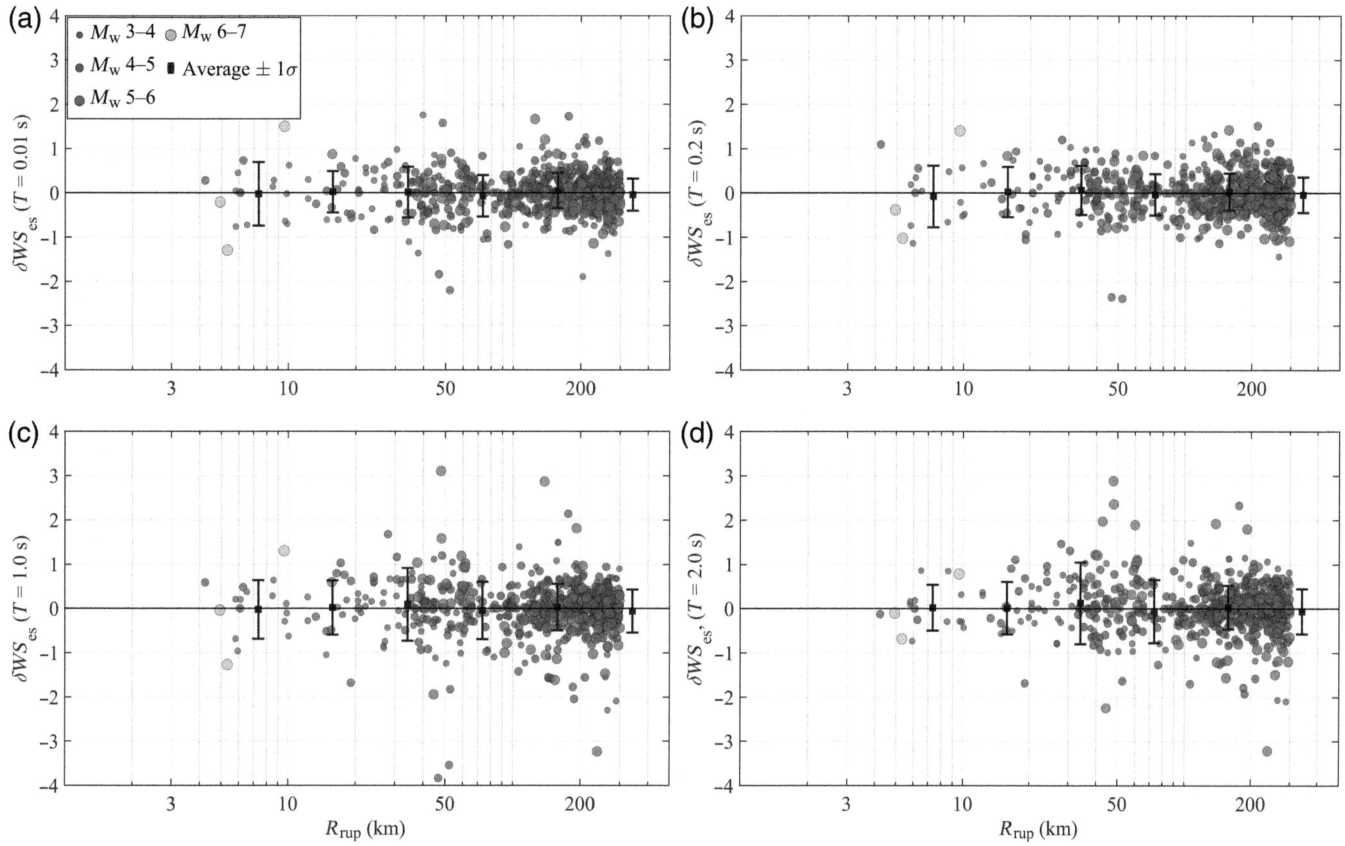

Figure 8. δWS_{es} as a function of R_{rup} for spectral periods (a) 0.01, (b) 0.20, (c) 1.00, and (d) 2.00 s. Red circles and vertical bars (error bars) represent the average residuals within equally log-spaced R_{rup} bins and their corresponding standard deviations. The color version of this figure is available only in the electronic edition.

Figure 10 and Figures S11 and S12 provide a comparison of the proposed GMM (vertical response spectra) and the reference model (average reference models) as a function of period across varying **M**, R_{rup}, and V_{S30}. The adjustment factors for CENA shift the peak of the vertical response spectrum from longer to shorter periods compared to the average reference model. In addition, the vertical response spectrum is generally higher on soil than on rock, especially at short-spectral periods. This behavior may stem from the functional form used to derive adjustment factors for modifying predictions of the reference model. As a result, similar to the average reference model, the proposed model exhibits greater sensitivity to site conditions at higher frequencies (shorter periods). For a more detailed comparison, Figure S13 contrasts the proposed vertical model with the V/H ratio model of Pezeshk *et al.* (2022) for CENA. A scenario with **M** 7.55, $R_{rup} = 54.75$ km, and $V_{S30} = 760$ m/s is considered. To convert the V/H ratios to vertical components, we used the Pezeshk *et al.* (2018) horizontal GMM along with the site amplification models by Stewart *et al.* (2020) and Hashash *et al.* (2020) to adjust the site condition from $V_{S30} = 3000$ m/s to $V_{S30} = 760$ m/s. Figure S13 shows that the model developed in this study aligns well with the Pezeshk *et al.* (2022) V/H ratio-derived vertical model at longer periods (greater than approximately 0.10 s), whereas slightly lower values are obtained at shorter periods (less than approximately 0.10 s). We believe that part of the discrepancy between our model and Pezeshk *et al.* (2022) may arise from the use of the horizontal GMM of Pezeshk *et al.* (2018) to convert V/H ratios to vertical components, as well as from site adjustments that introduce additional uncertainty into the results. Using different methodologies and functional forms may also contribute to the observed discrepancy between the two models. However, we believe the two models are reasonably comparable and can be used in a logic tree to capture epistemic uncertainties.

CONCLUSIONS

In this study, we developed a vertical GMM for the data-poor region of CENA using the REM outlined by Atkinson (2008). Vertical GMMs are essential for creating vertical design spectra, which are crucial for seismic design in critical infrastructure such as dams, nuclear power plants, and highway bridges. Our REM is based on the average of three vertical GMMs from the NGA-West2 project, specifically those developed by Bozorgnia and Campbell (2016), Gülerce *et al.* (2017), and Stewart *et al.* (2016). The selection of these three models, along with the provision of confidence bounds for the adjustment

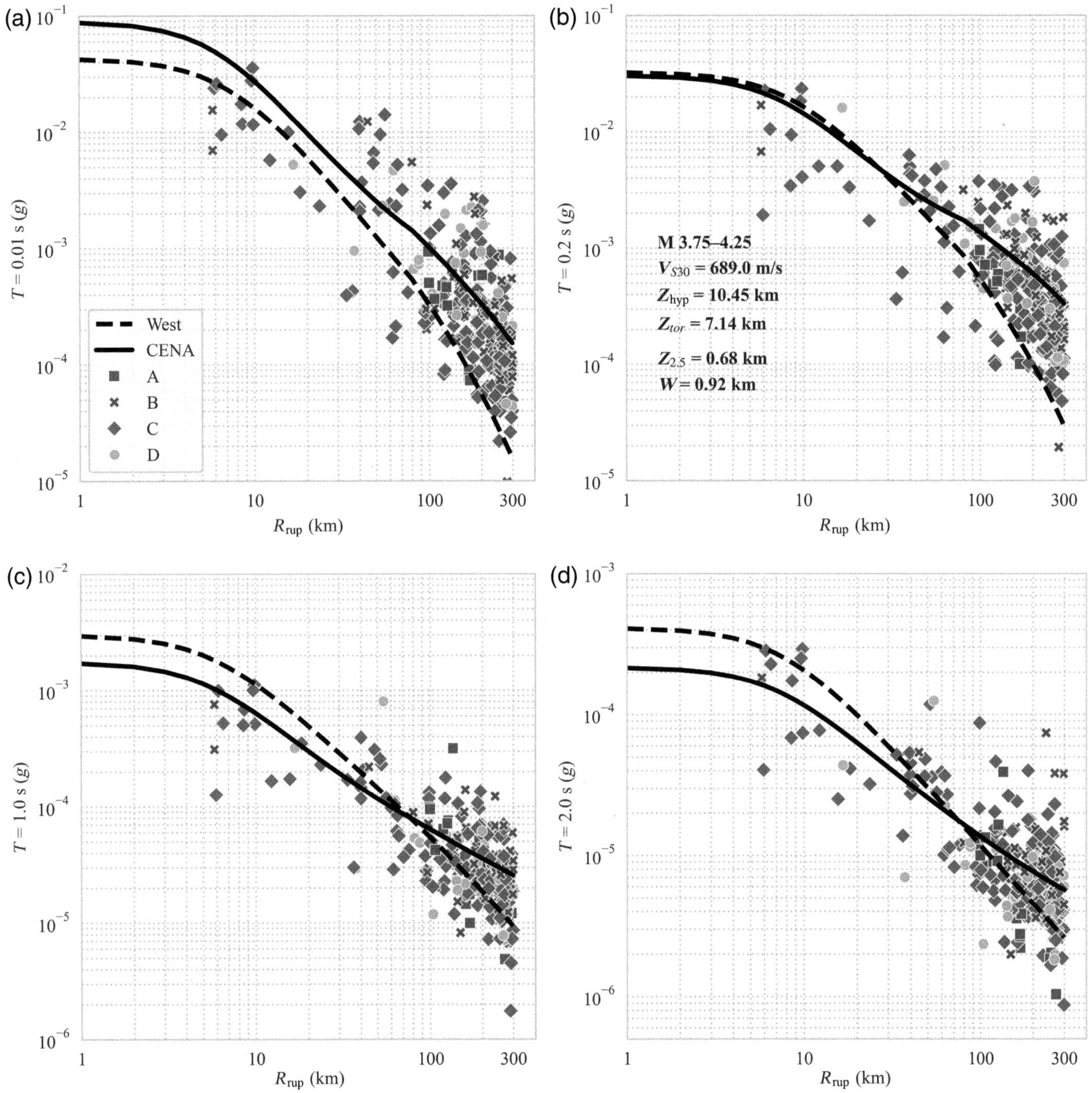

Figure 9. Comparison of the distance scaling of the proposed ground-motion model (GMM) for central and eastern North America (CENA) with the reference GMM (west) for a strike-slip fault ($\delta = 90°$) at periods of (a) 0.01, (b) 0.20, (c) 1.00, and (d) 2.00 s. Models are plotted for the observed data's median magnitude within the specified bin (**M** 4.0) and the corresponding average hypocentral depth and shear-wave velocity. Observed data points are categorized by respective National Earthquake Hazard Reduction Program (NEHRP) site class. The magnitude range of the observed data is **M** 3.75–4.25. The color version of this figure is available only in the electronic edition.

factors, ensures that epistemic uncertainty in the choice of reference model is effectively captured.

Furthermore, the NGA-West2 and NGA-East data sets contain abundant data from small-to-moderate magnitude events at regional distances, making their comparison with the referenced empirical model and the average reference model meaningful. This study's proposed REM closely aligns with CENA observed data across various seismological parameters, including shear-wave velocity, magnitude, and distance, over spectral periods ranging from 0.01 to 10 s. Moreover, the model exhibits no significant residual trends with respect to these parameters, confirming its suitability for ground-motion predictions

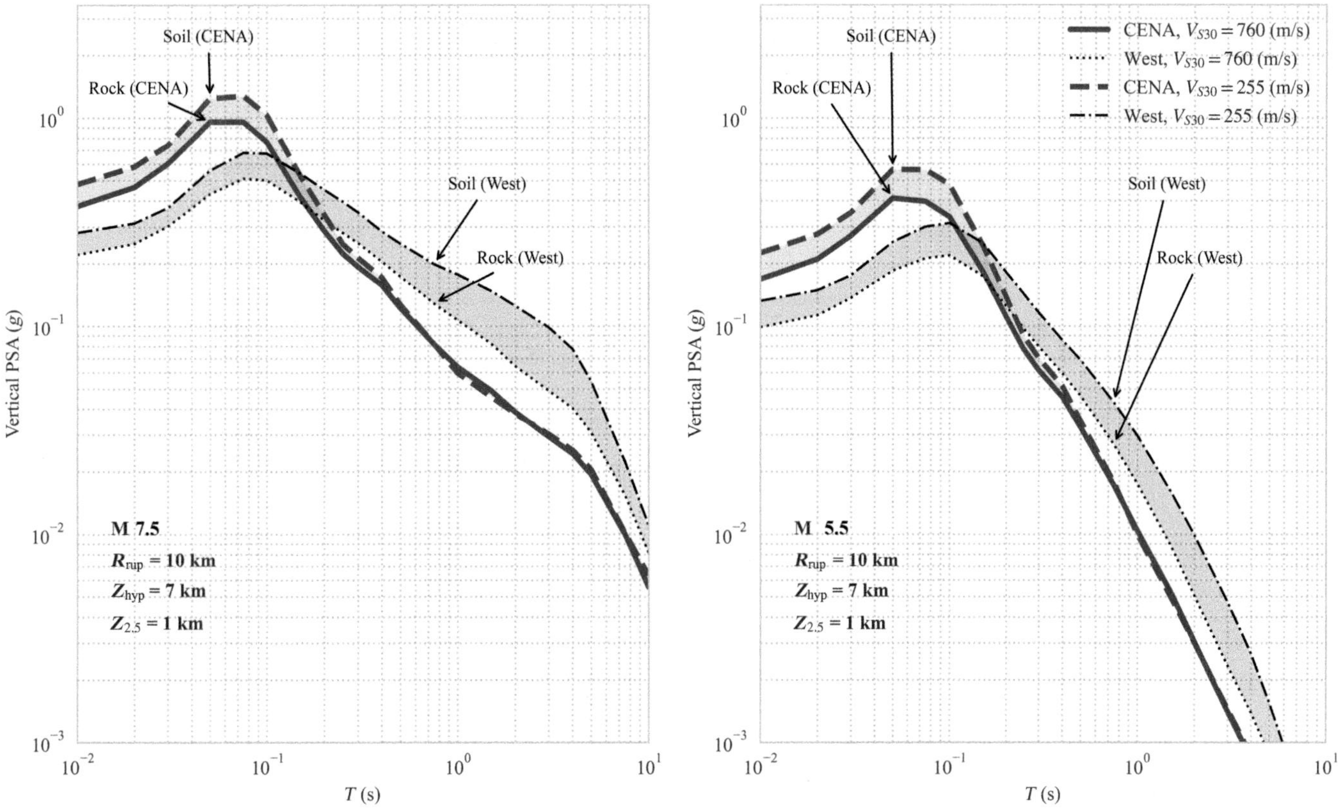

Figure 10. Comparison of the vertical response spectrum of the proposed GMM for CENA with the reference GMM (west) for a strike-slip fault ($\delta = 90°$) for different magnitudes and site conditions. PSA, pseudospectral acceleration. The color version of this figure is available only in the electronic edition.

in the CENA region. Our model can be applied to the design of critical infrastructure, regional hazard maps, and site-specific PSHA for CENA sites to develop vertical response spectra. The data set used in this study is sparse at near distances and for larger magnitudes. Future studies are needed to formulate vertical GMMs using updated data sets with more near-source recordings and alternative methodologies. The model developed here, together with other relevant GMMs, can be incorporated into a logic tree to capture epistemic uncertainties.

DATA AND RESOURCES

The Next Generation Attenuation-East Project (NGA-East) flat-file used in this study could be accessed from (www.peer.berkeley.edu, last accessed October 2019). In addition, we used the acceleration time histories to compute the vertical-component pseudospectral accelerations (PSAs) that were not presented in the NGA-East database. We used ArcMap 10.5.1 to plot Figure 1. For other figures, we used Python 3.7 libraries: numPy, pandas, seaborn, Matplotlib, and statsmodels to perform linear mixed-effects regression and make the remaining figures. The supplemental material to this article includes 14 figures and 2 tables. Table S1 summarizes the earthquakes used in this study to develop the ground-motion model (GMM) for vertical response spectra. Figures S1–S4 illustrate Δ as a function of distance for spectral accelerations at periods of 0.01 (Fig. S1), 0.2 (Fig. S2), 1.0 (Fig. S3), and 2.0 (Fig. S4) s. Figure S5 presents a comparison of the sigma estimated in this study with those reported by previous studies. Figure S6 and Table S2 show the regression coefficients as a function of period, together with their 95% confidence intervals. Figures S7 and S8 depict the spatial distribution of $\delta S2S_s$ and the standard error (SE) of $\delta S2S_s$. Figures S9 and S10 compare the distance scaling of the proposed central and eastern North America (CENA) GMM with that of the reference GMM, whereas Figures S11 and S12 compare vertical response spectra as a function of period.

DECLARATION OF COMPETING INTERESTS

The authors acknowledge that there are no conflicts of interest recorded.

ACKNOWLEDGMENTS

The authors would like to thank Editor-in-Chief Martin Mai, Associate Editor Sanjay Singh Bora, Emel Seyhan, and the anonymous reviewer for their thoughtful comments and constructive reviews of this article.

REFERENCES

Akhani, M., M. Davatgari-Tafreshi, and S. Pezeshk (2024). Adjusting Central and Eastern United States ground-motion models for use in the Coastal Plain, considering the sediment thickness, *Earthq. Spectra* **40,** no. 4, 2669–2691.

Atik, L. A. (2015). NGA-East: Ground-motion standard deviation models for Central and Eastern North America, *PEER Rept. 2015-07,* Pacific Earthquake Engineering Research Center, University of California, Berkeley, California, available at https://peer.berkeley.edu/ (last accessed April 2025).

Atik, L. A., N. Abrahamson, J. J. Bommer, F. Scherbaum, F. Cotton, and N. Kuehn (2010). The variability of ground-motion prediction models and its components, *Seismol. Res. Lett.* **81,** no. 5, 794–801.

Atkinson, G. M. (2008). Ground-motion prediction equations for eastern North America from a referenced empirical approach: Implications for epistemic uncertainty, *Bull. Seismol. Soc. Am.* **98,** no. 3, 1304–1318.

Atkinson, G. M. (2010). Ground-motion prediction equations for Hawaii from a referenced empirical approach, *Bull. Seismol. Soc. Am.* **100,** no. 2, 751–761.

Atkinson, G. M., and D. M. Boore (1995). Ground-motion relations for eastern North America, *Bull. Seismol. Soc. Am.* **85,** no. 1, 17–30.

Atkinson, G. M., and D. M. Boore (2006). Earthquake ground-motion prediction equations for eastern North America, *Bull. Seismol. Soc. Am.* **96,** no. 6, 2181–2205.

Atkinson, G. M., and D. M. Boore (2011). Modifications to existing ground-motion prediction equations in light of new data, *Bull. Seismol. Soc. Am.* **101,** no. 3, 1121–1135.

Atkinson, G. M., and D. Motazedian (2013). Ground-motion amplitudes for earthquakes in Puerto Rico, *Bull. Seismol. Soc. Am.* **103,** no. 3, 1846–1859.

Bates, D., M. Mächler, B. Bolker, and S. Walker (2015). Fitting linear mixed-effects models using lme4, *J. Stat. Softw.* **67,** 1–48.

Bommer, J. J., and N. A. Abrahamson (2006). Why do modern probabilistic seismic-hazard analyses often lead to increased hazard estimates? *Bull. Seismol. Soc. Am.* **96,** no. 6, 1967–1977.

Bommer, J. J., S. Akkar, and Ö. Kale (2011). A model for vertical-to-horizontal response spectral ratios for Europe and the Middle East, *Bull. Seismol. Soc. Am.* **101,** no. 4, 1783–1806.

Boore, D. M. (2005). SMSIM—Fortran programs for simulating ground motions from earthquakes: Version 2.3—A revision of OFR 96-80-A, available at http://www.daveboore.com/smsim (last accessed March 2024).

Boore, D. M., and S. Akkar (2003). Effect of causal and acausal filters on elastic and inelastic response spectra, *Earthq. Eng. Struct. Dynam.* **32,** no. 11, 1729–1748.

Boore, D. M., J. P. Stewart, E. Seyhan, and G. M. Atkinson (2014). NGA-West2 equations for predicting PGA, PGV, and 5% damped PSA for shallow crustal earthquakes, *Earthq. Spectra* **30,** no. 3, 1057–1085.

Bozorgnia, Y., and K. W. Campbell (2004). Engineering characterization of ground motion, in *Earthquake Engineering: From Engineering Seismology to Performance-Based Engineering,*Y. Bozorgnia and V. V. Bertero (Editors), CRC Press, Boca Raton, Florida, 215–315.

Bozorgnia, Y., and K. W. Campbell (2013). Ground motion model for the vertical component of PGA, PGV, and pseudo acceleration response spectra, Chapter 4, *Pacific Earthquake Engineering Research Center (PEER) Rept. No. 2013/24.*

Bozorgnia, Y., and K. W. Campbell (2016). Vertical ground motion model for PGA, PGV, and linear response spectra using the NGA-West2 database, *Earthq. Spectra* **32,** no. 2, 979–1004.

Bozorgnia, Y., N. A. Abrahamson, L. A. Atik, T. D. Ancheta, G. M. Atkinson, J. W. Baker, A. Baltay, D. M. Boore, K. W. Campbell, B. S. J. Chiou, *et al.* (2014). NGA-West2 research project, *Earthq. Spectra* **30,** no. 3, 973–987.

Campbell, K. W. (2003). Prediction of strong ground motion using the hybrid empirical method and its use in the development of ground-motion (attenuation) relations in eastern North America, *Bull. Seismol. Soc. Am.* **93,** no. 3, 1012–1033.

Campbell, K. W., and Y. Bozorgnia (2003). Updated near-source ground-motion (attenuation) relations for the horizontal and vertical components of peak ground acceleration and acceleration response spectra, *Bull. Seismol. Soc. Am.* **93,** no. 1, 314–331.

Campbell, K. W., and Y. Bozorgnia (2014). NGA-West2 ground motion model for the average horizontal components of PGA, PGV, and 5% damped linear acceleration response spectra, *Earthq. Spectra* **30,** no. 3, 1087–1115.

Chiou, B. S. J., and R. R. Youngs (2013). Ground motion prediction model for vertical component of peak ground motions and response spectra, Chapter 5, *Pacific Earthquake Engineering Research Center (PEER) Rept. No. 2013/24.*

Chiou, B. S. J., and R. R. Youngs (2014). Update of the Chiou and Youngs NGA model for the average horizontal component of peak ground motion and response spectra, *Earthq. Spectra* **30,** no. 3, 1117–1153.

Davatgari-Tafreshi, M., and S. Pezeshk (2025a). Hybrid empirical ground-motion model for the Alborz region of northern Iran, *Soil Dynam. Earthq. Eng.* **192,** 109,292.

Davatgari-Tafreshi, M., and S. Pezeshk (2025b). A ground-motion model for the shallow crustal earthquakes in New Zealand, *Earthq. Spectra* **41,** 2460–2486.

Davatgari-Tafreshi, M., and S. Pezeshk (2025c). Analysis of single-station standard deviation based on empirical data set from the Central and Eastern United States, *Bull. Seismol. Soc. Am.* **115,** no. 5, 2507–2521, doi: 10.1785/0120240191.

Davatgari-Tafreshi, M., and S. Pezeshk (2025d). Analysis of repeatable source and path effects on the ground-motion median and standard deviation based on an empirical dataset from the Central and Eastern United States, *Earthq. Spectra* doi: 10.1177/87552930251348484.

Dawood, H. M., A. Rodriguez-Marek, J. Bayless, C. Goulet, and E. Thompson (2016). A flatfile for the KiK-net database processed using an automated protocol, *Earthq. Spectra* **32,** no. 2, 1281–1302.

Douglas, J., and B. Edwards (2016). Recent and future developments in earthquake ground motion estimation, *Earth Sci. Rev.* **160,** 203–219.

Douglas, J., H. Bungum, and F. Scherbaum (2006). Ground-motion prediction equations for southern Spain and southern Norway obtained using the composite model perspective, *J. Earthq. Eng.* **10,** no. 1, 33–72.

Douglas, J., G. Aldama-Bustos, S. Tallett-Williams, M. Daví, and I. J. Tromans (2024). Ground-motion models for earthquakes occurring in the United Kingdom, *Bull. Earthq. Eng.* 1–38.

Dreiling, J., M. P. Isken, W. D. Mooney, M. C. Chapman, and R. W. Godbee (2014). NGA-East regionalization report: Comparison of four crustal regions within central and eastern North America using waveform modeling and 5%-damped pseudo-spectral acceleration response, *PEER Rept. 2014,* 15 pp.

Elnashai, A. S., and A. J. Papazoglou (1997). Procedure and spectra for analysis of RC structures subjected to strong vertical earthquake loads, *J. Earthq. Eng.* **1,** no. 1, 121–155.

Gülerce, Z., and N. A. Abrahamson (2011). Site-specific design spectra for vertical ground motion, *Earthq. Spectra* **27,** no. 4, 1023–1047.

Gülerce, Z., R. Kamai, N. A. Abrahamson, and W. J. Silva (2013). Ground motion prediction equation for the vertical ground motion component, *Pacific Earthquake Engineering Research Center (PEER) Rept. No. 2013/24.*

Gülerce, Z., R. Kamai, N. A. Abrahamson, and W. J. Silva (2017). Ground motion prediction equations for the vertical ground motion

component based on the NGA-W2 database, *Earthq. Spectra* **33,** no. 2, 499–528.
Goulet, C. A., T. Kishida, T. D. Ancheta, C. H. Cramer, R. B. Darragh, W. J. Silva, Y. M. Hashash, J. Harmon, J. P. Stewart, K. E. Wooddell, *et al.* (2014). Pacific earthquake engineering research center (PEER), *Rept. No. 2014/17.*
Goulet, C. A., Y. Bozorgnia, N. A. Abrahamson, N. Kuehn, L. Al Atik, R. R. Youngs, and G. M. Atkinson (2018). Central and eastern North America Ground-motion characterization (NGA-east), *No. DOE-UC-08314,* University of California, Berkeley, California.
Goulet, C. A., T. Kishida, T. D. Ancheta, C. H. Cramer, R. B. Darragh, W. J. Silva, and R. R. Youngs (2021). PEER NGA-east database, *Earthq. Spectra* **37,** no. 1_suppl, 1331–1353.
Goulet, C. A., Y. Bozorgnia, N. Kuehn, L. Al Atik, R. R. Youngs, R. W. Graves, and G. M. Atkinson (2021). NGA-East ground-motion characterization model part I: Summary of products and model development, *Earthq. Spectra* **37,** no. 1_suppl, 1231–1282.
Haji-Soltani, A., S. Pezeshk, M. Malekmohammadi, and A. Zandieh (2017). A study of vertical-to-horizontal ratio of earthquake components in the Gulf Coast Region, *Bull. Seismol. Soc. Am.* **107,** no. 5, 2055–2066.
Hassani, B., and G. M. Atkinson (2015). Referenced empirical ground-motion model for eastern North America, *Seismol. Res. Lett.* **86,** no. 2A, 477–491.
Hashash, Y. M., O. Ilhan, J. A. Harmon, G. A. Parker, J. P. Stewart, E. M. Rathje, K. W. Campbell, and W. J. Silva (2020). Nonlinear site amplification model for ergodic seismic hazard analysis in Central and Eastern North America, *Earthq. Spectra* **36,** no. 1, 69–86.
Hollenback, J., C. A. Goulet, and D. M. Boore (2015). Adjustment for source depth, chapter 3 in NGA-east: Adjustments to median ground-motion models for central and eastern North America, *PEER Rept.* 8 pp.
Kuehn, N. M., N. A. Abrahamson, and M. A. Walling (2019). Incorporating nonergodic path effects into the NGA-West2 ground-motion prediction equations, *Bull. Seismol. Soc. Am.* **109,** no. 2, 575–585, doi: 10.1785/0120180260.
Kunnath, S. K., E. Erduran, Y. H. Chai, and M. Yashinsky (2008). Effect of near-fault vertical ground motions on seismic response of highway overcrossings, *J. Bridge Eng.* **13,** no. 3, 282–290.
Landwehr, N., N. M. Kuehn, T. Scheffer, and N. Abrahamson (2016). A nonergodic ground-motion model for California with spatially varying coefficients, *Bull. Seismol. Soc. Am.* **106,** no. 6, 2574–2583, doi: 10.1785/0120160118.
Lavrentiadis, G., N. A. Abrahamson, K. M. Nicolas, Y. Bozorgnia, C. A. Goulet, A. Babič, J. Macedo, M. Dolšek, N. Gregor, A. R. Kottke, *et al.* (2023). Overview and introduction to development of non-ergodic earthquake ground-motion models, *Bull. Earthq. Eng.* **21,** no. 11, 5121–5150.
Lin, P. S., C. T. Lee, C. T. Cheng, and C. H. Sung (2011). Response spectral attenuation relations for shallow crustal earthquakes in Taiwan, *Eng. Geol.* **121,** nos. 3/4, 150–164.
McGuire, R. K., W. J. Silva, and C. J. Costantino (2001). Technical basis for revision of regulatory guidance on design ground motions: Hazard-and risk-consistent ground motion spectra guidelines, *U.S. Nuclear Regulatory Commission NUREG/CR-6728,* Division of Engineering Technology, Office of Nuclear Regulatory Research, Washington, D.C., 1020 pp.
Pezeshk, S., A. Zandieh, and B. Tavakoli (2011). Hybrid empirical ground-motion prediction equations for eastern North America using NGA models and updated seismological parameters, *Bull. Seismol. Soc. Am.* **101,** no. 4, 1859–1870.
Pezeshk, S., A. Zandieh, K. W. Campbell, and B. Tavakoli (2018). Ground-motion prediction equations for central and eastern North America using the hybrid empirical method and NGA-West2 empirical ground-motion models, *Bull. Seismol. Soc. Am.* **108,** no. 4, 2278–2304.
Pezeshk, S., A. Farhadi, and A. Haji-Soltani (2022). A new model for vertical-to-horizontal response spectral ratios for central and Eastern North America, *Bull. Seismol. Soc. Am.* **112,** no. 4, 2018–2030.
Pezeshk, S., M. Davatgari-Tafreshi, and A. Haji-Soltani (2024). Hybrid empirical ground-motion models for the Island of Hawaii based on an updated strong ground-motion database, *Bull. Seismol. Soc. Am.* **114,** no. 4, 2186–2201.
Pinheiro, J. C., and D. M. Bates (1996). Unconstrained parametrizations for variance-covariance matrices, *Stat. Comput.* **6,** 289–296.
Rodriguez-Marek, A., G. A. Montalva, F. Cotton, and F. Bonilla (2011). Analysis of single-station standard deviation using the KiK-net data, *Bull. Seismol. Soc. Am.* **101,** no. 3, 1242–1258.
Shahjouei, A., and S. Pezeshk (2016). Alternative hybrid empirical ground motion prediction equations for Central and Eastern North America using hybrid simulations and NGA-West2 Models, *Bull. Seismol. Soc. Am.* **106,** no. 2, 734–754, doi: 10.1785/0120140367.
Silva, W., N. Gregor, and R. Darragh (2002). Development of regional hard rock attenuation relations for central and eastern North America, *Technical Rept.* Pacific Engineering and Analysis, El Cerrito, California.
Stewart, J. P., D. M. Boore, E. Seyhan, and G. M. Atkinson (2016). NGA-West2 equations for predicting vertical-component PGA, PGV, and 5%-damped PSA from shallow crustal earthquakes, *Earthq. Spectra* **32,** no. 2, 1005–1031.
Stewart, J. P., E. Seyhan, D. M. Boore, and G. M. Atkinson (2013). Vertical component ground motion prediction equations for active crustal regions, *Pacific Earthquake Engineering Research Center (PEER) Rept. No. 2013/24.*
Stewart, J. P., G. A. Parker, G. M. Atkinson, D. M. Boore, Y. M. Hashash, and W. J. Silva (2020). Ergodic site amplification model for central and eastern North America, *Earthq. Spectra* **36,** no. 1, 42–68.
Strasser, F. O., N. A. Abrahamson, and J. J. Bommer (2009). Sigma: Issues, insights, and challenges, *Seismol. Res. Lett.* **80,** no. 1, 40–56.
Tavakoli, B., and S. Pezeshk (2005). Empirical-stochastic ground-motion prediction for eastern North America, *Bull. Seismol. Soc. Am.* **95,** no. 6, 2283–2296.
Toro, G. R., N. A. Abrahamson, and J. F. Schneider (1997). Model of strong ground motions from earthquakes in central and eastern North America: Best estimates and uncertainties, *Seismol. Res. Lett.* **68,** no. 1, 41–57.
Villani, M., and N. A. Abrahamson (2015). Repeatable site and path effects on the ground-motion sigma based on empirical data from southern California and simulated waveforms from the CyberShake platform, *Bull. Seismol. Soc. Am.* **105,** no. 5, 2681–2695, doi: 10.1785/0120140359.

Manuscript received 9 June 2025
Published online 6 January 2026

A Combined PGD–PGV Scaling Law with R_{proxy} Distance for the G-FAST Earthquake Early Warning Module

Jensen V. DeGrande*[1] and Brendan W. Crowell[2]

ABSTRACT

Early estimation of strong ground motions and earthquake magnitude is essential for earthquake and tsunami early warning systems and rapid response. We present a new magnitude scaling law relating peak ground velocities (PGVs) and peak ground displacements (PGDs) derived from Global Navigation Satellite Systems (GNSS) data based on a global dataset of real earthquake observations. We used high-rate (1-Hz) GNSS observations for earthquakes ranging in magnitude from M_w 4.9 to 9.1. With this dataset, we explored the evolution of PGV and formally combined it with the PGD scaling law that forms the core of the geodetic first approximation of size and time (G-FAST) module in ShakeAlert, by computing a new distance metric based directly on the PGV and ground-motion model equations developed from a very-high-rate GNSS dataset. We assess the validity of this new distance metric and its performance within the scaling law by comparing it with the performance of the scaling law when using other distance metrics, such as hypocentral distance and mean rupture distance. Moreover, we investigate four case study events with unique rupture characteristics and explore the potential to determine earthquake magnitude from PGV and PGD observations. We find that our newly developed distance metric characterizes true ground motion better than traditionally used distance metrics, including hypocentral distance, which is currently used in early warning operations. We finish by discussing the downstream impacts of improved ground-motion characterization in the context of operational early warning.

KEY POINTS

- We compute a proxy distance metric from geodetic ground velocities for use in a magnitude scaling law.
- Ground motions are better characterized with the proxy distance and can account for rupture characteristics.
- Using the proxy distance reduces the need for modeling faulting extent in an operational context.

Supplemental Material

INTRODUCTION

Earthquake early warning systems (EEWSs) around the world utilize observations of ground motion from strong-motion accelerometers and broadband seismometers. These observations can be used to estimate the magnitude, hypocenter, and other earthquake source parameters as soon as possible to distinguish the location and intensity of strong shaking. Early warning systems work exceedingly well for magnitude estimation of small-to-moderate-size events (Allen and Melgar, 2019). However, inertial-only sensors in general have difficulty recording the full dynamic range of ground displacements, especially at low frequencies during large earthquake events ($M_w > 7.5$) that are dominated by near-field body forces generated from the earthquake source (Melgar *et al.*, 2013; Crowell, 2024). This presents an issue for seismic-only early warning algorithms attempting to estimate earthquake source parameters in real time, especially for these extremely damaging, large-magnitude events.

Geodetic data, specifically GNSS displacements, have recently been incorporated into early warning algorithms (Crowell *et al.*, 2009, 2016; Grapenthin *et al.*, 2014; Minson *et al.*, 2014; Murray *et al.*, 2018, 2023) and ground-motion models (GMMs; Goldberg *et al.*, 2021; Crowell *et al.*, 2023) as a complement to traditional seismic approaches. Typically, peak ground displacement (PGD) is diagnostic of total moment release (Aki and Richards, 1980;

1. Department of Earth and Space Sciences, University of Washington, Seattle, Washington, U.S.A., https://orcid.org/0000-0003-4142-2587 (JVD); 2. School of Earth Sciences, The Ohio State University, Columbus, Ohio, U.S.A., https://orcid.org/0000-0001-7096-601X (BWC)

*Corresponding author: jdegran@uw.edu

Cite this article as DeGrande, J. V., and B. W. Crowell (2025). A Combined PGD–PGV Scaling Law with R_{proxy} Distance for the G-FAST Earthquake Early Warning Module, *Bull. Seismol. Soc. Am.* **116**, 770–785, doi: 10.1785/0120250168

Mai and Thingbaijam, 2014; Melgar *et al.*, 2015; Hayes, 2017), and peak ground velocity (PGV) is diagnostic of earthquake damage (Worden *et al.*, 2012); both are crucially important for earthquake source estimation. GMMs relate earthquake properties, such as magnitude or slip area, to a predicted ground-motion observation, such as PGD, peak ground acceleration (PGA), PGV, and spectral acceleration (SA). GMMs will commonly include additional terms regarding distance attenuation, site amplification, and source terms to model the physical characteristics of the relationship as well. They are often derived from real earthquake observations; in this study, we reference a GMM developed from very-high-rate GNSS PGV observations of real earthquakes. Simpler empirically derived scaling relationships are often used in EEWS, and their implications have been explored in both seismic studies (Olson and Allen, 2005; Noda and Ellsworth, 2016) and geodetic studies (Crowell *et al.*, 2013; Melgar *et al.*, 2015; Fang *et al.*, 2021; Goldberg *et al.*, 2021), including the fruition of the geodetic first approximation of size and time (G-FAST) module of ShakeAlert, where a PGD-only scaling law is the core of the geodetic module:

$$\ln(\mathrm{PGD}) = A + BM_{\mathrm{w}} + CM_{\mathrm{w}}\ln(R). \quad (1)$$

The G-FAST algorithm currently uses either PGDs to determine the magnitude or rapidly computed coseismic displacements to determine slip on the fault (Crowell *et al.*, 2016; Murray *et al.*, 2018, 2023). Although G-FAST performs well when assessed against current seismic algorithms and working in combination with those algorithms in the ShakeAlert early warning system (Murray *et al.*, 2023), there are areas for potential improvements. These areas are related to the noise in real-time GNSS displacement time series, location errors from the seismic system, the logic filters built into the backend of G-FAST, and potential lack of site-specific metrics/corrections (e.g., Crowell, 2024).

In this study, we explore the utility of incorporating PGVs, also recorded on GNSS instruments, into the existing PGD-only scaling law (equation 1) through direct inclusion in the distance metric term. GNSS velocities inherently have a lower noise level than displacements because the processing method removes signal delays between satellite and receivers that do not change rapidly; this approach is known as either the variometric approach or the time-differenced carrier-phase method (Colosimo *et al.*, 2011; Benedetti *et al.*, 2014; Crowell *et al.*, 2023). In addition, PGVs recorded on GNSS do not have a dynamic range limitation, in contrast to broadband seismometers, which will clip in the near field of large earthquakes. The implications of using PGVs alone in scaling laws for magnitude estimation have already been explored, specifically in one study by Fang *et al.* (2021), where they presented a scaling law based directly on GNSS-derived PGVs for magnitude estimation. The concept of PGVs scaling with magnitude was further verified by the work presented in Dittmann *et al.* (2022). Note that these studies only looked at the scaling between magnitude, distance, and PGV.

We focus on estimating a new measure of distance, based on recorded PGV and previously determined GMM relationships, to be used in the existing PGD scaling law within G-FAST. Moreover, we explore the applications of this new distance metric to act as a proxy for the generalized mean rupture distance (R_p), a slip-scaled distance to account for the heterogeneity in slip distributions (Thompson and Baltay, 2018). Multiple studies suggest that R_p provides one of the more accurate representations of distance from slip patch to earthquake origin when compared to other distance metrics, such as hypocentral distance (Thompson and Baltay, 2018; Goldberg *et al.*, 2021; Goldberg and Haynie, 2022). However, R_p is oftentimes not available when an earthquake ruptures. Rather, it is determined post-event from the finite-fault model to directly compute the distance of each slip patch. Goldberg *et al.* (2022) demonstrate the reliability and increased timeliness of finite-fault models when utilizing joint inversion modeling of a variety of data sources, dependent on regional availability. However, even with these advancements, finite-fault models, and thus R_p, are still not available within the tens of minutes of a rupture, making it difficult for this metric to be viable in rapid magnitude estimation through a typical scaling law relationship (Goldberg and Haynie, 2022; Goldberg *et al.*, 2022). A more rapid, although less accurate finite-fault model can be obtained from G-FAST itself, however, solutions are generally not stable for 10s of seconds after a PGD magnitude (Crowell *et al.*, 2018). A formal relationship between PGV and the generalized mean rupture distance (R_p) may be a better solution to modulate distance in real time with no prior knowledge of the faulting extent.

We consider the preliminary GMM presented by Crowell *et al.* (2023) based entirely on validated observations of real earthquakes on very-high-rate GNSS instruments (5, 10, 20, and 100 Hz). The coefficients for the GMM equations (c_0, c_{R0}, c_{R1}, c_{M1}, and c_{M2}) were determined empirically through a simple least-squares regression, and they were computed for two different distance measures: the mean rupture distance (R_p) and the rupture distance (R_{rup}). We utilize the equations and coefficients from the GMM for R_p to derive a new distance metric, R_{proxy}, and assess its performance within the scaling law:

$$R_{\mathrm{proxy}} = \exp\left(\frac{\ln(\mathrm{PGV}) - c_0 - F_M}{c_{R0} + c_{R1}M}\right). \quad (2)$$

See the Derivation of R_{proxy} distance section for further details regarding equation (2). We note that the dataset used in this study and the dataset used for GMM development in Crowell *et al.* (2023) are nearly the same. In addition, because we use the same magnitudes and GMM coefficients as the Crowell *et al.* (2023) study, the difference between R_{proxy} and R_p at each station–event pair should be indicative of the site effects, event terms, and directivity. This means R_{proxy} is not only a distance metric but rather condenses a higher order of complexity (site

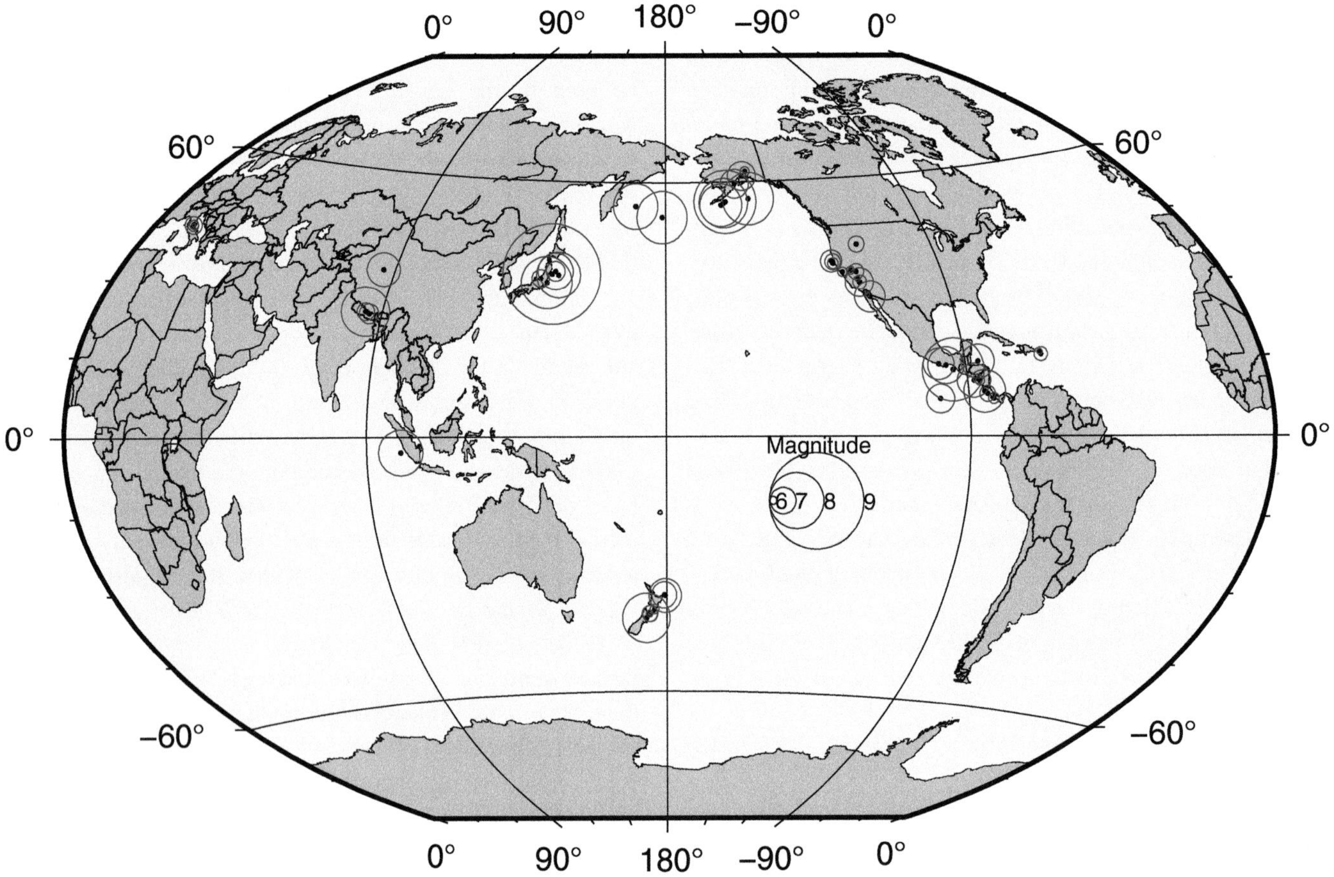

Figure 1. Map indicating all earthquakes used in this study. The black solid circles represent the official epicentral location per the U.S. Geological Survey (USGS) event page, and the red circles indicate the size of the event by magnitude. The color version of this figure is available only in the electronic edition.

effects, event terms, and directivity) into one term. It acts as a rupture distance that is modulated by these other terms.

An analog to R_{proxy} would be the finite-fault detector (FinDer) algorithm in ShakeAlert, which uses a map of the spatial distributions of PGAs and images matches these motions to precomputed distribution templates to estimate an earthquake's magnitude, length, and orientation of the rupture (Böse *et al.*, 2012, 2018). This algorithm specifically helps with defining the fault zone and understanding ground-motion distributions for larger-magnitude events with potentially intricate rupture patterns. We utilize R_{proxy} to mimic the results from FinDer, specifically the variability in ground motions, using scaling laws, ground-motion modeling equations, and GNSS waveforms. Using our approach, we are only dependent on station waveform data (i.e., PGV) and an initial magnitude estimate to understand ground-motion distribution for large-magnitude events.

Through analysis of ground-motion residuals, we compare the performance of the scaling law when using R_{proxy} against the performance when using two commonly used distance metrics—hypocentral distance (R_{hyp}), which is currently used in the G-FAST version of the scaling law, and the mean rupture distance (R_p), which is difficult to obtain in real time due to the requirement of slip distribution (Thompson and Baltay, 2018; Goldberg and Haynie, 2022; Goldberg *et al.*, 2022). In addition, we demonstrate the performance of R_{proxy} in the scaling law on four case studies of events in different regions with different mechanisms and data availability. We use these findings to demonstrate the value in using R_{proxy} in the existing geodetic scaling law, especially for complicated rupture styles where hypocentral distance does not include enough information and larger magnitude events where seismic-only methods saturate. Finally, we demonstrate how to determine earthquake magnitude from PGV and PGD observations by utilizing a grid search due to the nonlinear nature of the scaling law and discuss potential downstream impacts for operational EEW.

DATA AND METHODS

This study uses high-rate (1-Hz) data from 59 earthquakes ranging in magnitude from 4.9 to 9.1, shown in Figure 1 with their respective magnitudes, and with a varying number of stations per event, depending on the location of the event and nearby station networks. Information on each event, including the number of stations and mechanisms, can be found in Table S1, available in the supplemental material to this article. The magnitude for each event is based on the U.S. Geological Survey (USGS) published magnitude. We use a total of 2352 station–event pairs. All station–event pairs have been visually inspected to validate that a true seismic signal, or surface wave, is present in the waveform greater than the white-noise level associated with GNSS displacements (1 cm for North/East components and 3–5 cm for the Up component; see Melgar *et al.*, 2020). Station–event pairs where a seismic signal is not present are discarded.

For each station–event pair, we initially compute the three-component displacement and velocity waveforms from the raw observation data obtained in Receiver Independent Exchange Format (RINEX) (see Data and Resources). To compute displacements, we use GipsyX (Bertiger *et al.*, 2020), a precise point positioning code that requires rapid or final orbits and satellite clocks from the International GNSS Service, and differential code biases from the Jet Propulsion Laboratory to increase the precision of the position estimate. Final orbits and clocks were available and used for all events in this study. To compute the velocities, we use the Satellite Navigation-derived Instantaneous Velocities (SNIVEL) algorithm (Crowell *et al.*, 2023), which uses the variometric or time-differenced carrier phase approach. GNSS velocities are computed by taking a single difference in time between phase observables (in this case, the narrow-lane combination of L1 and L2) and satellite positions (Colosimo *et al.*, 2011; Benedetti *et al.*, 2014; Grapenthin *et al.*, 2018; Shu *et al.*, 2018; Crowell, 2021). Because of this processing method, many of the errors associated with the observation equation are eliminated, and the noise level of the velocity observable is greatly reduced compared to that of the displacement (roughly a factor of 5–10; see Shu *et al.*, 2018). We calculate the total maximum displacement, or 3D displacement, by taking the maximum of the Euclidean norm of the North, East, and Up components for a certain amount of time after the origin time, dependent on the magnitude of the event. For the purposes of the scaling law, we use the total maximum displacement value as the PGD at the station. We compute the total maximum velocity using the same methodology on the velocity component waveforms; the total maximum velocity is used as the PGV at the station.

Using the PGD-only scaling law (equation 1), our computed PGDs, and the official magnitude for each event, we perform a least-squares regression to determine the coefficients A, B, and C. Here, the least-squares solution minimizes the Euclidean 2-norm. We did not perform any reweighting or resampling of the binned observations because we intend for this to be a first-order analysis. We focus on a fixed-effects regression with a simple least-squares determination, which does not account for random effects or the multiple levels of variability between events that may introduce bias to the model. Because the scaling law currently operates using the hypocentral distance, or the distance from the earthquake origin to the station, we perform the regression using the hypocentral distance as R.

TABLE 1
Coefficients for Least Squares Regression of Equation (1)

Distance Metric	A	B	C
Scaling law with hypocentral distance, R_{hyp} (G-FAST)	−7.865	1.913	−0.1008
Scaling law with mean rupture distance, R_p	−7.977	1.937	−0.1027
Scaling law with proxy distance, R_{proxy}	−7.317	1.867	−0.1040

Each row indicates the distance metric used in regression. G-FAST, geodetic first approximation of size and time.

From this, we obtain the coefficients presented in the first row of Table 1. Note this is equivalent to the approach used by Goldberg *et al.* (2021), but we replace log base 10 with natural log for both the PGD and the distance term in the equation to be consistent with the PGV GMM in Crowell *et al.* (2023) and traditional seismic GMMs. We predict the PGDs from this relationship by substituting the newly computed coefficients, the official magnitude, and the hypocentral distance as R. We compare the predicted PGDs output from this computation with the observed PGDs, directly obtained from the waveform, to assess the performance through natural log residuals.

For events where the slip model is available, we compute the mean rupture distance, R_p, using $p = -2.0$ as the power law weighting and weight each subfault by slip amplitude. These are the same methods by Crowell *et al.* (2023) used to compute R_p for the GMM development and a similar power of the mean, p, to that used in Goldberg *et al.* (2021); In addition, Thompson and Baltay (2018) note that a p of −2.0 is within the optimal range for velocities. We use the official finite-fault models (Hayes, 2017) from the National Earthquake Information Center (NEIC) by extracting them directly from the geoJSON files on the USGS event overview pages for each earthquake where available (see Table S1). We treat events without an official finite-fault model available as point sources. Using the previously described methodology and equation (1), we regress new coefficients A, B, and C using the R_p as R within the least-squares regression (see Table 1, second row). Again, we compute the predicted PGDs by substituting these new coefficients and R_p into equation (1) and compare with the observed PGDs through natural log residuals.

Derivation of R_{proxy} distance

To derive the proxy distance, R_{proxy}, we reference the ground-motion modeling equations presented by Crowell *et al.* (2023) as a starting point for exploring the relationship between PGV and the mean rupture distance, R_p. Equations (3)–(5) of our study are adopted from the preliminary GMM (CDDG22) based on PGVs recorded on very-high-rate GNSS presented by Crowell *et al.* (2023; see equations 4–6) with slight modifications described subsequently. Similar to GMMs presented in Thompson and Baltay (2018) and Goldberg *et al.* (2021), only the magnitude scaling (F_M) and distance scaling (F_R) terms are considered for the GMM relationships:

$$\ln(\mathrm{PGV}) = c_0 + F_M + F_R. \quad (3)$$

For mathematical simplicity, we ignore the anelastic attenuation term originally included in the Crowell *et al.* (2023) formulation and only consider the geometrical spreading/magnitude-dependent attenuation term ($c_{R0} + c_{R1}M$) of the distance-scaling term (F_R), resulting in the following equation:

$$F_R = (c_{R0} + c_{R1}M)\ln(R). \quad (4)$$

We recognize the importance of the anelastic attenuation term ($c_{R2}R$); however, if we were to include it in the above term, it would significantly increase the difficulty of isolating R; it would require a complicated series expansion that would not be generalized and only useful for certain ranges, which is not ideal. For consistency, we attempted to derive new GMM coefficients that also exclude the anelastic attenuation term, but we found that this degraded the quality of the results and increased biases for some cases. However, the standard deviations were nearly the same as when we did include the anelastic attenuation term in the GMM coefficients, so we opted to adopt the GMM coefficients from Crowell *et al.* (2023), which include the anelastic attenuation term. We postulate that when the anelastic attenuation term is included in the GMM coefficient regression, it better offsets the impacts of aliasing, which we discuss in further detail later on. As this is a simple, first-order analysis R_{proxy}, future work is still needed to determine the optimal scaling and aliasing corrections.

In a similar fashion to Crowell *et al.* (2023) and Goldberg *et al.* (2021), we use a magnitude-scaling term that is simplified to ignore the small-magnitude terms and is as follows:

$$F_M = c_{M1}M + c_{M2}\ln(1 + \exp(-M)). \quad (5)$$

Coefficients c_0, c_{R0}, c_{R1}, c_{M1}, and c_{M2} were originally solved for through a simple least-squares regression based on the generalized mean rupture distance (R_p) in Crowell *et al.* (2023). We directly adopt these coefficients, which can be found in Table 2. With these equations and the GMM coefficients, we substitute the equations for F_R (equation 4) and F_M (equation 5) into equation (3) and rearrange to solve for the distance, R, to formalize a relationship between R and PGV:

$$\ln(R_{\mathrm{proxy}}) = \frac{\ln(\mathrm{PGV}) - c_0 - F_M}{c_{R0} + c_{R1}M}. \quad (6)$$

After rearranging, we can plug in the observed PGVs from our 1-Hz dataset, derived directly from the processed waveforms, to calculate a proxy distance metric, R_{proxy}, for each

TABLE 2
Ground-Motion Model Coefficients Using R_p

Coefficient	Value
c_0	−13.485
c_{R0}	1.338
c_{R1}	−0.3396
c_{M1}	2.835
c_{M2}	206.078

Coefficients for the CDDG22 ground-motion model (GMM), determined by Crowell *et al.* (2023) using R_p and a very-high-rate Global Navigation Satellite System (GNSS) global catalog.

station–event pair. This metric is based directly on the PGV waveform data and the previously determined ground-motion relationship from Crowell *et al.* (2023) shown in equations (3)–(5), effectively eliminating the need for earthquake source modeling in this application.

After solving for R_{proxy}, we can assess its performance within the scaling law (equation 1) in terms of ground motion by directly substituting it into the original PGD-only scaling law as R. We first substitute R_{proxy} into equation (1) using the coefficients A, B, and C determined from the regression using hypocentral distance as is practice in G-FAST (Table 1, first row). We then substitute using the coefficients A, B, and C determined using the mean rupture distance to explore the effects of using coefficients developed with a more accurate distance metric (Table 1, second row). However, because R_p is unavailable in real time, this is mainly a comparison point to evaluate the performance of the proxy distance.

As a final point, we perform another least-squares regression similar to the two described in the previous section, except we use the proxy distance itself to determine a new set of coefficients A, B, and C (Table 1, third row). Again, we substitute these coefficients and R_{proxy} into equation (1) to determine the predicted ground motions (PGDs) from this new distance metric and newly regressed coefficients to compare with the observed values.

Similar to predicting the PGDs from equation (1), we can rearrange to solve for magnitude,

$$M_{\mathrm{w}}\text{-estimated} = \frac{\ln(\mathrm{PGD}) - A}{B + C\ln(R_{\mathrm{proxy}})}, \quad (7)$$

and use this to assess the performance of each distance metric and coefficient combination by comparing the output with the official post-event magnitude. We explore the results of magnitude estimation with the four case studies (Fig. S1). A variety of factors, for example, style of faulting, near-source distance scaling, near-surface geology, and other source/path/site effects, impact the realized magnitude of an earthquake event (Chiou and Youngs, 2008, 2014; Sahakian *et al.*, 2018, 2019). Most of these factors cannot be accurately estimated from ground-motion data alone.

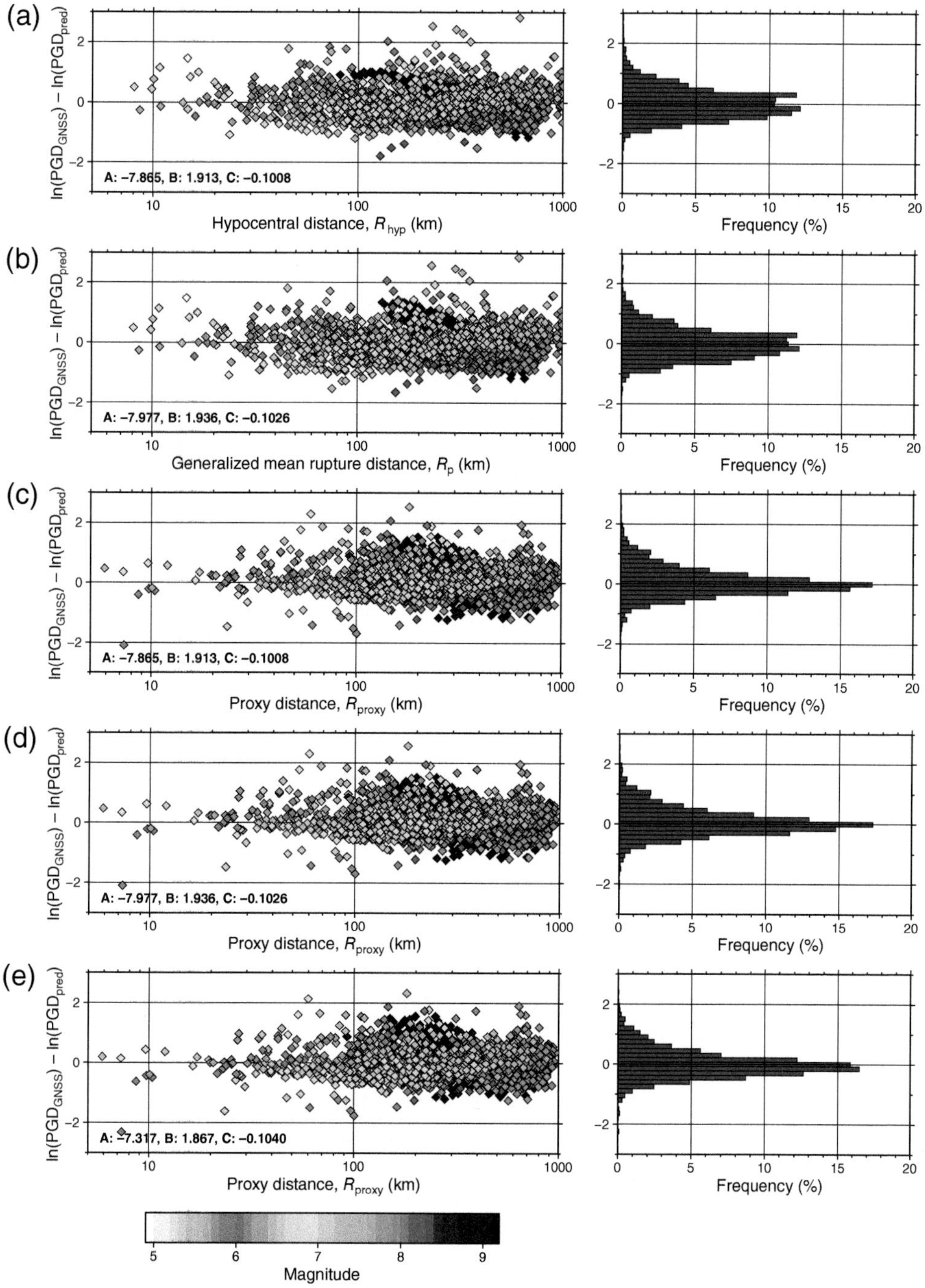

Figure 2. Natural log residuals between peak ground displacement (PGD) from Global Navigation Satellite System (GNSS) and predicted from the scaling law. Panels on the left side are the residuals as a function of the distance metric, and panels on the right are the percent frequency histograms of the residuals for all observations. Residuals are defined as $\ln(PGD_{GNSS}) - \ln(PGD_{predicted})$. (a) The performance of the original scaling law using the hypocentral distance on the 1 Hz dataset. (b) The performance of the scaling law when using the post-computed generalized mean rupture distance for each station–event pair based on the event's official finite-fault model. (c) The results of plugging in the proxy distance, computed with the modified ground-motion model (GMM) equations from Crowell *et al.* (2023) and peak ground velocity (PGV) values from this study's data catalog, to the original scaling law using coefficients determined with the hypocentral distance. (d) The results of substituting the proxy distance into the scaling law using coefficients determined with R_p. (e) The result of substituting the proxy distance and using the coefficients determined with R_{proxy} in the least-squares regression. The color version of this figure is available only in the electronic edition.

Because the combination of equations (1) and (2) is nonlinear with respect to magnitude, we cannot simply invert for earthquake magnitude in real time as is done with PGD-only scaling in G-FAST. To determine magnitude, we perform a grid search between magnitude 6 and 10 in 0.01 magnitude unit increments and then determine the L1 norm of the log residuals between true and predicted PGD. For predicted PGD values, we use the proxy distance computed from PGV (equation 2) and the Crowell *et al.* (2023) coefficients and then insert this value into equation (1) for each magnitude step. The chosen magnitude is the one that minimizes the L1 norm of the residuals.

RESULTS

Ground-motion estimation performance

The log residuals between the observed PGD values and the scaling law-predicted PGD values are calculated as $\ln(PGD_{GNSS}) - \ln(PGD_{predicted})$ and shown in Figure 2 as a function of each distance metric examined in this comparison. These residuals represent the fit of the coefficients to the dataset when using each distance metric. Because we are looking at the displacements, this visualizes how each instance of the scaling law characterizes ground motion for each earthquake event based on these coefficients and each distance metric used. The results shown in Figure 2a,c use scaling law coefficients that were estimated using R_{hyp} (Table 1, first row). The results in Figure 2b,d use coefficients estimated using R_p (Table 1, second row). Figure 2e shows results with coefficients estimated using R_{proxy} (Table 1, third row). In addition to the spread of residuals as a function of distance, we plot the histogram of the residuals for each distance metric.

Upon examining each residual panel, we observe a slightly tighter distribution for the three bottom panels where the proxy distance is used; that is, there are a smaller number of residuals beyond the range of 2 log units when compared to the scaling law instances that use the hypocentral distance or mean rupture distance. With all five, we generally see a larger spread of observations in the near field, particularly between 0 and 110 km, particularly for station–event pairs from events less than M_w 6.5, based on the color of the symbols. Based on the histograms, there does not seem to be a strong trend in under- or overprediction of the ground motions for any of the distance metrics. The histograms for each of the three proxy distance instances show a distinct peak just below zero and a tighter distribution of the residuals. We see a roughly normal distribution curve with significant peaks exceeding 15%, outperforming both scaling laws using hypocentral or mean rupture distance, where, whereas still a normal distribution, a broader peak is present between −0.5 and 0.5 log units at a frequency slightly over 10% for both metrics.

Although it seems our new distance metric is performing fairly well in terms of ground-motion residual distributions, we must also consider the impact of noise within GNSS observations and the threshold at which these observations accurately represent the surface wave from a rupture event. Although our processing method and sampling rate of 1 Hz mitigate some of the noise within the observation equation itself, we must account for the impacts of temporal aliasing based upon the frequency content of the event and how that scales with magnitude, given a sampling rate of 1 s. In terms of our sampling rate, this typically becomes an issue for events with a moment magnitude less than 6.5, where the corner frequency, or frequency at which the spectral field begins to decrease, is at approximately M 6.5 (Joyner, 1984). Lower magnitude events sampled at 1 Hz will have reduced peak velocity values than those obtained using data sampled at a very high rate with sub-second sampling. This is to be expected given the corner frequency dependence on magnitude detailed by Joyner (1984). To better understand the nuance between small- and large-magnitude events in terms of our dataset and newly developed distance metric, we split the dataset into two subsets for analysis, where events with an official magnitude greater than or equal to 7.5 are considered as large-magnitude events and those with magnitudes less than 7.5 are considered small–moderate-magnitude events. The majority of the observations in this dataset are between M_w 9.1 and 6.0, with only a few observations below M_w 6.0 (<30 observations). Because of this, we selected M_w 7.5 as the division point, rather than M_w 6.5, as it is nearly the midpoint of the magnitude range and splits the data observations more equally among the two subsets. We again plot the natural log residuals (Fig. 3) between the observed PGDs and the scaling law predicted PGDs for each of the five instances for these two subsets.

Segregating the residuals by magnitude allows us to see a more detailed performance of these scaling law instances and the three tested distance metrics for large-magnitude events, and the full potential of GNSS-derived data when incorporated into scaling laws. Again, we see a distinct peak centered around zero for all three instances that use the proxy distance developed in this study (Fig. 3c–e), whereas the two traditionally used distance metrics plateau with no notable peak (Fig. 3a,b). We see a similar range of residuals with no worsening or bias within the proxy distance cases. When considering only small–moderate-magnitude events (Fig. 3, right column), we see a distinguishable peak for the proxy distance cases, but this peak is slightly to the left of zero, indicating an overprediction bias from the scaling law for events of this magnitude range. This makes sense given the previous indication about the change in corner frequency with smaller magnitude events, so the recorded PGVs are smaller in value due to the sampling rate. For the hypocentral or mean rupture distance for small–moderate-magnitude events, we do see a better centering of the data around zero with a smaller bias. We also present the statistics for these subsets in Table 3, including the mean, median, standard deviation, and interquartile range for each scaling law instance.

For large-magnitude events, the mean and medians are closer to zero for all instances using the proxy distance compared to those using the hypocentral or mean rupture distance. Based on mean and median alone, the proxy distance using its own coefficients leads to the closest fit to zero with −0.0029 and −0.0315, respectively. This is a notable difference between the values for hypocentral distance, −0.0399 and −0.0689, and even the mean rupture distance, −0.0444 and −0.0648, reducing the mean by a factor of 10 and the median by half. The instances using the proxy distance and either the coefficients from hypocentral distance or mean rupture distance regressions still outperform both instances using the traditional distance metrics and their respective coefficients. In addition, the standard deviation between all five instances does not vary significantly, indicating the range of residuals does not change depending on the distance metric and we are not increasing the number of outliers or residual distribution with our newly computed metric. We also see a reduction in the interquartile range for the instances using the proxy distance. For small-to-moderate-magnitude events, we see a more complicated trend where the instance using the proxy distance and its own coefficients is still performing best in terms of mean, with a value of 0.0048; however, the hypocentral and mean rupture distance instances outperform all three proxy distance instances in terms of median. This is as expected with the trends presented in the histograms of Figure 3 for the small–moderate-magnitude events. However, we do note a slightly smaller range of standard deviations for the proxy distance instances as well as smaller interquartile ranges.

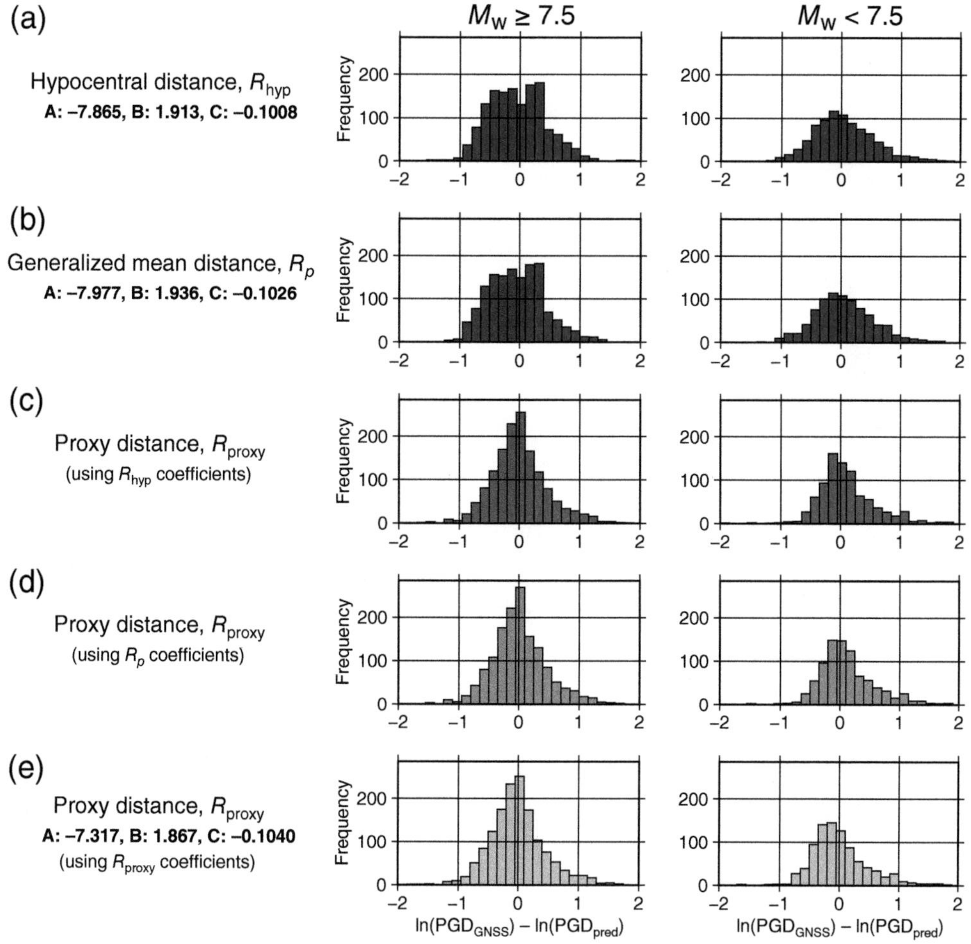

Figure 3. Natural log residuals between PGD from GNSS and predicted from the scaling law, segregated by magnitude. Plots on the left side are for events with magnitudes greater than or equal to M_W 7.5, and plots on the right side are for events with magnitudes less than M_W 7.5. Panel order of each instance (a–e) is the same as described in Figure 2. The color version of this figure is available only in the electronic edition.

Although we now have a better grasp on the nuance between small- and large-magnitude events, we also must consider the limitations associated with using a dataset of real earthquake observations. The events used vary in rupture mechanism, tectonic and geologic settings, and station/observation distribution and quantity. Because we are using a fixed-effects regression, we cannot fully capture the significance of these factors because they vary from event to event. To better understand some of these limitations, we examine four unique case studies.

Exhibit case studies

The performance of the ground-motion estimation ability of these scaling laws can be better assessed through case studies of specific events where all sites are experiencing the unique effects of each rupture. Of the data used in this study, 11 events had 30+ observations of ground motion. We examine four of these events of different magnitudes, mechanisms, and regions of the world to understand the performance of R_{proxy} in a singular rupture where site effects, rupture directivity, and other event-specific effects may impact the performance of the scaling law. For each event, R_{proxy} is calculated using only the NEIC magnitude, whereas R_{hyp} and R_p are computed using the NEIC location or slip model, respectively.

TABLE 3
Mean, Median, Standard Deviation, and Interquartile Range for Each Combination of Distance Metric and Coefficient

Distance and Coefficient Combination	Mean	Median	Standard Deviation	Quartile
Hypocentral distance, R_{hyp} (≥7.5)	−0.0399	−0.0689	0.4737	0.6809
Hypocentral distance, R_{hyp} (<7.5)	0.0667	−0.0095	0.5426	0.6740
Mean rupture distance, R_p (≥7.5)	−0.0444	−0.0648	0.4743	0.6709
Mean rupture distance, R_p (<7.5)	0.0741	0.0190	0.5436	0.6467
R_{proxy} and coefficients$_{Rhyp}$ (≥ 7.5)	0.0078	−0.0221	0.4580	0.5189
R_{proxy} and coefficients$_{Rhyp}$ (<7.5)	0.1188	0.0369	0.4942	0.5092
R_{proxy} and coefficients$_{Rp}$ (≥7.5)	0.0170	−0.0148	0.4561	0.5265
R_{proxy} and coefficients$_{Rp}$ (<7.5)	0.1343	0.0441	0.4978	0.5084
R_{proxy} and coefficients$_{Rproxy}$ (≥7.5)	−0.0029	−0.0315	0.4616	0.5189
R_{proxy} and coefficients$_{Rproxy}$ (<7.5)	0.0048	−0.0783	0.4859	0.4990

Data are separated by magnitude. Hypocentral and mean rupture distance use their respective coefficients, whereas three different combinations are used for the proxy distance (see Table 1 for coefficients).

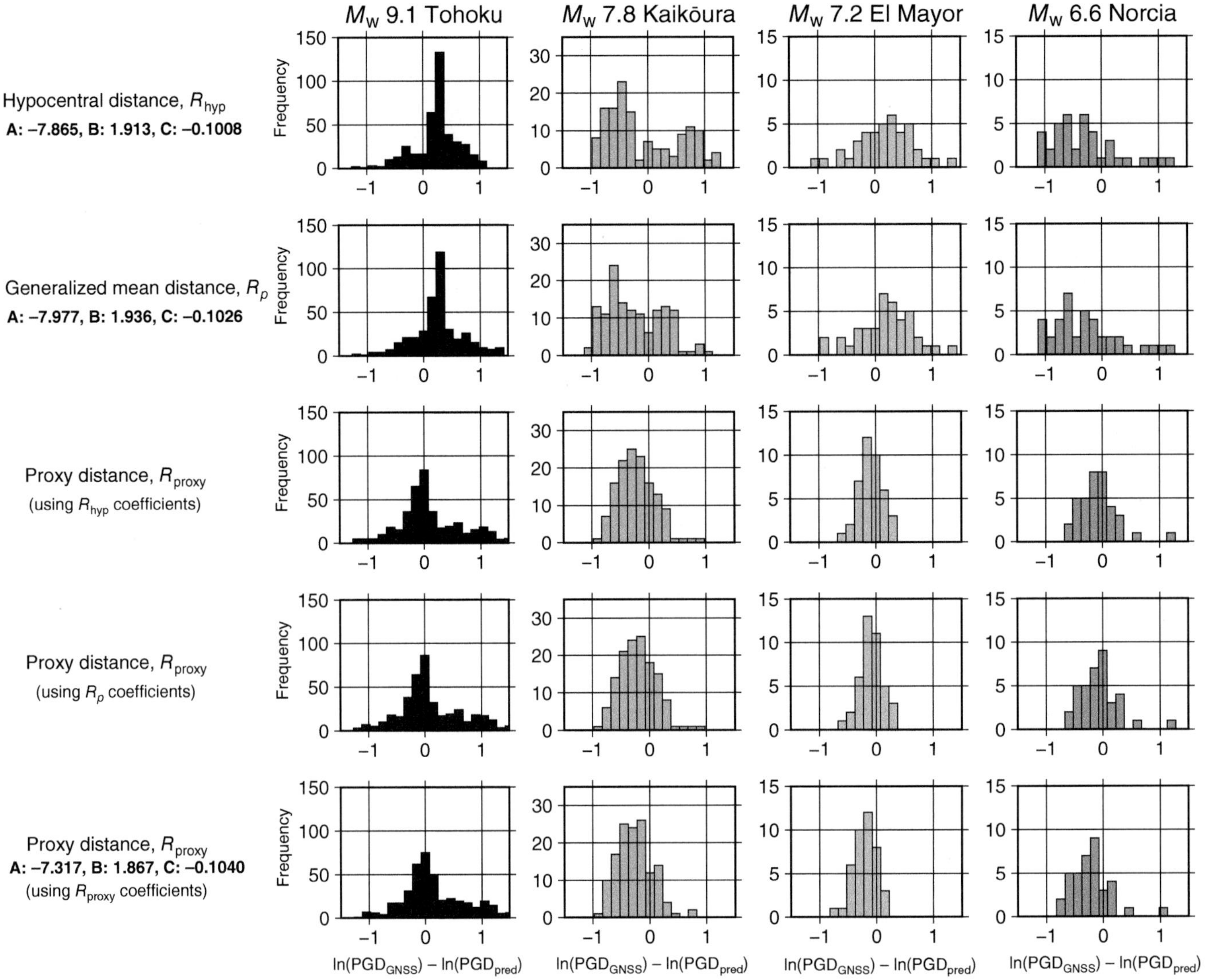

Figure 4. Log residuals for the ground motion, PGD, for the four case studies included in this study (M_w 9.1 Tohoku, M_w 7.8 Kaikōura, M_w 7.2 El Mayor, and M_w 6.6 Norcia) where residuals are defined as $\ln(PGD_{GNSS}) - \ln(PGD_{predicted})$. The color version of this figure is available only in the electronic edition.

2011 M_w 9.1 Tohoku, Japan

With a dense network of geodetic observations and one of the largest events of this century, the 2011 M_w 9.1 Tohoku megathrust event was a suitable case study to further understand the newly developed distance metric for large rupture. Geodetic observations from the Geonet network operated by the Geospatial Information Authority of Japan were processed through GipsyX and SNIVEL to yield GNSS displacement and velocity waveforms, respectively. Of our global catalog, 404 observations are from this event (approximately 17%). The maximum displacement and velocity were recorded on station 0550 as 621 cm and 35 cm/s at a hypocentral distance of 81 km.

The natural log residuals for M_w 9.1 Tohoku are shown in Figure 4, column 1. For instances where the hypocentral or the mean rupture distance is used, rows 1 and 2, we see an apparent underprediction bias. That is, the scaling laws are underpredicting the expected ground motion compared to the actual ground motion recorded on the GNSS instrument. For the most part, the residuals are contained within 1 log unit of zero. Because this is the largest event of the catalog and the only event with a magnitude greater than 9, we postulate that using only the distance from the source itself is not enough to properly characterize ground motions from large-magnitude events with large rupture lengths. However, when we incorporate the PGVs into the distance metric by means of our proxy distance (rows 3–5 in Fig. 4), we see a closer peak to zero. It is important to note that the spread of the residuals now extends beyond 1 log unit, and for each case using the proxy distance, we see a notable number of observations at 1 log unit. In addition, while the histogram peaks are closer to zero for the instances using the proxy distance, they are not directly centered over zero. Instead, we see a slight overprediction trend where the scaling law is predicting a slightly larger amplitude of ground motion than recorded on the instrument. Again, with this being the only event of this magnitude in the catalog, we view this as a limitation of the catalog and available real-world data that the scaling law coefficients were based upon. Statistically, we see the same trend as described earlier; the mean is farther from zero when using hypocentral and mean rupture distance, but the standard deviation is much better, and the cases using the proxy distance have a mean closer to zero but a much larger standard deviation and distribution of residuals (see Table S2).

One of the issues for Japan's EEWS was that the magnitude of the Tohoku event was underpredicted due to the large extent of the fault rupture (Hoshiba and Aoki, 2015). As a seismic-only system at the time, the magnitude was initially estimated as M_w 8.1, and thus the strength of the predicted ground motions was also underestimated, and inadequate warnings were issued, specifically for the Tokyo region (Hoshiba *et al.*, 2011). Hoshiba *et al.* (2011) state the estimated magnitude of 8.1 was near the upper limit of the system due to the effects of magnitude saturation for events greater than M_w 8. Even with GNSS observations, we see the same underprediction trend in the PGD log residuals of Figure 4 when only using the hypocentral distance or mean rupture distance in the scaling law. However, we see a closer estimate of the ground motions when utilizing the proxy distance. We performed the same analysis predicting the magnitude from the scaling law and noticed a different trend where the magnitude is overestimated for cases using the hypocentral or mean rupture distance. For the cases using the proxy distance, we again see a better fit to zero, and compared to the ground-motion residuals, we even see a better constraint on the range of residuals. The residuals between the observed magnitude and the predicted magnitude from the scaling law when using equation (7) are shown in Figure S1.

2016 M_w 7.8 Kaikōura, New Zealand

We selected the 2016 M_w 7.8 Kaikōura strike-slip event as one of the case studies to further assess the proxy distance metric because of the interesting rupture characteristics of this event. Hamling *et al.* (2017) detail the complex, multi-fault rupture where more than a dozen crustal faults are thought to have ruptured, causing the entirety of the country to experience shaking and extensive damage that had not been seen in the past 150 yr. In addition, evidence of strong northward directivity is thought to be involved due to the damage caused by this historic event, with large, enhanced ground motions observed at the north end of the South Island. Crowell *et al.* (2023) noted that this event was the only one to have a strong negative residual between the recorded ground motions and four GMMs assessed in that study, including the CDDG22 GMM for which we use the equations to derive the proxy distance.

With 136 1 Hz observations in our data catalog, the majority of which overlap with the very-high-rate catalog used in Crowell *et al.* (2023), we assess the performance of each distance metric in the scaling law for the M_w 7.8 Kaikōura event. The velocity and displacement waveforms were directly computed from the 1-Hz RINEX obtained from GeoNet operated by Earth Sciences New Zealand. Where 1-Hz data were not available, 10-Hz data were downloaded and resampled to the 1 s interval prior to processing with GipsyX or SNIVEL. The results for the natural log residuals of ground motion for this event are shown in Figure 4, column 2. For the scaling law using hypocentral distance (row 1 in Fig. 4), we see a bimodal distribution in the ground-motion residual histograms. We also see a bimodal trend when using the mean rupture distance. This complex distribution indicates the rupture directivity referenced in both Hamling *et al.* (2017) and Crowell *et al.* (2023). We see peaks both on the negative side of the histogram, or trends of overprediction, and on the positive side of the histogram, trends of underprediction. That is, some regions of the island experienced more ground motion and thus shaking intensity than others because the energy released from the earthquake did not propagate evenly from the epicenter but rather had a directional component to it that is present in the statistical analysis of this event. The scaling laws using the traditional distance metrics cannot compensate for this directivity and uniqueness. However, when we consider the histograms for the scaling laws that use the proxy distance (rows 3–5 in Fig. 4), we see one singular, distinct peak, indicating the ability to compensate for the directivity of this rupture. However, it is important to note that while a peak is apparent, this peak is centered slightly less than zero (approximate mean values of −0.21, −0.20, and −0.26, respectively for each proxy distance instance; refer to Table S3 for additional statistics), even more than we saw in the Tohoku example, indicating an overprediction of ground motion for this event. The range of residuals is a slightly better fit, within 1 log unit for the proxy distance cases, whereas it is slightly wider for the cases using hypocentral and mean rupture distance. We use equation (7) to compute an estimated magnitude for each station–event pair and plot these results in Figure S1 (column 2), where we note a similar trend to that of the ground-motion residuals with bimodal distribution in the hypocentral and mean rupture distance cases, but an underprediction of magnitude in the proxy distance cases.

With the uniqueness of the rupture, station availability, and bimodal distribution present in the ground motion and magnitude residuals for the Kaikōura event, we took this as an opportunity to explore how the proxy distance is working in terms of PGV and hypocentral distance (Fig. 5). We plot the difference between the newly computed proxy distance and the hypocentral distance of each station, or $R_{proxy} - R_{hyp}$. The symbol type, circle or square, indicates whether the difference is positive or negative; if there is a positive difference, circle symbol, then the proxy distance is greater than the hypocentral distance, and if there is a negative difference, square symbol, then the proxy distance is less than the hypocentral distance. The size of the symbol indicates the numerical size of the difference; larger symbol sizes mean a large difference between proxy and hypocentral

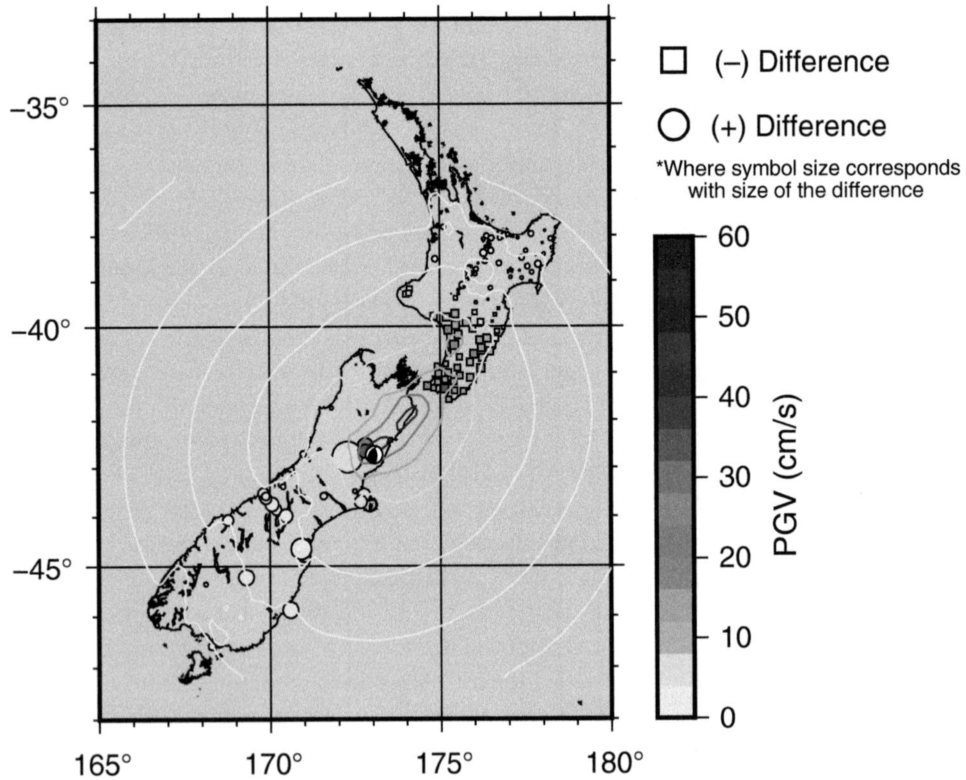

Figure 5. Map view of M_w 7.8 Kaikōura event, where symbols denote GNSS station observations used in this study. The color intensity indicates PGV in cm/s at each station, and the symbol type indicates whether a positive or negative difference results from $R_{proxy} - R_{hyp}$. A positive difference is indicated by a circle, and a negative difference is indicated by a square. The symbol size is indicative of the size of the difference. Contour lines represent official ShakeMap PGV contours in cm/s in the same color scale as the stations. The color version of this figure is available only in the electronic edition.

distance, whereas smaller symbols mean a small difference. We color each symbol by the PGV at each station, where lighter red hues indicate a lower PGV and deeper red hues indicate a higher PGV, as well as plot the PGV contours from the published ShakeMap for comparison. Based on the numerical sign of the difference and the actual PGV recorded at each station, we can get a better grasp on the relationship between R_{proxy} and observed PGV. We can think of this as when there is a positive difference, the proxy distance is mimicking a farther away station, or a station that recorded a lower PGV, whereas a negative difference would mean the proxy distance is mimicking a closer station, or a station that recorded a higher PGV. Based on this thinking, the stations to the south of the moment tensor indicate a positive difference, mimicking a farther away distance. This makes sense with the given northward directivity associated with this event; that is, these stations did not record a high PGV despite being relatively close to the hypocenter. There is a distinct trend where a cluster of stations directly to the northeast of the event has negative differences. In the same line of thinking, these stations are mimicked to be closer to the hypocenter based on the high PGV they recorded. Stations further north of the island, which coincide with lower levels of PGV contours, have relatively small positive differences, which is consistent with the indicated propagation direction and official magnitude of the event.

2010 M_w 7.2 El Mayor, Mexico

The geographic context and station network distribution for the M_w 7.2 El Mayor strike-slip event that occurred in 2010 make it another noteworthy case study. The majority of the observations of this event in our catalog are in southern California, or to the northwest of the epicenter of the event that struck the northern end of Baja California. All these stations are to the north of the international border, resulting in no observations of ground motion from GNSS to the east, west, or south of this event. The surface geology, fault geometry, and complexity of this rupture and the subsequent propagation of seismic waves has been further assessed in studies by Hauksson *et al.* (2010), who analyzed the entire earthquake sequence including foreshocks and aftershocks, and Wei *et al.* (2011) using geodetic, remote sensing, and seismological data to understand the fault geometry and history of slip in this region. We explore the performance of the scaling law when all the stations are in one spatial direction from the hypocenter. For this event, we downloaded 1-Hz observations for 41 regional geodetic stations from the EarthScope Consortium and processed them with GipsyX and SNIVEL to compute the displacement and velocity waveforms.

In Figure 4, column 3, we see a slight tendency for underprediction of PGD when hypocentral or mean rupture distance is used. There is a general peak around 0.18 and 0.18, respectively, and residuals span between approximately −1 and 1 log units. For the instances of the scaling law that use the proxy distance (rows 3–5 in Fig. 4), we see a notable peak slightly less than zero (approximately at −0.09, −0.09, and −0.21; see Table S4). Again, we see the overprediction bias that we saw in both the M_w 9.1 Tohoku and the M_w 7.8 Kaikōura case studies. The histograms for El Mayor indicate a narrow peak with steep drop-offs on either side. Similar to Kaikōura with the directivity aspect, the spatial location or distribution of ground-motion observations does not negatively impact the performance of the scaling law when proxy distance is used. Although there is an overprediction trend in the ground motions computed from the proxy distance scaling law instances, we note a significant reduction in the spread of residuals, well contained within −1 and +1 log units, and related standard deviation values (see Table S4). As with the previous two case study events, we compute the magnitude residuals using equation (7), and those results are shown in Figure S1. For the magnitude residuals, there is a drastic improvement in magnitude estimation when using the proxy distance, with a very notable peak centered over zero and minimal spread of residuals. We conclude that even with an asymmetric station distribution, using the proxy distance in the scaling law still leads to improved characterization of ground motion, and in this case, improved magnitude estimation, than using the hypocentral distance or mean rupture distance.

2016 M_w 6.6 Norcia, Italy

The 2016 M_w 6.6 Norcia earthquake is the final case study that we consider. It was the final and largest of a sequence of five earthquakes that shook the Italian peninsula and a normal-faulting event along a shallow fault in the Central Apennines mountain range. Although the smallest of the showcased case studies, this event has an even distribution of stations, with a handful of them very close to the main rupture. When compared to seismic networks in the region, we see there are many more GNSS stations in the near field, resulting in observations of higher ground motions and shaking intensities. We downloaded 39 geodetic observations from the Rete Integrata Nazionale (RING) Working Group and processed them with GipsyX and SNIVEL to compute the displacement and velocity waveforms for each station. Where 1-Hz data were not available, 10- or 20-Hz data were downloaded and resampled to the 1 s interval prior to processing with GipsyX or SNIVEL. The closest station, ARQT, was 16 km from the rupture and had a recorded PGD of 49 cm and PGV of 32 cm/s when sampled at 1 Hz.

The ground-motion residual results are presented in Figure 4, column 4. We see little to no trend in residuals when using the hypocentral or mean rupture distance in the scaling law; however, we do note that the majority of the data are within the negative log space with a few irregular peaks. For the instances using the proxy distance in the scaling law, we see a more consistent clustering of residuals near zero, but the peaks of the histogram are not as large as some of the other higher-magnitude events showcased in this study. In addition, the centering of data is again to the left of zero, indicating an overprediction bias. We also note an outlier with all these instances, where one residual was over a full +1 log unit. We postulate that the results for the M_w 6.6 Norcia event are heavily influenced by the aliasing effects with the 1-Hz GNSS observations. Although not perfect, we see a closer characterization of ground motion for the instances that use the proxy distance than we see with traditional distance metrics like hypocentral distance or mean rupture distance. As for the magnitude residuals, we actually see an underprediction in the magnitude for the scaling law using the proxy distances, but we again see a more distinct peak closer to zero than those of the instances using hypocentral or mean rupture distance.

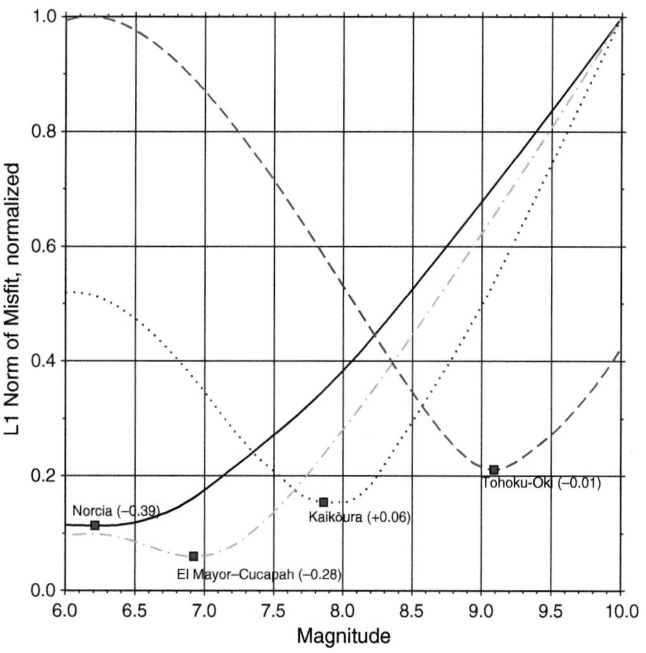

Figure 6. Results of the magnitude grid search for the four test events. The location of the minimum L1 norm is shown with the red squares, and the difference between the predicted and actual magnitudes is shown in parentheses. The L1 norm is normalized for each event for clarity. The color version of this figure is available only in the electronic edition.

Magnitude estimation with case study events

For the four test events, we determined the magnitude based upon a grid search and the coefficients from Crowell *et al.* (2023) and the values in Table 1 using proxy distance (Table 1, row 3). The results are shown in Figure 6. For the Tohoku and Kaikōura earthquakes, we find magnitudes in line with the published values, 9.09 for Tohoku and 7.86 for Kaikōura. That is, when the scaling law is used to estimate the magnitude with R_{proxy} as the distance metric, a grid search is employed, and the magnitude used to calculate R_{proxy} is consistent with the resulting magnitude from the grid search. For the Norcia and El Mayor earthquakes, the impact of aliasing on the PGV observations becomes apparent, and there is an underprediction of 0.39 and 0.28 magnitude units, respectively. A similar bias is observed in Figure S1 when looking at the single station magnitude residuals for Norcia and El Mayor earthquakes (columns 3 and 4, rows 3–5); it is worth noting that, even with the aliasing in the velocity observations used to compute R_{proxy}, the PGD-only magnitude residuals (i.e., the ones for hypocentral distance or mean rupture distance, rows 1–2 in Fig. S1) have a greater spread and bias than that of the proxy distance instances.

With regard to ground-motion prediction for early warning, the predicted magnitude is modulated by the proxy distance, so an underestimate in magnitude does not necessarily lead to a reduced ground motion. Even with aliasing and magnitude underestimation, the correction with R_{proxy} can potentially reduce the distance to the source over the hypocentral distance, and in certain cases, lead to a higher ground-motion prediction. Because the problem is nonlinear, it is difficult to generalize this argument to specific scenarios; however, examples throughout the early warning and ground-motion modeling literature show that the source finiteness is often a stronger driver of ground-motion prediction than the magnitude. Still, there is a trade-off between aliasing of the PGV observations, predicted magnitude, and ground-motion prediction that needs to be addressed prior to use in G-FAST.

DISCUSSION

The results for the scaling law using the proxy distance and any combination of coefficients give reasonable results for the entire 1 Hz GNSS catalog used in this study. However, the improvement in ground-motion characterization becomes apparent when the results are split between large-magnitude events and small-to-moderate-size events. We see that the instances of the scaling law using the proxy distance drastically outperform the instances using either hypocentral distance or mean rupture distance for large-magnitude events. Specifically for large-magnitude events, the mean is reduced by a factor of 10 and the median by a factor of 2 with no increase in residual spread distribution, additional bias, or outliers, indicating the validity of this distance metric.

The individual case study events with unique ruptures also yield reasonable results; however, there is a trend of overprediction of ground motions. This general trend of overprediction is present across all magnitudes, but when using the proxy distance, the scaling law is not impacted by complicated rupture characteristics, such as rupture directivity as shown in the Kaikōura example, or challenges with geographic and/or station distribution around an event, as shown in the El Mayor example. Very large-magnitude events, such as the Tohoku example, are still difficult to characterize in terms of both magnitude and ground motions, but we view this as a limitation due to a lack of real-world observations of events of this size. Moreover, Tohoku had a much smaller rupture zone with larger-than-expected slip when compared with scaling laws (Blaser *et al.*, 2010; Thingbaijam *et al.*, 2017).

We see a different limitation for smaller magnitude events in the catalog. Smaller magnitude events may see issues arise due to the fundamental constraints on GNSS observation data and the impacts of aliasing. The installation of geodetic networks was primarily executed for measuring crustal deformation related to strain accumulation and the surveying community, so many of these stations are evenly distributed for the most part. However, because they were installed with the idea that locations would be determined on longer timescales than, say, an earthquake rupture, they typically have a sampling rate of 15 s. A number of these stations sample at a high rate, or in this case, 1 Hz or one sample per second. Because we are using 1-Hz data to understand earthquake source processes, though, we must consider the corner frequency and magnitude range for which these GNSS observations are valid. Typically, this converges to geodetic velocities being valuable for large-magnitude events, reflecting the decrease in corner frequency with increasing magnitude (Joyner, 1984). Essentially, for lower magnitude events, the velocities need to be at a higher sampling rate to properly reflect ground motion. Ideally, sample rates in excess of 5 Hz are needed for smaller magnitude events. Some networks have varying degrees of very-high-rate GNSS data available, which is the data catalog described by Crowell *et al.* (2023) and used for the GMM development. However, this is not a common practice at present, and the majority of historical observations are at 1 Hz or lower. Thus, GNSS observations have a trade-off between a higher quantity of lower sampling rate observations or a lesser quantity of higher sampling rate observations. Because the observations used in this study were sampled at 1 Hz, the peak velocity values inherently contain aliasing and are scaled-down versions of the true ground motion, particularly for magnitudes less than M_w 6.5. To properly represent ground motion, we need higher sampling rates on GNSS instruments, but this leads to a high telemetry load that makes it difficult to consistently broadcast the raw data in real time. Modifications to GNSS receivers to allow onboard velocity calculations is feasible because the method only relies on broadcast ephemeris information, which would reduce the telemetry load for higher sample rates.

Velocity observations can be utilized in an advantageous way to better estimate ground motions, especially for large-magnitude events that are not impacted by aliasing. The utility of this method is further demonstrated by the fact that GNSS velocity observations are easily accessible and computationally scalable in real time due to the processing approach. Compared to methods that utilize only GNSS displacements, which are often very noisy in real time, the velocity approach does not require external corrections and can be easily obtained because it uses broadcast orbital information from satellites. In addition, we note that this study was entirely GNSS-based, but in future work, we can utilize the ground motions recorded at seismic stations that are collocated with GNSS stations to further expand and verify the results from using R_{proxy} in the geodetic scaling law.

Given the potential issues with a seismic-only approach to magnitude estimation or even the existing GNSS displacement approach, we make a case for our new distance metric, R_{proxy}, specifically for events larger than M_w 7.5, where we see a drastic improvement in mean, median, and standard deviation of ground-motion residuals when compared to traditional distance metrics. We also see that using R_{proxy} is not impacted by complicated rupture characteristics; that is, it can account for specifics of a rupture even without finite-fault modeling. As indicated previously, R_{proxy} reduces a higher order of complexity (site effects, event terms, and directivity) into a single term represented as the distance metric. A caveat to this is for small enough events that can be considered as a point source rather than a finite fault. With an event as a point source, one could argue that R_{proxy} would be reduced to the hypocentral distance. However, based on the results presented here, even in these cases, R_{proxy} performs better than the hypocentral distance because it still represents a scaled distance that inherently captures a portion of the site and directivity effects due to its direct derivation from PGV.

In an operational context, with the ease of computation of velocities, proxy distance can be determined in real time and used in the existing early warning systems. G-FAST currently has four conditional thresholds for it to be used for magnitude estimation in ShakeAlert: (1) the estimated magnitude from G-FAST must be greater than M_w 7.0, (2) the estimated seismic magnitude must be at least M_w 6.0, (3) the G-FAST magnitude uncertainty must be no greater than 0.5 units, and (4) at least three GNSS stations must report PGD above a time-dependent PGD threshold (Murray *et al.*, 2023). Given the results of this study for events larger than M_w 7.0, using proxy distance in these cases resulted in improved residual ground motions when compared to the results using the hypocentral distance. Because the minimum magnitude requirement is already employed in G-FAST, and it is known that GNSS is particularly relevant for larger-magnitude events rather than smaller magnitude events, this new distance metric would be particularly beneficial for large events, especially those with complicated rupture styles that include directivity and unusual propagation of energy as demonstrated by the M_w 7.8 Kaikōura case. We also reduce the need for knowledge of the faulting extent in the operational context, given that we can compute initial estimates by using proxy distance. We do want to note that all analysis presented in this study was performed with final GNSS displacement solutions. In real time, the quality of the displacement solutions would be reduced in comparison to the results presented here. However, there is a general understanding of the noise characteristics of real-time GNSS displacements that could be leveraged in an EEWS (Melgar *et al.*, 2020). Relatedly, we also would like to mention the velocity solutions used in this study, which can be computed using broadcast orbits, making velocity solutions of the same quality presented here available in real time. Ultimately, this approach and the prospect of applicability in an EEW will need to be further assessed. In the future, we aim to evaluate the best approach to incorporating R_{proxy} into existing methods and assess the timing aspects related to using the proxy distance in an operational sense, including modeling the growth of the estimated magnitude when using R_{proxy}, and any residual impacts on the precision of the method when using real-time displacement streams.

CONCLUSIONS

We develop and test a new distance metric that acts as a proxy for the mean rupture distance with readily available real-time data through GNSS observations, namely the velocities. This effective distance is determined through GMM relationships originally presented by Crowell *et al.* (2023) and adapted for this study. By taking the existing geodetic PGD scaling law presented by Crowell *et al.* (2013) and substituting our proxy distance for hypocentral distance, we yield better results in terms of characterizing ground motion compared with traditional distance metrics. In addition, through examination of unique case study events, we determined that by incorporating velocities into the distance metric directly, we are able to account for unusual rupture characteristics, leading to better ground-motion characterization of large ruptures for which simple distance metrics could not capture the complexities. We successfully modulate an effective distance with no prior knowledge of the faulting extent of a rupture, which has implications for early warning systems, GMMs, and rapid ShakeMap generation for post-event response.

DATA AND RESOURCES

For all events in the United States, Central America, and a handful of other major events in Asia, raw Global Positioning System (GPS) data were obtained from EarthScope Consortium, formerly UNAVCO, Inc., in Receiver Independent Exchange Format (RINEX) (https://data.unavco.org/archive/gnss/highrate/1-Hz/, last accessed December 2023). For Japan events, data were obtained from the GeoNet network operated by Geospatial Information Authority of Japan (GSI, 2022; https://www.gsi.go.jp/ENGLISH/geonet_english.html, last accessed December 2023). For New Zealand events, RINEX data were obtained through GeoNet, operated by Earth Sciences New Zealand (GNS Science, 2022; https://data.geonet.org.nz/gnss/event.highrate/, last accessed December 2023). For Italian events, RINEX data were obtained through the Istituto Nazionale di Geofisica e Vulcanologia (INGV) Rete Integrata Nazionale (RING) Working Group, which is licensed under a Creative Commons Attribution 4.0 International License (http://ring.gm.ingv.it/, last accessed December 2023) (INGV RING Working Group, 2016). The SNIVEL codebase is freely available on GitHub (https://github.com/crowellbw/SNIVEL, last accessed February 2024). GipsyX is licensed by Jet Propulsion Laboratory (JPL) to institutions, and the version used in this study is licensed to the University of Washington. The final orbits were obtained from JPL (https://sideshow.jpl.nasa.gov/pub/JPL_GNSS_Products/, last accessed February 2024), and precise orbits and clocks were obtained from the International Global Navigation Satellite System (GNSS) Service (https://igs.org/products/#about, last accessed February 2024). For manipulating raw RINEX data, we used TEQC (Estey and Meertens, 1999), which is freely available from UNAVCO, Inc. (https://www.unavco.org/software/data-processing/teqc/teqc.html, last accessed February 2024). The finite-fault models for each event were extracted from the geoJSON files on each event's U.S. Geological Survey (USGS) event page (USGS and Earthquake Hazards Program [EHP], 2017). Finite-fault availability is indicated for each event in the last column of Table S1. The GNSS velocity records in Seismic Analysis Code (SAC) format from SNIVEL, the GNSS displacement records in TXT format from GipsyX, and a spreadsheet of the events, peak ground motions, and event information are available on Zenodo (DeGrande, 2025). The supplemental material includes Figures S1 and S2 and Tables S1–S5.

DECLARATION OF COMPETING INTERESTS

The authors acknowledge that there are no conflicts of interest recorded.

ACKNOWLEDGMENTS

This work is funded under the National Aeronautics and Space Administration (NASA), Research and Opportunities in Space and Earth Science (ROSES-2022), Program element A.23: Earth Surface and Interior, Grant Number 22-ESI22-0004 to the University of Washington. The material used in this study is based upon data and services provided by the GAGE facility, operated by EarthScope Consortium, formerly UNAVCO, Inc., with support from the National Science Foundation (NSF), NASA, and the U.S. Geological Survey under National Science Foundation Cooperative Agreement EAR-1724794. In addition, the authors acknowledge New Zealand GeoNet and its sponsors, Rete Integrata Nazionale (RING) Global Positioning System data by Istituto Nazionale di Geofisica e Vulcanologia, and the GeoNet network operated by GSI in Japan for the Global Navigation Satellite System data used in this study. The authors would like to thank one anonymous reviewer and Dara Goldberg for their reviews of this work, which helped improve the article, as well as the associate editor who handled their reviews, and Editor-in-Chief P. Martin Mai for their helpful comments.

REFERENCES

Aki, K., and P. G. Richards (1980). *Quantitative Seismology*, Second Ed., University Science Book, Sausalito, California.

Allen, R. M., and D. Melgar (2019). Earthquake early warning: Advances, scientific challenges, and societal needs, *Annu. Rev. Earth. Planet. Sci.* **47,** 361–388, doi: 10.1146/annurev-earth-053018-060457.

Benedetti, E., M. Brazanti, L. Biagi, G. Colosimo, A. Mazzoni, and M. Crespi (2014). Global navigation satellite systems seismology for the 2012 M_w 6.1 Emilia earthquake: Exploiting the VADASE algorithm, *Seismol. Res. Lett.* **85,** 649–656, doi: 10.1785/0220130094.

Bertiger, W., Y. Barsever, A. Dorsey, B. Haines, N. Harvey, D. Hemberger, M. Heflin, W. Lu, M. Miller, A. W. Moore, *et al.* (2020). GipsyX/RTGx, a new tool for space geodetic operations and research, *Adv. Space. Res.* **66,** 469–489, doi: 10.1016/j.asr.2020.04.015.

Blaser, L., F. Krüger, M. Ohrnberger, and F. Scherbaum (2010). Scaling relations of earthquake source parameter estimates with special focus on subduction environment, *Bull. Seismol. Soc. Am.* **100,** 2914–2926, doi: 10.1785/0120100111.

Böse, M., T. H. Heaton, and E. Hauksson (2012). Real-time finite fault rupture detector (FinDer) for large earthquakes, *Geophys. J. Int.* **191,** 803–812, doi: 10.1111/j.1365-246X.2012.05657.x.

Böse, M., D. E. Smith, C. Felizardo, M. A. Meier, T. H. Heaton, and J. F. Clinton (2018). FinDer v.2: Improved real-time ground-motion predictions for M2–M9 with seismic finite-source characterization, *Geophys. J. Int.* **212,** 725–742, doi: 10.1093/gji/ggx430.

Chiou, S. J., and R. R. Youngs (2008). An NGA model for the average horizontal component of peak ground motion and response spectra, *Earthq. Spectra* **24,** 173–215, doi: 10.1193/1.2894832.

Chiou, S. J., and R. R. Youngs (2014). Update of the Chiou and Youngs NGA model for the average horizontal component of peak ground motion and response spectra, *Earthq. Spectra* **30,** 1117–1153, doi: 10.1193/072813EQS219M.

Colosimo, G., M. Crespi, and A. Mazzoni (2011). Real-time GPS seismology with a stand-alone receiver: A preliminary feasibility demonstration, *J. Geophys. Res.* **116,** doi: 10.1029/2010JB007941.

Crowell, B. W. (2021). Near-field strong ground motions from GPS-derived velocities for 2020 Intermountain western United States earthquakes, *Seismol. Res. Lett.* **92,** 840–848, doi: 10.1785/0220200325.

Crowell, B. W. (2024). Earthquake and tsunami early warning with GNSS data, in *GNSS Monitoring of the Terrestrial Environment: Earthquakes, Volcanoes, and Climate Change*, Y. Aoki and C. Kreemer (Editors), Elsevier, Amsterdam, Netherlands, 111–174.

Crowell, B. W., Y. Bock, and M. B. Squibb (2009) Demonstration of earthquake early warning using total displacement waveforms from real-time GPS networks, *Seismol. Res. Lett.* **80,** 772–782, doi: 10.1785/gssrl.80.5.772.

Crowell, B. W., J. V. DeGrande, T. Dittmann, and J. N. Ghent (2023). Validation of peak ground velocities recorded on very-high rate GNSS against NGA-West2 ground motion models, *Seismica* **2,** 1–14, doi: 10.26443/seismica.v2i1.239.

Crowell, B. W., D. Melgar, Y. Bock, J. S. Haase, and J. Geng (2013). Earthquake magnitude scaling using seismogeodetic data, *Geophys. Res. Lett.* **40,** 6089–6094.

Crowell, B. W., D. A. Schmidt, P. Bodin, J. E. Vidale, B. Baker, S. Barrientos, and J. Geng (2018). G-FAST earthquake early warning potential for Great earthquakes in Chile, *Seismol. Res. Lett.* **89,** 542–556, doi: 10.1785/0220170180.

Crowell, B. W., D. A. Schmidt, P. Bodin, J. E. Vidale, J. Gomberg, R. Hartog, V. C. Kress, T. I. Melbourne, M. Santillan, S. E. Minson, *et al.* (2016). Demonstration of the Cascadia G-FAST geodetic earthquake early warning system for the Nisqually, Washington, earthquake, *Seismol. Res. Lett.* **87,** 930–943, doi: 10.1785/0220150255.

DeGrande, J. V. (2025). A combined PGD-PGV scaling law from GNSS for the G-FAST earthquake early warning module [Data set], *Zenodo*, doi: 10.5281/zenodo.15741738.

Dittmann, T., K. Hodgkinson, J. Morton, D. Mencin, and G. S. Mattioli (2022). Comparing sensitivities of geodetic processing methods for rapid earthquake magnitude estimation, *Seismol. Res. Lett.* **93,** 1497–1509, doi: 10.1785/0220210265.

Estey, L. H., and C. M. Meertens (1999). TEQC: The multi-purpose toolkit for GPS/GLONASS data, *GPS Sol.* **3,** 42–49, doi: 10.1007/PL00012778.

Fang, R., J. Zheng, J. Geng, Y. Shu, C. Shi, and J. Liu (2021). Earthquake magnitude scaling using peak ground velocity derived from high-rate GNSS observations, *Seismol. Res. Lett.* **92,** 227–237, doi: 10.1785/0220190347.

GNS Science (2022). GeoNet Aotearoa New Zealand Stations Metadata Repository [Dataset], *GNS Science, GeoNet*, doi: 10.21420/RXKE-AZ44.

Goldberg, D. E., and K. L. Haynie (2022). Ready for real time: Performance of Global Navigation Satellite System in 2019 M_w 7.1 Ridgecrest, California, rapid response products, *Seismol. Res. Lett.* **93,** 517–530, doi: 10.1785/0220210278.

Goldberg, D. E., P. Koch, D. Melgar, S. Riquelme, and W. L. Yeck (2022). Beyond the teleseism: introducing regional seismic and geodetic data into routine USGS finite-fault modeling, *Seismol. Res. Lett.* **93,** 2208–3323, doi: 10.1785/0220220047.

Goldberg, D. E., D. Melgar, G. P. Hayes, B. W. Crowell, and V. J. Sahakian (2021). A ground motion model for GNSS peak ground displacement, *Bull. Seismol. Soc. Am.* **111,** 2393–2407, doi: 10.1785/0120210042.

Grapenthin, R., I. A. Johanson, and R. M. Allen (2014). Operational real-time GPS-enhanced earthquake early warning, *J. Geophys. Res.* **119,** 7944–7965, doi: 10.1002/2014JB011400

Grapenthin, R., M. West, C. Tape, M. Gardine, and J. Freymueller (2018). Single-frequency instantaneous GNSS velocities resolve dynamic ground motion of the 2016 M_w 7.1 Iniskin, Alaska, earthquake, *Seismol. Res. Lett.* **89,** 1040–1048, doi: 10.1785/0220170235.

GSI (2022). High-rate GNSS data from the GNSS Earth Observation Network System (GEONET), Geospatial Information Authority of Japan, available at https://www.gsi.go.jp/ENGLISH/geonet_english.html (last accessed December 2023).

Hamling, I. J., S. Hreinsdóttir, K. Clark, J. Elliott, C. Liang, E. Fielding, N. Litchfield, P. Villamor, L. Wallace, T. J. Wright, *et al.* (2017). Complex multifault rupture during the 2016 M_w 7.8 Kaikōura earthquake, New Zealand, *Science* **356,** doi: 10.1126/science.aam7194.

Hauksson, E., J. Stock, K. Hutton, W. Yang, J. A. Vidal-Villegas, and H. Kanamori (2010). The 2010 M_w 7.2 El Mayor-Cucapah earthquake sequence, Baja California, Mexico and southernmost California, USA: Active seismotectonics along the Mexican Pacific margin, *Pure Appl. Geophys.* **168,** 1255–1277, doi: 10.1007/s00024-010-0209-7.

Hayes, G. P. (2017). The finite, kinematic rupture properties of great-sized earthquakes since 1990, *Earth Planet. Sci. Lett.* **468,** 94–100, doi: 10.1016/j.epsl.2017.04.003.

Hoshiba, M., and S. Aoki (2015). Numerical shake prediction for earthquake early warning: Data assimilation, real-time shake mapping, and simulation of wave propagation, *Bull. Seismol. Soc. Am.* **105,** 1324–1338, doi: 10.1785/0120140280.

Hoshiba, M., K. Iwakiri, N. Hayashimoto, T. Shimoyama, K. Hirano, Y. Yamada, and H. Kikuta (2011). Outline of the 2011 off the Pacific coast of Tohoku earthquake (M_w 9.0)—Earthquake early warning and observed seismic intensity, *Earth Planets Space* **63,** 547–551, doi: 10.5047/eps.2011.05.031.

Istituto Nazionale di Geofisica e Vulcanologia (INGV) Rete Integrata Nazionale (RING) Working Group (2016). Rete integrata Nazionale GNSS, doi: 10.13127/RING.

Joyner, W. B. (1984). A scaling law for the spectra of large earthquakes, *Bull. Seismol. Soc. Am.* **74,** 1167–1188.

Mai, P. M., and K. K. S. Thingbaijam (2014). SRCMOD: An online database of finite-fault rupture models, *Seismol. Res. Lett.* **85,** 1348–1357, doi: 10.1785/0220140077.

Melgar, D., Y. Bock, D. Sanchez, and B. W. Crowell (2013). On robust and reliable automated baseline corrections for strong motion seismology, *J. Geophys. Res.* **118,** 1177–1187, doi: 10.1002/jgrb.50135.

Melgar, D, B. W. Crowell, J. Geng, R. M. Allen, Y. Bock, S. Riquelme, E. M. Hill, M. Protti, and A. Ganas (2015). Earthquake magnitude calculation without saturation from the scaling of peak ground displacement, *Geophys. Res. Lett.* **42,** 5197–5205, doi: 10.1002/2015GL064278.

Melgar, D., B. W. Crowell, T. I. Melbourne, W. Szeliga, M. Santillan, and C. Scrivner (2020). Noise characteristics of operational real-time high-rate GNSS positions in a large aperture network, *J. Geophys. Res.* **125,** e2019JB019197, doi: 10.1029/2019JB019197.

Minson, S. E., J. R. Murray, J. O. Langbein, and J. S. Gomberg (2014). Real-time inversions for finite fault slip models and rupture geometry based on high-rate GPS data, *J. Geophys. Res.* **119,** 3201–3231, doi: 10.1002/2013JB010622.

Murray, J. R., B. W. Crowell, R. Grapenthin, K. Hodgkinson, J. O. Langbein, T. Melbourne, D. Melgar, S. E. Minson, and D. A. Schmidt (2018). Development of geodetic component for the U.S. West Coast earthquake early warning system, *Seismol. Res. Lett.* **89,** 2322–2336, doi: 10.1785/0220180162.

Murray, J. R., B. W. Crowell, M. H. Murray, C. W. Ulberg, J. J. McGuire, M. A. Aranha, and M. T. Hagerty (2023). Incorporation of real-time earthquake magnitudes estimated via peak ground displacement scaling in the ShakeAlert earthquake early warning system, *Bull. Seismol. Soc. Am.* **113,** 1286–1310, doi: 10.1785/0120220181.

Noda, S., and W. L. Ellsworth (2016). Scaling relation between earthquake magnitude and departure time from P wave similar growth, *Geophys. Res. Lett.* **43,** 9053–9060, doi: 10.1002/2016GL070069.

Olson, E. L., and R. M. Allen (2005). The deterministic nature of earthquake rupture, *Nature* **438,** 212–215, doi: 10.1038/nature04214.

Sahakian, V., A. Baltay, T. Hanks, J. Buehler, F. Vernon, D. Kilb, and N. Abrahamson (2018). Decomposing leftovers: Event, path, and site residuals for a small-magnitude Anza region GMPE, *Bull. Seismol. Soc. Am.* **108,** 2478–2492, doi: 10.1785/0120170376.

Sahakian, V. J., A. Baltay, T. C. Hanks, J. Buehler, F. L. Vernon, D. Kilb, and N. A. Abrahamson (2019). Ground motion residuals, path effects, and crustal properties: A pilot study in southern California, *J. Geophys. Res.* **124,** 5738–5753, doi: 10.1029/2018JB016796.

Shu, Y., R. Fang, M. Li, C. Shi, M. Li, and J. Liu (2018). Very high-rate GPS for measuring dynamic seismic displacements without aliasing: Performance evaluation of the variometric approach, *GPS Sol.* **22,** doi: 10.1007/s10291-018-0785-z.

Thingbaijam, K. K. S., P. M. Mai, and K. Goda (2017). New empirical earthquake source-scaling laws, *Bull. Seismol. Soc. Am.* **107,** 2225–2246, doi: 10.1785/0120170017.

Thompson, E., and A. S. Baltay (2018). The case for mean rupture distance in ground-motion estimation, *Bull. Seismol. Soc. Am.* **108,** 2462–2477, doi: 10.1785/0120170306.

U.S. Geological Survey (USGS) Earthquake Hazards Program (EHP) (2017). Advanced National Seismic System (ANSS) comprehensive catalog of earthquake events and products: Various, doi: 10.5066/F7MS3QZH.

Wei, S., E. Fielding, S. Leprince, A. Sladen, J. Avouac, D. Helmberger, E. Hauksson, R. Chu, M. Simons, K. Hudnut, *et al.* (2011). Superficial simplicity of the 2010 El Mayor-Cucapah earthquake of Baja California in Mexico, *Nature* **4,** 615–618, doi: 10.1038/NGEO1213.

Worden, C. B., D. A. Gerstenberger, D. A. Rhoades, and D. J. Wald (2012). Probabilistic relationships between ground-motion parameters and modified Mercalli intensity in California, *Bull. Seismol. Soc. Am.* **102,** 204–221, doi: 10.1785/0120110156.

Manuscript received 7 July 2025
Published online 9 December 2025

Capturing the Uncertainty of Seismicity Observations in Earthquake Rate Estimates: Implications for Probabilistic Seismic Hazard Analysis and the USGS National Seismic Hazard Model

Andrew J. Michael*[1] and Andrea L. Llenos[2]

ABSTRACT

The rate of earthquakes in a region is a fundamental input to Probabilistic Seismic Hazard Analysis. We present a Monte Carlo method for computing that rate from seismicity catalogs while including a range of data and analysis uncertainties. This method is applied to regions for which the b value is assumed to be spatially invariant. Each region is broken down into epochs for which each epoch is estimated to have a uniform magnitude of completeness (M_c). The distribution of earthquake rates for $M \geq M_c$ is determined for each epoch by considering the Poisson likelihood of rates given the number of observed earthquakes with $M \geq M_c$. We use a Monte Carlo process to include the uncertainty in b, M_c, and individual event magnitudes. The result for each epoch is the joint distribution of the Poisson rate of earthquakes with magnitudes larger than the minimum value used to calculate hazard (M_1) and the Gutenberg–Richter b values, which control the extrapolation to other magnitudes. The rate for each region is either the duration-weighted average over the epochs or, to better capture temporal variations, we also consider mixture models. The mixture models also provide an avenue to allow temporal variations in b values. To implement this joint distribution in a logic tree, we use the mean and 95% confidence branches, each of which is parameterized with an $M \geq M_1$ rate and b value. We explore different ways of defining those branches, as well as non-Gutenberg–Richter branches, and their impact on hazard estimates. The mean hazard, but not the fractiles, is robust with respect to these choices. To illustrate these new methods, we use synthetic data and catalogs from recent U.S. Geological Survey National Seismic Hazard Models for the Central and Eastern United States and for Puerto Rico and the U.S. Virgin Islands.

KEY POINTS

- We present a new methodology for determining seismicity rates for probabilistic seismic hazard analysis.
- This methodology improves the consideration of epistemic uncertainty in b, completeness, and magnitudes.
- We discuss the impact on hazard of converting from the full distribution of rate and b to logic tree branches.

INTRODUCTION

We present a flexible method for estimating the total rate of seismicity, including uncertainty, from an earthquake catalog using a Monte Carlo process. This method is intended as part of creating an earthquake rupture forecast (ERF) for use in probabilistic seismic hazard analysis (PSHA). For that application, it is important to fully assess epistemic uncertainty for use in a logic tree (Kulkarni *et al.*, 1984). As implemented in this article, we consider uncertainty in the Gutenberg–Richter (GR)

1. U.S. Geological Survey, Earthquake Science Center, Moffett Field, California, U.S.A., https://orcid.org/0000-0002-2403-5019 (AJM); 2. Geologic Hazards Science Center, U.S. Geological Survey, Denver, Colorado, U.S.A., https://orcid.org/0000-0002-4088-6737 (ALL)

*Corresponding author: ajmichael@usgs.gov

Cite this article as Michael, A. J., and A. L. Llenos (2025). Capturing the Uncertainty of Seismicity Observations in Earthquake Rate Estimates: Implications for Probabilistic Seismic Hazard Analysis and the USGS National Seismic Hazard Model, *Bull. Seismol. Soc. Am.* **116**, 786–809, doi: 10.1785/0120240245

b value (Gutenberg and Richter, 1944), individual event magnitudes, the magnitude of completeness, and the effect of observing the seismicity over a limited time interval. We incorporate both the systematic bias of earthquake rate due to magnitude uncertainty considered by previous efforts (Electric Power Research Institute [EPRI], 1988; Rhoades and Dowrick, 2000; Electric Power Research Institute/Department of Energy/Nuclear Regulatory Commission [EPRI/DOE/NRC], 2012) and random uncertainty in the rates due to magnitude uncertainty.

This method was developed for the U.S. Geological Survey (USGS) National Seismic Hazard Model (NSHM). That PSHA effort begins with an ERF that gives the time-independent distribution of earthquake rates as a function of space and magnitude (Petersen *et al.*, 2024). The full ERF is a complex combination of earthquake rates on faults determined from paleoseismology, geologic slip rates, geodetic deformation models, and direct observations of seismicity (Field *et al.*, 2023). For the 2023 update of the NSHM for the conterminous United States (CONUS) (Petersen *et al.*, 2024) and Alaska (Powers *et al.*, 2024), and the upcoming update of the NSHM for Puerto Rico and the U.S. Virgin Islands (PRVI), the seismicity rate models are broken into two parts: spatial kernels that give the relative distribution of seismicity rates across a region (Llenos *et al.*, 2024) and a total rate model that gives the joint likelihood distribution of rate (λ) assuming a Poisson process and GR slope b. A similar approach was used for the Third Uniform California Earthquake Rupture Forecast (Felzer, 2013a,b; Field *et al.*, 2014), but that study used a fixed value of $b = 1$ and did not include as many sources of uncertainty. The total rate models are the focus of this article; the spatial kernel methodology and results for CONUS are discussed by Llenos *et al.* (2024) and for PRVI by Llenos *et al.* (2025).

The underlying philosophy for the total rate models is that the behavior of frequently occurring small earthquakes can be used to forecast the future occurrence rate of potentially damaging earthquakes. That will be true if the seismicity conforms to a known magnitude–frequency distribution such as the GR distribution with rate parameter a and slope b:

$$\log(N(m \geq M)) = a - bM, \quad (1)$$

in which N is the number of earthquakes with magnitude m greater than or equal to a threshold M (Gutenberg and Richter, 1944). Instead of a, we often refer to the Poisson rate λ for events of magnitude $m \geq M$ for a given duration. This rate can be determined with equation (1) and the probability of N events as follows:

$$P(N;\lambda) = \frac{\lambda^N e^{-\lambda}}{N!}. \quad (2)$$

Symbols are defined in Table 1.

Because we are working within the evolving NSHM framework, we make a few assumptions that are consistent with past models (e.g., Petersen *et al.*, 2020). We determine the rate for regions that are assumed to have a constant b value, but in which the magnitude of completeness varies between epochs. Following Felzer (2008), we determine the rate in epochs with a constant M_c and then (as a first approach) compute an average rate, weighted by the duration of each epoch. Felzer's goal for this procedure was to include the variation of rates across the epochs and prevent the most recent epoch, with the lowest M_c and therefore the most data, from dominating the result (as occurs with the method from Weichert, 1980). However, taking an average assumes that we have independent observations of the same quantity. We will show that an alternative approach of combining the epochs into a mixture distribution, analogous to separately including each epoch as a logic tree branch, gives greater emphasis to possible variations in rate and can allow for temporal variations in b value.

Observations of seismicity with magnitudes larger than the magnitude of completeness ($m \geq M_c$) are used to determine the joint distribution of rate and b. That joint distribution is then used to infer the joint distribution of the rate $\lambda(m \geq M_1)$ and b, in which M_1 is the minimum magnitude used to compute the ground-motion hazard. We will notate that joint distribution as $J(\lambda(m \geq M_1),b)$ or just as $J(\lambda(M_1),b)$.

Because the joint distribution is determined by many samples of a Monte Carlo process and has a complex shape in λ and b space, it would be unwieldy to include the full joint distribution in a logic tree. To overcome this issue, we explore multiple approaches for sampling the quantiles of the joint distribution to build a limited set of logic tree branches. For the 2023 update of the NSHM, three logic tree branches were used: a mean branch, a low-rate branch at the 0.025 quantile, and a high-rate branch at the 0.975 quantile (note: all quantiles in this article are out of 1 unit). The mean branch is given a weight of 0.74, whereas the low- and high-rate branches are each given a weight of 0.13. Other quantiles and weights can be chosen (Keefer and Bodily, 1983; Miller and Rice, 1983) for different hazard analyses without affecting the general approach and conclusions of this article. A five-branch approach will be explored in the section on branches and hazards. These branches can be parameterized with a single pair of λ and b values or as a more general distribution of rate with respect to magnitude, which we notate as $P(\lambda(m \geq M))$ or more compactly as $P(\lambda(M))$. We also explore the impact of these alternatives on estimating the mean hazard and the distribution of hazard with respect to uncertainty in earthquake rate and b.

The separation of the spatial kernels and total rate models is a new approach for the 2023 update. Through the 2018 update of the NSHM for CONUS (Petersen *et al.*, 2020) and the 2021 update of the NSHM for Hawaii (Petersen *et al.*, 2022), the spatial kernel and the total rate model were combined by spatially smoothing a declustered catalog in an approach that

TABLE 1
Symbols

Symbol	Definition
β	Gutenberg–Richter distribution slope with respect to natural logarithms
ΔM	Magnitude correction for uncertainty
ΔM_c	Minimum magnitude difference used for the *b*-positive method
λ	Earthquake rate
σ	One standard deviation, subscripted as *b* for *b* values, m for magnitudes
a	Gutenberg–Richter distribution intercept
b	Gutenberg–Richter distribution slope with respect to base 10 logarithms
$J(\lambda(m \geq M),b)$, $J(\lambda(M),b)$	The joint distribution of the rate of earthquakes with magnitudes greater than or equal to *M* and *b*
$L(\lambda\|N)$	Poisson likelihood of λ given *N* observations
m, M	Magnitude
M_1	Minimum magnitude used to compute hazard
M_c	Magnitude of completeness
M_{est}	Estimated earthquake magnitude from observations
M_{max}	Maximum magnitude used to compute hazard
M_T	True earthquake magnitude
M^*	Magnitude corrected for uncertainty
N	Number of earthquakes
N^*	Counting correction, when subscripted *e* is the sum over the epoch
Norm(x,σ)	The normal distribution with mean *x* and standard deviation σ
$P(\lambda(m \geq M))$, $P(\lambda(M))$	Probability distribution of the rate of earthquakes with magnitudes greater than or equal to *M*
$P(N(m \geq M))$, $P(N(M))$	Probability distribution of the number of earthquakes with magnitudes greater than or equal to *M*, during a given time period, including Poisson variability
T	Duration of an epoch
Subscript *e*	The subscript *e* refers to a single epoch
Subscript *i*	The subscript *i* refers to a single Monte Carlo trial
Subscripts avg and mix	The subscript avg refers to doing a weighted average over epochs, while mix refers to doing a weighted mixture of epochs

evolved from the 1997 update (Frankel, 1995) with the addition of adaptive smoothing (Helmstetter *et al.*, 2006) for the 2014, 2018, and 2021 updates (Petersen *et al.*, 2014; Moschetti, 2015). Separating the spatial kernels and total rate models allows us to better isolate and account for the epistemic uncertainty in each of the two components.

This separation also allows us to follow the advice of Marzocchi and Taroni (2014) to base the spatial kernels on declustered catalogs to avoid spatial bias from recent, large aftershock sequences, while including all earthquakes, including aftershocks, in determining the total rate of earthquakes. Using the full catalog to provide a Poisson rate provides a more accurate assessment of the hazard at low probabilities of exceedance (e.g., ≤10% in 50 yr) (Marzocchi and Taroni, 2014; Michael and Llenos, 2022).

Using the full catalog also allows us to determine the GR *b* values without the biases introduced by declustering methods. For instance, the Gardner and Knopoff declustering method (Gardner and Knopoff, 1974), which has been a mainstay of PSHA, significantly reduces the *b* values, producing the seemingly paradoxical result of lower rates at M_c and higher hazard than when using other declustering methods (Llenos and Michael, 2020). For this study, the *b* values were determined using the traditional maximum-likelihood method (Aki, 1965) and the *b*-positive method (van der Elst, 2021).

METHOD

To illustrate the methods used to determine earthquake rates for the recent NSHM updates, we generated a synthetic seismicity catalog (Fig. 1). This catalog was created with a rate of 0.1 $M \geq 5$ events per year, a GR distribution with $b = 1$, and normally distributed magnitude errors with a standard deviation of $\sigma_m = 0.2$. Incompleteness was applied in two epochs. From 1900 to 1960, the magnitude of completeness is $M_c = 4$, and from 1960 to 2000, the magnitude of completeness is $M_c = 3$. In both cases, incompleteness was applied to the catalog using a probabilistic scheme where the probability of detection is proportional to a cumulative normal distribution with a standard deviation of 0.1, with the detection probability set to 0.5 at two standard deviations below M_c. Thus, the probability of detection is 0.5 at $M_c - 0.2$ and 0.977 at M_c. For the synthetic catalog, the minimum magnitude used to compute hazard is $M_1 = 5$.

The first step to determine the earthquake rates is to determine a uniform GR *b* value for the region. This was done with two methods: the *b*-positive method (van der Elst, 2021) and the more traditional approach. The *b*-positive method is based on differences in magnitude between successive events and is robust with respect to both long-term changes in completeness due to network improvements and short-term degradations in completeness after large earthquakes. This allows us to

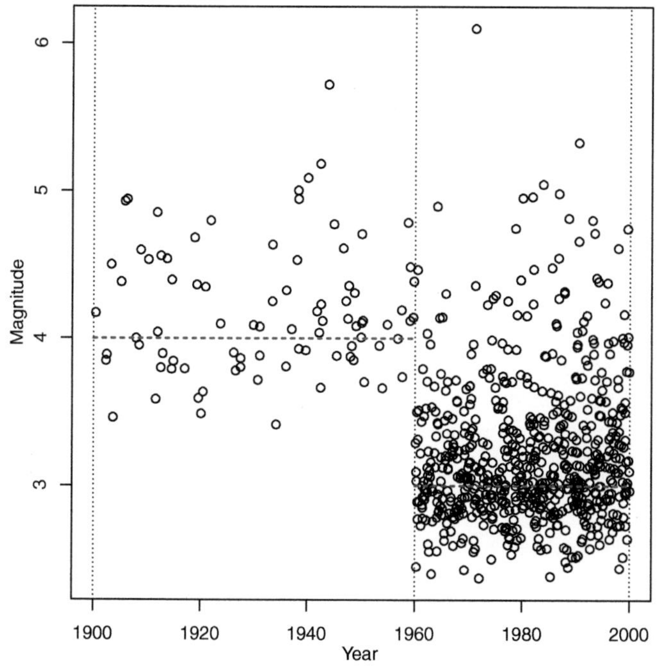

Figure 1. Magnitude–time plot of the synthetic catalog. Vertical dotted lines show the boundaries of the epochs. Horizontal dashed lines show M_c during each epoch. The color version of this figure is available only in the electronic edition.

compute the b value over the entire duration of the catalog for the region. Although this method does not require setting a magnitude of completeness (M_c), it does require setting a threshold for the minimum magnitude difference (ΔM_c) used. For very consistent seismicity catalogs, such as those from a single aftershock sequence, ΔM_c around 0.3 has been used (van der Elst, 2021). Uncertainty in the b value is determined with nonparametric bootstrap resampling, with replacement, of the entire data set. We include the uncertainty in ΔM_c by randomly choosing a new ΔM_c from a normal distribution with mean equal to the ΔM_c selected for the entire data set and a standard deviation of $\sigma = 0.3$ magnitude units, truncated at $\pm 3\sigma$. The uncertainty was chosen subjectively based on the b-positive results as a function of ΔM_c. The more traditional approach involves setting a magnitude of completeness, using the maximum-likelihood method (Aki, 1965), with a binning correction (Utsu, 1966), and determining uncertainties with nonparametric bootstrap resampling (Amorese *et al.*, 2010).

The application of both b-positive and the traditional approach to determining b of the synthetic catalog is shown in Figure 2. With $\Delta M_c = 0.4$, a value chosen subjectively from Figure 2b where the b-positive result is first stable, and with $M_c = 4$ for the traditional approach, both methods give a value very close to the input value of $b = 1$. Because $M_c = 4$ is an objective choice because we know how the catalog was created, for the synthetic example, we use the traditional approach with $b = 0.98$ and $\sigma_b = 0.08$.

Next, we need to determine a rate for the region (λ), which is divided by time in epochs with a constant M_{ce} for a duration T_e. Note that we use a subscript of e to denote an epoch and i to denote a single trial of the Monte Carlo process. If the e subscript is not used, then the value applies to the region for the

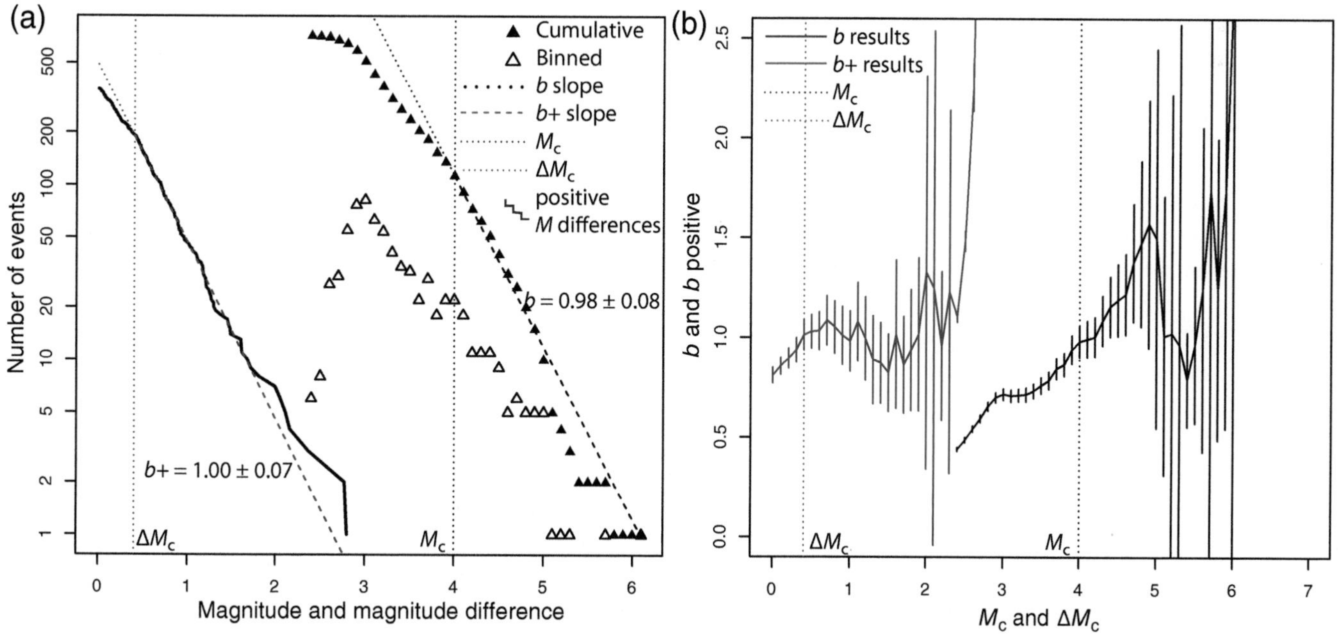

Figure 2. Magnitude distribution analysis plots for the synthetic example. (a) Magnitude–frequency plot showing both the distribution of magnitudes as 0.1-unit bins and the cumulative distribution and the cumulative distribution of positive forward-time magnitude differences. The vertical lines show the ΔM_c and M_c, sloped lines show the results of the b value analysis using both the traditional approach and b positive. (b) Stability of b value analysis showing the results as a function of ΔM_c and M_c with 1 standard deviation uncertainties. The color version of this figure is available only in the electronic edition.

TABLE 2
Results for the First Trial of the Application to the Synthetic Catalog

Row	Parameter	Epoch 1		Epoch 2
1	Epoch duration in years (T_e)	60		40
2	Randomly chosen b_i		0.91	
3	Randomly chosen M_{cei}	4.07		3.02
4	$N(M_{est} \geq M_{cei})$	47		369
5	$N(M* \geq M_{cei})$	41		337
6	Number of earthquakes with randomly chosen magnitudes $\geq M_{cei}$	45		349
7	$\sum N^*$ for earthquakes on the line above	49.12		380.99
8	Randomly chosen rate per epoch given $\sum N^*$ referenced to M_{cei}	38.9		371.9
9	Rate from line above extrapolated to $M \geq M_1$ and normalized to the rate per year	0.0935		0.146
10	Averaged rate weighted by epoch durations		0.115	
11	Rate and weight for mixture distribution	0.0935, 0.6		0.146, 0.4

entire time period. These epochs form our basic building blocks for determining the joint distribution of b value and rate ($J(\lambda(M), b)$) using a Monte Carlo approach with 100,000 trials.

For the region, we randomly select a b value (b_i) for each trial from a normal distribution using the mean b value and its standard deviation (σ_b), trimmed to $\pm 3\sigma_b$, and requiring that $0 < b_i < 1.5$. The limit of $b_i < 1.5$ is to avoid cases where the total moment rate is larger for small earthquakes than for large earthquakes. For each of the 100,000 trials, the single randomly selected b_i value is used to determine the rates for each epoch and allows us to average the rates across epochs. For example, in the first trial applied to the synthetic catalog, $b_1 = 0.91$ (Table 2).

To include observational uncertainties more fully in the rates for the NSHM, we add two sources of uncertainty not considered in previous models: the random effects of magnitude uncertainty and the magnitude of completeness uncertainty. Prior NSHM efforts included only the systematic effect of magnitude uncertainty. To include uncertainty in the magnitude of completeness (M_c) in the process, for each trial we determine a completeness value M_{cei} by adding normally distributed noise with $\sigma_c = 0.2$, and trimmed to $\pm 3\sigma_c$, to M_{ce}. The values used for the uncertainty of M_c are based on a subjective examination of the magnitude–frequency distributions. For the 2025 update of the NSHM for Puerto Rico and the U.S. Virgin Islands, we changed this to a one-sided distribution so that the noise can only increase M_c. This better conforms to our experience that M_c is more likely to be underestimated than overestimated. In addition, the one-sided uncertainty may be a good approach because allowing for two-sided uncertainty risks, including magnitudes where the catalog is incomplete and systematically decreasing the rates. Fortunately, the results for CONUS, which were done with the two-sided distribution, are robust with respect to this choice. For the PRVI crustal classification using a two-sided distribution would reduce the mean rate by about 10%, which is much smaller than the overall uncertainties. For the synthetic example, we use one-sided uncertainties, and the M_{ce1} values for the two epochs are 4.07 and 3.02, respectively (Table 2).

To include magnitude uncertainty in the rate estimation process, we consider the probability distribution of the true magnitude of each earthquake (M_T). We start with the magnitude information in the catalog, which is a distribution of the estimate of the magnitude (M_{est}) based solely on the observations (e.g., seismograms or intensities) of that individual earthquake. This is given in the NSHM catalogs as a magnitude (M_{est}) and a standard deviation (σ_m). The distribution of our best estimate of the magnitude based solely on these observations is Norm(M_{est},σ_m), in which Norm is the normal distribution. The distribution of M_T is the Bayesian combination of any prior information we have with Norm(M_{est},σ_m). That prior information is the GR distribution and incorporating it is necessary to correct for the systematic biases in rate caused by magnitude uncertainty. The distribution of M_T is Norm($M_{est} - \beta\sigma_m^2$,$\sigma_m$), in which $\beta = b \cdot \ln(10)$ (Rhoades, 1996). A way to understand the shift in the mean magnitude is to consider how an earthquake with magnitude M_{est} wound up in the catalog due to an earthquake occurring with magnitude M_T. M_T could have been bigger than M_{est} with an error that reduced the magnitude. Or M_T could have been smaller than M_{est} with an error that increased the magnitude. The latter is more likely because the GR distribution tells us that there are more earthquakes with magnitudes smaller than M_{est} than larger than M_{est}. Therefore, the distribution of M_T is shifted lower than the distribution of M_{est}. However, counting the earthquakes by the mean of M_T overcorrects for the effects of the magnitude uncertainty (Rhoades, 1996). The correct shift is based on the method of Tinti and Mulargia (1985), who derived how to correct the rate under the assumption that all the magnitudes have the same uncertainty. That was extended to the general case of variable uncertainties by the EPRI (1988), and more explicitly by Rhoades and Dowrick (2000). Those works showed that adjusting the magnitudes by $M^* = M_{est} - \Delta M$, in which $\Delta M = \beta\sigma_m^2/2$ results in an unbiased estimate of the rate. When estimating the rates, for each trial we select magnitudes that randomly sample from Norm(M^*,σ_m) truncated to $\pm 3\sigma_m$. Doing so includes both the

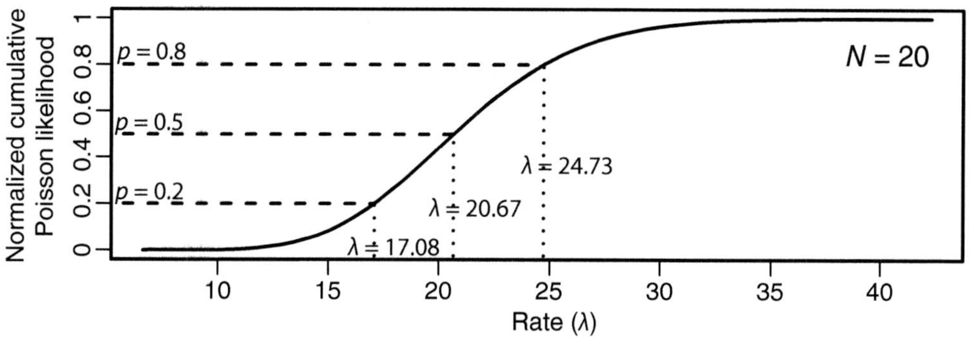

Figure 3. Normalized cumulative Poisson likelihood function given 20 observations and examples of the rates selected if the random uniform numbers are 0.2, 0.5, and 0.8.

random and systematic effects of magnitude uncertainty. If no magnitude uncertainty (σ_m) is listed in the NSHM seismicity catalog, then σ_m is set to 0.2, the median of the listed σ_m values.

There are some exceptions to using $M^* = M_{\text{est}} - \Delta M$. For magnitudes converted from one type to another using ordinary least squares, the magnitudes are biased such that it can be better to use $M^* = M_{\text{est}} + \Delta M$ (EPRI, 1988). And for events with an uncertain or complex magnitude history, it can be better not to use any correction (Musson, 2012). That is done for most of the magnitudes in the CEUS catalog (Mueller, 2018) and we use those corrections, or lack thereof, as provided by that process (Llenos *et al.*, 2024). For the PRVI catalog, magnitude corrections were always calculated with $M^* = M_{\text{est}} - \Delta M$. In many cases, σ_m had to be set to 0.2, and all magnitude corrections were computed as part of the rate estimation process rather than taken from the catalog.

We illustrate this process with the application of the method to the synthetic catalog. For that trial, there were 47 earthquakes with $M_{\text{est}} \geq M_{cei}$ in the first epoch and 369 in the second epoch. After the systematic magnitude correction, there were 41 earthquakes with $M^* \geq M_{cei}$ in the first epoch and 337 such events in the second epoch. After adding random errors to the M^* values, there were 45 earthquakes with magnitudes $\geq M_{cei}$ in the first epoch and 349 such earthquakes in the second epoch (Table 2).

In real catalogs, the term ΔM slightly overcorrects for the effect of the GR distribution because it is based on the theoretical GR distribution, and our data set is incomplete, particularly below the magnitude of completeness (M_c). Thus, there are fewer earthquakes with $M_T < M_{\text{est}}$ than theoretically expected. Because ΔM reduces the magnitudes by too large an amount, the resulting rates are biased low. This has been addressed by increasing the count of each earthquake from 1 to a count of N^* (EPRI/DOE/NRC, 2012). The N^* adjustment is approximate because it depends on how incomplete the catalog is below M_c, and the incompleteness is different for each catalog. EPRI/DOE/NRC (2012) found that $N^* = \exp(\beta^2\sigma_m^2/2)$ was an adequate adjustment based on their tests using synthetic data.

For $b = 1$ and $\sigma_m = 0.2$, $N^* = 1.1$. Thus, the N^* adjustment increases the rates by about 10%. For the CEUS catalog, most events have N^* between 1.0 and 1.3, whereas about 5% of the events have N^* around 1.8 due to high-magnitude uncertainty. For the PRVI crustal catalog, almost all events have the default value of $\sigma_m = 0.2$ and $N^* = 1.1$. For each epoch and trial, we sum N^* for the N_{ei} earthquakes with $M \geq M_{cei}$ to get N^*_{ei}.

For the first trial applied to the synthetic catalog, if we sum N^* for the events identified on row 6, we get $N^*_{ei} = 49.12$ and 380.99 for the two epochs, respectively (Table 2, row 7).

To get the distribution of rates, we sample rates proportional to the Poisson likelihood function given N^*_{ei} to get λ_{ei}. The Poisson likelihood function given N events is $L(\lambda|N) = e^{-\lambda}\lambda^N/N!$. Because the Poisson distribution is an integer distribution, we first round N^*_{ei} and then calculate the cumulative Poisson likelihood distribution as a function of λ and normalize so that the cumulative distribution goes from 0 to 1. To select a random rate proportional to that distribution, we select a random uniform number from 0 to 1 and then select the value of λ that corresponds to that quantile on the cumulative distribution. For example, Figure 3 shows the normalized cumulative Poisson likelihood given 20 observations. If the random numbers drawn from the uniform distribution are 0.2, 0.5, and 0.8, then the corresponding random rates would be 17.08, 20.67, and 24.73. Because the likelihood function has the same term as the probability of observing N events given λ, the cumulative Poisson probability function in packages such as R (R Core Team, 2022) provides a convenient way to calculate the normalized cumulative likelihood distribution. For the first trial of the synthetic example, the randomly chosen rates λ_{e1} are 38.9 and 371.9 earthquakes with $M \geq M_{cei}$ for the two epochs, respectively (Table 2, row 8).

Thus, for each of the 100,000 random values of b_i, we get a value of λ_{ei} for the epoch, and repeat that for each epoch. The rates are for $M \geq M_{cei}$. Because M_{cei} is different for each epoch and trial, we extrapolate the 100,000 rates from λ_{ei} ($m \geq M_{cei}$) to λ_{ei} ($m \geq M_1$), the minimum magnitude used to compute hazard, using that trial's b value. Because the duration of each epoch (T_e) is different, we also normalize the rates by T_e to get an annual rate. For the synthetic example, these rates are 0.0935 and 0.146 events with $M \geq M_1$ per year, respectively (Table 2, row 9). Taking the 100,000 samples together, we notate the joint distribution as $J_e(\lambda(M_1), b)$ for each epoch. The distributions for the two epochs of the synthetic example are shown in Figure 4a,b. To illustrate $J(\lambda(M_1),b)$ with a plot,

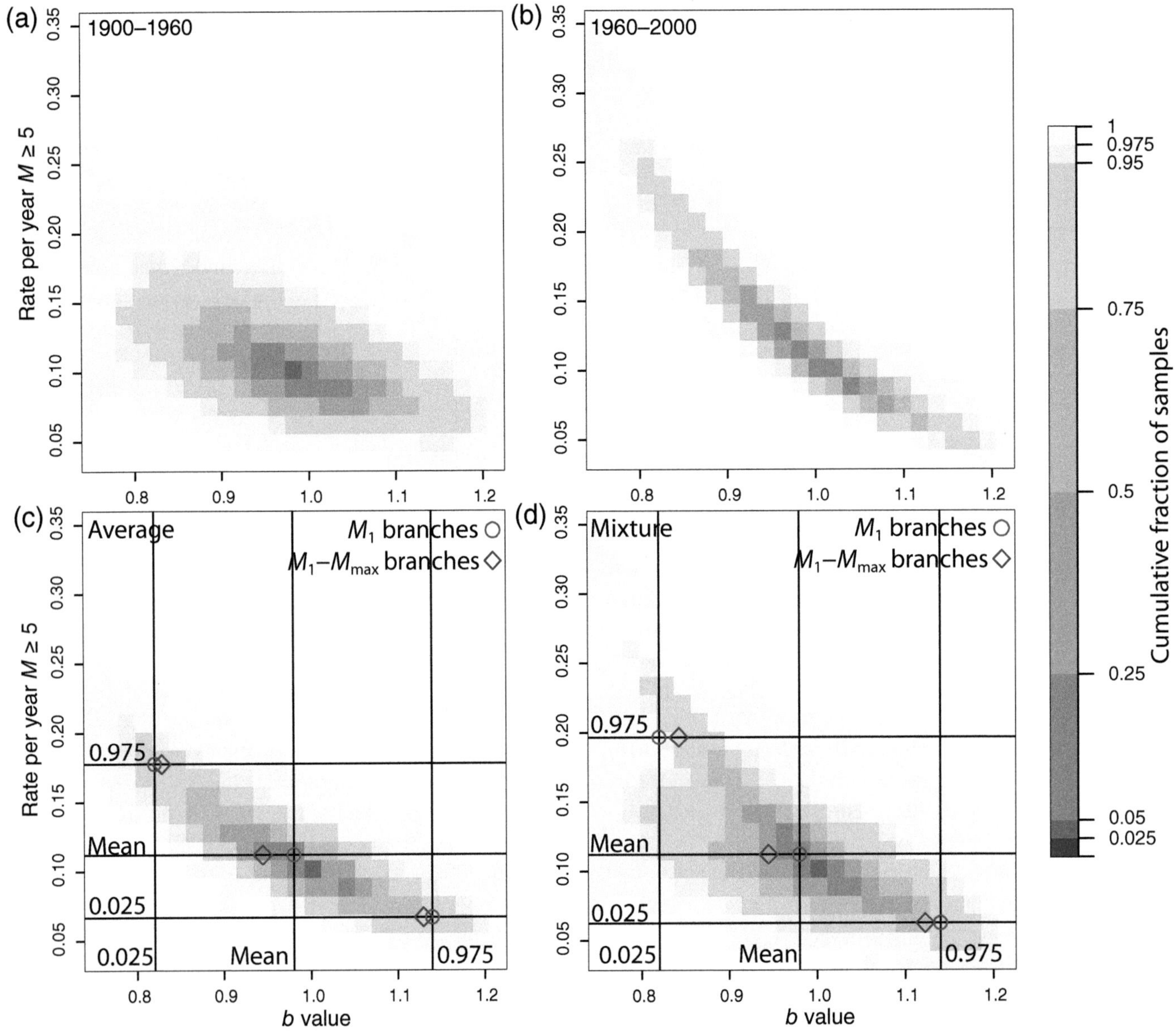

Figure 4. Joint distribution of rate and b value ($J(\lambda(m \geq M))$ for epochs of the synthetic data set: (a) 1900–1960 and (b) 1960–2000 and with the epochs merged as the (c) average approach ($J_{avg}(\lambda(m \geq M))$ and (d) mixture approach ($J_{mix}(\lambda(m \geq M))$. The cumulative fraction is the minimum area that contains a given fraction of the 100,000 samples. For example, the color associated with a 0.95 cumulative fraction and all darker colors can be interpreted as the 95% confidence region. In (c) and (d), vertical lines show the mean and the 0.025 and 0.975 quantiles of the b values. Horizontal lines show the mean and 0.025 and 0.975 quantiles of the rate. Symbols show the locations of the logic tree branches. The color version of this figure is available only in the electronic edition.

we show the minimum area of the space occupied by a given fraction of the samples. Thus, the area encompassed by the 0.95 fraction (and all smaller fractions) can be interpreted as the 95% confidence region of the distribution. That these are very peaked distributions can be seen by comparing the amount of the space occupied by the fraction from 1 to 0.5 versus from 0.5 to 0, or by comparing the space occupied by the two tails from 1 to 0.95 versus from 0.05 to 0. Although these plots are used to illustrate the distributions, all calculations were done with the full sets of samples. For the synthetic example, the second epoch has a tighter distribution due to the lower magnitude of completeness, despite the shorter duration.

To determine the rate for the trial ($\lambda_i(m \geq M_1)$), over all epochs, we average $\lambda_{ei}(m \geq M_1)$ over the epochs, weighted by the durations of each epoch (T_e), $\lambda_i(m \geq M_1) = (\sum_e \lambda_{ei}(m \geq M_1)T_{ei})/\sum_e T_e$. Taking the 100,000 samples together, we notate this average joint distribution as $J_{avg}(\lambda(M_1), b)$. For the first trial of the synthetic example, this would be the rate in row 10 and the b value in row 2 of Table 2, and the full distribution is shown in Figure 4c.

Instead of averaging over the epochs, we can combine the 100,000 samples for each epoch into a mixture distribution of 100,000 samples times the number of epochs, with each sample weighted proportionally to the length of the epochs. We notate

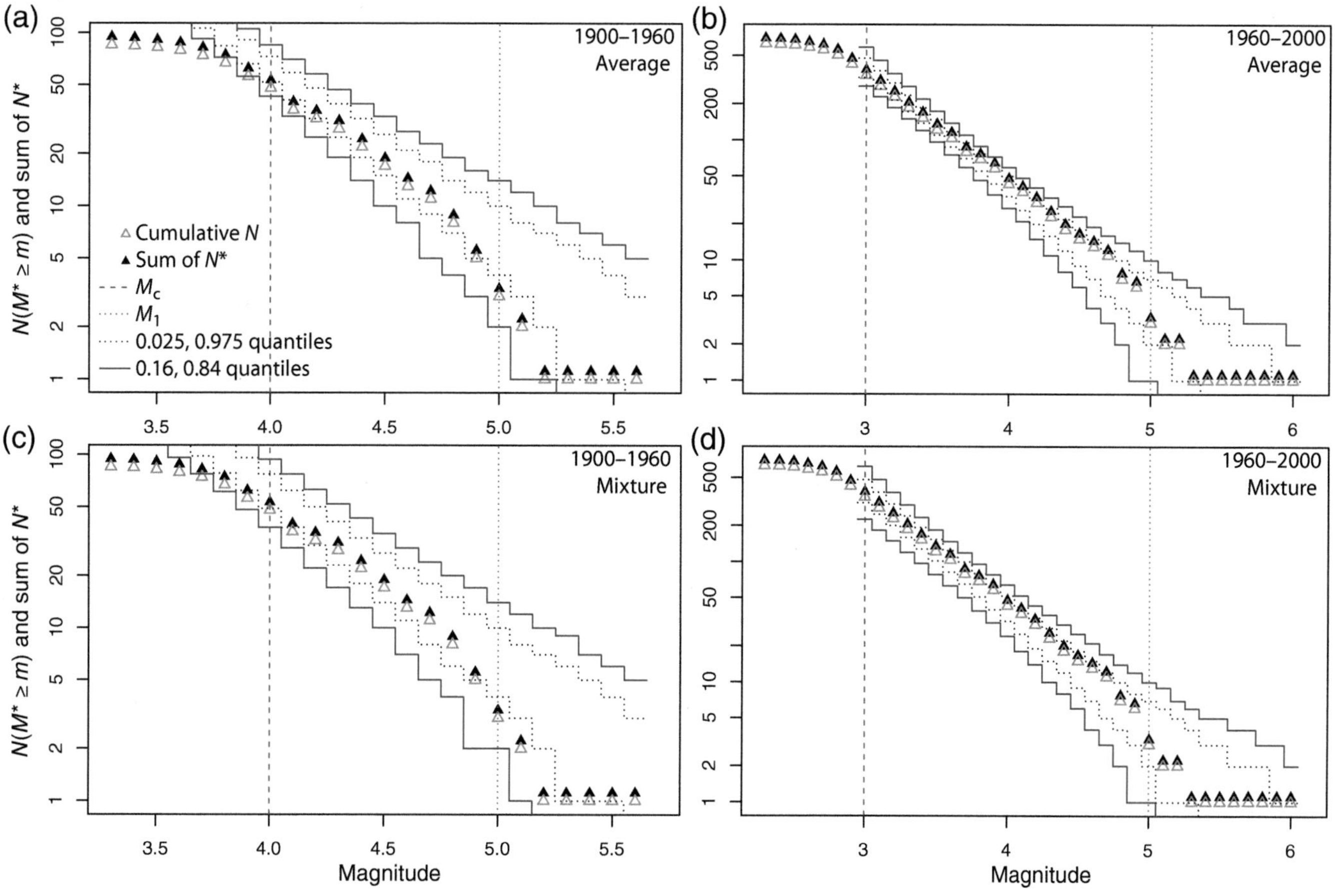

Figure 5. Magnitude–frequency distributions for the epochs of the synthetic example. These plots compare the observations as the cumulative distribution of $N(m \geq M)$ and the sum of N^* to the joint distributions: (a, b) $J_{avg}(\lambda(m \geq M)$ and (c,d) $J_{mix}(\lambda(m \geq M))$. Vertical dashed lines show M_c and M_1. The color version of this figure is available only in the electronic edition.

this mixture distribution as $J_{mix}(\lambda(M_1),b)$. The difference is that $J_{avg}(\lambda(M_1),b)$ assumes that the different epochs are measurements of the same underlying rate, whereas $J_{mix}(\lambda(M_1),b)$ assumes that each epoch is a measurement of the underlying rate during that epoch and that the overall underlying rate is contained within the union of these measurements. For the synthetic example, $J_{mix}(\lambda(M_1),b)$ gets a sample from each epoch for each trial (a total of 200,000 samples), and these would be the rates and weights shown in row 11 of Table 2. $J_{mix}(\lambda(M_1),b)$ is shown in Figure 4d. Compared to $J_{avb}(\lambda(M_1),b)$ (Fig. 4c), $J_{mix}(\lambda(M_1),b)$ (Fig. 4d) has a broader distribution. This is due to the difference in completeness between the two epochs because there is no underlying difference in rate or b value between the two epochs of the synthetic example. In real examples with truly varying seismogenic processes, the differences could be larger.

To compare with the observed seismicity during a given time period, the rates of $J_{avg}(\lambda(M_1),b)$ and $J_{mix}(\lambda(M_1),b)$ are scaled to the duration of the time period used and then Poisson variability is convolved with the joint distribution in order to get the distribution of the observed numbers of events as a function of magnitude, notated as $P(N(m \geq M))$ or $P(N(M))$. The $P(N(M))$ distribution is plotted by showing the quantiles 0.025, 0.16, 0.84, and 0.975. The data are shown both as the cumulative number of events with $N(M^* \geq m)$ and the sum of N^* for those events. Note that there is very little difference between those two views of the data because N^* is a small correction (Mueller, 2018). Figure 5a,b compares the synthetic data from each epoch to the predictions from $J_{avg}(\lambda(M_1),b)$. The fit is good from the overall magnitudes of completeness. The number of synthetic events falls off at lower magnitudes due to incompleteness and at high values due to the vagaries of this particular synthetic catalog. The mixture distribution, $J_{mix}(\lambda(M_1),b)$, provides wider uncertainties, as expected (Fig. 5c,d).

To approximate $J(\lambda(M_1),b)$ in the NSHM logic tree, we select three branches that represent the mean and 95% confidence limits of the distribution. The central branch uses the mean rate and b value. Using the mean rate, rather than the maximum-likelihood estimate (MLE), is especially appropriate in regions of low seismicity. Consider an epoch for which no earthquakes were observed with $M \geq M_{ce}$ and, therefore, $N_e^* = 0$. In that case, the MLE gives $\lambda_{se} = 0$. But the mean of the distribution of rates proportional to the likelihood

$L(\lambda_e|N_e^*)$ will be $\lambda_e(m \geq M_{ce}) = (N_e^* + 1)/T_e$. This mean is more reasonable because observing 0 events does not require that the rate is 0. Using the median, instead of the mean, rate would have a similar but slightly smaller effect because the median rate is about 0.67 units larger than the MLE (Fig. 3). For the synthetic example, the mean and median rates of the average model at M 5 are 0.112 and 0.109, respectively. These are close to the expected values given an input rate of 0.1 and the fact that the mean and median rates are slightly higher than the MLE.

For the low- and high-rate branch values the NSHM uses the 0.025 and 0.975 quantiles of the distribution of $\lambda(m \geq M_1)$. The rates at these quantiles will be associated with the full range of b values in the joint distribution of b value and rate. How to choose a b value for the high and low branches is a valid question. A conservative choice, yielding the widest range of rates when extrapolated to magnitudes above M_1, is to associate the 0.975 quantile of b with the low-rate branch (0.025 rate quantile) and 0.025 quantile of b with the high-rate branch (0.975 rate quantile). We call these the M_1 branches because they are set solely at that magnitude value. In some cases, this choice of b values may produce a range of rates for $M > M_1$ that exceeds the actual distribution if we extrapolate the rates to those higher magnitudes. Another choice would be to calculate the rate quantiles at M_1 and some higher value of magnitude (M_{max}) and then pick a b value that connects the same quantiles at the two magnitude thresholds. We call these the $M_1 - M_{max}$ branches because they are determined using both magnitudes. The locations of these branches for the synthetic example are shown on the joint distributions in Figure 4c and as a magnitude-rate plot in Figure 6. For the synthetic example, the M_1 and $M_1 - M_{max}$ branches are similar.

A third choice for how to construct branches is to project $J(\lambda(M_1),b)$ into the distribution of $\lambda(m \geq M)$ or $P(\lambda(M))$. This is done by extrapolating from $J(\lambda(M_1),b)$ to other magnitudes yielding $J(\lambda(M),b)$ and then taking the λ marginal distribution of $J(\lambda(M),b)$. That marginal distribution is $P(\lambda(M))$. The branches are curves that connect the mean or various quantiles of the rate from one magnitude to another. These can be parameterized simply as mean and quantile rates for each 0.1 units of magnitude from M_1 to M_{max} and we call them the exact branches. Although these curved branches are not GR, they are the result of the uncertainty structure of the analysis and not an underlying assumption that GR behavior is violated by the region. The exact branches for the synthetic example are also shown in Figure 6 and are similar to the M_1 and $M_1 - M_{max}$ branches.

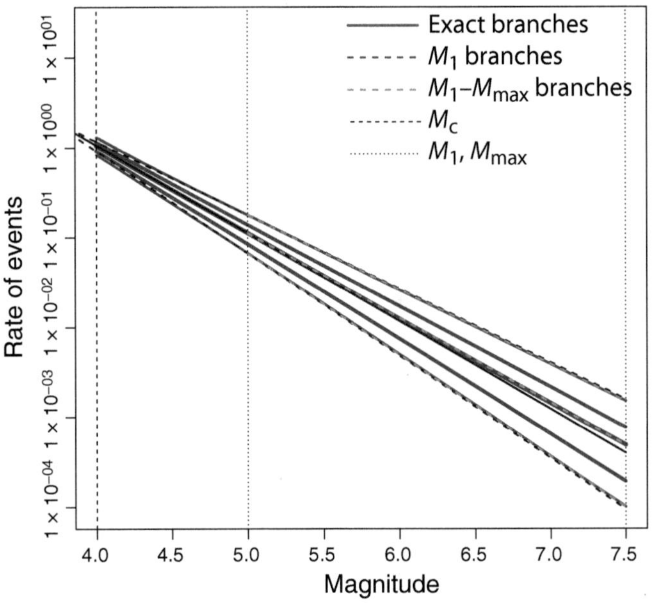

Figure 6. Branch choices for a synthetic example using the averaged approach for the joint distribution of rate and b value. The exact branches are the mean and quantiles of $P_{avg}(\lambda(m \geq M))$ with the mean shown as the thickest line, the 0.16 and 0.84 quantiles as intermediate thickness lines, and the 0.025 and 0.975 quantiles as the thinnest lines. The standard and alternate branches are shown as dashed lines of different shades. The mean and 0.025 and 0.975 quantiles are shown. Vertical dashed lines show M_c, and vertical dotted lines show M_1 and M_{max}. The color version of this figure is available only in the electronic edition.

RESULTS

Determination of the joint distributions

For each NSHM study, the area was divided into regions or tectonic classifications and the joint distribution of λ and b value was determined for each region or classification. To focus on the methods and implications for hazard, this article will focus on the CEUS region and the earthquakes classified as crustal (note that in this article, the crustal classification refers to the upper plate) within the PRVI model. These two regions provide differing examples of how best to choose logic tree branches from the joint distributions.

CEUS. The CEUS seismicity catalog was compiled following the methods of Mueller (2018) and starts in 1568 and goes through the end of 2022 (Petersen *et al.*, 2023). Earthquakes likely to be induced by anthropogenic activities were removed using a set of polygons and time periods (Llenos *et al.*, 2024). For the CEUS, the minimum magnitude used to compute hazard is $M_1 = 4.7$ (Field *et al.*, 2023). The CEUS was analyzed as a single region (Fig. 7a) with three completeness epochs adopted from the most conservative choices for subregions within the CEUS from the 2018 NSHM (Petersen *et al.*, 2020). These are $M_c = 4.7$ from 1850 to 1920, $M_c = 3.7$ from 1920 to 1980, and $M_c = 2.7$ from 1980 until the end of 2022 when the catalog was compiled (Fig. 7b). Note that when a year is given, it refers to the start of the year such that 2023 refers to the boundary between 2022 and 2023. A decimal year refers to part way through the years; for example, 2004.5 refers to halfway through 2004.

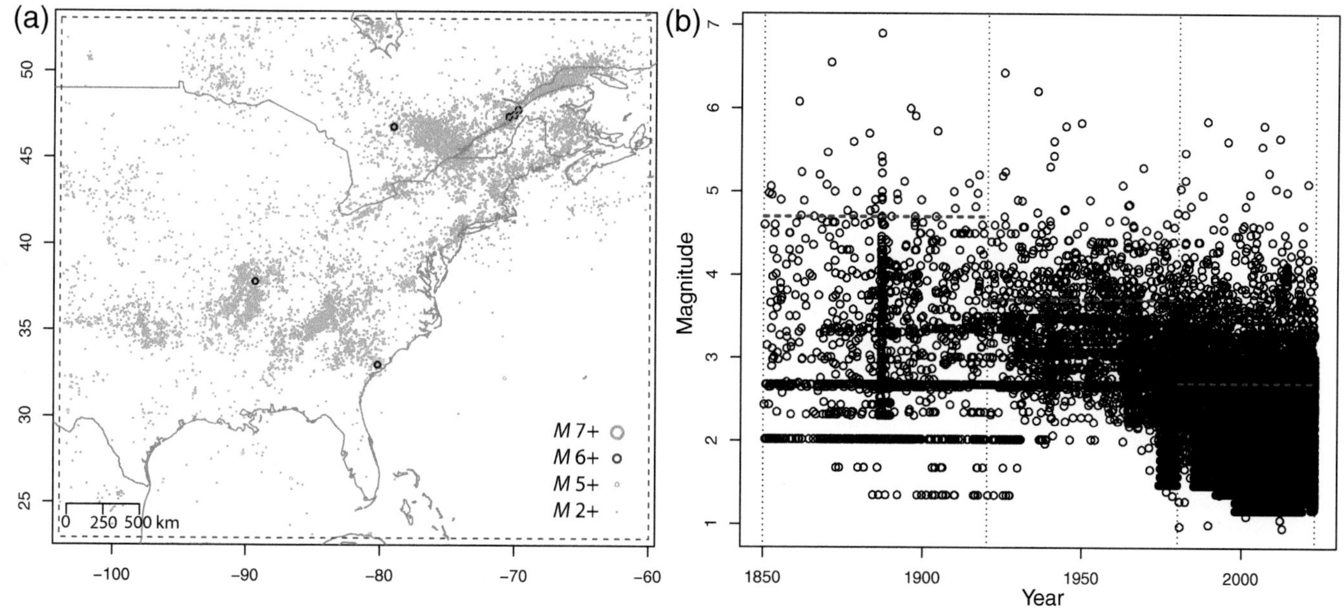

Figure 7. Seismicity analyzed in the Central and Eastern United States (CEUS). (a) Map showing the earthquake epicenters from 1850 onward. The dashed line shows the limits of the region. (b) Magnitude–time plot from 1850 onward. Vertical dotted lines show the boundaries of the epochs. Horizontal dashed lines show M_c during each epoch. The color version of this figure is available only in the electronic edition.

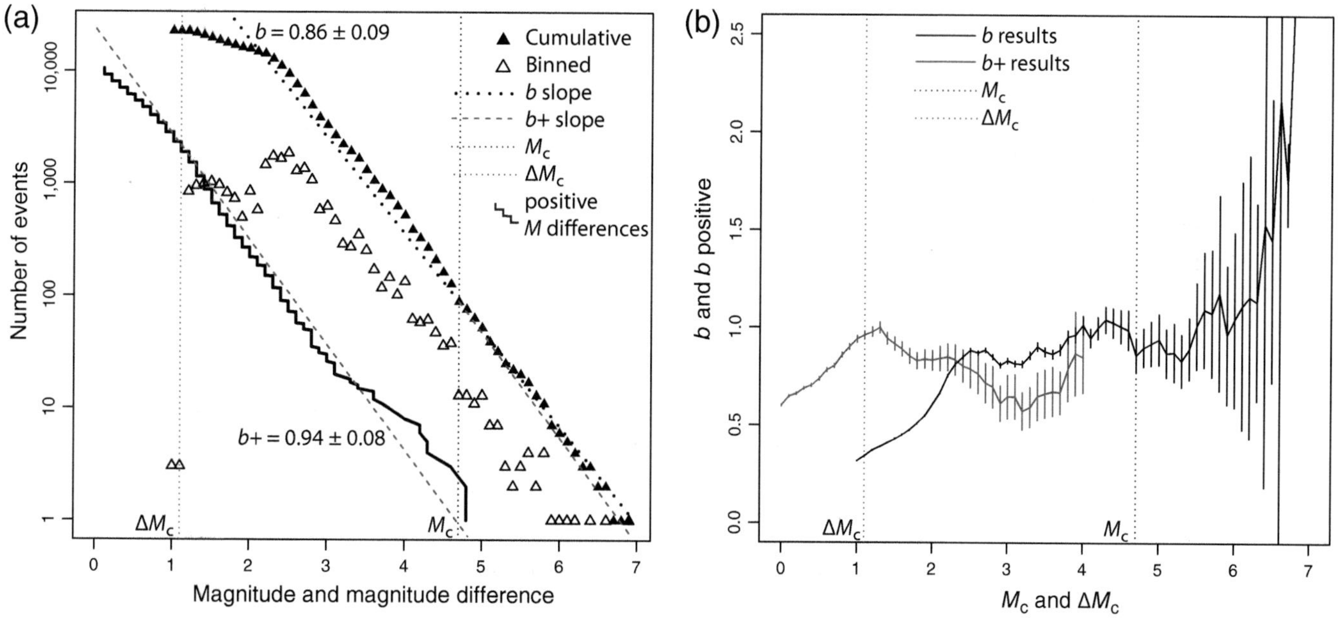

Figure 8. Magnitude distribution analysis plots for the CEUS. (a) Magnitude–frequency plot showing both the distribution of magnitudes as 0.1-unit bins and cumulative distribution and the cumulative distribution of positive forward-time magnitude differences. Vertical lines show the ΔM_c and M_c, sloped lines show the results of b value analysis using both the traditional approach and b positive. (b) Stability of b value analysis showing the results as a function of ΔM_c and M_c with 1 standard deviation uncertainties. The color version of this figure is available only in the electronic edition.

Using the b-positive method, the b value for the full region was determined using all the data from 1850 onward, and $\Delta M_c = 1.1$ based on achieving stability of the results with respect to ΔM_c (Fig. 8). We note that $\Delta M_c = 1.1$ is higher than the values of $\Delta M_c = 0.3$ that are often used for more consistent earthquake catalogs that cover a smaller region and/or a shorter period of time. The b-positive method yielded $b = 0.94 \pm 0.081$ (1σ). Applying the traditional methods to the data

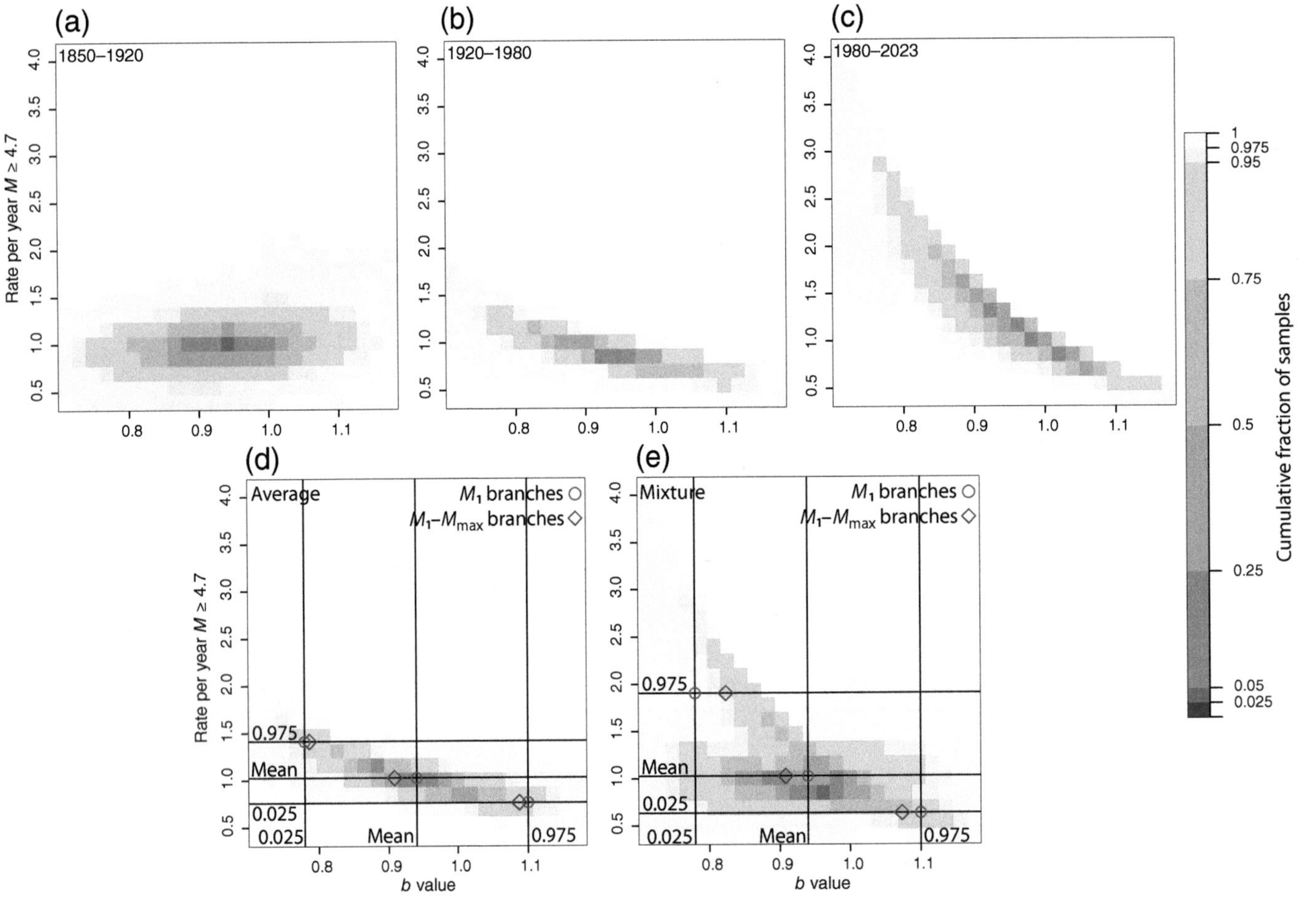

Figure 9. Joint distribution of rate and b-value ($J(\lambda(m \geq M))$ for epochs of the CEUS: (a) 1850–1920, (b) 1920–1980, and (c) 1980–2023 and with the epochs merged as the (d) average approach ($J_{avg}(\lambda(m \geq M))$ and (e) mixture approach ($J_{mix}(\lambda(m \geq M))$. The cumulative fraction is the minimum area that contains a given fraction of the 100,000 samples. For example, the color associated with a 0.95 cumulative fraction and all darker colors can be interpreted as the 95% confidence region. In (d) and (e), vertical lines show the mean and the 0.025 and 0.975 quantiles of the b values. Horizontal lines show the mean and 0.025 and 0.975 quantiles of the rate. Symbols show the locations of the logic tree branches. The color version of this figure is available only in the electronic edition.

from 1850 onward, with $M_c = 4.7$, yielded $b = 0.86 \pm 0.085$. We prefer the result from the b-positive approach because it is robust with respect to temporal changes in completeness and utilizes more data, with 2119 magnitude differences versus 86 magnitudes for the traditional method.

The joint distributions of b value and rate ($J(\lambda(M_1),b)$) for the three epochs have overlapping distributions but different uncertainty structure due to the varying M_c values (Fig. 9a–c). The peak rate for the final epoch is also higher than the peak rates for the prior epochs. For the full time period, $J_{avg}(\lambda(M_1),b)$ is determined by averaging the rates for the three epochs on a sample by sample basis, weighted by the duration of each epoch (Fig. 9d). This is the joint distribution used in the 2023 NSHM because the weighted average follows the practice from UCERF3 (Felzer, 2008). Alternatively, the mixture distribution, $J_{mix}(\lambda(M_1),b)$, better respects rate variations between the epochs because it avoids averaging and results in a broader distribution (Fig. 9e).

Figure 10a–c compares the average model to the data for the three epochs. For 1850–1920, the observed seismicity at $M_c = 4.7$ is at the 0.16 quantile of $P_{avg}(N(M))$ but is closer to the center of the distribution at higher magnitudes. For 1920–1980, the observations from $M_c = 3.7$ to $M_1 = 5$ are at or below the 0.025 quantile of $P_{avg}(N(M))$, but are closer to the center of the model higher magnitudes. For 1970–2023, the model fits well at $M_c = 2.7$, but at intermediate magnitudes the observations go below the 0.025 quantile. At the magnitudes used to compute hazard, $M > 5$, the observations are within the confidence bounds. The reason that the model seems biased high with respect to some of the observations is a curvature of the magnitude–frequency distribution, particularly for the latter two epochs. The rates are determined at M_c, in which the magnitude–frequency distribution is steeper than the mean b value. That brings up the rate for the final epoch (Fig. 10c). The steep slope then reduces the observed number of events in the intermediate magnitudes. For $M \geq 4.5$, the magnitude–frequency distribution has a shallower slope, bringing the observations back into the middle of the distribution. The complexity of the

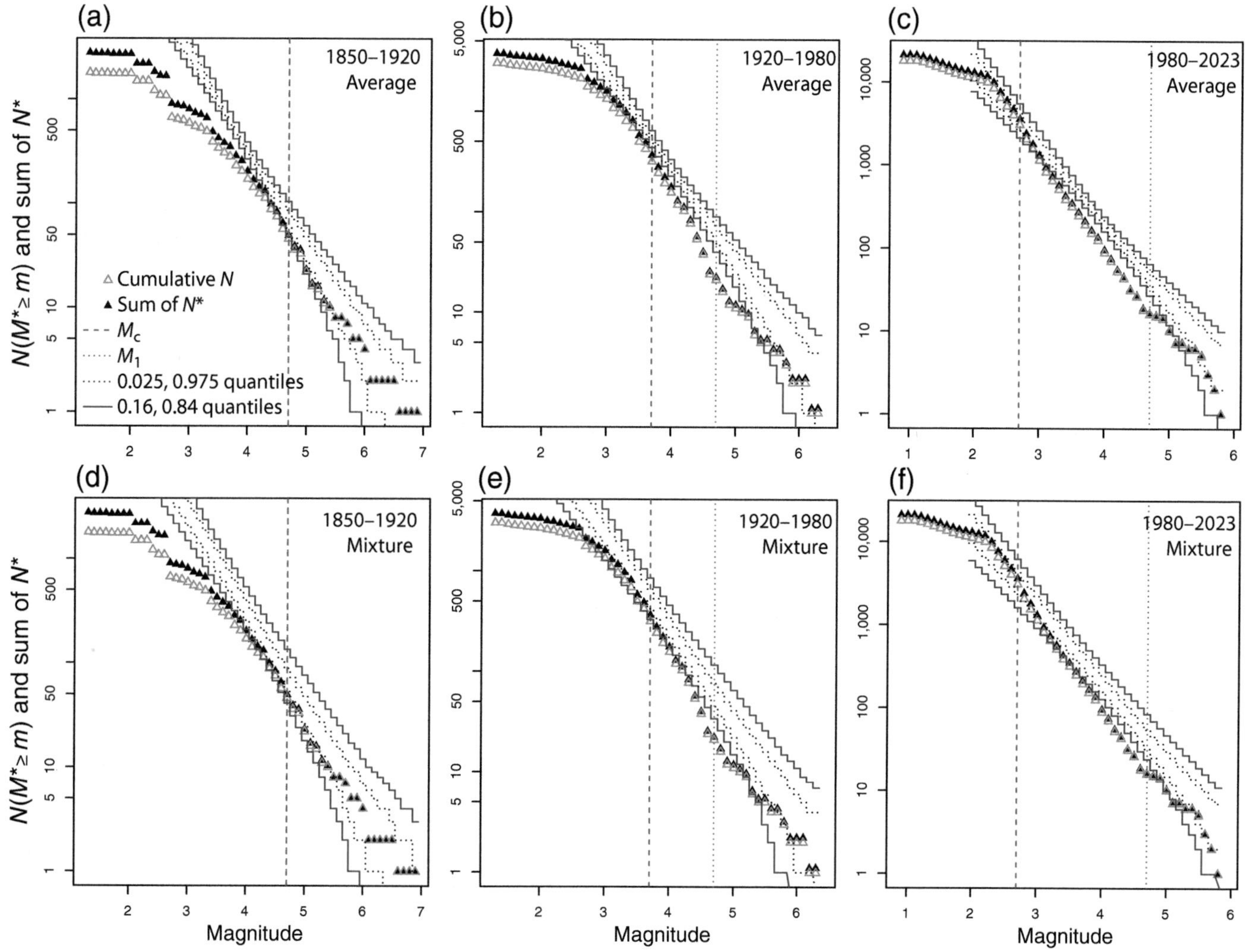

Figure 10. Magnitude–frequency distributions for the epochs of the CEUS. These plots compare the observations as the cumulative distribution of $N(m \geq M)$ and the sum of N^* to the joint distributions: (a–c) $J_{avg}(\lambda(m \geq M)$ and (d–f) $J_{mix}(\lambda(m \geq M))$. Vertical dashed lines show M_c and M_1. The color version of this figure is available only in the electronic edition.

magnitude–frequency distribution could be due to the vagaries of a catalog compiled from different networks and magnitude types. The three epochs are also compared to $P_{mix}(N(M))$ (Fig. 10d–f). Because the mixture distribution is just slightly broader than the average distribution, the observations are slightly closer to the center of the mixture distribution.

Crustal PRVI. For the 2025 PRVI NSHM, the catalog is described in Llenos *et al.* (2025), following the methods of Mueller (2018), and goes from 1615 to the end of 2023 (Shumway *et al.*, 2025). For the PRVI, the minimum magnitude used to compute hazard is $M_1 = 5$. The catalog was separated into tectonic classifications based on the Slab 2.0 model (Hayes *et al.*, 2018) using a catalog separation code (Haynie, 2024; Haynie *et al.*, 2025).

For the PRVI NSHM, the b value was determined for all earthquakes in the region, and not for specific tectonic classifications (Fig. 11a). These earthquakes were analyzed with two completeness epochs, which were determined by exploring spatiotemporal subsets of the seismicity. These are $M_c = 6$ from 1900 to 1973 and $M_c = 5$ from 1973, when the USGS National Earthquake Information Center (NEIC) began operations, until the end of 2023 when the catalog was compiled (Fig. 11b). The $M_c = 6$ during the early part of the twentieth century is lower than observed globally (Michael, 2014) but is apparent in the magnitude–frequency distribution for this catalog from 1900 to 1973 (Fig. 12a). Attempts to use lower magnitudes of completeness with additional epochs were judged not to be useful. This may be due to an issue within the area where the Puerto Rico Seismic Network dominates the combined catalog (Fig. 11a). Within this region from the middle of 2004 onward, there is a nonlinear magnitude–frequency distribution with an excess of events with $M < 4.5$ (Fig. 12b). This could be due to either an unusual seismogenic process or a bias in the magnitudes of these events which were converted from duration magnitudes to moment magnitude for this catalog (Llenos *et al.*, 2025). In either case, the excess events and steeper slope of the magnitude–frequency

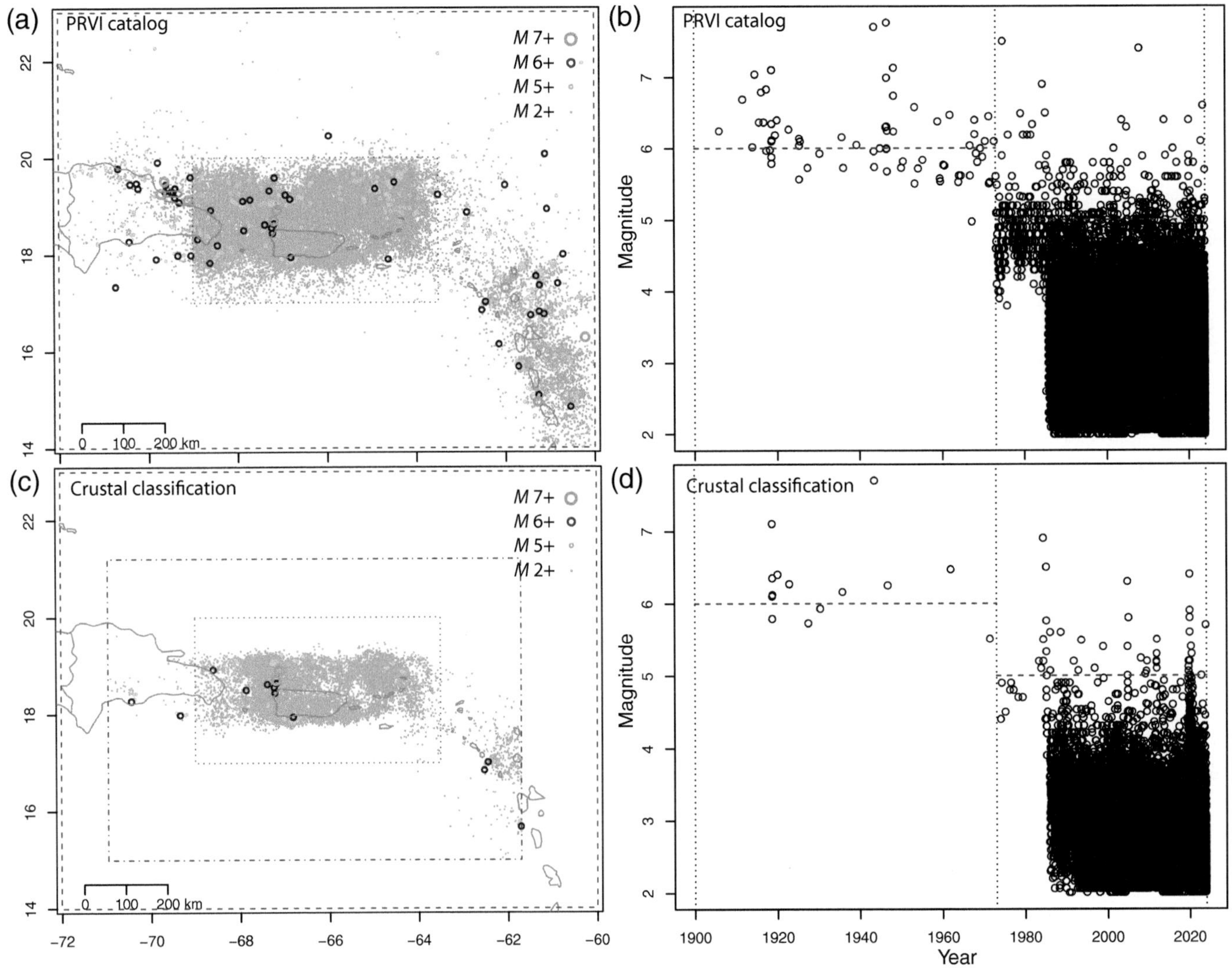

Figure 11. Complete Puerto Rico and the U.S. Virgin Islands (PRVI) catalog that was analyzed for the PRVI b value (a,b) and seismicity analyzed for the PRVI crustal classification (c,d). (a,c) Map showing the earthquake epicenters from 1900 onward. The dashed line shows the limits of the region. The dotted line shows the PRSN area of responsibility. In (c), the dashed–dotted line shows the limits of the polygon within which rates were calculated for the crustal classification. (b,d) Magnitude–time plot from 1900 onward. Vertical dotted lines show the boundaries of the epochs. Horizontal dashed lines show M_c during each epoch. The color version of this figure is available only in the electronic edition.

distribution preclude using it to estimate the rate of events with $M \geq 5$ that are used to compute the hazard for the PRVI.

Application of the b-positive method to the data from 1900 onward results requires $\Delta M_c = 1.3$ to obtain a stable result that is quite high at $b = 1.3 \pm 0.026$ (Fig. 13). This b value does not work to extrapolate from the rates of small events to the rates of the larger earthquakes of interest for hazard. This could be due to the catalog issues discussed in the previous paragraph. To compute a b value that is useful for the NSHM, we applied the traditional approach to the data from 1900 onward with $M_c = 6$ and obtained $b = 0.97 \pm 0.12$ (Fig. 13). We did not apply M_c uncertainty to the b value determination because the data set was already sparse with only 64 events of $M \geq 6$. This b value works fairly well for the second epoch from 1973 onward with $M_c = 5$, although it slightly overpredicts the number of events with magnitudes between about 5.3 and 6.9, but the number of these events is close to a slope of 1σ below the mean (Fig. 12c). If we tried to use $M_c = 4.5$ for the PRSN area from 2004.5 to 2024, the number of events for $M \geq 5$ is overpredicted at above the $1 - \sigma$ level (Fig. 12b). Thus, we concluded that these two epochs provide the best compromise between predicting the rates of the largest events and not overly limiting the amount of data available.

The rates for the PRVI crustal classification were computed for a region judged to be sufficiently close to Puerto Rico and the U.S. Virgin Islands to contribute to the hazard there (Fig. 11c). Figure 14a,b shows $J(\lambda(M_1),b)$ for the two epochs. The joint distribution is broader during the earlier epoch due to the few data available to constrain it. Comparing $J_{avg}(\lambda(M_1),b)$ and $J_{mix}(\lambda(M_1),b)$ (Fig. 14c,d) shows that the average approach provides a more focused distribution, but the mixture

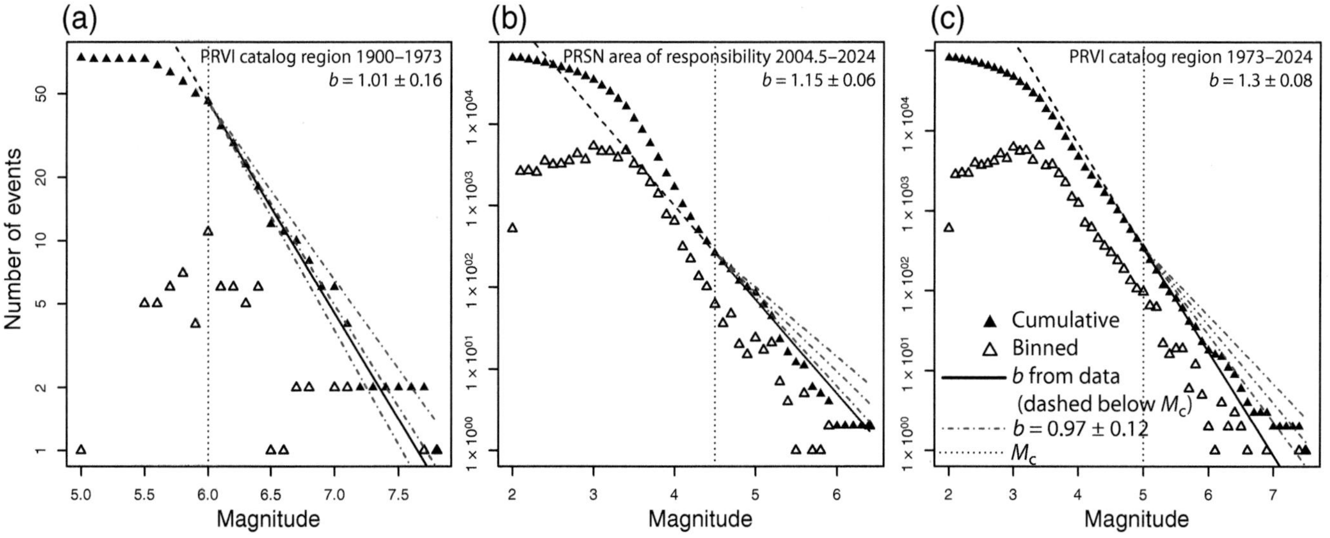

Figure 12. Magnitude–frequency plots for the PRVI. (a) The entire region from 1900 to 1973. (b) The PRSN Area of Responsibility from the middle of 2004 to the end of the catalog. (c) The entire region from 1973 to 2004. Each plot shows the distribution of magnitudes as 0.1-unit bins and the cumulative distribution. The result of traditional b value analysis on the data in each plot is shown as the diagonal line, which is dashed below the M_c used. The b value, and its uncertainty, used for the PRVI analysis is shown as the dashed–dotted lines. The color version of this figure is available only in the electronic edition.

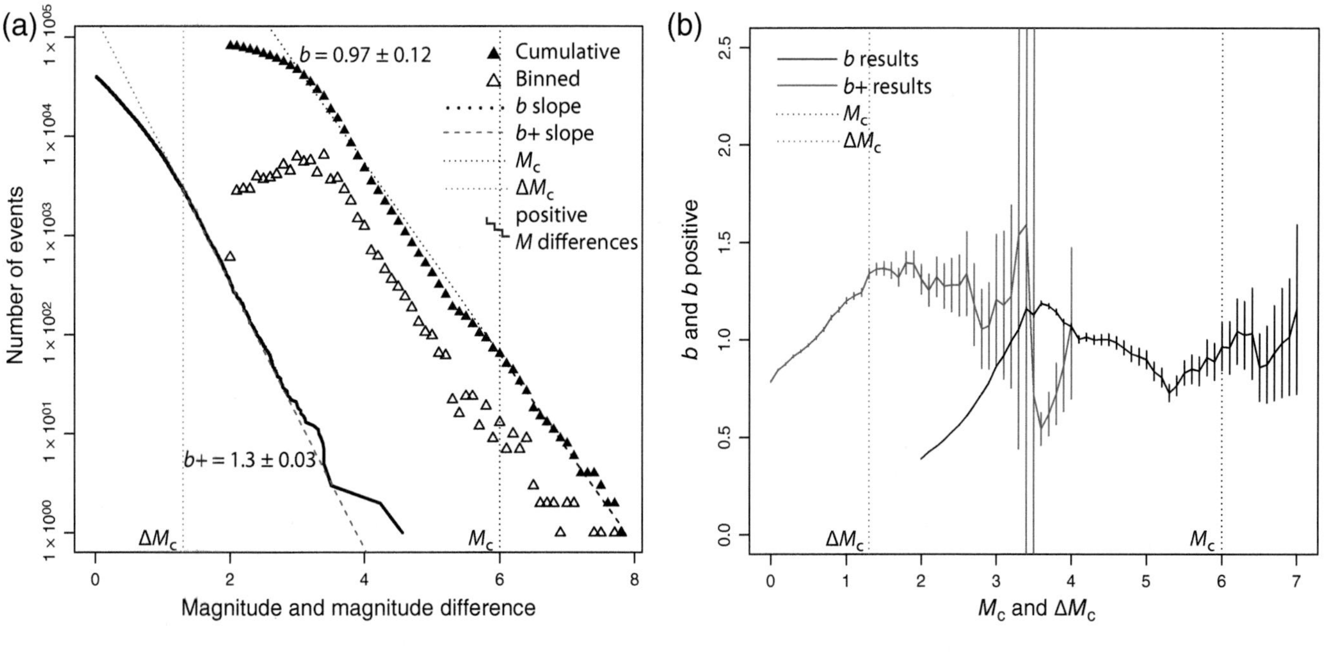

Figure 13. Magnitude distribution analysis plots for the PRVI. (a) Magnitude–frequency plot showing both the distribution of magnitudes as 0.1-unit bins and the cumulative distribution and the cumulative distribution of magnitude differences. Vertical lines show the ΔM_c and M_c, sloped lines show the results of b value analysis using both the traditional approach and b positive. (b) Stability of b value analysis showing the results as a function of ΔM_c and M_c with 1 standard deviation uncertainties. The color version of this figure is available only in the electronic edition.

distribution may better respect differences in rate over time. The observed seismicity during both epochs is within the 95% confidence limits of both $P_{avg}(N(M))$ and $P_{mix}(N(M))$ for $M \geq M_c$ (Fig. 15). The observations for the second epoch are near the lower limits of the confidence range because the earlier epoch's joint distribution includes higher rates than observed during the second epoch. The wider limits of $P_{mix}(N(M))$ prevent the data from ever quite reaching the 95% limits.

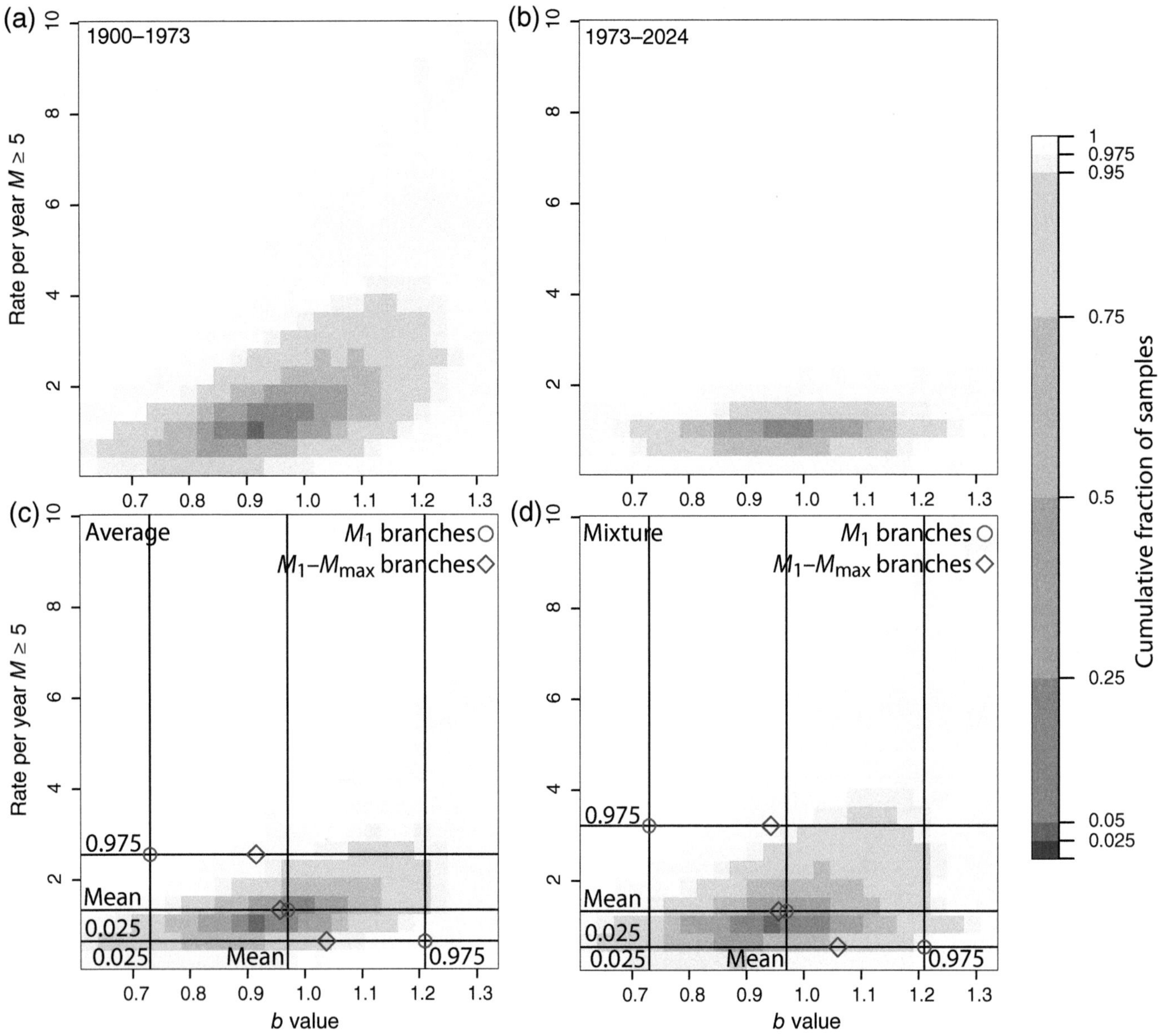

Figure 14. Joint distribution of rate and *b* value ($J(\lambda(m \ge M))$ for epochs of the PRVI crustal classification: (a) 1900–1973 and (b) 1973–2024 and with the epochs merged as the (c) average approach ($J_{avg}(\lambda(m \ge M))$ and (d) mixture approach ($J_{mix}(\lambda(m \ge M))$. The cumulative fraction is the minimum area that contains a given fraction of the 100,000 samples. For example, the color associated with a 0.95 cumulative fraction and all darker colors can be interpreted as the 95% confidence region. In (c) and (d), vertical lines show the mean and the 0.025 and 0.975 quantiles of the *b* values. Horizontal lines show the mean and 0.025 and 0.975 quantiles of the rate. Symbols show the locations of the logic tree branches. The color version of this figure is available only in the electronic edition.

Branches and hazards

To produce earthquake rates for use in the NSHM, we project the joint distributions, $J_{avg}(\lambda(M_1),b)$ and $J_{mix}(\lambda(M_1),b)$, into the probability distribution of rate as a function of magnitude $P_{avg}(\lambda(m \ge M))$ and $P_{mix}(\lambda(m \ge M))$ (or more compactly as $P_{avg}(\lambda(M))$ and $P_{mix}(\lambda(M))$), and present that probability distribution as quantiles on a magnitude-rate plot. Note that $P(\lambda(M))$ does not include the effects of a maximum magnitude because considerations of M_{max} are taken into account later in the NSHM process (Field *et al.*, 2023). The quantiles of both $P_{avg}(\lambda(M))$ and $P_{mix}(\lambda(M))$ are quite linear for the CEUS (Fig. 16a), with the mixture distribution being slightly wider. For the PRVI, $P_{mix}(\lambda(M))$ also provides slightly wider quantiles than $P_{avg}(\lambda(M))$, but the quantiles now have an hourglass shape (Fig. 16b). The difference between the two regions is that for the CEUS $M_c \le M_1$, whereas for the PRVI crustal region $M_c \ge M_1$. We make our observations of the rate at M_c and then extrapolate to other magnitudes using the *b* value and its uncertainty. Thus, at M_c, the *b* value and its uncertainty have no impact, and the uncertainty in the rate is smaller than at other magnitudes. As expected, the mixture distribution gives slightly wider quantiles than the average distribution for both regions. But the effect for these two regions is somewhat modest, suggesting that there are no large rate changes between the epochs. For the rest of the article, we will focus

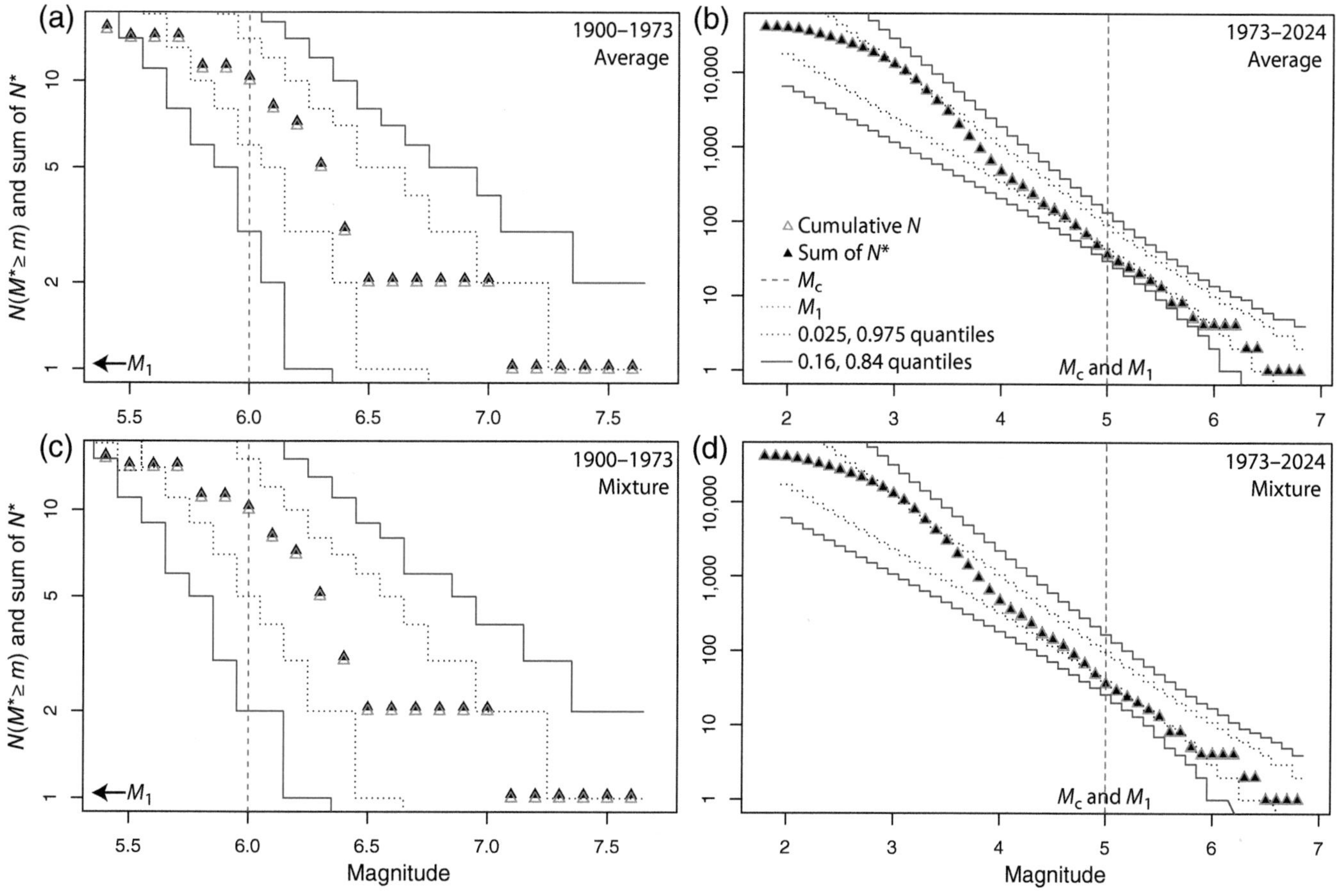

Figure 15. Magnitude–frequency distributions for the epochs of the PRVI crustal classification. These plots compare the observations as the cumulative distribution of $N(m \geq M)$ and the sum of N^* to the joint distributions (a,b) $J_{avg}(\lambda(m \geq M))$ and (c,d) $J_{mix}(\lambda(m \geq M))$. Vertical dashed lines show M_c and M_1. The color version of this figure is available only in the electronic edition.

on the average joint distributions that were used in the recent NSHM updates.

The next step is to select mean, low-, and high-rate branches for use in the NSHM logic tree. These branches are parameterized as a rate for events with $M \geq M_1$ and a b value. As described in the Methods section, our initial approach, called the M_1 branches, is to select the mean, 0.025, and 0.975 quantile rates for $M \geq M_1$ and associate them with the mean, 0.025, and 0.975 quantile b values. That approach does an excellent job of approximating the mean, 0.025, and 0.975 quantiles of $P_{avg}(\lambda(M))$ for the CEUS (Fig. 16c), and the M_1 branches were used for the recent CONUS (Petersen *et al.*, 2024) and Alaska (Powers *et al.*, 2024) NSHM efforts. However, due to the hourglass shape of $P_{avg}(\lambda(M))$, the M_1 branches produces low- and high-rate branches that are outside of the quantiles of $P_{avg}(\lambda(M))$ for the PRVI crustal classification (Fig. 16d). Comparing the branches to $J_{avg}(\lambda(M_1),b)$ shows that the M_1 branches fall within $J_{avg}(\lambda(M_1),b)$ for the CEUS (Fig. 9d), but the low- and high-rate branches are outside the distribution for the PRVI crustal classification (Fig. 14c).

To produce branches that more closely approximate the mean and quantiles of $P_{avg}(\lambda(M))$, our second branch approach, called the $M_1 - M_{max}$ branches, is to connect the mean and quantiles of $P_{avg}(\lambda(M))$ at M_1 and M_{max}. The recent CEUS NSHM updates use the same logic tree with three values of $M_{max} = 7.3$, 7.6, and 7.9. The $M_1 - M_{max}$ branches are robust with respect to small variations in M_{max}, and so we produce the $M_1 - M_{max}$ branches with a single value of $M_{max} = 7.5$ for the CEUS and use $M_{max} = 7.9$ for PRVI. These $M_1 - M_{max}$ branches are almost identical to the M_1 ones for the CEUS (Fig. 16c). For the PRVI crustal classification, the $M_1 - M_{max}$ branches match $P_{avg}(\lambda(M))$ much better than the M_1 branches (Fig. 16d). The $M_1 - M_{max}$ branches are closer to the bulk of $J_{avg}(\lambda(M_1),b)$ than the standard M_1 for the PRVI crustal class (Fig. 14c), but there is little difference in the two sets of branches for the CEUS (Fig. 9d).

An even better match between the logic tree branches and $P_{avg}(\lambda(M))$ can be achieved by relaxing the requirement that the branches be parameterized by a single rate and b value. We can produce branches that exactly match $P_{avg}(\lambda(M))$ by simply using the mean and quantiles of that distribution as branches. These exact branches can be parameterized as $\lambda(m \geq M)$ at 0.1 intervals of M. Including such branches in PSHA is computationally trivial because the integration of the ground-motion models (GMMs) over magnitude is generally done numerically, even for GR rate branches.

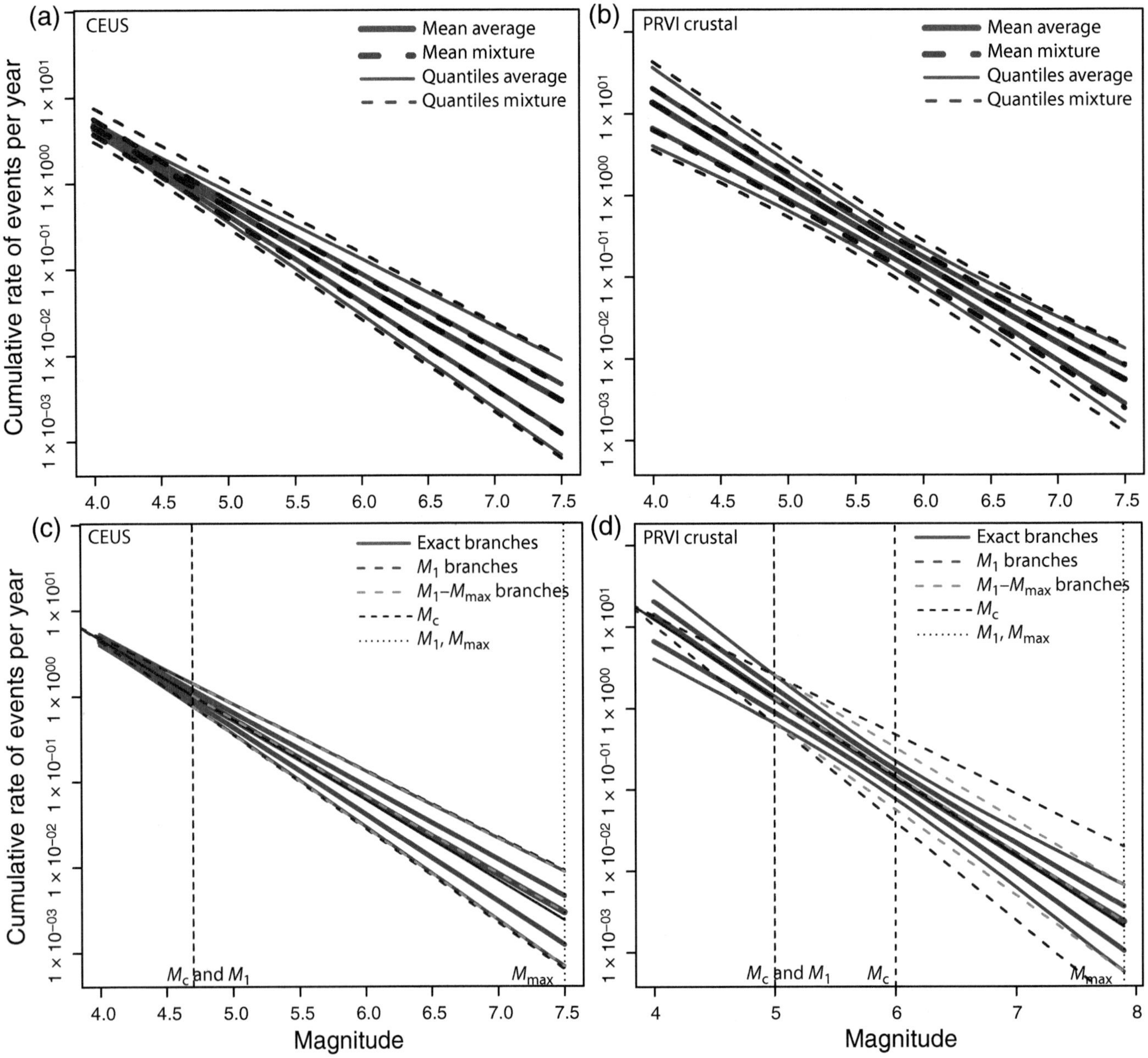

Figure 16. Average and mixture joint distributions shown as quantiles of the probability of rate as a function of magnitude ($P(\lambda(m \geq M))$) for (a) the CEUS and (b) the PRVI crustal classification. The average distribution is shown as solid lines, and the mixture distribution is shown as dashed lines. For each distribution, the mean is shown as the thickest line, the 0.16 and 0.84 quantiles as intermediate thickness lines, and the 0.025 and 0.975 quantiles as the thinnest lines. The branch choices for (c) the CEUS and (d) the PRVI crustal classification using the averaged approach for the joint distribution of rate and b value. The exact branches are the mean and quantiles of $P_{avg}(\lambda(m \geq M))$ as in (a) and (b). The standard and alternate branches are shown as dashed lines of different shades. The mean and 0.025 and 0.975 quantiles are shown. Vertical dashed lines show M_c, and vertical dotted lines show M_1 and M_{max}. The color version of this figure is available only in the electronic edition.

To understand the impact of these branch choices on the NSHM, we use a simplified Poisson hazard calculation. The advantage of calculating hazard is that it combines the impacts of the branch rates and b values. This simplified calculation considers all the events to be at a single point and calculates the peak ground acceleration (PGA) at a single site that is $d = 50$ km away with the GMM model from Cornell *et al.* (1979): $\ln \overline{\mathrm{PGA}} = -0.152 + 0.859M - 1.803 \ln(d + 25)$ with $\sigma = 0.57$. Although this is a simplistic GMM and spatial distribution, the goal of this analysis is to compare the effects of the branches rather than the absolute values of the ground motions. Hence, the conclusions reached here will be the same for any log-normal distribution and integration of the mean ground motion over space. The hazard is computed for the branches discussed earlier, along with branches using the same approaches at the 0.16 and 0.84 quantiles. Mean hazard and the distribution of hazard are computed

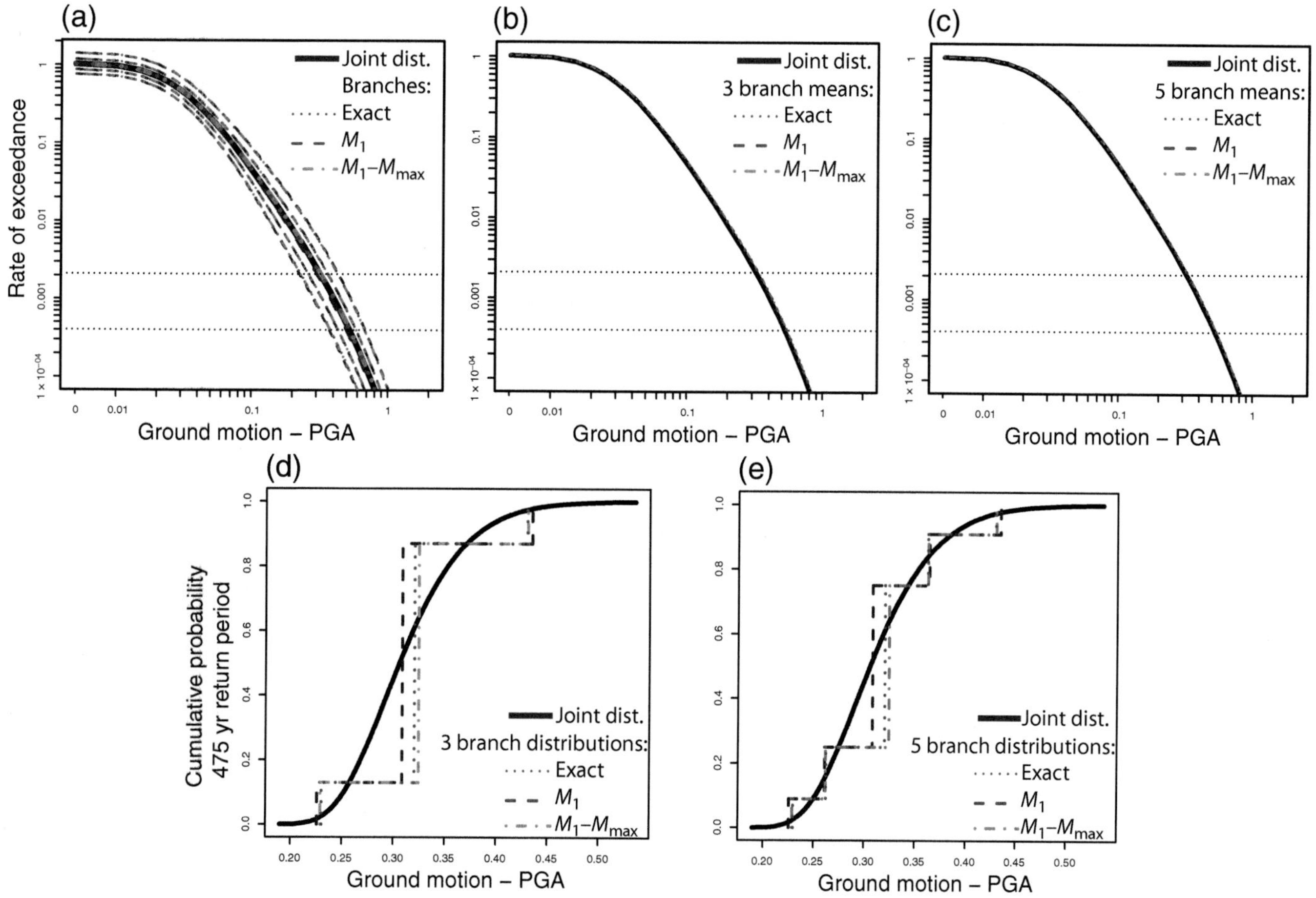

Figure 17. Simplified hazard results for the CEUS. (a) Rate of exceedance for peak ground acceleration (PGA) showing the mean hazard over the joint distribution $J_{avg}(\lambda(m \geq M))$ and the hazard computed from the mean and 0.025, 0.16, 0.84, and 0.975 quantiles for the exact, M_1, and M_1–M_{max} branches. (b) Mean hazard computed by averaging over $J_{avg}(\lambda(m \geq M))$ and the mean and 0.025 and 0.975 quantiles of the exact, M_1, and M_1–M_{max} branches. (c) Mean hazard computed averaging over $J_{avg}(\lambda(m \geq M))$ and the mean and 0.025, 0.16, 0.84, and 0.975 quantiles of the exact, M_1, and M_1–M_{max} branches. (d) Cumulative probability distribution of hazard computed for a 475 yr return period for $J_{avg}(\lambda(m \geq M))$ and the mean and 0.025 and 0.975 quantiles of the exact, M_1, and M_1–M_{max} branches. (e) Cumulative probability distribution of hazard computed for a 475 yr return period for $J_{avg}(\lambda(m \geq M))$ and the mean and 0.025, 0.16, 0.84, and 0.975 quantiles of the exact, M_1, and M_1–M_{max} branches. The color version of this figure is available only in the electronic edition.

from the mean branches as well as the logic trees of the branches. The latter is done in two ways. The first uses the 0.025 quantile, mean, and 0.975 quantile branches with weights of 0.13, 0.74, and 0.13, respectively. These quantiles and weights are standard for the NSHM. The second way uses the 0.025 quantile, 0.16 quantile, mean, 0.84 quantile, and 0.975 quantile branches with weights of 0.09, 0.16, 0.5, 0.16, and 0.09, respectively (Working Group on California Earthquake Probabilities, 2003). Both sets of weights match the mean and variance of a normal distribution (Miller and Rice, 1983). The results of the branches are compared to the mean hazard and distribution of hazard computed directly from the 100,000 samples of $J_{avg}(\lambda(M_1),b)$.

For the CEUS, there is little difference between the hazard computed from the M_1, $M_1 - M_{max}$, and exact branch approaches. In addition, for each approach, the hazard from the mean branch closely approximates the mean hazard computed from the 100,000 samples (Fig. 17a). Computing the mean hazard from three-branch and five-branch logic trees also produces a close approximation to the true mean hazard (Fig. 17b,c). Comparing the distribution of hazard for 475 yr recurrence computed from the 100,000 samples and a three-branch logic tree shows little difference between the three approaches to choosing branches (Fig. 17d). However, the three-branch approach does overestimate the probability of high and low ground motions and is fairly crude with only three steps in the distribution. This can be seen because the joint distribution crosses the vertical steps of the three-branch distribution near the bottom of the first steps and at the top of the last steps. Using five branches (Fig. 17e) produces a better approximation of the distribution of hazard, with the joint distribution crossing the vertical steps closer to their midpoints, and somewhat less overestimation of the probabilities of high and low ground motions.

For the PRVI crustal classification, there is more difference in the hazard computed from the branches determined with the M_1, $M_1 - M_{max}$, and exact approaches (Fig. 18a). As

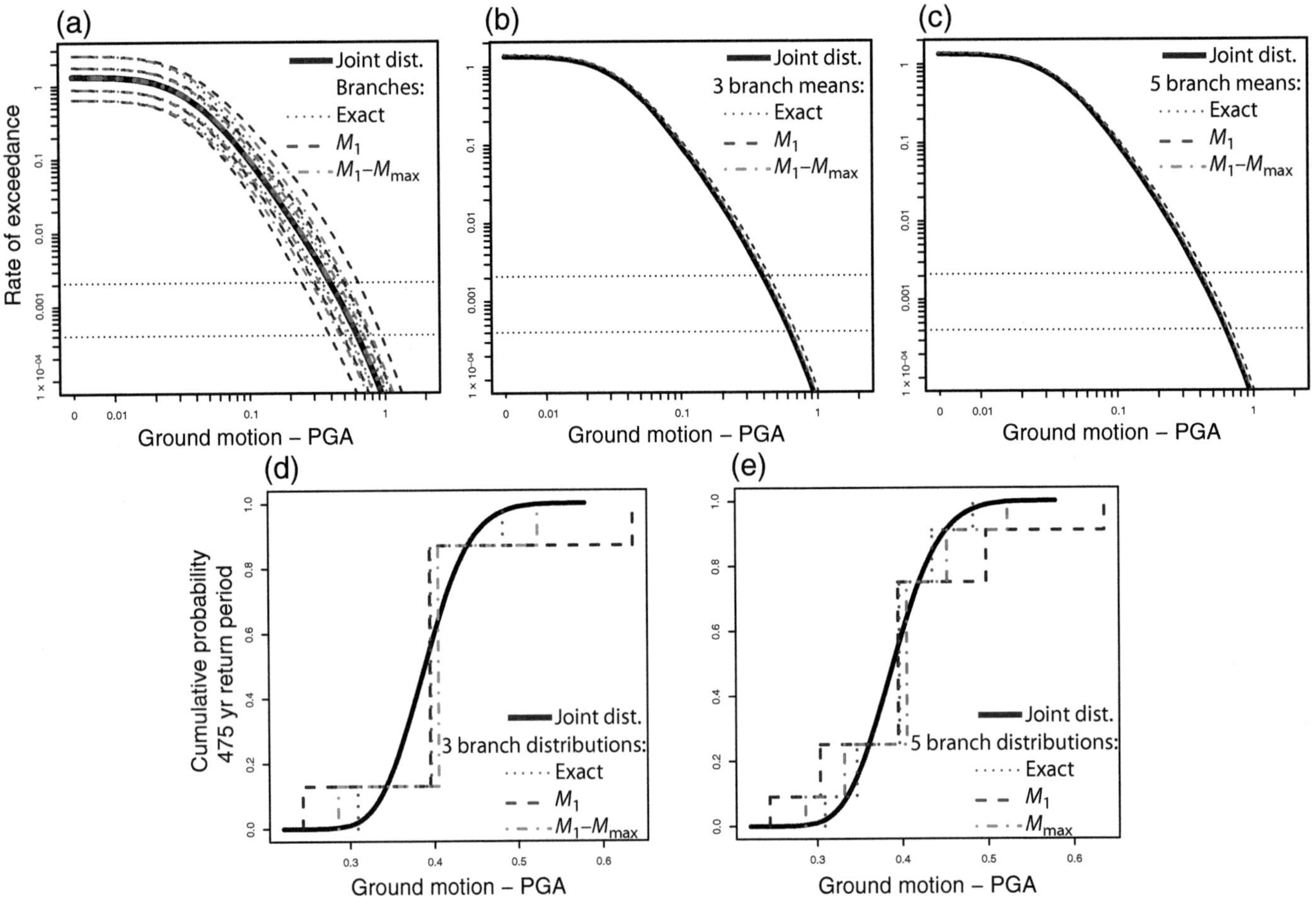

expected, the M_1 branches produce the widest range of hazard, and the exact approach produces the narrowest range. However, the mean branches from each approach closely approximate the mean hazard computed from the 100,000 samples. The three-branch and five-branch logic trees yield good approximations of the mean hazard, but the M_1 approach is slightly worse than the $M_1 - M_{max}$ and exact approaches for this metric (Fig. 18b,c). The hazard distribution computed with the three-branch logic tree and the M_1 branches greatly overestimates the probability of high and low ground motions, whereas the $M_1 - M_{max}$ and exact branches do better but still somewhat overestimate the probability of high and low ground motions (Fig. 18d). For the five-branch logic tree, the M_1 branches still greatly overestimates the probability of high and low ground motions, whereas the $M_1 - M_{max}$ and exact approaches do a better job of approximating the true distribution (Fig. 18e).

Figure 18. Simplified hazard calculations for the PRVI crustal classification. (a) Rate of exceedance for PGA showing the mean hazard over the joint distribution $J_{avg}(\lambda(m \geq M))$ and the hazard computed from the mean and 0.025, 0.16, 0.84, and 0.975 quantiles for the exact, M_1, and M_1–M_{max} branches. (b) Mean hazard computed by averaging over $J_{avg}(\lambda(m \geq M))$ and the mean and 0.025 and 0.975 quantiles of the exact, M_1, and M_1–M_{max} branches. (c) Mean hazard computed averaging over $J_{avg}(\lambda(m \geq M))$ and the mean and 0.025, 0.16, 0.84, and 0.975 quantiles of the exact, M_1, and M_1–M_{max} branches. (d) Cumulative probability distribution of hazard computed for a 475 yr return period for $J_{avg}(\lambda(m \geq M))$ and the mean and 0.025 and 0.975 quantiles of the exact, M_1, and M_1–M_{max} branches. (e) Cumulative probability distribution of hazard computed for a 475 yr return period for $J_{avg}(\lambda(m \geq M))$ and the mean and 0.025, 0.16, 0.84, and 0.975 quantiles of the exact, M_1, and M_1–M_{max} branches. The color version of this figure is available only in the electronic edition.

DISCUSSION

We have presented a new approach to considering observational uncertainties when determining earthquake rates for PSHA. We consider four types of uncertainty:

1. the uncertainty in the rate given the observed number of earthquakes over a given magnitude,
2. the uncertainty in b value,
3. the uncertainty in event magnitudes, and
4. the uncertainty in the magnitude of completeness.

The uncertainty in the rate is implemented using the Poisson likelihood function. This helps account for the uncertainty due to a limited-duration catalog because we do not assume that the observed number of earthquakes, over a limited period of time, provides an exact estimate of the rate. The uncertainty in b value impacts the extrapolation from the magnitude of completeness to magnitudes of interest for computing hazard. The uncertainty

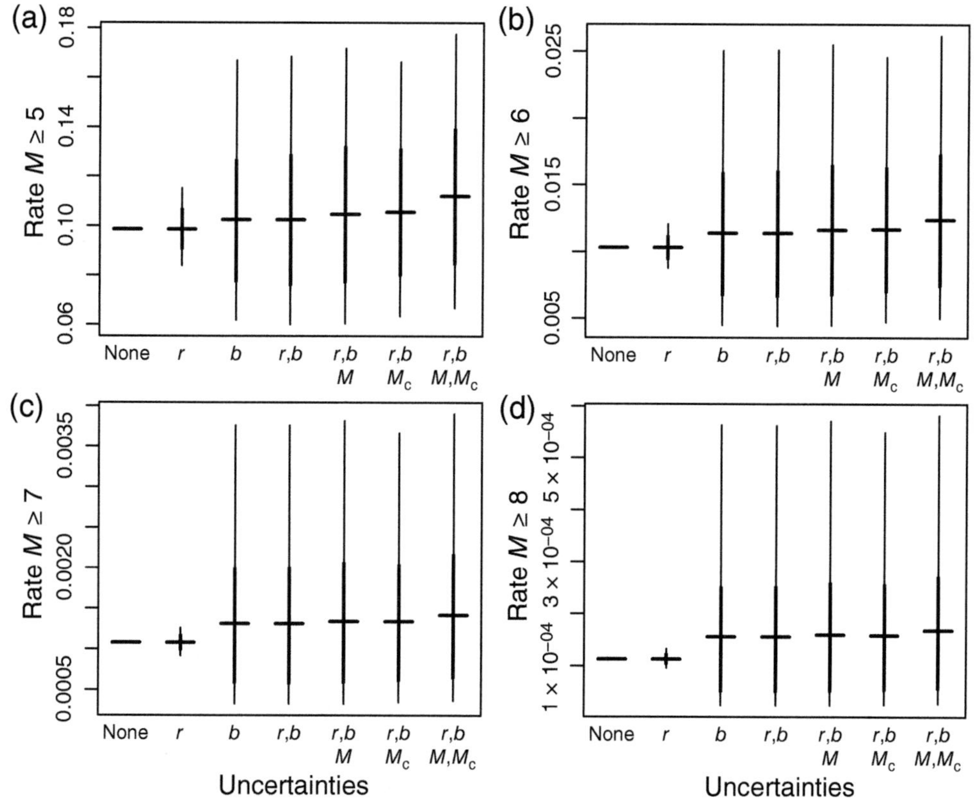

Figure 19. Estimated rate for $M \geq 5$, 6, 7, and 8 events in the synthetic test from $J_{avg}(\lambda(m \geq M))$ versus the types of uncertainty included. The types of uncertainty are b, $b$value; M, event magnitude; M_c, magnitude of completeness; r, rate. (a) $M \geq 5$, (b) $M \geq 6$, (c) $M \geq 7$, and (d) $M \geq 8$. Mean rates are shown by the horizontal lines, 1 and 2 standard deviation ranges are shown by the thin and think vertical lines, respectively.

in event magnitudes addresses random effects of uncertainty in individual events, and the uncertainty in the magnitude of completeness addresses the uncertainty in determining the best magnitude at which to measure rates. These four types of uncertainty are combined using a Monte Carlo process that allows us to determine the distribution of rates for a region by combining the results from a set of epochs with their own magnitudes of completeness.

But which of these four types of uncertainty has the greatest impact on the results? Figure 19 shows the distribution of rate at M 5, 6, 7, and 8 for the synthetic example while including different uncertainties. The biggest increase in the distribution of the rate comes from the addition of uncertainty in b value. The relative contribution of b value uncertainty, as compared to rate uncertainty, increases as the magnitude of interest gets further from M_c.

Figure 20 shows the distribution of the rate at M 5, 6, 7, and 8 for the CEUS. Again, the biggest increase in the distribution of the rate comes from the addition of uncertainty in the b value. Uncertainty in b value was not included in the NSHM through the 2018 update (Petersen *et al.*, 2020). Thus, this methodology is an important step forward. There is also an increase in the CEUS mean rate when the random effect of magnitude uncertainty is included. This does not occur for the synthetic example or the PRVI, and so it does not seem to be an artifact of the method.

Figure 21 shows the same information for the PRVI crustal classification. The inclusion of rate uncertainty is larger than for the synthetic example or the CEUS due to the small size of the data set with $M \geq M_c$. Which uncertainty makes the most difference varies a great amount depending on the magnitude of interest, because M_c is within this range of magnitudes. At M 5 and 6, the impact of uncertainty in b value is suppressed because we are close to the magnitude of completeness. But it makes a large difference at M 7 and 8. At M 5 and 6, the addition of uncertainty in M_c makes a noticeable difference in the range of rates. At no magnitude does the addition of uncertainty in event magnitude appear to make a large difference. However, splitting the gridded seismicity model into separate total-rate and spatial-kernel components and using the Monte Carlo process presented here makes it simple to include all of these uncertainties.

Although different methods were used, the 2022 Aotearoa New Zealand NSHM also considered uncertainty in rate, b value, and the magnitude of completeness (Rollins *et al.*, 2024). Their approach used logic tree branches for each uncertainty. This limits them to using a few values for each, whereas our Monte Carlo process allows us to determine the full distributions.

Another aspect of accounting for variations in earthquake rates relates to whether to average over epochs or to use a mixture model. Although averaging was meant to better account for temporal rate variations (Felzer, 2013a), taking an average fundamentally assumes that we have multiple observations of the same quantity. Using the mixture approach to produce the overall joint distribution from the epochs better respects temporal variations and produces a broader distribution of rates. If this approach is adopted in the future, it may be important to reconsider how we choose the epochs. Currently, they are chosen based on the history of M_c, which changes because seismic networks improve. To better consider temporal variations in rate, we should also consider searching for changes in rate

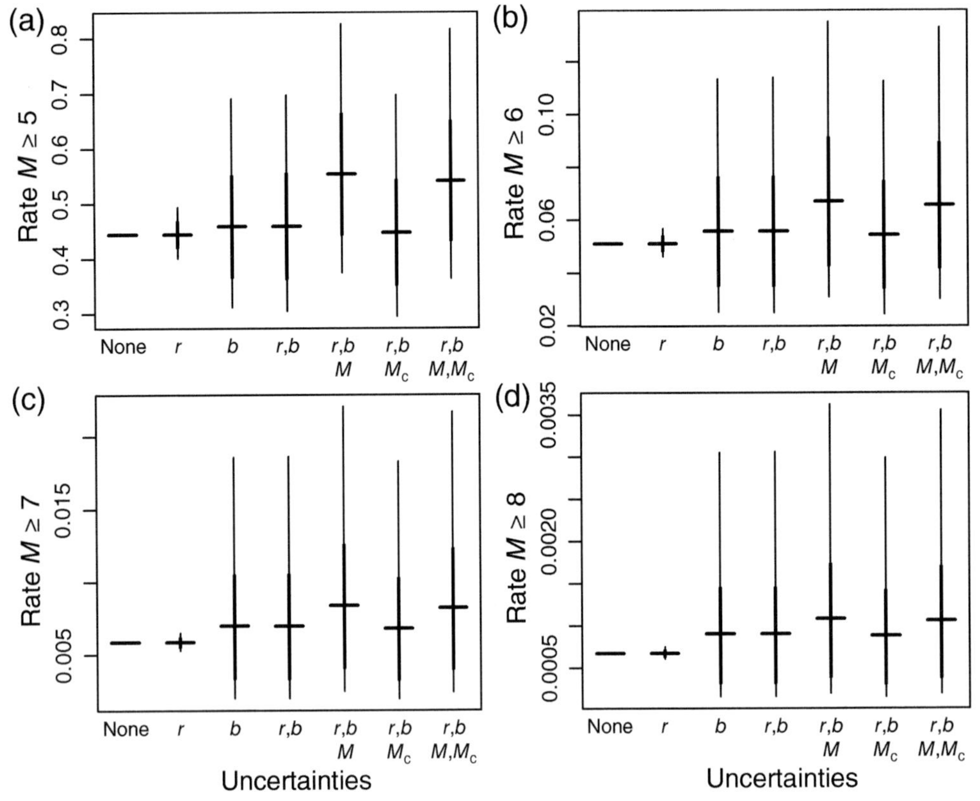

Figure 20. Estimated rate for $M \geq 5$, 6, 7, and 8 events in the CEUS from $J_{avg}(\lambda(m \geq M))$ versus the types of uncertainty included. The types of uncertainty are *b*, *b* value; *M*, event magnitude; M_c, magnitude of completeness; *r*, rate. (a) $M \geq 5$, (b) $M \geq 6$, (c) $M \geq 7$, and (d) $M \geq 8$. Mean rates are shown by the horizontal lines, 1 and 2 standard deviation ranges are shown by the thin and think vertical lines, respectively.

and separating the epochs based on both changes in M_c, rate, and *b*. That will make the process of choosing epochs more complex. In addition, complexities in the CEUS and PRVI magnitude–frequency distributions suggest changing from considering apparent catalog completeness to considering the magnitude at which the rates best extrapolate to the higher magnitudes used to calculate hazard. Instead of M_c perhaps we should be looking for M_{useful}.

How best to weight the epochs, in either the average or mixture approaches, presents an interesting question. In this study, we weight the epochs by their duration. This was proposed by Felzer (2008) to avoid giving a high weight to recent epochs with low M_c and therefore high numbers of observations with $M \geq M_c$. The latter occurs with the Weichert method (Weichert, 1980), which was used in the 1996 and 2002 NSHM (Frankel, 1995) when M_c decreases over time. If we are using the mixture approach to better capture rate variations and the application is to forecast the rate for the next 50 yr, then perhaps we should give a higher weight to more recent epochs. That would implement a philosophy that the recent past is the best guide to the near future. Even if a decision is made to give higher weight to the recent past, using the Weichert method may still not be optimal. The weighting in that method is based on the amount of data in each epoch, which is heavily influenced by the magnitude of completeness. Instead, it may be better to choose weights that are based on ideas about the variability of seismicity rather than our ability to record small earthquakes.

Because we consider the full distribution of uncertainties in our Monte Carlo process, we need an additional step to reduce the full distribution of rates as a function of magnitude to logic tree branches. Our M_1 approach works well when the magnitude of completeness is less than the minimum magnitude used for estimating hazard and avoids having the branches depend on the maximum magnitude. But the M_1 approach overestimates the range of rates when the magnitude of completeness is within the range of magnitudes used to compute hazard. In that case, at the expense of having to specify the maximum magnitude, the $M_1 - M_{max}$ approach of determining branches produces a better fit between the branches and the distribution of rates as a function of magnitude. For computing hazard directly from the gridded seismicity model, the exact branches (which do not rely on a GR distribution but follow the quantiles of the probability of rate as a function of magnitude) may be the best choice. Whether these non-GR branches are appropriate for other applications, such as the full ERF used for the NSHM, requires further examination by those carrying out each application. For instance, if each logic tree branch is meant to represent a possible reality, then people who conclude that the world displays GR behavior may argue that each branch should be GR. We do start with an initial assumption of GR behavior, and that is used to extrapolate from M_c to other magnitudes within a single sample of the joint distribution. The non-GR behavior of the resulting distribution of rate as a function of magnitude is due to the interaction of the various uncertainties. The exact branches best capture the impact of these uncertainties. If capturing these uncertainties is the primary goal, then the exact branches may be the best choice.

Although choosing branches involves some choices, it is fortunate that the mean hazard is generally robust with respect to how the branches are chosen and whether averages are taken over three- or five-branch logic trees. However, these are

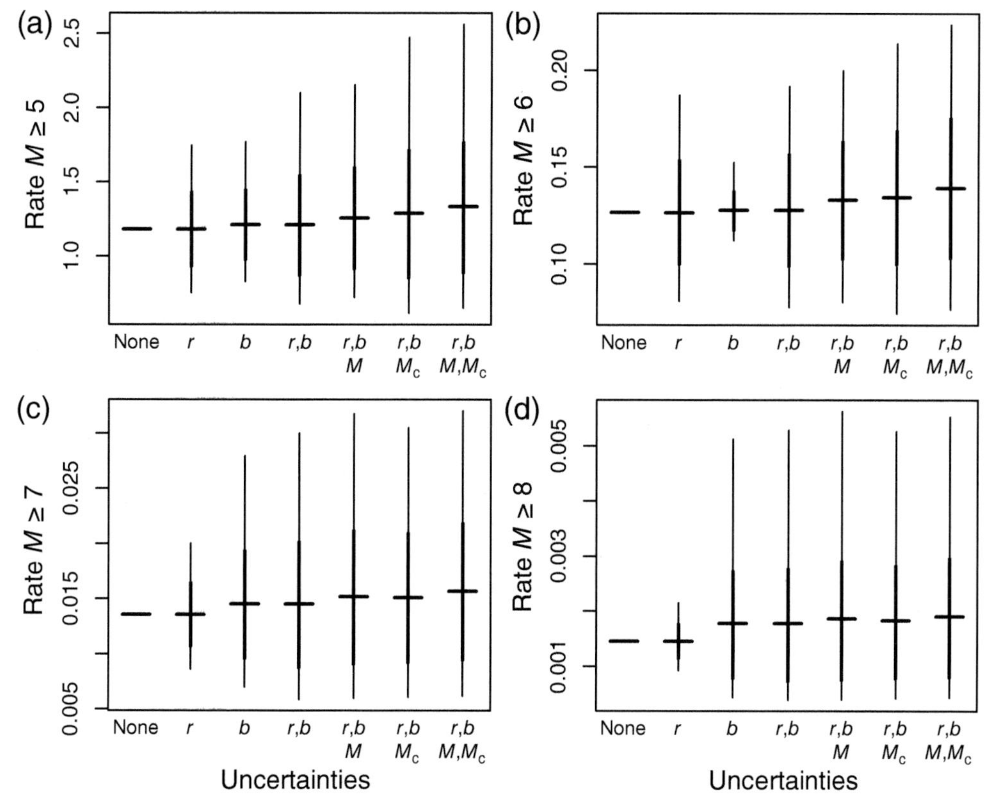

Figure 21. Estimated rate for $M \geq 5$, 6, 7, and 8 events in the PRVI crustal classification from $J_{avg}(\lambda(m \geq M))$ versus the types of uncertainty included. The types of uncertainty are b, b value; M, event magnitude; M_c, magnitude of completeness; r, rate. (a) $M \geq 5$, (b) $M \geq 6$, (c) $M \geq 7$, and (d) $M \geq 8$. Mean rates are shown by the horizontal lines, 1 and 2 standard deviation ranges are shown by the thin and think vertical lines, respectively.

important choices for applications that use fractiles of the hazard and thus depend on an accurate representation of the full distribution of hazard rather than just the mean.

In addition to changing the methodology for computing the gridded seismicity model by separating the total rates from the spatial kernel, we also use the full seismicity catalog, including foreshocks and aftershocks, to compute the seismicity rates. One concern that has been raised by including aftershocks in hazard calculations is that some aftershocks have lower ground motions than their mainshocks (Wooddell, 2014). However, their result applies only to nearby aftershocks that are on the same rupture plane as the mainshock. A more general look at aftershocks reveals that they have a broad range of stress drops and ground motions that are both smaller and larger than those for their respective mainshocks (Baltay *et al.*, 2019). Perhaps some adjustment to the ground-motion modeling from the gridded seismicity model is appropriate, but this requires more consideration before implementation.

Calculating hazard with rates determined from either a declustered or full catalog or a Poisson assumption can overestimate the hazard at higher probabilities, depending on the degree of clustering in the seismicity. A Poisson model is also incapable of accurately determining the hazard if we are interested in the probability of multiple exceedances of a given ground motion (Michael and Llenos, 2022). Overcoming these shortcomings requires abandoning the Poisson model to include clustering in the distribution of earthquake rates. The 2022 Aotearoa New Zealand NSHM improved on using a Poisson process to estimate rate uncertainty by considering the impact of non-Poisson rate changes and clustering on the variance of the seismicity process (Rastin *et al.*, 2024). This increases the range of rates, but it is not yet clear if the shape of that distribution overcomes the issues with computing hazard at high probabilities or for multiple exceedances.

Finally, a starting assumption for this study was using a b value that does not vary over a region or between epochs. That has been the practice for past NSHM efforts. It would be relatively simple to divide a region into multiple regions with different b values and simply carry out the hazard analysis separately for each region. Having the b value vary between epochs would conflict with the averaging approach to combining epochs. This is because the b value must be the same for each epoch in each trial so that averaging the rates across a single trial is meaningful. However, it would be possible to allow for b value variations in the mixture models.

CONCLUSIONS

Separating the gridded seismicity model into the total rates and spatial kernel has allowed us to better capture the epistemic uncertainties in both the total rate model and spatial kernel (Llenos *et al.*, 2024). Determining the joint distribution of earthquake rate and b value using a Monte Carlo approach allows us to consider a broad range of uncertainties. Currently, we consider uncertainty in rate, b value, event magnitudes, and the magnitude of completeness. Because the Monte Carlo approach is flexible, we can easily include other uncertainties or change the form of the uncertainties already under consideration. To best capture variability in rate over time for use in the next 50 yr, our process allows us to explore multiple ways of combining the information from different epochs into the joint distribution, such as averaged or mixture joint distributions, and weighting schemes. The mixture models would also allow for b value variations between epochs.

Once we have the joint distribution, represented as a large set of samples of rate and b value, there are multiple choices for how to include this information in the NSHM logic tree. Because the NSHM logic tree is extremely large, a compact representation of the total rates is helpful. A small number of branches can be selected after projecting the joint distribution into the probability of rate as a function of magnitude. The simple M_1 approach gives GR branches parameterized with a rate and b value and avoids having to specify a maximum magnitude. But the M_1 approach can overestimate the range of rates when the magnitude of completeness is above the minimum magnitude used to compute the hazard. The $M_1 - M_{max}$ approach avoids this issue at the expense of having to specify the maximum magnitude but maintains the simplicity of using GR branches. If non-GR branches are acceptable, then the exact approach of specifying the branches as the quantiles of rate as a function of magnitude is simple in concept, and each branch only requires giving a rate at reasonable magnitude steps, such as 0.1 units.

Fortunately, the mean hazard computed directly from the gridded seismicity is robust with respect to how we choose the rate branches and whether we use a single mean rate branch or three or five branches that span the 95% confidence limits. However, for applications that utilize fractiles of the hazard, these choices are important and should be considered in light of how best to support such applications.

DATA AND RESOURCES

All data used in this article came from published sources listed in the references. All calculations were done with the open-source statistical package R (https://www.R-project.org/, last accessed July 2025).

DECLARATION OF COMPETING INTERESTS

The authors acknowledge that there are no conflicts of interest recorded.

ACKNOWLEDGMENTS

The authors thank Ned Field, Kirstie Haynie, Warner Marzocchi, Kevin Milner, Charles Mueller, Peter Powers, Sepi Rastin, David Rhoades, Chris Rollins, and Allison Shumway for helpful discussions. Kevin Milner, Chris Rollins, and an anonymous reviewer provided useful comments. Any use of trade, firm, or product names is for descriptive purposes only and does not imply endorsement by the U.S. Government.

REFERENCES

Aki, K. (1965). Maximum-likelihood estimate of b in the formula log N=a-bM and its confidence limits, *Bull. Earthq. Res. Inst.* **45,** 237–239.

Amorese, D., J. R. Grasso, and P. A. Rydelek (2010). On varying b-values with depth: Results from computer-intensive tests for southern California, *Geophys. J. Int.* **180,** 347–360, doi: 10.1111/j.1365-246X.2009.04414.x.

Baltay, A. S., T. C. Hanks, and N. A. Abrahamson (2019). Earthquake stress drop and Arias intensity, *J. Geophys. Res.* **124,** 2018JB016753, doi: 10.1029/2018JB016753.

Cornell, C. A., H. Banon, and A. F. Shakal (1979). Seismic motion and response prediction alternatives, *Earthq. Eng. Struct. Dynam.* **7,** 295–315, doi: 10.1002/eqe.4290070402.

Electric Power Research Institute/Department of Energy/Nuclear Regulatory Commission (EPRI/DOE/NRC) (2012). *Central and Eastern United States Seismic Source Characterization for Nuclear Facilities, Final Report*, Palo Alto, California, 3176 pp., available at www.ceus-ssc.com (last accessed October 2022).

Electric Power Research Institute (EPRI) (1988). *Seismic Hazard Methodology for the Central and Eastern United States*, Palo Alto, California, 324 pp., https://www.epri.com/research/products/NP-4726-CCMLV3R1 (last accessed September 2024).

Felzer, K. R. (2008). Calculating California seismicity rates, Appendix I in The Uniform California Earthquake Rupture Forecast, version 2 (UCERF 2), *U.S. Geol. Surv. Open-File Rept. 2007-1437I*, 42 pp.

Felzer, K. R. (2013a). Appendix I: Calculating California seismicity rates, *U.S. Geol. Surv. Open-File Rept. 2007-1437I*, 44 pp.

Felzer, K. R. (2013b). Appendix L—Estimate of the seismicity rate and magnitude-frequency distribution of earthquakes in California from 1850 to 2011, *U.S. Geol. Surv. Open-File Rept. 2013-1165-L*, 13.

Field, E. H., R. J. Arrowsmith, G. P. Biasi, P. Bird, T. E. Dawson, K. R. Felzer, D. D. Jackson, K. M. Johnson, T. H. Jordan, C. Madden, *et al.* (2014). Uniform California Earthquake Rupture Forecast, Version 3 (UCERF3)-The Time-Independent Model, *Bull. Seismol. Soc. Am.* **104,** 1122–1180, doi: 10.1785/0120130164.

Field, E. H., K. R. Milner, A. E. Hatem, P. M. Powers, F. F. Pollitz, A. L. Llenos, Y. Zeng, K. M. Johnson, B. E. Shaw, D. McPhillips, *et al.* (2023). The USGS 2023 conterminous U.S. time-independent earthquake rupture forecast, *Bull. Seismol. Soc. Am.* **114,** 523–571, doi: 10.1785/0120230120.

Frankel, A. (1995). Mapping seismic hazard in the Central and Eastern United States, *Seismol. Res. Lett.* **66,** 8–21.

Gardner, J. K., and L. Knopoff (1974). Is the sequence of earthquakes in southern California, with aftershocks removed, Poissonian? *Bull. Seismol. Soc. Am.* **64,** 1363–1367.

Gutenberg, B., and C. F. Richter (1944). Frequency of earthquakes in California, *Bull. Seismol. Soc. Am.* **34,** 185–188.

Hayes, G. P., G. L. Moore, D. E. Portner, M. Hearne, H. Flamme, M. Furtney, and G. M. Smoczyk (2018). Slab2, a comprehensive subduction zone geometry model, *Science* **362,** 58–61, doi: 10.1126/science.aat4723.

Haynie, K. L. (2024). *Subduction Zone Earthquake Catalog Separation Code, Version 1.0.0: U.S. Geological Survey Software Release*, U.S. Geological Survey, Reston, Virginia, doi: 10.5066/P13E7CAY.

Haynie, K. L., E. M. Thompson, M. Hearne, G. P. Hayes, D. R. Shelly, A. M. Shumway, A. L. Llenos, A. J. Michael, and P. M. Powers (2025). Subduction zone earthquake catalog separation tool: Implementation in the USGS 2025 Puerto Rico and U.S. Virgin Islands National Seismic Hazard Model, *Seismol. Res. Lett.*, 10 pp., doi: 10.1785/0220250078.

Helmstetter, A., Y. Y. Kagan, and D. D. Jackson (2006). Comparison of short-term and time-dependent earthquake forecast models for southern California, *Bull. Seismol. Soc. Am.* **96,** 90–106.

Keefer, D. L., and S. E. Bodily (1983). Three-point approximations for continuous random variables, *Manage. Sci.* **29,** 595–609.

Kulkarni, R. B., R. R. Youngs, and K. J. Coppersmith (1984). Assessment of confidence intervals for results of seismic hazard analysis, *Eight World Conf. on Earthquake Engineering*, San Francisco, California, 21–28 July 1984, 263–270.

Llenos, A. L., and A. J. Michael (2020). Regionally optimized background earthquake rates from ETAS (ROBERE) for probabilistic seismic hazard assessment, *Bull. Seismol. Soc. Am.* **110,** 1172–1190, doi: 10.1785/0120190279.

Llenos, A. L., A. J. Michael, K. L. Haynie, A. M. Shumway, K. L. Haynie, and J. A. Herrick (2025). Using gridded seismicity to forecast the long-term spatial distribution of earthquakes for the 2025 Puerto Rico and U.S. Virgin Islands National Seismic Hazard Model, *Seismol. Res. Lett.*, 33 p (in press).

Llenos, A. L., A. J. Michael, A. M. Shumway, J. L. Rubinstein, K. L. Haynie, M. P. Moschetti, J. M. Altekruse, and K. R. Milner (2024). Forecasting the long-term spatial distribution of earthquakes for the 2023 U.S. National Seismic Hazard Model using gridded seismicity, *Bull. Seismol. Soc. Am.* **114,** 2028–2053, doi: 10.1785/0120230220.

Marzocchi, W., and M. Taroni (2014). Some thoughts on declustering in probabilistic seismic-hazard analysis, *Bull. Seismol. Soc. Am.* **104,** 1838–1845, doi: 10.1785/0120130300.

Michael, A. J. (2014). How complete is the ISC-GEM global earthquake catalog? *Bull. Seismol. Soc. Am.* **104,** 1829–1837, doi: 10.1785/0120130227.

Michael, A. J., and A. L. Llenos (2022). An efficient, analytic solution using order statistics for probabilistic seismic-hazard assessment without the Poisson assumption, *Bull. Seismol. Soc. Am.* **112,** 1678–1693, doi: 10.1785/0120210216.

Miller, A. C. I., and T. R. Rice (1983). Discrete approximation of probability distributions, *Manage. Sci.* **29,** 352–362.

Moschetti, M. P. (2015). A long-term earthquake rate model for the Central and Eastern United States from smoothed seismicity, *Bull. Seismol. Soc. Am.* **105,** 2928–2941, doi: 10.1785/0120140370.

Mueller, C. S. (2018). Earthquake catalogs for the USGS National Seismic Hazard Maps, *Seismol. Res. Lett.* **90,** 251–261, doi: 10.1785/0220170108.

Musson, R. M. W. (2012). The effect of magnitude uncertainty on earthquake activity rates, *Bull. Seismol. Soc. Am.* **102,** 2771–2775, doi: 10.1785/0120110224.

Petersen, M. D., M. P. Moschetti, P. M. Powers, C. S. Mueller, K. M. Haller, A. D. Frankel, Y. Zeng, S. Rezaeian, S. C. Harmsen, O. S. Boyd, *et al.* (2014). Documentation for the 2014 update of the United States National Seismic Hazard Maps, doi: 10.3133/ofr20141091.

Petersen, M. D., A. M. Shumway, P. M. Powers, E. H. Field, M. P. Moschetti, K. S. Jaiswal, K. R. Milner, S. Rezaeian, A. D. Frankel, A. L. Llenos, *et al.* (2023). *Data Release for the 2023 U.S. 50-State National Seismic Hazard Model—Overview, U.S. Geol. Surv. Data Release*, doi: 10.5066/P9GNPCOD.

Petersen, M. D., A. M. Shumway, P. M. Powers, E. H. Field, M. P. Moschetti, K. S. Jaiswal, K. R. Milner, S. Rezaeian, A. D. Frankel, A. L. Llenos, *et al.* (2024). The 2023 US 50-State National Seismic Hazard Model: Overview and implications, *Earthq. Spectra* **40,** 5–88, doi: 10.1177/87552930231215428.

Petersen, M. D., A. M. Shumway, P. M. Powers, M. P. Moschetti, A. L. Llenos, A. J. Michael, C. S. Mueller, A. D. Frankel, S. Rezaeian, K. S. Rukstales, *et al.* (2022). 2021 U.S. National Seismic Hazard Model for the State of Hawaii, *Earthq. Spectra* **38,** 856–916, doi: 10.1177/87552930231223995.

Petersen, M. D., A. M. Shumway, P. M. Powers, C. S. Mueller, M. P. Moschetti, A. D. Frankel, S. Rezaeian, D. E. McNamara, N. Luco, O. S. Boyd, *et al.* (2020). The 2018 update of the US National Seismic Hazard Model: Overview of model and implications, *Earthq. Spectra* **36,** 5–41, doi: 10.1177/8755293019878199.

Powers, P. M., J. M. Altekruse, A. L. Llenos, A. J. Michael, K. L. Haynie, P. J. Haeussler, A. M. Bender, S. Rezaeian, M. P. Moschetti, J. A. Smith, *et al.* (2024). The 2023 Alaska National Seismic Hazard Model, *Earthq. Spectra* **40,** 2545–2597, doi: 10.1177/87552930241266741.

R Core Team (2022). *R: A Language and Environment for Statistical Computing*, R Foundation for Statistical Computing, Vienna, Austria, available at https://www.R-project.org (last accessed July 2025).

Rastin, S. J., D. A. Rhoades, C. Rollins, and M. C. Gerstenberger (2024). Estimation of uncertainty in the average rate of earthquakes exceeding a magnitude threshold, *Seismol. Res. Lett.* **95,** 201–213, doi: 10.1785/0220230242.

Rhoades, D. A. (1996). Estimation of the Gutenberg-Richter relation allowing for individual earthquake magnitude uncertainties, *Tectonophysics* **258,** 71–83, doi: 10.1016/0040-1951(95)00182-4.

Rhoades, D. A., and D. J. Dowrick (2000). Effects of magnitude uncertainties on seismic hazard estimates, *12WCEE 2000: 12th World Conf. on Earthquake Engineering, 1179*, Aukland, New Zealand, 30 January–4 February 2000, 1–7.

Rollins, C., M. C. Gerstenberger, D. A. Rhoades, S. J. Rastin, A. Christophersen, K. K. S. Thingbaijam, R. J. Van Dissen, K. Graham, C. DiCaprio, and J. Fraser (2024). The magnitude–frequency distributions of earthquakes in Aotearoa New Zealand and on adjoining subduction zones, using a new integrated earthquake catalog, *Bull. Seismol. Soc. Am.* **114,** 150–181, doi: 10.1785/0120230177.

Shumway, A. M., K. R. Milner, J. M. Altekruse, J. A. Herrick, A. L. Llenos, A. J. Michael, K. L. Haynie, R. W. Briggs, K. S. Jaiswal, P. M. Powers, *et al.* (2025). Datasets for the 2025 USGS National Seismic Hazard Model for Puerto Rico and the U.S. Virgin Islands, *U.S. Geol. Surv. Data Release* (in press), doi: 10.5066/P14ATJLJ.

Tinti, S., and F. Mulargia (1985). Effects of magnitude uncertainties on estimating parameters in the Gutenberg-Richter frequency-magnitude law, *Bull. Seismol. Soc. Am.* **75,** 1681–1697.

Utsu, T. (1966). A statistical significance test of the difference in b-value between two groups of earthquakes, *J. Phys. Earth* **14,** 34–40.

van der Elst, N. (2021). A robust estimator of aftershock magnitude distribution in transiently incomplete catalogs, *J. Geophys. Res.* **126,** e2020JB021027, doi: 10.1029/2020JB021027.

Weichert, D. H. (1980). Estimation of earthquake recurrence parameters for unequal observation periods for different magnitudes, *Bull. Seismol. Soc. Am.* **70,** 1337–1356.

Wooddell, K. E. (2014). Classification of main shocks and aftershocks in the NGA-West2 database, *Earthq. Spectra* **30,** 1257–1267, doi: 10.1193/071913EQS208M.

Working Group on California Earthquake Probabilities (2003). Earthquake probabilities in the San Francisco Bay region: 2002-2031, *U.S. Geol. Surv. Open-File Rept., 03-214*, doi: 10.3133/ofr03214.

Manuscript received 16 October 2024
Published online 31 December 2025

Paleoseismology of the Zougahana Fault, Northern Aso Outer Rim, and Its Role in the Tectonics of Northern Kyushu

Keitaro Komura*[1], Hiroshi P. Sato[2], Hiroshi Yagi[3], Takayuki Nakano[4], and Hiroshi Une[5]

ABSTRACT

The Kumamoto earthquake (M_{JMA} 6.5 and 7.3) occurred on 14 and 16 April 2016, with the epicenter on the Futagawa and Hinagu faults, central Kyushu Island, southwest Japan. Differential Interferometric Synthetic Aperture Radar analyses detected many phase discontinuities in the source region. Phase discontinuities and ruptures were also confirmed at the Zougahana fault on the northeastern rim of Aso caldera, ~14 km northeast of the Futagawa fault. In this study, we conducted topographic interpretations, field surveys, outcrop descriptions and interpretations, and coring investigations of the Zougahana fault. We clarified that at least four earthquakes have occurred since 10 ka, including the 2016 earthquake. Among the events preceding the 2016 earthquake, the ages of the most recent three were estimated to be 5760–2750 cal B.P., 8700–5000 cal B.P., and 9330–7550 cal B.P. based on tephra and radiocarbon ages in the sediments. However, we note the possibility of missing events around 2 ka. Comparison with the paleoseismic history of the primary Futagawa fault and surrounding secondary faults suggests that the Zougahana fault is among the secondary faults that have repeatedly interacted with the Futagawa fault. The distribution of aftershocks and our analysis of seismic intensity and Coulomb stress change indicate that the trigger for the Zougahana fault may have been strong ground motions. However, seismogenic rupture of the fault during an aftershock 1.5 hr after the mainshock cannot be ruled out, implying that secondary faults around Aso caldera, including the Zougahana fault, may have slipped because of various triggers. Furthermore, within the transtensional tectonics model, which views the complex of volcanoes, grabens, and strike-slip faults that fan out across central Kyushu as a single unit, the Zougahana fault may not be a simple secondary fault on the surface but rather part of the main shear structure.

KEY POINTS

- The Zougahana fault, ~14 km northeast of the primary fault, ruptured during the 2016 Kumamoto earthquake.
- Six earthquakes, including the 2016 earthquake, were identified on the Zougahana fault.
- The 2016 rupture was likely triggered by the mainshock or seismogenic rupture by an aftershock.

Supplemental Material

INTRODUCTION

The Futagawa and Hinagu faults are active faults in central Kyushu Island, Japan, and are located on the southern edge of the Beppu-Shimabara graben zone (BSGZ) (Matsumoto, 1979) (Fig. 1a,b). In 2016, successive earthquakes of M_{JMA} 6.5 (M_w 6.2) at 21:26 JST on 14 April and of M_{JMA} 7.3 (M_w 7.0) at 01:25 JST on 16 April occurred along the Futagawa and Hinagu faults (the 2016 Kumamoto earthquake sequence; Earthquake Research Committee, the Headquarters for Earthquake Research Promotion, 2016). In this contribution, we use "the 2016 Kumamoto earthquake" or "the 2016 earthquake" to refer to the mainshock that occurred on 16 April. During this earthquake, a 30–34-km-long right-lateral rupture occurred along the Futagawa and northern part of the Hinagu faults from

1. Central Research Institute of Electric Power Industry, Abiko-shi, Japan, https://orcid.org/0000-0001-8715-5053 (KK); 2. Nihon University, College of Humanities and Science, Tokyo, Japan, https://orcid.org/0000-0003-2350-9478 (HPS); 3. Fukada Geological Institute, Tokyo, Japan; 4. Geospatial Information Authority of Japan, Tsukuba, Japan, https://orcid.org/0000-0001-9170-4377 (TN); 5. Ochanomizu University, Tokyo, Japan, https://orcid.org/0000-0002-4455-772X (HU)

*Corresponding author: komukeit@criepi.denken.or.jp

Cite this article as Komura, K., H. P. Sato, H. Yagi, T. Nakano, and H. Une (2025). Paleoseismology of the Zougahana Fault, Northern Aso Outer Rim, and Its Role in the Tectonics of Northern Kyushu, *Bull. Seismol. Soc. Am.* **116**, 810–836, doi: 10.1785/0120250184

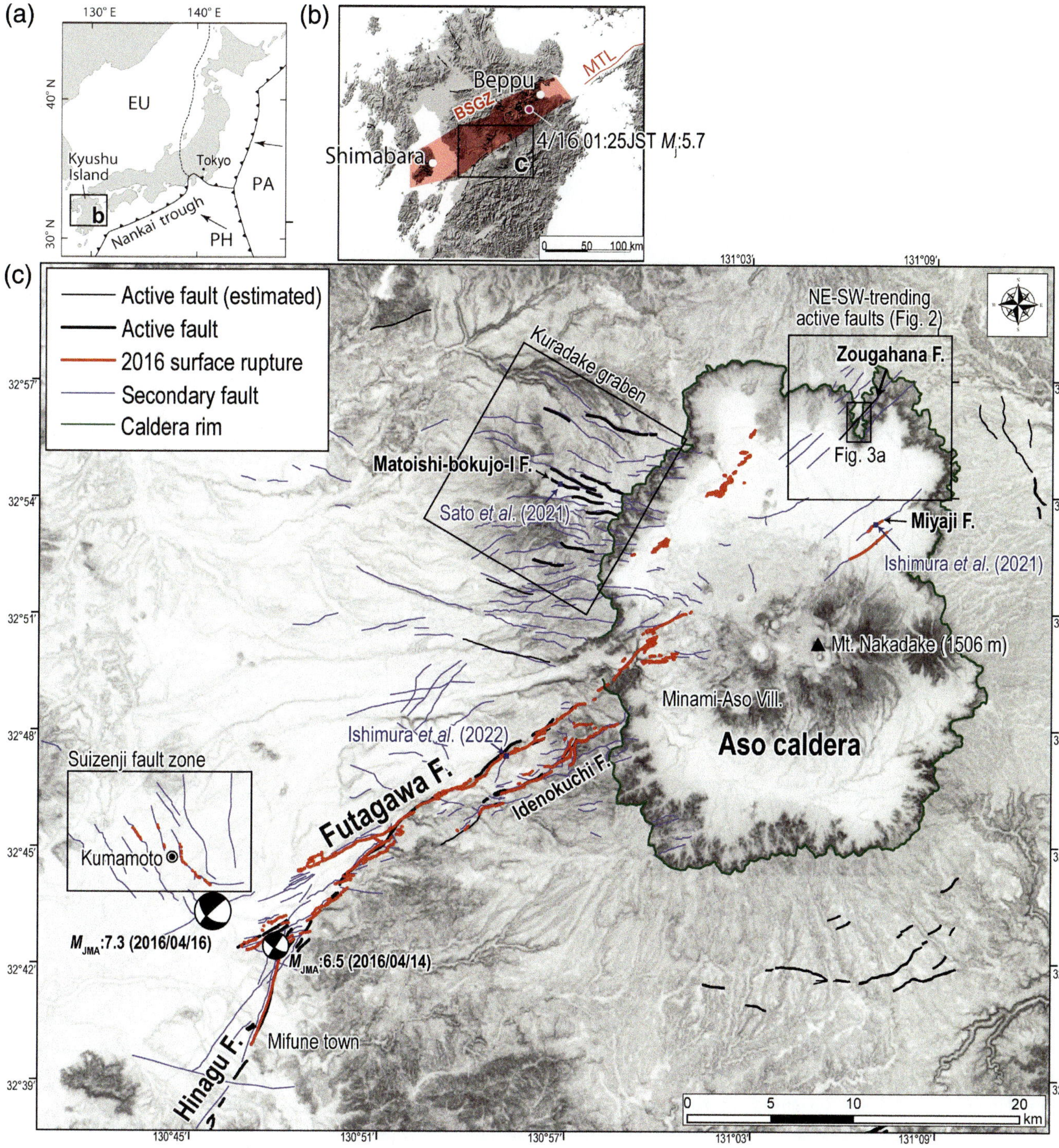

Mifune town in the southwest to Minami-Aso village in the northeast (Fig. 1c; Shirahama *et al.*, 2016; Kumahara *et al.*, 2022). Interferometric Synthetic Aperture Radar (InSAR) analysis of the 2016 earthquake confirmed numerous phase discontinuities around the Futagawa and Hinagu faults (Fujiwara *et al.*, 2016). Field surveys also revealed that some phase discontinuities had caused surface deformations (Goto *et al.*, 2017; Ishimura *et al.*, 2021; Une *et al.*, 2022). In this study, we refer to phase discontinuities confirmed in the field as secondary faults that are distinct from the primary fault (here the Futagawa fault) following the definition by Ishimura *et al.* (2021). Based on

Figure 1. (a) Location of the study area in Kyushu, southwestern Japan. (b) Topography and location of the study area in Kyushu. (c) Location and topographic map of the epicentral area of the 2016 Kumamoto earthquake. The black lines indicate traces of active and inferred active faults from Nakata and Imaizumi (2002), red lines indicate surface rupture traces of the 2016 Kumamoto earthquake from Kumahara *et al.* (2022), and blue lines represent phase discontinuities identified by Fujiwara *et al.* (2016). The trace of the Zougahana fault, the main target of this study, is based on Watanabe (1984). The background slope map was created from the Geospatial Information Authority of Japan (GSI) 10-m-mesh digital elevation model (DEM). BSGZ, Beppu–Shimabara graben zone; EU, Eurasia plate, MTL, median tectonic line; NE, northeast; PA, Pacific plate; PH, Philippine Sea plate; SW, southwest.

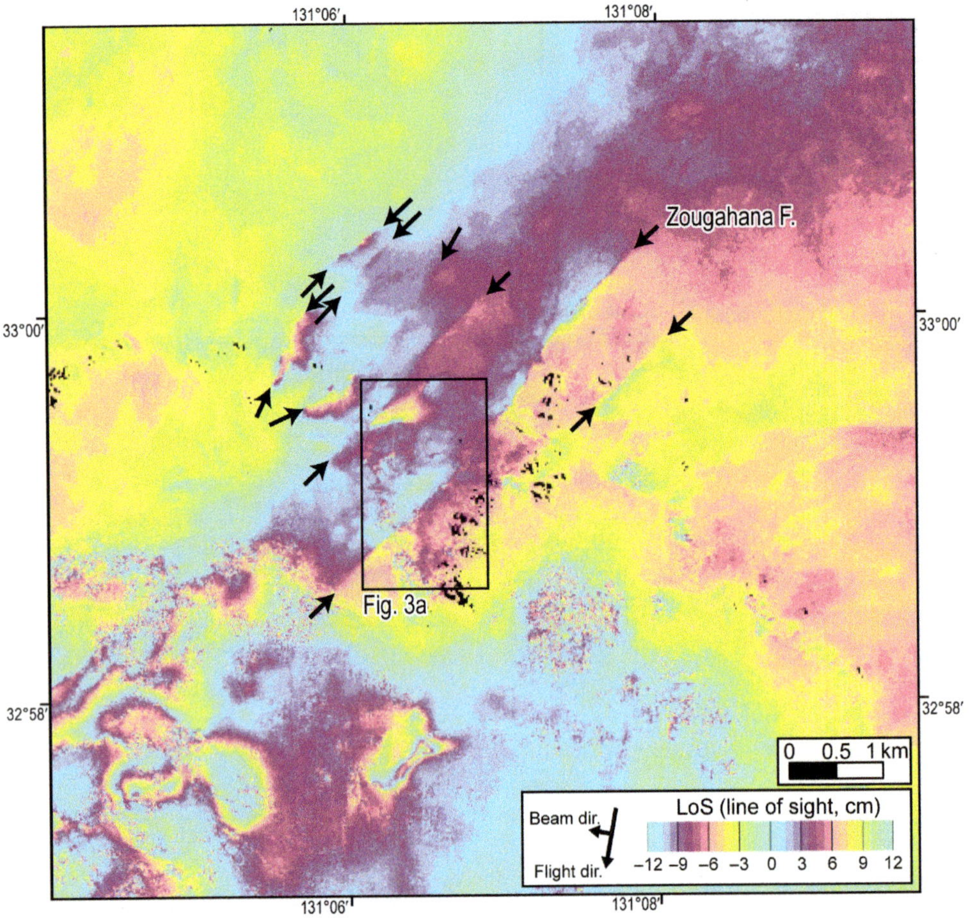

Figure 2. Interferogram of the Zougahana fault area from before and after the 2016 earthquake (location shown in Fig. 1c). The images were taken on 7 March and 18 April 2016 looking south and were created based on Geospatial Information Authority of Japan (GSI) maps.

subsequent coring data and trench surveys, it is becoming clear that some of these secondary faults have been activated repeatedly in the past (Goto *et al.*, 2017; Inoue *et al.*, 2020; Ishimura *et al.*, 2021; Sato *et al.*, 2021).

Several interpretations have been offered for the triggering of secondary faults associated with the 2016 Kumamoto earthquake in different regions. In the area of Kumamoto city west of the Futagawa fault, the Suizenji fault zone (Fig. 1c) is thought to have slipped because of the Coulomb stress change (ΔCFF, e.g., King *et al.*, 1994) associated with the rupture of the Futagawa fault (Goto *et al.*, 2017). Many secondary faults with a normal fault sense appeared in the Kuradake graben northwest of Aso caldera (Fig. 1c) (Fujiwara *et al.*, 2016; Une *et al.*, 2022) and have been attributed to the release of background north–south tensile stress triggered by the strong ground motions of the 2016 earthquake (Fujiwara *et al.*, 2020). Furthermore, multiple northeast–southwest-trending phase discontinuities were identified extending from the Futagawa fault's northeastern end to the northeastern rim of Aso caldera. The Miyaji fault (Fig. 1c), which has the same right-lateral sense as the Futagawa fault, is estimated to have repeatedly interacted with the Futagawa fault in the past (Ishimura *et al.*, 2021), although the triggering mechanism is not yet understood. Toda and Ishimura (2019) showed that two secondary faulting mechanisms occurred during the 2016 Kumamoto earthquake: ΔCFF triggering and dynamic triggering, both caused by the rupture of the Futagawa fault. The articles listed earlier suggest that secondary faulting can be triggered by diverse mechanisms, even for a single earthquake.

Clarifying the triggers of secondary faulting is important for assessing the potential for off-fault displacements and impacts on important structures (e.g., International Atomic Energy Agency [IAEA], 2010; Petersen *et al.*, 2011). In particular, secondary faults occurring along the direction of extension of a strike-slip fault provide important data for evaluating the characteristics of the fault tips, such as dispersion, extension, and step (King and Nábělek, 1985; Wesnousky, 1988, 2006; Lettis *et al.*, 2002; Kim and Sanderson, 2006; Biasi and Wesnousky, 2016, 2017). Together with this insight, central Kyushu Island has a unique geological structure, featuring multiple active volcanoes and grabens attributed to the oblique subduction of the Philippine Sea plate (e.g., Matsumoto, 1979; Hatanaka and Shimazaki, 1988; Chida, 1992; Oohashi *et al.*, 2020). Understanding whether secondary faulting that occurred in this tectonic setting is common or unique compared with typical strike-slip fault systems will also contribute to a more accurate evaluation of off-fault displacement hazards.

In this study, we focused on a 4.8-km-long phase discontinuity that appeared ~14 km northeast of the Futagawa fault along its direction of extension (Fig. 2) and that was previously interpreted by Fujiwara *et al.* (2016). This phase discontinuity appears to have been caused by activity on the Zougahana fault, a short fault ~3.5 km long (Fig. 1c; Obata, 1998) that roughly matches the trend of the phase discontinuity. The Zougahana fault occurs in a relatively fault-free area of the BSGZ (Fig. 1b) and may be an important factor in understanding the tectonics of the central Kyushu. Therefore, we conducted a paleoseismic

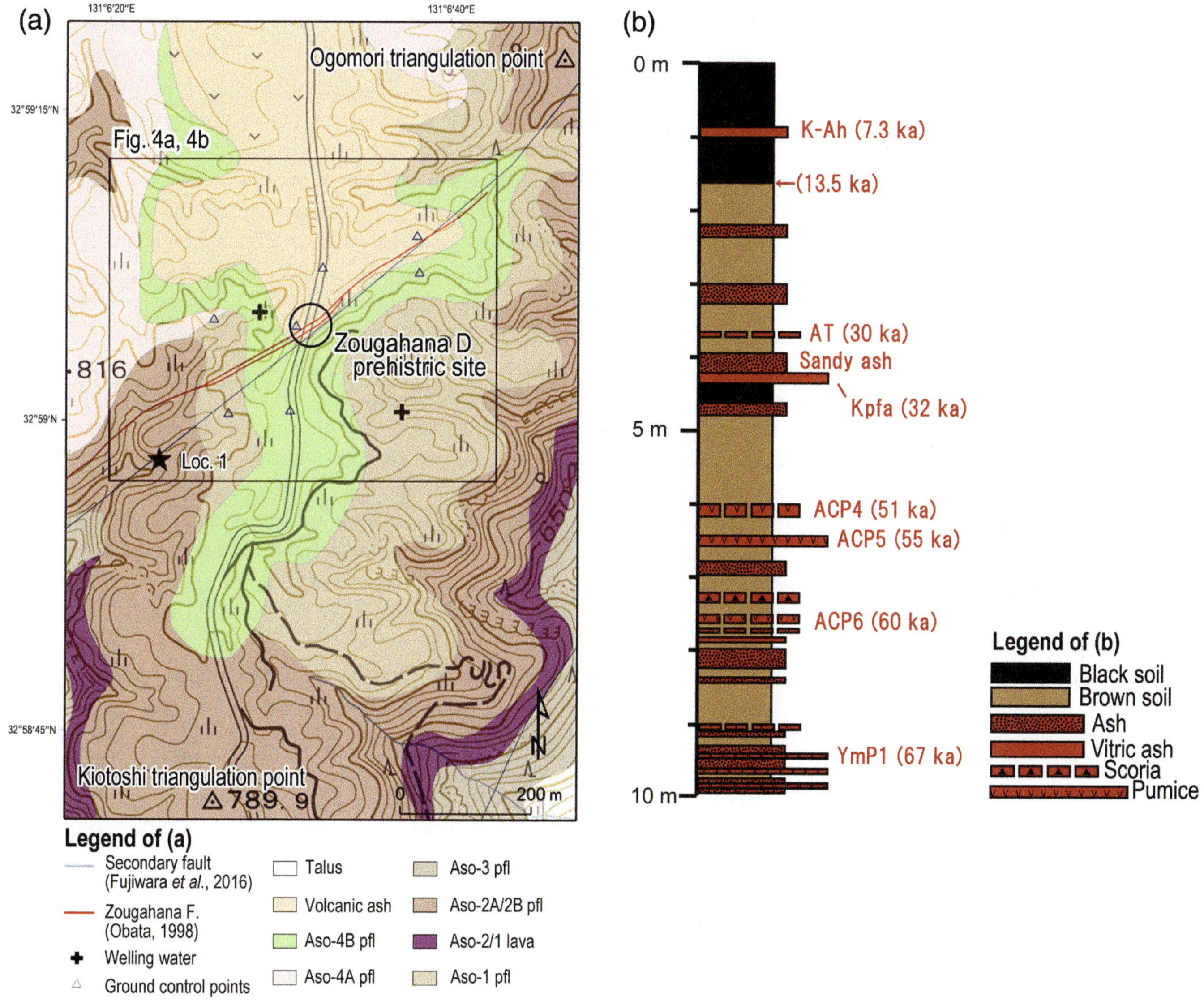

Figure 3. (a) Geological map of the area around the Zougahana D prehistoric site based on Ono and Watanabe (1985) and Obata (1998) (location shown in Fig. 1c). The traces of phase discontinuities and the Zougahana fault are after Fujiwara *et al.* (2016) and Obata (1998), respectively.
(b) Representative stratigraphic log showing the tephra stratigraphy of the northeastern part of Aso caldera, based on Miyabuchi and Sugiyama (2011).

field survey targeting the Zougahana fault to clarify its activity and association with the Futagawa fault. We also examined the trigger of the 2016 activity on the Zougahana fault from the perspectives of seismology and geology. Based on our results, we considered the role of this fault in the overall tectonics of central Kyushu.

OVERVIEW OF THE ZOUGAHANA D PREHISTORIC SITE AND GEOMORPHOLOGY IN THE NORTHEASTERN PART OF ASO CALDERA

The Futagawa fault, which was the main source of the 2016 Kumamoto earthquake, is an active fault with a northeast–southwest strike that extends from Kumamoto city center to Aso caldera (Fig. 1c). In addition, several other relatively short active faults have been identified around Aso caldera (e.g., Watanabe, 1984; The Research Group for Active Tectonics in Kyushu, 1989; Suzuki *et al.*, 2017). Of these, Watanabe (1984) identified a group of northeast–southwest-trending active faults in the northeastern part of Aso caldera (Fig. 1c). This group includes the Zougahana fault, which crosses the Zougahana D prehistoric site (Fig. 3a), containing relics from the late Paleolithic era (33–13 ka in Japan, Tsutsumi, 2003), as a northeast–southwest-striking fault, with the northwest being the downthrown side (Obata, 1998). They did not explicitly state whether this fault is a normal fault or a reverse fault but noted that the displacement cannot be explained by gravitational slumping toward the northwest.

The Zougahana D prehistoric site is located on a plateau that juts southward into Aso caldera at ~800 m elevation (Fig. 1c), and it encompasses a circular area of ~100 m in diameter, including the roadside outcrop described in detail later (Fig. 3a). Whereas the plateau is situated ~300 m above the caldera floor and the lower part of the caldera wall (below 650 m elevation) is a moderate scarp, the upper part of the caldera wall (650–800 m elevation) forms a steep scarp. According to Ono and Watanabe (1985), this steep scarp is composed of ejecta from past large-scale eruptions at Aso caldera (Fig. 3a), including the lower Aso-1 pyroclastic flow deposits (about 280–250 ka; Matsumoto *et al.*, 1991), the Aso-2/1 lava (about 260–190 ka and 150–140 ka; Matsumoto *et al.*, 1991), the Aso-2 pyroclastic flow deposits (about 140 ka; Matsumoto *et al.*, 1991), the Aso-3 pyroclastic flow deposits (about 130–120 ka; Matsumoto *et al.*, 1991), and the Aso-4 pyroclastic flow deposits (about 87 ka; Aoki, 2008). Most of the pyroclastic flow deposits are welded tuffs. In particular, the numerous black obsidian lithics found at the Zougahana D prehistoric site have been confirmed to originate from the Aso-2 welded tuff of this caldera wall (Watanabe *et al.*, 2001). The upper part of the plateau is covered by thick volcanic ash and aeolian loam that accumulated after the Aso-4 pyroclastic flow deposits.

The volcanic ash stratigraphy in the northeastern part of Aso caldera, including the Zougahana D prehistoric site, was investigated in detail by Miyabuchi *et al.* (2003) and Miyabuchi and Sugiyama (2011). They integrated the results of tephra surveys at multiple locations surrounding the Zougahana D prehistoric site and summarized the tephra stratigraphy and vegetation changes over the past 90,000 yr. Figure 3b is an excerpt from their schematic column up to 10 m depth. About 20 ash, vitric ash, scoria, and pumice layers exist, but most are petrographically similar minor tephras (e.g., YmS series; Miyabuchi, 2009) from the central cone in Aso caldera. They are therefore difficult to distinguish as chronological indicators in the stratum.

Nonetheless, three tephras described subsequently can be used as key age markers. The most versatile is the Kikai Akahoya (K-Ah) tephra, which erupted from the Kikai caldera in southern Kyushu at around 7.3 ka and is widely distributed from the Kyushu region to western Japan; this tephra is easily identifiable and useful for dating Holocene soils (e.g., Machida and Arai, 2003). In the Aso region, it occurs as a distinct orange layer in the black soil just below the surface (e.g., Miyabuchi and Sugiyama, 2011) and is easily identified by eye (Machida and Arai, 2003). The Aira Tn (AT) tephra was erupted from the Aira caldera in southern Kyushu about 30 ka and is also a highly versatile marker tephra that is used to date glacial deposits throughout Japan (e.g., Machida and Arai, 2003). In the Aso region, it is often recognized as being slightly lighter in color than the surrounding brown soil (e.g., Miyabuchi, 2009; Miyabuchi and Sugiyama, 2011). Although more difficult to identify by eye than the K-Ah tephra, the AT tephra is easily identified based on the refractive index of bubble-wall glass and major element analysis (Machida and Arai, 2003). Another local tephra distributed around Aso caldera is the Aso-Kusasenrigahama pumice (Kpfa; Watanabe *et al.*, 1982); distal deposits are also referred to as "Aso-K" (Machida and Arai, 2003). In the Aso area, it is recognized as a distinct orange pumice layer directly below the AT tephra (e.g., Miyabuchi, 2009; Miyabuchi and Sugiyama, 2011). Recent research on varves in Suigetsu Lake (central Japan) has constrained the eruption ages of the K-Ah and AT tephras to 7303–7165 cal B.P. and 30,009 ± 189 cal B.P., respectively (Smith *et al.*, 2013), and the eruption age of the Kpfa has been estimated as 32,647–32,376 cal B.P. (McLean *et al.*, 2020).

Obata (1998) classified the strata at the Zougahana D prehistoric site based on the results of outcrop and pit excavations and clarified that the strata included the K-Ah, AT, and Kpfa tephras. They also described multiple faults cutting through these tephra layers, displacing the Kpfa tephra by ~1.7 m vertically. Because all these faults cut the loam layer containing the 7.3 ka K-Ah tephra, they are certainly active faults. However, Obata (1998) did not provide more detailed information related to the displacement, such as the specific displacement amount of each layer and the timing of fault activity. Maps and databases of active faults around Aso caldera published since Obata (1998) do not include the trace of the Zougahana fault (e.g., Nakata and Imaizumi, 2002; Suzuki *et al.*, 2017; Imaizumi *et al.*, 2018; National Institute of Advanced Industrial Science and Technology, 2025), and detailed paleoseismic investigations have not been conducted to this day.

Methods

Geomorphologic and geologic surveys

To understand the detailed topography around the Zougahana fault, we created a morphometric protection index red relief image map (MPI-RRIM; Kaneda and Chiba, 2019) from a 1-m-resolution airborne light detection and ranging digital elevation model acquired by the Kyushu Regional Development Bureau of the Ministry of Land, Infrastructure, Transport, and Tourism in 2010, that is, before the 2016 Kumamoto earthquake (Fig. 4a). We made topographic interpretation using this MPI-RRIM (Fig. 4b,c). Furthermore, to map the topography at the Zougahana D prehistoric site in more detail, aerial photographs were acquired after the 2016 earthquake using a DJI Phantom 4 Pro unmanned aerial vehicle (UAV), from which a topographic map was generated (Fig. 5a). Before the UAV photography, we set eight real-time kinematic-Global Navigation Satellite System reference points (Fig. 3a). Using these reference coordinates, we generated a 3D image using structure from motion and multiview stereo (SfM-MVS) photogrammetry software (Agisoft Metashape, professional version) and generated a contour map. We also cut as much grass as possible over the 2016 rupture trace before the UAV photography. In addition, the wall of the surveyed outcrop and the location of the hand-coring survey described

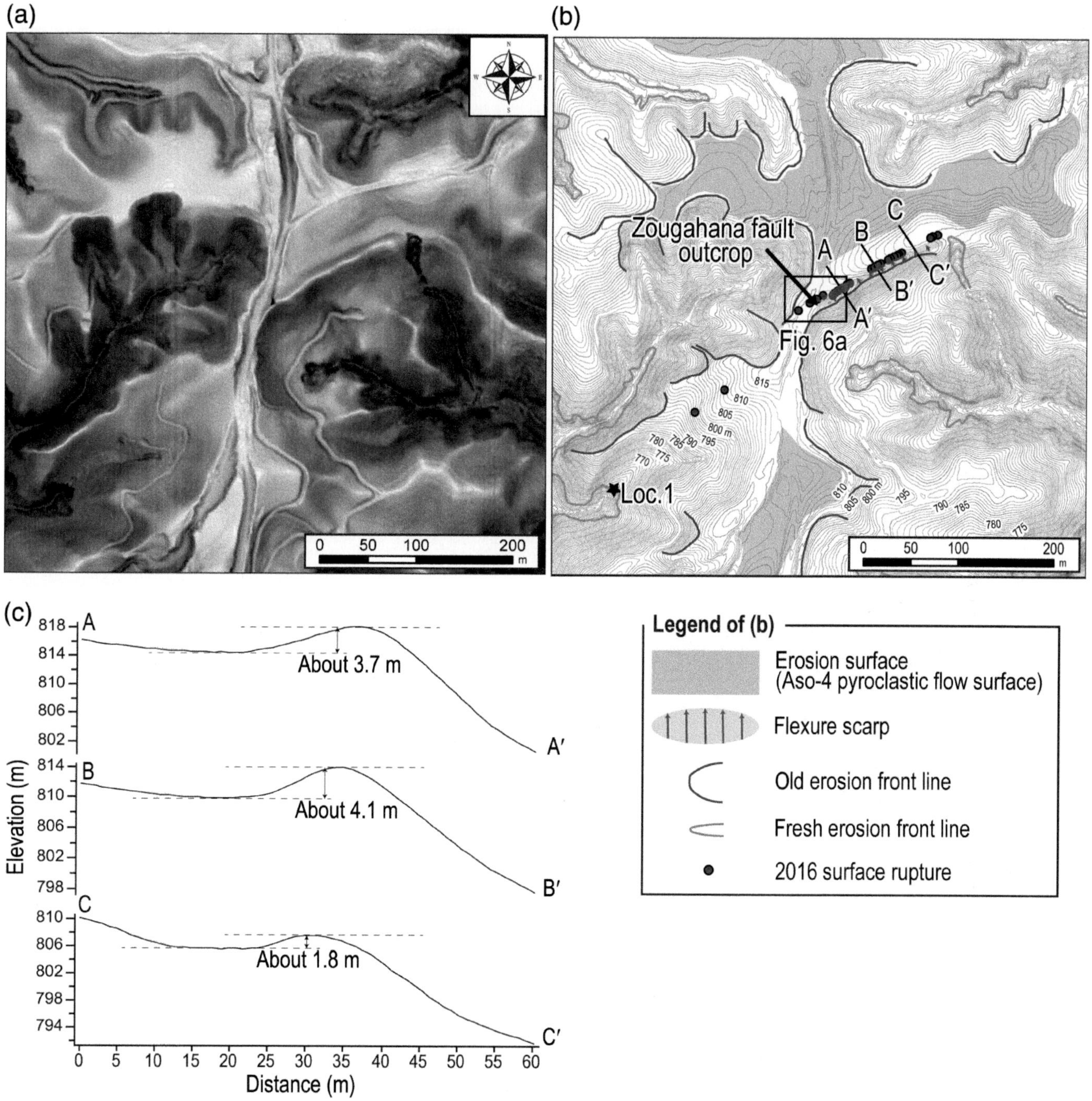

Figure 4. (a) MPI-RRIM of the area around the Zougahana D prehistoric site based on a 1-m-mesh lidar detection and ranging (LiDAR) digital elevation model (DEM) (location shown in Fig. 3a). (b) Geomorphic map of the same area. Background contours at 1 m intervals were created from the same LiDAR DEM. (c) Topographic cross sections of the scarp along the Zougahana fault (see (b) for location of the cross sections). The color version of this figure is available only in the electronic edition.

subsequently were measured using a total station (Nikon DTM-503) based on the aforementioned reference points. Furthermore, we conducted a surface survey of the area around the Zougahana D prehistoric site to track the 2016 rupture, search for fault outcrops, and confirm the surface geology (Fig. 5b–d).

Measurement of 2016 rupture fault displacement

Shirahama *et al.* (2016), Suzuki *et al.* (2017), and Kumahara *et al.* (2022) comprehensively mapped surface ruptures of the 2016 Kumamoto earthquake but did not recognize surface ruptures along the Zougahana fault. However, our field survey after the 2016 earthquake revealed a rupture in the paved road within the Zougahana D prehistoric site (Fig. 5a,b). The rupture was not visible in the Google Earth image taken before the earthquake, suggesting that this displacement formed during

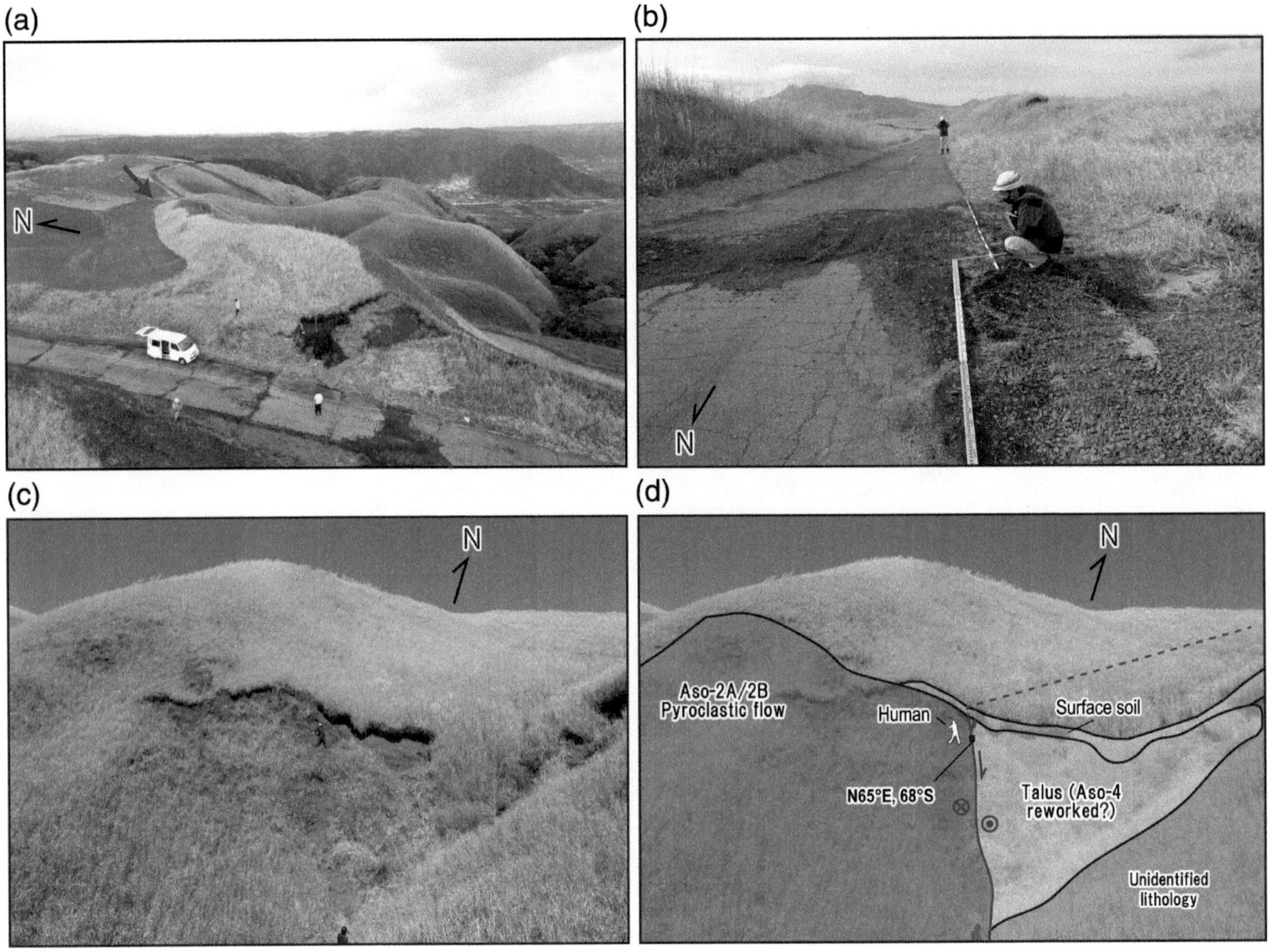

Figure 5. (a) Unmanned aerial vehicle (UAV) image of the Zougahana fault outcrop viewed from the west. Intermittent cracks created by the 2016 earthquake apparent in this view are indicated by red arrows.
(b) Photograph of the 2016 rupture across the paved road in front of the Zougahana fault outcrop. (c) Fault outcrop found ~290 m southwest of the Zougahana fault outcrop (Loc. 1 shown in Figs. 3a and 4b). (d) Geologic interpretation of the outcrop in (c). The color version of this figure is available only in the electronic edition.

the 2016 earthquake. To accurately evaluate this rupture's vertical and horizontal displacement, we surveyed a paved road surface using a total station, referring to the reference points shown in Figure 3a. The sideline's length was 50 m, and the distance between measurement points was 0.5 m. However, in areas with rapid displacement, more narrowly spaced points were used to measure displacement. The final measured displacement, reported as a value with a plus or minus error, was determined by the method of Kaneda *et al.* (2008) by creating best-fit lines with $\pm 1\sigma$ uncertainty drawn from the upthrown and downthrown sides and then reading the minimum and maximum values within ±20 m of the fault and setting them as values with ± error (Fig. 6a,b).

Detection of the up–down component of fault deformation using InSAR

To clarify the vertical movements around the Zougahana D prehistoric site caused by the 2016 Kumamoto earthquake, a Synthetic Aperture Radar (SAR) interferogram was generated from PALSAR-2 data (Table 1) acquired before and after the earthquake along ascending and descending orbits, from which we estimated the quasi-vertical and horizontal movements around the Zougahana fault (Fig. 7). We used RINC version 0.43 (Ozawa *et al.*, 2016) to process the PALSAR-2 data and followed the 2.5D analysis method of Fujiwara *et al.* (2000) to calculate the quasi-vertical and horizontal movements. In detail, each plane includes two line-of-sight deformation vectors perpendicular to (to the right of) the ascending and descending orbits at all ground points in the SAR image. The quasi-vertical component was calculated as the 2D deformation on the plane approximately vertical to the ground point. Note that because of atmospheric delay errors and residual east–west components, this method can introduce general vertical errors of several centimeters (~1–3 cm) and locally up to ~5 cm (Fujiwara *et al.*, 2000).

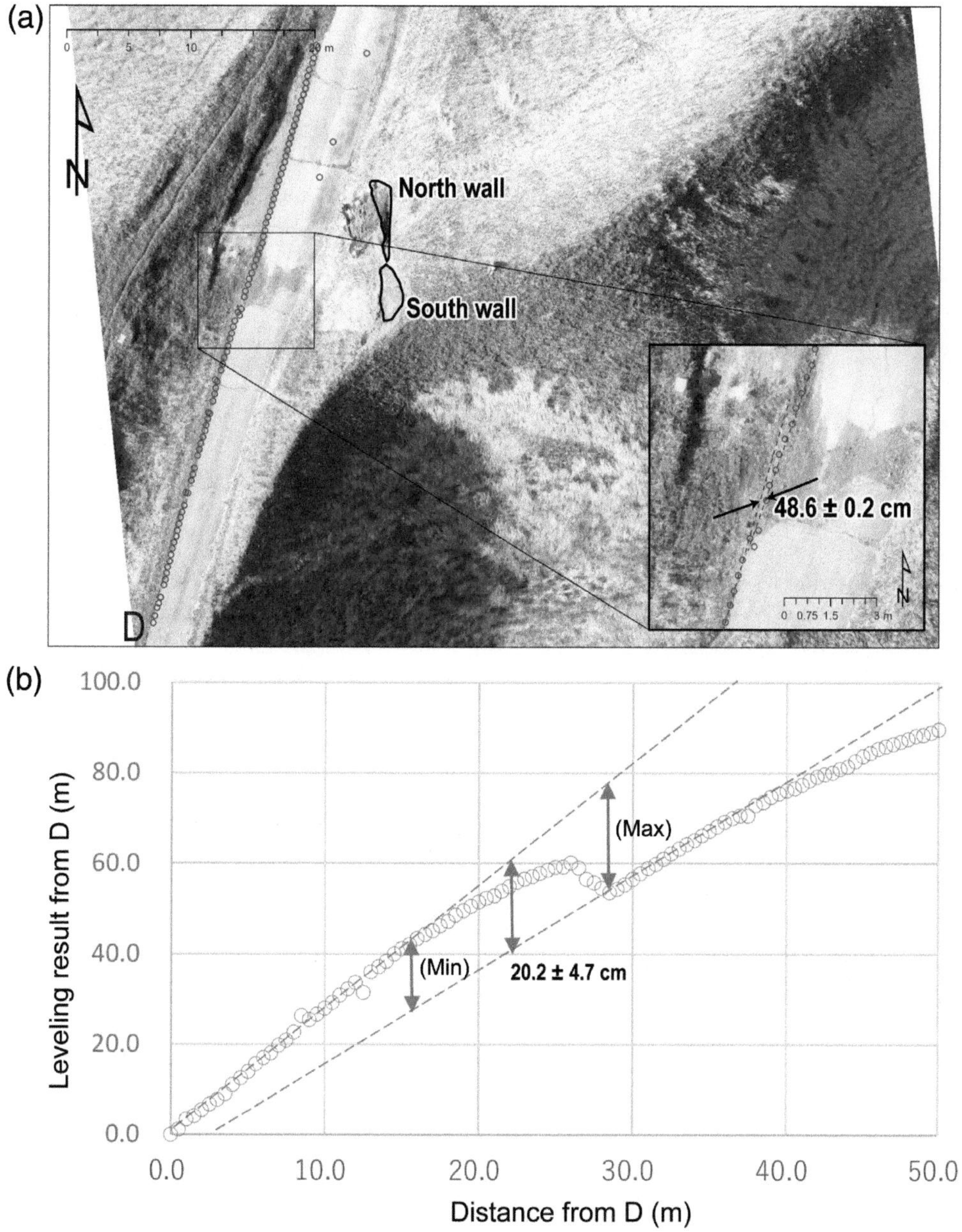

Figure 6. (a) Results of horizontal deformation measurements based on the total station survey along the paved road. The background image is an aerial photo taken by UAV in April 2021 (location shown in Fig. 4b). (b) Measured vertical deformation along the transect shown in (a). The color version of this figure is available only in the electronic edition.

Log of the Zougahana fault outcrop

Obata (1998) described the Zougahana fault outcrop located east of the paved road running north–south through the Zougahana D prehistoric site (Fig. 5a). The Zougahana fault outcrop was covered by vegetation and alluvial soil at the time of our survey. Although we planned to widen the outcrop using heavy machinery, it is in a culturally protected area by local government, and we could not do so. Therefore, we could only remove the surface vegetation and sediment from the existing outcrop and observe and describe the outcrop to reconstruct the 2016 rupture and prior displacements. While exposing the outcrop, we did not find any archaeological artifacts.

We exposed two walls: the north wall, ~4-m-high and 7.5-m-long north to south, and the south wall, ~4-m-high and 3.5-m-long north to south. Although the north and south walls are offset by ~1 m in the direction perpendicular to the wall's surfaces (i.e., the north wall is further back when looking at the walls toward the east), they are treated as continuous sections overlapping over a 1-m-long section. Our final log diagram connects the two walls accordingly.

TABLE 1
Specifications of the Advanced Land Observation Satellite (ALOS)-2 Data Used in This Study

Path	Frame	Orbit	Range	Observation Date (yyyy/mm/dd, yyyy/mm/dd)	Polarization	Mode	Off Nadir Angle
130	50	Ascending	Right	2015/11/19, 2016/10/20	HH	SM1 (3 m)	32.4°
23	950	Descending	Right	2019/03/07, 2016/04/18	HH	SM1 (3 m)	32.4°

outcrop to a depth of 4 m at two locations; from these cores, we collected samples for tephra analysis. We performed a similar hand auger survey at two sites along the paved road to the northwest of the fault outcrop and at two sites along the paved road to the southeast (Fig. 9a,b). A detailed description of hand cores and a detailed description of the stratigraphy of the Zougahana fault outcrop are provided in supplement 2.

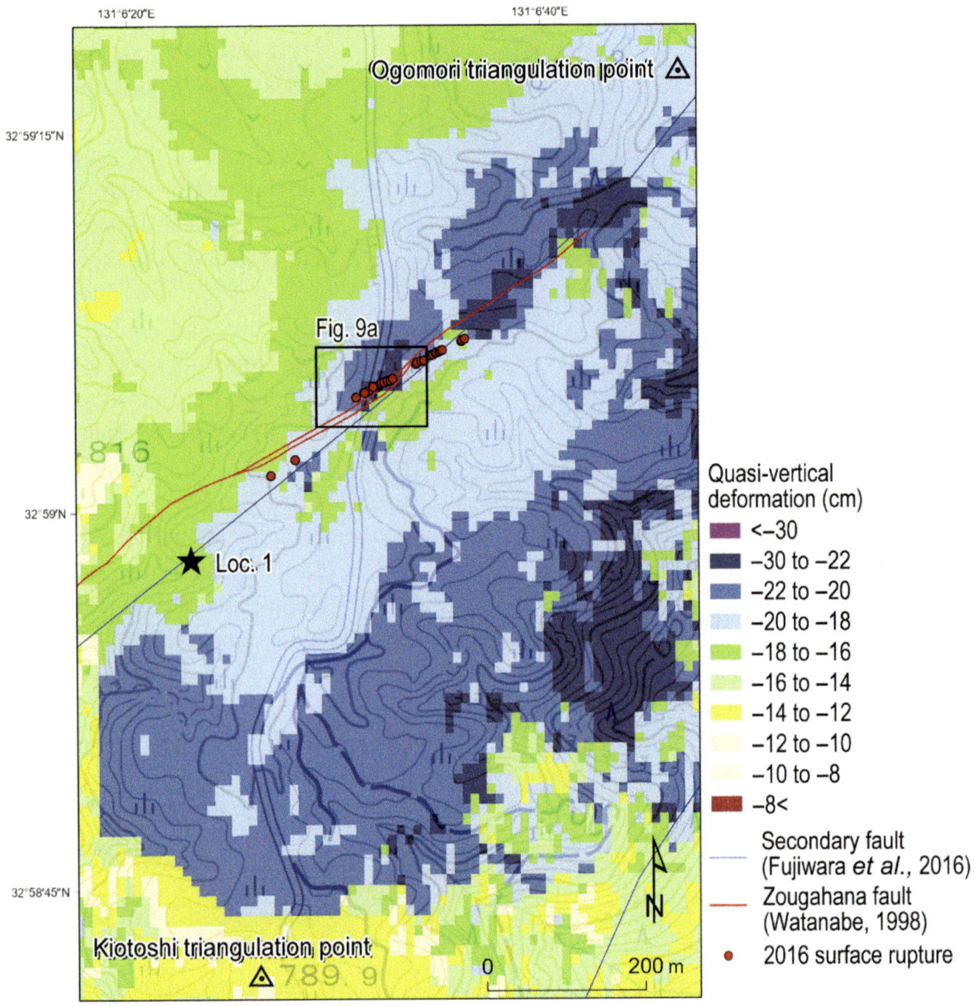

Figure 7. Quasi-vertical deformation calculated from the Interferometric Synthetic Aperture Radar (InSAR) image of the same area shown in Figure 3a.

Radiocarbon dating and tephra analysis

To estimate the ages of the sedimentary layers, we collected charcoal and organic soil samples from the outcrop wall for radiocarbon dating and blocks of soil measuring ~3 cm from the hand augers for tephra analysis. The latter were collected from locations where tephra was identified by eye.

Radiocarbon ages (Table 2) were obtained by accelerator mass spectrometry at the Yamagata University High-Sensitivity Accelerator Mass Spectrometry Center after acid and alkali treatment and sieving through a 250 μm sieve. We obtained and report in the outcrop descriptions conventional radiocarbon age, yr B.P. (CRA).

The auger soil samples were sieved using a mesh cloth and an ultrasonic cleaner to extract very fine ash particles (62.5–125 μm) for tephra analysis. The extracted particles were observed under a polarizing microscope, and the volcanic glass shards were counted. For samples in which a significant number of volcanic glass fragments were detected, the refractive index was measured using a RIMS2000 refractometer (Kyoto Fission Track Co., Ltd., Kyoto, Japan) at the department of civil and environmental engineering, Chuo University, Tokyo, Japan. In addition, we analyzed the major element compositions of some glass samples by wavelength dispersive spectroscopy using a JEOL-JXA-8800 electron probe microanalyzer (EPMA) at the Central Research Institute of Electric Power Industry, Chiba, Japan. We used the same analytical conditions as Takeuchi *et al.* (2021), using the AT tephra as the standard. The tephra analysis results, including the

Using string, we constructed a grid at 50 cm increments both walls and observed and described the detailed strata of the wall surface and the location of the 2016 rupture. In addition, we took high-resolution photographs of each grid cell to construct a 3D model and mosaic image of the wall surface using SfM-MVS (Agisoft Metashape, professional version).

The photographic mosaic and log of the Zougahana fault outcrop are shown in Figure 8a,b, respectively. The north and south walls overlap at 6.5–7.5 m horizontally across the outcrop (H6.5–H7.5), but the north wall is 1 m behind the south wall in the east–west direction (into the page). A 3D data and detailed description of the stratigraphy of the Zougahana fault outcrop are shown in supplement 1 and 2, available to this article, respectively.

Hand-coring survey

To describe the stratigraphy of the formations below the Zougahana fault outcrop and to identify key tephra layers, we used a hand auger to core down from the top of the fault

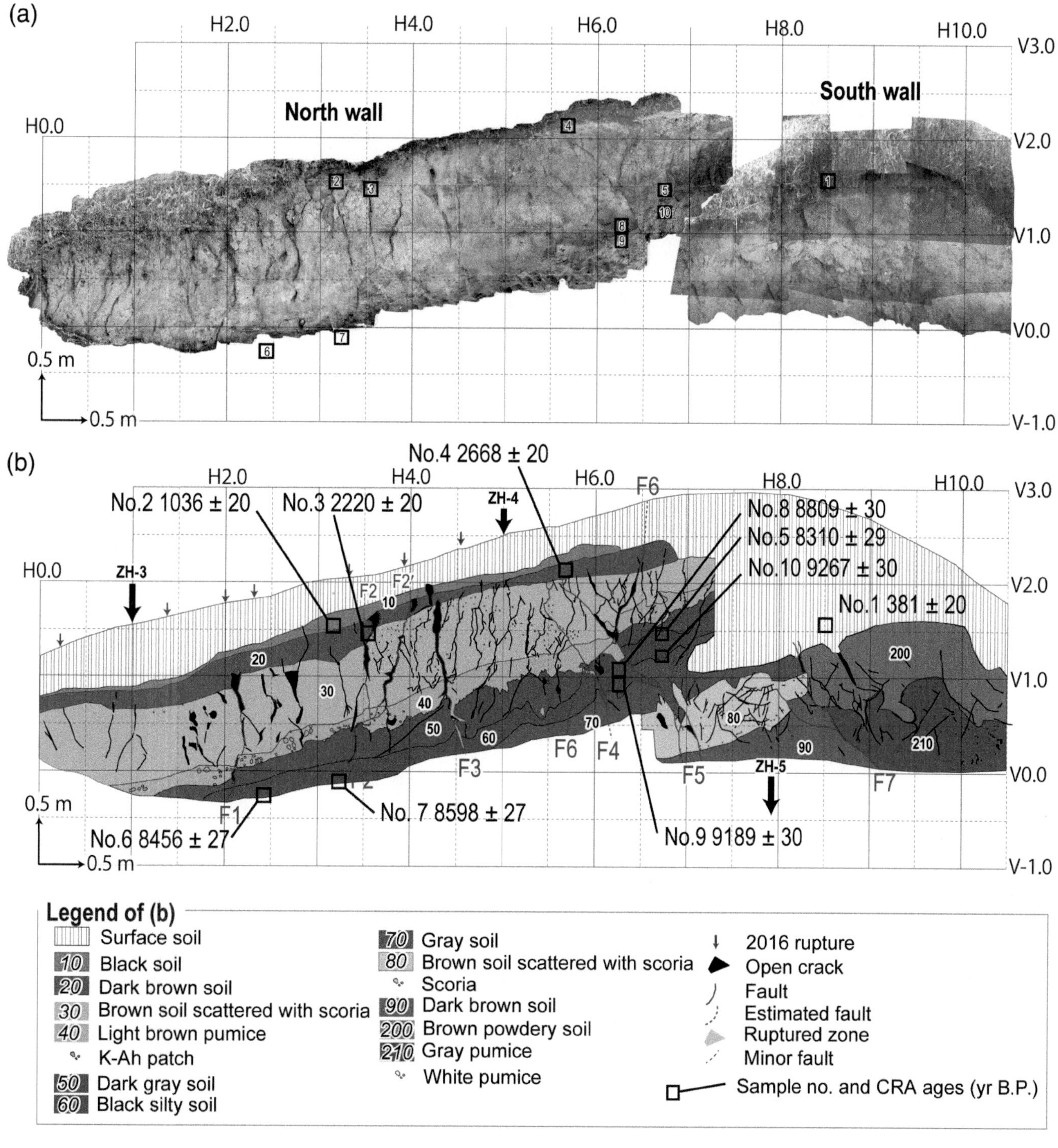

Figure 8. (a) Photomosaic of the Zougahana fault outcrop. Numbers in the open squares correspond to the radiocarbon sample numbers in Table 2. (b) Log of the Zougahana fault outcrop. Sample numbers and mean values of the conventional radiocarbon ages (CRA) (yr B.P.) are also shown. The color version of this figure is available only in the electronic edition.

mineral composition, refractive index, major element compositions of glass shards measured by EPMA, and microphotographs of particles in each tephra sample, is shown in supplement 2 and 3, along with detailed description of hand cores.

Based on the ages obtained from radiocarbon dating and tephra analysis, we used OxCal v.4.4 (Bronk Ramsey, 2024) and the IntCal20 calibration curve (Reimer *et al.*, 2020) to perform Bayesian estimation of the age of the event that displaced the strata. In this study, we used the sequence model (Bronk Ramsey, 1995) to impose constraints on the relative age of each age value when the lower strata were certainly older than the upper strata and the phase model (Bronk Ramsey, 2009) to treat age values for which the relative ages were unclear (disturbed sediments or sampling locations) as a uniform group.

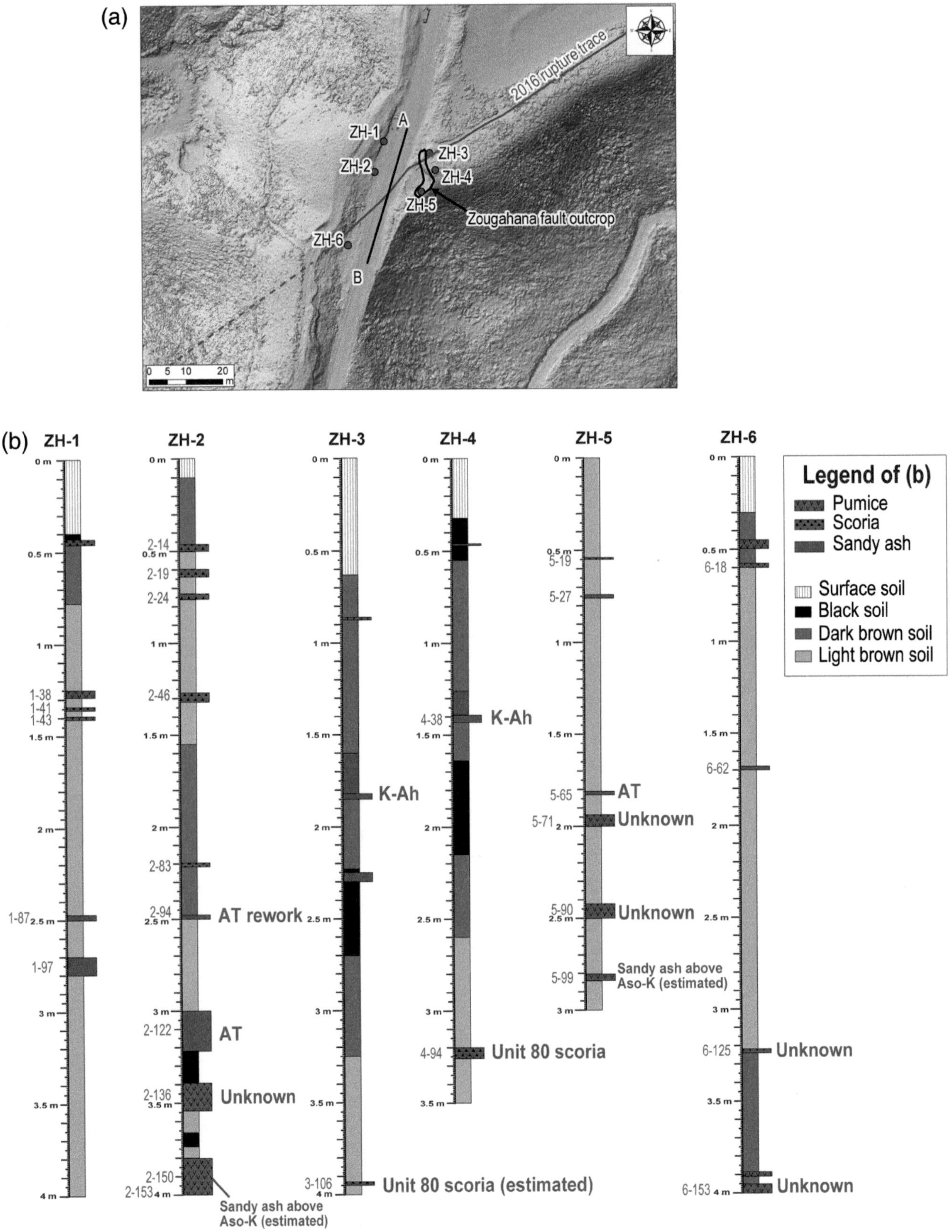

Figure 9. (a) Hand-coring locations (blue circles) adjacent to the Zougahana fault outcrop. The extent of this map is the same as in Figure 6a. The background image is an altitude step-color map created based on UAV aerial photography images. (b) Stratigraphic columns of the hand auger cores. Sample numbers (in red text; results in supplement 2) and correlated tephras are also shown. The color version of this figure is available only in the electronic edition.

TABLE 2
Radiocarbon Ages from the Outcrop Wall

Wall	Unit	Position	Sample Number	Materials	$\delta^{13}C$ (‰)	CRA (yr B.P.)	2σ Calibrated Age (cal B.P.)	Laboratory ID
S	Surface soil	H8.5, V1.5	1	Organic soil	24.45 ± 0.35	381 ± 20	500–320	YU-16059
N	10	H3.2, V1.5	2	Organic soil	21.53 ± 0.33	1036 ± 20	960–910	YU-13816
N	20	H3.5, V1.5	3	Organic soil	22.95 ± 0.33	2220 ± 20	2330–2140	YU-16619
N	20	H5.7, V2.2	4	Organic soil	23.83 ± 0.37	2668 ± 21	2850–2740	YU-16060
N	60	H7.7, V1.5	5	Organic soil	23.92 ± 0.26	8310 ± 29	9440–9140	YU-14994
N	60	H2.4, V-0.3	6	Organic soil	23.89 ± 0.30	8456 ± 27	9540–9440	YU-13815
N	60	H3.2, V-0.1	7	Organic soil	22.86 ± 0.37	8598 ± 27	9660–9490	YU-13814
N	60	H6.3, V1.1	8	Organic soil	24.31 ± 0.28	8809 ± 30	10120–9680	YU-14996
N	60	H6.3, V0.9	9	Organic soil	24.82 ± 0.27	9189 ± 30	10490–10240	YU-14997
N	60	H6.7, V1.2	10	Organic soil	25.10 ± 0.28	9267 ± 30	10570–10290	YU-14995

CRA, conventional radiocarbon age.

The calendar year calibration and model age values are reported rounded to the nearest 10 yr (cal B.P.) with a confidence interval of $\pm 2\sigma$. The code for the constructed OxCal model is shown in Text S1 in supplement 4.

RESULTS

Geomorphology, geology, and characteristics of the 2016 rupture around the Zougahana D prehistoric site

The geological map (Fig. 3a) shows that most of the plateau in the Zougahana D prehistoric site area is covered by the Aso-4 pyroclastic flow, and the MPI-RRIM and geomorphological maps show that the plateau is being eroded from east to west (Fig. 4a,b). The erosion front can be divided into two parts: an older erosion front and a younger, fresher-looking erosion front that erodes the older part. Part of the fresh erosion front coincides with the geological boundary between the Aso-2 and the Aso-3 pyroclastic flow (Fig. 3a), which may be a geomorphological feature associated with different degrees of welding. To the northeast of the Zougahana fault outcrop is a linear scarp with a N60°E–N70°E strike and a height of 1.8–4.1 m (Figs. 4b,c and 5a). Although it is not possible to rule out the possibility that these linear scarp features were formed by fluvial erosion, the linear valley morphology is unusual in this area, where a horseshoe-shaped erosion front dominates (Fig. 4b); therefore, the linear valley morphology is likely due to repeated fault displacement.

The mapped location of the 2016 rupture (Fig. 4b) shows a rupture with a strike of N70°E, and relatively northwest-downward displacement was observed on the paved road (Fig. 5a,b). Many 2016 ruptures were observed directly above the Zougahana fault outcrop, and only two ruptures were found to the east of the outcrop (Fig. 4b). Nonetheless, in the gorge on the southwest side of the Zougahana fault outcrop (Loc. 1 shown in Figs. 3a and 4b), we discovered a new fault outcrop that had not been described in previous studies (Fig. 5c,d). Although this location is situated on Aso-2A/2B pyroclastic flow deposits (Fig. 3a), scarp deposits consisting mainly of secondary or reworked deposits of the more recent Aso-4 eruptive phase are exposed on the south side of the fault (Fig. 5d). On the valley floor, a small amount of welded tuff was exposed on the south side of the fault, although the lithology of this deposit was unclear. The fault at the boundary between the Aso-2A/2B pyroclastic flow deposit and the scarp deposits strikes N65°E and dips 68° S (Fig. 5d), consistent with the strike of the rupture observed on the paved road immediately adjacent to the Zougahana fault outcrop. The fault identified at Loc. 1 is a south-dipping normal fault characterized by an open rupture near the surface. The direction of vertical displacement is opposite that of the northwest-dipping rupture identified on the paved road directly below the Zougahana fault outcrop. Accordingly, we interpret the Zougahana fault as characterized by lateral movement, with the apparent direction of vertical displacement changing locally.

Figure 6 shows the results of the total station survey of the 2016 rupture on the paved road directly below the Zougahana fault outcrop. The horizontal displacement shows 48.6 ± 0.2 cm of right-lateral slip (Fig. 6a), and the vertical displacement shows the north side of the rupture dropping by 20.2 ± 4.7 cm (Fig. 6b). Therefore, the horizontal right-lateral slip is more than twice the vertical displacement, consistent with our previous interpretation that the dominant sense of slip is horizontal and that the apparent vertical displacement direction changes locally.

The quasi-vertical deformation InSAR analysis shows that the northwest side of the fault subsided by up to 11 ± 5 cm compared with the southeast side (Fig. 7). This is slightly smaller than the measured vertical displacement of the paved road (Fig. 6b). The difference may be explained by afterslip. Hashimoto (2020) presented an afterslip fault model with velocities of 0–5 cm/yr around the Zougahana fault based on InSAR observations during the two years following the earthquake. Because our field measurements were taken more than five years after the earthquake, it is entirely plausible that the difference exceeding 10 cm could have been accommodated during that period, even accounting for afterslip attenuation. Figure 7 includes two public triangulation points, Ogomori and Kiotoshi. According to Global Navigation Satellite System (GNSS) surveying by the Geospatial Information Authority of Japan before and after the earthquake (Ootaki *et al.*, 2016), the relative displacement of the Ogomori point relative to the Kiotoshi point was ~3 cm to the north and ~76 cm to the east, with 5 cm of subsidence. These survey results further support that the right-lateral horizontal displacement was much greater than the vertical displacement.

Zougahana fault outcrop stratigraphy

Obata (1998) conducted outcrop and small-scale pit excavation surveys around the Zougahana fault outcrop and identified 25 stratigraphic units cut by 15 faults, and we were able to re-expose layers 1–9 in the outcrop. We note that the stratigraphic divisions, numbers, and fault names used herein are newly reclassified and differ from those of Obata (1998). In identifying the units, we focused on the color, consistency, powderiness, and continuity of the strata observed in the field. In our classification, we recognized 12 units: the topsoil and units 10, 20, 30, 40, 50, 60, 70, 80, 90, 200, and 210. Units 10–60 were observed in the north face and units 80–210 in the south face, with unit 70 being common to both faces (Fig. 8b).

The stratigraphic sequence consists of multiple soil units with varying color, thickness, and organic content. The surface dark brown soil (sample 1: 381 ± 20 yr B.P.) overlies several organic-rich layers, including black unit 10 (sample 2: 1036 ± 20 yr B.P.), dark brown unit 20 (samples 3–4: 2220–2668 ± 20 yr B.P.), and brown unit 30 containing orange scoria. Below these, unit 40 is a light brown layer including the K-Ah tephra, and unit 50 is a clayey dark gray soil deformed by faulting. Unit 60 (samples 5–10: 9297–8281 yr B.P.) is a black clay-rich layer, underlain by grayish unit 70 and brownish unit 80 that contains the scoria-type volcanic ashes from Aso central cones and also shows deformation. The deeper dark brown unit 90 includes white scoria, whereas units 200 and 210 are inorganic brown to gray soils with powdery or crunchy textures, scattered scoria, and deformation structures at their boundaries. Their composition and light color suggest glacial deposits, and because the AT tephra (~30 ka) lies below unit 210, all overlying units are younger than 30 ka.

Faults on the outcrop walls

Numerous faults and open cracks were observed in the outcrop wall (Fig. 8a) and we number the main faults extending from the bottom of the wall surface and displacing the units F1–F7 from north to south (Fig. 8b). Although we observed the 2016 rupture directly above the surface soil in the range of H0.0–H4.5, no clear faults were observed within the surface soil. It is possible that the displacement was dispersed by unconsolidated soil and existing vegetation, making it difficult to trace the displacement through the surface soil. We note that the fault names used herein are distinct from those of Obata (1998), and we identified the faults independently.

Fault F1 was observed in the north wall, displacing the unit 30–20 boundary by ~13 cm to the north. This displacement opened a crack up to 10 cm wide and 40 cm tall. Although we could not trace the fault upward of unit 20, 2016 ruptures were distributed on the ground surface above the top of F1. The unit 40–30 boundary was also vertically displaced by about 4–15 cm, but it was not possible to determine whether a clear vertical displacement occurred in the units below. We also observed an open crack 3 cm wide and 10 cm tall near the unit 50–40 boundary (H2.1, V−0.1), and the patchy K-Ah tephra contained in unit 40 had fallen out of place.

Fault F2 was observed on the north wall, and an open crack 5–10 cm wide and up to 50 cm tall was observed near the unit 30–20 boundary. Slightly open cracks were also observed in units 40–60. The clear open crack was in unit 20 but could not be traced into unit 10. However, 2016 ruptures were distributed on the ground surface, extending from the upper end of F2. F2 deformed the top of unit 20 by ~7 cm to the north and displaced the top of unit 30 by ~12 cm to the north; it did not displace strata below unit 30.

In addition, a subordinate fault F2′ splits off F2 toward the top of unit 40 and developed into an open crack 10 cm wide and 10 cm tall near the top of unit 20. Like F1 and F2, the 2016 ruptures are distributed on the ground surface extending upward from F2′. A small opening was observed in units 30–50 but became unclear near the bottom of unit 60. We measured a northward displacement of about 3.6 cm at the top of unit 30.

Fault F3 was observed in the north wall, characterized by an open crack up to 10 cm wide and 10 cm tall cutting units 10 and 20 and another open crack up to 10 cm wide and about 100 cm tall cutting units 30 and 40. The displacement was observed up to the top of unit 10, and the 2016 rupture was observed on the ground extending from the upper end of F3. Although there was no clear vertical displacement at the unit boundaries, the top of unit 50 was displaced southward by 4.2–12.5 cm, and the top of unit 60 was displaced southward by 4.2–16.7 cm. In addition, we observed a fissure-fill structure, in which units 50 and 60 open along F3 and the opening was filled by material from unit 40.

Fault F4 was observed in the north wall. We traced a slight crack in units 30–40 to at least the unit 30–20 boundary. Near the unit 60–50 boundary (H5.9, V1.2), F4 was displaced 1–2 cm to the north (i.e., to the left of the wall surface) by fault F6 (discussed in a later paragraph). We traced F4 to the base of the north wall, where it displaced the top of unit 60 by 9.2–36.7 cm to the north and the top of unit 70 by up to 9.2 cm to the south. We attribute this apparent reversal of the sense of displacement to the lateral offset of the units in 3D. Fissure-fill structures were observed in two locations in the lower units, with unit 40 filling the opening in units 50 and 60 and unit 60 filling the opening in unit 70.

Fault F5 is the longest fault in the exposed wall, extending from the base of the south wall to the unit 30–20 boundary on the north wall. An open Y-shaped crack was visible near the unit 40–30 boundary (H6.3, V1.4), and the fault showed a complex, nested form. Fault F6, described in detail in the next paragraph, has displaced F5 ~3 cm to the north (to the left side of the wall). Localized openings also appeared near the top of unit 80 (H6.7, V0.6), below which the fault showed complex branching in units 80 and 90. The fault displaced the top of unit 40 by ~13 cm, unit 50 by ~18 cm, unit 60 by ~18 cm, and unit 70 by ~17 cm, all in a down-to-the-north sense. Although faults F1–F4 are steeply dipping, F5 showed characteristics of a reverse fault, dipping 50°–60° S. In addition, we observed a fissure-fill structure, with unit 40 dropping into units 50 and 60, unit 60 dropping into the opening in unit 70, and unit 70 also dropping into the opening in unit 80.

Fault F6 was observed as a north-dipping fault on the north wall, and the crack extended upward to the top of unit 20; although unclear, it seemed to continue into the surface soil and near surface. However, we did not observe any 2016 rupture on the surface directly above F6. We also traced a clear fracture to the base of the north wall. F6 appeared to have caused a northward displacement of ~9–16 cm at the top of unit 40, displacing fault F5 by about 3 cm and fault F4 by 1–2 cm in the same direction. Therefore, F6 must postdate faults F4 and F5.

Fault F7 was observed to be a south-dipping fault separating units 70–90 from units 200 and 210 in the south wall. Because units 200 and 210 are interpreted to be last glacial period deposits, their juxtaposition next to units 70–90 implies that F7 is a reverse fault that uplifted units on the south side (the right side of the wall). F7 branched off gradually at H8.7 and V0.5, and the leftmost branch terminated in unit 80. The top edge of F7 showed an opening ~5–10 cm wide, and we confirmed that F7 reaches the surface soil. Unit 80, which contains the scoria band in its lower portions, was displaced vertically in multiple locations by F7, with northward displacement of ~3–17 cm at the unit 80–70 boundary and ~10–12 cm at the unit 90–80 boundary. Unit 80 was tilted ~20° northward toward the F7 fault from around H7.0, and we estimated the total vertical displacement resulting from this tilting to be >60 cm.

Shallow fault structure from the hand auger cores

Cores ZH-1 and ZH-2 (Fig. 9b), taken near a paved road (Fig. 9a), likely lost their uppermost layers during construction; both contain multiple scoria and volcanic ash layers, with ZH-2 including a 22-cm-thick AT tephra and orange-colored layers correlated with or slightly younger than the Kpfa tephra (about 30–32 ka). Cores ZH-3 and ZH-4 (Fig. 9b), obtained from the fault outcrop wall (Fig. 9a), show dark to light brown soils with several ash and scoria layers, including a 17–25 cm sandy volcanic ash correlated to the K-Ah tephra and deeper scoria correlated to unit 80 of the wall section. Core ZH-5 (Fig. 9b), from the base of the wall (Fig. 9a), consists mainly of light brown soil containing several thin ash layers; the 1.82-m-deep sandy ash corresponds to the AT tephra, and deeper orange ash may relate to tephra above Kpfa. Core ZH-6 (Fig. 9b), south of the fault (Fig. 9a), contains multiple thin ash layers but no major identifiable tephra, suggesting older deposits than AT and Kpfa. Together, these cores record multiple tephra horizons (K-Ah, AT, and possibly Kpfa) useful for constraining the depositional and history of the Zougahana fault.

Figure 10 presents the elevations and positions of the hand auger cores relative to the Zougahana fault outcrop sketches as a cross section based on the total station survey projected along the paved road (line A–B; Fig. 9a). In the outcrop, unit 40 and the K-Ah tephra were displaced 4–16 cm vertically by each of the F1, F5, and F6 faults (Fig. 8b) for a total displacement of 26–31 cm. However, the displacements of the volcanic ash and scoria layers below the K-Ah tephra were greater, recording cumulative fault displacements. The relative heights of the scoria layers in unit 80 in the south wall and in core ZH-4 (and perhaps ZH-3) indicate a vertical offset of 2.9 m across faults F1–F6 (Fig. 10). In addition, the relative heights of the AT tephra in cores ZH-2 and ZH-5 indicate a vertical offset of ~2.6 m across faults F1–F6 (Fig. 10). However, if the units were originally dipping north, the actual vertical offset would likely be smaller than these. In fact, although the measurement methods and criteria are unclear, Obata (1998), who conducted pit excavation at a point several tens of meters northeast of this outcrop, noted that a 1.7 m vertical displacement had occurred in the Kpfa tephra. Including their estimates, we inferred that the vertical displacement of the overlying AT tephra to be between 1.7 and 2.9 m. Regardless of its uncertainty, our results clearly highlight a cumulative displacement between the deposition of the AT tephra (about 30 ka) and the K-Ah tephra (about 7.3 ka). In addition, given that the F7 reverse fault exists between cores ZH-5 and ZH-6 (Fig. 10), the sediments identified in ZH-6 likely correspond to the hanging wall of the fault, representing material upthrown from units even older than the AT tephra and Kpfa tephra. Furthermore, because there were no traces of faults in ZH-6, it is also unlikely that F7 passes even farther south (right side of Fig. 10) of ZH-6.

DISCUSSION

Paleoearthquakes and age constraints for the Zougahana fault outcrop

The Zougahana fault outcrop records multiple displacement events based on faultings and deformation structures such as fissure-fill, deformed-horizon, undulation, and unconformity observed at the top surface of each unit. In addition, the deformation structures of faults F5, F7, and the surrounding areas (Fig. 8b), which had the best continuity and were the most straightforward to interpret, were useful for recognizing

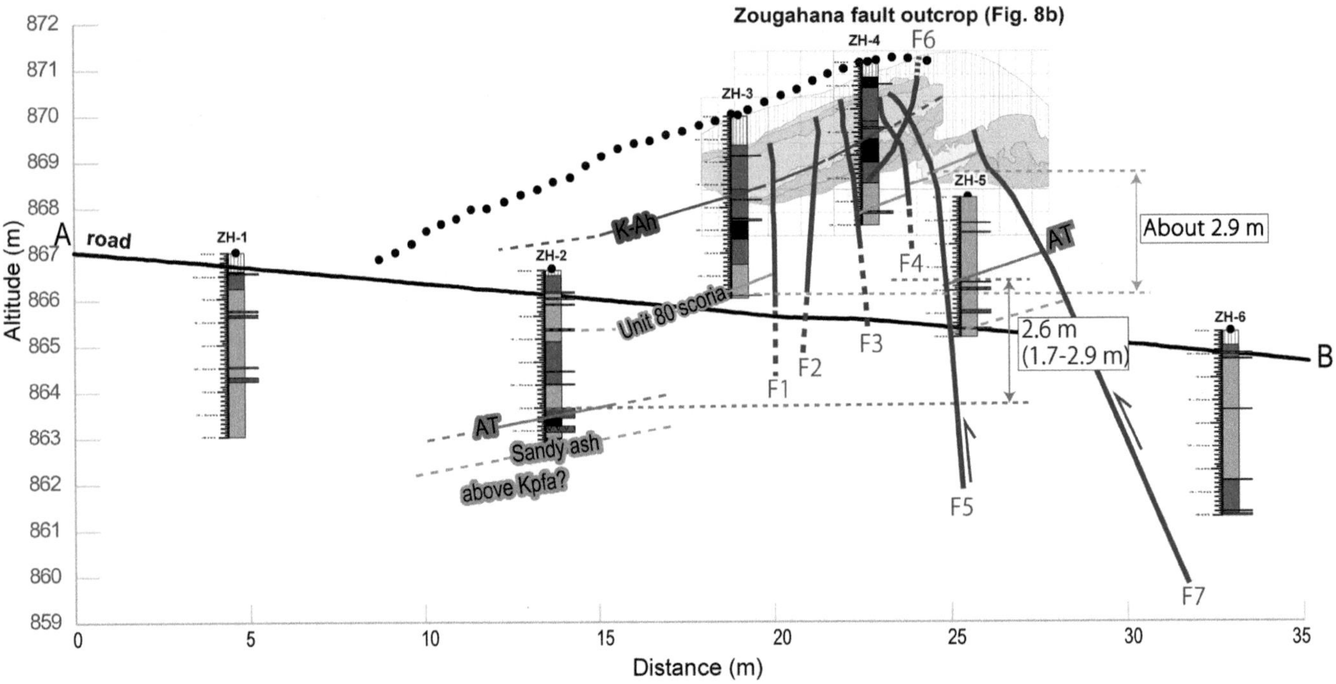

Figure 10. Inferred subsurface structure along line A–B (located in Fig. 9a) from the hand cores and the outcrop log. The black circles indicate the total station survey points and the locations of the hand cores. The color version of this figure is available only in the electronic edition.

events. In this subsection, we identify events, including the 2016 earthquake, from the most recent to the oldest.

The 2016 rupture at the ground surface was distributed over a width of about 4.5 m (H0.0–H4.5), but there was no clear fault corresponding to the 2016 rupture in the outcrop (Fig. 8b). Accordingly, we interpret that the displacements observable in the outcrop are part of a positive flower structure (e.g., Fossen, 2016) associated with right-lateral offset and that this distributed displacement is expressed as flexural displacement at the ground surface. The outcrop also showed many fresh open cracks and fissures that had not yet been filled with sediment, which we attribute to the 2016 earthquake, consistent with a trench survey of the Futagawa fault conducted after the 2016 earthquake (Ishimura *et al.*, 2022). Because all faults in the outcrop were accompanied by fresh open cracks and fissures, it is likely that all faults moved during the 2016 earthquake. In particular, faults F1–F3 on the north side have large apertures and are consistent with the locations of the 2016 ruptures at the ground surface, suggesting that most of the displacement during the 2016 earthquake occurred along these faults. Figure 11a is a close-up view of the Zougahana fault outcrop log (Fig. 8b) focused on the area around faults F5 and F7 in the range H5.0–H9.0, V0.0–V3.0. By removing all open cracks and fissures thought to have formed because of the 2016 earthquake, we estimate the pre-2016 earthquake wall surface appeared as in Figure 11b. Fault F6, which reached the surface and displaced fault F5 by about 3 cm and fault F4 by 1–2 cm to the north (left side of the outcrop) as a result of the 2016 earthquake, and we have retrodeformed this displacement in Figure 11b.

We estimate that the penultimate event occurred before the deposition of unit 20 because faults F4 and F5 are interrupted at the unit 30–20 boundary, and the displacement at the unit 40–30 boundary caused by fault F5 cannot be attributed to the 2016 displacement. Hereafter, we refer to this event as "Event 1." Figure 11c shows the estimated wall surface immediately after event 1. In addition, the deformed horizon at the unit 40–30 boundary on the hanging wall of F5 is presumed to have been deformed by event 1. At that time, the surface of unit 30 may also have been deformed, but it was likely eroded away or flattened by the time unit 20 began to deposit (Fig. 11b). By retrodeforming the displacement of fault F5 to zero displacement at the unit 40–30 boundary, we obtain the estimated pre-event 1 wall surface shown in Figure 11d.

We estimate that the antepenultimate event ("Event 2") occurred before or during the deposition of unit 40. Although the unit 50–40 boundary is characterized like a fissure-fill structure, the top surface of unit 40 is inconsistently relatively flat, suggesting that deformation occurred when the unit 50–40 boundary was at the surface or the invisible surface within the unit 40. This interpretation is based on the textbook interpretation of paleoseismology (Allen, 1986; Allen and Wallace, 1986; McCalpin *et al.*, 2009). In the latter case, the steps or cracks that formed within unit 40 can be interpreted as having subsequently been eroded away. Furthermore, material from unit 40 fills fissures along faults F4 and F5 in units 50 and 60. Figure 11e shows the estimated wall surface immediately after event 2, assuming the event horizon was

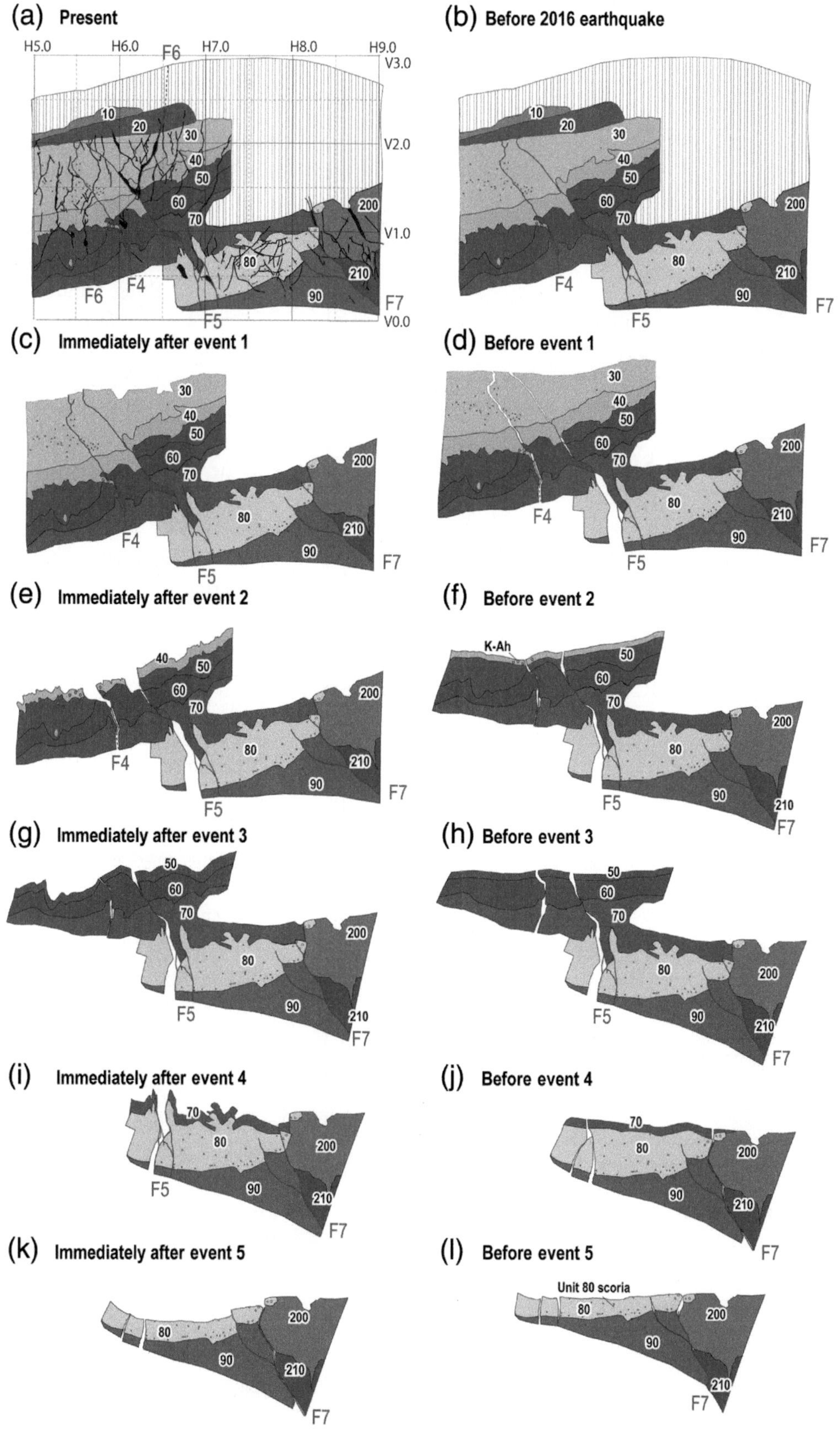

Figure 11. (a–l) Retrodeformation sequence of faulting and sedimentation around faults F4–F7 in the wall log (Fig. 8b). The color version of this figure is available only in the electronic edition.

within unit 40. By restoring the deformation at the surface of unit 50 as well as along the fissures, we estimate that the pre-event 2 wall surface was as shown in Figure 11f. This reconstruction means that it is impossible to determine whether the K-Ah ashfall occurred before or after the event.

According to Figure 11f, unit 50 (dark gray soil layer) is thicker to the north (left) and appears to abut unit 60. Therefore, when the deposition of unit 50 began or during the deposition of unit 50, it is possible that the ground surface to the south (right) was already uplifting, and we estimate that the preceding event ("Event 3") occurred before the deposition of unit 50. We consider that the deformed horizon at the unit 60–50 boundary also supports the occurrence of event 3 when the unit 60–50 boundary was at the surface or the invisible surface within the unit 50. Figure 11g shows the estimated wall surface immediately after event 3, assuming the event horizon was within unit 50. By correcting the deformation of units 60 and 50 and rotating the section to have a flat surface, we obtain the pre-event 3 wall surface shown in Figure 11h.

We estimated the event preceding event 3 ("Event 4") based on the clear fissure-fill structure and undulation caused by fault F5, which occurred when the unit 80–70 boundary was at the surface or the invisible surface within the unit 70. We interpret that event 4 caused the ground surface to open; the subsequent deposition of unit 70 filled the fissure. Figure 11i shows the terminate within unit 80. Therefore, it is possible that an event occurred during the deposition of unit 80 ("Event 5"). Figure 11k shows the estimated wall surface immediately after event 5, from which we obtained the pre-event 5 wall surface by restoring deformation and tilting until we achieved a flat surface for unit 80 (Fig. 11l) is estimated. Furthermore, because white scoria is scattered below unit 80, event 5 must have occurred after deposition of this scoria.

To the south of fault F7, older deposits (units 200–210) extend farther south (Fig. 8b). Furthermore, we estimated 1.7–2.9 m of cumulative vertical displacement of the AT tephra from our hand-core results (Fig. 10), but this displacement cannot be explained by the cumulative vertical displacements of events 1–5 estimated so far. Therefore, numerous events must have preceded event 5.

In summary, we identified six past events (the 2016 event and events 1–5) in the Zougahana fault outcrop. The vertical displacements measured on faults F1–F7 at each stratum boundary on the wall of the Zougahana fault outcrop (Fig. 8b), as well as the unit levels of events 1–5 and the 2016 earthquake, are shown in Figure S5 in supplement 5. We constructed a chronological model of these events using OxCal based on the CRA ages (yr B.P.) obtained from the wall and ages of 7303–7165 cal B.P. and 30,009 ± 189 cal B.P. for the K-Ah and AT tephras, respectively (Smith *et al.*, 2013) (Fig. 12). According to the model chronology, event 1 (thought to have occurred at the unit 30–20 boundary) is estimated to have occurred at 5760–2750 cal B.P., event 2 (unit 50–40 boundary or during the deposition of unit 40) at 8700–5000 cal B.P., and

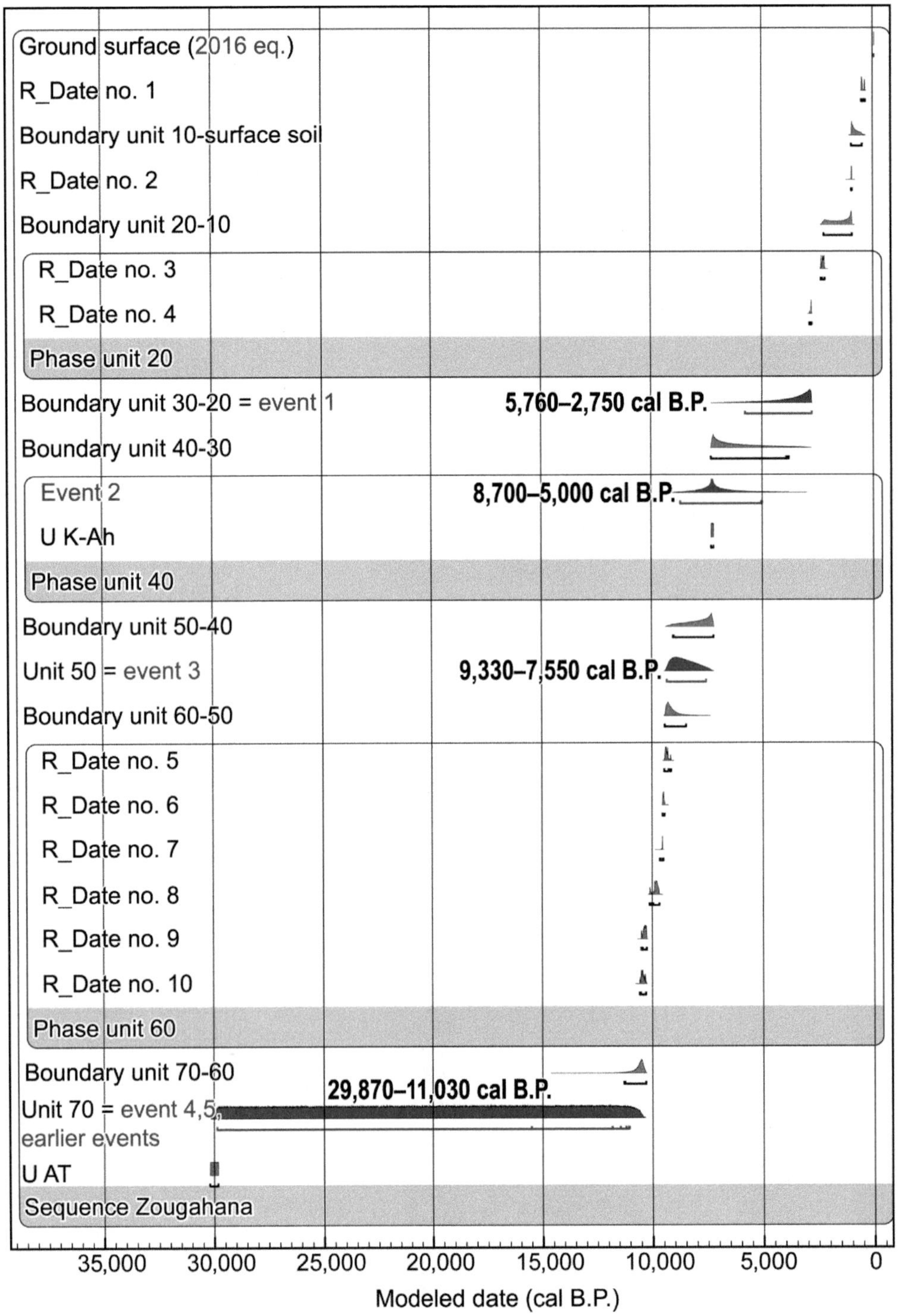

Figure 12. Earthquake age model of the Zougahana fault outcrop constructed with OxCal software based on CRAs, tephras, and constrained ages for each event. "R_date" indicates the radiocarbon age of each sample number (Fig. 8b, Table 2), and "U" indicates tephra ages. Event ages are rounded to the nearest decade and presented with a 2σ (95.4%) confidence interval. The color version of this figure is available only in the electronic edition.

estimated wall surface immediately after event 4, assuming the event horizon was within unit 70, from which we obtained the pre-event 4 wall surface by restoring deformation (Fig. 11j).

The F7 fault in the south wall displaced the upper surface of unit 90, and at least one of the branches of this fault appears to

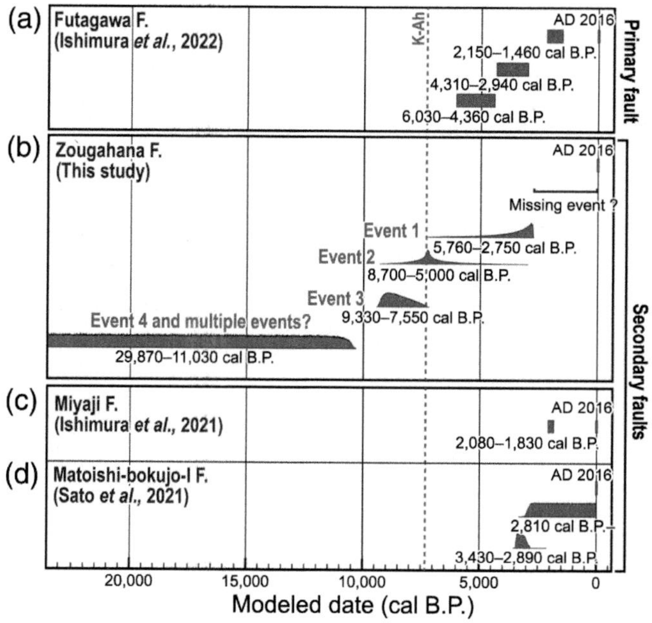

Figure 13. Comparison of the paleoseismic histories of (a) the primary fault (Futagawa fault; Ishimura *et al.*, 2022) and its secondary faults: (b) the Zougahana fault (this study), (c) the Miyaji fault (Ishimura *et al.*, 2021), and (d) the Matoishi-bokujo-I fault (Sato *et al.*, 2021). The color version of this figure is available only in the electronic edition.

event 3 (unit 60–50 boundary or during the deposition of unit 50) at 9330–7550 cal B.P. Events 4 (unit 80–70 boundary or during the deposition of unit 70), 5 (during deposition of unit 80), and the multiple earlier events for which constraining radiocarbon ages and tephra are not available are collectively estimated to have occurred between 29,870 and 11,030 cal B.P. (Fig. 12) assuming the AT tephra as the oldest age constraint.

Comparison with paleoseismic events on the Futagawa fault and other secondary faults

We interpreted at least six earthquakes, including the 2016 earthquake, on the Zougahana fault in the last ~30 ka, including four in the last 10 ka (Fig. 12). The average recurrence interval of events from just before the occurrence of event 3 to just after the 2016 earthquake, which were estimated with relatively high accuracy, was calculated to be ~2500–3200 yr. Assuming these average recurrence intervals to have remained constant, these values correspond to the occurrence of 9–12 events since the deposition of the AT tephra about 30 ka. The dominant sense of slip is strike slip, and the displacement amount may vary for each event (e.g., Petersen *et al.*, 2011). Therefore, although this is a reference calculation, we will examine the cumulative vertical displacement here. The vertical displacement in the 2016 earthquake measured on the paved road in front of the Zougahana fault outcrop was 20.2 ± 4.7 cm (Fig. 6b); if this is characteristic vertical slip during a single event, the cumulative displacement since the AT tephra fall is 2.19 ± 0.80 m. This calculated value overlaps within the margin of error with the vertical displacement of the AT tephra, ranging from 1.7 to 2.9 m, based on our group-sequence coring (Fig. 10). Because no cumulative lateral offset, such as offset channels, has been found, it is difficult to discuss about cumulative lateral displacement.

Multiple trench surveys have been carried out on the Futagawa fault, the source fault of the 2016 Kumamoto earthquake (Fig. 1c), since the 2016 earthquake (Kumahara *et al.*, 2017; Okamura *et al.*, 2018; Tsutsumi *et al.*, 2018; Ueta *et al.*, 2018; Toda *et al.*, 2019; Ishimura *et al.*, 2022; Iwasa *et al.*, 2022). Among these, Ishimura *et al.* (2022) reconstructed a reliable paleoseismic history of the Futagawa fault based on multiple pit excavation surveys. They concluded that four earthquakes (including the 2016 event) occurred after the K-Ah tephra fall, and they estimated the ages of the three events preceding the 2016 event to be 2150–1460 cal B.P., 4310–2940 cal B.P., and 6030–4360 cal B.P. (Fig. 13a). In particular, their penultimate event (2150–1460 cal B.P.) has been confirmed in several other trench surveys along the Futagawa fault (Toda *et al.*, 2019; Iwasa *et al.*, 2022). In this study, we did not identify any events corresponding to the penultimate event on the Futagawa fault, and we only found evidence for one or two events (events 1 and 2) since the deposition of the K-Ah tephra (Fig. 13b). Accordingly, we suspect there may have been a possible missing event around 2150–1460 cal B.P. (Fig. 13). This age corresponds to the vicinity of the unit 20–10 boundary on the outcrop wall (Fig. 8b). The F2 fault has imposed displacement on this unit 20–10 boundary, which we inferred resulted from the 2016 earthquake. Some of this displacement on the F2 fault may correspond to the missing penultimate event. Of course, it is not certain that activity on the Zougahana fault has always accompanied activity of the Futagawa fault, and it may have reacted only once or several times. Nonetheless, similarly timed events were identified on the Miyaji fault (a secondary fault about 5 km south of the Zougahana fault; Fig. 1c) at 2080–1830 cal B.P. (Ishimura *et al.*, 2021; Fig. 13c) and on the Matoishi-bokujo-I fault (a secondary fault ~10 km away and belonging to the Kuradake graben on the northwest side of the outer rim of Aso caldera; Fig. 1c) some time since 2810 cal B.P. (Sato *et al.*, 2021; Fig. 13d). The paleoseismic histories of these secondary faults are also consistent with the penultimate event along the Futagawa fault in 2150–1460 cal B.P., ~2 ka, implying the existence of possible missing event on the Zougahana fault. Additional trench surveys to better determine the paleoseismic history of the Zougahana fault should yield further data for comparison.

What is the driving force of the Zougahana fault?

The paleoseismic record shows that the Zougahana fault has repeatedly interacted with the Futagawa fault in the past. But what drove the movement on the Zougahana fault during

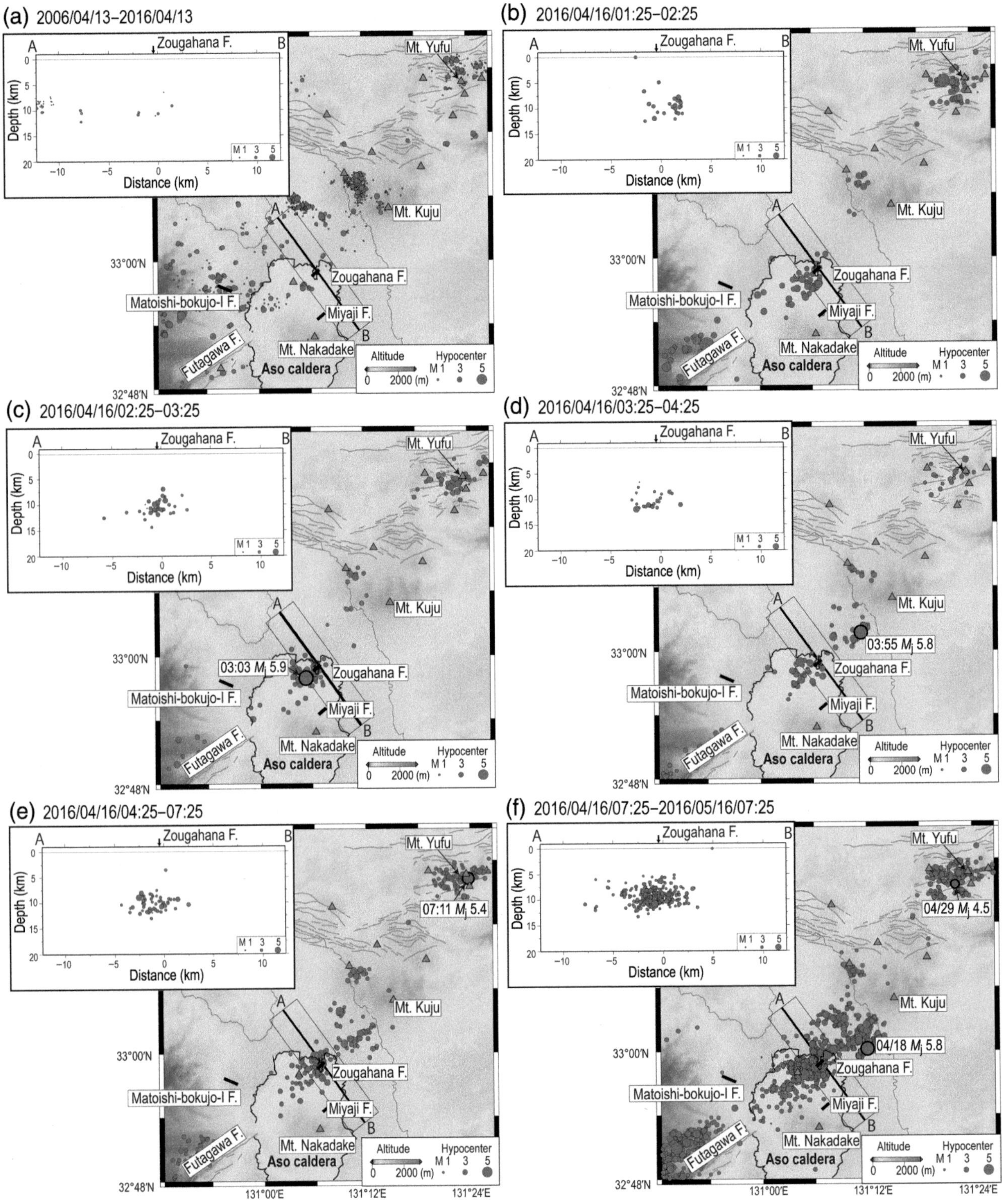

Figure 14. (a) Background seismicity from Aso caldera to Mt. Yufu in the 10 yr preceding the 2016 Kumamoto earthquake. Cross sections to 20 km depth orthogonal to the Zougahana fault are shown. The targeted earthquakes are those shallower than 20 km depth and stronger than M_{JMA} 2, and hypocenters are based on the All-Japan hypocenter catalog by the Japan Meteorological Agency (JMA). The source determination accuracy for inland shallow crustal earthquakes within Japan is <1 km (Tamaribuchi, 2018). The gray lines in the figure are active fault traces from the National Institute of Advanced Industrial Science and Technology (2009), and the red triangles indicate the locations of Quaternary volcanoes, from Nishiki *et al.* (2012). We use the visualization system for subsurface structures at the National Institute of Advanced Industrial Science and Technology (AIST) to make this panel. (b–f) The distribution of aftershocks in the same area: (b) up to 1 hr after the mainshock, (c) 1–2 hr after the mainshock, (d) 2–3 hr after the mainshock, (e) 3–6 hr after the mainshock, and (f) 6 hr to 1 month after the mainshock. The color version of this figure is available only in the electronic edition.

the 2016 Kumamoto earthquake? This pressing question needs to be answered to better evaluate the behavior of active strike-slip faults. In this section, we will consider this question from the perspectives of the aftershock distribution, strong ground motions, and ΔCFF associated with the mainshock.

Relationship of the Zougahana fault to the background seismicity and the 2016 earthquake aftershock distribution

Figure 14 shows shallow background seismicity (<20 km depth) from the northeastern part of the source region of the 2016 Kumamoto earthquake to Mt. Yufu, Oita Prefecture, as well as the distribution of aftershocks since the mainshock on 16 April 2016 based on the All-Japan hypocenter catalog by the Japan Meteorological Agency (JMA). This figure includes the locations of the Zougahana, Matoishi-bokujo-I, and Miyaji faults, which are considered to have triggered slip during the 2016 Kumamoto earthquake and may have repeatedly interacted in the past.

During the 10 yr preceding the 2016 Kumamoto earthquake, earthquakes occurred only sparsely along the Futagawa fault and in the northern part of the caldera (Fig. 14a). In addition, shallow earthquakes of volcanic origin occurred around the active volcanoes Mt. Yufu and Mt. Kuju. However, there is no linear distribution of seismic sources along the strike of the Zougahana fault.

After the mainshock occurred at 01:25 JST on 16 April, active aftershocks were observed at ~10 km depth in the northern part of Aso caldera, including the Zougahana fault, without any time lag (Fig. 14b). In contrast, there exists a gap in aftershocks from the northeastern end of the Futagawa fault to the area around the Zougahana fault, known as the "Aso gap" (Uchide *et al.*, 2016; Yoshida *et al.*, 2017). The Aso gap has traditionally been attributed to the existence of a low-density body underground (Miyakawa *et al.*, 2016); recent InSAR analyses and precise gravity observations have revealed that a hydrothermal system has created a low-stress state that prevented the propagation of the rupture (Kobayashi *et al.*, 2025). In addition, an M_{JMA} 5.7 earthquake occurred near Mt. Yufu, ~55 km northeast of the Futagawa fault, at the same time as the mainshock. It is clear in Figure 14b that aftershock activity near Mt. Yufu had begun at that time. Indeed, numerous studies have shown that the seismic ground motions accompanying the mainshock of the 2016 Kumamoto earthquake triggered this earthquake near Mt. Yufu (Miyazawa, 2016; Uchide *et al.*, 2016; Yoshida, 2016; Saito *et al.*, 2025).

One to two hours after the mainshock, aftershocks continued around the Zougahana fault at ~10 km depth, with the largest (M_{JMA} 5.9) occurring at 03:03 JST (Fig. 14c). Then, within 2–3 hr after the mainshock, aftershock activity around the Zougahana fault extended farther to the northeast, and at 03:55 JST, an M_{JMA} 5.8 aftershock occurred southwest of Mt. Kuju (Fig. 14d). Three to six hours after the mainshock, aftershocks continued along the Zougahana fault and near Mt. Kuju, and at 07:11 JST, a relatively large M_{JMA} 5.4 aftershock again occurred near Mt Yufu (Fig. 14e). Figure 14f shows the distribution of aftershocks that occurred over the following month. Aftershocks along the Zougahana fault and near Mt. Kuju and Mt. Yufu continued. On 18 April, an M_{JMA} 5.8 aftershock occurred southwest of Mt. Kuju, and on 29 April, an M_{JMA} 4.5 aftershock occurred southeast of Mt. Yufu (Fig. 14f).

Based on the aftershock distribution, aftershock activity occurred immediately after the mainshock at ~10 km depth directly below the Zougahana fault, and aftershocks propagated northeasterly from there to southwest of Mt. Kuju during the 2–3 hr following the mainshock. Mt. Kuju appears to be an obstacle (the "Mt. Kuju wall") to aftershocks heading farther northeast. In addition, aftershock activity increased near Mt. Yufu, even farther from the epicenter. Given the gap in aftershock activity between Mt. Kuju and Mt. Yufu, the aftershocks from the Zougahana fault did not propagate there.

Focusing on the Matoishi-bokujo-I and Miyaji faults, some shallow seismicity occurred around the Matoishi-bokujo-I fault before the mainshock, but no aftershocks occurred there, and almost no background earthquakes or aftershocks occurred around the Miyaji fault. Therefore, two secondary fault patterns occurred during the 2016 Kumamoto earthquake: one with aftershocks, including the Zougahana fault, and one without.

Relationship of the Zougahana fault to the 2016 Kumamoto earthquake seismic intensity distribution

Figure 15a shows the estimated seismic intensity distribution associated with the mainshock of the 2016 Kumamoto earthquake. The center of the Futagawa fault experienced strong ground motions >6+ on the JMA seismic intensity scale, and it is estimated that the Zougahana and Matoishi-bokujo-I faults were also hit by stronger ground motions compared with the surrounding areas that experienced JMA seismic intensity 6−. In particular, the Zougahana fault outcrop is within an isolated hill, and ground motions could be further amplified by the topographic effect (e.g., Boore, 1972). In contrast, the Miyaji fault, which was also triggered by the mainshock, did not experience strong ground motions compared with surrounding areas, registering JMA seismic intensities of 5− to 5+. In comparison, some areas in the Mt. Yufu region experienced strong ground motions at JMA seismic intensities of 6− to 6+, considered to result from the M_{JMA} 5.7 earthquake that occurred almost simultaneously with the mainshock (Miyazawa, 2016; Uchide *et al.*, 2016; Yoshida, 2016).

Coulomb stress changes (ΔCFF)

We investigated the effect of ΔCFF on the secondary fault group, including the Zougahana fault located northeast of the Futagawa fault. Many fault models have been proposed for the Futagawa fault rupture associated with the mainshock, as well as various

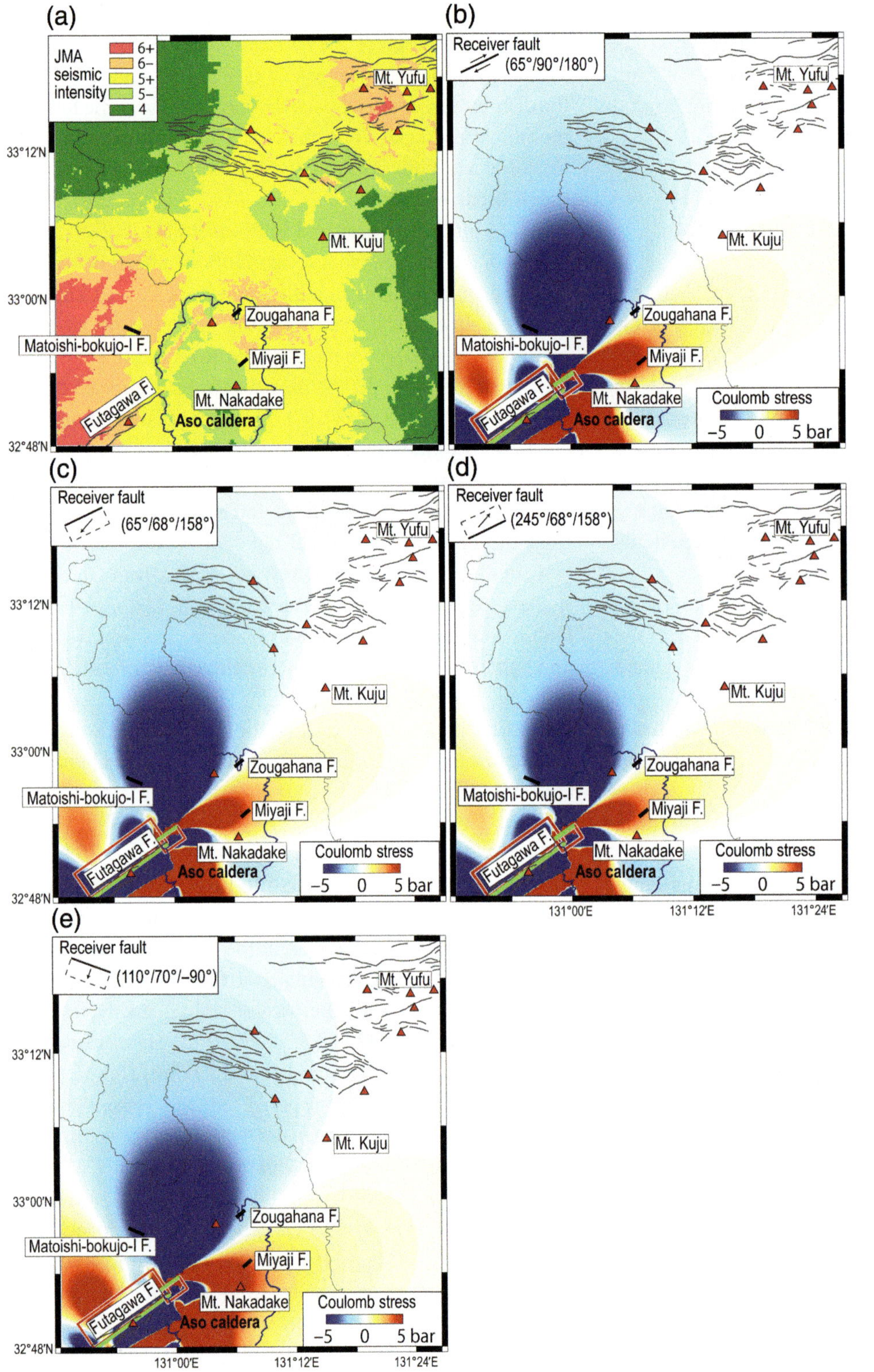

Figure 15. (a) Estimated seismic intensity distribution of the mainshock of the 2016 Kumamoto earthquake by the National Research Institute for Earth Science and Disaster Prevention, based on the Japan real-time information system for earthquake (J-RISQ) homepage. (b–e) Coulomb stress change (ΔCFF) in the northeastern part of the epicentral area associated with the slip of the Futagawa fault. The fault model was adopted from Yarai *et al.* (2016). (b–d) ΔCFF resolved (b) onto a pure dextral strike-slip fault, (c) onto a dextral and oblique-slip with south-dipping fault, and (d) onto a dextral and oblique-slip with north-dipping fault. In (b–d), the strike of the receiver fault set is the Zougahana fault. (e) ΔCFF resolved onto a normal fault with the same strike and dip as the Matoishi-bokujo-I fault. All the above panels, gray thin lines indicate active faults, and red triangles indicate the locations of Quaternary volcanoes, whose sources are the same as in Figure 14.

theories about the northeast end of the rupture (e.g., Asano and Iwata, 2016; Himematsu and Furuya, 2016; Ozawa *et al.*, 2016; Kobayashi *et al.*, 2017, 2025; Yoshida *et al.*, 2017; Yue *et al.*, 2017; Zhang *et al.*, 2018). Some models include the Zougahana fault and the surrounding area as the source fault, crossing Aso caldera (Kubo *et al.*, 2016; Uchide *et al.*, 2016). Here, however, we adopted the fault model estimated from GNSS and InSAR data acquired by the Geospatial Information Authority of Japan (Yarai *et al.*, 2016) and analyzed ΔCFF. This model focuses on the explanation of crustal movement along the Futagawa fault and does not include the Zougahana fault. Because this aligns with the northeastern end of the surface rupture (Shirahama *et al.*, 2016; Kumahara *et al.*, 2022) (Fig. 1c), we judged it to be a reasonable model. The northeastern end of this fault model is also where the surface rupture dispersed, like the tip of a broom (e.g., Kim and Sanderson, 2006). We used Coulomb 3.3 software (Toda *et al.*, 2011) to calculate ΔCFF, with Poisson's ratio set to 0.25 and Young's modulus to 80 GPa and assume that the Zougahana fault is a pure right-lateral strike-slip fault.

The results of the calculations showed that the Zougahana fault lies within an area of slightly negative coulomb stress from 0.1 to −0.7 bars (Fig. 15b). In addition, Figure 15c,d shows the results of our analysis when the Zougahana fault was assumed as the south- and north-dipping oblique-slip fault, considering the vertical displacement from the 2016 earthquake (Fig. 6). The shape of the negative ΔCFF area is almost identical in both cases, with a slight negative value (−0.1 to −0.7 bar). A significant discovery is that the Zougahana fault is not in an area clearly characterized by positive ΔCFF; accordingly, static stress cannot have been an active trigger of the Zougahana fault. In contrast, the Miyaji fault, which has a strike nearly parallel to that of the Zougahana fault, is in a region clearly characterized by positive ΔCFF values of at least 3 bars (Fig. 15b–d). Even if the Futagawa fault repeatedly ruptured with the Zougahana and Miyaji faults, the triggering factors for the two secondary faults might have differed. Figure 15e shows the same analysis results but when the receiver fault is set to have the sense of movement of the Matoishi-bokujo-I fault. We took the strike of the Matoishi-bokujo-I fault as the value measured on the map and assumed the fault to be a pure normal fault with a 70° S dip. This assumption is based on the previous interpretation of the fault group northwest of Aso by Fujiwara *et al.* (2016). The results show that the Matoishi-bokujo-I fault clearly lies within an area of the negative ΔCFF region (<−5.0 bar) regardless of the orientation of the receiver fault. Therefore, static stress cannot be said to be the active trigger of the Matoishi-bokujo-I fault, just as it is not for the Zougahana fault.

Trigger of secondary faulting at the northeast end of the Futagawa fault

Several factors in the previous sections suggest that the ground motions caused by the mainshock of the Futagawa fault (Fig. 15a) were the most likely trigger of at least the Zougahana fault, rather than static triggering. However, another consideration is that an M_{JMA} 5.9 earthquake occurred around the Zougahana fault ~1.5 hr after the mainshock (JST 03:03) (Fig. 14c). According to the F-net mechanism solution, this earthquake had M_w 5.5, a hypocentral depth of 5 km, an N29°E strike, and a slip plane dipping 60° to the northwest. This slip plane sense broadly corresponds to the typical sense of slip for faults in the study area, including the Zougahana fault. For reference, when using the scaling law for strike-slip faults of Wells and Coppersmith (1994), an M_w 5.5 earthquake can produce a subsurface rupture length of ~3.31 km and an average displacement of 0.04 m. In addition, if we adopt the scaling laws updated in recent years, the earthquake can produce a subsurface rupture length of ~6.35 km and an average displacement of 0.10 m (Thingbaijam *et al.*, 2017), 6.42 km, and 0.21 m, respectively (Brengman *et al.*, 2019) (for details of these calculations, see supplement 6). The length of the phase discontinuity that appeared along the Zougahana fault was ~4.8 km (Fig. 2), with a field horizontal displacement of 48.6 ± 0.2 cm and a vertical displacement of 20.2 ± 4.7 cm (Fig. 6a,b). Such displacement amounts are approximately consistent with the scaling laws, suggesting another possibility, that the Zougahana fault was activated as a seismogenic fault rupture with the aftershock ~1.5 hr after the mainshock rather than simultaneously with the mainshock. Unfortunately, there were no satellite observations between the mainshock and this aftershock. Because the area around the Zougahana D prehistoric site is uninhabited, it is difficult to obtain residents' testimonies; accordingly, it remains difficult to determine whether the Zougahana fault was activated at the time of the mainshock or the aftershock.

Similar to the Zougahana fault, the trigger of the Matoishi-bokujo-I fault rupture cannot be explained by ΔCFF (Fig. 15e), and there is no aftershock distribution in this area (Fig. 15b–f). The Matoishi-bokujo-I fault rupture was therefore likely triggered by strong ground motions at the same time as the mainshock. Fujiwara *et al.* (2020) pointed out that the phase discontinuities to the northwest of Aso caldera, including the Matoishi-bokujo-I fault, did not reflect stress changes associated with the mainshock, but rather that the displacement was caused by strong ground motions, reflecting the background north–south tensile stress field; we consider their interpretation to be valid. In contrast, the results for the Miyaji fault indicate that ΔCFF is a strong candidate as a trigger for displacement there (Fig. 15b–d). Therefore, although ruptures on secondary faults around Aso caldera are synchronized to activity on the Futagawa fault, their triggers are diverse. Accordingly, when evaluating secondary faults at the edge of the main fault, assessments based on only one factor will lead to underestimations of the displacement probability of that fault.

Role of the Zougahana fault in the tectonics of central Kyushu

The tectonics of the central Kyushu region, including the Futagawa fault, have been the subject of several studies that have produced various models and interpretations. Hatanaka and Shimazaki (1988) interpreted the north–south extensional movement of the BSGZ (Matsumoto, 1979) as a phenomenon in which central and northern Kyushu are displaced dextrally, parallel to the median tectonic line (Fig. 1b). They inferred that the BSGZ was formed by the Philippine Sea plate dipping obliquely to the west of the median tectonic line and that the graben group, which runs in an en echelon pattern, formed to relieve the local strain of east–west compression and north–south tension. Chida (1992) divided this graben group into seven individual grabens (including the Beppu Bay, Yufudake, Kuehirayama, Haneyama, and Kuradake grabens) and proposed that these grabens formed because of the local east–west compressive stress field within the broader, north–south tensile stress field caused by right-lateral movement along the Oita–Kumamoto tectonic line, which forms the southern limit of these grabens. Furthermore, Oohashi *et al.* (2020) discussed the tectonic history of central Kyushu by summarizing the strain field of the Futagawa fault and surrounding areas as determined by geological and geodetic methods, as well as the stress field as determined by seismological methods, in the context of existing data. They newly

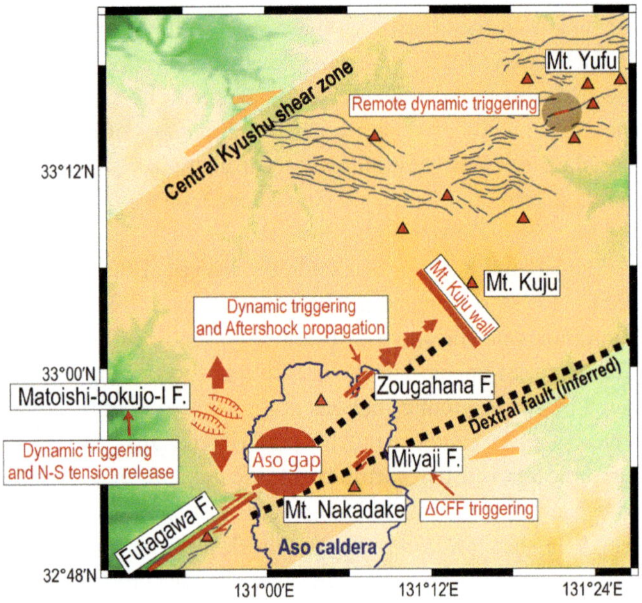

Figure 16. Schematic map showing the characteristics of secondary faults and illustrating the relationship between the tectonics of Central Kyushu and the tectonics from Aso caldera to Mt. Yufu. The Central Kyushu shear zone and the dextral fault (inferred) are drawn from Oohashi *et al.* (2020). The gray thin lines indicate active faults, and the red triangles indicate the locations of Quaternary volcanoes, whose sources are the same as in Figure 14. N-S, north–south.

defined the BSGZ as the Central Kyushu shear zone, a complex of volcanoes, grabens, and strike-slip faults formed under a transtensional tectonic regime running parallel to the larger structure of the BSGZ. The 2016 Kumamoto earthquake is considered to be a tectonic movement in which dextral slip on the Futagawa-Hinagu fault zone (i.e., the southern boundary fault of the Central Kyushu shear zone), the formation of a graben, and the areal subsidence of the Kumamoto Plain to the north boundary of the Central Kyushu shear zone occurred simultaneously.

The Central Kyushu shear zone model proposed by Oohashi *et al.* (2020), which incorporates results from the 2016 Kumamoto earthquake and recent geodetic research, is the most consistent with our interpretation. In this case, the activity of the Matoishi-bokujo-I fault, which is part of the Kuradake graben, can be explained reasonably by transtensional tectonics. However, how should the Zougahana and Miyaji faults be positioned within the model? As revealed by our survey of the Zougahana fault outcrop, the Zougahana fault has repeatedly and similarly slipped since the deposition of the AT tephra about 30 ka. In addition, the fault outcrop at Loc. 1 (Figs. 3a and 4b) clearly shows that the fault separates the Aso-2A–2B pyroclastic flow deposit (deposited about140 ka; Matsumoto *et al.*, 1991) (Fig. 5c,d); accordingly, the Zougahana fault may have been active since the Middle Pleistocene. The Aso-4 eruption (about 87 ka; Aoki, 2008), which formed the present-day Aso caldera, must have destroyed and buried all active geomorphic structures around Aso caldera, including the Zougahana fault. Still, we may be witnessing a snapshot of the old scarp gradually re-emerging because of ground motions on the Futagawa fault (or other surrounding earthquakes) or the addition of static strain. In other words, the Zougahana and Miyaji faults may not be simple secondary faults in the shallow layer but may be the main shear structures that make up the Central Kyushu shear zone. Figure 16 is a schematic diagram showing the locations and characteristics of the secondary faults caused by the 2016 Kumamoto earthquake superimposed on the Central Kyushu shear zone model of Oohashi *et al.* (2020). Although the accuracy of the locations is not sufficient, Oohashi *et al.* (2020) drew inferred dextral faults that pass through Aso caldera, and we suspect that these faults are related to the Zougahana and Miyaji faults. In the future, it will be necessary to clarify whether structures corresponding to these secondary faults are hidden beneath the Aso caldera and Mt. Kuju volcanic zones using seismic reflection surveys and detailed aftershock observations. In addition, future studies should consider that secondary faults can form at the contact between active faults and volcanic zones because of various factors.

CONCLUSIONS

Following the 2016 Kumamoto earthquake, phase discontinuities were confirmed by InSAR analyses that aligned with the Zougahana fault, which is ~14 km northeast of the primary Futagawa fault, and a surface rupture was confirmed by a field survey after the 2016 earthquake. In this study, we investigated paleoseismic activity on the Zougahana fault by conducting topographic interpretations, field surveys, and interpretations of fault outcrops and multiple cores. As a result, we were able to identify at least six paleoearthquakes, including the 2016 earthquake, on the Zougahana fault. The ages of the four most recent events, which were estimated with relatively high accuracy, were constrained by tephra analyses and the OxCal model using radiocarbon dating, as the AD2016 earthquake and events at 5760–2750 cal B.P. (event 1), 8700–5000 cal B.P. (event 2), and 9330–7550 cal B.P. (event 3). Furthermore, it is also thought that multiple events occurred in the period from 29,870 to 11,030 cal B.P. after deposition of the AT tephra around 30 ka, including events 4 and 5. Compared with the paleoseismic history of the Futagawa fault and other secondary faults around Aso caldera, it became clear that the number of events recognized at the Zougahana fault was likely to be an underestimate, supporting possible missing events at the Zougahana fault outcrop around 2 ka.

Based on the distribution of aftershocks, seismic intensity, and a Coulomb stress change (ΔCFF) analysis of the 2016 Kumamoto earthquake, we interpreted the Zougahana fault's trigger to have been strong ground motions associated with the mainshock. However, it is currently impossible to determine whether it was triggered at the same time as the mainshock or by the M_{JMA} 5.9 aftershock that occurred around the Zougahana fault ~1.5 hr later. In contrast, within the same secondary fault, the Matoishi-bokujo-I fault in the northwest of the Aso caldera may have produced normal fault displacement without an aftershock caused by strong ground motions. The Futagawa fault's ΔCFF may have triggered the Miyaji fault inside the caldera. Even if the secondary faults around Aso caldera rupture at the same time as the Futagawa fault in the past, the specific triggers of their fault motions are diverse. When evaluating secondary faults at the ends of primary faults, assessments based on only one type of factor will likely lead to underestimates of the displacement probability of that fault.

Within the transtensional tectonics model (Central Kyushu shear zone), which views the larger structure of the Beppu–Shimabara Graben as a complex of volcanoes, grabens, and en echelon strike-slip faults, the Zougahana fault may not be a simple surface secondary fault. Instead, it may belong to a main transtensional shear structure. In the future, it will be necessary to carry out detailed geophysical surveys and aftershock observations to determine whether structures corresponding to surface secondary faults are buried underground in the volcanic zone.

DATA AND RESOURCES

Advanced Land Observation Satellite (ALOS)-2 data were provided by Japan Aerospace Exploration Agency (JAXA) within the framework of ERI JURP 2024-B-02 in the Earthquake Research Institute, the University of Tokyo. The 1-m-mesh light detection and ranging (LiDAR) digital elevation model (DEM) used for geomorphic interpretation was obtained in 2010 by the Unzen Reconstruction Office of the Kyushu Regional Development Bureau of the Ministry of Land, Infrastructure, Transport, and Tourism and was used with the permission of the Geospatial Information Authority of Japan (GSI). The 10-m-mesh DEM used to create Figure 1 was also provided by GSI. The interferogram in Figure 2 was created by GSI map (https://maps.gsi.go.jp). A visualization system for subsurface structures (https://gbank.gsj.jp/subsurface/english/ondemand.php) of AIST was used for aftershock distribution mapping (Fig. 14). Hypocenters in Figure 14 are based on the All-Japan hypocenter catalog by the Japan Meteorological Agency (JMA). The Japan Real-time Information System for earthQuake (J-RiSQ; https://www.j-risq.bosai.go.jp/report/en/R-20240323083201-0057) was used to map the seismic intensity distribution (Fig. 15a). All websites were last accessed in December 2025. The supplemental material for this article includes a 3D Zougahana fault outcrop PDF (supplement 1), detailed description the stratigraphy of the Zougahana fault outcrop, hand cores, and the result of tephra analysis (supplement 2), a data sheet of major element compositions of glass shards measured by EPMA (supplement 3), code for the OxCal chronological model of faulting events (supplement 4), and the vertical displacements measured on faults F1–F7 at each stratum boundary on the wall of the Zougahana fault outcrop (Fig. 8b), as well as the unit levels of events 1–5 and the 2016 earthquake (supplement 5) and calculation of the surface rupture length and average displacement of the Zougahana fault predicted from moment magnitude and scaling laws (supplement 6).

DECLARATION OF COMPETING INTERESTS

The authors acknowledge that there are no conflicts of interest recorded.

ACKNOWLEDGMENTS

In carrying out the fault outcrop survey, the authors were helped by Shiraishi, the land manager of the Kiotoshi Pastural Cooperatives, and Toshikuni Miyamoto of the Aso City Board of Education; the authors obtained permission in advance from the Aso-Kujyu National Park Management Office of the Ministry of the Environment in accordance with the relevant laws and regulations. The authors thank Yasuo Miyabuchi, Ryuichi Teshima, Yuji Goto, Tatsuya Konoo, Hajime Fukami, Ryukei Fukushima, Daiki Nishioka, and Miki Tokumaru from Kumamoto University for their cooperation in this fault outcrop survey. Akihiro Yamada of Ceres Corporation and Hidenobu Takahashi of the Central Research Institute of Electric Power Industry assisted with the hand auger coring survey. Yukiko Suwa of Ceres Corporation provided valuable advice on electron probe microanalyzer (EPMA) analysis. The authors are also grateful to Associate Editor Nicola Litchfield and to the two reviewers, James Muirhead, and an anonymous reviewer for their constructive comments. This work was supported by JSPS KAKENHI Grant Numbers JP20K01141 and JP23K00972 (principal investigator, Hiroshi Une).

REFERENCES

Allen, J. R. L. (1986). Earthquake magnitude-frequency, epicentral distance, and soft-sediment deformation in sedimentary basins, *Sediment. Geol.* **46,** nos. 1/2, 67–75.

Allen, C. R., and R. E. Wallace (1986). Seismological and paleoseismological techniques of research in active tectonics, in *Active Tectonics*, R. E. Wallace (Editor), National Academies Press, Washington, D.C., 148–154.

Aoki, K. (2008). Revised age and distribution of ca. 87 ka Aso-4 tephra based on new evidence from the northwest Pacific Ocean, *Quat. Int.* **178,** no. 1, 100–118.

Asano, K., and T. Iwata (2016). Source rupture processes of the foreshock and mainshock in the 2016 Kumamoto earthquake sequence estimated from the kinematic waveform inversion of strong motion data, *Earth Planet Space* **68,** no. 1, 147, doi: 10.1186/s40623-016-0519-9.

Biasi, G. P., and S. G. Wesnousky (2016). Steps and gaps in ground ruptures: Empirical bounds on rupture propagation, *Bull. Seismol. Soc. Am.* **106,** no. 3, 1110–1124.

Biasi, G. P., and S. G. Wesnousky (2017). Bends and ends of surface ruptures, *Bull. Seismol. Soc. Am.* **107,** no. 6, 2543–2560.

Boore, D. M. (1972). A note on the effect of simple topography on seismic SH waves, *Bull. Seismol. Soc. Am.* **62,** no. 1, 275–284.

Brengman, C. M. J., W. D. Barnhart, E. H. Mankin, and C. N. Miller (2019). Earthquake-scaling relationships from geodetically derived slip distributions, *Bull. Seismol. Soc. Am.* **109,** no. 5, 1701–1715, doi: 10.1785/0120190048.

Bronk Ramsey, C. (1995). Radiocarbon calibration and analysis of stratigraphy: The OxCal program, *Radiocarbon* **37,** no. 2, 425–430, doi: 10.1017/s0033822200030903.

Bronk Ramsey, C. (2009). Bayesian analysis of radiocarbon dates, *Radiocarbon* **51,** no. 1, 337–360, doi: 10.1017/S0033822200033865.

Bronk Ramsey, C. (2024). OxCal 4.4, available at https://c14.arch.ox.ac.uk/oxcal/OxCal.html# (last accessed April 2024).

Chida, N. (1992). Active faults in Central Kyushu, southwest Japan - Quaternary faulting along the median tectonic line in Kyushu, *Memoir. Geol. Soc. Jpn.* **40,** 39–51 (in Japanese with English abstract).

Earthquake Research Committee, Headquarters for Earthquake Research Promotion (2016). Evaluation of the 2016 Kumamoto earthquake, available at http://www.static.jishin.go.jp/resource/monthly/2016/2016_kumamoto.pdf (last accessed April 2024) (in Japanese).

Fossen, H. (2016). *Structural Geology*, Second Ed., Cambridge University Press, 377–400.

Fujiwara, S., T. Nakano, and Y. Morishita (2020). Detection of triggered shallow slips caused by large earthquakes using L-band SAR interferometry, *Earth Planets Space* **72,** no. 1, 1–23, doi: 10.1186/s40623-020-01239-6.

Fujiwara, S., T. Nishimura, M. Murakami, H. Nakagawa, M. Tobita, and P. A. Rosen (2000). 2.5-D surface deformation of M6.1 earthquake near Mt Iwate detected by SAR interferometry, *Geophys. Res. Lett.* **27,** no. 14, 2049–2052, doi: 10.1029/1999GL011291.

Fujiwara, S., H. Yarai, T. Kobayashi, Y. Morishita, T. Nakano, B. Miyahara, H. Nakai, Y. Miura, H. Ueshiba, Y. Kakiage, *et al.* (2016). Small-displacement linear surface ruptures of the 2016 Kumamoto earthquake sequence detected by ALOS-2 SAR interferometry, *Earth Planets Space* **68,** no. 1, 160, doi: 10.1186/s40623-016-0534-x.

Goto, H., H. Tsutsumi, S. Toda, and Y. Kumahara (2017). Geomorphic features of surface ruptures associated with the 2016 Kumamoto earthquake in and around the downtown of Kumamoto City, and implications on triggered slip along active faults, *Earth Planets Space* **69,** no. 1, 26, doi: 10.1186/s40623-017-0603-9.

Hashimoto, M. (2020). Postseismic deformation following the 2016 Kumamoto earthquake detected by ALOS-2/PALSAR-2, *Earth Planets Space* **72,** no. 1, 154, doi: 10.1186/s40623-020-01285-0.

Hatanaka, Y., and K. Shimazaki (1988). Rupture process of the 1975 central Oita, Japan, earthquake, *J. Phys. Earth* **36,** no. 1, 1–15.

Himematsu, Y., and M. Furuya (2016). Fault source model for the 2016 Kumamoto earthquake sequence based on ALOS-2/PALSAR-2 pixel-offset data: Evidence for dynamic slip partitioning, *Earth Planets Space* **68,** no. 1, 169, doi: 10.1186/s40623-016-0545-7.

Imaizumi, T., T. Miyauchi, H. Tsutsumi, and T. Nakata (2018). *Digital Active Fault Map of Japan, [Revised Edition]*, University of Tokyo Press, Tokyo.

Inoue, N., N. Kitada, N. Shibuya, M. Omata, T. Takahama, M. Tonagi, and K. Irikura (2020). Probabilistic evaluation of off-fault displacements of the 2016 Kumamoto earthquake, *Pure Appl. Geophys.* **177,** no. 5, 2007–2019, doi: 10.1007/s00024-019-02345-7.

International Atomic Energy Agency (IAEA) (2010). Seismic hazards in site evaluation for nuclear installations, *IAEA Safety Standards Series No. SSG-9*, IAEA, Vienna.

Ishimura, D., Y. Iwasa, N. Takahashi, R. Tadokoro, and R. Oda (2022). Paleoseismic events and shallow subsurface structure of the central part of the Futagawa fault, which generated the 2016 M_w 7.0 Kumamoto earthquake, *Geomorphology* **414,** 108,387.

Ishimura, D., H. Tsutsumi, S. Toda, Y. Fukushima, Y. Kumahara, N. Takahashi, T. Ichihara, and K. Takada (2021). Repeated triggered ruptures on a distributed secondary fault system: An example from the 2016 Kumamoto earthquake, southwest Japan, *Earth Planets Space* **73,** no. 1, 39, doi: 10.1186/s40623-021-01371-x.

Iwasa, Y., Y. Kumahara, H. Goto, D. Ishimura, and T. Hosoya (2022). Faulting history of the Futagawa fault zone based on trenching survey at Komori, Nishihara Village, Kumamoto Prefecture, *Active Fault Res.* **56,** 47–58, doi: 10.11462/afr.2022.56_47 (in Japanese with English abstract).

Kaneda, H., and T. Chiba (2019). Stereopaired morphometric protection index red relief image maps (Stereo MPI-RRIMs): Effective visualization of high-resolution digital elevation models for interpreting and mapping small tectonic geomorphic features, *Bull. Seismol. Soc. Am.* **109,** no. 1, 99–109, doi: 10.1785/0120180166.

Kaneda, H., T. Nakata, H. Tsutsumi, H. Kondo, N. Sugito, Y. Awata, S. S. Akhtar, A. Majid, W. Khattak, A. A. Awan, *et al.* (2008). Surface rupture of the 2005 Kashmir, Pakistan, earthquake and its active tectonic implications, *Bull. Seismol. Soc. Am.* **98,** no. 2, 521–557, doi: 10.1785/0120070073.

Kim, Y., and D. J. Sanderson (2006). Structural similarity and variety at the tips in a wide range of strike–slip faults: A review, *Terra Nova* **18,** no. 5, 330–344, doi: 10.1111/j.1365-3121.2006.00697.x.

King, G., and J. Nábělek (1985). Role of fault bends in the initiation and termination of earthquake rupture, *Science* **228,** no. 4702, 984–987, doi: 10.1126/science.228.4702.984.

King, G. C., R. S. Stein, and J. Lin (1994). Static stress changes and the triggering of earthquakes, *Bull. Seismol. Soc. Am.* **84,** no. 3, 935–953.

Kobayashi, H., K. Koketsu, and H. Miyake (2017). Rupture processes of the 2016 Kumamoto earthquake sequence: Causes for extreme ground motions, *Geophys. Res. Lett.* **44,** no. 12, 6002–6010, doi: 10.1002/2017GL073857.

Kobayashi, T., K. Matsuo, R. Ando, T. Nakano, and G. Watanuki (2025). High-resolution image on terminus of fault rupture: Relationship with volcanic hydrothermal structure, *Geophys. J. Int.* **240,** no. 2, 1196–1214.

Kubo, H., W. Suzuki, S. Aoi, and H. Sekiguchi (2016). Source rupture processes of the 2016 Kumamoto, Japan, earthquakes estimated from strong-motion waveforms, *Earth Planets Space* **68,** no. 1, 161, doi: 10.1186/s40623-016-0536-8.

Kumahara, Y., H. Kaneda, and H. Tsutsumi (Editors) (2022). *Surface Ruptures Associated with the 2016 Kumamoto Earthquake Sequence in Southwest Japan*, Advances in Geological Science, Springer Nature Singapore, Singapore, doi: 10.1007/978-981-19-1150-7.

Kumahara, Y., M. Torii, T. Nakata, H. Goto, Y. Iwasa, Y. Suzuki, M. Watanabe, S. Toda, N. Takahashi, and M. Okuno (2017). Fault history of the northern part of Futagawa-Hinagu fault zone based on trench survey at Dozon, Mashiki Town and at Kawayo, Minami-Aso Village, *Program and Abstracts JSAF 2017 Fall Meeting*, Hiroshima University, Higashi-Hiroshima, 24–25 November 2017 (in Japanese).

Lettis, W., J. Bachhuber, R. Witter, C. Brankman, C. E. Randolph, A. Barka, W. D. Page, and A. Kaya (2002). Influence of releasing stepovers on surface fault rupture and fault segmentation: Examples from the 17 August 1999 Izmit earthquake on the North Anatolian fault, Turkey, *Bull. Seismol. Soc. Am.* **92,** no. 1, 19–42.

Machida, H., and F. Arai (2003). *Atlas of Tephra in and Around Japan [Revised Edition]*, University of Tokyo Press, Tokyo (in Japanese).

Matsumoto, A. (1979). Some problems on volcanic activities and depression structures in Kyushu, Japan, *Memoir. Geol. Soc. Jpn.* **16,** 127–139 (in Japanese with English Abstract).

Matsumoto, A., K. Uto, K. Ono, and K. Watanabe (1991). K-Ar age determinations for Aso volcanic rocks: Concordance with volcano stratigraphy and application to pyroclastic flows, *Program Abstracts Volcanol. Soc. Jpn.* **2,** 73 doi: 10.18940/vsj.1991.2.0_73 (in Japanese).

McCalpin, J. P., T. K. Rockwell, and R. J. Weldon II (2009). Paleoseismology of strike-slip tectonic environments, *Int. Geophys.* **95,** 474.

McLean, D., P. G. Albert, T. Suzuki, T. Nakagawa, J.-I. Kimura, Q. Chang, Y. Miyabuchi, C. J. Manning, A. MacLeod, S. P. E. Blockley, *et al.* (2020). Constraints on the timing of explosive volcanism at Aso and Aira Calderas (Japan) between 50 and 30 ka: New insights from the Lake Suigetsu sedimentary record (SG14 Core), *Geochem. Geophys. Geosys.* **21,** no. 8, e2019GC008874, doi: 10.1029/2019GC008874.

Miyabuchi, Y. (2009). A 90,000-year tephrostratigraphic framework of Aso volcano, Japan, *Sediment. Geol.* **220,** nos. 3/4, 169–189.

Miyabuchi, Y., and S. Sugiyama (2011). 90,000-year phytolith record from tephra section at the northeastern rim of Aso Caldera, Japan, *Quat. Int.* **246,** nos. 1/2, 239–246.

Miyabuchi, Y., H. Hoshizumi, H. Takada, K. Watanabe, and S. Xu (2003). Pumice-fall deposits from Aso volcano during the past 90,000 years, southwestern Japan, *Kazan* **48,** no. 2, 195–214 (in Japanese with English abstract).

Miyakawa, A., T. Sumita, Y. Okubo, R. Okuwaki, M. Otsubo, S. Uesawa, and Y. Yagi (2016). Volcanic magma reservoir imaged as a low-density body beneath Aso volcano that terminated the 2016 Kumamoto earthquake rupture, *Earth Planets Space* **68,** no. 1, 208, doi: 10.1186/s40623-016-0582-2.

Miyazawa, M. (2016). An investigation into the remote triggering of the Oita earthquake by the 2016 M_w 7.0 Kumamoto earthquake using full wavefield simulation, *Earth Planets Space* **68,** no. 1, 205, doi: 10.1186/s40623-016-0585-z.

Nakata, T., and T. Imaizumi (2002). *Digital Active Fault Map of Japan*, University of Tokyo Press, Tokyo (in Japanese).

National Institute of Advanced Industrial Science and Technology (2009). Active fault database of Japan, June 23, 2009 version, available at https://gbank.gsj.jp/activefault/index_e_gmap.html (last accessed March 2025).

National Institute of Advanced Industrial Science and Technology (2025). Active fault database of Japan, February 14, 2025 version, available at https://gbank.gsj.jp/activefault/index_e_gmap.html (last accessed March 2025).

Nishiki, K., J. Itoh, and T. Ueno (2012). Database of Quaternary volcanic and intrusive rock bodies in Japan, *Geol. Surv. Jpn. Interim Rept. 60* (in Japanese).

Obata, H. (Editor) (1998). The Zougahana D prehistoric site in Ichinomiya Town, Aso Country, Kumamoto Prefecture, in *Summary Report on First Excavation*, Board of Education, Ichinomiya Town (in Japanese with English Abstract).

Okamura, Y., S. Abe, Y. Miyashita, T. Azuma, T. Togo, Y. Shirahama, Y. Awata, T. Maruyama, T. Ogami, R. Imura, *et al.* (2018). Survey of detailed position and shape of active faults to understand the fault segments and observation to reveal the paleoseismic history and slip rates, in *Research Report of a Comprehensive Active Fault Survey After the 2016 Kumamoto Earthquake*, 2017 Fiscal Year, Ministry of Education, Culture, Sports, Science and Technology and Kyushu University (in Japanese).

Ono, K., and K. Watanabe (1985). Geological Map of Aso volcano, *Geological Map of Volcanoes 4*, Geological Survey of Japan (in Japanese with English abstract).

Oohashi, K., M. Otsubo, S. Matsumoto, K. Kobayashi, K. Sato, and T. Nishimura (2020). The quaternary tectonics of Central Kyushu and the 2016 Kumamoto earthquake: From a multifaceted viewpoint combining geology, seismology, and geodesy, *J. Geogr.* **129,** no. 4, 565–589, doi: 10.5026/jgeography.129.565 (in Japanese with English abstract).

Ootaki, O., T. Inoue, I. Ueda, T. Yamashita, K. Yamaguchi, H. Shirai, A. Suzuki, and K. Mikihara (2016). Revision of the results of control points after the 2016 Kumamoto earthquake, *J. Geos. Inf. Auth. Jpn.* **128,** 177–187 (in Japanese).

Ozawa, T., E. Fujita, and H. Ueda (2016). Crustal deformation associated with the 2016 Kumamoto earthquake and its effect on the magma system of Aso volcano, *Earth Planets Space* **68,** no. 1, 186, doi: 10.1186/s40623-016-0563-5.

Petersen, M. D., T. E. Dawson, R. Chen, T. Cao, C. J. Wills, D. P. Schwartz, and A. D. Frankel (2011). Fault displacement hazard for strike-slip faults, *Bull. Seismol. Soc. Am.* **101,** no. 2, 805–825.

Reimer, P. J., W. E. Austin, E. Bard, A. Bayliss, P. G. Blackwell, C. B. Ramsey, M. Butzin, H. Cheng, R. L. Edwards, and M. Friedrich (2020). The IntCal20 northern hemisphere radiocarbon age calibration curve (0–55 cal kBP), *Radiocarbon* **62,** no. 4, 725–757.

Saito, K., H. Takahashi, M. Ohzono, and Y. Ohta (2025). Dynamic stress estimation during the M 5.7 remotely triggered earthquake caused by the 2016 M 7.0 Kumamoto earthquake, Kyushu, Japan, using dense strong-motion and high-rate GNSS data, *Seismol. Res. Lett.* **96,** no. 5, 2848–2855, doi: 10.1785/0220240311.

Sato, H. P., K. Komura, H. Une, T. Nakano, and H. Yagi (2021). Study on cumulative activities of passively ruptured faults through a trenching survey at the Matoishi Bokujo I fault, northwest side of the Aso Caldera, southwestern Japan, *Geog. Rev. Jpn. Ser. A* **94,** no. 4, 250–264, doi: 10.4157/grj.94.250 (in Japanese with English abstract).

Shirahama, Y., M. Yoshimi, Y. Awata, T. Maruyama, T. Azuma, Y. Miyashita, H. Mori, K. Imanishi, N. Takeda, T. Ochi, *et al.* (2016). Characteristics of the surface ruptures associated with the 2016 Kumamoto earthquake sequence, central Kyushu, Japan, *Earth Planets Space* **68,** no. 1, doi: 10.1186/s40623-016-0559-1.

Smith, V. C., R. A. Staff, S. P. E. Blockley, C. Bronk Ramsey, T. Nakagawa, D. F. Mark, K. Takemura, and T. Danhara (2013). Identification and correlation of visible tephras in the Lake Suigetsu SG06 sedimentary archive, Japan: Chronostratigraphic markers for synchronising of east Asian/west Pacific palaeoclimatic records across the last 150 ka, *Quat. Sci. Rev.* **67,** 121–137, doi: 10.1016/J.QUASCIREV.2013.01.026.

Suzuki, Y., D. Ishimura, Y. Kumaki, Y. Kumahara, N. Chida, T. Nakata, and T. Nakano (2017). 1:25,000 active fault map, Futagawa-Hinagu fault zone and its Vicinity "Aso", Geospatial Information Authority of Japan, Ibaraki (in Japanese).

Takeuchi, S., K. Toshida, D. Miura, H. Ito, and S. Uesawa (2021). Relationships between magmatic properties and eruption magnitude of explosive eruptions at Japanese arc volcanoes during the last one hundred thousand years, *J. Volcanol. Geotherm. Res.* **419,** 107,345.

Tamaribuchi, K. (2018). Evaluation of automatic hypocenter determination in the JMA unified catalog, *Earth Planets Space* **70,** no. 1, 141, doi: 10.1186/s40623-018-0915-4.

The Research Group for Active Tectonics in Kyushu (1989). *Active Tectonics in Kyushu,* University of Tokyo Press, Bunkyo-ku, Tokyo (in Japanese).

Thingbaijam, K. K. S., P. Martin Mai, and K. Goda (2017). New empirical earthquake source-scaling laws, *Bull. Seismol. Soc. Am.* **107,** no. 5, 2225–2246.

Toda, S., and D. Ishimura (2019). Evaluation of short active faults reflected from distributed minor surface breaks found at recent inland large earthquakes including the 2016 Kumamoto earthquake, *Quat. Res. (Daiyonki-Kenkyu)* **58,** no. 2, 121–136 (in Japanese with English Abstract).

Toda, S., R. S. Stein, V. Sevilgen, and J. Lin (2011). Coulomb 3.3 Graphic-rich deformation and stress-change software for earthquake, tectonic, and volcano research and teaching—user guide, 63 pp., available at https://pubs.usgs.gov/of/2011/1060/ (last accessed April 2024).

Toda, S., M. Torii, M. Okuno, A. Konno, H. Ono, and N. Takahashi (2019). Evidence for Holocene paleoseismic events on the 2016 Kumamoto earthquake rupture zone within the Aso caldera, *Active Fault Res.* **51,** 13–25, doi: 10.11462/afr.2019.51_13 (in Japanese with English abstract).

Tsutsumi, T. (2003). Upper paleolithic lithic industries and adaptation strategy to a cold climate, *Quat. Res. (Daiyonki-Kenkyu)* **42,** no. 3, 205–218, doi: 10.4116/jaqua.42.205.

Tsutsumi, H., S. Toda, H. Goto, Y. Kumahara, D. Ishimura, N. Takahashi, K. Taniguchi, M. Omata, Y. Kohriya, M. Gomi, *et al.* (2018). Paleoseismic trenching across the surface rupture of the 2016 Kumamoto earthquake at Jichu, Mashiki Town, Kumamoto Prefecture, *Active Fault Res.* **49,** 31–39, doi: 10.11462/afr.2018.49_31 (in Japanese with English abstract).

Uchide, T., H. Horikawa, M. Nakai, R. Matsushita, N. Shigematsu, R. Ando, and K. Imanishi (2016). The 2016 Kumamoto–Oita earthquake sequence: Aftershock seismicity gap and dynamic triggering in volcanic areas, *Earth Planets Space* **68,** no. 1, 180, doi: 10.1186/s40623-016-0556-4.

Ueta, K., R. Miyawaki, K. Iemura, T. Yokoyama, and A. Miyawaki (2018). Paleoseismological study on surface fault ruptures produced by the 2016 Kumamoto earthquake, *Japan Geoscience Union Meeting 2018,* Makuhari Messe, Chiba, 20–24 May 2018 (in Japanese with English abstract).

Une, H., T. Nakano, S. Fujiwara, H. P. Sato, and H. Yagi (2022). Surface Ruptures in the Northwest of the Outer Aso Caldera, in *Surface Ruptures Associated with the 2016 Kumamoto Earthquake Sequence in Southwest Japan,* Y. Kumahara, H. Kaneda, and H. Tsutsumi (Editors), Advances in Geological Science, Springer Nature, Singapore, Singapore, 205–211, doi: 10.1007/978-981-19-1150-7_15.

Watanabe, K. (1984). Active faults in and around Kumamoto, *J. Kumamoto Geosci. Assoc.* **76,** 9–16 (in Japanese) (Translated by KK).

Watanabe, K., K. Ono, and S. Hiratsuka (1982). Pumice eruption at Kusasenrigahama volcano, *Bull. Vol. Soc. Jpn.* **27,** 337–339 (in Japanese).

Watanabe, K., K. Taguchi, H. Obata, and S. Okamoto (2001). Examination of obsidian and its gemstones excavated from the Zougahana D prehistoric site, Aso, Japan (Preliminary Report), *J. Kumamoto Geos. Assoc.* **127,** 2–9 (in Japanese) (Translated by KK).

Wells, D. L., and K. J. Coppersmith (1994). New empirical relationships among magnitude, rupture length, rupture width, rupture area, and surface displacement, *Bull. Seismol. Soc. Am.* **84,** no. 4, 974–1002.

Wesnousky, S. G. (1988). Seismological and structural evolution of strike-slip faults, *Nature* **335,** no. 6188, 340–343, doi: 10.1038/335340a0.

Wesnousky, S. G. (2006). Predicting the endpoints of earthquake ruptures, *Nature* **444,** no. 7117, 358–360.

Yarai, H., T. Kobayashi, Y. Morishita, S. Fujiwara, Y. Hiyama, S. Kawamoto, H. Ueshiba, Y. Miura, and B. Miyahara (2016). Source fault models of the 2016 Kumamoto earthquake inverted from crustal deformation, *Bull. Geos. Inf. Auth. Jpn.* **128,** 169 (in Japanese).

Yoshida, S. (2016). Earthquakes in Oita triggered by the 2016 M 7.3 Kumamoto earthquake, *Earth Planets Space* **68,** no. 1, 176, doi: 10.1186/s40623-016-0552-8.

Yoshida, K., K. Miyakoshi, K. Somei, and K. Irikura (2017). Source process of the 2016 Kumamoto earthquake (M_j 7.3) inferred from kinematic inversion of strong-motion records, *Earth Planets Space* **69,** no. 1, 64, doi: 10.1186/s40623-017-0649-8.

Yue, H., Z. E. Ross, C. Liang, S. Michel, H. Fattahi, E. Fielding, A. Moore, Z. Liu, and B. Jia (2017). The 2016 Kumamoto $M_w = 7.0$ earthquake: A significant event in a fault–volcano system, *J. Geophys. Res.* **122,** no. 11, 9166–9183, doi: 10.1002/2017JB014525.

Zhang, Y., X. Shan, G. Zhang, W. Gong, X. Liu, H. Yin, D. Zhao, S. Wen, and C. Qu (2018). Source model of the 2016 Kumamoto, Japan, earthquake constrained by InSAR, GPS, and strong-motion data: Fault slip under extensional stress, *Bull. Seismol. Soc. Am.* **108,** no. 5A, 2675–2686.

Manuscript received 31 July 2025
Published online 31 December 2025

Erratum to Characterizing Lithospheric Transverse Isotropy Using Moment Tensors—On the Origin of the Non-Double-Couple Components of Global CMT Solutions

Hitoshi Kawakatsu*[1]

This article reports an error of Kawakatsu (2024) in the adaptation of the newly introduced *r-projection* methodology to replace it with the corrected one. The resulting modifications of the content are also discussed.

In the section "Projection of the isotropic component" (page 3001), the author introduces the concept of *r-projection* that defines how the isotropic component is projected into the vertical compensated linear vector dipole (CLVD) component when the trace-free constraint is imposed in the moment tensor (MT) inversion. From line 15 of the right column, it reads: "In our case for shallow earthquakes, … the long-period surface wave excitation due to the isotropic MT $\boldsymbol{I} = [1,1,1]$ and the vertical CLVD MT $\boldsymbol{C} = [0.5,0.5,-1]$ … are nearly equal in magnitude and opposite in sign. . . ." This statement is mistaken, and the sign is the same for $\boldsymbol{I}$ and $\boldsymbol{C}$. This view is consistent with the statement of Kawakatsu (1996) (at line 4 of the right column of page 529) that "The correlation matrix for a shallow event using long-period surface-wave data (fig. 4a) indicates an almost complete correlation between the $\boldsymbol{I}$ and $\boldsymbol{C}$ components," supplemented with their figure 4a showing −0.99 for the correlation coefficient, that is, nearly complete negative correlation, which was later confirmed by Shuler *et al.* (2013). The confusion in Kawakatsu (2024) is partially caused by the error in Kawakatsu (1996) in which the isotropic component $\boldsymbol{I} = [1,1,1]$ was presented consistently in their figures by an open (white) circle, when it should be presented by a closed (black) circle.

Accepting this view, M_I will be converted to M_C as $M_C^* = M_C + M_I$ (and $M_I^* = 0$, such that the summation of two components are conserved) that requires $r = 4$ and $\alpha = -2.0$, $\beta = -0.5$ (*r4-projection*), resulting in

$$
\begin{aligned}
M_{11}^* &= M_{11} - 0.5\boldsymbol{I} \\
M_{22}^* &= M_{22} - 0.5\boldsymbol{I} \\
M_{33}^* &= M_{33} - 2.0\boldsymbol{I},
\end{aligned}
\quad (1)
$$

which should replace equation (23) of Kawakatsu (2024). It is worth noting that this conversion occurs in the source side geographical coordinate but not in the principal coordinates of the original MT (Kawakatsu, 1996, 2024). Subsequently, the discussions based on equation (23) need to be made based on this new equation (1).

Figure 1 is the result of the bootstrap analysis of the entire Global Centroid Moment Tensor (Global CMT) dataset (quality controlled) for the period of January 1976–November 2023. Although the general pattern of the misfit function map is not so changed, the slope of the minimum valley is steeper, indicating a slightly larger uncertainty for ξ. The location of the minimum valley is also slightly shifted toward the other side of the PREM sub-Moho (at a depth of 24.4 km) model. This shift modifies some of the discussions presented in Kawakatsu (2024), but the conclusion that the PREM sub-Moho VTI model serves as a suitable initial model for further investigation is unchanged. The related modifications for the other figures (original figures 5, 6, 8–10, S2, S4–S7) and a table (the bottom seven rows of Table 2) are given in the supplemental material.

DATA AND RESOURCES

The Global Centroid Moment Tensor (Global CMT) data analyzed in this article are downloaded from the source in the public domain: Global CMT webpage (https://www.globalcmt.org, last accessed February 2024). Most of the computations and figures are made using the MATLAB software (https://jp.mathworks.com, last accessed December 2025). The supplemental material contains how other related figures and a table might be affected by this erratum.

DECLARATION OF COMPETING INTERESTS

The author acknowledges that there are no conflicts of interest recorded.

ACKNOWLEDGMENTS

The author thanks Akiko Takeo for the discussion.

1. Earthquake Research Institute, The University of Tokyo, Tokyo, Japan, https://orcid.org/0000-0001-9161-5024 (HK)

*Corresponding author: hitosi@eri.u-tokyo.ac.jp

Cite this erratum as Kawakatsu, H (2026). *Erratum to* Characterizing Lithospheric Transverse Isotropy Using Moment Tensors—On the Origin of the Non-Double-Couple Components of Global CMT Solutions, *Bull. Seismol. Soc. Am.* **116**, 837–838, doi: 10.1785/0120250271

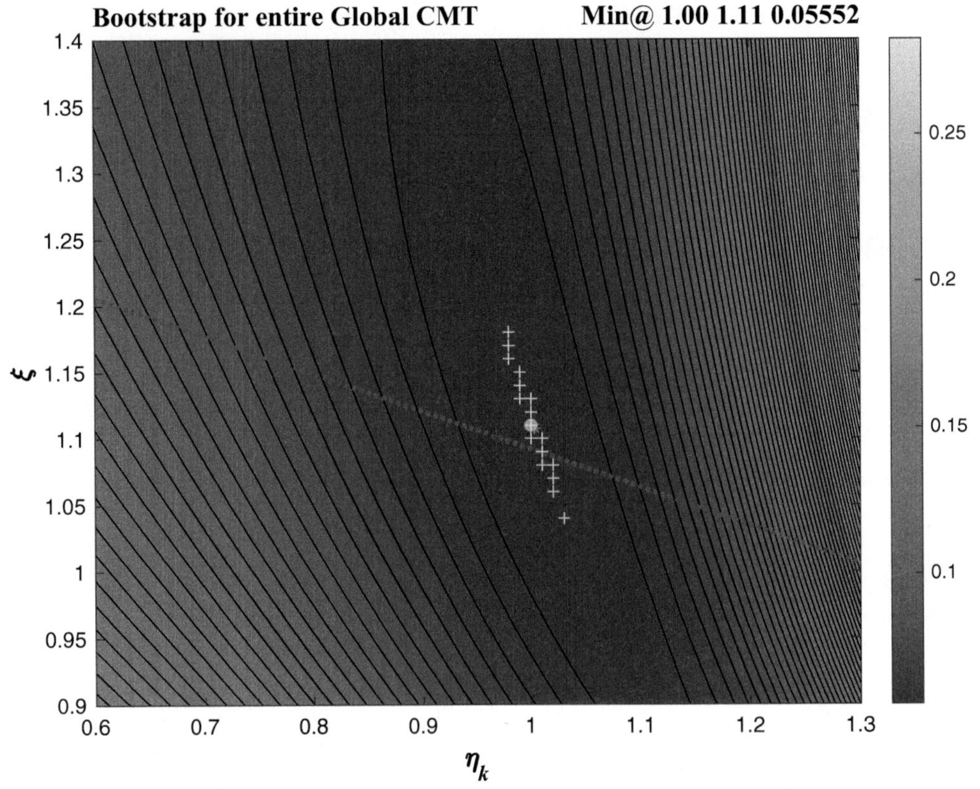

Figure 1. (Corresponds to figure 7 of Kawakatsu, 2024 with *r4-projection*) Bootstrap error estimate for the entire Global Centroid Moment Tensor (Global CMT) dataset. Results of 500 bootstrap resampling are shown by yellow plus marks. The point in cyan color gives the minimum const-function location, and the red asterisk denotes the preliminary reference Earth model (PREM) sub-Moho point as a reference. The green asterisk indicates the bootstrap average, which almost overlaps with the minimum const-function location. Note that the resampling minimum points are mostly scattered along the minimum valley of the misfit map, indicating the lack of the resolution along the valley. The formal bootstrap estimates are $\eta_\kappa = 1.003 \pm 0.009$ and $\xi = 1.108 \pm 0.022$ with a correlation coefficient of Cor = −0.960. The *S-P* scaling 1.0 is use. The three digits at the top give the minimum point (η_κ, ξ) and the corresponding misfit value in equation (28) of Kawakatsu (2024). The color version of this figure is available only in the electronic edition.

REFERENCES

Kawakatsu, H. (1996). Observability of the isotropic component of a moment tensor, *Geophys. J. Int.* **126,** 525–544.

Kawakatsu, H. (2024). Characterizing lithospheric transverse isotropy using moment tensors–On the origin of the non-double couple components of Global CMT solutions, *Bull. Seismol. Soc. Am.* **114,** 2995–3010, doi: 10.1785/0120240136.

Shuler, A., G. Ekstrom, and M. Nettles (2013). Physical mechanisms for vertical-CLVD earthquakes at active volcanoes, *J. Geophys. Res.* **118,** 1569–1586.

Manuscript received 2 December 2025
Published online 21 January 2026

The Seismological Society of America is an international scientific society devoted to the advancement of seismology and the understanding of earthquakes for the benefit of society.

www.seismosoc.org
www.bssaonline.org

SSA
Seismological
Society of America